Intent in Competition Law

Maya-Salomé Garnier

Foreword by David Bosco
Introduction by Catherine Prieto

Concurrences

2025

Paris – New York – London

First prize, Faculty of Law and Political Science of Aix-en-Provence

Concurrences Ph.D. Award

Garrigou Prize, Académie de legislation

Prize from Aix-Marseille University

Accessit to the Lassier Prize LIDC

(Ligue internationale de droit de la concurrence)

106 West 32nd Street, Suite 144 New York, NY, 10001, USA
www.concurrences.com
book@concurrences.com

First Printing, Septembre 2025
978-1-954750-15-9 (Paperback)
Library of Congress Control Number: 2025943325

Cover Design: Yves Buliard, www.yvesbuliard.fr
Book Design and Layout implementation: Nord Compo

Concurrences Books

Tributes

James F. Rill – A Life in Antitrust, *2024*

Eleanor M. Fox – Antitrust Ambassador to the World, *2021*

Herbert Hovenkamp – The Dean of American Antitrust Law, *2021*

Frédéric Jenny – Standing Up for Convergence and Relevance in Antitrust, (Vol. I & II), *2019 & 2021*

Albert Foer – A Consumer Voice in the Antitrust Arena, *2020*

Richard Whish – Taking Competition Law Outside the Box, *2020*

Douglas H. Ginsburg – An Antitrust Professor on the Bench (Vol. I & II), *2018 & 2020*

Wang Xiaoye – The Pioneer of Competition Law in China, *A. Emch, W. Ng (eds.), 2019*

Ian S. Forrester – A Scot without Borders (Vol. I & II), *A. Komninos (eds.), 2015*

William E. Kovacic – An Antitrust Tribute (Vol. I & II), *2013 & 2014*

Practical Books

Competition Law and the Challenges of Insular Economies – A Focus on French Polynesia and the Pacific Region, *J. Peyre, E. Silvestro, V. Terrien, T. Emen, Y. Lecornu (eds.), 2025*

Competition Inspections under EU Law, 2nd Edition, *N. Jalabert-Doury, 2025*

Navigating the DMA: Application Across National Jurisdictions, *G. Muscolo & A. Massolo (eds.), 2025*

Artificial Intelligence and Competition Policy, *A. Abbott, T. Schrepel (eds.), 2024*

State Aid & National Enforcement, *J. Derenne, D. Jouve, C. Lemaire, F. Martucci (eds.), 2024*

The 2023 U.S. Merger Guidelines: *A Review, Sean Sullivan (ed.), 2024*

Competition Inspections in 25 Jurisdictions 2nd Edition – A Practitioner's Guide, *N. Jalabert-Doury (ed.), 2024*

EU Antitrust Enforcement – Law, Economics, History, *Policy & Practice, Wouter P. J. Wils, 2024*

The EU Foreign Subsidies Regulation, *Andreas Reindl, Isabelle Van Damme, 2024*

Compendium of Antitrust Damages Actions – ICC – 2nd edition, *J.W.H. Denton AO, F. Brunet, S. Williams, C. Inthavisay (eds.), 2023*

Pharmaceutical Antitrust: An Analysis of U.S. and EU Law, *M. Thill-Tayara, G. Gordon (eds.), 2023*

Innovation Paradox in Merger Control, *G. Gurkaynak, 2023*

Antitrust and the Digital Economy, *Y. Katsoulacos (ed.), 2023 (in collaboration with CRESSE)*

Judicial Review of Competition Cases, *D. Ginsburg, T. Eicke (eds.), 2023*

Competition Law Treatment of Joint Ventures, *B. Bleicher, N. Campbell, A. Hamilton, N. Hukkinen, A. Khan, A. Mordaunt (eds.), 2022 (in collaboration with the IBA)*

Information Exchange & Related Risks, *Z. Marosi, M. Soares (eds.), 2022 (in collaboration with the IBA)*

Rulemaking Authority of the U.S. Federal Trade Commission, *D. Crane (ed.), 2022*

The International Competition Network at Twenty, *D. Anderson & P. Lugard (eds.), 2022*

Competition Case Law Digest – 5th Edition, *F. Jenny, N. Charbit (eds.), 2022*

Competition Inspections in 21 Jurisdictions – A Practitioner's Guide, *N. Jalabert-Doury (ed.), 2022*

Perspectives on Antitrust Compliance, *A. Riley, A. Stephan, A. Tubbs (eds.), 2022 (in collaboration with the ICC)*

Turkish Competition Law, *G. Gürkaynak, 2021*

Competition Law – Climate Change & Environmental Sustainability, *S. Holmes, D. Middelschulte, M. Snoep (eds.), 2021*

Merger Control in Latin America – A Jurisdictional Guide, *P. Burnier da Silveira, P. Sittenfeld (eds.), 2020*

Competition Inspections under EU Law – A Practitioner's Guide, *N. Jalabert-Doury, 2020*

Gun Jumping in Merger Control – A Jurisdictional Guide, *C. Hatton, Y. Comtois, A. Hamilton (eds.), 2019 (in collaboration with the IBA)*

Choice – A New Standard for Competition Analysis? *P. Nihoul (ed.), 2016*

PhD Theses

The Economics of Digital Markets – Essays in Theoretical and Empirical Industrial Organization, *E. Arnaud-Joufray, 2024*

Abuse of Platform Power, *F. Bostoen, 2023*

Reform of Chinese State-Owned Enterprises, *X. Bai, 2023*

Competition & Regulation in Network Industries – Essays in Industrial Organization, *J-M. Zogheib, 2021*

The Role of Media Pluralism in the Enforcement of EU Competition Law, *K. Bania, 2019*

Buyer Power, *I. Herrera Anchustegui, 2017*

General Interest

Why Competition? Voices from the Antitrust Community and Beyond, *D. Crane, D. Gerard, R. Tritell (eds.), 2024*

Competition Law Dictionary, *D. Healey, R. Whish, W. E. Kovacic, P. Trevisán (eds.), 2024*

The 5 Labours of Europe, *P.-E. Partsch, 2024*

Great Antitrust Enforcers, *W. E. Kovacic, 2023*

Competition – How to Speak Like an Expert, *E. Combe, 2023*

Women and Antitrust – Voices from the Field (Vol I & II), *E. Kurgonaite & K. Nordlander, 2020*

e-Book versions available for **Concurrences+** subscribers

SUMMARY

FOREWORD

Is an understanding of competition law still possible? Its fundamental concepts – undertaking, restriction of competition, relevant market, abuse… – have never seemed as unstable as they do in our contemporary legal context. The Court of Justice of the European Union has failed to illuminate the path: its case law is opaque. For about fifteen years, judgments have followed one another without pointing toward any clear direction. Consider, in agreements law, the evolution of the notion of "by object" restriction, which has become so elusive that one must always await the next "landmark decision" to understand the constructions only sketched by the previous one. Turn also to the law of abuse, subject to the incessant flux of case law regarding the criteria for qualifying anticompetitive conduct. As for the European Commission's decision-making practice, it falls within an ever-changing administrative doctrine. In less than half a century, it has already shifted three times: from a legalistic method of analyzing firm behaviors – where the prohibition is formally stated – to an economic approach in which the effects of such behaviors are assessed. Today, it culminates in an imprecise synthesis; embedded within is a political perception of business conduct, making competition rules a mere tool in service of various – and variable – societal objectives. As for the academic world, which ought to bring order to the subject, it is riven by contradictory, sometimes irreconcilable, currents, and can no longer agree even on the essentials. Yet it should be a force for proposals – if not *reconciliation* – in competition law: a reconciliation with itself, as it were, gathering the scattered fragments of its identity.

It is to this immense task that, with remarkable audacity, the author of this thesis, Maya-Salomé Garnier, has set herself. Intellectual courage is evident throughout the work and produces some remarkable pages of legal theory. The title of the research may mislead by its modesty: while the work does indeed study *intent in competition law*, the doctrinal approach is in fact far more ambitious. First, to approach the concept and role of intent in competition law, the author develops a *general* theory of intent that goes well beyond this field – one from which other areas may also draw inspiration. This theory draws upon history to rediscover a concept that permeates the entire legal system, particularly criminal law. Furthermore – and above all – the thesis does not merely aim to encourage positive law on anticompetitive practices to give greater visibility to a rethought concept of intent. It revisits the entire edifice – and in doing so, shakes it, from the foundations to its most seemingly accomplished structures. The effects-based approach, on which agreements and abuse classifications supposedly rest? A myth. The consumer welfare standard, deemed by the Court of Justice to be the essential aim of competition law? A mere formula, devoid of normative force. The distinction between "by object" and "by effect" restrictions? A hollow and elusive dichotomy. Ms. Garnier quite simply makes intent one of the fundamental concepts – if not the essential criterion – for defining competition infringements. This approach is all the more compelling in that it attempts to chart a distinctively *legal* path for competition law. In this, it is certain to appeal to jurists who have experienced a sense of powerlessness since economic analysis came to dominate the field.

Will the thesis convince its readers? Like any heterodox work, it is unclassifiable – almost revolutionary – even though the author claims merely to reveal what has always been present. It will undoubtedly challenge many deeply held convictions. But it promises a rare intellectual journey, one that will lead readers from ancient law to the Digital Markets Act, from Diocletian to Margrethe Vestager, from Aristotle to Posner, from criminal law to modern economic theory. And it will, without question, prompt them to reconsider their most settled beliefs about competition law – and to envision another path for its future.

David Bosco
Law Professor, Aix-Marseille University

INTRODUCTION

From the outset, Maya-Salomé Garnier's thesis is iconoclastic, ultimately reflecting a sense of saturation and even exasperation brought on by the complexity and uncertainties of the new industrial economy. This economy was a major source of inspiration for the effects-based approach during the modernization of competition policy in the late 1990s. The effects-based approach has failed to fulfill its promises of more reliable application through predictive analyses of the rationality of actors. The outcome of this "new economic approach" is far from flattering, as it has proven to be barely functional due to its complexity, often exploited by well-resourced companies, and associated with stagnation or even capture.

Therefore, it is no surprise that the European Commission has actively relied on the classification of restrictions by object in its decision-making practice, at the risk of self-contradiction. This has resulted in tensions during judicial review that the Court of Justice has poorly managed. As for the classification of abuse, which was supposed to be the preferred domain of the effects-based approach, the failure is even more pronounced. The European Commission's decision-making practice has come under heavy scrutiny, and the Court of Justice's preliminary rulings have even contributed to erratic case law. We even now have abuse by object. The loss of clarity has gradually descended into great intellectual disorder. Scholars have attempted to follow its twists and turns, find guiding principles, and explain shifts, all in vain. Maya-Salomé Garnier denounces the limits of these efforts in her incisive analyses.

In contrast, her thesis contributes to the construction of a general theory of intent for the purposes of simplification, clarity, efficiency, and adaptability of competition rules. This requires us to move beyond the contemporary perception of intent, which is steeped in subjectivity. By referring to pre-19th century analysis, she instead defends an objective concept of intent, justifying a significant role for presumptions.

Highly scholarly and "engaged", Maya-Salomé Garnier's work is both destabilizing and invigorating. She invites us to rediscover competition law in a bold, inspired and inspiring vision.

Catherine Prieto

Law Professor, University Paris 1 Panthéon-Sorbonne

ABBREVIATIONS AND LATIN LOCUTIONS

a contrario	by contrast, on the contrary
adde	add
ADLC	French Competition Authority
art., arts.	article, articles
ass. plén.	Assemblée plénière
CA	Court of Appeal
Cass.	Court of Cassation
cf.	compare
ch. acc.	indictment division
ch. civ.	*chambre civile* [Civil Division]
ch. com.	*chambre commerciale* [Commercial Division]
ch. crim.	*chambre criminelle* [Criminal Division]
chron.	chronicle
CJEU	Court of Justice of the European Union
Comm. CE	Commission of the European Communities
comm.	comment
Cons. conc.	Competition Council
contra	the opposite
de lege ferenda	the law as it ought to be
de lege lata	as the law stands
disp.	*disputatio*
doctr.	doctrine
e.g.	for example
EC Treaty	Treaty establishing the European Community
ECHR	European Convention for the Protection of Human Rights and Fundamental Freedoms
ECJ	Court of Justice of the European Communities
ECtHR	European Court of Human Rights
ed., eds.	edition, editor, editors
EESC	European Economic and Social Committee
erga omnes	with respect to all
esp.	especially
et al.	et al.
et seq.	and the following
Eur. Comm.	Commission of the European Union
ex multis	among many others
fasc.	fascicule
gr. ch.	Grand Chamber
i.e.	that is

id.	in the same place
in abstracto	in the abstract
in	in
infra	below
inter alia	among others
inter partes	between the parties
ipso facto	as a consequence
JCP E	La Semaine Juridique Entreprise et Affaires
JCP G	La Semaine Juridique General Edition
JORF	Official Journal of the French Republic
LGDJ	General library of law and jurisprudence
no.	number
nota bene	please note that
O.J.	Official Journal of the European Communities/European Union
OECD	Organisation for Economic Co-operation and Development
op. cit.	*opus citatum*, quoted work
p., pp.	page, pages
para., paras.	paragraph, paragraphs
per se	in and of itself
ratione materiae	by reason of the subject matter
ratione personae	by reason of the person
repub.	republished
resp.	respectively
RSC	Journal of Criminal Science and Comparative Criminal Law
RTD Civ.	Quarterly Review of Civil Law
RTD Com.	Quarterly Review of Commercial Law
RTD Eur.	Quarterly review of European law
SCOTUS	Supreme Court of the United States
SSRN	Social Science Research Network
stricto sensu	in the strict sense
supra	above
TFEU	Treaty on the Functioning of the European Union
TLFi	Computerized French Language Treasury
trans.	translator
vol.	volume

AUTHOR'S NOTES

We have chosen to limit the use of abbreviations when citing journal titles. Given their variety and, in some cases, their age, we felt it preferable to mention their names *in extenso*. Similarly, in order to improve access to the sources used, we have avoided frequent use of the term "*op. cit.*" When several pages separate the first mention of a reference from the next, the full citation is repeated.

All references cited have been consulted directly, with the exception of a few German-language sources, which are followed by the note "cit. by" or "cit. and trans. by." While these are not included in our bibliography, we considered it helpful to mention them for the benefit of German-speaking readers.

To avoid repetition, we have treated the expressions "competition law" and "law of anticompetitive practices" as synonyms – although the latter is more restrictive, as it only covers agreements and abuses of dominant position, and excludes merger control and State aid law.

Cross-references in footnotes refer to paragraph numbers.

"Use real life and its rich variety!
They're living it, but unreflectingly;
They'll notice this or that they didn't know.
Colourful changing scenes and little sense,
Much error, mixed with just a grain of truth –
That's the best drink for such an audience;
They'll be refreshed and edified."*

*

* *

Self-evidence is the hardest to prove.
Everyone knows it – yet few are moved.
Convincing them is no small feat:
A host of arguments must be arranged,
A touch of logic, artfully exchanged,
To challenge prejudice and prompt defeat.

* J. W. Goethe, *Prelude on the Stage*, *in* FAUST, PART ONE (D. Luke trans., Oxford Univ. Press 1987)(1790).

INTRODUCTION

1. **"Nothing is worth finding but what has always existed."**[1] In the heart of Babel, men set about building a tower so high that it would pierce the sky. From its summit, it would have been possible to know everything, foresee everything and direct everything. Icarus' dream led to discord: the construction collapsed before it was completed, and its builders, who had quarreled so much, would never again speak the same language.

Don't human beings constantly reproduce their myths?[2] The modern mind hunts down chance, rejects the unknown and dreams of control.[3] The legal edifice is based on a science that has taken the place of transcendence; jurists have built a skyscraper of rationality, smooth and uncluttered. At the height of their ambition, they believe they can see beyond the horizon, and are burning to outline the future. No longer able to perceive the earth clearly, they have to use more and more precision to try and grasp a distant reality, resorting to a complex novlanguage, hermetic to the uninitiated. Their proud building is of a singular architecture:[4] erected on ancient foundations, the first floor is made of Renaissance walls, onto which a multitude of glass and steel stories have since been superimposed. The tower bends but still holds.

A curious man ventured in, and soon lost his way in the labyrinth. He sought advice from everyone he met, but no one had a map. "We'd have to design one!" he thought. "There is no science except that which is hidden," whispered a wise old man.[5] Pondering these words, he first imagined drawing each corridor, but realized that his map would be as vast as the territory. So he thought, with a reforming impulse, of proposing an innovative architecture that would solve the problem. The wise man told him that others had come up with the same idea before him: all it did was add another floor to the edifice, making the situation worse.

Discouraged, he gave up and left. Barely out of the door, he nearly tripped: he had stumbled on a buried Roman vestige, flush with the

---

1 G. Cornu, *Aperçu de la pensée juridique française contemporaine*, *in* 1 Extrait des annales de l'Université de Poitiers 15, 28 (1960): "The essential, but what else? It is ineffable, I know. Invisible to the eye... [N]othing is worth finding but what has always existed. To catch a glimpse of this, the jurist could usefully draw inspiration from the diver in the Mediterranean. On the surface, the crest of the waves tosses and irritates him, the foam blurs his vision. Everything is movement. But if, on a breath, he sinks into deep waters, into a place where no eddies stir, then, before surfacing again, he discovers, in complete vertigo, the clarity of the sea and the calm of the Gods. The sea will always be the sea, the sea always beginning again."

2 G. Tournier, Babel ou le vertige technique (1959).

3 D. Villey, Notes de philosophie économique (1958–59): Le jeu des intérêts 172 (1965).

4 The architectural metaphor was used in the eighteenth century by Blackstone to describe developments in the common law, *see* W. Blackstone, A Disclosure on the Study of the Law (1758); or by Wittgenstein to describe those of language, *see* L. Wittgenstein, Tractatus logico-philosophicus – Suivi de Investigations philosophiques 121 (P. Klossowski trans., Gallimard 1961), aphorism 18.

5 G. Bachelard, Le rationalisme appliqué 38 (2004).

ground. He understood. Since the building was built on the roots of the past, perhaps the solution lay in its history. So he began digging, in the hope of finding a Rosetta Stone to decipher what had become complex, to reunite what had been disjointed, to restore what had drifted from the bedrock of law.

2. **An itinerary: from intuition to theory.** Wherever jurists look, if they are interested in a major legal concept, they will see that the monolith that it was yesterday has today cracked, giving way to scattered fragments, buried under an avalanche of layers of special national or supra-state rules, "innovative" theories that forget or ignore tradition, technical terms devoid of a past,[6] to such an extent that if researchers are asked the question: "Is the law still based on the reasoning, principles and notions of yesteryear?" they will be placed on dry land – that of paradox. Their intuition will lead them to believe that, despite the increasing complexity of the legal order, the scattered elements before their eyes are still linked by something essential, albeit invisible. The picture will take on the trappings of a vast enigma, which they hope to solve in order to restore the meaning, coherence and values of the law.

Intention is one of those notions whose apparent indeterminacy, or supposed obliteration, is matched only by its central place in the legal system.[7] Yet, in competition law, it is most often relegated to being just one index among others, or rejected in the name of the "objective" nature of offenses. In criminal law, its conceptualization is uncertain: it varies from pen to pen – to the point of being described as an "untraceable notion."[8] It must be acknowledged that the law has grown labyrinthine, even for the well-versed – owing in part to Byzantine debates that lend undue gravitas to a legislative and jurisprudential output often lacking considerably in substance.

Nevertheless, we took the gamble of believing in the permanence of certain legal constants, in order to explore the hypothesis that, despite its claimed scientificity and objectivity, competition law could be theorized in terms of a legal notion: intention.

Between this first intuition and the elaboration of a theory, many obstacles had to be overcome, both in terms of the discipline and the concept studied. Since the path is as important as the point of arrival, the aim here is to retrace the path – and the choices and uncertainties that accompanied

---

6 P.-Y. Gautier, *Quelle langue parle le droit?*, 186 Pouvoirs 99, 100 (2023): "[F]or private law, nothing is worse than sloppy concoctions and vulgates drafted by technocrats whose words and phrases have been blown around by all sorts of pressure groups. …In the European Union, the loss of legal language has reached its peak." *Adde*, F. Zenati-Castaing, Le savoir des lois: Essai sur le droit romaniste 176–77 (2021).

7 Cf. the words of Paul Amselek, *L'interpellation actuelle de la réflexion philosophique par le droit*, Droits 123, 126 (1986): "[T]he things we are most familiar with, and to whose presence we gradually pay less attention, are precisely those that play the greatest role."

8 I. Moine-Dupuis, *L'intention en droit pénal: Une notion introuvable?*, Recueil Dalloz 2144 (2001).

the research,[9] and served as a blueprint for the study. In order to develop a theory of intent in competition law (**VII**), it was first necessary to conceptualize the notion itself (**VI**), and to delve into the history of the discipline in order to rediscover the principles that originally underpinned it (**V**). This detour into the past has made it possible to overcome the current uncertainties surrounding the definition of intent (**IV**), and to confirm the initial idea that, despite the minimization of its role (**III**), it offers a means of deciphering competition law (**II**). However, in view of the monument of complexity it has become (**I**), this assertion is not self-evident, since it no longer seems to care about traditional legal concepts – sometimes vilified as lacking rigor[10] – and its methods and objectives may today appear autonomous from ordinary law.

Section I

3. **Initial observations: competition law, a monument to complexity.** If there is one discipline that provides a topical illustration of the technocratic drifts[11] affecting contemporary law,[12] it is competition law. The hard core of "economic law," it is characterized by its strong links with economic science, which "'delivers' a field and concepts,"[13] dictates the objectives to be pursued[14] and reveals the behaviors to be sanctioned.[15] "Without economic theory, there can be no competition law!"[16] This remark is all the more true today: since the 2000s, under the influence of the "modernization"

9 As Emmanuel Gaillard has remarked, "one might think of presenting a theory … as complete as possible, disregarding the hesitations that have marked both the history of the notion and the author's research. This would undoubtedly be to deprive oneself of an interesting dimension and a useful precaution." E. Gaillard, Le pouvoir en droit privé 16 (1985), no. 15.

10 On the subject of "competition on the merits," *see, inter alia*, OECD, *Competition on the Merits: Key findings, summary and notes* 47 (OECD Roundtables on Competition Policy Papers, No. 56, 2006): "Competition policy would be strengthened if courts and agencies were to abandon the use of empty phrases like 'competition on the merits.'"

11 According to Habermas, technocratic systems shift the locus of decision-making in favor of a "scientific intelligentsia," and conceal, under the veneer of a supposedly objective and axiologically neutral logic, "what is in truth, however, only politics, as it has always been done." *See* J. Habermas, La technique et la science comme "idéologie" 100–103 (1973).

12 The observation of a decline, or regressive trends in law, is not new. *See inter alia*: G. Ripert, Le déclin du droit: Études sur la législation contemporaine (1949); B. Oppetit, Droit et modernité 118–19 (1998). Despite the warnings issued since the last century, the legal system continues to grow ever heavier, as if driven by the law of entropy.

13 G. Farjat, *La notion de droit économique*, 37 Archives de philosophie du droit 27, 60 (1992).

14 On the economic point of view regarding the aims of competition law, *see* in particular: A.-L. Sibony, Le juge et le raisonnement économique en droit de la concurrence 86–135 (2008), nos. 109–78.

15 L. Idot, *La qualification de la restriction de concurrence: À propos des lignes directrices de la Commission concernant l'application de l'article 81, § 3 CE, in* La modernisation du droit de la concurrence 85 (G. Canivet & M.-A. Frison-Roche eds., 2006): "The definition of what constitutes a restriction of competition will mainly depend on the economists' judgment of the merits of the behavior."

16 L. Vogel, *L'économie, serviteur ou maître du droit?, in* Une certaine idée du droit : Mélanges offerts à André Decocq 606 (2004).

movement inspired by an American school of thought,[17] the ambition has been to bring the solutions adopted fully into line with economic theories, in order to promote the effective implementation of European competition rules, and to make economic efficiency an objective in itself.[18]

But new theories are always conquerors, and only succeed in imposing themselves by calling into question their elders, claiming that they make up for their supposed shortcomings. This is why legal reasoning has been caricatured,[19] with an accusation that would not convince any legal theorist:[20] that it is too "formalistic," and leads to miscarriages of justice by repressing behavior which, because it has no harmful effect on competition or consumers, should be deemed lawful. The "economic nature" of the discipline therefore implies, by definition, its "consequentialism."[21] Competition law is thus driven by a chronic[22] epistemological doubt about the relevance of legal reasoning alone to identify infringing behavior.[23] The relationship between the jurist and the economist is said to have been inverted: normativity is said to derive mainly from the teachings of economic analysis, set up as a new source of law, with the jurist, deploying his technique but no longer his art, tasked with integrating and arranging the economist's doxa in the manner of a dogma.[24]

A dogma deemed immutable, but hardly intelligible: if the center of gravity of the competition infringement now seems to be the restrictive *effect* on competition or the *effect* on the consumer, the contours of these notions, foreign to the legal vocabulary, are still, to this day, uncertain.[25] How could it be otherwise? Economic theory is not a stabilized field of knowledge, as evidenced by the debates on the foundations, methods and risks

17 Namely, the Chicago School. On the Chicagoan inspiration of the "effects approach" induced by the modernization of the discipline, *see*, in particular: D. M. B. Gerard, *The Effects-Based Approach Under Article 101 TFEU and its Paradoxes: Modernisation at War with Itself?*, *in* Ten Years of Effects-Based Approach in EU Competition Law: State of Play and Perspectives 17, 18–31 (J. Bourgeois & D. Waelbroeck eds., 2012).

18 Effectiveness "qualifies a means that enables the desired result to be achieved," while efficiency "qualifies a relationship between means and an end in terms of costs." The economic approach to competition law has made "economic efficiency" a goal in itself, to be pursued "effectively," cf. A.-L. Sibony, *Du bon usage des notions d'efficacité et d'efficience en droit*, *in* L'efficacité de la norme juridique: Nouveau vecteur de légitimité 62, 66, 77 resp. (M. Fatin-Rouge Stefanini, L. Gay & A. Vidal-Naquet eds., 2012).

19 D. Bosco & C. Prieto, Droit européen de la concurrence 477 (2013), no. 558.

20 For an illuminating comparison between the supposed formalism of legal reasoning in competition law and the study of legal formalism by American theorist Frederic Schauer, *see* J. Lindeboom, *Formalism in Competition Law*, 18 Journal of Competition Law & Economics 832 (2022).

21 F. Hoffmann, *Probabilité et droit de la concurrence*, Revue française de droit administratif 531 (2011).

22 For an epistemological approach to competition law, *see* N. Petit, *Épistémologie du droit de la concurrence*, *in* 1 Laurence Idot: Concurrence et Europe – Liber Amicorum 557 (C. Lemaire & F. Martucci eds., 2022).

23 F. Castillo de la Torre, *Is the Effects-Based Approach Too Cumbersome? Taking Stock of Recent Practice and Case Law on Article 102 TFEU*, *in* The Transformation of EU Competition Law: Next Generation Issues 145, 146 (A. Claici, A. Komninos & D. Waelbroeck eds., 2023).

24 *See* M. van der Woude, *La métamorphose d'un droit*, Concurrences no. 2-2022, art. no. 106134.

25 *Ex multis*, P. Stoffel-Munck, L'abus dans le contrat: Essai d'une théorie 446, 451 (2000), nos. 602, 610; D. Waelbroeck & D. Slater, *The Scope of Object vs Effect under Article 101 TFEU*, *in* Ten Years of Effects-Based Approach in EU Competition Law: State of Play and Perspectives 131, 138 (J. Bourgeois & D. Waelbroeck eds., 2012).

of ideological misrepresentation associated with this "science,"[26] which, because it is human, cannot be exact, let alone objective.[27] Despite such uncertainties, which do not sit well with the principle of legal certainty,[28] reference to and recourse to economic analysis have become widespread over the past two decades. Under the aegis of what specialists call the "effects approach" or the "more economic approach," there is no longer an article of doctrine, a Commission decision or a Court of Justice ruling that does not mention or mobilize here a "counterfactual analysis" or an "as-efficient competitor" test, there a "damage scenario," constantly using a vocabulary hinged on the nebulous notion of "effect."[29]

Competition law now gives the impression of being like the ink blots on a Rorschach test,[30] made up of random and abstract figures left to the free interpretation of the observer, offering more to assess the personality of the interpreter than the real meaning of the task – so much so that one dares to ask the question: "Is competition law 'law'?"[31] so much so that it can seem, in some respects, to consist of a jumble of decisions of expediency. And if the intelligibility of competition rules is necessarily diminished, their effectiveness – the hobbyhorse of proponents of the economic approach – fails to materialize. As a result of the unprecedented increase in the burden of proof incumbent on competition authorities, which mobilize vast economic analyses to prove the harmful effects produced by litigious behavior, the cost of implementing the rules has never been so high, decisions and rulings so long, and the speed of proceedings so compromised. Above all, the readability and adaptability of competition law have been undermined, as evidenced by the current debates on the criteria for classifying anticompetitive behavior, which are resurfacing more than sixty years after the birth of European competition law, due to the supposedly new practices of companies operating in digital markets.[32]

---

26 On this theme, *see inter alia* H. Brochier, *Fondements idéologiques et visée scientifique en économie*, 10 ÉCONOMIES ET SOCIÉTÉS 169 (Oct. 1988); A. Beres, *Entretien sur l'économie avec Sir Karl Popper*, 1 REVUE FRANÇAISE D'ÉCONOMIE 55 (1986); A. BOYER ET AL., LA PENSÉE DE KARL POPPER ET LA SCIENCE ÉCONOMIQUE (1987) ; D. M. HAUSMAN, THE INEXACT AND SEPARATE SCIENCE OF ECONOMICS 123–240 (1992).

27 Yet, as Christian Atias has remarked, "[u]nself-conscious subjectivity is less to be feared than an illusion of objectivity," *see* C. ATIAS, THÉORIE CONTRE ARBITRAIRE 21 (1987).

28 On this subject, *see* C. Prieto, *La sécurité juridique dans le droit de la concurrence*, *in* SÉCURITÉ JURIDIQUE ET DROIT ÉCONOMIQUE 299, 311–17 (L. Boy, J.-B. Racine & F. Siiriainen eds., 2010).

29 The source of unlawfulness is said to reside mainly in the "effects" of behavior on the market, L. Vogel, *Où va le droit de la concurrence? in* LE DROIT FRANÇAIS DE LA CONCURRENCE, TRENTE ANS APRÈS, L'ORDONNANCE DU 1ER DÉCEMBRE 1986: RÉTROSPECTIVES ET PERSPECTIVES 37, 38 (C. Arens, M. Chagny & J.-L. Fourgoux eds., 2017).

30 The point is made by the European Commission's principal legal adviser (DG COMP), F. Castillo de la Torre, *Is the Effects-Based Approach Too Cumbersome? Taking Stock of Recent Practice and Case Law on Article 102 TFEU*, *op. cit.* at 196.

31 H. First, *Is Antitrust "Law"?*, 10 ANTITRUST 9 (1995).

32 The *Google Android*, *Google AdSense* and *Google Shopping* cases provide an illustration of this: in the Commission's decisions, legal reasoning plays a lesser role than economic analysis, which inevitably gives rise to debates as to why this or that novel practice should, or should not, be qualified as anticompetitive behavior. On this subject, *see inter alia* A.-S. Choné-Grimaldi, *Les abus de position dominantes dans le secteur numérique (réflexions à partir de la décision* Google-Android*)*, RECUEIL DALLOZ 343 (2020).

While the solution could, and most certainly should, have consisted of theoretical reflection aimed at simplifying the application of existing texts, the path taken was quite different: the European legislator opted to adopt a new regulation, as technical as it is difficult to understand, the Digital Markets Act,[33] with the illusory aim of remedying the alleged shortcomings of the prohibition of agreements and abuses of dominant position.[34]

However, in recent years, some have noted that "there is reason to believe that the economic approach has largely remained within the doctrinal field,"[35] and voices are being raised to denounce the deceptions, or at the very least the limitations, of the economic prism.[36] Today, however, we are witnessing not a return to sound principles, but an increased politicization of competition law, driven by a debate on the plurality of its economic, social, and now societal[37] objectives.[38] The discussion is certainly becoming less rigorous, and some authors rightly call for a remobilization of presumptions,[39] or a "return to the legal."[40] If we now speak of "postmodernization"[41] or "second modernization"[42] to designate the new era in which competition law is entering, perhaps the most pertinent course of action would be to return to tradition, by definition insusceptible of neologism – in other words, to return to classic legal reasoning.

---

33 Regulation (EU) 2022/1925 of the European Parliament and of the Council of Sept. 14, 2022, on Contestable and Fair Markets in the Digital Sector, 2022 O.J. (L 265) 1.

34 One author has rightly remarked that the shortcomings of Articles 101 and 102 TFEU may have been exaggerated in order to strengthen the legitimacy of the new instrument, *see* J.-C. Roda, *Le Digital Markets Act (1re partie) – Contrôler les contrôleurs d'accès,* Communication Commerce électronique (Feb. 2023), étude 4, esp. nos. 8–9.

35 Bosco, *Regard sur la postmodernisation de l'abus de position dominante*, *in* 1 Laurence Idot: Concurrence et Europe – Liber Amicorum 25, 27 (C. Lemaire & F. Martucci eds., 2022); *adde* R. Maulin, *L'approche par les effets en droit de la concurrence: Le devoir d'inventaire*, Concurrences no. 3-2015, art. no. 73845, 24.

36 Note that in 2015, a round table was entitled (in its French version): "Faut-il brûler les économistes?" *See* L. Idot, M. van der Woude & J. Philippe, *Why Bother with Economists?*, Concurrences no. 3-2015, art. no. 74831, 62. On this theme, the following preface is of interest: P. Maistre du Chambon & P. Conte, *Préface*, *in* Analyse économique du droit et matière pénale xiii, xvi (C. Claverie Rousset ed., 2018): "[I]t is up to law, including criminal law, to seek first and foremost to promote a social order, stemming from a reflection on the ideal conception of man, of his place in a society based on values that are more humanistic than merely economic… Because law is axiological, the questions it raises cannot be resolved simply by equations." *Adde*, C. Atias, *Sur E. Mackaay et St. Rousseau,* Analyse économique du droit, *Paris, Dalloz, Éditions Thémis, 2008*, Revue de la recherche juridique: Droit prospectif 2469 (2008). More generally, *see* P. Malaurie, *Le droit et l'esprit: Dernière leçon*, 67 Commentaire 609, 611 (1994): "[N]o science can make perfect law, because, say the good people, perfection is not of this world and the good people are kindly right. Or, say the jurists, because justice and injustice and all human values are beyond scientific evaluation."

37 The environment, gender equality, democratic pluralism, equity – few themes are spared, as competition law now seems to be seen as a tool for perfecting the social order.

38 Among a wealth of literature, *see* N. Mathey, *Les finalités du droit de la concurrence: Essai de téléologie du droit,* Contrats concurrence consommation (Dec. 2020), dossier 13.

39 C. Prieto, *Source économique du droit de la concurrence: Quelle efficacité?*, Contrats concurrence consommation (June 2020), dossier 3, nos. 20–21; *adde* J. B. Baker, The Antitrust Paradigm: Restoring a Competitive Economy 71–80 (2019).

40 D. Bosco, *Regard sur la postmodernisation de l'abus de position dominante*, *op. cit.* at 36.

41 *Id.* at 25–36.

42 P. Ibáñez Colomo, The (Second) Modernisation of Article 102 TFEU, Reconciling Effective Enforcement, Legal Certainty and Meaningful Judicial Review (Oct. 2023), https://ssrn.com/abstract=4598161.

Section II

4. **The initial hypothesis: intention, a key to deciphering competition law.** Relying on legal reasoning to provide a unitary and coherent theoretical foundation for the discipline clearly establishing the constituent elements of competition infringements. However, in a discipline deemed "objective" and focused on economic effects, what could be the role of a legal concept such as intention? The first intuition is that of the philistine, who doubts the possibility of unintentionally fomenting a cartel or abusing one's dominant position. The second intuition comes from the jurist: competition infringements are criminal offenses,[43] and the principle of culpability[44] requires the characterization of a mental element.[45] While this argument may be convincing to the criminal lawyer, the competition law specialist is not necessarily of the same opinion – some perceiving criminal law and its rigorous principles as a tool ill-suited to economic matters,[46] which require more agile regulation. The first obstacle, which is both the starting point for the research and a source of curiosity for the researcher, lies in the minimization, or even rejection, of the role of intention, the reasons for which need to be understood.

Section III

5. **A contradicted hypothesis: the rejection of intention in competition law – the result of confusion between intention and motive.** From the earliest years of Community construction, the fate of intention seemed sealed: the majority doctrine rejected it in the name of the "objective" nature of the discipline.[47]

43 A. Bailleux, The Fiftieth Shade of Grey Competition Law, "Criministrative Law" and "Fairly Fair Trials," *in* Do Labels Still Matter? Blurring Boundaries Between Administrative and Criminal Law: The Influence of the EU 137 (F. Galli & A. Weyembergh eds., 2014). With fines having increased exponentially over the past twenty years, it is all the more important to ensure that the principles of criminal law are respected. In this respect, *see* W. P. J. Wils, *The Increased Level of EU Antitrust Fines, Judicial Review and the ECHR*, 33 World Competition 5 (2010).

44 On this subject, *see* R. Sicurella, Nulla poena sine culpa*: Un véritable principe droit européen?*, Revue de science criminelle et de droit pénal comparé 15 (2002).

45 Sud Fondi v. Italy, App. no. 75909/01, ¶ 116 (ECtHR Jan. 20, 2009): Article 7 of the Convention requires "a link of an intellectual nature (conscience and will) making it possible to detect an element of responsibility in the conduct of the material perpetrator of the offence" (unofficial translation); for a commentary, *see* R. Sicurella, *Développer une culture pénale européenne: De l'européanisation des principes fondamentaux du droit pénal à une théorie "européenne" de la responsabilité pénale*, 1 Revue de science criminelle et de droit pénal comparé 1, 14–15 (2020).

46 J.-B. Perrier & J.-C. Roda, *Droit pénal et droit de la concurrence*, *in* Le droit pénal et l'éthique des affaires 127, 127–28 (J.-B. Perrier ed., 2018): "Economic law has often been distanced from the ethical concerns [of criminal law], the emphasis being placed on the primary objective of ensuring market efficiency. As for criminal law, it has long been considered a tool ill-suited to economic matters, with some authors seeing in its use 'a sign of the immaturity' of the market."

47 For a summary of these debates, *see* L. Focsaneanu, *La notion d'abus dans le système de l'article 86 du Traité instituant la Communauté économique européenne*, *in* La réglementation du comportement des monopoles et entreprises dominantes en droit communautaire 324, 362–63 (J. A. Van Damme ed., 1977). At the time, the author remarked that "citations in support of the alleged objective character of abusive exploitation could easily be multiplied, as they reflect the predominant doctrine," *id.* at 363. A few decades earlier, in tort

Now that the debate has been settled, it has temporarily died down. The subject has, however, been the subject of renewed attention, albeit discreet,[48] over the last twenty years or so. The number of French works on the subject remains relatively small,[49] while the majority of studies on the subject have focused on U.S. law.[50] It is worth taking a closer look, as American authors have profoundly influenced, and at the same time led astray, European doctrine.

As early as 1890, Senator John Sherman declared that requiring intent would impose an impossible condition and defeat the purpose of antitrust law.[51] Subsequently, the most influential opponent of taking intention into account was Richard Posner,[52] initiator and promoter of the economic approach to competition law, who believed that "any doctrine that relies on proof of intention will be, at best, erratically applied."[53] Intention should be irrelevant, as only the procompetitive or anticompetitive effects generated by conduct would matter in deciding whether it was infringing.[54] The case law of the U.S. Supreme Court has fluctuated with regard

---

law, Paul Roubier had similarly excluded the criterion of intention from his theory of unfair competition, *see* P. Roubier, *Théorie générale de l'action en concurrence déloyale*, RTD COM. 541, 560 (1948).

48 Although countless symposia have been organized on the "economic approach" or its avatars, none has ever focused on intention, and the studies dedicated to it are only rarely cited by legal scholars.

49 V. Dobre, L'intention fautive en droit européen de la concurrence (2020) (Ph.D. dissertation, Université Paris X Nanterre); *see also* the developments in the following thesis: A.-S. CHONÉ-GRIMALDI, LES ABUS DE DOMINATION: ESSAI EN DROIT DES CONTRATS ET EN DROIT DE LA CONCURRENCE 163–94, 259–61 (2010), nos. 236–274 and nos. 396–400; S. Bringuier-Fau, *La volonté en droit de la concurrence, in* DE LA VOLONTÉ INDIVIDUELLE 166 (M. Nicod ed., 2010); R. Bouscant, *La faute dans les infractions aux règles de concurrence en droit européen*, RTD EUR. 67 (2000). In 2004, the Conseil de la concurrence [Competition Council] published a study on intent, but this was confined to cartels, and more specifically to the place of intent in the alternative between "object" and "effect," *see* Cons. conc., *Études thématiques: Objet, effet et intention anticoncurrentiels, in* RAPPORT D'ACTIVITÉ 55 (Mar. 30, 2004). *Adde* a commentary on the judgment: Case C-549/10 P, Tomra, ECLI:EU:C:2012:221: A.-L. Sibony, *La CJUE précise la pertinence de l'intention pour la qualification d'abus de position dominante*, CONCURRENCES no. 3-2012, art. no. 48339, 101.

50 *See, inter alia*, J. H. Bishop, *Criminal Intent as Applied to Conspiracy Under the Sherman Act*, XI VIRGINIA LAW REVIEW 417 (Apr. 1925); M. C. Quinn, *Predatory Pricing Strategies: The Relevance of Intent Under Antitrust, Unfair Competition, and Tort Law*, 64 ST. JOHN'S LAW REVIEW 607 (Spring-Summer 1990); W. S. Comanor & H. E. Frech, *Predatory Pricing and the Meaning of Intent*, 38 THE ANTITRUST BULLETIN 293 (Summer 1993); R. A. Cass & K. N. Hylton, *Antitrust Intent*, 74 SOUTHERN CALIFORNIA LAW REVIEW 657 (Jan. 2001); O. Odudu, *The Role of Specific Intent in Section 1 of the Sherman Act: A Market Power Test?*, 25 WORLD COMPETITION 463 (2002). M. Lao, *Reclaiming a Role for Intent Evidence in Monopolization Analysis*, 54 AMERICAN UNIVERSITY LAW REVIEW 151 (2004); M. Lao, *Aspen Skiing and Trinko: Antitrust Intent and "Sacrifice,"* 73 ANTITRUST LAW JOURNAL 171 (2005); M. E. Stucke, *Is Intent Relevant?*, 8 JOURNAL OF LAW, ECONOMICS & POLICY 801 (Autumn 2012). *Adde*, for a comparative analysis of U.S. and EU law, *see* M. João Melícias, *Use and Abuse of Intent Evidence in Antitrust Analysis*, 33 WORLD COMPETITION 569 (2010).

51 E. W. KINTNER, 1 THE LEGISLATIVE HISTORY OF THE FEDERAL ANTITRUST LAWS AND RELATED STATUTES 115 (1978).

52 Richard Posner has also proposed an economic analysis of intent. According to the author, "the concept of intent in criminal law serves three economic functions: identifying pure coercive tranfers, estimating the probability of apprehension and conviction, and determining whether the criminal sanction will be an effective (cost-justified) means of controlling undesirable conduct." *See* R. Posner, *An Economic Theory of the Criminal Law*, 85 COLUMBIA LAW REVIEW 1193, 1221 (1985).

53 R. POSNER, ANTITRUST LAW 214–15 (2nd ed., 2001). The author continues: "Judges and juries do not always understand that the availability of evidence of illegitimate intent is often a function of the defendant's luck and legal sophistication, not the underlying reality. A company whose executives are sensitized to competition law will not leave a documentary trail of improper intent; a company whose executives lack such sensitivity will often create ample evidence of such intent simply by a clumsy choice of words to describe innocent behavior."

54 Stucke, *Is Intent Relevant?*, *op. cit.* at 820.

to the role attributed to intent,[55] to which both criticism of the concept and uncertainty about its boundaries[56] have undoubtedly contributed. In *Olympia*,[57] the opinion of Judge Richard Posner is edifying: he considers that the intention reflected in the bellicose language used by a representative of the respondent company towards its competitor[58] should not be taken into account, since the ferment of competition is rivalry, which postulates the desire to oust one's competitors.[59] At this point, doesn't the jurist immediately perceive an elementary confusion between intention and motive?[60] Intention alone is a constitutive element – the mental element must be proven – and, clearly, a motive is not sufficient to characterize an offense. The rejection of intent thus appears to be the result of a semantic error that mixes two clearly distinct notions.

However, despite the fragile, if not erroneous, nature of the argument put forward to exclude the relevance of the concept, the terms of the American debate nonetheless sowed the seeds of a perennial misunderstanding in Europe.[61] Likewise, doctrine and jurisprudence[62] *confused* intent *with motive*,[63] and treated it not as a constitutive element, but as an unreliable clue, sometimes relevant, but never sufficient to qualify an anticompetitive practice. According to the prevailing view, reference to intent "adds virtually nothing to the analysis," it is an "imprecise and elusive concept," and its proof "by its very nature suspect (if not vain or inept)."[64] Sometimes set up as a "qualification test" to corroborate

55 *See* Lao, *Aspen Skiing and Trinko: Antitrust Intent and "Sacrifice," op. cit.* at 171–208.

56 The mental element, "*mens rea*" in English, is subject to a wide variety of interpretations in the United States. R. Batey, *Judicial Exploitation of Mens Rea Confusion, at Common Law and under the Model Penal Code*, 18 Georgia State University Law Review 341, 355–59 and 380–81 (2001).

57 Olympia Equipment Leasing Co. v. Western Union Telegraph Co., 797 F.2[d] 370 (7th Cir. 1986).

58 In this case, "These turkeys ought to be flushed!" – an expression that needs no translation.

59 In *Olympia*, Judge Posner expressed himself as follows in his opinion: "Most businessmen don't like their competitors, or for that matter competition. They want to make as much money as possible and getting a monopoly is one way of making a lot of money. That is fine, however, so long as they do not use methods calculated to make consumers worse off in the long run." In French unfair competition law, *see* the following article: A. Pirovano, *La concurrence déloyale en droit français*, 26 Revue internationale de droit comparé 467, 487 (1974): it would be impossible to distinguish good from bad intent, since "competition, which is competition, postulates the commission of prejudices!"

60 Intention being the objective pursued, and motive the subjective reasons why the individual pursues this goal.

61 European studies on the subject systematically refer to American positions.

62 *See, inter alia*, Case C-680/20, Unilever Italia, ECLI:EU:C:2023:33, para. 45: "[P]roof of an anti-competitive intention ... constitutes an indication of the nature and objectives pursued by the strategy of that undertaking and, on that basis, may be taken into account. ...However, *demonstration of the existence of such an intention is neither necessary nor sufficient*, in itself, to establish the existence of an abuse of a dominant position, since the concept of 'abuse', within the meaning of Article 102 TFEU, is based on an *objective assessment* of the conduct in question" (emphasis added).

63 To our knowledge, the only study that clearly distinguishes intention from motive in competition law is the following: P. L. Parcu, *Considerazioni sulla rilevanza del movente nella valutazione delle violazioni antitrust*, *in* ix Antitrust Between EU Law & National Law 341, 370–80 (E. A. Raffaelli ed., 2011).

64 B. Hawk, *À propos de la "concurrence par les mérites": Regards croisés sur l'article 82 CE et la Section 2 du Sherman Act*, Concurrences no. 3-2005, art. no. 231, 33, 34–35, esp. nos. 13–14.

the existence of an anticompetitive effect,[65] or castigated for creating a useless legal category,[66] its role is said to vary from case to case, making the notion resistant to any unitary theorization. Indeed, the study of intent is almost systematically confined to abuses of dominant position,[67] particularly predatory pricing practices.[68] Very few comprehensive studies have been carried out,[69] and these have studied infringements in succession, without developing a general theory or avoiding the aforementioned pitfalls.

There is, however, a textual argument in favor of taking intention into account: the Regulation on the implementation of the rules on competition stipulates that a fine may only be imposed on an undertaking if it has committed the infringement "intentionally or negligently"[70] – negligence being, in practice, treated as an attenuating circumstance, and systematically confused with an error of law[71]. As for the reference to "deliberate intent," it would imply, as it is inserted in the chapter on sanctions, that intention is taken into consideration only at the stage of imposing the fine, but not at the stage of characterizing the offense[72] – which presupposes

---

65 *Ex multis*: P. Akman, *The Role of Intent in the EU Case Law on Abuse of Dominance*, 39 European Law Review 316, 319 (2014); A. Bavasso, *The Role of Intent Under Article 82 EC: From "Flushing the Turkeys" to "Spotting Lionesses in Regent's Park,"* 11 European Competition Law Review 616, 619 (2005); Bringuier-Fau, *La volonté en droit de la concurrence, op. cit.* at 166: "In competition law, voluntariness is taken into account in the analysis of an economic process. …It is apprehended… by the economist, who uses it as a starting point for a prospective search for market harm."

66 R. Nazzini, The Foundations of European Union Competition Law: The Objectives and Principles of Article 102, 58 (2011).

67 The only study devoted to the role of intention in agreement matters is the following: O. Odudu, *Interpreting Article 81(1): Object as Subjective Intention*, 26 European Law Review 62 (2001). However, it limits the role of intention to "by object" agreements, excluding "by effect" infringements from its scope.

68 T. Eilmansberger, *How to Distinguish Good From Bad Competition Under Article 82 EC: In Search of Clearer and More Coherent Standards for Anti-Competitive Abuses*, 42 Common Market Law Review 129, 146–52, 170–77 (2005); Bavasso, *The Role of Intent Under Article 82 EC: From "Flushing the Turkeys" to "Spotting Lionesses in Regent's Park," op. cit.* at 616–23; T. Eilmansberger, *Dominance – The Lost Child? How Effects-Based Rules Could and Should Change Dominance Analysis*, 2 European Competition Journal 15 (2006); Akman, *The Role of Intent in the EU Case Law on Abuse of Dominance, op. cit.*; C. O'Grady, *The Role of Exclusionary Intent in the Enforcement of Article 102*, 37 World Competition 459 (2014); on Italian decision-making practice on abuse of predation, M. Siragusa, *Italy – New Forms of Abuse of Dominance and Abuse of Law*, *in* Abuse of Dominance in EU Competition Law: Emerging Trends 119 (P. L. Parcu et al. eds., 2017); P. L. Parcu & M. L. Stasi, *The Role of Intent in the Assessment of Conduct under Article 102 TFEU*, *in* Abuse of Dominance in EU Competition Law: Emerging Trends 12 (P. L. Parcu et al. eds., 2017).

69 Three recent theses should be mentioned, dealing with both agreements and abuse of dominant positions: Dobre, L'intention fautive en droit européen de la concurrence, *op. cit.*; F. Costa-Cabral, Intent in EU Competition Law: The Judicial Assessment of Anti-Competitive Strategies (2014) (Ph.D. dissertation, King's College London); J. Blockx, *Mens Rea* in EU Antitrust Law: When Intentions Matter (2020); for a synthesis, J. Blockx, *Revaluing the Role of Intent Evidence in EU Antitrust Law*, 3 European Competition and Regulatory Law Review 354 (2019).

70 Council Regulation (EC) No. 1/2003 of Dec. 16, 2002, on the Implementation of the Rules on Competition Laid Down in Articles 81 and 82 of the Treaty, 2003 O.J. (L 1) 1, art. 23(2).

71 Blockx, *Mens Rea* in EU Antitrust Law: When Intentions Matter, *op. cit.* at 153, no. 502; L. Bernardeau & J.-P. Christienne, Les amendes en droit de la concurrence: Pratique décisionnelle et contrôle juridictionnel du droit de l'Union 181 (2013), no. 380.

72 In this regard, *see* Bouscant, *La faute dans les infractions aux règles de concurrence en droit européen, op. cit.* at 67.

admitting that an offense that would not be the product of any intention suddenly requires a mental element, depending on the stage of reasoning. Such an assertion would, however, run counter to the analysis frequently adopted by case law, more or less explicitly, when judges use terms or expressions from the lexical field of intention, such as "strategy," "plan," "with the aim of," "on purpose," "with the objective of," to qualify the litigious conduct.

In short, since competition law is, at first glance, neither a very hospitable ground for intention nor, because of the confusion it conveys, a field of exploration offering a clear picture of it, a detour along the path of criminal law, which is marked out by rigorous principles, appeared necessary – although it was also fraught with pitfalls.

Section IV

6. **A new direction: in search of a definition of intent – a detour via criminal law.** Although criminal law should have made it easy to define intent, the disappointment lived up to expectations. Intention is among the most challenging subjects,[73] and while difficulty, like a challenge, can spark interest,

73 André Decocq had alerted his doctoral student Adrien-Charles Dana, who was about to undertake a doctorate involving the study of intention: "The project was enough to worry a thesis supervisor. M. Dana's supervisor shared his fears with him, pointing out that, among other things, such a project implied a reading program far out of proportion to what the preparation of a thesis ordinarily requires," A. Decocq, *Préface*, *in* A.-C. Dana, Essai sur la notion d'infraction pénale xi, xii (1982); G. Levasseur, *Étude de l'élément moral de l'infraction*, xvii Annales de la Faculté de droit et de sciences économiques de Toulouse 81, 84–85 (1969), fasc. 1: "Doctrine finds itself ... in a particularly difficult position when it attempts to construct a coherent, comprhensive and logical system capable of accounting for very concise legislative texts and case law that is at once varied, confused on many points and evolving for certain offenses"; J. B. Herzog, *La prévention des infractions involontaires contre la vie et l'intégrité de la personne humaine*, *in* 1 La prévention des infractions contre la vie humaine et l'intégrité de la personne 207, 215 (A. Besson & M. Ancel eds., 1956): "Criminal science undoubtedly has no problem more delicate to resolve than that of guilt"; Y. Mayaud, *L'intention dans la théorie du droit pénal*, xii Problèmes actuels de science criminelle 57, 57 (1999): "[I]f the reference to intention is constant, giving the illusion of a familiar concept, it must nonetheless be acknowledged that the realities unfolding under the cover of intention are far from certain. One can be convinced of this from the outset by consulting doctrine and analyzing case law. Not everything aligns: major differences exist from one author to another, from one decision to the next, revealing a certain unease – at times bordering on uncertainty – so evident are the contradictions and profound the divergences"; P. Mimin, *L'intention et le mobile*, *in* La chambre criminelle et sa jurisprudence: Recueil d'études en hommage à la mémoire de Maurice Patin 114, 115 (1965): "The difficulty, the impossibility perhaps, of giving a satisfactory definition of intent ... embarrasses any mind that studies the works of criminal law scholars"; R. Merle & A. Vitu, Traité de droit criminel 719 (7th ed. 1997), no. 572: the mental element has "become an inexhaustible field of controversy comparable in certain respects to civil law discussions on the notion of cause in obligations"; J. Lebret, *Essai sur la notion de l'intention criminelle*, Revue de science criminelle et de droit pénal comparé 438, 451–52 (1938): "[We] had to draw up a sort of report of shortcomings. The theory of intent, when considered in its practical applications, is as narrow and as disappointing as possible. ... Common expressions ... refer to a diluted notion, perhaps even ... quite empty." M. Puech, Droit pénal général 183 (1988), no. 510: "The theory of intent is one of the least enlightened subjects in criminal law"; E. Wagner, La notion d'intention pénale dans la doctrine classique et la jurisprudence contemporaine 1–3 (1976) (Ph.D. dissertation, Université de Clermont-Ferrand): "Undertaking a study of intent immediately places the person who engages in it on one of the most uncomfortable terrains of thought: that of paradox. ...It is as if everyone were simultaneously convinced of its intellectual beauty and its utter uselessness," and while "ancient authors were already complaining about the difficulty of the study" and that "difficulty attracts the daring mind," it is nevertheless "rather fear that prevails"; B. Mercadal, *Recherches sur l'intention en droit pénal*, 1 Revue de science criminelle et de droit pénal comparé 1, 8 (Jan.–Mar. 1967): "Not only is the necessity itself of the intentional element not legally determined, but the content of this element is also ambiguous"; M. Benillouche, *La subjectivisation de l'élément moral de l'infraction: Plaidoyer pour une nouvelle*

it can also mislead, discourage, or even cause one to lose a sense of proportion.[74] While the classic definition of the concept is uncontroversial, as intent presupposes both knowledge and the will[75] of a result,[76] it was gradually subdivided into various forms of *dol* – general, special, eventual, preterintentional, simple, aggravated, etc. – the number of which increases if we add the French subdivisions to those of other countries[77] – even though these numerous categories, based on a psychological approach to the agent, do not systematically lead to differences in regime in practice.[78] In addition, the principle laid down in all European penal codes, according to which crimes and offenses are intentional, unless the legislator has made an exception,[79] has been rightly criticized since, depending on the definition of intent, several crimes would not be intentional, while certain contraventions would require intent.[80] In addition to these debates on the definition and regime of intention, its scope was also narrowed in favor of competing notions such as imputability, capacity and causality, the boundaries of the latter being highly variable according to the authors.[81]

---

théorie de la culpabilité, Revue de science criminelle et de droit pénal comparé 529 (2005): the mental element is a concept that "remains obscure to this day"; J.-H. Robert, Droit pénal général 320 (6th ed. 2005): "[M]odern literature as a whole offers a picture of great disharmony. The different forms and varieties of intent are classified into various '*dols*,' each assigned an adjective… This system of vocabulary is unfortunately quite unusual in the writing of repressive texts," giving the overall impression of being in the middle of a great "labyrinth."

74 Ludwig Harscher von Almendingen, for example, concludes his long years of research into intention in a style similar to that of the German Romantics: "I believe I have placed a valuable offering on the altar of truth. A new light has dawned on me, a new horizon has opened up before my eyes; I know this, and I welcome it for the guardian angel of humanity. Posterity will have to judge whether the dawn of truth has been revealed or only the deceptive glow of an illusion formed of vain vapors," L. H. von Almendingen, Untersuchungen über das kulpose Verbrechen 250 (1804), quoted and translated in French by R. Griffon, De l'intention en droit pénal 29 (1911).

75 E. Garçon, i Code pénal annoté 8 (2nd ed. 1952), no. 77; H. Donnedieu de Vabres, Traité élémentaire de droit criminel et de législation pénale comparée 70 (2nd ed. 1943), no. 126; R. Garraud, i Traité théorique et pratique du droit pénal français 571, 574 (3rd ed. 1913), nos. 287 and 288; J. Verhaegen, *La définition de l'intention coupable dans les codes pénaux modernes*, *in* i Liber amicorum Frédéric Dumon 527, 529 (1983); J. Pradel, Droit pénal comparé 104 (4th ed. 2016), no. 67.

76 But are we talking about the legal result (i.e., the will to knowingly break the law), or the material result (the will to achieve a concrete result)? On this distinction, *see* E. Villey, *De l'intention en matière pénale*, i La France judiciaire 1 (1876), doctrine.

77 For an enumeration in Latin, *see* J. Jimenez De Asua, *La faute consciente et le "dolus eventualis,"* Revue de droit pénal et de criminologie 603, 610 (1959–1960).

78 Even the most classic subdivision, between general and special *dol*, has been the subject of pertinent criticism, cf. Puech, Droit pénal général, *op. cit.* at 185, no. 513; or R. Legros, L'élément moral dans les infractions 333 (1952).

79 Pradel, Droit pénal comparé, *op. cit.* at 103, no. 66; *adde*, in the same vein, J. Verhaegen, *L'exigence de l'intention coupable dans les infractions aux lois et règlements particuliers*, Revue de droit pénal et de criminologie no. 12, 947, 947 (1986).

80 Legros, L'élément moral dans les infractions, *op. cit.* at 98–100: "[T]he will to achieve the result is required only when the law necessarily provides for it. Apart from these exceptional cases, simple will is all that is required… The will to achieve the result is not required in principle, even in the case of crimes and offenses: it is only required when the law demands it."

81 R. Merle, Droit pénal général complémentaire 180 (1957): "The greatest anarchy presides over the doctrinal delimitation of the very similar concepts of responsibility, imputability and culpability"; *adde*, in the same vein, G. Levasseur, *L'imputabilité des infractions en droit français*, Revue de droit pénal et de criminologie nos. 5–6, 387, 388–89 (1969): "It must be said that the issue of imputability is one of the least well clarified in French law. … 'Responsibility,' 'culpability,' 'imputability,' and 'criminal capacity'

Finally, in line with the general trend towards objectivization of legal techniques, theories were developed that had their counterpart in tort law,[82] giving rise to the idea of "objective," "no-fault" criminal liability,[83] which, while ultimately only a passing fad, did little to clarify the meaning of a concept that had gradually become obscure.

So, regardless of the direction the jurist takes, whether in competition law or criminal law, they struggle to find a way out – as positive law offers few landmarks for those who dream of a blueprint. The way out, then, consisted of a temporary retreat into the past, where the difficulties gradually dissipated, thanks to the discovery of the "underlying sedimentary layers" of contemporary theories.[84]

Section V

7. **A historical discovery: the original recognition of the role of intent in competition law, and the reasons for its gradual disappearance.** Although the birth of competition law is generally traced back to the Sherman Act, passed in 1890, the discipline has much older ancestors.[85] Interest in the notion of rivalry, and the distinction between desirable competition and that which leads human beings and society to their ruin, can already be found in Hesiod's poem, *Works and Days.*[86] As far back as antiquity, hoarding and monopolies were severely punished, and intent required, as evidenced by both Roman law and the first trial to have survived, recorded in Lysias' speech *Against the Corn Dealers.*[87] Aristotle, in particular in his *Nicomachean Ethics*,[88] undertook a comprehensive reflection on trade, not dissociating economic and legal perspectives, and placed

are notions whose use by authors is not without some confusion"; R. Ottenhof, *Imputabilité, culpabilité et responsabilité en droit pénal*, 2 Archives de politique criminelle 71, 72 (2000): "The concept of imputability is one of the vaguest and most controversial in French criminal law. Its complexity only increases when, as is the case here, we try to situate it in relation to the concepts of culpability and responsibility."

82 M. Planiol, Traité élémentaire de droit civil 304–305 (1931), no. 863 ter: according to Marcel Planiol, the idea of basing civil liability no longer on fault but on risk was a "new idea" that "appealed to young minds both because it presented the problem of liability with apparent scientific rigor and because it appealed to the idea of social solidarity."

83 *Ex multis, see* A. Legal, *La responsabilité sans faute, in* La chambre criminelle et sa jurisprudence: Recueil d'études en hommage à la mémoire de Maurice Patin 130, 131 (1965): the author considers that "we are thus moving towards a rapprochement between the principles of criminal law and the solutions of civil law, which tend to base the obligation to make reparation no longer on fault, but on the creation of a risk."

84 C. Atias, Théorie contre arbitraire 217 (1987).

85 For a history of competition law, *see* D. Bosco & C. Prieto, Droit européen de la concurrence 17–109 (2013), nos. 3–118.

86 Hesiod, Theogony and Works and Days (M. L. West trans., Oxford Univ. Press 2008).

87 Lysias, Against the Corn Dealers (W. R. M. Lamb trans., Harvard Univ. Press 1930).

88 Aristotle, Nicomachean Ethics (H. Rackham trans., Harvard Univ. Press 1926).

intention at the heart of the division between good and bad chrematistics. The Stagirite is also the first to offer a theory of intent that is both simple and singularly modern. Subsequent rediscovery of ancient teachings enabled Scholastics – notably Thomas Aquinas, Lessius, Olivi, and Molina – as well as doctors of law, to refine theories and extend traditions. A *continuum* thus unites antiquity and old law, the gradual sedimentation of principles having conditioned the formation of a *common ius*, both with regard to the notion of intention itself and its central role in the repression of hoarding and monopoly.

Nevertheless, from the eighteenth onwards, economic science, detaching itself from philosophy, became autonomous and claimed the same objectivity and accuracy as the natural sciences. Under the impetus of Bentham and Mill, the utilitarian current, which today serves as an ersatz philosophy for competition law,[89] undertook a complete overhaul of morality, breaking with tradition,[90] supposedly to provide a "scientific" foundation for this notion suddenly deemed "anarchic."[91] Such an ambition implied measuring the lawfulness of an act by its *results* on the "greatest happiness of the greatest number"[92] – such a utility calculation being, despite the growing sophistication of economic analysis, no more possible today than it was three centuries ago.[93] However, whereas the known origins of the discipline, only maneuvering constituted an offense and aroused a strong moral stigma, contemporary competition law was born in the twentieth century in an entirely different landscape and has since been perceived as a discipline where *outcomes matter more than intentions* – functioning as a tool that must be "efficient" in deploying an economic policy aimed at fostering the greatest happiness of the consumer.

At the same time, the nascent codification movement led each country to retreat into its own legal system. The result was a gradual fragmentation of theories on the most established notions, foremost among which was intention, and a relative neglect of past solutions. Intention seemed to lose importance, but only in appearance. It was gradually buried under a superimposition of layers, due to the increasing complexity of doctrinal theorizations of the concept, as well as to the consequentialist perspective

---

89 Indeed, the vast majority of contemporary economic analysis is utilitarian. Moreover, the connection between Benthamian utilitarianism and Posnerian economic theories has been noted by a number of authors, *see, e.g.*, R. Dworkin, Taking Rights Seriously vii, ix, 97–98 (1977); H. L. A. Hart, *American Jurisprudence Through English Eyes: The Nightmare and the Noble Dream*, 11 Georgia Law Review 969, 987–88 (1977); R. A. Epstein, *The Next Generation of Legal Scholarship*, 30 Stanford Law Review 635, 645 (1978).

90 On this theme, *see* D. Baranger, Penser la loi: Essai sur le législateur des temps modernes 210–60 (2018).

91 E. Halévy, 3 Le radicalisme philosophique : La formation du radicalisme philosophique 226 (PUF 1996) (1901–1904).

92 The formula was originally coined by Helvétius, Treatise on Man, His Intellectual Faculties and His Education (W. Hooper trans., 1777); it was later taken up by Bentham, Beccaria and John Stuart Mill.

93 J.-P. Cléro, *Le calcul benthamien des plaisirs et des peines: Calcul introuvable ou seulement indéfiniment différé?*, 78 Archives de Philosophie 229 (2015).

adopted by competition law. Nevertheless, like a groundswell, and despite the contemporary dogma of effects, the concept continued to underpin the discipline's solutions, creating a contradiction between the image it conjures up and the reasoning it implicitly mobilizes. Having traced the first lineaments of a theory of intent, it was now time to go beyond the controversies surrounding the concept and transform the hypothesis into a thesis in order to demonstrate its continuing role in competition law.

Section VI

8. **The need for a general theory of intent.** The initial aim of conceptualizing intent was to demonstrate the concept's *autonomy* in competition law. In the first place, it was autonomous *ratione personae*: since the subject of competition law is the company, it was necessary to determine whether it could be recognized as having its own intention, and in what specific ways this intention could be attributed to it. However, the links between the liability of legal entities and that of the company became apparent, and the impression of autonomy faded. The aim was then to identify the irreducible differences between civil liability law and criminal law, but once again, at the end of the research, it was the conceptual identity that stood out. However, a final vector of autonomization seemed undeniable. As competition law is part of European Union law, the concept of intent had to have been conceptualized autonomously from those of the Member States.[94] However, on the one hand, the concept had not been clearly theorized by European judges[95] and, on the other, a concept could not be accepted by Member States if it clashed with their legal traditions, with the result that its elaboration at the Union level remained dependent on national theoretical constructs.[96] It was therefore necessary to have recourse to comparative law[97] to overcome the artificial oppositions between countries and establish the parallels uniting them[98] in order to

94 Opinion of Advocate General Y. Bot, Case C-72/11, Mohsen Afrasiabi, ECLI:EU:C:2011:737, paras. 43–44: the Advocate General notes that the definition of the terms "knowingly" and "intentionally" "must be interpreted given an autonomous and uniform interpretation throughout the Union." The autonomy of the notion of "intent" is also clearly expressed in the ECN+ Directive, *see* Directive (EU) 2019/1 of the European Parliament and of the Council of Dec. 11, 2018, to Empower the Competition Authorities of the Member States to be More Effective Enforcers and to Ensure the Proper Functioning of the Internal Market, 2019 O.J. (L 11) 3, recital 42.

95 J. Blomsma, Mens Rea and Defences in European Criminal Law 6 (2012).

96 On this subject, *see* P. Pescatore, *Le recours, dans la jurisprudence de la Cour de justice des communautés européennes, à des normes déduites de la comparaison des droits des États membres*, Revue internationale de droit comparé 337 (1980).

97 This comparison has taken a two-pronged approach, confronting both contemporary and ancient theories, and different legal systems – as the following book invites us to do: R. Sacco, La comparaison juridique au service de la connaissance du droit (1991).

98 According to Rodolfo Sacco, this is the role of doctrine, *see* R. Sacco, *Droit commun de l'Europe, et composantes du droit*, *in* Nouvelles perspectives d'un droit commun 95, 103 (M. Cappelletti ed., 1978).

develop a theory of intent. Although this theory was initially intended to apply only to competition law, the path we followed ultimately contradicted the idea that intention had characteristics specific to this discipline. On the contrary, the study revealed the *transversal nature of* the concept, which necessitated the development of a *general theory* that, by transcending the divisions between countries and different areas of the law, proposes a new classification of offenses according to their moral element. This has served as a reading grid and theoretical foundation for discovering and demonstrating that, despite its apparent rejection, intent plays a fundamental role in positive competition law.

Section VII

9. **A thesis: the fundamental role of intent in competition law.** Once the principles that originally founded the law of anti-competitive practices were rediscovered, and after the concept of intent was conceptualized through a general theory, the role of the latter became clear. It made it possible to approach the discipline through the prism of classic legal reasoning, and to take a fresh look at some of the most hotly debated theoretical issues – notably the alternative between object and effect, and the concept of restriction of competition. A paradox emerged: while the constant, if not exclusive, concern of competition law seems to be the "effects" produced by litigious behavior, it would be possible, as proposed at the end of the research, to remove the notion of effect, and all the related theories, from competition analysis, without altering the established solutions. Indeed, despite the influence of U.S. antitrust law on European law, the position of EU judges has not changed substantially in the wake of the "modernization" wave: case law has not endorsed the consequentialist perspective advocated by supporters of the more economic approach. As the guardian of continuity, the Court of Justice, unlike the U.S. Supreme Court, did not yield to the siren calls of the Chicago School, preserving the identity of the European model, whose superiority over its American counterpart is today affirmed by some.[99] European competition law has remained focused on behavior rather than results, and has continued, more or less explicitly, to rely more on legal presumptions than on economic analysis. Competitive *legal reasoning*, the study of which is often neglected, thus calls for rediscovery. *De lege lata*, the thesis demonstrates that intent plays a role in the characterization of anticompetitive practices, as a constitutive element, unlike effects, which do not require proof. Intent

99 The U.S. Supreme Court is far more sensitive to political changes than the Court of Justice. However, it is now argued that the so-called more economic or effects-based approach has led to an under-application of competition rules and, consequently, to an unprecedented concentration of economic power in U.S. markets. On this subject, *see* J. B. Baker, The Antitrust Paradigm: Restoring a Competitive Economy 1–7 (2019).

also plays a part in defining offenses – abuse of a dominant position and agreement offenses having been defined, in a unified manner, as "*dol* with market power." *De lege ferenda*, it is argued that adopting the theory of intent would simplify competition law, thereby improving its readability, effectiveness, and adaptability to contemporary issues.

Ultimately, the thesis calls for a significant paradigm shift, which, although it may appear to represent a break from the current theoretical frameworks of competition law, nonetheless makes coherent and systematic reference to positive law and constitutes a reconnection with its traditional foundations. The choice of plan was thus conditioned by a hopeful determination to win over readers despite the distance separating the proposed theory from the dominant paradigm. To this end, the plan adopts a dynamic approach, tracing the evolution of the research and enabling readers to assess their adherence to the statements made at each stage.[100] The itinerary of the thesis is thus similar to that of its introduction: the conceptualization of intent (**Part I**) precedes the theorization of its role in competition law (**Part II**).

100 For a similar approach, *see* E. Gaillard, Le pouvoir en droit privé 18 (1985), no. 17.

PART I

THE CONCEPT OF INTENT

10. **Discover the historical and conceptual foundations of intent in competition law.** The complexity of contemporary competition law makes it difficult to grasp the underlying legal principles and reasoning clearly and unequivocally. The discipline seems to leave more room for economic and political considerations than for major legal concepts. Thus, in a field reputed "objective," the place of intention is apparently minimal,[1] even though it is in fact fundamental. Only a genealogy of the link between intention and competition law can account for both its antiquity and its persistence. Once this link has been re-established, however, the researcher is faced with a major problem: intention, once theorized in a simple, unitary way, now counts among the most difficult subjects, so controversial is the notion.[2] It is therefore inconceivable to discuss its role in positive competition law without first untangling the threads that, as things stand, prevent us from precisely weaving the contours of the concept.

Knowledge of the historical development of intent (**Title I**) is therefore essential to justify the relevance of the subject, both because it attests to competition law's ongoing consideration of intent, and because it offers keys to understanding contemporary law. The conceptualization of intention in positive law, leading to the proposal of a general theory of intent (**Title II**), is a necessary prerequisite for the study, insofar as it will serve as a foundation and reading grid for developing a theory of intent in competition law.

1 *See supra*, no. 5.

2 *See supra*, no. 6.

Title I

The historical evolution of intent

11. **"The detour is the true path":[1] in search of principles.** Legal reasoning is never completely new: "[J]ust as newborn babies are inscribed in a society that precedes them," certain rules may appear innovative, but are no less interwoven "in an ancient fabric whose appearance they contribute to altering, and more rarely the weave."[2] The study of an institution cannot, therefore, do without the study of its historical continuity.[3] Yet research into the history of competition law is rare:[4] often, the birth of the discipline is presented as dating back to the passage of the Sherman Act in 1890. In fact, it has much older ancestors, whose knowledge is essential to understanding the essence of competition offenses,[5] as it reveals principles that have not been substantially altered since then. The same is true of intent: if doctrinal theorizations today are scattered and fragmentary – diverging within the same country, and from one country to another – the historical approach offers the opportunity to discover the lowest common denominator from which contemporary conceptualizations have developed.

---

1 V. Jankélévitch, L'aventure, l'ennui, le sérieux 217 (Flammarion 2017) (1963).

2 R. Libchaber, L'ordre juridique et le discours du droit: Essai sur les limites de la connaissance du droit 195 (2013).

3 C. Atias, *Une crise de légitimité seconde*, Droits 21, 29 (1986). *Adde* C. Atias, Le traitement des délinquants 24 (1991): according to the author, the definition of a crime is not reducible to the few lines of the incriminating text: it is the fruit of a history that is generally known by few and mastered by none.

4 However, the following important study should be noted: D. Bosco & C. Prieto, Droit européen de la concurrence 17–109 (2013), nos. 3–118.

5 In this sense, *see* R. Piotrowski, Cartels and Trusts: Their Origin and Historical Development From the Economic and Legal Aspects 363 (1933). For a discussion of the French, German, Italian and English debates on whether it is relevant to compare ancient monopolistic practices with contemporary anticompetitive practices, *see* pp. 117–30. The author regrets that, despite several attempts to demonstrate the depth of the link between ancient and contemporary law, general opinion remains reluctant to admit the usefulness of the historical approach in competition law: "The current science of cartels and trusts passes over in silence the whole history of the old movement up to the middle of the nineteenth century as being outside its scope."

12. **Semantic clarifications.** The term "*droit de la concurrence*" (competition law) is an anachronism for practices that were repressed in antiquity and the Middle Ages. The word "*concurrence*" (competition) did not appear until the seventeenth century,[6] and became widespread in the eighteenth century.[7] The choice to use this term stems from a linguistic convention: the terms "*accaparement*" (hoarding) and "*monopole*" (monopoly), which refer to the fraudulent practices of merchants, were often used synonymously, and could refer to both individual and collective behavior. For the sake of clarity, it therefore seemed appropriate to refer to them as "anticompetitive practices" or "competition law," even though these terms did not exist. Similarly, although contemporary authors sometimes distinguish between intention and will, the two terms will be used interchangeably here, as they were considered equivalent at the time.[8]

13. **Epistemological clarifications.** The historian Paul Veyne describes history as a narrative: just as a narrative never reaches the event in all its dimensions, "history sorts, simplifies, organizes, fits a century into a page" – this synthesis being no less spontaneous and forgetful than that of memory, when we try, in a few minutes, to relate several years of a life.[9] For this reason, the only requirement to be met by anyone embarking on a historical process is the veracity of the facts recounted, and the reliability of the sources.[10] And if we ask "What should the historian be interested in?" any answer is illusory, insofar as "it is impossible to fix a scale of importance that is not subjective."[11] The historical narrative is always incomplete, a construction produced by the "back-and-forth of inferences" that marks the limits of historical objectivity.[12]

    When it is the jurist who is interested in the past, their quest is guided by the search for what, in yesterday's law and philosophy, could shed light on today's legal system. Thus, it appears that intention was explicitly taken into account from the birth of competition law until the eighteenth

---

6 https://classiques-garnier.com/index.php/grand-corpus-des-dictionnaires-ixe-xxe-s.html. In the seventeenth century, the word "*concurrence*" was used synonymously with "*concourir.*" By the end of the seventeenth century, it gained a partly autonomous meaning: "*Prétention réciproque à la même charge, dignité, ou autre avantage. Souvent une cause de l'exclusion de l'un ou l'autre des prétendants.*" ["Reciprocal claim to the same office, dignity, or other advantage. Often a cause for the exclusion of one or other of the contenders."]

7 In a more modern sense, it appears in Montesquieu's *Esprit des Lois* (1748), which states: "[I]t is competition which sets a just value on merchandise, and establishes the relation between them" (The Spirit of Laws, bk. xx, at 352 (T. Nugent trans., 1752, Batoche Books 2001)); *see* R. de Roover, La pensée économique des scolastiques: Doctrine et méthode 16 (1971).

8 L. A. Zaibert, *Intentionality, Voluntariness, and Culpability: A Historical-Philosophical Analysis*, 1 Buffalo Criminal Law Review 459, 464 (1998).

9 P. Veyne, Comment on écrit l'histoire: Essai d'épistémologie 14 (1971).

10 *Id.* at 26.

11 *Id.* at 41.

12 *Id.* at 191. *Adde* W. Durant, 13 Histoire de la civilisation 262 (1963): "The historian always oversimplifies and hastily selects a manageable minority of facts and faces from a crowd of souls and events whose immense complexity they could never embrace or understand."

century (**Chapter 1**). It was not until the modern era that the principles of the past began, not to disappear, but rather, under the influence of scientific thought, positivism and the utilitarian trend, to fade into the background behind new theories that relegated them to a secondary position, although intention continued to *implicitly* underpin the solutions and spirit of competition law (**Chapter 2**).

Chapter 1
EARLY RECOGNITION

14. **A *continuum*, a tradition: the gradual sedimentation of principles.** Legal thought has its origins in distant forebears who have passed through the ages: studying the origins of a concept or rule thus provides access to an important phase in the development of principles, that of "common sense."[1] A form of competition law has existed since antiquity, and there was no doubt that intent was taken into account to repress the maneuvers of merchants (**Section 1**). From the thirteenth century onwards, following the rediscovery of Roman law and Aristotle's thought, ancient solutions were taken up, commented on, and clarified by Scholastics and doctors of law throughout Europe, enabling them to be disseminated and sedimented – thus constituting the common cultural heritage of European countries (**Section 2**).

Section 1
Recognizing intent in antiquity

15. **Anticompetitive practices in antiquity: criminal behavior.** From the very beginnings of civilization, just as writing was taking shape, the earliest mythological accounts reveal a veritable obsession with the profusion of foodstuffs and the abundance of means of subsistence: Sumerian literature never ceases to describe rivers of grain heaped up, orchards heavy with fruit, stables and sheepfolds filled to overflowing.[2] It is hardly surprising, then, that in later times, in Greece as in Rome, practices that

---

1 W. James, Pragmatism: A New Name for Some Old Ways of Thinking (1907) (N.B.: the author is not referring to law, but to thought in general).

2 S. N. Kramer, Le mariage sacré à Sumer et à Babylone 57–63 (J. Bottéro trans., 1983).

hindered trade by creating scarcity through *fraudulent means*, in order to take dishonest *advantage* of it, were considered atrocious crimes and severely punished. What was at stake was not the comfort of consumers who craved non-essential goods, but the survival of entire peoples. Such morally iniquitous behavior was systematically punished by criminal law.

16. **Severe criminal repression necessitating the existence of legal safeguards.** Penalties provided for under ancient criminal law were commensurate with the seriousness of such behavior: they ranged from temporary banishment to life imprisonment and, depending on the period, even the death penalty. It was therefore imperative to ensure that such punishments were not inflicted unjustly. For this reason, intent, taken into account from the very birth of criminal law (**Paragraph 1**), made it possible, as far as possible, to ensure a balance in the repression of anticompetitive practices (**Paragraph 2**).

Paragraph 1 – Characteristics of intent in ancient criminal law

17. **Intent, a functional concept.** Consideration of intent coincided with the birth of criminal law: as soon as a state was formed, there was a break with the archaic system, which was concerned only with damage. Intention made it possible to condemn only those individuals who had intended to do harm, and, in the event of damage, to mitigate the punishment of those who had not sought it. It is thus the symbol of the humanization of repression and the ethical foundation of the right to punish, as it offers the possibility of inflicting the fairest possible sentences (**I**). “As just as *possible*”: the limits of intention are precisely the limits of possibility. Adopting this criterion implies not only considering that humans are free but also positing that it is possible to discern their intentions. But nothing is less certain. The question of human freedom is an enigma and will always remain so; knowing the thoughts of others is impossible and, moreover, hardly desirable. Intention, however, was never based on *truths*, but on *postulates*, which are by their very nature unprovable. It is therefore a *pragmatic* elaboration, whose only function is to get closer to reality, without ever claiming to reach it (**II**).

I. A concept at the service of justice

18. **The transition from objective reaction to harm to subjective responsibility for fault.** Before human beings formed a society, and delegated the right to punish to the third-party arbiter, the State, the reaction to harm involved another form of evil: revenge. Revenge is blind, violent

and usually unjust. The one who avenges their family or tribe does not concern themselves with whether the offender acted on purpose but soothes their pain by retaliating against the offender in kind: they, too, become an executioner. The primitive reaction to crime was thus objective – the adjective could, in this context, only be pejorative (**A**). The birth of criminal law opened the door to taking account of the individual's state of mind – placing intention at the heart of its concerns from the outset (**B**).

A. Objective liability, characteristic of primitive societies

19. **The place of individuals in primitive societies.** In primitive societies, individuals count for very little – they blend into the group whose daily life is marked by a belief in the supernatural's influence on everyday life. These two characteristics – the predominance of the collective over the individual and mysticism – have a considerable influence on the reaction to crime.[3] The figure of the criminal does not yet exist. Since they did not act freely, but under the influence of the gods, holding human beings guilty would be meaningless. Individuals are responsible for nothing, guilty of nothing: they are *actors* in a chain of *events* beyond their control, not the *authors* of a *fault*.[4] Attention is focused entirely on the damage[5] – an external manifestation that breaks with order and is more the result of the will of the gods than of human wickedness. Vengeance and composition are thus an objective *reaction* against crime, not a subjective search for individual *responsibility*. Its function is neither punishment nor deterrence. It is not a matter of amending or rehabilitating the offender, but of erasing a stain[6] common to the entire offended clan.

20. **The objective, collective reaction to the damage suffered.** To use the term "responsibility" and then qualify it as "objective and collective" is a misuse of language, as the notion does not fit well with these two adjectives. The word "reaction" is more appropriate. This reaction is, on the one hand, *objective*[7]: automatic, indifferent to culpability, proportionate

---

3 H. Lévy-Bruhl, *Le point de vue de l'historien du droit*, VIII ANNALES DE LA FACULTÉ DE DROIT ET DE SCIENCES POLITIQUES ET ÉCONOMIQUES DE STRASBOURG 35, 35–37 (1961).

4 J. Poirier, *Les caractères de la responsabilité archaïque*, VIII ANNALES DE LA FACULTÉ DE DROIT ET DE SCIENCES POLITIQUES ET ÉCONOMIQUES DE STRASBOURG 19, 22 (1961).

5 Indeed, primitive tribes had not yet drawn the distinction between criminal law and civil liability law, and reparation was confused with punishment, *see* J.-L. Gazzaniga, *Les métamorphoses historiques de la responsabilité*, *in* LES MÉTAMORPHOSES DE LA RESPONSABILITÉ, SIXIÈMES JOURNÉES RENÉ SAVATIER 3, 7 (1997); in the same vein, Lévy-Bruhl, *Le point de vue de l'historien du droit*, *op. cit.* at 38–39.

6 Notably through purification rituals, *see* M. Mauss, *La religion et les origines du droit pénal, d'après un livre récent*, 34 REVUE D'HISTOIRE DES RELIGIONS 269, 287 (1896).

7 Among a wealth of literature: P. FAUCONNET, LA RESPONSABILITÉ 105 (1920): "[I]n the history of criminal law, we are gradually approaching pure objective responsibility; the relative importance of the internal moral element diminishes, that of the external element increases: at the limit, the act committed without any moral failure and the accident are exactly assimilated to the intentional act"; E. GARÇON, LE DROIT PÉNAL: ORIGINES – ÉVOLUTION – ÉTAT ACTUEL 19–20 (1922); L. Gernet, *Le droit pénal de la Grèce Ancienne*,

solely to the result and not to the fault. Neither unintentional damage nor accident is accepted as an excuse for the criminal – even in the case of homicide. Moreover, the reaction is *collective*: identification of the culprit is not required, and the principle of "individual responsibility" is nonexistent. Revenge can be exacted, or payment made, impersonally against anyone belonging to the tribe of the perpetrator. And if the victim clan does not know where the damage originated, its members will resort to divinatory practices to locate the source of the evil and trigger their reprisals.[8]

21. **The absence of criminal law in primitive societies.** This archaic system of vengeance and composition bears little relation to criminal law, understood as a *society*'s punitive reaction to behavior deemed antisocial. This is because primitive tribes do not form a "society," while the existence of a *right* to punish is inextricably linked to that of a superior, third-party authority in the dispute, which is not vengeful but dispenses *justice* in the name of all. But tribes, independent of one another, act only in their own name – they are guided neither by the idea of justice nor by a desire to pacify. Revenge is exercised on behalf of the clan's sovereignty, and in this sense is analogous to war,[9] and has more in common with public international law than with criminal law.[10] It must therefore be admitted that it is inappropriate to speak of "primitive criminal law" and, consequently, of "objective" criminal law, as this system does not fall within the scope of criminal law.

If there were an ancestor of criminal law in these times, it would have to be found where there was organized social power, i.e., within the tribe itself, where the head of the family or clan inflicted, in addition to vengeance or composition, an *individual* punishment on the actual perpetrator of the harmful behavior, proportionate to their *fault*.[11] It is in these intra-

---

in Du châtiment dans la cité. Supplices corporels et peine de mort dans le monde antique 9, 16–17 (1984): "Two aspects in particular are characteristic of the most ancient liability: it can be collective and it can be contracted involuntarily"; J. Gaudemet, *Le problème de la responsabilité pénale dans l'Antiquité*, *in* ii Studi in onore di Emilio Betti 483, 483 (1961); R. Griffon, De l'intention en droit pénal 3–4 (1911); J. Pinatel, *L'apport de l'ethnographie à la criminologie et au droit pénal*, xxi Revue de science criminelle et de droit pénal comparé 646, 647 (1966); A. Lebigre, Quelques aspects de la responsabilité pénale en droit romain classique 55 (1967); A. Laingui, Histoire du droit pénal 20 (2nd ed. 1993); H. Parent, *Histoire de l'acte volontaire en droit pénal anglais et canadien*, 45 McGill Law Journal 975, 979–80 (2000); Mauss, *La religion et les origines du droit pénal, d'après un livre récent*, *op. cit.* at 285; Lévy-Bruhl, *Le point de vue de l'historien du droit*, *op. cit.* at 48; Poirier, *Les caractères de la responsabilité archaïque*, *op. cit.* at 19; Gazzaniga, *Les métamorphoses historiques de la responsabilité*, *op. cit.* at 7–8.

8 Lévy-Bruhl, *Le point de vue de l'historien du droit*, *op. cit.* at 44.

9 Mauss, *La religion et les origines du droit pénal d'après un livre récent*, *op. cit.* at 285.

10 This point of view is defended by Garçon, Le droit pénal: Origines – évolution – état actuel, *op. cit.* at 11–22. At the end of his demonstration, he concludes: "We have just shown that vengeance and compositions are, in their original origin, nothing more than a kind of international law between patriarchal, independent and sovereign families. It is wrong that many historians have seen in them a primitive system of criminal law… And isn't this the very system still practiced today by the nations most proud of their civilization in their relations with one another? …Is the indemnity stipulated in so many peace treaties in fact very different from the very old composition of primitive peoples?" *Id.* at 22.

11 *Id.* at 23.

family practices, and these alone, that the premises of criminal law[12] could be detected, for, incidentally, nothing is further removed from criminal punishment than private vengeance.

22. **Criminal law was not originally objective.** This is an important point, as it refutes the common syllogism that the system of "archaic responsibility" is the ancestor of criminal law; that this system is objective; and that criminal law was therefore objective at its inception. Conversely, considering that the birth of criminal law occurred further back in history, when a state authority was established, demonstrates that criminal responsibility was subjective from the outset.

B. Subjective liability, concomitant with the birth of criminal law

23. **The birth of criminal justice, in opposition to the archaic system of responsibility.** The system of "objective responsibility" – the archaic system – is found whenever two sovereignties coexist without a higher authority playing the role of arbiter.[13] When tribes that had lived in isolation eventually drew closer together and established increasingly numerous social and commercial relationships, a society emerged, making public punishment possible.[14] And as soon as criminal justice became public, it became a state monopoly.[15] The authorities then had to establish the legitimacy of their punitive action. The aim was no longer to avenge a group of individuals, but to ensure the peace and stability of the city as a whole.[16] This new punitive power gave rise to an unprecedented concern: citizens had to be protected against arbitrariness in order to ensure order. This concern had already appeared in Greek mythology, notably in Hesiod's *Theogony*, which is the earliest source of ideas underlying the notion of the rule of law.[17]

With the emergence of state authority, it is now a third party that makes decisions, and not the victim who retaliates: justice is rendered in the name of all, and cannot strike at a community. Responsibility becomes individual, and the individual becomes solely responsible to society. But making the individual *responsible* implies knowing to what *extent* they are

---

12 A. Lebigre believes that individual responsibility was precisely introduced by the system of noxal surrender, an intra-family punishment inflicted by the head of the family following the commission of a crime by a member of the clan. *See* Lebigre, Quelques aspects de la responsabilité pénale en droit romain classique, *op. cit.* at 5–8.

13 Garçon, Le droit pénal: Origines – évolution – état actuel, *op. cit.* at 20.

14 Mauss, *La religion et les origines du droit pénal d'après un livre récent*, *op. cit.* at 288.

15 One author notes that "there is a crime in the penal sense when the sanction is administered by the State and on its behalf," *see* Gernet, *Le droit pénal de la Grèce Ancienne*, *op. cit.* at 34.

16 Garçon, Le droit pénal: Origines – évolution – état actuel, *op. cit.* at 32.

17 L. B. Tremblay, *L'origine mythique de la primauté du droit: Hésiode et les dieux*, 52 Revue juridique Thémis de l'Université de Montréal 425, 456 (2018).

responsible. Given that ancient crimes shared the severity of the punishments they incurred, it became necessary to make their infliction subject to a more precise assessment of the criminal act.[18] Taking intention into account appeared to be the best way to "approach the reality of the unlawful act."[19] *The function* of intent has remained the same since the outset: to achieve fairer results, in proportion to the seriousness of the conduct.

24. **Taking the defendant's intentions into account: a means of ensuring fairer punishment.** In ancient Greece, towards the end of the seventh century and the beginning of the sixth century BC, the city began to adopt a state justice system. Draco's law, passed around 620 BC, provided for the public punishment of murder, and "nowhere is there an earlier or clearer preoccupation with determining and measuring guilt in the law,"[20] as Greek criminal law was built on the distinction between voluntary and involuntary.[21] As evidenced by Lysias' speech *Against Simon*, intention is already more important than the result:

> Why, it is clear that even the makers of our laws did not think well, when people happened in a fight to break each other's heads, to make it a case for banishment from their country; else they would have exiled a goodly number. But in the case of any persons who, designing to kill, wounded others without being able to kill them, they appointed the punishment in that degree of severity, judging it meet that where they had shown design and premeditation they should pay the penalty: though if they might not have succeeded, none the less their best efforts had been exerted.[22]

In Roman times, the laws attributed to Numa also distinguish between voluntary and involuntary homicide: to be found guilty, one must have killed "*dolo sciens*" – knowingly.[23] The principle of subjective repression also prevails in the Law of the Twelve Tables, which punishes with different penalties depending on whether or not the offense was committed with intent.[24] The *Digest* contains numerous references attesting to the consideration given to the accused's state of mind: a rescript from

---

18 Lebigre, Quelques aspects de la responsabilité pénale en droit romain classique, *op. cit.* at 60.

19 *Id.* at 63.

20 Gernet, *Le droit pénal de la Grèce Ancienne*, *op. cit.* at 24.

21 A. Laingui & M. Crépin, *La philosophie du droit pénal dans l'Antiquité grecque et romaine*, 53 Revue internationale de droit pénal, 597, 611 (1982); in the same vein, Laingui, Histoire du droit pénal, *op. cit.* at 16. In the same vein, *see* B. Winiger, Responsibility, Restoration and Fault 24–25 (2018).

22 W. R. M. Lamb trans. (Harvard Univ. Press 1930); *see* C. Viano, *Causalité et responsabilité chez Lysias et Aristote*, *in* Aitia: Causalité juridique, causalité philosophique 69, 76 (2015).

23 J.-M. Carbasse, Histoire du droit pénal et de la justice criminelle 49 (3rd ed. 2014), no. 21.

24 *Id.* In the same vein, *see* B. Perrin, *Le caractère subjectif de la répression pénale dans les xii Tables*, 28 Revue historique de droit français et étranger 383, 383–84, 390–403 (1951); Lebigre, Quelques aspects de la responsabilité pénale en droit romain classique, *op. cit.* at 56, and Y. Jeanclos, Droit pénal européen: Dimension historique 33–35 (2009).

Emperor Hadrian states that "[i]n the perpetration of crime, the intention, and not the event, is considered";[25] Callistratus affirms that punishment can easily be determined by determining the guilty party's intention;[26] Paul confirms that "the wish and intention of the culprit make a distinction in the case of crime."[27]

The principle of subjective responsibility was thus established at the very birth of criminal law: judges began to pay attention to defendants' intentions as soon as judicial bodies were set up. There is thus a concomitance between the birth of criminal law and the recognition of intent. It remains to be seen what legal consequences this has had.

II. A legal abstraction

25. **The development of the notion of intention, a pragmatic construct autonomous from beliefs.** Intention embodies the idea one forms of oneself – a notion accompanied by a host of philosophical and religious representations. However, since ancient times, Greek and Roman rationality has made it possible to distinguish between the Cosmos and the City, and thus to separate the order of beliefs from the legal order.[28] The point is an important one: attesting to the fact that beliefs did not influence the legal concept of intention demonstrates that it is a notion determined solely by a pragmatic objective – ensuring fairer repression. Thus, even though free will was not believed to exist in antiquity (**A**), it was nevertheless *postulated in law* to enable the development of the regime of intention (**B**).

A. The lack of belief in the existence of free will in the ancient world

26. **Fate in Greco-Latin culture.** Mythology, tragedies, and epics provide insight into the beliefs of the Greco-Roman civilization.[29] To point out that determinism is omnipresent here is an understatement. The criminal appears systematically predestined – this is the central theme of tragedy, which is precisely tragic because the outcome seems fatal, whatever the

25 Digest, 48, 8, 14.

26 *Id.*, 47, 21, 2.

27 *Id.*, 47, 2, 55.

28 P. Ricœur, ii Philosophie de la volonté: Finitude et culpabilité 318–19 (Points 2009) (1960).

29 "Myth," from the Greek *mythos*, means "story." Poets claimed to "recount the lives of the gods and heroes of the past," and mythology was "a central aspect of Greek religion." *See* Tremblay, *L'origine mythique de la primauté du droit: Hésiode et les dieux*, *op. cit.* at 444. According to Jean-François Revel, Greek religion "was not based on revelation, it professed no religious dogma, it was a collection of myths, the essence of which was due to poets – Homer, Hesiod," J.-F. Revel, Histoire de la philosophie occidentale 25 (2003). To the question: "Did the Greeks believe in their myths?" historian Paul Veyne replies: "[O]f course they did!" P. Veyne, Les Grecs ont-ils cru à leurs mythes? 138, 454 (1983).

protagonist's efforts, heroic heart, and goodwill.[30] Life unfolds like a play written in advance, written by someone else, in which the characters are driven by higher forces.[31]

And so it is in the Homeric universe, where the inexorability of things and human impotence[32] are constantly brought to the fore, with the hero having little choice but to set out on his quest and accomplish the mission assigned to him. At the beginning of both *The Iliad*[33] and *The Odyssey*,[34] Achilles' fate is already sealed by the will of Zeus, and Hector himself admits that "no man hath ever escaped, be he coward or valiant, when once he hath been born."[35]

The figure of destiny is also embodied by the three Moirai,[36] who were later renamed the Parcae by the Romans.[37] They embody a law that even the gods cannot transgress, and regulate the existence of every mortal with the help of a thread[38] that one spins, the second winds, and the third cuts off when life comes to an end. According to Hesiod's *Theogony*, the Moirai "[w]ho give mortals at birth good and evil to have."[39]

But if both virtue and vice come from the gods, isn't it unfair to hold us responsible for our faults and reward our good deeds? Ancient philosophers, whose aim was to encourage virtue and promote the good life, were quick to address this fundamental question.

27. **The insoluble quarrel of free will: the opposition between the Stoics and the Epicureans.** The problem with determinism is that it denies human responsibility. This stumbling block led to a school war between the Stoics, who maintained that every event is the product of a cause that is

30 In this sense, *see* J. Gaudemet, *Le problème de la responsabilité pénale dans l'Antiquité*, *in* II Studi in onore di Emilio Betti 483, 487–88 (1961).

31 For a detailed account of the role of fate in the major ancient epics, *see* D. Arnould, Les figures du destin dans l'épopée antique gréco-latine (2016).

32 P. Larrieu, Mythes grecs et droit: Retour sur la fonction anthropologique du droit 138–39 (2017).

33 Homer, The Iliad (A. T. Murray trans., Harvard Univ. Press 1924), I, 5: "The wrath sing, goddess, of Peleus' son, Achilles … thus the plan of Zeus came to fulfillment."

34 Homer, The Odyssey (A. T. Murray trans., Harvard Univ. Press 1919), I, 78–81: "But come, let us who are here all take thought of his return … for he will in no wise be able, against all the immortal gods and in their despite, to contend alone." Paradoxically, as Zeus deliberates Achilles' fate, he harshly judges the humans who accuse the gods: "Look you now, how ready mortals are to blame the gods. It is from us, they say, that evils come, but they even of themselves, through their own blind folly, have sorrows beyond that which is ordained," *id.*, I, 32–34.

35 Homer, The Iliad, *op. cit.*, VI, 485–487.

36 Atropos, Clotho, and Lachesis, P. Grimal, Dictionnaire de la mythologie grecque et romaine 300 (15th ed. 2002). Moirai are sometimes presented as the daughters of Zeus and Themis, or of Nyx, the primordial goddess of night. On this double filiation, *see* V. Pirenne-Delforge & G. Pironti, *Les Moires entre la naissance et la mort: de la représentation au culte*, 3–4 Études de lettres 93, 103–105 (2011).

37 Nona, Decima, Morta – the *tria fata*, the "three Fates," Grimal, Dictionnaire de la mythologie grecque et romaine, *op. cit.* at 348; J. Schmidt, Dictionnaire de la mythologie grecque et romaine 160 (1993).

38 Moirai appear forty-eight times in *The Iliad*, sixty-one times in *The Odyssey*, *see* Arnould, Les figures du destin dans l'épopée antique gréco-latine, *op. cit.* at 24.

39 Hésiode, La Théogonie, Les Travaux et les Jours et autres poèmes 34–35 (P. Brunet trans., Livre de Poche 1999). Hesiod, Works and Days and Theogony (S. Lombardo trans., Hackett Pub. Co. 1993).

both prior and external[40] – as Cleanthes put it: "In sin and sorrow what I might have done. In noble virtue. Aye, the willing soul. Fate leads, but the unwilling drags along"[41] – and the Epicureans, who could not resign themselves to admitting that we could be no more than the puppets of fate. Lucretius thus put the Stoics to the test, asking: if the world is predetermined, then how can we explain "this free will down here that drives beings where pleasure calls them, that makes them change course at the whim that carries them away?"[42] Accusing the Stoics of fatalism, the Epicureans criticized them for inciting men to laziness and inertia – why act if everything happens?[43] – and for making them irresponsible, since fault loses its meaning if fate is master of everything.[44]

An attempt at reconciliation was undertaken by Chrysippus, Aulus Gellius, and Cicero, who strove – not without difficulty – to make destiny and freedom compatible. Their argument is as follows. Take two accessories: a cone and a cylinder. These inert objects will only be activated by an external impulse, but once launched, they will each follow a movement of their own – the cone will turn in circles, while the cylinder will advance straight ahead. In short, destiny provides the impetus, but humans act according to their own nature.[45] A new obstacle! Do we ever choose who we are, are we ever free to determine our own personality and desires? Plato, in the *Myth of Er*,[46] maintains that souls decide on their incarnation, while Aristotle believes that the gifts of nature "obviously do not depend on us" but on "divine causes…"[47]

The controversy seems insurmountable, and the question "Is the human being free?" appears impossible to settle definitively. Fate – *anankè* for the Greeks, *fatum* for the Romans – is rooted in belief. Philosophers, for their part, seek to challenge its omnipotence for pragmatic reasons – to make people accountable and to encourage virtue – but by means of purely

---

40 Democritus, Zeno, Cleanthes, Seneca, Epictetus and Marcus Aurelius all asserted that there is neither chance nor freedom for the individual. For a detailed study, *see* Arnould, Les figures du destin dans l'épopée antique gréco-latine, *op. cit.* at 50–56.

41 Quoted in Seneca, 3 Moral letters to Lucilius 229 (R. Mott Gummere trans., Loeb Classical Library 1925), letter cvii.

42 Lucrèce, De la nature 27 (C. Nisard trans., Firmin Didot 1868), bk. ii, 256–260.

43 "Lazy reasoning" is a classic argument against the fatalistic thesis. Here it is: you get sick. In a predestined world, whatever you do, it is either your destiny to die, or to get better. Conclusion: since everything is already written, there is no need to consult a doctor! *See* Cicéron, Traité du destin 15 (A. Yon trans., Les Belles Lettres 2018), xiii.

44 Aulu-Gelle, Nuits Attiques 84–85 (R. Marache trans., Les Belles Lettres 1978), bk. v–x.

45 This example comes from Chrysippus, whose *Treatise on Destiny* has not been preserved. It is reproduced and commented on by Aulu-Gelle, Nuits Attiques, *op. cit.*, bk. vii, 11–12, at 85–86; and Cicéron, Traité du destin, *op. cit.* at 22–23, xix.

46 Platon, *La République – Livre X*, *in* x Œuvres de Platon 234 (V. Cousin trans., Pichon et Didier 1834).

47 Aristotle, Nicomachean Ethics (H. Rackham trans., Harvard Univ. Press 1926) However, Aristotle did not really set out to resolve the question of free will, *see* M. Frede, *Aristotle on a Choice without a Will*, *in* A Free Will: Origins of the Notion in Ancient Thought 19 (2012); for which he was criticized as "hesitant and superficial" by A. Schopenhauer, Essai sur le libre arbitre 114–15 (S. Reinach trans., Rivages Poche 2018).

verbal distinctions, unsuited to elucidating a mystery destined to remain unsolved. But while the philosopher may be content to speculate, the jurist must act. This is why, despite the enigma of human freedom, free will has been postulated in law to enable the judge to establish the guilt of individuals.

B. The free will postulated in law in order to elaborate the regime of intention

28. **Bypassing the problem of free will through law.** On the outskirts of the City, Clinias talks to the Stranger from Athens:[48]

> THE STRANGER – All the wicked, in all their faults, are wicked against their will. The unjust is, I suppose, wicked, but the wicked is wicked against his will. Now, it is absurd to say that an act that was not committed willingly could have been done willingly; and it goes without saying that at this hour my duty is to agree with myself, and I am of the opinion that it is never willingly that a man commits injustice.
>
> CLINIAS – Will you distinguish between injustices that are not committed willingly and those that are committed willingly, and will we inflict harsher punishments for the former, and lesser ones for the latter? Or will the penalties be equal for all, since there are absolutely no injustices that are committed willingly?
>
> The STRANGER – In every city, every legislator who has ever lived has legislated these two faults as two species of injustice. Should we proceed in this way without having found a way out of the embarrassment in which this difficulty has placed us, acting as if it were something that emanated from a god, without proving in any way the correctness of this distinction? On the contrary, before legislating, we need to show that there are two offences here, and that there is a difference between them, so that when the time comes to assign punishment to one or the other, anyone can agree with the reasons given and be able to judge whether the punishment is appropriate or not.

It does not matter! Plato tells us, that it is impossible to resolve the question of whether we commit injustice voluntarily or not: justice demands that we admit such a distinction, and on this basis develop a theory to distinguish what is intentional from what is not *in law*.[49]

---

48 Platon, *Lois*, *in* PLATON: ŒUVRES COMPLÈTES 903–907 (Brisson ed., Flammarion 2008), bk. IX, 860c to 863d. For another translation, *see* PLATON, VII-VIII ŒUVRES DE PLATON 162–66 (V. Cousin trans., Pichon et Didier, 1832), bk. IX.

49 In this sense, *see* J. Gaudemet, *Le problème de la responsabilité pénale dans l'Antiquité*, *in* II STUDI IN ONORE DI EMILIO BETTI 483, 487–93 (1961). According to the author, by distinguishing, against belief, between voluntary and involuntary offenses, Greek thought achieves "a purely secular notion of responsibility," *id.* at 493.

29. **Aristotle's *Nicomachean Ethics*: the first traces of the regime of intention.** If the characterization of intention does not involve a quest for metaphysical truth or futile psychological investigations, the question of its legal regime remains. And it was Aristotle, a keen observer of jurisprudence, who first sketched[50] its broad outlines.[51] It was studied and commented on by Thomas Aquinas,[52] and then by numerous jurists.[53]

Aristotle considers that the classification of a crime is determined less by the nature of the act performed than by the intention expressed by that act,[54] from which it follows that it is important not to confuse voluntary and involuntary acts.[55] The Stagirite then *postulates* that *man acts intentionally by nature*, i.e., for Aristotle, *with full knowledge*[56] and *after deliberation.*[57]

This is the case, except in certain hypotheses. Firstly, behavior is involuntary if it is *forced* or caused by *accident*,[58] since in this case, no personal contribution is made to the action – for example, when we "are carried somewhere, either by the wind, or by people who hold you in their power."[59] The act is still involuntary if it results from the *inability to deliberate*, which is found in beings "devoid of reason."[60] It is also involuntary if it results from *ignorance*,[61] but not just any ignorance: error will not constitute a valid excuse whenever it appears to result from negligence, for it depends on those concerned not to remain naive and to apply themselves to learning.[62] Such is the case for

---

50 Indeed, Aristotle was the first to conceptualize precisely the distinction between the voluntary and the involuntary, *see* L. A. Zaibert, *Intentionality, Voluntariness, and Culpability: A Historical-Philosophical Analysis*, 1 Buffalo Criminal Law Review 459, 467 (1998); Aristotle having analyzed more closely the conditions under which an act can be considered intentional than Plato, *see* D. Agretelis, *Mens Rea in Plato and Aristotle*, 1 Issues in Criminology 19, 30 (1965).

51 Clearly dissociating theological thought from legal thought, *see* M. Villey, Leçons d'histoire de la philosophie du droit 27 (1962); M. Villey, La formation de la pensée juridique moderne 84 (2003).

52 *See infra*, nos. 54–58.

53 *See infra*, no. 69

54 Aristote, *Rhétorique*, *in* Aristote: Œuvres complètes 2634–37 (P. Pellegrin ed., 2014), bk. i, ch. x, 1368b. *See also* Aristotle, Nicomachean Ethics (H. Rackham trans., Harvard Univ. Press 1926), bk. v, 10, 1135b, p. 275: "[T]he debate is not whether or not a harmful fact has occurred, but whether it has been justly caused. ...If a man has deliberately caused a wrong, he is acting unjustly."

55 It should be noted that there is a dispute among Hellenists as to whether Aristotle is speaking of intention or will in the *Nicomachean Ethics*, but that these are not of decisive importance at this stage, since the two words are considered synonymous at this time. In this sense, *see* Zaibert, *Intentionality, Voluntariness, and Culpability: A Historical-Philosophical Analysis*, *op. cit.* at 464.

56 Aristotle, Nicomachean Ethics (H. Rackham trans., Harvard Univ. Press 1926), bk. iii, 4, 1111a, pp. 135–36.

57 *Id.*, bk. iii, 4, 1111b, pp. 137–38. Note that Aristotle already distinguishes intention from "motives," the latter being the reasons why man acts. He specifies that they can be taken into account: motives can, in fact, lead to indulgence or reinforce blame, *see id.*, bk. iii, 1, 1110a, pp. 128–29.

58 *Id.*, bk. v, 10, 1135a, p. 271.

59 *Id.*, bk. iii, 1, 1110a, p. 127.

60 *Id.*, bk. iii, 4, 1111b, p. 138.

61 *Id.*, bk. iii, 1, 1110a, p. 127.

62 *Id.*, bk. iii, 7, 1114a, p. 152.

those who claim not to know "those legal provisions whose knowledge is compulsory and presents no difficulty,"[63] or for the reckless who adopt a course of conduct leading to "*reasonably foreseeable*" damage.[64] Despite the alleged error – about the law, the fact or the consequences of the act – a *fault* can then be characterized, which, for Aristotle, renders the voluntary action.[65]

In short, *human beings act voluntarily by nature*. Since they can choose virtue, they are responsible for their evil inclinations if their personality leads them towards vice.[66] If they cannot put forward a legitimate excuse, they are deemed to have acted intentionally. The original definition of intention is therefore essentially *negative*: the law postulates in a general way that every act is intentional, before checking whether there is any reason to believe that it is not.

30. **Roman casuistry and the refinement of the regime of intent.** The Greek heritage is tangible in Roman criminal law.[67] The Romans borrowed from the Greeks the two conditions of criminal responsibility – knowledge (*sciens*) and will (*voluntas*)[68] – as well as the causes that render intent, and hence the offense, disappear.[69] However, the pragmatic Romans never arrived at a general theory of intent.[70] It is nevertheless possible to detect a refinement of its regime.[71] Roman law gave rise to new concepts: *dol* (*dolus*), fraud *(fraus*), negligence (*culpa*), accident (*casus*), chance (*fortuna*), and result (*exitus*)[72] – all of which made it possible to apprehend the offense more precisely, and to rank its seriousness in order to proportion the penalty more finely. Fraud, for example, appears to be a specific case of *dol*: when an offense involves *fraus*, the judge is seeking to ascertain not only whether or not the individual has behaved intentionally but more specifically, whether or not they have used maneuvers or artifices to achieve their ends.[73] While the first three con-

---

63 *Id.*

64 *Id.*, bk. v, 10, 1135b, p. 273.

65 *Id.*

66 *Id.*, bk. III, 7, 1113b, pp. 149–50.

67 J.-C. Genin, La répression des actes de tentative en droit criminel romain: Contribution à l'étude de la subjectivité répressive à Rome 16 (1968) (Ph.D. dissertation, Université de Lyon), and references cited.

68 Carbasse, Histoire du droit pénal et de la justice criminelle, *op. cit.* at 49, no. 21.

69 For example, lunatics, children and animals are excused for not being able to form an intention, *see* Lebigre, Quelques aspects de la responsabilité pénale en droit romain classique, *op. cit.* at 53; and the Greek conception of error of fact and error of law is also taken up, *see* Carbasse, Histoire du droit pénal et de la justice criminelle, *op. cit.* at 52–53, no. 21.

70 Carbasse, Histoire du droit pénal et de la justice criminelle, *op. cit.* at 48, no. 20. Nevertheless, the Romans provided the material on which this theorization could later be based, from the twelfth century onwards, in the writings of doctors of law and theologians.

71 Lebigre, Quelques aspects de la responsabilité pénale en droit romain classique, *op. cit.* at 55.

72 Carbasse, Histoire du droit pénal et de la justice criminelle, *op. cit.* at 49, no. 21.

73 In the Middle Ages, the concept was taken up by jurists to qualify theft and its derivative offenses, *see infra*, no. 69. We shall also see that fraud is the characteristic moral element of a large number of offenses in business criminal law, which derive to a greater or lesser extent from theft, *see infra*, no. 245.

cepts – *dolus*, *fraus* and *culpa* – pertain to intentional acts,[74] accident and chance preclude conviction, and very little attention is paid to the outcome of offenses. This is borne out by the importance of repressing attempts in Roman law,[75] which can be found in a variety of offenses such as murder, poisoning, electoral fraud, currency forgery, as well as monopoly or hoarding.[76] This refinement of intent did not, however, lead to insurmountable theoretical difficulties: Roman law, resolutely focused on practical application, considered that the judge did not have to carry out in-depth psychological investigations in order to characterize the defendant's intent. This was inferred from the facts, as the completion of an act and the circumstances surrounding it revealed the author's intent, according to the adage "*res in se dolum habet*."[77] Finally, an interesting phenomenon occurred during the Late Roman Empire. Under the reign of Emperor Justinian, intent took on an even greater importance than in the classical period,[78] which went hand in hand with harsher repression.[79] This can be explained by the increasing use of presumptions of intent,[80] and points to an important characteristic of the concept: it is a malleable notion that can be used to enhance the effectiveness of repressive policy.

Intention thus held a central place in ancient criminal law. As competition law was criminal in nature, it too placed this concept at the core of its reasoning

Paragraph 2 – The place of intent in ancient "competition law"

31. **Continuity in the criminal repression of anticompetitive practices in the ancient world.** The repression of anticompetitive practices was a major concern of both Greek (**I**) and Roman (**II**) criminal law. While there is continuity between these two periods, the sources available on the subject differ. Philosophy and the art of oratory played a predominant role

74 Carbasse, Histoire du droit pénal et de la justice criminelle, *op. cit.* at 49, no. 21. Whereas *dolus* implies the intention of the result, *culpa* implies only the will to adopt a given behavior without having considered the consequences. Today, these two notions correspond to the distinction between intentional and voluntary acts, which will be developed further *infra*, no. 189.

75 *Id.* at 54–56, no. 23.

76 Genin, La répression des actes de tentative en droit criminel romain : Contribution à l'étude de la subjectivité répressive à Rome, *op. cit.* at 45 *et seq.*

77 Digest, 45, 1, 36. On this adage, *see* A. Laingui & A. Lebigre, I Histoire du droit pénal : Le droit pénal 28 (1979).

78 *Id.* at 243.

79 *Id.* at 245–52; in the same vein, Carbasse, Histoire du droit pénal et de la justice criminelle, *op. cit.* at 51, no. 21.

80 *Id.*

in Greece, while legal data abounded in Roman times. From these two types of sources, an overall picture emerges, enabling us to grasp the place occupied by intention in the repression of hoarding and monopoly during this period, which, although very distant, proves enlightening in understanding the original meaning of competition law.

I. Greek law

32. **Intention plays both a theoretical and practical role.** The interest in studying the Greek period is twofold. From a theoretical perspective, mythology and philosophy teach that the criterion for distinguishing fair exchange from unfair exchange was intention, thereby informing the definition of competition offenses (**A**). From a practical perspective, the first recorded trial of an anticompetitive practice attests to the fact that intention was at the core of the reasoning used to characterize the offense (**B**).

A. Intent as a criterion for distinguishing between good and bad trade

33. **A first pre-philosophical reflection: Hesiod's *Works and Days*.** Given that commerce is the lifeblood of the city, it is hardly surprising that it was addressed early on in mythological stories. Hesiod's poem *Works and Days*[81] addresses the themes of wealth and work, and "engraved the precepts of justice and wisdom in the souls of the peoples."[82] Indeed, Hesiod is regarded by some as one of the earliest thinkers on economics.[83] In the course of this text, we already find a reflection on competition, then called "strife," as well as an essential distinction, which, once drawn, will never disappear, between good and desirable rivalry and that which, on the contrary, leads man and society to their ruin: "So, after all, there was not one kind of *Strife* alone, but all over the earth there are two. As for the one, a man would praise her when he came to understand her; but the other is blameworthy: and they are wholly different in *nature*."[84]

---

81 Hésiode, *Œuvres d'Hésiode*, *in* Les petits poèmes grecs 113 (M. A. Bignan trans., M. Aimé-Martin ed., 1838). For another translation, *see* Hésiode, Les Travaux et les Jours (P. Mazon trans., Les Belles Lettres 2018). In the French version of this book, we reproduced extracts from M. A. Bignan's translation, having taken care to compare the two versions to check that there were no notable differences between them altering the meaning of the text. Here, we used H. G. Evelyn-White's translation: Hesiod, The Homeric Hymns and Homerica (Harvard Univ. Press 1914).

82 Introduction to Hesiod's poem by M. A. Bignan, *Œuvres d'Hésiode*, *op. cit.* at 113.

83 B. Gordon, Economic Analysis Before Adam Smith: Hesiod to Lessius 3 (1975), p. 3; *adde* M. N. Rothbard, 1 Economic Thought Before Adam Smith: An Austrian Perspective on the History of Economic Thought 8 (1995).

84 Hésiode, *Œuvres d'Hésiode*, *op. cit.* at 140 (emphasis added).

The poem teaches wise principles: we must seek to enrich ourselves, because poverty is a ruin for man, and because he who lives well attracts the envy of others, turns them away from idleness, and drives "even the shiftless to toil."[85] Individuals, thus stimulated by the spirit of competition, ward off famine and ensure abundance for the entire people. Hesiod warns, however, that one must not enrich oneself through evil deeds – and beware of those who seize "many treasures by the strength of their hands" or usurp them "by the skill of their tongue, as happens all too often when the love of gain seduces the spirit of man."[86] Wealth, far from being condemned in itself, is on the contrary encouraged, with Hesiod going so far as to offer advice on how to get rich, notably through maritime trade – he even assures the reader that through his work, he will "soon have amassed a great fortune."[87] Profit from trade is not demonized; what is demonized is undeserved enrichment, as "dishonorable gains are equivalent to losses."[88] The poet thus teaches that gain can be pursued, provided that unjust *methods* are not used.[89]

34. **Aristotle's distinction between good and bad commerce.** Contrary to the popular belief that trade and the pursuit of profit were long considered reprehensible in their own right, Aristotelian thought, like that of Hesiod, is highly nuanced. Roman law owes him a debt of gratitude, and his writings were an important source of inspiration for Augustine, as well as Thomas Aquinas and all the Scholastics, all of whom commented on the Stagirite's texts, drawing from them the foundations of their economic doctrine.[90] If the study of Aristotelian thought has historical value, it also offers a relevant and still topical reflection on competition law[91] in two respects. Firstly, from a substantive point of view, Aristotle makes distinctions that enable us to think about the dividing line between competition on the merits and unfair competition. Secondly, from a methodological point of view, Aristotle's thought makes us realize that there was a time when moral, legal and economic analyses were not separated, but joined together in an overall reflection with justice as the guiding principle.

35. **Intention: the criterion for distinguishing between good and bad trade.** Aristotle – and he is not the only one[92] – dissociates two forms of justice:

---

85 *Id.*

86 *Id.* at 144.

87 *Id.*

88 *Id.*

89 Gordon, Economic Analysis Before Adam Smith: Hesiod to Lessius, *op. cit.* at 4–5.

90 *See infra*, no. 60.

91 For an analysis of competition law in the light of Aristotle's thought, *see* G. Decocq, *Éthique et droit de la concurrence*, Contrats concurrence consommation (Jan. 2020), repère 1.

92 Plato already distinguished two forms of justice in his *Laws* (757), as did Isocrates in his *Areopagitic Discourse* (vii, 21–22). The distinction was taken up by Cicero, notably in the *Topica* (4, 23), *see* J. Gaudemet, *Justice distributive*, Encyclopædia Universalis.

one corrective, the other distributive.[93] The first, corrective justice, does not distinguish between individuals; it corresponds to equality before the law and aims to restore a disrupted order. The law does not discriminate; it must apply to everyone in the same way, otherwise justice would be broken.[94] The second form of justice, distributive justice, is of an entirely different nature. It consists of attributing to individuals the share of goods and honors that is their due, in proportion to their merit, which implies treating *unequally* individuals who are *unequally deserving*. It follows that some may be wealthier than others or hold a higher social status. In short, to each according to their qualities and efforts. The judgment made on personal gain depends not on an egalitarian vision of wealth distribution but, as Aristotle teaches us, on the *means* used to enrich oneself and the *end* pursued by this enrichment.

The end pursued by the merchant – enrichment – is not decried per se. In this respect, the Aristotelian doctrine of chrematistics[95] makes enlightening distinctions. If, in modern parlance, the term has acquired a pejorative meaning[96] – today it is defined as "the greatest possible production of consumer goods, regardless of their utility"[97] – the original meaning of the word was richer.[98] Chrematistics concerned the administration of things and the management of goods, in other words, the art of acquiring.[99] It was subdivided into two types: on the one hand, enrichment aimed at powering domestic life or the expansion of the city; on the other, enrichment aimed solely at itself – enrichment for enrichment's sake.[100] Excessive hoarding of money is seen as a threat to the city, for if everyone hoards until they no longer need it, the people will cease to be motivated to

93 This distinction is developed in *Nicomachean Ethics*, and also in *Politics*. *See also* Aristote, Éthique à Nicomaque (J. Tricot trans., Librairie philosophique J. Vrin 2007), bk. v, at 229–52; Aristote, La politique (J. Tricot trans., Librairie philosophique J. Vrin 2019), bk. iii, 9, at 203–11. Aristotle, Nicomachean Ethics (H. Rackham trans., Harvard Univ. Press 1926) and Aristotle, Politics: A New Translation (C. D. C. Reeve trans., Hackett 2017).

94 Aristotle writes: "It matters little whether it is a good man who has robbed a dishonest man, or a dishonest man a good man…: the law takes into account only the distinctive character of the wrong done, and treats the parties equally, asking only whether one has committed, and the other has suffered, an injustice," Aristotle, Nicomachean Ethics, *op. cit.*, bk. v, 7, 1131b, at 248. On this form of equality, theorized by the Greeks under the name of "isonomy," notably by Solon and Herodotus, *see* F. A. Hayek, The Political Ideal of the Rule of Law 6–9 (1955). Corrective equality is the basis for theories of "formal" justice, according to which justice means equal treatment. On the limits of this assertion and the difficulties it raises, *see* C. Perlman, De la justice 22–42 (1945).

95 The theme of chrematistics is mainly developed in Book v of Nicomachean Ethics, *op. cit.* and Book i of Politics, *op. cit.*

96 The fact that this term has acquired a pejorative meaning is not unrelated to Marx's use of the theory of chrematistics in support of his theses, notably in *Capital: A Critique of Political Economy*. On this subject, *see* A. Jaulin, *Marx lecteur d'Aristote*, 1 Les Études Philosophiques 105, 120 (2016).

97 TLFi. Lalande also points out that this term is generally used in a pejorative sense in contemporary times, cf. A. Lalande, Vocabulaire technique et critique de la philosophie 140–41 (2002).

98 For a detailed study, *see* J. Moreau, *Aristote et la monnaie*, 82 Revue des Études Grecques 349 (1969), fasc. 391–393. The author also notes that the term "chrematistics" was "diverted from its normal meaning, at the same time as the notion of wealth was altered," *id.* at 353–54.

99 *Id.* at 352–53.

100 A. Piettre, Histoire de la pensée économique et des théories contemporaines 14–15 (7th ed. 1979).

produce, and famine will soon follow despite everyone's virtual wealth: think of the unfortunate Midas, who starved to death because everything he touched turned to gold. These two kinds of chrematistics are in direct opposition to each other and, from an ethical perspective, are not judged in the same way. The starting point lies in their purpose: both aim at the acquisition goods, "but not with the same *intention*; one directed toward an *end*, the other seeks only increase."[101] Thus, the merchant can, without risking reproach, amass a large fortune[102] if he needs it to acquire a ship, pay his sailors, or even just to secure his status as a notable.[103] As a result, Aristotle does not consider gain to be an unjust excess in itself, except in cases where maneuvers are involved.

36. **An illustration: the legitimate enrichment of Thales through the creation of a monopoly.** To illustrate his point, Aristotle tells the story of Thales,[104] who was criticized for his poverty, which was seen as proof of the futility of philosophy. To counter the slanderers, he devised a strategy to enrich himself, thanks to his fine knowledge of astronomy. He predicted an abundant olive harvest, and paid a deposit to rent all the oil presses in the region in advance. The harvest proved to be just what the philosopher expected, and he was able to take advantage of his monopoly to sublet the works on whatever terms he wished, making a substantial profit.[105] Far from condemning this practice, Aristotle praises it, even though Thales benefited from a monopoly and made a considerable profit. There are two reasons for this: firstly, the gain resulted from an investment, a risk-taking, a gamble on the future, rather than from dishonesty; secondly, even though he was the only seller, Thales did not abuse the monopoly or "raise prices excessively."[106]

The Stagirite concludes that, even for private individuals, it is useful to know how to make one's property bear fruit, as this will improve one's finances, those of the family and, consequently, those of the city.[107] He even multiplies the examples of the different procedures recommended for enriching oneself in *The Economics.*[108] In short, and to use contemporary

---

101 Moreau, *Aristote et la monnaie*, *op. cit.* at 354 n.18 (emphasis added).

102 Neither Aristotle nor Plato advocated an ascetic lifestyle. *See* Gordon, Economic Analysis Before Adam Smith: Hesiod to Lessius, *op. cit.* at 29: "Neither philosopher is an advocate of poverty as a way of life. Plato, for example, sees it as a threat to social stability, a prime source of revolution. Aristotle associates poverty with degradation for the individual."

103 Some Scholastics, in particular Pierre de Jean Olivi, took up this idea in the Middle Ages, *see infra*, no. 61.

104 Aristotle, Politics, *op. cit.*, bk. i, ch. xi, at 69–71.

105 A profit equivalent to twice the initial investment, "of one hundred talents for an initial investment of fifty," *id.*

106 *Id.*

107 *Id.*

108 Aristote, Économiques (J. Tricot trans., Librairie philosophique J. Vrin 2004), bk. ii, at 31–66. Aristotle, 18 Aristotle in 23 Volumes (G. C. Armstrong trans., Harvard Univ. Press 1935) It should be noted that there is nevertheless some controversy among ancient Greek specialists as to the attribution of certain passages in the work to Aristotle; *see* the foreword by Jules Tricot.

terms, being in a position of monopoly[109] is not condemned in itself, as long as the acquisition of this position is based on merit, and the monopolist does not abuse it. It is not, therefore, the monopolistic position in a market as such that is blameworthy, but the means by which it is obtained and the use to which it is put.

37. **Economics: a knowledge inseparable from ethics and law.** Aristotle's second teaching is methodological. In Greek times, economics had little in common with the econometric models and sophisticated calculations we know today.[110] This is because *economics was not an independent science*, let alone an *exact* one. Ethical, legal and economic considerations were brought together in a single, comprehensive[111] reflection of a metaphysical nature.[112] Such a *unitary* approach implies that no question is treated independently of the others, and cannot be isolated from an overall analysis.[113] The ideal of justice serves as a focal point and a goal to be achieved through the triptych of "ethics-law-economics." In the Aristotelian system, justice cannot be thought of in the legal, moral or economic senses, i.e., in a vacuum. For Aristotle, it is a matter of questioning reality in the light of higher *values* and *ends*,[114] in order to discover the *rules of conduct* that enable people to live happily together.[115] The focus is on honest, virtuous human action, the rectitude of intentions and actions – in other words, on the *process* of exchange, not its *outcome*. The question was not what the "optimal" market structure or prices might be. It was a matter of determining the conditions of a *just* exchange, and the answer boiled down to this: what is just is what is free from dishonest behavior.[116]

It is hardly surprising, then, that the criterion of intent was at the heart of the first surviving competition case.

---

109 We understand monopoly here in the contemporary economic sense of the term – a situation in which there is only one supplier in a market.

110 The mathematization of economics is a phenomenon that began between the seventeenth and eighteenth centuries; *see infra*, no. 116.

111 S. Trifilio, Esprit mathématique et pensée économique dans l'Antiquité et au Moyen Âge 252–53 (2010) (Ph.D. dissertation, Aix-Marseille University): "It was through the intermediary of law that economics made its entry onto the stage of ideas; it was under its wing that it gradually took shape and grew until it acquired… the status of an autonomous discipline in the eighteenth century. Reflections on justice and the just led… to economic considerations in the modern sense of the term."

112 D. Villey, Notes de philosophie économique (1958–59): Le jeu des intérêts 83 (1965): according to the author, what "is striking about the Ancients is the unity of the great adventure." We shall see that this union between different types of knowledge would later result in a divorce between science and philosophy, and the prevalence of scientific reasoning over metaphysical reasoning; *see infra*, no. 82.

113 As K. Polanyi, *Aristotle Discovers the Economy*, *in* Trade and Markets in the Early Empires 64, 79 (K. Polanyi, C. M. Arensberg & H. W. Pearson eds., 1957): "Whenever Aristotle touched on a question of the economy he aimed at developing its relationship to society as a whole."

114 *Compare with infra*, nos. 423–425, on the contemporary lowering of the ends of law to material stakes.

115 Gordon, Economic Analysis Before Adam Smith: Hesiod to Lessius, *op. cit.* at 35.

116 From the eighteenth century onwards, the debate will no longer be posed in the same terms, *see infra*, nos. 78 *et seq.*

B. Intent as a criterion for punishing anticompetitive behavior

38. **An introductory note: trade in Athens, between dirigisme and freedom.** In primitive tribes, food transactions were forbidden, as foodstuffs were considered sacred.[117] Subsequently, trade, particularly in cereals, enabled the expansion of cities, notably Athens, where it became widespread. As the city was not self-sufficient, its survival depended on trade.[118] A phenomenon that can already be observed in the ancient world and persists to this day is the oscillation between periods when trade is left relatively free and others when it is more heavily administered by the state. Indeed, following each crisis, whether due to famine, war or political unrest, the state took control of the economy by setting price quotas, or even by partially or totally replacing merchants to supply the city.[119] These measures were always arbitrary and often ineffective. On the other hand, when merchants were allowed to operate freely, they did so only insofar as they did not behave dishonestly. From antiquity onward, there existed a fundamental difference in the nature of two forms of trade regulation: the setting of prices or quotas – according to contemporary categorizations – fell under administrative regulation, while the repression of hoarding and monopolies fell within the scope of criminal law. In the first case, the authorities substituted themselves for the natural play of the market, setting the conditions of exchange directly; in the second, they left the market free, but punished the abusive use of that freedom.

39. **Lysias' speech *Against the Corn Dealers*: the first surviving record of a trial condemning an anticompetitive practice.** Lysias' speech *Against the Corn Dealers*,[120] delivered in 386 BC,[121] is the first surviving record of a trial condemning an anticompetitive practice.[122] If this is the first evidence of the existence of this offense, it is certainly not the first time it was perpetrated, nor punished, as Lysias attests at the very beginning of his speech:

> How many times . . . have we seen ourselves besieged by these usurers, and languishing in the midst of the abundance they hid from us? All this, gentlemen, is nothing new; our ancestors have long had sad

117 K. Polanyi, La subsistance de l'homme: La place de l'économie dans l'histoire de la société 127 (Flammarion 2011) (1977).

118 *Id.* at 146.

119 *See* M. Finley, Économie et société en Grèce ancienne (1984).

120 For a complete transcription of the speech, *see* M. Bizos & L. Gernet, ii Lysias: Discours, (xvi-xxxv et fragments) 81 (1962) or N. Delamare, i Traité de la Police 297–300 (1705). The quotations reproduced below are taken from Lysias, Against the Corn Dealers (W. R. M. Lamb trans., Harvard Univ. Press 1930).

121 T. Figueira, "Sitopolai" *and* "Sitophylakes" *in Lysias' "Against the Graindealers": Governmental Intervention in the Athenian Economy*, 40 Phoenix 149, 150 (1986).

122 W. Dunham, *Cold Case Files: The Athenian Grain Merchants, 386 B.C.*, 28 Cato Journal 495, 495 (2008); L. Kotsiris, *An Antitrust Case in Ancient Greek Law*, 22 International Lawyer 451, 451 (1988).

> experiences of it. The *tricks*, *frauds* and *malice* of these regrattiers were well known to them.[123]

Human greed, leading some merchants to maneuver for undue gain, is indeed nothing new. In ancient Egypt, papyri dating back 3,000 BC reveal that coalitions already existed, operating to fix the price of various products, such as wool and clothing.[124] Even further back in history, the first known code of laws, promulgated by the Sumerian king Ur-Nammu and predating Hammurabi's Code by around three hundred years,[125] already mentions the existence of these "rapacious individuals" who approppriated oxen, sheep and donkeys.[126] It is therefore highly probable that the practice of hoarding existed and was sanctioned from the very birth of trade, in all civilizations.[127]

In ancient Greek times, the grain trade was divided between two types of merchants: the traders, who transported wheat by ship from faraway lands to the port of Piraeus in Athens, and the city merchants, who sold the wheat to Athenians in the markets. As the land of Attica was arid, its cultivation alone could not feed the inhabitants. Unable to obtain supplies from local farmers alone, merchants turned to fairground traders. But they did not simply buy the right amount of wheat – enough to feed the population. They forced the latter to sell them their entire cargo, then stored these goods, waiting patiently for the people to cry famine. Only then would they sell the wheat at the price they wished.

To put an end to these practices, a law was passed imposing a maximum purchase quota: on pain of death, merchants were forbidden to buy as much wheat as they wished from the fairground, to prevent them from building up excessive reserves.[128] This law, poorly enforced, proved ineffective, and merchants were able to continue their iniquitous maneuvers. The Senate was informed by the magistrates. The people demanded that the accused be sentenced to death without trial. Lysias opposed: he convinced the crowd that it was necessary, according to the laws of equity, to hear them before executing them. Justice had to be done: they were tried before eleven judges – the panel reserved for the most serious crimes. The defendants had indeed broken the law setting a quota for purchases, but it was not this charge that was upheld. Discussions focused

---

123 Delamare, I Traité de la Police, *op. cit.* at 299 (emphasis added).

124 N. Green, *The Road to Conviction – The Criminalisation of Cartel Law*, *in* 30 Annual Proceedings of the Fordham Corporate Law Institute: International Antitrust Law & Policy 13, 13 (2003).

125 S. N. Kramer, L'histoire commence à Sumer 76–77 (2017).

126 *Id.* at 77–80.

127 One author points out that there were severe sanctions against such maneuvers in India, several centuries before our era; *see* R. Piotrowski, Cartels and Trusts: Their Origin and Historical Development From the Economic and Legal Aspects 89–90 (1933).

128 Figueira, "Sitopolai" *and* "Sitophylakes" *in Lysias' "Against the Graindealers": Governmental Intervention in the Athenian Economy*, *op. cit.* at 152–53.

on the hoarding perpetrated by the merchants. On the eve of his speech, Lysias alerted his audience: "You will see very clearly all the *tricks* they used to perpetuate public misery and profit from it."[129]

The indictment clearly focused on the merchants' intentions. Describing their strategy in detail, the speaker tried to prove that their "excessive purchases of wheat [had] been made *deliberately* … and *with the sole aim of* increasing the price." The possibility that their intention was laudable, and not unjust, was then scrupulously examined before being dismissed:

> Perhaps they will say … that they made these wheat purchases out of their attachment and inclination for the city, and to have a reason to sell them to us very cheaply. Gentlemen, we still have to push them to the limit, and convince them that they are lying. Is it not true that if they had acted in this way for our sake, having bought a lot of wheat at once and at the same price, they would have displayed a reasonable quantity every day in the markets, and would not have sold it more expensively one day than the next! However, it is known to us, Messieurs, and to all of us, that they hid its abundance from us, and that not only from one day to the next, but in the same day from morning to evening, they had raised the price … as if they were ready to run out.[130]

It should be noted that, far from giving undue credence to the good intentions of the merchants, their fraudulent intent is deduced from their behavior, and not from any futile psychological investigation. There can be no doubt about the intentional nature of the offense. Indeed, by this time, the distinction between intent and negligence was already well known. For example, public inspectors responsible for monitoring commerce in Athens were often given heavy sentences for professional negligence. Lysias used this example to bolster his argument and justify the infliction of exemplary – in this case, capital – punishment on merchants. Addressing the magistrates, he pointed out: "If you have punished [inspectors] with death for simple negligence in discovering faults and reporting them, what penalties will you not pronounce against the real culprits? … It is not possible for you to absolve them."[131]

Lysias called for the death penalty for two reasons. Firstly, because he felt it was proportionate to the cruelty of the merchants,[132] who could not have been unaware that they were enriching themselves unfairly at the

---

129 N. Delamare, I Traité de la Police, *op. cit.* at 298 (emphasis added).

130 *Id.* at 298–99.

131 *Id.* at 300.

132 N.B.: a death sentence is obviously never proportionate, whatever the offense, and this assertion needs to be seen in the context of the time.

expense of the people, nor that their designs were likely to cause famine: "So many good citizens, so many poor people have died of hunger because of the monopolies and other bad practices of these people!"[133]

Secondly, the merchants could not but be aware that by behaving in this way, they were breaking the law, which, *even if it was not written down*, was dictated by natural equity, and therefore immanent to human reason: "Didn't they know that by doing so against the Laws, they were exposing their lives?"[134]

Conscientiousness and willpower were combined, and even at the heart of this trial, which bears the seeds of future developments in competition law. Lysias' speech also makes it clear that penalizing an offense has a pedagogical virtue and a dissuasive function. Condemning the merchants is a warning that a standard of behavior has been established, a boundary between what is permitted and what is forbidden that becomes valid for everyone else:

> All the people whom these prevaricators have caused so much suffering, are convinced that if you condemn them to death, it will make the others more restrained, more faithful in their trade, and more exact observers of the Laws; that on the contrary if you release them, it is to give to all by this impunity, the license to do in the future whatever they please.[135]

For Lysias, the best strategy for ensuring abundance was to make sure that merchants refrained from such maneuvers and adhered to sound trade practices:

> If these prevaricators are condemned to death as they have deserved, this will bring in the bulk of the grain trade, make us more fond of the fair traders, and attract abundance to us; if, on the contrary, these culprits are absolved, what merchants thus despised will want to trade with us? [Condemning them is] the only way to bring back wheat, otherwise it is quite certain that the extreme dearness in which it is at present will continue forever.[136]

The apprehension of unfair behavior was thus already aimed at avoiding the harmful long-term consequences of hindered commercial exchange, the most effective remedy for achieving this end being criminal law, which educates and prevents future infringements by deterring unscrupulous traders. The use of criminal law to punish anticompetitive practices was therefore also to be found in Roman law.

---

133 Delamare, i Traité de la Police, *op. cit.* at 299 (emphasis added).

134 *Id.*

135 *Id.*

136 *Id.*

II. Roman law

40. **The repression of anticompetitive practices in written and unwritten Roman law.** While the study of the Roman period is complementary to that of the Greek era, we must be wary of a positivist reading of Roman law: such an approach would be tantamount to observing the past through a distorting mirror.[137] Roman law is not limited to the *Corpus Juris Civilis*. The late Justinian compilation stems from an arbitrary choice[138] that fails to reflect not only the full range of offenses punished in ancient Rome[139] but – more importantly – the Roman way of reasoning, inherited from Greek dialectic.[140] Nevertheless, written law allows us to attest to the profusion of laws repressing anticompetitive practices (**A**), while the study of unwritten law enables us to grasp the spirit of this repression and to attest to the central role of intention (**B**).

A. Recognition of intent in written law

41. **Introductory note: trade in Rome, between dirigisme and freedom (again).** As in ancient Greece,[141] dirigisme coexisted with commercial freedom in Roman times. In fact, there was an annona service – a public service managed by the prefect of the annona to provide the people with a sufficient quantity of wheat, sometimes free of charge, sometimes at a modest price[142] – as well as, to complete the frumentary canon, a share of free trade left to merchants. Nevertheless, whenever prices rose excessively or foodstuffs became too scarce, measures were taken that were as drastic as they were ineffective:[143] establishing state monopolies;[144] forcing individuals to sell all their wheat[145] and forbidding them to stock up for

---

137 This distorted vision of Roman law, which fails to understand it by reducing it to written law alone, has been disseminated since the seventeenth century by the modern school of natural law and then by the Pandectists, who wanted to make Roman law "a science, a system of fixed rules, whereas it was a research, an art," *see* M. Villey, Le droit romain 132 (2012).

138 A. Schiavone, Ius: L'invention du droit en Occident 37–53 (G. & J. Bouffatigue trans., Belin 2008).

139 The traces we have of Roman criminal law as reproduced in the *Digest* are reduced to a catalog, which has "the defect that all catalogs have, i.e., of never being complete," M. Dequeux de Saint-Hilaire, De l'influence du christianisme sur le droit pénal des Romains 39 (1861).

140 M. Villey, *Logique d'Aristote et droit romain*, 28 Revue historique de droit français et étranger 309–28 (1951).

141 *See supra*, no. 38.

142 This service already existed in ancient Greece. The institutions of the Greek period, notably the prefect of the annona, were adopted with similar powers and competences in Roman law, *see* H. Babled, Droit romain: De la cura annonae chez les Romains 6–7 (1892). For a detailed examination of the operation of the annona service under the Roman Republic and Empire, *see id.* at 11–157.

143 According to Titus Livius, History of Rome, iv, 2, 3, 12, quoted by Babled, Droit romain: De la cura annonae chez les Romains, *op. cit.* at 169; in the same vein, N. Green, *The Road to Conviction – The Criminalisation of Cartel Law*, *in* 30 Annual Proceedings of the Fordham Corporate Law Institute: International Antitrust Law & Policy 13, 14 (2003).

144 O. Descamps & R. Szramkiewicz, Histoire du droit des affaires 68–68 (2nd ed. 2013).

145 Babled, Droit romain: De la cura annonae chez les Romains, *op. cit.* at 168.

more than a month;[146] ordering sellers to remain standing at the market, hoping that, exhausted, they would lower their prices to sell faster;[147] or setting maximum prices.[148] Diocletian's edict thus set Empire-wide prices for over a thousand products – from lupins and fenugreek to pork, peacock and gold – as well as wages, depending on the profession: mosaicist, blacksmith, barber, baker, notary…[149] The penalty, death, nevertheless seemed excessive. As a result, it was rarely pronounced.[150] The edict was rarely enforced, and failed to achieve its aim, with prices far exceeding those set.[151] In short, its only effect was to dissuade merchants from selling and producers from producing, and to encourage the growth of the black market.

42. **The profusion of Roman laws sanctioning anticompetitive practices.** Although the *Digest* reproduces only one of the laws proscribing anticompetitive practices, it is far from being the only provision of this nature to have been in force in Roman times.[152] This law, which is the best known, is reproduced in Book 48 of the *Digest*, which lists public crimes, in other words, those that harm not private interests but the general interest.[153] This is the *Lex Iulia de annona*, known as the "Julian Law on Provisions." It punished with a fine of twenty gold coins those merchants who diverted foodstuffs intended for the people, or sought to have them unduly bid upon – as well as those who, *through fraudulent maneuvers*, withheld ships destined to supply Rome.[154] The *Lex Iulia de annona* was enforced by the prefect of the annona,[155] to whom anyone, including women,[156] could lodge an accusation. However, as the crime committed is very serious, the prefect of the annona must, after investigation, refer the case to the prefect of the city, who alone is competent to impose the penalty.[157]

---

146 *Id.* at 162.

147 Under the reign of Emperor Nero, *id.*

148 During the reign of Emperor Tiberius, *id.* at 163; Emperor Diocletian, *id.* at 169–70; and Emperor Julian, *id.* at 171.

149 R. Rees, Diocletian and the Tetrarchy 139–46 (2004).

150 Babled, Droit romain: De la cura annonae chez les Romains, *op. cit.* at 170.

151 G. Depeyrot, Le Bas Empire romain: Économie et numismatique 97–98 (1991).

152 In this sense, R. Piotrowski, Cartels and Trusts: Their Origin and Historical Development From the Economic and Legal Aspects 104 (1933).

153 T. Mommsen, i Le droit pénal romain 9–10 (J. Duquesne trans., Albert Fontemoing 1907).

154 Fieffé-Lacroix, ii La clef des lois romaines, ou dictionnaire analytique et raisonné de toutes les matières contenues dans le Corps de Droit 252 (1810).

155 On the various responsibilities of the prefect of the annone, *see* Babled, Droit romain: De la cura annonae chez les Romains, *op. cit.* at 56–64; Delamare, i Traité de la Police, *op. cit.* at 54; Fieffé-Lacroix, ii La clef des lois romaines, ou dictionnaire analytique et raisonné de toutes les matières contenues dans le Corps de Droit, *op. cit.* at 352.

156 Digest, 48, 12, 3, 2.

157 Delamare, i Traité de la Police, *op. cit.* at 54.

Nevertheless, even before the reign of Emperor Augustus, during which the *Lex Iulia de annona* was enacted, town councilors already had a duty under the Republic to suppress any *attempt* at hoarding,[158] whether committed by a single person or by an agreement between several merchants.[159] This offense was still punished under the reign of Valentinian III.[160] Emperor Zeno passed the *Jubemus* law, which was enshrined in the Code *De Monopolis*, prohibiting agreements by which merchants agreed to sell goods such as foodstuffs, wood or clothing at a certain price, and also forbidding any *attempt* to constitute a monopoly – the penalties could go as far as confiscation and perpetual exile.[161] Pliny the Elder thus attests that there is no behavior that has provoked more *senatus consulta* than monopoly and hoarding.[162]

43. **The repression of anticompetitive practices, involving the consideration of merchants' intent.** Several factors demonstrate that the anticompetitive practices punished by the Roman laws mentioned above require an element of intent. Firstly, the offenses fall into the category of public crimes, requiring the characterization of intent.[163] Secondly, the punishment for attempt, as provided in certain texts, is only possible in the case of intentional offenses.[164] Thirdly, the Code of Justinian describes the offense as practices, meetings or actions aimed at *artificially* altering prices.[165] Finally, the only example mentioned by the *Digest* in relation to the *Lex Iulia de annona*, the withholding of a ship, notes that this maneuver presupposes "the use of fraud."[166] There is thus no doubt that intent was required by written law.

While Theodor Mommsen regrets the lack of written sources on this offense,[167] turning to unwritten Roman law helps complete the picture already outlined.

---

158 Titus Livius, History of Rome, xxxviii, 35, quoted by Babled, Droit romain: De la cura annonae chez les Romains, *op. cit.* at 162.

159 Piotrowski, Cartels and Trusts: Their Origin and Historical Development From the Economic and Legal Aspects, *op. cit.* at 105.

160 Valentinien iii, De Pantapolis ad Urbem Romam revocandis, cit. and trans. by Babled, Droit romain: De la cura annonae chez les Romains, *op. cit.* at 167.

161 On this law, *see* Babled, Droit romain: De la cura annonae chez les Romains, *op. cit.* at 167–68; D. Bosco & C. Prieto, Droit européen de la concurrence 22 (2013), no. 9; N. Meusy, ii Code de la religion et des mœurs, ou Recueil des principales ordonnances, depuis l'établissement de la monarchie françoise, concernant la religion et les mœurs 59 (1776); P.-F. Muyart de Vouglans, Institutes au droit criminel 607 (1757); Green, *The Road to Conviction – The Criminalisation of Cartel Law*, *op. cit.* at 14; N. Green, *From Rome to Rome: The Evolution of Competition Law into a Twenty-First Century Religion*, 9 Competition Law Journal 7, 11, 16 (2010).

162 Pline l'Ancien, I Histoire naturelle (E. Littré trans, Firmint-Didot et Cie 1877), bk. viii, lvi, at 240–241.

163 Carbasse, Histoire du droit pénal et de la justice criminelle, *op. cit.* at 50, no. 21.

164 This statement will be justified *infra*, no. 250.

165 Justinien, ii Les douze livres du Code de l'empereur Justinien 159–60 (P.-A. Tissot trans., A. Metz, 2nd ed. 1807).

166 Digest, 48, 12, 2, 1.

167 T. Mommsen, III Le droit pénal romain, bk. iv, 177–79 (J. Duquesne trans., Albert Fontemoing 1907).

B. Non-written law takes intention into account

44. **Anticompetitive practices repressed by means of an extraordinary action: the "stellionate."** As in Greece, on the basis of Solon's laws, Ulpian mentions the possibility, in Roman law, of forming *societas*, provided these associations are not *fraudulent.*[168] Several passages in the *Digest* also attest to the existence, in Rome, of the principle now known as "freedom of enterprise."[169] Now, when a freedom is recognized, it is only within certain limits and must be protected: it is therefore logical that any maneuver that hinders the freedom of commerce should be sanctioned – in this case, through a *cognitio extraordinaria.*[170] An extraordinary action is one that can be brought even in the absence of a written text.[171] This type of action only makes it possible to seize offenses that are obviously contrary to natural law; in other words, it only offers to punish behavior that is so bad in itself that citizens do not need a text to know that it is proscribed.[172] Moreover, since the rule was not specified by a text, the punishment was left to the arbitration of the judge,[173] who proportioned it to the guilt of the accused[174] and could therefore impose capital punishments:[175] ban on trade for time or life, relegation to an island, forfeiture of dignity, or even condemnation to public works.[176]

The extraordinary action, which enabled anyone, including women and slaves,[177] to lodge a complaint to have an anticompetitive practice punished,

---

168 Delamare, i Traité de la Police, *op. cit.* at 301.

169 In this sense, A. Wacke, *Freedom of Contract and Restraint of Trade Clauses in Roman and Modern Law*, 11 Law and History Review 1, 3–5 (1993) *See also* Digest, 1, 18, 6, 4: "The Governor of a province must make it his especial care that no one shall be prevented from transacting any lawful business, and that nothing prohibited shall be done, and that no punishment shall be inflicted upon the innocent."

170 *Extra ordinem* justice became established during the transition from the Republic to the Empire, cf. Y. Rivière, Histoire du droit pénal romain: De Romulus à Justinien 22–23 (2021).

171 Carbasse, Histoire du droit pénal et de la justice criminelle, *op. cit.* at 42–43, no. 16.

172 The system of "extraordinary actions" was revived during the medieval period. In this respect, *see* Carbasse, Histoire du droit pénal et de la justice criminelle, *op. cit.* at 76–77, no. 33.

173 Ulpian uses the expression "arbitrary punishment" in the Digest, 47, 10, 2. 11 It should be noted that the term "arbitrary" did not carry a pejorative meaning at the time; that connotation would only emerge after the French Revolution. In this sense, F. Saint-Bonnet, *Arbitraire*, *in* Dictionnaire des droits de l'homme 58, 60 (J. Andriantsimbazovina et al. eds., 2008).

174 And also according to the offender's social rank: *humiliores* received the most severe punishments, *honorati* the least infamous. For an account of this system, *see* Dequeux de Saint-Hilaire, De l'influence du christianisme sur le droit pénal des Romains, *op. cit.* at 45–46.

175 In Roman law, capital punishment was not confined to the death penalty. The term also encompasses other punishments, divided into three degrees: punishments that cause loss of life; those that do not take life but deprive the individual of liberty, such as a sentence to public works; and finally, those that affect the reputation of the condemned, such as relegation. *See* Fieffé-Lacroix, ii La clef des lois romaines, ou dictionnaire analytique et raisonné de toutes les matières contenues dans le Corps de Droit, *op. cit.* at 248–49.

176 Babled, Droit romain: De la cura annonae chez les Romains, *op. cit.* at 164; Fieffé-Lacroix, ii La clef des lois romaines, ou dictionnaire analytique et raisonné de toutes les matières contenues dans le Corps de Droit, *op. cit.* at 739.

177 Babled, Droit romain: De la cura annonae chez les Romains, *op. cit.* at 164.

was called *stellionate.*[178] Linked to public crimes, stellionate is the counterpart in criminal law of the action for *dol* in civil law.[179] The term refers to "any kind of atrocious *dol* or *deceit* that had no particular name."[180] The criterion for triggering this action is dishonest intent, the will to deceive. This characteristic of stellionate is directly linked to the origin of the term – derived from the Latin *stelio* and designating the deceitful, the swindler.

45. **The etymology of the word "*stellionate*": the story of a small speckled lizard.** The *stelio* owes its name to a small mottled lizard to which Pliny the Elder dedicated vast developments in his *Natural History.*[181] He lists the medicinal uses of the gecko's skin: it was used to treat epilepsy, for example, and as a remedy for many other ailments – its molt was a rare and highly sought-after commodity. So how is it that, despite the virtuous uses to which the animal's leather was put, its name took on such a pejorative connotation? There is a good reason: after losing its skin, the reptile always swallowed its molt, selfishly refusing to contribute to the preservation of human health. This behavior prompted the naturalist Pliny to write that the saurian was more cunning than any other animal when it came to frustrating man.[182] It is because of this evil intention attributed to the reptile that the word *stelio* has come to designate a dishonest, cunning individual[183] – one who prefers to jealously keep for themselves a good they do not need instead of providing it in abundance every season to those who lack it. The parallel with the offense of hoarding is obvious: merchants who, in order to enrich themselves beyond reason, use maneuvers to deny the people the foodstuffs they need for their subsistence correspond faithfully to the personality of the *stelio.*

46. **From the speckled lizard to the magician Dardanus.** Hoarders were the dread of the people and their rulers, so much so that they were thought to have evil powers – evidenced by the very name used to describe them: *dardanarii.* The term is derived from the name of the magician Dardanus, as it was believed that the artificial price manipulation achieved by merchants

---

178 It should be noted that the meaning of the term *stellionate* in Roman times differs from its current meaning. Today, stellionate refers to a "civil offense consisting of selling or mortgaging to someone, through false claims or omissions, a property that had already been sold or mortgaged to another person," Vocabulaire juridique 991 (G. Cornu ed., 11th ed. 2016).

179 So Ulpian writes: "It must be remembered that those who have committed any fraudulent act can be prosecuted for this crime … for what in private law gives rise to an action for fraud is the basis for a criminal prosecution in an accusation of *Stellionatus.* Hence, whenever where the offence lacks a name, we designate it *Stellionatus.*" Digest, 47, 20, 3. Stellionate is thus the "generic term under which Roman laws encompassed all types of fraud and deception … for which the law had not assigned a specific designation," B. d'Argis, *Stellionat*, xv L'Encyclopédie de Diderot et d'Alembert 509 (1751).

180 J.-B. Delaporte & P. N. Riffé-Caubray, xiv Les pandectes françaises, ou recueil complet de toutes les lois en vigueur 366 (1806) (emphasis added).

181 Pline l'Ancien, ii Histoire Naturelle (E. Littré trans., J. Dubochet 1850), bk. xxx, tit. xviii–xlix.

182 *Id.*, tit. xxvii, para. 2.

183 *See* the article by a Hellenist who has devoted several studies to *stelio*, S. Byl, *Notule relative au glissement de sens de "stelio,"* 45 Latomus 143 (1986), fasc. 1.

was the result of magical maneuvers or spells[184]. Ulpian uses this term to designate hoarders.[185] Beyond the anecdotal nature of these two nicknames – *stelio* and *dardanarii* – they show that the essential characteristic of anticompetitive behavior in Roman law is to be a maneuver, an artifice, a fraud, a dishonest sleight of hand.

*

* *

47. **Conclusion to Section 1: the clear affirmation of principles since antiquity.** Going back to the origins of criminal law and the earliest traces of competition law, we can observe two key points. Firstly, intent was central to the emergence of criminal law. The definition of this concept, both by Aristotle and through Roman casuistry, appears eminently modern – likely because it was passed down through the Scholastics and jurisconsults of the Ancien Droit. Secondly, the law of anticompetitive practices has a very ancient ancestor. At the time, the repression of monopoly and hoarding was not dependent on complex economic analyses. These offenses were the subject of legal, moral, and philosophical reflection, focusing on the intentions of merchants, their behavior, and their disloyalty rather than on the effects their practices had on the market.

48. **The temporary neglect of principles: 5th–12th centuries.** After the fall of the Roman Empire at the end of the fifth century, influenced by barbarian invasions, the law became fragmented and previously accepted principles disintegrated until the rediscovery of ancient thought during the Renaissance. Frankish law saw a return to the objectivity of repression,[186] characteristic of the archaic period.[187] Once again, facts judged man:[188] responsibility reverted to being both objective and collective.[189]

In 426, Augustine published *The City of God*, a forward-looking work in which he predicted that if Rome were to perish, the Church would be ready to take over. The period that followed was marked by religious ascendancy, which led to confusion between the temporal and spiritual orders until the twelfth century.[190] This dissolution of law into religion had a direct impact on the concept of criminal liability, as well as on

184 C. Daremberg, E. Saglio & E. Pottier, II Dictionnaire des Antiquités grecques et romaines 26 (1892).

185 Digest, 47, 11, 8 6.

186 J.-A. Roux, I Cours de droit criminel français 145–46 (2nd ed. 1927).

187 Studied *supra*, nos. 18–21, *see* J. Gaudemet, *Le problème de la responsabilité pénale dans l'Antiquité*, *in* II Studi in onore di Emilio Betti 483, 506 (1961).

188 O. Descamps, *Histoire du droit de la responsabilité dans le monde occidental*, *in* Prendre la responsabilité au sérieux 37, 46 (A. Supiot ed., 2015).

189 A. Laingui & M. Crépin, *La philosophie du droit pénal du Moyen Âge à l'époque moderne*, 53 Revue internationale de droit pénal 613, 615 (1982).

190 A. Laingui, *Le premier grand traité de responsabilité pénale: Le* "De Poenis Temperandis" *d'André Tiraqueau (1559)*, *in* Mélanges en l'honneur du Doyen Pierre Bouzat 179, 190 (1980).

economic provisions. In the penal sphere, judges henceforth relied on God to provide proof of the accused's intentions. This was determined by the use of ordeals, which were not banned until the twelfth century[191] and consisted in subjecting the accused to a physical ordeal believed to reveal their innocence or guilt through divine intervention.[192] This conflation of religion and law can also be seen in the rules governing the economy, which in the Carolingian period were laid down in royal texts that also addressed questions of faith.[193] It is then difficult to distinguish between purely economic measures and those of a religious nature, as in the capitularies adopted during Charlemagne's reign, such as those of Frankfurt (794),[194] Nijmegen (806),[195] or the capitularies of Thionville (805), which, promulgated during a famine, require that we "immediately begin to pray for divine mercy."[196]

This period, nicknamed the "Dark Ages,"[197] led to a momentary neglect of the principles developed in antiquity, and had no influence on contemporary law.[198] It was not until the rediscovery and dissemination of Roman law and Aristotle's thought that these principles resurfaced, developed and subsequently spread to all European countries.

*

* *

Section 2
The consolidation of intent from the 13th to the 18th century

49. **The rediscovery of ancient sources and the emergence of a general law.** From the eleventh to the thirteenth centuries, a veritable "renaissance of commerce" occurred,[199] generating cultural exchanges throughout Europe. Roman law was rediscovered from the eleventh century onwards, and its

191 A. Morin, *De l'étude des racines chrétiennes des droits pénaux français, britannique et canadien*, 32 Revue générale de droit 213, 275–76 (2002).

192 For a discussion of the different types of ordeals (fire, water or boiling water ordeals), *see id.* at 274–75.

193 M. Cândido da Silva, *L'économie morale carolingienne (fin VIIIe – début IXe siècle)*, 66 Médiévales 159, 177 (2014).

194 *Id.* at 169–70.

195 *Id.* at 173.

196 *Id.* at 176.

197 W. Durant, 11 Histoire de la civilisation 131–390 (1963) bk. iv.

198 Morin, *De l'étude des racines chrétiennes des droits pénaux français, britannique et canadien*, *op. cit.* at 265.

199 W. Durant, 12 Histoire de la civilisation 73–95 (1963).

study quickly gained "recognition almost equal to that of theology."[200] In the thirteenth century, Aristotle's work was exhumed. Although it was initially banned,[201] the fate of Aristotelian doctrine during the Renaissance was nevertheless "due to its scope, an almost unique phenomenon in the history of the revival of ideas."[202] It influenced not only developments relating to criminal responsibility, but also the theorization of commercial exchange. Roman law and Aristotelian theories play a key role in the writings of both the Scholastics and the jurisconsults of the Modern Era. The unity of the period studied (13th–18th centuries) is thus due to the emergence and persistence of a shared foundation of legal sources, which combines customary rules that vary according to place but are similar in spirit, canon law, and a flourishing doctrine[203] – doctors of law describing "a criminal law common to the whole of Europe."[204]

50. **The reaffirmation of the central role of intention by the Scholastics and the doctors of law.** The transmission of ancient writings to posterity takes place through the convergence of two distinct sources, which, by allowing us to trace the final features of this historical sketch, reveal the central role of intention. Initially, it was the Scholastics who took up and extended the Greco-Roman analyses (**Paragraph 1**). Their reflections were widely commented on by doctors of law, contributing to their influence (**Paragraph 2**).

Paragraph 1 – Scholastic theorization of intention

51. **The contribution of the Scholastics to the theorization of criminal responsibility and commercial exchange.** The contribution of the Scholastics is fundamental: their treatises dealt not only with theological matters, but also with law and economics, in the spirit of Aristotelian thought, which did not separate the various forms of knowledge.[205] Drawing a clear distinction between the temporal and religious orders, they developed a genuine theory of intention (**I**), and offered insightful views on its role in commercial exchange (**II**).

---

200 A. Schiavone, Ius: L'invention du droit en Occident 27 (G. & J. Bouffatigue trans., Belin 2008).

201 W. Durant, 13 Histoire de la civilisation 214–15 (1963).

202 J.-F. Revel, Histoire de la philosophie occidentale 247 (2003). *Adde* M. Villey, Philosophie du droit: Définitions et fins du droit, Les moyens du droit 40–41 (repub. 2001), no. 26: Michel Villey considers it necessary to return to the origins of law, where one encounters Aristotle – "an author whom the general public considers out of the running, struck from the register," yet who exerts a "profound influence on European thought," right up to the Middle Ages, where he "was 'the philosopher.'"

203 Carbasse, Histoire du droit pénal et de la justice criminelle, *op. cit.* at 141, no. 66. The author dedicates the second part of his work to the period spanning from the thirteenth to the eighteenth century.

204 *Id.* at 145, no. 68.

205 *See supra*, no. 37.

I. An essential criterion for incurring criminal liability

52. **Intention, a source of confusion between law and morality?** While predestination is pervasive in ancient beliefs,[206] free will, by contrast, is established as an axiom of Christianity.[207] Thomas Aquinas takes a clear-cut view: "Man has free will: otherwise counsels, exhortations, commands, prohibitions, rewards, and punishments would be in vain.[208] Man, marked by original sin, can therefore seek good, but also choose evil. For all his misguided actions, as for all his impious thoughts, he is fully guilty – a sinner seeking redemption with every confession.[209] Has this demanding conception of human freedom[210] had an impact on the role of intention in criminal law? Has intention, under the influence of theologians, become the Trojan horse of confusion between law and morality? This is one of the criticisms often leveled at the concept of intention today: granting it a place in law would involve taking vague moral considerations into account, and would therefore be a source of legal uncertainty. However, while religion has undoubtedly had a considerable influence on criminal law,[211] theologians themselves, as early as the twelfth century,[212] took care to distinguish between sin and offense,[213] between

---

206 *See supra*, nos. 26–27.

207 There are, however, unresolvable controversies as to the origin of this free will and its compatibility with God's grace. Two main positions stand in opposition: either freedom comes from man himself – as argued by the Pelagians, Thomas Aquinas, the Jesuits and Erasmus – or, if it is considered a gift from God, freedom is only partly autonomous – as argued by Augustine, the Jansenists and Martin Luther and his "*servo arbitrio*" theory. *See*, among a vast body of literature: O. Descamps, *Histoire du droit de la responsabilité dans le monde occidental*, *in* PRENDRE LA RESPONSABILITÉ AU SÉRIEUX 37, 44 (A. Supiot ed., 2015); M. Frede, *Augustine: A Radically New Notion of a Free Will?*, *in* A FREE WILL: ORIGINS OF THE NOTION IN ANCIENT THOUGHT 153 (2012); M. Huftier, *Libre arbitre, liberté et péché chez saint Augustin*, 33 RECHERCHES DE THÉOLOGIE ANCIENNE ET MÉDIÉVALE 187 (1966); O. Lottin, *La preuve de la liberté humaine chez saint Thomas d'Aquin*, 23 RECHERCHES DE THÉOLOGIE ANCIENNE ET MÉDIÉVALE 323 (1956); ÉRASME, LUTHER, LUTHER: DU SERF ARBITRE. ÉRASME, DIATRIBE: DU LIBRE ARBITRE (Gallimard 2001); BOSSUET, TRAITÉ DU LIBRE ARBITRE (Manucius 2006).

208 THOMAS AQUINAS, SUMMA THEOLOGICA, Ia Pars, qu. 83.

209 On the subject of original sin, Cioran, with his usual cynicism, writes: "That sin is your livelihood. Without it you would starve to death, for your ministry would have no further meaning," *Aveux et anathèmes*, *in* CIORAN, ŒUVRES 1656 (Gallimard 1995).

210 Affirmed by the Council of Trent as a "dogma of the Church." *See* A. LAINGUI, HISTOIRE DU DROIT PÉNAL 105 (2nd ed. 1993).

211 A. Morin, *De l'étude des racines chrétiennes des droits pénaux français, britannique et canadien*, 32 REVUE GÉNÉRALE DE DROIT 213 (2002); M. Villey, *La responsabilité chez St Thomas*, VIII ANNALES DE LA FACULTÉ DE DROIT ET DES SCIENCES POLITIQUES ET ÉCONOMIQUES DE STRASBOURG 117, 118 (1961); L'abbé Metz, *La responsabilité pénale dans le droit canonique médiéval*, VIII ANNALES DE LA FACULTÉ DE DROIT ET DE SCIENCES POLITIQUES ET ÉCONOMIQUES DE STRASBOURG 83, 85, 91 (1961); A. Laingui, *Le droit pénal canonique, source de l'ancien droit pénal laïc*, *in* ÉGLISES ET POUVOIR POLITIQUE 213 (1987); A. LAINGUI, LA RESPONSABILITÉ PÉNALE DANS L'ANCIEN DROIT (XVIE – XVIIIE SIÈCLES) 13 (1970).

212 From the Gratien Decree onwards, *see* CARBASSE, HISTOIRE DU DROIT PÉNAL ET DE LA JUSTICE CRIMINELLE, *op. cit.* at 281, no. 137.

213 It should be noted that Christian influence nevertheless burdened criminal law with religiously based offenses that gradually disappeared with its secularization; *see* J.-M. Carbasse, *Sécularisation et droit pénal*, 60 DROITS: REVUE FRANÇAISE DE THÉORIE JURIDIQUE 13, 37 (2014).

earthly justice and divine justice[214] and thus clearly dissociated the religious conception of intention from its legal meaning. This distinction (**A**), which may seem dated in an age marked by secularism, is nonetheless an important step, since it demonstrates that intention is not an unfathomable, moralistic notion, but a clearly defined legal concept – as evidenced by its theorization by Thomas Aquinas (**B**).

A. The clear distinction between religious and legal conceptions of intention

53. **The clear distinction between religious and legal conceptions of intention.** Contrary to popular belief,[215] the Church has not confused crime with sin. Indeed, the judgment and repression of sin pertain to the interior forum – the forum of conscience. This is the task of the priest confessor, who inflicts a penance voluntarily accepted by the sinner in order to lead them to redemption.[216] Human justice is quite different: the judgment passed on a criminal offense relates to the external forum, the realm of the visible. Punishment is pronounced by the courts, and forcibly administered with the more modest aim of maintaining the social order.[217] As a result, the key characteristic of intention – which in law is an *abstraction*[218] – has endured even under the influence of canon law. The confessor judges *loco Dei*, in the place of God: he must fathom the soul, and the slightest intention, even if it is not followed by an act, is referred to him for sentence. Conversely, it is neither the role nor the capacity of the judge to set himself up as the inquisitor of consciences.[219] Thus, while both temporal and divine orders require intention to establish sin or offense,[220] respectively, intention is not apprehended in the same way. It is *absolute* for the *priest*, *relative* for the *judge*.

Thomas Aquinas thus admits that "[i]n the business affairs of men, there is no such thing as demonstrative and infallible proof, and we must be content with a certain conjectural probability."[221] The judge, for whom

214 R. Eckert, *Peine judiciaire, pénitence et salut entre droit canonique et théologie (xIIe s. - début du xIIIe s.)*, 4 Revue de l'histoire des religions 483 (2011); Villey, *La responsabilité chez St Thomas*, *op. cit.* at 127–28 and 132–33; L. Kahn, Étude sur le délit et la peine en droit canon V, 19 (1898) (Ph.D. dissertation, Université de Nancy); L'abbé Metz, *La responsabilité pénale dans le droit canonique médiéval*, *op. cit.* at 87; A. Laingui & M. Crépin, *La philosophie du droit pénal du Moyen Âge à l'époque moderne*, 53 Revue internationale de droit pénal 613, 615–16 (1982).

215 For a discussion of the frequent confusion between offense and sin, *see* Kahn, Étude sur le délit et la peine en droit canon, *op. cit.* at 13–15.

216 *Id.* at 18.

217 *Id.*

218 *See supra*, nos. 25 *et seq*.

219 Kahn, Étude sur le délit et la peine en droit canon, *op. cit.* at 19.

220 *Id.* at 36.

221 Thomas Aquinas, Summa Theologica, I-IIae, qu. 105, art. 2.

it is impossible to know intention, can only ever *presume* it on the basis of material acts and circumstances.[222] Two consequences follow. Firstly, mere intention is never reprehensible unless followed by an external manifestation,[223] precisely because it can only be revealed through that externalization. Secondly and consequently, intention is not, in law, an entirely *subjective* concept. It is, from an ontological point of view, because it relates to the individual, *the subject*. It is not so from a technical point of view, since the means of proving it are always, necessarily, *objective* – deduced from material findings, mainly *behavior*.

The distinction, which dates back to antiquity,[224] between the realm of beliefs and the legal order was thus maintained under the influence of theologians. It enabled Thomas Aquinas to elaborate a secular legal theory of intention, which was subsequently taken up and developed by jurists and which, in many respects, prefigures the contemporary conception of intention in criminal law.

B. Thomas Aquinas's legal theorization of intention

54. **Thomas Aquinas's refinement of the theory of intention.** For canonists, intention is the prerequisite for criminal responsibility.[225] The basis of their analysis is a passage from Saint Augustine, cited in Gratian's Decree: "So true is it that every sin is voluntary, that unless it be voluntary, it is no sin at all."[226] This axiom underpins the theoretical constructs of criminal law: from attempts to fortuitous events, including ignorance, insanity and minority.[227] Given that the principles of criminal liability revolve around intention, it is hardly surprising that many developments have been devoted to it. And it is without doubt Thomas Aquinas who has offered the richest analyses on this subject.[228] His *Summa Theologica*[229] is considered a veritable source of law, for both canonical and secular criminal law.[230] Aristotle's mark

---

222 Kahn, Étude sur le délit et la peine en droit canon, *op. cit.* at 19.

223 *Compare with* the theory of intention developed by the doctors of law, *infra*, no. 69.

224 *See supra*, nos. 25 *et seq.*

225 L'abbé Metz, *La responsabilité pénale dans le droit canonique médiéval*, *op. cit.* at 87.

226 *Id.* at 92. Gratian's Decree itself refers to a text in Justinian's Code (*C.*, 9, 16, 1), *id.* at 93.

227 *Id.* at 92.

228 According to A. Laingui and M. Crépin, Thomas Aquinas "left both canon law and secular law the richest legacy on the causes of fault." *See* Laingui & Crépin, *La philosophie du droit pénal du Moyen Âge à l'époque moderne*, *op. cit.* at 616.

229 Thomas d'Aquin, Somme Théologique (F. Lachat trans., Louis Vivès, 16 volumes, 1854–1861) (1266–1273); for a more recent edition in 4 volumes: Somme Théologique (Les éditions du Cerf 2021).

230 Note that a clear distinction is made in the *Summa Theologica* between evangelical law and the temporal order, with legal rules deriving not from "revealed dogma" but from secular reasoning based on Roman law and Aristotle. *See* M. Villey, *De laïcité du droit selon saint Thomas*, *in* Leçons d'histoire de la philosophie du droit 203, 203, 208, 215 (1962). The juridical themes addressed by Thomas Aquinas are mainly – but not exclusively – found in the *Secunda Secundae*, qu. 57 *et seq.*; *adde* Villey, *La responsabilité chez St Thomas*, *op. cit.* at 118.

is visible:[231] on error, for example, the adoption of his doctrine is almost literal.[232] But the scholastic goes further, and takes a decisive step forward in the theorization of intention in three respects: first, by distinguishing between the intention of the act and the intention of the result;[233] second, by questioning the conditions under which a result can be considered to have been intentionally sought; and third, by distinguishing the principal intention from the accessory effect – i.e., that which is not directly intended, but which nevertheless constitutes one of the consequences of the behavior.

55. **The characterization of intention in the presence of an *act that is inherently evil.*** For Thomas Aquinas, intention is defined as "that which moves towards the end,"[234] which can be either the act itself or the result of that act. The scholastic states that, in all cases, intention can only be determined a posteriori, from the act – the latter being the only element accessible.[235]

He then argues that intention is evil not only when it seeks an evil *outcome*, but also when it is directed toward an *act* that is evil in itself.[236] In this second case – the intention of an evil act – few questions arise. Indeed, since intention can only be judged based on outward behavior, if that behavior is bad, the intention will unquestionably be held to be bad. For example, when the legislator prescribes certain standards for weights and measures, the mere fact of not complying with them makes the merchant guilty – because the act itself, regardless of any result, is unlawful.[237]

56. **Characterizing intent in the presence of a *result detachable from the act.*** A far more complex question is under what conditions someone can be held responsible for the *result of their act.*[238] In theory, things are simple: if the negative outcome is intended, the intention is itself bad. But in practice, since intention can only be known from behavior, how can we know whether the result caused by that behavior was intended? Is this not an insurmountable impasse? If we can presume with any hope of accuracy that behavior X is caused by intention X, then behavior X can

---

231 In this sense, *see* Laingui & Crépin, *La philosophie du droit pénal du Moyen Âge à l'époque moderne, op. cit.* at 617.

232 To the question "Whether ignorance excuses from sin altogether?" Thomas Aquinas answers that it can happen that it cannot be excused, notably if it is willed, "as when a man wishes of set purpose to be ignorant of certain things that he may sin the more freely," or when one neglects to learn what one is bound to know and can know. Ignorance is an excuse only if it is "entirely involuntary," which is the case if it is "invincible." Thomas Aquinas, Summa Theologica, IIae Iae, qu. 76, art. 3; *compare with* Aristotle's theory, *supra*, no. 29.

233 We will take up this *summa divisio* in our own conceptualization of intention, *see infra*, no. 233.

234 Thomas Aquinas, Summa Theologica, IIa IIae, qu. 12, art. 1.

235 *Id.*, IIa IIae, qu. 20, art. 1.

236 *Id.*, IIa IIae, qu. 20, art. 2.

237 *Compare with* positive law, discussed *infra*, no. 158.

238 This question is dealt with in Thomas Aquinas, Summa Theologica, IIa IIae, qu. 20, art. 5.

also produce results Y or Z, or even A. So how can we say that Y or Z is caused by intention X? How, then, can we state with any certainty that Y, Z or A is the result of an intention X?

Thomas Aquinas proposed a landmark response. He distinguished between "*essential effects*" and "*accidental effects.*" According to him, if the effect follows the act "by itself and most often," the effect is *foreseeable* and therefore *must be anticipated.* In other words, if the effect is foreseeable, the intention of the effect is presumed. Conversely, if the effect "happens only by accident and very rarely" it cannot be considered to have been foreseen. For example, if someone dies from intoxication, and the administered substance is known to be a deadly poison, the perpetrator was aware that its ingestion would result in death. If they were unaware, they cannot invoke ignorance to exonerate themselves – given the nature of the substance, they should have known, as the outcome was self-evident. On the other hand, if a berry is offered to a friend who unfortunately turns out to be allergic to it, since most people do not die from consuming it, it is not possible to foresee the occurrence of death – the effect is accidental. Thomas Aquinas concludes: the virtue of intention is assessed "according to its essential effects, and not according to its accidental effects."[239] Echoing Aristotle, he considers that "accidental results are not intentional," but that, conversely, a bad intention can be characterized in someone who does not take the precautions required to prevent the occurrence of the negative outcome.[240]

57. **The distinction between primary intention and accessory effect.** Illustrating his point with the example of self-defense, Thomas Aquinas notes that "[n]othing prevents the same act from having two effects, only one of which is intended, while the other is not." This is the case of a person defending themselves: they seek only to protect themselves – which is legitimate – but this may result in injuring or even killing their aggressor. However, actions are essentially judged based on their primary intention, not on their incidental effects. If the main intention is legitimate, then the collateral effect cannot establish guilt. However, there is one important condition: proportionality. Indeed, "an act performed with a good intention can become bad when it is not proportionate to its end."[241] It follows, *a contrario* and in general, that a bad effect can sometimes be justified if it is the accessory and proportionate consequence of a good intention.[242]

58. **Legacy of Thomas Aquinas' doctrine.** Thomas Aquinas' doctrine is of major importance, as it was adopted by jurists[243] and later, in modern

239 *Id.*, IIa IIae, qu. 68, art. 8.

240 *Id.*

241 *Id.*, IIa IIae, qu. 68, art. 7.

242 The theories of self-defense and legitimate ground proceed from this reasoning, *see infra* nos. 338–341.

243 *See supra*, no. 69.

times, served as the basis for the German theory of intention, which centered on the concept of foreseeability.[244] However, the contribution of the Scholastics was far from limited to the conceptualization of intention: they also made a decisive contribution to the theorization of harm to competition.

II. The single criterion for identifying an infringement on competition

59. **The modernity of scholastic economic theories.** Why dwell for a moment on the Scholastics' view of economics? We might well assume that their doctrine is no more than a distant echo of the issues of our time. Did they not simply condemn usury outright and advocate a charity too pious to be of interest to modern economics? To limit ourselves to these prejudices would be to judge them unfairly.[245] Their doctrine is much closer to certain contemporary theories than is generally believed[246] and, contrary to popular belief, the Scholastics did not sacrifice analysis to moral concerns.[247] According to De Roover, the economic ideas underpinning contemporary law on anticompetitive practices have their roots in the Scholastics.[248] In Schumpeter's view, they are the founders of modern economic analysis, and offered tools for reflection so relevant that some later work, because it relies on complexities that are not very useful, constitutes an unnecessary detour.[249]

---

244 *See supra*, no. 193.

245 The doctrine of the Scholastics was re-explored from the 1950s and 1960s, thanks to the pioneering work of Joseph Schumpeter and Raymond de Roover, which helped to debunk misconceptions and highlight the richness and contemporary relevance of their theories. *See* Rothbard, 1 Economic Thought Before Adam Smith: An Austrian Perspective on the History of Economic Thought, *op. cit.* at x; *adde* on Raymond de Roover's contribution to the history of scholastic thought: J. Kirshner, *Les travaux de Raymond de Roover sur la pensée économique des scolastiques*, 30 Annales 318 (1975). Finally, *see* S. Trifilio, Esprit mathématique et pensée économique dans l'Antiquité et au Moyen Âge 270 (2010) (Ph.D. dissertation, Aix-Marseille University): "The great merit (and originality of the Scholastics in relation to Aristotle) undoubtedly lies in their ability to bring together in a coherent manner, under the banner of justice, more than their predecessors. … They were led, for some … to put their finger on what we have called since the seventeenth century 'competition.' In this way, they were able to identify and relate, through an ethic of commerce, a whole set of objects that would later become those of political economy."

246 In this sense, *see* R. De Roover, *Monopoly Theory Prior to Adam Smith: A Revision*, 65 The Quarterly Journal of Economics 492, 524 (1951).

247 R. De Roover, La pensée économique des scolastiques: Doctrine et méthode 9 (1971).

248 R. De Roover, *The Concept of Just Price: Theory and Economic Policy*, 18 The Journal of Economic History 418, 427 (1958).

249 J. A. Schumpeter, History of Economic Analysis 97 (1954): "It is within their systems of moral theology and law that economics gained definite if not separate existence, and it is they who come nearer than does any other group to having been the 'founders' of scientific economics. And not only that: it will appear, even, that the bases they laid for a serviceable and well-integrated body of analytic tools and propositions were sounder than was much subsequent work, in the sense that a considerable part of the economics of the later nineteenth century might have been developed from those bases more quickly and with less trouble than it actually cost to develop it, and that some of that subsequent work was therefore in the nature of a time- and labor-consuming detour."

60. **The continuity between Scholastic economic theorization and that of Aristotle.** In addition to religious sources, the Scholastics all commented on Aristotle's texts,[250] but hardly any on Plato's.[251] They remained faithful to the Aristotelian method[252] and did not dissociate ethical, legal and economic thinking.[253] The aim of their teaching was to determine the rules that should govern economic relations. The focus is on the *process* of exchange, the *behavior* and *intentions* of merchants, not on the *results*. The central question of their thinking is under what conditions exchange can be considered fair. According to them, the price is fair provided that it has been determined by the free interaction between the will of the buyer community and that of the sellers. Conversely, the price is unjust when it is not freely determined, i.e., when it is the result of fraud, manipulation or coercion. For this reason, the Scholastics unanimously condemn monopoly, which they interpret not in the strict sense,[254] but in a much broader sense.[255] For them, the term encompasses any maneuver directed against transaction *freedom*, with the aim of gaining market control.[256] In the name of the common good and natural law,[257] it is severely condemned because it necessarily prevents the formation of a just price. To understand the Scholastics' condemnation of monopoly (**B**), we must first outline their doctrine of the just price (**A**).

A. The just price: a natural consequence of the free meeting of wills

61. **The positive definition of a just price: common estimation.** *A priori*, we might think that, for theologians, the price is just if it does not exceed the requirements of charity or social justice. This is not so: in economic matters, we find again the distinction between internal and external forums, as already explained in relation to criminal responsibility.[258]

250 They extended Aristotle's thinking on the question of the right price, which he addressed only indirectly through his analysis of the different forms of justice. Indeed, Aristotle never used the term "just price," nor did he engage in any detailed analysis of value, *see* M. Finley, Économie et société en Grèce ancienne 267–68 (1984); Schumpeter, History of Economic Analysis, *op. cit.* at 57; S. Trifilio, Esprit mathématique et pensée économique dans l'Antiquité et au Moyen Âge 113 n.436 (2010) (Ph.D. dissertation, Aix-Marseille University).

251 De Roover, La pensée économique des scolastiques: Doctrine et méthode, *op. cit.* at 21.

252 *See supra*, no. 37.

253 G. Erner, *La morale économique chrétienne: Le tournant médiéval*, 3 Revue internationale des sciences sociales 513, 514 (2005); De Roover, La pensée économique des scolastiques: Doctrine et méthode, *op. cit.* at 18–20.

254 Strictly speaking, monopoly refers to a market situation where a single seller faces a multitude of buyers.

255 Just as in Roman times, when the term "monopoly" was sometimes used as a synonym for "hoarding," "coalition," or "stellionate."

256 R. de Roover, *La doctrine scolastique en matière de monopole et son application à la politique économique des communes italiennes*, *in* I Studi in onore di Amintore Fanfani nel venticinquennio di cattedra universitaria 149, 161 (1962).

257 W. Decock, Le marché du mérite: Penser le droit et l'économie avec Léonard Lessius 124 (2019).

258 *See supra*, no. 53.

Theologians certainly advocate virtue, charity and sharing, but this concerns individual consciences – the internal forum. Exchange is also theorized in terms of earthly justice. The Scholastics were well aware that the aim of any commercial enterprise is profit, and that it is profit that encourages merchants to do their best, which, in turn, has positive consequences for the community – it is then up to the Church to aid the needy and hear the confessions of merchants seeking repentance.[259] The price is thus considered fair, from a legal point of view, if it is the result of a *common estimate*.[260] Put another way, the just price is simply the "prevailing market price."[261]

How does this common assessment arise? In other words, what enables us to determine the value of something? Pierre de Jean Olivi distinguishes five criteria: utility, scarcity, labor, risk, and the offices and dignities associated with them.[262] The price is not linked to the cost of production.[263] Instead, the just price is the result of a contractual analysis on the part of the Scholastics.[264] This has several consequences. First, the high price of a good cannot be contrary to morality if the exchange takes place voluntarily: as everyone is free to buy and sell, a merchant may charge a higher price for a rare good or one deemed useful by the community.[265] Consequently, even if the price seems exorbitant, this is not a problem if the buyer is aware of the excess affecting the transaction and nevertheless agrees to it.[266] This was already the case in the luxury goods market: the price was irrelevant as long as an enthusiast was willing to spend on an antique bust or a hunting falcon.[267] Second, neither profit nor commercial activity is decried in itself,[268] just as in

---

259 On this subject, *see* S. Piron, *Marchands et confesseurs. Le Traité des contrats d'Olivi dans son contexte*, *in* L'Argent au Moyen Âge 289, 293–94 (1998).

260 The Scholastics are unanimous on this point, cf. De Roover, La pensée économique des scolastiques: Doctrine et méthode, *op. cit.* at 25; Rothbard, 1 Economic Thought Before Adam Smith: An Austrian Perspective on the History of Economic Thought, *op. cit.* at x–xi.

261 However, some Scholastics held – and this has been the subject of much controversy, notably between Franciscans and Dominicans – that the just price stems from common estimation, but may also be set by the state. *See* De Roover, *Monopoly Theory Prior to Adam Smith: A Revision*, *op. cit.* at 496; and B. Gordon, Economic Analysis Before Adam Smith: Hesiod to Lessius 228 (1975).

262 Olivi, Traité des contrats 113–15 (S. Piron trans., Les Belles Lettres 2012). For a detailed analysis of these criteria, *see* De Roover, La pensée économique des scolastiques: Doctrine et méthode, *op. cit.* at 46–50.

263 De Roover, *Monopoly Theory Prior to Adam Smith: A Revision*, *op. cit.* at 496.

264 S. Trifilio, *The Economic Theory of the Scholastics as a Contractual Analysis*, 24 Journal des Économistes et des Études Humaines 4 (2018): "The economic developments of the Scholastics are ordinarily reduced to the problem of 'just price', but compared to the origin and to the goal of their reflections, this problem appears indeed to be secondary. Their method, which consists in an authentic contractual analysis, is what is more surely the sign of their School. The 'just price' is only the condition of the 'just contract' (transaction or *commutatio*)."

265 Olivi, Traité des contrats, *op. cit.* at 95–101.

266 *Id.* at 105.

267 De Roover, La pensée économique des scolastiques: Doctrine et méthode, *op. cit.* at 70–71.

268 A. Lapidus, Le détour de valeur 23 (1986).

Aristotle's works.[269] Profit is viewed as a driving force that generates benefits for the community and is a fair reward for the "perils, expenses, industries and vigilant foresight" of merchants.[270]

It follows from this definition that the just price cannot be determined mathematically.[271] It depends on so many ever-changing circumstances, specific to the parties involved in the exchange, to each place, each product, each community, that *it is impossible to objectively theorize the value of a good*. Thus, Scholastics believed that the *pretium mathematicum* – "the mathematical price" – depended on so many particular factors "that it could never be known to man but was known only to God."[272]

62. **The negative definition of just price: the absence of maneuvering.** While the determination of a just price cannot be known in advance, nor can it be objectively fixed with the aid of calculations, it is bounded by clear limits. In other words, while in the abstract the just price cannot be defined positively, it can be defined negatively. For this reason, deception is condemned,[273] as are the abuse of the buyer's or seller's weakness or personal necessity,[274] fraud and *dol*.[275] Discrimination is also frowned upon. Olivi asks: "If a medicinal herb can save me from death, can the person selling it to me demand from me a price equivalent to the cure, i.e. inappreciable?" His reasoning is clear: if the remedy is rare, it can be sold at a high price, but it must not be sold at a higher price to the person who needs it.[276] The seller cannot legitimately set discriminatory prices according to the respective needs of buyers.

Thus, a price is always just when it is freely agreed; it is unfair, however, when dishonesty is involved. And if there is one form of dishonesty that the Scholastics condemned in unison, precisely because it represents the most serious obstacle to the formation of a just price,

---

269 *See supra*, no. 35. Thomas Aquinas, in his *Summa Theologica*, takes up Aristotle's distinction between the two chrematistics, and concludes: "Nevertheless gain which is the end of trading, though not implying, by its nature, anything virtuous or necessary, does not, in itself, connote anything sinful or contrary to virtue: wherefore nothing prevents gain from being directed to some necessary or even virtuous end, and thus trading becomes lawful. Thus, for instance, a man … and seek gain, not as an end, but as payment for his labor." *Secunda Secundae*, qu. 77, art. 4, in answer to the question "Whether, in trading, it is lawful to sell a thing at a higher price than what was paid for it?"

270 Olivi, Traité des contrats, *op. cit.* at 139.

271 Decock, Le marché du mérite: Penser le droit et l'économie avec Léonard Lessius, *op. cit.* at 96.

272 F. A. Hayek, referring to Molina and de Lugo. Hayek is quick to point out that he would "sometimes wish that our mathematical economists would take this to heart," F. A. von Hayek, *The Pretence of Knowledge*, 79 The American Economic Review (1989) 3, 5.

273 Olivi, Traité des contrats, *op. cit.* at 97.

274 *Id.* at 123–25.

275 De Roover, *La doctrine scolastique en matière de monopole et son application à la politique économique des communes italiennes*, *op. cit.* at 165.

276 Olivi, Traité des contrats, *op. cit.* at 109–17.

it is monopoly. Molina writes that "when, in the absence of fraud, monopolies and other malpractices, it is customary in any region or place for a thing to be commonly sold at one price, that price must be taken as the measure and rule for judging the just price of that thing in that region or place, so long as cyclical variations neither raise nor lower that price."[277] Monopolists are unjust because they impose the conditions of exchange on others by exercising a constraint which, because it breaks with the principle of the free meeting of wills, hinders the establishment of a just price.

B. Fraudulent intent, an obstacle to the formation of a just price

63. **The Scholastics' unanimous condemnation of monopoly.** *Monopolium est injustum et rei publicae injuriosum* – "monopoly is unjust and harmful to the public good": such was the saying.[278] Between the thirteenth and seventeenth centuries, a large number of Scholastics – French, Italian, Spanish, German, Belgian… – devoted studies to monopoly, primarily in their treatises on contracts.[279] All condemned it without a single dissenting voice.[280] According to Gratien's Decree, profits derived from the exercise of a monopoly would be considered *turpe lucrum*, i.e., shameful gains.[281] And when Pierre Jean de Olivi justifies the money earned by merchants, he immediately points out that, conversely, they will be damned if, carried away by greed – the root of all sins[282] – they behave like criminals by engaging in fraudulent monopoly.[283]

64. **Justifying the condemnation of monopoly.** While it goes without saying that monopolies are condemned, we need to ask ourselves why they are considered unjust. The monopolist has many faces: the walker, who goes out on the road to meet country folk and buy their livestock before they reach the market, thus limiting the number of

277 L. De Molina, 2 De iustitia et de iure: De contractibus 392 (Mylius 1602), disp. 348 (we thank Professor Laurent Calvié for his translation of the following extract: "*quando absque fraude, monopoliis, atque aliis versutiis, communiter res aliqua vendi consuevit pretio in aliqua regione, aut loco, idhabendum est pro mensura et regula judicandi pretium iustum rei illius in ea regione, aut loco, interim dum circumstantiæ non variantur, quibus meritò pretium accrescat, vel decrescat*").

278 De Roover, *Monopoly Theory Prior to Adam Smith: A Revision*, *op. cit.* at 498.

279 *Ex multis*: Henry of Susa, John Duns Scotus, Pierre de Jean Olivi, Bernardine of Siena, Antoninus, Thomas Aquinas, John Nider, Conrad Summenhart, Domingo de Soto, Thomas de Vio, Leonard Lessius. *See* the numerous references cited by De Roover, La pensée économique des scolastiques: Doctrine et méthode, *op. cit.* at 26–30.

280 Erner, *La morale économique chrétienne: Le tournant médiéval*, *op. cit.* at 514; De Roover, *La doctrine scolastique en matière de monopole et son application à la politique économique des communes italiennes*, *op. cit.* at 160.

281 Gratian's Decree, *Corpus Juris Canonici*, causa xiv, qu. 4, can. 9, quoted by De Roover, La pensée économique des scolastiques: Doctrine et méthode, *op. cit.* at 67.

282 Thomas Aquinas, Summa Theologica, Ia IIae Pars, qu. 84, art. 1.

283 Olivi, Traité des contrats, *op. cit.* at 145–47.

competitors;[284] the Gargantua, who stores up provisions in order to create an artificial shortage;[285] the tailor, innkeeper, secondhand dealer, baker, wool comber or hemp maker who foments a coalition with his peers to fix prices;[286] or bosses willingly agreeing among themselves on the need for a general reduction in wages.[287] Behaviors may vary greatly, as the cunning of dishonest individuals knows no bounds, but they all share the same characteristic: *artifice*. Commercial exchange is a "natural" process, the Scholastics said.[288] Conversely, artifice is that which comes from the hand of man, rather than occurring spontaneously. The market, in essence, is beyond the control of the individual who takes part in it: according to Scholastic doctrine, neither the buyer nor the seller has the slightest control over the conditions of exchange – they are imposed on them by the market, by the blind encounter of supply and demand.[289]

But what is *the intention* of monopolists? It is to dominate the rules of the game – and to free themselves from them in order to win by cheating. That is where the fault lies. Imagine a game of chess in which a player, frustrated by a losing position, suddenly grants themselves the right to move their king as many squares as they please and make their queen invincible. In doing so, they ensure victory by placing themself, like a demiurge, above the rules that bind every other player. The monopolist is the one who plays the merchant in the same way as he would play this game of chess. Yet the market is a game that everyone plays, and that benefits everyone – a game of public interest. That is why the monopolist is not a tough opponent, but the enemy of the game itself. They are not the one who takes advantage of tactical superiority or a favorable opening; they are the one who *distorts* the chessboard to achieve their ends. In short, it does not matter who wins or how much they win, as long as the game has not been rigged.

65. **An illustration: the Rhodes merchant, or the legitimacy of opportunism.** If the result itself does not count, if the only reprehensible behavior is that which consists of distorting the rules of the game, this means, *a contrario*, that provided the merchant has not dishonestly influenced the conditions of exchange, he can legitimately take advantage of a market situation that is favorable to him.

---

284 De Roover, La pensée économique des scolastiques: Doctrine et méthode, *op. cit.* at 67–68.

285 *Id.*

286 In response to these maneuvers, Italian municipal statutes and corporate regulations contained provisions prohibiting monopolies, *see* De Roover, *La doctrine scolastique en matière de monopole et son application à la politique économique des communes italiennes*, *op. cit.* at 172–78.

287 *Id.* at 159.

288 De Roover, *The Concept of Just Price: Theory and Economic Policy*, *op. cit.* at 423.

289 De Roover, La pensée économique des scolastiques: Doctrine et méthode, *op. cit.* at 54.

This assertion is confirmed by the case of the Rhodes merchant, studied by several Scholastics.[290] A merchant transports provisions to a region affected by food scarcity. He is then the sole seller, and will certainly take advantage of this to charge high prices. But he is also the only one with crucial information: he knows that other merchants are following the same route as him, and will soon arrive with more supplies – probably bringing prices down considerably. The question is: can the merchant lawfully charge high prices by taking advantage of the shortage tormenting the people, or must he reveal to them the imminent arrival of unexpected provisions, even if it means cutting into his profit? The answer given by both Thomas Aquinas[291] and Leonardo Lessius[292] is unequivocal. The merchant has simply been lucky and has not maneuvered to delay his competitors,[293] so he is not the cause of the situation and can legally take advantage of it. Admittedly, it would be more virtuous to reveal the information, but this concerns his conscience alone: he is not obliged to do so under the rules of earthly justice.

The contribution of the Scholastics thus appears fundamental in both respects: in direct continuity with ancient principles, they established the centrality of intention in both criminal and competition law. Their reflections were widely commented on by doctors of law and helped to spread its influence across Europe.

Paragraph 2 – The influence of intention across Europe

66. **The formation of a European tradition through the *ius commune*.** From the Middle Ages to modern times, each legal system had its own local and customary rules, but this pluralism was balanced by the existence of an *ius commune*[294] – a body of learned general law taught in the great universities of Europe, which helped maintain "unity in diversity."[295]

---

290 The *casus* of the Rhodes merchant was discussed by Thomas Aquinas and Leonardo Lessius, among others. However, this example is much older: in antiquity, Diogenes, Antipater and even Cicero discussed it. *See* Decock, Le marché du mérite: Penser le droit et l'économie avec Léonard Lessius, *op. cit.* at 84–86.

291 Thomas Aquinas, Summa Theologica, IIa IIae, qu. 77, art. 3, esp. obj. 4.

292 Leonardo Lessius, De iustitia et iure, quoted by Decock, Le marché du mérite: Penser le droit et l'économie avec Léonard Lessius, *op. cit.* at 85.

293 Let's recall the behavior which, under Roman law, was punished as hoarding – namely, the deliberate delaying of ships at the entrance to Rome, *see supra*, no. 42.

294 The notion of "general law" can take on many meanings, *see* N. Balat, Essai sur le droit commun 3–6 (2016), nos. 6–9. We use it here in the historical sense of a legal tradition common to European countries.

295 B. Oppetit, *Retour à un droit commun européen, in* Droit et modernité 73, 74–75 (1998).

Doctrine played a crucial role at the time: it had a direct influence on the judicial decisions and on the development of the law, with doctors of law frequently serving as advisors to kings.[296] The *ius commune* is not, however, a body of norms in the sense we understand it today;[297] it lays down general principles, elaborates concepts and generates ways of reasoning.[298] In this sense, it is perhaps more valuable, because it is less contingent: it materializes a cross-border agreement on values,[299] which themselves stem from the past and which, by virtue of their continuity, can be considered inherent to the legal system of European countries.

This general law is, in essence, relative to a given institution.[300] Among European countries with a long legal tradition, all share a common vision: from Germany to France, from England[301] to Italy, there is unanimous agreement on both the central role of intent in criminal law (**I**) and the condemnation of anticompetitive practices[302] (**II**).

I. The existence of a common criminal law

67. **Continuity between the ancient and medieval periods.** Intention was at the heart of reflections on criminal liability in antiquity. As European criminal law was rooted in Greco-Roman traditions (**A**), it is hardly surprising

---

296 H. Coing, *European Common Law: Historical Foundations*, *in* Nouvelles perspectives d'un droit commun 31, 32–33 (M. Cappelletti ed., 1978). In the same vein, *see* A. Laingui, La responsabilité pénale dans l'Ancien droit (xvie – xviiie siècles) 8 (1970): according to the author, criminal law was essentially determined "by the authority of authors and the jurisprudence of rulings, based on Roman law."

297 Indeed, it is doubtful whether there has ever been a "unified system of norms." Indeed, the unity of law cannot be overestimated, and research into the *ius commune* is more fruitful and accurate if it confines itself to seeking out the common features that unite the different legal orders. In this sense, and for a historiography of studies on *ius commune*, *see* J.-L. Halpérin, *L'approche historique et la problématique du* jus commune, 52 Revue internationale de droit comparé 717 (2000).

298 R. David, *Le droit continental, la* Common Law, *et les perspectives d'un* jus commune *européen*, *in* Nouvelles perspectives d'un droit commun 113, 114 (M. Cappelletti ed., 1978).

299 R. Sacco, *Droit commun de l'Europe, et composantes du droit*, *in* Nouvelles perspectives d'un droit commun 95, 95 (M. Cappelletti ed., 1978).

300 Balat, Essai sur le droit commun, *op. cit.* at 105–29, nos. 151–186.

301 The study of English law could have been omitted for two reasons: first, because the United Kingdom is not a founding member of the European Union and has since left it; second, because the influence of Roman law on common law is a matter of controversy. Nevertheless, we felt it important to include it in our study for two other reasons. On the one hand, U.S. competition law, which is the subject of many contemporary comparisons with its European counterpart, has its origins in British law, *see* N. Green, *The Road to Conviction – The Criminalisation of Cartel Law*, *in* 2003 Annual Proceedings of the Fordham Corporate Law Institute 13, 28 (2004). On the other hand, the idea that common law is isolated from Roman precedent is often exaggerated, *see* P. Brand, *The Beginnings of the English Common Law (to 1350)*, *in* The Oxford Handbook of European Legal History 430 (H. Pihlajamäki, M. D. Dubber & M. Godfrey eds., 2018). Indeed, when perusing English criminal law treatises of the period, no one can fail to notice the very many references made by authors to Roman law, and sometimes to Greek philosophers.

302 David Gerber highlights the major influence of the *ius commune* on the emergence of modern competition law, Law and Competition in Twentieth Century Europe: Protecting Prometheus 34–36 (2nd ed. 2001).

that the role played by intent was the subject of a consensus among European countries (**B**).

A. The reception of ancient criminal law

68. **The decisive influence of ancient law on European criminal law.** The principles, foundations and axioms of criminal law have not changed substantially since ancient times. This is largely due to the influence of canon law,[303] which was itself inspired by Roman law and Aristotle.[304]

The Holy Roman Empire adopted Roman law,[305] the *Lex Carolina*, a synthesis of ancient sources and Germanic culture,[306] being, in many respects, a literal translation of ancient provisions.[307] The contributions of Roman law to Anglo-Saxon legal thought are more significant than is generally thought,[308] and the claim that common law is impervious to outside influences is more myth than reality.[309] One hardly needs to convince the reader of Rome's influence in Italy.[310] Finally, the treatises of French jurisconsults of the Modern Era appear as "centos of ancient texts."[311] There is thus a definite continuity, giving rise to a genuine tradition. In the absence of a break in the doctors of law's sources of inspiration, it is not surprising that they drew from this common fund the same principles regarding the requirements for criminal liability.[312]

B. Consensus on the need for and definition of intent

69. **The expansion of intention's role and the refinement of its theory.** Following the rediscovery of Roman law, the principles developed in ancient times

303 M. Villey, Le droit romain 52–53 (2012).

304 *See supra*, no. 54.

305 O. Descamps, *Histoire du droit de la responsabilité dans le monde occidental*, *in* Prendre la responsabilité au sérieux 37, 49 (A. Supiot ed., 2015).

306 C. Levitta, Précis de l'histoire du droit pénal allemand depuis la Caroline jusqu'à nos jours 6–7 (M. L. Bonneville de Marsangy trans., Cotillon 1862).

307 P.-F. Muyart de Vouglans, Les loix criminelles de France dans leur ordre naturel xxiv–xxv (1780).

308 H. S. Maine, Ancient Law: Its Connection with the Early History of Society and its Relation to Modern Ideas vii–viii (1906).

309 *See* in this regard A. Schiavone, Ius: L'invention du droit en Occident 28–32 (G. & J. Bouffatigue trans., Belin 2008). Maitland has also argued that English jurists have for centuries exaggerated the particularism of English legal history to contrast with the triumph of Roman law on the continent. For an in-depth study, *see* J. A. Escudero, *L'historiographie générale du droit anglais*, 9 Les Cahiers de droit 117, 129–30, 158, 168, 172 (1967–1968).

310 R. Sorice, *La rilevanza penale della colpa nel Medioevo: Ricerche sulla Doctrina Bartoli*, 31 Rivista internazionale di dirrito comune 199, 199 (2020).

311 A. Laingui & M. Crépin, *La philosophie du droit pénal du Moyen Âge à l'époque moderne*, 53 Revue internationale de droit pénal 613, 618–19 (1982).

312 Contrary to Savigny's view that, unlike Roman civil law, we have borrowed "only a small number of principles of secondary importance" from its criminal component, I Traité de droit romain 2 (C. Guenoux trans., Firmin Didot Frères 1855); on the contrary, we believe that its study should be encouraged, as it is so fruitful. In this sense, *see* F. Walter, Histoire du droit criminel chez les Romains vi (J. Picquet-Damesme trans., A. Durand 1863).

were adopted by European countries. Great significance was attributed to intent, which became the *Alpha* and *Omega* of criminal responsibility. Without exception, the treaties adopted the Roman distinctions between *dolus*, *culpa*, *casus* and *fraus*.[313] Roman texts feature prominently in these treaties, serving as the "adages of classical law."[314] All the hypotheses preventing the characterization of intention are taken up: insanity, age, ignorance, constraint, order of the law, command of legitimate authority, legitimate defense.[315]

In Germanic law, liability is subjective:[316] the *Lex Carolina* of 1532 requires the magistrate to investigate whether the crime was committed intentionally, prescribes different penalties according to the seriousness of the *dol*, and authorizes prosecution of a simple attempt.[317] The Germans incorporated Roman concepts and the distinction between *dolus* and *culpa*.[318]

In England, as early as the end of the twelfth century, Henry de Bracton took up the Roman maxims and gave a central place to intention.[319] It was at this time that the saying that is still a cardinal principle of Anglo-Saxon criminal law appeared: "*actus non facit reum nisi mens sit rea*" – "An act is not guilty if the mind is not guilty."[320] This focus on intention can also be found in Edward Coke's *Institutes of the Laws of England*[321] and the work of criminal lawyer Matthew Hale.[322] The emphasis is on excuses, called "defences," which remove intention – the English having an essentially negative conception of its regime. Hale dedicates the first chapters of his seminal work *On the Laws and Customs of England* to the causes that defeat the will.[323] William Blackstone does the same,[324] and concludes by

313 On these concepts, *see supra*, no. 30.

314 A. Laingui, Histoire du droit pénal 88–89 (2nd ed. 1993)

315 *Id.* at 90 and 99. In the same vein, Y. Bongert, 1 Cours d'histoire du droit pénal: Le droit pénal français médiéval de la seconde moitié du xiiie siècle à l'ordonnance de 1493, 353–55 (1973).

316 P. Fauconnet, La responsabilité 115 (1920).

317 Y. Jeanclos, Droit pénal européen: Dimension historique 61–63 (2009).

318 H. D. J. Bodenstein, *Phases in the Development of Criminal Mens Rea*, 36 South African Law Journal 323, 325–27 (1919).

319 H. de Bracton, 2 On the Laws and Customs of England 290 (S. E. Thorne trans., Harvard Univ. Press 1968): "We must consider with what mind or with what intent a thing is done … for take away the will and every act will be indifferent, because your state of mind gives meaning to your act, and a crime is not committed unless the intent to injure intervene, nor a theft is committed except with intent to steal."

320 F. B. Sayre, *Mens Rea*, 45 Harvard Law Review 974, 974 (1932).

321 H. Parent, *Histoire de l'acte volontaire en droit pénal anglais et canadien*, 45 McGill Law Journal 975, 993–99 (2000).

322 *Id.*

323 M. Hale, 1 The History of the Pleas of the Crown 14–57 (1800), ch. ii–ix.

324 W. Blackstone, Commentaries on the Laws of England 13–21 (Oxford Univ. Press 2016), ch. ii.

writing that what protects against punishment "may be reduced to this single consideration, the want or defect of will."[325]

In French legal doctrine, the principles of Roman law were faithfully adopted again.[326] The first treatise on criminal responsibility, written by André Tiraqueau, continually invokes examples from antiquity.[327] Hugo Grotius borrows his theory of error directly from Aristotle,[328] whom he also quotes extensively.[329] Muyart de Vouglans considers that, like the Stagirite, error in law is not admissible against "natural law," as it is sufficient to "go within oneself and consult one's own reason"[330] in order to learn from its precepts. The same is true of major legal concepts such as abuse, fraud and theft: there is no need for a text to recognize that these are offenses. Under the Ancien Droit, intention was such an important factor, presupposing freedom and will,[331] that most unintentional offenses fell under civil rather than criminal law.[332] Penalties are imposed according to the seriousness of the intent.[333] Grimaudet writes that intent is presumed from the material fact, with the onus on the accused to prove their good faith;[334] and that while simple intent is not punishable, attempt is "deemed for the fact."[335]

The most refined theorization of the concept, however, comes from Italy, in the writings of Bartolus de Saxoferrato. His theory was subsequently taken up and commented on by German jurists in the nineteenth century.[336] Bartolus' influence would prove to be immense: he can indeed be considered one of the founders of the doctrine of *foreseeability*. Drawing on the theories of Thomas Aquinas,[337] he developed the idea

325 *Id.* at 20.

326 Thus, the notion of intentional fault in Ancien Droit appears very clearly as early as the thirteenth century, *see* Y. Bongert, 1 Cours d'histoire du droit pénal: Le droit pénal français médiéval de la seconde moitié du xiiie siècle à l'ordonnance de 1493, 338 (1973).

327 A. Laingui, *Le premier grand traité de responsabilité pénale: Le "*De Poenis Temperandis*" d'André Tiraqueau (1559), in* Mélanges en l'honneur du Doyen Pierre Bouzat 179, 203 (1980).

328 H. Grotius, ii Le droit de la guerre et de la paix 617–18 (J. Barbeyrac trans., Pierre de Coup 1724), bk. ii, ch. xx, § xliii.

329 R. Legros, *Une lecture pénale de Grotius*, 73 Bulletin de la classe des lettres et des sciences morales et politiques 424, 445–46 (1987).

330 Muyart de Vouglans, Les loix criminelles de France dans leur ordre naturel, *op. cit.* at xxxiii.

331 A. Laingui & A. Lebigre, i Histoire du droit pénal : Le droit pénal 28 (1979).

332 Laingui & Crépin, *La philosophie du droit pénal du Moyen Âge à l'époque moderne*, *op. cit.* at 626.

333 A. Laingui, La responsabilité pénale dans l'Ancien droit (xvie – xviiie siècles) 35 (1970).

334 F. Grimaudet, *Traité des causes qui excusent de dol*, *in* Œuvres 390, 402 (Robert Foüet 1669).

335 *Id.* at 405.

336 Sorice, *La rilevanza penale della colpa nel Medioevo: Ricerche sulla Doctrina Bartoli*, *op. cit.* at 204.

337 In this sense, *see* Bodenstein, *Phases in the Development of Criminal Mens Rea*, *op. cit.* at 342. For a discussion of Thomas Aquinas' theory, *see supra*, nos. 54–57.

that intent should be assessed based on the likelihood of the result occurring.[338] If an outcome is probable, it is foreseeable – and thus, it can be presumed to have been foreseen. The key criterion distinguishing guilt from non-guilt thus becomes foreseeability.[339]

70. **The existence of a simple, unitary theory of intent in criminal law.** At that time, there was a common perception of criminal responsibility, entirely organized around the concept of intent. There was no divergence of views in its theorization. This is no longer the case today:[340] the codification movement and the nationalization of law have led to the development of doctrinal currents that are distinct from one country to another, and even within the same country – and the original simplicity of reasoning has given way to great complexity. The same can be said of competition law: beginning in the eighteenth century, general law gave way to a fragmented approach to repressing anticompetitive behavior.

II. The emergence of a common "competition law"

71. **The outcome of several millennia of history: the existence of a European tradition.** The first part of this brief history is drawing to a close. It has resulted in a shared European perspective, both on the need to repress anticompetitive practices (**A**), and on the consideration of intention in this repression (**B**).

A. The consensus on the repression of anticompetitive behavior

72. **Between freedom and dirigisme (time and again).** As in the past, the repression of anticompetitive practices entails that a certain amount of trade is left free, and the State has never abandoned its desire to regulate prices – whether in the Middle Ages or Modern Times.[341] Haphazard, ineffective, and arbitrary,[342] these policies, as usual, have proven strikingly ineffective in combating high prices.[343]

---

338 Bodenstein, *Phases in the Development of Criminal Mens Rea*, *op. cit.* at 347–49.

339 Sorice, *La rilevanza penale della colpa nel Medioevo: Ricerche sulla Doctrina Bartoli*, *op. cit.* at 206.

340 *See infra*, nos. 179 *et seq*.

341 *See* no. 38 for the Greek period, no. 41 for the Roman period.

342 R. De Roover, *The Concept of Just Price: Theory and Economic Policy*, 18 The Journal of Economic History 418, 429–30 (1958): "The history of price regulation remains to be written, but we know it to be a tale of woe," as price regulation was "haphazard, vexatious, inefficient, and arbitrary."

343 A. Liautey, La hausse des prix et la lutte contre la cherté en France au xvie siècle 166 (1921). For a critique of the royal pricing policy, *see id.* at 324–34.

73. **The repression of anticompetitive practices in Europe: the state of play.** In England, a collection of statutes mentions that even before the Norman Conquest in the tenth century, ancient English law already contained rules against anticompetitive practices.[344] Broadly defined, monopoly is prohibited as it goes against the "fundamental laws of the realm," even in the absence of a written rule: it is an offense *malum in se* – wrong in itself, even if it is not expressly punished by a law.[345] Several treatises are devoted entirely to these practices,[346] and leading English law scholars often dedicate a study to them.[347] In addition, numerous statutory laws passed under the reigns of Edward III, Edward IV, Edward VI and Henry VIII severely repressed these practices, depicting hoarders as oppressors, or even as enemies of the country.[348]

In the Holy Roman Empire, the best-known legislation is that adopted under the reign of Charles V in 1540,[349] but it is far from the only one.[350] A German treatise on fraudulent monopolies uses the Roman term "dardanarius."[351] In Belgium and the Netherlands, several ordinances explicitly condemn monopolies.[352] The jurisconsult Dominique-François de Sohet also mentions their prohibition in his *Institutes*, placing monopoly among the crimes alongside theft and fraudulent bankruptcy.[353] In Italy, Balde attests to having seen these same laws strictly applied in his own time, in the fourteenth century.[354]

In France, Nicolas Delamare notes, in his important *Traité de la police*, that the "vice of monopoly" was felt throughout Europe and

---

344 S. Browne, The Laws Against Engrossing, Forestalling, Regrating, and Monopolizing: Containing All the Statutes and Adjudged Cases Concerning Them 22 (1767).

345 *Id.* at 84.

346 *See* in particular E. Morris, Short Inquiry Into the Nature of Monopoly and Forestalling With Some Remarks on the Statutes Concerning Them (1795).

347 *See* in particular W. Blackstone, Commentaries on the Laws of England 101–105 (Oxford Univ. Press 2016), ch. xii.

348 For an account of the content of these laws, *see* N. Green, *The Road to Conviction – The Criminalisation of Cartel Law*, *in* 2003 Annual Proceedings of the Fordham Corporate Law Institute 13, 13–15 (2004); and N. Green, *From Rome to Rome: The Evolution of Competition Law into a Twenty-First Century Religion*, 9 Competition Law Journal 7, 11–18 (2010).

349 W. Decock, Le marché du mérite: Penser le droit et l'économie avec Léonard Lessius 133–34 (2019).

350 For an account of the various competition laws in the Holy Roman Empire, *see* R. Piotrowski, Cartels and Trusts: Their Origin and Historical Development From the Economic and Legal Aspects 176–84 (1933).

351 Mentioned in N. Delamare, ii Traité de la Police 302 (1722).

352 C. Laurent, J. Lameere & H. Simont, Recueil des anciennes ordonnances de la Belgique 234 (1907), quoted by R. De Roover, *Monopoly Theory Prior to Adam Smith: A Revision*, 65 The Quarterly Journal of Economics 492, 506 n.6 (1951).

353 J. Constant, *Dominique-François de Sohet, jurisconsulte liégeois*, Journal des tribunaux no. 4761, 673, 681 (Nov. 20, 1971).

354 P.-F. Muyart de Vouglans, Institutes au droit criminel 607 (1757).

was severely punished by the laws of all nations.[355] Jean Domat mentions an "infinite number of ordinances and regulations" prohibiting hoarding.[356] Pierre-François Muyart de Vouglans observes that the law forbidding such practices is "so wise that it will never be abolished."[357] The Sens and Angers rulings of 1556 and 1611 even classified them as royal cases.[358]

Not only were anticompetitive practices repressed throughout Europe, but the criterion for this repression – intent – was also at the heart of the debate.

B. Reception of the criterion of intention

74. **The criterion for the repression of anticompetitive practices: fraudulent intent.** As with the Scholastics and the ancient world, monopoly is considered synonymous with hoarding, and is understood in a very broad sense. According to Muyart de Vouglans: "Any *enterprise* or *association* tending to *hinder* or *destroy* the *freedom of* trade."[359]

Jousse links monopoly to *fraud*, defining it as an "agreement to the detriment of the public good, in order to obtain an advantage."[360] Noting that there are different kinds of monopolies, he distinguishes six distinct types, and specifies that even lords may be guilty of the offense.[361] He goes on to state that when bodies or communities commit a crime, the penalty, consisting of a fine, is inflicted on their leaders or syndics.[362] Finally, he mentions a particularly interesting principle, noting that the penalty for monopoly does not apply when it contributes to the "public interest."[363]

75. **Violations of competition law: *crimes* derived from *theft*.** In two major treatises, Jean Domat's *Loix* and Nicolas Delamare's *Traité de la police*, monopoly is associated with the concept of "police."[364] Does this mean

---

355 Delamare, ii Traité de la Police, *op. cit.* at 302.

356 J. Domat, iv Les loix civiles dans leur ordre naturel: Le droit public 220 (1701). *See*, in the same vein, L. de Jaucourt, *Loi*, *in* ix D. Diderot, Encyclopédie, ou dictionnaire raisonné des sciences, des arts et des métiers 643, 652 (Briasson).

357 Muyart de Vouglans, Institutes au droit criminel, *op. cit.* at 607.

358 N. Meusy, ii Code de la religion et des mœurs, ou Recueil des principales ordonnances, depuis l'établissement de la monarchie françoise 56–59 (1776). In the same vein, D. Jousse, iii Traité de la justice criminelle de France 831 (1771), para. iv, tit. xxxvi.

359 P.-F. Muyart de Vouglans, Les loix criminelles de France dans leur ordre naturel 340 (1780), bk. iii, tit. iv, art. iii: "Du Monopole" (emphasis added).

360 Jousse, iii Traité de la justice criminelle de France, *op. cit.* at 831.

361 *Id.* at 831–32.

362 *Id.* at 832.

363 *Id.* at 833.

364 Monopoly is studied in Domat, iv Les loix civiles dans leur ordre naturel: Le droit public, *op. cit.*, bk. i: "Du gouvernement de la police générale d'un État."

that, in the Ancien Droit, the prohibition of monopoly was simply a matter of what we would today call "market policing"? In modern times, the term "*droit de police*" refers to a form of administrative interventionism with various objectives.[365] However, before the French Revolution, the word "police" was defined as "all laws and regulations aimed at preserving public order, as opposed to rules governing private interests only."[366] It was a very broad term, actually designating criminal law itself,[367] as opposed to civil law.

In criminal law treatises, notably that of Muyart de Vouglans, the offense of monopoly is systematically categorized under the section on theft. In his *Traité des crimes*, it is mentioned in Title V: "Du vol et de ses différentes espèces," Chapter VII: "Des vols qualifiés comme contraires à la sûreté du commerce." The remark is important. Firstly, it shows the strong moral stigma attached to this crime, considered atrocious by all jurisconsults of the Ancien Droit. Secondly, this kinship between theft and anticompetitive practices has an impact on the structure of the latter, both being intentional offenses where the unlawfulness arises solely from the means employed.[368]

76. **Monopoly: an extraordinary crime.** In the tradition of Roman law,[369] monopoly belongs to the category of *extraordinary crimes*, i.e., those "for which neither the name nor the penalty is determined by any law, but are left to the arbitration of the judge to punish them according to the circumstances."[370] On the one hand, this means that, whatever the tactics employed, there is no need for a specific text to punish them. On the other hand, it attests to the fact that monopoly is such a dishonest offense that no one can validly plead an error of law to escape punishment: the rule is immanent to every human being's sense of right and wrong.[371]

*

*   *

77. **Conclusion to Chapter 1: the uncontroversial consideration of intention in competition law from antiquity to the eighteenth century.** Intention, which has always been the ethical basis of the right to punish, was theorized

---

365 E. Picard, La notion de police administrative 222–53 (1984).

366 *Id.* at 54

367 *Id.* at 26–27.

368 *See infra*, no. 245.

369 *See supra*, no. 44.

370 Muyart de Vouglans, Institutes au droit criminel, *op. cit.* at 30–31.

371 M. Meccarelli, *Criminal Law: Before a State Monopoly*, *in* The Oxford Handbook of European Legal History 632, 643–44 (H. Pihlajamäki, M. D. Dubber & M. Godfrey eds., 2018).

in a simple, unitary way: it was not the subject of doctrinal controversy. The characterization of anticompetitive behavior was based exclusively on the distinction between honest commercial practices and fraudulent maneuvers: it was the intention and behavior of merchants that constituted the offense. From the eighteenth century onwards, European criminal law began to lose its way "in the twists and turns of national laws," leading to a fragmentation of doctrine and practice.[372] The utilitarian trend also led to a radical change in the perception of competition law. In short, hitherto accepted principles gave way to new theories that broke with tradition.

*

* *

372 Jeanclos, Droit pénal européen: Dimension historique, *op. cit.* at 70.

Chapter 2
CONTEMPORARY ERASURE

78. **A disruption: the persistence of intention despite opposing currents.** From the eighteenth century onwards, under the influence of utilitarian and positivist currents, the way in which law was perceived and conceived was disrupted. The major legal concepts, foremost among them intention, were suddenly accused of being based on unscientific doctrines and supported by an idea of morality deemed too uncertain, which should be replaced by a "science of legislation" in order to eradicate the subjectivive aspect of law in favor of greater "objectivity." Intention then seems to be losing importance (**Section 1**). But this decline is only apparent. If intention was made less visible by surface agitation, it sank into deep waters and, indifferent to contrary currents, continued, like a groundswell, to underpin the reasoning and solutions of competition law (**Section 2**).

Section 1
Causes of the decline of intent from the 18th century onward

79. **A break with the past.** The eighteenth century was characterized by a desire to wipe the slate clean – to break with the order of *beliefs*, and usher in the age of *scientific reason.* Hitherto established principles appeared suspect, irrational and arbitrary: they were subjected to doubt and critical scrutiny.[1] Morality, in particular, whose knowledge was deemed immanent

1 C. Perelman, Le raisonnable et le déraisonnable en droit: Au-delà du positivisme juridique 152 (1984): "The philosophical tradition of the West, at least since the seventeenth century, has been profoundly influenced by the development of mathematical physics and the natural sciences based on experience, measurement, weighing and calculation. Anything that could not be reduced to quantifiable quantities was, by the same token, regarded as vague and confused, as foreign to clear and distinct knowledge."

to every human being, was considered too vague to serve as the basis for legal rules. The classical utilitarians thus attempted to *establish a scientific basis for morality*, in order to give it a rational foundation, by deeming moral any act that produces *beneficial effects* for the happiness of the greatest number (**Paragraph 1**). Utilitarianism exerted an important influence on the law, and in particular on the conception of competition law, as evidenced by the fact that from the nineteenth century onwards, the mere existence of a fraudulent maneuver was no longer sufficient for the litigious behavior to be sanctioned: the law required, in addition, that it produce a certain effect on the market (**Paragraph 2**).

Paragraph 1 – The emergence of a utilitarian morality focused on effects

80. **Scientific progress and state action.** The undeniable progress of the natural sciences has encouraged the emergence of human "sciences": the aim was to discover the laws that govern human action (**I**). Far from being merely descriptive, the ambition was also normative,[2] for if it is possible to understand the mechanisms of action, it is also conceivable – and even, in the minds of its promoters, desirable – to propose a new science of legislation, presumed to be more rational because based on "scientific" foundations (**II**).

I. The ambition to discover the laws of humanity through scientific reasoning

81. **The human sciences: adopting the deterministic postulate of the natural sciences.** The natural sciences originally developed on the basis of a deterministic postulate (**A**), which was quickly adopted by those studying the human sciences (**B**).

A. The natural sciences: based on a deterministic premise

82. **The new hegemony of scientific thought.** While science and philosophy have been inseparable since antiquity,[3] their alliance gradually broke down from the seventeenth century onwards. With the advent of the experimental method of Galileo and Newton,[4] physical science developed by emancipating

---

2 G. Levasseur, *Étude de l'élément moral de l'infraction*, XVII ANNALES DE LA FACULTÉ DE DROIT ET DE SCIENCES ÉCONOMIQUES DE TOULOUSE 81, 82 (1969), fasc. 1.

3 *See* the Aristotelian model, *supra*, no. 37.

4 A. Boutot, *Science and philosophy*, ENCYCLOPÆDIA UNIVERSALIS.

itself from metaphysics.[5] The autonomy of science had two consequences: one positive, the other negative. On the one hand, it has led to the specialization of knowledge in particular fields, resulting in decisive progress in our understanding of the world and major technical advances. At the same time, however, it has led to the emergence of a new attitude toward the world, which humans believed could be *entirely* deciphered through reason. The improvement of the scientific method led the greatest minds to believe that it could achieve *absolute* rigor and certainty,[6] and lead to virtually limitless results – in other words, a *perfect*, *objective*, and *true* understanding of the world. Philosophy, which offered the field of knowledge only uncertain and provisional speculations, was relegated to the status of a brilliant second, condemned to commenting on the only form of knowledge now valued: scientific knowledge.[7] Thus, reasoning not based on "rational" grounds was suddenly judged to be subjective, arbitrary and alien to true knowledge – which was required to be objective[8] or, failing that, condemned not to be.[9] This new scientific method has had a decisive influence on the human sciences and, *ultimately*, on the way in which the law is developed and interpreted – which is why it is worth examining its postulates.

83. **The aim of the natural sciences: to isolate laws.** The natural sciences aim to understand phenomena in order to isolate *recurring patterns*. *If* I drop a pen a meter above the ground, the pen will *necessarily* fall to the ground. There is a link of *necessity* between cause and effect – the same cause *always* leads to the same effect. The experimental method consists of discovering and then describing these causal relationships, which Newton called "laws."[10] A defining trait of a natural law is its inevitability; that is, it leaves no room for chance: gravity exists, everywhere and at all times. No one can escape it. Since a scientific law is always *true*, it allows us to make *certain* predictions: when I drop my pen, I can predict with certainty that it will fall.

The hard sciences were thus built[11] on a *deterministic postulate*. Indeed, science is deterministic not only *a priori*, since it postulates the absence

5 A. Koyré, *De l'influence des conceptions philosophiques sur l'évolution des théories scientifiques*, A. Koyré, Études d'histoire de la pensée philosophique 253, 261–62 (1971).

6 G. Bachelard, Le nouvel esprit scientifique 11 (PUF 2020) (1934).

7 J.-F. Revel, Histoire de la philosophie occidentale 255 (2003); *adde* D. Villey, Notes de philosophie économique (1958–59): Le jeu des intérêts 85 (1965): the author speaks of a "secession" between philosophy and the natural sciences, then the social sciences.

8 On the emergence of objectivity in science, *see* J. Feldman, *Objectivité et subjectivité en science. Quelques aperçus*, XL Revue européenne des sciences sociales 85 (2002); L. Daston & P. Galison, Objectivité (2012).

9 Nevertheless, the revolt came from art. On this subject, *see* E. Sabato, *Le règne de la science et la révolte romantique* and *La subjectivité de l'art contre l'objectivité de la science*, *in* L'écrivain et la catastrophe 11 and 34 (1986).

10 Newton mentions the existence of "laws of motion" in his *Philosophiæ Naturalis Principia Mathematica*, published in 1687.

11 Notably following the discoveries of quantum physics, the deterministic postulate has gradually been called into question by the hard sciences themselves, *see infra*, no. 115.

of randomness in order to exist, but also a posteriori, since, by discovering laws, it demonstrates the existence of determinism with each of its advancements.[12] As the scientific method's breakthroughs were as numerous as they were decisive, it soon aroused great fascination among those who studied not natural phenomena but human ones.[13]

The human sciences then imported the scientific method into the study of human beings and, along with it, the deterministic postulate of the natural sciences.

B. The adoption of a deterministic postulate by the human sciences

84. **The human sciences' emulation of the natural sciences.** The temptation to establish a scientific foundation for the study of human beings was significant: if it is now possible to decipher nature, why should it be impossible to predict human action? Condorcet put it this way:

> If man can predict with near certainty the phenomena whose laws he knows... why should one regard as a chimerical enterprise the attempt to outline, with some degree of probability, the future destinies of the human species based on the results of its history? The sole foundation of belief in the natural sciences lies in the idea that the general laws – whether known or unknown – that govern the phenomena of the universe are necessary and constant; and for what reason should this principle be any less true for the development of man's intellectual and moral faculties than for the other operations of nature?[14]

This summarizes the idea that, since the natural sciences are rigorous, their method should be imported into the study of humans, which will henceforth be referred to as the "sciences." It was then deemed possible to determine the great regularities of human action, reifying humans in the process and denying their free will[15] in order to make them the object of studies claiming, on the model of hard sciences, scientific accuracy and truth.

Montesquieu put forward the idea of a causal relationship between a region's climate and the laws adopted by its people.[16] Criminology, for

12 H. Poincaré, Dernières pensées 244 (1920).

13 F. A. Hayek, Scientisme et sciences sociales: Essai sur le mauvais usage de la raison 8 (R. Barre trans., Plon 1995).

14 Condorcet, *Dixième époque: Des progrès futurs de l'esprit humain, in* Esquisse d'un tableau historique des progrès de l'esprit humain 265, 265 (GF Flammarion 1988) (1794).

15 X. Martin, *Du temps des Lumières à 1810: Anthropologie et droit criminel*, Bicentenaire du Code pénal – 1810-2010, Paris, Les colloques du Sénat 65, 65 (2010).

16 Montesquieu, ii De l'esprit des lois 33 (Dabo 1824) (1748), para. 3, bk. xiv "Des lois dans le rapport qu'elles ont avec la nature du climat."

its part, has developed on a deterministic basis[17] – criminological analyses focus on the study of biological or social conditioning that can lead to crime.[18] The deterministic presupposition has also been adopted by certain sociologists,[19] as well as by most psychiatrists.[20] In economics, the physiocrats set out to discover "the natural laws of society, valid for all times and all countries."[21] Following in their footsteps, most modern economic theories sought to construct a *pure*, mathematical economy,[22] based "exclusively on the observation of regular sequences of economic phenomena."[23] Economics thus eliminated all randomness, all free will[24] and all subjective elements.[25]

85. **The normative ambition of the human sciences.** Science is essentially descriptive – it aims to enhance our understanding of the world. But if it is possible to know that, in the presence of a cause X, human beings react in a way Y, then it becomes possible to consciously influence human action through incentives and sanctions. And if human beings can be steered like a train on tracks, why not ensure that society as a whole moves in the direction of "progress"? Auguste Comte, the founder of positivism, built his thought on this intellectual foundation. His aim was to rebuild anew what the Revolution had undermined: a moral and religious edifice.[26] To achieve this, his theories had to be based on a world of objective truths,[27] establishing an anti-metaphysical and anti-theological society built on the

---

17 Indeed, it was "elsewhere than in philosophy that the positivist school went looking for the raw material of determinism, favorable to its entire theory: in science," P.-J. Delage, *L'apport de la philosophie dans la théorisation du droit pénal*, *in* FAUT-IL RETHÉORISER LE DROIT PÉNAL? 17, 22 (J. Leroy ed., 2017). *See*, in the same vein, A. El Khouri, Le courant néo-classique dans la pensée et le droit pénal en France 16–17 (1994) (Ph.D. dissertation, Paris II).

18 J. Pinatel, *Responsabilité et criminologie*, VIII ANNALES DE LA FACULTÉ DE DROIT ET DE SCIENCES POLITIQUES ET ÉCONOMIQUES DE STRASBOURG 159, 160–62 (1961).

19 A. HAMON, DÉTERMINISME ET RESPONSABILITÉ (1898). In the introduction to his book, the sociologist writes that "all of us, or almost all of us, have been nourished by the idea that man possesses free will. This explains how difficult it is to eradicate this false conception from our mentalities, for it is in contradiction with all human phenomena." *Id.* at 4.

20 P. A. Baan, *La notion de discernement au point de vue psychiatrique*, *in* XVIII ANNALES DE LA FACULTÉ DE DROIT ET DE SCIENCES POLITIQUES ET ÉCONOMIQUES DE STRASBOURG 183, 183 (1961).

21 D. VILLEY & C. NÊME, PETITE HISTOIRE DES GRANDES DOCTRINES ÉCONOMIQUES 57 (1996).

22 *Id.* at 75.

23 *Id.* at 230.

24 Indeed, Shackle has shown that classical economic analysis is based on a deterministic view of the world, cf. G. L. S. SHACKLE, EPISTEMICS AND ECONOMICS: A CRITIQUE OF ECONOMIC DOCTRINES 155–65 (Routledge 2017) (1972); G. L. S. SHACKLE, TIME & CHOICE (1976); for an introduction to Shackle's thought, *see* P. Beaugrand, *Le temps, l'imagination, l'incertitude dans la théorie du professeur G. L. S. Shackle*, 33 REVUE ÉCONOMIQUE 297 (1982); *compare with* H. BERGSON, L'ÉVOLUTION CRÉATRICE 340–41 (1941): "Time is invention or it is nothing at all."

25 VILLEY & NÊME, PETITE HISTOIRE DES GRANDES DOCTRINES ÉCONOMIQUES, *op. cit.* at 232.

26 G. CHABERT, UN NOUVEAU POUVOIR SPIRITUEL: AUGUSTE COMTE ET LA RELIGION SCIENTIFIQUE AU XIXE SIÈCLE 12 (2004).

27 Referring to Auguste Comte, Hayek points out that the scientistic attitude "has found its most characteristic expression in the various attempts to dispense with our subjective knowledge of the working of the human mind," SCIENTISME ET SCIENCES SOCIALES: ESSAI SUR LE MAUVAIS USAGE DE LA RAISON, *op. cit.* at 66.

idea that the moral and political sciences are capable of achieving as much precision as the mathematical sciences.[28] From then on, by discovering the laws of human evolution, it became possible and desirable to master this evolution and take control of the social order. To what end? *Progress* will be the goal.[29] Who will decide what progress is if philosophy no longer exists? The answer has yet to be found.[30]

86. **The illusory ambition of a science of human behavior.** In the scientific sense, law is an observed regularity in facts, a constant. But is there anything less constant than human action? There is more than an incompatibility between human beings and scientific law – there is an antinomy. The human mind is not an observable object of study in the same way as a physical or biological fact.[31] Human action, inherently subjective, resists scientific experimentation;[32] thus, asserting knowledge of the laws of existence amounts to nothing more than a revolt against reason.[33] No law can fully account for human evolution, because it depends on so many unpredictable factors that they are impossible to know in their entirety, and therefore unfit to serve as a basis for valid predictions about the future.[34] By ignoring this contradiction, the idea that society could be rebuilt from scratch, for its own good, gradually took root – without anyone recognizing the astonishing presumption[35] of this ambition, or its dangers. It transfers religious absolutism to its scientific equivalent.[36]

---

28 *Id.* at 82.

29 Auguste Comte's famous phrase is: "Love as principle, order as basis, progress as goal."

30 Michel Villey puts it remarkably well: "As for *ends*, what do the technocrats who govern us propose? They lull us to sleep with words, speaking of expansion, of developing production – production for what, and of what? And when they play at being philosophers, they come to preach change, 'progress.' Progress for what?" M. Villey, *Critique de l'utilitarisme juridique*, Revue de la recherche juridique: Droit prospectif 166, 171 (1981-1982), no. vi-9.

31 The social sciences deal, not with the relations between things, but with the relations between men and things or the relations between man and man. They are concerned with man's actions, and their aim is to explain the unintended or undesigned results of the actions of many men." F. A Hayek, The Counter-Revolution of Science: Studies on the Abuse of Reason, *op. cit.* 25 (1955).

32 *Id.* at 41: "Unless we can understand what the acting people mean by their actions any attempt to explain them, i.e., to subsume them under rules which connect similar situations with similar actions, are bound to fail." *Id.* at 31.

33 The expression is borrowed from Ludwig von Mises who, in L'action humaine: Traité d'économie (R. Audouin trans., Institut Coppet 2011), devotes a section entitled "La révolte contre la raison" ["The revolt against reason"] (at pp. 83–86), to denouncing belief in the unlimited powers of reason.

34 F. A. Hayek, Droit, Législation et Liberté: Une nouvelle formulation des principes libéraux de justice et d'économie politique 100–101 (R. Adouin trans., PUF 2013). Hayek concludes that these so-called laws of evolution "assert a purely mystical necessity, pushing evolution in a certain predetermined direction."

35 The idea is now "so widely held that few people are at all aware what an astonishing claim it really implies," *see* Hayek, The Counter-Revolution of Science: Studies on the Abuse of Reason, *op. cit.* at 74. Bruno Leoni is of a similar opinion: "The mythology of our time is not religious but political," one of its main myths being "the pretension of political leaders who think they hold the truth and act according to it." B. Leoni, La Liberté et le droit 52 (2006).

36 It is worth noting that Auguste Comte himself aspired to create a religion, the "Religion Totale." In a letter to the public prosecutor M. de Thoulouze dated April 22, 1851, he wrote: "I am convinced that, before the year 1860, I will preach positivism at Notre-Dame, as the only real and complete religion." Proof, if proof were needed, of the eternal return to the idea of the absolute. This letter is quoted in Georges Chabert's Un nouveau pouvoir spirituel: Auguste Comte et la religion scientifique au xixe siècle, *op. cit.* at 196. Since

Offering the sovereign the role, if not the duty, of determining, in the name and on behalf of each individual, what is best for them, it reinforces his power.[37] This is undoubtedly why this idea remained so persistent[38] – and gave rise to the ambition to base state action on scientific reasoning.

II. The desire to base state repression on scientific reasoning

87. **The emergence of a new form of morality and its influence on the conception of competition law.** The normative ambitions of the new human "sciences" could have remained a dream of theorists, confined to the realm of ideas. But this was not to be: they exerted a concrete and lasting influence on the legal system. Despite their weak – if not false – assumptions, they gave rise to a consequentialist, instrumentalist and utilitarian vision of law – law as a tool in the service of specific, material objectives, devoid of transcendence.[39] But who is to tell the law what its objectives are? The human sciences, in particular economics, which is deemed exact, rational and objective. Thus, the utilitarians had to scientifically define an *ersatz* morality, breaking away from its classical conception **(1)**, in order to determine the law "objectively" and "rationally" and, ultimately, to found a "science of legislation"[40] **(2)**.

---

the critical posture of the Enlightenment calls for radical doubt – not only of all beliefs but also of the teachings of tradition – it paradoxically leads to a form of relativism rooted in skepticism, making it impossible to identify indisputable truths. The re-establishment of religion then appears as a necessary counterweight to the downfall of the idea of certainty, a means of halting the state of permanent doubt, in order to lay the stable foundations necessary for the people's government. In this sense, *see* M. Fumaroli, *Anciens et modernes, décadence ou progrès: Le "retour à l'Antique" au XVIIIe siècle*, *in* Exercices de lecture: De Rabelais à Paul Valéry 498, 501 (2006).

37 Ludwig von Mises wrote of Auguste Comte, for example: "He knew precisely what the future held in store for mankind. And naturally, he considered himself the supreme legislator." Mises, L'action humaine: Traité d'économie, *op. cit.* at 83.

38 For Hayek, belief in the possibility of constructing social order legitimizes the action of "those who seek an outlet for their creative imagination, and burn to draw the contours of the future," F. A Hayek, La Constitution de la Liberté 171 (R. Audouin & J. Garello trans., LITEC 1994).

39 On this subject, *see infra*, nos. 418 *et seq*.

40 It should be noted that the idea of a "science of legislation" resurfaces later in Kant's *Doctrine of Right*, about which Michel Villey is sharply critical. He writes that Kantian rationalism had the "naive ambition… to deduce *everything*, following the example of mathematics," and the disastrous aim of leaving jurists – now mere "pure technicians" – to carrying out only "tasks of execution," thus marking "the height of a period in which the philosophy of law was *forgotten*" that would continue with Kelsen – "the greatest prophet of legal rationalism." *See* M. Villey, La Doctrine du droit *dans l'histoire de la science juridique*, pref. to Kant, Métaphysique des mœurs, Première partie: Doctrine du droit 7, 11–16, 33 (A. Philonenko trans., Librairie philosophique J. Vrin 2011).

A. From classical intention-based morality to utilitarian morality

88. **The utilitarian utopian project.** The Enlightenment was all about "progress,"[41] a utilitarian and pragmatic[42] aim.[43] To achieve this goal, utilitarians laid the foundations of a utopian program aimed at perfecting the world.[44] While ancient philosophers and theologians alike drew a clear distinction between the temporal and divine orders,[45] and recognized that the human world was condemned to imperfection, the utilitarians' dream was to eradicate crime and found a perfect society.[46] To realize their project, an omnipotent, omniscient legislator was needed to compel the will of mankind. The idea was to found a theocracy without God, in which science would take the place of transcendence, and the State would replace Providence. This current of thought inspired a new conception of penal sanction,[47] and prescribed a method of lawmaking that broke with tradition[48] – now seen as nothing more than a series of "prejudices born of ignorance."[49]

The first step in this project consisted in rejecting the classical notion of morality – that we discover through our senses and intuition – and replacing it with a morality grounded in "scientific" foundations.

89. **Utilitarians' rejection of "sensualist" morality.** What is morality? A host of "anarchic principles," according to Bentham.[50] Or, in the opinion of his disciple John Stuart Mill, a question on which philosophers have been divided into "sects and schools, carrying on a vigorous warfare against one another" in vain for over two thousand years.[51] For Mill, criminal law rests – wrongly – on "the popular theory of a natural faculty, a sense or

---

41 While improved material conditions and medical discoveries constitute "progress," none of the sovereign goods – nature, the soul, the arts or justice – ever progress. Therefore, proposing "progress" as the end of law is a subversion of law, which has only justice in its sights. On this theme, *see* W. Hazlitt, *Pourquoi les arts ne progressent-ils pas? – Un fragment*, *in* Sentiment et raison 133 (J. Zanetta trans., Sorbonne Université Presses 2019).

42 M. J. De Soto, *Les philosophes du xviiie siècle et la Révolution française*, viii Annales de la faculté de droit et des sciences politiques et économiques de Strasbourg 137, 152–53 (1961).

43 J.-H. Robert, *Politique pénale: Ressorts et évolution*, 128 Revue Pouvoirs 103, 103 (2009).

44 D. Baranger, Penser la loi: Essai sur le législateur des temps modernes 232 (2018).

45 *See supra*, no. 25 and no. 53.

46 P. Malaurie, *Le droit et l'esprit: Dernière leçon*, 67 Commentaire 609, 610–11 (1994): "It was one of the great illusions of the Enlightenment and the French Revolution to place exclusive faith in Reason… Even if one day we were to discover a prodigious legal law-making machine, which would make it possible to know *all the* factors (and I do mean *all*) that dominate human relations … it would not be capable of creating perfect law."

47 Michel Villey notes that legal utilitarianism is not "one of those paper constructions that rise within the walls of an academic chapel; it is the air we breathe." *Préface*, *in* M. El Shakankiri, La philosophie juridique de Jérémy Bentham i, v (1970).

48 Baranger, Penser la loi: Essai sur le législateur des temps modernes, *op. cit.* at 195–96.

49 A. Leca, La genèse du droit: Essai d'introduction historique au droit 255 (2nd ed. 2000).

50 E. Halévy, 3 Le radicalisme philosophique : La formation du radicalisme philosophique 226 (PUF 1996) (1901–1904).

51 J. Stuart Mill, Utilitarianism 1 (3rd ed. 1867).

instinct, informing us of right and wrong."[52] Italian philosopher Beccaria teaches us that we need to emancipate ourselves from an "emotional" search for the rule, and to dispense with the dangerous and overly subjective criterion of intention.[53] Indeed, the morality of a behavior should not be judged on the basis of *good* or *bad* intention, since individuals all have a different conception of good and evil, and because the same individual may today consider as good what they will tomorrow condemn as evil.[54] Intention, morality, fault, disloyalty, fraud, maneuvering – all these vague, indeterminate notions, which had hitherto formed the ethical basis of the right to punish, ought henceforth to be set aside.[55] They are criticized for leaving room for interpretation, doubt and randomness. The method used by the legislator to draw up the rule, and by the magistrate to implement it, is judged to be "arbitrary"[56] because it is not based on anything concrete other than an overly vague "feeling" of justice.[57] The *art of* law, an obsolete vestige of the past, was to fade into the background and become a *science.*[58]

90. **The development of a "science" of morality.** However, neither Beccaria, Bentham, nor Mill intended to disregard the notion of "morality." Their project was to replace classical morality with a new morality – a *utilitarian* morality.[59] The paradigm shift is radical. The utilitarian vision implies judging the *morality* of an act *solely* in terms of its *result*: this is what is known as "consequentialist" morality. Notions of right and wrong are not dismissed,[60] but the *timing* and *criterion* for this evaluation differ.

---

52 *Id.* at 3.

53 C. Beccaria, Des délits et des peines 75–77 (M. Chevallier trans., GF Flammarion 1991): "The foregoing reflections authorize me to assert that the true, the *only* measure of offenses is the *harm done to the nation*, and not, as some *mistakenly think*, the intention of the guilty party" (emphasis added).

54 *Id.* Beccaria believes that if intent were taken into consideration, "a particular code would have to be established for each citizen."

55 Naturally, this proposal met with outright opposition from jurisconsults. Muyart de Vouglans, noting the immense popularity of the Italian's "little treatise," dedicated part of his *Institutes* to its refutation. In his opinion, and quite rightly, Beccaria's comments – *who was not a jurist* – were the fruit of a profound misunderstanding of the principles of criminal law, and his theory constituted a grave danger. *See* P.-F. Muyart de Vouglans, *Réfutation du traité des délits et des peines, in* Les loix criminelles de France dans leur ordre naturel, *op. cit.* at 811–31. *Adde* on their opposition, *see* A. Laingui, *P.-F. Muyart de Vouglans ou l'anti-Beccaria*, 39 Archives de philosophie du droit 169 (1995).

56 Note that it was only in the eighteenth century that the term "arbitrary" acquired a pejorative meaning, precisely because it was vehemently denounced by the philosophers of the Enlightenment, *see* F. Saint-Bonnet, *Arbitraire, in* Dictionnaire des droits de l'homme 58, 60 (J. Andriantsimbazovina et al. eds., 2008).

57 As Denis Baranger writes for Bentham, "[w]hoever has not acquired a scientific knowledge of the sources of human action falls into the errors of 'custom,' which is a bad advisor, for lack of an analytical study of the principles governing the human mind." Baranger, Penser la loi: Essai sur le législateur des temps modernes, *op. cit.* at 245. *Compare with* Dean Carbonnier's valorization of "feeling" *infra*, no. 412.

58 *Id.* at 22–23. The idea of a "science of legislation" is central to the Enlightenment: it is also present in Adam Smith, David Hume, Condorcet, Turgot, Destutt de Tracy, Voltaire and Cabanis. *See id.* at 184–88 and 210.

59 Villey & Nême, Petite histoire des grandes doctrines économiques, *op. cit.* at 68.

60 Utilitarianism does not seek to dispense with the notions of right and wrong, but to resolve the debate on the criterion of right and wrong, i.e., to establish morality on a scientific basis.

In the utilitarian perspective, the morality of an act is established a posteriori, once the result has been achieved, regardless of whether the individual was aware of the consequences of their behavior at the moment they acted. Intention, free will and choice, Bentham tells us, are "fictions of language," imaginary characters entirely fabricated.[61] Man is rational: his decisions are wholly determined by his two masters – pleasure and pain – and are thus predictable and subject to influence. Since he has no more free will than a stone falling from the top of a cliff, it is conceivable to treat him like an automaton, expected to produce certain results designed and desired by the state in advance – failing which he will be considered deficient.

Once it has been established that the focal point of moral judgment should be the result, not the intention, it is still necessary to determine the *criterion* for distinguishing between a "good" and a "bad" result. At this point, morality boils down to utility: the result is *morally good* if it is *materially useful*. But what is utility? "The greatest happiness of the greatest number!"[62] Utilitarian morality rests on the cardinal principle that pleasure[63] is *the sole end* of human life – and that we must renounce proposing any other.[64] Now that we have accepted this principle, we need to answer a final question. How do we know if the majority of people are satisfied? The method is simple: all we need to do is perform a "*calculus* of felicity."[65] And if we immediately think of doubting the practical feasibility of such a calculation,[66] it is, in the minds of utilitarians, possible, rational, exact, objective – in a word: *scientific*.[67]

61 M. El Shakankiri, La philosophie juridique de Jérémy Bentham 246 (1970).

62 The formula was originally coined by Helvétius, Treatise on Man, His Intellectual Faculties and His Education (W. Hooper trans., 1777); it was later taken up by Bentham, Beccaria and John Stuart Mill.

63 *Compare with* S. Trifilio, Esprit mathématique et pensée économique dans l'Antiquité et au Moyen Âge 100 (2010) (Ph.D. dissertation, Aix-Marseille University): "According to Aristotle, happiness is man's ultimate end, the sovereign good to which he aspires: Book I of the *Nicomachean Ethics* demonstrates this. *But this happiness is not equivalent to pleasure, nor is it even attained by means of pleasure*" (emphasis added).

64 E. Goblot, Essai sur la classification des sciences 263 (1898).

65 This calculation is one of the central aspects of utilitarian theory. The question of the calculation of pleasures and pains is "moreover absolutely central to understanding how classical economics developed from Bentham onwards in the nineteenth century." *See* E. de Champs, *Utilitarisme et liberté. La pensée politique de Jeremy Bentham*, 78 Archives de Philosophie 221, 225 (2015).

66 *See also* Halévy, 3 Le radicalisme philosophique, *op. cit.* at 226–27: the author wonders why the principle of utility should not also fall into the category of "anarchic principles," among which Bentham ranks sensualist morality. *Adde*, D. Villey, Notes de philosophie économique (1958–59): Le jeu des intérêts 230 (1965): "Since general utility is the sum of individual utilities, anything that increases the sum of the satisfactions of any given individual ... can only be favorable to the general interest. We can see where the fallacy lies here: it may be that, in order to serve their own interest, subject A engages in behavior that diminishes the sum of pleasures devolved to B, to C... In this case, there is no reason to assert that what improves A's situation is necessarily favorable to the general interest, even as defined by Bentham."

67 Bentham considers this calculation possible, as he bases his philosophy on a deterministic postulate, discussed *supra*, no. 84, and believes that human knowledge is rapidly advancing towards "perfection." *See* J. Bentham, A Fragment on Government 93 (1891): "The age we live is in a busy age; in which knowledge is rapidly advancing towards perfection."

B. The influence of utilitarian morality on the development of competition law

91. **The development of a science of criminal law.** The ambition of this new "moral science" is not only theoretical but also practical. It does not merely *describe* phenomena but aims to *prescribe* the results to be achieved by the legal system, as well as the means to achieve them. To "moral science" thus corresponds a "legislative science." Indeed, the dream of most thinkers at the end of the eighteenth century was "that utility should take shape in law, and that law should be built entirely on a calculation of utility."[68] Bentham therefore drew up a project for the codification of criminal law, with the aim of completely reforming its foundations and reasoning.[69] In his *Theory of Legislation*, an act is deemed an offense due to its harmful consequences for the greatest number.[70]

The question the legislator must ask is: in terms of the amount of punishment, are the effects of an act greater than the expected aggregate of collective happiness? If this *utility test* is passed, i.e., if the positive effects outweigh the negative effects, then there is no crime,[71] and vice versa. The main criterion for government action is no longer *behavior* or *intention*, but the *results* of individual behavior on individuals, considered as a whole. The gap between utilitarian theory and classical criminal law is abysmal. Criminal law becomes an instrument, a technique in the literal sense of the term – i.e., "a set of procedures designed to produce certain results deemed useful."[72] From now on, recourse to punishment should be justified by a scientific analysis of its effects, since the standard prescribed by utilitarians is basically nothing more than their economic theories, applied as an imperative.[73]

92. **The influence of utilitarianism on the right to punish.** The penal codes adopted at the end of the eighteenth century and the beginning of the nineteenth obviously did not embrace the utilitarian doctrine,[74] the revolutionary upheavals having "affected ideology before legal reality."[75]

---

68 M. Foucault, Naissance de la biopolitique: Cours au Collège de France, 1978-1979, 256 (2004).

69 Bentham vindicates this rupture by considering that "[t]he vulgar nomenclature of offenses is not only incomplete, it is misleading. It was necessary to begin by reforming it, or to leave science in the obscurity in which it was found," J. Bentham, Traités de législation civile et pénale 252 (Dalloz 2010).

70 For Bentham, a crime is nothing other than "an act which we think ought to be prohibited on account of some evil which it causes, or tends to cause." *Id.* at 253.

71 Baranger, Penser la loi: Essai sur le législateur des temps modernes, *op. cit.* at 244.

72 A. Lalande, Vocabulaire technique et critique de la philosophie 1106 (2002).

73 El Shakankiri, La philosophie juridique de Jérémy Bentham, *op. cit.* at 249.

74 A. Laingui & M. Crépin, *La philosophie du droit pénal du Moyen Âge à l'époque moderne*, 53 Revue internationale de droit pénal 613, 620 (1982).

75 A. Decocq, Droit pénal général 29 (1971).

Although hardly perceptible at first glance, utilitarianism nevertheless had a real and profound impact over the long term.

If criminal law initially remained more or less impervious to it, it gradually became burdened by a multitude of offenses that were more preventive than repressive, detached from any moral stigma. Penal sanctions were gradually mobilized for instrumental rather than retributive purposes, to such an extent that contemporary criminal law may now appear, to a certain degree, artificial.[76] Moreover, while the classical rule of law is generally negative – it marks a limit without indicating a direction[77] – the utilitarian conception of the rule takes the result as its starting point, draws a line to get there, and punishes those who fail to follow the line. And we know how many offenses today stem from this second logic. Lastly, the extremely technical and precise wording of the offenses,[78] as intended by Bentham,[79] coupled with the principle of a strict interpretation of the text of the law, has led to a materialistic conception of the offense, leaving less room for intention – now often presumed almost automatically by the judge.[80] Thus, even if the immediate impact of utilitarianism is not obvious at first glance, contemporary criminal law is nonetheless inspired by two contradictory sources – one Romano-Canonical, the other utilitarian.[81]

The most significant influence of utilitarianism, however, lies elsewhere. The aim of Benthamian criminal law was to establish a "system of social control"[82] that was as "efficient" as possible;[83] in other words, to reduce the cost of suppressing behaviors deemed harmful to society.[84] The result was a new way of looking at state action, to which a new method of intervention had to correspond. Sound management – the "*management* of happiness," as Bentham called it[85] and which prefigured later welfare

---

76 Foucault, Naissance de la biopolitique: Cours au Collège de France, 1978-1979, *op. cit.* at 69.

77 J. Rivero, *Droit public et droit privé: Conquête, ou* statu quo *?*, Recueil Dalloz 69, 69 (1947), chron. xviii.

78 On this theme in contemporary law, *see infra*, no. 237.

79 According to Denis Baranger, Bentham is indeed one of the "midwives of the new world of legislative positivity," Baranger, Penser la loi: Essai sur le législateur des temps modernes, *op. cit.* at 212.

80 Indeed, the more precise the incriminating text, the less important the role of intention.

81 In this sense, *see* J.-H. Robert, *La faute et la peine dans la philosophie du nouveau Code pénal français*, *in* La faute, la peine et le pardon 99, 101 (J.-B. D'Onorio ed., 1999).

82 M. Bozzo Rey, A. Brunon-Ernst & E. de Champs, *Préface*, *in* Bentham, Traités de législation civile et pénale, *op. cit.* at xxiii.

83 C. Laval, *Jeremy Bentham et le gouvernement des intérêts*, 1 Revue du Mauss 289, 289 (2006). This efficiency involved, among other things, the implementation of a system of generalized surveillance, dubbed the *Panopticon* by Bentham. This system is masterfully analyzed by M. Foucault, *Le panoptisme*, *in* Surveiller et punir: Naissance de la prison 228 (1975). Panopticism was originally a method of designing prisons. Nevertheless, far from being limited to the prison context, its scope constitutes "a general political formula that characterizes a type of government." Foucault, Naissance de la biopolitique: Cours au Collège de France, 1978-1979, *op. cit.* at 68–69.

84 Foucault, Naissance de la biopolitique: Cours au Collège de France, 1978-1979, *op. cit.* at 254. *Compare with* contemporary economists' theories on criminal law, *see infra*, no. 121.

85 Baranger, Penser la loi: Essai sur le législateur des temps modernes, *op. cit.* at 244–53.

theories[86] – meant finding alternatives to criminal law, which was too cumbersome to handle: the shift had to be toward administrative law. The nationalization of contemporary society and the changes in administrative activity have their origins precisely in the late eighteenth century.[87] Since then, we have witnessed a redeployment of the right to punish toward forms of social control beyond the penal sphere.[88] This is precisely what has occurred in competition law.

93. **The influence of utilitarianism on competition law.** The link between Bentham's theory and contemporary competition law is so obvious that competition law specialists reading these lines will surely not find themselves in unfamiliar territory.[89] Utilitarianism serves as its fertile ground, providing the philosophical underpinning for the emergence of the notion of effect in the field.[90]

In antiquity, as under the Ancien Droit, the repression of anticompetitive practices focused exclusively on merchants' conduct and intent: the question of "effects" simply did not arise. The analysis was behavioral in nature and grounded in legal concepts shaped by a long-standing tradition. The judge sought to characterize fraud and maneuvering – a criterion that was not only necessary, but above all *sufficient*. The paradigm shift brought about by utilitarianism should not be underestimated. On the one hand, it has led to the gradual discrediting of legal notions[91] and, on the other, to the dissociation of behavior from results, requiring, in addition to the fraudulent nature of the behavior, proof of an effect on the market. However, the presumed accuracy of predictions in social sciences is an illusion.[92] How do you calculate an effect? Two centuries later, scientists have yet to reach a consensus on the issue. The result has been an alarming increase in complexity, the emergence of contradictory theories and, consequently, a loss of reference points.

---

86 *See infra* nos. 356–357.

87 F. Audren, A.-S. Chambost & J.-L. Halpérin, Histoires contemporaines du droit 180–88 (2020).

88 M. Girot, La dépénalisation: Un instrument au service du droit pénal 87 (1994) (Ph.D. dissertation, Université de Poitiers).

89 We shall see, *infra*, no. 119, that the idea of a link between Benthamite utilitarianism and contemporary competition law is not merely hypothetical, as utilitarianism shares a certain kinship with the economic analysis of law commonly employed in this field.

90 Indeed, one author has noted that the dominance of positivism, and the exacerbated rationalism it promotes, has influenced the legal understanding of monopoly, since it leads to considering law as a mere "instrument" for achieving "economic objectives." *See* C. Salomão Filho, Histoire critique des monopoles: Une perspective juridique et économique 15 (2010).

91 Think of today's fierce criticism of the notion of "competition on the merits" (*see infra*, no. 363). *See* in particular F. Castillo de la Torre, *Is the Effects-Based Approach Too Cumbersome? Taking Stock of Recent Practice and Case Law on Article 102 TFEU, in* The Transformation of EU Competition Law: Next Generation Issues 145, 149 (A. Claici, A. Komninos & D. Waelbroeck eds., 2023) (*nota bene*: the author does not agree with the criticism): "It is fashionable to say that the expression 'competition on the merits' has no content or is not useful because one man's competition on the merits or 'normal competition' is another man's 'unfair' or 'abnormal' competition." Is this not the same reproach that utilitarians generally level at the notion of morality (*see supra*, no. 89)?

92 The idea that the possibilities of economic science are limited will be developed further, *infra* nos. 115–117.

The sudden introduction of the notion of effect in competition law in article 419 of the 1810 French Penal Code caused a significant theoretical upheaval, and a break with tradition. Competition law gradually became an instrumental, technical, consequentialist law, progressively evolving into a specialized field. Utilitarianism has thus shaped the "philosophy" of contemporary competition law.

Paragraph 2 – The introduction of effects in competition law

94. **An economic and legal paradigm shift.** The industrial revolutions led to structural changes in the economy. The growth of industry, the possibility of forming corporations, access to large-scale capital, the improvement of tools and production techniques, and the discovery of new engines were all factors that greatly increased factory productivity, to the point of increasing production beyond consumer needs. The shortages of the past gave way to crises of overproduction: while scarcity was the scourge of ancient times, excess has become the endemic evil of the modern era.

The repression of anticompetitive practices – once considered morally iniquitous and legally illicit beyond question – is now the subject of controversy. Indeed, when the population is not starving, is it still legitimate to criminally sanction the maneuvers of merchants? Do agreements truly undermine the proper functioning of the economy to such an extent as to justify recourse to criminal law? Might the effects of agreements not, in certain circumstances, prove beneficial? In the past, such questions were never raised: the maneuver was punished for its own sake, as it was deemed inherently unjust. These are questions of the modern age – and they remain as relevant as ever.

95. **A shift in the focus from intent to effect.** It was indeed necessary to ask whether the repression of the past remained relevant after such a transformation of the economic structure; in other words, to ask whether anticompetitive practices were still likely, in this new context, to harm the common good. In this sense, questioning the economic effects of agreement is not in itself open to criticism. However, the emergence of such considerations has caused considerable doctrinal upheaval. The reason is as follows: economic analyses have not always sought to *coexist* with traditional legal reasoning – economic reasoning has sometimes overshadowed legal reasoning.

96. **The transition from criminal to administrative competition law.** Between 1810 and the adoption of the Treaty of Rome in 1957, competition law underwent a period of transition from a millennia-old criminal tradition to administrative law.

Article 419 of the Penal Code, which for the first time required proof of an effect on prices to characterize the offense, would prove largely ineffective (**I**). In other European countries, the criminal repression of anticompetitive practices is gradually falling into disuse. Debates became highly technical: competition law gradually became a specialist field, raising some of the most difficult problems in economics. Economic theories began to contradict one another, which led either to doubts about the very relevance of the discipline or to the view that it amounted to nothing more than a tool of economic policy – its moral stigma toward merchants' maneuvers reduced to a mere shadow of what it once was. The idea of administrative enforcement of competition rules, supposed to foster the implementation of economic policies, dates back to a lecture given in 1894, in which Adolf Menzel advocated this turn.[93] The first legislation to introduce administrative competition law[94] was a German law of 1923.[95] It bears a strong resemblance to the French system adopted thirty years later. The latter, which was to exert a strong influence on the drafting of the Treaty of Rome,[96] marked the emergence of the now-famous "by object or by effect" alternative (**II**).

I. The emergence of effects in the 1810 penal code

97. **The first steps towards "effects": between complexity and inefficiency.** The criterion of "effects" appeared for the first time in competition law with the adoption of article 419 of the Penal Code, which required the judge to establish, in addition to the coalition itself, a concrete impact on prices.[97] In practice, this new requirement proved to be an obstacle to the characterization of offenses: criminal judges refused to resort to presumptions of effect, and encountered immense difficulties in establishing a causal link between the agreement and its effect on prices. The introduction of effects thus led to the ineffectiveness of article 419 (**A**). Moreover, the question

---

93 Gerber, Law and Competition in Twentieth Century Europe: Protecting Prometheus, *op. cit.* at 54–55.

94 For an overview of the first competition mechanisms adopted by European countries after the Second World War, *see* A. Kuenzler & L. Warlouzet, *National Traditions of Competition Law: A Belated Europeanization Through Convergence?*, *in* The Historical Foundations of EU Competition Law 89 (K. K. Patel & H. Schweitzer eds., 2013). On the situation in Belgium, *see* M. Van de Kerchove, Le droit sans peines: Aspects de la dépénalisation en Belgique et aux États-Unis 252–73 (1987).

95 Gerber, Law and Competition in Twentieth Century Europe: Protecting Prometheus, *op. cit.* at 109 and 115. On this law, its application and the criticism it provoked, *see id.* at 125–48.

96 *See infra*, no. 109

97 It should be noted that the first country to introduce a post-codification provision criminalizing cartels was Austria in 1803. Unlike article 419 of the French Penal Code, the Austrian text made no mention of the effect on the market: "The agreement of several or all of the business people in a particular business *for the purpose of* increasing the price of a good without work and to the disadvantage of the public, or to reduce such price for their own purposes, or to create shortages is to be punished as a serious criminal violation," cit. and trans. by Gerber, Law and Competition in Twentieth Century Europe: Protecting Prometheus, *op. cit.* at 53 n.36 (emphasis added).

of the effects of agreements and their economic harmfulness gave rise for the first time to complex debates, resulting in the adoption of diametrically opposed doctrinal positions, which contributed to overshadowing legal considerations on anticompetitive practices (**B**).

A. The cause of the ineffectiveness of article 419

98. **The background to the adoption of article 419 of the Penal Code.** After the 1789 Revolution, the assemblies, having just abolished corporations,[98] feared that they would reappear in another form. They passed the Le Chapelier law on June 14, 1791, prohibiting all industrial and commercial groupings, followed by the "*loi sur l'accaparement*" [law against hoarding] on July 26, 1793, making the offense punishable by death. The origin of article 419 of the Penal Code is to be found in the combination of these two laws,[99] which explains its complex wording.[100] The article is inserted in Book III: "Of Crimes and Delicts, and of their Punishment," Title II: "Crimes and Delicts against Individuals," Chapter II: "Crimes and Delicts against Property." As evidenced by the debates preceding the adoption of the 1810 Penal Code,[101] the coalition "causes significant harm not only to the interests of a few individuals in particular, but also to those of commerce in general."[102] In line with the criminal law treatises of the Ancien Droit,[103] article 419 is presented as a particular type of theft, alongside fraudulent bankruptcy, fraud, and breach of trust.[104] The moral stigma attached to the offense of coalition was still clearly perceptible

---

98 By Allarde Decree of Mar. 2 and 17, 1791.

99 As evidenced by the explanatory memorandum preceding its adoption. *See* in this regard H. Babled, Droit français: Les syndicats de producteurs et détenteurs de marchandise au double point de vue économique et pénal 132–33 (1892); *adde*, A. Chauveau, F. Hélie & E. Villey, V Théorie du Code pénal 599–603 (1888), nos. 2385–2387.

100 Article 419, as drafted in 1810, states: "Those who, by false or slanderous reports, purposely spread among the people; or by offering higher prices than those which were asked by the venders themselves; or by coalitions or combinations among the principal holders of the same kind of merchandize or provisions, tending to prevent such goods being sold at all, or being sold under a certain price; or by any fraudulent ways or means whatever, shall have effected the enhancement or reduction of the price of provisions or merchandize; or of the public securities and stocks, above or below the prices which would have been determined by the free and natural competition of trade; shall be punished with an imprisonment of not less than one month, nor more than one year, and a fine of from 500 to 10,000 francs. The offenders may, moreover, be placed, by sentence or judgment, under the superintendence of the high police, during not less than two years, nor more than five years." The Penal Code of France, Translated Into English; with a Preliminary Dissertation and Notes (Butterworth 1819) For a detailed analysis of the incriminating text, *see* no. 124.

101 For references to the debates and speeches preceding the adoption of article 419 of the 1810 Penal Code, *see* J.-G. Locré, xxxi La législation civile, commerciale et criminelle de la France 17–18 (1827).

102 M. Le conseiller d'État L.-J. Faure, *Rapport au Corps législatif: séance du 9 février 1810*, Archives parlementaires de 1787 à 1860, 2e série (1800 à 1860), Tome X, du 21 janvier 1808 au 5 juin 1810, 549, 553 (1867).

103 *See supra*, no. 75. The continuity between the 1810 Penal Code and the Ancien Droit is hardly surprising. Indeed, the codifiers sought to articulate "the principles of a rejuvenated *jus commune*, adapted to the conditions and needs of nineteenth-century men," and to commit to writing "a renewed common law." R. David, C. Jauffre-Spinosi & M. Goré, Les grands systèmes de droit contemporain 51 (12th ed. 2016), no. 51.

104 This historical proximity between competition offenses and crimes such as theft, fraud, and breach of trust is coupled with a structural identity among these offenses. *See infra*, no. 245.

in 1810, as evidenced by the speech given by State Councilor L.-J. Faure in his report to the Corps législatif: "Nor did escape the foresight of the Code these guilty *maneuvers* employed by *greedy* speculators *in bad faith* to raise or lower the price of commodities or goods ... above or below the prices that natural and free competition in commerce would have determined."[105] Mr. Louvet shared this view when, after presenting the offense as being highly "dangerous," he exclaimed: "Well, gentlemen! These maneuvers *of greed* and *intrigue* ... have not been forgotten in the draft."[106] If, at the dawn of the nineteenth century, the need to repress hoarding was not yet in doubt, the structure of the text nevertheless limited its practical effectiveness.

99. **The judge's new obligation to qualify an *effect on prices*.** The break between article 419 of the Penal Code and the Ancien Droit is complete. The article imposes an *unprecedented* obligation on the judge to provide proof of a *concrete result on the market*, by making the rise or fall in prices resulting from the coalition a *constitutive element* of the offense.[107] It should be remembered that, until then, any hoarding was deemed, *in and of itself*, to undermine free competition, and thus to distort prices.[108] In any case, this new requirement prevented the criminal judge from characterizing the offense, making article 419 of little practical use.[109] Indeed, whereas Roman law and the Ancien Droit allowed for "extraordinary actions," after the French Revolution, the principle of legality "*nullum crimen sine lege*" became dogma.[110] From this stems a rule from which judges cannot deviate: the strict interpretation of criminal law.[111] Under the strictness of principle, the legislator's will – to repress hoarding – cannot override the textual application of article 419. The letter prevails over the spirit, even when the letter contradicts the spirit.

100. **The literal interpretation of article 419 by the Criminal Division of the Court of Cassation.** To facilitate the qualification of the effect on prices,

---

105 Faure, *Rapport au Corps législatif: séance du 9 février 1810*, *in* ARCHIVES PARLEMENTAIRES DE 1787 À 1860, *op. cit.* at 553.

106 M. Louvet, *Rapport au Corps législatif: séance du 10 février 1810*, *in* ARCHIVES PARLEMENTAIRES DE 1787 À 1860, *op. cit.* at 613 (emphasis added).

107 CHAUVEAU, HÉLIE & VILLEY, THÉORIE DU CODE PÉNAL, *op. cit.* at 605.

108 *See* the doctrine of the Scholastics on this subject, *supra* nos. 63–65.

109 F. Deak, *Contracts and Combinations in Restraint of Trade in French Law – A Comparative Study*, 21 IOWA LAW REVIEW 397, 418–19 (1936).

110 Post-revolutionary criminal law is no longer "built around the judge but from the law." P. Robert, *La crise de l'économie répressive*, 1 REVUE DE SCIENCE CRIMINELLE ET DE DROIT PÉNAL COMPARÉ 69, 72 (1986); *adde*, in the same vein, R. MERLE, LA PÉNITENCE ET LA PEINE 78 (1985): "The great initiators of penal change" aimed to "return the power to punish to the law and take it away from the judges," considering only "the utility of penalties."

111 Indeed, the judge is not authorized to extend "a clear text to facts that it does not cover, even if the preparatory work indicates that it was the legislator's intention to incriminate such acts," nor even to rectify a material error that may have crept into a text. P. Coste-Floret, *L'interprétation des lois pénales*, 1 REVUE DE SCIENCE CRIMINELLE ET DE DROIT PÉNAL COMPARÉ 4, 9–10 (1937).

the criminal judge could have resorted to presumptions of effect in the presence of manifestly fraudulent agreements. However, this was not the case: in constant jurisprudence, from the adoption of article 419 until its reform in 1926, the Criminal Division of the Court of Cassation systematically refused to presume that an agreement had an impact on prices. For example, in the *Durand v. Gontié* case,[112] merchants had joined forces to set their prices collectively. Proof of the agreement had been established to the requisite legal standard, but the judge still had to demonstrate that "without the effect of the coalition, prices would have been lower than they would have been had the coalition not existed."

How do you prove such a causal link? Judges must first determine the price that would result from "natural and free competition in commerce." In the majority of decisions, the price retained is that which prevailed prior to the formation of the coalition.[113] Secondly, they are required to establish the existence of a price variation *attributable* to the agreement. Here, things get more complicated. The Criminal Division considers that the absence of a price increase or decrease does not mean that the agreement had no effect, since the price fall could have been greater in the absence of the coalition. It also considers that the rise, stagnation, fall or absence of a fall in prices may equally be the result of accidental causes, or of local circumstances not attributable to the parties to the agreement...[114] Proving the effect thus appears to be extremely difficult to provide, if not a *probatio diabolica*. However, the Court of Cassation has ruled that article 419 "does not apply to coalitions whose result is *possible* or even *presumed*, but only to those whose *justified result* is to raise prices or, what amounts to the same thing, to prevent prices from falling."[115] The plaintiff in the appeal argued in this case that "once the coalition was known, the rise or prevention of the fall were the necessary consequences; that, in any case, such was the presumption, and that it was up to the defendants to destroy this presumption by proof to the contrary."[116] The appeal was rejected on the grounds that such a presumption would be tantamount to punishing the attempt, which is not provided for in article 419.[117]

The introduction of the notion of price effect did not shed any new light on the repression of anticompetitive practices; on the contrary, it whittled away the effectiveness of the text. Few convictions were handed down by

112 Cour de cassation [Cass.] [supreme court for judicial matters] crim., Feb. 1, 1834, Rec. Sirey 1834, t. xxxiv, pp. 81–84 (Fr.).

113 L. Pfister, *Contrat, libre concurrence et ordre public : la sanction des ententes dans la jurisprudence française du XIXe siècle*, 2 Revue des contrats 349 (2012).

114 Cass. crim., Feb. 1, 1834, Rec. Sirey 1834, t. xxxiv, p. 83 (Fr.).

115 *Id.* (emphasis added).

116 *Id.*

117 *Id.* at 84.

the criminal courts, except when the increase was concomitant with the agreement, and so significant that the causal link became indisputable. This was the case in *Duclos and Mille*.[118] Sieur Mille had devised an ingenious system enabling him to control the price of soda ash – an essential ingredient in soap manufacture – on the Marseilles market. He had leased six unoccupied local factories, not to bring them back into operation, but to prevent any manufacturer refusing to join his coalition from setting up there. If the judges were able to establish the effect on prices, it was due to the lack of subtlety on the part of the Provençal Mille, who suddenly raised his rates after putting his maneuver into effect. According to the Royal Court of Aix-en-Provence, it was in fact only "the *suddenness* and *enormity* of this increase" that demonstrated that "the new prices [had] been imposed by the coalition."[119]

101. **The extensive interpretation of article 419 by the Civil Division of the Court of Cassation.** In order to corroborate the assertion that without this condition of effect, article 419 could have served as a powerful tool in the fight against anticompetitive practices, it is of interest to turn to the jurisprudence of the Civil Division. Indeed, when seized with requests to annul an agreement, the civil court – which was not bound by the principle of legality of offenses and penalties – departed from a literal reading of the conditions set out in Article 419. It took the opportunity to disregard the requirement of a concrete effect on prices, and thus held, through an expansive interpretation of the text, that coalitions could be annulled solely on the basis of their *illicit cause*. Thus, in *Bonneau-Létang v. Enfert*,[120] the Court of Cassation endorsed the reasoning of the Bourges Court, which had used a presumption of effect on prices, considering that by their arrangement, the earthenware merchants had "placed the purchasers in their immediate dependence," thereby "significantly undermining public order, which requires the utmost freedom for commerce," and *ipso facto* "ruling out competition, the only means of putting the true price on the various goods."[121] In this case, despite the agreement, prices had remained relatively low, which did not prevent its annulment.

In *Gombaud v. Petit*, the Civil Division then expressly held that "in commercial matters, it is not necessary for the decision establishing the coalition to state expressly that the result of the agreement was to produce the increase or decrease [in prices] of the merchandise."[122] This jurisprudential approach not only yielded more effective outcomes, but also aligned with

118 Cass. crim., Aug. 31, 1838, Rec. Sirey 1838, t. xxxiii, pp. 988–90 (Fr.).

119 *Id.* at 989 (emphasis added).

120 Cass. civ., June 18, 1828, Rec. Dalloz 1833, t. xxxiii, pp. 174–75 (Fr.).

121 *Id.*

122 Cass. civ., June 26, 1850, Rec. Sirey 1850, pp. 726–31 (Fr.).

the longstanding notion that the mere act of fraudulent agreement necessarily impedes the formation of a just price. Thanks to this presumption, which made it possible to circumvent the difficult task of proving effects, throughout the nineteenth century litigants tended to turn more frequently to the civil courts, to such an extent that, paradoxically, article 419 was more successful before the civil courts than before the criminal courts.[123]

102. **The welcome but unimplemented reform of article 419: repression of attempts.** Aware of the practical ineffectiveness of article 419, the legislator reformed it in 1926. Guillaume Poulle, rapporteur for the Legislation Commission, remarked that the criminal judge was "disarmed because article 419 only made it possible to reach the consummated offense."[124] The Minister of Justice Louis Barthou, for his part, felt that "it was a question of making applicable a penal law that was not likely to be applied."[125] To this end, the solution adopted was to sanction the attempt, which should have allowed the criminal judge to bypass the thorny issue of qualifying a concrete result. In this way, the judge could, just like the civil court, limit the analysis to establishing the fraudulent intent of the parties to the disputed coalition in order to convict. This reform was undoubtedly designed to give a new lease of life to the criminal prosecution of agreements. The reform provided for higher penalties, those of 1810 having been deemed insufficient[126] – as if the legislator had, in a belated burst, become convinced of the relevance of severely punishing coalitions. But by 1926, article 419 had already been a controversial text for several decades, deemed useful and necessary by a minority, while the majority considered it outdated, an "anachronism written under the influence of the Emperor, in one of his days of anger."[127] Since the nineteenth century, the repression of agreements has been the subject of lively doctrinal controversy, as to whether they produce harmful effects.

B. The source of endless doctrinal controversy

103. **Doctrinal hesitations on the harmful effects of agreements.** From both a moral and legal point of view, agreements were still considered harmful when the 1810 Penal Code was adopted.[128] But as some authors have noted, while the subject "raises the most complex questions of political economy," it is enough "to refer to the motives expressed by the legislator of 1810...

123 Deak, *Contracts and Combinations in Restraint of Trade in French Law – A Comparative Study*, *op. cit.* at 424.

124 Adoption of a Bill to Amend Articles 419 and 420 of the French Penal Code, Journal Officiel de la République Française [JORF] [Official Gazette of France] Débats parl., Sénat, Nov. 19, 1926, pp. 1648–55, at 1649 (Fr.).

125 *Id.* at 1650.

126 *Id.*

127 These are the words of the appellant's lawyer in Cass. civ., June 26, 1850, Rec. Sirey 1850, pp. 726–31, at 730 (Fr.).

128 *See supra*, no. 98.

to be convinced that he had not even glimpsed the economic problems he was touching on in passing."[129] At the dawn of the nineteenth century, economic thinking on competition was in its infancy.[130] Despite the still-fragile foundations of economic theory, the focus of the debate had shifted. It is no longer a question of whether the coalition is at fault or dishonest. Economics now has a say in the relevance of repression, and agreements must now be assessed based on their effects.

The consensus was therefore short-lived, as debates about the harmful or beneficial nature of agreements multiplied. Very soon, voices were raised calling for the repeal of article 419 of the Penal Code. Skillful writers, using a variety of arguments[131] and largely incompatible with each other, argued in favor of abandoning the repression of agreements. For example, a socialist, author of a much-discussed study on trade unions, called for the repeal of article 419 in the name of the right to protect oneself from the ruin caused by free competition:[132] since competition produces disastrous effects on small merchants, they should be able to join forces, sheltered from the reprimands of the criminal judge. At the other end of the spectrum, some liberals believe that coalitions should be permitted because they produce no real effect: time will erase them of its own accord and, in the meantime, agreements will only cause relative and temporary harm to competition.[133] Another argument is that repressing coalitions is tantamount to unduly instituting a regime of "compulsory competition."[134] In the opinion of one economist, the harmful effects of hoarding practices are now no more than a "prejudice to be combated" that "hardly exists today except in the minds of the totally uneducated."[135] A thick doctrinal fog is forming. As Louis Wolowski writes, he sees, "a strange thing, everyone speaking at the same time about free

---

129 Chauveau, Hélie & Villey, Théorie du Code pénal, *op. cit.* at 585–86.

130 Nineteenth-century economists still reasoned within the framework of a pre-industrial, agricultural economy, and for the most part focused more on the question of exchange value than on the phenomenon of competition itself. At the time, competition was seen primarily as a condition of value formation (as in Ricardo, Say and Stuart Mill), and not as such. In this sense, *see* R. Le Moal, I Contribution à l'étude d'un droit de la concurrence: Nature du droit sur les valeurs concurrentielles 60–62 (1972) (Ph.D. dissertation, Université de Rennes).

131 As Daniel Villey notes: "Political economy in the nineteenth century essentially consisted of a long controversy between liberals on the one hand, and interventionists, reformists and revolutionaries on the other." *See* D. Villey, Notes de philosophie économique (1958–59): Le jeu des intérêts 189 (1965).

132 C. Jannet, *Les syndicats industriels pour régler la production en France*, La Réforme Sociale 121 (Jan. 1895).

133 "If coalitions sometimes disrupt the effect of these natural laws, it is at least only in certain exceptional cases, or for a very short time. … If their industry were open to competition, their coalition would soon be broken by newcomers, who would re-establish the fair prices in spite of them. … These principles are, in their general expression, those professed by all economists. … Some have admitted, or seemed to admit, [that competition] can sometimes give way, even in a fairly lasting way, under the pressure exerted by coalitions. We think they have given this irregular pressure more force than it has." A.-F. Cherbuliez & C. Coquelin, *Coalitions*, *in* i Dictionnaire de l'économie politique: Contenant l'exposition des principes de la science 382, 385 (C. Coquelin & G.-U. Guillaumin eds., 1852).

134 C.-F. Waelbroeck, De la liberté des coalitions industrielles et commerciales en Belgique 123 (1867).

135 A. Clément, *Accaparement*, *in* i Dictionnaire de l'économie politique: Contenant l'exposition des principes de la science 5, 5 (C. Coquelin & G.-U. Guillaumin eds., 1852).

competition, and the same arguments, put forward by both sides, leading to diametrically opposed consequences."[136]

Thus, the impression that emerges from a reading of nineteenth-century doctrine is one of compartmentalization. Economists think like economists, focusing on consequentialist considerations that they consider scientific;[137] while jurists tend to take positions partly determined by their political views, whether liberal or socialist. Economics and politics take over the debate, so much so that reflections on the *legal* definition of anticompetitive *behavior* are partly eclipsed.

104. **Political considerations enter the scene.** At the beginning of the twentieth century, new considerations, this time of a political nature, legitimized a new interpretation of article 419, allowing the judge not to sanction all coalitions.[138] This evolution is due to the fact that it is now taken for granted in public opinion that American economic prosperity is due "in large part to the action of trusts... [which] contribute powerfully to the economic expansion of the great American republic."[139] Indeed, abroad more than in France, producer groups – trusts in the United States, *Kartells* in Germany, syndicates in Italy – tend to organize themselves more effectively.[140] What was forbidden in 1810 was now "not only accepted, but established as an intangible dogma, encouraged and protected by the public authorities."[141] Agreements aimed at regulating production or even agreeing on prices became commonplace, and sometimes benefited from the benevolent gaze of the state.[142] The word "hoarding," which "once aroused the strongest emotions... no longer frightens people today, but rather makes them smile." Consequently, to prohibit all agreements as a matter of principle "would be to close one's eyes to the light."[143] Article 419, becoming weighed down with political stakes in a context of rising nationalism,[144] became the subject of divergent interpretations, compromising its credibility.

---

136 L. Wolowski, *La concurrence et la coalition*, x Revue de législation et de jurisprudence 367, 370 (Apr.-Sept. 1839).

137 This is reflected in the title of one of the leading economic works of the time: *Dictionnaire de l'économie politique: Contenant l'exposition des principes de la science* which can be translated as *Dictionary of Political Economy: Containing an Exposition of the Principles of the Science.*

138 We will examine this new line of jurisprudence *infra*, no. 125.

139 Observations by Conseiller rapporteur Michel-Jaffard under Cass. civ., May 3, 1911, Rec. Dalloz 1912, pp. 32–45 (Fr.), at 40–41.

140 *Id.*

141 *Id.*

142 One author argues that "[b]y getting to the heart of the matter, we realize that this whole theory is quite unsound, and that if case law has rallied to it, it is no doubt only to give a legal appearance to its legitimate desire to restrict the scope of application of article 419." J. Percerou, *Des syndicats de producteurs: Essai sur leur fonctionnement et leur forme juridique*, Annales de droit commercial 271, 284 (1897).

143 *Id.*

144 One author observes that the turnaround in French case law is perhaps not unconnected with the concomitant cartelization of German industry, which was then encouraged by the public authorities, Deak, *Contracts and Combinations in Restraint of Trade in French Law – A Comparative Study*, *op. cit.* at 434; on the phenomenon of cartelization in Germany and Austria, *see* D. J. Gerber, Law and Competition in Twentieth Century Europe: Protecting Prometheus 51–53 and 91–95, resp. (2nd ed. 2001).

105. **The introduction of the offense of illicit price increases in 1936: the bureaucratic turning point.** At the same time, history was once again repeating itself:[145] as with every crisis, the state authorities sought to regain control of the economy. Clearly, article 419 was not the most effective tool for this purpose. A first turning point was taken in 1936 with the adoption of the offense of illicit price increases, which had the same objective as article 419, namely, to combat price rises, this time by means of bureaucratic regulation, prefiguring the shift to administrative competition law.

To counter galloping inflation, the government passed a law in 1936 aimed at controlling the prices of staple foods. The rapporteur of the Legislation Commission (the "Commission") began his remarks by expressing regret that the Assembly had been called upon to deliberate under such rushed conditions on a text permitting considerable interference by the State.[146] The Commission wanted to make the offense intentional, which would have meant that merchants could justify raising their prices and escape condemnation.[147] This did not happen. As the aim of the text is precisely to overcome the difficulties of applying article 419 and to circumvent its controversies, it is stipulated that civil servants will be responsible for setting a "normal" price for each product, monitoring each merchant, and automatically punishing any offender who exceeds the price set by the experts. While economists have long been skeptical about the success of such measures,[148] the Commission's rapporteur was of a different opinion when he challenged the Minister: "I have confidence in your subtlety. I am sure that, in a moment, you will give us an illuminating demonstration of how you envision the application of the law."[149]

106. **The abandonment of criminal law and the shift to administrative competition law.** In France, the time has now come, willingly or not, for economic dirigisme.[150] It follows naturally that criminal law, with its rigidity and principles, is no longer the panacea for rapid, targeted intervention in response to capricious economic conditions. Thus, in most other European countries, the use of criminal law against agreements, when it was still the

---

145 *Compare with* antiquity, *supra*, no. 38 for Greek law, no. 41 for Roman law; and with Ancient Droit, *supra*, no., 72.

146 Adoption of a Bill on the Repression of Unjustified Price Increases, JORF, Débats parl., Sénat, Aug. 13, 1936, pp. 1337–49 (Fr.), at 1338–39.

147 *Id.* at 1339.

148 "Despite the inevitable failure of these disastrous attempts, there are still today in this world, as we know, a few unfortunate spirits, a few fevered minds who dream from time to time of fixing the relative value of things through public regulation." C. Coquelin, *Concurrence*, *in* I Dictionnaire de l'Économie politique: Contenant l'exposition des principes de la science 448, 452 (C. Coquelin & G.-U. Guillaumin eds., 1852).

149 Adoption of a Bill on the Repression of Unjustified Price Increases, *op. cit.* at 1344.

150 Claude Champaud notes that from 1914 onwards, "for 40 years, except for a few brief periods of respite, regulation, dirigisme, interventionism and Malthusianism will take precedence over entrepreneurial freedom… Prices, contracts and commercial transactions will be regulated. …Malthusian agreements will be encouraged, and sometimes made compulsory." C. Champaud, *Les sources du droit de la concurrence au regard du droit commercial et des autres branches du droit applicable en France*, *in* Études offertes à Roger Houin: Problèmes d'actualité posés par les entreprises 61, 75 (1985).

norm, was abandoned,[151] with the stated aim of counterbalancing the economic power of the United States. Manufacturers are now encouraged, and sometimes obliged, to come together and concentrate their forces, replacing free competition considered anarchic with "reasoned" production through coalitions, in order to more effectively counter foreign competition.[152]

Thus ended[153] a millennia-old tradition of using criminal law to protect competition. The aim was to show that, as soon as we discard traditions, start thinking in terms of results or effects, and subordinate the law to economics and politics, the result bears nothing fertile, except for fields of insoluble debate – in other words, weeds for those who wish to cultivate their own garden. The transition from criminal law to administrative law will do nothing to clarify what has become progressively obscure since 1810.

II. The persistence of effects in the 1945 ordinance

107. **The introduction of the expression "for object or for effect," a source of uncertainty regarding the mental element of the offense.** After much debate and several aborted projects,[154] a new administrative framework for regulating agreements[155] was finally introduced in 1953 by decree.[156] The text was hastily adopted, "without glory, a little '*on the sly*'."[157] and drafted by two

---

151 Babled, Droit français: Les syndicats de producteurs et détenteurs de marchandise au double point de vue économique et pénal, *op. cit.* at 186–94.

152 A. Colliez, Les coalitions industrielles et commerciales d'aujourd'hui: trusts, cartels, corners 471 (1904).

153 It should be noted that article 419 of the French Penal Code remained in force until 1986, being applied only in very exceptional circumstances following the creation of the Commission Technique des Ententes in 1953. For an account of the "extraordinary complexity" of the relationship between article 419 of the Penal Code and the 1945 Ordinance on prices, *see* A. Decocq, *L'article 419 du Code pénal est-il devenu un texte historique?*, Revue de jurisprudence commerciale 77 (1980).

154 For a detailed presentation of the debates and projects that preceded the adoption of the 1953 decree, *see* A. Chatriot, *Les ententes: Débats juridiques et dispositifs législatifs (1923-1953), La genèse de la politique de concurrence en France*, Histoire, économie & société nos. 1, 7 (2008). During this period, notes Michel Debré, economic disorder went hand in hand with legal disorder, *Pour une administration de l'économie française*, Sciences politiques 246, 259 (June 1938). *Adde*, on this intermediary period, M. Kipping, *Concurrence et compétitivité: Les origines de la législation* anti-trust *française après 1945*, *in* vi Études & documents 429 (1994); on the first decades of administrative competition law and the impact of Regulation No. 17/62 on domestic law, *see* D. Brault, L'État et l'esprit de concurrence en France 37 (1987).

155 At this stage, we do not intend to study the abuse of a dominant position. Its prohibition was not enacted until 1967, by means of an amending finance law (Loi de finances rectificative no. 63-328 du 2 juillet 1963, JORF no. 0154, July 3, 1963). For a summary of the preparatory work, *see* L. Laugier, *La prohibition des abus de position dominante*, Gazette du palais no. 345–348, 1 (Dec. 11–14, 1965). Moreover, the author premonitatively predicts that abuses of dominant positions "will be examined with greater severity in Community law than in domestic law" (*id.* at 3). In fact, they were not the subject of a developed decision-making practice over the period studied here. In this sense, V. Sélinsky, L'entente prohibée, à travers les avis de la Commission technique des ententes et des abus de position dominante 9–10 (1979): "[T]he material is too limited to prompt a thorough examination of its contribution."

156 Décret no. 53-704 du 9 août 1953 relatif au maintien ou au rétablissement de la libre concurrence industrielle et commerciale, JORF, Aug. 10, 1953, p. 7045.

157 This is the expression used by one of the decree's two authors, Louis Franck. We reproduce below the full extract, which describes the conditions under which the antitrust regulations were adopted. *See* L. Franck, 697 ministres: Souvenirs d'un directeur général des prix, 1947-1962, 84 (1989): "Long and fruitless debates had unfolded before the Assembly on the control of restrictive economic practices. My colleague

senior civil servants – France having been compelled to adopt provisions protecting competition in order to comply with the international obligation[158] contracted when signing the Havana Charter in 1948.[159] However, it was to inspire the drafting of the 1957 Treaty of Rome.[160] A study of article 59 *bis* is important, as it marks the appearance of the alternative between object and effect (**A**), which was from the outset, and remains to this day,[161] a source of uncertainty in the interplay between intention and result (**B**).

A. The emergence of the expression "for object or for effect"

108. **The new competition law, the product of conflicting political influences.** The decree provides for the insertion into the 1945 Ordinance on prices[162] of a Section IV devoted to the "maintenance of free competition." It is no small paradox that the birth of the modern system of competition law took place in the midst of a dirigiste ordinance. Prominent authors did not fail to comment on this mixture of genres. Claude Champaud observed that "[t]he resurgent waters of liberalism are mingled with dirigisme,"[163] and that if we analyze "the circumstances, political motivations and economic aims of the promulgation [of the decree], it is a paradox, not to say a hoax."[164] Gérard Farjat wrote that "[t]he French regulation was not intended… to enforce a *principle* of free competition" but was "an *instrument* in the service of an economic policy."[165] Lastly, Jean-Jacques Burst and Robert Kovar noted that "[t]he conditions under which French competition law was formed undoubtedly did not help

---

Yves Le Portz and I thought that special powers might provide us with some means to act: this was the origin of the decree of August 9, 1953… The Secretary of State for Trade was really only interested in prohibiting price fixing and discriminatory practices, but *the three of us* put *the finishing touches* to a text that we presented to a surprised and wary Laniel, wondering what galley he was being taken on board. Thus was born, without glory and somewhat 'on the sly,' this *embryonic* form of antitrust regulation. Admittedly, it never aroused the passion of the masses, and this approach to tackling 'economic powers' did not arouse the same interest in France as it did in the United States, or even in Federal Germany. When, three or four years later, we presented Paul Ramadier with our first report on the activities of our Commission Technique des Ententes, *we were greeted with polite but total indifference*: the Commission's efforts could hardly have had any influence on our price index" (emphasis added).

158 Article 46(1) of the Havana Charter required each state party to take appropriate measures to prevent trade practices that "restrain competition, limit access to markets, or foster monopolistic control." United Nations Conference on Trade and Employment, Apr. 1948, E/CONF.2/78, p. 86.

159 A. D'Angio-Barros, *Affaires économiques - Concurrence et pratiques anti-concurrentielles: 1931-1985*, Service des archives économiques et financières (May 2012), https://www.economie.gouv.fr/saef/affaires-economiques-concurrence-et-pratiques-anti-concurrentielles; in the same vein, Gerber, Law and Competition in Twentieth Century Europe: Protecting Prometheus, *op. cit.* at 187.

160 *See infra*, no. 109.

161 *See infra*, no. 304.

162 Ordonnance no. 45-1483 du 30 juin 1945 relative aux prix, JORF, July 8, 1945, no. 160, p. 4150.

163 Champaud, *Les sources du droit de la concurrence au regard du droit commercial et des autres branches du droit applicable en France*, *op. cit.* at 75.

164 *Id.* at 76.

165 G. Farjat, Droit économique 504 (2nd ed. 1982) (emphasis added).

to ensure its homogeneity."[166] In its first report to the Minister, the newly established Commission Technique des Ententes [Technical Commission on agreements][167] observed that the adoption of these competition rules by decree "contributes to giving the text a modest character that is worth emphasizing: we are not dealing here with one of these ambitious legislations... [but with] a form of experimental legislation."[168]

In just a century, the law has become *consequentialist* and *utilitarian*, serving political and economic interests. It is hardly surprising, then, that article 59 bis of the Decree, which prohibits agreements, did not set its sights on preserving the purity of principles. On the contrary, it sowed the seeds of ever-growing complexity, disregarding past traditions in favor of technical language, hardly conducive to conferring philosophical meaning and sound legal logic on contemporary competition law.

109. **Article 59 bis of the 1945 Ordinance, a source of inspiration for the Treaty of Rome.** The temporary often tends to linger. Such was the case with article 59 bis, which, even though it was quickly drafted, served as the inspiration for the 1957 Treaty of Rome.[169] Its content is clearly reminiscent of the future article 85,[170] now article 101 of the Treaty on the Functioning of the European Union (TFEU). Article 59 bis states:

> Subject to the provisions of article 59 ter, all concerted actions, agreements, express or tacit understandings, or coalitions in any form and for any reason whatsoever, *having the object or likely to have the effect*

---

166 J.-J. Burst & R. Kovar, Droit de la concurrence 4 (1981).

167 By article 59 quater of Décret no. 53-704 of Aug. 9, 1953.

168 Commission technique des ententes, *Rapport au ministre chargé des affaires économiques: années 1954 et 1955*, JORF Documents administratifs, Jan. 14, 1960, no. 1, pp. 1–14, at 2.

169 According to Lazar Focsaneanu, it served as a "model for the drafters of article 85(1)." *See Pour objet ou pour effet*, 87 Revue du marché commun 862, 868 (Jan. 1966). The alternative "for object or for effect" does indeed appear in the French drafting proposal for the said article, reproduced in the following study: J. A. Ellis, *L'interprétation du mot 'affecter' dans l'article 85, § 1er, du Traité de la Communauté économique européenne par rapport aux mots 'empêcher', 'restreindre', ou 'fausser' le jeu de la concurrence*, Recueil Dalloz 221, 225–26 (1963), chron. xxxiii. In the same vein, *see* L. F. Pace & K. Seidel, *Drafting and the Role of Regulation 17: A Hard-Fought Compromise*, *in* The Historical Foundations of EU Competition Law 54, 62 (K. K. Patel & H. Schweitzer eds., 2013): "[T]he proposed rule would contain the same principles as Articles 59 *bis* and 59 *ter* of the French decree of 1953"; as well as G. Levasseur, *Les sanctions dans le traité constitutif du Marché Commun*, *in* Les problèmes juridiques et économiques du Marché Commun 95, 105 (H. Batiffol et al. eds., 1960): according to the author, the competition rules adopted in Community law "appear to be in harmony with the regime established by the decree-laws of 1953." This is not surprising, given the words of Dean Rivero: "Compared with private law, which is rooted in centuries-old traditions, administrative law is a latecomer. ...The influence of France, because of the historical priority that circumstances have conferred on the development of its administrative law, has long been predominant. A characteristic sign: Otto Mayer, before undertaking his systematization of German administrative law, thought it necessary to begin by writing a work devoted to French administrative law; and he wrote in 1896: 'We Germans play above all, vis-à-vis France, the role of one who imitates and receives'." *See* J. Rivero, *Vers un droit commun européen: Nouvelles perspectives en droit administratif*, *in* Nouvelles perspectives d'un droit commun 389, 393–94 (M. Cappelletti ed., 1978).

170 As a reminder, article 85(1) of the EC Treaty states that "all agreements between undertakings... which have as their object or effect the prevention, restriction or distortion of competition within the common market" are "incompatible with the common market" and "prohibited"; article 85(2) states that "agreements or decisions prohibited pursuant to this Article shall be automatically void." Finally, article 85(3) states that the provisions of paragraph 1 "may however be declared inapplicable" to all agreements "which contribut[e] to improving the production or distribution of goods or to promoting technical or economic progress, while allowing consumers a fair share of the resulting benefit."

> of hindering the full exercise of competition by preventing the lowering of cost or selling prices, or by encouraging an artificial rise in prices, are prohibited.

Article 59 ter[171] introduces a mechanism enabling the parties to the agreement to put forward justifications – similar to that provided for in the German law of July 27, 1957, which stipulates that agreements may be justified in the name of the common good[172] – which will later be known as exemptions.

There is a clear change here from the text of article 419 of the Penal Code. Administrative vocabulary replaces the semantics of criminal law. The gap between article 419 of the Penal Code and article 59 bis thus appears greater than between article 419 and the texts of Roman law.[173] The vocabulary has shifted dramatically: exit the coalitions resorting to "fraudulent means" under Article 419; now there are agreements "having the object or likely to have the effect of hindering" competition. This expression is bound to give rise to immense difficulties in determining the constituent elements of the offense.

B. The uncertain relationship between intent and effect

110. **The emergence of the "object" or "effect" alternative: the rise of difficulties concerning criteria for imputability.** The origins of this alternative between "object" and "effect," which is still the subject of much debate in jurisprudence and doctrine today,[174] lie in the 1953 decree. In the past, neither the Sherman Act of 1890, nor article 46(1) of the Havana Charter of 1948, nor article 65 of the Treaty of Paris establishing the European Coal and Steel Community (ECSC Treaty) of 1951, nor subsequently the German anti-agreement law adopted in 1957[175] made such a distinction. Perhaps it was inspired by certain rulings handed down by the Supreme Court of the United States at the beginning of the twentieth century, in which the Court made a tripartite analysis, not easily understood by the continental jurist,

---

171 "The provisions of article 59 bis do not apply to concerted actions, agreements or understandings:
1. Resulting from the application of a legislative or regulatory text;
2. The authors of which are able to *justify that they have the effect* of improving and extending the outlets for production, or of ensuring the development of economic progress through rationalization and specialization."

172 A. Pirovano, *Progrès économique ou progrès social (ou les contradictions du droit de la concurrence)*, RECUEIL DALLOZ-SIREY 145, 154 (1980), chron. XXII.

173 V. SÉLINSKY, L'ENTENTE PROHIBÉE, À TRAVERS LES AVIS DE LA COMMISSION TECHNIQUE DES ENTENTES ET DES ABUS DE POSITION DOMINANTE 1 n.1 (1979).

174 For a discussion, in positive law, of the alternative between "object" and "effect," *see infra*, no. 304.

175 In this sense, R. JOLIET, THE RULE OF REASON IN ANTITRUST LAW: AMERICAN, GERMAN AND COMMON MARKET LAWS IN COMPARATIVE PERSPECTIVE 124 (1967). Section 1(1) of the Anticartel Act reads as follows: "Agreements made for a *common purpose*... are of no effect insofar as they are *likely to influence, by restraining competition*, production or markets conditions." *Id.* at 74 n. 1 (emphasis added).

between the purpose, intention and effect of the conduct in question.[176] We will, of course, have to ask ourselves what this expression[177] means, if anything at all. At this stage, let's just point out that the insertion of the phrase "having the object or likely to have the effect" in article 59 bis has given rise to a number of additional quibbles concerning the question of whether the impediments to competition can be attributed to the disputed agreements. This imputability was early recognized by the Commission Technique des Ententes as a necessary condition for their repression.[178] At issue was the meaning of the terms "object" and "effect," and whether these conditions were cumulative or alternative. In its second report to the Minister of Economic Affairs, the Commission Technique des Ententes provided a clear-cut answer, albeit one that was not consistent with the principles of logic:

> According to the terms of article 59 bis, imputability may be based either on *intent* (agreement (agreement "having as its object"), or *on a contravention* or even *a hypothetical* agreement (agreement "which may have as its effect"), with both criteria potentially being combined.[179]

Like Schrödinger's cat, the agreement is a quantum infraction. Sometimes intentional, sometimes contraventional, even "hypothetical," it would be situated, before being observed, somewhere between these two incompatible statements. Indeed, not only is the word "object" the antonym of the word "effect,"[180] but more importantly, in criminal law, there exists no offense that is *simultaneously* intentional *and* contraventional. Indeed, even in the case of contraventions, it is inadmissible to hold an individual criminally liable for a purely hypothetical – i.e., unforeseeable – result.[181]

This distinction between object and effect has given rise to lasting uncertainty as to the role of intention: if the intentional criterion is only necessary in the presence of an "agreement whose object is to restrict competition," this could mean – and this has been the interpretation of some legal scholars[182] – that the

176 *See* in particular: Standard Oil of New Jersey v. United States, 221 U.S. 1 (1911); United States v. American Tobacco, 221 U.S. 106 (1911).

177 *See infra*, no. 305.

178 Commission technique des ententes, *Rapport au ministre chargé des affaires économiques: année 1956*, J.O., Documents administratifs, Jan. 14, 1960, no. 2, pp. 15–28, at 17 (emphasis added).

179 *Id.*

180 In its legal sense, the word "effect," "as opposed to object" means: "consequence not sought by the author of the act"; whereas the word "object" refers to the "purpose pursued." *See* R. Rouquette, Dictionnaire droit administratif 293 and 542, resp. (2002).

181 In this sense, *see infra*, no. 311.

182 B. Goldman, Cours de droit du commerce et de la concurrence dans les communautés européennes 354 (1964). *See also*, *ex multis*, G. Levasseur, *Les sanctions dans le traité constitutif du Marché Commun*, *in* Les problèmes juridiques et économiques du Marché Commun 95, 112 (H. Batiffol et al. eds., 1960): "[U]nlike traditional criminal law, the assessment of the fault committed by the individual or the defaulting company appears to be of relatively secondary importance. It makes no difference whether the *object of* the prohibited

infringement can also be characterized in the event that "the anticompetitive effect it produces was not intended by the participants."

*

* *

111. **Conclusion of Section 1: taking stock of the emergence of the notion of effect in competition law.** *Disruption* and *paradox* – these are the words that seem to best describe the birth of contemporary competition law.

A *disruption*, first and foremost. Economics and law no longer look quite the same as they did yesterday. The emergence of the natural sciences, which relegated philosophy to a secondary role, led to a progressive compartmentalization of knowledge. Under the influence of utilitarianism, economic thought tended to separate itself from the legal perspective. The notion of competition became more autonomous, with economists theorizing about the influence of agreements on the market, and questioning their positive or negative effects, whereas in the past, all that mattered was the existence of a maneuver.

This development marks the emergence of a *paradox*. While the economic debate has begun to adopt a consequentialist perspective, and the law seems to have followed suit – on the one hand, by making price manipulation a constituent element of the offense under article 419 of the Penal Code, and on the other, by inserting the alternative "for object or for effect" into article 59 bis of the 1945 Ordinance – this development has not removed the need for intention. Although the need to take intent into account is becoming less and less visible, paradoxically, it remains just as present as before. This is because the law has not been able to do without this criterion, which from the outset has served as the basis for the repression of anticompetitive practices.

*

* *

---

cartels was to distort competition within the common market, as long as they had this *effect*; this objective criterion is sufficient to justify conviction. The 'moral element' of the offense is very limited." *Adde* P. Barbry & R. Plaisant, *Libre concurrence et ententes industrielles*, Recueil Dalloz 67, 68 (1954), chron. xi: "Article 59 *bis* applies whether the action has the object or may have the effect of hindering the full exercise of free competition. Fraudulent intent is therefore not required. Moreover, it would appear that an action or agreement that is originally lawful, but fails to produce the intended effect, may become unlawful as a result of a change in the market beyond the control of those involved. Moreover, certain authors, who equate cartels by object with *per se* prohibited offenses have, argued in favor of the preponderance of the effect over the object." *See* M.-C. Boutard Labarde & G. Canivet, Droit français de la concurrence 38 (1994). Finally, the notion of "effect" has sometimes been confused with that of "effectiveness." *See* J.-J. Burst & R. Kovar, Droit de la concurrence 236 (1981): "As soon as the anticompetitive object is established, the qualification of illegal agreement is retained without having to consider the effectiveness of the practices."

Section 2
Reasons for maintaining the intention of 1810 in the twenty-first century

112. **Law, certainty and principles.** The legal system is based on a principle that is firmly anchored in its tradition: predictability – for it would not be fair to hold an individual liable for the unforeseeable consequences of their behavior. If competition law had fully embraced the consequentialist perspective, sanctioning behavior only if it produced harmful effects on competition, or more broadly on markets, it would quickly have been confronted with a major problem: the economic criterion of "effects" is unsuitable for providing certainties, since economic science, unlike law, is not a stabilized field of knowledge based on centuries-old values (**Paragraph 1**). While the economic and political debates surrounding competition law have gradually taken center stage, to the point of becoming omnipresent today, the law has nevertheless remained faithful to its principles, and has continued, more or less explicitly, to require intention – whether on the basis of article 419 of the 1810 Penal Code, or article 59 bis of the 1945 Ordinance (**Paragraph 2**).

Paragraph 1 – The shortcomings of the economic effects criterion

113. **Foundations and philosophy of contemporary economic analysis.** There is much debate about the epistemological foundations of economic analysis. What does economics allow us to understand? Is it truly, as some have argued, a science capable of objectivity – one that provides precise, neutral knowledge of reality and makes reliable predictions? (**I**) In addition to these debates, it is worth noting the philosophical origins of most contemporary economic approaches, particularly those on which competition law is based. Most of these derive largely from classical utilitarianism and inherently carry its same limitations (**II**).

I. The foundations of contemporary economic analysis

114. **Postulates and refutability of economic theories.** For the most part, economic theories provide models of reality that are supposed to enable reliable forecasts. Among economists, this postulate is the subject of a major debate between those who advocate the realism of economic analysis and

those who take an instrumental view of it (**A**). However, when a discipline cannot agree on its foundations, consensus on the criteria for refuting its theories is compromised (**B**).

A. Between realism and instrumentalism

115. **Epistemological controversies concerning the scientific status of economic analysis.** In contemporary times, the sciences have been accused of neglecting the question of the meaning of human existence, in order to effectively advance an increasingly complex, specialized and scattered knowledge of the world. They are thus said to be going through a crisis that began in the twentieth century.[183] Since then, the hard sciences themselves have ceased to think of themselves as totally objective,[184] and have introduced a degree of relativity and uncertainty,[185] making room once again for the subject[186] and intuition.[187] However, economic analysis has not given up its claim to a scientific aim that has been asserting itself and developing since the eighteenth century.[188] The question is whether economics can truly be considered a science, understood as a discipline capable of objectively establishing stable and exact laws, and therefore of predicting economic phenomena with a certain degree of certainty, or *at least* probability. This question is at

---

183 On this subject, *see* E. Husserl's fundamental work, LA CRISE DES SCIENCES EUROPÉENNES ET LA PHÉNOMÉNOLOGIE TRANSCENDANTALE (G. Granel trans., Gallimard 1989). Husserl traces the origins of the divorce between philosophy and science, and the failure of the latter to provide an exhaustive representation of the world, i.e., to fulfill its promise of absoluteness. The author demonstrates that the scientific method rests on a subjective foundation that has been masked, then forgotten; and calls for its meaning to be rediscovered through the transcendental method, which leaves room for the subject without renouncing scientific reasoning. Michel Villey believes that the path opened up by Husserl would make it possible to overcome the quarrel between science and natural law, provided that science agrees to open itself up to "the experience of the just." *See* M. VILLEY, LEÇONS D'HISTOIRE DE LA PHILOSOPHIE DU DROIT 100 (1962).

184 C. ATIAS, ÉPISTÉMOLOGIE JURIDIQUE 102 (1985). Quantum or wave physics, the theory of relativity, the introduction of the concepts of chance and disorder, have in effect imposed a revision of so-called positive or objective science. On how these new theories called into question previous scientific postulates and gave rise to the "new scientific spirit" at the beginning of the twentieth century, *see* G. BACHELARD, LA FORMATION DE L'ESPRIT SCIENTIFIQUE (5th ed. 1967).

185 Nobel Prize-winning chemist Ilya Prigogine indeed observes "the emergence of a science that is no longer limited to simplified, idealized situations, but confronts us with the complexity of the real world." *See* I. PRIGOGINE, LA FIN DES CERTITUDES 15 (1996).

186 In this sense, *see* G. BACHELARD, LE NOUVEL ESPRIT SCIENTIFIQUE 150–51 (PUF 2020) (1934): the author argues that scientific description is not immediate, as assumed by Cartesian evidence, but necessarily mediated by the person of the observer.

187 Henri Poincaré thus writes that if "[w]e believe that our reasoning no longer calls on intuition, philosophers will tell us that this is an illusion. Pure logic would never lead us to anything but tautologies; it could not create anything new; it is not from it alone that any science can emerge." H. POINCARÉ, LA VALEUR DE LA SCIENCE 20 (1911). One may find it worthwhile to consult the whole of the first chapter, "Intuition and Logic in Mathematics," which the author concludes by stating that "logic and intuition each have their necessary role. Both are indispensable. Logic, which alone can give certainty, is the instrument of demonstration; intuition is the instrument of invention."

188 H. Brochier, *Fondements idéologiques et visée scientifique en économie*, 10 ÉCONOMIES ET SOCIÉTÉS 169, 170 (Oct. 1988).

the root of a major controversy[189] among economists, between advocates of economic *realism* and those who promote an *instrumentalist* vision of economic analysis.

116. **The realist and instrumentalist theses in economics.** If we consider that economic analysis must be realistic, i.e., able to provide a description as close as possible to the real world, then its scientific nature may be open to debate. Indeed, the postulate on which economic theories are based is that of the rationality of agents – a premise that reduces them to cold calculators seeking at all times to optimize their means to achieve their ends. This premise is refutable, as it fails to take into account the psychological reality of individuals.[190] Nevertheless, rationality is the central assumption of economic theory.[191] Its value lies in the fact that it makes it possible to model human behavior, using an approximation that enables forecasts to be made via mathematical processing.[192] Described in this way, economic analysis appears disconnected from reality due to its excessive degree of abstraction and formalism.[193] Paradoxically, this modeling confers on it "a considerable knowledge effect," and therefore a strong authority; even though economics is "based on a weak conceptualization," formulating "often tautological" propositions, resulting "to this extent, [in] a pseudo-science."[194]

If, on the other hand, we believe that economic analysis does not have to be faithful to reality, then it would be possible to found "positive economics." This "instrumentalist" position was championed by Milton Friedman. He believes that the classic and "perennial" criticism accusing economics of being unrealistic misses its target.[195] In his view, an economic theory should be considered relevant as soon as it enables valid and meaningful predictions.[196] Since reality is out of reach for economics, the question of whether a theory is relevant should be

---

189 There can be no claim to exhaustiveness here. For an overview of epistemological issues in economics, *see*, in particular, D. M. Hausman, The Inexact and Separate Science of Economics 123–240 (1992).

190 It should be noted, however, that in response to this objection, concerning the lack of realism of the rationality postulate, complexifications of the rational agent model have been proposed. On the different ways of conceiving rationality, *see* M. Lagueux, Rationality and Explanations in Economics (2014). The author points out that approaches that tend to relativize the postulate of rationality are resistant to mathematical formalization, which explains why most economists find it relevant to opt for a postulate of total rationality (at 113). *See also*, on the need to revise the rationality postulate in the light of advances in neuroscience, C. Schmidt, Neuroéconomie (2010).

191 H. Brochier, *Rationalité économique*, Encyclopædia Universalis. According to the author, the postulate of rationality is the foundation of all modern marginalist and *welfare* theory.

192 The mathematization of economics originated in the eighteenth and nineteenth centuries with Quesnay and Cournot, and has since developed continuously. *See* T. Pouch, *La science économique sous le regard de Husserl*, 1 L'homme & la Société 165, 172–73 (2010).

193 H. Brochier, *La science économique est-elle une science?*, Les études philosophiques 229, 229–30 (Apr.-June 1978)

194 *Id.* at 231–32.

195 M. Friedman, *The Methodology of Positive Economics*, *in* Essays in Positive Economics 3, 30–31 (1996).

196 *Id.* at 5.

resolved solely by examining whether the predictions it produces are "good enough for the purpose in hand" or, *at the very least*, "better than predictions from alternative theories."[197] This implies that the realism of the postulates is irrelevant, as theories should only be tested on the basis of the predictions they allow.[198] In this sense, Milton Friedman believes that economics can be an objective science, in the same sense as the physical sciences.[199]

This controversy between realists and instrumentalists shows that economic analysis is not a settled field of knowledge. On the contrary, there seems to be a permanent hesitation as to its scientific foundations,[200] with economists "unable to define unambiguously, in its day-to-day operation, what is 'scientific' and what is not."[201] This results not only in significant instability within economic theories, but also in the potential to mask ideological biases as scientific assertions.

B. The refutability of economic theories

117. **The impossibility of empirically verifying the validity of economic theories.** The reluctance of some economists to admit that economic analysis can ever produce "scientific" predictions is linked to the fact that the community of economists does not agree on the criteria for the *refutability* of theories.[202] The problem lies in the impossibility of unequivocally verifying the results obtained empirically. Indeed, the immense complexity of economic phenomena makes it difficult to establish the validity of the laws proposed – human history is not a "reproducible experiment"[203] – unless we deny the existence of a degree of free will.[204] Friedman's instrumentalism bypasses the question of the validity of the premise, but still fails to overcome the essential issue of the uncertainty of results. This approach

197 *Id.* at 41.

198 P. Mongin, *L'instrumentalisme dans l'Essai de M. Friedman*, Économies et sociétés 73, 75 (Oct. 1987).

199 Friedman, *The Methodology of Positive Economics*, *op. cit.* at 4. Note that this is also the opinion of Vilfredo Pareto, who considered that "among the social sciences, the science of ophelimity [i.e., the science of subjective utility felt by an agent] is the only one whose results have reached a degree of precision and certainty comparable to that of the propositions of the other natural sciences, such as chemistry and physics." V. Pareto, Cours d'économie politique 6 (Librairie Droz 1964) (1896).

200 In this sense, *see* Brochier, *La science économique est-elle une science?*, *op. cit.* at 233.

201 *Id.*

202 J. Lallement, *Popper et le principe de rationalité*, Économies et sociétés 25, 29 (Oct. 1987). The author believes that it is "the vacuity of the principle of rationality that makes its strength: its factual content is so weak that it thereby excludes any possibility of refutation."

203 H. Brochier, *Les théories économiques sont-elles réfutables?*, Économies et sociétés 107, 116 (Oct. 1987): economic analysis, in fact, "does not have, unlike the natural sciences, the final check that is the effectiveness of statements in reality."

204 *See* A. Beres, *Entretien sur l'économie avec Sir Karl Popper*, 1 Revue française d'économie 55, 57–60 (1986); *adde*, D. Villey, Notes de philosophie économique (1958–59): Le jeu des intérêts 121 (1965): "If there is no science except of the determinate, to what extent can economic facts, which result from human choices, be held to be such?"

bypasses the debate, as it does not seek to defend the scientific interest of using a false premise, and simply exonerates itself from the task of engaging in this debate.[205] Such a method is therefore opposed to conceptual revision – which is questionable from a scientific point of view – and is not conducive to ensuring the stability of theories.

The instrumentalist approach, largely dominant,[206] can also give way to stratagems designed to protect a theory from any possibility of falsification. Indeed, it can allow ideological statements to be scientifically disguised, as long as an empirical test confirming the initial hypothesis is all that is needed to make the theory valid.[207] Indeed, when studying the main economic theories, it is easy to notice that they are almost always caught up in "ideological battles and discourses."[208] Yet the trend is towards more complex statements which, owing to their increasing technicality and formalization, appear to be axiologically neutral.[209] The paradox is as follows: even though economics has always been grounded in *doctrines*, it now appears to claim neutrality, while still resting on various ideologies concealed behind mathematical complexities inaccessible to non-specialists.[210]

Finally, in the absence of knowing whether and according to what criteria a theory is refuted, the validity of all theories is upheld, even though they are extremely varied, competing, and even incompatible with each other. The result is a state akin to the anarchy of knowledge.[211] One economist admitted that his greatest dilemma was feeling torn between his attraction to economic theory and his doubts as to its relevance.[212] Believing that the work of economists consists essentially in amusing themselves with "toys called models,"[213] he thinks that there is not a single theory that does not lead to absurd conclusions when applied to circumstances far

205 Mongin, *L'instrumentalisme dans l'Essai de M. Friedman*, *op. cit.* at 96–97.

206 *See*, in this sense, *id.* at 97: the author believes that economists have been "all the more willing to indulge in Friedmanian recommendations" because it was a doctrine "flattering to the epistemological conscience of economists." *Adde*, Hausman, The inexact and separate science of economics, *op. cit.* at 1: while the author acknowledges that the axioms on which economics is based are inexact, he considers that economic methods are scientifically acceptable. Richard Posner himself subscribes to this trend, considering that economic analysis models are valid as *useful* approximations, even if the hypothesis on which they are based is false. *See* R. A. Posner, The Overcoming Law 17 (1995).

207 C. Le Pen, *'Falsifiabilité' et théorie économique, ou comment rendre une théorie économique infalsifiable*, Économies et sociétés 119, 124–25 (Oct. 1987).

208 Brochier, *Fondements idéologiques et visée scientifique en économie*, *op. cit.* at 171.

209 *Id.* at 172.

210 *See* P. Salin, *L'école 'autrichienne' et l'esprit scientifique*, 177 Liberté économique & progrès social 2, 6 (Fall 2021): "[T]he more complex the explanation, the more scientific it seems. And, quite often, the more mathematical it is, the closer it seems to the natural sciences, and the more serious it appears."

211 Brochier, *Les théories économiques sont-elles réfutables?*, *op. cit.* at 113.

212 A. Rubinstein, *Dilemmas of an Economic Theorist*, 74 Econometrica 865, 866 (2006).

213 *Id.* at 865. *Compare with* J. Tirole, Théorie de l'organisation industrielle 12 (1993): the author writes that in "the field of economics, the best developed and *most aesthetically pleasing* model is the competitive equilibrium paradigm of Arrow and Debreu" (emphasis added).

removed from the framework in which it was conceived.[214] The ambition to provide forecasts that are, if not exact, then *at least* plausible, thus appears illusory.[215] In short, the only certain prediction that science can provide is that it will never provide a perfect prediction.[216]

That economics advances through a process of error and correction is clearly not open to criticism. Nevertheless, the unstable, unpredictable, and potentially biased nature of economic analyses makes it necessary to reflect critically on the normative objective of economic reasoning in competition law[217] – all the more so as the latter stems from a school of thought that is itself debatable:[218] utilitarianism.

II. The utilitarian heritage of contemporary economic analysis

118. **The continuing problem of utilitarianism: the moral question.** There is a connection between the classical utilitarianism of Jeremy Bentham and the economic analysis of Richard Posner (**A**). Both currents have *attempted to* replace the so-called sensualist morality[219] with a scientific vision of human problems – an attempt that has proved unsuccessful, insofar as the moral question cannot be evacuated (**B**).

A. A continuum from Jeremy Bentham to Richard Posner

119. **A direct link between contemporary economic analysis and classical utilitarianism.** In certain respects, economic analysis as used in the law of anti-competitive practices appears[220] – and not least – to be an *extension of*

214 Rubinstein, *Dilemmas of an Economic Theorist*, *op. cit.* at 871.

215 In this sense, *see*: "Unless we can understand what the acting people mean by their actions any attempt to explain them, i.e., to subsume them under rules which connect similar situations with similar actions, are bound to fail." F. A. Hayek, The Counter-Revolution of Science: Studies on the Abuse of Reason 31 (1955), https://ia803403.us.archive.org/10/items/counterrevolutio030197mbp/counterrevolutio030197mbp.pdf.

216 H. Poincaré, La valeur de la science 219 (1911): "Science is imperfect, and if I add that it will always remain so, I am certain that this is a prediction that, for its part at least, will never be contradicted."

217 *See infra*, nos. 437–438.

218 *See infra*, nos. 420 *et seq*.

219 *See supra*, no. 89.

220 Even if the majority of contemporary economic theories are utilitarian, it would be unfounded to assert, without qualification, that economic analysis as *a whole* is a modernized form of Benthamian utilitarianism. Indeed, the scope of economic analysis is far broader than that of classical utilitarianism: far from being confined to the study of market exchanges or crime, virtually everything today seems subject to the scrutiny of economic theory. For an illustration of the considerable broadening of the field of economic analysis, *see* S. D. Levitt & S. J. Dubner, Freakonomics: A Rogue Economist Explores the Hidden Side of Everything (2005); or more recently, P. T. Leeson, WTF?! An Economic Tour of the Weird (2017). For this reason, it is impossible to compare Bentham's utilitarianism with the whole of economic analysis, which is so varied and subdivided into distinct, even opposing schools, in terms of both scope and methods (as in the case of the Austrian school, which, in opposition to the methodology adopted by the other schools, is the perfect illustration of the diversity that reigns in this field). On this subject, *see* the reference work, P. Larouche,

Jeremy Bentham's utilitarian doctrine.[221] Firstly, the deterministic postulate of utilitarianism[222] is identically present in the economic approach.[223] Like Bentham's theory, the latter is based on the assumption that human beings behave rationally[224] – which implies that man is a predictable, predetermined being. A second point in common is their *consequentialist* vision:[225] they judge the relevance of an act, law, or decision by its *effects.*[226] Finally, both reject moral philosophy[227] as a weak discipline, unable to achieve consensus[228] and, more generally, the role of tradition in the development and application of legal rules.[229] Their difference lies in a few developments,[230] which are nonetheless decisive for understanding the philosophical underpinnings of the economic approach used in competition law today. The main difference between economic analysis and classical utilitarianism lies in the replacement of the criterion of "the greatest happiness of the greatest number" with that of "wealth maximization." While this change is supposed to make the economic approach a

---

E. Mackaay, A. Parent & S. Rousseau, Analyse économique du droit (3rd ed. 2021). Our perspective here is more limited: we will focus on the economic approach adopted in competition law (which conveys a reductive vision of economic analysis, *see infra*, no. 436), and whose filiation with Benthamian utilitarianism is obvious, with a few differences – a child is not a faithful copy of its parents.

221 Richard Posner himself initially recognized that Bentham's utilitarianism was another name for economic theory, before retracting his own assertion. *See* R. A. Posner, Economic Analysis of Law 357 (1972): "Bentham's utilitarianism, in its aspect as a positive theory of human behavior, is another name for economic theory. Pleasure is value, and pain cost." The existence of a kinship between contemporary economic analysis and the utilitarian theories of the eighteenth and nineteenth centuries has also been noted by many authors. *See, e.g.*, R. Dworkin, Taking Rights Seriously vii, ix, 97–98 (1977); H. L. A. Hart, *American Jurisprudence Through English Eyes: The Nightmare and the Noble Dream*, 11 Georgia Law Review 969, 987–88 (1977); R. A. Epstein, *The Next Generation of Legal Scholarship*, 30 Stanford Law Review 635, 645 (1978). Other leaders in the economic analysis of law, such as Gary Becker, more readily acknowledge the filiation between their work and Bentham's theory. *See Crime and Punishment: An Economic Approach,* 76 The Journal of Political Economy 169, 209 (1968); T. Kirat, *Économie et droit: De l'analyse économique du droit à de nouvelles alliances?*, 49 Revue économique 1057, 1059–60 (1998).

222 *See supra*, no. 90.

223 For a study highlighting the need for economic analysis to move in the direction of methodological individualism (a minority economic trend that takes human freedom into account), *see* E. Mackaay, *La règle juridique observée par le prisme de l'économiste: Une histoire stylisée du mouvement de l'analyse économique du droit*, Revue internationale de droit économique 43, 87–88 (1986).

224 A. Strowel, *Utilitarisme et approche économique dans la théorie du droit: Autour de Bentham et de Posner*, 18 Revue interdisciplinaire d'études juridiques 1, 7, 11 (1987).

225 *Id.* at 14.

226 Larouche et al., Analyse économique du droit, *op. cit.* at 5.

227 On the rejection of so-called sensualist morality by classical utilitarians, *see supra*, no. 89.

228 In this sense, *see* R. A. Posner, *Law and Economics is Moral*, 24 Valparaiso University Law Review 163, 166 (1990): "I regard moral philosophy as a weak field, a field in disarray, a field in which consensus is impossible to achieve in our society."

229 *See* R. A. Posner, Frontiers of Legal Theory 145–69 (2001).

230 It should be noted that Richard Posner has redoubled his efforts to sever the links between the economic analysis of law and utilitarianism, in order to defend himself against severe criticism, particularly from Dworkin, Epstein and Hart, who have assimilated the two currents (*see* the references cited *supra*, no. 119). In response, Richard Posner published an article criticizing the shortcomings of utilitarianism and attempting to distinguish his approach. However, this attempt at distanciation is unconvincing; so much so that the article in question tends rather to comfort the reader in the idea that, as Posner himself maintained in 1972, his theories are a form of utilitarianism. *See* R. A. Posner, *Utilitarianism, Economics, and Legal Theory*, 8 Journal of Legal Studies 103 (1979).

theory that produces results in line with our moral conceptions, it fails to eliminate the ethical question, and provides only an unsatisfactory answer.

B. The impossibility of dismissing the moral question

120. **Is wealth maximization an "ethical" theory?** Utilitarianism has been criticized for failing to clarify the method of calculating the "greatest happiness of the greatest number,"[231] a calculation that proves difficult because the preferences of individuals are, in practice, impossible to know.[232] Modern economic analysis has therefore proposed another, more reliable criterion: that of "wealth maximization." In this case, the calculation of the "right outcome" must be assessed against the standard of *a single* preference: wealth.[233] The reasoning is as follows. If everything can be bought, then every preference has a monetary value, so every preference can be calculated in terms of price. Put another way, we all want to satisfy our desires, and these desires have a price, from which it follows that the more money we have, the more desires we can satisfy – and therefore the greater our well-being.[234] Where classical utilitarianism assessed the value of a legal rule in terms of its capacity to realize a variety of ends, the contemporary economic approach still reduces the order of ends to wealth alone.

In Richard Posner's view, such a worldview is nonetheless "ethical." Wealth maximization as a criterion would counter the "utility monster" criticism that utilitarianism fails to distinguish clearly between good and morally questionable preferences. According to Richard Posner, taking into account only the preference for wealth would make the results of the economic approach align with our "*common moral intuitions*" – in other words, bring his theory into line with ethics.[235] The author illustrates his point with the example of "torturers." According to him, sadists who derive immense pleasure from the suffering of others would not be able to maximize their wealth since, in order to indulge in their hobby, they would have to buy the consent of their victims; which, quite logically, would rapidly impoverish them – with the exception, however, of the

---

231 Posner, *Utilitarianism, Economics, and Legal Theory*, *op. cit.* at 113. On the difficulties of the Benthamian calculation of happiness, *see* J.-P. Cléro, *Le calcul benthamien des plaisirs et des peines: Calcul introuvable ou seulement indéfiniment différé?*, 78 Archives de Philosophie 229 (2015).

232 Posner, *Utilitarianism, Economics, and Legal Theory*, *op. cit.* at 111–19.

233 Strowel, *Utilitarisme et approche économique dans la théorie du droit: Autour de Bentham et de Posner*, *op. cit.* at 16–18. Anne-Lise Sibony has also pointed out the logical dependency between the goal of wealth maximization and the price system. *See* A.-L. Sibony, Le juge et le raisonnement économique en droit de la concurrence 94 (2008), no. 121.

234 However, we must be careful not to interpret this schema in a caricatured way, and not see it as a straightforward transformation of the human being into a consumer. Indeed, since everything can be converted into monetary terms, this means that desires that are not aimed at market commodities can also be included in the calculation. For example, making ecological choices has a price, even if it is not necessarily "marketable."

235 Posner, *Utilitarianism, Economics, and Legal Theory*, *op. cit.* at 119.

wealthiest.[236] In this way, the goal of wealth maximization would produce a natural sorting, and would in fact automatically limit morally deviant behavior.

121. **The impossibility of abandoning the ethical criterion.** Apart from the absurd and iniquitous nature of such an example, it also highlights two essential problems with the utilitarian economic approach. Firstly, it is based on the most outdated value system,[237] far removed from contemporary societal aspirations, not to say alien. Economic analysis presupposes the *legitimacy* of the goal of wealth maximization[238] in order to draw descriptive and normative conclusions. It is therefore more than necessary to ask whether this objective is desirable, and whether it should constitute the sole and ultimate societal project from which to derive rules of law.[239] Secondly, this illustration demonstrates – if proof were needed – that a utilitarian approach cannot, in the final analysis, dispense with a moral analysis of human affairs, which is all the more essential given that economic reasoning tends to reduce the symbolism of the right to punish to very little. For Gary Becker, the purpose of punishment is reduced to the simplest device – the means of limiting "the negative externalities of certain acts"[240] while for George Stigler, the objective of criminal law is limited to achieving the "degree of compliance with the rule of prescribed (or proscribed) behavior that the society believes it can afford,"[241] taking into account the cost of its implementation. At times, economic analysis has also led to shocking results: for example, Isaac Ehrlich's highly modeled demonstration that the death penalty is an "effective" punishment.[242]

It should also be pointed out that Richard Posner, far from simply dispensing with the notion of morality, is also trying, where classical utilitarians have failed, to establish a *science of objective morality*, devoid of transcendence, that would enable us to build an optimal world.

---

236 We reproduce Richard Posner's text in full, to assure the reader that we are not misrepresenting what he said: "I turn now to the question whether the economic approach, like the utilitarian, yields results violently inconsistent with our common moral intuitions. I believe not. The 'utility monster' has no place in a system of ethics founded on wealth maximization. The fact that I might derive so much gusto from torturing people as to exceed their misery in a felicific weighing would not make me a good man or give me the right to torture people. I would have to *buy* my victims' consent, and these purchases would soon deplete the wealth of all but the wealthiest sadists." *Id.* at 131. *Adde, see* Richard Posner's unconvincing reasoning when he tries to justify the fact that the economic analysis of law leads to results in line with morality. POSNER, *Law and Economics is Moral*, *op. cit.*

237 In this sense, *see* VILLEY & NÊME, PETITE HISTOIRE DES GRANDES DOCTRINES ÉCONOMIQUES, *op. cit.* at 256–57.

238 SIBONY, LE JUGE ET LE RAISONNEMENT ÉCONOMIQUE EN DROIT DE LA CONCURRENCE, *op. cit.* at 92, no. 119.

239 Indeed, Posner's project, far from being limited to a description, is, like that of the classical utilitarians, *normative*. *See infra*, no. 437.

240 Becker, *Crime and Punishment: An Economic Approach*, *op. cit.* at 201.

241 G. J. Stigler, *The Optimum Enforcement of Laws*, 78 JOURNAL OF POLITICAL ECONOMY 526, 526 (1970).

242 I. Ehrlich, *The Deterrent Effect of Capital Punishment: A Question of Life and Death*, 65 THE AMERICAN ECONOMIC REVIEW, 397 (1975).

However, morality cannot be scientific[243] because it is human – and therefore evolving, like society. Resolving a moral problem is never a definitive or certain operation, and this is precisely why it is a "problem."[244] Morality renews itself: it is neither fixed nor determinable once and for all.[245] In any case, it will never be accessible through mathematical calculations.[246]

The objectivity promoted by utilitarian currents became an obsession, as it was the solution par excellence, in the opinion of its promoters, to remove the supposed unpredictability, irrationality and arbitrariness of the legal system. Objectivity was a reaction of defiance towards the criterion of justice, which until then had always involved ethical reflection.[247] Indeed, utilitarianism was born at a time when it was thought possible to muzzle both legislators and judges by forcing them to respect the dogma of scientific rationality. The rules of law,[248] which call on indeterminate notions[249] such as fault, *dol*, unfairness and abuse, should therefore be based on something other than moral analysis – deemed "anarchic."[250] However, it is impossible to found a law without some degree of philosophy,[251] transcendence and interpretation, without denying the notion of law itself – for where discussion ends, there is no longer any law.[252] It is undoubtedly the inadequacies of the economic perspective[253] that have

---

243 E. Goblot, Essai sur la classification des sciences (1898). After presenting the two ways of understanding morality, metaphysical and utilitarian (at 253–63), the author concludes that "[w]e do not have to assign morality any place in our classification of the sciences. …[T]he theoretical doctrine on which morality is based is not scientific, but metaphysical." *Id.* at 269.

244 E. Blondel, Le problème moral 2–3 (2000).

245 *Id.* at 47.

246 S. Trifilio, Esprit mathématique et pensée économique dans l'Antiquité et au Moyen Âge 110 (2010) (Ph.D. dissertation, Aix-Marseille University): "In the ethical sciences… no reality primarily manifests in quantitative form. The size, (external) shape, number and dimensions of the objects of the practical sciences are always variable and accidental; they tell us nothing about what these objects *are*. Their quality alone must therefore be taken into account, as it alone tells us about their true substance. We can therefore understand why the idea of 'mathematization' (*id est* the fact of making subject to mathematics what is not mathematical in essence, or does not appear to be mathematical according to experience) is totally foreign to the epistemology developed by Aristotle."

247 *See supra*, Aristotle's and the Scholastics' way of reasoning, resp. no. 37 and no. 51.

248 According to Dean George Ripert, the classical rule of law contrasts with regulatory law, which is endowed with a "mathematical rigor that leaves no room for discussion." Conversely, in "the application of the great legal rules, will and cause, good faith and fraud, correct conduct and fault play a role. In modern law, on the other hand, the text applies automatically. We could almost do without jurists for this application." *See* G. Ripert, Le déclin du droit: Études sur la législation contemporaine 71 (1949).

249 On the notion of "indeterminate notions," *see infra* nos. 410–412.

250 *See supra*, no. 89.

251 In his *Leçons d'histoire de la philosophie du droit*, Michel Villey's first axiom is that "philosophical reflection is the irreplaceable instrument of legal *progress*." M. Villey, Leçons d'histoire de la philosophie du droit 13–14 (1962).

252 C. Atias, De la difficulté contemporaine à penser en droit: Leçons de philosophie du droit 25 (2016).

253 On this subject, *see* V. Malabat, *Le droit pénal a-t-il encore une utilité ?*, *in* Analyse économique du droit et matière pénale 91, 102 (C. Claverie Rousset ed., 2018): "If we reason… on its purely utilitarian function of sanction (and sanction can be conceived as something other than utilitarian), then criminal law is probably not indispensable, without this meaning that it is not useful. But if we see criminal law as the expression of a society's strong values, which are its cement because they are binding on all, then criminal law is probably more useful today than ever before, whatever economic analysis we make of it."

led the legal system not to fully embrace it, and to remain founded on principles with a long tradition.

Paragraph 2 – The persistence of the legal criterion of intent

122. **Reasons for the persistence of the criterion of intent.** Whether in the Penal Code of 1810, or at the dawn of adopting administrative competition law, the criterion of intent has been maintained (**I**). Indeed, decriminalization does not exempt one from adhering to the reasoning and principles inherent to the field, insofar as – even when the sanction is imposed by an administrative authority – its punitive nature necessitates the incorporation of comparable safeguards (**II**).

I. Intention, from the penal code of 1810 to the ordinance of 1945

123. **The need to establish intent, both under article 419 of the Penal Code and on the basis of article 59 bis of the 1945 Ordinance.** Although article 419 of the Penal Code establishes the effect of a price-fixing agreement as a constitutive element of the offense, it continues to explicitly require the element of intent (**1**). Subsequently, the decision-making practice of the Commission Technique des Ententes confirmed that intention remained required, albeit implicitly this time (**2**). There is a real interest in studying the latter's decisions, as the jurisprudence of the early European bodies closely resembles it.[254] The jurisprudence of the Court of Justice is characterized by great deference to its own precedents, and the main principles of its reasoning were determined as early as its first judgments.[255]

A. Asserted recognition of intent in criminal competition law

124. **The definition of the intentional element required by article 419 of the Penal Code: an undefined element, as it cannot be determined in advance.** The offense provided for by article 419 of the Penal Code is clearly an intentional one. Émile Garçon, in his note under the article, writes that "[c]onforming to general principles, intent will be realized when the agent

254 V. Sélinsky, L'entente prohibée, à travers les avis de la Commission technique des ententes et des abus de position dominante 268 (1979).

255 L. Navel, L'argument de continuité jurisprudentielle dans la jurisprudence de la Cour de justice de l'Union européenne 38–53 (2021). *Adde, see infra*, no. 302.

acts with knowledge, knowing that the means he employed were intended to have the effect of suppressing competition."[256] Two essential elements must therefore be differentiated: the means of perpetrating the offense and the result. The fraud employed constitutes the "moral evil" of the offense, while the price rise or fall it produced constitutes the "material evil."[257] As the difficulties involved in characterizing the result have already been discussed,[258] it is now time to define the mental element. The article provides three examples[259] – mentioned by *way of illustration* – the legislator having recognized that it was "impossible to determine all the forms that fraud and greed can take"[260] – the means of defrauding being so numerous, "that it would hardly be easier to detail them than to foresee them."[261] By adding the expression "any fraudulent means whatsoever," the text has extended the scope of incrimination to all fraudulent maneuvers likely to alter prices. It is thus "*in this fraud*, a necessary element of the various modes of perpetration, *that all the criminality of the offense lies.*"[262] From this perspective, article 419 is not legislative innovation on the part of the legislator: the words have certainly changed, but there is no substantive difference between hoarding or monopoly in Ancien Droit and ancient law, and the behaviors sanctioned by the Penal Code of 1810.[263] Since time immemorial, it has been fraud that makes the offense, and fraud alone that characterizes the infringement of competition: "Free competition is that which is exercised *through work* and *without fraud*; as soon as it employs *fraudulent maneuvers*, it is no longer competition, it is a monopoly. The interest of free industry demands its repression."[264]

The fraudulent element in question is, by its very nature, *indeterminate*, since it varies with each case, depending on the fraudulent means employed.[265] The offense is thus virtually adaptable to all new situations,

---

256 E. Garçon, iii Code pénal annoté 395 (2nd ed. 1959). Cf. the classic definition of intent, *infra*, no. 188.

257 Chauveau, Hélie & Villey, Théorie du Code pénal, *op. cit.* at 605.

258 *See supra*, nos. 99–100.

259 The three examples are as follows: false or slanderous facts spread among the public; overbids made at the prices asked by the sellers themselves; meetings or coalitions among the principal holders of the same merchandise or commodity. All three modes of execution require intent: false or slanderous facts must be spread "*deliberately*"; overbids made "*with the intention* of driving up prices"; and the parties to the coalitions must have acted "knowingly, with awareness of their mutual coordination." *See* Chauveau, Hélie & Villey, Théorie du Code pénal, *op. cit.* at 606–607.

260 *Id.* at 605.

261 *Id.* In the same vein, H. Babled, Droit français: Les syndicats de producteurs et détenteurs de marchandise au double point de vue économique et pénal 133 (1892): referring to article 419, the author writes that "fraud can disguise itself in a thousand other forms; and the legislator did not care to foresee them all, he only spoke of the most frequent."

262 Chauveau, Hélie & Villey, Théorie du Code pénal, *op. cit.* at 620 (emphasis added).

263 *Id.* at 599.

264 *Id.* at 622, no. 2399.

265 Babled, Droit français: Les syndicats de producteurs et détenteurs de marchandise au double point de vue économique et pénal, *op. cit.* at 133.

which allows for an important observation. It is now commonplace to state that when an authority punishes an agreement *by object*, or an abuse of a dominant position *per se*, it is not required to establish effects, but that in the absence of conduct falling into either of these categories, it would have to adopt an "effects" approach to characterize the infringement.[266] Such reasoning is illogical, as it stems from confusion as to the object of proof. Indeed, certain forms of behavior may appear *prima facie* fraudulent – as in the case of the three examples given in article 419. If a judge is called upon to rule on one of these cases, the characterization will be made without further examination: the judge will not have to provide specific proof of fraudulent means, since experience, or even common sense, attest to the fraudulent nature of such conduct. On the other hand, when faced with a practice that is either unprecedented or ambiguous, the judge will have to *give reasons for* classifying the conduct in question as "fraudulent maneuvers." This will require a closer examination of the *context* in which the behavior takes place, and a detailed analysis of the strategy at work. But such an analysis will not be aimed at characterizing the result – in other words, the effect – on the contrary, the judge will have to prove the fraud – and hence the intentional element.

125. **Intent in the service of jurisprudential adaptation: the distinction between "good" and "bad" agreements.** The end of the nineteenth century was marked by the adoption of the Waldeck-Rousseau law of 1884 on freedom of association, which some authors at the time wrongly argued had tacitly abrogated article 419.[267] This stems from a reasoning error: just because it is lawful to group together does not mean that any association is legitimate. In Ancien Droit, guild statutes frequently included anti-monopoly provisions, showing that the existence of a corporatist regime was not incompatible with the sanctioning of hoarders.[268] This law did, however, lead to a turning point in jurisprudence, as well as an interesting renewal of legal debates. Indeed, once an association is permitted, how can it be distinguished from an illicit coalition? This question was already being asked by the Romans,[269] and is still relevant in contemporary law: it is sometimes difficult to distinguish between behavior that comes under the heading of competition on the merits and that which is alien to it. To establish the boundary between what is permitted and what is prohibited, a doctrinal movement later emerged, led by Henri Savatier and Léon Mazeaud. Their aim was to provide *legal* criteria to enable judges to distinguish between "good" and "bad" agreements.

---

266 *See infra*, no. 298.

267 As noted by J. Percerou, *Des syndicats de producteurs: Essai sur leur fonctionnement et leur forme juridique*, Annales de droit commercial 271, 278 (1897). Moreover, French law does not recognize the tacit abrogation of a law.

268 *See supra*, no. 64.

269 *See supra*, no. 44.

Pointing out that article 419 is an "uncertain text"[270] drafted under "contradictory impressions,"[271] Henri Savatier denounces the "complete oblivion of the principles of yesteryear."[272] For him, the problem lies in the fact that we no longer know how to distinguish licit and virtuous cooperation from iniquitous and unfair practices. He criticizes "the hypocrisy and duplicity of legal assumptions about free competition."[273] In his opinion, there is something Pharisaical about claiming to protect free competition by prohibiting coalitions verbatim, when in practice they are "prohibited, unless they are coalitions of capital"; repressing professional companies when financial companies are permitted;[274] and judging that hoarding vanishes as if by magic, when the coalition takes the form of commercial companies.[275] He concludes that "the concern of the interpreters of the law seemed to be not to apply the Penal Code to hoarders."[276]

The proposed criterion of distinction is not the effects of the agreements, but the parties' *intention*: either the coalition aims at "preserving competitors" or "destroying them."[277] Léon Mazeaud considers that the criterion for making the distinction lies in the *pursued aim*,[278] the *artifice*,[279] the *abuse*, or even the *abnormality*.[280] Deciding otherwise, in his view, would go against equity, as it would result in the suppression of legitimate and virtuous intentions.[281] Legal rationality dictates that only agreements whose aim is "not the protection of its members, but the oppression of others" should be repressed.[282] This approach is not novel; it aligns with a longstanding tradition. In ancient times, association was permitted as

---

270 H. Savatier, La concurrence déloyale, l'accaparement et l'organisation moderne du commerce et de l'industrie 17 (1896).

271 *Id.* at 18.

272 *Id.* at 11–12. The author adds that "[t]he fault that still weighs on our time was not understanding that it was necessary, not to sacrifice the tradition of the past regarding the limits of competition, but to better grasp its essential principles." *Id.* at 15–16.

273 *Id.*

274 *Id.*

275 *Id.* at 19. For an example, *see* the *Duroux v. Bimar* case, in which the Criminal Division did not classify a cartel as an illicit coalition, as it had been formed through a trading company created for the occasion, Cass. crim., Jan. 26, 1838, Rec. Sirey 1838, t. xxxviii, pp. 241–43 (Fr.).

276 Savatier, La concurrence déloyale, l'accaparement et l'organisation moderne du commerce et de l'industrie, *op. cit.* at 19. The author goes on to condemn "the ingenious indulgence to protect the calculations of greed from the rigors of criminal law." *Id.* at 20.

277 *Id.* at 23.

278 L. Mazeaud, i Le régime juridique des ententes industrielles et commerciales en France 90 (1928).

279 *Id.* at 97.

280 *Id.* at 123.

281 *Id.* at 141.

282 Babled, Droit français: Les syndicats de producteurs et détenteurs de marchandise au double point de vue économique et pénal, *op. cit.* at 228–29.

long as it was not fraudulent.[283] Similarly, in the Ancien Droit, coalition was not sanctioned if it was justified by a reason of public interest.[284] This principle was also central to common law, which was familiar with the standard of unreasonable restraints,[285] subsequently adopted in the form of the "rule of reason" in the United States, on the basis of the Sherman Act.[286] At the end of the nineteenth century, similar considerations were also to be found in German case law.[287]

This view aligns with the new jurisprudence that took hold in France from the 1890s onwards.[288] Indeed, judges now distinguish between coalitions that stem from fraudulent intent and those that pursue an objective deemed legitimate. For example, coalitions whose aim is not to artificially increase prices (although the price increase is the consequence of the agreement), but to prevent the bankruptcy of their members, are deemed lawful.[289] The reasoning is identical to that which would later justified the individual exemptions granted by the Commission of the European Communities in the case of "crisis agreements."[290] This approach to agreements has not disappeared: it was transposed into article 59 ter of the 1945 Ordinance[291] and foreshadows the future exemption mechanism.[292]

126. **The deletion of the expression "*manœuvre frauduleuse*" by the 1926 reform, subject to debate in the Senate.** In 1926, at the time of the adoption of the

---

283 *See supra*, no. 44.

284 *See supra*, no. 74.

285 One author has noted that the French distinction between good and bad agreements is a transposition of the English doctrine of unreasonable restraints. *See* Deak, *Contracts and Combinations in Restraint of Trade in French Law – A Comparative Study*, *op. cit.* at 400–401.

286 T. C. Bartholomae, *The Common Law on Restraint of Trade*, 1 The University Journal of Business 451, 451–56 (1923); *adde*, G. Marenco, *La notion de restriction de concurrence dans le cadre de l'interdiction des ententes*, *in* ii Mélanges en hommage à Michel Waelbroeck 1217, 1226–28 (1999). *Nota bene*: the rule of reason nowadays has a different meaning, since it implies an "effects-based" approach, *see infra*, no. 344.

287 *See* not. Reichsgericht, Dec. 4, 1897, 38 RGZ 155, 157: "[I]f the firms of a particular brand band together to eliminate or control price reduction among themselves, their co-operation can be seen not only as… a service to the public, provided that such prices really are continuously so low that economic ruin threatens the firms," quoted and translated by Gerber, Law and Competition in Twentieth Century Europe: Protecting Prometheus, *op. cit.* at 92.

288 Deak, *Contracts and Combinations in Restraint of Trade in French Law – A Comparative Study*, *op. cit.* at 434–35; Pfister, *Contrat, libre concurrence et ordre public: la sanction des ententes dans la jurisprudence française du xixe siècle*, *op. cit.* at 349.

289 Cass. civ., May 3, 1911, Rec. Dalloz 1912, pp. 32–42 (Fr.). For another example of the admission of a justification based on intention, *see* Cass. civ., Oct. 26, 1921, Rec. Dalloz 1925, p. 120 (Fr): "The agreement between various merchants, whose purpose was not to bring about an artificial increase in coal prices but to put an end to the degradation of prices caused by the competition they engaged in among themselves – at a time when competition could and did occur through the importation of foreign coal – does not constitute the offense provided for in Article 419 of the Penal Code and is not even contrary to public order." (unofficial translation) For numerous other case law references, *see* A.-A. Al-Sanhoury, *Le standard juridique*, *in* ii Recueil d'études sur les sources du droit en l'honneur de François Gény 144, 154–55, 156, n.14 & 16 (1934).

290 *See infra*, no. 346, and decisions cited.

291 *See infra*, no. 109.

292 *See infra*, no. 285.

reform to article 419, an interesting debate took place between the Senators and the Minister of Commerce and Industry Maurice Bokanowski. Senator Joseph Courtier was troubled by a concern. The law voted in removes the expression "*manœuvre frauduleuse*" (fraudulent maneuver). It is true that the offense, at least on the surface, appears to be slightly more "objective":

> All those who… by exercising or attempting to exercise, either individually, or through assembly or coalition, an action on the market with the aim of obtaining a gain that would not be the result of the natural interplay of supply and demand… shall be punished.[293]

Fearing that the intentional element might disappear or diminish in importance, the senator suggested adding the word "abusively" to "better show what the legislator had in mind."[294] Rapporteur Guillaume Poulle replied:

> We are dealing with an offense that is not a contraventional offense. Consequently, *culpable intent is essential.* …How do you expect it to be necessary, useful, to add the word "abusively," when everything in the text cries out forcefully, to be heard by everyone and, first and foremost, by the judge, that culpable intent is required?[295]

The Minister of Justice, Louis Barthou, shared the rapporteur's opinion, considering that adding the adverb "abusively" would not have contributed anything precise to the text.[296] The Minister of Commerce and Industry concluded that "it is unnecessary to introduce the word 'abusive,' as the notion of abuse is implied in every line of the text under discussion."[297] So, regardless of the words used to describe anticompetitive behavior, their *nature* is to be intentional infringements.

127. **The removal of the result condition by the 1926 reform: the beginnings of modern jurisprudence.** The main aim of the 1926 reform was to make it possible to punish attempts – the need to characterize the market result having hampered the effectiveness of article 419 since 1810.[298] However, the repression of attempts completely changes the situation.[299] Indeed, if the result no longer needs to be characterized, this means that the mere manifestation of the intention to obtain "a gain that would not be the

293 Adoption of a Bill to Amend Articles 419 and 420 of the French Penal Code, JORF, Débats parl., Sénat, Nov. 19, 1926, pp. 1648–55, at 1654. *Compare with* former article 419: "Those who … by any fraudulent ways or means whatever, shall have effected the enhancement or reduction of the price … above or below the prices which would have been determined by the free and natural competition of trade."

294 *Id.* at 1651.

295 *Id.* (emphasis added).

296 *Id.*

297 *Id.*

298 *See supra* nos. 99–100.

299 At least in theory, as article 419 of the Penal Code has not been widely applied following the reform – for the reasons set out *supra*, no. 102.

result of the natural interplay of supply and demand" may now constitute the offense. A legitimate question then arises: what is such a gain? The question was raised by Senator Anatole Manceau, and was the subject of lively discussion:[300]

> The Chairman of the Commerce Committee, Senator Louis Serre – Gain that is not the result of the natural functioning of competition is that which results from fraudulent maneuvers.
>
> Senator Anatole Manceau – Say it!
>
> Senator Louis Serre – It's in every line of the text…
>
> Senator Joseph Vallier – (*addressing Senator Anatole Manceau*) As a businessman, you should understand this, because it's a question of common sense…
>
> Senator Jean Coignet – Right now, we're working on the impossible task of defining an indefinable offense.
>
> The Minister of Trade and Industry Maurice Bokanowski – This is one of the issues that legislators throughout the ages, and in all countries, have had the most difficulty in achieving through precise texts. In the presence of an offense, which, I admit, is a little uncertain, judges will above all have to draw inspiration, alongside the text, from the *travaux préparatoires* and the words spoken here. This jurisprudence will develop in the same way as that which has interpreted article 419, and it is quite clear that it can scarcely deviate from that which the courts of appeal and the Court of Cassation have established in the years since 1810. The difference established by jurisprudence between frank and loyal agreements – as Chevalier Faure said at a session in February 1810 – and the others, is clearly and specifically defined in the explanatory memorandum of the bill we are discussing.

In short, and in line with the thinking of the scholastics,[301] the result – the acquisition of an illegitimate gain – depends on the existence of *fraudulent intent*. If there is no fraud, then the interplay between supply and demand is not affected, and therefore there is no illicit gain.[302] This solution is still valid, and even, contrary to what one might think at first glance, *a fortiori*, albeit implicitly, in the case of the offense defined by article 59 bis of the 1945 Ordinance.

300 Adoption of a Bill to Amend Articles 419 and 420 of the French Penal Code, *op. cit.* at 1653–54. The following is an unofficial translation of the debate held in the Senate.

301 *See supra*, nos. 63–65.

302 It will be shown *infra*, no. 379, that this assertion is still valid in contemporary law on anticompetitive practices.

B. Implicit recognition of intent in administrative competition law

128. **Textual arguments: the irrelevance of the result and the importance of intention in article 59 bis.** Article 419 required the combination of two constituent elements: the fraudulent maneuver *and* the effect on the market – the effect in question being a *result on prices*. Until attempts were made punishable from 1926 onwards, the offense in the Penal Code was therefore a so-called material or result offense,[303] i.e., an offense that is only consummated if the result is actually achieved.[304]

Article 59 bis of the 1945 Ordinance marks an important shift. Its wording calls for a different interpretation from that of article 419. Article 59 bis prohibits agreements "having the object or likely to have the effect of *hindering the full exercise of competition.*" The effect here is linked to the competition *process* itself, which means that the effect in question is not an effect on the market,[305] and therefore not a result,[306] but *the effect on competition*, independently of the consequences of this restriction of competition.[307]

A close examination of the letter of the article thus provides unequivocal information on the structure of the offense. It is no longer a material offense, but a so-called formal offense, i.e., one that is *consummated independently of the achievement of any result.*[308] This does not amount to punishing the attempt, but to establishing it as an autonomous offense.[309] Thus, the introduction of the notion of "effect" in the text of incrimination is not decisive, as the material element of a formal offense[310] is significantly diminished, with the mental element playing a more important role. Paradoxically, the introduction of the notion of effect has, in theory, obscured and set aside debates on the role of intention, while in practice, intention would,

---

303 From 1926 onwards, however, the offense remains material, but the attempt is assimilated to the completed offense, *see supra*, no. 102.

304 B. Bouloc, Droit pénal général 243 (27th ed. 2021), no. 248.

305 The rest of article 59 bis cannot be interpreted in the opposite way: "having the object or likely to have the effect of hindering the full exercise of competition *by preventing* the lowering of cost or selling prices, or by encouraging an artificial rise in prices." Indeed, the use of the expression "by preventing" indicates unequivocally that the two statements that follow are examples of illicit behavior, not results.

306 It should be noted, however, that there are several ways of conceiving the result in criminal law. It is possible to argue that any offense, even a material one, produces an unlawful result, if we define the result as "an infringement of a legal interest protected by criminal law." This is the position taken by J.-Y. Maréchal, Essai sur le résultat dans la théorie de l'infraction pénale 10 (2003). Here, we take a more restrictive view of the term "result," in the sense of a separate and distinct consequence of the prohibited conduct.

307 This textual argument is equally valid for the current article 101 TFEU, *see infra*, no. 272.

308 Bouloc, Droit pénal général, *op. cit.* at 243, no. 248. For a detailed definition of the concept of "formal offense," and how cartels and abuses of dominant positions fall within this category in positive law, *see* nos. 271–275.

309 On this legislative process, *see infra*, no. 158 and no. 272.

310 On the notion of formal infringement, *see infra*, no. 271.

at the same time, acquire a predominant place – more important than in article 419 of the Penal Code.

Moreover, the use of the word "effect" is highly misleading. It leads to a regrettable confusion between "effect on competition" and "effect on the market," i.e., between two things that should be clearly distinguished.[311] The effect on the market would consist, for example, in the exclusion of a competitor, a rise in prices, or a drop in product quality. The effect on competition is quite different. But what exactly is the effect? Nothing all that different from anticompetitive intent – that indefinable thing the senators debated in 1926,[312] before concluding that it was obviously nothing more than a matter of common sense. A question to which no one has had an answer since antiquity, except the following: competition is no longer free if it is hindered by unfair behavior, fraudulent maneuvers, or dishonest strategies. These expressions may not have a specific, precise, or scientific meaning, but they are nonetheless the subject of a long tradition.

129. **Arguments resulting from the decision-making practice of the Commission Technique des Ententes: the effect, at most, an element of proof of intent.** In practice, did the Commission Technique des Ententes consider the effect a constitutive element of the infringement? The answer is negative: according to established case law,[313] even if the absence of an effect is established, the existence of anticompetitive intent is sufficient to bring the agreement within the scope of the prohibition.[314] This means that the effect is not required to characterize the offense, and therefore cannot be considered a constitutive element. At most, it can, to a certain extent, serve as *evidence* of anticompetitive intent.[315] But it is important to know what is meant by "effect." The practice of the Commission shows that the "effects-based" approach is nothing more than a poorly chosen technical expression referring to the classic legal operation of linking new or ambiguous cases to an indeterminate notion.[316] The alternative is thus as follows: (i) either the conduct itself provides clear evidence of anticompetitive intent, and the effects play no role at the qualification stage; (ii) or the conduct is new or ambiguous, and the intent must be characterized by means of an "effects-based" approach.

---

311 *See infra*, no. 355.

312 *See infra*, no. 127.

313 As we shall *see*, *infra*, nos. 279–281, this is also a consistent solution in the case law of the Court of Justice of the European Union.

314 V. Sélinsky, L'entente prohibée, à travers les avis de la Commission technique des ententes et des abus de position dominante 248–49 (1979).

315 In the same sense, in positive law, *see infra*, no. 330.

316 The reasoning here is the same as that set out for article 419, *see supra*, no. 124.

In the first hypothesis, the intentional element is presumed almost irrefutably in the case of all strategies that clearly appear to restrict competition.[317] The Commission then writes that the practices in question "generally have as their *object*," "have a well-known *role*," "*aim to hinder* the development of any business," "can only *aim to prevent*," "*aim to* give the *appearance of* effective competition."[318] Obviousness and flagrancy prove intent, without the need for highly developed motivation, as the companies could not have been unaware that they were breaking the rules of the game. And while many opinions focus on the practices implemented without mentioning intent, this does not mean that intent is absent – it is simply presumed.[319] Examples of practices deemed to undermine competition are those aimed at limiting the number of competitors, creating barriers to entry, or restricting competitors' freedom of action.[320] Presuming intent on the basis of the material element is a classic phenomenon in criminal law: when the facts obviously fall within the scope of a given qualification, the conduct irrefutably presumes intent.[321] For example, in the case of fraud, the judge is not required to specifically justify the finding of intent to defraud if the defendant has used a false name or capacity, since such a practice is, according to established case law, deemed to fall within the scope of deception.[322]

In the second case, if there is any doubt as to whether a behavior falls into the category of a "maneuver," further proof and justification are required. For example, in the case of refusal to enter into a contract, such a practice cannot *prima facie* be considered a maneuver aimed at restricting competition – since freedom of contract implies the right to enter into a contract as well as the right not to enter into one. However, if the prosecuting authority demonstrates, in the light of the circumstances of the case, that a collective refusal to contract has the character of a boycott,[323] then the practice will be deemed to harm competition. To prove this, the authority adopts an inverted reasoning: it starts from the restriction of competition to *infer* the existence of a maneuver. In other words, it starts "from the effect" and goes back to the cause – proof of the restrictive effect *retrospectively* presuming anticompetitive intent. In so

---

317 Sélinsky, L'entente prohibée, à travers les avis de la Commission technique des ententes et des abus de position dominante, *op. cit.* at 247.

318 *Id.* (emphasis added).

319 *Id.* at 268.

320 For a complete typology, *see id.* at 129–215.

321 This is particularly true in business criminal law, where the professional's negligence is sufficient to prove their intention to commit an offense, *see infra* nos. 156–157.

322 M.-L. Rassat, *Escroquerie*, JurisClasseur Pénal des Affaires (June 2022), fasc. 10, no. 49.

323 *See* Commission technique des ententes et des abus de position dominante, *Rapport au ministre chargé des affaires économiques: années 1970 et 1971*, JORF, Documents administratifs, 1972, avis du 18 décembre 1970, *Groupement lainier mazamétain*, p. 425.

doing, it does nothing more than link ambiguous behavior to an identified category: anticompetitive strategy.

This interpretation is supported by the fact that the Commission has never limited itself to *merely* noting the "effect on competition," but has always verified that such an effect was *foreseeable*[324] – which amounts to establishing proof that the company had foreseen it, and therefore had intended it.[325] The Commission's decision-making practice attests to the fact that agreement offenses "always presuppose anticompetitive intent – that is, at least awareness of the anticompetitive effect of the practices in question. And while such awareness is easily presumed from the said effect, this is merely a classic phenomenon in criminal jurisprudence."[326] Herein lies the limit of the effect: it can only be taken into consideration insofar as it is reasonably foreseeable, since it is on this condition that it can be considered intentional.

It should also be noted that, at the same time, the decision-making practice of the Commission Technique des Ententes was identical to that of the German competition authority. In its 1961 annual report, the Bundeskartellamt stated that the effects could not be attributed to the parties to a agreement if they occurred "against all likelihood and contrary to everyday experience," since in such cases they "could not have been foreseen by the participating companies."[327]

In short, the distinction between object and effect, like that between the per se approach and the effects approach, cannot, from a logical point of view, correspond to a distinction between intentional and non-intentional behavior – competition offenses being, by their very nature, intentional. The alternative refers to the distinction between behavior whose fraudulent nature is obvious, and behavior whose fraudulent nature is ambiguous. The effect must therefore be considered, insofar as it is foreseeable, as a means of proving intention,[328] and not as an independent element of proof.

Assigning a different meaning to the notion of effect than the one just explained would necessarily lead to absurd reasoning. It would indeed be strange, not to say inconceivable, to imagine that it would be possible to devise a plan

---

324 Sélinsky, L'entente prohibée, à travers les avis de la Commission technique des ententes et des abus de position dominante, *op. cit.* at 256.

325 This assimilation of foresight and intention aligns with the ancients' thinking, notably Thomas Aquinas (*supra*, no. 56) and the Italian jurisconsult Bartole (*supra*, no. 69).

326 A. Decocq, *L'article 419 du Code pénal est-il devenu un texte historique?*, Revue de jurisprudence commerciale 77, 80 (1980) (*nota bene*: the author writes this not in relation to article 419 of the Penal Code, but in commenting on the decision-making practice relating to article 59 bis of the 1945 Ordinance).

327 Report quoted and translated in French by A. Deringer, *Les règles de la concurrence au sein de la C.E.E. (Analyse et commentaire des articles 85 à 94 du Traité)*, Revue du Marché Commun no. 3284, 87 (Feb. 1963).

328 In this regard, *see* Sélinsky, L'entente prohibée, à travers les avis de la Commission technique des ententes et des abus de position dominante, *op. cit.* at 268. We will show that this analysis also applies to positive law, *infra*, no. 330.

to restrict competition that did not have such an object, but only such an effect. This would imply admitting that it is possible to devise an aimless strategy that accidentally turns out to be dishonest and unfair, regardless of any intention – an assertion that defies logic, and ignores the fundamental role of presumptions in criminal law.[329] The idea of holding a company liable for the unforeseeable effects of its behavior would also run counter to the principles established in criminal law, whereas administrative law, when it is repressive, must respect them.

II. Intention, from criminal law to repressive administrative law

130. **The impossibility of departing from criminal law principles.** Whenever the law assumes a repressive function – as is the case with certain branches of administrative law (**A**) – it must, in order to comply with constitutional and conventional principles, respect the guarantees pertaining to criminal law (**B**).

A. Repressive administrative law as part of criminal law

131. **Contemporary competition law's lack of autonomy from criminal law.** Does the shift in competition law from criminal to administrative law imply a radical change in reasoning and applicable principles? The adoption of article 59 bis, despite a significant semantic change, did not put aside the intentional criterion, as confirmed by the decision-making practice of the Commission Technique des Ententes. *A priori*, however, one might think that the fact that competition law has been decriminalized would lead to differences in legal frameworks. It would be a new "branch of law," involving the combination of principles or methods hitherto covered by different branches,[330] since competition law has specific procedures and escapes the distinction between public and private law.[331] This would give rise to a "new law" which, as soon as it is attached to the administrative sphere, would become more "objective," as it pursues "economic policing" goals reflecting an "economic policy,"[332] constituting "regulation" rather than repression. If this were the case, it would mean that competition law would have become autonomous from criminal law reasoning. Yet, while it reforms old techniques "in an effort to adapt them in a way that

---

329 *See infra*, no. 197.

330 G. Farjat, *La notion de droit économique*, 37 Archives de philosophie du droit 27, 31 (1992).

331 *Id.* at 36.

332 A. de Laubadère & P. Delvolvé, Droit public économique 49 (5th ed. 1986).

makes them unrecognizable," these "coexist with the body of traditional legal rules," which cannot be suddenly extinguished.[333]

132. **Do administrative offenses carry less of a moral stigma than criminal offenses?** Some academics believe that decriminalizing a norm leads to the "progressive anesthesia of its symbolic significance" attached to criminal law.[334] Administrative law would thus serve as the instrument of a purely utilitarian form of regulation, detached from any moral dimension,[335] and aimed at punishing so-called artificial criminality insofar as it does not imply any sense of guilt,[336] as opposed to classical criminal law, which punishes so-called natural crimes and offenses. This distinction between two types of repression – one genuine, the other artificial – has rightly been criticized:[337] indeed, if a sanction is imposed for the violation of a artificial prohibition, with no link whatsoever to morality, there is a great risk of trivializing and multiplying the misguided use of the repressive tool,[338] leading ultimately to the ineffectiveness of an overly fussy law, accustoming minds not to respect it.[339]

White-collar crime[340] has provided fertile ground for the development of this idea: the increasing number and technical nature of business offenses can lead one to believe that their moral dimension is diminishing, or even disappearing,[341] from which it follows that certain offenses should

333 C. Champaud, *Contribution à la définition du droit économique*, Recueil Dalloz 215, 216–17 (1967), chron. xxiv.

334 M. Van de Kerchove, *Symbolique et instrumentalité: Stratégies de pénalisation et de dépénalisation dans une société pluraliste*, Revue de l'Université de Bruxelles nos. 1–3, 123, 123 (1984). *Adde*, M. Delmas-Marty & G. Giudicelli-Delage, Droit pénal des affaires 18–20 (4th ed. 1990) and references cited: the authors refer to public indifference to "white-collar" crime, and to the "moral anomie of economic life" described by Émile Durkheim.

335 This can sometimes lead to confusion: if there is no moral stigma attached to an offense, it is easy to deduce (wrongly) that no "moral element" is required. However, as intention is a technical concept, the two are clearly not linked. *See*, in this respect, *infra*, no. 194.

336 P. Caeiro, *The Influence of the EU on the 'Blurring' Between Administrative and Criminal Law*, *in* Do Labels Still Matter? Blurring Boundaries Between Administrative and Criminal Law: The Influence of the EU 171, 177 (F. Galli & A. Weyembergh eds., 2014).

337 *Ex multis*: M. Girot, La dépénalisation: Un instrument au service du droit pénal 221–22 (1994) (Ph.D. dissertation, Université de Poitiers): "The distinction whereby offenses with a high moral value would be qualified as natural and others as artificial no longer holds. Consumer protection belongs just as much to morally based protection as does the offense of theft"; S. H. Kadish, *Some Observations on the Use of Criminal Sanctions in Enforcing Economic Regulations*, 30 University of Chicago Law Review 423, 445 (1963); H. L. A. Hart, *The Aims of the Criminal Law*, 23 Law and Contemporary Problems 401, 404–405 (Summer 1958): Hart believes that a sanction is justified only if the repressed behavior is the object of common disapproval by society; S. P. Green, *Why It's a Crime to Tear the Tag Off a Matress: Overcriminalization and the Moral Content of Regulatory Offenses*, 46 Emory Law Journal 1533, 1563–69 (Fall 1997): the author mentions several statistical studies of public opinion, attesting to the fact that supposedly amoral business offenses are in fact as poorly perceived by society as traditional crimes.

338 On this theme, *see* M. Delmas-Marty, *Pour des principes directeurs de législation pénale*, Revue de science criminelle et de droit pénal comparé 225 (1985).

339 G. Ripert, Aspects juridiques du capitalisme moderne 243–47 (2nd ed. 1951).

340 The classic definition was given by E. H. Sutherland, White Collar Crime 7 (1983): white-collar crime is an offense committed by a person belonging to a higher socio-economic class, or involving professionals working in a company, as well as its management.

341 J. Coffee, *Does Unlawful Mean Criminal: Reflections on the Disappearing Tort/Crime Distinction in American Law*, 71 Boston University Law Review 193, 198 (1991).

be decriminalized, as the administrative sanction would be more effective and would not entail any moral condemnation.[342] It is clear, however, that there is a business morality,[343] which the law, whether criminal or administrative, aims to uphold, and whose violation is no less serious than that of other so-called classic offenses.[344]

133. **Theorizing repressive administrative law and linking it to the principles of criminal law.** While administrative law has traditionally met the needs of the general interest by two means – public service and policing[345] – the contemporary proliferation of administrative offenses, and their often repressive nature, has not failed to attract the attention of legal scholars.[346] Alerted by the trend towards the decriminalization of certain offenses, from the 1990s onwards,[347] the doctrine has endeavored to demonstrate that when administrative law assumes functions similar, or even identical, to those of criminal law – repression, deterrence – it must respect, by virtue of constitutional principles and in the name of respect for the European Convention on Human Rights (ECHR), the rules pertaining to criminal matters. It follows that

342 It should be noted that there is no unanimous agreement as to whether white-collar crime should be punished by means of criminal law or administrative law, *see* in this sense K. Tiedemann, *Tendances mondiales d'introduction de sanctions nouvelles pour les crimes en col blanc*, XLIV REVUE INTERNATIONALE DE CRIMINOLOGIE ET DE POLICE TECHNIQUE 226, 226, 231–40 (Apr.-June 1991); J. Pradel, *Les sanctions en matière de délinquance économique*, *in* THE SANCTIONS IN THE FIELD OF ECONOMIC CRIMINAL LAW 85, 86 (1984).

343 In this sense, *see* R. Legros, *L'influence des lois particulières sur le droit pénal général*, REVUE DE SCIENCE CRIMINELLE ET DE DROIT PÉNAL COMPARÉ 233, 236–41 (1968); R. Legros, *Imputation pénale et entreprise économique*, REVUE DE DROIT PÉNAL ET DE CRIMINOLOGIE NOS. 5–6, 365, 369 (Feb.-March 1969). *Adde*, *id.* at 367–68: "In truth, morality was evolving at the same time as the law: from being individual, it was gradually becoming social. However, in doctrinal terms, we have both recognized the evolution of law and ignored that of morality. ...We have failed to see that, just as classical criminal law necessarily bore the moral coloring of its time, the new criminal law – born from new social, economic, fiscal, technical, and international demands – is neither artificial nor material, but organically reflects the spirit of the new times, of a society with its own morality, values, and ideals." *Adde*, A. LEPAGE, P. MAISTRE DU CHAMBON & R. SALOMON, DROIT PÉNAL DES AFFAIRES 2 (6th ed. 2020): "Contrary to a commonly held opinion, too widely widespread, there is a business morality for which criminal law is accountable." Finally, for an illustration in financial markets law, *see* B. Mercadal, *Éthique financière*, *in* L'ÉTHIQUE DES MARCHÉS FINANCIERS 23 (J.-V. Louis & D. Devos eds., 1996).

344 Indeed, the characteristic of certain business offenses, sometimes infringements of the law on anticompetitive practices, is to cause slight harm to a large number of victims, who are often unaware of it. While the seriousness of these offenses may go unnoticed at first glance, it is easily detected when all the damage is added up – which leads us to believe that, on reflection, they are among the most harmful to society. In this sense, *see* S. P. Green, *Moral Ambiguity in White Collar Criminal Law*, 18 NOTRE DAME JOURNAL OF LAW, ETHICS & PUBLIC POLICY 501, 508, 519 (2004).

345 J. RIVERO, DROIT ADMINISTRATIF 387 (2011) (1960).

346 J. Larguier, *Mort et transfiguration du droit pénal*, *in* II ASPECTS NOUVEAUX DE LA PENSÉE JURIDIQUE. RECUEIL D'ÉTUDES EN HOMMAGE À MARC ANCEL 123, 139 (1975): "After the effacement of the legislator, aren't we going to witness the effacement of judges, to the benefit of the administration? ...In the disappearance of criminal law, it is clearly not severity for its own sake that we dread seeing die: administrative criminal law... can easily be more severe than another; ... [it] is arbitrariness that we must fear."

347 It should be noted, however, that it was at the beginning of the twentieth century in Germany (a forerunner in the use of administrative law for repressive purposes, *see supra*, no. 96) that the author James Goldschmidt coined the notion of "criminal administrative law." *See* DAS VERWALTUNGSSTRAFRECHT 1902, cited by M. D. Dubber, *The Comparative History and Theory of Corporate Liability*, 16 NEW CRIMINAL LAW REVIEW 203, 216 n.36 (2013). It was also in Germany, with the Act on Regulatory Offenses (the OWiG), that a law was adopted for the first time aimed at "reconciling the imperatives of efficiency of administrative action with the necessary guarantees surrounding the issuance of judicial sanctions." *See* A. Benmakhlouf & F. Falletti, *Les* Ordnungswidrigkeiten *en République Fédérale d'Allemagne*, 7 ARCHIVES DE POLITIQUE CRIMINELLE 74, 74 (1984).

when administrative law imposes sanctions, it is "in the same vein" as criminal law;[348] decriminalization does not exempt the administrative authority from respecting the procedural and substantive guarantees of the criminal justice system.[349] Thus, while one might have expected "repressive administrative law"[350] to be marked by a certain objectivity, the concepts of fault and mental element of the offense have nevertheless been transposed to into this area.[351]

The degree of severity of the administrative sanction must therefore correspond to the degree of guarantees provided to those subject to the law;[352] in European law on anticompetitive practices, this was only ultimately recognized at the cost of an ambiguity as carefully as it was enduringly maintained[353] – even though, despite its decriminalization, it is "still marked by criminal law, both in form and substance."[354]

---

348 Y. Gaudemet, *Préface*, *in* G. Dellis, Droit pénal et droit administratif: L'influence des principes du droit pénal sur le droit administratif répressif xix (1997); A. Varinard & E. Joly-Sibuet, *Les problèmes juridiques et pratiques posés par la différence entre le droit pénal et le droit administratif pénal*, 59 Revue internationale de droit pénal 189, 193–99 (1988): the authors stress the difficulty of distinguishing the two subjects. *Adde*, for an illustration in the field of market abuse law (a discipline in which administrative and criminal law still coexist), F. Stasiak, J.-M. Brigant & A. Bellezza, *Le droit répressif des abus de marché: Un exemple de confusion des genres?*, Revue de science criminelle et de droit pénal comparé 375 (2020); and in the law of anticompetitive practices, C. Babusiaux, *La répression et le contrôle administratif de la régulation concurrentielle*, *in* Les enjeux de la pénalisation de la vie économique 113, 117–18 (M.-A. Frison-Roche ed., 1997).

349 In this sense, *see* Council of Europe, Report on decriminalization 65–66 (1980).

350 Or "administrative criminal law," expressions both used to designate "a system that is not penal in the legal sense, but whose philosophical basis is nonetheless retributive," *see* M. Delmas-Marty, *Les problèmes juridiques et pratiques posés par la différence entre le droit criminel et le droit administratif pénal*, 59 Revue internationale de droit pénal 15, 15 (1988).

351 M. Delmas-Marty & C. Teitgen-Colly, Punir sans juger? De la répression administrative au droit administratif pénal 55–57 (1992). In the same vein, *see* J. Mourgeon, La répression administrative 181 (1967): "[T]he subjectivity of the offense is no less important in repressive administrative law than in repressive judicial law as a basis for the moral imputability of the act"; indeed, "it is inevitable that the two forms of repression should be very similar as far as the moral element is concerned," since with "the moral element of the offense, we enter the realm of the general principles of repressive law. There are no data or considerations specific to the secondary administrative institution to influence the principles of repressive technique: repressive administrative law can therefore be aligned with repressive judicial law."

352 G. Dellis, Droit pénal et droit administratif: L'influence des principes du droit pénal sur le droit administratif répressif 53 (1997). *Adde*, the recommendations of the XIVth Congress of the International Association of Penal Law, whose members voted unanimously in 1989 in favor of full recognition of the applicability to "criminal administrative law" of the principles of substantive criminal law and fair trial: International Association of Penal Law, *XIVe Congrès international de droit pénal (Vienne, 2-7 octobre 1989)*, 86 Revue internationale de droit pénal 129, 130 (2015). The Court of Justice of the European Communities recognized this early on, applying certain principles specific to criminal law to administrative sanctions; *see*, for example, for an implicit recognition of the applicability of the principle of legality, Case 117/83, Könecke, ECLI:EU:C:1984:288, para. 11: "[I]t must be emphasized that a penalty, even of a non-criminal nature, cannot be imposed unless it rests on a clear and unambiguous legal basis"; *adde*, along the same lines, Case 137/85, Maizenai, ECLI:EU:C:1987:493, para. 15.

353 Philippe Conte has made a general observation on the relationship between criminal law and competition law. *See* P. Conte, *Droit pénal et concurrence*, JCP - Cahiers de droit de l'entreprise no. 3, 21, 21 (2000): "[T]he intervention of criminal law in competition law is rich in lessons: everything is ambiguous, since one has the feeling that the legislator condescends to repress on condition, however, that there is no repression."

354 F. Stasiak, *Droit pénal et droit de la concurrence: Regards croisés*, *in* Droit pénal et autres branches du droit: Regards croisés 267, 267 (J.-C. Saint-Pau ed., 2012).

B. The obligation to respect criminal law principles

134. **The initial ambiguity surrounding the applicability of criminal law principles to anticompetitive practices.** The initial failure to acknowledge the criminal or "quasi-criminal" nature of the law on anticompetitive practices stems from a paradox: while the Commission, in order to enforce Community economic legislation, had to be competent to impose sanctions, the European Community had no competence in criminal matters.[355] What is more, in 1962, no Member State admitted the criminal liability of legal persons, so the imposition of criminal fines on companies would have been in direct contradiction with their position.[356] It is not surprising, therefore, that the first European regulation on anticompetitive practices stipulated that decisions taken on its basis were not "of a penal nature"[357] – the same formula having been transposed to the regulation currently in force.[358] However, the Community legislator's characterization of these decisions as "administrative sanctions" has not escaped criticism. Some scholars saw it as pure fiction, guided by a desire to avoid the problem of the criminal liability of legal persons and to avoid recognizing the applicability of the principles of criminal law, although the sanctions in question were unquestionably punitive in nature.[359] Initially, this ambiguity was maintained by the Advocates General who, in unison, considered the infringements to be

---

355 G. Levasseur, *Les sanctions dans le traité constitutif du Marché Commun*, *in* Les problèmes juridiques et économiques du Marché Commun 95, 99 (H. Batiffol et al. eds., 1960): "Under these conditions, the necessary sanctions cannot be truly penal in nature, even though they appear distinctly repressive." In the same vein, *see* L. Idot, *Réflexions sur l'application de certains principes et notions du droit pénal en droit des pratiques anticoncurrentielles*, *in* Les droits et le droit: Mélanges dédiés à Bernard Bouloc 457, 458 (2007) (the study focuses on the *non bis in idem* principle).

356 M. Guyomar, Les sanctions administratives 18 (2014).

357 Regulation (EC) No. 17/62, First Regulation Implementing Articles 85 and 86 of the Treaty, 1962 O.J. (13) English special edition: Series I Vol. 1959–1962, 87, art. 15(4)

358 Council Regulation (EC) No. 1/2003 of Dec. 16, 2002, on the Implementation of the Rules on Competition Laid Down in Articles 81 and 82 of the Treaty, 2003 O.J. (L 1) 1, art. 23(5).

359 In this sense, *see* F. Ost & M. Van de Kerchove, De la pyramide au réseau? Pour une théorie dialectique du droit 237–38 (2002), and references cited. *Adde*, R. Legros, *L'arrêt BMW et le droit pénal européen*, Cahiers de droit européen 206, 222, 223 resp. (1980): "For my part, I have always thought that these were genuine *criminal* sanctions. …I would even venture to suggest that, paradoxically, this haughty and useless pretension on the part of the regulatory power to take a doctrinal position in a regulatory text could well be the index of a baseless and futile declaration." The author goes on to note that an analysis of Court of Justice rulings shows that judges use "real criminal language" to punish competition offenses. Also, in the same vein, C. Smits & D. Waelbroeck, *Le droit de la concurrence et les droits fondamentaux*, *in* Les droits de l'homme dans les politiques de l'Union européenne 135, 139–40 (M. Candela Soriano ed., 2006): the assertion that fines imposed by the Commission are not of a criminal nature "suffers, however, from excessive formalism, making its fragility all the more evident"; W. P. J. Wils, *La compatibilité des procédures communautaires en matière de concurrence avec la Convention européenne des droits de l'homme*, Cahiers de droit européen, 329, 333–34 (1996); Y. Auguet, *Droit pénal et droit de la concurrence: 'La transformation du fait répressif en droit de la concurrence'*, *in* Droit pénal et autres branches du droit: Regards croisés 279, 283 (J.-C. Saint-Pau ed., 2012): "The decriminalization of competition law cannot be denied; however, it is only relative. …[O]ther sanctions, often described as administrative, do not escape the influence of '*criminal law*.'" Finally, it should be noted that competition law is thoroughly examined in J. Pradel & G. Corstens, Droit pénal européen (2nd ed. 2002), as well as in certain business criminal law manuals. *See inter alia*, A. Lepage, P. Maistre du Chambon & R. Salomon, Droit pénal des affaires (6th ed. 2020).

administrative in nature,[360] while at the same time, the Court of Justice was already admitting the punitive nature of the fines imposed by the European Commission.[361]

135. **This ambiguity has become untenable with the growing importance of fundamental rights.** Like Monsieur Jourdain[362], the European judge is thus unknowingly composing criminal law, timidly resisting the temptation before giving in to it,[363] in an unassuming manner, always under the sign of a little more or less.[364] Indeed, since the European Union is not a party to the ECHR,[365] the Court of Justice has never been called upon to rule directly on whether European law on anticompetitive practices falls within the scope of "criminal law." This concept, forged by the ECHR,[366] is of major importance, since once an offense falls within the scope of criminal law, it must be prosecuted and punished with due respect for fundamental rights. Criminal matters are autonomous

---

360 *Ex multis*: Opinion of Advocate General K. Roemer, Case 14-18, Walt Wilhelm, ECLI:EU:C:1968:55, pp. 25–27: the Advocate General compares the fines provided for in Regulation (EC) No. 17/62 with those provided for in the German Competition Act, which also deals only with administrative infringements; Opinion of Advocate General J. Gand, Case 41-69, ACF Chemiefarma, ECLI:EU:C:1970:51, pp. 726–29: describing the question of the administrative or criminal nature of fines as "delicate," the Advocate General's argument is based on the fact that "the Member States have not delegated to the Community any powers of a criminal law nature, properly so-called," p. 722; Opinion of Advocate General H. Mayras, Case 40/73, Suiker Unie, ECLI:EU:C:1975:78, pp. 2068–69 and 2119. A comparison with more recent opinions highlights the stark contrast and confirms that the criminal nature of competition infringements is now beyond doubt. *See*, for example, Opinion of Advocate General N. Wahl, Case C-194/14 P, AC-Treuhand, ECLI:EU:C:2015:350, paras. 16 and 25. It should be noted that in this case, the Commission nevertheless still contested the attachment of anticompetitive practices law to the hard core of criminal law, *see id.*, para. 24.

361 Under ECSC law, for example, the Commission had argued in two cases that the "automatic" calculation of fines ruled out their criminal nature and the application of the principle of culpability. The Court of Justice did not follow this line of reasoning, and substantially reduced the fines imposed by the Commission. *See* Case 188/82, Thyssen, ECLI:EU:C:1983:329; Case 270/82, Estel, ECLI:EU:C:1984:84. Recognition of the repressive nature of fines was also expressly recognized in anticompetitive practice law. *See* Case 41/69, ACF Chemiefarma, ECLI:EU:C:1970:71, para. 173: the fines provided for by Regulation (EC) No. 17/62 are intended "to suppress illegal activities and to prevent any reference"; *adde*, in the same vein, Case 100/80, SA Musique Diffusion française, ECLI:EU:C:1983:158, para. 105. For a detailed case law analysis concluding that "Community fines are always punitive sanctions," *see* K. Tiedemann, *Principes généraux applicables aux sanctions communautaires: Projet de rapport général*, *in* II ÉTUDE SUR LES SYSTÈMES DE SANCTIONS ADMINISTRATIVES ET PÉNALES DANS LES ÉTATS MEMBRES DES COMMUNAUTÉS EUROPÉENNES: RAPPORTS DE SYNTHÈSE 7, 19 (1994).

362 It is a reference to Molière's *Le Bourgeois gentilhomme*, in which Monsieur Jourdain famously discovers he has been speaking prose all his life without knowing it.

363 Fines have risen exponentially over the past twenty years, which should make us all the more attentive to the principles of criminal law. In this respect, *see* W. P. J. Wils, *The Increased Level of EU Antitrust Fines, Judicial Review and the ECHR*, 33 WORLD COMPETITION 5 (2010).

364 In this vein, L. Bernardeau & T. Étienne, *Principes généraux du droit et contrôle juridictionnel en droit de la concurrence – M. Jourdain: juge pénal?*, CAHIERS DE DROIT EUROPÉEN 365, 366, 369 (2016).

365 Negotiations for its forthcoming accession are still underway, *see* the Council of Europe website: https://www.coe.int/fr/web/human-rights-intergovernmental-cooperation/accession-of-the-european-union-to-the-european-convention-on-human-rights; *adde*, the position of Advocate General J. Kokott delivered on June 13, 2014, in relation to opinion procedure 2/13 initiated by the European Commission. It should be noted, however, that as early as 1979, the Court of Justice stressed the importance it attached to respect for fundamental rights. *See* ECJ, Memorandum concerning the accession of the EC to the Convention for the Protection of Human Rights and Fundamental Freedoms, SJ/229/79, 1979.

366 For a jurisprudential study on the notion of "accusation in criminal matters," *see* COUNCIL OF EUROPE, EUROPEAN COURT OF HUMAN RIGHTS, GUIDE TO ARTICLE 6 OF THE EUROPEAN CONVENTION ON HUMAN RIGHTS: RIGHT TO A FAIR TRIAL (CRIMINAL SECTION) 11–13 (2022), nos. 17–27; *adde*, Engel v. Netherlands, App. no. 5100/71 (ECtHR June 8, 1976); for an account of the criteria for determining which offenses fall within the scope of "criminal matters" and an examination of their respective weight in the qualification, *see* M. Delmas-Marty & C. Teitgen-Colly, *Annexe sur la matière pénale (au sens de l'article 6, CESDH)*, *in* PUNIR SANS JUGER? DE LA RÉPRESSION ADMINISTRATIVE AU DROIT ADMINISTRATIF PÉNAL, *op. cit.* at 165–69.

from national qualifications – an offense decriminalized in domestic law may therefore be "criminal" within the meaning of the Convention[367] – the very purpose of this autonomy being to prevent State Parties from excluding certain offenses from its scope of application.[368]

Nevertheless, the European Court of Human Rights (ECtHR) has ruled in favor of including the law on anticompetitive practices in "criminal matters" in several cases where it had to assess the conformity of certain national competition laws with article 6 of the Convention.[369] The fact that the subject of competition law is not an individual but a company is not an obstacle, despite the individualistic nature of fundamental rights: it is in fact accepted that legal entities,[370] and by extension companies,[371] are also holders of these rights, albeit with some differences from the protection afforded to natural persons.[372]

Once the criminal nature of competition law had been acknowledged,[373] the debate shifted to another arena. Indeed, "criminal law" is not a monolithic concept: it consists of shades of gray – from light gray to dark

---

367 Very often, administrative offenses fall under the heading of "criminal law," which has led some authors to write, quite rightly, that criminal law is "now merged with the notion of criminal law." *See* Lepage et al., Droit pénal des affaires, *op. cit.* at 2.

368 *See* Öztürk v. Germany, App. no. 8544/79), ¶ 49 (ECtHR Feb. 21, 1984); *adde*, M. Daury-Fauveau, Des principes constitutionnels ou internationaux, protecteurs des droits de l'homme, considérés dans leur application aux mesures punitives prononcées par une autorité autre que la justice pénale 131 (1992) (Ph.D. dissertation, Université Paris ii Panthéon-Assas).

369 Regarding the criminal nature of economic offenses under French Ordinance No. 45-1483 of June 30, 1945: Société Stenuit v. France, App. no. 11598/85, ¶ 67 (ECtHR May 30, 1991); regarding Finnish competition law (law on abuse of dominant position): Fortum Corporation v. Finland, App. no. 32559/96, ¶ 40 (ECtHR July 15, 2003); regarding French competition law (law on abuse of dominant position): Lilly v. France, App. no. 53892/00, ¶ 26 (ECtHR Oct. 14, 2003); regarding Italian competition law (agreement law): Menarini Diagnostics v. Italy, App. no. 43509/08, ¶ 44 (ECtHR Sept. 27, 2011). André Decocq thus considered that proceedings instituted on the basis of Regulation No. 17/62 "must undoubtedly be regarded as 'criminal charges' within the meaning of article 6." *See* A. Decocq, *De l'application de la Convention européenne aux procédures communautaires de concurrence pouvant aboutir à des amendes ou à des astreintes*, *in* Mélanges en hommage à Louis Edmond Pettiti 289, 298 (1998).

370 H. Kouamé-Koki, i Les droits fondamentaux des personnes morales dans la Convention européenne des droits de l'homme: De l'impensable à l'indispensable 32, 46 (2014). Although the legal person does not appear in the ECHR, certain fundamental rights have nevertheless been expressly recognized, notably the right to respect for property, in article 1 of the First Additional Protocol to the ECHR of Mar. 20, 1952.

371 For an in-depth study of the possibility for a company to mobilize certain fundamental rights through the mediation of the legal person, *see* T. Bombois, La protection des droits fondamentaux des entreprises en droit européen répressif de la concurrence 18–23 (2012).

372 Protection of the right to marry, the prohibition of torture, and freedom of religion, to name but a few, are irrelevant to the needs of legal entities. The effect or scope of certain fundamental rights is also more limited for legal persons than in the case of natural persons, notably the right to remain silent or the right to privacy. On these two topics, *see* N. Ida, *Abus de marché et droit de garder le silence*, JCP E nos. 16–17, 36 (Apr. 22, 2021), comm. 1226; G. Eveillard, *La vie privée des personnes morales*, Droit administratif 38 (Jan. 2023), comm. 4; *adde*, more generally, B. Faure, *Les droits fondamentaux des personnes morales*, Revue du droit public 233 (Jan. 2008).

373 *See*, *inter alia*, Opinion of Advocate General E. Sharpston, Case C-272/09 P, KME Germany, ECLI:EU:C:2011:63, para. 64: the Advocate General "readily concludes" that the infringement of article 81(1) EC "falls under the 'criminal head' of Article 6 ECHR as progressively defined by the European Court of Human Rights. The prohibition and the possibility of imposing a fine are enshrined in primary and secondary legislation of *general application*; the offense involves engaging in conduct which is generally *regarded as underhand*, to the detriment of the public at large, a feature which it shares with criminal offenses in general and which entails a *clear stigma*; a *fine* of up to 10% of annual turnover is undoubtedly *severe*, and may even put an undertaking out of business; and the intention is explicitly to *punish* and *deter*, with no element of compensation for damage" (emphasis added).

gray. Its darkest part, known as the "hard core," is made up of traditional criminal offenses – those that, for example, may result in imprisonment – while the further you move away from it, the lighter the color becomes, through the effect of a gradient. These different tones correspond to varying degrees of protection.[374] The key question is: to which shade of gray does the repression of agreements and abuses of dominant positions belong? The majority of legal writers today hold that, particularly in view of the exponential increase in the amount of fines imposed, the law on anticompetitive practices is clearly a dark gray.[375]

136. **The necessary role of intent in competition law.** The stakes are high. Indeed, the full, albeit belated, recognition of the criminal nature of competition offenses has direct consequences for the degree of protection that should be afforded to companies, and all the more so since the adoption, in 2012, of the Charter of Fundamental Rights of the European Union. This requires the Union to ensure, as a minimum, a level of protection equivalent to that of the ECHR,[376] which has led to a strong convergence between the case law of the Luxembourg and Strasbourg courts.[377] Respect for certain principles, first and foremost, the principles of legality, foreseeability, and culpability, as well as the presumption of innocence, leads to the need to take account of intent in competition law enforcement. The law of anticompetitive practices is certainly an *economic* law, using technical language and economic concepts; it is nonetheless a *repressive* law, and must therefore allow certain principles and reasoning specific to criminal law to *coexist* with its legal-economic methods.

*

* *

137. **Conclusion to Chapter 2: the apparent erasure but implicit persistence of intent in competition law.** "A legal system does not easily digest foreign bodies. A posteriori, phenomena of rejection occur within it."[378] The temptation was

374 *See* Jussila v. Finland, App. no. 73053/01, ¶ 43 (ECtHR Nov. 23, 2006): "Notwithstanding the consideration that a certain gravity attaches to criminal proceedings, it is self-evident that there are criminal cases which do not carry any significant degree of stigma. There are clearly 'criminal charges' of differing weight."

375 A. Bailleux, *The Fiftieth Shade of Grey Competition Law, "Criministrative Law" and "Fairly Fair Trials," in* Do Labels Still Matter? Blurring Boundaries Between Administrative and Criminal Law: The Influence of the EU 137, 151 and numerous references cited (F. Galli & A. Weyembergh eds., 2014).

376 Charter of Fundamental Rights of the European Union, 2012/C 326/02, 2012 O.J. (C 326) 391, art. 52(3): "In so far as this Charter contains rights which correspond to rights guaranteed by the Convention for the Protection of Human Rights and Fundamental Freedoms, the meaning and scope of those rights shall be the same as those laid down by the said Convention. This provision shall not prevent Union law providing more extensive protection."

377 In this sense, *see* P. Caeiro, *The Influence of the EU on the 'Blurring' Between Administrative and Criminal Law, in* Do Labels Still Matter? Blurring Boundaries Between Administrative and Criminal Law: The Influence of the EU 171, 177, 190 (F. Galli & A. Weyembergh eds., 2014).

378 J.-L. Bergel, *La relativité du droit?*, Revue de la recherche juridique: Droit prospectif no. 3, 13, 16 (1986).

great to subordinate the conception of competition law to the achievements of economic science, and to relegate traditional, sensualist morality to the past, in favor of a utilitarian morality based on the effects resulting from human action. However, the law has been unable to fully embrace this consequentialist perspective, insofar as it contradicts legal principles deeply rooted in the tradition of European countries. While the discipline has evolved considerably over the last two centuries, becoming more "objective" and giving more room to political and economic considerations, it has not abandoned the criterion of intention, not even at the birth of contemporary competition law. Thus, changes to the "superficial layers of the law" must not lead to "conceal[ing] the permanence and universality of the fundamental elements of the legal system."[379]

*

* *

138. **Conclusion of Title I: the contemporary complexification of the law – the history of a progressive compartmentalization.** The contemporary complexification of the law, and of competition law in particular, has its origins in a number of *compartmentalizations*.

First and foremost, a *temporal compartmentalization*: under the influence of positivism, the law was gradually assimilated to the law, itself conceived not as a *discovery* made possible by the study of tradition, the search for higher principles and the quest for the just, but as rules *decreed* by the will of the State. Law, which used to be a form of *knowledge*, has become a *power*[380] based on a *science*.[381] As a result, reference to the solutions of Roman law and the Ancien Droit, particularly in criminal law, has become the exception[382] following the codification movement of the nineteenth century,[383] even though most contemporary institutions can still easily be traced back to the past,[384] revealing the legal foundations common to European countries.

379 *Id.* at 22.

380 On this subject, *see* C. Atias, De la difficulté contemporaine à penser en droit: Leçons de philosophie du droit 50–53 (2016).

381 On this subject, *see* C. Atias, Science des légistes, savoir des juristes (3rd ed. 1993).

382 A. Laingui, La responsabilité pénale dans l'Ancien droit (xvie - xviiie siècles) 5 (1970): André Laingui notes the notable exception of Chauveau, Hélie and Villey's *Théorie du Code pénal*, which "contains references to the old criminalists on every page," and considers that "closer to the present day, E. Garçon's *Code pénal annoté* (1901) does not ignore the old law, but the quotations are rare and, on the whole, only very general references are made." Finally, the author judges that "moderns often seem to know only the picturesque, anecdotal or terrible side of the old criminal law."

383 R. David, C. Jauffre-Spinosi & M. Goré, Les grands systèmes de droit contemporain 2 (12th ed. 2016), no. 2: "It was not until the nineteenth century, and the break-up of this *jus commune*, replaced by national codifications, that the notion of a Law of universal value fell into disrepute."

384 Laingui, La responsabilité pénale dans l'Ancien droit (xvie - xviiie siècles), *op. cit.* at 5.

This *ius commune* was nevertheless lost from view: starting in the eighteenth century, criminal law gradually underwent the consequences of *geographical compartmentalization*. Each country retreated into its own legal system, and tried to assert its superiority.[385] The result was a fragmentation of common law, with the emergence of laws and doctrinal theories that sometimes broke, or at least appeared to break, with the unity of yesteryear.[386]

The period was also marked by the *compartmentalization of disciplines*. In the past, economics did not claim exactitude, nor did it consider itself capable of predicting the future. It was not dissociated from philosophy, and was therefore part, along with law, of a global reflection aimed at a good and just life in society. Economic analysis[387] has, under the influence of the natural sciences, detached itself from metaphysics, and believed itself capable of achieving the same rigor and objectivity – which is, however, nothing more than an illusion. It now aspires, specifically in economic law, to dictate solutions to the law, even if this means upsetting long-established principles.

Finally, we are witnessing a *compartmentalization of the different areas of law*. Whereas in Roman times, Ulpian wrote that *dol* is equipollent in criminal and civil law, today's legislators and legal writers tend to multiply legal concepts, using numerous new, technical terms, often devoid of history, and deemed to be specific to each discipline. Specialists battle over the scope and definition of these new terms, multiplying subdivisions and creating – sometimes artificially – oppositions that obscure the unity, universality and transversality of legal reasoning.

Intention is an excellent illustration of this: for the researcher, few fields are as fraught with difficulty. While it was theorized in a way that was both simple and unified in the era of *ius commune*, it is now one of the most difficult subjects. It would therefore be inconceivable to study its role in the law of anticompetitive practices without first developing a theoretical framework for the concept in positive law

385 David, Jauffret-Spinosi & Goré, Les grands systèmes de droit contemporain, *op. cit.* at 51, no. 50: instead of seeing in codification "the expression of a renewed common law, as their proponents had envisioned, we saw in it the instruments of a 'nationalization of law,' as a result of which the very idea of common law has nearly disappeared in Europe."

386 *Id.*: "An attitude of legislative positivism, aggravated by nationalism, was engendered by the codes, contrary to the idea that had inspired them. For jurists, law has now become their national law. Jurists retreated into their codes, and ceased to consider that law, as a norm of social conduct, was in essence supranational."

387 With the notable exception of certain currents, known as "heterodox," which have not renounced this unitary approach, *see infra*, no. 478.

Title II
Conceptualizing intent

139. **A conceptualization based on a comparative law approach.** Under the influence of the Europeanization of law,[1] it is now necessary to "free ourselves [from] national laws"[2] – which implies moving beyond the theoretical constructs of in domestic law[3] – in order to conceptualize legal institutions in a unitary way. Such an approach implies recourse to comparative law,[4] to make known the solutions adopted by different countries sharing a common culture, and thus reconstitute the *ius commune* of yesteryear.[5] The point is to realize that the legal divergences separating Member States are often more apparent than real, and that while they may use different techniques or doctrinal presentations, "a fundamental unity reigns in the law."[6] Indeed, legal comparison leads us to question the origin and justification of concepts used by positive laws, and requires us to give up "attributing to them a character of necessity" when their existence is underpinned only by temporal contingencies and artificial oppositions.[7] Such an undertaking

---

1 David, Jauffret-Spinosi & Goré, Les grands systèmes de droit contemporain, *op. cit.* at 2, no. 2: "The development of comparative law is a reaction against the nationalization of law that took place in the nineteenth century. Moreover, it has become necessary and urgent due to the unprecedented expansion of relations of all kinds in international life, making a rapprochement of laws desirable."

2 R. David, *Droit comparé et systèmes socio-politiques*, Revue internationale de droit comparé no. 2, 263, 263 (1970).

3 According to René David, the main obstacle to such an undertaking is related to "the routine of jurists." R. David, *Le droit continental, la* Common Law, *et les perspectives d'un* jus commune *européen, in* Nouvelles perspectives d'un droit commun 113, 124 (M. Cappelletti ed., 1978).

4 Indeed, the development of Union law has prompted numerous comparative law studies aimed at rediscovering a common legal tradition among the Member States. *See* in particular. B. Oppetit, *Retour à un droit commun européen, in* Droit et modernité 73, 73 (1998).

5 David, *Le droit continental, la* Common Law, *et les perspectives d'un* jus commune *européen, op. cit.* at 133–34.

6 *Id.*

7 David, Jauffret-Spinosi & Goré, Les grands systèmes de droit contemporain, *op. cit.* at 4, no. 5. *Adde*, in the same vein: R. Sacco, La comparaison juridique au service de la connaissance du droit 7 (1991):

is three-dimensional. On the one hand, it involves overcoming two compartmentalizations: the first, which seems to separate national laws, and the second, which gives the impression that reasoning is dissimilar from one area of law to another; and, on the other, it involves integrating the historical perspective, as it offers the opportunity to rediscover models which, "because of the values on which they are based," survive the passage of time.[8]

Essentially, the aim is to identify the constants in legal reasoning,[9] in order to reveal the transversal nature of the intention (**Chapter 1**), which will then enable us to propose a general theory that transcends national differences, while remaining acceptable to all Member States, as it stays true to tradition (**Chapter 2**).

This work is essential in order to examine the role of intent in competition law. Indeed, even though EU law has not yet given rise to a genuine theory of intent,[10] it has now evolved into an independent concept[11] that competition authorities and national courts must interpret in accordance with the case law of the Court of Justice[12] when applying articles 101 and 102 TFEU. Since it is difficult to find any trace of a definition of intent and the rules governing it, the competition authorities and judges of the Member States run the risk of interpreting it in accordance with their

---

"One of the tools that enable comparison to prepare the unification of law consists in denying certain artificial or only apparent differences, which seem to oppose the various national solutions." The author adds that, while doctrine could "point to the parallels already existing between the laws of different countries," it has not, to date, "always done so." *See* R. Sacco, *Droit commun de l'Europe, et composantes du droit*, *in* NOUVELLES PERSPECTIVES D'UN DROIT COMMUN 95, 103 (M. Cappelletti ed., 1978).

8 SACCO, LA COMPARAISON JURIDIQUE AU SERVICE DE LA CONNAISSANCE DU DROIT, *op. cit.* at 117.

9 These constants, which Rodolfo Sacco, borrowing from linguistics, has called "cryptotypes," are implicit and informal patterns of immense importance to legal reasoning, and which can be discovered through the operation of comparison. *See* SACCO, LA COMPARAISON JURIDIQUE AU SERVICE DE LA CONNAISSANCE DU DROIT, *op. cit.* at 105–106. Friedrich Hayek was no different when he recognized the existence of unconscious and incommunicable thought processes, which nevertheless guide and enable human interaction. *See* F. A. Hayek, *Rules, Perception and Intelligibility*, *in* 15 THE COLLECTED WORKS OF F. A. HAYEK 232, 251 (B. Caldwell ed., 2014): "[E]verything we can express is intelligible to others only because their mental structure is governed by the same rules as ours." *Adde*, J. Verhaegen, *Notions floues et droit pénal*, *in* LES NOTIONS À CONTENU VARIABLE EN DROIT 7, 10 (C. Perelman & R. Vander Elst eds., 1984): the author notes that authors who have studied the implementation of flexible notions by interpreters have focused on "the process of seeking out and highlighting 'specifying concepts' by which the law's implementing bodies, eliminating the vagueness of the notion, manage to identify certain concrete, or at any rate less abstract, determinations." Finally, *see* J. Carbonnier, *Les notions à contenu variable dans le droit français de la famille*, *in* LES NOTIONS À CONTENU VARIABLE EN DROIT 98, 105 (C. Perelman & R. Vander Elst eds., 1984): "[E]ven in a society where writing reigns supreme, there are other normative and regulatory systems beyond written law. If a legal norm refers to one of these normative systems that, not being written, do not have the same rigidity as the law, it will acquire a variable content. Its surface will reflect the interplay of external norms, an interplay that is shifting by nature: it is as if a strange mirror had been embedded in the text." In short, whatever words are used to describe this phenomenon, jurists intuitively senses that something hidden guides their reasoning – perhaps this is the intuitive sense of the law.

10 In this sense, J. BLOMSMA, MENS REA AND DEFENCES IN EUROPEAN CRIMINAL LAW 6 (2012).

11 A. Rosanò, *Some Developments of the Principle of* Mens Rea *in the Case Law of the Court of Justice of the European Union*, 7 NEW JOURNAL OF EUROPEAN CRIMINAL LAW 302, 314 (2016).

12 Directive (EU) 2019/1 of the European Parliament and of the Council of Dec. 11, 2018, to Empower the Competition Authorities of the Member States to be More Effective Enforcers and to Ensure the Proper Functioning of the Internal Market, 2019 O.J. (L 11) 3, recital 42.

national – and in some respects disparate – conceptions,[13] which could lead to divergent solutions[14] and compromise the principle of primacy and the objective of harmonizing Union law.

13 *See* BLOMSMA, MENS REA AND DEFENCES IN EUROPEAN CRIMINAL LAW, *op. cit.* at 8–11.

14 P. L. Parcu & M. L. Stasi, *The Role of Intent in the Assessment of Conduct under Article 102 TFEU*, *in* ABUSE OF DOMINANCE IN EU COMPETITION LAW: EMERGING TRENDS 12, 14 (P. L. Parcu et al. eds., 2017): it is hard "to identify a common European definition of intent, and thus a common role to be attributed to it by national authorities, courts and practitioners while applying EU competition law."

Chapter 1
THE TRANSVERSALITY OF INTENTION

140. **Intention, a constant in legal reasoning.** Over the last two centuries, as a result of a growing distrust of free will, and under the influence of the materialist philosophy inherited from the Enlightenment, objectivist currents have sought to do away with the notion of intention, suddenly deemed too subjective, inefficient and uncertain. Theories of risk, of material offenses, of no-fault or strict liability, then suggested that it was possible and necessary, on certain occasions, to emancipate oneself from the ethical basis that, until then, had justified state sanction. In spite of these tendencies, which were unfavorable to the persistence of intent and undoubtedly contributed to compromising its intelligibility by weighing it down with theoretical quarrels, it remained present, sometimes under "various technical disguises,"[1] foremost among which is presumption. The situation is paradoxical: while the place of intention has not changed, its appearances are now discreet, as it continues to guide reasoning without always coming out from behind the scenes. It also no longer seems to have any claim to universality, as its domain seems to have been reduced by the emergence of special regimes and competing theories and concepts. Yet we need to rehabilitate the intention, by overcoming false oppositions and distancing ourselves from doctrinal quarrels. It will then be easy to see that intention has remained the foundation of all liability, in all areas of the law – because it radiates throughout the entire legal system (**Section 1**) – and in all Member States sharing the same cultural background – because intention permeates all legal systems (**Section 2**).

---

1 P. Rémy, *Critique du système français de responsabilité civile*, 1 DROITS ET CULTURES 31, 37 (1966).

Section 1
A concept that radiates throughout the entire legal system

141. **Transversality *ratione personae* and *ratione materiae*.** Whenever the law establishes liability and imposes sanctions, it calls upon, explicitly or implicitly, the concept of intention, whatever the discipline concerned – the notion is transversal *ratione materiae* (**Paragraph 1**). *Ratione personae*, intention is not the prerogative of the natural person. Since, in law, intention is not a psychological reality, but a technical concept based on a legal abstraction, it is relevant to recognize that legal persons, and by extension companies, are endowed with an intention of their own (**Paragraph 2**).

Paragraph 1 – Transversality *ratione materiae*

142. **The transversality of intention: a concept that spans various legal disciplines.** Intention is not a concept exclusive to criminal law. The legal system as a whole is founded on the premise that human beings are free and autonomous, and therefore responsible for their voluntary acts. Intention is therefore found in civil, criminal and administrative law alike. While doctrine tends to distinguish between numerous types of fault, and to use Specialized terms for each discipline, creating the impression of compartmentalized notions and reasoning, it is on the contrary important to highlight the conceptual identity of intention (**I**), its modes of proof differing, however, depending on whether the law deals with a layperson or a professional (**II**).

I. The conceptual identity of intention

143. **The transversality of intention: criminal law and tort law.** Civil fault and criminal culpability are traditionally considered to be relatively impervious, conceptually speaking, to each other.[2] Indeed, civil fault is said to admit no gradations and to be unitary in nature, since the slightest fault is sufficient to incur the liability of its perpetrator, whereas intention is said to be the queen of criminal fault.[3] However, on closer examination, this assertion

---

2 All the more so, in the case of unintentional offenses, since Law no. 2000-647 of July 10, 2000, which clarifies the definition of unintentional offenses (JORF, no. 159 of July 11, 2000); the judge can now find fault where the criminal judge has judged that there was none. On this subject, *see* P. Bonfils, *Consécration de la dualité des fautes civile et pénale non intentionnelles*, Recueil Dalloz 721 (2004).

3 In this sense, *see* A. Pirovano, Faute civile et faute pénale, 115 (1966), no. 109.

is not so easily confirmed.[4] Apart from the existence of different rules of evidence,[5] the notion of intention transcends the conceptual distinctions generally made between disciplines. Thus, under the guise of the apparent autonomy of intention in tort law, it is the conceptual identity of intention in tort law and criminal law that shines through (**A**); an identity that is particularly evident in matters of unfair competition (**B**).

A. The identity of intent in tort and criminal law

144. **Doctrinal assertion of a "retreat from fault" in tort law.** Since the *Lex Aquilia*,[6] liability in tort has long been closely tied to fault,[7] but from the end of the nineteenth century onwards, a new doctrinal trend emerged,[8] which sought substitute risk for fault. The rise in accidents necessitated ensuring victims were compensated, and this led to the gradual expansion of liability cases,[9] while the widespread use of insurance also made it possible to limit the financial consequences for the designated person responsible.[10] Demonstrating *causality* took precedence over proving *fault*, with the occurrence of the *event* seemingly more important than the person *at fault*. Alternative concepts replaced that of fault to explain the phenomenon, which affected both French and other legal systems[11]: "objective fault," "risk theory," "strict liability," or "no-fault liability." At the time, a significant proportion of legal scholars sought to restrict the notion of

---

4 Some authors consider, for example, that civil fault has certain distinctive features compared to criminal fault, but is not totally distinct from it, notably in that it requires, like the latter, a moral element. *See* F. Terré, P. Simler, Y. Lequette & F. Chénedé, Droit civil: Les obligations 1078 (13th ed. 2022), nos. 950–951.

5 Indeed, there are more presumptions of fault in civil law than in criminal law, and these are more difficult to rebut (sometimes giving rise to the idea of "strict liability," or "no-fault liability," which, in our view, amounts to confusing the nature of liability – which is always, to a greater or lesser extent, justified by wrongful conduct – and the means of proving it, as we shall *see infra*, no. 151). Thus, in the event of a "vehicle malfunction, the driver does not incur strict criminal liability, which would be modeled on that which, in civil matters, results from the law of July 5, 1985; the prosecuting authorities will have to prove the fault (lack of maintenance, for example) accounting for this malfunction." *See* P. Conte, Droit pénal spécial 58–59 (6th ed. 2019), no. 80.

6 Of which "no legislation can repudiate inheritance" according to M. Planiol, Traité élémentaire de droit civil 304 (1931), no. 863 bis.

7 B. Starck, Essai d'une théorie générale de la responsabilité civile considérée en sa double fonction de garantie et de peine privée 6 (1947).

8 It should be noted, however, that the novelty of the hypotheses of liability for the actions of things or vicarious liability (hypotheses that do not *a priori* require fault) is questionable, given that they were not unknown in Roman law. In our view, therefore, this is rather a new doctrinal theorization of an old phenomenon. On this subject, *see* A. Ruelle, *Les responsabilités du fait d'autrui en droit romain dans la ligne de mire de Domat et de Pothier*, *in* Le fait d'autrui: Responsabilités contractuelles et extracontractuelles 9, 12–15 (C. Delforge & J. Van Zuylen eds., 2021).

9 G. Viney, *Rapport de synthèse*, *in* Les métamorphoses de la responsabilité, Sixièmes journées René Savatier 323, 327–33 (1997).

10 The burden of compensation is often borne by the insurer, who compensates the victim for the (sometimes very minor) fault of the insured party, who, although theoretically liable, can in practice escape the consequences of liability by securing adequate insurance. *See* R. Savatier, *Personnalité et dépersonnalisation de la responsabilité civile. La foi en la liberté de la personne et la responsabilité fondée sur la faute*, *in* Mélanges de droit, d'histoire et d'économie offerts à Marcel Laborde-Lacoste 321, 342 (1963).

11 For a comparative law study, *see* J. Knetsch, *La place de la responsabilité sans faute dans le système de responsabilité civile. Étude de droit comparé*, Revue des contrats no. 4, 196 (Dec. 2019).

culpability to criminal law, arguing that progress consisted in separating criminal and civil fault, with civil liability law no longer aiming so much to punish wrongful conduct as to compensate for damage.[12] At the same time, the risks created by commercial activities similarly shook the doctrinal theories established in criminal law. It was argued that the need to prove the guilt of offenders undermined the effectiveness of law enforcement, leaving many dangerous and reprehensible acts unpunished. The response from criminal doctrine was much the same as in civil law.[13] Gradually, a general and profound movement took shape, which has stood the test of time: that of objectivization.[14]

145. **The doctrinal refutation of the "retreat of fault" in tort law.** Against this backdrop, what remains of fault in tort law? Did those who defended these new theories of risk,[15] who claimed that one could be liable without committing a fault, and who saw in fault only inconveniences, fail to consider whether this notion had served a valuable purpose?[16] The supposed disappearance of this notion has created enormous confusion as to the basis of civil liability.[17] Since then, many authors have taken issue with the very idea of liability detached from fault.[18] This would be a return to the objective system of archaic times,[19] a sign of the regressive tendency of the law,[20] having in the process encouraged the legislator to adopt a host of special regimes, which are so many

---

12 In this sense, *see* P. Ancel, *Rapport de M. Ancel sur la responsabilité sans faute*, Travaux de l'Association Henri Capitant 65, 66–67 (1946).

13 In fact, modern developments linked to industrialization have made it necessary to impose criminal penalties on risky behavior causing significant damage, even if unintentional, i.e., solely due to recklessness or failure to comply with safety obligations, whereas historically, negligence was generally relegated to the sidelines of criminal law. This led one author, critical of this trend, to observe that we were "moving towards a convergence between the principles of criminal law and the solutions of civil law, which tend to base the obligation to pay compensation no longer on fault, but on the creation of a risk." *See* A. Legal, *La responsabilité sans faute*, *in* La chambre criminelle et sa jurisprudence: Recueil d'études en hommage à la mémoire de Maurice Patin 130, 131 (1965).

14 This phenomenon of objectivization, which can be observed in French and foreign criminal law, especially in relation to offenses committed by professionals, will be examined *infra*, nos. 152 *et seq.*

15 For an overview, *see* Planiol, Traité élémentaire de droit civil, *op. cit.* at 304–305, no. 863 ter.

16 Henri Mazeaud answers this question in the affirmative, and continues: "Theorists can construct no-fault liability and do whatever they like, but when they are faced with practice… [and they] have to ask themselves in what cases compensation for damage should be awarded, there is only one possible criterion, and that is fault." H. Mazeaud, *Discussion du Rapport de M. Ancel sur la responsabilité sans faute*, Travaux de l'Association Henri Capitant 76, 77 (1946).

17 In this regard, Paul Esmein writes that we "cannot imagine a greater confusion over the basis of liability than that which currently exists in France. In the presence of a conviction without a finding of fault, it is impossible to say whether it involves liability for fault or a guarantee of risk." P. Esmein, *La faute et sa place dans la responsabilité civile*, RTD civ. 481, 487 (1949).

18 Among an abundant body of doctrine, Philippe Le Tourneau is one of the authors who has argued most strongly in favor of the "universality of subjective civil liability." *See* in particular, P. Le Tourneau, *Les métamorphoses contemporaines et subreptices de la faute subjective*, *in* Les métamorphoses de la responsabilité, Sixièmes journées René Savatier 19 (1997); from the same author, *La verdeur de la faute dans la responsabilité civile*, RTD civ. 505 (1988).

19 On the objective reaction to damage in archaic societies, *see supra*, nos. 19–20.

20 B. Oppetit, Droit et modernité 118–19 (1998).

obligations "imagined for the sole pleasure of having them violated."[21] Objective fault also has the disadvantage of depriving liability of its moral and punitive functions.[22] Abroad, liability appears at worst an anomaly, at best a mirage.[23] Yet there are many reasons to support the thesis of the *trompe-l'œil* dissipation of fault. While fault may appear to have been sidelined by legal technique – through the increasing use of legal or jurisprudential presumptions of fault – it nonetheless remains the rational basis of all liability.[24]

146. **Demonstrating the permanence of civil fault.** Theoretically, civil fault, like criminal fault, always requires a material element, a legal element and a mental element[25] – the question being what this last element covers. Classically, fault is defined simply as a "breach of a pre-existing obligation, for which the law orders reparation when it has caused damage to another."[26] Intention, on the other hand, is understood as "the agent's will to commit the delict as determined by the law."[27] If we agree on these two definitions, the problem is quickly solved: as soon as civil law imposes a certain course of conduct, which it depends on the will of its author to follow or not to follow, it seems undeniable that any civil liability rests on a *voluntary* fault, even if it is minimal or an omission.[28]

If we draw the logical conclusions from this reasoning, the hypotheses of no-fault liability, i.e., "vicarious liability" or "liability for things," should be analyzed as *voluntary* breaches of a general duty imposed by the legal system: act as a responsible custodian.[29] Fault has not disappeared; rather, it is presumed in order to relieve the victim of the burden of proof. However, this presumption is still based on the idea that everyone is responsible for what they have in their custody, and that they are at

---

21 P. Hébraud, *Rôles respectifs de la volonté et des éléments objectifs dans les actes juridiques*, *in* II Mélanges offerts à Jacques Maury 420, 464 (1960).

22 G. Viney, Le déclin de la responsabilité individuelle 306 (1965).

23 Knetsch, *La place de la responsabilité sans faute dans le système de responsabilité civile. Étude de droit comparé*, *op. cit.* at 199–202.

24 Philippe Rémy thus considers that objective liability continues to leave "room for fault, under various technical disguises – requirement of an active role for the thing, definition of custody as power of use, control and direction, etc." P. Rémy, *Critique du système français de responsabilité civile*, I Droits et cultures 31, 37 (1966). *Adde*, in the same vein, C. Radé, *L'impossible divorce de la faute et de la responsabilité civile*, Recueil Dalloz 301 (1998).

25 This assertion is uncontroversially accepted in doctrine. *Ex multis*, J. Carbonnier, 4 Droit civil: Les obligations 405 (16th ed. 1992), no. 220; F. Terré et al., Droit civil: Les obligations, *op. cit.* at 1077, no. 950.

26 Planiol, Traité élémentaire de droit civil, *op. cit.* at 302, no. 863. On the (many) other possible meanings of the word "faute." *See* P. Jourdain, *Droit à réparation - Responsabilité fondée sur la faute*, JurisClasseur Notarial (Oct. 2022), fasc. 120-10, nos. 7–19.

27 This is the traditional definition provided by E. Garçon, I Code pénal annoté 8 (2nd ed., 1952), no. 77. This will be explored further *infra*, nos. 188–193.

28 Carbonnier, 4 Droit civil: Les obligations, *op. cit.* at 405, no. 220; in the same vein, Planiol, Traité élémentaire de droit civil, *op. cit.* at 304–305, no. 863 ter.

29 *See* Radé, *L'impossible divorce de la faute et de la responsabilité civile*, *op. cit.* at 303.

fault when they cause damage to others. In practice, this presumption is difficult to rebut,[30] but if there is a presumption, it is proof that there is something to presume – fault. Moreover, criminal law itself is not averse to the hypotheses of vicarious liability.[31] More open to criticism, on the other hand, are the solutions accepted over the last few decades by the Court of Cassation, which now recognizes the civil liability of persons with mental disorders and children.[32] By assuming their delictual capacity, the law no longer relies on a presumption but rather invokes a legal fiction,[33] enshrining an anomaly with no historical precedent,[34] and whose validity is open to question.[35]

147. **Demonstrating the relevance of fault gradation in civil liability.** Once the persistence of fault, and with it that of the mental element, has been accepted, in spite of objectivist trends, the relevance of its gradation remains to be demonstrated. This is far from self-evident. Indeed, since the adoption of the Civil Code in 1804, a dogma has run through civil

---

30 F. Terré et al., Droit civil: Les obligations, *op. cit.* at 1097–1102, nos. 978–983, for liability for damage caused by things, and at 1200–1207, nos. 1081–1087, for vicarious liability. In the case of liability for damage caused by things, case law oscillates between presumption of fault, which is difficult to rebut in practice, and presumption not of fault but simply of "liability," implying that liability is objective. However, in the case of liability for damage caused by things as in the case of vicarious liability, certain justifying facts still allow liability to be ruled out: extraneous cause, order of the law, command of legitimate authority, non-liability agreements, fault of the victim, acceptance of risk, or force majeure. This solution is accepted by all legal systems. For a comparative law analysis of defenses to a finding of no-fault liability: S. Steel, *Les défenses en matière de responsabilité contractuelle et extracontractuelle en droit français*, Revue des contrats no. 4, 262 (Dec. 2019).

31 Nor even, according to one author, to the hypothesis of criminal liability for acts caused by things. On the subject of vicarious liability in criminal law, *see infra*, no. 166. For an overview: F. Chabas, Responsabilité civile et responsabilité pénale 51 (1975).

32 For a detailed study of the historical development of the law, jurisprudence and doctrine on the liability of children and persons with mental disorders, *see* Y. Le Magueresse, Des comportements fautifs du créancier et de la victime en droit des obligations 95 (2007). From Roman times until the second half of the twentieth century, children and mentally impaired individuals were considered incapable of engaging their tortious liability. Following a jurisprudential shift by the Court of Cassation in 1964 (Cass. 2e civ., Dec. 18, 1964, JCP 1965, ii, 14304 (Fr.)), the Court has accepted, through an *in abstracto* assessment of the fault of the mentally impaired person, that it is possible to incur liability – a solution enshrined in the law of January 3, 1968, which abolished the principle of civil irresponsibility of the insane. However, article 489-2 of the French Civil Code, which states that: "[a] person who has caused damage to another while under the influence of a mental disorder is nonetheless obliged to make reparation" (unofficial translation), does not admit the existence of fault, or even liability, but simply of an obligation to make reparation. With regard to children, the turnaround came in 1984 with five rulings by the Assemblée plénière (Cass., ass. plén., May 9, 1984, no. 80-14.994), in which the Court of Cassation decided to invoke the child's own fault in order to reduce or exclude his or her right to compensation – a solution much criticized by the doctrine.

33 While fictions may prove convenient in that they enable, on a transitory basis – until doctrine proposes other solutions – certain legal effects to be produced in order to ensure greater justice, they prove in certain cases (including, in our view, this one) to be no more than an artificial device for dispensing with the need to recognize errors in reasoning. For a critical study of fictions, *see* R. Houin, *Le problème des fictions en droit civil*, Travaux de l'Association Henri Capitant 242, 242–46 (1947).

34 S. Vallar, *Folie et droit romain – Quelques observations*, Criminocorpus: Revue d'Histoire de la justice, des crimes et des peines 16 (2016), http://journals.openedition.org/criminocorpus/3146.

35 It should be noted, however, that the liability of persons deprived of discernment can only be engaged on the basis of quasi-delict, and not because of faults that require the intention to cause damage. Thus, "[t]he abandonment of moral imputability is not the abandonment of culpability." P. Pierre, *La place de la responsabilité objective: Notion et rôle de la faute en droit français*, Revue Juridique de l'Ouest no. 4, 403, 413 (2010).

liability: that of the unity of fault.[36] Indeed, if the slightest fault is deemed to engage the liability of its author, why burden ourselves with distinctions? Yet doctrine has continued to distinguish between different types of civil fault,[37] and not without reason. It is generally accepted that, even if damages are in principle a function of the harm suffered alone, the existence of intentional fault generally leads the judge to increase the amount, using a method sometimes hidden;[38] intention can also have an impact on the reparability of harm.[39] The characterization of intentional fault also results in a shift from contractual liability to extra-contractual liability.[40] Any intentional or deceitful fault is, moreover, uninsurable due to a legal exclusion.[41]

Nevertheless, intention has an additional interest that, although fundamental, is not sufficiently highlighted. Contrary to the principle that any

36 On the origin of the unitary conception of fault in tort law, *see* L. Sichel, La gravité de la faute en droit de la responsabilité civile 6 (2022), no. 6. The author describes the opposition between Pothier, who in 1848 developed the "theory of the three faults," adopted by the majority of the doctrine; and Le Brun, who saw in this gradation of civil faults a misreading of the *Digest* as well as an inexhaustible source of practical difficulties. Domat, who considered that "any fault, even unintentional, engages liability if it causes damage," had an influence on the final wording of the former articles 1382 and 1383 (now articles 1240 and 1241). The drafters of the Civil Code then decided to penalize all harmful faults, intentional and unintentional, in the same way – thus evacuating the theory of the gradation of faults, long-established before 1804.

37 In this respect, it is paradoxical that, despite the monistic conception of fault, doctrine has been so divided on the criteria for distinguishing between the different types of fault, and even on their number. Indeed, while authors generally adopt a tripartite classification (intentional, gross and inexcusable fault) (*see* Sichel, La gravité de la faute en droit de la responsabilité civile, *op. cit.* at 31, no. 22, and the many references cited), others have introduced additional degrees, one of them proposing a gradation of up to seven types of fault (very slight, slight, deliberate, inexcusable, gross, fraudulent and intentional): H. Lalou, *La gamme des fautes*, Recueil Dalloz 17, 18 (1940), chron. v.

38 In this sense, *see* A. Vignon-Barrault, Intention et responsabilité civile 335–437 (2000) (Ph.D. dissertation, Université du Maine), nos. 352–463; Carbonnier, 4 Droit civil: Les obligations, *op. cit.* at 409, no. 222.

39 Sichel, La gravité de la faute en droit de la responsabilité civile, *op. cit.* at 176–98, nos. 132–150.

40 Intentional or fraudulent misconduct renders legal ceilings and contractual clauses ineffective, and makes the entire loss reparable, even if it is unforeseeable (or *at least* leads to the award of additional damages). *See* Sichel, La gravité de la faute en droit de la responsabilité civile, *op. cit.* at 34, no. 25; *adde*, A. Vignon-Barrault, Intention et responsabilité civile, *op. cit.* at 331, no. 350.

41 This exclusion is provided for in article L113-1 of the French Insurance Code. Intention in insurance law is a vast subject, on which there is an abundance of doctrine and controversy. *See, ex multis*: Sichel, La gravité de la faute en droit de la responsabilité civile, *op. cit.* at 260–66, nos. 201–204; D. Bakouche, *Aléa et faute intentionnelle*, Responsabilité civile et assurances 26 (Mar. 2014), dossier 7; F. Leduc, *Retour sur les fautes de l'assuré faisant disparaître l'aléa*, Revue des contrats 59 (Sept. 2020); J. Bigot, *Faute intentionnelle, faute dolosive, faute volontaire: Le passé, le présent, l'avenir*, Revue générale du droit des assurances 75 (Feb. 2015); L. Mayaux, *Faute intentionnelle, dolosive… ou frauduleuse: L'art d'ajouter du flou au flou*, Revue générale du droit des assurances 147 (Mar. 2014); N. Charbit, *L'intention de la faute*, Petites affiches 14 (Mar. 14, 2003). These debates call for two comments. Firstly, they show that the judge always takes a pragmatic view of intention. If the notion of intention seems to vary from case to case, this is because it constitutes the abstract criterion that gives judges a certain margin of discretion, enabling them to assess the legitimacy of the interests involved. This criterion is used to strike a *balance* between the interests of the victim (who runs the risk of not being compensated if an intentional fault is found), those of the insurer (who only undertakes to compensate for a hazard, which is non-existent in the presence of an intention to cause damage), and those of the insured (who agrees to pay for an insurance policy in order to avoid bearing the cost of unintentional damage). It would nevertheless be possible and relevant to systematize the role of intention in insurance law. By means of a study of case law, it would be possible to isolate cases in order to draw up a typology of hypotheses in which the judge defines intention generously and those in which a stricter definition is applied. Secondly, the study of intent in insurance law reveals a principle that is also found in tort and criminal law: when judges are dealing with a professional (a notary, a builder or a doctor), they are more likely to presume intentional fault, even in cases of simple negligence. This observation will be developed in relation to criminal law *infra*, nos. 156–157.

fault, even the slightest carelessness, is sufficient to engage the tortious liability of its author, it appears that, in certain cases, only an intentional fault can do so. Thus, intention plays a role not only in determining the *quantum of* the penalty but also, in certain cases, in determining the nature of the liability itself. This is the case whenever, without *dol*, no prejudice is conceivable. There are many examples of this. In the pre-contractual phase, if the intention to deceive the contracting party is not demonstrated, *dol* or fraudulent concealment cannot be characterized. Moreover, conduct that may fall simultaneously under civil and criminal law only constitutes a tort to the extent that the judge discerns an element of intent[42]. In such cases, it is the nature of the means employed and the aim pursued that are sanctioned[43] – it is the fraud, and through it the intention, that causes the damage and gives rise to liability. Finally, whenever criminal law incriminates an intentional offense, in the civil action that may ensue, it is essentially an intentional fault that justifies the engagement of the civil liability of the perpetrator of the offense. It should therefore be recognized that, as in criminal law, there are different types of "pre-existing obligations" in civil law,[44] some of which require the existence of an intentional fault in order to incur liability.[45]

148. Demonstrating the conceptual identity of intention in tort and criminal law. The thesis of the conceptual identity of intention in tort law and criminal law is of great interest in today's world. At play is a dual dynamic: the penalization of civil liability and the civilization of criminal liability.[46] The law of civil liability is stepping beyond its traditional bounds to punish rather than merely repair,[47] while criminal law is seizing a growing number of simple

---

42 In criminal law, for example, deception and swindling are punishable under civil liability law as conduct consisting in creating an error in another's mind so as to induce them to make a decision they would not otherwise halve made.
On this subject. See P. Laurent, Contrat et droit pénal (2001) (Ph.D. dissertation, Université d'Aix-Marseille) at 63–72 for swindling, and at 173–79 for deception.

43 In this sense, M. Planiol, *Dol civil et dol criminel*, xx Revue critique de législation et de jurisprudence 545 & 643, 550 (1893).

44 We refer to Marcel Planiol's definition of fault cited *supra*, no. 146.

45 Marcel Planiol, in his *tableau des obligations légales dont l'article 1382 est la garantie* [Table of Legal Obligations for which Article 1382 Serves as Guarantee], distinguishes four types of obligation: "1. To refrain from any *violence* toward objects or persons. 2. To refrain from any *fraud*, i.e., any act intended to deceive another. 3. To refrain from any act requiring a certain level of *strength* or *skill* that one does not possess to the required degree. 4. To exercise sufficient *supervision* over dangerous objects in one's possession or over persons under one's care." Planiol, Traité élémentaire de droit civil, *op. cit.* at 306, no. 865. It goes without saying that the first two types of obligation require proof of intentional fault.

46 C. Dubois, Responsabilité civile et responsabilité pénale. À la recherche d'une cohérence perdue 243 (2016).

47 However, this is not a new phenomenon: in Roman law, it was possible for an action to have a mixed character, at the boundary between civil and criminal law. *See* M. Jacquemin, Droit romain: De la loi Aquilia - Droit français: De l'intention en droit pénal 31–45 (1888). With regard to the contemporary period, the dual function of civil liability – remedial and punitive – was demonstrated by B. Starck's thesis, Essai d'une théorie générale de la responsabilité civile considérée en sa double fonction de garantie et de peine privée, *op. cit.* Also attesting to the current relevance of the phenomenon is the proposal – since abandoned – put forward in the context of the civil liability reform to introduce a "civil fine" for deliberate faults committed with a view to obtaining a gain or a saving, with the stated aim of reviving the punitive

imprudences in its talons. This mechanically reinforces the porosity between the two disciplines, and encourages us to conceptualize intent in a unitary, cross-disciplinary way, building a theory applicable to all repressive laws.[48]

In tort law, as in criminal law, there are two main categories of fault: *intentional fault in the strict sense* and *intentional fault in the broad sense*. Intentional fault in the strict sense implies the characterization of the will to achieve a result;[49] intentional fault in the broad sense requires only the characterization of the will to act, to the exclusion of the will to cause the resulting damage.[50] According to these definitions, negligence is an intentional fault in the broad sense, since every individual is free not to be negligent, and being so is therefore a manifestation of their will.[51] The need to characterize one or other category of fault depends on the nature of the pre-existing obligation;[52] in the same way as in criminal law, the need to characterize one or other category of mental element depends solely on the nature of the offense described by the incriminating text.[53] The difference between a pre-existing obligation in civil law and an offense in criminal law lies in the fact that the former is indeterminate,[54] whereas the latter must necessarily be written,[55] in accordance with the principle of legality. However, this difference in the *source* of liability in no way affects the conceptual identity of the *criterion* for liability.[56]

Moreover, historically, intent was apprehended in a unified manner in both disciplines: Ulpian writes that the action for *dol* in civil law is the

---

function of civil liability. On this subject, *ex multis*: M. Bacache, *Responsabilité civile: Une réforme a minima?*, JCP G (Sept. 14, 2020), art. 1007; E. Dreyer, *La sanction de la faute lucrative par l'amende civile*, Recueil Dalloz no. 9, 1136 (2017); F. Rousseau, *Projet de réforme de la responsabilité civile : L'amende civile face aux principes directeurs du droit pénal*, JCP G 1177 (June 11, 2018), art. 686; J. Prorok, *L'amende civile dans la réforme de la responsabilité civile: Regard critique sur la consécration d'une fonction punitive générale*, RTD civ. 327 (2018).

48 This is the path we will be taking *infra*, nos. 212 *et seq*.

49 We therefore reject the doctrinal conception of intentional fault, which defines it as requiring proof of an "intention to harm." Not only is this view overly reductive, but it also confuses motive with intention. In the same vein, *see* Sichel, La gravité de la faute en droit de la responsabilité civile, *op. cit.* at 246–47, no. 192. For a contractualist, confusing motive and intention would be tantamount to confusing objective cause and subjective cause. *See*, for example, A. Bénabent, Droit des obligations 159–61 (19th ed. 2021), nos. 184–186. The distinction between intention and motive will be examined *infra*, no. 191

50 This distinction is made by Carbonnier, 4 Droit civil: Les obligations, *op. cit.* at 409, no. 222.

51 *See* negligent offenses in criminal law, *infra*, no. 195. Note that Roman law defined negligence as follows: "It is a fault not to foresee what a sensible man would foresee, or to warn only when it is no longer possible to avoid the danger." Digest, 9, 2, 31, concerning the *Lex Aquilia*.

52 In the sense of Marcel Planiol, *see supra*, no. 146.

53 *See infra*, nos. 222–223.

54 The civil law standard of conduct implies a fault that will only be named once it has been committed. *See* J. Combacau, *L'illicite et le fautif*, 5 Droits: Revue française de théorie juridique 3, 5 (1987).

55 That said, a pre-existing civil law obligation may be written; and the notion that criminal law allows no room for indeterminacy must be qualified. *See infra*, no. 198.

56 It could be argued that, unlike criminal law, civil law always requires prejudice. While it is true that this is a difference between civil and criminal law, we shall nevertheless see, through the example of unfair competition, that this prejudice can sometimes only be potential, *infra*, no. 150; moreover, certain criminal offenses also require, as a constitutive element, the occurrence of damage, *see infra*, nos. 238–239.

counterpart of the action for *stellionate* in criminal law.[57] Since then, doctrine has struggled to find a satisfactory criterion for distinguishing between civil and criminal *dol*,[58] which raises doubts as to the relevance of such a distinction.

However, how is it that the civil judge can sanction certain instances of negligence, or even certain intentional behaviors, that the criminal judge leaves unpunished? Would this not be a sign of a difference in nature between the mental element apprehended by the civil judge and the one known to the criminal judge? Three explanations, showing that this objection does not call into question the conceptual unity of intention, can be advanced.

First, the criminal legislator does not incriminate all wrongful conduct, leaving it to civil law to fill in the gaps.[59] Second, even if the criminal legislator incriminates a behavior, the public prosecutor may choose not to pursue the offense committed, or the victim may strategically decide to bring their action only before the civil judge.

A third argument involves a detour via negligence. Many negligent acts remain outside the scope of criminal law.[60] This is due not to the different *nature* of civil and criminal negligence, but to a difference in their *degree* of seriousness. Roman law already distinguished between *culpa levis* (slight negligence) and *culpa levissima* (very slight negligence), and isolated the hypothesis of *casus* (accident).[61] While the latter could never give rise to any liability,[62] the first could be subject to either private or public action, and the second was the exclusive domain of civil law. This is still the case today. Conduct of lesser seriousness falls exclusively within the scope of civil liability; conduct of established seriousness is classified as a criminal offense and generally prosecuted by the public prosecutor; finally, conduct of intermediate seriousness is generally criminal in nature, but in practice is more often sanctioned under civil liability than by means of criminal proceedings.

---

57 Digest, 47, 10, 3. On stellionate, *see supra*, nos. 44–45.

58 Marcel Planiol thus considers that the dividing line between civil and criminal *dol* has never been clearly drawn. He criticizes authors for making artificial distinctions, such as defining criminal *dol* as requiring the use of "culpable maneuvers," whereas civil *dol* would be committed through "deception and artifices." *See* Planiol, *Dol civil et dol criminel*, *op. cit.* at 547 and 549.

59 Terré et al., Droit civil: Les obligations, *op. cit.* at 1078, no. 951.

60 Since the establishment of the duality of civil and criminal non-intentional faults. *See supra*, no. 143.

61 The *culpa lata* (serious fault), on the other hand, had a special fate, following the adage "*culpa lata dolo aequiparatur*" ("gross negligence is equivalent to *dol*"). On these three faults, *see* J.-A. Roux, obs. under Cass. crim., Oct. 21, 1926, Sirey 1927, pp. 33–35, at 34. These observations are of major interest: the author offers a remarkable critique of the unity of civil and penal fault, which was the order of the day at the time, drawing on the history of the distinction between civil and penal liability in the case of unintentional fault.

62 *Id.* The solution has remained identical, even in the case of so-called no-fault or strict liability – insofar as the invocation of an external fact beyond the defendant's control may enable them to escape liability, *see supra*, no. 146.

The difference between these types of fault lies in their degree of seriousness, on the one hand, and in the standard of behavior to which the judge compares the defendant, on the other. In the case of a slight fault, the judge assesses the fault by reference to diligent behavior; in the case of a very slight fault, by reference to highly diligent behavior – which will make it virtually impossible to rebut the presumption of fault. Thus, between *culpa levis* and *culpa levissima*, the object of proof is the same, the method of proof is the same, the variant being the degree of exigency in assessing fault.[63]

The affirmation of the conceptual unity of the notion of intent is particularly evident in the case of fraudulent conduct, such as unfair competition. Indeed, although neither doctrine nor jurisprudence recognizes the need for intent – unlike most foreign systems – this constitutes an anomaly, and a source of inconsistency.

B. A demonstration based on the example of unfair competition

149. **The doctrinal and jurisprudential rejection of intent in unfair competition law.** Unfair competition belongs to the category of profitable wrongdoings,[64] and is a deliberate form of behavior adopted by "cunning and unscrupulous" individuals.[65] Although it is punishable under tort law,[66] it nevertheless shares a common spirit with the law on anticompetitive practices,[67] both stemming from the same origins. Moreover, legal writers subscribe to the view that unfair competition and anticompetitive practices inspire a sense of mutual belonging – the demand for loyalty[68] on the part of market players being their common foundation.[69] Acts of unfair competition can also be referred to the French Competition Authority, which considers itself competent to classify them as anticompetitive practices if they result

63 Moreover, even in civil law, some authors recognize that there is more a difference in degree than in nature between these two types of assessment. *See* Terré et al., Droit civil: Les obligations, *op. cit.* at 1081, no. 957; *adde*, *contra*, an author according to whom *in concreto* analysis is the prerogative of criminal law while *in abstracto* analysis characterizes civil law, J. Verhaegen, *Faute pénale et faute civile*, 28 Archives de philosophie du droit 17, 20 (1983).

64 Sichel, La gravité de la faute en droit de la responsabilité civile, *op. cit.* at 181, no. 137.

65 B. Starck, H. Roland & L. Boyer, 1 Obligations: Responsabilité délictuelle 534 (5th ed. 1996), no. 1336.

66 Unlike Germany and Italy, which have adopted special laws and do not sanction unfair competition under general law. *See* H. C. Eugen Ulmer, i La répression de la concurrence déloyale dans les États membres de la Communauté économique européenne: Droit comparé avec des propositions pour le rapprochement des législations 8–12 (1967), nos. 9–17.

67 According to one author, unfair competition is also based on the idea "that there is no fault when economic advantage is derived from competition on the merits." W. Chaiehloudj, *La percée de la responsabilité civile dans le droit des pratiques anticoncurrentielles*, RTD civ. 21, 22 (Jan.-Mar. 2023).

68 The element of unfairness is also found in other countries: unfair competition in the UK, *unlautere Wettbewerb* in Germany, cf. P. Roubier, *Théorie générale de l'action en concurrence déloyale*, RTD com. 541, 560 (1948).

69 F. Picod, *Droit du marché et droit commun des obligations: Rapport introductif*, RTD com. 1 (1998); *adde*, in the same vein, Y. Picod & N. Dorandeu, *Concurrence déloyale*, Répertoire de droit commercial (Apr. 2022), nos. 32–33.

from an agreement or emanate from a company in a dominant position.[70] What is more, in the past, the Court of Cassation has accepted that damage caused by a cartel can be compensated on the basis of civil liability.[71] From this it can be deduced that the civil courts and the competition authorities are dealing, under different labels, with similar behavior – the only difference between unfair competition and anticompetitive practices being one of degree,[72] since the latter presuppose the possession of market power, and cause damage not only *inter partes*, but *erga omnes* – i.e., potentially harming all players in a market.[73]

In the same way that an anticompetitive practice committed through "negligence" offends common sense,[74] it is difficult to conceive that it is possible to compete unfairly with others without having formed the intention to do so. However, legal writers are unanimous in rejecting the need for intent.[75] For a long time, case law nevertheless required that the conduct in question be motivated by fraudulent intent.[76] This solution was maintained[77] until a terse reversal ruling in 1958. The Court of Cassation then affirmed that an act of unfair competition could constitute "a *quasi-delict* that does not require an intentional element."[78] At issue was a retailer's use of the name of a homonym in a way that created confusion between two establishments. In this case, the trial judges refused to hold the professional liable, as the plaintiff had not *provided proof* of facts establishing that the defendant had "intentionally created confusion

---

70 ADLC [French Competition Authority], decision no. 12-D-19 of Sept. 26, 2012, regarding practices in the teeth whitening and lightening sector (Fr.). At issue in this case was a disparagement practice. On this decision, *see* D. Bosco, *Quarante millions d'euros pour un dénigrement abusif de médicaments génériques*, CONTRATS CONCURRENCE CONSOMMATION (July 2013), comm. 161.

71 Cass. com., Mar. 1, 1982, no. 80-15.834 (Fr.).

72 Moreover, this difference in degree is likely to diminish. In the recent decision of the Paris Court of Appeal in the *UberPop* case, the judges considered that the litigious practices "had the consequence of *disrupting the market.*" *See* Cour d'appel [CA] [regional court of appeal] Paris, Oct. 4, 2023, 21/22383, *UberPop* (Fr.) (emphasis added). The Court of Cassation's ruling is eagerly awaited, and will be most interesting in this respect.

73 On the distinction between *dol inter partes* and *dol erga omnes*, *see infra*, no. 404.

74 *See infra*, nos. 384 *et seq.*

75 *Ex multis*, Roubier, *Théorie générale de l'action en concurrence déloyale*, *op. cit.* at 565–66; A. Pirovano, *La concurrence déloyale en droit français*, 26 REVUE INTERNATIONALE DE DROIT COMPARÉ 467, 491 (1974); Picod & Dorandeu, *Concurrence déloyale*, *op. cit.* nos. 94–98; Y. Picod, *Concurrence déloyale et parasitisme: L'indifférence de la nature intentionnelle de la faute*, CONCURRENCES no. 1-2016, art. no. 77744, 1; D. Legeais, *Concurrence déloyale et parasitaire*, JURISCLASSEUR COMMERCIAL (Aug. 2021), fasc. 254, no. 51: "The fault to be taken into consideration may be intentional or unintentional. Proof of bad faith or intent to harm is therefore not required"; C. Tilloy, *Concurrence déloyale*, JURISCLASSEUR PROCÉDURES (Jan. 2021), fasc. 10, no. 52: "*Indifférence de l'élément intentionnel.*"

76 Pirovano, *La concurrence déloyale en droit français*, *op. cit.* at 490–91, and cases cited.

77 A breach was nevertheless created by the distinction drawn by certain courts, beginning in the early 1950s, between competition carried out in bad faith (considered unfair) and competition that is simply wrongful (considered unlawful). This distinction has been criticized on the grounds that, since the action for unfair competition is based on articles 1240 and 1241 of the French Civil Code (formerly articles 1382 and 1383), the requirement of intent is superfluous, since any negligence is sufficient to incur liability. *See* Pirovano, *La concurrence déloyale en droit français*, *op. cit.* at 468; *Adde*, Roubier, *Théorie générale de l'action en concurrence déloyale*, *op. cit.* at 546–50.

78 Cass. com., Apr. 18, 1958, no. 58-04.997 (Fr.) (emphasis added).

with the aim of taking advantage of his reputation and credibility."[79] Numerous subsequent rulings have reiterated this solution, using the same formula[80] almost word for word. It should be noted, however, that these rulings are virtually all decisions of cassation, indicating that trial judges are resisting the Court of Cassation's solution and continue to require intentional fault.[81] In Germany, on the other hand, "case law is based on the principle" that an action for unfair competition "presupposes that the act was performed with knowledge of the circumstances that constitute its unfair character"[82] – and has always maintained the requirement of intent.

150. **Paradoxes and inconsistencies relating to intent in unfair competition law.** As is the case whenever intent is mentioned, the notion polarizes the doctrine: unfair competition law has not escaped the phenomenon.[83] However, authors have unanimously decided to adopt a very narrow definition – intent to harm or bad faith.[84] On the one hand, such a concept is far too restrictive, and on the other, it leads to confusion between intent and motives.[85] While the existence of an intention to harm[86] may certainly lead the judge to increase the amount of damages and interest,[87] it is clear that this is not a criterion for qualifying unfair competition. Moreover, the confusion between intent and intention to harm leads to the same positions as those adopted in the law on anticompetitive practices.[88] Intent would be a moralizing concept, unsuited to the needs of economic life; it would give rise to circular and contradictory reasoning: it would be impossible to distinguish good from bad intention, since "competition, by its very nature, entails harm!"[89]

---

79 *Id.*

80 "The action for unfair competition finds its basis in the provisions of articles 1382 and 1383 of the Civil Code, and the quasi-delict provided for in these articles does not require an intentional element" or, more succinctly: "Unfair competition only presupposes a fault within the meaning of articles 1382 and 1383 of the Civil Code." *See* Picod & Dorandeu, *Concurrence déloyale*, *op. cit.* no. 95 and case law cited.

81 *Id.* The authors are astonished by this "reservation" and explain it by "the concern not to restrict too much the freedom of competition."

82 H. C. Eugen Ulmer, i La répression de la concurrence déloyale dans les États membres de la Communauté économique européenne: Droit comparé avec des propositions pour le rapprochement des législations 41 (1967), no. 65.

83 Pirovano, *La concurrence déloyale en droit français*, *op. cit.* at 486.

84 *See* references cited *supra*, no. 149.

85 *See supra*, no. 148.

86 For a definition of, and distinction between, intent and intention to harm (intention to cause *ad hominem* damage), and an explanation of why the latter is systematically sanctioned under the law of delict, *see* P. Stoffel-Munck, L'abus dans le contrat: Essai d'une théorie 47–58 (2000), nos. 37–52.

87 As is generally the case in tort law, *see supra*, no. 147.

88 On the confusion between motive and intent in anticompetitive practices law, and the need for a distinction, *see infra*, nos. 265–267

89 Pirovano, *La concurrence déloyale en droit français*, *op. cit.* at 487. This assertion is widespread in the doctrine relating to anticompetitive practices. However, in this field, harm only exists in the presence of disloyalty, which cannot be imagined to be unintentional. Moreover, while there may be *damage* (e.g., loss of clientele) without disloyalty, linked to the normal course of business, in this case there will be no

However, by defining intentional fault as the *will* to achieve a *result* and, more precisely, the fault required in matters of unfair competition as "the will to obtain undue gain by recourse to unlawful means,"[90] it then becomes possible to highlight a doctrinal paradox, as well as a jurisprudential inconsistency.

On the doctrinal side, we should mention the seminal study by Paul Roubier, who theorized the various categories of unfair competition in an article published in 1948 – which continue to be presented today according to his classification. He writes that the term "unfairness" is ambiguous, as it implies asking the following question: "Must there be *unfair intent*? Or is it sufficient for the defendant to have resorted to *means that are unfair* in themselves, quite apart from the intention of the person who used them?"[91] After stating that intent is not required, as only the use of "unfair means" is relevant, the author proceeds to outline the various types of sanctionable conduct. Although highly diverse, they all share one feature: without exception, they are described using a term rooted in intentionality – namely, that of "maneuver". For example, "confusion maneuvers," "denigration maneuvers," "internal disorganization of a rival company maneuvers," "general market disorganization maneuvers."[92] That a maneuver can be unintentional is surprising; that a person who resorts to unfair means has no unfair intention, surprising. This reasoning is based on an overly restrictive definition of intent, and stems from confusion between the *nature* of unfair competition and the methods of *proof*.[93]

Jurisprudence is no more at ease when it comes to tackling the question of intent. It chooses to take refuge in incoherence rather than question its categorical rejection of intent, as illustrated by its hardly tenable position

---

reparable *harm*. *See*, for example, P. Le Tourneau, *Les métamorphoses contemporaines et subreptices de la faute subjective*, *in* Les métamorphoses de la responsabilité, Sixièmes journées René Savatier 19, 27–28 (1997): "The legal criterion of unfair competition is disloyalty, not customer poaching. The latter may be a consequence, but it is not necessary." In this respect, it should be noted that judges find it extremely difficult to quantify the damage resulting from an act of unfair competition (loss of a potential market, of clientele, decline in revenue), since such a result is very difficult to isolate from other factors linked to the vagaries of the market. This makes it difficult for judges to distinguish between losses resulting from normal competition and those attributable to unfair conduct. Moreover, jurisprudence sometimes dispenses with the requirement of proven prejudice, contenting itself with characterizing a merely possible prejudice – in which case the fault counts for more than the result. Breaking with an established principle of tort law – the need for certainty of prejudice – judges are moving closer to the solutions adopted by competition authorities. *See* Sichel, La gravité de la faute en droit de la responsabilité civile, *op. cit.* at 181–83, nos. 137–138. Lastly, it should be noted that the same difficulties associated with the judicial assessment of damages are encountered when a victim seeks to obtain compensation for damage caused by anticompetitive behavior. For a recent example, *see* Cass. com., Mar. 1, 2023, no. 20-18.356 (Fr.), comm. D. Bosco, *Le préjudice de développement et le préjudice financier devant la Cour de cassation*, Contrats concurrence consommation (May 2023), comm. 85.

90 For a justification of this definition, *see* the attachment of unfair competition to the category of "offenses of means," *infra*, no. 245.

91 Roubier, *Théorie générale de l'action en concurrence déloyale*, *op. cit.* at 560 (emphasis added).

92 *Id.* at 565–66.

93 *See infra*, no. 151. This theme will be explored in greater depth in criminal law, *infra*, no. 156.

on parasitism. While there is no doubt that parasitism falls within the broader category of unfair competition, the particular treatment it receives nonetheless sets it apart from its kin. While the Court of Cassation recognizes that unfair competition can constitute a quasi-delict, thereby allowing recourse to article 1241 of the Civil Code, it only ever accepts article 1240 as a basis for parasitism.[94] It commonly defines parasitism as "the will to position oneself in the wake of another party," and even goes so far as to explicitly require intentional fault, noting the absence of "*malicious* slavish copying"[95] in order to refuse to hold the respondent liable. Parasitism stands alone within the realm of unfair competition as the only instance where intentional fault is required.[96] This specificity can be explained by the nature of parasitism, which implies a will to follow in the wake of a third party.[97] However, according to Paul Roubier's reasoning, parasitism does not require intent any more than other forms of unfair competition: the *mere fact* of placing oneself in the wake of a third party should suffice. The justification put forward therefore does not stand up to scrutiny, and one wonders why the Court of Cassation treats cases of the same nature differently, when it would be more consistent to invoke, for all hypotheses of unfair competition, only the basis of the tort, to the exclusion of the quasi-delict.

What is more, the reason given for extending unfair competition to cases of negligence is not the most convincing. The doctrinal explanations put forward, and the economic vocabulary used, are also to be found in the law of anticompetitive practices: "[A]ccepting the application of the theory of unfair competition, not only when there is intent to harm, but also in cases of mere negligence or recklessness, contributes to increasing the penetration rate of unfair competition in the market."[98] The adoption of a purely "objective" approach would therefore make it possible "to achieve healthy and effective competition."[99] This position once again demonstrates that there is confusion between the nature of unfair competition and its methods of proof. Indeed, effective enforcement cannot be achieved by distorting the notion of unfair conduct, which loses all meaning if we accept that it may stem from negligence.

---

94 C. Guettier al., Droit de la responsabilité et des contrats 2021/2022, 924 (2020), no. 2215.07.

95 Cass. com., Jan. 15, 2002, no. 99-21.547 (Fr.) (emphasis added).

96 In this sense, *see* J.-J. Frion, L'agissement parasitaire 94–96 (2001) (Ph.D. dissertation, Nantes), nos. 90–92.

97 Guettier et al., Droit de la responsabilité et des contrats 2021/2022, *op. cit.* at 924, no. 2215.07. *Adde*, M. Malaurie-Vignal, *La Cour de cassation distingue l'action en concurrence déloyale et l'action en concurrence parasitaire*, Contrats concurrence consommation (June 2014), comm. 127. For a critique of the requirement of intentional fault in parasitism, *see* Picod, *Concurrence déloyale et parasitisme: L'indifférence de la nature intentionnelle de la faute*, *op. cit.* at 3.

98 Y. Picod & N. Dorandeu, *Concurrence déloyale*, Répertoire de droit commercial (Apr. 2022), no. 95.

99 *Id.*, no. 85.

151. **On the confusion between the nature of unfair competition and its methods of proof, and the need to distinguish between them.** Let's leave it to Paul Roubier one last time:

> We are therefore in a position to assert that what jurisprudence pursues under the name of unfair competition is a set of means that are deemed unfair in business relationships. Unfair intent will undoubtedly be the most frequent case, but its demonstration is not necessary: what is ultimately targeted is confusion, denigration, etc., rather than the intention to confuse or denigrate. ...[T]he element of unfairness does not necessarily consist in unfair intent; it exists from the moment when there has been use of means deemed unfair.[100]

The example chosen by the author is that of confusion,[101] and we must recognize with him that it is possible not to "deliberately" create confusion between one's own products and those of a third party. Conversely, the hypothesis that denigration or disorganization is not accompanied by unfair intent seems to be fairly rare, not to say a textbook case.[102] These random statistics on the psychology of entrepreneurs, although undoubtedly accurate, cannot reasonably justify a conceptual divergence between different types of unfair competition, consisting in maintaining that it can sometimes be tortious, sometimes quasi-delictual, depending on the circumstances of the case. The law seeks simplicity and coherence: for the same theory, it is advisable to adopt unitary reasoning, and to group identical cases under a single umbrella in order to treat them in the same way. However, taking the point of view of the individual, and asking what they intended to do, not only runs counter to the distinction between the internal forum and the external forum drawn by theologians,[103] but also leads to the slippery slope of unnecessary distinctions.[104]

The logical impasse in case law and doctrine stems from confusion between the nature of unfair competition, which is essentially intentional, and its proof. Intent is *always* inferred from conduct and the surrounding circumstances. When an individual engages in unfair behavior, they must be presumed to have had corresponding unfair intent, until proven otherwise. What is more, when the individual in question

---

100 Roubier, *Théorie générale de l'action en concurrence déloyale*, *op. cit.* at 563.

101 "When it comes to cases where criticized competition manifests through facts that lead to confusion between establishments or their products, more often than not, this confusion is unintentional." *Id.* at 562.

102 *Id.*

103 Indeed, theologians have affirmed that, unlike the confessor who judges *loco Dei*, the judge never search hearts and minds, but is content simply to presume intentions from behavior, *see supra*, no. 53.

104 We shall see that, in criminal law, the adoption of a viewpoint centered on the agent and not on the nature of the offenses, which is very common in doctrine, similarly leads to errors of reasoning and superfluous distinctions, *infra*, no. 193.

is a professional, the presumptions resorted to by the judge carry a normative character:[105] they do not merely describe what *is*, but take as their starting point what the professional *should have done*. While we are critical of the use of article 1241 as a basis for punishing unfair competition, we nevertheless endorse the solutions adopted in case law. For example, in a case of poaching,[106] the lower courts refused to find unfair competition, as there was no evidence in the case file to show that the company had "knowingly" poached the employees of another company. The Court of Cassation, in line with its position, overturned the decision on the grounds that the required fault "does not require the establishment of intentional behavior."[107] However, since it is incumbent upon professionals not to poach, they are obliged not to do so; and if they nevertheless engage in these practices, it is established case law that they cannot plead good faith to escape the penalty.[108] Moreover, this is the solution adopted in corporate criminal law (droit penal des affaires), where negligence presumes intent.[109] Thus, in the case of denigrating behavior,[110] the defendant company argued that its letter was not intended to denigrate others. Once again, the trial judges accepted this argument, but the Court of Cassation overturned the decision. The excuse of good faith cannot be accepted, for the same reasons as above, but also because it is far more likely that the company in question had the intention to denigrate, so that it would be inappropriate to accept such a defense solely on the basis of the defendant's statements.[111] Indeed, to rebut a presumption, evidence to the contrary must be produced with sufficient probative force. Asserting that one is acting in good faith is tantamount to creating one's own proof, which is rarely convincing to judges.

Sanctions for unfair competition should therefore be based on a single legal foundation – article 1240 of the Civil Code – and decisions would benefit from a clearer and more unified set of reasons, admitting, for all cases of unfair competition: firstly, the need for intent as defined above; secondly, the use of presumptions of intent inspired by criminal case law on business offenses.

---

105 We will develop this assertion with regard to business offenses, *infra*, no. 156.

106 Cass. com., Mar. 11, 2003, no. 01-02.310 (Fr.).

107 *Id.* For another example, *see* Cass. com., Jan. 27, 1982, no. 80-14.175 (Fr.). In this case, an employer had refrained from verifying the sales representatives he had hired had informed their former employer of their acceptance of the new card.

108 Cf. the comments made *infra* in criminal law, nos. 156–157.

109 For an illustration based on the offense of deception, *see infra*, no. 157.

110 Cass. com., May 12, 2004, no. 02-19.199 (Fr.).

111 *See also* Cass. com., Oct. 17, 1984, no. 82-16.666 (Fr.). In matters of disorganization, if the actions have led to disorganization, additional proof that they were motivated by a desire to disorganize is not required. This can be explained by the fact that the most likely explanation is that they were intended to disorganize the business of others, and also by the irrelevance of motive.

Proof of intent in business criminal law is, to some extent, independent of general criminal law. This distinction reduces the burden of proof on the public prosecutor, allowing intent to be more easily presumed from negligent conduct, thereby ensuring greater enforcement effectiveness.

II. Techniques for proving intent

152. **The paradox of intent in business criminal law: pervasive in theory, yet seemingly subtle in practice.** Business criminal law illustrates the various techniques employed by the law to prove the mental element of offenses, which appear identically in the law of anticompetitive practices.

The function of business criminal law is to "protect us against the fraud of others."[112] The expression is eloquent. The flagship offenses of business crime[113] are composed of cunning, guile, and wit, of schemes long prepared and carefully thought through.[114] It is undeniable that business criminal law, by its very nature, generally punishes offenses of an intentional nature. However, it is marked, more so than general criminal law,[115] by a very strong sense of *objectivity*. In practice, intent seems almost absent. Judges do not seem to pay much attention to it, preferring to focus on the material elements of the offense rather than on the supposedly difficult mental element. Does this mean that intent plays no part in the matter? We must not fall into the trap of thinking so. Although very discreet, intent is omnipresent – hidden in the shadows of presumptions that only serve to bring it to light. So, while there is no autonomy in the definition of intent in business criminal law vis-à-vis general criminal law, there is a certain autonomy with regard to its proof.[116] Indeed, judges are often satisfied with simple negligence

112 M. Delmas-Marty, 1 Droit pénal des affaires 3 (3rd ed. 1990).

113 By "flagship offenses," we mean the classic offenses of business criminal law, which are historically (*see supra*, no. 75) derived from theft: fraudulent bankruptcy, swindling, misappropriation of corporate assets, breach of trust.

114 P.-A. Pageaud, *La notion d'intention en droit pénal*, JCP G 35, 36 (1950), i, doctr. 876: the "so-called 'clever' offenses require the elaboration of an intelligent, often very clever plan" – they are the archetype of intentional behavior.

115 B. Mercadal, *Recherches sur l'intention en droit pénal*, Revue de science criminelle et de droit pénal comparé 1, 28–32 (Jan.–Mar. 1967): the author considers that jurisprudence maintains a "pure" conception of intention in matters of assassination, murder, intentional bodily harm, arson – in short, in all offenses characterized by the intention to cause bodily and material harm. This is reminiscent of the distinction drawn by Boris Starck between Aquilian and non-Aquilian damages: the former being precisely bodily and material injuries, the latter economic or moral damages whose "licit or illicit character only becomes apparent after examination of the defendant's rights, the latter being able in certain cases to invoke a legitimate right to cause harm." *See* B. Starck, Essai d'une théorie générale de la responsabilité civile considérée en sa double fonction de garantie et de peine privée 47–48 (1947).

116 A further difference should be mentioned: business criminal law also has its own imputation techniques, based on case law, which can lead the judge to impute to the decision-maker an act committed by one of their employees – in other words, an act that they did not actually commit personally. This hypothesis will be examined *infra*, no. 166.

to prove intent[117] (**A**), as illustrated by the example of the offense of deception (**B**).

153. **The accepted definition of business criminal law.** Defining business criminal law would prove to be a chimerical undertaking,[118] as its scope would be an artificial construction based on poorly identified criteria.[119] Since the aim here is to study the particularities of proving the mental element of business offenses, business criminal law will be understood in a sense defined by reference to its subject: an offense falls within this category whenever the accused is a *professional* – whether a natural or legal person – acting in the course of their activities.[120]

A. The objective qualification of intent in the presence of a professional

154. **The strange idea of "no-fault criminal liability": a brief history of the concept of "material offenses" (19th century–1992).** In much the same way, and for much the same reasons, as in tort law,[121] criminal law had to contend with attacks on its oldest foundation: culpability. While we have refused to admit that extra-contractual liability can be detached from fault,[122] it goes without saying that, *a fortiori*, we could not conceive of a criminal law without it. However, from the nineteenth century onwards, in France and abroad,[123] doctrine, encouraged by bold jurisprudence, systematized the notion of "material offense" – defined as that exposes its author to criminal punishment independently of the search for fault.[124] These offenses, whose preferred field of application was business criminal

---

117 A similar solution can be found in the case of complicity in the commission of a crime against humanity (art. 213-4-1 of the Penal Code). According to Philippe Conte, the wording of the text, which provides for an alternative between the accomplice "who knew or, because of the circumstances, should have known," seems to enshrine a "complicity that can be committed intentionally but also through imprudence." The author then rightly observes that "this text, in fact, blends substantive and evidentiary rules," and proposes, "to bring it back into the fold of classic complicity…, to consider that the first branch of the alternative ('who knew') lays down a substantive rule and the second a rule of evidence." *See* P. Conte, *Quelques observations sur la distinction des règles substantielles et des règles de preuve en droit pénal*, *in* Mélanges en l'honneur de Philippe Théry: Les coutures du droit 195, 197–98 (2022). This is the same distinction we draw between the object of proof and the methods used to establish it.

118 The formula is that of Frédéric Stasiak: "Business criminal law is a chimera." F. Stasiak, Droit pénal des affaires 1 (2nd ed. 2009).

119 A. Lepage, P. Maistre du Chambon & R. Salomon, Droit pénal des affaires 3 (6th ed. 2020); in the same vein: Delmas-Marty, 1 Droit pénal des affaires, *op. cit.* at 4–9.

120 For a thesis on the subject, which uses the respondent's status as a professional to define the field of business criminal law, *see* N. Goldenberg, L'élément moral en droit pénal des affaires 6 (1995) (Ph.D. dissertation, Université Paris I Panthéon-Sorbonne).

121 *See supra*, no. 144.

122 *See supra*, no. 145.

123 The phenomenon is not unique to France: "no-fault" criminal offenses, or even strict liability offenses, have similarly developed abroad. In this respect, *see* J. Pradel, Droit pénal comparé 124–27 (4th ed. 2016), no. 81. For a study of the phenomenon in American law, *see* D. K. Brown, *Criminal Law's Unfortunate Triumph over Administrative Law*, 7 Journal of Law, Economics & Policy 657, 671–72 (2011).

124 J.-P. Marty, *Les délits matériels*, Revue de science criminelle et de droit pénal comparé 41, 41 (1982).

law,[125] paradoxically included certain offenses whose intentional nature was not in doubt.[126] To justify the existence of such offenses, the Court of Cassation was stingy with detail, most often content to assert, without any reasoning, that this or that offense constituted a material offense.[127] In reality, the aim was to bring certain offenses into line with the system of *contraventions*.[128] The criterion for designating material offenses, put forward by Ortolan and subsequently adopted by most authors, was that of the "police objective" guiding their repression.[129] Material offenses would thus be those whose function is to ensure collective discipline,[130] and which did not involve the transgression of a moral rule.[131]

The inflation of technical criminal legislation, combined with the perseverance of the Court of Cassation, divided the doctrine. On the one hand, some suggested that the principle of criminal culpability should no longer be treated as an intangible dogma and invited acceptance that intent should only be required for offenses "involving a positive and characterized attack on the social order."[132] On the other hand, the majority of doctrine was very hostile to the very notion of material offenses, and critical of the exclusion of all psychological elements.[133] This trend towards objectification nonetheless caused such a disturbance in criminal theory

---

125 In this regard, *see* P. Conte, *La dépénalisation: Réalité ou mirage? L'exemple de l'élément moral des infractions d'affaires*, *in* PEINES, DANGEROSITÉ, QUELLES CERTITUDES? 23, 27 (2010).

126 Such as deceit, counterfeiting, breach of trust, defamation, or receiving stolen property. For a detailed study of these examples: B. Mercadal, *Recherches sur l'intention en droit pénal*, REVUE DE SCIENCE CRIMINELLE ET DE DROIT PÉNAL COMPARÉ 1, 24–28 (Jan.–Mar. 1967). The author thus considers that in certain cases, despite the intentional nature of the offenses, jurisprudence "reduces the scope of intent to zero." *Id.* at 24.

127 *Id.* at 42. In the same vein, *see* A. Legal, *La responsabilité sans faute*, *in* LA CHAMBRE CRIMINELLE ET SA JURISPRUDENCE: RECUEIL D'ÉTUDES EN HOMMAGE À LA MÉMOIRE DE MAURICE PATIN 130, 132–33 (1965).

128 It should be noted at this point that we reject the idea according to which *contraventions* do not require a mental element, as some of them are even intentional in the strict sense, *see infra* no. 194.

129 M. ORTOLAN, I ÉLÉMENTS DE DROIT PÉNAL 251–55 (3rd ed. 1863), nos. 609–615.

130 Is this not also, *inter alia*, the aim of criminal law as a whole?

131 In this sense: R. GARRAUD, I TRAITÉ THÉORIQUE ET PRATIQUE DU DROIT PÉNAL FRANÇAIS 233–34 (3rd ed. 1913), nos. 108–109.

132 *Ex multis*: Legal, *La responsabilité sans faute*, *op. cit.* at 152: "It is to be expected that offenses of this kind can only increase in number at a time when social and economic interventionism tends to encircle individual activity within an increasingly complex network of legal and administrative prescriptions. In this way, the principle that there can be no liability without fault, understood in the traditional sense, will by necessity find itself pushed back into the realm of offenses involving a positive and characterized attack on the social order, where it retains its full value. But to pretend to treat it as an intangible dogma is to risk losing everything by trying to win"; E. Wagner, La notion d'intention pénale dans la doctrine classique et la jurisprudence contemporaine 377 (1976) (Ph.D. dissertation, Université de Clermont-Ferrand): "We continue to repeat the same theoretical and historically outdated scheme. We continue to ... base punishment on the idea of personal fault, whereas in reality liability is based on a committed act, and punishment is explained by sectoral and preventive policies. ...The reluctance to admit the idea of no-fault liability stems from the same rigid attachment to a philosophy whose meaning we refuse even to reconsider." In 1981, Henri Batiffol rightly remarked that "it is truly surprising that great minds have claimed to proscribe the search for intent," since "the fundamental principle of criminal law is the search for intent," cf. H. Batiffol, *Observations sur la preuve des faits*, *in* LA PREUVE EN DROIT 303, 310 (C. Perelman & P. Foriers eds., 1981).

133 *Ex multis*: A. Chavanne, *Le problème des délits involontaires*, REVUE DE SCIENCE CRIMINELLE ET DE DROIT PÉNAL COMPARÉ 241, 247 (1962): "I fear that the application in our field of a theory of risk, of an objectification of liability, leads us into the presence of the same difficulties as the theory of risk in matters of civil liability, and ultimately leads to a quite analogous impasse"; Marty, *Les délits matériels*, *op. cit.* at 45, and references

that it gave rise to enduring errors of reasoning, which have persisted right up to contemporary theories of intent.[134]

Nevertheless, the adoption of the 1994 Penal Code has, in part, reestablished the order of things: article 121-3 now states that, unless otherwise specified by law, crimes and offenses are intentional.[135] However, for most of the former material offenses, the legislator has not departed from the requirement of intent[136] – which inevitably raises the question of what fate the criminal judge has in store for them. Without sparing any suspense, let's say from the outset that the solutions have remained more or less the same. Indeed, the Court of Cassation has remained faithful to its previous line of jurisprudence, through the use of presumptions of intent.[137] The technique of presumption has thus made it possible to preserve the theoretical coherence of business offenses by recognizing their intentional nature, while maintaining the repressive effectiveness that had served to justify the theory of material offenses.

155. **The distinction between two types of business offense: intentional in the strict sense and intentional in the broad sense.** Certain business offenses, most of which correspond to offenses arising from so-called technical legislation,[138] require only *intentional* fault *in the broad sense*[139] in order to be characterized. They have the characteristic of not requiring

---

cited; R. Legros, *L'influence des lois particulières sur le droit pénal général*, Revue de science criminelle et de droit pénal comparé 233, 239–40 (1968); strongly criticizing Alfred Legal's doctrine, the author writes that it is advisable "on the one hand, to consider new offenses with their underlying moral foundation, and, on the other hand, to rebel against any idea of automatic, material, no-fault liability."

134 The consequences of this disruption will be studied *infra*, nos. 179 *et seq.*

135 We will, however, discuss the limits of the principled wording contained in article 121-3 of the Penal Code *infra*, no. 194.

136 Conte, *La dépénalisation: Réalité ou mirage? L'exemple de l'élément moral des infractions d'affaires*, *op. cit.* at 28; *adde*, in the same vein, M. Pralus, *Réflexions autour de l'élément moral des délits*, Droit pénal (Dec. 2002), chron. 41.

137 Conte, *La dépénalisation: Réalité ou mirage? L'exemple de l'élément moral des infractions d'affaires*, *op. cit.* at 28. The author considers that the Court of Cassation has thus "reduced to nothing the condition relating to the mental element" of these former material offenses. *Adde*, in the same vein: B. Bouloc, *Nécessité de l'intention en droit pénal*, Revue de science criminelle et de droit pénal comparé 847 (1996); J. Pradel, *La responsabilité pénale en droit français depuis le Code pénal de 1994: Permanence ou changements?*, *in* Les métamorphoses de la responsabilité, Sixièmes journées René Savatier 155, 167–68 (1997): "And so almost nothing has changed with the new code, since to obtain a conviction, the process of intentional qualification of the offense is almost as effective as that of material qualification. Today and tomorrow, as in the past, defendants accused of an offense formerly known as a material offense will therefore be quite easily punishable, with only the basis for punishment having changed."

138 Here are a few examples: inciting a minor to excessive alcohol consumption (art. 227-19 of the French Penal Code); having a borrower or buyer subscribe to, accept, or endorse bills of exchange or promissory notes (art. L. 341-14 of the French Consumer Code); direct or indirect propaganda or advertising in favor of tobacco (art. L. 3511-3 of the French Public Health Code); abandoning, depositing, or causing waste to be deposited in a manner contrary to environmental law (art. L. 541-46 of the French Environmental Code). More generally, we may include most offenses relating to customs and indirect taxation, as well as violations of labor law and transportation regulations. Lastly, it should be noted that all of these offenses are punishable by criminal penalties, and that some of them may result in imprisonment – demonstrating that the requirement of intent is not linked to the seriousness of the penalty incurred. *See* in this respect, *infra*, no. 194.

139 As a reminder (the distinction has already been set out in relation to tortious liability, *supra*, no. 148): intention in the broad sense refers to the will to behave, to the exclusion of the will to achieve the result. For further details, *see infra*, no. 233.

a result that can be separated from the sanctioned conduct:[140] the judge must therefore only characterize the will to adopt the offending conduct. This is the case for the offense of holding fraudulent weights or measuring instruments,[141] which, because it only targets conduct (possession), is punished independently of any result.[142] In practice, this category of offense is marked by a high degree of objectivity: the offense is presumed to have been committed intentionally as soon as the offending behavior is adopted[143] – the only way for the accused to escape punishment being to invoke a ground of justification or a cause of non-imputability.[144] In the case of these offenses, the question of intent is rarely mentioned in decisions[145] – which is explained by the fact that, in such cases, the mental element merges with a material element[146] described very precisely by the incriminating text.[147] It follows that the characterization of culpable intent most often results *automatically*[148] from a simple material finding.

Conversely, the most "classic" business offenses, namely, those that are closely or remotely related to theft in that they all involve the use of *unlawful means to obtain undue gain*:[149] receiving stolen property, breach of trust, misuse of corporate assets, blackmail, money laundering, corruption, bankruptcy, forgery, tax fraud, swindling, obstruction, counterfeiting, deception, market abuse and anticompetitive practices are all *intentional in the strict sense*,[150] and differ in many respects from the above.[151] Indeed, they involve, on the one hand, a result separable from

---

140 In this regard, M. Puech, Droit pénal général 195 (1988), no. 539.

141 Art. L. 413-2 of the French Consumer Code, punishable by up to two years' imprisonment and a fine of up to 300,000 euros (arts. L. 451-3 and L. 451-4 of the French Consumer Code).

142 For further details on the notion of criminal outcome, *see infra*, no. 189.

143 *See infra*, no. 237.

144 On this subject, *see infra*, nos. 217–219.

145 The judge sometimes simply notes that the respondent has violated the norms prescribed by law "with full knowledge of the facts." *See infra* no. 196.

146 R. Maman, Contribution à l'étude de l'élément intentionnel en droit pénal des affaires 343 (2007) (Ph.D. dissertation, Université de Toulouse) no. 500.

147 This indicates that the material element is itself confused with the legal element. Intent is then lost in a "hypertrophied legal element." In this sense, *see* Maman, Contribution à l'étude de l'élément intentionnel en droit pénal des affaires, *op. cit.* at 27, no. 32. *Adde*, for a distinction between objective and subjective drafting of incriminating texts, illustrated by examples, *see* Goldenberg, L'élément moral en droit pénal des affaires, *op. cit.* at 20–25.

148 According to one author, business criminal law is characterized by the almost automatic triggering of the professional's criminal liability: W. Jeandidier, *L'élément matériel des infractions d'affaires ou la prédilection pour l'inconsistance*, *in* Mélanges offerts à Raymond Gassin: Sciences pénales & sciences criminologiques 245, 245 (2007).

149 *See infra*, no. 245.

150 Intention in the strict sense is understood as the will to perform the conduct *and* to achieve a certain result. *See infra*, no. 243.

151 These will be clarified and systematized *infra*, nos. 243–254.

the conduct;[152] on the other, they require the characterization of a fraudulent means – in other words, they comprise an abstract notion with indeterminate content.[153] In theory, such offenses should entail a greater degree of subjectivity than intentional offenses in the broad sense. Yet in business criminal law, the reasoning underlying the characterization of intentional offenses in the strict sense is, in practice, marked by inconsistency – ranging from "the most abstract routine automatism"[154] to highly developed argumentation when the accused contests the existence of the mental element.

This phenomenon gives the impression that criminal responsibility is objective, whereas it is merely objectified.[155] Intent, though seemingly a constant theoretical concern, is in practice treated *implicitly*[156] – creating the impression that its very existence is in doubt.[157] Yet this apparent objectivity stems from the use of presumptions of intent, which merit closer examination. It is particularly important to understand how business criminal law qualifies the mental element of so-called offenses of means,[158] since cartels and abuses of dominant position fall within this same category.[159]

156. **Proof of intentional business offenses in the strict sense: negligence presumes intent.** Once again, let's distinguish between two hypotheses: one where intent (understood in the strict sense) to commit the offense seems obvious, and one where it is only probable.

Where the conduct in question clearly demonstrates the existence of a fraudulent strategy, it is sufficient to infer the existence of intent from the description of the defendant's conduct.[160] In other words, if the conduct at issue falls within the category of fraudulent means, according to established case law, intent will automatically be inferred from the latter.[161] This procedure is not unique to business offenses. As intent is a psychological

---

152 Result achieved or virtually achievable in the hypothesis of repression of the attempt, *see infra*, no. 272.

153 On concepts with indeterminate content, *see infra*, nos. 410–412.

154 W. Jeandidier, Droit pénal des affaires 220 (1991).

155 Goldenberg, L'élément moral en droit pénal des affaires, *op. cit.* at 67–68.

156 We shall see that the same applies to anti-competitive practices law, *infra*, nos. 260 *et seq*.

157 Maman, Contribution à l'étude de l'élément intentionnel en droit pénal des affaires, *op. cit.* at 11, no. 4.

158 On this category of offense, *see infra*, nos. 244–245.

159 *See infra*, nos. 271–275.

160 In this case, "as soon as the material element is demonstrated, the offense exists *ipso facto*. Sometimes, moreover, the Court of Cassation indicates that the mental element is deduced from the factual circumstances, for if the procedure used is complex, it is hard to see how it could not have been developed by a conscious person who intended it." B. Bouloc, *Présomption d'innocence et droit pénal des affaires*, Revue de science criminelle et de droit pénal comparé, 465, 467 (July–Sept. 1995). The author then cites the examples of counterfeiting and defamation.

161 For an illustration in the area of swindling, *see infra*, no. 198.

fact, it can never be *proven*, but only *presumed* based on tangible material elements – be they behavior or circumstances.[162]

If, on the other hand, intent does not appear to be fully established based on external evidence, but is merely *probable*, business criminal law presents an important particularity compared to general criminal law. In such cases, and as a matter of course,[163] *the judge presumes culpable intent based on negligence* – to the point of elevating this evidentiary mechanism into a substantive rule.[164] This solution is not unique to French law: it is also found in other countries, notably Germany.[165] Its justification lies in the *professional status* of the accused. As specialists in a given branch of activity, they are deemed to be familiar with the laws, regulations and rules of the art pertaining to it – and supposed to respect them.[166] In cases of breach of trust, bankruptcy, receiving stolen property, fraud,[167] or counterfeiting, it is common for judges to treat negligence as sufficient to characterize intent.[168] For example, an importer accused of counterfeiting the "Bic" trademark defended himself on the grounds of negligence. The trial judges did indeed find that no checks had been carried out when the goods were delivered from Hong Kong – which supported the theory that the importer was unaware that the products were counterfeit – but, dashing the accused's hopes, they seized upon this shortcoming to presume his culpable intent. Their reasoning was upheld by the Court of Cassation.[169] This case calls for a few remarks, and allows us to formulate three arguments in favor of the relevance of such presumptions.

Firstly, while nothing proves that the importer knew his goods were counterfeit, nothing confirms that he was unaware of it either. Generally speaking, the most frequent hypothesis remains that of intentional fraud.

---

162 Nor is this a new procedure. Thomas Aquinas, himself relying on Roman law and Aristotelian writings, already referred to it in his legal theory of intention, *see supra*, no. 53.

163 V. Saint-Gérand, La culpabilité dans la théorie de la responsabilité pénale 546–47 (2000) (Ph.D. dissertation, Université Jean Moulin Lyon III).

164 In this sense, *see* X. Pin, *La non-intention est-elle vraiment l'exception?*, *in* Le nouveau Code pénal, 20 ans après: État des questions 79, 86 (L. Saenko ed., 2014). *Adde*, on this theme, *see* P. Conte, *Quelques observations sur la distinction des règles substantielles et des règles de preuve en droit pénal*, *in* Mélanges en l'honneur de Philippe Théry: Les coutures du droit 195, 195–202 (2022).

165 German criminal lawyers, however, approach the problem not from the angle of negligence, but from that of omission. For a study, *see* G. Dannecker, *La responsabilité pénale pour les délits d'omission, notamment dans le domaine de l'économie et de l'environnement*, Revue de science criminelle et de droit comparé 379, 389 (Apr.–June 1987).

166 In this sense, *see* J. Berréville, *Quelques réflexions sur l'élément moral de l'infraction*, Revue de science criminelle et de droit pénal comparé 865, 875 (1973).

167 In this sense, *see* G. Levasseur, *Le droit de la preuve en droit pénal français*, *in* La preuve en droit 175, 193 (C. Perelman & P. Forier eds., 1981); *adde*, for example, E. Dreyer, Droit pénal général 758–60 (6th ed. 2021), nos. 938–940.

168 V. Peltier, *L'élément moral de la contrefaçon de marque*, Propriété industrielle (Apr. 2017), étude 12, no. 30.

169 Cass. crim., Feb. 29, 2000, no. 98-88.175 (Fr.).

Moreover, the existence of negligence reinforces the *likelihood* of intent, since if the importer had been genuinely concerned not to counterfeit, he would have carried out the necessary checks. In this sense, the definition of a presumption is respected: it consists in "holding an unknown fact to be proven on the basis of a known fact that is an indication of it."[170] However, considering that negligence most often points to fraud does not misrepresent reality.

A second argument in favor of these presumptions is that without them, the effectiveness of punitive enforcement would be compromised. Not resorting to them would imply that every time a defendant invoked negligence, they could evade liability altogether.[171] Indeed, since the offenses in question are intentional in nature, mere negligence would not suffice to establish the requisite mental element, and hence the offense. Moreover, the theoretical possibility of opening up these offenses to negligence would present two disadvantages.[172] The first is logical: it is illogical to recognize that a maneuver can be devised through negligence – the two terms being antinomic. The second is that it would be inappropriate to reduce the liability of defendants solely on the basis of the excuse of negligence – as this would diminish the deterrent function of the offenses, the penalty necessarily being, by virtue of the principle of proportionality, of lesser importance in the case of negligence.

A final argument relates to the existence – particularly important for professionals – of pre-existing obligations.[173] The presumption of intent used for them can then be analyzed as a normative presumption, aimed at sanctioning non-compliance. This makes it possible not only to *describe* the most probable hypothesis, but also to *prescribe* a devoir-être.[174] In doing so, it gives professionals a sense of responsibility, encouraging them to be highly vigilant.

Some authors have argued that these presumptions distort business offenses, transforming the infraction into a hybrid concept that lies

170 Vocabulaire juridique 799 (G. Cornu ed., 11th ed. 2016).

171 P. Conte, L'apparence en matière pénale 321–22 (1984) (Ph.D. dissertation): according to the author, such solutions can "be based, sociologically speaking, on solid reasons. The rigor of unfailing repression is essential in an era where we have all too often seen victims abandoned to the actions of these 'businessmen'... for whom the pursuit of profit appears to be a universal justification... .How can we accept that individuals who have, at times, shown an obvious talent for taking advantage of the benefits of their positions, on the other hand claim to have been totally deprived of them when it came to carrying out their obligations and fulfilling their duties, and, in short, plead their own negligence as an excuse?" (*Nota bene*: from a legal point of view, the author is nonetheless critical of this evidentiary practice).

172 We shall see that this is nevertheless the choice made by the European legislator with regard to fraud against the Community budget (*infra*, no. 205) and anticompetitive practices (*infra*, no. 268).

173 These pre-existing obligations may either be written into texts other than the incriminating text (specifically in the technical legislation mentioned *supra*, no. 155); or they may be assessed, as in tort law, by reference to the general notion of fault and the various extra-legal sources to which it refers (think, for example, of professional practices). In this case, the intentional element is deduced from the breach of these pre-existing obligations. In this sense, *see* P. Merle, Les présomptions légales en droit pénal 212 (1970).

174 *Id.* at 77.

halfway between negligent offenses and intentional offenses.[175] For all the reasons set out above, however, we can only endorse their use: they make it possible to affirm the intentional nature of certain business offenses while also facilitating the proof of their mental element, which can sometimes be challenging in practice. As we shall see from the illustration of the offense of deception, this evidentiary technique helps to ensure a certain repressive *balance*.

B. A demonstration based on the example of the offense of deception

157. **Proof of intent based on negligence: a rebuttable presumption.** The offense of deception[176] is clearly an intentional offense – this is clear both from the structure of the incriminating text,[177] from the preparatory work for the 1905 law,[178] and from the constant position of the Court of Cassation.[179] However, the latter has ruled that "the fact that an importer, *who knows that* a product of foreign origin intended for cattle feed is likely, with a very high probability coefficient, to contain ricin,... *delivers* such a product without having subjected it to numerous analyses, the *necessity of* which *he is not unaware* ... constitutes the mental element of the offense."[180] This example is just one of many[181] illustrating the frequent use of a presumption of intent based on simple negligence.[182] The judges also noted that "total good faith would have required not only that samples be taken, but also that the results of the analyses be known before delivery to the client – with certainty as to the integrity

175 *See*, in particular, W. Jeandidier, *L'élément moral des infractions d'affaires ou l'art de la métamorphose*, *in* Une certaine idée du droit: Mélanges en l'honneur d'André Decocq 369, 375–77 (2004). The author concludes: "The standard business fault is thus a hypertrophied general *dol*, of low intensity, situated at the margins of lesser faults that it has ultimately absorbed but that have also distorted it." *Id.* at. 383; *adde*, B. Mercadal, *Recherches sur l'intention en droit pénal*, Revue de science criminelle et de droit pénal comparé 1, 24 (Jan.–Mar. 1967): citing deception in sales and counterfeiting as examples, the author denounces the fact that, in such cases, "jurisprudence purely and simply distorts the notion of intent. Not only is it unconcerned with whether or not there is a desire for a result, but it even dispenses with the agent's awareness of the act committed. It sees culpable intent in the very fact of imprudence, clumsiness or negligence"; J.-L. Costa, *Les infractions involontaires du point de vue de la responsabilité pénale en France*, Revue de science criminelle et de droit pénal comparé 731, 733–39 (1963). As in unfair competition law (*see supra*, no. 151), such an analysis arises from a confusion between the nature of the offense and the methods of proof.

176 Art. L. 441-1 of the French Consumer Code.

177 In our view, this criterion is one of the two that must be taken into account to determine the nature of the moral element required to characterize an offense (*see infra*, nos. 222–223).

178 E. Verny, *Fraudes: Tromperies et falsifications*, JurisClasseur Concurrence - Consommation, (June 2021), fasc. 1010, no. 48.

179 *Id.*

180 Cass. crim., May 8, 1968, no. 67-90.684 (Fr.) (emphasis added) (unofficial translation).

181 Fraud is indeed a prime area for this phenomenon. In this sense, *see* Berréville, *Quelques réflexions sur l'élément mental de l'infraction*, *op. cit.* at 873.

182 The use of this presumption is so frequent in cases of deception that the doctrine has turned it into a case of "commission by omission," considering that a simple abstention is sufficient to characterize the offense. *See* Jeandidier, *L'élément matériel des infractions d'affaires ou la prédilection pour l'inconsistance*, *op. cit.* at 251.

of the goods."[183] This attests to the fact that such a presumption is not merely a description of what is, but the prescription of what ought to be.

However, this presumption is not irrebuttable. The accused may escape sanction either by invoking a justification[184] or by demonstrating that they were not negligent. A rather unusual case[185] illustrates this point: a consumer found a field mouse in a bag of Panzani pasta. The characterization of the material element was indisputable: it goes without saying that the presence of a rodent in tagliatelle affects the substantial qualities, composition, and quantity of the product. In addition to the material element, however, the trial judges recalled that "to be punishable, deception must be based on *fraudulent intent*," which can be "*deduced* from the absence or inadequacy of checks on the product by the manufacturer, before it is put on sale." In this case, however, the seller was able to prove that he had taken preventive measures and implemented *serious* and *sufficient* controls. The offense was therefore not established. Indeed, the cause of the material fact – the sale of rodent pasta – could not be considered intentional, since in the absence of negligence, it was accidental. This case thus serves as a reminder that, even if the material element is established, this does not always *automatically* entail proof of the mental element,[186] which constitutes an important difference in regime between intentional offenses in the strict sense and intentional offenses in the broad sense.[187]

158. **The existence of a legal presumption of culpable intent as an autonomous offense.** The offense of deception has another interesting feature. Article L. 454-2 of the French Consumer Code establishes a *legal presumption* of culpable intent when the offense is committed "with the aid of false or inaccurate weights or instruments"; their mere possession, without any legitimate reason,[188] also making it possible to characterize the attempted deception.[189] This is an interesting mechanism, in that it reduces the burden of proof on the public prosecutor. It is also frequent: for example, article 101(1)(a) TFEU presumes that cartels are anticompetitive agreements.

The legislator has also criminalized the possession of false weights and measures as *a distinct offense.*[190] This illustrates a more general phenomenon that will come under critical scrutiny in competition law: more and more

183 Cass. crim., May 8, 1968, no. 67-90.684 (Fr.) (unofficial translation).

184 As these defenses apply to all criminal offenses, whether intentional in the strict or broad sense, *see infra*, nos. 217–219.

185 CA Grenoble, ch. corr. 1, Apr. 30, 2007 (Fr.).

186 In this regard, *see* G. Raymond, *Le mulot mort était dans le sachet de pâtes alimentaires*, CONTRATS CONCURRENCE CONSOMMATION (Dec. 2007), comm. 311.

187 Among others, *see infra*, nos. 249–254.

188 On the theory of legitimate grounds, *see infra*, nos. 338–342.

189 MERLE, LES PRÉSOMPTIONS LÉGALES EN DROIT PÉNAL, *op. cit.* at 66–67.

190 Art. L. 413-2 of the French Consumer Code.

laws are being enacted[191] that merely criminalize conduct that until then could already be captured by more general offenses. The process consists in breaking down an intentional offense in the strict sense into distinct sub-infractions, aimed at much more specific cases, and which are intentional offenses in the broad sense. The question is whether this legislative practice leads to more "effective and efficient" justice. This question is all the more important as the phenomenon is not unique to competition law, but affects the whole of criminal law, if not the whole of the law.

Conversely, if there is one thing that truly belongs to competition law, and which highlights the transversality of the concept of intent, it is its subject – the company. We shall now examine the recognition of intent specific to legal persons, and by extension to companies, as well as the particularities of its imputation to this distinct legal subject.

Paragraph 2 – Transversality *ratione personae*

159. **Are legal persons and companies endowed with intent of their own?** Intent is a transversal concept, in that it is not the exclusive domain of natural persons. Indeed, when dealing with a legal person – *a fortiori* a company[192] – there is a disconnect between the *material perpetrator* of the offense and its *legal author*. Nevertheless, imputing an offense to a disembodied entity does not constitute a case of vicarious penal liability: since it is deemed to be endowed with intent of its own (**I**), an offense committed by a person acting on its behalf is imputed to it as if it had committed the offense itself (**II**).

---

191 Cf., in competition law, the Digital Markets Act. *See infra*, nos. 448–449.

192 We have excluded from the scope of this study the hypothesis of the criminal liability of individuals on the basis of competition rules. Member States may decide to make individuals criminally liable for their involvement in anticompetitive practices. Several have done so, including France, Greece, Estonia, and Ireland. *See* W. P. J. Wils, *Is Criminalization of EU Competition Law the Answer?*, 28 World Competition 117, 129–30 (2005). In France, article L. 420-6 of the Commercial Code makes it a criminal offense for a natural person to "fraudulently take a personal and decisive part in the conception, organization or implementation" of anticompetitive practices. This provision has given rise to many doubts as to the interpretation of the mental element, which doctrine nevertheless considers to be intentional. *See ex multis*: M.-P. Lucas de Leyssac & C. Lucas de Leyssac, *L'inquiétant article L. 420-6 du Code de commerce et comment se rassurer*, *in* Les droits et le Droit: Mélanges dédiés à Bernard Bouloc 651, 661–66 (2006); *adde*, J.-B. Blaise, *La sanction pénale*, JCP E no. 12, 30, 31 (Mar. 21, 2013), comm. 1170, no. 7. Given the limited litigation to which this provision gives rise (in this sense, R. Saint-Esteben, *Une repénalisation du droit de la concurrence en France? À propos de l'utilisation de l'article 40 du code de procédure pénale par les services d'instruction de l'Autorité*, Concurrences no. 2-2019, art. no. 90001, 54, 55, no. 2) and the lack of specificity of the mental element of this offense vis-à-vis that of offenses under the law of anticompetitive practices, we will not devote any particular developments to it. Indeed, we will demonstrate that anticompetitive offenses must be classified as "offenses of means," in the same way as theft or swindling, although some authors have rightly pointed out that article L. 420-6 of the French Commercial Code "ultimately incriminates nothing other than conduct akin to swindling." *See* A. Decocq & M. Pédamon, L'ordonnance du 1er décembre 1986 relative à la liberté des prix et de la concurrence 18 (1987), no. 50. It should be noted, however, that in 2020, the General Rapporteur of the French Competition Authority once again referred a case to the public prosecutor's office. *See* D. Bosco, *Pénal et concurrence: La nouvelle donne*, Contrats concurrence consommation (Feb. 2020), repère 2.

I. Recognition of a disembodied entity's own intent

160. **Can a disembodied entity form intent?** The legal person,[193] whatever form it takes in the various legal systems, has the particularity of not being human: it embodies the collective action of several individuals, without having – at least at first sight – its own *autonomous* reality. It would be an object with "no soul to be damned, and no body to be kicked,"[194] unfit to commit offenses, since it would be devoid of a will of its own. Although the criminal liability (or at least administrative liability) of legal persons is now accepted, the controversy has long stalled over whether it is possible, or relevant, to recognize their intent[195] (**A**) – a recognition that appears particularly justified[196] (**B**).

A. The controversial history of legal person criminal liability

161. **Recognition of the criminal liability of groups (Roman law–18th century).** *Societas delinquere non potest!* Such is the established formula, the historical precedent often invoked as an authoritative argument against the capacity of legal persons to commit offenses. A "pseudo-Roman" adage,[197] yet nowhere to be found in the *Digest*. However, this assertion has been widely contested,[198] and the reality appears to be more nuanced: Roman

---

193 An English author, considering with a touch of irony the conflicts engendered by this question on the continent, writes that the number of jurists who have tackled it is so great that it is possible to classify authors into two categories: those who have written on the nature of legal persons, and those who have not …*See* M. Wolff, *On the Nature of Legal Persons*, 54 Law Quarterly Review 494, 494 (1938). It would therefore be out of the question to claim any form of exhaustiveness. *Ex multis*: L. Michoud, *La notion de personnalité morale*, Revue du droit public et de la science politique en France et à l'étranger 193 (1899); L. Michoud, La théorie de la personnalité morale et son application au droit français (2020); R. Demogue, *La notion de sujet de droit: Caractères et conséquences*, RTD civ. 611 (1909); J. Dewey, *The Historical Background of Corporate Legal Personality*, 35 Yale Law Journal 655 (1926); J. Hamel, *La personnalité morale et ses limites*, Recueil Dalloz 141 (1949), chron. xxxiv; P. A. French, *The Corporation as a Moral Person*, 16 American Philosophy Quarterly 207 (1979); E. Richard, *'Mon nom est personne': La construction de la personnalité morale ou les vertus de la patience*, 4 Entreprises et histoire 14 (2009); finally, for a summary of the "reality *versus* fiction" debate, as well as numerous references, *see* S. François, Le consentement de la personne morale 32–40 (2020), nos. 36–49.

194 In the famous words of Lord Chancellor Edward Thurlow, pronounced at the end of the eighteenth century: "No soul to be damned, and no body to be kicked", quoted by J. C. Coffee, *No Soul To Damn, No Body To Kick: An Unscandalized Inquiry Into the Problem of Corporate Punishment*, 79 Michigan Law Review 386, 386 (1981).

195 Indeed, "[t]he requirement of intent in criminal law appears to be the only serious obstacle to the criminal liability of legal persons." *See* P. Faivre, *La responsabilité pénale des personnes morales*, Revue de science criminelle et de droit pénal comparé, 547, 553 (July–Sept. 1958).

196 The majority doctrine today adopts the anthropomorphic thesis, *see*, *inter alia*, E. Dreyer, Droit pénal général 915 (6th ed. 2021), no. 1180: "Legal persons have neither flesh nor blood; yet they have organs. They have no feelings; yet they have a will. They are invisible, yet they act and can even be reproached for their inaction."

197 K. Tiedemann, *La responsabilité pénale dans l'entreprise: Vers un espace judiciaire européen unifié?*, Seminar of the Association de recherches pénales européennes under the patronage of the European Commission (Paris, Dec. 13, 1996 – Court of Cassation), Introductory report, Revue de science criminelle et de droit pénal comparé 259 (1997).

198 Savigny's idea of the absence of delictual capacity of groupings in France was contested by Otto von Gierke, Theodor Mommsen and Georg Beseler. On this controversy, *see* A. Mestre, Les personnes morales et le problème de leur responsabilité morale 9–12 (1899).

law is said to have gradually recognized that a collective entity may possess a capacity to offend distinct from that of its members,[199] and may even be punished for intentional offenses.[200]

When Roman law was rediscovered, canonists followed suit, recognizing the existence of a *universitas* that was distinct from the personhood of its members.[201]

Jurisconsults, for their part, considered that the will of the members of a *universitas* constituted the will of the *universitas* itself, this *autonomy* rendering it capable of committing offenses in its own right.[202] Bartolus had a far-sighted vision and put forward a landmark argument:[203] the fiction that makes a collective an artificial being also can serve to suppose it has a soul – thus allowing it to be considered guilty and punishable.[204] In the fourteenth century, Italian criminal law scholars continued to affirm the delictual capacity of such entities, exerting a significant and lasting influence across Europe.[205]

162. **Questioning the criminal liability of groups since the French Revolution.** While the criminal liability of groups was recognized and widespread on the European continent, the French Revolution swept away these solutions. Its individualist, anti-corporate philosophy, and its intangible principle of personal criminal liability, were to lead to the denial of the legal personality of collective entities, and hence of their criminal liability.[206] The legal personality of the legal person was reduced to a fictitious favor granted by the law to certain groups, with the human being deemed the sole true bearer of legal personality, the only real subject of law.[207]

From the time of codification, the conflict between supporters of the social reality of the legal person and those who considered it to be a mere

---

199 M. Lizee, *De la capacité organique et des responsabilités délictuelle et pénale des personnes morales*, 41 McGill Law Journal 131, 134 (1995).

200 In this sense, *see* R. Valeur, La responsabilité pénale des personnes morales dans les droits français et anglo-américains 9–10 (1931); *adde*, in the same vein, Mestre, Les personnes morales et le problème de leur responsabilité morale, *op. cit.* at 34, 39.

201 This recognition dates back to Innocent IV's commentary on Gregory IX's *Decretals* in the 1250s. *See* Mestre, Les personnes morales et le problème de leur responsabilité morale, *op. cit.* at 66–74; Y. Thomas, *L'extrême et l'ordinaire: Remarques sur le cas médiéval de la communauté disparue*, *in* Y. Thomas, Les opérations du droit 207, 207 (2011); Dewey, *The Historical Background of Corporate Legal Personality*, *op. cit.* at 665.

202 Mestre, Les personnes morales et le problème de leur responsabilité morale, *op. cit.* at 47–52.

203 In the same way that he offered a reflection on intent destined for a lasting legacy, *see supra*, no. 69.

204 Mestre, Les personnes morales et le problème de leur responsabilité morale, *op. cit.* at 93.

205 *Id.* at 116–27. Title xxi of the Criminal Ordinance of 1670 (which remained in force until the French Revolution), listing the various methods of "instituting proceedings," is thus entirely devoted to criminal procedure against corporate bodies and communities. Muyart de Vouglans, Grotius, Pufendorf and Blackstone all agree on the recognition of the delictual capacity of groups.

206 Tiedemann, *La responsabilité pénale dans l'entreprise: Vers un espace judiciaire européen unifié?*, *op. cit.* at 259. The criminal liability of collective entities was abolished not for scientific considerations, but for reasons of political expediency. In this sense, *see* J. Radulesco, *La responsabilité pénale des personnes morales*, Revue internationale de droit pénal no. 1, 286, 293 (1929).

207 A. Paynot-Rouvillois, *Personne morale et volonté*, 28 Droits: Revue française de théorie juridique 17 (1999).

creature of the law has long animated the doctrine.[208] This dispute has always run up against the same difficulty: whether or not the collective entity has *its own autonomous will.* If this is not the case, how can we accept that it can commit an offense – which is only conceivable if its perpetrator is endowed with free will and discernment? Moreover, what would be the purpose of a sentence that cannot lead to repentance or cause suffering for the one subjected to it?[209] Free will or necessity, autonomy or subjection of the will, real or imagined existence – how to decide? The quarrel has since died out, without having been settled.[210] The history of the criminal liability of legal persons has been an eventful one. Departing from the relative unity of past principles, the nineteenth century marked the beginning of fragmentation. Each legal system has adopted a variety of approaches, ranging from one extreme to the other,[211] such that the development of contemporary law in this area appears neither settled nor fully achieved.[212]

163. **A return to recognizing the criminal liability of legal persons: a first step in Anglo-Saxon law.** It was the English who first reopened the path toward recognizing the criminal liability of legal persons. Pragmatic in their approach, they gave little weight to metaphysical considerations regarding whether collective entities possess a will of their own, instead implicitly presuming it for clear practical reasons.[213]

Initially, as early as the eighteenth century in England, corporations were held criminally liable for offenses of omission causing *public nuisance*[214] by borrowing from the theory of vicarious responsibility found in tort law, which was regarded as more "objective" than intentional offenses.[215] From the second half of the nineteenth century, the English extended this liability to unintentional commission of offenses.[216]

---

208 *See* P. Durand, *L'évolution de la condition juridique des personnes morales de droit privé*, *in* I Le droit privé français au milieu du XXe siècle: Études offertes à Georges Ripert 138, 140 (1950), and doctrinal references cited.

209 These classic arguments are set out and opposed by G. Levasseur, *Les personnes morales victimes, auteurs ou complices d'infractions en droit français*, Revue de droit pénal et de criminologie 827, 840 (1954-1955).

210 R. Libchaber, *Réalité ou fiction? Une nouvelle querelle de la personnalité est pour demain*, RTD civ. 166 (2003).

211 G. Viney, *Conclusions*, Actes du colloque du 7 avril 1993 sur "La responsabilité pénale des personnes morales", Revue des Sociétés 381, 381 (1993).

212 R. Legeais, Grands systèmes de droit contemporains: Approche comparative 430 (3rd ed. 2016).

213 P. Kenel, La responsabilité pénale des personnes morales en droit anglais: Un modèle pour la Suisse 65 (1991).

214 K. F. Brickey, *Corporate Criminal Liability: A Brief History and an Observation*, 60 Washington University Law Quarterly 393, 401–403 (1982).

215 R. Legeais, *Les réponses du droit anglais et du droit allemand aux problèmes de la responsabilité pénale des personnes morales*, Actes du colloque du 7 avril 1993 sur "La responsabilité pénale des personnes morales", Revue des Sociétés 371, 372 (1993); *adde*, in the same vein, M. D. Dubber, *The Comparative History and Theory of Corporate Liability*, 16 New Criminal Law Review 203, 225 (2013).

216 J. R. Spencer, *La responsabilité pénale dans l'entreprise en Angleterre*, Revue de science criminelle et de droit pénal comparé 289 (1997).

The door had been opened: once it was accepted that omissions could be punished, there was no theoretical reason why positive acts should not also be punished.[217]

The third stage – the admission of corporate criminal liability for intentional offenses – was reached in the United States in an antitrust case. This took place in 1909,[218] with a Supreme Court ruling[219] based on the Elkin Act.[220] New York Central was accused of having granted rebates to sugar refineries in violation of federal law. Defense counsel argued that punishing the company itself, and not the individual perpetrators, was contrary to the U.S. Constitution, as it violated the presumption of innocence and unfairly harmed innocent shareholders. The Supreme Court considered that the antitrust law could only be effectively enforced if the company that had benefited from the offense was the target of the proceedings.[221] It held that Congress would lose all power if it could not reach corporate entities directly, "holding them responsible for the *intent and purposes of the agents* to whom they have delegated the power to act."[222] It was then recognized that corporations could be subject to criminal prosecution for any violation of antitrust laws.[223] The admission of the criminal liability of corporations for intentional offenses was then gradually accepted in general.[224]

164. **The recent widespread acceptance of criminal or administrative liability for legal persons.** In Europe, besides England, the Netherlands was the first to reintroduce the criminal liability of legal persons, as early as 1870 in customs law, and then generally in economic offenses in 1950.[225]

In 1991, the Court of Justice adopted a neutral stance, stating that Community law did not oblige Member States to introduce the criminal liability of legal persons into their national law[226] – seeming to recognize *a*

217 Brickey, *Corporate Criminal Liability: A Brief History and an Observation*, *op. cit.* at 407–408.

218 B. Wendzel, M. Angelo, M. Jantz & A. Peterson, *Corporate Criminal Liability*, 56 American Criminal Law Review 671, 679–80 (2019).

219 New York Central & Hudson River Railroad v. United States, 212 U.S. 481 (1909).

220 The Elkin Act, passed in 1903, was an amendment to the Interstate Commerce Act of 1887.

221 The U.S. Supreme Court went on to state: "[T]he great majority of business transactions in modern times are conducted through these bodies, and particularly interstate commerce is almost entirely in their hands. To give them immunity from all punishment because of the old and exploded doctrine that a corporation cannot commit a crime would virtually take away the only means of effectually controlling the subject matter and correcting the abuses aimed at." *New York Central & Hudson River Railroad* at 495–96.

222 *Id.* at 496 (emphasis added).

223 Brickey, *Corporate Criminal Liability: A Brief History and an Observation*, *op. cit.* at 411–12.

224 *Id.* at 421–22.

225 Respectively with the Algemene Wet op de Douane of 1870 and the Wep op de Economische Delicten of 1950, *see* J. A. E. Vervaele, *La responsabilité pénale de et au sein de la personne morale aux Pays-Bas. Mariage entre pragmatisme et dogmatisme juridique*, Revue de science criminelle et de droit pénal comparé 325 (1997).

226 Case C-7/90, Paul Vandevenne, ECLI:EU:C:1991:363, para. 12.

contrario that a State could admit such liability.[227] Subsequently, in 1997,[228] the European Union[229] nevertheless obliged Member States to introduce criminal liability, or at least administrative liability, for legal persons, by mandating that they take the necessary measures to ensure that they can be held liable for fraud, active corruption, and money laundering.[230] At the same time, the authors of the *Corpus juris*[231] considered that the refusal to recognize the criminal liability of legal persons was "historically outdated."[232]

In 2012, the European Commission published a substantial comparative law report on this topic.[233] The report notes that all Member States have now introduced either criminal or administrative liability for legal persons.[234] In a study published in 2021, the Council of Europe concurs.[235]

Germany presents an interesting example. The country still does not admit the criminal liability of legal persons for a reason of principle: the prevailing view is to deny that a collective entity is endowed with a will of its own and, consequently, can be held criminally responsible.[236] However, since 1968, legal persons can be held administratively liable under section 30 of the Ordnungswidrigkeiten (OWiG), and may be subjected to fines of a punitive nature.[237] Offenses under the OWiG require intent as a matter of principle, and, by exception, negligence[238] – in other words, a mental

227 In this regard, *see* J. Pradel, *La responsabilité des personnes morales en droit pénal comparé*, *in* STRAFJUSTIZ UND RECHTSSTAAT: JUSTICE PÉNALE ET ÉTAT DE DROIT 49, 51 (M. A. Niggli & N. Queloz eds., 2003).

228 By adopting the Council Act of June 19, 1997, drawing up the Second Protocol of the Convention on the protection of the European Communities' financial interests (97/C 221/02).

229 It should be noted that the Council of Europe has likewise undertaken to compel States to introduce criminal or administrative liability for legal persons. *See* G. De Vel, *La responsabilité pénale des personnes morales dans les instruments juridiques du Conseil de l'Europe*, *in* LA RESPONSABILITÉ PÉNALE DES PERSONNES MORALES EN EUROPE 343 (S. Adam, N. Colette-Basecqz & M. Nihoul eds., 2008).

230 EC Comm., *Green Paper on the approximation, mutual recognition and enforcement of criminal sanctions in the European Union*, COM(2004)334 final (Apr. 30, 2004), at 21.

231 A large-scale comparative law project led by Mireille Delmas-Marty in 1996, aimed at proposing harmonization measures to align national laws.

232 CORPUS JURIS: PORTANT DISPOSITIONS PÉNALES POUR LA PROTECTION DES INTÉRÊTS FINANCIERS DE L'UNION EUROPÉENNE 72–73 (M. Delmas-Marty ed., 1997).

233 G. VERMEULEN, W. DE BONDT & C. RYCKMAN, LIABILITY OF LEGAL PERSONS FOR OFFENCES IN THE EU, Eur. Comm. - DG Justice (JLS/2010/JPEN/PR/1009/E4) (2012).

234 *Id.* at 10.

235 Council of Europe, Thematic Monitoring Review of the Conference of the Parties to CETS No.198 on Article 10 (1 and 2), ("Corporate Liability") C198-COP(2021)6_HR (Nov. 19, 2021), at 5–6.

236 *See also* H.-H. Jescheck, *Die strafrecthliche Verantwortlichkeit der Personenverbände*, 65 ZEITSCHRIFT FÜR DIE GESAMTE STRAFWISSENSCHAFT 213 (1953); G. Stratenwerth, *Strafrechliche Untermehmenshaftung? in Festschrift für Rudolf Schmitt* 302 (K. Geppert, J. Bohnert & R. Rengier eds., 1992). Both references are cited in VERMEULEN ET AL., LIABILITY OF LEGAL PERSONS FOR OFFENCES IN THE EU, *op. cit.* at 22.

237 D. Dölling & C. Laue, *Corporate Criminal Liability in Germany – A Never Ending Story?*, *in* LA RESPONSABILITÉ PÉNALE DES PERSONNES MORALES EN EUROPE 25, 28–29 (S. Adam, N. Colette-Basecqz & M. Nihoul eds., 2008). On the (permeable) boundary between criminal law and repressive administrative law, *see supra*, nos. 130–136.

238 H. J. Hirsch, *Rapport allemand*, *in* LA CRIMINALISATION DU COMPORTEMENT COLLECTIF: XIVe CONGRÈS INTERNATIONAL DE DROIT COMPARÉ 31, 60 (H. De Doelder & K. Tiedemann eds., 1996).

element attesting to guilt. Can we not see the artifice in refusing to impose criminal sanctions on legal persons in the name of the constitutional principle of culpability, while at the same time imposing administrative sanctions, which also require culpability?[239] The admission of corporate criminal liability appears nonetheless justified for several reasons.

B. Justified admission of corporate criminal liability

165. **Legal theory argument: observations on the nature and function of legal concepts.** The debate as to whether the will of a legal person is real or fictitious is, by its very nature, insoluble – as is the question of whether human beings are capable of self-determination.[240] Yet, since the origins of criminal law, legislators have never attempted to settle the question of whether human beings possess a free, autonomous will. They have always *postulated* free will as the necessary basis for incurring liability.[241] However, particularly since the nineteenth century, the legal concept of the legal person has been obscured by extralegal considerations of a popular, political, moral, philosophical, or even theological nature.[242]

Legal practitioners have thus fallen into the "realism trap," believing that "the quality of a legal concept is measured by its ability to describe raw reality," forgetting that its function is "to prompt the application of appropriate solutions."[243]

While it must be acknowledged that there is an obvious element of fiction in admitting that a disembodied entity can be endowed with will, fictionality is nonetheless, to some extent, inherent in any legal concept. Indeed, by its very nature, a concept is an abstract construction based on a part of reality, but it is always added to this reality in order to produce certain legal consequences. The example of legal personality is topical in this respect: etymologically, the word "person" means "mask" – the latter being no more than a screen, a concept used by the law to attribute rights and duties to its subjects.[244] The concept of the natural person is no less fictional than that of the legal person. Do we not decide that the criterion of legal death is the end of brain activity rather than the end of vital functions, thus anticipating the end of personality as opposed to the end of life, for purely pragmatic reasons?[245] Is the natural person truly more "real" than

---

239 In this sense, *id.* at 39.

240 Cf. *supra*, nos. 26–27.

241 *See supra*, no. 28.

242 Dewey, *The Historical Background of Corporate Legal Personality*, *op. cit.* at 655.

243 C. Atias, Épistémologie juridique 154 (1985), no. 82.

244 In this sense, *see* A. Amalfitano, La responsabilité pénale des personnes morales en Europe: Une recherche pour la construction d'un modèle commun 38–45 (2015).

245 R. Libchaber, *Réalité ou fiction? Une nouvelle querelle de la personnalité est pour demain*, RTD civ. 166 (2003).

the legal person?[246] Legal personality is a construct: reducing human beings to the abstraction of the natural person should naturally "pave the way for the recognition, under the idea of person, of companies and other groupings."[247] Finally, the argument of coherence leads us to argue in favor of recognizing the criminal liability of legal persons, since in civil law, the latter are deemed to be endowed with a will of their own,[248] justifying their capacity to consent.[249]

166. **An argument of principle: the need to curb cases of vicarious criminal liability.** Recognition of the criminal liability of legal persons could (and undoubtedly should) have helped to curb an emerging phenomenon of the twentieth century: the establishment of a form of vicarious criminal liability, the mere mention of which "gives rise to unease."[250] In order to compensate for the delictual incapacity of legal persons, judges have held corporate executives liable for the actions of their subordinates,[251] both in France and abroad.[252] This practice was even enshrined in law with the 1945 ordinance on prices,[253] which made the following punishable:

> All those who, in any capacity whatsoever, are responsible for the management or administration of any enterprise, establishment, company, association, or public entity, have either personally contravened *or, as principal, have allowed any person under their authority or control to contravene the provisions of the present ordinance.*[254]

---

246 The saying that "no one has lunch with a legal person, but it often picks up the tab" applies just as much to the natural person: you do not share a meal any more with the lawyer's natural person than with a legal one. In this sense, *see* M. Germain, *L'apport du droit de l'entreprise au droit des personnes*, Colloque du 25e anniversaire de la FNDE, JCP E 11, 12 (1997), suppl. 2.

247 R. Libchaber, *Le juriste et ses objets: Trois exemples de construction en droit privé*, 7 Enquête 5 (1999), http://enquete.revues.org/1583.

248 This prompted one author to write that, while civil law treats the legal person with benevolence, criminal law mistreats it. *See* P. Morvan, *La personne morale maltraitée par le droit pénal*, *in* Code pénal et Code d'instruction criminelle – Livre du bicentenaire 171, 176 (2010).

249 The capacity of a legal person to give consent is justified by the fact that it entails a "structured organic process," and that the "legal person's own will" is "determined and subsequently expressed through its corporate bodies." *See* François, Le consentement de la personne morale, *op. cit.* at 365, no. 593.

250 J. Salvaire, *Réflexions sur la responsabilité pénale du fait d'autrui*, Revue de science criminelle et de droit pénal comparé, 307, 307 (Apr.-June 1964). For a perspective, *see* E. Dreyer, *Que reste-t-il du principe de responsabilité personnelle des personnes physiques?*, *in* Le nouveau Code pénal, 20 ans après: État des questions 97 (L. Saenko ed., 2014).

251 It was Robert Badinter's wish, at the time of the adoption of the 1994 Penal Code, to do away with this hypothesis of vicarious criminal liability by introducing the criminal liability of legal persons. *See* H. Matsopoulou, *Extension de l'imputabilité des personnes morale*, *in* Dix ans après la réforme de 1994: Quels repères dans le Code pénal 67, 67 (M. Danti-Juan ed., 2005).

252 Notably in Germany, where, to avoid having to admit that this was a case of vicarious criminal liability, the doctrine mobilized the theory of commission by omission. *See* J. Pradel, Droit pénal comparé 79 (4th ed. 2016), no. 48; *adde*, in the same vein, G. Dannecker, *La responsabilité pénale pour les délits d'omission, notamment dans le domaine de l'économie et de l'environnement*, Revue de science criminelle et de droit comparé 379, 390 (Apr.–June 1987).

253 For a commentary on this ordinance, *see supra*, nos. 108–109.

254 Art. 56, first paragraph of Ordinance No. 45-1483 du 30 juin 1945 relative aux prix, JORF, July 8, 1945, no. 160, pp. 4150–4155 (emphasis added) (unofficial translation). Commenting on this article, Georges Levasseur wrote that "case law solutions are extremely severe, to the point of sometimes shocking fairness." cf. G. Levasseur, *L'imputabilité des infractions en droit français*, 5–6 Revue de droit pénal et de criminologie 387, 395 (1969).

The imputation of the offense was then based on the act actually committed by a third party.[255] The solution was justified by the use of either the "theory of power"[256] – as the company director has prerogatives to control their employees, it is their responsibility to ensure that they do not commit an offense[257] – or the theory of risk – the director's liability being the trade-off for the benefits gained from their employees' services.[258] Thus, in a case concerning the offense of minimum price fixing, the Court of Cassation went so far as to refuse to exonerate the company director from liability, even though he had demonstrated the existence of a delegation of authority, and the trial judges had not established the defendant's "conscious and voluntary" participation in the offense.[259] The Criminal Division has consistently ruled out as inadmissible the defense that the accused had taken all precautions to ensure compliance with the law by their subordinates.[260] However, since in business criminal law, negligence is often sufficient to prove intent,[261] this means that a director can be found guilty of an intentional offense on the grounds of their negligence in preventing the negligence of their subordinate[262] – in which case their liability is upheld at the cost of a "double denaturation."[263]

167. **Economic and sociological arguments: the autonomy of will of the collective entity and the subordination of its agents.** Finally, given that offenses most

---

255 Doctrine has attempted to justify this solution by drawing a distinction between "two rules that must never be confused: on the one hand, an absolute principle, without exception, that of the personality of penalties; on the other hand, the principle of imputability of the offense to the material perpetrator of the act, a principle that is subject to exceptions." *See* R. Legros, L'élément moral dans les infractions 34 (1952).

256 D. Rebut, L'omission en droit pénal: Pour une théorie de l'équivalence entre l'action et l'inaction 605–609 (1993) (Ph.D. dissertation, Université Jean Moulin Lyon iii). One author has also argued that this theory could hypothetically form the basis for criminal liability for damage caused by things. *See* S. Detraz, *L'hypothèse d'une responsabilité pénale du fait des choses*, *in* Mélanges en l'honneur du professeur Jacques-Henri Robert 229, 239 (2012): "[N]othing would prevent the company director from being held liable for an intentional offense committed by means of an object which, by virtue of [their] duty of care, they were responsible for."

257 M. Delmas-Marty, *Le droit pénal, l'individu et l'entreprise: culpabilité 'du fait d'autrui' ou du 'décideur'?*, JCP G no. 45 (Nov. 20, 1985), doctr. 3218; C. Cohen, *Le chef d'entreprise est-il délinquant ordinaire ?*, *in* Les enjeux de la pénalisation de la vie économique 71, 75–77 (M.-A. Frison-Roche ed., 1997).

258 In this sense, and for a critical look, *see* M. Puech, Droit pénal général 362 (1988), no. 999.

259 Cass. crim., June 25, 1979, no. 78-93.259 (Fr.).

260 A. Legal, *La responsabilité pénale du fait d'autrui dans son application au chef d'entreprise*, *in* Mélanges offerts à Jean Brethe de la Gressaye 477, 484 (1967). It should be noted that, conversely, in civil liability law, the Court of Cassation has refused to recognize that the principal can be held liable for damage caused by their agent's faults, even if they are fraudulent. *See* Cass., ch. mixte, Oct. 29, 2021, no. 19-18.470 (Fr.), comm. P. Stoffel-Munck, JCP G no. 24 (June 20, 2022), doctr. 759.

261 *See supra*, nos. 156–157.

262 On the use of presumptions of negligence in this area, and its virtually irrefutable nature in practice, *see* V. Ligny, La responsabilité pénale du chef d'entreprise: Essai de théorisation d'une responsabilité pénale en mutation 90–109 (2021). The author also notes a "shift in criminal repression from the person of the director to the company." *Id.* at 361.

263 B. Schütz, Le principe de la personnalité des peines en droit pénal français 234 (1967) (Ph.D. dissertation, Université de Nancy); *adde*, Rebut, L'omission en droit pénal: Pour une théorie de l'équivalence entre l'action et l'inaction, *op. cit.* at 622–23: "The reasoning goes from induction to induction to arrive at a presumption of intention: if the abstentionist did not oppose the offense that was being committed … although he could have done so, it is because he wished not to oppose it, from which it can be presumed that he wanted to associate himself with it."

often benefit legal persons,[264] and that they are always committed because of their lack of supervision, equity requires that sanctions be imposed on them personally,[265] which also encourages them to prevent their commission more effectively.[266] However, the most convincing argument in favor of the criminal liability of legal persons is not their punishment's economic efficiency.[267]

Indeed, what justifies collective entities being punished in their own right is a reality that can be glimpsed from a sociological perspective: a company is not merely made up of the sum of the wills of the individuals who make it up. It is endowed with an autonomous "sociological reality."[268]

As a cultural environment,[269] an organized structure regulated by ad hoc procedures,[270] or even a legal order in its own right,[271] the company imposes a social framework on individuals that conditions their decision-making,[272] with the result that the latter, partly deprived of their autonomy due to their subordinate status, respond to its orders more than they influence it. While the company's agents have only relative autonomy when acting on its behalf, logic dictates that the company itself is endowed with an autonomous will, since it is precisely this will that enables it to constrain the will of its members.

This reality is all the more striking in the modern age, marked by tertiarization and the growing importance of so-called intellectual professions. Whereas, at the beginning of the industrial era, companies exercised control over their employees' bodies, today their aim is to channel their

---

264 In addition, offenses committed by large-scale businesses can have a far greater impact than those that might be perpetrated by individuals. *See* S. Sun Beale, *A Response to the Critics of Corporate Criminal Liability*, 46 American Criminal Law Review 1481, 1484 (2009).

265 B. Fisse & J. Braithwaite, *The Allocation of Responsibility for Corporate Crime: Individualism, Collectivism and Accountability*, 11 Sydney Law Review 468, 508 (1988).

266 C. M. V. Clarkson, *Kicking Corporate Bodies and Damning their Souls*, 59 The Modern Law Review 557, 566 (1996). It should be noted, however, that some authors question the relevance of criminal liability for legal persons, arguing in particular that sanctioning them is tantamount to imposing the consequences of punishment on innocent third parties (shareholders, creditors, employees, consumers) and may jeopardize the entity's survival. Furthermore, as the adoption of compliance policies does not exonerate companies from liability, nor can it prevent the commission of offenses with any certainty, the criminal liability of legal persons is unlikely to encourage them to prevent offenses. On this theme, *ex multis*: A. W. Alschuler, *Two Ways to Think About the Punishment of Corporations*, 46 American Criminal Law Review 1359, 1367 (2009); A. Hamdani & A. Klement, *Corporate Crime and Deterrence*, 61 Stanford Law Review 271 (2008).

267 On the inadequacy of economic analyses in conceptualizing the company, *see* S. Schweitzer, *Du mécanicisme à l'émergence de l'humain dans la théorie contemporaine de la firme*, *in* Éthique en entreprise 77, 88 (2001).

268 According to Jean Pradel, this is what justifies the criminal liability of legal persons. *See* J. Pradel, *La responsabilité des personnes morales en droit pénal comparé*, *in* Strafjustiz und Rechtsstaat: Justice pénale et État de droit 49, 50 (M. A. Niggli & N. Queloz eds., 2003).

269 This is the opinion of two authors who have taken up the fascinating work of ethnologist Bronislaw Malinowski (*Crime and Custom in Savage Society*, 1926). *See* J. Conley & W. O'Barr, *Crime and Custom in Corporate Society: A Cultural Perspective on Corporate Misconduct*, 60 Law and Contemporary Problems 5, 13 (1997).

270 C. Hannoun, Le droit et les groupes de sociétés 164 (1991).

271 S. Romano, L'ordre juridique 91–96 (L. François & P. Gothot trans., Dalloz, 2nd ed. 2005).

272 In this sense, *see* M. Olson, Logique de l'action collective 77–83 (M. Levi trans., Éditions de l'Université de Bruxelles 2018).

mental energy[273] – thereby reducing their decision-making power. But what independence is left to the employee when their function, the rules governing their work, and the objectives are determined outside them? The company leads those who operate within it to adopt behaviors that become habitual, routine, and automatic, reducing them to being mere tools in the service of ends that it predetermines.[274] The same applies, in the case of a group of companies, to the relationship between the parent company and its subsidiaries: the decentralization of decision-making is only achieved through the centralization of decision-making procedures, so that the autonomy of subsidiaries is never more than apparent.[275] What is more, as the figure of the big boss has faded with the shareholder dilution of capital, the bonds of subordination are becoming increasingly impersonal and disembodied,[276] leaving even less room for negotiation, or even for challenging rules that no one seems to control.[277] And if guilt is "omnipresent and consubstantial with life in the organization,"[278] it is not linked to non-compliance with the law, but to non-compliance with the company's internal rules.[279]

The phenomenon is intensifying: rules and procedures have become ubiquitous in companies, and IT tools facilitate stricter control of compliance.[280] The use of artificial intelligence also raises questions about the role of humans in the internal decision-making process. Some software programs are reportedly capable of making better choices than employees, leaving the latter even less free, since they merely validate a course of action predetermined by a software program,[281] and henceforth acting

273 M. Pagès, M. Bonetti, V. De Gauléjac & D. Descendre, L'emprise de l'organisation 16–17 (7th ed. 2019). The company thus develops as a site of ideological production, enabling it to develop a psychological hold on workers – a hold of which they are often unaware. *See Id.* at 60–61. This evolution is reinforced by the fact that the managerial model used is no longer, as in the past, based on coercion, prohibition, and constraint (the so-called paternal model), but on the offer and withdrawal of love (the so-called feminine model). *See id.* at 62. For an illustration, *see* H. Weber, *L'adhésion des employés à l'organisation chez McDonald's*, 1 Nouvelle revue de psychosociologie 117 (2006). On the psychological impact of managerial methods and the resulting loss of decision-making autonomy for agents, *see* J. Chapoutot, Libres d'obéir: Le management, du nazisme à aujourd'hui (2020).

274 *Id.* at 84–88 and 137.

275 *Id.* at 75.

276 A. Eraly, *Le pouvoir sans l'incarnation: L'empire de la domination impersonnelle*, 1 Nouvelle revue de psychosociologie 223, 226–29 (2021).

277 Indeed, far from being at the origin of this phenomenon of internalization of the corporate culture and its rules, managers are portrayed as "the most complete victims, psychologically and ideologically, of the system they promote." Pagès et al., L'emprise de l'organisation, *op. cit.* at 253.

278 *Id.* at 242.

279 Some authors have noted that the company creates a psychic investment similar to that analyzed by Freud in the army or the Church. *See* V. De Gauléjac, *L'emprise à IBM, 1979-2019: De l'adhésion à la répression*, 1 Nouvelle revue de psychosocologie 13, 15 (2021).

280 J. Vandewattyne & D. Ndahabonimana, *Quarante ans après* L'emprise de l'organisation*: Un retour sur le terrain*, 1 Nouvelle revue de psychosociologie 23, 32 (2021).

281 Y. Ferguson, *Puissance de calcul, force de l'emprise? Critique de l'organisation augmentée*, 1 Nouvelle revue de psychosociologie 157, 158–59 (2021).

under the rigid and flawless supervision of robots operating a "micro-management"[282] of their every move.[283]

If the criminal liability of a legal person thus appears justified, insofar as it is not entirely fictitious to acknowledge its own intent, it should be noted that the imputation of an offense to a disembodied entity presents certain specific features.

II. A technique specific to the company: imputing intent to an entity without legal personality

168. **Imputing an offense to a disembodied entity.** In the presence of a disembodied entity, it is necessary to distinguish two elements: on the one hand, the commission of the offense, and on the other, its imputation.[284] Admitting the criminal liability of legal persons should not lead us to deny the obvious: offenses are always *materially* committed by human beings. Indeed, while it is possible and relevant to admit that a legal person has a will, it would be misleading to claim that it has a body. Condemning a legal person therefore requires determining the conditions under which the acts and intentions of those working for or within it can engage its liability, in other words, how the offense committed by one or more persons acting on its behalf can be imputed to it. These rules of imputation, designed for entities with legal personality (**A**), have been extended to those without – namely, the company, which is subject to competition law (**B**).

In this respect, the legitimacy of imputing liability to a parent company for the actions of one of its subsidiaries is the subject of considerable debate, particularly as regards whether parent companies are, in fact, sanctioned "independently of their culpability."[285] Thus, establishing that the basis for sanctioning the company is identical to that justifying the sanction of the legal person provides a theoretical basis for legitimizing the solutions

---

282 On this theme, *see* S. Head, Mindless: Why Smarter Machines are Making Dumber Humans 16 (2014).

283 On the phenomenon of delegation of decision-making from man to machine, *see* C. Villani, Donner un sens à l'intelligence artificielle 186 (2018); on the emergence of a "technological paternalism," involving the multiplication of alerts, recommendations, warnings, prohibitions or injunctions, *see* the work by philosopher E. Sadin, L'intelligence artificielle ou l'enjeu du siècle. Anatomie d'un anti-humanisme radical 16 (2018); finally, on the emergence of new professions, notably that of "ethicist" (a profession consisting of designing algorithms that function, in their learning modalities, in accordance with sound values), *see* Ferguson, *Puissance de calcul, force de l'emprise? Critique de l'organisation augmentée, op. cit.* at 165.

284 Conversely, in the case of natural persons, the notion of imputation is superfluous insofar as it merges with the concept of intent, *infra*, no. 184.

285 P. Whelan, *Parental Antitrust Liability and the Pressing Issue of the Legitimacy of EU Competition Law*, Concurrences no. 2-2021, art. no. 100086.

adopted with regard to the company – which cannot be justified solely by the argument that the concept is "functional," nor by the sole objective of deterrence and effective enforcement of competition rules.

A. A technique designed for entities with legal personality

169. **The variety of models for imputing offenses to legal persons.** Comparative law shows that different countries apply different models for imputing offenses to legal persons.[286] These range between two extremes, from the most rigid to the most flexible: either imputation requires (i) identification of a natural person as the perpetrator, (ii) occupying a managerial positions, as well as (iii) a failure of supervision on the part of the legal person; or imputation is "automatic" from the moment when (i) the offense has been committed (ii) by a person acting on behalf of the legal person.

It is important to note that the adoption of either model depends directly on the way in which the legal person[287] is considered. If we accept that it has a will distinct from that of its members, it is not absolutely necessary to identify a culpable natural person. Conversely, if we consider that the legal person has no will of its own, and that it acts only through that of its members, it is logical to require the identification of the material perpetrator of the offense.[288] The disadvantage of the second view is that it allows a form of vicarious criminal liability to persist,[289] thereby contravening the criminal law principles recognized by most countries; whereas the first respects the principle of personal criminal liability, and is also effective.[290]

---

286 These models vary in number depending on the author. Some classify them into categories and subcategories to capture the nuances specific to each model, while most recognize only two or three, and some go so far as to identify up to five different models. On this subject, *see ex multis*: G. Vermeulen, W. De Bondt & C. Ryckman, Liability of Legal Persons for Offences in the EU, Eur. Comm. - DG Justice (JLS/2010/JPEN/PR/1009/E4) 56–59 (2012); K. Tiedemann, *Introduction*, *in* La criminalisation du comportement collectif: XIVe Congrès international de droit comparé 6, 27–29 (H. De Doelder & K. Tiedemann eds., 1996); K. Tiedemann, *La responsabilité pénale dans l'entreprise: Vers un espace judiciaire européen unifié?*, Seminar of the Association de recherches pénales européennes under the patronage of the European Commission (Paris, Dec. 13, 1996 – Court of Cassation), Introductory report, Revue de science criminelle et de droit pénal comparé 259 (1997); S. Adam, N. Blaise & N. Colette-Basecqz, *Conclusions*, *in* La responsabilité pénale des personnes morales en Europe 433 (S. Adam, N. Colette-Basecqz & M. Nihoul eds., 2008); J. Pradel, *La responsabilité des personnes morales en droit pénal comparé*, *in* Strafjustiz und Rechtsstaat: Justice pénale et Etat de droit 49, 59–63 (M. A. Niggli & N. Queloz eds., 2003); M. Hornman & E. Sikkema, *Corporate Intent: In Search for a Theoretical Foundation for Corporate Mens Rea*, *in* Overarching Views of Crime and Deviancy: Rethinking the Legacy of the Utrecht School 287 (F. De Jong ed., 2015); S. Geeroms, *La responsabilité pénale de la personne morale: Une étude comparative*, 48 Revue internationale de droit comparé 533, 539–54 (1996); M. Pieth & R. Ivory, *Emergence and Convergence: Corporate Criminal Liability Principles in Overview*, *in* Corporate Criminal Liability: Emergence, Convergence and Risks 3, 6–7, 48–53 (M. Pieth & R. Ivory eds., 2011); finally, for a detailed account of the *identification doctrine*, the *senior management test*, the *aggregation doctrine*, the *corporate culture doctrine* and the *structural negligence doctrine*, and a critical assessment of their relevance (based on criteria such as certainty of proof, conformity with jurisprudential practice and fairness), *see* N. Cavanagh, *Corporate Criminal Liability: An Assessment of the Models of Fault*, 75 The Journal of Criminal Law 414 (2011).

287 In this regard, Y. Mayaud, *L'articulation des responsabilités pénales entre personne morale et personnes physiques – Une logique d'artifices...*, Actualité juridique Pénal 546 (2018).

288 C. Wells, *Corporate Criminal Responsibility*, *in* Research Handbook on Corporate Legal Responsibility 147, 148–49 (S. Tully ed., 2005).

289 *Id.*

290 Pradel, *La responsabilité des personnes morales en droit pénal comparé*, *op. cit.* at 59–60.

Today, there seems to be a consensus in favor of recognizing that, while a legal person necessarily acts through the intermediary of human beings, it nonetheless has a will of its own, and the imputation of an offense on its behalf is justified by its independence from its members.[291]

170. **The gradual unification of the rules governing the imputation of offenses to legal persons: towards the abolition of the requirement to identify a natural person.** The direction of legal developments indicates a trend toward the abolition of the requirement to identify a natural person as the guilty party. In the U.S., this requirement was dropped at the beginning of the twentieth century.[292] In German law, the OWiG, which initially stipulated that only the organs of a legal person could be held criminally liable, broadened the scope of liability to include all those authorized to act on its behalf.[293] In France, while article 121-2 of the Penal Code makes the liability of a legal entity conditional on the identification of the natural person, organ or representative, who has committed the offense, in practice, the courts of appeal and the Court of Cassation often consider this condition to be met, even in the case of intentional offenses.[294] French legal writers are therefore right to call for the article to be reworded to require only that the offense be "committed on behalf of the legal person," without the material perpetrator having to be identified.[295] Finally, it should be noted that the European Commission's fifth recommendation, in its 2012 report on the liability of legal persons, recommends that Member States consider that it is no longer necessary to prove that the offense was committed by a natural person.[296] This is precisely the solution that has been adopted in anticompetitive practices law, for the purpose of imputing the infringement committed to the entity devoid of legal personality that is the enterprise. It could, moreover, make a valuable contribution to the ongoing French debate on whether it would be appropriate to extend article 121-2 of the Penal Code to corporate groups.[297]

---

291 F. Rousseau, L'imputation dans la responsabilité pénale 389–418 (2009), nos. 356–382.

292 J. A. E. Vervaele, *La responsabilité pénale de et au sein de la personne morale aux Pays-Bas. Mariage entre pragmatisme et dogmatisme juridique*, Revue de science criminelle et de droit pénal comparé 325 (1997).

293 H. J. Hirsch, *Rapport allemand*, *in* La criminalisation du comportement collectif: XIVe Congrès international de droit comparé 31, 55 (H. De Doelder & K. Tiedemann eds., 1996).

294 J.-Y. Maréchal, *Plaidoyer pour une responsabilité pénale directe des personnes morales*, JCP G no. 38, 46, 48–49 (Sept. 14, 2009), étude 249. The Court of Cassation states that "the offense could only have been committed, on behalf of the company, by its organs or representatives." For involuntary manslaughter, *see* Cass. crim., June 20, 2006, no. 05-85.255 (Fr.); and concerning the offense of forgery, Cass. crim., June 25, 2008, no. 07-80.261 (Fr.).

295 J.-C. Saint-Pau, *Faut-il repenser la responsabilité pénale des personnes morales ?*, *in* Faut-il rethéoriser le droit pénal? 101, 111 (J. Leroy ed., 2017); *adde*, Maréchal, *Plaidoyer pour une responsabilité pénale directe des personnes morales*, *op. cit.* at 50–51.

296 Vermeulen et al., Liability of Legal Persons for Offences in the EU, *op. cit.* at 13.

297 On this subject, *see* J. Chacornac, *L'article 121-2 du Code pénal et les groupes de sociétés: Les sociétés mères sont-elles des personnes morales comme les autres?*, *in* Mélanges en l'honneur du Professeur Philippe Conte 271 (2023).

B. A technique extended to entities without legal personality

171. **The *relative* autonomy of the undertaking-specific imputation technique compared to the one used for legal person.** The notion of undertaking[298] is unique in the legal landscape: lacking legal personality, sometimes described as a "new subject of law"[299] or a "theoretical *no-man's-land*,"[300] it is said to have acquired, over decades of jurisprudential clarification, a genuine "conceptual autonomy."[301] The reality, however, is more nuanced. Admittedly, the undertaking displays significant specificities compared to legal persons, if only because it transcends the formal boundaries of legal personality.[302] Moreover, since it is more nebulous than the legal person, its delimitation is flexible, and can fluctuate within the same corporate group from one case to another, depending on the offense in question.[303] Unlike a legal person, the existence of an undertaking requires the exercise of economic activity.[304] Finally, it should be noted that it is possible for an enterprise to consist of a natural person,[305] or a single legal person, whether large or small – making it a notion that, while theoretically unitary, encompasses fundamentally distinct realities.[306]

---

298 Among a vast body of literature, two theses specifically address the company. *See* L. Arcelin, L'entreprise en droit de la concurrence français et communautaire (2003); and more recently, E. Thomas, L'entreprise contrevenante en droit des pratiques anticoncurrentielles: Variations autour de la distinction entre société et entreprise (Union européenne et France) (2021).

299 This is the view taken by O. Mach, L'entreprise et les groupes de sociétés en droit européen de la concurrence 8 (1974). For a contrary view, *see* J. Paillusseau, *Les apports du droit de l'entreprise au concept de droit*, Colloque du 25e anniversaire de la FNDE, JCP E 3, 8 (1997), suppl. 2: the author considers that the enterprise is neither a subject nor an object of law, but rather an "object of legal structuring."

300 G. Lagarde, *Propos de commercialiste sur la personnalité morale: Réalité ou réalisme?*, *in* Études offertes à Alfred Jauffret 429, 436–37 (1974); *adde*, in the same vein, G. Friedel, *À propos de la notion d'entreprise…*, *in* Études dédiées à René Roblot: Aspects actuels du droit commercial français 97, 106–107 (1984).

301 L. Arcelin, *La conquête du droit du marché par la notion d'entreprise*, RTD com. 575 (2018).

302 According to the famous statement of principle stating that "concept of an undertaking encompasses every entity engaged in an economic activity, regardless of the legal status of the entity and the way in which it is financed." Case C-41/90, Klaus Höfner and Fritz Elser, ECLI:EU:C:1991:161, para. 21.

303 Case C-170/83, Hydrotherm Gerätebau, ECLI:EU:C:1984:271, para. 11.

304 On this subject, *see* O. Odudu, The Boundaries of EC Competition Law: The Scope of Article 81, 23 (2006).

305 Provided that the individual qualifies as an enterprise. In this sense, *see* W. P. J. Wils, *Is Criminalization of EU Competition Law the Answer?*, 28 World Competition 117, 125–27 (2005); *adde*, the conclusions of Advocate General B. Vesterdorf, July 10, 1991, in Case T-1/89, Rhône-Poulenc, ECLI:EU:T:1991:38, at 916. For an example, *see* Case C-180/98, Pavel Pavlov, ECLI:EU:C:2000:428, para. 77: "The self-employed medical specialists who are members of the LSV therefore carry on an economic activity and are thus undertakings within the meaning of Articles 85, 96 and 90 of the Treaty. The complexity and technical nature of the services they provide and the fact that the practice of their profession is regulated cannot alter that conclusion."

306 The unitary approach to the enterprise, whatever its size, is not without its problems in terms of principle: how can we justify treating a large group, an individual, or a small family structure in the same way, particularly when it comes to assessing error of law, in a field as complex as competition law? On this subject, *see infra*, no. 466.

These four particularities aside, it is clear that the technique used to define an undertaking is not based on purely economic criteria,[307] but rather on a line of reasoning that is an *extension* of that which underpins the criminal liability of legal persons. Indeed, the foundation is the same whether liability is assigned to a legal person or to the undertaking, and only the method of imputation has been broadened in competition law.

172. **The basis for imputing the offense to the undertaking: *autonomy* and its corollary, *personal* liability.** Autonomy underpins the personal liability of the individual, just as it justifies that of the legal person and the undertaking. However how "modern" or "economic" the law may be, it never abandons certain structures of reasoning: liability remains tied to the (postulated) existence of free will. If parent company and subsidiary[308] are treated as one, this is because the latter "does not decide *independently upon its own conduct* on the market, but carries out, in all material respects, the instructions given to it by the parent company,"[309] as if it were merely its extension.[310]

For the same reason, employees are considered to be "auxiliary *organ* forming an integral part of the [enterprise],"[311] as long as they perform their functions "for [it] and under [its] direction."[312] Judges thus focus on the nature of employment contracts to justify the fact that employees generally cannot be qualified as an undertaking, owing to their lack of autonomy.[313]

This also explains why case law does not distinguish between offenses committed by governing bodies or senior executives, and imputes to the

307 On the limits of the "economic unity" doctrine, *see* O. Odudu & D. Bailey, *Single Economic Entity Doctrine in EU Competition Law*, 51 Common Market Law Review 1721, 1747, 1747–54 (2014). The authors point out that the doctrine of economic unity would imply that any legal person within a corporate group could be held liable for the offenses committed by another entity forming part of the same economic unit. However, case law clearly shows that this is not the case. This is evidenced by the fact that belonging to a corporate group is not determinative in defining the perimeter of the enterprise. *See* Case 30/87, Corinne Bodson, ECLI:EU:C:1988:225, para. 20; *adde*, more recently and along the same lines, Case C-65/02 P, ThyssenKrupp Stainless, ECLI:EU:C:2005:454, para. 66. On this subject, *see also* with interest: E. Claudel, *Autonomie et notion d'entreprise*, Contrats concurrence consommation (June 2020), dossier 7.

308 Or, more generally, principal and agency, branch, representative, or independent service provider. *See* A. Decocq & G. Decocq, Droit de la concurrence: Droit interne et droit de l'Union européenne 103 (9th ed. 2021), no. 57.

309 Case 48/69, Imperial Chemical Industries, ECLI:EU:C:1972:70, para. 133.

310 The expression was used in the Opinion of Advocate General A. Rantos, Case C-680/20, Unilever Italia, ECLI:EU:C:2022:586, para. 49; comm. D. Bosco, *L'article 102 du TFUE, le réseau de distribution et la notion d'unité économique*, Contrats concurrence consommation (Oct. 2022), comm. 158. This was a particular case in which only the head of a distribution network was held liable for the anticompetitive behavior of its independent distributors, the latter being merely the "instrument" by which the dominant undertaking implemented its exclusionary practice. *See* Case C-680/20, Unilever Italia, ECLI:EU:C:2023:33, para. 30; comm. D. Bosco, *Réseaux de distribution exclusive et abus de position dominante*, Contrats concurrence consommation (Mar. 2023), comm. 48.

311 Case 40/73, Suiker Unie, ECLI:EU:C:1975:174, para. 539.

312 Case C-22/98, Jean Claude Becu, ECLI:EU:C:1999:419, para. 26.

313 For a detailed study of case law relating to employees of the enterprise, *see* C. Townley, *The Concept of an 'Undertaking': The Boundaries of the Corporation – A Discussion of Agency, Employees and Subsidiaries*, *in* EC Competition Law: A Critical Assessment 3, 4–16 (G. Amato & C.-D. Ehlermann eds., 2007).

undertaking the offense perpetrated by any or all of its employees.[314] This imputation requires neither that principal partners or managers took part in the infringement, nor even that they were aware of it, but simply the "action by a person who is authorized to act on behalf of the undertaking"[315] – which would make it possible, in the hypothesis that anticompetitive behavior was adopted by an artificial intelligence, to impute it to the undertaking[316] without giving rise to insurmountable theoretical difficulties. This condition is, moreover, interpreted flexibly by the Court of Justice, which attaches little importance to the agent's *power* to act on behalf of the undertaking,[317] nor to the argument that the employee acted alone, without informing their superiors and against their orders.[318] This is an appropriate solution, because since the commission of an offense is most often a clandestine activity, and always a prohibited act, it is rare for an undertaking's agent to do so "with a mandate."[319]

Competition law thus adopts the anthropomorphic thesis, taken to its extreme: the undertaking is seen as the sole brain, its subsidiaries and employees being merely its arms, its acting members – a brain capable of surviving even after the body perishes, and of infiltrating another still-living body...[320]

When several legal entities are encompassed within an undertaking's, they are held personally liable for an offense that they themselves are deemed to have committed.[321] From the undertaking's point of view, however, this is neither vicarious liability nor no-fault liability; on the contrary, it is

314 *See* I. Luc, *La responsabilité pénale des personnes morales en droit de la concurrence*, *in* Dépénalisation de la vie des affaires et responsabilité pénale des personnes morales 119, 121 (M. Benillouche & M. Daury-Fauveau eds., 2009).

315 Case 100/80, SA Musique Diffusion française, ECLI:EU:C:1983:158, para. 97. *Adde*, along the same lines, Case T-373/10, Villeroy & Boch Austria, ECLI:EU:T:2013:455, para. 244; Case T-389/10, SLM, ECLI:EU:T:2015:513, para. 410.

316 *See infra*, nos. 515–516.

317 W. Wils, *The Undertaking as Subject of E.C. Competition Law and the Imputation of Infringements to Natural or Legal Persons*, 25 European Law Review 99, 106 (2000), and references cited.

318 *See* in this respect, *inter alia*, Opinion of Advocate General B. Vesterdorf, Case T-1/89, Rhône-Poulenc, ECLI:EU:T:1991:38, at 1002–1006.

319 Case C-68/12, Protimonopolny úrad Slovenskej republiky, ECLI:EU:C:2013:71, para. 26. *Adde*, in the same spirit: Case T-373/10, Villeroy & Boch Austria, ECLI:EU:T:2013:455, para. 243: the General Court rejects the argument that the mere fact the undertaking was no longer active in a sector is not sufficient to invalidate the finding that its employee continued to take part in illicit discussions in that sector.

320 Here, we focus on the more controversial hypothesis of economic continuity. Among the abundant literature on this subject, *see* L. Idot, *La responsabilité pénale des personnes morales: Les leçons du droit européen de la concurrence*, Concurrences no. 1-2012, art. no. 41768, 55, 68–72, nos. 50–72. Note that this solution is now accepted even in criminal law. *See* Cass. ass. plén., Nov. 25, 2020, no. 18-86.955 (Fr.), comm. P. Conte, *Le cas des fusions-absorptions de sociétés*, Droit pénal (Jan. 2021), comm. 2; L. Donnedieu de Vabres-Tranié & M. de Walsche, *Interprétation systématique de la notion d'entreprise et responsabilité pénale des personnes morales*: *Quand le droit de la concurrence bouscule le droit pénal des personnes morales*, Gazette du Palais no. 11, 74 (May 5, 2022).

321 Case C-294/98 P, Metsä-Serla Oyj, ECLI:EU:C:2000:632, para. 34.

"*liability for its own misconduct and personal in nature.*"[322] The punitive nature of the fines imposed means that infringements must be attributed in accordance with the principle of personal liability.[323] Thus, the fact that a parent company can be held liable for offenses committed by its subsidiaries is in no way an exception to this principle, but "is the expression of that very principle," for if "the parent company's involvement in the commission of the offence may not have been directly apparent outwardly,... that does not detract from its personal (co-)responsibility for the offence," given that it is the parent company that "pulls the strings within the group of companies."[324]

It is therefore the intent of the undertaking that is characterized, since its hold over its subsidiaries and employees deprives them of autonomy. To identify an enterprise – i.e., to draw a face over a body – the criterion is logically that of decisive influence, since it proves the absence of autonomy of its acting members. This reasoning also underpins the criminal liability of legal persons: when an offense committed by a natural person is imputed to a legal person, we recognize that the employee's will is, in reality, that of the "brain" that employs them.

173. **The undertaking delimitation criterion: the parent company's ability to exert decisive influence.** The criterion most often used to delimit an undertaking, in order to include a parent company that has not participated directly in the infringement,[325] is the decisive influence it exercises over its subsidiaries. This is based on the existence of economic, organizational, and legal links between the various entities.[326] In practice, either the formal organization of the group, as expressed in its bylaws or contracts, allows for the characterization of a capacity to control, or this is not the case and the judge must then prove this capacity.[327] To do this, the judge may use

---

322 Case T-372/10, Bolloré, ECLI:EU:T:2012:325, para. 51 (emphasis added); *Adde*, along the same lines, Case T-104/13, Toshiba, ECLI:EU:T:2015:610, para. 136. The Court of Justice has itself recognized that "there is no principle of strict liability in Community competition law, since the Commission's decisions do not impute liability to companies without its proof being established." *See* Case C-97/08 P, Akzo Nobel, ECLI:EU:C:2009:536, para. 71.

323 Opinion of Advocate General J. Kokott, Case C-97/08 P, Akzo Nobel, ECLI:EU:C:2009:262, paras. 38–39.

324 *Id.*, paras. 97–99.

325 Or, since the Cour of Justice ruling of Oct. 6, 2021, Case C-882/19, Sumal SL, ECLI:EU:C:2021:800, to include in a private action the subsidiary that was not being sued by the competition authority. However, this solution does not undermine the unity of the concept of the undertaking, nor does it enshrine a "liability of the subsidiary for the conduct of the parent company," which would be illogical and detrimental to the principle of personal liability, given that the subsidiary has no power of control over its parent company. For an argument along these lines, *see* M.-S. Garnier, *'Un pour tous, et tous pour un!': L'arrêt Sumal précise le périmètre de la notion d'entreprise pour faciliter les actions privées*, Contrats concurrence consommation (Dec. 2021), comm. 186.

326 Case C-628/10 P, Alliance One International, ECLI:EU:C:2012:479, para. 43; Case C-521/09 P, Elf Aquitaine, ECLI:EU:C:2011:620, para. 53.

327 For example, the Court of Justice has ruled that the exercise of joint control over a subsidiary by two independent parent companies does not preclude the establishment of an economic unity between one of them and their joint subsidiary, and has therefore focused on demonstrating its ability and interest in exercising decisive influence over the said subsidiary. *See* Case C-293/13 P, Fresh Del Monte, ECLI:EU:C:2014:2439, paras. 75–99.

the "body of evidence" method,[328] or a presumption of decisive influence. This presumption is sometimes referred to as the "capitalistic presumption," which seems to indicate – wrongly – that it is intended to provide proof of a simple economic unit. However, this is not the purpose of the proof, which consists not in economic ownership, but in the existence of a *determining influence*, which can be established on the basis of criteria other than capital ownership, such as, for example, the holding of voting rights[329]. Indeed, the Court of Justice has recognized that it is "not the mere holding of all or virtually all the capital of the subsidiary in itself that gives rise to the presumption…, but the *degree of control* of the parent company over its subsidiary that this holding implies."[330] Indeed, when a parent company holds one hundred percent of a subsidiary's capital, even if it does not participate directly in the offense committed by its subsidiaries, it exercises a decisive influence over them.[331]

Verification of the actual exercise of influence therefore appears superfluous, since the subsidiary then "necessarily follows a policy laid down by the same bodies as, under its statutes, determine [the parent company's] policy."[332] The presumption leads to a reversal of the burden of proof: the competition authority is not required to adduce "additional indicia relating to the actual exercise of influence by the parent company"[333] – which means, *a contrario*, that the mere *capacity* to influence is sufficient. In order to rebut the presumption, it is then up to the parent company to demonstrate that the subsidiary behaves autonomously on the market[334] – proof that is extremely difficult to provide, and has been described by some as *probatio diabolica.*[335]

When parent company and subsidiary form part of the same unit, the competition authority can issue a decision imposing a fine on the parent company "without having to establish the personal involvement of the

328 For examples of elements taken into account by the judge to characterize decisive influence, *see* Arcelin, L'entreprise en droit de la concurrence français et communautaire, *op. cit.* at 269–301.

329 *See* Case C-595/18 P, The Goldman Sachs Group, ECLI:EU:C:2021:73; comm. D. Bosco, *La Cour de justice confirme une extension de la présomption capitalistique*, Contrats concurrence consommation (Mar. 2021), comm. 46. In this judgment, the Court of Justice aptly renamed the "capitalistic presumption," replacing it with the expression "presumption that the parent company actually exercises decisive influence," para. 36.

330 Case C-595/18 P, The Goldman Sachs Group, ECLI:EU:C:2021:73, para. 35 (emphasis added).

331 Case C-97/08 P, Akzo Nobel, ECLI:EU:C:2009:536, para. 77.

332 Case 107/82, AEG-Telefunken, ECLI:EU:C:1983:293, para. 50.

333 Case C-97/08 P, Akzo Nobel, ECLI:EU:C:2009:536, para. 62.

334 Case C-286/98 P, Stora Kopparbergs Bergslags, ECLI:EU:C:2000:630, para. 29. *See*, to the same effect, Case C-97/08 P, Akzo Nobel, ECLI:EU:C:2009:536, para. 61.

335 On this subject, *see* E. Claudel, *Responsabilité au sein des groupes en droit de la concurrence: Un exemple à suivre?*, Cahiers de droit de l'entreprise no. 5 (Sept. 2017), dossier 27: according to the author, a large part of the doctrine and certain Advocates General consider that this is an irrebuttable presumption of fact, violating fundamental rights (rights of defense, presumption of innocence, equality of arms, *non bis in idem*, legal certainty, proper administration of justice). All these arguments were rejected by the Court of Justice. For Emmanuelle Claudel, "[t]hese criticisms are indicative of a very low level of acceptability of praetorian solutions. And yet, even if questionable, this jurisprudence has its virtues."

latter in the infringement."[336] The ability to exercise decisive influence thus carries with it a presumption of involvement in the infringement.

174. **The consequences of this imputation with regard to the mental element of the offense: rejection of the parent company's argument of negligence.** Since the Court of Justice recognizes that each legal entity encompassed within an undertaking is personally liable for its own fault, it seems logical that a parent company should have tried to argue that it had not "deliberately" committed the infringement in question, but only "through negligence," since it claimed to have been unaware of its subsidiary's conduct.[337] The General Court's reasoning in response to this argument is noteworthy. The judges began by establishing intentional commission of the cartel at issue by the subsidiary.[338] They then reject the plea put forward by the parent company, considering that since the latter is "regarded as having itself committed the infringement," it "cannot invoke a mitigating circumstance relating to infringements committed as a result of negligence."[339] The subsidiary's intent is *automatically imputed* to the enterprise, which includes the parent company.

175. **Is the existence of a "code of conduct" an obstacle to imputing intent to the undertaking?** Can the parent company exonerate itself by demonstrating that it put in place the necessary controls to prevent the infringement from occurring? This was the claimant's argument in *Schindler*: it held that the parent company of the group could not be accused of any fault of its own, resulting from "its own participation in an infringement" or "breach of certain organisational obligations existing within the group," since it "did its utmost" to avoid the commission of infringements by its subsidiaries "by establishing and developing a compliance programme which is a model of its kind."[340] However, the Court ruled that the adoption of a compliance program and a code of conduct not only "does not alter the reality of the infringement,"[341] but rather suggests "that the parent company did in fact supervise the commercial policy of its subsidiaries."[342] The solution is severe,

336 Case C-97/08 P, Akzo Nobel, ECLI:EU:C:2009:536, para. 59.

337 Case T-399/09, Holding Slovenske Elektrarne, ECLI:EU:T:2013:647, para. 137.

338 *Id.*, para. 141: "[I]t is obvious that the members of TDR's [the subsidiary] personnel or management who participated on its behalf in various meetings organised in connection with the cartel, and who subsequently implemented the decisions taken at those meetings, could not have been unaware that their conduct had as its object the restriction of competition in the common market. ...It follows that the Commission was correct in not finding, in the contested decision, that TDR had committed the infringement as a result of negligence ... ."

339 *Id.*, para. 142.

340 Case C-501/11, Schindler, ECLI:EU:C:2013:522, para. 90.

341 *Id.* para. 113.

342 *Id.*, para. 114. The Opinion of Advocate General J. Kokott is enlightening as to the reasons behind the Court of Justice's solution. It rightly considers that a compliance program "which 'functions' must be capable of effectively preventing serious, long-term cartel offences and of uncovering and promptly rectifying any infringements of the law committed"; however, in view of the findings in this case (duration and seriousness of participation in the cartel), it can "cannot therefore be assumed that Schindler 'did its utmost' to prevent the contested cartel offences." *See* Opinion of Advocate General J. Kokott, Case C-501/11 P, Schindler,

but pertinent: it would be too easy to escape punishment by arguing that precautions may have been taken merely as a façade.[343] It is also consistent with the Court's other pronouncements, notably its refusal to acknowledge that seeking legal advice can exonerate.[344]

*

* *

176. **Conclusion to Section 1: the transversality of intent.** While doctrinal disputes over intent, and the legal techniques used to characterize it, may have given rise to the impression that it is sometimes removed from reasoning, a comparative approach reveals that it is, in fact, a foundational condition for liability to be incurred – whether in tort law or criminal law, and whether the fault is attributed to a physical person or a disembodied entity. Beyond radiating throughout the entire legal system, it is now necessary to demonstrate that intent also permeates all countries sharing a common cultural heritage, which could enable EU law to develop a clear, unitary theory of intent.

*

* *

Section 2
A concept that permeates all legal systems

177. **The European construction of concepts: striking a balance between autonomy and dependence.** Numerous studies have sought to develop a methodology and identify the issues involved in the construction of Europe.[345] The legislator drafts laws, the judges interpret them, and their decisions, by virtue of the principle of primacy and the requirement of conforming interpretation, penetrate the domestic legal order of the Member States. Consequently, the terms used and the solutions adopted at the European Union level must not contradict the theoretical constructs of the countries that make up the Union. The concepts used in Union law are thus both

ECLI:EU:C:2013:248, para. 99.

343 Referring to the sociological approach, mentioned *supra*, no. 167.

344 *See infra*, no. 466.

345 On this topic, *see inter alia*: S. Cimamonti & J.-B. Perrier, *Perspectives européennes: L'avenir de la justice pénale de l'Union européenne*, XXIV LES NOUVEAUX PROBLÈMES ACTUELS DE SCIENCES CRIMINELLES 139 (2013).

autonomous – since they are defined by the European legislator or courts, and are binding on national judges – and dependent on national constructions – since a concept could not be accepted by the Member States if it clashed head-on with their tradition. This dual characteristic of autonomy and dependence calls for comparative law[346] in order to find either the lowest common denominator or the prevailing orientation.[347] It is also giving rise to a growing phenomenon of "denationalization of criminal law theory," with the aim of achieving a "conceptual syncretism,"[348] i.e., to adopt a broader view of national practice and theories – to go beyond their dissimilarities, which are often only apparent,[349] and focus on their similarities.

178. **The lack of a satisfactory conceptualization of intent in both domestic criminal law and European Union law.** To pinpoint the concept of intent as it is understood in European Union law, it is impossible to disregard the solutions adopted in the domestic laws of the Member States.[350] However, national theories of intent are extremely complex, to the point of making the concept difficult to grasp (**Paragraph 1**), which undoubtedly explains why the European Union has yet to develop a genuine theory of intent[351] (**Paragraph 2**).

346 Among abundant literature, *see*: on the importance of comparative law in the praetorian interpretation of EU law, K. Lenaertz & J. A. Gutierrez-Fons, Les méthodes d'interprétation de la Cour de justice de l'Union européenne 93–105 (2020), nos. 102–111; A. Bernardi, *Stratégies pour une harmonisation des systèmes pénaux européens*, 24 Archives de politique criminelle 195, 216 (2002); J. Pradel, *Les grandes tendances de l'européanisation des systèmes pénaux nationaux*, 50 Les Cahiers de droit 1015, 1030 (2009); finally, it should be noted that references to comparative law are rare and subtle in CJEU judgments, but appear more explicitly in the Opinion of Advocates General and in the Commission's contributions. *See* P. Pescatore, *Le recours, dans la jurisprudence de la Cour de justice des communautés européennes, à des normes déduites de la comparaison des droits des États membres*, Revue internationale de droit comparé 337, 338 (1980). An additional difficulty has emerged with the integration of new States into the Union – necessarily expanding the scope of comparison. *See id.* at 350.

347 Bernardi, *Stratégies pour une harmonisation des systèmes pénaux européens*, *op. cit.* at 205–207.

348 A. Bernardi, *L'européanisation de la science pénale*, 26 Archives de politique criminelle 3, 33 (2004).

349 According to R. Sacco, *Droit commun de l'Europe, et composantes du droit*, *in* Nouvelles perspectives d'un droit commun 95, 106–107 (M. Cappelletti ed., 1978): "The task of doctrine" is to "prevent the formation of artificial conceptions, leading to the belief in the existence of insurmountable barriers between the laws of different countries. ...It must become aware of the parallels that really exist between the different rights, and emphasize them. ...Generalizations should be the conclusion of a comparison of detailed rules concerning a given problem. The common core of systems would thus be highlighted"; *adde*, P. Hébraud, *Rôles respectifs de la volonté et des éléments objectifs dans les actes juridiques*, *in* II Mélanges offerts à Jacques Maury 420, 428 (1960): the internationalization of law is intended "to dig institutions down to their fundamental nature in order to resolve the conflicts they give rise to"; F. Ost & M. Van de Kerchove, De la pyramide au réseau? Pour une théorie dialectique du droit 18, 99–100 (2002): the authors observe that the construction of Europe requires a creative effort to rediscover and interpret general and shared principles, and underscore the pivotal role played by the judge of the European Union in this work of unification.

350 In this sense, *see* Opinion of Advocate General H. Mayras, Case 26/75, General Motors Continental, ECLI:EU:C:1975:141, at 1388: "Although in the strict sense of the term the fines prescribed by Regulation No 17 are not in the nature of criminal-law sanctions, I do not consider it possible, in interpreting the term 'intentionally', to disregard the concepts which are commonly accepted in the penal legislation of the Member States."

351 *See* in particular R. Legros, *L'arrêt BMW et le droit pénal européen*, Cahiers de droit européen 206, 228–29 (1980): "There is, therefore, certainly a 'penal' lacuna in Community law: with rare exceptions, there is no indication of general principles. ...In most cases, we have been satisfied with a superficial, formalistic recourse to principles."

Paragraph 1 – The inextricable complexity of national theories of intent

179. **The disadvantages of complex theories of intent.** Intent is reputed to be one of the most obscure subjects in criminal law[352] – which has the disadvantage of making it impossible to pinpoint either the scope of intent (**I**) or its content (**II**).

I. Complexity creates uncertainty about the scope of intent

180. **Two forms of challenge.** Initially, intent was challenged directly – some authors went so far as to deny the relevance of the concept (**A**) – which undoubtedly contributed to the reduction, in contemporary times, of the scope of intent (**B**).

A. Direct challenges: denying the relevance of intent

181. **The questioning of free will and its unprecedented influence on the legal theory of intent.** From the seventeenth century onwards,[353] free will was called into question in Europe.[354] It is of little importance, one might

352 *See supra*, no. 6.

353 We invite the reader to make the connection between what follows and the rupture between science and philosophy that occurred at the same time, studied *supra*, nos. 80 *et seq*.

354 In France, key figures among the Encyclopedists, including Diderot, "were convinced determinists who expressed ideas comparable to those we find a century later among the Italian positivists," *see* C. Debuyst, *Les conceptions criminologiques de la criminalité*, *in* XXIV ANNALES DE L'UNIVERSITÉ DE SCIENCES SOCIALES DE TOULOUSE 151, 154 (1976), fasc. 1 et 2. Across the Channel, Hobbes, Bentham, Locke and Mill strongly opposed the classical doctrine of intention upheld by Blackstone, Coke and Hale, which they considered artificial, and to which they intended to substitute a mechanistic, materialist conception based on a deterministic vision of man, *see* H. Parent, *Histoire de l'acte volontaire en droit pénal anglais et canadien*, 45 MCGILL LAW JOURNAL 975, 1000–1002 (2000). Among Germans, the front against free will is composed of the most brilliant writers. Nietzsche, for example, writes: "Today we have no sympathy anymore for the concept of 'free will': we know only too well what it is – the most disreputable of all the theologians' tricks, designed to make humanity 'responsible' in the theologians' sense, that is, to make it dependent on them ...... All the old psychology, the psychology of will, is predicated on the fact that its originators, the priests in the elites of ancient communities, wanted to create a right for themselves to inflict punishments . . . . Human beings were thought to be 'free' so that they could be ruled, so that they could be punished ... ." *See* F. W. NIETZSCHE, TWILIGHT OF THE IDOLS 35 (R. Polt trans., Hackett Publishing Company 1997). Schopenhauer, for his part, wishes to disillusion his readers: there is no such thing as free will, the will is a prime site of enslavement, for we do not decide what we want – the residual question being whether such an awareness is sufficient to indicate a relative degree of freedom. *See* A. SCHOPENHAUER, ESSAI SUR LE LIBRE ARBITRE (S. Reinach trans., Rivages Poche 2018). In contemporary times, the field is dominated by analytic philosophy (a current founded by Frege and Russel, focused on the internal logic of discourse and intended to shed light on classical philosophical questions through purely logical reasoning). The quarrel now revolves around two questions. First, "What is freedom?" – a question at the origin of discussions focused on the notion of "alternative possibility." On this subject, *see* the seminal study: H. G. Frankfurt, *Alternate Possibilities and Moral Responsibility*, 66 THE JOURNAL OF PHILOSOPHY 829–39 (1969). The author seeks to determine in which cases it is possible to assert that there is such an alternative, which is supposed to be the basis of responsibility. A second, no less thorny issue is "Are determinism and responsibility compatible?" Here we are confronted by compatibilists, for whom moral responsibility is compatible with causal determinism; and incompatibilists, for whom moral responsibility is not compatible with causal determinism. The literature on this subject is

retort: we know that the law, from its earliest known origins, has postulated it for pragmatic reasons, without being able to furnish proof.[355] A significant difference nevertheless separates earlier times from the present. This time, the challenges to free will have not remained without influence on legal thought. The jurist seems to have lent an ear to the siren calls of materialist philosophy and a science reputed to be exact; and interdisciplinarity – though so often fruitful – has led to a frontal challenge to the very relevance of intent. Admittedly, the notion has not been abandoned by positive law. But these doctrinal disputes gave rise, on one hand, to misunderstandings, and on the other, to reasoning that was foreign to legal logic, to such an extent that they led to a profound and lasting disruption of the theory of intent. This theory, though simple, is subtle: it does not take much to obscure it and plunge it into inextricable metaphysical meanderings.[356]

182. **The impact of deterministic philosophy on theories of intent: Beccaria, the Italian positivists, and the French school of social defense.** If we renounce free will as the foundation of responsibility, we must logically abandon consideration of intent. This is what was proposed by writers as authoritative as they were influential.[357] As early as 1764, Beccaria argued that intention should be dispensed with[358] – a criterion which, in his view, led inevitably to miscarriages of justice and opened the door to arbitrariness.[359] Whereas the Ancien Droit regarded the commission of evil as the product of deliberate will, this principle came under sustained attack from the nineteenth century onwards.[360] These discussions took on an "inordinate importance,"[361] even though

---

difficult to access for non-specialists: the demonstrations call on logical arguments often taking the form of mathematical language. For an overview, *see* C. Michon, Qu'est-ce que le libre arbitre? (2011); *adde*, J.-B. Lebohec, *La responsabilité est-elle incompatible avec le déterminisme* ?, 63 Archives de philosophie du droit 83 (2021); for arguments in favor of the "incompatibilist" thesis, *see* the now-classic work by P. Van Inwagen, Essai sur le libre arbitre (C. Michon trans., Librairie philosophique J. Vrin 2017); for a detailed account of the opposing theses (compatibilist and incompatibilist), *see* G. Le Gousse, Le pouvoir d'agir autrement: Essai sur le libre arbitre (2017); *adde*, F. De Monneron, Le déterminisme et la responsabilité morale (2011) (Ph.D. dissertation, Université de Nantes).

355 *See supra*, nos. 26–27 for the ancient period, no. 53 for the Ancien Droit.

356 Questions such as "Does free will exist?" and "What are will and intention?" are destined to remain without a definitive answer, freedom being "the most contentious question of metaphysics, the most contentious science." D. Hume, An Enquiry Concerning Human Understanding 98 (The Open Court Publishing Co. 1900) (reprinted from the posthumous edition of 1777).

357 For a detailed historical study, *see* A. Frambéry-Iacobone, La recherche de l'intention en droit pénal contemporain (xixe-xxe siècles) 267–345 (2022) (Ph.D. dissertation, Université de Bordeaux).

358 On this theme, *see* X. Martin, Beccaria, Voltaire et Napoléon: Ou l'étrange humanisme pénal des Lumières (1760-1810) 20 (2018): "[I]f intent counts for nothing,… the penal question becomes demoralized. Its law becomes objective, and recognizes social utility as its sole aim."

359 The arguments of Beccaria, who, let us recall, was not a jurist, would appear specious to any criminal law specialist. On Muyart de Vouglans' refutation of Beccaria's theses, *see supra*, no. 89.

360 A. Laingui, *L'Homme criminel dans l'Ancien Droit*, Revue de science criminelle et de droit pénal comparé 15, 30 (Jan.-Mar. 1983).

361 A. Laingui & M. Crépin, *La philosophie du droit pénal du Moyen Âge à l'époque moderne*, 53 Revue internationale de droit pénal 613, 614 (1982).

they concerned a concept which, for several millennia, had been deeply rooted in legal traditions.[362] Indifferent to the legacy of the past, the proponents of the Italian positivist school nevertheless sought to hold criminal law specialists to account: why continue to base criminal law on intent, when we know that freedom is an illusion?[363] The wish of these criminologists was to see the emergence of an "objective" form of responsibility based not on guilt, but on the prevention of danger.[364] Convinced of the idea that human beings do not act voluntarily, but are predetermined by their physiological and psychological make-up as much as by the influence of their environment, these authors sought to replace the criterion of intent with that of periculosity, i.e., the danger represented by the individual.[365] This movement also had its heyday in France in the twentieth century with the school of social defense, whose program was similar.[366] It led certain authors to propose new theories of intent,[367] breaking with the classical theory:[368] it was necessary to stop presuming an empty intent, too abstract, unfaithful to reality, in order to focus on the personality of the offender, and take into consideration their "anti-social motives."[369]

183. **The critical evaluation of intent theories in the light of scientific analysis.** Under cover of and in the name of a thirst for objectivity,[370] these currents gave rise to a new approach to intent, consisting in "scientifically" verifying the psychological truth of the concept,[371] or its relevance from

---

362 *See supra*, no. 77.

363 "The positive school of criminology does not accept this unanimous reasoning of jurists," because "positive physio-psychology has completely annihilated this belief in free will or moral freedom," Enrico Ferri tells us in 1905, still convinced, twenty-seven years after the publication of his book *Négation du libre arbitre et responsabilité*. *See also* E. Ferri, La sociologie criminelle 318–19 (L. Terrier trans., Alcan 1905), no. 42.

364 P. Nuvolone, *Lombroso et le droit pénal*, Revue de science criminelle et de droit pénal comparé 291, 292 and 295 (1977).

365 R. Bernardini, L'intention coupable en droit pénal 14–17 (1974) (Ph.D. dissertation, Université de Nice).

366 Its leader, Marc Ancel, puts it this way: "Once brought back to human reality, this concrete responsibility seems liberated from its former weight. Traditional doctrine was, in fact, burdened by a metaphysical free will that lay beyond its proper domain. Thus, after proclaiming it imperiously, it made only very limited practical use of it. This freedom, posited as a principle of the delinquent, was nothing more than a postulate transformed into a legal presumption." M. Ancel, La défense sociale nouvelle 254–55 (3rd ed. 1981).

367 In the latest edition of his précis, Bernard Bouloc contrasts the "classical and abstract" conception of intention with a "realist and positivist" conception, the latter being that of the Italian school, which testifies to the persistence, even if only doctrinal, of these theories. *See* B. Bouloc, Droit pénal général 265 (27th ed. 2021), no. 278.

368 On the classic theory, *see infra*, no. 189.

369 J. Lebret, *Essai sur la notion de l'intention criminelle*, Revue de science criminelle et de droit pénal comparé 438, 475–83 (1938).

370 The paradox is obvious: these supposedly objective theories are the ones that fall into total subjectivism. *See* J. Pinatel, *Responsabilité et criminologie*, viii Annales de la faculté de droit et de sciences politiques et économiques de Strasbourg 159, 166–67 (1961).

371 The jurist is now expected to hear and heed the point of view of the criminologist, the philosopher, and even the psychologist ... In this sense, *see* R. Merle, *La culpabilité devant les sciences humaines et sociales*, Revue de science criminelle et de droit comparé 29, 29 (1976).

the point of view of economic analysis,[372] and examining the conformity of legal solutions against extralegal theories that were unverified and unverifiable. The doctrine began to adopt a perspective centered on the agent and their psyche, which naturally led to a multiplication of the forms and degrees of intent.[373] Inspired by a metaphysical conception of the intentional act,[374] jurists have made an originally simple concept extremely complex, breaking it down into ever more precise subcategories whose boundaries and practical scope remain uncertain.[375] Captivated by advances in neuroscience,[376] they have occasionally used them to re-examine the basis of criminal responsibility.[377] It is then only a small step to conclude that "classical criminal law is based on an outdated anthropology that bears no relation to current data from the human sciences," and that the "theory of intent is pretty much empty," a "pure fiction."[378] Thus, considering the complexity of the concept, its scientific inaccuracy

---

372 R. Posner, *An Economic Theory of the Criminal Law*, 85 Columbia Law Review 1193, 1221 (1985): "The subjective intentions, or state of mind, of the accused criminal are a pervasive consideration in the criminal law. This is puzzling to the economist: one can read many books on economics without encountering a reference to 'intent.' But in fact *the concept of intent in criminal law serves three economic functions*: identifying pure coercive tranfers, estimating the probability of apprehension and conviction, and determining whether the criminal sanction will be an effective (cost-justified) means of controlling undesirable conduct" (emphasis added). For an in-depth analysis, *see id.* at 1221–31. In the same vein, *see* J. S. Parker, *The Economics of Mens Rea*, 79 Virginia Law Review 741 (1993).

373 *See infra*, no. 190

374 It was the Germans, in the nineteenth century, who were the first to adopt a metaphysical approach to intent, *see infra*, no. 193. Of course, this is not to criticize the philosophy of intent per se: the subject is fascinating, and the role of metaphysics is not to produce statements that are applicable. It should, however, remain foreign to the legal conceptualization of intent, since the jurist must be practice-oriented, insofar as such an approach leads to the introduction of legal distinctions lacking practical relevance, and thus does not contribute to making the concept of intent clear and operational. For anyone interested in the contemporary philosophy of intent, it is worth mentioning the essay by Anscombe, a disciple of Wittgenstein who founded the "philosophy of action" movement. Her work can be meaningfully compared to that of Hart and Hegel. All three philosophers agree that intent can only be discovered through action, which ultimately signifies a return to Aristotelian and Scholastic pragmatism. *See* G. E. M. Anscombe, Intention (1957); S. Hampshire, H. L. A. Hart, *Decision, Intention and Certainty*, 67 Mind 1 (1958); R. B. Pippin, Hegel's Practical Philosophy: Rational Agency as Ethical Life 147–79 (2008).

375 *See infra*, no. 190.

376 *See* L. Pignatel, L'émergence d'un neurodroit: Contribution à l'étude de la relation entre les neurosciences et le droit, 87–163 (2019) (Ph.D. dissertation, Université d'Aix-Marseille). The author writes that, following the Italian theory of the "innate criminal," current neuroscientific research falls within "this paradigm of the biological explanation of behavior … in terms of determination by the structure and functioning of the brain." *Id.* at 87. *Adde*, for a legal perspective on a collective work bringing together recent works by leading neuroscientists, Y. Poullet, *À propos de* Free Will, Causality and Neuroscience, 62 Archives de philosophie du droit 565 (2020). The risk, if we push this interference of neuroscience in law to its extremes, would be to end up proceeding, in order to judge an individual, to a control of their thoughts, of their inner self, "thus relegating man to the rank of a laboratory animal." *See* M. Puech, Droit pénal général 171 (1988), no. 477.

377 For an example, *see* H. Parent, *L'imputabilité pénale. Mort d'un mythe, naissance d'une réalité*, 35 Revue juridique Thémis, 191, 239 (2001): "Today, thanks to the progress of science and the refinement of psychological observation, many people are questioning the idea that the capacity to choose is the sole property of man. Indeed, a growing number of studies tend to demonstrate the importance of willpower in the insane, in children and in animals. If the capacity to choose is no longer unique to man, then what is the basis for criminal accountability?"

378 J. Pinatel, *La théorie pénale de l'intention devant les sciences de l'homme*, *in* L'évolution du droit criminel contemporain: Recueil d'études à la mémoire de Jean Lebret 181, 181 and 185, resp. (1968).

and its questionable usefulness,[379] we have dared to wonder "whether the whole of positive law could not do without it."[380]

These extreme tendencies have since been marginalized, but like innocent seeds planted in fertile ground, they are no strangers to a fundamental movement that, over the past two centuries, has tended to artificially reduce the scope of intent and its practical importance.

B. Indirect challenges: reducing the scope of intent

184. **The emergence of new notions disrupting the classic theory of intent: imputability, causality, capacity.** One need only consult a recent textbook to realize that the notion of intent is no longer central to the theory of criminal liability. Only a few pages, ten or twenty at best, are devoted to it, classically detailing the different forms of intent, then distinguishing it from simple fault and motive.[381] The study is now occupied by other notions, foremost among which are imputability, capacity and causality. In other words, in addition to culpability, which was originally the sole basis for the right to punish, doctrine has superimposed other notions – and the theories that inevitably accompany them. A perusal of doctrinal writings thus gives the impression of great confusion, not to say anarchy;[382] the role and boundaries of each of these new institutions being defined in a highly variable manner from one author to the next.[383] This phenomenon of complexification has directly contributed to pushing intent into the background, and making it extremely difficult to define it, understand its function, and circumscribe its role.

379 Jean Lebret, for example, criticizes the classical theory of intent for failing to take satisfactory account of the will, since the law automatically postulates its freedom, from which it follows that the theory of intent is "Spurious" and therefore useless. *See* Lebret, *Essai sur la notion de l'intention criminelle*, *op. cit.* at 455–57.

380 The author continues: "Isn't a safe way of enforcing the rule … to punish transgression without regard to lack of intent?" *See* P. Mimin, *L'intention et le mobile*, *in* La chambre criminelle et sa jurisprudence: Recueil d'études en hommage à la mémoire de Maurice Patin 114, 120 (1965).

381 As we shall see *infra*, nos. 194–198, these statements are essentially definitional, and provide little information on the regime of the concept of intent.

382 R. Merle, Droit pénal général complémentaire 180 (1957): "The greatest anarchy presides over the doctrinal delimitation of the very similar concepts of responsibility, imputability and culpability"; in the same vein, G. Levasseur, *L'imputabilité des infractions en droit français*, 5–6 Revue de droit pénal et de criminologie 387, 388–89 (1969): "It must be said that the issue of imputability is one of the least well clarified in French law. …'Responsibility,' 'culpability,' 'imputability,' and 'criminal capacity' are notions whose use by authors is not without some confusion." R. Ottenhof, *Imputabilité, culpabilité et responsabilité en droit pénal*, 22 Archives de politique criminelle 71, 72 (2000): "The concept of imputability is one of the vaguest and most controversial in French criminal law. Its complexity only increases when, as is the case here, we try to situate it in relation to the concepts of culpability and responsibility." *Adde*, for a critique of the classic definition of imputability, which, according to the author, is full of contradictions, J.-H. Robert, *Imputation et complicité*, JCP G 33, 33–34 (1975), I, Doctrine, chron. 2720. The latter considers that the usefulness of the notion of imputation, rather than imputability, only becomes apparent when the offense is committed by multiple individuals, as we have argued *supra*, no. 168.

383 J. Pradel, *La responsabilité pénale en droit français depuis le Code pénal de 1994: Permanence ou changements?*, *in* Les métamorphoses de la responsabilité, Sixièmes journées René Savatier 155, 156–57 (1997): "Going through the doctrine gives the impression of a certain mess, an intellectual waste, so varied is the presentation of the conditions of responsibility." *See also* the doctrinal references cited by the author on the different theories relating to the relationship between imputability, culpability and responsibility.

Indeed, a new notion is often a conqueror: it only succeeds in imposing itself on the theoretical landscape by challenging its neighbors, claiming that it fills the gaps better than its predecessors.[384] The lure of novelty regularly outweighs the stability of old constructs, and as we enthusiastically embrace new trends, we forget to ask ourselves whether the dusty notions we intend to relegate to the attic have not served us well. Such is the image conjured up by the emergence of the notion of imputability – only two centuries old.[385] It stems from the tendency, the offspring of Descartes and Kant,[386] to dissociate the objective from the subjective,[387] and spread due to the interest it received from Italian positivists, who intended to replace the notion of culpability,[388] as well as the attraction of German doctrine for objectification.[389]

Imputability and other concepts such as capacity and causality have gradually reduced the role of intent in criminal liability.[390] Their undeniable rise legitimately raises the difficult question of the place of the mental element, which has become lost in their maze.[391] Indeed, the dominant trend is now to confine the study of intent to that of culpability, itself

384 In this sense, E. Gaillard, Le pouvoir en droit privé 17 (1985), no. 16.

385 R. Bernardini & M. Dalloz, ii Droit criminel: L'infraction et la responsabilité 149 (4th ed. 2020), no. 405: in the Ancien Droit, "imputability, culpability, and responsibility were considered synonymous, in a conception that combined the search for the offense, the judgment of reproach against its author, and the punishment addressed to them"; *adde*, in the same sense, G. Levasseur, *L'imputabilité en droit pénal français*, Revue de science criminelle et de droit pénal comparé 3, 3 (Jan.–Mar. 1983). Even in the early twentieth century, the three terms were still often considered synonymous. *See* R. Garraud, i Traité théorique et pratique du droit pénal français 553 (3rd ed. 1913), no. 267.

386 On this theme, *see* M. Villey, La Doctrine du droit *dans l'histoire de la science juridique*, preface to Kant, Métaphysique des mœurs, Première partie: Doctrine du droit 7, 10–12 (A. Philonenko trans., Librairie philosophique J. Vrin 2011).

387 Imputability is deemed objective, and culpability subjective. On the sterility of the distinction between object and subject, *see* C. Atias, De la difficulté contemporaine à penser en droit: Leçons de philosophie du droit 37–39 (2016).

388 In this sense, *see* Garraud, i Traité théorique et pratique du droit pénal français, *op. cit.* at 555, nos. 270–271. Along with Ortolan, Garraud is one of the first to set out the distinction between imputability and culpability in a French treatise, and believes that focusing on the notion of imputability would constitute a "step backwards" – a regression to archaic forms of objective responsibility.

389 Pufendorf had already paved the way in the seventeenth century; in the early nineteenth century, an influential doctrine began to distinguish the mental element (subjective notion) from illegality (objective notion), and to favor the objective element, ultimately rendering the notions of fault and intent purely formal. In this sense, *see* H.-H. Jescheck, *The Doctrine of Mens Rea in German Criminal Law: Its Historical Background and Present State*, 8 Comparative and International Law Journal of Southern Africa 112, 113–17 (1975).

390 Theses on causality, capacity or imputability either greatly minimize the role of intent in order to increase the scope of the notion under study, or overlay it onto culpability and multiply distinctions whose actual practical scope is difficult to grasp. *See*, for example, A. Nasri, Contribution à l'étude de la notion de causalité en droit pénal 145 and 148 (2006) (Ph.D. dissertation, Université Paris i Panthéon-Sorbonne), resp. no. 154 and no. 156: the author questions "the very usefulness of the concept of culpability," which fulfills "no pragmatic function"; C. Margaine, La capacité pénale 151 (2011) (Ph.D. dissertation, Université Montesquieu Bordeaux iv), no. 207: criminal capacity is presented as an indispensable prerequisite to culpability, but it is difficult to understand how it differs in practice from imputability; finally, *see* E. Gomez, L'imputabilité en droit pénal 25 (2017) (Ph.D. dissertation, Université de La Rochelle).

391 G. Levasseur, *Étude de l'élément moral de l'infraction*, xvii Annales de la faculté de droit et de sciences économiques de Toulouse 81, 86 (1969), fasc. 1: "Not only are the levels of the mental element multiplying and blending into each other, but the exact legal scope of this element is losing its clarity. What is the place of the mental element in the interplay between these concepts, whose exact scope is not clear at first glance, and which are difficult to explain to students: responsibility, imputability, culpability, criminal capacity?"

marginalized, and then to study, under the theory of either the offense or imputability, or both, or, or … the other conditions of liability.[392] The majority of doctrine thus considers that imputability is distinct from the mental element, or even impervious to it; while dissenting voices continue to defend the opposite.[393]

This maelstrom has two drawbacks. Firstly, it hinders comparative law analyses. Other European countries are experiencing the same kind of bickering,[394] which makes it difficult to draw fruitful parallels between unstable concepts that are interpreted differently, not only within a single country, but also from one country to another[395] – resulting in "dogmatic exasperation."[396] All this, while courts and penal codes remain indifferent to these Byzantine debates.[397] Secondly, this imbroglio has led to the intent losing its meaning, and part of its scope of action.

185. **Imputability's conquest of a domain belonging to intent: knowledge and will.** In all European countries, intent is classically defined as the *knowledge* and *will* to commit the offense.[398] However, imputability is just as classically defined as intelligence and will, or capacity, or freedom, or discernment, or knowledge.[399] Imputability and intent are like twin sisters,

---

392 *Id.* at 89.

393 V. Saint-Gérand, La culpabilité dans la théorie de la responsabilité pénale 75 (2000) (Ph.D. dissertation, Université Jean Moulin Lyon III) and numerous references cited. Conversely, some minority authors consider that imputability is part of the mental element, notably M.-L. Rassat, Droit pénal général 348 and 367 (2nd ed. 1999), resp. no. 248 and no. 260; and P. Conte & P. Maistre du Chambon, Droit pénal général 189 (5th ed. 2000), no. 381. The following excerpt provides ample evidence of the inextricable nature of this debate, and justifies our not dwelling on it any further. *See* Bernardini & Dalloz, II Droit criminel: L'infraction et la responsabilité, *op. cit.* at 150–51, no. 407: "Some authors often place the offense within the study of criminal liability, as the 'generating fact' of this liability, sometimes asserting that 'it would be more accurate to speak of the material and intellectual elements, not of the offense, but of criminal liability.' Furthermore, they address imputability, conceived as 'the capacity of the person to answer for the offense,' under the determination of responsible persons or the subjective causes of irresponsibility. Sometimes, the doctrine situates, within the study of culpability, both the materiality of the act and imputability, as well as the intentional or unintentional modalities of the offense. Other authors position the study of culpability within that of the offense, as its moral dimension, and refer the analysis of imputability to the examination of subjective causes of criminal responsibility. Some place imputability as a prerequisite for responsibility and culpability among the characteristics of the offense. Exceptionally, the offense is analyzed solely from an objective perspective, with imputability, culpability, and responsibility referred to the study of the offender. At the very least, extreme theoretical diversity still prevails, *necessitating a reformulation of offense subjectivity*" (emphasis added). *Adde*, for a proposal to "re-theorize" the distinction between culpability and imputability, J.-B. Perrier, *La distinction culpabilité/imputabilité*, *in* Faut-il rethéoriser le droit pénal 69, 76–80 (J. Leroy ed., 2017).

394 With the exception of Anglo-Saxon countries, which are more pragmatic and averse to excessive theorizing, and have remained outside these debates.

395 D. Oehler, *La conception juridique allemande de la culpabilité*, *in* XXIV Annales de l'Université de sciences sociales de Toulouse 73, 73 (1976), fasc. 1 and 2.

396 P. Nuvolone, *La conception juridique italienne de la culpabilité*, *in* XXIV Annales de l'Université de sciences sociales de Toulouse 59, 59, 71 (1976), fasc. 1 and 2.

397 As the legislator and the judges have remained faithful to the old idea that "in a broad sense, culpability is nothing other than the entirety of the conditions of criminal responsibility." *See* J. Vidal, *La conception juridique française de la culpabilité*, *in* XXIV Annales de l'Université de sciences sociales de Toulouse 45, 45 (1976), fasc. 1 et 2.

398 *See infra*, no. 188, and references cited.

399 André Decocq writes: "[I]f one refuses to play with words … is the distinction between intelligence, will, and discernment not thereby ruined?" A. Decocq, Droit pénal général 202 (1971).

almost indistinguishable.[400] The consequence of the overlap between the definitions of imputability and intent is important: since most authors now place imputability in the foreground,[401] causes that abolish knowledge or will are henceforth deemed to affect imputability[402] and not to remove the mental element.[403] This divorce, which is merely the spoiled fruit of a historical contingency, led an influential doctrine to drastically reduce the scope of intent in favor of imputability, before asserting that, upon reflection, intent was not so useful. Indeed, if intent and imputability are carved from the same wood (conscience and will), a struggle for control of this domain inevitably ensues.

People are deemed to act voluntarily, presumed to know the law and to be aware of their actions – unless they provide evidence to the contrary, such as insanity, minority, or error of law or fact. However, many offenses, and in particular the so-called material offenses of the past,[404] do not require proof of a particular mental element in addition to proof of the offending behavior, with the result that judicial observation of the behavior suffices to establish the corresponding mental element and, consequently, the offense – the only way for the accused to evade punishment being to prove the existence of a justifying cause.[405] Since most of these defenses are linked to imputability – which is defined in the same terms as the classical conception of intent – it takes but a single step to defend the idea that, because it adds nothing to imputability, intent is useless, erroneous,

400 There is an abundance of doctrine on this subject. *See inter alia*: E. Wagner, La notion d'intention pénale dans la doctrine classique et la jurisprudence contemporaine 84 (1976) (Ph.D. dissertation, Université de Clermont-Ferrand); A.-C. Dana, Essai sur la notion d'infraction pénale 455 (1982), no. 457; Rebut, L'omission en droit pénal: Pour une théorie de l'équivalence entre l'action et l'inaction, *op. cit.* at 162; E. Dreyer, Droit pénal général 757 (6th ed. 2021), no. 938.

401 *See supra*, no. 184.

402 In the same spirit, justificatory facts are often treated as causes that make the offense itself disappear, rather than the mental element; whereas, logically and for the sake of simplicity, we should consider that, since justificatory facts are all based on a form of constraint (that of legitimate authority, that of the aggressor who forces the victim to defend themselves legitimately), they therefore abolish the will and, consequently, the intent to commit the offense. For a demonstration of the possible assimilation between duress and justificatory grounds, *see* Dana, Essai sur la notion d'infraction pénale, *op. cit.* at 174–249, nos. 166–237. Some authors, despite distinguishing between causes of non-imputability and causes of non-culpability, recognize that the legal effects of the former are similar to those of the latter. *See* Saint-Gérand, La culpabilité dans la théorie de la responsabilité pénale, *op. cit.* at 96–129, esp. 129.

403 Yves Mayaud is one of the most influential advocates of the impermeability between imputability and culpability. *See* Y. Mayaud, *L'intention dans la théorie du droit pénal*, xii Problèmes actuels de science criminelle 57, 58 (1999): for the author, "[c]onscience is not specific to intent, and invoking it stems from a confusion between imputability and culpability. ... Indeed, conscience is nothing other than the manifestation of free will, without which there can be no responsibility, for lack of imputability"; *adde*, Y. Mayaud, *De l'article 121-3 du Code pénal à la théorie de la culpabilité en matière criminelle et délictuelle*, 37 Recueil Dalloz (1997): "Criminal responsibility is made up of imputability and culpability, the former referring to the philosophical dimension of the matter, for what it presupposes in terms of free will and discernment, the latter presenting a more technical aspect, by taking into account psychological differences that are at the origin of behaviors"; Y. Mayaud, *La volonté à la lumière du nouveau Code pénal*, *in* Mélanges en l'honneur du professeur Jean Larguier: Droit pénal, procédure pénale 203, 215–16 (1993): the will is an "element of imputability" in that it represents an "aptitude for freedom," which underlies the existence of the traditional causes of non-imputability, namely, insanity and duress.

404 On the concept of "material offense," *see supra*, no. 154.

405 *See infra*, nos. 217–219.

purely fictitious, artificial, vanished, abstracted from legal reality.[406] This is how the battle was won by imputability, whereas common sense should have led us to recognize and value the anteriority of intent over its rival, its greater stability due to its progressive sedimentation, its less questionable philosophical foundations – and therefore to fight imputability, a superfluous notion, a source of complexity, devoid of scope.

186. **Reducing the role of intent by emphasizing the other "elements of the offense."** This first victory against intent was accompanied by a second, which is merely the consequence of the first success. At the same time, the scope of intent was being eroded by the breakdown of the offense into "elements."[407] A comparative study of German and French doctrines on this subject conveys the impression of a competition in which the escalation of subtlety seems to be a guarantee of excellence.[408] The theory of the constitutive elements of the offense is one of the finest Franco-German tournaments:[409] while a few authors maintain that the offense comprises only a single constitutive element (the theory of the unique constitutive element), most respond that it comprises two (the classic material and mental elements), whereas others – quite numerous across the Rhine – have added one (the legal element), or even two (the wrongfulness element).[410] The merit of this debate is that it has given everyone considerable latitude to defend their own doctrine, and thus to show their originality; it has also enabled everyone to contradict each other on the respective relevance and scope of

---

406 The argument is made repeatedly by R. Legros, L'Élément moral dans les infractions 66, 115, 125, 137–38, 141–42, 330 (1952). *Adde*, Dana, Essai sur la notion d'infraction pénale, *op. cit.* at 463, no. 466: "Thus conceived, intent necessarily loses all specificity. It no longer accounts for this or that form of guilt. It corresponds to the very definition of the concept of offense, situated within a legalistic system… . It is its generality, which is incompatible with the selection that is its raison d'être, that underlines the uselessness of general *dol.*" Wagner, La notion d'intention pénale dans la doctrine classique et la jurisprudence contemporaine, *op. cit.* at 19; I. Moine-Dupuis, *L'intention en droit pénal: Une notion introuvable?*, Recueil Dalloz 2144 (2001): "Reduced to awareness of the unlawful nature of the act (combined with the will to carry it out), abstracted from the material facts, does intent in criminal law still evoke an autonomous element of the offense?"

407 J.-H. Robert, *L'histoire des éléments de l'infraction*, Revue de science criminelle et de droit pénal comparé 269, 270 (1977).

408 Thus, the theory of the offense remains, to this day, a mystery. *See* R. Ollard, *Essai sur l'élément qualifiant de l'infraction*, *in* Mélanges en l'honneur du Professeur Philippe Conte 605, 605 (2023): "Unless criminal law doctrine deliberately maintains a certain mystery, out of a taste for *disputatio* or in order to preserve the very object of its study, the theory of criminal offense may not yet have revealed all its secrets, as attested by the many controversies to which it is still subject." The author then offers an analysis of "the qualifying element of the offense."

409 For a detailed account, *see* K. Ambos, *Réflexions sur la théorie française de l'infraction pénale du point de vue allemand*, *in* Vers un nouveau procès pénal? Neue Wege des Strafprozesses 147, 147–50 (J. Leblois-Happe ed., 2013).

410 We have oversimplified: we should point out the debates over the term "mental element," which some prefer to rename "psychological" or "intellectual" element; furthermore, some retain three constitutive elements, but replace the legal element with the unjust element (considering that breaking the law is in principle unjust, and that it is therefore appropriate to highlight this original idea through a new denomination); let's also note that the "objective theory of the single constitutive element" assigns the subjective dimension of the act to another category, that of the "offender" offender is good or, as the case may be, that of "imputation"; let's finally mention the "objectivo-subjective" theory, which recognizes, after a necessary effort of synthesis, that the offense mixes objective *and* subjective elements…

these new concepts, which have been handled with great skill, even though the practical repercussions of these theoretical controversies are hard to perceive. These complications once again stem from the desire to separate the object from the subject: fearing the hypothetical subjectivity of the theory of responsibility, one reassures oneself by asserting and prioritizing the objectivity of the theory of the offense. However, this distinction is not only artificial, but above all misleading: the material element is, as we shall see,[411] intrinsically linked to the mental element, both of which are (and always have been) apprehended "objectively" by judges.

A final tour de force must be mentioned. Weakened, assailed from all sides, intent has been reduced to almost nothing: indeed, what remains of it once knowledge and will have been stripped away? If criminal liability is merely a matter of imputability, and imputability is objective; if, moreover, a significant number of offenses can be characterized solely on the basis of a material finding; this would imply the existence of either: "strictly material offenses" or "offenses devoid of any mental element," "objective faults" or "no-fault criminal liability."[412] While this line of reasoning may seem absurd, and its conclusion shocking, it was nevertheless fashionable in European countries in the nineteenth century.[413] Since then, part of the doctrine[414] has criticized the very notion of objective fault, particularly in light of the growing importance of fundamental rights, and recognizes that the characterization of an offence, whatever its nature, always implies establishing the culpability of its perpetrator, even if this culpability is presumed.[415] After two centuries of uncertainty, the modern age seems ready to embrace intent once again.

Nevertheless, disrupted, weighed down and obscured by attacks on its scope, the content of intent has itself become elusive: the various attempts to define intent have proved largely incompatible with one another, and sometimes unfaithful to jurisprudential reality.

---

411 *See* Appendix no. 2 *infra*.

412 For an illustration in business criminal law, *see supra*, no. 154.

413 J. Pradel, Droit pénal comparé 127–31 (4th ed. 2016), nos. 82–84.

414 However, an absolute consensus has yet to be reached. *See* Dana, Essai sur la notion d'infraction pénale, *op. cit.* at 290–91, no. 279: the author notes that, in the field of *contraventions*, there is great uncertainty as to the nature of the mental element required, since a *faute contraventionnelle* has, in his view, a strictly material content.

415 *Ex multis*: for a comparative law analysis, *see* J. Verhaegen, *L'élément fautif en matière de contraventions aux règlements*, Revue de droit pénal et de criminologie no. 3, 289, 290 (1988); *adde*, along the same lines in Belgian law, Legros, L'élément moral dans les infractions, *op. cit.* at 8–11; for France, Levasseur, *L'imputabilité des infractions en droit français*, *op. cit.* at 389; Decocq, Droit pénal général, *op. cit.* at 225–26; H. Donnedieu de Vabres, Traité élémentaire de droit criminel et de législation pénale comparée 67 (2nd ed. 1943), no. 122: "Will is an indispensable mental element in the constitution of all offenses… This holds true even for minor offenses, simple police *contraventions*, which are wrongly called *purely material* offenses"; and in common law countries, M. Budd & A. Lynch, *Voluntariness, Causation and Strict Liability*, Criminal Law Review 74, 77 (Feb. 1978).

II. A complexity that leads to uncertainty about the content of intent

187. **Intent: an unfathomable concept?** The difficulties associated with the study of intent stem from the fact that today there is a great deal of confusion surrounding this concept, both in terms of its definition (**A**) and its regime (**B**).

A. Confusion as to the definition of intent

188. **The simplicity of the classic definition: "knowledge and will."** At first glance, the requirement of intent gives the impression of a perfect consensus: today's criminal codes all recognize the rule that any offense implies "intent, except in exceptional cases where it presupposes imprudence or negligence."[416] The definition adopted, often in the silence of the codes, is moreover virtually the same from one country to another. Intent presupposes the combination of two elements: knowledge and will.[417] This definition is faithful to that proposed by the classical criminal law specialists;[418] it is also in line with the spirit of the preparatory work for the 1810 Penal Code,[419] whose influence on European countries is well known. It is nonetheless general and abstract. And yet, if we try to make it more precise, the veneer of simplicity is soon chipped away.

189. **The etymological controversy surrounding intent: *intendere*, "to tend towards."** A first difficulty arises from the etymology of the word "intent," from the Latin *intendere*: "to tend towards." Authors unanimously recognize that intent implies a will directed towards a certain result.

---

416 Pradel, Droit pénal comparé, *op. cit.* at 103, no. 66; *adde*, in the same vein, J. Verhaegen, *L'exigence de l'intention coupable dans les infractions aux lois et règlements particuliers*, Revue de droit pénal et de criminologie no. 12, 947, 947 (1986).

417 J. Verhaegen, *La définition de l'intention coupable dans les codes pénaux modernes*, *in* i Liber amicorum Frédéric Dumon 527, 529 (1983); Pradel, Droit pénal comparé, *op. cit.* at 104, no. 67.

418 The best-known formula is that of Émile Garçon: "Intent, in its legal sense, is the agent's will to commit the offense as determined by the law; it is the guilty party's awareness of violating the legal prohibitions (which they are always deemed to know)." E. Garçon, i Code pénal annoté 8 (2nd ed. 1952), no. 77. Other criminal law specialists of the time retained essentially the same definition. *See ex multis*: Donnedieu de Vabres, Traité élémentaire de droit criminel et de législation pénale comparée, *op. cit.* at 70, no. 126; R. Garraud, i Traité théorique et pratique du droit pénal français 571, 574 (3rd ed. 1913), nos. 287 and 288.

419 In 1810, Chevalier Faure expressed his views on the subject before the Corps législatif as follows: "Another rule common to all defendants ... is that one cannot declare guilty someone who was in a state of insanity at the time of the act, or who, despite the strongest resistance, could not refrain from yielding to force. Every crime or offense consists of both the act and intent: in the two cases we have just discussed, no criminal intent could have existed on the part of the defendants, since one did not enjoy his moral qualities, and in the case of the other, constraint alone directed the use of his physical strength." *See Exposé des motifs du Livre II du Code pénal dans la séance du Corps Législatif du 3 février 1810*, *in* J.-G. Locré, xxix La législation civile, commerciale et criminelle de la France 260, 264 (1831), no. 6. It is worth noting that the excerpt refers to what legal doctrine generally examines under the concept of imputability; however, Chevalier Faure makes no mention of this, and studies the two cases of "non-imputability," namely insanity and duress, from the angle of intent.

But what result are we talking about?[420] The "criminal outcome" i.e., the infringement of the interest protected by the legislator? Such an extensive approach implies that any offense, including those that do not provide for a result detachable from the act, virtually entails a result: that of infringing the penal law. Or, more restrictively, do we mean the result in the ordinary sense of the term – i.e., the aim pursued by the perpetrator of the conduct in question?[421] Such an understanding has the advantage of precision, but the disadvantage of paradox: many incriminating texts do not provide for results distinct from the incriminated conduct, and therefore would not presuppose any intent.[422] For this reason, many criminal law specialists have proposed a distinction between will and intent:[423] will would be limited to the conduct, while only intent would imply a distinct result. There would thus be offenses that were merely voluntary: if a person sped, they would be convicted, even if their behavior caused no accident; and some intentional offenses: when an individual shoots another person at point-blank range, their act will result in the death of the victim. According to this view, many offenses would be unintentional, which would infringe the principle that all crimes and offenses, unless expressly exempted by the legislator, presuppose intent;[424] and conversely, some *contraventions*

---

420 For a discussion of the different meanings of the term "result" in criminal law, *see* J.-Y. Maréchal, Essai sur le résultat dans la théorie de l'infraction pénale 415–25 (2003), nos. 622–634, and the doctrinal references cited.

421 Philippe Conte has rightly pointed out that it is "not certain that these conceptions are irreconcilable: in reality, everything depends on the result on which we reason. In particular, it is clear that when the result of the offense practically merges with the material element, to the point where it becomes difficult to distinguish one from the other, the desire for the result is identical to the will to commit the incriminated material act." *See* P. Conte, L'apparence en matière pénale 272 (1984) (Ph.D. dissertation), no. 231.

422 In this sense, *ex multis*: E. Villey, Précis d'un cours de droit criminel 119–20 (2nd ed. 1880): "[T]he question of intent does not arise in all cases: it is only when the offense consists of a certain harm, a certain prejudice caused, that we can ask whether the agent intended to produce this harm, to cause this prejudice. In all cases where the law incriminates, not the prejudicial result of an act, but an action or inaction in itself, apart from its consequences, the question of intent, as we understand it, does not arise"; P.-A. Pageaud, *La notion d'intention en droit pénal*, JCP G 35, 37 (1950), i, doctr. 876: "[T]he question of culpable intent will only arise in cases where the criminal law punishes the act on the basis of a certain result, but in no way in cases where the act is in itself prohibited, independently of any idea of result"; Rebut, L'omission en droit pénal: Pour une théorie de l'équivalence entre l'action et l'inaction, *op. cit.* at 229 (and in the same vein, at 252): "The notion of intent has a place only for those offenses that include a detachable result. ...The notion of intent should not be used when it is reduced to the mere desire for material conduct."

423 *Ex multis*: E. Villey, *De l'intention en matière pénale*, i La France judiciaire 1, 4–5 (1876), doctrine: "Are *intent* and *will* synonymous? Yes, in everyday language; yes, sometimes in legal language and in legal texts. However, this is a source of confusion, and it is useful to distinguish theoretically between the two terms in order to assign each its own meaning... [T]he will to do an act is quite different from the will to obtain the consequences of that act; the former in no way implies the latter. Should we not distinguish them by different names? Let's give the first the name of *will*, and the second the name of *intent*," for there are "many cases where intent is really distinct from will"; Mayaud, *La volonté à la lumière du nouveau Code pénal*, *op. cit.* at 206: "[I]f intent passes through will, will may not necessarily be accompanied by intent"; M. Berthe, Le rôle de la volonté en droit pénal 17–19 (2010) (Ph.D. dissertation, Université Paris viii Vincennes), nos. 20–24. This distinction is justified by the fact that while "the act performed is almost always in conformity with the act planned, the consequences of the latter are not always the same as those intended by the perpetrator. ...The act does not always achieve the aim of the intention; it may have other results." *See* J.-M. Thévenon, L'élément objectif et l'élément subjectif de l'infraction: Contribution à l'étude de leurs définitions et de leurs rapports 120–21 (1942).

424 For examples, *see infra*, no. 194.

would be intentional,[425] whereas simple fault is normally required in such cases. To break the deadlock, many authors now consider will to be synonymous with intent,[426] but this has the disadvantage of making it impossible to distinguish between offenses of different kinds.[427]

Although the definition of intent, which is so far elementary and incomplete, gives the impression of a Chinese puzzle, we are only at the first level of the game – a kind of training to learn how to solve other, more sophisticated tangrams.

190. **The breakdown of intent into different forms of *dol*.** In fact, intent has been broken down into an impressive number of sub-categories of "*dol*," which obviously increases when French and foreign classifications are combined:[428] *dol général, dol simple, dol spécial, dol présumé, dol manifeste, dol déterminé, dol indéterminé, dol réfléchi, dol aggravé, dol prémédité, dol direct, dol indirect, dol oblique, dol éventuel, dol praeterintentionnel…*[429] The tangle of these nebulous notions and their theoretical indeterminacy have prompted criticism from a minority of legal scholars, who argue in favor of a unitary conception of intent.[430] In any case, legislators and case law alike

---

425 Since some *contraventions* involve a result detachable from the conduct, *see* Pageaud, *La notion d'intention en droit pénal*, *op. cit.* at 36; J.-Y. Maréchal, *Élément moral de l'infraction*, JURISCLASSEUR PÉNAL CODE (Nov. 2022), fasc. 20, no. 8 and no. 16; E. Villey, *De l'intention en matière pénale*, *op. cit.* at 8.

426 G. Blanc-Jouvan, *La frontière entre le volontaire et l'involontaire: L'exemple de la délinquance routière*, *in* CODE PÉNAL ET CODE D'INSTRUCTION CRIMINELLE: LIVRE DU BICENTENAIRE 485, 485–86 n.2 (2010) and the numerous doctrinal references cited; S. Berté Puel, L'intention en droit pénal 81 (2005) (Ph.D. dissertation, Université Paris x Nanterre): "For the majority, intent and will are the expression of the same reality. This view is further endorsed by the Penal Code, which uses the term 'will' to describe intentional offenses and employs the term 'involuntary' to refer to unintentional offenses." Authors are encouraged in this by the Penal Code itself, which, "like the old code, constantly fosters confusion between terms. Out of habit and convenience, its drafters have indeed retained the expression '*involuntary manslaughter*' and distinguished between '*voluntary*' and '*involuntary*' attacks on life and bodily integrity." *See* A. Giudicelli, *Incertitudes sur les frontières de l'intention*, *in* DIX ANS APRÈS LA RÉFORME DE 1994: QUELS REPÈRES DANS LE CODE PÉNAL? 25, 32–33 (M. Danti-Juan ed., 2005).

427 LEGROS, L'ÉLÉMENT MORAL DANS LES INFRACTIONS, *op. cit.* at 106: "It is often asserted by doctrine and jurisprudence that … the criminal intent required in principle for crimes and offenses is the will to break the law. Once again, we are faced with a purely verbal formula. …The will to break the law is invariably required in all offenses." However, as André Decocq rightly writes, a distinction must be made between two types of offense: "[I]n some, the result is *inextricably linked to the material conduct that produces it*; in others, the *result is detachable from the conduct and presents a random character in relation to it*." DECOCQ, DROIT PÉNAL GÉNÉRAL, *op. cit.* at 211; *adde*, in the same vein, M. PUECH, DROIT PÉNAL GÉNÉRAL 189–90 (1988), no. 526.

428 We should also mention, for information, the classification of different types of *mens rea* in common law countries – an autonomous island in the turbulent ocean of continental quarrels: to be characterized, certain offenses must be committed *purposely*, others *knowingly*, or *recklessly* or *negligently*. These four categories are the most classic, and there are of course many more (without being exhaustive: *subjective intent, objective intent, direct intent, indirect intent, oblique intent*, etc.), but they are the ones retained and defined by the American Model Penal Code (§ 2.02) in order to provide as much guidance as possible for judges, who nevertheless continue to interpret the mental element required for the same offense in different ways from one state to another, and even within the same state, from one case to another. On this issue, *see* R. Batey, *Judicial Exploitation of Mens Rea Confusion, at Common Law and under the Model Penal Code*, 18 GEORGIA STATE UNIVERSITY LAW REVIEW 341, 355–59, 380–81 (2001).

429 For an enumeration in Latin, *see* J. Jimenez De Asua, *La faute consciente et le "dolus eventualis"*, REVUE DE DROIT PÉNAL ET DE CRIMINOLOGIE 603, 610 (1959–1960).

430 BERNARDINI & DALLOZ, II DROIT CRIMINEL: L'INFRACTION ET LA RESPONSABILITÉ, *op. cit.* at 188, no. 439; *adde*, PUECH, DROIT PÉNAL GÉNÉRAL, *op. cit.* at 185, no. 513: the author challenges the distinction between *dol spécial* and *dol général*, which he describes as "unscientific." It is worth noting that even this distinction, despite being the most traditional, is subject to criticism from the doctrine. *See* in particular LEGROS, L'ÉLÉMENT MORAL DANS LES INFRACTIONS, *op. cit.* at 333.

remain largely impervious to the finesse of these divisions.[431] Moreover, these notions are foreign to the original meaning of dol, which implies the intent to deceive, the use of a maneuver or a ruse[432] – to require dol for all offenses would therefore mean, according to this understanding, that they would require a form of fraud to be characterized, which is clearly not the case.[433]

191. **The occasional confusion between intent and motive.** Theoretical disputes extend even to the most established principles, such as the irrelevance of motives.[434] Intent is the objective pursued; motives are the reasons for action[435] – a feeling, an emotion, a desire, a need.[436] Eminently subjective, if they can be taken into account at the stage of individualizing the punishment,[437] they should, on the other hand, be disregarded at the stage of characterizing the offense. Nevertheless, it has been argued that motive is sometimes used as a constituent element of the offense, in the form of a "*dol spécial*,"[438] which is then "confused with intent."[439] The offense of gathering information with a view to handing it over to a foreign power[440] would be an illustration of this phenomenon. But in this case, should we not consider that, as the incriminated aim is nothing other than the result of the offense, the mental element is simply intent, and not a motive[441]

192. **The ambiguous link between intent and lack of intent.** There is another complication to note. At the opposite end of the spectrum from intent is lack of intent[442] – both maintaining a relationship that is as ambiguous as it is

431 J.-H. Robert, Droit pénal général 320 (6th ed. 2005). A glance at the codes and case law shows that, apart from the notions of "*dol général*" and "*dol spécial*" sometimes used by judges, the other expressions are nowhere to be found.

432 J. Gaudemet & E. Chevreau, Droit privé romain 384–85 (3rd ed. 2009); *adde*, on *dol*, *infra*, no. 400.

433 For example, "*dol éventuel*" and "*dol praeterintentionnel*" do not require any maneuvering.

434 A principle recognized both in France and abroad, *see* Pradel, Droit pénal comparé, *op. cit.* at 110, no. 71.

435 L. Josserand, Les mobiles dans les actes juridiques de droit privé 10 (2nd ed. 2006): "Intent is a matter of purpose, unmasking the ends pursued; motives are the driving forces of the will, which put it into action." For a study in English law, *see* A. Kenny, *Intention and Purpose*, 63 The Journal of Philosophy 642 (1966).

436 Thévenon, L'élément objectif et l'élément subjectif de l'infraction: Contribution à l'étude de leurs définitions et de leurs rapports, *op. cit.* at. 118–19.

437 *See infra*, nos. 230–232.

438 *Ex multis*: J.-L. Soulignac, L'élément moral dans les infractions en droit pénal français 108 (1955) (Ph.D. dissertation, Université de Nancy); Mimin, *L'intention et le mobile*, *op. cit.* at 118: "Distinguishing indifferent motive from intent, and especially from *dol spécial*... will sometimes be challenging."

439 In this regard, P. E. Trousse, *Le mobile justificatif*, Revue de droit pénal et de criminologie 418, 433 (1962–1963).

440 Art. 411-7 of the French Penal Code.

441 Several authors support this argument, which we endorse: Pageaud, *La notion d'intention en droit pénal*, *op. cit.* at 38–39; Legros, L'élément moral dans les infractions, *op. cit.* at 230.

442 As the negative of intent, lack of intent is equally difficult to define. Is it involuntary? Does it imply guilt, even if reduced? It has been said that lack of intent is present whenever the result of an offense is unintended. *See* Y. Mayaud, *Retour sur la culpabilité non intentionnelle en droit pénal... (À propos de la loi no. 2000-647 du 10 juillet 2000)*, Recueil Dalloz 603 (2000). But as with intent, to be complete, this simple definition would require agreement on the notion of result (*see supra*, no. 189). It has also been distinguished from

contradictory. As in the world of intent, in the realm of lack of intent, there is a whole host of terms to describe criminal misconduct:[443] ordinary, characterized, deliberate, simple, conscious, unconscious, with foresight, without foresight, negligent, imprudent, clumsy, inattentive, reckless… And at the boundary of the two universes, there is a common ground, where intent and lack of intent mix until they merge in a region called "*dol éventuel.*"

Its contours are fluid: they vary from one country to another,[444] with debates focusing on whether or not *dol éventuel* (the scope of which is itself quite variable[445]) falls within the realm of intentional (or voluntary?) fraud. *Dol éventuel* differs from *dol* (general or special?) in that, in the

---

intent by the view that the latter is a "manifestation of hostility to social values," while lack of intent is a "manifestation of indifference to these values." *See* A. Decocq, Droit pénal général 207 (1971). This presentation has been taken up by many authors, but is now criticized for lacking realism: "The reference to the protected value was too abstract, even metaphysical; conversely, the distinction between hostility and indifference implied an overly subjective approach to the agent's behavior." *See* Dreyer, Droit pénal général, *op. cit.* at 749–50, no. 929. Moreover, the notion of value is itself open to debate. Indeed, if we consider the term "value" in a broad sense, we are led to consider that any offense, by its very nature, infringes a value: the interest protected by the legislator. Even at a time when offenses are multiplying and may be losing some of their symbolic significance, each and every one of them, including offenses falling under so-called technical legislation, protects an underlying value, however remote, questionable or new.

443 Here again, we combine both French and foreign legal terminology. In France, we primarily recognize three types of fault: *faute simple* (ordinary fault), *faute délibérée* (deliberate fault), and, since the year 2000, *faute caractérisée* (qualified fault). For further details on these three types of fault, *see* Mayaud, *Retour sur la culpabilité non intentionnelle en droit pénal… (À propos de la loi no. 2000-647 du 10 juillet 2000)*, *op. cit.* at 603; F. Rousseau, *Tentative d'éclaircissements de l'obscur article 121-3, alinéa 4 du Code pénal, in* Mélanges en l'honneur du Professeur Philippe Conte 733 (2023); Y. Mayaud, *Les délits non intentionnels en matière pénale*, Revue de droit sanitaire et social 49 (2008). For a critical approach to the complexity of these different forms of fault, *see* A. Varinard, *Le déplacement des critères de la faute*, *in* Dix ans après la réforme de 1994: Quels repères dans le Code pénal 45, 55–57 (M. Danti-Juan ed., 2005): the author, noting a "splintering" of criminal fault, considers that case law solutions in this area "leave one perplexed"; *adde* J. B. Herzog, *La prévention des infractions involontaires contre la vie et l'intégrité de la personne humaine*, *in* 1 La prévention des infractions contre la vie humaine et l'intégrité de la personne 207, 215 (A. Besson & M. Ancel eds., 1956): "[I]t must be noted that the concept of fault gives rise to numerous contradictions and that the doctrines relating to fault … prove to be fragmented and debatable"; *adde*, P. Conte, *Le lampiste et la mort*, Droit pénal (Jan. 2001), chron. 2: the author criticizes, in particular, the link between types of fault and the alleged differences in assessment of the causal link (direct or indirect) between fault and damage.

444 X. Pin, *La non-intention est-elle vraiment l'exception?*, *in* Le nouveau Code pénal, 20 ans après: État des questions 79, 88 (L. Saenko ed., 2014). The authors do not, however, arrive at the same answers when they ask which countries equate *dol éventuel* with intent, *compare with* the previous article and the following references: Jimenez De Asua, *La faute consciente et le "dolus eventualis"*, *op. cit.* at 605–606; Pradel, Droit pénal comparé, *op. cit.* at 116–17, no. 75; for an in-depth analysis, at the end of which the author considers that it would be appropriate to recognize that possible fraud belongs to the realm of intent, *see* F. Negrel-Filippi, Le dol éventuel, vers la reconnaissance d'une intention atténuée 29–30 and 302 resp. (2010) (Ph.D. dissertation, Université Paris i Panthéon-Sorbonne).

445 Doctrinal writers use this expression to refer to very different practical realities: involuntary manslaughter – which raises the question of how "*dol éventuel*" differs from simple negligence; proof of intent through negligence in business criminal law (*see supra*, nos. 158–159); or even deliberate endangerment – which is paradoxical, as it does not require the occurrence of any result in the strict sense – (note that this new category has caused further doctrinal disruption, and encouraged the doctrine to put the mental element back on the drawing board: *see* Blanc-Jouvan, *La frontière entre le volontaire et l'involontaire: L'exemple de la délinquance routière*, *op. cit.* at 492–95 and the numerous references cited; for a critical approach, *see* M. Puech, *De la mise en danger d'autrui*, Recueil Dalloz 153 (1994)). Generally speaking, on the subject of *dol éventuel*, *see* J. Cedras, *Le dol éventuel: Aux limites de l'intention*, Recueil Dalloz 18 (1995); Jimenez De Asua, *La faute consciente et le "dolus eventualis"*, *op. cit.*; Giudicelli, *Incertitudes sur les frontières de l'intention*, *op. cit.* at 37; J. Pradel, Droit pénal général 487–88 (22nd ed. 2019), no. 570. It should also be noted that a comparison is generally made between *dol éventuel* and *dol praeterintentionnel*, since in the presence of either, "the result, as realized, was not intended," but they would nevertheless be distinguished because "whereas in *dol éventuel*, the result that was not foreseen, or was foreseen merely as a possibility, was not intended either in the form in which it was realized, or in a less serious form, in the praeterintentional offense, the result was partially intended." *See* B. Bouloc, Droit pénal général 254 (24th ed. 2015), no. 286.

case of dol (the real kind!), "the perpetrator wants the result and considers it certain, or knows that it is almost certain," whereas in the case of *dol éventuel*, "they envisage it as merely possible, not seeking it, but not excluding it either."[446] And so we have to imagine the judge, an unwitting catechist,[447] practicing the art of divination to establish the exact state of mind of the accused.[448]

193. **The origin of complexity: the psycho-metaphysical approach to intent.** Herein lies the problem, burying any possibility of conceptual coherence: the definition of intent is based on a psycho-metaphysical approach consisting of a gradation (vain because impracticable) of the individual's mental states. When studying works on the mental element, one frequently encounters expressions such as "the agent wills," "intends to," "aims to," the individual "represents themselves," they "consider possible," "conceivable," "probable," "certain" – a sign that the theory of intent focuses on the agent's point of view. This tendency originated with the German authors[449] who, throughout the nineteenth century, fought over the criterion of intent: does it lie in the will to achieve the result (*Willenstheorie*), or in the mental representation of this result (*Vorstellungstheorie*)?[450] Human beings themselves often struggle to understand what they want: how can we aspire to build a legal theory on such shifting sands as volition?

A closer look at Roman law and the treatises of the Ancien Droit reveals a clear contrast with post-revolutionary literature. The Romans were pragmatic: *res in se dolum habet* – "intent is deduced from the facts."[451] As for the jurists of the Ancien Droit, they confined themselves to theorizing the achievements of antiquity, and drew a simple line: there is intent if there is foreseeability, *objectively* assessed in the light of the facts of the case.[452]

Is there anything more to say? Improper language always leads astray. It is hardly surprising that such major semantic uncertainties should have led to further confusion, this time more serious, as it affects the very regime of intent.

---

446 Pradel, Droit pénal comparé, *op. cit.* at 111, no. 73.

447 This is Marc Puech's criticism of what he sees as an excessively subtle approach to intent: "[W]hat makes all these analyses conjectural is that they are based on plausible inferences from subjective interpretations," and proceed "from the idea that intent is a notion of moral order," which would transform the judge "into a catechist," whereas the latter can only grasp the individual's intent "in their behavior and through their behavior, and not in all its psychological complexity." *See* M. Puech, *Scolies sur la faute pénale*, 5 Droits: Revue française de théorie juridique, 77, 81–83 (1987).

448 It is for this reason that Robert Legros calls for the pure and simple deletion of the notion of *dol éventuel*. *See* Legros, L'élément moral dans les infractions, *op. cit.* at 212: "This notion must be rejected from the legal vocabulary because it needlessly complicates a simple problem, it runs counter to an essential problem of interpretation, and it creates a source of confusion."

449 Renowned for having pioneered a "metaphysical" approach to intent. In this sense, *see* Ambos, *Réflexions sur la théorie française de l'infraction pénale du point de vue allemand, op. cit.* at 150.

450 For a nuanced account of these two theories, and numerous references (in German), *see* R. Griffon, De l'intention en droit pénal 13–18, 30–59 (1911).

451 *See supra*, no. 30.

452 *See supra*, no. 69.

B. The existence of confusion regarding the regime of intent

194. **The absence of an operational method for determining the nature of the mental element specific to each offense.** As we have seen, intent can be defined in several ways. In the broadest sense, it can refer to the knowledge and will to engage in the conduct; in the strictest sense, the will to achieve a specific result, distinct from the conduct; in an intermediate sense, the acceptance of a foreseeable but unintended result.[453] In practice, different forms of intent coexist, and each has its own specific legal regime.[454] The jurists' task is therefore to distinguish: when they detect a difference in regime, their role is to deduce a difference in notion.[455]

Today, however, judges and doctrine alike do not need to take this step: the legislator has already decided for them. In European countries, the rule that crimes and offenses are intentional is now accepted, unless the legislator has made an exception.[456] In France, article 121-3 of the French Penal Code, adopted in 1994, contains this principle: "There is no crime or offense without intent to commit it."[457] In the old Penal Code, although such a rule already implicitly existed,[458] no guidance was given on the mental element specific to each offense: it was up to practitioners to consult the incriminating texts to determine the nature of the required intent, on a case-by-case basis,[459] by means of a study of the structure of the incriminating text and its jurisprudential interpretation.[460]

The stakes were high and the task difficult, as the French Penal Code uses no fewer than twenty-five expressions to evoke intent:[461] *volontairement* (voluntarily), *de mauvaise foi* (in bad faith), *sciemment* (knowingly), *en connaissance* (with knowledge), *intentionnellement* (intentionally), *en vue de* (with the aim of), *dans le dessein de* (with the purpose of), *tendant à* (tending to), *frauduleusement* (fraudulently), etc. Such terms would be welcome if they provided clarity. However, this is not the case: their presence does not systematically reflect the requirement of intent in the strict sense; their

---

453 This distinction is made in the following work: Soulignac, L'élément moral dans les infractions en droit pénal français, *op. cit.* at 5-6.

454 As we shall see *infra*, no. 214.

455 J.-L. Bergel, *Différence de nature (égale) différence de régime*, RTD civ. 255, 257–58 (1984), no. 3.

456 Pradel, Droit pénal comparé, *op. cit.* at 103, no. 66; *adde*, in the same vein, Verhaegen, *L'exigence de l'intention coupable dans les infractions aux lois et règlements particuliers*, *op. cit.* at 947.

457 The legislator cannot waive the requirement of intent for crimes, but only for offenses.

458 *See* the *travaux préparatoires* of the 1810 Penal Code, cited *supra*, no. 188.

459 Mayaud, *L'intention dans la théorie du droit pénal*, *op. cit.* at 57–66, esp. at 64; Maréchal, *Élément moral de l'infraction*, *op. cit.*, nos. 3–5.

460 *See infra*, nos. 222–223.

461 Puech, Droit pénal général, *op. cit.* at 187, no. 520.

absence does not always imply its nonexistence;[462] furthermore, with each successive reform, the legislator has shown inconsistency in designating the mental element of the same offense.[463]

The legal distribution set out in article 121-3 was therefore, *a priori*, timely. But only *a priori*. The text, which is extremely poorly drafted,[464] gives rise to difficulties of interpretation that are marked by both absurdity and seriousness.[465] The reason is simple: like foreign laws, it makes the required mental element dependent on the tripartite classification of offenses (*crimes*, *délits*, *contraventions*).[466] This classification distributes offenses according to their seriousness, leading to differences in sentencing, procedure, and jurisdiction. On the other hand, this classification provides no information on the intent required, which depends solely on the structure of the offense.[467] Nevertheless, many authors, as encouraged by the legislator, defend the idea that the requirement of intent should be reserved only for the most serious offenses[468] – thus making the seriousness of the offense the criterion

---

462 On this point, *see* Thévenon, L'élément objectif et l'élément subjectif de l'infraction: Contribution à l'étude de leurs définitions et de leurs rapports, *op. cit.* at 125–29. Let us add that the legislator is sometimes inconsistent, for example in matters of swindling, "the Penal Code reproduced the provision of article 405 of the law of 1791 with important modifications (the article stated that 'those who, *par dol*... would have ... swindled'). ...The words '*par dol*,' from which all the trouble stemmed, were removed, and only the enumeration of the means of deception – already present in the Constituent text – was retained and slightly expanded." *See* M. Planiol, *Dol civil et dol criminel*, xx Revue critique de législation et de jurisprudence 545 & 643, 561 (1893).

463 For example, in the case of swindle, "the Penal Code reproduced the provision of article 405 of the law of 1791 with important modifications (the article stated that 'those who, *par dol* ... would have ... swindled'). ...The words '*par dol*,' from which all the evil stemmed, were removed, and the enumeration of the means of deception already contained in the text adopted by the Constituent Assembly was retained, but slightly expanded." *See* Planiol, *Dol civil et dol criminel*, *op. cit.* at 561. In the opinion of Marcel Planiol, this accumulation of terms cannot provide a serious definition of the required intent, as these terms have "no technical value" and can only be used as "synonyms for maneuvers." *See id.* at 555.

464 We will spare the reader from its full reproduction. Article 121-3, which has expanded from fifty words in its initial drafting to two hundred and fifteen today, is made up of redundancies, repetitions, subordinate propositions, adverbs, epithets, conjunctions, circumstantial clauses, present tense, imperfect tense, past tense ... It combines all the ingredients "to introduce the student of legislative drafting to what should not be done in matters of legislation." *See* F. Sobo, L'article 121-3 du Code pénal 385 (2006) (Ph.D. dissertation, Université de Poitiers), no. 312. For a clear-sighted critique, *see* P. Conte, *Les Messieurs Jourdain dans les palais de la République: Variations sur l'article 121-3 du Code pénal et ses avatars*, *in* Mélanges en l'honneur du professeur Jacques-Henri Robert 137 (2012).
Puech, Droit pénal général, *op. cit.* at 187, no. 520.

465 P. Conte, *L'obscur article 121-3 du Code pénal*, Recueil Dalloz 1317 (2014): "Legal doctrine is trying to untangle the decisions that attempt to introduce, as best they can, a little rationality into article 121-3 of the Penal Code. ...Also, and in view of a multitude of nebulous solutions whose commentary is perhaps not essential, is it not giving a toot much of seriousness to a text that is singularly lacking it?"

466 The terms "crimes", "délits", "contraventions" are used here to reflect the tripartite classification under French criminal law. These categories do not correspond directly to Anglo-American distinction such as felonies or misdemeanors. The term "contravention" is retained in French due to the absence of an exact equivalent in English legal terminology.

467 *See infra*, nos. 222–223.

468 *Ex multis*, W. Jeandidier, *L'élément moral des infractions d'affaires ou l'art de la métamorphose*, *in* Une certaine idée du droit: Mélanges en l'honneur d'André Decocq 369, 369 (2004): "Intent or *dol*, which represents the most developed form of fault, pertains to the most serious offenses"; Mayaud, *L'intention dans la théorie du droit pénal*, *op. cit.* at 63; Wagner, La notion d'intention pénale dans la doctrine classique et la jurisprudence contemporaine, *op. cit.* at 379–85.

for determining the mental element it requires.[469] Others, encouraged by the expression "mental element," believe that intent would not be required in the presence of offenses devoid of moral stigma.

A study of case law shows, however, that even simple *contraventions* sometimes require intent in the strict sense (the will to achieve the result), while many *fautes contraventionnelles* and certain crimes are satisfied with intent in the broad sense (the mere will to engage in the conduct),[470] in other words, a simple "*faute contraventionnelle*."[471] It follows that, in practice, and contrary to the letter of article 121-3, there is no link between the criminal, delictual or contraventional nature of an offense and the nature of its mental element.[472] The absence of clearly defined criteria between the different categories of the mental element prevents coherent theorization of the practical differences between them.[473]

The rule that crimes and offenses are always intentional has proved to be misguided in theory and erroneous in practice in two respects. It states either too much: in the strict sense (the will to achieve the result), not all crimes and offenses are intentional;[474] or too little: in the broad sense (the will to engage in the conduct), all criminal offenses are, without exception, intentional.[475]

---

469 But this criterion is wrong. Take drunk driving, for example: it is punishable as a *contravention* when the blood alcohol level is less than 0.8 grams per liter (art. R. 234-1 of the Highway Code), and as a *délit* if the level is higher or in the event of a repeat offense (art. L. 234-1 of the Highway Code); even though the behavior is identical in both cases. However, the Court of Cassation considers that the *délit* in question requires intent within the meaning of article 121-3 of the French Penal Code, unlike the corresponding *contravention*. In this respect, *see* Y. Mayaud, *Entre le dit et le non-dit, ou les leçons de droit pénal du Conseil constitutionnel*, Recueil Dalloz 589 (1999).

470 For examples, *see infra*, nos. 233 *et seq*.

471 A *faute contraventionnelle* is defined as a fault that is characterized as soon as material conduct has been established. *See* Bouloc, Droit pénal général, *op. cit.* at 260, no. 295. It occurs whenever the incriminating text describes only material conduct, without regard to the result (*see infra*, no. 236).

472 This is what Robert Legros demonstrated in his thesis on the mental element. As a Belgian judge, he adopted a practical approach to the mental element, which enabled him to make decisive advances in the theory of intent. On this point, *see* Legros, L'élément moral dans les infractions, *op. cit.* at 152–55. *Adde*, F. Chabas, *La notion de contravention*, Revue de science criminelle et de droit pénal comparé 1, 1–3 (1969): the author argues that the criterion of penalty does not imply a distinct regime with respect to the mental element.

473 To cite just one example at this stage: attempt is inconceivable for certain types of offense because "one can only attempt [those] which presuppose a goal, an intention. Otherwise, one would admit the attempt of offenses of negligence, which is inconceivable." B. Mercadal, *Recherches sur l'intention en droit pénal*, Revue de science criminelle et de droit pénal comparé 1, 13 (Jan.–Mar. 1967). The repression of the attempt also leads to a sugnificant reduction in the material element in favor of the mental element, since "[a]s soon as materiality diminishes in intensity, compensation occurs through a stronger reliance on intent, with the attempt being more an expression of the latter than of a well-established materiality." Mayaud, *L'intention dans la théorie du droit pénal*, *op. cit.* at 65.

474 Legros, L'élément moral dans les infractions, *op. cit.* at 98–100: "[T]he will to achieve the result is required only when the law necessarily provides for it. Apart from these exceptional cases, simple will is all that is required … . The will to achieve the result is not required in principle, even in the case of crimes and offenses: it is only required when the law demands it."

475 Frédéric Stasiak was quick to point out the harmful consequences of this general confusion between mental element and intent in the strict sense (the will to achieve the result) in relation to stock market violations. Analyzing the case law in this area, he notes that failure to distinguish between the two makes it impossible to answer important practical questions (notably definitional and evidentiary), and leads to differences of interpretation between jurisdictions, while equating the two constitutes a semantic error. *See* F. Stasiak, *Infractions boursières*, Revue de science criminelle et de droit pénal comparé 113 (Jan.-Mar. 2011).

195. **Intent in negligent offenses.** Not all offenses are intentional, some may argue. What about negligence? Offenses of negligence (or imprudence, or clumsiness, or lack of foresight, or...[476]) are most often referred to as "unintentional," or even "involuntary." There is considerable confusion on this point,[477] but the difficulty is more apparent than real.

Negligent offenses[478] share a common characteristic: they all presuppose the occurrence of damage.[479] In order to distinguish them from intentional offenses, the doctrine puts forward the fact that the result is not desired by the agent. While it is undeniable that in this case the result is not intended,[480] this approach obscures the question of the regime governing these offenses. All we need to do to break the deadlock is to change our perspective and ask the following question: What must be proved in order to characterize a negligent offense? The agent's foresight or lack thereof? If this were the case, we would return to an issue already raised:[481] How can the judge know what the defendant did or did not foresee? If the agent's prediction of the result were the criterion for qualification, it would be extremely difficult to prove the mental element.

The pitfall of the classic doctrinal presentation of negligent offenses is that, by emphasizing the absence of intent to cause the result, the voluntary nature of the behavior that led to it is omitted.[482] If an individual is driving at 69 km/h on boulevard Carnot and hits a pedestrian, they would certainly not have wished for the pedestrian's death, but they would nonetheless have voluntarily behaved in a reckless manner that caused the accident (which is no longer an accident in the legal sense of the term, since the driver's will had a part to play in it[483]). The difference between

---

476 Jean Pradel, after demonstrating that the various terms in use were "very similar," identified a cross-cutting notion common to all so-called unintentional offenses: "lack of foresight," defined as "the agent's awareness of committing an unlawful act, without intending to cause harm." He therefore proposed grouping together the various negligence offenses under the heading of offenses of lack of foresight. *See* J. Pradel, *Le défaut de prévoyance en droit pénal français*, Revue de droit pénal et de criminologie 435, 437–38 (Mar.-Apr. 1994).

477 *See*, for example, F. Desportes & F. Le Gunehec, Droit pénal général 452 (16th ed. 2009): "In the case of imprudence or negligence, there is no intent to violate criminal law. Since the occurrence of the damage was not foreseen by the perpetrator, they did not intend to cause the damage. There is no *dol spécial*. In most cases, this person was not even aware that they were committing an offense of imprudence or negligence. There is therefore no *dol général* either. This absence of intent does not, however, equate to absence of will, even though the expression '*délits involontaires*' ["involuntary offenses"] is sometimes used, which can be misleading."

478 The reasoning does not apply to deliberate endangerment, as, contrary to the majority doctrine, we do not classify it in this category. *See infra*, no. 236.

479 P. Salvage, *L'imprudence en droit pénal*, JCP G no. 50, 3984 (Dec. 11, 1996); Desportes & Le Gunehec, Droit pénal général, *op. cit.* at 452, no. 488.

480 For if it were, it would no longer be possible, for example, to distinguish between voluntary and involuntary manslaughter.

481 *See supra*, no. 192.

482 Herzog, *La prévention des infractions involontaires contre la vie et l'intégrité de la personne humaine*, *op. cit.* at 217.

483 Decocq, Droit pénal général, *op. cit.* at 201: "In the absence of a will, a human act does not constitute an action, but an event." In the same vein, for an analogy with the Roman notion of *casus* (fortuitous event), *see* J.-A. Roux, obs. under Cass. crim., Oct. 21, 1926, Sirey 1927, pp. 33–35, at 34 (Fr.).

voluntary and involuntary manslaughter lies solely in the fact that, in the case of voluntary manslaughter, the will relates to the result; whereas, in the case of so-called involuntary manslaughter, the will relates only to the behavior that caused the result,[484] which, on reflection, is not so involuntary after all.[485]

To qualify as an offense of negligence, therefore, it is not necessary to prove that the result was foreseen or foreseeable, but simply that a *fault* was *deliberately committed*[486] and that there was an *objective causal link* with the damage. The fault in question consists in behaving in a short-sighted manner, which is tantamount to not respecting the pre-existing obligation[487] imposed on everyone not to cause damage to others.

In this sense, there is no difference in nature between the mental element of intentional offenses in the broad sense (will to act regardless of the result) and negligent offenses,[488] since both presuppose engaging in conduct prohibited by criminal law.[489] As negligence offenses can thus be included in the category of intentional offenses in the broad sense, our assertion that "all offenses are intentional" is not called into question.

196. **The excuse of negligence or error.** Another confusion stems from a line of reasoning that appears here and there, but can be dismissed after a brief analysis. Here we are, attending a trial:

> THE ACCUSED – I didn't do it on purpose!
>
> THE JUDGE – That's precisely what we're accusing you of!

If the offender uses this magnanimous excuse, one wonders whether they actually knew they were violating criminal law, with its sometimes

---

484 Herzog, *La prévention des infractions involontaires contre la vie et l'intégrité de la personne humaine*, *op. cit.* at 218.

485 Contrary to what the term "involuntary" manslaughter might suggest. In this sense, *see* Giudicelli, *Incertitudes sur les frontières de l'intention*, *op. cit.* at 32–33. Indeed, since the famous *Laboube* ruling, jurisprudence has recognized that "any offense, even unintentional, presupposes that its perpetrator acted with intelligence and will", which was not the case here, as the defendant was none other than a six-year-old child. In his note on the judgment (M. Patin, note under Cass. crim., Dec. 13, 1956, no. 55-05.772, Rec. Dalloz, II, Jurisprudence, 1957, pp. 349–50, at 350 (Fr.)), Maurice Patin justifies this solution by arguing that the absence of intelligence and will prevents the characterization of the offense, as it prevents the mental element from being established.

486 This fault can be either written (a driver violating the Highway Code causes an accident; an employee is injured because of a breach of a written obligation of prudence or safety); or non-written – in which case it is assessed in the same way as civil fault, since the law of civil liability imposes a general duty not to cause damage to others.

487 On the notion of "pre-existing obligation" in law of civil liability, *see supra*, no. 148.

488 This thesis, which argues in favor of "the unity of criminal intent between fraud and fault," is very much in the minority in doctrine. It is, however, defended by J. B. Herzog, *La prévention des infractions involontaires contre la vie et l'intégrité de la personne humaine*, *op. cit.* at 220 and 243; *adde*, PUECH, DROIT PÉNAL GÉNÉRAL, *op. cit.* at 195, no. 540: the author believes that the distinction between negligent offenses and *contraventions* is overstated, as both stem from a single, unified concept.

489 In this sense, LEGROS, L'ÉLÉMENT MORAL DANS LES INFRACTIONS, *op. cit.* at 174; *adde*, in the same vein, A. Chavanne, *Le problème des délits involontaires*, REVUE DE SCIENCE CRIMINELLE ET DE DROIT PÉNAL COMPARÉ 241, 246 (1962): when it comes to so-called involuntary offenses, what criminal law punishes "is behavior, not a result."

meticulous prescriptions and thousands of rules that legislative inflation has rendered Kafkaesque.[490]

And the Court of Cassation has consistently replied,[491] with all the rigor of an unequivocal formula: "[T]he mere violation, with full knowledge of the facts, of a legal or regulatory prescription implies, on the part of the perpetrator, the guilty intent required by article 121-3, paragraph 1, of the Penal Code."[492] Yet, one must acknowledge that in a society like ours, anyone can, like Monsieur Jourdain, commit an offense without knowing it.

And the Court of Cassation has consistently held that a professional's guilty intent is proved to the requisite legal standard when it is established that they did not take the necessary care to ensure that they did not commit the offense;[493] it follows that they will be convicted of an intentional offense, even though they may really only have been guilty of negligence.[494] However, it must be recognized that a company director, exhausted by their responsibilities, may be negligent, but devoid of malice.

Doctrine concludes that, in such cases, intent is not taken into account,[495] since the excuse of good faith is not received,[496] since the defendant cannot

---

490 Wagner, La notion d'intention pénale dans la doctrine classique et la jurisprudence contemporaine, *op. cit.* at 373: "So-called artificial criminality will gradually become the primary concern of criminal authorities." These words are almost fifty years old, but they have not aged a day – they have the eternal youth of premonition.

491 This formula has been consistently applied in case law. In this sense, *see* Mayaud, *Entre le dit et le non-dit, ou les leçons de droit pénal du Conseil constitutionnel, op. cit.* at 589, and the numerous judgments cited in tort matters. It appears, among other things, in most offenses governed by so-called technical legislation, such as breaches of the Town Planning Code, destruction of a protected plant species, hunting offenses, usurpation of the title of in-house counsel, illegal practice of a profession, acquisition of birds of protected species, irregular cabotage… For other examples, *see* Maréchal, *Élément moral de l'infraction, op. cit.,* no. 34.

492 *Ex multis, see* Cass. crim., July 12, 1994, no. 93-85.262 (Fr.), in urban planning law; Cass. crim., Mar. 22, 2016, no. 15-84.949 (Fr.), in environmental law.

493 On this subject, *see supra*, nos. 156–157.

494 For example, if a jar of homemade tomato sauce is found to contain something other than tomato sauce, the artisan will be condemned for deception if they failed to carry out the necessary checks, even if they were unaware that they were selling a non-compliant product and were therefore only guilty of negligence.

495 Observing the phenomenon of legislative inflation, and noting that the new criminal law offenses were aimed more at objective and precise behaviors than at states of mind, it was possible to deduce that intent was disappearing. *See* Mercadal, *Recherches sur l'intention en droit pénal, op. cit.* at 33; *adde*, Wagner, La notion d'intention pénale dans la doctrine classique et la jurisprudence contemporaine, *op. cit.* at 4; Rebut, L'omission en droit pénal: Pour une théorie de l'équivalence entre l'action et l'inaction, *op. cit.* at 229: the author notes that while "an ideal conception would aim to understand [intent] as 'the will to achieve the result'…, it has long been known that jurisprudence has definitively shattered these hopes, often contenting itself with a significantly reduced version of this model"; S. Detraz, *L'intention coupable est-elle encore le principe ?, in* LE NOUVEAU CODE PÉNAL, 20 ANS APRÈS: ÉTAT DES QUESTIONS 63–65 (L. Saenko ed., 2014): according to the author, the increase in the number of offenses and the jurisprudential assimilation of negligence into intent would thus de facto neutralize intent without the need to formally undermine it. Quantitatively, the number of offenses requiring intent in the broad sense (the will to engage in the conduct) is indeed significantly greater than the number of offenses requiring intent in the strict sense (the will to achieve the result).

496 We shall see that it is, in fact, never admissible – even in cases of murder – where the materiality of the facts is sufficient, in itself, to reflect the accused's state of mind. *Infra*, no. 197.

successfully defend themselves by showing that they did not have the intent to commit the offense,[497] since, in short, it matters little whether the violation of criminal law "was intentional, voluntary, committed recklessly, in ignorance of the regulation."[498] Such reasoning leads to the acceptance that an intentional offense can be "committed negligently" – which may make sense in common parlance, but is legally inappropriate.

Indeed, there is an adage that everyone knows, including non-lawyers: "No one is supposed to be ignorant of the law." Its corollary can be traced back to an ancient tradition:[499] knowledge of the law is systematically presumed, since it is already a fault not to know what is forbidden, and not to inform oneself. We can (and, of course, must) condemn the consequences of this modern adage,[500] which does not sit well with an excessively meticulous criminal law;[501] but it is illogical to deduce that intent is abstracted from legal reality. Indeed, if something is presumed, it is because it has to be proved. Intent is therefore implicitly present, even if it disappears through a rigorous and sometimes excessive presumption.[502]

197. **The origin of confusion: the trial scene, the backstage of presumption.** Intent does not play the leading role, rarely makes an appearance on stage, and is seldom seen by the audience, except in the first few performances, when

---

497 This was also the criticism leveled at the classic theory of intent by authors sympathetic to the ideas of social defense: the judge would apply it too abstractly, too mechanically, too detached from the offender's actual reality. *See supra*, no. 182 and corresponding footnotes, in particular the study by Jean Lebret.

498 Bouloc, Droit pénal général, *op. cit.* at 260, no. 295.

499 Aristotle, the scholastics, and the jurisconsults of the Ancien Droit said no different.

500 This presumption of intent may turn into fiction. For a critique in this sense of the presumption of knowledge of the law. *See* A. Bayart, *Peut-on éliminer les fictions du discours juridique?*, *in* Les présomptions et les fictions en droit 27, 32 (C. Perelman & P. Forier eds., 1974).

501 Aristotle, like the Scholastics, had already drawn a distinction between behaviors so obviously contrary to morality that no law was needed for them to be recognized as forbidden, and other behaviors, which could be forbidden for good reasons, but which required a law so that their addressees knew what they should not do.

502 The presumption of knowledge of the law is extremely difficult to rebut. In France, case law requires the existence of an "invincible error," which is very strictly assessed. On this subject, *see, e.g.*, Levasseur, *L'imputabilité des infractions en droit français*, *op. cit.* at 391; Maréchal, *Élément moral de l'infraction*, *op. cit.*, no. 26 and cases cited; for an analysis of a case in which invincible error was upheld, *see* Decocq, Droit pénal général, *op. cit.* at 215. *Adde*, Legros, L'élément moral dans les infractions, *op. cit.* at 52–53: the author notes that there is no difference in the regime for errors of law between *contraventions* and other offenses. It should also be noted that most foreign laws (and, as we shall see, the law of anticompetitive practices – *see infra*, no. 269), adopt a different approach to errors of law, treating them as mitigating circumstances. This allows for greater nuance: an error of law does not prevent a finding of infringement, but may lead to a reduction in the penalty; and as the effect attached to the error of law is then less, it is assessed more flexibly, and no doubt in a manner more in line with reality. For comparative law studies: J.-P. Doucet, *Une discussion sur l'erreur de droit*, Revue de science criminelle et de droit pénal comparé 497, 500 (1962); *adde*, more recently, J. Blomsma, Mens Rea and Defences in European Criminal Law 464–76 (2012). Finally, there is a problem of great practical importance (which will be examined *infra*, nos. 461–467): in the presence of an incriminating text containing a general and abstract notion (fraudulent maneuvers, abuse, restriction of competition…), the question may arise as to whether the jurisprudential interpretation of the norm is foreseeable. This question is particularly important in common law countries and in European Union law, even if it is not foreign to written law countries. Indeed, a legal provision leaving a margin of appreciation to the judge may give rise to interpretative case law creating "for the litigant at least an intellectual doubt as to the scope of the law." *See* Legros, L'élément moral dans les infractions, *op. cit.* at 58–59.

it comes out to greet the audience at the end of the show. Yet it is intent that guides the actors' steps and dictates many of their words. But it is only when the play is new, the case unheard of, the affair ambiguous, that it shows up to remind us that, however long it may have been away, it was always there, lurking in the wings. The rest of the time, spectators, tired of waiting for it, end up thinking it is like the ghosts of the theater – an old legend no longer believed.

Intent, far from being just another rising star, spinning with the species, is the quiet director setting the rules of reasoning. To do this, it uses its favorite tool: presumption.

Presumptions of intent, which more often than not make it disappear from court decisions while tacitly manifesting its existence, have not prompted the doctrinal reflection deserved.[503] This gap in legal theory prevents us from grasping, with the requisite coherence, the concept's regime. The result is a blurring of the boundaries between the different categories of offense and the corresponding forms of mental element.

To convince ourselves, let's take a look at three classic acts:

Act I – The contravention and "material offenses." Intent sticks to every movement of the actors, fully merging with them. The offense does not require a result, only the adoption of a specific course of conduct,[504] from which it follows that, unless a valid justification is put forward and the question of intent arises,[505] the facts speak for themselves and (de facto) irrebuttably presume the mental element.[506]

Act II – Business crime. Most characters – breach of trust, misuse of corporate assets, fraud, deception – appear to be driven entirely by intent. But in this case, as we know,[507] intent is established by simple negligent behavior

503 Note that this topic has been the subject of a Ph.D. dissertation in progress since 2020: M. Cabantous, La preuve de l'intention en droit civil et pénal: Contribution à la théorie de la *probatio diabolica* (F. Rouvière & A. Sériaux supvs., Université d'Aix-Marseille). One author has also pointed out that the use of presumptions is essential to establish the mental element of offenses under monetary and financial law. *See* N. Ida, La preuve devant l'Autorité des marchés financiers 317–18 (2019) (Ph.D. dissertation, Université d'Aix-Marseille), no. 267.

504 This logically leads to the idea that "*dol général* and *faute contraventionnelle* share certain common traits." R. Merle & A. Vitu, Traité de droit criminel 727 (7th ed. 1997), no. 577.

505 This defense, which is the only admissible argument to defeat the characterization of the mental element with respect to material offenses and contraventions, can also be invoked for all others. The mental element system has a "pyramid" structure, with justifying causes forming the common foundation of all criminal offenses. In this sense, *see* Wagner, La notion d'intention pénale dans la doctrine classique et la jurisprudence contemporaine, *op. cit.* at 18.

506 Mayaud, *Entre le dit et le non-dit, ou les leçons de droit pénal du Conseil constitutionnel*, *op. cit.* at 589: culpability then "need not be proven, which renders it a presumption.... It therefore matters little what the offender's state of mind is, provided their conduct is sufficiently manifested"; Decocq, Droit pénal général, *op. cit.* at 226–27 and 212–13: these offenses "all consist of an extremely simple element, bearing in itself its result" and "generally explained solely by the intent or ordinary fault of its author," from which it follows that "proof is singularly facilitated"; Bouloc, Droit pénal général, *op. cit.* at 260, no. 296: "[O]nce the material fact is established, the *faute contraventionnelle* exists; by proving the fact, one proves the fault"; Merle & Vitu, Traité de droit criminel, *op. cit.* at 747, no. 594: regarding material offenses, "the fault is included in the facts."

507 *See supra*, nos. 156–157.

or by presumed knowledge of the material elements of the offense[508] – two occasional stand-ins which (de facto) irrebuttably presume it.[509]

Act III – Murder. Let's end with the central theme of tragedy – a register in which respect for custom should dictate that intent be omnipresent. And yet! While in this case, the will to murder – the *animus necandi* – must be specifically demonstrated, in practice it is most often deduced, without very thorough examination, from the behavior.[510] Indeed, trial judges do not look for the precise, psychological, truthful intent of the accused, but ask whether the "normal" consequence of their act is to cause death.[511] It is only when the material element is "equivocal" that they must provide further reasons for characterizing the intent[512] and bring in other evidence – factual, documentary, circumstantial, testimonies, confessions, etc.[513]

---

508 This is the case in matters of concealment, where the judge must establish the intent to conceal items whose fraudulent origin is known to the perpetrator. However, proof of this knowledge is usually deduced from the circumstances in which the accused obtained the items, their concealment or the low price paid. Once these circumstances have been established by the court, it is virtually impossible for the defendant to escape a finding of infringement. In a case involving the concealment of misappropriated corporate assets, for example, the Court of Cassation ruled that intent had been proven to the requisite legal standard, since the defendant had received the sums in a concealed account whose existence he had concealed and could not justify, implying that he was "necessarily" aware of the criminal origin of the funds (Cass. crim., Sept. 24, 2008, no. 08-80.113 (Fr.)). For a commentary on this ruling, *see* M. Véron, *Recel d'abus de biens sociaux*, DROIT PÉNAL (Nov. 2008), comm. 139: "Confronted with such factual circumstances, proof of good faith and ignorance that the sums held came from a crime or misdemeanor proves impossible. By referring to a 'necessary' awareness drawn from factual elements, jurisprudence is not far from making it an *irrefragable presumption*" (emphasis added).

509 Presumption here assumes a normative role, enabling proof of intent to be adapted to the needs of law enforcement. *See* Mercadal, *Recherches sur l'intention en droit pénal*, *op. cit.* at 7 and 46: "Jurisprudence does not have a theory of intent; it has a criminal policy on intent," with the plasticity of intent serving repressive action.

510 *See*, for example, Cass. crim, June 18, 1991, no. 91-82.033 (Fr.). The defense put forward the argument that "murder presupposes not only the will to hit the victim" – the material will to engage in the conduct – "but also the will to kill him" – the will to achieve the result – from which it follows "that by limiting itself to holding that the accused had the will to hit his brother without establishing that he had the will to kill him, the Court of Appeal, which did not characterize the will to kill, did not legally justify the charge." The Court of Cassation dismissed the appeal, ruling that, since the trial judges had noted the use of a weapon and the vulnerability of the area of the body concerned, their reasoning was free of insufficiency. For a commentary on this ruling. *See* G. Levasseur, *Homicide volontaire:* Animus necandi, REVUE DE SCIENCE CRIMINELLE ET DE DROIT PÉNAL COMPARÉ 73 (1992): "[P]roof of criminal intent can scarcely be reported other than through a *combination of presumed facts*; … it will be difficult for the accused to bring out the contrary evidence, and simple denials will no doubt be deemed insufficient" (emphasis added). *Adde* DECOCQ, DROIT PÉNAL GÉNÉRAL, *op. cit.* at 212–13: the author gives the example of "the use of a firearm in the direction of a perfectly visible person and in the absence of any other target."

511 GRIFFON, DE L'INTENTION EN DROIT PÉNAL, *op. cit.* at 133–35: the judge qualifies intent on the basis of material facts "because they have no other more direct means of arriving at a conviction. …In particular, when the agent denies having foreseen that their action would have such a result or would have it in a certain way, the judge, in the absence of significant facts, will admit or not the assertion according to the likelihood or implausibility of the *objective causal relationship* that linked the act and the result. …It is therefore understandable that the Court rarely has to set aside judgments [on the grounds of lack of intent] and is hardly led to clarify the notion of intent, since on the other hand it rightly recognizes that the question of intent is one of pure fact" (emphasis added). *Adde*, Maréchal, *Élément moral de l'infraction*, *op. cit.*, no. 26 and decisions cited.

512 Pageaud, *La notion d'intention en droit pénal*, *op. cit.* at 35.

513 Soulignac, L'élément moral dans les infractions en droit pénal français, *op. cit.* at 178–79; *adde*, R. Maman, Contribution à l'étude de l'élément intentionnel en droit pénal des affaires 229 (2007) (Ph.D. dissertation, Université de Toulouse), no. 334: the author rightly notes that intent, which cannot be proven directly, can only be established through presumption.

The moral of the story is self-evident: if intent is rare on stage, it plays a major role behind the scenes. A crucial yet discreet mechanism, without it, the play could not be performed.

Moreover, these three acts are linked by a common thread: the material and mental elements are intrinsically linked to the point of often becoming one[514] under the effect of the presumption mechanism – the objectifying prism of criminal liability.

198. **The hidden link between presumptions of intent, behavioral standards, and the jurisprudential interpretation of offenses with indeterminate content.** The manifest objectivity with which judges apprehend intent in practice contrasts with criminal doctrine, which more often than not describes it as a "subjective" notion. This is certainly the case from an ontological point of view – it relates to the subject – but not from a legal point of view – legal technique has always enabled judges to apprehend it objectively.

Indeed, intent does not involve psychological inquiry, and therefore in no way implies the probing of hearts and minds: its legal apprehension does not have to be "*true*,"[515] but only *reasonable.*[516] Without recourse to presumption, however, the characterization of intent would be impossible, for nothing is less obvious than knowing what is going on and, *a fortiori* when time has passed, what has happened in the mind of another. Presumption is based precisely on the idea that evidence is rare, which makes it necessary, in law, to "transform hesitations into certainties," by reasoning on the basis of what happens in the normal course of things.[517] By shifting the burden of proof onto factual elements that are easier to demonstrate, presumptions make it possible to consider proven what is

514 Thévenon, L'élément objectif et l'élément subjectif de l'infraction: Contribution à l'étude de leurs définitions et de leurs rapports, *op. cit.* at 55.

515 The law as a whole is not bound to the truth. *See* P. Louis-Lucas, *Vérité matérielle et vérité juridique*, *in* Mélanges offerts à René Savatier 583, 583 and 594 resp. (1965): "Undoubtedly, law has a duty, not only to describe, but as its name implies, to direct… . Legally, not all truth is good to respect. …[Unlike] the chemist or the naturalist, the jurist's direct objective is not to scrutinize matter. Since they must know it, they must go beyond knowledge of it." *Adde*, Wagner, La notion d'intention pénale dans la doctrine classique et la jurisprudence contemporaine, *op. cit.* at 81–84: "[I]t is forbidden to contest the voluntary nature of the act as long as one does not contest having possessed [a] state of consciousness and freedom. …But having a faculty does not imply that one uses it. … In reality, law is indifferent to this truth, to this hidden face of man. Its deduction makes no claim to experimental truth, but to a dogmatic and normative value"; *compare with* P. Amselek, *Les règles juridiques en tant qu'objets mentaux*, 79 Archives for Philosophy and Social Philosophy 311, 317–19 (1993).

516 Otherwise, it would be akin to fiction. On the distinction between presumption and fiction, no one has written better than François Gény: "[W]hereas legal presumption is based on verisimilitude, and merely generalizes, somewhat rashly, even contrary to the uneven course of things in life, at least, in the normal direction, and with an optimistic conception of the world order, of isolated and fragmentary solutions, fiction more clearly confronts nature, or what we hold to be natural, and, with a bias, it ignores it, turns it upside down or overturns it, it violently challenges what the world view seems to impose on us, to achieve … a result in harmony with our desires." F. Gény, iii Science et technique en droit privé positif: Élaboration technique du droit positif 261 (1921), no. 228.

517 P. Roubier, Théorie générale du droit: Histoire des doctrines juridiques et philosophie des valeurs sociales 114 (2nd ed. 1951), no. 13.

only highly probable,[518] and to combat the abusive mobilization of ill-considered evidence[519] – thus facilitating the judge's task.[520]

Nevertheless, presumption can, on a case-by-case basis, run counter to probabilities[521] to varying degrees depending on the role the law intends to attribute to it: it then becomes *normative*,[522] and plays a role in the development of substantive rules.[523] One example is the presumption of intent based on simple negligence in business criminal law, already mentioned.[524] Furthermore, certain presumptions of fact are used so often that they become "quasi-legal" presumptions.[525] Although unwritten, they acquire, through constant use, a force equivalent to that of legal presumptions, even though they do not appear in any legal text and are seldom mentioned in the reasons for decisions. It is therefore absolutely essential that they be highlighted and verified by doctrine,[526] since they *implicitly* shape the judge's reasoning and determine the conclusion they reach.

This type of presumption is intrinsically linked to two other legal phenomena: standards and jurisprudential interpretation of offenses with

---

518 Gény, iii Science et technique en droit privé positif, *op. cit.* at 265, no. 230.

519 *Id.* at 227–28, no. 232. With regard to proof of intent, unsubstantiated evidence includes all evidence based on nothing other than the defendant's own statements, such as "I didn't know" or "I didn't do it on purpose."

520 C. Perelman, *Présomptions et fictions en droit, essai de synthèse*, *in* Les présomptions et les fictions en droit 339, 340–41 (C. Perelman & P. Foriers eds., 1974).

521 Criminal evidence is not just a matter of truth, but also of persuasion. In this sense, *see* M. Delmas-Marty, *La preuve pénale*, 23 Droits: Revue française de théorie juridique 53, 53 (1996). For some authors, "the purpose of judicial presumption is to persuade the judge's mind of a truth." *See* H. Lécuyer, *Des effets à la cause: la présomption maltraitée*, *in* Études en l'honneur du professeur Marie-Laure Mathieu – Comprendre: Des mathématiques au droit 425, 430 (2019).

522 J. Wróblewski, *Structure et fonctions des présomptions juridiques*, *in* Les présomptions et les fictions en droit 43, 55–56 (C. Perelman & P. Forier eds., 1974). The following passage is enlightening: "The presumption is applied in situations where: (a) the Court must make a decision; (b) the decision requires the recognition of evidence; (c) the evidence is hard to establish; (d) it is desired to place the burden of proof in a special way; (e) *the presumption standard* determines the direction of the decision when there is no evidence to the contrary, and the conditions laid down by this standard are met" (emphasis added).

523 P. Merle, Les présomptions légales en droit pénal 128 (1970).

524 *See supra*, nos. 156–157.

525 The notion of "quasi-legal presumption" was theorized by magistrate Pierre Mimin. *See* P. Mimin, *Les présomptions quasi-légales*, JCP G 43, 43–44 (1946), i, Doctrine, doctr. 578: "Near these legal presumptions, judicial law shows an order of other presumptions. Far stronger than presumptions of fact, presumptions of man, or indicators – which are not always admissible and, when admissible, are freely weighed – they resemble legal presumptions. They have the same energy. Agreed to be true *a priori*, they generally admit proof to the contrary; but, until then, cannot be disregarded. … Case law states them as principles, and the Court of Cassation has often overturned rulings that treated them as mere presumptions of fact, believing they could be set aside without proof to the contrary. We call them quasi-legal presumptions because, although they are not written into the law, they nevertheless have the force of law. …[This type of presumption] is found in criminal law when, on the material element of many offenses, the Court of Cassation grafts the presumption of malignity …, the Court of Cassation annulling judgments which, on the vague ground that intent is not established, dismiss, without discussion, this presumption of *dol* implied in the fact."

526 In fact, it is necessary to "constantly monitor their play, by assessing the influence [they] exert on the superior and substantive interests [they] are intended to protect" and, if necessary, to "make them more flexible, so as to ensure that the just prevails in all cases." Gény, iii Science et technique en droit privé positif, *op. cit.* at 447, no. 253.

indeterminate content.[527] While intent is generally presumed on the basis of the mere materiality of the facts, this may sometimes not be sufficient to establish the mental element of the offense. When the material element is too *ambiguous* to demonstrate, to the requisite legal standard, the existence of a corresponding intent, additional evidence must be provided. And since intent is unattainable, it is therefore necessary to supplement the reasoning by means of a standard.

The *standard*[528] offers the possibility of approximating the accused's state of mind through abstract analysis: it is a measuring instrument in terms of "normality," aiming to reason from what is "reasonable."[529] It can be detected by the use of words such as "normally," "abnormally," "rationally," "abusively," "excessively," "significantly," etc.[530] At first glance, one might think that criminal law, so concerned with legality, would be impervious to this technique implying a certain margin of interpretation.[531] However, recourse to the standard method is very common in this field, due to the large number of concepts with indeterminate content that it involves (such as abuse, maneuvers, fraud, etc.).[532] This is because the law, even criminal law, cannot foresee everything. Words are imperfect tools, never able to capture reality in all its complexity.[533]

The standard thus acts as a bridge between a legal text that does not say enough and the judge's duty to decide on a concrete problem. However, the normality to which it refers is not merely descriptive: it is normative. To fill the gaps left by the written rule, the law sets an unwritten standard of behavior – that which is expected of individuals – and then passes a judgment of reproach when it finds that the agent has not conformed to this standard,[534] using formulas such as: the agent "should have known," "could not have been unaware," "was necessarily aware."

---

527 On this subject, *see infra*, nos. 413–414.

528 A technique known and used since antiquity, it was theorized in the United States by Roscoe Pound, before being imported to France by Stéphane Rials and his 1978 thesis: *Le juge administratif français et la technique du standard (Essai sur le traitement juridictionnel de l'idée de normalité)*.

529 G. Khairallah, *Le raisonnable en droit privé français*, RTD civ. 439, 461 (1984): "[R]easonableness should not be seen as subjectivism, intuition or an appeal to a vague sense of justice. The judge's main concern is to avoid arbitrariness and to find coherent solutions. ...It is true to say that the reasonable solution is the one most in line with tradition."

530 S. Rials, *Les standards, notions critiques du droit*, *in* Les notions à contenu variable en droit 39, 43 (C. Perelman & R. Vander Elst eds., 1984).

531 M. Delmas-Marty, *Les standards en droit pénal*, Revue de la recherche juridique: Droit prospectif no. 4, 1019, 1020 (1988).

532 For numerous examples, *see* F. Haid, Les notions indéterminées dans la loi: Essai sur l'indétermination des notions légales en droit civil et pénal 109–20 (2005) (Ph.D. dissertation, Aix-Marseille Université), nos. 60–72; *adde*, R. Legros, *Les notions à contenu variable en droit pénal*, *in* Les notions à contenu variable en droit 21 (C. Perelman & R. Vander Elst eds., 1984).

533 On the ineffable aspect of law, *see infra*, nos. 411–412.

534 In this sense, Delmas-Marty, *Les standards en droit pénal*, *op. cit.* at 1020: "Through the prohibitions that are criminal offenses, [the standard] establishes a 'duty to be,' thus an ideal of behavior and not an average."

The majority of doctrine, however, consider that the criminal judges, modeling their attitude on that of the civil judges, would resort to the standard only in the presence of a negligent offense, established *in abstracto*; but would not use it to presume intent, which would have to be characterized by means of an analysis *in concreto*.[535] This opposition is excessive: on the one hand, the distinction between *in abstracto* and *in concreto* assessments is questionable – they are distinguished by a difference in degree, not in nature;[536] and on the other hand, even in the case of intentional offenses in the strict sense (the will to achieve a result detachable from the conduct), intent is still detected by reference to the model of the rational and diligent individual.[537]

However, if the law considers us to be in full possession of our mental capacities and free to make our own choices, and requires us to be reasonable, prudent, and diligent at all times, we still need to be able to identify precisely which behaviors are prohibited. However, abstract penal norms inevitably raise the question of the identification of the concrete cases that relate to them – in other words, they involve a major qualification issue. This problem arises whenever the case before the judge is new: either because the situation to be governed appears new in itself, or because the solution applied to a situation already known seems required to be new.[538] Jurisprudential interpretation thus plays a major role in defining the offense, as it clarifies and develops it with each new instance.[539]

This phenomenon[540] is directly linked to proof of intent. Indeed, one cannot punish someone who could not reasonably foresee the forthcoming

---

535 The point is a classic one. *See ex multis*: Puech, Droit pénal général, *op. cit.* at 197–99, nos. 545–551; Pradel, Droit pénal comparé, *op. cit.* at 119–20, no. 77; Pradel, *Le défaut de prévoyance en droit pénal français*, *op. cit.* at 438; Rebut, L'omission en droit pénal: Pour une théorie de l'équivalence entre l'action et l'inaction, *op. cit.* at 231–32; Dana, Essai sur la notion d'infraction pénale, *op. cit.* at 339–47, nos. 328–334; Verhaegen, *La définition de l'intention coupable dans les codes pénaux modernes*, *op. cit.* at 529; A. Sériaux, *L'appréciation de la faute pénale d'imprudence en droit français contemporain*, Revue de science criminelle et de droit pénal comparé 231, 238 (Apr.-June 2017).

536 In this regard, *see* Terré et al., Droit civil: Les obligations, *op. cit.* at 1081, no. 957.

537 It is worth noting that doctrine in this sense is very much in the minority. For a convincing study, *see* Pageaud, *La notion d'intention en droit pénal*, *op. cit.* at 39: "To judge is to compare, and often – an idea perhaps too hidden – proof of intent results from a visible discrepancy between the reprehensible conduct and that which a man normally aware of what is permitted or forbidden would have adopted in the same circumstances. This reference to a general type of prudent man is, in fact, a crucial element when it comes to searching for 'fraudulent intent' on the part of the agent on the occasion of equivocal offenses. ...[T]he proof of intent ... is deduced from an abnormal, unusual attitude, i.e., one that does not conform to accepted rules."

538 C. Atias, Juris dictio: *Redire l'inédit*, Recueil Dalloz 281 (1992), no. 5.

539 *See infra*, nos. 413–414.

540 As frequent as it is ancient, this phenomenon is, in fact, immanent to legal practice. *See* R. von Jhering, III Études complémentaires de l'Esprit du droit romain: Du rôle de la volonté dans la possession: Critique de la méthode juridique régnante 129 (O. de Meulenaere trans., A. Marescq 1891): "When the legislator, as is the most frequent case, has not himself made known his X, it is up to science to seek it in the data provided by the law. This path has always been followed by jurisprudence in order to extend by analogy the limited scope of legislative ideas when they first appear. *a, b, c*, make him find X, and this, in turn, indicates *d, e, f*. If a comparison may be made, it does not move in a straight line, as is often

jurisprudential solution, as it would then be fictitious and artificial to consider that the accused had the intent to infringe the law.[541]

Let's take the example of swindle, which illustrates the presence of indeterminate norms in criminal law, since it presupposes the existence of a "fraudulent maneuver."[542] Everyone, whether or not they know the law, can easily imagine what this expression covers; no one, including those who do know, can provide a general, perfect, and precise definition. We will reason by example,[543] we will pick out a few common features, but we will always miss the mark in part. It is only by multiplying concrete cases that we will naturally and progressively[544] discover the provisional scope of the notion. The concept will be continually slightly renewed by "borderline cases," i.e., instances at the boundaries of a definition, which raise the question of whether they should be included or excluded from the definition.

A motorist parks his car in a paying space. Not wanting to pay a few euros for regular parking, but not wanting to be fined either, the clever individual substitutes a worthless token for a valid coin to trigger the parking meter mechanism. Is this a fraudulent maneuver? The Court of Cassation answers with certainty, as such an act, which consists in obtaining discharge from the parking fee while persuading inspectors of its payment, shows a clear spirit of cheating.[545]

This jurisprudential interpretation has a direct impact on proof of intent. Since intent is deduced from the facts, when new conduct is linked to a criminal qualification, the intent to break the law will still be presumed, even if no prior decision has ruled on the question. Most of the time,

---

erroneously admitted, from the known to the unknown; but knowingly or unknowingly, it makes a detour via the principle, via X, and goes first upwards from *a, b, c*, to X, then downwards from X to *d, e, f*." This is, according to Jhering, one of the "fundamental operations" of law, which is reproduced "in all legal systems."

541 We will see that this problem is very prevalent in anticompetitive practices law, *infra*, no. 467.

542 A study of case law on swindling does in fact make it possible to realize the balance sought by the judge between respect for the principle of the legality of offenses and penalties, on the one hand, and the interpretation necessary for the application and evolution of the notion of "fraudulent maneuvers," on the other. *See* A. Chavanne, *Le délit d'escroquerie et la politique criminelle contemporaine (Étude de jurisprudence)*, *in* Les principaux aspects de la politique criminelle moderne: Recueil d'études en hommage à la mémoire du Professeur Henri Donnedieu de Vabres 147, 149 (1960).

543 This highly fruitful method was theorized by F. Rouvière, *La méthode casuistique: L'apport des cas critiques pour la construction des catégories juridiques*, Revue de la recherche juridique: Droit prospectif no. 5, 1985 (2018).

544 On the theme of the "sedimentation" of norms, and the inevitable shift from the relative effect of decisions to a "normative effect," even in countries governed by written law, *see* J.-L. Bergel, *Le processus de transformation de décisions de justice en normes juridiques*, Revue de la recherche juridique: Droit prospectif no. 4, 1055, 1058–59 (1993).

545 *See* the following note on this decision: R. Gassin, note under Cass. crim., Dec. 10, 1970, no. 70-91.155 (Fr.), JCP G (1972), II, Jurisprudence, no. 17277. Raymond Gassin rightly points out an argument that could have been used against classifying the offense as swindling: the fact that the conduct in question was not very serious, and perhaps did not merit criminal prosecution. Wondering whether a special text was needed, he replied that in "these times of regrettable inflation," it was better to apply mitigating circumstances in favor of the accused, rather than pass a new law.

this poses no problem, as the linking operation is usually *reasonable* and *predictable* – provided, however, that it takes place in a country with a well-trained judiciary.

On the other hand, if the interpretation is unpredictable, or if motivation is absent or faulty, the presumption of intent becomes a fiction that must be fought – because we must demand from judges the same thing they demand from defendants: reason.

199. **The need for a new theorization of the concept of intent: hope arising from European Union law.** A reassessment is necessary. The neglect of the major role of presumptions, its insufficiently studied links with standards and jurisprudential interpretation, the uncertain definition and categorization of intentional offenses: all of these factors prevent doctrine from arriving at a general and coherent theorization of the regime of intent.

Whereas in the seventeenth century, the concept was understood in a simple and unified manner,[546] since then, each country seems to have withdrawn into internal theoretical disputes, multiplying essays and studies, without succeeding in clarifying a subject today unanimously considered obscure.[547]

Nevertheless, the fact that more and more countries have joined the European Union since 1957 was a source of hope – that of reviving the tradition of *ius commune.*[548] The construction of the Community, which has prompted extensive comparative law studies,[549] and necessitated agreement on common definitions and principles, could have helped to unravel the mystery of intent. However, this has not been the case: the European Union has yet to develop a comprehensive theory of this concept, even though it now recognizes its fundamental importance.

Paragraph 2 – The unfinished emergence of a European theory of intent

200. **Intent in European Union law: in search of a theory.** The initial task – to create not only a common economic area, but also a unified community of law[550] – was immense, and it is understandable that the drafters of

546 *See supra*, no. 77.

547 *See supra*, no. 73.

548 On the *ius commune*, *see supra*, no. 66.

549 B. Oppetit, *Retour à un droit commun européen*, *in* Droit et modernité 73, 73 (1998): "Is Europe, after a parenthesis of a century and a half, about to revive one of its great legal traditions, that of *jus commune*? This question is increasingly being asked in scientific circles." On this theme, *see* M.-F. Renoux-Zagamé, *Le droit commun entre providence divine et raison*, *in* Du droit de Dieu au droit de l'homme 50 (2003).

550 Case 294/83, Parti écologiste "Les Verts", ECLI:EU:C:1986:166, para. 23.

the treaties, the legislator, and the Community judges, at the dawn of this adventure, neglected to develop a genuine theory of intent. This gap could have been gradually filled. Alas, a study of the concept of intent in EU law gives the impression of a disorderly accumulation of incoherent and often incomprehensible decisions and positions, despite the fact that it was incumbent on the European judges to provide a definition, since the mental element "must be interpreted given an autonomous and uniform interpretation throughout the Union."[551] There are several reasons for this.

Firstly, criminal lawyers have not always welcomed the Europeanization of criminal science, since it means abandoning the view that national legal dogma is sacrosanct,[552] and calling into question long-established frameworks. In this respect, unintelligibility offers the advantage of unanimity – the accumulation of abstruse definitions makes it possible to give up taking sides in favor of one or other national theory.

The absence of a satisfactory conceptualization of intent is undoubtedly also due to the drafting style specific to the European Union. Indeed, whereas criminal law specialists use the same lexical field, and sometimes employ an almost literary style when addressing the question of the mental element, European Union law, which bears the hallmark of administrative law,[553] resorts to extremely technical formulas that are more difficult to systematize.

Finally, from the outset, the European Union's action seems to have been guided, like that of the French administration, by a concern for efficiency, yet the notion of intent has the bad, albeit false, reputation of thwarting repressive activism. This prejudice has led European legislators and judges alike to periodically rule in favor of no-fault liability systems, and to objectify the characterization of intent to the point of sometimes claiming to abstract it from judicial reasoning – these attempts, fortunately thwarted, nevertheless do little to clarify the subject. Despite this supranational imbroglio, the principle of culpability has gradually found its place in European Union law, to the point where it is now unanimously recognized (**I**). There is no longer any doubt that the mental element must be taken into account, while the theory of intent is struggling to emerge (**II**), as it consists of a jumble of scattered and scarcely intelligible definitions.

551 Opinion of Advocate General Y. Bot, Case C-72/11, Mohsen Afrasiabi, ECLI:EU:C:2011:737, para. 44.

552 A. Bernardi, *L'européanisation de la science pénale*, 26 Archives de politique criminelle 3, 33 (2004).

553 "[I]n the field of administrative law, the diversity of techniques, inherited from national history, is at first sight more striking than the common features. In fact, the problem has hardly been studied." *See* J. Rivero, *Vers un droit commun européen: Nouvelles perspectives en droit administratif*, *in* Nouvelles perspectives d'un droit commun 389, 391, 393–94 (M. Cappelletti ed., 1978).

I. The gradual recognition of the principle of culpability in union law

201. **From implicit to explicit, from unstable to permanent: the rise of the culpability principle in Union law.** Recognition of the need to characterize a mental element in order to impose a sanction, whether criminal or administrative, was discreet and ad hoc during the first decades of Community law (**A**); indeed, it is only since the 1990s that the principle of culpability has come to be unanimously and expressly accepted (**B**).

A. An initially ad hoc and implicit recognition

202. **Initially hesitant and inconsistent positions adopted by European legislators and judges.** As early as the Treaty of Paris establishing the ECSC, the Court of Justice indirectly recognized that the imposition of sanctions, even administrative ones, implied compliance with the principle of culpability,[554] despite some statements to the contrary by the Commission of the European Communities.[555] By 1962, the legislator had stipulated that fines could only be imposed for cartels and abuses of dominant positions if these offenses were committed "intentionally or negligently."[556]

While these beginnings were encouraging, in a resolution adopted in 2012, the European Parliament regretted that a "fragmented approach [has been] followed so far" in this area.[557] Indeed, both legislators and judges have sometimes been ambiguous about respecting the principle of culpability. Some legislative proposals have thus provided that sanctions may be imposed for breaches of regulations, either for intentional acts, or for negligence, or finally, "if the correct functioning of the legislation in question" so requires, "irrespective of the existence of any subjective factor."[558] The Court of Justice was no less ambivalent, on several occasions admitting that Member States were entitled, in order to ensure compliance with a European regulation and where justified by a general interest, to adopt

554 In this regard, K. Tiedemann, *Principes généraux applicables aux sanctions communautaires: Projet de rapport général, in* II Étude sur les systèmes de sanctions administratives et pénales dans les États membres des communautés européennes: Rapports de synthèse 7, 28 (1994), and cases cited.

555 *See, inter alia*, Comm. EC, June 2, 1971, IV/26.760, II, C, 6: "[D]iscrimination is an objective constitutive element of an offense that does not imply guilt" (unofficial translation). For a critique of this decision, *see* L. Focsaneanu, *La notion d'abus dans le système de l'article 86 du Traité instituant la Communauté économique européenne, in* La réglementation du comportement des monopoles et entreprises dominantes en droit communautaire 324, 342–43, 362–64 (J. A. Van Damme ed., 1977), and the references cited.

556 Regulation (EC) No. 17/62, First Regulation Implementing Articles 85 and 86 of the Treaty, 1962 O.J. (13) English special edition: Series I Vol. 1959–1962, art. 15. For a commentary, *see* Tiedemann, *Principes généraux applicables aux sanctions communautaires: Projet de rapport général, op. cit.* at 28.

557 European Parliament Resolution of May 22, 2012, on a European Union Approach to Criminal Law (2013/C 264 E/02), 2013 O.J. (CE 264)7, para. 11.

558 *Proposal for a Council Regulation (EEC) on controls and Penalties Applicable to the Common Agricultural and Fisheries Policies*, COM(90) 126 final (June 6, 1990), art. 4(4).

"a system of strict criminal liability."[559] Moreover, there is no express reference to the principle of culpability in primary legislation, neither in the EU Charter of Fundamental Rights nor in the ECHR.

This shortcoming did not escape criticism, which gradually led to the rise in prominence of the "*nulla poena sine culpa*" principle, now unanimously accepted.

B. A now unanimous and explicit recognition

203. **The recent recognition of the principle of culpability in European Union law.** All Member States now acknowledge the necessity of the mental element[560] – the principle of culpability even having constitutional status for most of them.[561] It is therefore hardly surprising that the *Corpus Juris* – a comparative law work published in 1997 by a group of experts commissioned by the European Commission to identify harmonization measures aimed at reducing disparities between national standards[562] – established culpability as the foundation of criminal liability.[563] Beyond EU criminal law,[564] the principle was also recognized in repressive administrative law.[565] A report published in 1994, also overseen by the Commission, recommended that this principle be enshrined in writing, and that a written rule be adopted to the effect that "there is no liability without proof of dol or recklessness," the latter being punishable "only when expressly provided for in the texts,"

559 Case C-326/88, Hansen & Soen, ECLI:EU:C:1990:291, para. 19. Advocate General W. van Gerven, in his Opinion delivered on Dec. 5, 1989, justifies recourse to strict criminal liability by emphasizing its "effectiveness" (para. 8), while admitting such "derogations" from the principle of culpability only in a "number of – as a rule fairly exceptional – cases" (para. 13). *See*, to the same effect, Case C-177/95, Ebony Maritime, ECLI:EU:C:1997:89, paras. 36–39. Advocate General F. G. Jacobs, in his Opinion delivered on Oct. 19, 1996, para. 46, justifies the solution by the importance of the public interest at stake. Finally, certain judgments link respect for the principle of culpability to the criminal nature of the provision at issue, admitting the possibility of objective criminal liability in matters of administrative regulation: Case C-210/00, Käserei Champignon Hofmeister, ECLI:EU:C:2002:440, para. 44. The Court followed the Opinion of Advocate General C. Stix-Hackl, delivered on Nov. 27, 2001, para. 59. Cf. Salabiaku v. France, App. no. 10519/83, ¶¶ 27–28 (ECtHR Oct. 7, 1988): the Court held that States may, under certain conditions, render a material act punishable, whether or not it results from criminal intent or negligence. Nonetheless, these were *presumptions of guilt* – attesting to the fact that the mental element had not disappeared. The Court also considered that article 6(2) of the ECHR (which sets out the principle of the presumption of innocence) requires States to keep such presumptions within reasonable limits.

560 *See supra*, no. 188.

561 Either explicitly or implicitly, by linking the principle of culpability to other principles of expressly constitutional value. *See* R. Sicurella, *Développer une culture pénale européenne: De l'européanisation des principes fondamentaux du droit pénal à une théorie "européenne" de la responsabilité pénale*, Revue de science criminelle et de droit pénal comparé 1, 12–13 (Jan.– Mar. 2020).

562 Corpus Juris: Portant dispositions pénales pour la protection des intérêts financiers de l'Union européenne 29 (M. Delmas-Marty ed., 1997).

563 *Id.* at 66–67.

564 For an overview of EU criminal law provisions, *see* S. de Biolley, H. Labayle & A. Weyembergh, Criminal Law of the European Union (4th ed. 2020).

565 In this sense, Tiedemann, *Principes généraux applicables aux sanctions communautaires: Projet de rapport général, op. cit.* at 29: "The case law of the Court of Luxembourg has enshrined the breadth of this principle, which, given its frequent foundation in national constitutional law, must today be regarded as a general principle of Community law. …[O]ne can no longer doubt the existence of the principle of culpability."

whatever the nature of the punishment – criminal or administrative.[566] This is a clear development: the European Union now explicitly recognizes the need for a mental element,[567] as illustrated by three recent examples.

The European legislator, in a resolution adopted in 2012, acknowledged that it recognized "the principle of individual culpability (*nulla poena sine culpa*)."[568]

In customs law, renowned for its objectivity, a proposed directive initially provided for "strict liability" offenses, which could be characterized "independently of any element of fault." The article in question was quickly amended to remove any trace of objective liability;[569] indeed, in 2016, the European Economic and Social Committee (EESC) affirmed the need to respect the principle of culpability, including in customs matters.[570]

Finally, in competition law, the ECN+ Directive, which came into force in 2019, initially contained no reference to the mental element of infringements. However, at the request of the European Parliament,[571] an amendment added an important recital: "In accordance with the Charter of Fundamental Rights of the European Union,... fines should be imposed where the infringement has been committed intentionally or negligently"[572] – implying that consideration of the mental element is required by the said Charter. The following sentence also states that "[t]he notions of intent and negligence should be interpreted in line with the case law of the Court of Justice of the European Union on the application of Articles 101 and 102 TFEU."[573]

---

566 *Id.* at 33 and 40.

567 *See ex multis*: R. Sicurella, Nulla poena sine culpa*: Un véritable principe droit européen?*, Revue de science criminelle et de droit pénal comparé 15 (2002): the author considers that strict liability is a "drift" that can in no way be justified by "imperatives of efficiency"; T. Elholm, *Guilt / Fault, in* General Principles for a Common Law Criminal Framework in the EU: A Guide for Legal Practitioners 41, 42 (R. Sicurella et al. eds., 2017); *adde*, for an in-depth study, G. Panebianco, *The* Nulla Poena Sine Culpa *Principle in European Courts Case Law: The Perspective of the Italian Criminal Law, in* Human Rights in European Criminal Law: New Developments in European Legislation and Case Law After the Lisbon Treaty 47, 68, 73 (S. Ruggeri ed., 2015).

568 European Parliament Resolution of May 22, 2012, on a European Union Approach to Criminal Law (2013/C 264 E/02), 2013 O.J. (CE 264)7, recital J and para. 4.

569 *See* the procedure sheet for the *Proposal for a Directive of the European Parliament and of the Council on the Union Legal Framework for Customs Infringements and Sanctions*, 2013/0432(COD), and the related amendments to article 3. The proposal was finally withdrawn by the Commission in 2020.

570 EESC Opinion on the Proposal for a Directive of the European Parliament and of the Council on the Union Legal Framework for Customs Infringements and Sanctions (2016/C 487/08), para. 3.1.

571 *See* the report by MEP A. Schwab, (COM(2017)01 42 – C8-0119/2017 – 2017/0063(COD)); and the table of proceedings, COM(2017)0142 (2017/0063 (COD)). We contacted the Archives Service of the European Union to request access to the debates that gave rise to this amendment, but these have not been made public.

572 Directive (EU) 2019/1 of the European Parliament and of the Council of Dec. 11, 2018, to Empower the Competition Authorities of the Member States to be More Effective Enforcers and to Ensure the Proper Functioning of the Internal Market, 2019 O.J. (L 11) 3, recital 42.

573 *Id.* It should be noted that the rest of the recital strangely and illogically leaves Member States free to resort to the "criterion of objective liability," which is highly open to criticism. On the one hand, Member States have long since abandoned no-fault criminal liability, making the statement anachronistic (*see supra*, no. 186); on the other hand, it is hard to understand how a national judge could interpret the expression "intentionally or negligently" in line with EU case law, while at the same time introducing a system of objective liability, the two being, to say the least, antinomic.

If the necessity of the mental element is recognized, and national judges are required to interpret it in line with their European counterparts, it is still necessary to agree on a definition. Such a definition struggles to emerge – the definitions provided by EU law being rare, scattered, and not very intelligible.

II. The continuing proliferation of definitions of intent in union law

204. **Theoretical and praetorian attempts at definition.** European Union law frequently refers to intent, but its judges have never clearly determined what can be qualified as such.[574] The doctrinal definitions that have been proposed appear insufficient (**A**), while the few definitional attempts made by the Court of Justice are largely unsatisfactory (**B**).

A. Insufficient doctrinal definitions

205. ***Corpus Juris*' attempt to define intent: a critical examination of an attempt at theorization.** It is an arduous task to propose a clear definition of intent, compatible with the domestic laws of Member States, even though doctrine has been at war over the issue for several centuries. While the task is certainly a difficult one, it is nonetheless surmountable:[575] it is advisable not to oversimplify, and to build a theory on the basis of generally accepted solutions,[576] in order to preserve national legal identities.[577]

---

574 In this sense, J. Blomsma, Mens Rea and Defences in European Criminal Law 6 (2012); *adde*, in the same sense, P. L. Parcu & M. L. Stasi, *The Role of Intent in the Assessment of Conduct under Article 102 TFEU*, *in* Abuse of Dominance in EU Competition Law: Emerging Trends 12, 14 (P. L. Parcu et al. eds., 2017): it is hard "to identify a common European definition of intent, and thus a common role to be attributed to it by national authorities, courts and practitioners while applying EU competition law." For an overview, *see* A. Rosanò, *Some Developments of the Principle of* Mens Rea *in the Case Law of the Court of Justice of the European Union*, 7 New Journal of European Criminal Law 302 (2016). Note that the same question arises in international criminal law, *see* the study by S. Glaser, *Élément moral de l'infraction internationale*, Revue Général de droit international public 537, 542 (1955): the author considers that the mental element is an integral part of the international offense, and attempts to identify the rules generally accepted in doctrine in order to theorize the concept. Article 30(1) of the Rome Statute of the International Criminal Court now provides that "Unless otherwise provided, a person shall be criminally responsible and liable for punishment for a crime within the jurisdiction of the Court only if the material elements are committed with intent and knowledge." Rome Statute of the International Criminal Court, July 17, 1998, 2187 U.N.T.S. 3, entered into force July 1, 2002, at 20. However, the interpretation of this provision is proving extremely difficult. On this subject, *ex multis*: P. Currat, *L'interprétation du Statut de Rome*, 20 Revue québécoise de droit international 137, 145–48 (2007); for a detailed study, M. Elewa Badar, The Concept of Mens Rea in International Criminal Law 417 (2013): the author considers that the question of the mental element remains one of the most complex in international criminal law, which can be explained by the use of a large number of vague and imprecise terms to define it.

575 *See* our conceptualization, *infra*, nos. 212 *et seq*.

576 Sicurella, *Développer une culture pénale européenne: De l'européanisation des principes fondamentaux du droit pénal à une théorie "européenne" de la responsabilité pénale*, *op. cit.* at 19.

577 J. Pradel, *Les grandes tendances de l'européanisation des systèmes pénaux nationaux*, 50 Les Cahiers de droit 1015, 1030 (2009).

However, we must be careful not to go down the wrong path by adopting definitions that either provide no information at all on the regime of intent or are inspired by a single legal tradition, thereby running the risk of the theory not being accepted by other European countries. Unfortunately, *Corpus Juris*, the only major work on the subject, has not avoided these two pitfalls.

Although in its second version, and at the request of several national reports, it defined the notions of intent, gross negligence and imprudence, it did so on the basis of Anglo-Saxon law[578] – a surprising choice, to say the least. English law is pragmatic, and has never developed a real theory of the mental element. Unaffected by doctrinal quarrels, it has developed almost autonomously from continental law over the last two centuries,[579] which means that it is unlikely to be compatible with the legal systems of the Member States. Furthermore, like national theories of intent, the *Corpus Juris* definitions focus on the agent's point of view[580] – an approach that has proven to be both misleading and inadequate for providing information on the regime of intent.[581]

It should also be noted that, while the *Corpus Juris* requires intent for all offenses relating to the protection of the EU's financial interests, it admits an exception in the case of fraud against the Community budget, for which it requires only gross negligence. This provision is the one that has attracted the most criticism from Member States,[582] many of whom do not accept that fraud can be an offense of negligence.[583] This alternative – identical to that used in anticompetitive practices law[584] – has nevertheless been retained, as in the opinion of the editors of *Corpus Juris*, restricting repression to intentional offenses would have risked "considerably weakening the effectiveness of the text."[585] This assertion is not at

578 The editors of *Corpus Juris* acknowledge that the "definitions given follow the English Law Commission because *Corpus Juris* itself refers to English law." III La mise en œuvre du Corpus Juris dans les États membres: Dispositions pénales pour la protection des finances de l'Europe 281 (M. Delmas-Marty & J. A. E. Vervaele eds., 2000).

579 To be convinced of this, it suffices to look at the degrees of *mens rea* it retains: these are far removed from the different types of *dol* retained by continental law. *See supra*, no. 190.

580 III La mise en œuvre du Corpus Juris dans les États membres: Dispositions pénales pour la protection des finances de l'Europe, *op. cit.* at 281: "There is intentional fault or *dol* if the offender seeks out the circumstances leading to the existence of the constituent elements of the offense, or knows or believes that these circumstances exist. Serious recklessness is constituted if the perpetrator knowingly takes a risk leading to the commission of the offense, and if this risk appears unreasonable in view of the circumstances. Gross negligence is constituted when the risk is obvious in light of circumstances known to the perpetrator, even if they are unaware of it."

581 *See* for a demonstration, *supra*, no. 194; and for a solution, *infra*, nos. 222–223.

582 Sicurella, Nulla poena sine culpa*: Un véritable principe droit européen? op. cit.* at 15.

583 For a table summarizing Member States' positions on article 10 ("mental element"), a summary of the national reports and details of the criticisms of this article country by country, *see* III La mise en œuvre du Corpus Juris dans les États membres: Dispositions pénales pour la protection des finances de l'Europe, *op. cit.* at 128–29 (for the table), 260–61 (for the summary), and 287–315 (for a country-by-country analysis).

584 *See infra*, no. 268.

585 III La mise en œuvre du Corpus Juris dans les États membres: Dispositions pénales pour la protection des finances de l'Europe, *op. cit.* at 75.

all convincing, since we know that when criminal law deals with offenses committed by professionals, it presumes intent on the basis of negligence, a solution found in most Member States.[586]

B. Unsatisfactory legal definitions

206. **The various names given to the mental element in European Union texts.** In the same way as national legislators,[587] the European legislator uses numerous expressions to which judges have difficulty in finding an enlightening definition. Indeed, European texts contain numerous terms to designate the mental element: offense committed "with intent, recklessly or by serious negligence,"[588] "intentionally or negligently,"[589] "knowingly and intentionally,"[590] etc.

It should be noted that, in French, the expression used in anti-competitive practices law ("*de propos délibéré ou par négligence*") differs from that recently adopted by the Digital Markets Act ("*volontairement ou par négligence*"[591]). Did the legislator intend to distinguish between the mental element required to characterize an infringement of either regulation? There are two reasons to doubt this. Firstly, the section in question was not the subject of any amendment during the legislative procedure preceding the adoption of the Digital Markets Act – which indicates that this point was not open to debate. Secondly, if we refer to the English version of the regulation, we notice that the expression used is the same in both texts: both stipulate that the offense must be committed "intentionally or negligently." There is thus a major translation issue: while the English texts invariably mention "intent," the French texts refer to "*propos délibéré*" or "*volonté.*" As we know, these terms are not systematically held to be synonymous by the doctrine.[592] It should

586 *See supra*, nos. 157–158. A counter-argument could be that failing to distinguish between intent and negligence violates the principle of proportionality, since intent should lead to the imposition of a harsher penalty than mere negligence. In this sense, *see* Sicurella, Nulla poena sine culpa*: Un véritable principe droit européen?*, *op. cit.* at 15. Nevertheless, a distinction must be drawn between the nature of the offense (which logically cannot be both intentional and non-intentional) and the criteria used to determine the penalty (which may leave room for negligence, which is then taken into account not as a constitutive element, but as a mitigating circumstance). Proportionality *and* logic are thus preserved.

587 *See supra*, no. 195.

588 Directive 2005/35/EC of the European Parliament and of the Council of Sept. 7, 2005, on Ship-Source Pollution and on the Introduction of Penalties for Infringements, 2005 O.J. (L255) 11, art. 4. In interpreting this directive, the European Court of Justice, after recalling the principle of legality and the resulting obligation of clarity, has merely stated that these various concepts are intended "to apply to an indeterminate number of situations that it is impossible to envisage in advance and not to specific conduct capable of being set out in detail in a legislative measure." Case C-308/06, Intertanko, ECLI:EU:C:2008:312, paras. 71 and 73, resp. The litigant should therefore understand the scope of a text that the judges fail to explain.

589 Regulation (EU) 2022/1925 of the European Parliament and of the Council of Sept. 14, 2022, on Contestable and Fair Markets in the Digital Sector, 2022 O.J. (L 265) 1, art. 30(1) and (3).

590 Council Regulation (EC) No. 423/2007 of Apr. 19, 2007, Concerning Restrictive Measures against Iran, 2007 O.J. (L 103) 1, art. 7(4).

591 Regulation (EU) 2022/1925, art. 30(1) and (3).

592 *See supra*, no. 189.

also be noted that this alternative between intent and negligence is found identically in all competition law infringements: cartels, abuse of dominant position, procedural violations, early completion of a gun jumping, breaches of the Digital Markets Act. In the same way as the letter of article 121-3 of the French Penal Code, which states: "There is no crime or offense without the intent to commit it," the European formulas that are supposed to designate the mental element of offenses do not make it possible to identify the important differences in nature between different categories of offense.[593]

Union law also tends to provide for several types of mental element simultaneously for the same offense – generally intent and negligence[594] – from which it follows, according to the "logic" of the legislator, that an offense could be either intentional or non-intentional, depending on the circumstances.[595] This drafting practice, inspired by Anglo-Saxon law, is undoubtedly motivated by the desire to make it easier to characterize offenses, by not requiring actual proof of a conscious violation of the law. This is not, however, a relevant legislative strategy, since no matter how a text is drafted, such proof need not be produced – knowledge of the law always being presumed.

Given this uncertainty, it is unsurprising that the Court of Justice has struggled to establish a clear, unified definition of the mental element in EU law infringements.

207. **The attempts to define by the Court of Justice of the European Union.** The Court of Justice's first attempt at a definition dates back to 1981: "[O]ffences which were intentionally committed, if they are to be punishable, require an intent to commit them on the part of the person concerned."[596] It is not particularly conclusive, as the wording is tautological: an intentional offense is, obviously, one that requires intent.

Thirty years later, a second attempt was offered to the judges, who had to interpret the following provision: "The participation, knowingly and intentionally, in activities the object or effect of which is, directly or indirectly, to circumvent the measures referred to in paragraphs 1, 2 and 3 shall be prohibited."[597] Here's what they tell us:

> The terms "knowingly" and "intentionally" imply … firstly an element of knowledge and secondly an element of intent. …Those two

593 Concerning article 121-3 of the French Penal Code, *see supra*, no. 194; for a breakdown of offenses according to the mental element they require, *see infra*, nos. 222–223.

594 *Ex multis*: Regulation (EC) No. 1/2003, art. 23(1) and (2); Regulation (EU) 2022/1925, art. 30(1) and (3); Commission Regulation (EC) No. 1975/2006 of Dec. 7, 2006, Laying Down Detailed Rules for the Implementation of Council Regulation (EC) No. 1698/2005, as Regards the Implementation of Control Procedures as well as Cross-Compliance in Respect of Rural Development Support Measures, 2006 O.J. (L368) 74, art. 23; Regulation (EU) 2022/2554 of the European Parliament and of the Council of Dec. 14, 2022, on Digital Operational Resilience for the Financial Sector, 2022 O.J. (L333) 1, art. 51(2).

595 This way of reasoning stems from a common error that is explained and challenged *infra*, no. 304.

596 Case 157/80, Siegfried Ewald Rinkau, ECLI:EU:C:1981:120, para. 15.

597 Regulation (EC) No. 423/2007, art. 7(4).

> cumulative requirements ... are met where the person participating in an activity covered by Article 7(4) of Regulation No 423/2007 deliberately *seeks* the object or the effect, direct or indirect, of circumvention connected therewith. They are also met where the person in question is aware that his participation in such an activity can have that object or effect and *accepts* that possibility.[598]

Make of that what you will![599] It was not until 2014 that the judges were once again able to attempt a definition. The plaintiff argued that the administration had unduly reduced the amount of his agricultural subsidy, after he had violated his obligations regarding the spreading of manure, which he claimed was unintentional – thereby raising the question of the intent required to qualify this breach.[600] This is the Court's answer: "The concept of 'intentional non-compliance' ... must be interpreted as requiring an infringement of the rules on cross-compliance by a beneficiary of aid who *seeks* a state of non-compliance with those rules or who, without seeking such a state, *accepts* the possibility that it may occur."[601]

If we disregard the "European" style of drafting and attempt a synthesis, we note that both of these last two definitions share the idea that an offense is committed intentionally when the agent *seeks* the result, or at least *accepts* its possibility.[602] However, they also have the disadvantage of providing no information on the regime of intent[603] – there is no indication of the conditions under which the judge may consider that the agent actually sought or accepted the result, or to which result reference is made.[604]

Nor is the EU judges' sole proposal for defining "gross negligence" any more enlightening. According to them, this implies: "[A]n *unintentional*

598 Case C-72/11, Mohsen Afrasiabi, ECLI:EU:C:2011:874, paras. 66–67 (emphasis added).

599 We will analyze this judgment in greater detail *infra*, no. 305, as part of our study of the meaning of the alternative "for object or for effect" in the law of anticompetitive practices.

600 Advocate General Juliane Kokott notes in this regard that the "concept of intent must be given an independent and uniform interpretation for the purposes of European Union law," but that while it "does occasionally appear in the case-law, neither the legislature nor the Court of Justice has as yet developed a universally valid definition." *See* her Opinion in Case C-396/12, A.M. van der Ham, ECLI:EU:C:2013:698, paras. 32–33. *Adde*, mention should be made of the attempted definition by Advocate General Henri Mayras, in Case 26/75, General Motors Continental, ECLI:EU:C:1975:141, at 1388–89: he proposed to define intent as "the will to commit an act" which the agent "knew was unlawful ... and conscious of the unlawful consequences of his behaviour"; whereas negligence should be considered "where the author of the infringement, although acting without any intention to perform an unlawful act, has not foreseen the consequences of his action in circumstances where a person who is normally informed and sufficiently attentive could not have failed to foresee them." This definition of intent, identical to those of classic authors, suffers from the same shortcomings; while the definition proposed for negligence, as it mixes in the same sentence awareness of breaking the law, foresight of a result (apparently, the result consisting in breaking the law?), and a standard of diligence, is incomprehensible to say the least.

601 Case C-396/12, A.M. van der Ham, ECLI:EU:C:2014:98, answer to the first preliminary question (emphasis added).

602 This, according to established doctrinal classifications, amounts to recognizing that *dol éventuel* belongs to the domain of intent. *Compare with supra*, no. 192.

603 For the reasons explained *supra*, no. 193.

604 On the different meanings of the term "result," *see supra*, no. 189.

act or omission by which the person responsible commits a *patent* breach of the duty of care which he *should have* and *could have* complied with in view of his attributes, knowledge, abilities and *individual situation.*"[605] This definition has two shortcomings: firstly, it conflates the terms "involuntary" and "unintentional";[606] secondly, it suggests that fault of negligence should be characterized by an analysis *in concreto*, whereas doctrine unanimously recognizes that criminal negligence is assessed *in abstracto.*[607]

In short, these definitions are so all-encompassing that they seem to voluntary avoid taking any clear stance. The judge seeks to cover all possible situations, even if this is to the detriment of conceptual clarity and rigor. The aim pursued – the effective implementation of European rules – is understandable, but it does not require distorting the notion of intent in order to be achieved, as long as the latter is sufficiently plastic to adapt to repressive needs.

208. **Union judges' terse definition of intent in anticompetitive practices law.** In competition law, the problem was quickly settled. In the name of the objectivity of infringements,[608] the relevance of "subjective intent," "good faith," or even "intent to harm"[609] – expressions that have never been defined[610] – has been rejected. However, since cartels and abuses of dominant positions must be committed "intentionally or negligently" to be punishable, it remains necessary to determine what this requirement entails. To do so, judges systematically use the same formula, which invariably reappears from case to case, to define intent; whereas no definition of negligence[611] has ever been provided.[612] The infringement is thus considered to have been committed "intentionally" when the accused company "cannot be unaware of the anti-competitive nature of its conduct, whether or not it is aware that it is infringing the competition rules of the Treaty."[613]

This recurring formula has the disadvantage of grounding the definition of intent on knowledge of the law – yet, such knowledge is systematically

605 Case C-308/06, Intertanko, ECLI:EU:C:2008:312, para. 77; similarly, Case C-47/07 P, Masdar (UK), ECLI:EU:C:2008:726, para. 90.

606 Like national legislators, *see supra*, no. 195.

607 *See supra*, no. 198.

608 Since 1979, the Court has tirelessly repeated the formula that "[t]he concept of abuse is an objective concept." Case 85/76, Hoffmann-La Roche, ECLI:EU:C:1979:36, para. 6. *Adde*, for example, Case C-52/09, TeliaSonera Sverige, ECLI:EU:C:2011:83, para. 27. Even in the most recent decisions, this sentence is still frequently used to justify the rejection of intent.

609 *See infra*, no. 265.

610 We will see that this expression is used to refer to motives, which, effectively and by definition, are never taken into account at the stage of characterizing an offense. *See infra*, nos. 266–267.

611 "Gross negligence" has been defined (*see supra*, no. 207), but not just "negligence."

612 In any case, we have not found any, nor has Advocate General Juliane Kokott; *see* her Opinion in Case C-308/06, Intertanko, ECLI:EU:C:2007:689, para. 103.

613 The formula is longstanding, and the case law is well established: *see* paragraph 268, and the case law cited. It is paragraph 268

presumed until proven otherwise.[614] Furthermore, it could be applied to both intentional and negligent offenses, and therefore fails to distinguish between these two types of offense, despite their different natures.

209. **The enigmatic case of the mental element of market abuse.** The law of market abuse and the law of anticompetitive practices have a common history[615] and are, in terms of the mental element, of the same nature – the offenses they enact being the result of a maneuver.[616] A priori, there is therefore no reason why intent should be treated differently from one subject to another.[617] However, in the latest European regulation on market abuse, no reference is made to intent or even negligence, the only "infringement" of the regulation allowing for the imposition of an administrative fine.[618] Nevertheless, there is one occurrence of the word "deliberate"[619] as well as a multitude of terms that fall within the lexical field of intent: "manipulation" appears fifty-two times, "attempt" nine times, "false or misleading information" nine times.

Equally strange is the "logic" behind the important *Spector* ruling on insider trading. In order to "objectify" the offense, the European legislator had taken care to substitute the expression "*use* of inside information" for the old, supposedly too subjective, term "*taking advantage of.*"[620] The question was therefore whether the offense, as newly defined, still implied any intent whatsoever. The judges' reasoning was perplexing. First, they acknowledge that this semantic change was made with the aim of "remov[ing] any element of purpose or intention from the definition of insider dealing,"[621] only

614 *See infra*, no. 219.

615 Indeed, the articles dealing with illicit coalitions and the forerunner of stock exchange law were placed consecutively in the 1810 Penal Code, precisely because they stemmed from the same rationale. *See* A. Chauveau, F. Hélie & E. Villey, V Théorie du Code pénal 626–27 (1888), nos. 2403–2404: "The legislator, after having foreseen and punished the various frauds that can taint commercial operations, had wanted to banish stock market games from commerce, when those who engage in them offer no guarantees, and when bad faith can mislead the odds." The contrast between the style of these authors, as precise as they were erudite, and European Union law is striking.

616 *See infra*, no. 245.

617 *Contra*, for a comparative analysis arguing that intent is not taken into account in either case, *see* M.-A. Frison-Roche, *Peut-on établir des analogies opératoires entre droit de la concurrence et droit boursier?*, 144 Petites affiches 9 (July 19, 1999).

618 Regulation (EU) No. 596/2014 of the European Parliament and of the Council of Apr. 16, 2014, on Market Abuse, 2014 O.J. (L173) 1, art. 30.

619 *Id.*, recital 44.

620 This semantic change was intended to result in the objectification of the mental element of insider dealing, thereby enabling greater effectiveness in the enforcement of insider trading offenses. *See* Opinion of Advocate General J. Kokott, Case C-45/08, Spector Photo Group, ECLI:EU:C:2009:534, paras. 57–58. This amendment has not, in fact, changed the accepted solutions. *Compare*, before the reform, *with* Opinion of Advocate General P. Mengozzi, Case C-391/04, Ypourgos, ECLI:EU:C:2006:669, para. 50 & n.7: the mental element of the offense "does not presuppose an intention to profit therefrom"; and after the reform, Case C-45/08, Spector Photo Group, ECLI:EU:C:2009:806, para. 55: "[C]ertain situations may require a thorough examination of the factual circumstances enabling it to be ensured that the use of the inside information is actually unfair…." Proof, if any were needed, that one can never entirely objectify an offense which, by its very nature, presupposes fraud.

621 Case C-45/08, Spector Photo Group, ECLI:EU:C:2009:806, para. 34, comm. F. Stasiak, *L'utilisation d'une information privilégiée par un initié primaire*, Revue de science criminelle et de droit pénal comparé 156 (Jan.–Mar. 2010); *adde*, L. Idot, *Opérations d'initiés*, Europe (Feb. 2010), comm. 75.

to assert, a few paragraphs later, that "[o]nce the constituent elements of insider dealing ... are satisfied, it is ... possible to assume an intention on the part of the author of that transaction,"[622] since "intention ... can be inferred implicitly from the constituent material elements"[623] – such reasoning does little to clarify the concept of intent.

*

* *

210. **Conclusion of Section 2: the difficulty of defining and grasping the regime of intent.** Despite the unanimous acceptance of the principle that any crime or offense presupposes, in principle, the intention to commit it, neither national theories nor Union law provides a clear definition of the concept. Intent, whose study is widely regarded as one of the most difficult,[624] is not a stabilized field of knowledge – which, in its current state, prevents us from using it to determine the role the notion plays in competition law.

*

* *

211. **Conclusion to Chapter 1: the need to propose a general theory of intent.** The cross-cutting nature of intent, which is recognized by all Member States and transcends disciplines, opens up a fruitful avenue of research. In order to overcome the theoretical obstacles that obscure the understanding of the concept, and to show the unity of the reasoning behind liability, it seems necessary to propose a theory that, while new, is not innovative, as it aligns with the continuity of traditions common to the Member States, and proposes a return to the unity that prevails in law. This exploration of a general theory of intent will then serve as a foundation for building a theory of intent in competition law.

*

* *

622 Case C-45/08, Spector Photo Group, ECLI:EU:C:2009:806, para. 38.

623 *Id.*, para. 44.

624 *See supra*, no. 6.

Chapter 2
TOWARD A GENERAL THEORY OF INTENT

212. **The aim: to develop a general theory of intent.** In the museum of doctrinal theories, there is one work that cannot be ignored: the painting of intent. The closer you look at it, the clearer you see the strangeness of its composition – made up of overlapping thick layers, no doubt due to its age and successive restorations. The majestic frame surrounding the painting, indicating that it belongs to the class of "major themes," may discourage the formulation of the slightest proposal, for fear of altering such a solemn theme. The only way out is for the researcher to take a blank sheet of paper[1] and draw a few lines in pencil. The aim is not to create a work of art: the process is more akin to the work of an architect than that of a painter. The aim of the[2] "system builder" is to compartmentalize the space into several rooms, assigning each a specific function, while simultaneously emphasizing the unity of the overall structure.

213. **The method: a pragmatic approach.** The pragmatic approach we have adopted[3] implies renouncing any attempt to establish the philosophical or psychological

---

1 Apart from its introductory remarks, this chapter will contain no doctrinal references. However, we will refer the reader to our previous demonstrations if needed.

2 The expression is that of Dean Rivero, *Apologie pour les 'faiseurs de système'*, Recueil Dalloz 99 (1951), i, Doctrine, chron. xxiii.

3 This method was inspired by the work of two American philosophers: Charles Sanders Peirce and his pupil William James. *See* in particular: W. James, Pragmatism: An Old Name for Some New Ways of Thinking (1907); C. S. Peirce, À la recherche d'une méthode (J. Deledalle-Rhodes & M. Balat trans., Presses Universitaires de Perpignan 1993). For an introduction to the thought of William James, *see* S. Malderieux, William James: L'attitude empiriste (2008). The intuition that the most fruitful method for apprehending intent is a practical approach was also that of Robert Legros, who himself chose this path in his thesis: R. Legros, L'élément moral dans les infractions (1952). Reading the article *Tû-tû* by Danish legal philosopher Alf Ross was also of major importance in our reflections. *See* A. Ross, *Tû-tû*, 7 Enquête 263 (E. Millard & E. Matzner trans., 1999). After delving into the Noît-cif tribe, in which the abstract expression "Tû-tû" was used to designate a set of rules, the author demonstrates, by drawing an analogy with what was happening in this primitive society, that our legal concepts are irrelevant when understood in themselves, from which it follows that it is, in practice, useless to attempt

meaning of intent. For the jurist, such an undertaking would be counterproductive. A concept is relevant if, and only if, it reflects genuine differences in regime, for it is on this condition that it enables a rational and coherent presentation of legal rules. This requires us to move away from widespread approaches, which consist either in defining intent from the point of view of the agent's psyche,[4] or in determining the requisite mental element on the basis of the tripartite classification of offenses (*crimes, délits, contraventions*)[5] or, in European Union law, in using various stylistic formulas to ensure formal respect for fundamental rights.[6] It is therefore appropriate to examine these classifications and theories. The first step was to identify the differences in the way jurisprudence treats the mental element of all offenses, in order to draw up a new classification of offenses according to their mental element and the specific regime relating to it.[7] This quadripartite classification is thus applicable whatever the nature of the offense – *crimes, délits, contraventions* – or the discipline concerned – competition law, administrative law, criminal law, European Union law, tort law – and whatever the country.[8]

214. **The result: the pyramidal structure of intent.** The theory rests on the postulate that all offenses are intentional – the law invariably requires both the will to break the law and knowledge of it in order to hold a person liable. There is therefore a regime common to all offenses (**Section 1**), forming the universally accepted basis of liability; coupled with regimes specific to different categories of offense (**Section 2**) – the regime of intent being pyramidal in structure.

---

to investigate their meaning, and misleading to treat them as principles or empirical truths that could serve as a basis for deducing solutions. The function of the concept, for Alf Ross, is to set out legal rules in a coherent way, in order to provide a rational presentation of the law in force. We believe, however, that the technical undertaking of conceptualization should not dispense with a critical look at the content of the law, as this would run the risk of falling into a positivist approach. In this sense, *see* C. Atias, Épistémologie juridique 154 (1985), no. 82; *adde*, J. Parain-Vial, *La nature du concept juridique et la logique*, 11 Archives de philosophie du droit 45, 57 (1966): "Behind the problems of legal logic, metaphysical problems always loom. This is why the ideal of law cannot be that of mathematics." Put another way, the following discussion, which aims to shed light on the structure of reasoning, will not exempt us from adopting a substantial and critical approach to the definition of intent in the law of anticompetitive practices (*see infra*, nos. 260 *et seq.*). Rodolfo Sacco's work on legal comparison has also shown us just how fertile this method can be. It aims to go beyond doctrinal descriptions and apparent divergences in solution, to seek out what, in practice, is common to different legal systems. *See* R. Sacco, La comparaison juridique au service de la connaissance du droit (1991). Finally, even before we began our research, we were aware of the limits of words, of their inability to fully grasp reality, and of the inevitable deformation they inflict on it. This led us, from the outset, to reason not according to what they suggest, but rather what they purport to designate. Our reading of a thesis on the contributions of Wittgenstein's philosophy to legal reasoning has confirmed this: *see* E. Silva-Romero, Wittgenstein et la philosophie du droit 108–29 (2002), nos. 88–100. According to the author, the function of doctrinal activity is to clarify ambiguous propositions in law, through a logical analysis of language.

4 *See supra*, no. 193.

5 *See supra*, no. 194.

6 *See supra*, nos. 200 *et seq*.

7 *See* our summary table of the quadripartite classification of offenses according to their mental element, *infra*, Appendix no. 1; and our diagram of the relationship between the different elements of the offense, Appendix no. 2. It should be noted that competition offenses are found exclusively in categories no. 1 (offense of commission) and no. 3 (offense of means). This classification does not call into question the relevance of the tripartite classification of offenses, nor is it intended to replace it, insofar as the latter has implications for sentencing, procedure, and jurisdiction. It would also benefit from further work specifically focused on tort law: for this reason, we have indicated, for each type of offense, which type of civil fault it might correspond to.

8 We have deliberately set aside the doctrinal vocabulary used in the various countries, in order to propose simple, clearly defined terms capable of being received by all legal systems.

Section 1
A common framework for all offenses

215. **The reasoning behind the characterization of all offenses.** Proof of intent is not *probatio diabolica.* Judges have always approximated the state of mind of those they have had to judge. We therefore need to shed some light on the way they proceed, by theorizing proof of intent (**Paragraph 2**). To do this, it is first necessary to circumscribe the object of proof, by setting out the method for determining the requisite intent (**Paragraph 1**).

Paragraph 1 – Determining the required intent

216. **A regime applicable to all offenses, coupled with a specific regime for each category of offense.** In order to be characterized as an offense, it presupposes that the agent has the capacity to *be aware* of the prohibitions and to *wish* to infringe them. This dual requirement is common to all offenses (**I**). However, a second step is necessary to identify the specific intent of certain offenses. Since each category of offense has its own specific regime, it is necessary to determine the criteria for assigning them appropriately (**II**).

I. Intent required for all offenses

217. **The two elements forming the basis of intent.** The foundation of intent consists of two elements: *knowledge* (**A**) and *will* (**B**),[9] whose probative regime needs to be examined.

A. A common requirement: will to commit the offense

218. **Proof of will to commit the offense.** In order to incur liability, the law requires the existence of an offense committed voluntarily. This requirement applies to all offenses.[10] However, as free will is postulated by law, the legal system establishes a presumption: when the agent is judged, they

9 This is the "classic" definition of intent, *see supra*, no. 188. We have retained it because it attains a cardinal point that is indispensable; and because all national laws, as well as European Union law, invariably require these two elements. We reject their association with the notion of imputability for the reasons set out *supra*, no. 185. In our theory, these two conditions belong to the realm of intention.

10 Including so-called negligent offenses, *see supra*, no. 195. However, it should be remembered that, contrary to a long-standing tradition, for only a few decades, civil liability law has held incapable persons responsible, *see supra*, no. 146.

are presumed to have acted voluntarily; it follows that the prosecuting authority does not have to prove this will.

However, this presumption is rebuttable, and it is up to the defendant to show that their will was either non-existent (insanity, minority)[11] or forced (order of the law, command of legal authority, constraint, necessity). If they succeed, no offence can be attributed to them. On the other hand, if this is not the case, their behavior *will irrebuttably presuppose, de facto*, the corresponding intent.[12] The reasoning is as follows: if an adult of sound mind and under no compulsion raises their arm, the law deems they have done so voluntarily.

Proof of will is more than straightforward. Most of the time, it does prompt any debate. The same applies to proof of knowledge of the law.

B. A common requirement: knowledge of the law

219. **The probative regime for knowledge of the law.** In order to hold an individual liable for an offense, the legal system always requires that they be aware of violating its prohibitions.[13] However, to ensure that this requirement does not become tolerance for those who, more or less knowingly, prefer to remain uninformed in order to behave as they please with impunity, the law presumes knowledge of the law. Thus, when an agent commits an offense, they are deemed to have knowingly infringed the rules, without the prosecuting authority having to prove it.

However, if they succeed in demonstrating the existence of a reasonable doubt as to the scope of the law, they will remain guilty of violating it, but a mitigating circumstance may be taken into account in their favor.[14] On the other hand, if they fail to rebut this presumption, they will be irrebuttably presumed to have intended to violate the law.

Proof of these two conditions is the first step in establishing liability. However, in certain cases, it may be necessary for the judge to provide additional evidence to establish the mental element of the offense. In order to determine what this evidence consists of and how it can be adduced, we will now describe the criteria for identifying the specific intent required for certain offenses.

---

11 These two defenses are clearly not applicable to legal persons or businesses.

12 On the difference between presumptions of fact and presumptions of law, and the existence of "quasi-legal" presumptions governing the characterization of intent, *see supra*, no. 198.

13 Except, *a priori*, in civil liability law, because of a particularity linked to the definition of fault: fault may be extralegal. However, criminal law is not entirely contained in the law, and includes concepts as abstract as that of "civil fault," implying, as in civil law, a significant degree of interpretation on the part of the judge, *see supra*, no. 198. It is therefore possible to consider, by departing from a narrow vision of legality, that the norm is not entirely contained in the text of the law, but is also sometimes defined by case law – which is the norm in common law countries, and is also in line with the ECHR's interpretation of the principle of legality. It follows that, even in civil liability law, the notion of fault is also "legally defined by law," if case law is included.

14 This is not the system adopted in France, but it is the one adopted by most Member States and by European Union law (particularly in competition law, *see* nos. 461–467); and it is, in our view, the most relevant for the reasons set out *supra*, no. 196.

II. The specific intent required according to the structure of the offense

220. **A method for identifying the requisite intent based on the structure of the offense.** As the tripartite classification of offenses (*crimes*, *délits*, *contraventions*) does not imply any difference in terms of the mental element of the offense (**A**), it is necessary to propose operational distribution criteria. These are based on the structure of the offense (**B**).

A. Legal classification of the offense: an irrelevant criterion

221. **Justification for rejecting the criterion of legal classification of offenses: an inoperative criterion for establishing the requisite intent.** The legal classification of offenses is not a relevant criterion, since it does not systematically reflect the differences in the mental element between the three categories of offense it comprises.[15] In fact, all offenses are intentional in the broad sense of the term (will to engage in the conduct), in that they require a combination of the will to commit the offense and knowledge of the law, even if this is presumed. Moreover, many crimes do not require intent in the narrow sense,[16] nor do many offenses;[17] on the other hand, some *contraventions* do.[18] The same reasoning applies to infringements of European Union law. While it provides different expressions to designate the requires mental element, it nevertheless applies identical formulations to offenses of distinct natures.[19]

It is therefore necessary to propose another criterion for classifying offenses based on their requisite mental element.

B. The structure of the offense: an operational criterion

222. **The necessary distinction between the drafting of the incriminating text and the structure of the offense.** The wording of a legal text[20] does not

15 *See supra*, no. 194

16 *Ex multis*: ordering that no one survives or threatening an adversary with this (art. 416-8 of the Penal Code); desertion to the enemy (art. L. 321-13 of the Code of Military Justice); abandonment of a minor of fifteen years of age followed by the death of the latter (art. 227-2 of the Penal Code); enslavement (art. 224-1 A of the Penal Code); torture and acts of barbarism (art. 222-1 of the Penal Code).

17 *Ex multis*: indecent exposure (art. 222-32 of the Penal Code); violation or desecration of graves (art. 225-17 of the Penal Code); failure to obey a lawful order (art. L. 233-1 of the Highway Code); driving under the influence (art. L. 234-1 of the Highway Code); threatening to commit a crime or offense against persons, the attempt of which is punishable (art. L. 222-17 of the Penal Code); as well as most offenses belonging to so-called technical legislation (for examples, *see supra*, no. 155).

18 *Ex multis*: deliberately killing a domestic, tame, or captive animal (art. R. 655-1 of the Penal Code); willful violence resulting in total incapacity to work for up to eight days (art. R. 625-1 of the Penal Code).

19 *See supra*, no. 206.

20 We do not use the term "incriminating text," so as not to limit our vocabulary to criminal law alone. The expression "legal text" encompasses unwritten law, and reflects a reality that contemporary jurists can no longer deny: legicentrism is dead. It also enables us to adapt our theory to the law of civil liability, as it encompasses the "pre-existing obligation," the breach of which characterizes civil fault (*see supra*, no. 148).

always reveal the structure of the offense. Focusing on the wording, i.e., the words used, would lead to falling back into their trap. Indeed, the legislator employs a multitude of terms to define intent, without necessarily reflecting the required mental element. European Union law provides the best illustration of this,[21] while national laws are not to be outdone.[22] Identifying the structure of an offense therefore involves going beyond a mere analysis of words to break down the offense into its various elements.

To do this, it is first necessary to examine the incriminating text. For example, it is possible, *a priori*, to think that torture is an intentional crime in the strict sense (the will to achieve the result). However, since it does not require any result that can be detached from the conduct itself – the act of torturing[23] – it is an intentional offense in the broad sense (the will to engage in the conduct), like most minor offenses.

While in this example, a simple reading of the incriminating text is sufficient to classify the offense – as we shall see, this is also the case for cartels[24] – in other cases, it is not sufficient, and it is then necessary to refer to the elements required to characterize the offense, in order to infer its structure – this is the analysis we will carry out with regard to abuses of a dominant position.[25]

223. **The formula for classifying offenses according to their mental element.** In order to classify offenses, the following formula[26] should be applied:

> Does the offense have a detachable result?
>
> ✘ *No*. Then it is a "*offense of commission.*"
>
> ✓ *Yes*, but does the result have to be achieved voluntarily?
>
> ✘ *No*. Then it is a case of "*offense of lack of foresight*"
>
> ✓ *Yes*, but is the result achieved voluntarily unlawful solely because of the means used to achieve it?
>
> ✓ *Yes*, so it is a "*offense of means.*"
>
> ✘ *No*. Is the result achieved voluntarily illicit in itself?
>
> ✓ *Yes*, so it is a "*offense of result.*"

21 *See supra*, no. 206.

22 *See supra*, no. 194.

23 Art. 222-1 of the Penal Code.

24 *See infra*, no. 271 and no. 275.

25 *See infra*, no. 271 and no. 274.

26 This formula is based on conditional logic, which is widely used in algorithmic programming. It relies on a sequence of "if/then" reasoning, where a new input is displayed only if a specific condition is met.

Each of these four types of offense has its own partially autonomous regime,[27] although all are based on common probative reasoning.

Paragraph 2 – Modes of proof of intent

224. **Objectivity and subjectivity: two stages, two types of reasoning.** Intent is always established objectively by the judge. This assertion is true at the stage of characterizing the offense, but false at the sentencing stage, where subjectivity reigns supreme. Thus, the defendant's *intent is objectively proven* when it comes to characterizing the offense (**I**); whereas their *intentions* are *subjectively assessed* in order to adjust the sentence (**II**) – the reasoning consisting in the first case of proving the *offense*, and in the second of assessing the *degree of culpability*.

I. The objectivity of evidence at the stage of qualifying the offense

225. **Proof of Intent Through the Exclusive Use of Presumptions.** As the intent of others cannot be probed, it is impossible to *prove* – it can only be *presumed*. Although the probative mode of intent often leads to its disappearance from decisions, it would be hasty to conclude that it plays no role.[28] Not only does it constitute the ethical foundation of the right to punish, but it is also an object of proof that occupies a preponderant place in the reasoning governing the characterization of offenses.

Presumptions of intent are of two kinds: they can be based either on the *material elements of* the case (**A**) or on general, abstract *standards* (**B**). If the former are insufficient to establish intent, or if the accused succeeds in reversing the burden of proof – thereby requiring the judge to provide additional justification – the latter may be used.

A. Presumptive evidence based on material elements

226. **The definition of "material elements."** By the term "material elements," we are not referring to the "material element" of the offense, as opposed to the "mental element." Rather, in addition to the agent's conduct, we are referring to the factual circumstances surrounding their act – in other words, the context.

Behavior – because it manifests intent – and circumstances – because they explain it – are, in fact, the only elements likely to be apprehended by

27 These regimes are described *infra*, nos. 233 *et seq*.

28 For the reasons explained *supra*, no. 197.

judges to enable them to presume intent, *retrospectively*. Behavior is also indispensable to the existence of reprehensible intent, since mere intent is never reprehensible – the law is not the judge of consciences, but only of intentions translated into acts, even if they are only preparatory.

227. **The variable probative value of presumptions of intent.** Presumptions vary in their probative value. At the top of the scale is behavior, the ultimate proof of intent, which is sometimes even sufficient to establish the mental element.

However, when the defendant's behavior alone casts doubt on their intentions, other evidence must be adduced. In such cases, the judge will use the "body of evidence" method. Based, for example, on documentary evidence or witness testimony, the judge will form an opinion as to the existence or absence of an offense. If they decide to convict, they will then have to provide reasons for their decision – i.e., outline all the elements taken into account in their reasoning, and build a case. The latter will be more or less convincing, depending on the degree of plausibility of the evidence gathered.

In this respect, the statement of reasons is extremely important, as it is the only basis for a genuine review on appeal, and possibly in cassation. Indeed, even if the national or European Court of Cassation does not rule on the facts, it nonetheless checks whether the elements used to characterize the mental element have been brought together, the scope attributed to them, or the existence of contradictions or ambiguities in the grounds.[29]

Furthermore, in order to reinforce their motivation, or if they are forced to do so because the accused has succeeded in reversing the burden of proof, the judge may, if necessary, resort to standards.

B. Proof by presumptions based on standards

228. **Defining standards.** A standard is an instrument for measuring normality. It consists of abstract reasoning based on a predetermined model. The standard is always objective, since it does not involve an *in concreto* assessment of the accused's state of mind or abilities – the latter being systematically presumed until proven otherwise.[30] Nevertheless, certain standards are specific to a particular type of individual: for example, professionals are subject to a higher standard than non-professionals. This does not mean, however, that the analysis becomes subjective: once it has been established that the accused is a professional, the judge does not seek to determine whether they are more or less gifted or competent, but compares them, mechanically, to a demanding standard.

29 *See* notably *supra*, no. 198.

30 *See supra*, no. 198.

It should be noted that, generally speaking, the standard does not describe reality. The normality on which it is based is not the norm understood as an "average." Thus, just because the majority of individuals behave in a certain way does not mean that their behavior becomes, for the judge, a standard. The normality of the standard is normative: the standard is not a description of what is, but what ought to be. As such, it extends and completes the meaning of the offense.

229. **Written or unwritten, legal or extra-legal standards.** The reference model may be contained in the law (e.g., in the Highway Code or so-called technical legislation). In this way, a professional's negligence can easily be established if they have breached one of their legal safety obligations. However, standards are often unwritten: they are created by the judge and solidified through constant yet evolving case law. The characterization of fault in tort law is a case in point: the use of the standard of the loyal and prudent man makes it possible, by contrast, to characterize what is disloyal or short-sighted.

The two examples just given refer to legal standards. However, these coexist with other standards of an "extralegal" nature.[31] These include a profession's best practices, such as those of a surgeon, architect, lawyer, plumber, or airline pilot. Standards can also be economic. In this case, they are designed, through extralegal analyses, to establish the behavior that a "normal,"[32] "rational" operator would have adopted, for example, in order to determine whether their conduct reflects an anticompetitive strategy or competition on the merits.

Proof of intent is thus based, at the stage of characterizing the offense, on predefined rules of reasoning, from which the judge cannot depart; conversely, intentions are evaluated subjectively by the judge when determining the penalty to be imposed.

II. Subjective assessment when determining the penalty

230. **The exclusion of the sentencing stage from the theory of intent.** Why, when we have hitherto maintained that the assessment of intent is always objective, does the assertion that *intentions* are sometimes apprehended subjectively suddenly emerge for the first time? The reason is simple: we need to distinguish between two stages of reasoning, and exclude the second

31 The term "extralegal" is apt for the distinction, but it can be argued that since these standards, *a priori* of a non-legal nature, are received by the law, they themselves become legal. Furthermore, since a profession's best practices can be normative (in the sense that they can be sanctioned by disciplinary bodies), they constitute a form of law.

32 In the sense just explained, *supra*, no. 228.

from the scope of intent theory. Indeed, if intent is objectively presumed at the moment of qualification of the offense, in order to determine the penalty, judges must then assess, as best they can, the agent's real, lived guilt. To do this, they will no longer ask the rigorous question of whether the individual intended to break the law, but will examine, approximately and on a case-by-case basis, their intentions – that is, their state of mind, their inner disposition, their motives, their personality. It is only at the cost of this imprecise, partly discretionary method, and therefore resistant to theorization (**B**), that the law can attempt to be humane (**A**).

A. Justifying the subjective nature of sanction determination

231. **The principle and limits of the subjective approach at the stage of penalty individualization.** While the characterization of the mental element of the offense is marked by a high degree of objectivity, this rigor is offset by greater flexibility at the stage of individualizing the penalty – where the judge assesses, weighs and arbitrates, in order to adjust the penalty in proportion to the agent's culpability as much as possible. The law is strict for all; punishment should be severe only for those who deserve it.

However, this subjectivity is framed and limited by the legislator, who sets a maximum – and sometimes a minimum – penalty; it may be reduced or even eliminated by pre-established calculation methods[33] or automatic sanctions.[34] The penalty then depends not only on culpability, but also on the inherent gravity of the offender's conduct. In criminal law, the sentence is sometimes increased to take account of the normal, albeit undesired, consequences of an act. In civil liability law, although the judge may take the defendant's intent into account when modulating the amount of damages,[35] the damages are proportionate to the harm caused. In the latter two cases, the law requires that the damage suffered be taken into account in determining the penalty, not merely the wrongful conduct and the intent behind it – for it is only fair that those who should have avoided causing harm to others should be held accountable for it.

Determining the penalty, therefore, does not depend solely on a subjective approach. However, when that is the case, the judge will not consider "intent" in the sense we have understood it up to now – the austerity of a logical construction cannot have its place at a time when the judge must become less scientific, and more human.

---

33 This is the case in anticompetitive practices law: competition authorities calculate the fine according to a pre-established methodology set out in guidelines, *see* Comm. EC, Guidelines on the Method of Setting Fines Imposed Pursuant to Article 23(2)(a) of Regulation (EC) No. 1/2003, 2006 O.J. (C 210), 2; ADLC, Communiqué de l'Autorité de la concurrence relatif à la méthode de détermination des sanctions pécuniaires (July 30, 2021).

34 A thesis on this subject is in preparation for 2019: V. Martinez, *L'automaticité de la sanction en droit privé*, dir. C. Bloch, D. Poracchia, Université d'Aix-Marseille. *See*, on this subject, V. Martinez, L'automaticité de la sanction en droit privé (2024) (Ph.D. dissertation, Université d'Aix-Marseille).

35 *See supra*, no. 150.

B. A typology of intent taken into account

232. ***Intentions*, in their everyday sense.** A certain leniency may be shown to the first-time offender, because of a painful past or unfavorable circumstances, or to the manager of a small company who is unaware of their obligations, and whose bankruptcy would result from too severe a penalty. More severity may be shown to the repeat offender whose past record suggests that they will drag other souls down with them, or to the person whose sole purpose was clearly to harm others. Intentions, valorous or malicious, good or bad faith, loyalty or disloyalty, greedy or charitable motives, jealousy, passion, frustration, desire for revenge, determination to instigate an offense, willingness to actively participate in it or to repent of it, personality, antecedents – these intentions, these gray areas of being, are assessed when it comes to determining the penalty. No science can claim to provide the magistrate with a method for doing this, for it is to their *intuitive sense of* justice that they appeal. This is the limit of legal *reasoning*.

No theory can validly claim to describe, explain, break down, and classify such a phenomenon. It would be possible to undertake a statistical study, but it would reveal little beyond the boundless plurality of situations, which are as many stories as they are cases. This is why it is important not to confuse the concept of intent, whose regime can usefully be systematized at the qualification stage, with intentions, understood in their everyday sense and which, because they are assessed in all their diversity, cannot be theorized.

Section 2
A specific framework for certain offenses

233. **The distinction between intentional offenses *lato sensu* and intentional offenses *stricto sensu*.** The *summa divisio* of our theory lies in the distinction between *intentional offenses lato sensu* and *intentional offenses stricto sensu*. This distinction is based on a single criterion: the will to achieve the result. Either the text of the law requires only the characterization of the will to engage in the conduct, or it also requires the characterization of the will to achieve the result. These two categories of offense share a common regime, which has just been examined; in addition, one (**Paragraph 1**) and the other (**Paragraph 2**) have their own specific regime.

Paragraph 1 – Regime specific to intentional offenses *lato sensu*

234. **The definition of intentional offenses *lato sensu*.** The common feature of *lato sensu* intentional offenses[36] is that they require only the will to engage in the conduct, to the exclusion of the will to achieve a result. This characteristic gives rise to a common regime for this category (**II**), overlaid by a specific regime for the two sub-categories that make it up (**I**).

I. The distinction between offenses of commission and offenses of lack of foresight

235. The distinction between **offenses of commission and offenses of lack of foresight.** Among *lato sensu* intentional offenses, two subcategories are distinguished by a partly distinct regime: offenses of commission (**A**) and offenses of lack of foresight (**B**). Their distinction is based on a single criterion: the existence or absence of a result detachable from the conduct.

A. Regime specific to offenses of commission

236. Defining offenses of commission. When the offense consists of the will to engage in a course of conduct regardless of the outcome, it is an offense of commission.

The choice of this expression is justified by the fact that once the agent commits the offending act, and on this condition alone, they are held responsible.

The main, though by no means exclusive, breeding ground for these offenses is what legal writers often refer to as "police regulations" or "contraventional law," the aim of which is more to enforce a certain collective discipline, by means of precise (but often poorly drafted) texts, than to punish morally reprehensible behavior.[37] This form of legislation has seen exponential growth in recent decades, as it did some time before the fall of the Roman Empire.[38]

---

36 We have chosen to retain this dual appellation – "intentional *lato sensu*" or "voluntary" offense – for several reasons. It enables our theory to adapt to the definition of intent used in contemporary penal codes, and to preserve the relevant distinction made by a large body of doctrine between intent and will; at the same time, it removes from the legal vocabulary expressions that are a source of confusion, such as "involuntary offense" or "unintentional offense" – since it must be admitted that all offenses are intentional in the strict sense, or voluntary.

37 Recall the notion of "material offense," *supra*, no. 154.

38 We will criticize the fact that it is now a recurring legislative practice (recurring legislative practice) to resort to this category of offense, *see infra*, nos. 448. *et seq*.

This category includes, for example, the majority of *contraventions*, most breaches of technical legislation[39] and tax law, certain crimes and offenses,[40] and the deliberate endangerment of the lives of others.[41]

In law of civil liability, offenses of commission would find their counterpart in civil faults, which could be renamed "fault of commission," and which would include civil faults relating to offenses in this category,[42] as well as contractual breaches – the contract being the law of the parties, failure to respect it alone engages the liability of the defaulting debtor.

There are also offenses of commission under competition law: procedural offenses, violations of the Digital Markets Act[43] and all comparable regulations,[44] failure to fulfill commitments undertaken in a commitment procedure or following a merger, or gun-jumping in merger proceedings.

237. **Characteristics specific to offenses of commission.** Offenses of commission are characterized independently of any result. As a result, they do not require proof of any causal link, nor do they rely on any established standard. They result solely from the (presumed willful) violation of legal prescriptions, which makes them the easiest offenses to characterize, since the qualification operation is almost[45] automatic. Moreover, errors of law are rarely accepted,[46] as the texts are so precisely drafted that, even though they may be numerous and abstruse, the litigant is presumed (sometimes fictitiously) to know and understand them. Lastly, and because of their very precision, offense of commission do not adapt well to changes in reality, are quickly obsolete, and must be constantly reformed in order to keep up, often late, with the times. In this respect, they are open to

---

39 For examples, *see supra*, no. 155.

40 *See supra*, no. 221.

41 Despite the numerous doctrinal debates concerning the mental element of deliberate endangerment (*see infra*, no. 192), this offense, unlike offenses of lack of foresight (*see infra*, no. 239), does not require any detachable result of the conduct. The source of much of the dispute lies in the use of the term "deliberate" to describe the offense, which led part of the doctrine to consider that it was an intentional offense, and to consider that it was a legal consecration of the category of *dol éventuel*. However, in order to characterize the offense, no result is required, and the judge does not have to ask whether the accused actually foresaw that they could cause a risk to others; hence, the foreseeability of the result is not a criterion for characterizing the offense either.

42 Because they are punished independently of any result, offenses of commission *a priori* rarely cause harm to others. The possibility of civil consequences is not, however, a theoretical possibility, insofar as offenses of commission sometimes entail a prejudicial result included in the conduct itself: this is the case with torture, the desecration of graves or, in competition law, a company's failure to uphold its commitments (which may cause prejudice to a third party).

43 Regulation (EU) 2022/1925 of the European Parliament and of the Council of Sept. 14, 2022, on Contestable and Fair Markets in the Digital Sector, 2022 O.J. (L 265) 1.

44 Such as the Digital Services Act, Regulation (EU) 2022/2065 of the European Parliament and of the Council of Oct. 19, 2022, on a Single Market for Digital Services, 2022 O.J. (L 277) 1; and soon: the Data Act or the Artificial Intelligence Act.

45 "Almost," because as with all offenses, the respondent can escape a finding of infringement if they invoke one of the justifications mentioned *supra*, nos. 218–219.

46 Except in the (very rare) event that the law is so technical that it becomes obscure, and the respondent succeeds in demonstrating that they have been misled by the administration, for example in tax law.

criticism, insofar as their inevitable multiplication, their complexity, and the automaticity of their qualification sometimes lead to intent becoming a dangerous fiction, since the possibility of knowing them all exceeds the capacities of human understanding.

B. Regime specific to offenses of lack of foresight

238. **Defining offenses of lack of foresight.** When the law describes the will to engage in the conduct and the occurrence of an unintended but foreseeable result, the offense in question is an offense of lack of foresight.

The term used here is explained by the fact that what is sanctioned here is the agent's lack of foresight in adopting a course of action without regard to its likely harmful consequences.[47]

The scope of these offenses is the protection of life, physical integrity, and property.[48] They punish unintentional harm,[49] because even if the individual does not want the result, they must be held responsible for it, because they could and should have foreseen and avoided it, which has a pedagogical function – to indicate to everyone that it is advisable to be careful.

This category includes, for example: unintentional homicide, unintentional injury, unintentional fire, unintentional destruction, damage or deterioration of property belonging to others, or failure to assist a person in danger.

In civil liability law, it would include the civil faults corresponding to these infractions, which could be renamed "faults of lack of foresight," as well as quasi-delictual civil wrongs.[50]

Finally, there are no competition law offenses in this category.

239. **Characteristics specific to offenses of lack of foresight.** Offenses of lack of foresight are material offenses: they are characterized if, and only if, the conduct adopted in violation of the law produces a harmful result that is detachable from the conduct. It follows that the prosecuting authority must adduce two types of evidence. Firstly, that of the adoption of wrongful conduct, presumed to be voluntary.[51] Although offenses of lack of foresight do not require the will to achieve a result, they are nonetheless voluntary, since they require the will to engage in wrongful conduct. Indeed, if there is no will, there is an accident; if there is an accident,

---

47 *See* Jean Pradel's article, in which he groups the various faults of negligence, imprudence and clumsiness under the expression "lack of foresight," cited *supra*, no. 195.

48 What Boris Starck describes in his thesis as "Aquilian damages," *see supra*, no. 152.

49 And not "involuntary." It would make good legal sense to stop writing "involuntary manslaughter," for example, as the wrongful conduct leading to the death must be voluntary in order to be punished.

50 Some may be upheld even when criminal law refrains from intervening, the difference between the offense of lack of foresight and the fault of lack of foresight being, in this case, one of degree rather than of nature. *See supra*, no. 148.

51 For the reasons explained *supra*, no. 195.

there is no liability.[52] Secondly, they require proof of a *material causal link* between the conduct and the result. In contrast to *intellectual causation*, material causation refers to a causal relationship between material conduct and the material result; intellectual causation, on the other hand, presupposes a causal relationship between the will and the material result. For example, the prosecuting authority must establish that it was indeed the car driven by the defendant that, by striking the victim, injured or killed them; on the other hand, it does not have to prove specifically that the driver, by adopting reckless driving, actually foresaw that they were likely to cause damage. In fact, this condition is presumed, not by an analysis *in concreto*, but by recourse to a *due diligence standard.*

II. The common framework for offenses of commission and lack of foresight

240. **The very easy proof of the mental element in *lato sensu* intentional offenses.** It follows from the common characteristic of intentional offenses *lato sensu* – not to presuppose the will to achieve a result – that their lack of foresight element is reduced in comparison with intentional offenses *stricto sensu*. It is therefore easier to prove the mental element of these offenses, as intent is presumed from the wrongful conduct alone (**A**), and once this has been established, the presumption is irrebuttable (**B**).

A. An intention automatically presumed from the material element

241. **Complete overlap between the mental and material elements of the offense.** In the case of an offense of commission, the adoption of conduct prohibited by law alone constitutes the offense. In the case of an offense of lack of foresight, although a result is also necessary, the offense is characterized solely by the adoption of improvident conduct. In both cases, however, the conduct – the material element – is inseparable from the mental element. Indeed, the conduct is systematically presumed to have been adopted voluntarily, in the absence of proof to the contrary. It follows that the prosecuting authority, in proving the material element, automatically also proves the mental element of the offense.

Moreover, since it is impossible to attempt to commit an offense consisting solely in the adoption of a certain behavior, it follows that the attempt of intentional offenses *lato sensu* is not punishable – to commit or not to commit, that is the alternative.

---

52 Accident is understood here in its legal sense, rather than its everyday usage: a fortuitous event or accident occurs when damage arises without any human intervention.

B. A presumption of irrebuttable intent in fact

242. **The practical impossibility of proving the contrary once the material element has been established.** As a result of the overlap between the moral and material elements of an intentional offense *lato sensu*, once proof of the material element has been established, the accused cannot successfully rebut the presumption of the mental element. In practice, the presumption of intent is irrebuttable.

Paragraph 2 – The rules governing intentional offenses *stricto sensu*

243. **Defining intentional offenses *stricto sensu*.** The common feature of intentional offenses *stricto sensu*[53] is that they require, in addition to the will to perform a given act, the will to achieve a certain result. This characteristic gives rise to a regime that is partly common to this category (**II**), and which is overlaid with a regime specific to the two subcategories that make it up (**I**).

I. The distinction between offenses of means and of result

244. **The criterion for distinguishing between offenses of means and offenses of result.** Among intentional offenses *stricto sensu*, two subcategories are distinguished by a partly distinct regime: offenses of means (**A**) and offenses of result (**B**). Their distinction is based on a single criterion: the nature of the result. Either the result is unlawful in itself, i.e., it is, in all circumstances, prohibited *in principle*; or the result is unlawful only because of the *means* employed to achieve it.

A. The specific regime for offenses of means

245. **Defining offenses of means.** When the law describes the will to engage in conduct with a view to achieving a result that is unlawful solely due to the means used, the offense in question is an offense of means.[54]

---

53 We have chosen this term because of the etymology of the term "intent," from the Latin *intendere*, "to tend towards." In both its strict and everyday meaning, intent implies the adoption of behavior *aimed at* achieving a certain result (*see* the doctrine cited in this sense, *supra*, no. 189).

54 The notion of "offense of means" is not used here in its commonly accepted sense. In French criminal law, the notion of "*infraction de moyen*" is synonymous with formal offenses, and designates an offense that does not require the occurrence of any result in order to be characterized.

The choice to name this offense this way is explained by the desire to emphasize the stratagem, ruse, fraud, artifice, cunning, deception, surprise, maneuver – in short, the unlawful means used by the agent to achieve their objectives.

Historically,[55] these offenses stem from theft-related conduct and share similarities with it. They are most often[56] aimed at protecting property rights, either directly or indirectly.

These include theft, deception, fraud, forgery, corruption, influence peddling, abuse of power, fraudulent bankruptcy, swindling, misappropriation of corporate assets, breach of trust, insider trading and market abuse.

In civil liability law, this category covers civil faults that we might call "offenses of means." They consist of the civil faults associated with the offenses in this category, to which should be added, among others, abuse of rights, pre-contractual *dols* as well as unfair competition[57] and private actions for damages resulting from anticompetitive practices.

The notion of "offense of means" is very important for our demonstration, as we classify anticompetitive agreements and abuses of dominant position under it.[58]

246. **Characteristics specific to offenses of means.** The main feature of offenses of means is that the result they aim to achieve – the delivery of a good, a transfer of ownership, a gain, an advantage or a saving – is not, in principle, illegal. It can be, and most often is, the normal consequence of the conclusion of a contract, of a pertinent commercial strategy, of sharp business acumen. The result in question only becomes unlawful if it has been obtained by means that are themselves unlawful: misappropriation, concealment, disloyalty, fraud, maneuver, artifice. It follows that the result alone does not characterize the mental element of the offense: it is the unlawfulness of the means that lies at the heart of the proof. At most, the result enables the offense to be consummated, but the attempt to commit most offenses of means is also punishable. Whatever the hypothesis, the central element of offenses of means consists in the intention to use unlawful means to achieve one's ends, and not in the result potentially or actually achieved.

Moreover, proof of the causal link between the material element (the means) and the result (the economic advantage) is unnecessary: the unlawful means induce the unlawful result by themselves – they are one and

55 *See supra*, no. 75.

56 With the notable exception of rape, which falls into this category despite the fact that this offense punishes the physical and moral integrity of the victim.

57 *Compare with* our discussion of unfair competition and our criticism of its possible quasi-delictual basis, *supra*, nos. 149–151.

58 We will specifically demonstrate the inclusion of cartels and abuses of dominant positions in the category of offenses of means *infra*, nos. 271–275.

the same. Demonstrating the unlawful nature of the means presumes the existence of a potential or actual unlawful result, as well as the corresponding requisite intent.

At this stage, one might think that since proof of intent is, once again, deduced from conduct, intent is of no use in characterizing the offense, since it would, *in fine,* contribute nothing more than the material element. This reasoning is hasty. Indeed, whenever the illicit nature of the means in question is in doubt – either because it is new, or because it constitutes a borderline case,[59] or because the defendant claims that they have not used abnormal means to achieve their ends – it will be necessary to ask the question of intent to determine whether or not to include the case in question in the scope of the offense.[60] This also explains why offenses of means are the only ones that can be justified if the defendant successfully invokes a *legitimate ground.*[61]

To do this, judges most often use a *loyalty standard*: implicitly or explicitly, they seek to know what a "normal individual"[62] in the same situation would have known or done. If they consider that the individual's behavior deviates too far from the standard in question, they conclude that the most plausible explanation is that they intended to adopt unlawful means, and characterize the offense. The defendant may, however, attempt to avoid a finding of infringement by justifying their behavior. In this case, the defendant will have to demonstrate that there is another – albeit lawful – reason for their conduct, other than that put forward by the prosecuting authority. This type of reasoning can be applied explicitly or implicitly by the judge. It is very common in anticompetitive practices law.[63]

Finally, it should be noted that only offenses of means can be complex offenses – think of swindling and cartels.[64] In such cases, it is the overall strategy, the intention common to the various material acts, that enables them to be grouped together in a single offense report.

B. The regime specific to offense of result

247. **Defining offenses of result.** When the law describes the will to engage in conduct with a view to achieving a result that is unlawful in itself, the offense in question is an offense of result.

---

59 *See supra*, no. 198.

60 This defining dimension of intention will be studied specifically in competition law, *infra*, nos. 353 *et seq*.

61 We will study the theory of legitimate ground, which occupies an important place in the law of anticompetitive practices, *infra*, nos. 337–349.

62 Here we mean "normal" in the sense explained *supra*, no. 229.

63 *See infra*, no. 325.

64 On "complex" cartels, referred to in case law as "single and continuous infringements," *see infra*, no. 329.

This expression underlines the fact that these offenses are characterized by the unlawfulness in principle of the objective pursued, regardless of the nature of the means used.

They share the same domain as offenses of lack of foresight:[65] the protection of life, physical integrity, and material assets, with the difference that they punish intentional damage.[66]

Included in this category are intentional homicide, intentional assault and battery, intentional arson, intentional destruction, damage or deterioration of property belonging to others, and assault.

In civil liability law, the civil faults associated with these offenses could be renamed "faults of result." It would appear that no civil fault that is not at the same time an offense of result falls into this category; this is because such conduct is so serious that it always constitutes a criminal offense, and therefore leaves no room for an autonomous civil fault, unlike the other three types of offense.

248. **Characteristics specific to offenses of result.** The main feature common to all offenses of result is that the result in question is always unlawful in itself. Indeed, it is never lawful to intend or attempt to injure the life or body of another person, or to materially damage their property; the corollary being that it is never possible to justify the adoption of conduct that reasonably tends to produce such a result – except in the case of self-defense, a justification that is, moreover, admissible only in the case of an offense of result.[67]

The proof to be produced is thus that of the existence of an intellectual causal link between the conduct and the result. This means demonstrating that the conduct reasonably tends to produce the said result. Such proof may be self-evident: an individual shoots another person in the chest at point-blank range – it is then obvious that such conduct is intended to cause death, and no excuse will be admissible.[68] It may also require additional evidence and motivation, when the link between the conduct and the result does not in itself ensure that the individual intended to cause it. On a foggy day, a hunter shoots a person in the distance, half hidden by a tree, and causes their death. To determine whether *animus necandi* has occurred, the judge will have to ascertain whether the material elements[69]

---

65 *See supra*, no. 238.

66 Not "voluntary." In the same way as for offenses of lack of foresight (*see supra*, no. 238), changes should be made to the designation of offenses, to avoid confusion. For example, it would be advisable to write "intentional homicide" instead of "voluntary homicide" – the will refers to the conduct and not to the result, whereas murder is only characterized if proof of the will to achieve the result, i.e., intent *stricto sensu*, is provided.

67 *See infra*, no. 341

68 Except as justified *supra*, nos. 218–219.

69 As defined *supra*, no. 226.

are sufficient to establish an intellectual causal link. If, for example, it turns out that the defendant was a champion marksman, and that the victim was none other than his wife's lover, the accident theory may be called into question.

Offenses of result sometimes require recourse to a *standard of rationality*. The judge will have to ask whether or not the conduct adopted reasonably leads to the unlawful result. If this is the case, intent is presumed; if it is not, the case must either be dismissed, or further evidence must be adduced on the basis of the material facts of the case.

II. Common rules for offenses of means and results

249. **The easy proof of the mental element of intentional offenses *stricto sensu*.** Contrary to popular belief, proving intent is not difficult in the case of intentional offenses *stricto sensu*. It is slightly less straightforward than in the case of intentional offenses *lato sensu*, as it may sometimes require additional motivation on the part of the judge. However, as with all offenses, proof of intent is deduced objectively from the material evidence, with the difference that it is not systematically presumed, and leaves room for proof to the contrary – a guarantee of good justice and a more accurate assessment of the defendant's actual guilt (**B**). If we adopt a criminal policy point of view, and seek the greatest possible efficiency in the implementation of the norm, it should be noted that this disadvantage is nevertheless offset by the possibility, in the case of intentional offenses *stricto sensu*, of punishing the attempt, or even making it an autonomous offense (**A**).

A. The possibility of punishing the attempt and making it an autonomous offense

250. **Punishing attempts and making them autonomous offenses: two distinct yet complementary mechanisms.** Most intentional offenses *stricto sensu* are punished as attempts.

Sanctioning attempts, a penal policy choice already observed in Roman times,[70] is justified by the fact that the behaviors in question – because they not only manifest the will to engage in unlawful conduct, but also reflect malicious intent – must be apprehended by the law as soon as that intent is externalized through a beginning of execution. This applies to offenses such as murder and swindling: the absence of a result does not preclude a finding of an offense.

70 *See supra*, no. 30.

However, the legislator may also choose to make such an attempt an autonomous offense: the offense is then said to be "formal"[71] and the result, which is not a constitutive element of the offense, is always irrelevant at the stage of its characterization. The same applies to poisoning, which does not require the death of the victim, and to abuse of a dominant position, which does not require the production of an effect on the market.[72]

An attempt may also constitute an autonomous offense when it is collective. Indeed, if several people share the same intention and plan to carry it out together, their association becomes punishable even if they do not put their plan into effect. In this case, the materiality of the offense is reduced to a minimum, the agreement or simple concertation on a common intention being sufficient to create the offense. The offenses in question are criminal conspiracy and anticompetitive agreement – the latter being nothing other than an economic criminal conspiracy.[73]

251. **The merits of punishing attempts rather than adopting a special text.** The particularity of intentional offenses *stricto sensu* is that they consist of *general and abstract rules*, most often very old and describing in an indeterminate way the proscribed behaviors. Today's legislators, conditioned by the prevailing philosophy,[74] no doubt consider these rules insufficient, and prefer more precise ones. It is hardly surprising, then, that one of the most common contemporary legislative strategies is to identify one of the behaviors that is or could be covered by an existing offense and, by means of an additional law, to make it a new offense. The new offense is then derived from a main offense, drafted in a more precise (but rarely clearer) manner, and belonging to the category of offenses of commission[75] – for example, the possession of false weights and measures for the offense of deception, or some of the rules laid down by the Digital Markets Act to supplement offenses under the law of anticompetitive practices.[76]

The reasons put forward to justify the drafting of new texts are always the same: this procedure is deemed to make it possible to target the behavior in question more "effectively" by intervening more rapidly, before it causes the feared result; and to offer a pedagogical advantage: by creating a special offense, the legislator expressly indicates what is only implicit, as developed by case law, with regard to principal offenses. However, since

---

71 For a definition of formal offense, *see infra*, no. 272.

72 For a demonstration of this assertion: using textual arguments, *see infra*, no. 274; using a jurisprudential study, *see infra*, nos. 282–283.

73 *See infra*, no. 275. We will demonstrate that cartels and abuses of dominant positions are cut from the same cloth: the proscribed behavior is identical, the main difference between one and the other lying in the individual or collective nature of the infringement.

74 *See supra*, nos. 91–93.

75 *See supra*, no. 236.

76 For a critical look at the Digital Markets Act, *see infra*, nos. 448–452.

attempts to commit intentional offenses *stricto sensu* can be punished, the judge can, in certain cases, already reach the behavior that is the subject of a special text, without the latter needing to exist. Secondly, it would be possible to educate without resorting to legislation, which should always be used as a last resort, and sparingly. Indeed, using soft law tools would be just as "effective" in informing justiciables of the precise content of prohibitions, without adding yet another stone to an already titanic legislative edifice.

B. Intent not systematically presumed from the material element

252. **Intent: a guiding criterion in the search for and production of evidence.** Unlike intentional offenses *lato sensu*,[77] the mental element of intentional offenses *stricto sensu* does not systematically coincide with the material element. It must sometimes be proven by additional evidence or motivation.

This additional proof may involve taking into consideration all the material elements[78] to corroborate the proof of intent by means of a body of evidence. It may also involve giving reasons for linking the conduct in question to the legal definition – and therefore asking the judge to extend the legal definition.[79]

253. **Admissibility of motives as evidence.** Unlike intentional offenses *stricto sensu*, motives can be taken into account as evidence of intent. While they can never, on their own and to the requisite legal standard, be used to prove intent, they can nevertheless be accepted as an element of proof that is neither required nor sufficient, but which nevertheless makes it possible to corroborate a body of evidence – as is the case in anticompetitive practices law.[80]

254. **Admissibility of errors of fact as excuses.** As far as excuses specific to intentional offenses *stricto sensu* are concerned, it is worth mentioning the error or fact, an excuse that can enable a person to avoid being found guilty of an offense. The scope of this excuse is nevertheless limited by the theory of the impossible offense; while its effect is almost systematically neutralized, in business criminal law, by the set of demanding presumptions.[81]

*

* *

---

77 On this point, *see supra*, no. 240.

78 On the notion of material elements, *see infra*, no. 226.

79 On this subject, *see supra*, no. 198.

80 *See infra*, no. 326.

81 *See supra*, nos. 156–157.

255. **Conclusion of Chapter 2: some propositions.** Several propositions follow from our theory of intent. It would be appropriate to admit that:

1° All offenses, including *contraventions*, require intent *lato sensu* – i.e., knowledge and will.

2° The notion of imputability should be abandoned, since its scope is more or less identical to that of intent, and its appearance is subsequent to it.

3° Subdividing the mental element into multiple forms of *dol* or fault is unnecessary. Such categorizations are based on a psychological approach to the agent, obscure doctrinal debates and rarely reflect genuine differences in regime.

4° In Union law, great care should be taken in translating the terms used to define the mental element of offenses.

5° The nature of the mental element bears no relation to the seriousness of the offense, nor to the discipline to which it belongs: only the structure of the offense matters in determining the intent it requires.

6° The fact that it is possible, in the presence of a professional, to prove intent on the basis of negligence does not entail a denaturation of business offenses. To hold otherwise is to confuse the modes of proof of an offense with its nature.

*

* *

256. **Conclusion of Title II: overcoming theoretical oppositions to provide keys to reasoning.** Conceptualizing intent in positive law has meant studying the notion across several disciplines and in several legal systems. While intent appeared to be received in a transversal and universal way, the doctrinal controversies surrounding the notion made it difficult to discover its legal regime. It was therefore essential to propose a new theory, based on a pragmatic approach and in keeping with the legal traditions common to the Member States. This attempt at a general theory provides the keys to a better understanding of the conditions under which liability is incurred, whatever the country or discipline. In short, the aim is to restore a *ius commune* of intent, which could perhaps serve as a basis for reflection for other researchers, and which, in the context of this study, will make it possible to highlight its role in competition law.

*

* *

257. **Conclusion of Part I: laying the foundations for determining the role of intent in competition law.** The history of competition law teaches us that, from the outset, the discipline has embraced the notion of intent, and attributed to it a fundamental role. As the law evolved without abandoning its traditions and principles, the notion's disappearance from the eighteenth century onwards was only apparent: intent continued, like a deep current, to underpin the prohibition of competition offenses. At the same time, however, the concept of intent lost its original unity and clarity as a result of the compartmentalization of national laws and different areas of the law. It was therefore necessary, before proposing a theory of intent in competition law, to develop a general theory of intent. Now that the historical and conceptual foundations of the subject have been established, it is possible to theorize the role of intent in positive competition law.

*

* *

PART II

THE ROLE OF INTENT

258. **The omnipresence of effects, the neglect of intent.** In modern times, and particularly since the 2000s with the advent of the "more economic approach," otherwise known as the "effects-based approach," both the definition and the criteria for qualifying anticompetitive practices seem resolutely focused on their "effects" – so much so that we are now dealing with a consequentialist law,[1] The Commission's decision-making practice and communications, the case law of the European Court of Justice and the doctrine all use a vocabulary that suggests that behavior infringes the competition rules if it has a restrictive effect on competition, or produces a negative effect on consumers – their "well-being" being deemed to be the "ultimate objective" of the discipline.[2] Since these effects must be measured using economic analyses, the nature of the methods employed would require competition law to conform to economic doxa. Economic science would thus be of fundamental normative significance, both in the definition of rules and in their implementation.[3] The voice of economists would take precedence over that of jurists,[4] with concepts such as "unfairness" or "competition on the merits" being widely criticized as being too vague, if not "meaningless."[5] Having become extremely technical, the discipline is said to be "objective"[6] insofar as it has eliminated any risk of arbitrariness by replacing legal concepts with a range of economic tests.[7] Yet, if the effects carried more weight than the existence of a maneuver, the role of intent would be reduced to a bare minimum and, de facto, the concept seems to hold only a relative place in this field, and is often criticized by legal scholars.

259. **The central, if implicit, role of intent: the need to make visible what is hidden.** Intent plays a *fundamental*, albeit *implicit*, role *de lege lata*. It is a constitutive element of competition infringements and contributes to their definition, unlike effects, whose definitional scope is minimal, and

---

1 F. Hoffmann, *Probabilité et droit de la concurrence*, Revue française de droit administratif 531 (2011).

2 Case C-377/20, ENEL, ECLI:EU:C:2022:379, para. 46.

3 L. Vogel, Concurrence: 11 leçons 3 (2nd ed. 2020): "[T]he economy is growing in power to the point where a veritable 'economization' of competition law is taking place. …However, from an economic point of view, a company's behaviors matter far less than their effects on the market."

4 L. Idot, *La qualification de la restriction de concurrence: À propos des lignes directrices de la Commission concernant l'application de l'article 81, § 3 CE*, *in* La modernisation du droit de la concurrence 85 (G. Canivet & M.-A. Frison-Roche eds., 2006): "The definition of what constitutes a restriction of competition will mainly depend on the economists' judgment of the merits of the behavior."

5 OECD, Competition on the Merits, Policy Roundtables, DAF/COMP(2005)27 (Mar. 30, 2006), at 91: "Competition policies would be strengthened if courts and agencies refrained from using empty expressions such as 'competition on the merits'."

6 The judgment most frequently cited in support of this assertion is the following: Case 85/76, Hoffmann-La Roche, ECLI:EU:C:1979:36, para. 91: "The concept of abuse is an objective concept … ."

7 F. Castillo de la Torre, *Is the Effects-Based Approach Too Cumbersome? Taking Stock of Recent Practice and Case Law on Article 102 TFEU*, *in* The Transformation of EU Competition Law: Next Generation Issues 145, 146 (A. Claici, A. Komninos & D. Waelbroeck eds., 2023): "[T]he [effects-based] approach was often premised on a chronic epistemological doubt that could mainly be dispelled using a certain set of economic tools."

whose role at the enforcement stage is limited to that of an auxiliary clue, sometimes relevant, but not required to establish an agreement or an abuse of a dominant position (**Title I**). There is therefore a profound discrepancy between the rhetoric of competition law and the reality,[8] with numerous theories with no normative scope having been superimposed over time – which is not without giving rise to legitimate concerns about the predictability and readability of rules that nonetheless fall within the realm of criminal law. In addition, the aim of economic analysis, which is to make competition law more "efficient,"[9] has paradoxically led to an increase in the cost of its implementation and a reduction in the speed of proceedings, due to an unprecedented increase in the complexity of the discipline,[10] which is now struggling to adapt to contemporary issues, particularly in digital markets. Nevertheless, despite appearances, neither the spirit nor the accepted competition law principles have changed substantially since antiquity. *De lege ferenda,* by advocating a "return to the legal,"[11] it would suffice to abandon the effects-based approach in favor of the theory of intent, by making explicit the reasoning and principles accepted since the origin of the case law of the Court of Justice, in order to restore the coherence and intelligibility of competition law, and reweave the deep-rooted ties that connect it, both with its origins and with ordinary law (**Title II**).

8 D. Bosco, *Regard sur la postmodernisation de l'abus de position dominante, in* 1 Laurence Idot: Concurrence et Europe – Liber Amicorum 25, 27 (C. Lemaire & F. Martucci eds., 2022), according to the author, there is "reason to believe that the economic approach has largely remained in the doctrinal field."

9 Particularly under the influence of the Chicago School, *see* D. M. B. Gerard, *The Effects-Based Approach Under Article 101 TFEU and its Paradoxes: Modernisation at War with Itself?, in* Ten Years of Effects-Based Approach in EU Competition Law: State of Play and Perspectives 17, 18–31 (J. Bourgeois & D. Waelbroeck eds., 2012).

10 On this subject, *see* C. Prieto, *Source économique du droit de la concurrence: Quelle efficacité?,* Contrats concurrence consommation (June 2020), dossier 3.

11 Bosco, *Regard sur la postmodernisation de l'abus de position dominante, op. cit.* at 36: "[A] 'return to the legal' is what we should be inviting." *Adde,* J.-B. Blaise, *Une construction inachevée: le droit français des ententes et des positions dominantes, in* Aspects actuels du droit commercial français: Études dédiées à René Roblot 159, 161 (1984): "The development and greater practical effectiveness of competition law undoubtedly require a restoration of the role of the norm."

Title I
The implicit role of intent *de lege lata*

260. **The central role of intent in *characterizing* and *defining* competition infringements.** There are deceptive appearances that, far from giving a true picture of reality, conceal it: appearances can reveal what is real, or merely constitute an illusion.[1] The rejection of intent, and the emphasis on effect, is akin to a conjuring trick. Effects are placed center stage, when in fact they are merely incidental; intent is relegated to the wings, when in fact it plays the leading role. And yet, legal discourse has a duty to describe qualification criteria with precision, and to provide definitions that capture the essence of the institution under study. However, when appearance contradicts reality, when the explicit is opposed to the implicit, the clarity of the legal system is compromised.[2] It is therefore appropriate to make visible the reasoning that has been progressively masked, by demonstrating that, despite appearances, intent is a necessary constitutive element in the characterization of competition infringements (**Chapter 1**), and that it plays a part in their definition (**Chapter 2**). While definition generally precedes qualification,[3] it is nevertheless appropriate to approach the path in reverse. Indeed, since the process of qualification presupposes establishing the elements that contribute to its definition,[4] it is first

1 P. Conte, L'apparence en matière pénale 20–21 (1984) (Ph.D. dissertation), no. 16.

2 T. Ivainer, *Qu'est-ce qu'un texte clair?*, Histoire Épistémologie Langage no. 4, 23, 28 (1984): "[C]larity expresses a degree of adequacy between the explicit terms of a normative system and its implicit terms."

3 G. Cornu, *Les définitions dans la loi*, *in* Mélanges dédiés à Jean Vincent 77, 88 (1981): "Definition is reference, qualification is connection; definition is model, qualification is comparative act; definition is position, qualification is movement; definition is a general assertion in waiting, qualification is the interpreter's reasoning in a particular case; one is the stone, the other the throw."

4 Vocabulaire juridique 150 (G. Cornu ed., 11th ed. 2016).

necessary to demonstrate that effects are not a constitutive element of competition infringements, in order to convince the reader that they must be excluded from the definition of anticompetitive practices.

Chapter 1
THE ROLE OF INTENT IN ESTABLISHING OFFENSES

261. **The central role of intent in the characterization of competition infringements.** Unlike effects on competition or on the market, intent is a necessary constituent element in the characterization[1] of a cartel or abuse of a dominant position. The minimization of its role is the result of semantic confusion: when jurisprudence mentions the term "intent," it actually refers to motives, which are, in principle, irrelevant. A study of the structure of competition infringements teaches us that they are formal in nature: since they are attempts, established as autonomous offenses, their consummation does not require the occurrence of any result. It follows that defenses based on the absence of anticompetitive effects or the existence of pro-competitive effects, even when they are deemed admissible in theory, are systematically rejected by the judge in practice. The reasoning is, in fact, geared towards proving anticompetitive intent, as this is an element required to characterize infringements (**Section 1**). A study of the methods of proving such intent (**Section 2**) deconstructs the "effects-based approach," by demonstrating, using technical arguments,[2] that it does not

---

1 Apart from the study of the attenuating circumstance based on the existence of a reasonable doubt as to the scope of the law (*see infra*, nos. 464–467), we exclude from the scope of our study the role of intention at the stage of calculating the *quantum* of the sanction, insofar as, as we have already explained, the judge's assessment of intentions in measuring culpability is too subjective to be theorized (*see supra*, no. 232). On this subject, however, *see*: V. Dobre, L'intention fautive en droit européen de la concurrence 294–334 (2020) (Ph.D. dissertation, Université Paris X Nanterre).

2 The technical argument explains and justifies one rule through another, in order to discover, after having detached itself from all contingencies and risen above scattered cases, the substance of the institution studied, and the coherence with which it integrates into the whole of law, *see* F. Colonna d'Istria, *Qu'est-ce qu'un argument technique en droit? Étude aristotélicienne*, *in* PENSER LA TECHNIQUE JURIDIQUE 169, 178–80, 185–87 (A. Desrameaux & F. Colonna d'Istria ed., 2018). More generally, on legal argumentation, *see* F. Haid, *Les classes et sous-classes d'arguments utilisables pour répondre à une problématique juridique de droit privé: Contribution à l'élaboration des fondamentaux épistémologiques de la formation des juristes à l'argumentation*, 35 REVUE DE LA RECHERCHE JURIDIQUE: DROIT PROSPECTIF 1606 (2021).

shift the *focus* of proof,[3] but simply increases the *burden* of proof. It will therefore be shown that the distinction between "object" and "effect"[4] does not correspond to a difference in nature between practices that would be prohibited on the basis of their anticompetitive object, and others on the basis of their anticompetitive effects, but to a difference relating to the degree of thoroughness of the investigation and reasoning required to establish the infringement.

Section 1
Intent as the object of proof

262. **The need to characterize intent, the irrelevance of effects.** Delimiting the object of proof implies determining the structure of the offense.[5] As anticompetitive practices are offenses of means,[6] the required intent is the use of unlawful means to gain an undue advantage (**Paragraph 1**). Because of the formal nature of these offenses, they do not require, as a constitutive element, any result – the effects therefore not being an element required to characterize them (**Paragraph 2**).

Paragraph 1 – Intent, a necessary element for the characterization of the offense

263. **A necessary delimitation.** In order to circumscribe the object of proof for competition infringements, we need to make some important distinctions between intent and related concepts (**I**), before demonstrating that abuse of dominant position and agreements are formal offenses, falling into the category of offenses of means (**II**).

---

3 On the distinction between object of proof and method of proof, *see* A.-L. Sibony, *La preuve scientifique évitée. Inventaire de quelques techniques judiciaires*, *in* Preuve scientifique, preuve juridique 161, 162–67 (E. Truilhé-Marengo ed., 2011): the object of proof refers to what must be proven, while the method of proof designates how the proof must be presented.

4 This distinction is enshrined in article 101 TFEU, which prohibits agreements. Although article 102 TFEU does not expressly provide for this, doctrine generally draws a distinction between infringements "per se" and "by their effects" in relation to abuses of a dominant position, *see* in particular P. Ibáñez Colomo, *Beyond the More Economics-Based Approach: A Legal Perspective on Article 102 TFEU Case Law*, 53 Common Market Law Review 709, 712–13 (2016): "In the same way that Article 101(1) TFEU distinguished between agreements that restrict competition 'by object' and 'by effect', the Court takes the view that some practices are abusive by their very nature, while others are only caught by Article 102 TFEU where they have restrictive effects on competition."

5 According to the method proposed *supra*, nos. 222–223.

6 On the definition of "offense of means," *see supra*, no. 245.

I. Defining the required intent

264. **What intent is not: subjective intent and negligence.** In the law of anti-competitive practices, intent is often confused with motives – referred to as "subjective intention" – whereas the two concepts should be carefully distinguished (**A**). Furthermore, the distinction made by Regulation 1/2003 between intent and negligence appears superfluous (**B**), as the latter is, in practice, systematically confused with error of law.

A. The necessary distinction between subjective intent and intent

265. **The apparent rejection of intent: the origins of confusion.** Numerous decisions have affirmed that intent, whether anticompetitive or pro-competitive, is not a necessary element in the characterization of an offense.[7] It has been inferred that such intent would not be required at the stage of characterizing the infringement, but only at the stage of imposing the fine[8] – which would imply a rather paradoxical two-stage analysis: conduct that did not stem from any intent would suddenly presuppose a mental element, depending on the stage of reasoning.[9] While it is true that the Commission systematically, albeit very briefly, examines the mental element at the end of its decisions, it would be hasty to deduce that it plays no role beforehand.[10]

The first two judgments that are said to have rejected the relevance of intent at the qualification stage – *Miller* and *CRAM* – have since been frequently cited by the Court of Justice. A careful reading of these

---

7 *Ex multis*: Case T-128/98, Aéroports de Paris, ECLI:EU:T:2000:290, para. 173: "[T]he concept of abuse is an objective concept and implies no intention to cause harm"; Case C-551/03 P, General Motors, ECLI:EU:C:2006:229, para. 77: "[P]roof of that intention is not a necessary factor in determining whether an agreement has such a restriction as its object"; Case T-321/05, AstraZeneca, ECLI:EU:T:2010:266, para. 356: "[P]roof of the deliberate nature of the conduct and of the bad faith of the undertaking in a dominant position is not required for the purposes of identifying an abuse of a dominant position"; Case C-549/10 P, Tomra, ECLI:EU:C:2012:221, para. 22: "The existence of an intention to compete on the merits, even if it were established, could not prove the absence of abuse"; Case C-307/18, Generics (UK), ECLI:EU:C:2020:52, para. 162: "[F]or the purposes of application of Article 102 TFEU, there is no requirement to establish that the dominant undertaking has an anticompetitive intent"; Case C-377/20, ENEL, ECLI:EU:C:2022:379, answer to the third question referred: "A competition authority is not required to show intent on the part of the undertaking in question to exclude its competitors...." For two examples in French law, *see* Cons. conc. [French Competition Council] decision no. 94-D-21 of Mar. 22, 1994, concerning the practices of Office d'annonces, exclusive manager of advertising in France Télécom directories (Fr.), at 27; Cons. conc. decision no. 01-D-67 of Oct. 19, 2001, concerning practices identified in the award of public roadworks contracts in the Bouches-du-Rhône department (Fr.), at 9.

8 According to art. 23(2) of Council Regulation (EC) No. 1/2003 of Dec. 16, 2002, on the Implementation of the Rules on Competition Laid Down in Articles 81 and 82 of the Treaty, 2003 O.J. (L 1) 1, the Commission can only impose fines if the infringing conduct was done "intentionally or negligently."

9 *See* R. Bouscant, *La faute dans les infractions aux règles de concurrence en droit européen*, RTD Eur. 67 (2000).

10 This assertion is confirmed by the fact that the standard of proof required to characterize a competition infringement is identical, whether or not a fine is imposed. In this sense, F. Castillo de la Torre & E. Gippini Fournier, Evidence, Proof and Judicial Review in EU Competition Law 40 (2017), no. 2.031; *adde*, Case T-442/08, CISAC, ECLI:EU:T:2013:188, para. 94.

judgments reveals the true meaning and scope of this now traditional statement of principle.

In the first case, the company claimed that it had not been aware that it was infringing the competition rules. In response to this argument, the Court held that it could not have been unaware that its conduct was intended to restrict competition, and that it should therefore be held to have deliberately infringed article 85 EC (now art. 101 TFEU).[11] In the second, the applicant argued that the Commission could only find against it on the grounds of a agreement if it could demonstrate that the parties to the agreement had jointly set themselves an anti-competitive objective, which was clearly not the case here. The Court rejected this argument, holding that it was not necessary to prove that the companies had had a "common intent at the time when the agreement was concluded," but simply to examine "the *aims* pursued by the agreement as such."[12]

It is clear from these two judgments that the Court in no way rejected intent: in the first case, it presumed it, while in the second, it noted that intent had to be established objectively on the basis of the agreement, i.e., the conduct, and not the intentions of the parties – which is fully in line with the reasoning on intent.[13]

The *Hoffmann-La Roche* ruling is also frequently cited, and it is hastily deduced from its famous reasoning that "[t]he concept of abuse is an objective concept,"[14] that intent is not a constituent element. However, on the one hand, the formula does not directly rule it out,[15] since it could be argued that any infringement is "objective," in the sense that its interpretation or implementation does not depend on subjective considerations; on the other hand, the ruling follows on immediately from the *United Brands* case, in which the judges had expressly recognized the relevance of the objective pursued by the respondent company.[16]

266. **The reasons for the confusion: the lack of precision in the vocabulary used.** While jurisprudence insists that intent is not required to characterize an offense, it nonetheless occasionally admits its relevance as an element of

11 Case 19/77, Miller International, ECLI:EU:C:1978:19, paras. 17–18.

12 Case 29/83, Compagnie royale asturienne des mines, ECLI:EU:C:1984:130, paras. 25–26 (emphasis added).

13 Intent is always inferred objectively from conduct: if the latter establishes the offense to the requisite legal standard, intent is presumed and the defendant cannot validly maintain that they were unaware of committing the alleged offense, *see supra*, no. 226; *adde*, in the same sense, the Opinion of Advocate General A. Tizzano, Case C-551/03 P, General Motors, ECLI:EU:C:2005:639, para. 77.

14 Case 85/76, Hoffmann-La Roche, ECLI:EU:C:1979:36, para. 91.

15 In this sense, *see* T. Eilmansberger, *How to Distinguish Good From Bad Competition Under Article 82 EC: In Search of Clearer and More Coherent Standards for Anti-Competitive Abuses*, 42 Common Market Law Review 129, 146–47 (2005).

16 Case 27/76, United Brands, ECLI:EU:C:1978:22, para. 189.

proof.[17] By corroborating other clues, intent could thus play a part in qualifying anticompetitive behavior – it would be a criterion that is not mandatory, relevant but not sufficient.[18]

Criminal law reasoning might, at first glance, seem unrelated to the law of anticompetitive practices, because in criminal law, intent is an *object* of proof required to characterize an offense, not an *element* of proof of the offense itself. However, the Court of Justice seems to reduce it to a potential evidence, which can be mobilized in case of doubt as to whether the conduct in question constitutes an offense.[19]

However, a study of case law shows that judges never refer to intent when they confine it to a mere element of proof.

Although the Court of Justice has only once provided a semantic clarification of what it means by "intention,"[20] the General Court and the Advocates General have nonetheless specified that what is meant in this context is the "subjective intention"[21] – this expression being a literal translation of the English "*subjective intent*" which refers not to intent, but to motives.[22] The Court of Justice made this clear in 2012, in the *Tomra* case, where it expressly equated intent with motives.[23]

---

17 *Ex multis*: Case C-62/86, Akzo, ECLI:EU:C:1991:286, paras. 131–140; Case C-333/94 P, Tetra Pak ECLI:EU:C:1996:436, para. 42; Case C-551/03 P, General Motors, ECLI:EU:C:2006:229, para. 78: "[I]f the intention of the parties does not constitute a necessary factor in determining the restrictive character of an agreement, there is nothing to prohibit the Commission or the Community courts from taking that intention into account"; Case C-549/10 P, Tomra, ECLI:EU:C:2012:221, para. 20: "[T]he existence of any anti-competitive intent constitutes only one of a number of facts which may be taken into account in order to determine that a dominant position has been abused"; Case C-307/18, Generics (UK), ECLI:EU:C:2020:52, para. 162: proof of anticompetitive intent "constitutes a fact that may be taken into account in order to determine that a dominant position has been abused"; the latter formula is found in identical terms in Case C-377/20, ENEL, ECLI:EU:C:2022:379, answer to the third question referred for a preliminary ruling; Case C-680/20, Unilever Italia, ECLI:EU:C:2023:33, para. 45: "[P]roof of an anti-competitive intention" constitutes "an indication of the nature and objectives pursued by the strategy of that undertaking and, on that basis, may be taken into account. …However, demonstration of the existence of such an intention is neither necessary nor sufficient, in itself, to establish the existence of an abuse of a dominant position, since the concept of 'abuse', within the meaning of Article 102 TFEU, is based on an objective assessment of the conduct in question."

18 On the *Tomra* case, *see* A.-L. Sibony, *La CJUE précise la pertinence de l'intention pour la qualification d'abus de position dominante*, Concurrences no. 3-2012, art. no. 48339, 101, 102.

19 In this sense, *see* N. Zingales, *Antitrust Intent in an Age of Algorithmic Nudging*, 7 Journal of Antitrust Enforcement 386, 394–98 (2019).

20 This is not without its problems, since national competition authorities and courts need to be able to clearly interpret the concepts used by EU judges. In this instance, the same confusion between intent and motive is found in French domestic law, cf. Cour d'appel [CA] [regional court of appeal] Paris, pôle 5, ch. 7, Dec. 20, 2018, 18/07722 (Fr.), para. 42.

21 *Ex multis*: Case T-321/05, AstraZeneca, ECLI:EU:T:2010:266, para. 309; Case T-472/13, Lundbeck, ECLI:EU:T:2016:449, para. 519; Opinion of Advocate General P. Mengozzi, Case C-209/10, Post Danmark, ECLI:EU:C:2011:342, para. 51; Opinion of Advocate General A. Rantos, Case C-377/20, ENEL, ECLI:EU:C:2021:998, paras. 137–139. Finally, it should be noted that Advocate General A. Rantos, in his Opinion in Case C-42/21 P, Lietuvos geležinkeliai, ECLI:EU:C:2022:537, para. 137, draws a clear distinction between "intent" and "subjective intention" – the latter to be understood as referring to "subjective factors, such as the motives underlying the business strategy in question."

22 On the basis of the Sherman Act, we can observe the same confusion between intent and motive. *See*, for example, United States v. Trans-Missouri Freight Association, 166 U.S. 290, 342 (1897): "The necessary effect of the agreement is to restrain trade or commerce, *no matter what the intent was on the part of those who signed it*" (emphasis added). When a company signs an agreement that "necessarily" restricts competition, it will be presumed to have intended to restrict competition.

23 Case C-549/10 P, Tomra, ECLI:EU:C:2012:221, paras. 19–20.

267. **Dispelling the confusion: the distinction between intent and motive.** The problem becomes clearer: the apparent rejection, or ad hoc and partial admission, of intent is not actually aimed at intent, but at motives.[24]

Once this distinction has been made, it is clear that case law is in line with penal logic: motives are never taken into account to characterize the offense[25] – at most, they can be used, at the stage of qualifying the offense, as proof of intent,[26] and at the stage of determining the *quantum* of the penalty, as a mitigating or aggravating circumstance.[27]

While semantic rigor dictates that jurisprudence should clearly and systematically distinguish between intent and motive, this confusion should not lead us to believe that intent plays only a secondary role in the characterization of competition infringements.

Expressly required by Regulation 1/2003, it nevertheless shares the stage, in theory, with another concept: negligence. In practice, however, the distinction made by competition law between intent and negligence appears superfluous.

B. The superfluous distinction between negligence and intent

268. **The alternative between "intentional" or "negligent" infringement under Regulation 1/2003.** In order to impose a fine, the Commission must establish that the infringement was committed "intentionally or negligently"[28] – a stylistic formula found in all competition law regulations.[29] The presence of such an alternative implies the acceptance of two propositions that are, to say the least, rather peculiar: firstly, that the same infringement could be either intentional or negligent, depending on the circumstances; and secondly, that it would be possible to instigate a agreement or engage in abusive behavior out of carelessness.

One can easily understand what may have motivated such wording:[30] in the interests of efficiency, the legislator no doubt wanted to ensure that

---

24 For an in-depth study of the use of mobiles as evidence of competition infringements, *see* P. L. Parcu, *Considerazioni sulla rilevanza del movente nella valutazione delle violazioni antitrust*, *in* IX ANTITRUST BETWEEN EU LAW & NATIONAL LAW 341, 370–80 (E. A. Raffaelli ed., 2011). We will consider motives when we examine the means of proving intent, *infra*, no. 326.

25 *See supra*, no. 191.

26 *See supra*, no. 253.

27 *See supra*, no. 231.

28 Council Regulation (EC) No. 1/2003 of Dec. 16, 2002, on the Implementation of the Rules on Competition Laid Down in Articles 81 and 82 of the Treaty, 2003 O.J. (L 1) 1, art. 23(2); formerly art. 15(2) of Regulation (EC) No. 17/62.

29 Council Regulation (EC) No. 139/2004 of Jan. 20, 2004, on the Control of Concentrations between Undertakings, 2004 O.J. (L 24) 1, art. 14(1) and (2); Regulation (EU) 2022/1925 of the European Parliament and of the Council of Sept. 14, 2022, on Contestable and Fair Markets in the Digital Sector, 2022 O.J. (L 265) 1, art. 30(1) and (3).

30 It should be noted here that the alternative between intent and negligence was also retained by *Corpus Juris* with regard to the offense of fraud against the Community budget – this provision having been the subject of a great deal of criticism from Member States, reluctant to admit that fraud can be unintentional, *see supra*, no. 205.

companies could not invoke lack of intent to evade sanctions.[31] On the one hand, an offense by its very nature rests on a single mental element, which had to be determined on the basis of its structure – by means of an analysis of the incriminating text, potentially complemented by jurisprudential analysis[32] – which in this case will attest to the fact that competition infringements belong to the category of intentional offenses.[33] On the other hand, the accused can never invoke the fact that they did not intentionally break the law to avoid a finding of infringement – their intent being systematically presumed from the behavior adopted.[34] Moreover, in business criminal law, negligence on the part of a professional is always sufficient to prove intent.[35] Finally, the very broad definition of intent in anticompetitive practices law makes such an alternative purely superfluous. In the Court's view, an infringement is committed deliberately if "the undertaking concerned cannot be unaware of the anticompetitive nature of its conduct, whether or not it was aware that it was infringing the competition rules of the Treaty."[36] It follows that the company can never legitimately claim that it did not intend to infringe the rules,[37] as long as its conduct attests to the contrary and there is no reasonable doubt as to the scope of the law.[38]

---

31 It was, moreover, the desire for more effective implementation of the rules that led the authors of *Corpus Juris* to propose such an alternative, *see supra*, no. 205.

32 *See supra*, no. 222.

33 *See infra*, no. 272.

34 *See supra*, no. 196. The only admissible defense is that of demonstrating that the conduct in question is not itself unlawful, since "negligence" cannot compensate for insufficient reasoning. In the *General Motors* case, for example, the Commission relied exclusively on "deliberate intent," a ground contested by the applicant. In order for a fine to be imposed, the Commission requested that negligence be finally admitted by a substitution of grounds. The Court did not accept negligence, and annulled the Commission's decision after concluding that there had been no infringement, in the absence of abuse of a dominant position. *See also* Case 26/75, General Motors Continental, ECLI:EU:C:1975:150, paras. 24 and 20, resp.; *adde*, Opinion of Advocate General H. Mayras, Case 26/75, General Motors Continental, ECLI:EU:C:1975:141, at 1390–91.

35 *See supra*, nos. 156–157. However, the Court has sometimes used the alternative between "intentionally" or "negligently" to hold that the claimant's argument that the "clauses were inserted in the contracts through negligence cannot be taken into account"; it is irrelevant whether the insertion of the said clauses was intentional or not, since in the case of a professional, negligence is sufficient to prove intent, *see* Case C-89/85, Ahlström Osakeyhtiö, ECLI:EU:C:1993:120, para. 174.

36 The formula is a long-standing one and has been consistently applied in case law. *Ex multis*: Case 19/77, Miller International, ECLI:EU:C:1978:19, paras. 17–18; Case 100/80, SA Musique Diffusion française, ECLI:EU:C:1983:158, para. 112; Case 96/102, IAZ International Belgium, ECLI:EU:C:1983:310, para. 45; Case 322/81, Nederlandsche Banden Industrie Michelin, ECLI:EU:C:1983:313, para. 107; Case 246/86, Belasco, ECLI:EU:C:1989:301, para. 41; Case T-15/89, Chemie Linz, ECLI:EU:T:1992:37, para. 350; Case T-61/89, Dansk Pelsdyravlerforening, ECLI:EU:T:1992:79, para. 157; Case T-143/89, Ferriere Nord, ECLI:EU:T:1995:64, para. 41; Case T-141/89, Trefileurope, ECLI:EU:T:1995:62, para. 176; Case T-62/98, Volkswagen, ECLI:EU:T:2000:180, para. 334; Case T-99/04, AC-Treuhand, ECLI:EU:T:2008:256, para. 156; Case C-280/08 P, Deutsche Telekom, ECLI:EU:C:2010:603, para. 124; Case C-681/11, Schenker & Co., ECLI:EU:C:2013:404, para. 37; Case T-472/13, Lundbeck, ECLI:EU:T:2016:449, para. 762; Case C-614/16 P, Merck, ECLI:EU:C:2021:246, para. 122. In French law, *see* Cass. com., Jan. 29, 2020, no. 18-10.967 (Fr.), paras. 480–481.

37 *See, inter alia*, Comm. EC, Mar. 11, 2008, COMP/38.543, International removal services, paras. 563–565.

38 One may consult with interest the Opinion of Advocate General J. Mazák, Case C-280/08 P, Deutsche Telekom, ECLI:EU:C:2010:212, paras. 39–40. *Adde*, on the subject of error of law, *see infra*, nos. 461–467.

What is more, in practice, recourse to negligence is not only rare, but also unenlightening: in some of its decisions, the Commission is careful not to specify whether it is basing itself on intent or negligence, and retains both – leading to meaningless statements such as: "[The company] committed the infringement intentionally, or at least negligently."[39] And even in the infrequent case where it only mentions negligence, it still leaves open the possibility of intention, writing, for example, that companies are "at *least* negligent by being unaware,"[40] in which case the Court of Justice sometimes requalifies negligence in favor of intent.[41] Moreover, the latter does not even require the Commission to specify the nature of the mental element identified,[42] and the judges of the Union tend to dismiss simultaneously the arguments relating to the absence of intent and the lack of negligence.[43]

269. **Using the concept of "negligence" in practice: confusion with error of law.** While negligence is, in theory, one of the two conditions for the imposition of fines, in practice it is considered solely as a mitigating factor.[44] As such, it is systematically confused with another concept – error of law.[45] Apart from this unfortunate usage, the Commission never considers negligence as an autonomous mitigating circumstance.[46] The only role

---

39 *Ex multis*: Comm. EC, June 9, 1976, IV/29.020, Vitamines, para. 28; Comm. EC, Oct. 7, 1981, IV/29.491, Nederlandsche Banden-Industrie Michelin, para. 57; Comm. EC, Feb. 5, 1992, IV/31.572, Industrie de la construction aux Pays-Bas, para. 140; Comm. EC, July 4, 2007, COMP/38.784, Wanadoo España v. Telefónica, para. 764; Comm. EC, Jan. 30, 2008, COMP/B-1/39.326, E.ON Energie, art. 1; Eur. Comm., June 21, 2017, Case AT.40013, Lighting Systems, C(2017) 4100 final, para. 73; Eur. Comm., Oct. 2, 2017, C(2017) 6544 final, Baltic Rail, para. 371; Eur. Comm., Jan. 22, 2019, C(2019) 241 final, CaseAT.40049, MasterCard II, para. 94: "Mastercard committed an infringement intentionally, or at least negligently"; Eur. Comm., July 8, 2021, AT.40178, Car Emissions, para. 198.

40 EC Comm., Dec. 23, 1977, IV/29.146, BMW Belgium, para. 27 (emphasis added), concerning Belgian BMW dealers.

41 For the reason given above: the definition of intent is so broad that it encompasses negligence. For example, the Court reclassified the Commission's definition of negligence in favor of intent in Case 96/82, IAZ, ECLI:EU:C:1983:310, para. 45; *compare with* Comm. EC, Dec. 17, 1981, IV/29.995, NAVEWA-ANSEA, para. 75.

42 Case C-137/95 P, SPO, ECLI:EU:C:1996:130, para. 56: "[T]he case law of the Court of Justice ... draws no distinction between the two cases [deliberate intent and negligence] in which fines may be imposed, which are given as alternatives to each other."

43 *See* in particular Case T-259/02, Raiffeisen Zentralbank Österreich, ECLI:EU:T:2006:396, para. 211: "[T]he complaint that the infringement was not committed intentionally must be rejected. The applicants' arguments purporting to show the lack of any negligence are therefore irrelevant."

44 In para. 3 of the 1998 guidelines (Comm. EC, Guidelines on the Method of Setting Fines Imposed Pursuant to Article 15(2) of Regulation No. 17 and Article 65(5) of the ECSC Treaty, 1998, O.J. (C 9) 3) and in para. 29 of the 2006 guidelines (Comm. EC, Guidelines on the Method of Setting Fines Imposed Pursuant to Article 23(2)(a) of Regulation (EC) No. 1/2003, 2006 O.J. (C 210) 2), *see* L. Bernardeau & J.-P. Christienne, Les amendes en droit de la concurrence: Pratique décisionnelle et contrôle juridictionnel du droit de l'Union 163–64 (2013), nos. 337–339.

45 In this sense, J. Blockx, *Mens Rea* in EU Antitrust Law: When Intentions Matter 153 (2020), no. 502. For a comparative law approach to error of law, *see supra*, no. 196, and doctrinal references cited. For a study on the consideration of reasonable doubt as to the law in anticompetitive practices law, *see infra*, nos. 464–467.

46 In this respect, Bernardeau & Christienne, Les amendes en droit de la concurrence: Pratique décisionnelle et contrôle juridictionnel du droit de l'Union, *op. cit.* at 181, no. 380: "[U]nder the 2006 guidelines, an undertaking may benefit from an attenuating circumstance if it 'provides evidence that the infringement has been committed as a result of negligence'. To our knowledge, however, the Commission has never applied this attenuating circumstance as such." For an example, *see* Comm. EC, July 4, 2007, COMP/38.784, Wanadoo España v. Telefónica, paras. 727–729 and para. 765. In *Electrabel*, the applicant criticized the Commission

attributed to negligence in case law thus stems from a confusion between two notions that should be clearly distinguished. This supports the assertion that the notion of negligence is, in anticompetitive practices law as in the other European regulations in which it is mentioned,[47] a superfluous notion – the mental element required being, in practice, exclusively intent, which now needs to be determined.

II. Determining the required intent

270. **The nature of competition infringements.** Agreements and abuse of a dominant position fall into the category of offenses of means (**A**) and are, moreover, two infringements of a formal nature (**B**) – which implies that no result is required in order to characterize them.

A. Agreements and abuse of dominant position: offenses of means

271. **Competition infringements fall into the category of offenses of means.**[48] Abuse of a dominant position and agreement offenses both involve a result that is detachable from the conduct and deliberately sought: like other offenses in the same category,[49] this consists in obtaining an economic advantage. Such a result is not, of course, unlawful in itself: it is indisputable that a company can lawfully grow and make profits – the pursuit of gain being the very essence of commerce and the vector of competition. The offense is therefore only constituted if the company has used unlawful means[50] to achieve its ends: consequently, it is the unlawfulness of the means *alone* that renders the advantage obtained[51] undue and, therefore, unlawful itself.[52]

It remains to be seen whether the result – obtaining an undue advantage – must be achieved in order for the infringement to have been

---

for not taking into account its alleged negligence as a mitigating circumstance. The General Court rejected the argument, holding in particular that in view of "the applicant's experience," its argument that it had only been negligent was "unconvincing," *see* Case T-332/09, Electrabel, ECLI:EU:T:2012:672, paras. 229–258, esp. para. 252. *Adde*, for a comparative study of case law before and after the publication of the 2006 guidelines, *see* Blockx, *Mens Rea* in EU Antitrust Law: When Intentions Matter, *op. cit.* at 160–66, nos. 528–549.

47 *See supra*, no. 206.

48 The aim here is to apply our formula for classifying offenses according to the required mental element, in order to demonstrate that anticompetitive practices fall into the category of offenses of means.

49 Such as theft, deceit, fraud, forgery, corruption, influence peddling, abuse of power, fraudulent bankruptcy, misappropriation of corporate assets, breach of trust, swindling, insider trading, or market abuse, *see supra*, no. 245.

50 We use the term "illicit" here because of its neutrality: for a definition of anticompetitive intent, *see infra*, nos. 353 *et seq.*

51 Economic advantage resulting, for example, from higher prices, the exploitation of a business partner or consumers, or the elimination of one or more competitors.

52 In the same way, theft is only established in the case of *fraudulent* removal of another person's property.

committed. In other words, does the competition authority have to prove a concrete effect on the market to characterize an abuse or an agreement? We know that offenses of means have the particularity of being susceptible to attempt, which can be established as an autonomous infringement.[53] Such is the case with anticompetitive practices, which are formal offenses.

B. Agreements and abuse of dominant position: formal offenses

272. **Defining formal offenses: the example of poisoning.** A formal offense is one which sanctions a *means*, the consequence of which is an exclusively *legal* result[54] – i.e., the *risk* of the result feared by the legislator coming about.[55] Its scope is narrow: it can only concern intentional offenses *stricto sensu*,[56] as these are the only ones liable to be attempted.[57] However, the formal offense consists precisely in making the attempt an autonomous offense.[58] The most classic example is poisoning:[59] this is an attempt to commit murder that is punishable on its own, regardless of its outcome, provided that a substance "*of such a nature as to*" cause death is administered – the use of a means *likely* to produce the feared result being sufficient to characterize the offense. The particularity of formal offenses lies in the fact that their materiality is reduced to a minimum: in fact, *the mere intent to achieve the result*, expressed through a *means likely* to attain it, is sufficient to characterize the offense.

273. **Preliminary clarification: the "false friends" of legal vocabulary.** The use of expressions familiar to the law on anticompetitive practices,

---

53 *See supra*, no. 246.

54 This definition is that of P. Spitéri, *L'infraction formelle*, Revue de science criminelle et de droit pénal comparé 497, 513 (1966). There is much controversy about the definition of a formal offense. Some define it broadly: any offense that does not require a result as a constitutive element would be "formal," as opposed to so-called material offenses (Bouloc, Droit pénal général, *op. cit.* at 243, no. 248). This first definition covers all the offenses that we have grouped together in the category of "offenses of commission" (*see supra*, no. 236). Other authors define it more narrowly (*inter alia*, Spitéri, *L'infraction formelle*, *op. cit.*; M. Wagner, Les effets de l'infraction: Essai d'une théorie générale 83 (2011), nos. 182–183), and include in this category only a limited number of offenses, such as poisoning, criminal conspiracy, conspiracy or forgery. It is this second, more restrictive, view that we prefer: it allows us to give a precise designation to the legislative phenomenon of making the attempt to commit certain intentional offenses in the strict sense an autonomous offense.

55 In this sense, Wagner, Les effets de l'infraction: Essai d'une théorie générale, *op. cit.* at 319, no. 776.

56 *See supra*, no. 243.

57 *See supra*, no. 250.

58 In this sense, A. Prothais, *Plaidoyer pour le maintien de l'incrimination spéciale de l'empoisonnement*, Recueil Dalloz-Sirey 107, 109 (1982), chron. xviii. The conceptual proximity of the formal offense to the attempt led Jean Lebret to consider that the distinction between the two was unnecessary, *see* J. Lebret, i Cours de droit pénal général et de procédure pénale 63 (1964). It is true that, in practice, it amounts to the same thing to punish the attempt to commit an offense as to make it an autonomous offense: in both cases, the result is not required to characterize the offense, the mere commencement of execution, or even preliminary acts in the case of agreement or conspiracy, being sufficient for conviction. However, there is a major difference between the two concepts: whereas an attempt is only punishable if the legislator expressly provides for it, a formal offense punishes an attempt *by its very nature*, without the legislator specifying it – the formal nature of an offense being inferred from the structure of the incriminating text and its jurisprudential interpretation.

59 Art. 221-5 of the French Penal Code defines poisoning as "[m]aking an attack against the life of another person by the use or administration of substances *liable* to cause death" (emphasis added).

such as "of a nature to," "likely to," "having the effect of," "proper to", "capable of," since they designate an element subsequent to the conduct, seems *a priori* to require the occurrence of a result. However, this is not always the case:[60] in order to determine whether an infringement is of a formal nature, it is therefore necessary to ascertain to which referent the terms in question are attached.[61] However, these often refer solely to the legal result, i.e., the one *feared* by the legislator, but which does not have to be achieved for the offense to be characterized[62] – the fact that the conduct in question is *capable of* achieving the result in question being sufficient for conviction. The potentiality of effect described in this case is not, in fact, intended to designate the result and establish it as a constitutive element, but to specify the definition of the means employed, i.e., the material element and the corresponding intent.[63]

274. **Abuse of a dominant position as a formal offense.** Abuse of a dominant position is defined as "[a]ny abuse ... of a dominant position."[64] The incriminating text, which merely states that abuse is prohibited, is of no help in determining the constituent elements of the offense. It is therefore necessary to refer to the case law definition,[65] provided by the *Hoffmann-La Roche* judgment, which establishes that the offense is aimed at:

> the behaviour of an undertaking in a dominant position which is *such as to* influence the structure of a market ... and which, through *recourse* to *methods* different from those which condition normal competition ... has *the effect of* hindering the maintenance of the degree of competition still existing in the market or the growth of that competition.[66]

Three textual arguments allow us to deduce from this short extract that the result is not a constitutive element of the offense. Firstly, two expressions

---

60 Art. L. 121-1 of the French Consumer Code states: "A commercial practice is unfair where it is contrary to the requirements of professional diligence and alters or *is likely* to alter substantially the economic behaviour of the consumer" (emphasis added). The result – altering consumer behaviour – is not a constitutive element of the offense. Moreover, it would be extremely difficult to prove – which, according to Anne-Lise Sibony, implies opening up the law to the teachings of psychology, *see* A.-L. Sibony, *La porosité du droit: À propos des relations du droit avec d'autres disciplines*, 2 Revue de la Faculté de droit de l'Université de Liège 271, 274 (2010).

61 Wagner, Les effets de l'infraction: Essai d'une théorie générale, *op. cit.* at 136, no. 325.

62 *Id.* at 139, no. 335. For numerous examples illustrating "the uncertainty in which jurisprudence is plunged, through the fault of the legislator, who does not clearly distinguish" between the result as a constitutive element and the feared result, which need not be characterized, *see id.* at 150–58, nos. 371–388.

63 *Id.* at 136, no. 326.

64 Art. 102 TFEU (formerly art. 86 EC, then 82 EC).

65 Following the method we established *supra*, nos. 222–223.

66 Case 85/76, Hoffmann-La Roche, ECLI:EU:C:1979:36, para. 91 (emphasis added).

indicate the presence of a feared result: "such as to" and "the effect of." Secondly, the referent to which these two expressions refer is not the result on the market – for example, a price increase or foreclosure – but competition itself, i.e. a *process*. Thirdly, the effect on competition is only sanctioned if it results from "methods different from those which condition normal competition"; in other words, it is the use of such methods that causes the harm to competition.[67]

275. **The classification of agreements within the category of formal offenses.** An agreement is anticompetitive if it has its "object or effect the prevention, restriction or distortion of competition."[68] There are two arguments in favor of classifying agreements as formal offenses. First, as in the case of abuse of a dominant position, the effect refers not to an effect on the market, but to the effect on the "functioning of competition." Second, an agreement is, by its very nature, like a criminal conspiracy,[69] a formal offense. In fact, it is the formal offense par excellence: its materiality is even more limited than that of the other offenses in this category, since it does not even require a commencement of execution to be punishable – mere preparatory acts, i.e., coordination with an illicit aim,[70] being sufficient for the offense to be consummated.[71]

276. **The need for empirical verification.** Given the prominence of effects in competition law, both in the writings of legal scholars and in those of authorities and judges, the assertion that competition infringements do not require any actual result as a constitutive element may, at first glance, appear counterintuitive. This is why the theoretical arguments set out above need to be supplemented by empirical verification, aimed at confirming the idea that jurisprudence does not require an effect as a constitutive element.

---

67 This has an important logical consequence: harm to competition is not an autonomous concept that can be dissociated from the conduct itself – as we will demonstrate *infra*, nos. 368–377.

68 Art. 101 TFEU (formerly art. 85 EC, then 81 EC).

69 On the notion of criminal conspiracy in common law, *see* C. Angeloff, *Developments in the Law: Criminal Conspiracy*, 72 Harvard Law Review 920, 924 (1959): the author notes that the anticipatory repression of conspiracy (triggered at the moment of concertation, i.e., the exchange of criminal intent) is justified by the fact that when an intent shared by several people is directed towards an illicit goal, the risk of its realization is tenfold and potentially more harmful; *adde*, A. Harno, *Intent in Criminal Conspiracy*, 89 University of Pennsylvania Law Review 624, 646 (1941): in conspiracy, it is intent and intent alone that makes the crime; finally, more specifically in American antitrust law, *see* J. H. Bishop, *Criminal Intent as Applied to Conspiracy Under the Sherman Act*, xi Virginia Law Review 417 (Apr. 1925).

70 The Court of First Instance expressly recognized that the concertation was not a mere attempt, but an autonomous infringement, in Case T-53/03, BPB, ECLI:EU:T:2008:254, para. 87: "BPB's arguments that it was at most a *mere attempt at an agreement* must fail. The fact that BPB and Knauf expressed their common intention … constitutes an agreement."

71 A. Vitu & D. Beauvais, *Participation à une association de malfaiteurs*, JurisClasseur Pénal Code (Aug. 2022), fasc. 20, no. 22; *adde*, in the same vein, Spitéri, *L'infraction formelle*, *op. cit.* at 519.

Paragraph 2 – Effects, an element not required to characterize the offense

277. **The lack of normative impact of effects.** Case law generally considers the effects of the conduct at issue irrelevant at the stage of characterizing infringements (**I**), so it follows logically that when a company invokes an argument based on the absence of effect, it is systematically inoperative (**II**).

I. Jurisprudential indifference to effects

278. **Effects are not a constituent element of competition infringements.** The Union judges have consistently recognized, from the earliest rulings of the Court of Justice, that competition infringements are established regardless of the occurrence of any anticompetitive effect, whether in the case of agreements (**A**) or abuse of a dominant position (**B**).

A. The infringement, consummated independently of any effect in matters of agreements

279. **Consistent, unambiguous case law: market effects are not a constituent element of agreements.** Generally speaking, and as in American law,[72] in agreement cases, the competition authority does not have to prove anticompetitive effects,[73] as long as the anticompetitive object is established[74] – from which

---

72 On the basis of section 1 of the Sherman Act, proof of a market outcome is not required, once the conspiracy has been established, *see* for example United States v. Socony-Vacuum Oil Co., Inc., 310 U.S. 150, 255 (1940): "[A] conspiracy to fix prices violates § 1 of the Act though *no overt act is shown*, though it is *not established that the conspirators had the means available for accomplishment of their objective*" (emphasis added); *adde*, for a commentary, J. A. Rahl, *Symposium on 'Price Competition and Antitrust Policy': Price Competition and the Price Fixing Rule – Preface and Perspective*, 57 Northwestern University Law Review 137, 145–46 (1962).

73 In view of the alternative between object and effect provided for in article 101 TFEU, it would be appropriate to argue here that certain agreements, when characterized by means of an "effects-based" approach, logically require the demonstration of a result. We will demonstrate, *infra*, nos. 293 *et seq*., that the "effects-based" approach does not involve characterizing a result, but is intended to prove intent. At this point, let's simply recall the textual argument referred to *supra*, no. 275: the effect referred to in the incriminating text refers "to competition" and not to any effect on the market. Any interpretation to the contrary would, moreover, be inconsistent with the rulings cited below, in particular with the established solution whereby a agreement that has not been implemented, and which has therefore not been able to produce any effect, is nonetheless deemed to constitute an infringement; and with the jurisprudential solution whereby a company's demonstration of the absence of an effect cannot prevent a finding of infringement: if this were a constitutive element, the infringement could not be characterized without its presence.

74 The solution dates back to 1966, with the *Société Technique Minière* and *Consten and Grundig* rulings – the formulas they employ have since been used identically in almost all subsequent rulings, including the most recent ones: Case 56-65, Société Technique Minière, ECLI:EU:C:1966:38; Case 56-64, Consten and Grundig, ECLI:EU:C:1966:41, at 342: "[F]or the purpose of applying Article 85(1), there is no need to take account of the concrete effects of an agreement once it appears that it has as its object the prevention, restriction or distortion of competition," so that "the absence in the contested decision of any analysis of the effects of the agreement ... does not, of itself, constitute a defect in the decision." This is settled case law, *see, e.g.*, Case 123/83, Bureau national interprofessionnel du cognac, ECLI:EU:C:1985:33, para. 22; Case 45/85, Verband der Sachversicherer, ECLI:EU:C:1987:34, para. 39; Case C-277/87, Sandoz Prodotti Farmaceutici, ECLI:EU:C:1990:6, para. 15; Case T-141/89, Trefileurope, ECLI:EU:T:1995:62, para. 60; Case T-142/89, Usines Gustave Boël, ECLI:EU:T:1995:63, para. 89; Case T-144/89, Cockerill-Sambre, ECLI:EU:T:1995:65, para. 67;

it logically follows that the company cannot defeat a finding of infringement by demonstrating that the agreement produced no effect.[75] For example, in the *British Sugar* case, competitors argued that their participation in meetings had had no effect on prices.[76] The Commission admitted that it was unable to prove any anticompetitive effect,[77] but the Court of First Instance nevertheless held that once the anticompetitive purpose of the meetings had been established, it was not necessary to verify whether the agreement had produced any effects.[78]

280. **Characterization of the agreement despite the impossibility of any effect: the absence of implementation of the agreement does not prevent a finding of infringement.** Jurisprudence goes further and considers that not only is the absence of any concrete effect on the market, or even on competition,[79] not required, but that, in addition, proof of the agreement's implementation is not necessary.[80] The agreement is thus sanctioned not only independently

Case T-148/89, Trefilunion, ECLI:EU:T:1995:68, para. 79; Case C-219/95 P, Ferriere Nord, ECLI:EU:C:1997:375, para. 15: this case is particularly interesting. The applicants considered that the effects had to be demonstrated, since the Italian version of article 85 EC set out the expression "*per oggetto e per effetto*," a faulty translation having replaced "or" by "and," suggesting that object and effect were two cumulative conditions. The Court rejected the argument and upheld its case law, holding that the uniform interpretation of Community rules should prevail over the clerical error in the Italian version of the offending text. *Adde*, Case T-141/94, Thyssen Stahl, ECLI:EU:T:1999:48, para. 635; Case C-49/92 P, Anic Partecipazioni, ECLI:EU:C:1999:356, para. 99; Case C-199/92 P, Hüls, ECLI:EU:C:1999:358, para. 178; Case T-25/95, Cimenteries CBR, ECLI:EU:T:2000:77, para. 1531; Case T-62/98, Volkswagen, ECLI:EU:T:2000:180, para. 231; Case T-202/98, British Sugar, ECLI:EU:T:2001:185, para. 72; Case T-23/99, LR AF 1998, ECLI:EU:T:2002:75, para. 47; Case T-368/00, General Motors Nederland, ECLI:EU:T:2003:275, para. 104; Case T-50/00, Dalmine, ECLI:EU:T:2004:220, para. 147; Case T-49/02, Brasserie nationale, ECLI:EU:T:2005:298, para. 97; Case T-322/01, Roquette Frères, ECLI:EU:T:2006:267, para. 201; Case T-53/03, BPB, ECLI:EU:T:2008:254, para. 83; Case C-209/07, Beef Industry Development, ECLI:EU:C:2008:643, para. 15; Case T-450/05, Automobiles Peugeot, ECLI:EU:T:2009:262, paras. 44–45; Case C-501/06 P, GlaxoSmithKline, ECLI:EU:C:2009:610, para. 55; Case T-587/08, Fresh Del Monte, ECLI:EU:T:2013:129, para. 304; Case C-32/11, Allianz Hungária Biztosító, ECLI:EU:C:2013:160, paras. 33–34; Case C-382/12 P, MasterCard, ECLI:EU:C:2014:2201, para. 184; Case C-345/14, Maxima Latvja, ECLI:EU:C:2015:784, paras. 16–17; Case C-373/14 P, Toshiba Corporation, ECLI:EU:C:2016:26, paras. 24–25; Case T-691/14, Servier, ECLI:EU:T:2018:922, para. 219; Case C-228/18, Budapest Bank and Others, ECLI:EU:C:2020:265, paras. 33–34.

75 This is the logical consequence of the rulings cited in the previous footnote. Judges have sometimes expressly recognized this, for example in the following cases: Case T-23/99, LR AF 1998, ECLI:EU:T:2002:75, para. 47; Case T-44/00, Mannesmannröhren-Werke, ECLI:EU:T:2004:218, para. 130 and para. 196: "[U]undertakings which conclude an agreement whose purpose is to restrict competition cannot, in principle, avoid the application of Article 81(1) EC by claiming that their agreement should not have an appreciable effect on competition"; Case T-50/00, Dalmine, ECLI:EU:T:2004:220, para. 151: "[S]ince the Commission is not required to demonstrate an adverse effect on competition in order to establish an infringement of Article 81 EC ... Dalmine's arguments concerning the effects of the agreement are irrelevant in the present context"; Case T-49/02, Brasserie nationale, ECLI:EU:T:2005:298, para. 140.

76 Case T-202/98, British Sugar, ECLI:EU:T:2001:185, para. 69.

77 *Id.*, para. 70.

78 *Id.*, para. 73.

79 On the distinction between effect on the market and effect on competition, *see infra*, nos. 355 *et seq.*

80 This solution is also settled case law, *see, e.g.*, Case 86/82, Hasselblad, ECLI:EU:C:1984:65, paras. 45–46; Case C-277/87, Sandoz Prodotti Farmaceutici, ECLI:EU:C:1990:6, paras. 17–18; Case C-89/85, Ahlström Osakeyhtiö, ECLI:EU:C:1993:120, para. 175: "[T]he fact that a clause intended to restrict competition has not been implemented by the contracting parties is not sufficient to remove it from the prohibition in Article 85(1)"; Case T-66/92, Herlitz, ECLI:EU:T:1994:84, para. 40; Case T-77/92, Parker Pen, ECLI:EU:T:1994:85, para. 55; Case T-141/89, Trefileurope, ECLI:EU:T:1995:62, para. 60; Case T-148/89, Trefilunion, ECLI:EU:T:1995:68, para. 79; Case T-23/99, LR AF 1998, ECLI:EU:T:2002:75, para. 47; Case T-67/01, JCB Service, ECLI:EU:T:2004:3, para. 103; Case T-53/03, BPB, ECLI:EU:T:2008:254, para. 90; Case T-401/08, Säveltäjäin Tekijänoikeustoimisto Teosto, ECLI:EU:T:2013:170, paras. 65–66: "It follows that the Commission was not required to demonstrate that the applicant actually applied the membership clause."

of proof of its concrete effect, but also in the event that, not having been implemented, it was not even capable of producing any effect.[81]

In the important *Rhône-Poulenc* case,[82] the applicant argued that, in order to characterize a concerted practice, it was necessary to prove the existence of concerted action *and* behavior on the market.[83] Conversely, the Commission argued that accepting the applicant's argument would be tantamount to excluding from the scope of article 85 EC practices "having as their purpose, but not necessarily as their effect, the distortion of competition";[84] and that such a position would be inconsistent with the case law of the Court, which refers to the conduct actually adopted by undertakings, not as a constitutive element of the infringement, but as a "factual element from which the concerted action may be deduced."[85] According to the Court's case law, "no actual conduct on the market is required," but only "contact between economic operators."[86] The Court of First Instance followed the Commission's reasoning, holding that a concerted practice can be characterized as soon as there has been "direct or indirect contact" with an anticompetitive aim[87] – regardless, therefore, of the behavior actually adopted as a result of such a practice.

In another case, the applicants argued that such a position was tantamount to punishing "mere unlawful intentions which are not followed up by any implementing measures,"[88] which, in their view, was all the more unacceptable given that, in this case, the companies had submitted evidence – an audit and an econometric study—demonstrating that the concerted action had no effect.[89] Conversely, according to the Commission, the companies did not have to implement any concrete behavior as a result of their agreement, which was reprehensible "once *the intention* to substitute cooperation for the risks of

81 The absence of implementation could, at most, have an impact on the amount of the fine, *see, for example,* Comm. EC, May 16, 2000, IV/34.018, FETTCSA, recital 135. The Court of First Instance upheld the Commission's decision on this point, ruling that the failure to implement the agreement could, at most, have an impact on the calculation of the fine – which in this case was reduced by 20% due to this attenuating circumstance, Case T-213/00, CMA CGM, ECLI:EU:T:2003:76, paras. 293–294.

82 The Court's decision was eagerly awaited, as there was much debate in legal scholarship as to whether, in order to be characterized as a concerted practice, it had to be followed by parallel conduct (which does not constitute an effect in the sense of a result, but simply an implementation of the concerted action), or whether mere proof of the concerted action was sufficient. For a summary of the divergent views of legal scholars and Advocates General prior to the *Rhône-Poulenc* ruling, *see* Opinion of Advocate General B. Vesterdorf, Case T-1/89, Rhône-Poulenc, ECLI:EU:T:1991:38, at 933–39.

83 Case T-1/89, Rhône-Poulenc, ECLI:EU:T:1991:56, para. 115.

84 *Id.*

85 *Id.*

86 *Id.*

87 *Id.*, para. 121.

88 Case T-12/89, Solvay, ECLI:EU:T:1992:34, para. 238.

89 *Id.*, para. 239 and para. 266. The very idea of producing econometric studies to demonstrate that a agreement that was not implemented had no effect on the market is, moreover, rather surprising.

competition has materialized in cooperation."[90] The Court of First Instance agreed with the Commission's analysis, finding that the infringement was characterized by the fact that the company "pursue[d] the *aim* of eliminating in advance uncertainty about the future conduct of its competitors."[91]

Finally, the Court of First Instance ruled that a boycott could be imputed to an undertaking "without there being any need for it actually to participate, or even be capable of participating, in its implementation," since a contrary solution would lead to the result that "an undertaking which approved a boycott but did not have the opportunity to adopt a measure to implement it would avoid any form of liability for its participation in the agreement."[92]

281. **No need to examine the actual impact on the market when calculating the fine.** Even when determining the seriousness of the agreement in question in order to calculate the amount of the fine, the Commission[93] is not systematically required to examine the actual impact of the infringement on the market,[94] and in any case, this is never a decisive criterion,[95] as is

90 *Id.*, para. 247 (emphasis added). The solution is an old one, *see* Case 48/69, Imperial Chemical Industries, ECLI:EU:C:1972:70, 64: a concerted practice consists in "knowingly substitutes practical cooperation between [competing undertakings] for the risks of competition." In a commentary on this judgment, Robert Joliet defined a concerted practice as "a reciprocal communication of intent between competitors, prior to any action in the market, by which each of the undertakings concerned leads the others to expect that it will act in a particular way, thereby reducing market uncertainty," and logically considered that "there is a concerted practice as soon as there is concertation," regardless of its tangible consequences, *see* R. Joliet, *La notion de pratique concertée et l'arrêt ICI dans une perspective comparative*, CAHIERS DE DROIT EUROPÉEN 251, 285 (1974). For the author, to consider that effective implementation is required would be tantamount to confusing "the definition of the concerted practice and the problem of its proof," *id.* at 271; in the same vein, on the confusion, with regard to concerted practices, between their definition and their method of proof, *see* L. FOCSANEANU, LA JURISPRUDENCE DE LA COUR DE JUSTICE DES COMMUNAUTÉS EUROPÉENNES EN MATIÈRE DE CONCURRENCE: LES RÈGLES APPLICABLES AUX ENTREPRISES (ARTICLES 85 ET 86 DU TRAITÉ DE ROME) 110–11 (1977).

91 Case T-12/89, Solvay, ECLI:EU:T:1992:34, para. 256 (emphasis added). The Court of First Instance rejects the applicants' argument at paras. 270–273.

92 Case T-23/99, LR AF 1998, ECLI:EU:T:2002:75, para. 157.

93 Contrary to the Commission's decision-making practice, the Conseil de la Concurrence only imposed a "fine in principle" in the case of a agreement that had not produced any effects: Cons. conc., decision no. 08-D-03, Feb. 21, 2008. concerning practices implemented by the Fédération Nationale des Gîtes de France and the Bienvenue à la ferme network (Fr.), comm. D. Bosco, *Une 'amende de principe' pour une entente sans effets*, CONTRATS CONCURRENCE CONSOMMATION 39 (Apr. 2008), comm. 108. In the light of positive law, however, such a decision no longer seems conceivable: at the time of the dispute, the current version of article L. 464-2 of the French Commercial Code stipulated that financial penalties had to be proportionate "to the extent of the damage caused to the economy," but this criterion was abolished by article 2 of Ordinance no. 2021-649 of May 26, 2021, which transposed the ECN+ Directive into French law, and the latest guidelines issued by the French Competition Authority no longer mention it (*see* ALDC, Communiqué de l'Autorité de la concurrence relatif à la méthode de détermination des sanctions pécuniaires (July 30, 2021)).

94 Indeed, "the actual impact of the infringement on the market" *may* be one "criterion among others" for assessing the seriousness of the infringement, *see* Case C-511/06 P, Archer Daniels Midland, ECLI:EU:C:2009:433, para. 125; *adde*, Case C-534/07 P, William Prym, ECLI:EU:C:2009:505, para. 74. In this respect, it should be noted that contrary to the 1998 guidelines (Comm. EC, Guidelines on the Method of Setting Fines Imposed Pursuant to Article 15(2) of Regulation No. 17 and Article 65(5) of the ECSC Treaty, 1998, O.J. (C 9) 3, para. 1, A), which mentioned taking into account the "actual impact on the market, where this can be measured"; the 2006 guidelines no longer mention this (Guidelines on the Method of Setting Fines Imposed Pursuant to Article 23(2)(a) of Regulation (EC) No. 1/2003, 2006 O.J. (C 210) 2). For an analysis, *see* L. BERNARDEAU & J.-P. CHRISTIENNE, LES AMENDES EN DROIT DE LA CONCURRENCE: PRATIQUE DÉCISIONNELLE ET CONTRÔLE JURIDICTIONNEL DU DROIT DE L'UNION 48–53 (2013), nos. 151–159.

95 Case T-217/06, Arkema France, ECLI:EU:T:2011:251, para. 180: "In that regard, it has consistently been held that, by reason of their very nature, agreements merit the severest fines. Their possible concrete impact on the market, particularly the question to what extent the restriction of competition resulted in a market

borne out by consistent case law to the effect that "it would be disproportionate to require such proof, which would absorb considerable resources, given that it would necessitate making hypothetical calculations based on economic models whose accuracy it would be difficult for the Court to verify and whose infallibility is in no way proved."[96]

Conversely, what is decisive in examining the seriousness of the infringement is "whether the agreement members did all they could to give practical effect *to their intentions*."[97] What happened next, "at the level of the market prices actually obtained is liable to have been influenced by other factors outside the control of the members of the agreement"[98] – the latter could therefore not validly claim a reduction in the fine because of "external factors which counteracted their own efforts."[99]

Not only is *the effect on the market* not an important element of assessment, but the judges also unambiguously consider that "the effect which an agreement or concerted practice may have had *on normal competition* is not a conclusive criterion in assessing the proper amount of the fine"; the "factors relating to the intentional aspect" being "more significant than those relating to its effects."[100]

B. The infringement, consummated independently of any effect in matters of abuse of a dominant position

282. **Consistent, unambiguous case law: effect is not a constituent element of abuse of a dominant position.** As in the case of agreements, the position of the European Court of Justice is unambiguous. It is settled case law that the effect on competition or on the market is not a constituent element of abuse of a dominant position, since "the fact that the result sought is not achieved is not enough to avoid the practice being characterized as an abuse of a dominant position."[101] Accordingly, the Commission

---

price higher than would have obtained without the agreement, is not a decisive factor for determining the level of fines"; *adde*, to the same effect, Case T-127/04, KME Germany, ECLI:EU:T:2009:142, para. 64.

96 Case T-259/02, Raiffeisen Zentralbank Österreich, ECLI:EU:T:2006:396, para. 286. The same formula is used in the following judgments: Case T-73/04, Carbone-Lorraine, ECLI:EU:T:2008:416, para. 85; Case T-69/04, Schunk and Schunk, ECLI:EU:T:2008:415, para. 167; Case T-456/05, Gütermann and Zwicky, ECLI:EU:T:2010:168, para. 129; Case T-39/06, Transcatab, ECLI:EU:T:2011:562, para. 169.

97 Case T-456/05, Gütermann and Zwick, ECLI:EU:T:2010:168, para. 130.

98 *Id.*

99 *Id.*

100 Case T-141/94, Thyssen Stahl, ECLI:EU:T:1999:48, para. 636.

101 Case T-24/93, Compagnie maritime belge transports, ECLI:EU:T:1996:139, para. 149. The same formula is used in the following judgments, *ex multis*: Case T-228/97, Irish Sugar, ECLI:EU:T:1999:246, para. 191; Case T-340/03, France Télécom, ECLI:EU:T:2007:22, para. 196; Case C-280/08 P, Deutsche Telekom, ECLI:EU:C:2010:603, para. 254; Case C-52/09, TeliaSonera Sverige, ECLI:EU:C:2011:83, paras. 65–66; Case C-457/10 P, AstraZeneca, ECLI:EU:C:2012:770, para. 111; Case C-23/14, Post Danmark, ECLI:EU:C:2015:651, paras. 66–67. *See also*, more recently, Case C-538/18 P, České dráhy, ECLI:EU:C:2020:53, para. 70; Case T-612/17, Google and Alphabet, ECLI:EU:T:2021:763, paras. 440–442; Case C-680/20, Unilever Italia, ECLI:EU:C:2023:33, para. 41.

is not required to "demonstrate actual anticompetitive effects," but only to provide "proof of the creation of barriers to entry to the market and thus a demonstration of *potential* anticompetitive effects"[102] – a principle still upheld in the Court's most recent case law.[103]

Here, once again, we find the vocabulary specific to formal offenses:[104] to establish an abuse of a dominant position, "it is not necessary to show that the abuse under consideration had an actual impact on the relevant markets," "[i]t is sufficient in that respect to show that the abusive conduct of the undertaking in a dominant position *tends* to restrict competition or, in other words, that the conduct *is capable* of having that effect."[105]

283. **Consummation of the abuse of a dominant position at the commencement stage: the *AstraZeneca* case.** If no result is required to characterize an abuse of a dominant position, it remains to be seen at what point the offence can be established. Do mere preparatory acts suffice for the infringement to be consummated, or is a commencement of execution a minimum requirement?

The arguments put forward by the applicants in *AstraZeneca* (AZ) enabled the Court of First Instance to give a clear and unequivocal answer to these questions.[106]

AZ was accused of abusing its dominant position by making misleading statements before the patent offices of certain Member States, with the aim of obtaining supplementary protection certificates (SPCs) for a drug (Losec), granting AZ an extension of patent protection to which it was not actually entitled, or only entitled for a limited period. AZ's aim was to keep generic manufacturers out of the market.

In this case, the companies argued that "an intention to restrict competition" was not sufficient "to prove the requisite effect on competition, since the conduct intended to have that effect[107] *must have been engaged*

---

102 Opinion of Advocate General J. Mazák, Case C-280/08 P, Deutsche Telekom, ECLI:EU:C:2010:212, para. 64; *adde*, to the same effect, Opinion of Advocate General J. Mazák, Case C-52/09, TeliaSonera Sverige, ECLI:EU:C:2010:483, para. 39.

103 *See*, in particular, Case C-377/20, ENEL, ECLI:EU:C:2022:379, answer to second question. For a critique of the consideration of "potential effects" in abuse of dominance cases, which could lead the authorities to base their decisions solely on the size of the company being sued, thus leading to a populist drift, *see* T. Schrepel, *Les position dominantes bientôt sanctionnées?*, JCP E NO. 46, 36 (Nov. 15, 2018).

104 *See supra*, no. 272, for a reasoning by analogy with poisoning.

105 *Ex multis* (emphasis added): Case T-203/01, Manufacture française des pneumatiques Michelin, ECLI:EU:T:2003:250, para. 239; Case T-219/99, British Airways, ECLI:EU:T:2003:343, para. 293; Case T-155/06, Tomra Systems, ECLI:EU:T:2010:370, para. 289; Case C-549/10 P, Tomra, ECLI:EU:C:2012:221, paras. 68 and 79. In this regard, the Court of First Instance has stated that "[t]he "effect" referred to in the case-law … does not necessarily relate to the actual effect of the abusive conduct complained of." *See* Case T-203/01, Manufacture française des pneumatiques Michelin, ECLI:EU:T:2003:250, para. 239.

106 Note that the appellants' appeal was dismissed in its entirety by the Court of Justice, *see* Case C-457/10 P, AstraZeneca, ECLI:EU:C:2012:770.

107 Expressions such as intended to have that effect are, from a semantic point of view, pleonasms. An objective, a goal, a strategy, an intention, always aims at an effect, a consequence, a result. To specify this is no more effective than saying "to climb to the top": it would be preferable to write "a behavior whose objective is." On the pleonastic nature of certain expressions used in competition law, *see infra*, no. 485.

in."[108] In other words, the mere intention to restrict competition would not suffice: the company would also have to have *engaged* in conduct capable of achieving this objective for the infringement to be characterized. The companies thus felt that the Commission had erred in law in "alleging that AZ's dealings with its patent attorneys revealed *fraudulent conduct* from 7 June 1993, when AZ communicated instructions to them," i.e., before "before the SPC was applied for," since "neither AZ nor its attorneys had yet contacted the patent offices and since AZ had not yet obtained a right or enforced a right, its conduct could not have had any effect on competition."[109] To characterize the infringement before the *planned strategy* had been implemented or had prospered amounted, according to the applicants, to "the undertaking's liability being incurred" at a stage when its behavior was not yet capable of having any "direct effect on competition."[110] Such reasoning would have wrongly led the Commission to sanction mere "*preparatory acts* which were not abusive in themselves."[111]

The Commission, for its part, argued that article 82 EC (now 102 TFEU) covers "behaviour which is *aimed at* or *capable of* achieving anticompetitive effects, *regardless of its success*,"[112] since the consequences of abusive conduct depend on *factors outside the* company's *control* – in this case, the public authorities' decision to grant or refuse to grant SPCs. It follows that the infringement would have been established even if the public authorities had not issued the SPCs following AZ's misleading statements, precisely because "[t]he illegal nature of behaviour cannot depend on the contingencies of the behaviour of a third party."[113] The Commission went on to argue that, according to established case law, "behaviour whose purpose or object is to restrict competition" is unlawful "regardless of whether the aim is achieved," and further contested "that the contested decision is based on *mere intention* on the part of the applicants, since that decision identified *behaviour which was capable of* excluding competitors."[114]

The General Court partly adopted the Commission's arguments. Initially, it endorsed the Commission's reasoning, holding that where conduct is "*of such a nature* as to restrict competition, the question whether it is abusive in nature cannot depend on the contingencies of the reactions of third parties,"[115] from

108 Case T-321/05, AstraZeneca, ECLI:EU:T:2010:266, para. 309 (emphasis added).

109 *Id.*, para. 319 (emphasis added).

110 *Id.*

111 *Id.*, para. 322 (emphasis added).

112 *Id.*, para. 331 (emphasis added).

113 *Id.*, paras. 331–332.

114 *Id.*, para. 334 (emphasis added).

115 *Id.*, para. 360 (emphasis added).

which it follows that the infringement would have been constituted solely on the basis of AZ's misleading statements, even if the public authorities had not granted it any exclusive rights.[116] However, contrary to the Commission's view, the General Court rightly held that the infringement began, not when AZ gave its instructions to the patent agents, but when the company communicated its SPC applications to the national patent offices.[117]

The General Court's reasoning is fully in line with penal logic. Except in the case of agreement, conspiracy, or criminal conspiracy,[118] a formal offense cannot be characterized on the basis of mere preparatory acts: as in the case of an attempt,[119] the *commencement of execution* is required for conviction.[120] While the notion of commencement of execution is the subject of abundant and varied doctrine in criminal law[121] and of case law described as "elusive,"[122] it nevertheless receives a stable praetorian definition: a commencement of execution is characterized by "acts which tend directly towards the crime or misdemeanor *with the intent* of committing it."[123] These are distinguished from preparatory acts or mere "projects"[124] in that the latter "have as their object to facilitate the accomplishment of criminal thought"[125] – as in the case of instructions given to patent

116 *Id.*, para. 362.

117 *Id.*, para. 370. This point has been validated by the Court of Justice, *see* Case C-457/10 P, AstraZeneca ECLI:EU:C:2012:770, para. 64.

118 Agreements, like conspiracy or criminal conspiracy, may be characterized on the basis of mere evidence of concertation, even if this has not subsequently led to any commencement of execution, *see supra*, no. 275 on the theoretical level, *supra*, nos.279 *et seq*. for jurisprudential illustrations.

119 On the distinction between a formal offense and an attempt, *see supra*, no. 272, *adde*, no. 272. For a study of attempt in Roman criminal law, *see* J.-C. Genin, La répression des actes de tentative en droit criminel romain: Contribution à l'étude de la subjectivité répressive à Rome 16 (1968) (Ph.D. dissertation, Université de Lyon); and more recently, B. Auroy, La consommation de l'infraction (2021) (Ph.D. dissertation, Université Paris-Saclay).

120 *See* M. Segonds, *Tentative*, JurisClasseur Pénal Code (Nov. 2022), no. 1: "According to the classic analysis taken up by all contemporary doctrine, the criminal process, otherwise known as *iter criminis*, runs from the idea to the criminal resolution, from the criminal resolution to the preparation, from the preparation to the commencement of execution, ending with the consummation of the offense. As a matter of principle, in the name of respect for freedom of thought, but also because of its revocable nature and an insurmountable evidentiary hurdle, criminal resolution and, *a fortiori*, criminal thought are guaranteed impunity. The principle of impunity also prevails in the presence of preparatory acts, subject to the existence of autonomous offenses such as, in particular, the offenses of conspiracy and participation in a criminal conspiracy… . On the other hand, the commencement of execution constitutes the stage from which the perpetrator may attract repression."

121 *Ex multis:* M. Segonds, *Tentative*, *op. cit.* nos. 7–32; D. Rebut, *Tentative*, Répertoire de droit pénal et de procédure pénale (May 2009), nos. 8–32. On the whole, the doctrine appears to be divided between a *subjective* definition of commencement of execution, emphasizing the agent's *intent*, and an *objective* definition, prioritizing the existence of the agent's *act*. Let's make a simple observation: these debates seem to us to unnecessarily complicate a simple problem. Indeed, we have shown that the dissociation between the agent's behavior and intent is largely artificial, insofar as the two are inseparable: there is no reprehensible intent without behavior, and no reprehensible behavior without intent – behavior proves intent at the same time as it manifests it (*see supra*, no. 226).

122 Rebut, *Tentative*, *op. cit.*, no. 17.

123 *Id.*, no. 19 (emphasis added), and numerous case law references cited.

124 The Court of Justice recently ruled, quite rightly, that "a practice cannot be classified as abusive if it has remained at the planning stage," *see* Case C-680/20, Unilever Italia, ECLI:EU:C:2023:33, para. 43.

125 F. Hélie, A. Chauveau & E. Villey, i Théorie du Code pénal 386 (1887), no. 246.

agents, whereas the commencement of execution attests that the agent's intent is certain, and presumes that they would have completed their criminal design "if some accidental cause had not disturbed it,"[126] – such as a refusal by national patent offices to grant SPCs.

II. The inoperability of arguments based on effects

284. **A paradox: theoretical admissibility, but lack of acceptance in practice of arguments based on effects.** Generally speaking, any argument designed to prevent a finding of infringement by demonstrating the absence of any real effect on the market is unlikely to stand in the way of the characterization of infringements.[127] Paradoxically, the law on anticompetitive practices is filled with effect-based theories, which are supposed to enable companies to justify anticompetitive behavior if they can prove that the positive effects of their behavior outweigh its negative effects – a strange line of reasoning in the eyes of the criminal lawyer. Quite legitimately, companies leverage this to try and avoid a finding of infringement. This phenomenon leads to extensive litigation, lengthening the time taken to reach decisions, slowing down trials and, last but not least, increasing the cost of enforcement for the authorities and the cost of defense for the accused parties, both of whom have to produce economic expert reports in an attempt to prove that a given behavior has produced beneficial or harmful effects on the market, or even on consumers.

However, because of the formal nature of competition infringements, authorities and judges alike systematically reject such arguments. Such a situation is singular: while doctrine and jurisprudence recognize *in theory* the invocability of these defenses, *in practice* they are invariably ineffective, both in the case of abuse of a dominant position (**B**) and in the presence of a agreement (**A**).

A. Systematically ineffective arguments in matters of agreements

285. **The disappearance of individual exemption decisions since 2003 and their cause: the exclusive but ineffective consideration of market effects.** As early as the first regulation implementing the competition rules,[128] provision was made for the Commission to exempt restrictive agreements, i.e., not to prohibit or punish certain agreements that were deemed to be anticompetitive. A system of prior notification was introduced at the time, and the

126 *Id.* at 387, no. 247.

127 *See supra*, nos. 279–281 in agreement cases (mere concertation without effect is sufficient to characterize the infringement); nos. 282–283 in abuse of a dominant position cases (mere commencement of execution without effect is sufficient to characterize the infringement).

128 Regulation (EC) No. 17/62.

Commission, which had to rule on the legality of thousands of applications, was soon overwhelmed. Since the entry into force of Regulation 1/2003, companies are no longer required to notify their agreements: block exemption regulations continue to establish a presumption of legality,[129] and defendants may also, in the course of litigation, seek an individual exemption on the basis of article 101(3), after their conduct has been found to be unlawful on the basis of article 101(1).[130]

In the past, the Commission granted numerous exemptions, and an examination of its decision-making practice reveals that these were motivated by the existence of a legitimate ground.[131] However, in parallel with the abandonment of the notification system, another significant change was made by the Commission: since 2004, it has ceased to assess arguments based on the existence of an "objective justification" – and now only accepts defenses linked to "efficiency gains" benefiting consumers.[132] This notion is difficult to grasp, not only for jurists, but also for economists, as its assessment depends on "the welfare standard" applied[133] – itself a subject of controversy among specialists.[134] Such complexity is all the more problematic as national competition authorities can now also adopt exemption decisions: the indeterminacy and complexity of the economic concepts used are therefore likely to lead to fragmented and disparate implementation of the rules at the national level[135] – compromising the objective of harmonizing European Union law and the principle of legal certainty.[136]

What is more, consulting the Commission's guidelines on how to grant an exemption presents the reader with a paradox. While the effects of

---

129 We will consider block exemption regulations from this angle, in the context of the theory of legitimate grounds, *infra*, no. 345.

130 EC Comm., Guidelines on the Application of Article 81(3) of the Treaty, 2004 O.J. (C 101) 97, para. 11.

131 As to whether individual exemption decisions granted prior to 2003 fall under the theory of legitimate grounds, *see infra*, no. 346.

132 A. C. Witt, The More Economic Approach to EU Antitrust Law 167 (2019); *adde*, in the same sense, L. Idot, *L'intégration des considérations d'intérêt public dans le droit des ententes: Approche juridique*, Concurrences no. 2-2021, art. no. 99790, 12, 19, no. 32: "[U]nder the new so-called 'economic' approach, the interpretation of Article 101(3) TFEU has been clearly refocused on the so-called 'efficiencies' theory."

133 OECD, The Role of Efficiency Claims in Antitrust Proceedings, DAF/COMP(2012)23 (May 2, 2013), at 11: "[T]he fact that efficiencies play an ever more important role in competition law by no means implies that their assessment is easy and unproblematic… . [C]ompetition authorities may find it difficult to duly take into account efficiency claims put forward by the firms, or worse they may apply the concept in an imprecise and inconsistent manner… . For example, whether to accept certain types of efficiency gains (e.g. fixed-cost savings) or not depends on the welfare standard a specific competition authority applies."

134 On this subject, *see* A.-L. Sibony, Le juge et le raisonnement économique en droit de la concurrence 118–23 (2008), nos. 157–162; *adde*, L. Lovdahl Gormsen, A Principled Approach to Abuse of Dominance in European Competition Law 20–58 (2010).

135 For a study of the extent to which national competition authorities differ in their interpretation of article 101(3), *see* O. Brook, *Struggling with Article 101(3) TFEU: Diverging Approaches of the Commission, EU Courts, and Five Competition Authorities*, 56 Common Market Law Review 121 (2019).

136 In this sense, *see* C. Prieto, *La sécurité juridique dans le droit de la concurrence*, *in* Sécurité juridique et droit économique 299, 311 (L. Boy, J.-B. Racine & F. Siiriainen eds., 2010).

conduct on the market are not a constituent element of competition infringements,[137] an agreement could be exempted, i.e., justified, if its "*pro-competitive effects* outweigh *the anti-competitive effects*"[138] – which is illogical, to say the least, given that the said effects are not required to characterize the infringement. Moreover, the effects in question here are not effects on the competitive process itself, but on the market:[139] according to the Commission, they consist of "positive economic effects" such as lower prices, economies of scale, improved product or service quality, or technological progress.[140] Three additional conditions are laid down: the undertakings must reserve "a fair share" of the profits resulting from the agreement for "consumers"; the restrictions of competition must be indispensable; and the agreement "must not afford the parties the possibility of eliminating competition in respect of a substantial part of the products in question."[141] The analysis is uncertain, insofar as proof of these three conditions is very difficult, if not impossible, to provide;[142] and complex, since it mobilizes economic analyses, which, by their very nature, are based on conjectures and postulates that are open to debate.[143]

Are these analyses, at the very least, useful? In other words, are they likely to succeed in court? Let's put it bluntly: the answer is no. Since 2004, the Commission has never once granted an individual exemption.[144]

286. **The theory of "cumulative effect": a theory that is not one.** A second theory, based on effects, would make it possible to punish a vertical agreement[145] that only partially contributes to restricting competition, by taking into consideration the restrictive effect of the offending agreement, added to that of all the parallel agreements *entered into by third parties*. Such reasoning could lead, for example, to a finding that a contract concluded

---

137 *See supra*, nos. 279–281.

138 EC Comm., Guidelines on the Application of Article 81(3) of the Treaty, *op. cit.*, para. 11; *adde*, in the same vein, *id.*, paras. 40–41.

139 On the need to distinguish between effects on the competitive process and effects on the market, *see infra*, nos. 355 *et seq.*

140 For a complete typology of "efficiencies" that may be accepted on the basis of article 101(3), *see* EC Comm., Guidelines on the Application of Article 81(3) of the Treaty, *op. cit.*, paras. 59–72.

141 *Id.*, para. 34 b), c) and d). For an in-depth examination of these conditions, *see* in particular D. Bosco & C. Prieto, Droit européen de la concurrence 522–49 (2013).

142 Moreover, the Commission recognizes that even if an agreement were likely to produce efficiencies, the condition that its conclusion be indispensable for that purpose is unlikely to be met, *see* Eur. Comm., Observations of the Commission under Article 15, Paragraph 3, of Regulation No. 1/2003 (2020), no. 7764P, paras. 19–36.

143 *See supra*, nos.114 *et seq.*

144 In this sense, *see* Brook, *Struggling with Article 101(3) TFEU: Diverging Approaches of the Commission, EU Courts, and Five Competition Authorities*, *op. cit.* at 131; in the same vein, A. C. Witt, The More Economic Approach to EU Antitrust Law 167 (2019). For an example of a case in which the efficiencies argument was rejected, *see* Case T-168/01, GlaxoSmithKline, ECLI:EU:T:2006:265, paras. 214–308.

145 A vertical agreement is a concerted practice or agreement between companies operating at different levels of the production or distribution chain, for example between a producer and a distributor.

between a supplier and its distributor is anticompetitive, not only because of the restriction of competition attributable to it, but also because of the existence of agreements of the same type, to which the company in question is not a party – which is difficult to accept from a legal point of view,[146] since an agent is only responsible for their own behavior, not that of others. This theory is, however, deemed to have been enshrined in positive law,[147] and appears in the block exemption regulations for vertical agreements,[148] the accompanying guidelines,[149] and the Commission's *De Minimis* Notice.[150]

However, the theory of cumulative effect is based on a few isolated decisions, confined to beer contracts and, above all, nuanced to such an extent that it does not really seem to be a theory, but simply an application of the classic reasoning presiding over the characterization of agreements.

In fact, taking into consideration the foreclosure of the market due to the presence of parallel agreements is relevant to the assessment of the economic context in which the agreement takes place. Nevertheless, to maintain that an agreement may be anticompetitive solely because of effects that, "whether or not they were intended by the parties," result from a factual situation for which they are not responsible,[151] is contrary to the legal principle that only the *foreseeable consequences* of an act can engage the responsibility of its author.[152] However, this is not the position of the Court, which has ruled that the "cumulative effect" is "one among others" in assessing the context of the agreement in question,[153] and then specified in the *Delimitis*

146 E. Claudel, Ententes anticoncurrentielles et droit des contrats 109–10 (1994) (Ph.D. dissertation, Université Paris x Nanterre): the author stresses that in this case, "the causal link between concerted action and market disruption is distended."

147 M. Malaurie-Vignal, *Logique économique et logique juridique*, CONTRATS CONCURRENCE CONSOMMATION (Nov. 2005), étude 20.

148 In the presence of competition "limited by the cumulative effect of parallel networks of similar agreements," the theory of cumulative effect can theoretically allow the Commission to withdraw the benefit of the exemption, *see* Commission Regulation (EU) 2022/720 of May 10, 2022, on the Application of Article 101(3) of the Treaty on the Functioning of the European Union to Categories of Vertical Agreements and Concerted Practices, 2022 O.J. (L 134) 4, art. 6(1) and recitals 20–21; formerly, art. 6(1) and recitals 15–16 of Commission Regulation (EU) No. 330/2010 of Apr. 20, 2010, on the Application of Article 101(3) of the Treaty on the Functioning of the European Union to Categories of Vertical Agreements and Concerted Practices, 2010 O.J. (L 102) 1.

149 Eur. Comm., Guidelines on Vertical Restraints, 2022 O.J. (C 248) 1, paras. 257–261; formerly, Eur. Comm., Guidelines on Vertical Restraints, 2010 O.J. (C 130) 1, paras. 75–76.

150 EU Comm, Notice on Agreements of Minor Importance which Do Not Appreciably Restrict Competition under Article 101(1) of the Treaty on the Functioning of the European Union, 2014 O.J. (C 291) 1, para. 10: "A cumulative foreclosure effect is unlikely to exist if less than 30% of the relevant market is covered by parallel (networks of) agreements having similar effects."

151 This, however, was the position of the Wilkin-Janssen consorts, who sought annulment of the beer contract binding them to Brasserie de Haecht, *see* Case C-23/67, Brasserie de Haecht, ECLI:EU:C:1967:54, at 412.

152 It should be noted that the Commission did not fail to point out that accepting the reasoning of the Wilkin-Janssen consorts would produce "consequences *contrary to natural justice*, to the accepted rules governing *liability*, *wrongful activity* and *legal certainty* in respect of undertakings which, individually, are not necessarily responsible for the situation considered as a whole," *see* Case C-23/67, Brasserie de Haecht, ECLI:EU:C:1967:54, at 414 (emphasis added).

153 *Id.* at 415–16.

judgment that only agreements that "make an *appreciable* contribution" to the foreclosure of the market should be considered anticompetitive.[154]

B. Systematically ineffective arguments for abuse of a dominant position

287. **Theoretical recognition by the Court of Justice and the Commission of the possibility of invoking efficiency gains to justify an abuse of a dominant position.** When the first regulation implementing the competition rules was adopted,[155] the European Parliament wondered whether it would be appropriate, in the case of abuse of a dominant position, to provide for an exemption mechanism similar to that for agreements.[156] This procedure was not adopted, but very early on, the Court of Justice recognized the possibility for accused companies to justify their conduct by demonstrating the existence of an objective justification,[157] which, as in the case of agreements, is similar to the criminal concept of legitimate ground.[158]

However, case law went a step further in 2007. In the *British Airways* ruling, the Court of Justice held for the first time that, in addition to this type of justification, it was open to undertakings to prove "efficiencies," which implies "determine[ing] whether the *exclusionary effect* arising from such a system, which is disadvantageous for competition, may be *counterbalanced*, or outweighed, by *advantages in terms of efficiency* which *also benefit the consumer*"[159] – a "reasoning" directly inspired by merger law.[160]

In 2009, when it published its Guidelines, the Commission took up the theory of justification based on efficiencies, and specified that the burden of proof

---

154 Case C-234/89, Stergios Delimitis, ECLI:EU:C:1991:91, para. 24; *compare with* Case C-214/99, Neste Markkinointi Oy, ECLI:EU:C:2000:679, paras. 37–39. It should be noted that, in the latter case, the Commission stressed the risk of arbitrariness of such a theory, para. 24. For an application of the cumulative effect theory by the French Competition Authority, *see* ADLC, decision no. 15-D-06 of Apr. 21, 2015, regarding practices implemented by Booking.com B.V., Booking.com France SAS and Booking.com Customer Service France SAS in the online hotel booking sector (Fr.), paras. 136–141. In para. 137, in line with the case law of the Court of Justice, the Autorité states that "responsibility for the cumulative anticompetitive effect can be attributed only to those undertakings that contribute significantly to that effect" (unofficial translation).

155 Regulation (EC) No. 17/62.

156 Eur. Parl., Committee on the Internal Market, Minutes of the meeting of May 24–25, 1962, Milan, PE/V/62-6, p. 12: "The Commission notes that the notification forms referred to by Mr. Von der Groeben relate only to Article 85(1) of the Treaty and do not concern Article 86. One wonders whether it would not be appropriate, or even normal, for these forms to also relate to the provisions of Article 86 of the Treaty." (unofficial translation).

157 An *a contrario* reading of the *Hoffmann-La Roche* ruling already suggests the existence of such a defense: if an abuse was characterized, it was because the disputed exclusive supply commitment was not based on any "economic transaction which justifies this burden or benefit," *see* Case 85/76, Hoffmann-La Roche, ECLI:EU:C:1979:36, para. 90; cf. Case 311/84, CBEM, ECLI:EU:C:1985:394, para. 27.

158 In this sense, *see infra*, no. 349, and references cited.

159 Case C-95/04 P, British Airways, ECLI:EU:C:2007:166, para. 86.

160 As evidenced by the Opinion of Advocate General J. Kokott, Case C-95/04 P, British Airways, ECLI:EU:C:2006:133, n.63: Juliane Kokott notes that "[s]imilar considerations on the account to be taken of efficiency advantages can be found, in the area of merger control." Such a justification is clearly admissible in merger law, since in this area the authorities do not judge behavior, but intervene *ex ante* to regulate market structure, which implies forward-looking economic analyses.

rests with the undertaking, with the authority taking care of the "weighing-up of any apparent anti-competitive effects against any advanced and substantiated efficiencies,"[161] with the abuse being justified only if these appear to be "sufficient to guarantee that no net harm to consumers is likely to arise."[162]

288. **Lack of practical scope for justification based on efficiency gains.** Proof of the twofold condition laid down by case law is virtually impossible to provide: firstly, because of the vague and disputed nature of the economic notion of efficiency;[163] secondly, because it seems doubtful that it would be possible to provide proof that anticompetitive behavior could ever benefit consumers. Indeed, such reasoning is manifestly inconsistent, given that case law consistently presumes that harm to the competitive process is *deemed to be* detrimental to consumers.[164]

While it is debatable whether it is possible to prove efficiency gains,[165] its admissibility is now recognized. However, this line of jurisprudence is illogical: as the actual effects of anticompetitive behavior are not a constitutive element of the offense of abuse, it is hardly rational to consider that "efficiency benefiting the consumer" – an obscure expression, to say the least – can prevent a finding of infringement. Moreover, although several rulings have recognized this theory,[166] it has to be said that, to date, *no decision* has accepted such a defense, as efficiency gains have never been able to prevent the characterization of an abuse of a dominant position,[167] and some companies are now reluctant to invoke this argument.[168]

In short, *the efficiency argument is always ineffective* in both abuse of dominance and agreement, due to the incompatibility of these defenses

---

161 Comm. EC, Guidance on the Commission's Enforcement Priorities in Applying Article 82 of the EC Treaty to Abusive Exclusionary Conduct by Dominant Undertakings, 2009 O.J. (C 45) 7, paras. 28–31. For concrete illustrations of the (complex) assessment of efficiency-based defenses to abusive conduct in the case of: a rebate system, para. 46; tying or bundling, para. 62; predatory conduct, para. 74; refusal to supply, para. 89.

162 *Id.*, para. 30.

163 On the complexity of the concept of efficiency gains, *see supra*, no. 285.

164 In this sense, *see infra*, no. 361.

165 On the difficulties of assessing efficiency gains, *see* R. O'Donoghue, *What Makes a Unilateral Conduct Abusive: The Legal Perspective*, *in* The Notion of Restriction of Competition: Revisiting the Foundations of Antitrust Enforcement in Europe 169, 232–38 (D. Gerard, M. Merola & B. Meyring eds., 2017).

166 *Ex multis*: Case C-52/09, TeliaSonera Sverige, ECLI:EU:C:2011:83, para. 76; Case C-209/10, Post Danmark, ECLI:EU:C:2012:172, para. 41; Case C-413/14 P, Intel, ECLI:EU:C:2017:632, para. 140: an undertaking in a dominant position can demonstrate that "the exclusionary effect [brought about by its conduct] may be counterbalanced, or outweighed, by advantages in terms of efficiency which also benefit the consumer."

167 *See ex multis*: Case T-201/04, Microsoft, ECLI:EU:T:2007:289, para. 1125; Case T-612/17, Google and Alphabet, ECLI:EU:T:2021:763, paras. 586–590; Case T-604/18, Google, ECLI:EU:T:2022:541, paras. 601–619.

168 As the Court of First Instance noted in the *Tomra* case, *see* Case T-155/06, Tomra Systems, ECLI:EU:T:2010:370, para. 224: "[T]he applicants had every opportunity to put forward an objective economic justification of their practices which was not anti-competitive. They could have explained what efficiency gains they thought they might make from their exclusivity agreements, quantity commitments and individualised rebate schemes. However, the applicants do not maintain before the Court that their conduct gave rise to the least discernible efficiency gain, was otherwise justified or resulted in lower prices or any other benefits for consumers."

with the structure of the infringements: it is logically impossible to defeat the characterization of a formal offense using arguments based on effects. These theories are therefore superfluous, since they are at odds with the reality of litigation, and produce "negative effects" that are detrimental, not to consumers, but to the law of anticompetitive practices itself. On the one hand, they undermine the clarity of the law by giving the impression that certain arguments can be invoked even though they are inoperative. On the other hand, the hypothetical consideration of these arguments leads companies to invoke them almost systematically, which increases the cost of defending and enforcing competition rules[169] – from which it follows that the ineffectiveness of "efficiency" is obvious.

*

* *

289. **Conclusion of Section 1: competition infringements are intentional offenses.** Textual arguments, as well as an analysis of the Court of Justice's consistent case law, attest to the fact that competition infringements are intentional offenses. Given their formal nature, no result, in other words, no effect, is required as a constitutive element, and defenses based on demonstrating the absence of effects or the existence of "pro-competitive" effects, although deemed admissible in theory, are systematically rejected by the judge in practice. Given that intent is an object of proof for competition infringements, we now turn to the types of evidence that can be used to presume the existence of anticompetitive intent.

*

* *

169 *See* Witt, The More Economic Approach to EU Antitrust Law 191–92 (2019), *op. cit.*: "After so much debate about the importance of efficiencies and so much effort to introduce the efficiency defence…, this discrepancy between theory and practice is somewhat puzzling. In fact, the development even appears counterproductive. At the moment, the key effect of an efficiency defence is the generation of additional costs for all parties involved. The parties invoking the defence regularly require expert economic input to present the efficiencies in a way that complies with the Commission's guidelines. They often commission complex econometric analysis to prove and quantify the efficiencies expected… . The Commission regularly engages with these efficiency claims in depth, examining the validity of the data, the calculations and the very models used to predict the efficiencies. Efficiency defences are thus a costly and time-consuming business. Without realistic chances of success, this additional cost makes little sense." *Adde*, B. Smulders, *The Bifurcated Approach and Its Practical Impact on the Establishment of Harm to Competition*, *in* The Notion of Restriction of Competition: Revisiting the Foundations of Antitrust Enforcement in Europe 51, 61 (D. Gerard, M. Merola & B. Meyring eds., 2017). The author asks whether it makes sense for a company to rely on defenses based on the demonstration of "efficiencies," and remarks: "The Commission has been criticised occasionally that it does not effectively rely on efficiency defences, that Article 101(3) is a dead letter while Article 102 efficiency defence is a sham"; in the same vein, *see* J.-F. Bellis & T. Kasten, *Will Efficiencies Play an Increasingly Important Role in the Assessment of Conduct Under Article 102 TFEU?, in Competition Law and the Enforcement of Article 102*, 129, 135–37 (F. Etro & I. Kokkoris eds., 2010). *Contra*, for arguments in favor of this defense, which, according to the author, provides better consumer protection, *see* E. Rousseva, *Reflections on the Relevance and Proof of Efficiency Defences in Modern EU Antitrust Law*, *in* Ten Years of Effects-Based Approach in EU Competition Law: State of Play and Perspectives 290–91 (J. Bourgeois & D. Waelbroeck eds., 2012).

Section 2
Methods for proving intent

290. **The essential use of presumptions to characterize competition infringements.** Qualifying anticompetitive behavior requires, on the one hand, *proving the facts* – for example, the material existence of a concerted action – and, on the other, *linking* the disputed behavior *to a legal category*. Given the abstract nature of the value protected, namely, competition, this second operation can only be accomplished by mobilizing presumptions. Indeed, to demonstrate infringement of an *abstract value*, the *method* itself is *abstract*: it necessarily relies on a theoretical construction.[170] *Direct proof* is thus impossible: the judge cannot assert, without a detour through presumptive reasoning, that such behavior is anticompetitive, precisely because competition is neither a concrete object nor a person, but a value, i.e., something that exists only in the world of ideas. It is therefore essential to start from *known facts* – the litigious conduct and its context – to draw *unknown consequences* – the presumed infringement of an intangible value. *In anticompetitive practices law, the use of presumptions is therefore indispensable.*

291. **The quasi-legal nature of presumptions and their dual function: probative and definitive.** The presumptions used in anticompetitive practices law are quasi-legal in nature:[171] originating in case law, their repeated use gives them an important normative scope, to such an extent that they, *in fine,* contribute to refining the definition of the offense.[172] Presumptions thus have a dual function: they are both a means of proof and an extension of the norm.[173] Indeed, when the judge presumes that, unless there is a legitimate reason, a particular pricing practice is likely to restrict competition and therefore constitutes an abuse of a dominant position, this reasoning not only makes it possible to *characterize* the infringement, but also implies a bias in the *definition* of the restriction of competition.[174]

---

170 There is, in fact, a difference in the methods used to characterize offenses involving *material damage* and those involving *harm to intangible value*: the latter require a *theoretical construct* and *a consensus on values*, while the former can be established through a simple *factual observation*. Factual observation

171 On quasi-legal presumptions, *see supra*, no. 198.

172 This topic will be dealt with in the next chapter, *see infra*, nos. 353 *et seq.*

173 This is evidenced by the fact that certain presumptions are treated by the Court of Justice as substantive rules binding on national courts. Conversely, if they were rules of evidence, the principle of primacy of European Union law would not apply, due to the principle of procedural autonomy of Member States. For example, it has been held that the presumption that, in the event of an exchange of price information, undertakings are *deemed* to have taken account of the said information, is a substantive rule. *See* Case C-8/08, T-Mobile Netherlands, ECLI:EU:C:2009:343, paras. 44–53, and answer to the second question.

174 Laurence Idot has rightly emphasized the existence of a "distinction between the facts and the qualification of these facts," and noted that making the latter is "not always easy in competition law", *see* L. Idot, *Réflexions sur l'évolution de la preuve des pratiques anticoncurrentielles devant les autorités de concurrence*, CONCURRENCES no. 4-2017, art. no. 84879, 45, 48, no. 10. *Adde*, F. Castillo de la Torre, *Is the Effects-Based Approach Too*

292. **Evidentiary reasoning focused on proving intent.** In anticompetitive practices law, evidentiary reasoning does not focus on effects, but aims to presume intent.[175] To demonstrate this assertion, it is necessary to address the question of the standard of proof, in order to deconstruct one of the discipline's most difficult theoretical problems – namely, the so-called effects-based approach. It would appear that this approach does not shift the focus of proof, but consists in applying a classic evidentiary principle,[176] which has not changed despite the increased complexity brought about by the more economic approach:[177] when a practice does not *prima facie* appear capable of restricting competition, and the infringement is therefore not sufficiently characterized in law, more proof is required (**Paragraph 1**). The next step is to draw up a typology of the presumptions used by the courts, and to examine their probative value, thus corroborating the thesis that they are intended to prove the intent of the respondents, rather than the effects (**Paragraph 2**).

Paragraph 1 – The different standards of proof required

293. **The "effects-based approach": the source of a thorny logic problem.** The distinction between an agreement sanctioned on the basis of its object or its effect, and between abuse prohibited per se or by its effects,[178] is an

Cumbersome? Taking Stock of Recent Practice and Case Law on Article 102 TFEU, in The Transformation of EU Competition Law: Next Generation Issues 145, 152 (A. Claici, A. Komninos & D. Waelbroeck eds., 2023): the author notes that the definition of infringements and questions relating to their proof are often confused.

175 P. L. Parcu, *Considerazioni sulla rilevanza del movente nella valutazione delle violazioni antitrust, in* ix Antitrust Between EU Law & National Law 341, 341 (E. A. Raffaelli ed., 2011): "[N]o one can deny that any antitrust qualification is based on a presumption of anticompetitive intent."

176 In this respect, it should be noted that one author has defended the idea that the system of proof is uniform, and even transcends the distinction between civil and criminal law. *See* R. Legros, *La preuve légale en droit pénal, in* La preuve en droit 149, 158 (C. Perelman & P. Forier eds., 1981).

177 In this sense, A. La Pergola & L. Prete, *Burden of Proof in Competition Law: An Overview of EU and National Case Law,* e-Competitions Special Issue 1, 11 (Mar. 29, 2023), art. no. 111517: "[D]espite the basic principles [relating to the burden of proof] having remained relatively consistent and uncontested throughout the centuries…, their application in the specific competition cases may give rise to fierce battles. In particular, the reliability and persuasiveness of economic evidence is a topic that, especially in the last years, has given rise to great controversy… . That being said, the administrative and judicial developments surveyed in this contribution appear to remain within the confines of a relatively orthodox application of the basic principles."

178 Following the example of other authors, we will not distinguish between the alternative between object and effect in agreement cases, and that between infringement per se and infringement by effects in abuse of dominant position cases, *see inter alia,* P. Ibáñez Colomo, *Beyond the More Economics-Based Approach: A Legal Perspective on Article 102 TFEU Case Law,* 53 Common Market Law Review 709, 712–13 (2016): "In the same way that Article 101(1) TFEU distinguished between agreements that restrict competition 'by object' and 'by effect', the Court takes the view that some practices are abusive by their very nature, while others are only caught by Article 102 TFEU where they have restrictive effects on competition"; A. Meij & T. Baumé, *Balancing Object and Effect Analysis in Identifying Abuses of a Dominant Position under Article 102 TFEU, in* Ten Years of Effects-Based Approach in EU Competition Law: State of Play and Perspectives 159 (J. Bourgeois & D. Waelbroeck eds., 2012).

alternative well known to competition law specialists, but little known to the rest of the legal profession. It would mean having to characterize the anticompetitive effects of a practice, whenever its object – in other words, its objective – does not appear to be *prima facie* anticompetitive. Such reasoning suggests, on the one hand, that the effects are the object of the proof, and on the other hand, that the object is a presumption of effect – which is, however, in contradiction with case law. The alternative is thus of "false simplicity,"[179] insofar as, while the underlying rule is clear at first glance, on closer examination it poses a thorny logic problem. This is why it is necessary to deconstruct the effects approach (**I**) in order to understand what it means in practice, and then to determine its real function (**II**).

I. Deconstructing the "effects-based" approach

294. **Observable hesitations in the Commission's decision-making practice, in the case law of the European courts, and in legal doctrine.** There are many subjects under debate in competition law, but the alternative between object and effect is certainly one of the most talked about. Encouraged by a hesitant and often obscure jurisprudence, legal scholars, advocates general, and judges alike are constantly revisiting the issue with each new ruling. It is therefore appropriate to look at the meaning attributed to this alternative in the case law of the European courts and in the decision-making practice of the Commission (**A**), before taking a critical look at the way in which it has been theorized by doctrine (**B**).

A. History and current status of the alternative between object and effect in practice

295. **The first rulings by the Court of Justice:[180] the origin of a perennial confusion.** In the same way as the Commission Technique des Ententes, established under the French decree of 1953, which was the first to provide for the alternative between object and effect,[181] it is not surprising that the Court of Justice, in its very first judgments, "stumbled over such a

179 M. Debroux, *Restriction par objet: L'Avocat Général Bobek propose à la Cour de justice de l'Union européenne, saisie d'une question préjudicielle par la Cour suprême hongroise, une méthode d'analyse visant à déterminer si une pratique anticoncurrentielle peut être qualifiée de restriction par objet ou si l'examen de ses effets est nécessaire (*Gazdasági Versenyhivatal / Budapest Bank*)*, CONCURRENCES no. 4-2019, art. no. 92206, 87, 88: "Nothing is more misleading than the apparent simplicity of the distinction between a restriction of competition by object and by effects."

180 The first judgments studied dealt exclusively with agreements, with case law on abuse of dominant positions only appearing later.

181 *See infra*, nos. 109–110.

poorly drafted text."[182] However, as the first formulas of principle were to be found identically in all subsequent case law, they ended up giving substance to a problem that might never have existed, and which can easily be overcome.[183]

As early as the *Société Technique Minière* case, the embarrassment is palpable: the operative part mixes, in no particular order, arguments based on the harmfulness of the object of the agreement with formulas relating to its effects,[184] and the Court finally concludes by advocating an *overall contextual approach* aimed at determining whether the disputed agreement "is to be considered as prohibited by reason of *its object or of its effect*,"[185] making the alternative lose all meaning.[186] For his part, Advocate General Karl Roemer had mixed up object and effect in his analysis,[187] then criticized the Court, in *Consten and Grundig*, for not "being wholly consistent in its actions," since in his view, the object theory "implies ... an examination of the effects."[188]

One commentator noted that, in these two cases, the judges had given a narrow and overly literal interpretation of the incriminating text, while they should have taken the simpler view that an agreement could generally be deemed anticompetitive on the basis of its "reasonably foreseeable effects"[189]; meanwhile René Joliet considered that the European judges had implicitly accepted the solution advocated by Advocate General Karl Roemer, which was close to the rule of reason used on the basis of the Sherman Act.[190] Be that as it may, for several decades thereafter, the

182 Focsaneanu, La jurisprudence de la Cour de justice des communautés européennes en matière de concurrence: Les règles applicables aux entreprises (Articles 85 et 86 du Traité de Rome), *op. cit.* at 168.

183 For a deconstruction of the opposition between object and effect, *see infra*, nos. 294 *et seq.*

184 Case 56-65, Société Technique Minière, ECLI:EU:C:1966:38, at 359–60, 249–50: the Court begins its reasoning by stating that the object and effect of an agreement are alternative requirements; it then points out that the object of the agreement must be assessed in the light of the economic context in which it is situated; it then states that if the disputed clauses do not reveal a sufficient degree of harmfulness to competition, the effects of the agreement should be examined and it should be demonstrated that "competition has *in fact* been prevented" (which could lead to the erroneous conclusion that the effect is a constitutive element of the infringement); but finally it considers that if the aim of the agreement is for the undertaking to enter an area where it was not active, the alteration of competition could be questioned...

185 *Id.* at 250 (emphasis added).

186 *See* Focsaneanu, La jurisprudence de la Cour de justice des communautés européennes en matière de concurrence: Les règles applicables aux entreprises (Articles 85 et 86 du Traité de Rome), *op. cit.* at 170.

187 Opinion of Advocate General K. Roemer, Case 56-65, Société Technique Minière, ECLI:EU:C:1966:17, at 256: the Advocate General asks the question "In what circumstances may it be said that they have as their object or effect the restriction of competition?" without distinguishing between one hypothesis or the other.

188 Opinion of Advocate General K. Roemer, Case 56-64, Consten and Grundig, ECLI:EU:C:1966:19, at 516–17 358.

189 L. Focsaneanu, *Pour objet ou pour effet*, 87 Revue du marché commun 862, 866, 870 (Jan. 1966).

190 R. Joliet, The Rule of Reason in Antitrust Law: American, German and Common Market Laws in Comparative Perspective 11–12, 109–110 (1967).

Court abandoned its effort at conceptual distinction and, more pragmatically, required only proof of the influence of the disputed agreement on competition[191] – this reasoning being consistent with that governing the characterization of formal offenses.[192]

296. **The Commission's decision-making practice on agreements, from its origin to the advent of the "more economic" approach.** For the first thirty years of its decision-making practice, the Commission did not distinguish between the object and effect of behavior. More often than not, it referred to both terms without differentiating between them, using almost systematically the conjunction "and,"[193] rarely the conjunction "or,"[194] while sometimes it referred directly to neither the object nor the effect.[195] Whatever the terms used, there is no difference in the nature of the analysis carried out by the Commission:[196] it has always taken into consideration not only the form of the conduct, but also the context and the actual framework in

---

191 Focsaneanu, La jurisprudence de la Cour de justice des communautés européennes en matière de concurrence: Les règles applicables aux entreprises (Articles 85 et 86 du Traité de Rome), *op. cit.* at 170. *See ex multis*: Case 40-70, Sirena, ECLI:EU:C:1971:18, answer to the first preliminary question; Case 1-71, Cadillon, ECLI:EU:C:1971:47, para. 7; Case 78-70, Deutsche Grammophon, ECLI:EU:C:1971:59, para. 6; Case 22-71, Béguelin, ECLI:EU:C:1971:113, paras. 7–32; Case 8-74, Procureur du Roi, ECLI:EU:C:1974:82, para. 12.

192 On the definition of formal offenses, *see supra*, no. 272.

193 *Ex multis*: Comm. EC, July 16, 1969, IV/26.623, Entente internationale de la quinine, para. 21: the "agreements or concerted practices mentioned ... had the object and effect of restricting competition"; Comm. EC, Dec. 1, 1976, IV/29.018, Miller International, para. 11: "The object and effect of these agreements was to prevent exports of the goods to other Community countries. They thus had the object and effect of restricting such competition . . . ."; Comm. EC, Dec. 22, 1976, IV/24.510, Gerofabriek, II, (a), 3: "These agreements ... have the object and effect of perceptibly restricting and distorting competition"; Comm. EC, Sept. 21, 1978, IV/28.824, Droit d'obtention – Semences de maïs, II, 2: "[T]hese agreements had the object and effect of restricting competition"; Comm. EC, Dec. 12, 1978, IV/29.535, white lead, para. 24: "The object and effect of this cooperation was the restriction of competition"; Comm. EC, Sept. 28, 1981, IV/29.988, Italian flat glass, II, A, 3: the "agreements have as their object and effect the prevention, restriction and distortion of competition"; Comm. EC, Dec. 7, 1982, IV/30.070, National Panasonic, para. 48: "An export prohibition ... has as its object and effect a restriction of competition within the common market. Its object is to prevent dealers and their subsequent purchasers in other Member States from reselling the products in question and thus from competing with other established dealers"; Comm. EC, Dec. 7, 1984, IV/28.930, Milchförderungsfonds, para. 29: the decisions "have as their object and effect a distortion of competition"; Comm. EC, Dec.10, 1984, IV/30.717, Uniform Eurocheques, para. 33: "The agreements and decisions within the eurocheque system, which have as their object the fixing of the price of a service, represent restrictive practices… . They have as their effect the prevention of competition between the banks in any country. . . ."; Comm. EC, July 12, 1985, IV/4.204, Velcro-Aplix, B, II: "The agreement has the object and effect of restricting competition"; Comm. EC, Dec.18, 1987, IV/31.017, Fisher-Price/Quaker Oats, para. 20: "[T]he agreement had as its object and its effect the restriction and the distortion of competition . . . ."; Comm. EC, Dec. 18, 1987, IV/31.503, Konica, para. 41: "The export ban imposed ... had the object and effect of restricting competition… . Its aim was to restrain dealers ... from selling to customers in other Member States, so that these would not compete with dealers under contract to Konica Europe" Comm. EC, Dec. 4, 1991, IV/33.157, Eco System v. Peugeot, para. 23: the agreement "has as its object and effect the restriction of competition."

194 For example, in Comm. EC, Aug. 2, 1989, IV/31.553, Welded steel mesh, para. 175: the provisions had "as their object, or at least as their effect… ."

195 *Ex multis*: Comm. EC, Jan. 6, 1982, IV/28.748, AEG-Telefunken, para. 70; Comm. EC, Nov. 16, 1983, IV/30.696, Distribution system of Ford Werke AG – interim measure, para. 32; Comm. EC, Dec. 12, 1983, IV/30.389, Nutricia/de Rooij, para. 35; Comm. EC, Dec. 18, 1985, IV/30.739, Siemens/Fanuc, para. 24; Comm. EC, Sept. 25, 1986, IV/31.143, Peugeot, para. 34; Comm. EC, Nov. 26, 1986, IV/31.204, MELDOC, paras. 59–60.

196 A. C. Witt, The More Economic Approach to EU Antitrust Law 201 (2019).

which the disputed agreement took place,[197] in varying degrees of detail depending on the case in question. Moreover, in all cases, the effect taken into account has never been the effect on the market, but only *the effect on the competitive process.*[198]

297. **The Commission's decision-making practice on abuse of dominance, from its origin to the advent of the "more economic" approach.** The Commission's decision-making practice on abuse of a dominant position was similar, insofar as references to objectives and effects can be found throughout the decisions, without it being possible to give either term a specific meaning or to discern the existence of a particular regime.

As early as 1971, in its first case under article 86 of the EC Treaty, the Commission referred to the "discriminatory effects" of GEMA's articles of association.[199] Yet, if *discriminatory conduct* does indeed potentially produce a *discriminatory effect*, stating it explicitly amounts to a pleonasm. It would be like describing the *act* of throwing a stone at a pane of glass and then writing that the likely *effect* of this behavior is to throw the stone at the wall.[200]

It sometimes used the term "effect" to designate the ability of conduct to restrict competition.[201] More often than not, its use of this word was unexpected, and seems to stem from a linguistic tic, i.e., an unconscious way of writing using meaningless words, rather than from the implementation of reasoning. This is particularly apparent in the *Michelin* decision: the authority considers that the conduct at issue constitutes an abuse of a dominant position, since "[i]t restricts dealers' freedom of choice and results in inequality of treatment as between tyre dealers" and the "access of other tyre producers to the market is also restricted."[202] In this case, it is clear that the word "effect" does not provide any information, and could be removed from the sentence without altering its meaning.

---

197 Opinion of Advocate General Bobek, Case C-228/18, Budapest Bank, ECLI:EU:C:2019:678, para. 46: "[T]he Court's case-law has always been consistent on this point: the assessment of a practice under EU competition rules cannot be made in the abstract, but requires an examination of that practice in the light of the legal and economic conditions prevailing on the markets concerned. The importance of this principle is confirmed by the fact that it has been found to be valid with regard to both Article 101(1) TFEU and Article 102 TFEU. Not even when dealing with forms of conduct like price fixing, market sharing or export bans, which are generally recognised to be particularly harmful to competition, can the economic and legal context be totally ignored."

198 In this respect, *see* the excerpts from the decisions reproduced *infra*, no. 296, which all refer, without exception, to harm to competition and not to the effects produced on the market.

199 Comm. EC, June 2, 1971, IV/26.760, GEMA, II, C, 1, c.

200 This illustration will be developed further *infra*, no. 492.

201 *See* in particular: Comm. EC, June 9, 1976, IV/29.020, Vitamines, para. 24: the Commission considers that the conduct at issue is "by its very nature" to deprive customers of "all freedom of choice," which is described as a "restrictive effect." It should be noted that it would be possible to write, more simply, that such conduct restricts competition, without mentioning the term "effect."

202 Comm. EC, Oct. 7, 1981, IV/29.491, Nederlandsche Banden-Industrie Michelin, para. 37 (emphasis added).

Finally, it should be noted that the Commission has always linked the choice between object and effect to the competitive process, and not to the result produced on the market. In the *Decca* case, for example, it held that the undertaking "was not entitled to use *means* which were illegal" under article 86 "in as much as their *object and/or effect* were: the maintenance or the strengthening of its dominant position ... *in a manner which is restrictive of competition*, the *limitation of the access* of third parties to the market ... and of the *freedom of choice* of the consumer."[203]

298. **The interference of the "more economic" approach: the Commission's new doctrine.** With the adoption of the "more economic approach," the Commission profoundly amended its doctrine. Advocates of a greater role for economic analysis, whose main, if not exclusive, argument is to criticize legal reasoning for its "formalism,"[204] have caricatured previous case law in order to accuse the Court of having regard only to the form of agreements, whereas the judges had always, since 1966, required in addition a contextual analysis of the disputed practices.[205]

However, in 2004, in the Commission's guidelines on article 81, which, it should be remembered, are not binding on the Court of First Instance, the Court of Justice or the national competition authorities, and therefore express only its own doctrine, the Commission suddenly linked the distinction between object and effect to a highly significant difference in regime[206] – albeit without normative scope. The Commission announced that if the agreement did not have the object of restricting competition, it would need to be demonstrated that it impacts "actual or potential competition to such an extent that on the relevant market *negative effects on prices, output, innovation or the variety or quality of goods and services* can be expected with a reasonable degree of probability."[207] Similarly,

---

203 Comm. EC, Dec. 21, 1988, IV/39.979, Decca Navigator System, para. 112 (emphasis added).

204 This criticism, which stems from a misunderstanding of legal reasoning, will be examined *infra*, nos. 486–487.

205 D. Bosco & C. Prieto, Droit européen de la concurrence 477 (2013), no. 558 "From its very first rulings in response to preliminary questions, the Court of Justice has opted for a very concrete approach to the implementation of Article 101 TFEU. This should put into perspective the criticisms of the formal approach attributed to both the Court and the Commission, which have somewhat caricatured the period preceding the major project to modernize European competition policy." In the same vein, *see* F. Castillo de la Torre, *Is the Effects-Based Approach Too Cumbersome? Taking Stock of Recent Practice and Case Law on Article 102 TFEU*, *in* The Transformation of EU Competition Law: Next Generation Issues 145, 148 (A. Claici, A. Komninos & D. Waelbroeck eds., 2023): the author notes that the examination of the capacity to restrict competition (otherwise known as the "potential effects" or "capacity to produce anti-competitive effects" analysis) is not new, and does not date from the "more economic approach" – it was already present in decision-making practice before the Commission's change of doctrine.

206 Laurence Idot points out that the title "guidelines" is "misleading," as "the Commission is in fact undertaking a complete reinterpretation of Article 81 EC," *see* L. Idot, *La qualification de la restriction de concurrence: À propos des lignes directrices de la Commission concernant l'application de l'article 81, § 3 CE*, *in* La modernisation du droit de la concurrence 88 (G. Canivet & M.-A. Frison-Roche eds., 2006).

207 EC Comm., Guidelines on the Application of Article 81(3) of the Treaty, 2004 O.J. (C 101) 97, para. 24. For a critique of these guidelines, criticizing them, among other things, for the excessive complexity of the economic analyses required and their non-compliance with the case law of the Court of Justice, *see* N. Petit, *The Guidelines on the Application of Article 81(3) EC: A Critical Review* (IEJE Working Paper No. 4/2009), https://ssrn.com/abstract=1428558.

in its guidelines on priorities for the application of article 82 published in 2009, the Commission addresses the issue of restriction of competition under the following heading: "Foreclosure leading to consumer harm ('anti-competitive foreclosure')"[208] – suggesting, through the association of the two expressions, that the criterion for restricting competition lies in the harm suffered by consumers.[209]

In other words, this would mean that the "effects-based" approach would henceforth involve characterizing an effect, not only on the competition process, but also on the market and even on consumers – which would be manifestly incompatible with the Court's established case law, according to which concrete effect is not a constitutive element of infringements,[210] and this despite the fact that the Commission itself considers that its communication "is not intended to constitute a statement of the law and is without prejudice to the interpretation of Article 82" by the Court of First Instance and the Court of Justice.[211] For competition authorities, this would mean focusing their attention "more on the outcome of the competitive process than on the conditions under which it takes place"[212] and, in short, requiring the implementation of competition rules to produce results in line with the prescriptions of economic analysis.[213]

299. **The Commission's ambiguous decision-making practice since the "more economic" approach to agreements.** However, since 2004, while the Commission has made a point of assessing the "real economic effects" of the practices it has pursued, it has more often than not pursued agreements, which are clearly anticompetitive, and has therefore frequently adopted a "by object" approach.[214] In other cases, the results of its decision-making practice are paradoxical.

---

208 Comm. EC, Guidance on the Commission's Enforcement Priorities in Applying Article 82 of the EC Treaty to Abusive Exclusionary Conduct by Dominant Undertakings, 2009 O.J. (C 45) 7, III, B. For a commentary, *see* N. Petit, *From Formalism to Effects: The Commission's Communication on Enforcement Priorities in Applying Article 82 EC*, 32 World Competition 485, 491–93 (2009).

209 *See also* Comm. EC Press Release IP/08/1877, Antitrust: Consumer Welfare at Heart of Commission Fight Against Abuses by Dominant Undertakings (Dec. 3, 2008).

210 *See supra*, nos. 277 *et seq*. *Adde*, N. Petit, Droit européen de la concurrence 314–15 (3rd ed. 2020), no. 745: "[I]t is rumored in some Brussels circles that the Commission's Legal Service has drawn up an internal memo questioning the compatibility of the text [the aforementioned guidelines] with the case law of the CJEU."

211 Comm. EC, Guidance on the Commission's enforcement priorities in applying Article 82 of the EC Treaty to abusive exclusionary conduct by dominant undertakings, *op. cit.*, para. 3.

212 D. Bosco, *Regards sur la modernisation de l'abus de position dominante*, 133 Petites affiches 14 (July 3, 2008), no. 5; *adde*, A. C. Witt, The More Economic Approach to EU Antitrust Law 212 (2019): the author notes that, since modernization, the Commission now assesses the effect on consumer welfare rather than the effect on companies' commercial freedom.

213 G. Canivet, *La place des économistes dans les organes d'application du droit de la concurrence: Retour sur un malaise existentiel*, Concurrences no. 2-2019, art. no. 90116, 1, 2. For a critical look, *see infra*, nos. 435 *et seq.*

214 A. C. Witt, *The Enforcement of Article 101 TFEU: What Has Happened to the Effects Analysis?*, 55 Common Market Law Review 417, 426 (2018), and decisions cited; *adde*, L. Idot, *Le retour de l'objet anticoncurrentiel…*, Concurrences no. 4-2009, art. no. 29202, 1.

In the *Lunbeck*[215] and *Fentanyl*[216] cases, both involving practices that had never before been the subject of litigation, the authority characterized "restrictions by object" by means of an extremely detailed analysis – which legitimately raises questions about the boundary between "object" and "effects" approaches.

In the *Servier* case, the Commission recalled that the practices in question – settlement agreements relating to patents – could not be presumed unlawful, and that proof of their infringement depended on the specific circumstances of the case.[217] Having demonstrated, once again through a very detailed analysis, that the *object of* the contested agreements was to restrict competition, the authority decided that, even if the infringement had been established to the requisite legal standard, it would, "for the sake of completeness," undertake an analysis of the effects on the market.[218] It did the same in the *Groupement des cartes bancaires* case,[219] while in its *MasterCard I* decision, it avoided taking a position on the approach used[220] and successively analyzed the object, then the effect.

Finally, let's mention the *Visa* case: at issue was Visa's refusal to admit Morgan Stanley as a member, which prevented the latter from issuing Visa cards in Europe and excluded it from the card transaction market. While the decision is shorter than those just cited, and the company's behavior was – if we refuse to play with words – obviously aimed at preventing Morgan Stanley's penetration of the European market, and therefore at restricting competition, the Commission decided to consider a "restriction by effects."[221] In view of the in-depth examination of the practices that were analyzed through the prism of a "by object" approach in its other decisions, it seems difficult, if not impossible, to clearly distinguish this from the "effects-based" approach used in this case.

300. **The Commission's ambiguous decision-making practice since the "more economic" approach to abuse of dominance.** No less disconcerting are the decisions handed down on the few cases of abuse of dominant position

215 Eur. Comm., June 19, 2013, C(2013) 3803 final, Lundbeck.

216 Eur. Comm., Dec. 10, 2013, C(2013) 8870 final, Fentanyl.

217 Eur. Comm., July 9, 2014, C(2014) 4955 final, Servier, para. 1102.

218 *Id.*, para. 1213. The analysis of the effects of this decision takes up 212 pages!

219 Comm. EC, Oct. 17, 2007, COMP/D1/38606, Groupement des cartes bancaires, para. 252: "Although, according to Community case-law, there is no need to take account of the concrete effects of an agreement when it is established that it has as its object the restriction of competition, the Commission will examine the anticompetitive effects of the measures at issue in this section."

220 Comm. EC, Dec. 19, 2007, COMP/34.579, MasterCard, para. 407: at the end of its "by object approach," the Commission states that "given that it can be clearly established that the MasterCard MIF has the *effect* of appreciably restricting and distorting competition to the detriment of merchants in the acquiring markets it is not necessary to reach a definite conclusion as to whether the MasterCard MIF is a restriction by object." Such reasoning is, to say the least, abstruse: either the infringement has been proved to the requisite legal standard, or it has not – it seems strange that, in addition to asking whether the standard of proof has been met, we have to decide which "category" the infringement falls into.

221 Comm. EC, Oct. 3, 2007, COMP/D1/37860, Visa International, paras. 76–201.

that the Commission has dealt with over the same period. A curious habit now seems to animate the Commission: as when it prosecutes agreements, when faced with an abuse of a dominant position, the Commission first characterizes the infringement to the requisite legal standard, after numerous references to the Court's landmark judgments, by demonstrating the *capacity* of the behavior to restrict competition. Then, while taking the precaution of pointing out that *such an analysis is not required by case law*, it carries out a wide-ranging examination of the effects of the conduct in question, both on the market and on consumers – *which it considers to be excessive.*[222]

301. **Intermediate conclusion on the Commission's decision-making practice since the "more economic" approach.** In short, on the basis of both articles 101 and 102 of the TFEU, the Commission systematically carries out an in-depth analysis when the case requires it, including when it finds a "restriction by object," and then sometimes engages in an examination of the actual effects on the market, specifying that this is not required by the Court. This second practice is not only aberrant, insofar as it has no impact on the outcome of litigation,[223] and drastically increases the cost of enforcing competition rules, but above all, it introduces doubt as to the constituent elements of infringements. Indeed, when the Commission announces, in its communications, that the criterion for qualifying anticompetitive practices lies in the harmful effects they produce on the market or consumers, and when it devotes, in practice, vast developments aimed at proving them, it is quite legitimate for companies to believe, wrongly, that the said effects are a constitutive element.[224] It is not surprising, therefore, that they began to argue before the European courts that the Commission had not

222 *See ex multis* (emphasis added): Comm. EC, Mar. 29, 2006, COMP/E-1/38.113, Prokent-Tomra, paras. 285 and 332: "Although ... it is sufficient to 'show that the abusive conduct of the undertaking in a dominant position tends to restrict competition...', the Commission has completed its analysis in this case by considering the likely effects of Tomra's practices on the RVMs market"; Comm. EC, July 4, 2007, COMP/38.784, Wanadoo España v. Telefónica, paras. 543–544: "*Article 82 does not require the Commission to examine specifically whether the conduct of the dominant undertaking has caused prejudice to consumers.* In the present case however, the Commission has examined the impact of Telefónica's practices and has established that Telefónica's conduct was not only capable of restricting, or in other words, likely to restrict competition in the retail market, but it also had an actual impact on the competitive structure of the relevant market and a *detrimental impact for end users*" (emphasis added); Comm. EC, May 13, 2009, COMP/C-3/37.990, *Intel*, paras. 923–924: "Whilst the findings referred to in the preceding recital [the capacity of the rebates to restrict the companies freedom to choose], ...are in themselves sufficient to find an infringement under Article 82 of the Treaty according to the case law, the Commission will *in addition* demonstrate that, *on top of fulfilling the conditions of the case law*, [these practices] were capable of causing or likely to cause anticompetitive foreclosure (which is likely to result in consumer harm)." The additional analysis of effects, although not required by case law, runs to 200 pages in this case. *Adde*, Eur. Comm., June 22, 2011, COMP/39.525, Telekomunikacja Polska, para. 813: "In the present case, the Commission will establish that TP's conduct was *capable of restricting*, in other words, *likely to restrict competition* in the retail market. Moreover, *despite this not being necessary in order to prove an abuse of dominant position* it will also demonstrate that TP's conduct was likely to have detrimental effects for consumers."

223 In fact, contrary to the received idea that such overabundant analyses would protect the Commission's decisions from the risk of reversal, they can, on the contrary, weaken them, *see infra*, no. 444.

224 *See* L. Lovdahl Gormsen, *Why the European Commission's Enforcement Priorities on Article 82 EC Should Be Withdrawn* 1, 5 (2010), https://ssrn.com/abstract=2400402.

established the infringement to the requisite legal standard, because it had not established the effects.[225] And it is undoubtedly the increasing use of such a defense that has since given rise to the indigestible dispute over the distinction between the object and the effect, whereas the alternative had, for several decades, remained uncontroversial.

302. **The case law of the Court of Justice since the "more economic" approach: the quiet strength of continuity.** Despite a plethora of recent case law, some consider that, as early as the 1966 *Société Technique Minière* ruling, everything had already been established.[226] The Court of Justice is attached to its precedents, reverential towards its original decisions, to which it continues to refer even today: it is the guardian of continuity.

However, some judgments have been much talked about – such as *BIDS*, which has been interpreted as marking the advent of an "extensive conception of object."[227] Yet it appears to be of limited novelty. The excitement surrounding this case stems from a new recital, repeated verbatim in subsequent judgments: "The distinction between 'infringements by object' and 'infringements by effect' arises from the fact that certain forms of collusion between undertakings can be regarded, *by their very nature*, as being injurious to the proper functioning of normal competition."[228]

Taken on its own, this sentence does indeed seem to imply that an agreement could be deemed anticompetitive on the basis of its form alone. But placed in context, like a distant mirage, the appearance of novelty immediately evaporates: this point is placed after two others, which repeat *in extenso* the solution established by the *Société Technique Minière* and *Consten and Grundig* rulings – both requiring an assessment of the context.[229]

Six years later, during which the Court consistently endorsed by-object approaches submitted for its review, the *Groupement des cartes bancaires*

---

225 One author notes: "It was not surprising that some applicants typically argued before the EU Courts that the Commission had not followed its own Guidance," *see* F. Castillo de la Torre, *Is the Effects-Based Approach Too Cumbersome? Taking Stock of Recent Practice and Case Law on Article 102 TFEU*, *in* The Transformation of EU Competition Law: Next Generation Issues 145, 147 (A. Claici, A. Komninos & D. Waelbroeck eds., 2023).

226 J.-P. Kovar & R. Kovar, *L'objet anticoncurrentiel au sens de l'article 101, paragraphe 1, du TFUE: Un objet difficile à identifier*, Concurrences no. 1-2016, art. no. 77266, 48, 51.

227 For a more measured interpretation of the judgment, *see* O. Odudu, *Restrictions of Competition by Object – What's the Beef?*, 8 Competition Law Journal 11 (2009). Numerous authors have criticized the "lack of realism" and "excessive formalism" of anticompetitive practices law, both of which are linked to a supposedly insufficient consideration of the economic effects of litigious practices. *See ex multis*: D. Waelbroeck & D. Slater, *The Scope of Object vs Effect under Article 101 TFEU*, *in* Ten Years of Effects-Based Approach in EU Competition Law: State of Play and Perspectives 131, 133 (J. Bourgeois & D. Waelbroeck eds., 2012).

228 Case C-209/07, Beef Industry Development, ECLI:EU:C:2008:643, para. 17 (emphasis added). The same formula is used in the following judgments, *ex multis*: Case C-8/08, T-Mobile Netherlands, ECLI:EU:C:2009:343, para. 29; Case C-429/11 P, Gosselin, ECLI:EU:C:2013:463, para. 43; Case C-345/14, Maxima Latvja, ECLI:EU:C:2015:784, para. 18; Case C-307/18, Generics (UK), ECLI:EU:C:2020:52, para. 67; Case C-611/16 P, Xellia Pharmaceuticals, ECLI:EU:C:2021:707, para. 96.

229 Case C-209/07, Beef Industry Development, ECLI:EU:C:2008:643, paras. 15–16.

ruling reassured doctrinal commentators, who saw in it the salutary return of a "more restrictive" conception of object.[230] However, it seems to us that this case, too, did not upset the established order: after referring, once again, to its old judgments, the Court simply criticized the General Court for having confined itself to reproducing the Commission's decision, without checking, as the defendants had invited it to do, whether the practices in question "displayed a sufficient degree of harm to competition to be regarded as having as their object a restriction of competition."[231] Was this not a reproach linked to insufficient reasoning and a failure to reply to the conclusions, rather than a problem of substance? In fact, when the case was referred back to the General Court, the judges took the view that it could not be ruled out that the measures in question restricted competition, as they potentially led to the exclusion of new entrants to the market, or to the restriction of their acquisition activity;[232] and it is clear that what remains at the heart of the reasoning is not so much the notion of effect, as the question of whether competition has been restricted by the practice in question. One by one, the defendants' arguments were dismissed[233] – this jurisprudential saga, *in fine*, giving the impression of a mountain giving birth to a mouse.

The same sentiment emerges from a study of the *Intel* case.[234] Some have seen it as a landmark judgment, implicitly reversing[235] case law in that the Court imposed an examination of the exclusionary effects of the conduct at issue – a subtle indication that European judges were adopting the more economic approach advocated by the Commission.[236] Instead, we see a clarification of the distribution of the burden of proof.[237] Indeed, the *Intel* ruling is nothing more than a direct application of a classic evidentiary principle: when a company submits "supporting evidence[] that its conduct was not capable of restricting competition," the General

230 *See inter alia*: D. Bosco, *La Cour de justice appelle une interprétation restrictive de la notion de restriction par l'objet*, CONTRATS CONCURRENCE CONSOMMATION (Nov. 2014), comm. 250.

231 Case C-67/13 P, Groupement des cartes bancaires, ECLI:EU:C:2014:2204, para. 90.

232 Case T-491/07 RENV, Groupement des cartes bancaires, ECLI:EU:T:2016:379, para. 90.

233 In this regard, *see* L. Idot, *Mesures tarifaires d'adhésion à un groupement et effets anticoncurrentiels*, EUROPE (Aug. 2016), comm. 295.

234 Case C-413/14 P, Intel, ECLI:EU:C:2017:632; Case T-286/09 RENV, Intel, ECLI:EU:T:2022:19.

235 D. Bosco, *L'arrêt Intel, un 'grand arrêt'?*, CONTRATS CONCURRENCE CONSOMMATION (Nov. 2017), comm. 227: according to the author, the jurisprudential shift lies in the fact that rebates were prohibited per se under the *Hoffmann-La Roche* judgment, whereas the *Intel* case requires an assessment of their exclusionary effects. In our view, the notion of "per se" prohibition is misleading (*see infra*, no. 320): conduct is never sanctioned in the abstract, and if a company puts forward an argument that casts doubt on whether the practice constitutes an infringement, it is up to the Court to respond, as the burden of proof is reversed. On this subject, *see infra*, no. 321.

236 A. P. Komninos, *Intel: The ECJ Finally Speaks – Time to Listen*, 4 COMPETITION LAW & POLICY DEBATE 42 (2018).

237 In this sense, *see* L. Idot, *Une lecture de l'arrêt Intel*, CONCURRENCES no. 1-2018, art. no. 86053, 15, 19, no. 19.

Court is obliged to respond to the plea raised by the defendant,[238] which implies a thorough examination[239] – since failure to respond to the argument raised would mean that the right to be heard would not be respected.[240]

303. **Conclusion: the alternative between object and effect, or unnecessary complexity in otherwise straightforward reasoning.** The Court's original solutions do not seem to us to have been profoundly amended over time. However, it is clear that, as corporate behavior has become more diversified and complex, economic science can prove useful in identifying those that are likely to be harmful to competition. But this does not imply a shift in the object of proof.[241] At the very most, it is sometimes a matter of integrating economic appraisals into the analysis, as one *element of proof* among others.[242] As for the constituent elements of competition infringements and the reasoning behind their characterization, these have remained unchanged since the 1960s. However, on the theoretical level, confusion is now total: there is an inextricable mix of genres between effect and context (under what conditions does the study of context require the use of a counterfactual analysis, and is this counterfactual analysis the prerogative of the effects approach or can it be used within the framework of an object approach?); the actual, concrete or real effect, and the effect that is only foreseeable, probable or potential (do these different terms lead to the application of a particular regime?); the effect on competition, on the market and on the consumer (which: intermediate or final?); the effect and experience[243] (economic or legal?) – these many uncertainties invite us to take a critical look at the alternative between object and effect.

B. A critical look at the alternative between object and effect in theory

304. **Overview of doctrinal theorizations of the alternative between object and effect.** Since both the "by object" approach and the "by effect" approach require an assessment of context, the question is what distinguishes

238 In this sense, *see* F. Marty, *L'approche plus économique en matière d'application des règles de concurrence* 1, 26 (GREDEG Working Papers Series, No. 2020-16): "[I]t is not certain that this judgment in itself enshrines the Court of Justice's definitive adherence to the more economic approach, in that it simply requires the General Court to consider the parties' arguments as to the conclusions that the rebate scheme was indeed *such* as to exclude from the market a competitor as efficient as Intel" (emphasis added).

239 Case C-413/14 P, Intel, ECLI:EU:C:2017:632, paras. 138–139.

240 Case C-680/20, Unilever Italia, ECLI:EU:C:2023:33, para. 54.

241 On this subject, *see infra*, nos. 313 *et seq.*

242 In this sense, *see infra*, nos. 331–336.

243 *See* in particular Opinion of Advocate General N. Wahl, Case C-67/13 P, Groupement des cartes bancaires, ECLI:EU:C:2014:1958, paras. 55–56.

them – a theoretically delicate point,[244] especially since decision-making practice is not a model of consistency.

A question does arise, however. Do "by object or per se" and "by effect" infringements correspond to two different types of offense: one with the object, the other with the effect of restricting competition[245] – in criminal law terms, one formal, the other material?[246] The idea has already been put forward,[247] and "restriction by object" has sometimes been compared to the "offense of endangerment"[248] or to an "attempted offense."[249] This assertion must be rejected, however, insofar as, as we have shown, competition infringements are formal in nature, and not material.[250] The Court's settled case law also establishes, contrary to the Commission's guidelines and directives, that the effect taken into consideration is only ever the effect, actual or merely potential, on competition, and not on the market or consumers.[251] Consequently, the infringement cannot be an offense of result.

---

244 L. Idot, *La Cour de Justice revient une nouvelle fois sur la notion d''objet anticoncurrentiel'*, Revue des contrats no. 3, 955 (July 1, 2013): the author remarks, with regard to the *Allianz Hungária Biztosító* judgment, that "it is not certain that the national judge is really helped," as "between the definition of the restriction by object … and its identification by means of a multi-criterion method, close to, if not identical to, that which must be followed for the analysis of the effects, there is only one thread"; *adde*, in the same vein, L. Idot, *La distinction restriction de concurrence par objet / restriction de concurrence par effet et article 101 TFUE: Un sujet de* disputatio, *in* Mélanges en l'honneur du professeur Claude Lucas de Leyssac 243, 257–58 (G. Parléani ed., 2018); D. Bosco, *À propos de la notion de restriction par l'objet (encore…)*, Contrats concurrence consommation (Nov. 2019), comm. 183: commenting on Advocate General Bobek's Opinion in the *Budapest Bank* case, the author finds it difficult to separate the contextual analysis required under a restriction by object from that to be undertaken under an effects-based approach – "the contextual analysis recommended [under a restriction by object], because it is of the same nature as the effects-based analysis, does not have specific identifiable content."

245 This is in particular the interpretation of Advocates General Juliane Kokott and Melchior Wathelet, *see* Opinion of Advocate General J. Kokott, Case C-8/08, T-Mobile Netherlands, ECLI:EU:C:2009:110, para. 45; and the Opinion of Advocate General M. Wathelet, Case C-373/14 P, Toshiba Corporation, ECLI:EU:C:2015:427, para. 57.

246 As a reminder, a formal offense (in the broadest sense) is one that can be committed without the occurrence of any result, while a material offense is one that requires a result as a constitutive element.

247 Kovar & Kovar, *L'objet anticoncurrentiel au sens de l'article 101, paragraphe 1, du TFUE: Un objet difficile à identifier*, *op. cit.* at 49 and 59; *adde*, Petit, Droit européen de la concurrence, *op. cit.* at 313–24, nos. 743–764, and esp. at 315, no. 745: "[I]t is possible to envisage the restriction by effect as a 'consequentialist tort', totally distinct from the formal offenses captured by the condition of object."

248 The path was opened up by Juliane Kokott, in her Opinion delivered on Feb. 19, 2009, in Case C-8/08, T-Mobile Netherlands, ECLI:EU:C:2009:110, para. 47. *Adde*, M. Behar-Touchais, *Vers un retour à une conception stricte de la restriction par l'objet*, Concurrences, Workshop of Apr. 17, 2015: *Restriction par objet, restriction par effet: Quelle portée encore accorder à cette distinction?*; Kovar & Kovar, *L'objet anticoncurrentiel au sens de l'article 101, paragraphe 1, du TFUE: Un objet difficile à identifier*, *op. cit.* at 50. However, the comparison is not entirely faithful to criminal theory: unlike agreement offenses, deliberate endangerment offenses do not require the will to achieve the result, but simply the will to engage in dangerous conduct. These two offenses are not of the same nature, and are not subject to the same regime. *See supra*, nos. 233 *et seq.*

249 Cons. conc., *Études thématiques: Objet, effet et intention anticoncurrentiels*, *in* Rapport d'activité 55, 62 (Mar. 30, 2004): the notion of object would be tantamount to "punishing the attempt to undermine competition," but it would be advisable "not to confuse the attempt to undermine competition … with the attempt to conclude an anticompetitive agreement." This idea is hardly in line with the reasoning of criminal law: since an agreement is of the same nature as a criminal conspiracy, it is not, strictly speaking, an attempt, *see supra*, no. 275.

250 *See supra*, nos. 273–274.

251 *See supra*, nos. 277 *et seq.*

Some consider that the alternative "for object or for effect" corresponds to a probative problem. The object would establish a presumption, whereas the effect would require additional proof – the distinction between the two would thus be one of degree rather than of nature[252] – one author having remarked that the effects-based approach could make it possible to "complete" the qualification of restriction by object.[253] The proposition is relevant in theory, but does not faithfully reflect decision-making practice, since the effects-based approach does not systematically correspond to a more thorough analysis than that carried out on the basis of the object-based approach.[254]

Moreover, while most of the doctrine apprehends "object" as a presumption, the question of what this presumption proves is also open to debate. Some see it as a presumption of intent,[255] while others see it as a "presumption of effect on consumers."[256] The latter view, however, makes little sense, as the effect on the market or on consumers is not a constitutive element, and there is no point in presuming it or attempting to prove the contrary.[257]

The distinction between "object" and "effect" thus resembles a delicate crest line, whose theorization is subject to abundant case law[258] and

---

252 S. Gervasoni, *Une différence de degré plus que de nature, qui impose une approche prudente et pragmatique de la distinction*, Concurrences, Workshop of Apr. 17, 2015: *Restriction par objet, restriction par effet: Quelle portée encore accorder à cette distinction?*

253 C. Prieto, *La généralisation de l'analyse fondée sur les effets*, 239 Petites affiches 8 (Nov. 29, 2007). In the same vein, with reference to American law: M.-A. Frison-Roche & J.-C. Roda, Droit de la concurrence 362 (2nd ed. 2022), no. 447: "The whole question surrounding per se prohibition litigation is therefore often about determining which new practices fall into this category."

254 *See supra*, no. 299

255 O. Odudu, *Interpreting Article 81(1): Object as Subjective Intention*, 26 European Law Review 62, 64–71 (2001); Petit, Droit européen de la concurrence, *op. cit.* at 299, no. 722.

256 R. Whish, *Anticompetitive Object vs. Anticompetitive Effects: Does it Really Matter?*, Concurrences no. 2-2012 (New Frontiers of Antitrust Conference – Paris, Feb. 10, 2012), art. no. 45426, 59, 60; *adde*, in the same vein, D. Bailey, *Restrictions of Competition by Object under Article 101 TFEU*, 49 Common Market Law Review 559, 562–63 (2012); L. Peeperkorn, *Defining 'By Object' Restrictions*, Concurrences no. 3-2015, art. no. 74812, 40, 42, no. 12 & 44, no. 22: "It would be prudent to base the classification of a particular type of restriction as a by object restriction on sufficient experience or other empirical evidence that the restriction in question will normally have an *overall negative effect on competition and consumers*" (emphasis added); R. Nazzini, *Article 81 EC Between time Present and Time Past: A Normative Critique of Restriction of Competition in EU Law*, 43 Common Market Law Review 497, 504 (2006).

257 This is borne out by the Opinion of Advocate General J. Kokott, Case C-8/08, T-Mobile Netherlands, ECLI:EU:C:2009:110, para. 45: "[T]he prohibition on 'infringement by object' may not be interpreted as meaning that an anti-competitive object gives rise merely to some kind of presumption of unlawfulness which may be rebutted, however, if in the specific case no negative consequences for the operation of the market can be demonstrated."

258 *Ex multis*: Case C-8/08, T-Mobile Netherlands, ECLI:EU:C:2009:343, para. 43: "[A] concerted practice pursues an anti-competitive object … where, according to its content and objectives and having regard to its legal and economic context, it is *capable* in an individual case of resulting in the prevention, restriction or distortion of competition within the common market. It is not necessary for there to be actual prevention, restriction or distortion of competition or a direct link between the concerted practice and consumer prices" (emphasis added); Case C-501/06 P, GlaxoSmithKline, ECLI:EU:C:2009:610, para. 63: the Court held that the Court of First Instance had erred in law by making the existence of the anticompetitive object of the agreement subject to proof that it entailed disadvantages for consumers; Case C-403/08, Football Association Premier League, ECLI:EU:C:2011:631, paras. 134–146; Case C-32/11, Allianz Hungária Biztosító, ECLI:EU:C:2013:160, paras. 31–51; Case C-429/11 P, Gosselin, ECLI:EU:C:2013:463,

abundant commentary[259] – the "never-ending story"[260] of a tightrope walker in search of stability.

Let us rise above this wave of complexity to put forward a hypothesis: perhaps this distinction is impossible to draw *in abstracto*,[261] as it merely reflects an evidentiary rule that is not only not specific to the law of anticompetitive practices, but also does not require the object/effect alternative to exist.

This conjecture leads us into another terrain: that of meaning. Since neither the courts nor the doctrine has succeeded in conferring a clear content on the alternative, this could mean that it is devoid of one. It would be the fruit of a twofold contingency: poor legislative drafting, into which the Commission subsequently inserted itself to introduce, like a stowaway, a doctrine contrary to jurisprudence. The alternative is thus a commonplace that continues to be invoked out of habit, even though it is illogical and not based on any real reasoning.

---

paras. 40–57; Case C-286/13 P, Dole Food Company, ECLI:EU:C:2015:184, paras. 111–134: the Court considers that the General Court was entitled to find that the contested pre-pricing communications had the object of restricting competition insofar as they make it possible to reduce uncertainty as to competitors' behavior; Case C-172/14, ING Pensii, ECLI:EU:C:2015:484 paras. 26–56; Case C-373/14 P, Toshiba, ECLI:EU:C:2016:26, paras. 23-36; Case C-307/18, Generics (UK), ECLI:EU:C:2020:52, para. 111 on "restriction by object," and para. 122 on "restriction by effect"; Case C-228/18, Budapest Bank, ECLI:EU:C:2020:265, paras. 33–44 on whether conduct can have both the object *and* effect of restricting competition (the answer is positive), and paras. 51–86 for yet another review of case law on the criteria for qualifying as a restriction "by object." For an analysis of these rulings, *see* Petit, Droit européen de la concurrence, *op. cit.* at 296–329, nos. 718–777.

259 In addition to the doctrinal references already cited, *see* in particular: O. Odudu, *Interpreting Article 81(1): The Object Requirement Revisited*, 26 European Law Review 379 (2001); A. Jones, *Left Behind by Modernisation? Restrictions by Object under Article 101(1)*, 6 European Competition Law Journal 649 (2010); C. Grynfogel, *La notion d'"objet anticoncurrentiel' et la sécurité juridique des entreprises*, Revue de jurisprudence de droit des affaires nos. 8–9, 5 (2014), chron.; L. Vogel, *Une nouvelle venue sur la scène du droit de la concurrence: La restriction par objet*, Contrats concurrence consommation (May 2015), dossier 2: according to the author, the authorities have developed on the basis of "restriction by object" an "entirely new concept that falls fully within the framework of the effects theory, as the expression 'restriction by object' indicates." We admit to not understanding this reasoning. *Adde*, N. Petit, *La rationalisation au long cours de la restriction de concurrence par 'objet' dans la jurisprudence de la Cour de justice de l'Union européenne*, AJ Contrats d'affaires – Concurrence – Distribution 422 (2015); L. Idot, *Les suites de l'arrêt dit 'des cartes bancaires': La distinction 'restriction de concurrence par objet / restriction par effet' toujours au cœur des débats sur l'article 101 TFUE*, RTD Eur. 817 (2016); B. Amory, G. Van De Walle & N. A. Smuha, *The Object-Effect Dichotomy and the Requirement of Harm to Competition: On the Road to Clarity After* Cartes Bancaires*?*, *in* The Notion of Restriction of Competition: Revisiting the Foundations of Antitrust Enforcement in Europe 65 (D. Gerard, M. Merola & B. Meyring eds., 2017); T. Schrepel, *Pour une suppression en droit de la concurrence des restrictions 'par objet': L'innovation juridique peut aussi être conceptuelle*, *in* L'innovation juridique et judiciaire: Méthodologie et perspectives 321 (A. Masson & H. Bouthinon-Dumas ed., 2019); F. Olbrechts, *The Concept of Restriction of Competition 'By Object': An Endless Debate*, Competition Forum no. 0011 (2021); D. Bosco, *La Cour de justice confirme son approche des restrictions par l'objet applicable aux accords de règlement amiable dans l'affaire du Citalopram*, Contrats concurrence consommation (May 2021), comm. 87.

260 D. Bosco, *Restriction 'par l'objet': Une histoire sans fin*, Contrats concurrence consommation (June 2020), comm. 103: the author notes that the fact that the "restriction by object" litigation has not abated is perhaps "a sign that the Court has so far failed to give a clear direction to its case law," and doubts that the *Budapest Bank* judgment will make a useful contribution to this, as "many key passages are unclear and add to the impression of vagueness conveyed by the concept."

261 In this sense, J.-B. Blaise, *Ententes*, Répertoire de droit européen (Sept. 2017), no. 495: "The object is determined in relation to the economic and legal context of the agreement. Determining the object of the agreement is therefore a matter for the individual case, which presents itself differently in each particular case. In some cases, the restriction of competition is obvious from the terms of the agreement or the content of the decision. …In other cases, on the contrary, the determination of the restrictive object of competition requires more detailed research."

To test this hypothesis, we need to turn once again to history and comparative law, to discover where the expression comes from, how it is used in other disciplines, and how doctrine outside competition law views it.

305. **In search of the meaning of the alternative "for object or for effect": the origin of the expression, and its use outside competition law.** We know that the expression "for object or for effect" originated, in the law of anticompetitive practices, in article 59 *bis* of the French decree of 1953, a hastily drafted text that the Treaty of Rome nevertheless reproduced almost identically, despite the interpretive difficulties it gave rise to from the outset.[262] The alternative seems incongruous to the jurist,[263] as a single legal qualification is based on a single causality criterion: either the text requires the will to achieve a result, or it does not – and even when it does not make it necessary, the law only ever holds an individual responsible for the normal, and therefore foreseeable, consequences of their actions.

Readers will not be surprised to learn that this alternative originated in administrative law – a creation whose object (and effect?) was undoubtedly to capture reality in all its dimensions, for the sake of "efficiency."[264] Although it was initially confined to this field,[265] its success was subsequently exported to other domains, so that it is now present in virtually all areas of law – from labor law[266] to consumer law,[267] from crimi-

262 *See supra*, nos. 109–110.

263 As a reminder, in its legal sense, the word "effect" means: "consequence not sought by the author of the act"; while the word "object" refers to the "purpose pursued," *see* R. Rouquette, Dictionnaire droit administratif 293 and 542 (2002).

264 The same applies to the alternative between intent and negligence, which is found in many European law regulations – the European Union having borrowed heavily from French administrative law. In this respect, *see supra*, no. 206.

265 It is found in numerous administrative law texts, *see*, *e.g.*, art. L. 2224-31 of the General Code of Territorial Collectivities: "Actions relating to energy savings by final consumers of gas or electricity … must have the *object or effect* of avoiding or deferring the extension or reinforcement of public distribution networks"; art. L. 77-10-23 of the Code of Administrative Justice: "Any clause having the *object or effect* of prohibiting a person from taking part in a group action is deemed unwritten"; art. R. 5142-5 of the General Code of Public Property: "[N]o act whose *object or effect* is to engage the liability of the local authority or group of local authorities to third parties in its capacity as concessionaire may be set up against the State"; art. 187(2) of the General Tax Code: "The rate of withholding tax … is set at 75% … unless the debtor provides proof that the distribution of these products in this State or territory has *neither the object nor the effect* of enabling them to be located in such a State or territory *for tax evasion purposes*"; art. L. 442-9 of the Town Planning Code: "Any regulatory provision whose *object or effect* is to prohibit or restrict the right to build or to affect the use or purpose of the building … ceases to have effect"; art. L. 3511-3 of the Public Health Code: "Any sponsorship operation is prohibited when its *object or effect* is direct or indirect propaganda or advertising in favor of tobacco." *Adde*, in the words of the Conseil d'État (Council of State): CE, Nov. 21, 2001, no. 238214, Zhary (Fr.): "The referral to the interim relief judge ("juge du référé-liberté") must not have the *object or effect* of compensating for the litigant's omission to refer to the administrative judge a recourse on the merits within the allotted time"; CE, Apr. 4, 2019, no. 429370, Hamon (Fr.): "If certain discriminations may, given the *motives* that inspire them or the *effects* they produce on the exercise of such freedom" (emphasis added).

266 Art. L. 1152-1 of the French Labor Code: "No employee shall be subjected to repeated acts of mental harassment whose *object or effect* is to degrade their working conditions" (emphasis added).

267 Art. L. 132-1 of the French Consumer Code: "In contracts concluded between professionals and non-professionals or consumers, clauses are considered *abusive* if their *object or effect* is to create, to the detriment of the non-professional or consumer, a significant imbalance in the rights and obligations of the parties to the contract" (emphasis added).

nal law[268] to European Union law,[269] and even in certain international conventions.[270] Surprisingly, this highly inelegant "style clause" is also included in provisions that clearly punish intentional conduct *stricto sensu*, such as electoral fraud[271] and harassment.

306. **The perspective of criminal law doctrine on the alternative between the object and the effect in the incriminating text of the offense of harassment.** Specifically, the introduction of this phrasing into the definition of harassment in 2002 ("repeated remarks or behaviors having the *object or effect* of degrading working conditions"[272]) did not occur without controversy: criminal lawyers are accustomed to being sensitive to problems relating to the mental element. Some considered the wording to be "a bit convoluted,"[273] while others stressed that the judge would have to "use their imagination to give content" to the incrimination – *a priori* suggesting that the offense could be either formal or material in nature,[274] and Philippe Conte legitimately felt that this was "scribbled legislation."[275] Describing the alternative as "troubling," the author argues not only that "these difficulties in the form of argumentation owe everything to a highly ambiguous text," but also that they are "the fruit of dismaying reflection," given that the notion of an offense being committed either intentionally or recklessly is, to say the least,

268 Art. 222-33-2 of the French Penal Code criminalizes "the fact of harassing others through repeated remarks or behaviors having the *object or effect* of degrading working conditions" (emphasis added).

269 Council Regulation (EC) No. 423/2007 of Apr. 19, 2007, Concerning Restrictive Measures against Iran, 2007 O.J. (L 103) 1, art. 7(4): "The participation, *knowingly* and *intentionally*, in activities the *object* or *effect* of which is, directly or indirectly, to circumvent the measures referred to in paragraphs 1, 2 and 3 shall be prohibited." This text is highly inconsistent: since the terms "knowingly" and "intentionally" refer to the expression "the object or effect of which" as a whole, such wording should imply that even the effect must have been intended – making its presence superfluous. However, this was not the interpretation adopted by the Court of Justice, which, following the opinion of the Advocate General, held that mere negligence was sufficient to characterize the infringement, *see* Case C-72/11, Mohsen Afrasiabi, ECLI:EU:C:2011:874, paras. 66–67; *adde*, Opinion of Advocate General Y. Bot, Case C-72/11, Mohsen Afrasiabi, ECLI:EU:C:2011:73, paras. 78–95: he does not fail to conclude that, in the present case, the respondent "was perfectly well aware that he was committing an act contrary to the Regulation."

270 United Nations, Convention on the Elimination of All Forms of Discrimination against Women, New York, Dec. 18, 1979, art. 1: "For the purposes of the present Convention, the term 'discrimination against women' shall mean any distinction, exclusion or restriction made on the basis of sex which has the *effect or purpose* of impairing or nullifying the recognition, enjoyment or exercise by women ... human rights and fundamental freedoms... ." (emphasis added).

271 Art. L. 118-4 of the French Electoral Code: "Seized of a challenge to the election, the election judge may declare ineligible, for a maximum period of three years, the candidate who has carried out *fraudulent maneuvers whose object or effect* is to undermine the sincerity of the ballot" (emphasis added). It would be astonishing, to say the least, to consider that a fraudulent maneuver can be the result of no fraudulent intent!

272 Art. 222-33-2 of the French Penal Code (emphasis added), quoted *supra*, no. 305. It should be noted that the definition of sexual harassment, contained in art. 222-33 of the French Penal Code, which covers similar conduct (the means are identical, only the aim differs), does not contain such an alternative, and has therefore not given rise to any difficulty of interpretation with regard to the mental element. M.-L. Rassat, *Agressions sexuelles*, JurisClasseur Pénal Code (Feb. 2023), fasc. 20, no. 147.

273 C. Duvert, *Harcèlement moral*, JurisClasseur Pénal Code (Dec. 2022), fasc. 20, no. 3; *adde*, in the same vein, B. Platel & T. Viala, *Le fabuleux destin du concept de harcèlement moral*, JCP E no. 20, 762 (May 16, 2002).

274 V. Malabat, *À la recherche du sens du droit pénal du harcèlement*, Droit social 491 (2003).

275 P. Conte, *Harcèlement moral – Éléments matériel et moral*, Droit pénal (Apr. 2016), comm. 58.

a singular construct.[276] Jean Pradel and Michel Danti-Juan considered that the causality described by the article was "hypothetical, to say the least," as the mention of the effect suggests "that the legislator is relying here on the divinatory power of judges and that, consequently, arbitrariness is not far off."[277] Moreover, given that harassment is a formal offense requiring, as a constitutive element, no result distinct from the conduct itself,[278] mention of the mere "object" or "purpose" of the conduct would have been amply sufficient.[279]

307. **The alternatives "for object or for effect" and "per se" or "by effect": alternatives that run counter to legal logic.** For the same reason that led eminent criminal lawyers to consider that the effect is the intruder in harassment cases, it must be admitted that it is superfluous in anticompetitive practices law: the alternative could be replaced by another, more readable wording, without altering the long-established solutions.[280] To see this, we first need to identify the two possible meanings of the effects-based approach, before explaining why they are contrary to legal logic.

308. **The two possible meanings of "effect" in anticompetitive practices law.** Two distinct meanings can be attached to the notion of effect.

First – and this seems to be the definition currently adopted by the majority of economists, part of the doctrine and the Commission – the effects-based approach involves determining *the harmful consequences of practices on the market*: conduct will only be deemed anticompetitive if it has a concrete effect on the market (lower quality, higher prices,

---

276 *Id.* The author also notes that "this difference between the various forms of harassment is completely absurd in principle, because, in the legislator's logic (so to speak), nothing justifies that the repression should depend, here, on an actual infringement of the victim's rights, whereas, there, that consequence is treated as irrelevant."

277 J. Pradel & M. Danti-Juan, Droit pénal spécial: Droit commun, droit des affaires 343 (8th ed. 2020), no. 468.

278 *See*, in particular, the clear and unequivocal reasoning that justified the cassation, Cass. crim., Dec. 6, 2011, no. 10-82.266 (Fr.): the Cour de cassation ruled that the court of appeal had "added conditions to the law that it does not include," by "holding that the consequences of the deterioration in working conditions had to be proven, whereas *the mere possibility of this deterioration is sufficient to constitute the offense of moral harassment*" (emphasis added). *Adde*, more recently and in the same vein, Cass. crim., Jan. 23, 2018, no. 16-87.709 (Fr.). Case law also seems to deduce criminal intent from the actual occurrence of such deterioration (which seems difficult to characterize, however, since it refers to a psychological or health condition). *See*, for example, Cass. crim., Sept. 2, 2020, no. 19-82471 (Fr.), comm. E. Dreyer, *Harceler la fille, c'est aussi harceler la mère*, Gazette du Palais no. 40, 47 (Nov. 17, 2020).

279 In this sense, *see* M. Wagner, Les effets de l'infraction: Essai d'une théorie générale 143 (2011), no. 345, and more generally, for a critique of this article, at 141–44, nos. 341–345. In the author's view, it is difficult to accept that a text of incrimination could have provided, for the same qualification, two distinct forms of offense (one requiring a result, the other not). Marion Wagner considers that the effect in this context refers to "a mere consequence of the conduct," as "the deterioration in working conditions is in itself contained in the repeated conduct of the agent," and that there is therefore no need to require proof of a result distinct from the conduct itself. By way of analogy, we will develop the idea that the restriction of competition is in itself contained in the anticompetitive behavior *infra*, nos. 368 *et seq.*

280 For a proposal for new wording, *see* no. 503.

foreclosure of a competitor, etc.),[281] is not "efficient" or harms "consumer welfare."[282]

According to a second interpretation, the effect can be understood as the result produced by a behavior, not on the market or consumers, but on the competitive process[283] – i.e., *the influence of a behavior on the competitive process*. The effects-based approach would then require us to analyze whether competition has actually been restricted, or was likely to be restricted, even though this was not the aim of the practice in question. The effect would thus refer to *the unintended consequence – neither foreseen nor intended –* of a behavior on competition: a company adopts a certain course of action, which produces an effect on competition that could not have been foreseen. The notion of "effect" would make it possible to punish conduct for its unforeseeable consequences.

309. **Criticism of the first definition of "effect": it is contrary to case law and compromises legal certainty.** The first definition of "effect" – the effect on the market – although present in doctrinal debates and omnipresent in Commission communications, must be excluded from the outset. Indeed, it is fundamentally incompatible with the established case law according to which the result of anticompetitive practices is not a constitutive element of the infringements, and therefore does not have to be demonstrated.[284] Moreover, proof of a result would be extremely difficult, if not virtually impossible, to provide.[285] Moreover, little progress has been made since Bentham's time on the method of calculating the greatest happiness of the greatest number.[286] Such an analysis is highly speculative, if not outright divinatory[287] – and for that reason alone, it is disqualified by the legal system, as being irreconcilable with the principle of foreseeability.[288]

---

281 This is the isolated analysis of the General Court in the *Servier* case, which was however sharply criticized, in our view rightly so, by Advocate General Juliane Kokott. *See* Case T-691/14, Servier, ECLI:EU:T:2018:922, paras. 1107–1139; and Opinion of Advocate General J. Kokott, Case C-176/19 P, Servier, ECLI:EU:C:2022:576, paras. 254–330.

282 As one author has rightly remarked, "[t]he proponents of a 'more economic' and less 'formalist' approach seem to want to give the notion of 'effect' on competition a different meaning: from now on, the effect is no longer meant to concern competition understood as an ideal process…, but quantitative variations in the measurable parameters of a market's functioning (notably price levels or producer or consumer surplus)," *see* R. Maulin, *L'approche par les effets en droit de la concurrence: Le devoir d'inventaire*, CONCURRENCES no. 3-2015, art. no. 73845, 24, 26, no. 9.

283 *Ex multis, see* P. Marsden & P. Whelan, *"Consumer Detriment" and its Application in EC and UK Competition Law*, 27 EUROPEAN COMPETITION LAW REVIEW 569, 584 (2006): the authors rightly consider that neither the actual nor the potential effect of the disputed conduct on consumer welfare is required or even taken into consideration by case law.

284 *See supra*, nos. 278 *et seq.*

285 To be convinced of this, it is enough to refer to 19th-century case law: article 419 of the 1810 Penal Code required, as a constitutive element, that the judge provide proof of an effect on prices, which in almost all cases failed to establish an offense, *see supra*, nos. 99–100.

286 *See supra*, nos. 91 *et seq.* on the birth of this theory; nos.119 *et seq.* on its reception by modern economic analysis.

287 This speculative character is recognized by economists themselves, *see supra*, nos.114 *et seq.*

288 On the principle of foreseeability in competition law, *see infra*, nos. 461 *et seq.*

310. **Criticism of the second meaning of "effect": it adds nothing to the "object" if the effect is foreseeable.** The second meaning of "effect" – the effect on competition – is, at first glance, less directly conflicting with the spirit of the texts and case law. But it is no less illogical. Indeed, we know that in criminal law, and more specifically in business criminal law, the natural and thus foreseeable consequence of conduct systematically assumes that the result was deliberately sought.[289] Consequently, it is not necessary for a competition authority to prove that the restrictive effect was actually intended: it is sufficient to demonstrate that the conduct was liable to lead, or did in fact lead, to a certain result, in order to presume that this was its purpose, and therefore that this was the intent of the undertaking concerned.[290] The notion of effect therefore appears superfluous, since even if it were absent, the legal regime would be identical – the result presuming intent when it is foreseeable.

311. **Criticism of the second meaning of "effect": it does not allow unforeseeable effects to be sanctioned, and therefore adds nothing to the "object."** On the contrary, if the restrictive effect on competition is not *objectively foreseeable*, it cannot, under any circumstances, be attributed to the company. To admit the contrary would be tantamount to agreeing to punish a company for the unforeseeable consequences of its actions,[291] and the characterization of infringements would then become "a matter of pure chance, whose amoral nature would be intolerable."[292] This would also be in direct conflict with the principle of fault-based liability and the principle of legality, both of which are recognized as applicable in the law of anticompetitive practices.[293] It follows that the effect does not make it possible to punish acts that the object would be incapable of apprehending, and therefore does not broaden the scope of the offense, which makes it lose all raison d'être.

---

289 *See supra*, nos. 156–157 in criminal law.

290 In this sense, *see* R. Joliet, The Rule of Reason in Antitrust Law: American, German and Common Market Laws in Comparative Perspective 119 n.2 (1967): "As the conspirators must be regarded as intending the consequences of their action, intent will be inferred when there is an anticompetitive effect." "This is why it is difficult to perceive how an actual restraint of competition could be produced without intent." In our view, this reasoning is only valid when the restrictive effect in question is foreseeable.

291 What the doctrine rejects in unison, *see ex multis*: L. Focsaneanu, *Pour objet ou pour effet*, 87 Revue du marché commun 862, 864 (Jan. 1966): a restriction of competition is "not imputable to undertakings … when it has occurred against all probability and contrary to the experience of everyday life, and consequently could not have been foreseen"; B. Goldman, A. Lyon-Caen & L. Vogel, Droit commercial européen 385 (5th ed. 1994): while the probability of restrictive effects may be sufficient to establish an infringement, these effects must be objectively foreseeable; R. Blasselle, I Traité de droit européen de la concurrence 571 and 373, resp. (2002): the restriction of competition must "appear to be the reasonable consequence of the substance of the agreement," without necessarily having to "refer not to the parties' concrete forecast, but rather to what could reasonably have been foreseen."

292 L. Focsaneanu, La jurisprudence de la Cour de justice des communautés européennes en matière de concurrence: Les règles applicables aux entreprises (Articles 85 et 86 du Traité de Rome) 168 (1977). In the same vein, *see* Focsaneanu, *Pour objet ou pour effet*, *op. cit.* at 869: if the authorities could rely exclusively on the effect, the infringement could be characterized even though the parties "could not even foresee that their agreement could produce such consequences. A change in market conditions would suffice to render the parties' agreement unlawful… . A large number of commercial contracts would thus be plunged into a state of permanent uncertainty, their validity at the mercy of changing market conditions."

293 *See infra*, nos. 461 *et seq.*

To salvage the reasoning, it would be possible to appeal to the notion of negligence,[294] which would allow a company to be sanctioned for an unintended anticompetitive effect.[295] But, as a reminder, negligence also implies the will to engage in unlawful conduct,[296] and wrongful conduct only exists in the presence of a prior obligation and a *material causal link* between the conduct and the prejudicial result,[297] both of which are lacking here for two reasons. By definition, no prior obligation exists when the application of the "rule" – which no longer deserves the name – depends solely on the contingent and uncertain consequences of an act. What is more, negligent offenses are only constituted when the damage has actually occurred: unlike competition infringements, they are offenses of result. Precisely what justifies holding an agent liable for the damage they have caused without having intended to do so is the possibility, in the presence of *actual damage*, of inferring with any claim to certainty, or at least beyond a reasonable doubt, the link between damage and wrongful conduct. Given that anticompetitive behavior, on the one hand, is not an offense of result, and, on the other hand, only ever produces virtual damage, because it undermines a value[298] – competition – it is possible to make every conceivable conjecture without having the ability to check their veracity. For this reason, the characterization of a restriction of competition must be substantiated and not merely hypothetical, but *probable* – and therefore foreseeable.

312. **Conclusion: the paradox of the alternative between object and effect.** Since the notion of effect cannot, as we have just established, mean anything other than the *natural consequence* of the conduct adopted by a company, it is thereby stripped of any function: either the effect is not the natural consequence of the conduct, and thus cannot ground any liability; or the effect is the natural consequence of the conduct,[299] and it may be presumed to have been intentionally pursued.[300]

Either the effect has no effect at all; or the effect adds nothing to the object.

---

294 We have already shown how this concept is superfluous in the law of anticompetitive practices, *supra*, nos. 268–269.

295 However, this was the interpretation adopted by the Commission Technique des Ententes on the basis of the French Ordinance of 1945, as well as by a number of legal scholars, *see supra*, no. 110, and the doctrinal references cited.

296 *See supra*, no. 195.

297 Regarding the regime of "offenses of lack of foresight," *see supra*, no. 239.

298 *See supra*, no. 290.

299 We will also see, *infra*, nos. 368 *et seq.*, that the alternative between object and effect, by dissociating anticompetitive behavior and the restriction of competition, establishes an artificial causal link between one and the other.

300 A parallel with the offense of harassment is illuminating here. According to Philippe Conte, the legislator introduced into the definition of the offense the alternative between the object and the effect, in order to "nullify the usual defense of harassers, consisting in claiming that they did not intend the consequences of their acts," this initiative being however "useless since, by virtue of the principle of intimate conviction, the usual rules of evidence obviously already enabled the judge to overcome such denials," *see* P. Conte, *Quelques observations sur la distinction des règles substantielles et des règles de preuve en droit pénal*, *in* MÉLANGES EN L'HONNEUR DE PHILIPPE THÉRY: LES COUTURES DU DROIT 195, 201 (2022).

In short, the opposition – now considered established dogma in competition law – between "by object" or "per se" infringements, and "by effect" infringements, only requires, on examination, the application of a classic line of reasoning, which, far from being specific to the discipline, is to be found in every trial, and simply stems from the existence of a variation in the evidential burden, making it possible to characterize the same infringement, which is a function of the particular circumstances of each case.

II. Theorizing the function of the "effects-based" approach

313. **The function of the "effects-based" approach: a higher burden of proof, an identical object of proof.** *De lege lata*, the "effects-based" approach implies nothing other than a higher standard of proof. However, the expression "by effects" seems to imply that, when the competition authority engages in such an analysis, it must prove the existence of anticompetitive effects. However, this is not the case: the object of proof remains, in all cases, the "*capacity* to restrict competition" – which amounts to demonstrating the intent to restrict competition (**A**). It follows that the "effects-based" approach *does not shift the focus of proof*, but rather *increases the burden of proof* on the prosecuting authority in the case of conduct whose capacity to restrict competition is not obvious (**B**).

Given that such reasoning is not exclusive to the law of anticompetitive practices, but is generally applied in every trial, without the need for any written rule to specify it, and that it also leads to confusion as to the constituent elements of infringements, we consider, *de lege ferenda*, that it would be appropriate to stop using the term "effects-based approach" and, consequently, to abandon the alternative between the object and the effect.[301]

A. Identical evidentiary requirements: intent to restrict competition

314. **Is the approach *exclusively* based on effects a myth?** It is topical to note that doctrinal debates are concentrated on the method of designating restrictions "by object," while they remain rather silent, or at the very least evasive, when it comes to mentioning effects-based cases – some attribute this discretion to the difficult-to-operate nature, at the jurisdictional level, of such an approach.[302] The search for a decision basing a finding of infringement on effects alone leads to failure, so much so

301 *See infra*, no. 503.

302 R. Maulin, *L'approche par les effets en droit de la concurrence: Le devoir d'inventaire*, Concurrences no. 3-2015, art. no. 73845, 24, 35–37, nos. 59–66.

that the effects-based approach seems, at the end of the quest, to be the stuff of myth.[303]

Thus, after 2003, the *Visa* case is one of the few, if not the only, in which the Commission has engaged *exclusively* in an "effects-based" approach.[304] On the eve of its demonstration, the authority announced that it is about to establish that "the Rule as applied to Morgan Stanley prevented Morgan Stanley from entering the UK credit and deferred debit/charge card acquiring market," as such behavior "had *potential anticompetitive effects* in that market."[305] Let's ask ourselves: does the fact that, in this decision, the Commission did not, in line with its previous and consistent practice,[306] write "having as its object and effect," but merely mentioned effects, change the reasoning in any way?

This appears to be a classic case: the authority carried out a contextual analysis to establish that the practice in question had unjustifiably prevented a new competitor from entering the market. Once this has been demonstrated, does considering that this was the "effect" or "object" of the behavior have any impact on the outcome of the dispute? It is fair to doubt that: if this is the objective, but it has not been achieved, this is enough to convict; if this is the potential effect, it appears foreseeable, and can therefore be considered as having been intentionally pursued. In short, the alternative does not change the demonstration, nor the object of the proof: the ability to restrict competition.

With regard to abuse of a dominant position, although a distinction is usually made between practices prohibited per se and those involving an analysis of "effects," the point is the same: the two can easily merge into one another without this changing either the reasoning followed or the object of proof of the infringements – the Court of First Instance having, moreover, on several occasions recognized that the object merged with the effect on the basis of article 102 TFEU.[307]

If object and effect are not as distinct as they appear, they have nonetheless become a kind of imaginary creature, lending themselves to metaphor. Advocate General Bobek, for example, compared the alternative, not to the Loch Ness monster, but to a finless fish floating in the air, exhaling the scent of lilies. His tale is enlightening: it aims to explain why certain practices appear to be obviously anticompetitive, while others require

303 The same observation was made by Véronique Sélinsky with regard to the decision-making practice of the Commission Technique des Ententes, *see supra*, no. 129.

304 *See supra*, no. 299.

305 Comm. EC, Oct. 3, 2007, COMP/D1/37860, Visa International, para. 76.

306 *See supra*, no. 296.

307 Case T-203/01, Manufacture française des pneumatiques Michelin, ECLI:EU:T:2003:250, para. 241: "[F]or the purposes of applying Article 82 EC, establishing the anti-competitive object and the anti-competitive effect are one and the same thing." The formula is repeated in the following rulings, *ex multis*: Case T-340/03, France Télécom, ECLI:EU:T:2007:22, para. 195; Case T-286/09, Intel, ECLI:EU:T:2014:547, para. 203.

in-depth examination to reveal their true nature.[308] That said, if there is to be any dissection of the beast, it is invariably aimed at establishing that the floating, fragrant creature *is* indeed a fish, not that it *has the effect of* being a fish...[309]

In order to convince ourselves of this, it is relevant to reason by analogy with criminal law, making a detour via the offense of poisoning, before demonstrating that proof of competition infringements follows exactly the same logic, even though the text incriminating poisoning does not contain the alternative between object and effect.

315. **Illustration based on poisoning: strawberry juice flavored with arsenic.** Like anticompetitive practices, the offense of poisoning belongs to the category of formal offenses.[310] It does not require the death of the victim in order to be characterized, just as competition infringements do not require the demonstration of a result on the market.[311] On the other hand, both do require the use of a means "likely to," "capable of," or "liable to" causing death[312] or restricting competition, although this means is not exhaustively defined by the legislator. Using the example of poisoning to illustrate the alternative between object and effect, we can see that the reasoning followed in competition law is in no way different from that of criminal law – except that the latter is logical, straightforward, and thus easier to grasp. To illustrate this, let's set the scene. An individual hands their friend a glass of arsenic-laced strawberry nectar.

316. **Half strawberry juice, half arsenic: poisoning established *prima facie*.** Let us imagine two extreme cases. Either the glass contains only fruit juice: there is no poisoning, because no one dies from drinking such a beverage; or the glass is half-filled with a powerful, tasteless, odorless poison – arsenic – and poisoning is obvious. In this case, all the public prosecutor has to do is provide evidence of the conduct – the administration of such a cocktail – to prove the material and mental elements of the offense.

---

308 Opinion of Advocate General Bobek, Case C-228/18, Budapest Bank, ECLI:EU:C:2019:678, para. 51: "Simplified to a metaphorical extreme, if it looks like a fish and it smells like a fish, one can assume that it is fish. Unless, at the first sight, there is something rather odd about this particular fish, such as that it has no fins, it floats in the air, or it smells like a lily, no detailed dissection of that fish is necessary in order to qualify it as such. If, however, there is something out of the ordinary about the fish in question, it may still be classified as a fish, but only after a detailed examination of the creature in question."

309 We will demonstrate *infra*, nos. 368 *et seq.*, that the alternative between object and effect introduces a causal relationship that does not exist between the anticompetitive behavior and the restriction of competition – which explains why, just as it is absurd to write that a strange fish "has the effect of being a fish," the reasoning consisting in saying that "such behavior has the effect of restricting competition" is devoid of logic.

310 In this sense, *see supra*, no. 272.

311 As we have already demonstrated *supra*, nos. 277 *et seq.*

312 One criminal law specialist calls this criterion the "condition of effectiveness" of the means employed, which is reminiscent of competitive vocabulary... *See* A. Prothais, Tentative et attentat 170 (1985), nos. 246–247. The author notes, in particular, that the difficulty of the question "stems from the fact that one must evaluate the lethal character [of the substance], without being able to refer to its actual lethal effect, since the poisoning is consumed without waiting for the result" – a well-known problem in the law of anticompetitive practices.

317. **A drop of arsenic added to a glass: the need to *demonstrate* the ability to cause death to establish poisoning.** Let's now consider a more subtle hypothesis. The individual slips only a drop of poison into the glass. The question arises as to whether the quantity of arsenic is sufficient to be *capable* of causing death.[313] Given that the average lethal dose is 1.5 mg/kg body weight, the question would have to be asked whether it was large enough to be lethal, taking into account the context: 33 mg may be enough to kill a 50 kg individual, but not an 80 kg person. If the conduct – introducing poison into a glass – is *prima facie* a means likely to cause death, in certain cases it will be necessary to take into account the *circumstances of the case* in order to verify whether the conduct in question was genuinely *liable to achieve the intended objective.*

318. **Fruit juice offered to a person allergic to strawberries: a lethality that only becomes apparent on closer examination of the context.** Returning to our first example: strawberries, pure juice. If *further investigation* reveals that the victim is allergic to strawberries, and that the perpetrator knew this, a seemingly harmless act will suddenly take on a more sinister dimension.[314] Proving the offense would then involve a detailed analysis, which, while it would certainly involve attention to the *likely consequences* of its administration to the victim, would, in fact, be aimed at proving the intent that animated the perpetrator.

319. **Synthesis of the three cases: an identical object of proof – the ability to cause death.** Now that the glass is half-filled with arsenic, there is no need to wonder about the victim's build or the murderer's intent. The offense is proven by the evidence, and the evidence precludes any argument to the contrary.[315] Can you imagine a judge accepting the defendant's excuse of error? On the other hand, if the glass contains only a few drops of arsenic, the question arises as to whether the behavior is likely to cause death. Finally, in the

---

313 It should be noted that there is some debate as to whether or not the administration of an insufficient quantity of poison is sufficient to characterize the offense: some consider such a case to be an impossible crime, likely to receive no criminal qualification, while others believe that if the person prosecuted believed with certainty in the lethal nature of the substance administered, they could be found guilty, *see* H. Angevin, *Atteintes volontaires à la vie*, JurisClasseur Pénal Code (June 2021), no. 96; *adde*, E. Verny, *Empoisonnement*, Répertoire de droit pénal et de procédure pénale (Dec. 2016), nos. 28–30; finally, one author considers that the administration of a substance whose quality is to cause death is sufficient to characterize poisoning, the quantity actually administered being irrelevant, *see* Prothais, Tentative et attentat, *op. cit.* at 171, no. 248. According to Philippe Conte, in order to draw the (delicate) line between the qualifications of poisoning and administration of harmful substances, it is necessary to "take into consideration the potential result of the substances, by virtue of an assessment made *in abstracto*, according to whether the product is merely harmful or capable of causing the death of a victim… . Consequently, if the guilty party causes the victim to absorb a substance capable of causing death, but the victim, who is more resistant than the average, survives, the poisoning will nonetheless be consummated; conversely, if the victim dies due to a particular weakness, where anyone else would have survived, only article 222-15 of the Penal Code will be applicable, especially when the perpetrator did not have homicidal intent. But, precisely, it is appropriate not to take into account only the abstract nature of the substance: the intent of the offender, as with any formal offense, is also important," *see* P. Conte, Droit pénal spécial 15 (6th ed. 2019), no. 15.

314 Verny, *Empoisonnement*, *op. cit.* no. 34: the administration of the same substance to two different people may result in a finding of poisoning if the perpetrator "knows that the substance used is lethal" to the victim, even if its harmlessness to other people has been established.

315 If not, as we have established *infra*, nos. 217–219, defenses based on a lack of will or awareness of wrongdoing.

absence of any poison, i.e., if the behavior appears *a priori* to be harmless, it may still prove to be an offense if the public prosecutor demonstrates that the victim is allergic to the substance administered and that the accused knew this. In all cases, the circumstances must be studied: the analysis is of the same nature and aims to prove the same thing; only its degree varies. Some behaviors leave the intent of the perpetrator beyond doubt, while others are more subtle or ambiguous, requiring in-depth analysis.

In any event, the means employed must invariably be examined in order to provide proof of its *ability to achieve the intended goal*, since it is on this criterion that "all the constituent elements of the offense are defined"[316] – in other words, *if there is no ability, there is no intent.*

Finally, it should be noted that the definition of "lethal substance" has become more complex over time, and has begun to give rise to difficulties of interpretation due to the appearance of new substances, the effects of which are not yet fully known.[317] Scientific expertise, of a medical nature, may therefore be required to establish the lethality of these new substances. However, even if such lethality were scientifically demonstrated, the accused would still have to prove that it was either known to them or, at the very least, *reasonably foreseeable* – for what is not known cannot form the basis of any liability.

320. **Reasoning by analogy between poisoning and competition infringements.** Let's compare our examples with the evidentiary reasoning used in competition law.

Arsenic poisoning would be the equivalent of an anticompetitive practice falling within the "object box,"[318] or prohibited "per se."[319] It is worth mentioning here the origin of the expression "per se": it was first used in 1940 by the U.S. Supreme Court, in the *Socony-Vacuum Oil* case. The Court held that a price-fixing agreement was unlawful per se, implying only that no argument put forward by the company could *justify* such conduct.[320]

316 D. Mayer, *La notion de substance mortelle en matière d'empoisonnement*, Recueil Dalloz 325 (1994).

317 *Id.*

318 The expression is that of Richard Whish and David Bailey, *see* Competition Law 132–36 (10th ed. 2021), and the practices mentioned.

319 It should be noted that some authors reject the equivalence between "infringement by object" and "prohibited infringement per se," on the grounds that there is a significant difference between the two: while "infringements by object" could theoretically be exempted under European Union law, infringements per se would not be justifiable under American law. In practice, however, things are much less clear-cut, since "infringements by object" are never exempted, and the rule of reason can be invoked by the American judge even in the presence of a "per se infringement." Moreover, Advocate General Juliane Kokott, referring to an "infringement by object," used the expression "per se prohibition" (*see* Opinion of Advocate General J. Kokott, Case C-8/08, T-Mobile Netherlands, ECLI:EU:C:2009:110, para. 43) – which supports the idea that these two different terms designate a similar, if not identical, phenomenon. In this sense, *see* M.-A. Frison-Roche & J.-C. Roda, Droit de la concurrence 365–66 (2nd ed. 2022), no. 451.

320 United States v. Socony-Vacuum Oil Co., Inc., 310 U.S. 150, 218 (1940): "Agreements to fix prices in interstate commerce are unlawful *per se* under the Sherman Act, and *no showing* of so-called competitive abuses or evils which the agreements were designed to eliminate or alleviate *may be interposed as a defense*" (emphasis added).

Originally, therefore, the per se infringement was in no way opposed to an "effects-based" approach: it was simply a matter of asserting that certain conduct was unjustifiable – that is, insusceptible of evidence to the contrary. The solution is good jurisprudential policy: just as a judge would not accept any justification from a defendant who had half-filled a glass with arsenic, would a competition authority accept the excuse of good faith or error put forward by parties to agreements??

As for the dose of poison present in the glass of strawberry juice, this would refer to contextual elements: market concentration, economic power of the companies involved, coverage rate of the practice, etc. The nature of the behavior is established: arsenic is a substance by its very nature and is obviously capable of causing death, and certain practices are also inherently and evidently capable of restricting competition. But just as a drop of arsenic would only kill a butterfly, an exclusivity rebate covering only ten percent of the market would not restrict competition.

Lastly, some practices do not obviously restrict competition, but upon closer examination we may find that they are as harmful as a strawberry is to an allergic person. What is more, certain novel substances, like some unprecedented economic practices, will require even more detailed analysis to determine whether they are lethal – can a virus be qualified as a poison? – or anticompetitive – as in the first margin squeeze cases, or the "self-preference" in the *Google Shopping* decision.[321] The question of whether a virus can "cause death" will certainly be raised, but not in order to characterize an effect – since the result is not a constitutive element – but in order to determine whether the defendant intended to poison; similarly, the question will be asked whether such conduct "may restrict competition," but this will not be for the purpose of qualifying an actual restriction of competition, or an effect on the market, but to determine whether this was the intent of the company being sued.

So, in any case, *the object of proof never shifts*:[322] the only difference between the cases mentioned is that *the burden of proof is increased* in the case of ambiguous conduct, i.e., conduct that does not appear *prima facie* to be an offense.

---

321 *See* esp. *infra*, no. 520 and no. 524.

322 Neither in European Union law nor in U.S. law, as expressly recognized by the U.S. Supreme Court, *see* NCAA v. Board of Regents of University of Oklahoma, 468 U.S. 85, 103 (1984): "Our analysis of this case under the Rule of Reason, of course, does not change the ultimate focus of our inquiry. Both *per se* rules and the Rule of Reason are employed to form a judgment about the competitive significance of the restraint"; *adde*, in the same judgment, n.26: "[T]here is often no bright line separating *per se* from Rule of Reason analysis. *Per se* rules may require considerable inquiry into market conditions before the evidence justifies a presumption of anticompetitive conduct."

B. A heavier burden of proof in the case of ambiguous conduct

321. **Burden of proof and standard of proof for competition infringements.** The burden of proof[323] of a violation of competition rules lies with the party or authority alleging it.[324] The standard of proof, a concept borrowed from the common law,[325] "determines the requirements which must be satisfied for facts to be regarded as proven."[326] The two are intrinsically linked. In the first instance, the competition authority must gather all the relevant evidence to establish the existence of an infringement. If it succeeds in doing so, the ball is in the defendant undertaking's court. Depending on the probative value of the initial body of evidence, it will be more or less difficult for the accused to present effective counter-evidence and argument[327] – i.e., to shift the burden of proof once again and force the prosecuting authority to respond.[328]

The object of proof is always the same – namely, the existence of a means capable of restricting competition (the material element) and the corresponding intent (the mental element). The standard of proof is also always the same:[329] that of reasonable doubt, which benefits the company.[330] The only purpose of proof is to establish the "firm conviction" that an offense has been committed,[331] which presupposes that all its constituent elements are present. However, the longer the match lasts, the more thorough the investigation and the reasoning[332] – the prosecuting authority's burden of

323 On the different meanings of the concept of burden of proof, and for a comparison between the civil law perspective and the common law tradition, *see* A.-L. Sibony & E. Barbier de la Serre, *Charge de la preuve et théorie du contrôle en droit communautaire de la concurrence: Pour un changement de perspective*, 43 RTD Eur. 205, 208–12 (Apr.-June 2007).

324 Council Regulation (EC) No. 1/2003, art. 2. *Adde*, Case C-185/95 P, Baustahlgewebe, ECLI:EU:C:1998:608, para. 58; Case C-49/92 P, Anic Partecipazioni, ECLI:EU:C:1999:356, para. 86.

325 J.-C. Roda, *Le standard de preuve: Réflexions à partir du droit de la concurrence*, Recueil Dalloz 1297 (2021).

326 Opinion of Advocate General J. Kokott, Case C-8/08, T-Mobile Netherlands, ECLI:EU:C:2009:110, n. 60.

327 Cf. the definition of the burden of proof provided by H. Motulsky, Principes d'une réalisation méthodique du droit privé: La théorie des éléments générateurs des droits subjectifs 131 (2002), no. 117: "[I]t is the necessity, for each of the parties, to establish, on pain of losing the case, through widely accepted means, the judge's conviction as to the truth of those of the factual circumstances corresponding to the elements generating the right claimed by them, which have been validly contested by their adversary."

328 On this point, *see* Opinion of Advocate General J. Kokott, Case C-105/04 P, FEG, ECLI:EU:C:2005:751, para. 73: "A substantiated submission by the Commission can be overturned only by an at least equally substantiated submission by the parties. The rules governing the burden of proof are only applicable at all where both parties provide sound, conclusive arguments and reach different conclusions."

329 It should be noted that the standard of proof is identical, whether the practice in question is an agreement or an abuse of a dominant position. In this respect, *see* F. Castillo de la Torre & E. Gippini Fournier, Evidence, Proof and Judicial Review in EU Competition Law 53 (2017), no. 2.057.

330 *See*, *inter alia*, a recent judgment, Case T-235/18, Qualcomm, ECLI:EU:T:2022:358, para. 359: "Where the Court still has a doubt, the benefit of that doubt must be given to the undertaking accused of the infringement." *Adde*, Case T-321/05, AstraZeneca, ECLI:EU:T:2010:266, para. 475.

331 Case T-519/09, Toshiba, ECLI:EU:T:2014:263, para. 77; *adde*, Case C-12/03 P, Tetra Laval, ECLI:EU:C:2005:87, para. 41.

332 Indeed, since one "must only prove what is contested," the more a point is contested, the more it is necessary to accumulate evidence in order to convince, *see* C. Perelman, *La preuve en droit: Essai de synthèse*, *in* La preuve en droit 357, 358 (C. Perelman & P. Forier eds., 1981).

proof is proportional to the number of ball exchanges between the opponents.[333] Evidentiary reasoning is similar to a heated discussion between two people, where each aims to convince a third party. Either the arguments put forward first are so relevant that they will cut short any debate, or, if they are likely to be countered, the other will have to support their own,[334] and so on until the spectator of the joust is convinced by one or other thesis.

But just because a discussion is more in-depth does not mean that the *object of* the debate has changed. It is true that arguments will become increasingly detailed and complex, at the risk of forgetting what the original point was. However, it is inconceivable, in law, that the deepening of proof should lead to its displacement towards another object of proof. So, logically, the "effects-based" approach cannot aim to prove anything other than the "by object" approach. On the other hand, when material evidence is not sufficient to characterize the offense, it must be supplemented by presumptive reasoning.

322. **The relationship between material evidence and abstract presumptions.** From a schematic point of view, evidence can be grouped into two categories: *material* evidence and *abstract* presumptions. The purpose of the former is to demonstrate the existence of a *fact* – a behavior or circumstance: for example, documentary evidence can establish the existence of an agreement. The latter are based on presumptive reasoning aimed at interpreting established facts, in order to *qualify* them – for example, it is presumed that an information exchange on prices restricts competition.[335] The first, material evidence, which comes into play beforehand and is of crucial importance in practice, presents little theoretical difficulty.[336] On the other hand, the second, abstract presumptions, because they mix questions of proof and substance,[337] are of a more complex nature. Both are used by the prosecuting authority and the defendants. It is worth examining the relationship between the two.

---

333 This apparently simple process is extremely difficult to systematize in detail, as it is directly dependent on each case, and highly variable from one case to another. An American theorist has attempted to do so, by schematizing the different scenarios for apportioning the burden of proof. *See*, for example, the graph he produced to illustrate a murder case: J. H. Wigmore, Un jalon vers une "science de la preuve": La représentation graphique des raisonnements probatoires 32 (O. Leclerc trans, Dalloz 2019).

334 In this sense, *see* Case C-204/00 P, Aalborg Portland, ECLI:EU:C:2004:6, para. 79: "[T]he factual evidence on which a party relies may be of such a kind as to require the other party to provide an explanation or justification, failing which it is permissible to conclude that the burden of proof has been discharged"; along the same lines, Case T-426/10, Moreda-Riviere Trefilerías, ECLI:EU:T:2016:335, para. 109.

335 The distinction is borrowed from two authors who have distinguished between "fact-intensive" and "law-intensive" cases, cf. P. Ibáñez Colomo & A. Kalintiri, *The Evolution of EU Antitrust Policy: 1966–2017*, 83 The Modern Law Review 321, 325–27 (2020).

336 Even if proving the facts can prove extremely difficult in practice, for example when it comes to proving the duration of the practices in question.

337 *See supra*, no. 291.

When the Commission bases its finding of infringement on material evidence, which, on its own, establishes the infringement to the requisite legal standard, the defendants cannot present a plausible alternative to the Commission's argument,[338] but can only point to the inadequacy of the evidence retained.[339] Thus, in some cases, material evidence *presumes the infringement, in fact, irrefragable manner* – it closes the debate by *definitively* convincing the judge,[340] without always requiring in-depth analysis.[341] This reasoning is not peculiar to competition law: there are an extremely large number of unambiguous cases in which material evidence alone is sufficient to characterize the material and mental elements of the infringement.

However, this does not mean that a certain behavior will always and irrefragably presume infringement, so that there is no practice that is, in all cases and whatever the circumstances, punishable "per se."[342] Indeed, even an agreement is theoretically justifiable: just think of crisis agreements, which were once exempted, or price agreements, which may not be deemed infringing on the twofold condition that the parties to the agreement have no market power,[343] and put forward a legitimate reason.[344]

Conversely, if the material evidence leaves any doubt as to the anticompetitive nature of the conduct in question, it will be necessary to supplement it with a theoretical justification – in other words, with abstract presumptions. Such presumptions arise, or at least should arise, in novel cases, when the competition authority is required to justify the connection of new conduct to case law. In the presence of ambiguous cases, companies will then be

338 *See* in particular Case T-36/05, Coats, ECLI:EU:T:2007:268, para. 72: "[T]he case-law, according to which it is sufficient for the applicants to prove circumstances which cast the facts established by the Commission in a different light and thus allow another 'plausible explanation' of the facts to be substituted for the one adopted by the Commission, is applicable only where the Commission's reasoning is based on the supposition that the facts established cannot be explained [otherwise]. It is not, therefore, applicable where the Commission's findings are based on documentary evidence."

339 Case T-67/00, JFE Engineering, ECLI:EU:T:2004:221, para. 187.

340 Henri Batiffol believes that irrebuttable presumptions serve precisely to avoid the multiplication of evidence to the contrary, as this would lead to "trials that are impossible to judge," *see* H. Batiffol, *Observations sur la preuve des faits*, *in* La preuve en droit 303, 306 (C. Perelman & P. Forier eds., 1981).

341 Indeed, "the analysis of the economic and legal context of which the practice forms part may thus be limited to what is strictly necessary in order to establish the existence of a restriction of competition by object," *see* Case C-373/14 P, Toshiba Corporation, ECLI:EU:C:2016:26, para. 29; Case C-469/15 P, FSL, ECLI:EU:C:2017:308, para. 107.

342 In this sense, *see* W. P. J. Wils, *Judgment of the EU General Court in Intel and the So-Called More Economic Approach to Abuse of Dominance*, 37 World Competition 405, 426 n.115 (2014): "[C]ontrary to U.S. antitrust law, EU antitrust law does not contain any *per se* prohibitions"; *adde*, I. Lianos, La transformation du droit de la concurrence par le recours à l'analyse économique 1403 (2007), no. 1009: the author notes that the per se approach is not an "automatic" qualification, since it always implies taking the context into account.

343 On market power, which we analyze as a prerequisite for infringement, *see infra*, nos. 384 *et seq.*

344 For example, if price fixing is part of a group purchasing, specialization or research and development agreement. Eur. Comm., Guidance on Restriction of Competition "By Object" for the Purpose of Defining which Agreements May Benefit from the De Minimis Notice, C(2014) 4136 final (June 3, 2015), at 6–7. For other examples pointing to the possible justification of "restrictions by object" (including market sharing, output restrictions, bid rigging, collective boycott agreements, information sharing on price, etc.) when the parties to the agreement do not have significant market shares, *see Id.* at 7–17. On the theory of legitimate ground, *see infra*, nos. 337 *et seq.*

free to invoke an *alternative explanation* to that of the authority, in order to shed a different light on the established facts.[345] This will deepen the debate, but in no way shift the focus of proof: the issue will no longer be merely probative, but also substantive. For the authority will have to defend that a given behavior falls within the definition of anticompetitive practice, while the company will have to argue that this is not the case.

Paragraph 2 – The different types of evidence used

323. **The distribution of the burden of proof.** Strictly speaking, intentional offenses have a special feature: the material element does not *systematically* presume the mental element.[346] Thus, when conduct alone does not allow a presumption of corresponding intent beyond a reasonable doubt, the prosecuting authority is required to gather additional evidence to characterize the offense. This is precisely the reasoning followed in anticompetitive practices law. The proof focuses entirely on the conduct adopted and the objective pursued by the companies[347] and, if these do not sufficiently attest to the existence of an anticompetitive practice, it will be up to the Commission to gather additional evidence (**I**), and it will then be up to the defendants to provide proof of justifications that would defeat the finding of an infringement (**II**).

I. Behaviors and bodies of evidence presuming intent

324. **Primary and secondary evidence.** Material elements,[348] i.e., conduct and the circumstances surrounding it, are the main elements of proof of competition infringements (**A**). Contrary to popular belief, economic analyses[349] play only an ancillary role[350] in this matter as sometimes relevant evidence, but are not required to characterize an infringement (**B**).

---

345 In this spirit, by analogy, *see* Case 29/83, Compagnie royale asturienne des mines, ECLI:EU:C:1984:130, para. 16.

346 *See supra*, nos. 252–254

347 F. Castillo de la Torre & E. Gippini Fournier, Evidence, Proof and Judicial Review in EU Competition Law 47–48 (2017), no. 2.045.

348 As defined *supra*, no. 226.

349 As the role of economic analysis is far less prominent in anticompetitive practices law than in merger law, *see* L. Idot, *Réflexions sur l'évolution de la preuve des pratiques anticoncurrentielles devant les autorités de concurrence*, Concurrences no. 4-2017, art. no. 84879, 45, 55, no. 33; T. Valletti, *Economics in Competition Law - Working Together*, Concurrences no. 4-2017, art. no. 84876, 11, 12.

350 Recently, *see* Case C-680/20, Unilever Italia, ECLI:EU:C:2023:33, para. 44: "[A]lthough, for the purposes of assessing whether an undertaking's conduct is capable of restricting effective competition on a market, a competition authority may rely on the guidance from economic sciences, confirmed by empirical or behavioural studies, the taking into consideration of that guidance cannot, however, be sufficient." *Adde*, Opinion of

A. Material elements: the main elements of proof

325. **The varying probative value of evidence.** The methods of proof in anticompetitive practices law do not differ fundamentally from those used in other disciplines. As direct, unambiguous evidence is rare, the prosecuting authority usually has to assemble a body of evidence – i.e., a number of elements that corroborate each other.[351] Of course, there is no way we can discuss every possible mode of proof here. We will focus on those that demonstrate that the object of proof is intent, not anticompetitive effect.

In general, EU judges assume that companies act rationally: they therefore attach little credibility to facts that appear to run counter to "normal" commercial behavior.[352] The value of evidence differs according to whether it is oral or written,[353] with the probative value of documentary evidence itself varying according to a number of criteria.[354] For example, a document contemporaneous with the offense will play a more important role than one drawn up *ex post*, and will be deemed more or less reliable depending on who wrote it or its degree of precision.[355] But whatever the evidence used, the aim is always to approximate the defendant's intent. As the company is a disembodied entity, this will always be established on the basis of the acts of agents acting on its behalf,[356] which will be

Advocate General J. Kokott, Case C-23/14, Post Danmark, ECLI:EU:C:2015:343, para. 4: at a time when "there are mounting calls for European competition law to adopt a more economic approach," Advocate General Juliane Kokott had invited the Court not to "allow itself to be influenced so much by current thinking ('Zeitgeist') or ephemeral trends," but to "have regard rather to the legal foundations." In the same spirit, *see* E.-J. Mestmäcker, *The EC Commission's Modernization of Competition Policy: A Challenge to the Community's Constitutional Order*, 1 European Business Organization Law Review 401, 412 (2000): "Modernization is a dialectic concept and not very enlightening as a policy guideline. It suggests both an enlightened mind and a fascination with what is fashionable."

351 Case 48/69, Imperial Chemical Industries, ECLI:EU:C:1972:70, para. 68: "[T]he question whether there was a concerted action in this case can only be correctly determined if the evidence upon which the contested decision is based is considered, not in isolation, but as a whole"; Case T-141/94, Thyssen Stahl, ECLI:EU:T:1999:48, para. 175: "[T]he evidence must be assessed in its entirety, taking into account all relevant circumstances of fact"; Case T-321/05, AstraZeneca, ECLI:EU:T:2010:266, para. 477; Case T-375/06, Viega, ECLI:EU:T:2011:106, para. 57; Case T-519/09, Toshiba, ECLI:EU:T:2014:263, para. 77; Case T-286/09, Intel, ECLI:EU:T:2014:547, para. 64: the Court considers that this method of proof is valid for both agreement and abuse of a dominant position; Case C-74/14, Eturas, ECLI:EU:C:2016:42, para. 37: evidence may "be proven not only by direct evidence, but also through indicia, provided that they are objective and consistent."

352 Castillo de la Torre & Gippini Fournier, Evidence, Proof and Judicial Review in EU Competition, *op. cit.* at 43, no. 2.036, and case law references cited.

353 *Id.* at 164, no. 4.009. Oral evidence includes statements given during competition inspections, or confessions made during leniency proceedings.

354 *See* in particular Case T-566/08, Total Raffinage Marketing, ECLI:EU:T:2013:423, para. 66: "Particularly high probative value may be attached to statements which, first, are reliable, second, are made on behalf of an undertaking, third, are made by a person under a professional obligation to act in the interests of that undertaking, fourth, go against the interests of the person making the statement, fifth, are made by a direct witness of the circumstances to which they relate and, sixth, were provided in writing deliberately and after mature reflection"; *adde*, in the same sense, Case T-67/00, JFE Engineering, ECLI:EU:T:2004:221, paras. 205–210; Case T-348/08, Aragonesas Industrias y Energía, ECLI:EU:T:2011:621, para. 104.

355 Castillo de la Torre & Gippini Fournier, Evidence, Proof and Judicial Review in EU Competition, *op. cit.* at 175–82, nos. 4.026–4.041.

356 *See supra*, nos.168 *et seq.*

presumed to faithfully reflect its state of mind. However, it is important not to confuse intent and motive, as proof of the latter can, at most, serve to corroborate proof of intent.

326. **Motive or "subjective intent": a relevant but not required indicator, which can occasionally corroborate proof of anticompetitive intent.** In order to qualify predatory pricing, the competition authority compares the prices charged with the costs of the dominant company.[357] If prices are below average variable costs, the existence of an anticompetitive strategy is presumed. If they are higher than average variable costs, but lower than average total costs,[358] this is only a *prima facie* case, which the authority will have to supplement with other evidence – circumstances, documentary evidence, or "subjective intent"[359] (i.e., motive[360]). In both cases, the aim is to demonstrate the existence of anticompetitive intent. In most cases, however, the doctrine reverses the reasoning. It considers that, in the first case (prices below variable costs), the behavior is "by nature" anticompetitive, whereas in the second only (prices above variable costs but below total costs), it is necessary to prove the existence of a "strategy" – the term "strategy" often being confused with subjective intent.[361] However, the existence of an anticompetitive strategy, i.e., an anticompetitive intent, is the object of proof, not the method of proof.[362]

327. **Proof of concurrence of wills in agreement cases.** When a competition authority deals with an agreement, the proof is similar to that required for conspiracy under English law, or for *association de malfaiteurs* under French law,[363] which implies that the law of anticompetitive practices captures the concrete behavior of companies "far more than it focuses on the legal constructs of contract law."[364] The characterization of an

---

357 On this "cost test" and the "AEC test," *see infra*, nos. 335–336.

358 Total costs include fixed and variable costs.

359 Proof of motive is never essential (the same is true in criminal law, incidentally), as rightly notes D. Dittert, *Abus de position dominante: Vers une approche "plus économique"?*, REVUE DES AFFAIRES EUROPÉENNES NO. 1, 197, 200 (2012): "Far from contenting itself with the simple finding that Post Danmark's intent to oust its competitor Forbruger-Kontakt could not be established, the Court also looks at the objective circumstances characterizing the offending conduct. This exercise would have been irrelevant if only direct evidence of Post Danmark's subjective intent had been admissible."

360 In French, it would be more correct to write "*mobile*" (motive), rather than translate "subjective intent" as "*intention subjective*," as this expression does not exist in French criminal law. Moreover, motive is totally distinct from intent. However, doctrine and European judges systematically, albeit erroneously, equate these two concepts. *See supra*, nos. 265–267.

361 In such cases, intent is treated as a mere "criterion" for qualification, whereas it is the object of the proof, *see* in particular A.-L. Sibony, *La CJUE précise la pertinence de l'intention pour la qualification d'abus de position dominante*, CONCURRENCES no. 3-2012, art. no. 48339, 101, 102.

362 *See* Cass. com., June 9, 2021, no. 19-10.943 (Fr.), para. 11: "[T]he court of appeal, which did not seek to quantify a loss by carrying out the cost test but only to *characterize the dominant undertaking's intent to eliminate competition*" (emphasis added).

363 For the reasons given *supra*, no. 275.

364 B. Oppetit, *Le consentement sans l'échange: Le concours des consentements, le concours implicite*, REVUE DE JURISPRUDENCE COMMERCIALE 69, 70 (Nov. 1995), Special Issue: "L'échange des consentements."

agreement therefore does not require proof of consent in the civil law sense of the term,[365] but of the existence of a concurrence of wills in the criminal law sense[366] – which means, for example, that the form it takes is of no importance,[367] nor does it matter whether it is legally binding,[368] whether it is express or tacit, active or passive,[369] or whether or not a party has an interest in adhering to it.[370] Proof of the concurrence of wills is much less demanding, and therefore easier to provide, than that of genuine consent.[371]

328. **The complex, single and continuous offense: a plurality of behaviors united by a single intent.** Like criminal law,[372] the law of anticompetitive practices is familiar with the notion of a complex offense. This concept has long been recognized in the field of agreements, whereas it has only recently been accepted in the case of abuse of a dominant position.[373] Competition authorities use this classification when several practices are united by the same objective, as it would be "artificial" to subdivide behavior driven by "a single purpose" into several separate offenses.[374] In order to establish the existence of a single infringement, it is therefore necessary to demonstrate that the practices in question

---

365 On this subject, *see* E. Claudel, *Rôle et place des mécanismes fondamentaux du droit civil en droit des affaires*, RTD Com. 291 (1999); E. Claudel, Ententes anticoncurrentielles et droit des contrats (1994) (Ph.D. dissertation, Université Paris x Nanterre); *adde*, Y. Guenzoui, *Entente et contrat: Le trouble notionnel*, RTD Com. 273 (2006).

366 For an in-depth study, *see*: C. Grynfogel, *Le concours de volontés entre entreprises, une notion protéiforme en droit communautaire des ententes*, Revue de jurisprudence de droit des affaires 552 (2005).

367 *See* in particular Case C-74/04 P, Volkswagen, ECLI:EU:C:2006:460, para. 37; Case C-49/92 P, Anic Partecipazioni, ECLI:EU:C:1999:356, para. 131.

368 The recommendations of an association of undertakings can thus constitute agreements (Case 209/78, Van Landewyck, ECLI:EU:C:1980:248, para. 86; Case 96/82, IAZ, ECLI:EU:C:1983:310, paras. 19–20; Case T-325/01, Daimler Chrysler, ECLI:EU:T:2005:322, paras. 210–211), or a gentlemen's agreement (Case 41/69, ACF Chemiefarma, ECLI:EU:C:1970:71, paras. 112–113).

369 This situation is frequently found in vertical agreements, where distributors tacitly accept the policy pursued by their supplier: *see* in particular Case 107/82, AEG-Telefunken, ECLI:EU:C:1983:293, paras. 38–39; Case C-277/87, Sandoz Prodotti Farmaceutici, ECLI:EU:C:1990:6; conversely, in the *Bayer* case, the distributors had officially opposed their supplier's policy, which prevented an agreement from being characterized, *see* Case T-41/96, Bayer, ECLI:EU:T:2000:242, paras. 148–157.

370 Case 25/84, Ford Werke, ECLI:EU:C:1985:340, paras. 19–21.

371 For an in-depth study of proof of concurrence of wills, *see*: C. Prieto, *Ententes: Concours de volontés*, JurisClasseur Europe Traité (Oct. 2017), fasc. 1405, esp. nos. 48–71 for agreements, and nos. 76–79 for concerted practices.

372 Complex offenses generally include swindling, forgery and sometimes harassment, *see* M.-L. Rassat, *Escroquerie*, JurisClasseur Pénal des Affaires (June 2022), fasc. 10, no. 20; V. Malabat, *L'incrimination générale de faux*, Répertoire de droit pénal et de procédure pénale (Feb. 2017), no. 7; P. Mistretta, *Harcèlement*, Répertoire de droit pénal et de procédure pénale (Apr. 2022), no. 49. The complex offense is made up of a plurality of acts of a different nature, all working towards the same end. In our view, it is only conceivable in the case of an offense of means (*see supra*, no. 246).

373 For a detailed history, *see* L. Idot, *Réflexions sur la notion d'infraction unique et continue en droit européen de la concurrence*, *in* Humanisme et justice: Mélanges en l'honneur de Geneviève Giudicelli-Delage 549, 552–55 (2016), and case law references cited. On French decision-making practice, *see* with interest the report: ADLC, *L'infraction unique, complexe et continue*, *in* Rapport annuel 2015, 91, 102–105 (Mar. 2016).

374 Case T-1/89, Rhône-Poulenc, ECLI:EU:T:1991:56, para. 126; Case C-293/13 P, Fresh Del Monte, ECLI:EU:C:2014:2439, para. 156.

pursue "a single *aim*,"[375] an "overall plan."[376] In the case of abuse of a dominant position, this overall strategy may be aimed at eliminating a competitor and, in the case of agreements, at controlling a market or fixing prices.[377] In addition, the qualification of a complex offense requires demonstrating either that the undertaking was aware of the infringing behavior of the other undertakings involved in the agreement, or that it could reasonably have foreseen it and was prepared to accept the risk – this condition being most often presumed on the basis of the material contribution made by the undertaking in question to the complex infringement.[378] Here, we see that the two criteria characterizing a complex offense are, on the one hand, willingness and, on the other, knowledge, which is fully in line with criminal theory.

329. **Negligence presumes intent.** In the *Eni* case, an employee had attended around ten meetings, and subsequently claimed that he was convinced that they were legal.[379] The applicant then invoked negligence in an attempt to obtain a reduction in the fine. The Court found, however, that in view of the "manifestly anticompetitive content of the technical meetings,"[380] the question of whether the representative of the company being sued "had the correct impression of what was discussed" with its competitors was irrelevant.[381] The employee's alleged negligence thus presumes the intent of the company in whose name and on whose behalf he was acting. Thus, following the principle applied in business criminal law,[382] in anticompetitive practices law there is a presumption of intent based on simple negligence, so that a company cannot exonerate itself by putting forward an explanation ostensibly incompatible with the materiality of the facts established by the prosecuting authority.[383]

375 *Id. Adde*, Case T-53/03, BPB, ECLI:EU:T:2008:254, para. 257; Case T-27/10, AC-Treuhand, ECLI:EU:T:2014:59, para. 238: "[T]he notion of a single infringement covers a situation in which several undertakings participated in an infringement in which continuous conduct *in pursuit of a single economic aim* was intended to distort competition, and also individual infringements linked to one another by the same object (all the elements sharing the same *purpose*) and the same subjects (the same undertakings, who are *aware that they are participating in the common object*)" (emphasis added).

376 Case C-204/00 P, Aalborg Portland, ECLI:EU:C:2004:6, para. 258; Case T-53/03, BPB, ECLI:EU:T:2008:254, para. 256.

377 Idot, *Réflexions sur la notion d'infraction unique et continue en droit européen de la concurrence*, *op. cit.* at 556–57, and references cited. For a discussion of the various elements relevant to characterizing the existence of an overall plan, *see* ADLC, *L'infraction unique, complexe et continue*, *op. cit.* at 106–12.

378 To this end, *see* Case C-49/92 P, Anic Partecipazioni, ECLI:EU:C:1999:356, paras. 87–88; *adde*, Case C-441/11 P, Verhuizingen Coppens, ECLI:EU:C:2012:778, paras. 42–52; Case C-293/13 P, Fresh Del Monte, ECLI:EU:C:2014:2439, paras. 157–160.

379 On the subject of imputation of offenses committed by employees to the company, *see supra*, no. 172.

380 Case T-558/08, Eni, ECLI:EU:T:2014:1080, para. 269.

381 *Id.*, para. 270.

382 *See supra*, nos. 156–157.

383 This reasoning is, moreover, consistent with the theory of intent: since intent is systematically presumed based on the material element and the surrounding circumstances, if these make it reasonable to establish that the defendant had the intention to commit an offense, they will not be able to defeat the finding of an offense by arguing a lack of intent, unless the material elements themselves are challenged.

330. **The implementation of conduct and its effect on competition or the market: evidence of an infringement.** Because of their formal nature, neither the conduct actually adopted, nor the effect on competition or on the market, constitute constitutive elements of competition infringements.[384] On the other hand, they can play a role in corroborating the existence of an infringement. In such cases, it is relevant to take them into account, although this is neither necessary nor sufficient for conviction.

Firstly, taking into account the implementation of an agreement or its effect may have an impact on the duration of the infringement. The General Court has ruled that the fact that an undertaking "refrained from participating in further meetings" for a certain period does not imply that it ceased to participate in an agreement.[385] In such cases, the onus is on the company to demonstrate that it has adopted "fair and independent competitive conduct in the relevant market," in order to prove that it is no longer a party to the agreement.[386] Similarly, in the absence of direct evidence of illicit meetings held in any given year, the General Court justified the characterization of the infringement on the grounds that, given that an anticompetitive meeting had been held the previous year and that prices had remained uniform on the market, "the anti-competitive effects of the said discussions" continued to unfold.[387] In other words, the fact that prices remained in line with those agreed is an indication that the infringement was continuing.

Secondly, the effect may, on a case-by-case basis, strengthen the demonstration of the anticompetitive nature of the disputed practice. In the *Google Shopping* case, for example, the Commission sought to ascertain whether the company's conduct had the effect of making it more difficult for competing price comparison services to obtain requests from Internet users and data enabling them to improve their services, or whether it could have the effect of reducing incentives to innovate, or increasing barriers to entry.[388] This "close examination of the actual effects," described by the Court as a "further analysis," made it possible to support the reasoning, and thus to conclude that the conduct in question did not fall within the scope of "competition on the merits."[389] It was not a question of analyzing the effect for its own sake: the effect was merely an indication, in retrospect, of the company's anticompetitive intent.

384 This means that, in the case of an agreement, the infringement is constituted from the moment concerted action is established, and in the case of abuse of a dominant position, once there is even a mere commencement of execution. *See supra*, nos. 277 *et seq.*

385 Case T-132/07, Fuji Electric, ECLI:EU:T:2011:344, para. 115.

386 Case T-303/02, Westfalen Gassen Nederland, ECLI:EU:T:2006:374, para. 139.

387 Case T-373/10, Villeroy & Boch Austria, ECLI:EU:T:2013:455, para. 143 (unofficial translation). In the same spirit, *see* Case 96/75, EMI Records, ECLI:EU:C:1976:87, para. 15; Case 243/83, Binon, ECLI:EU:C:1985:284, para. 17.

388 Case T-604/18, Google and Alphabet, ECLI:EU:T:2022:541, para. 294.

389 *Id.*, para. 295.

It should be noted that, *a contrario*, the fact that conduct has not, in fact, produced a restrictive effect on competition cannot prevent a finding of infringement: at most, this circumstance – which is, by its very nature, outside the undertakings' control – may constitute evidence capable of reversing the burden of proof or casting doubt on the existence of an anticompetitive practice.[390] In several recent cases, the Court has also held that the "pro-competitive effects" of conduct may be taken into account, as elements of context, on the basis of paragraph 1, "in so far as they are capable of calling into question the overall assessment of whether the concerted practice concerned revealed a sufficient degree of harm."[391]

We can thus see that the effect occasionally plays a role as an element, taken into account among others, making it possible to corroborate or weaken the proof of the offense. And yet, never before have theories on effects played such a major role in legal doctrine, nor have expert reports played such a major role in litigation. This paradox raises a number of questions, given that economic analyses are no more than incidental evidence, and are sometimes used to excess.

B. Economic analyses: accessory or overabundant evidence

331. **The difficulty of identifying the scope of economic analysis.** In competition law, it is sometimes difficult to distinguish between what falls within the scope of economic analysis, and what is nothing more than a fact[392] or common sense reasoning.[393]

---

390 In this regard, *see* Case C-377/20, ENEL, ECLI:EU:C:2022:379, paras. 55–56 and answer to the second question: the fact that conduct has not produced "actual restrictive effects … may indicate that the conduct in question is unable to produce anti-competitive effects, although it must be supplemented by further items of evidence intended to demonstrate that inability."

391 Case C-307/18, Generics (UK), ECLI:EU:C:2020:52, paras. 103–104; *adde*, in the same sense, Opinion of Advocate General J. Kokott, Case C-307/18, Generics (UK), ECLI:EU:C:2020:28, para. 158; Case C-883/19 P, HSBC, ECLI:EU:C:2023:11, paras. 139–140; Case C-211/22, Super Bock Bebidas, ECLI:EU:C:2023:529, para. 36.

392 As Judge and President of the General Court M. van der Woude rightly points out, *A Curious Question: Why Bother with Economists?*, Concurrences no. 3-2015, art. no. 74831, 66, 66, no. 3: "[E]conomists tend to put the label 'economic' on issues, which lawyers simply regard as facts."

393 One example is the "counterfactual test" applied in the *Remia* case. In the case of non-competition clauses concluded with a view to the transfer of a business, the Court of Justice first ruled that it was necessary to examine "what would be the state of competition if those clauses did not exist." It went on to explain that if the buyer and seller remained in a competitive situation after the transfer, the latter, who knows the particularities of the business transferred, could "win back his former customers" and "drive the undertaking out of business." The Court concluded that the disputed clauses had the "merit of ensuring that the transfer has the effect intended," which contributed "to the promotion of competition because they lead to an increase in the number of undertakings in the market in question." *See* Case 42/84, Remia, ECLI:EU:C:1985:327, paras. 18–19. Apart from the last sentence, it is difficult to see how such an analysis is economic: the Court is stating the obvious – that *the clauses in question are justified by a principal and legitimate objective*, namely the transfer of a business – which is purely legal reasoning. More generally, on the theory of legitimate ground, *see infra*, nos. 337 *et seq.* On the other hand, some consider that certain economic theories, despite the fact that they arouse a form of fascination, produce no results that common sense could not achieve. *See*, for example, on game theory, S. Schweitzer, Le libéralisme: Autopsie d'une incompréhension 59 (2023): "Game theory is common sense theorized and now presented in such a sophisticated way that common sense, whose virtue lies precisely and justly in being accessible to all, has become reserved for only a few."

What is more, while the Commission and companies frequently refer to "economic studies,"[394] this expression, which is vague, to say the least, covers very different realities. These may be statistical or econometric studies (e.g., cost or market share analyses), or actual modeling (e.g., a sophisticated counterfactual test, or a prospective analysis of the possible effects of the litigious behavior). Expert reports range from simple data collection to the most complex evaluations.[395]

Economic analysis also often takes the form of "tests," which are as diverse as they are varied – without claiming to be exhaustive: counterfactual test, as-efficient competitor test, sacrifice test, consumer harm test, efficiency test, Elhauge test, foregone profits test, recoupment test[396] – some of which, although well represented in doctrine, are simply never used in practice, while others are overabundant, as they aim to demonstrate something that does not need to be proven.[397] It should also be noted that the term "test" can be misleading as to their actual role. In fact, they are usually presented as trials by fire – the (scientific) ordeals[398] of modern times. The reasoning is binary: either the test is passed, and the company is cleared; or it fails, and the blade of the sanction falls. But nothing could be further from the truth: as they are never more than clues, tests are at most, and only if they are relevant, elements of proof in broader evidentiary reasoning.[399]

Finally, it should be pointed out that not all the "tests" used in anticompetitive practices law are economic in nature. For example, when a case comes under the theory of essential facilities,[400] doctrine and case law[401] frequently focus on whether the "Bronner test" (named after the eponymous judgment) is "applicable." Such a test is not, strictly speaking, an economic one, since it merely repeats the criteria identified by the Court to determine whether,

394 This, moreover, does not date from the advent of the "more economic approach," *see* in this sense, F. Castillo de la Torre & E. Gippini Fournier, Evidence, Proof and Judicial Review in EU Competition Law 211 (2017), no. 4.105.

395 *Id.* at 211–12, no. 4.106: "They range from simple (observed past price correlation … based on available sales data) to extremely sophisticated (counterfactual estimates of market developments in alternative hypothetical scenarios)."

396 The literature on these tests is abundant, but not always accessible to non-economists. *See*, *ex multis*: OECD, Competition on the merits, Policy Roundtables, DAF/COMP(2005)27 (Mar. 30, 2006), at 65–78; P. Akman, *The Tests of Illegality under Articles 101 and 102 TFEU*, 61 Antitrust Bulletin 84 (2016); P. Rey, *Concurrence par les mérites*, *in* La modernisation du droit de la concurrence 151, 155–60 (G. Canivet ed., 2006).

397 In this sense, *see infra*, no. 333.

398 On the use of ordeals to establish guilt until the twelfth century, *see supra*, no. 48.

399 In this sense, *see* in particular Case C-23/14, Post Danmark, ECLI:EU:C:2015:651, para. 62; Case C-680/20, Unilever Italia, ECLI:EU:C:2023:33, para. 40.

400 An essential facility is "an equipment, resource or infrastructure … access to which is strictly necessary (or indispensable) to carry out an economic activity." In certain cases, the owner of such a resource may commit an abuse of dominant position if they refuse to grant access to third parties under transparent, fair and non-discriminatory conditions. *See* G. Decocq, *Facilité essentielle*, *in* Dictionnaire de droit de la concurrence 443–44 (M. Chagny & E. Combe eds., 2023). For an analysis of the *Magill*, *Oscar Bronner* and *IMS* Health judgments, *see* F. Marty & J. Pillot, *Des critères de l'application de la théorie des facilités essentielles dans le cadre de la politique de concurrence européenne*, l Reflets et perspectives de la vie économique 197, 213–15 (2011).

401 Judges are obliged to respond to the arguments put forward by the parties.

in the *Bronner* case,[402] the disputed practice was anticompetitive. However, by definition, the criteria deemed relevant in one case will not necessarily be decisive in subsequent cases, even if the facts are similar. Given that each case is at least partially different from the previous one, it would seem surprising for a legal expert to consider creating a "test" based on one judgment. And the Court of Justice tirelessly repeats an obvious point which, because it is self-evident, should not require a judge to use their pen: the Commission is not obliged to systematically apply the *Bronner* test,[403] because the criteria it sets out were justified by the "specific circumstances" of the case in question[404] – circumstances that obviously differ from case to case. Such a "test," as well as any similar test,[405] is therefore neither economic nor sensible from a legal point of view.

332. **The challenges of economic expertise: scientific rigor, bias, predictability.** In addition, several obstacles to the acceptance of economic analysis in the implementation of competition rules must be mentioned.

We have already shown that, from an epistemological point of view, economics is not free of flaws.[406] When reasoning is based on modeling, the conclusions drawn are by their very nature conjectural[407] – always questionable, often disputed.[408] In this respect, it is paradoxical that Union judges only exceptionally commission experts,[409] while the economic reports proposed by companies are often suspected of being biased, even

402 Case C-7/97, Oscar Bronner, ECLI:EU:C:1998:569.

403 *Inter alia*: Case C-52/09, TeliaSonera Sverige, ECLI:EU:C:2011:83, para. 58; Case T-612/17, Google and Alphabet, ECLI:EU:T:2021:763, para. 240.

404 Case C-152/19 P, Deutsche Telekom, ECLI:EU:C:2021:238, paras. 42–45, comm. D. Bosco, *Retour vers le futur de l'arrêt Bronner*, Contrats concurrence consommation (May 2021), comm. 85; *adde*, in the same sense, Case C-42/21 P, Lietuvos geležinkeliai, ECLI:EU:C:2023:12, para. 76, comm. D. Bosco, *Nouvelles précisions sur le champ d'application du test Bronner*, Contrats concurrence consommation (Mar. 2023), comm. 49.

405 By "analogous test," we mean any test that consists in gathering together the criteria deemed relevant in the context of one case, with the aim of subsequently applying them mechanically to other cases. The problem with this kind of "reasoning" is that it leads defendants to argue that "all the criteria relating to such and such a test" must be met, failing which the finding of infringement would be vitiated by an error of law. However, while each criterion can be validly discussed when the similarity between two cases justifies it, it is counterproductive, and contrary to the principles of legal qualification, to demand that all cases be resolved by applying the same recipe.

406 *See supra*, nos. 114 *et seq.*

407 For example, with regard to the AEC test and counterfactual analysis, *see* F. Castillo de la Torre, *Is the Effects-Based Approach Too Cumbersome? Taking Stock of Recent Practice and Case Law on Article 102 TFEU*, *in* The Transformation of EU Competition Law: Next Generation Issues 145, 165 and 168 (A. Claici, A. Komninos & D. Waelbroeck eds., 2023): "The AEC test is in essence an evaluative exercise where … it relies on assumptions for which, by definition, there is no certain and definitive answer, only a best or reasonable estimate"; "Counterfactuals … are difficult to 'prove' with any degree of certainty, for they require the fact finder to speculate what would have happened if the undertaking had not done what it actually did. If combined with a benefit of the doubt, it would be simply impossible to prove an infringement." *Adde*, D. Bosco, *Le test de l'opérateur aussi efficace: Une nouvelle ère?*, Concurrences no. 3-2013, art. no. 53042, 12, 14, no. 10.

408 *See, inter alia*, Opinion of Advocate General Darmon, Case C-89/85, Ahlström Osakeyhtiö, ECLI:EU:C:1992:293, paras. 397, 432 and 437: the Advocate General repeatedly notes the questionable and purely conjectural nature of the reports produced by the experts. On this subject, *see also* the Commission's guide to best practice: Eur. Comm., *Best Practices for the Submission of Economic Evidence and Data Collection in Cases Concerning the Application of Articles 101 and 102 TFEU and in Merger Cases*, Staff Working Paper, C(2011) 7329 final (Nov. 17, 2011).

409 In this respect, *see* the following study: E. Barbier de La Serre & A.-L. Sibony, *Expert Evidence before the EC Courts*, 45 Common Market Law Review 941, 949 (2008).

if only half-heartedly.[410] What is more, proponents of the "economic approach" themselves acknowledge that there is no such thing as a "perfect test," but only certain tests that are less imperfect than others.[411]

However, it is one thing to use economic reasoning to *corroborate* certain presumptions of illegality, taking note of the fact that economists consider that this or that behavior is likely to restrict competition. This is a substantial approach: economics aims to *help* define infringements.[412] But quite different is the willingness to grant it a significant role at the stage of rule implementation: in the courtroom, there is no time for conjecture – the sky must be clear if we are to arrive at a certainty and reach a decision. In other words, once the rule has been determined, it is not up to the experts, whoever they may be, to change it to suit the case in hand. If this were the case, the principle of foreseeability would be violated.[413]

It follows that economic analyses can only be relevant when they contribute to proving a constituent element – which, in practice, is not always the case.

333. **The frequent mismatch between economic tests and analyses and the constituent elements of competition infringements.** It is relevant to note that the current presentation of economic tests takes them not only to a high level of abstraction, but, above all, very far from the established jurisprudential principles.[414] Indeed, they are commonly defined as analyses designed to distinguish between practices "that increase consumer welfare in the long term and those that decrease it."[415] However, this is not the purpose of proof.[416]

---

410 *Id.* at 964–66. *Adde*, B. Bouloc, *Les techniques probatoires d'analyse des comportements économiques*, *in* Les enjeux de la pénalisation de la vie économique 81, 88 (M.-A. Frison-Roche ed., 1997); Castillo de la Torre & Gippini Fournier, Evidence, Proof and Judicial Review in EU Competition Law, *op. cit.* at 261, no. 5.069. On the probative value of these reports, *see id.* at 212–21, nos. 4.108–4.124.

411 This is the conclusion reached by the following report, following a presentation of the characteristics of the "ideal test" (as illusory as a political program: accuracy, reduction of false positives and negatives, ease of application, consistency, predictability, objectivity, transparency, etc.): OECD, Competition on the merits, *op. cit.* at. The idea that one economic model need not provide accurate forecasts, but simply be less bad than another, can usefully be paralleled with Milton Friedman's instrumentalism, studied *supra*, no. 116.

412 This topic will be addressed *infra*, nos. 354 *et seq.* However, we will demonstrate that economic analysis alone cannot define infringing behaviors.

413 *See infra*, nos. 458–460.

414 One author writes: "A test which looks at the objective tendency of the conduct of a dominant firm to achieve a certain purpose or effect is not a test of intent. It is a test of effect. In reality, the theory of 'objective' intent tries to conflate and solve two separate problems and it does so by *creating an unnecessary legal concept*" (emphasis added). *See* R. Nazzini, The Foundations of European Union Competition Law: The Objectives and Principles of Article 102, 58 (2011). On the one hand, this is contrary to the reasoning of criminal law; on the other, how can intent, such a fundamental concept in law, be described as an "unnecessary legal concept"?

415 F. Lévêque, *Quel test de preuve pour l'article 82?*, Revue Lamy de la concurrence no. 11, 111 (Apr. 2007). *Inter alia*, in the same vein: G. De Muizon, *Les tests de preuve économiques permettant de caractériser une pratique anticoncurrentielle*, Concurrences no. 4-2012, art. no. 49238, 25, 25, nos. 3-4; L. Peeperkorn, *Conditional Pricing and the AEC Test – A Happy Marriage or an Awkward Couple?*, Concurrences no. 2-2019, art. no. 90191, 40, 47–48, nos. 42–48. *See also* Comm. EC, Guidance on the Commission's Enforcement Priorities in Applying Article 82 of the EC Treaty to Abusive Exclusionary Conduct by Dominant Undertakings, 2009 O.J. (C 45) 7, para. 27.

416 *See supra*, nos. 262 *et seq.*

On the other hand, when the Commission devotes dozens of pages to demonstrating the effects on prices or consumers, it mobilizes economic analysis for a mostly useless purpose, while acknowledging, incidentally, that such an examination is overabundant.[417] This is because the evidence is essentially based not on substantial economic analysis, but on presumptions.[418] Similarly, when the competition authority or the companies themselves draw up counterfactual scenarios in order to demonstrate the actual effects of the disputed practice,[419] because these effects are not a criterion for condemnation. The same applies to counterfactual tests designed to determine whether efficiencies could have been achieved in the absence of the litigious conduct:[420] we know that this type of "pro-competitive effect" is never likely to defeat a finding of infringement.[421] It thus appears that anticompetitive practices law takes in useless evidence, which always proves detrimental, in the medium term, to the proper functioning of the legal system.[422]

Finally, even when proof of an effect may be relevant as a clue, it is neither required[423] nor sufficient,[424] which raises a legitimate question: are the efforts mobilized in this way well spent – is the game worth the candle?

334. **The ancillary role of economic analysis: the example of parallel behavior.** In order to characterize an agreement, the competition authority must first establish the existence of an agreement, or at least a concerted action. When evidence is lacking, but parallelism between the behaviors of several companies is observed, an expert appraisal may be commissioned to determine

---

417 *See supra*, nos. 299–300, and references cited.

418 L. Idot, *Argument économique et argument sociologique*, *in* L'ARGUMENT SOCIOLOGIQUE EN DROIT: PLURIEL ET SINGULARITÉ 43, 54 (D. Fenouillet ed., 2015); *adde*, *see supra*, no. 290.

419 In this sense, Castillo de la Torre, *Is the Effects-Based Approach Too Cumbersome? Taking Stock of Recent Practice and Case Law on Article 102 TFEU*, *op. cit.* at 169–70: "The case law supports the view that elaborate counterfactuals of the type recently proposed by certain applicants are not required. …[T]he *Generics UK* judgment makes it clear that the 'counterfactual' relates first of all to the *conduct* of the undertaking, not to the effects on the market, or how the market would operate or be structured." *See* Case C-307/18, Generics (UK), ECLI:EU:C:2020:52, paras. 120–122. *Adde*, Case T-612/17, Google and Alphabet, ECLI:EU:T:2021:763, paras. 377–379, esp. para. 378: "[T]he Commission cannot be required, either spontaneously or in response to a counterfactual analysis put forward by the undertaking being challenged, systematically to establish a counterfactual scenario… . That would, moreover, oblige it to demonstrate that the conduct at issue had actual effects, which … is not required in the case of an abuse of a dominant position, where it is sufficient to establish that there are potential effects."

420 On this type of counterfactual test, *see* D. Geradin & I. Girgenson, *The Counterfactual Method in EU Competition Law: The Cornerstone of the Effects-Based Approach*, *in* TEN YEARS OF EFFECTS-BASED APPROACH IN EU COMPETITION LAW: STATE OF PLAY AND PERSPECTIVES 217 (J. Bourgeois & D. Waelbroeck eds., 2012).

421 *See supra*, nos. 284 *et seq.*

422 In this sense, J. Wróblewski, *La preuve juridique: Axiologie, logique et argumentation*, *in* LA PREUVE EN DROIT 331, 341 (C. Perelman & P. Forier eds., 1981).

423 *See supra*, nos. 277 *et seq.*

424 Geradin & Girgenson, *The Counterfactual Method in EU Competition Law: The Cornerstone of the Effects-Based Approach*, *op. cit.* at 232: "Recent decisional practice suggests that when examining the infringement's effects, the Commission may simply compare the prices in the market where the abuse has been committed with prices in other markets and observe that the prices in the litigious market are, for instance, higher than in most other Member States. As such evidence is unlikely to be sufficient, the Commission will probably look at a range of other factors so as to create a body of evidence establishing anticompetitive foreclosure."

whether it is more likely to result from an agreement or from the normal functioning of the market. In practice, this type of analysis is of little use. Either concerted action has been sufficiently established, for example through e-mail exchanges attesting to the holding of meetings – in which case the expert opinion is of little use, other than to corroborate evidence that has already been established to the requisite legal standard – or concerted action has not been proven – in which case the economic analysis cannot compensate for the inadequacy of the evidence.[425] This type of study is, moreover, purely hypothetical. In the *Ahlström* case, the experts concluded that "the normal operation of the market [is] *a more plausible explanation* for the uniformity of prices than concertation,"[426] and the Advocate General stressed the questionable nature of their reports.[427] The jurist senses that such conjectures are not sufficient to characterize an infringement.[428]

335. **The ancillary role of economic tests: the example of the "as-efficient competitor test" (AEC).** Much ink has been spilled over the AEC test.[429] According to the Court:

> [T]hat concept refers to various tests which have in common the aim of assessing the ability of a practice to produce anti-competitive exclusionary effects by reference to the ability of a hypothetical competitor of the undertaking in a dominant position, which is as efficient as the dominant undertaking in terms of cost structure, to offer customers a rate which is sufficiently advantageous to encourage them to switch supplier, despite the disadvantages caused, without that causing that competitor to incur losses.[430]

Some have wondered whether its recognition might not herald a substantial upheaval in competition rules: perhaps from now on, only behavior capable of ousting competitors as efficient as the dominant firm would be deemed unlawful.[431] This reasoning once again conflates the proof of

---

425 In this sense, *see* M. J. Melícias, *Did They Do It: The Interplay Between the Standard of Proof and the Presumption of Innocence in EU Cartel Investigations*, 35 World Competition 471, 485 (2012), and case law cited.

426 Case C-89/85, Ahlström Osakeyhtiö, ECLI:EU:C:1993:120, para. 101 (emphasis added).

427 *See* the conclusions of Advocate General Darmon, cited *supra*, no. 332.

428 Yet there is much debate as to whether, *de lege ferenda*, in the age of so-called intelligent algorithms, such "collusive balances" should be sanctioned, even if there is no evidence of concerted action. S*ee* OECD, Roundtable on facilitating practices in oligopolies, DAF/COMP(2008)24 (Sept. 5, 2008). On this subject, *see infra*, no. 516.

429 Among a wealth of literature, *see* On-topic: A. Komninos et al., *Le test de l'opérateur aussi efficace: Une nouvelle ère?*, Concurrences no. 3-2013, art. no. 53042, 12.

430 Case C-680/20, Unilever Italia, ECLI:EU:C:2023:33, para. 56; comm. D. Bosco, *Réseaux de distribution exclusive et abus de position dominante*, Contrats concurrence consommation (Mar. 2023), comm. 48.

431 For a critical viewpoint, *see* Castillo de la Torre, *Is the Effects-Based Approach Too Cumbersome? Taking Stock of Recent Practice and Case Law on Article 102 TFEU*, *op. cit.* at 151: "One can interpret that the potential foreclosure of an as-efficient competitor is just one proxy for identifying conduct that is not based on competition on the merits. …The fallacy is the extrapolation of that dictum to assert that conduct (any conduct) cannot constitute an abuse *unless* it forecloses an equally efficient competitor. The condition requiring the dominant undertaking to use means of competition 'on the merits' is very often omitted."

infringement with its definition. Moreover, the importance of this test in evidentiary reasoning should not be exaggerated. The Court of Justice has repeatedly made this point very clear. The AEC test is only ever one of several indicators,[432] so failure to apply it does not constitute an error of law.[433] On the other hand, it has the disadvantages of being difficult to implement, and of being discarded when there is any doubt as to its accuracy,[434] thus mobilizing resources to no avail, as well as of basing the analysis exclusively on prices,[435] whereas the trend is now to extend it to other parameters of competition.[436] In any case, the Commission has recently clarified its doctrine on the use of this test, to bring it into line with the case law of the Court.[437]

336. **The complexity of economic analyses put to the test of common sense.** Complex economic analyses[438] often either aim to prove a point that is not required by law, or require considerable resources to demonstrate a fact that has value only as an incidental evidence, or unnecessarily complicate a simple line of reasoning.

For example, it is legitimate to ask what the notion of an "as-efficient competitor" adds to a simple analysis of a company's costs. It is well known that, when the prices charged by a dominant company are lower than its average variable costs, the judge, considering that the company has no economic interest in offering such prices, presumes that the only rational explanation for such behavior is the desire to eliminate its competitors[439] – which is deemed contrary to competition on the merits.[440]

---

432 Case C-23/14, Post Danmark, ECLI:EU:C:2015:651, para. 62; Case C-680/20, Unilever Italia, ECLI:EU:C:2023:33, para. 61.

433 Case C-549/10 P, Tomra, ECLI:EU:C:2012:221, paras. 73 and 80; *adde*, Opinion of Advocate General J. Kokott, Case C-23/14, Post Danmark, ECLI:EU:C:2015:343, para. 63; Case C-23/14, Post Danmark, ECLI:EU:C:2015:651, para. 57; Case C-680/20, Unilever Italia, ECLI:EU:C:2023:33, para. 58.

434 *See* recently, Case T-604/18, Google and Alphabet, ECLI:EU:T:2022:541, paras. 733–799, esp. para. 799: the Court concludes that there is "doubt as to the correctness of the result of the AEC test carried out by the Commission and, consequently, of the alleged exclusionary effect of the portfolio-based RSAs on a hypothetically at least as efficient competitor. Therefore, as conducted by the Commission, the AEC test does not support the finding of an abuse."

435 Case C-680/20, Unilever Italia, ECLI:EU:C:2023:33, para. 57.

436 *See infra*, nos. 433 *et seq.*

437 Eur. Comm., Amendments to the Communication from the Commission Guidance on the Commission's Enforcement Priorities in Applying Article 82 of the EC Treaty to Abusive Exclusionary Conduct by Dominant Undertakings, Annex, C(2023) 1923 final (Mar. 27, 2023), paras. 2–3; *adde*, Eur. Comm., *A Dynamic and Workable Effects-Based Approach to Abuse of Dominance*, Competition Policy Brief no. 1, 5 (Mar. 2023).

438 By referring only to "complex" economic analyses, we are excluding simple data collection or statistical studies, which are obviously relevant and not very debatable insofar as they constitute proven, concrete facts, and not a hypothetical, abstract argument: market share evaluations, for example, or an analysis of company costs.

439 It should also be noted that a competition authority is not required to demonstrate that the company has a chance of recovering its losses (*see* Case C-333/94 P, Tetra Pak, ECLI:EU:C:1996:436, para. 44), which makes the "recoupment test" superfluous.

440 Case C-62/86, Akzo, ECLI:EU:C:1991:286, para. 71; Case C-209/10, Post Danmark, ECLI:EU:C:2012:172, para. 27.

However, the (hypothetical) ability of the hypothetical as-efficient competitor "is generally determined in the light of the cost structure of the undertaking in a dominant position itself."[441]

This means that an imaginary character has been created from scratch, backed by the nebulous and controversial notion of "efficiency," so that, *in fine*, when asked to "sketch me that sheep…," the exercise consists of nothing more than sketching a look-alike of the dominant company. But for what purpose, and with what benefit? Why not confine the analysis to the dominant company and that company alone,[442] instead of complicating the reasoning by inventing a useless twin, as similar to the dominant company as its reflection in the mirror?[443]

In short, the role of economic analyses appears to be largely overestimated, given that they can corroborate broader probative reasoning as a clue, but are never sufficient on their own to characterize an infringement. Conversely, an essential defense available to companies has not been sufficiently theorized, even though it is of fundamental importance and practical significance – the *legitimate ground*, which, when accepted, enables the presumption of intent to be rebutted, and hence the finding of an infringement to be avoided.

II. Justifications for rebutting the presumption of intent

337. **A defense available to companies: legitimate ground.** Once the prosecuting authority has met its burden of proof and provided sufficient evidence to characterize an infringement of the competition rules, it is up to the defendant undertaking to put forward arguments likely to cast doubt on the existence of an infringement,[444] which means demonstrating that it did

---

441 Case C-680/20, Unilever Italia, ECLI:EU:C:2023:33, para. 56.

442 *Clearly*, a dominant company has the capacity to achieve economies of scale, and therefore to charge prices lower than those of its competitors while still being profitable; *clearly*, smaller operators are less likely to charge such prices; *clearly*, therefore, if the dominant company itself sells its goods or services at prices that do not enable it to cover its variable costs, a competitor that, by definition, is not dominant, has little chance of succeeding. Thus, the notion of an "as-efficient competitor" adds nothing to the analysis, and constitutes an excessively sophisticated detour.

443 On a more nuanced note, one author remarked that the concept of an as-efficient competitor was "perhaps little more than a tribute to the Commission's modernization efforts" – a tribute described as "cautious," *see* Bosco, *Le test de l'opérateur aussi efficace: Une nouvelle ère?*, *op. cit.* at 15, no. 13.

444 On the question – not clearly settled by positive law – of whether the burden of proof for the existence or absence of an exonerating circumstance falls on the company or the Commission, *see* A.-L. Sibony & E. Barbier de la Serre, *Charge de la preuve et théorie du contrôle en droit communautaire de la concurrence: Pour un changement de perspective*, 43 RTD Eur. 205, 220–25 (Apr.-June 2007). It should be noted, however, that in criminal law, "[t]he justification mechanism first requires a strong presumption of actual unlawfulness, at the risk of systematizing the reversal of the burden of proof," *see* M. Reix, Le motif légitime en droit pénal: Contribution à la théorie générale de la justification 342 (2012) (Ph.D. dissertation Université Montesquieu – Bordeaux iv), *adde*, at 419–23; in the same vein, J. Lasserre Capdeville, *Discriminations*, JurisClasseur Pénal Code (Dec. 2022), fasc. 20, no. 74. The Court of Justice has itself recognized, in anticompetitive practices law, that "it [is] for the undertaking … invoking the benefit of a defence against a finding of an infringement to demonstrate that the conditions for applying such defence are satisfied, so that the authority will then have to resort to other evidence," Case C-204/00 P, Aalborg Portland, ECLI:EU:C:2004:6, para. 78.

not intend to restrict competition.[445] While it cannot invoke minority or insanity, as such means are unthinkable for a company, it can, on the other hand, try to invoke the existence of a reasonable doubt as to the scope of the law. However, this will not enable it to overturn the finding of infringement: at most, in rare cases, it may be able to obtain a reduction in the fine imposed.[446] For this reason, the main line of defense available to companies to counter a finding of infringement lies in demonstrating legitimate ground (**B**), a concept borrowed from criminal law (**A**).

A. The theory of legitimate ground in criminal law: exculpatory intent

338. **Definition of legitimate ground.** A ground is a cause of justification, consisting either in a principled reason or in the invocation of specific circumstances, mobilized to justify conduct which, otherwise, would be considered as constituting an infringement.[447] Legitimacy, on the other hand, refers to "compliance with a higher legal or ethical standard."[448] Thus, for the defendant, to invoke a legitimate ground consists in arguing that their behavior pursued a licit end, in other words, in demonstrating that offending intent is lacking,[449] in order to defeat the finding of an offense.

339. **The difference between legitimate ground and motive.** Legitimate ground may appear, at first glance, to be very close to motive. In reality, it is intrinsically linked to intent. However, intent (the objective pursued) is distinct from motives (the reasons for acting).[450] While motives are eminently *subjective*, intent and legitimate ground are always objectively determined, since they involve only investigating whether the accused really wanted to infringe the *law*, and not asking why – jealousy, envy, anger, charity… – they did so.

We are referring here to law, not statute, because the legitimacy of a reason does not always stem from a text. It derives either from a legal principle, or from a reason deemed valid without being expressly enshrined. For example, the *principle* of entrepreneurial freedom justifies not condemning a vertical agreement aimed at organizing a selective distribution network, just as a safety *argument* may excuse certain forms of discrimination on the grounds of disability.[451] The legitimacy of an

445 It is also open to the company to challenge the material evidence adduced by the prosecuting authority, but for our part we will concentrate on the abstract evidence that is likely to defeat the finding of infringement.

446 *See infra*, no. 465.

447 Vocabulaire juridique 670 (G. Cornu ed., 11th ed. 2016).

448 *Id.* at 605.

449 Lasserre Capdeville, *Discriminations*, *op. cit.*, no. 73: according to the author, legitimate ground establishes "the absence of one of the constituent elements of the offense: the intentional element."

450 *See supra*, no. 191.

451 *See infra*, no. 342.

act is, in short, *objective* and *external* to the accused:[452] not all pretexts are accepted by the judge, who confines themselves to taking into consideration the motives deemed admissible by the legal system, expressly or implicitly.[453]

The difference in nature between legitimate ground and motive is coupled with a difference in regime. Whereas motive may, in certain cases, constitute a mitigating or aggravating circumstance leading to a modulation of the penalty, legitimate ground, if accepted, makes the offense disappear, and therefore exonerates the offender from all liability.[454]

340. **The difference in nature and regime between justificatory ground and other excuses.**[455] Unlike error, insanity or duress – which render a person irresponsible on the grounds of *absence of will* – legitimate grounds excuse based on the *lawful exercise of will.*

Here again, the distinct nature of these concepts is matched by an important difference in regime: while justifications based on lack of intent, if accepted, *automatically* excuse the accused, the invocation of a legitimate reason always implies reasoning in terms of *proportionality*.

Indeed, once the legitimate ground consists in demonstrating that the author's main intention was not to break the law, they must establish that their behavior was not only necessary, but also proportionate to the legitimate objective pursued.[456] In such a case, it is the primary intention that counts, and not the incidental effect.[457] The assessment of proportionality will then consist, for the judge, in verifying that the conduct at issue is genuinely aimed at achieving the lawful objective allegedly pursued – an objective that must be of at least equivalent value to that protected by the infringement in question.[458]

341. **Justificatory ground and self-defense: identical reasoning, distinct scope of application.** Self-defense, i.e., the "justified reaction to an unjustified

---

452 Lasserre Capdeville, *Discriminations*, *op. cit.* no. 76.

453 Reix, Le motif légitime en droit pénal: Contribution à la théorie générale de la justification, *op. cit.* 569.

454 As with all causes of justification, which confer "a licit character on facts that, apart from them and by themselves, would have constituted criminal offenses," *see* B. Perreau, De la qualification en matière criminelle 231–32 (1926).

455 For an account of the controversies in criminal doctrine concerning the notions of excuse, justifying fact and other grounds for non-guilt or non-imputability, *see*, in particular, A.-C. Dana, Essai sur la notion d'infraction pénale 152–249 (1982), nos. 144–237.

456 Reix, Le motif légitime en droit pénal : Contribution à la théorie générale de la justification, *op. cit.* at 523–44, nos. 543–571.

457 This reasoning is very old: the distinction between principal intention and accessory effect is already present in Thomas Aquinas, who himself draws inspiration from Aristotle, *see supra*, no. 57.

458 Reix, Le motif légitime en droit pénal : Contribution à la théorie générale de la justification, *op. cit.* at 535, no. 599. The author notes that "the balancing of the values at stake is guided by the purpose of the incrimination and by the overall coherence of the texts."

aggression,"[459] follows the same reasoning as legitimate ground, and also involves assessing the proportionality of the response.[460]

Similarly, neither self-defense nor legitimate ground can be invoked in the case of offenses of commission and offenses of lack of foresight: they can only be envisaged in relation to intentional offenses *stricto sensu.*[461] However, while self-defense is admissible in the case of offenses of result, it is inconceivable in the case of offenses of means; conversely, legitimate ground is inconceivable in the case of offenses of result, and only admissible in the case of offenses of means.[462] As competition infringements are offenses of means, this explains why, in anticompetitive practices law, the excuse of self-defense has never been accepted by the courts.[463]

342. **An illustration from criminal law: consideration of legitimate ground in discrimination matters.** Under criminal law, it is an offense to discriminate against certain individuals on the grounds of their actual or assumed membership of an ethnic group, race or religion, or on the grounds of their age, sexual orientation, gender or, in general, by applying criteria on which the law prohibits arbitrary distinctions.[464] However, certain forms of discrimination may be deemed legitimate, if they are justified by a reason of at least equivalent importance to the principle that the prohibition of discrimination protects – namely, equality – and are proportionate to this legitimate objective.[465] For example, it is not an offense to discriminate on the grounds of disability or state of health for the manager of a merry-go-round to refuse to allow an autistic child to take part, if they validly consider that their disability would compromise their own safety and that of the other participants.[466] After weighing the values at stake, the judge considers that equality must not take precedence over safety.

---

459 More precisely, "the state of one who, under the necessity of protecting their person or that of others, or even property, against an unjust aggression (actual or imminent) commits themselves an act prohibited by penal law, a situation which is, for them, a justifying fact, if at least the intensity of their response is *proportionate* to the seriousness of the attack," Vocabulaire juridique, *op. cit.* at 605 (emphasis added).

460 It is, moreover, from the example of self-defense that Thomas Aquinas developed his distinction between principal intention and accessory effect, *see supra*, no. 57.

461 On the definition of intentional offense *stricto sensu, see supra*, no. 243.

462 The terms "offenses of commission," "offenses of lack of foresight," "offenses of result" and "offenses of means" should be understood in the sense of our quadripartite classification, *see* our summary table, Appendix no. 1, *infra*.

463 *See infra*, no. 350.

464 Lasserre Capdeville, *Discriminations, op. cit.*, no. 1.

465 As noted by the European Court of Human Rights, "a difference of treatment is discriminatory ... if it 'has no objective and reasonable justification', that is if it does not pursue a 'legitimate aim' or if there is not a 'reasonable relationship of proportionality between the means employed and the aim sought to be realized'." *See* Gaygusuz v. Austria, App. no. 17371/90, ¶ 42 (ECtHR Sept. 16, 1996).

466 CA Limoges, ch. acc., May 14, 1991, no. 91-1048 (Fr.).

Such reasoning is quite simple. We shall see that, while it is implicitly accepted in the law of anticompetitive practices, it takes various forms and mobilizes more complex theories.

B. The implicit reception of the theory of legitimate ground in competition law

343. **An ancient and unanimously accepted reasoning: Roman law, common law, Ancien Droit, and 19th-century jurisprudence.** From the "*bon commerce*" of Roman law, to the reasonable restraints of common law, via the contribution to the common interest of the Ancien Droit, and the distinction between defensive and offensive agreements in the case law of the late nineteenth century:[467] everywhere and always, legal reasoning in the law of anticompetitive practices has welcomed the idea that a practice can be justified by a legitimate reason. This is because the value protected by the discipline – competition – is not the only one worthy of protection by the legal system.

First and foremost, it shares the territory with freedom of undertaking – the balance between freedom of undertaking and competition proving difficult to achieve in some cases. Indeed, without free undertaking, there can be no competition, but therein lies the paradox: preserving competition occasionally requires restricting the power of certain companies; and if this restriction is too great or unfounded, it is itself detrimental to competition. A constantly delicate, ever-evolving balance between freedom of undertaking and competition is therefore necessary.

Notwithstanding this first set of interests, which are distinct yet dependent on one another, many other values can justify behavior that would otherwise be deemed anticompetitive, escaping the clutches of the competition authorities. Think, for example, of environmental law, innovation, or the preservation of trade union or sporting models. In short, social, environmental and even societal issues can, here and there, disqualify the intervention of competition law. However, when competition law recognizes this, by deeming certain practices lawful on these grounds, it would be hasty to conclude that it integrates these values itself, or elevates them to objectives.[468] On the contrary, it steps aside to make way for other disciplines or rival principles,[469] whose raison d'être is precisely to compensate for the inadequacies of competition alone, which is clearly not sufficient to ensure the proper functioning of a society.[470]

---

467 *See supra*, no. 125.

468 On the "objectives of competition law," *see infra*, nos. 430 *et seq.*

469 We write "rival" because, in the cases we are looking at, two values are in competition, insofar as they cannot be simultaneously protected.

470 *See infra*, nos. 481–482.

344. **The subsequent fragmentation of the theory of legitimate ground into different "categories."** In competition law, it is always the same old story: what was once simple has now become complex – to the point where we lose sight of the unity of the reasoning behind seemingly scattered techniques and solutions. As a result, we quarrel over semantics, discuss the applicability of a particular theory to a given case, only to adopt another, ignoring the fact that, whatever the label attached to the procedure, we are still unknowingly doing the same thing: taking into account a legitimate ground.[471]

A case in point is the debate as to whether the rule of reason, reputedly specific to U.S. antitrust law, is accepted in European Union law. For some,[472] this is implicitly or partially the case; for others, it should be;[473] for others, it is not at all the case[474] – which the General Court and then the Court of Justice have upheld.[475] Moreover, European reasoning is indeed more compartmentalized than its American counterpart. Admittedly, we have a formidable arsenal at our disposal: on the one hand, block or individual exemptions based on article 101(3) TFEU; on the other, a case-by-case assessment based on paragraph 1 of the same article; not to mention the possibility of invoking objective justifications; and not forgetting the theory of ancillary restraints.

However, all these methods apply the same reasoning, and are justified by the structure of the competition infringement: given that anticompetitive intent is a constitutive element,[476] if it is lacking, there can be no finding of an infringement. This is the case when the primary intent is not to restrict competition, but to achieve another legitimate objective.

These assertions need to be verified, by examining exemptions, the theory of ancillary restraints, and objective justifications.

---

471 It should be noted that criminal law specialists equate exemptions and other objective justifications under competition law with justifying facts. *See* in particular A. Lepage, P. Maistre du Chambon & R. Salomon, Droit pénal des affaires 764–75 (6th ed. 2020), nos. 1349–73. *Adde*, P. Laurent, *L'entente: Une catégorie juridique ambivalente*, Recueil Dalloz-Sirey 307, 312–13 (1977), chron. xliii.

472 M.-A. Frison-Roche & J.-C. Roda, Droit de la concurrence 358 and 365–66 (2nd ed. 2022), nos. 445 and 451, resp.: the authors note that some have seen a "camouflaged rule of reason" in the "balancing test" based on article 101(1), and consider that the differences between the American and European systems should not be exaggerated. *Adde*, R. Kovar, *Le droit de la concurrence et la règle de raison*, Revue trimestrielle de droit européen no. 2, 237, 237 and 241 (1987): the author notes that several authors have expressed the idea that the rule of reason is included in the exemption regime.

473 M. Marquis, O2 (Germany) v Commission *and the exotic mysteries of Article 81(1) EC*, 32 European Law Review 29, 45–47 (2007): the author invites us to "re-re-visit" the rule of reason.

474 D. Bailey, *Règle de raison*, *in* Dictionnaire de droit de la concurrence 730, 731 (M. Chagny & E. Combe eds., 2023).

475 Case T-491/07 RENV, Groupement des cartes bancaires, ECLI:EU:T:2016:379, paras. 68–69: "It is true that, in a number of judgments, the Court and the General Court have expressed themselves in favor of a more flexible reading of the prohibition laid down in Article 81(1) EC," but "the judgments referred to in paragraph 68 cannot be interpreted as enshrining the existence of a rule of reason in Community competition law" (unofficial translation); *adde*, Case C-307/18, Generics (UK), ECLI:EU:C:2020:52, para. 104; Case C-883/19 P, HSBC, ECLI:EU:C:2023:11, para. 140; Case C-211/22, Super Bock Bebidas, ECLI:EU:C:2023:529, para. 36.

476 *See supra*, nos. 262 *et seq.*

345. **Block exemption regulations: simple legal presumptions of lawfulness justified by the existence of a legitimate ground.** As early as the 1980s, alongside the possibility of granting individual exemptions on the basis of article 101(3) TFEU, the Commission adopted block exemption regulations[477] enabling companies to benefit, outside any litigation procedure, from an "*a priori* exemption," provided that the agreement meets the conditions set out in these regulations.[478] However, the expression "*a priori* exemption" is somewhat misleading: for an exemption to be possible, an infringement must first have been identified[479] – otherwise, there is, strictly speaking, nothing to exempt.[480] However, by definition, when we consider in advance that a particular agreement or clause is not anticompetitive, we are establishing that there is no infringement. It would therefore be more accurate to speak, rather than of exemption, of *simple legal presumptions of lawfulness*.

To keep things simple, these presumptions can only be identified by means of a two-step process. First, it must be ascertained whether the agreement falls within the scope of a regulation, either by virtue of its nature (vertical agreement, specialization agreement, research and development agreement, etc.), or by virtue of the sector concerned (automotive sector, air transport sector, etc.).[481] Secondly, the relevant regulation must be read *a contrario*. Indeed, all exemption regulations are built on the same model, which consists in setting out the "hard-core restrictions" and "excluded

---

477 *Inter alia*: Commission Regulation (EU) 2023/1066 of June 1, 2023, on the Application of Article 101(3) of the Treaty on the Functioning of the European Union to Certain Categories of Research and Development Agreements, 2023 O.J. (L 143) 9; Commission Regulation (EU) 2023/1067 of June 1, 2023, on the Application of Article 101(3) of the Treaty on the Functioning of the European Union to Certain Categories of Specialisation Agreements, 2023 O.J. (L 143) 20; Commission Regulation (EU) 2022/720 of May 10, 2022, on the Application of Article 101(3) of the Treaty on the Functioning of the European Union to Categories of Vertical Agreements and Concerted Practices, 2022 O.J. (L 134) 4; Commission Regulation (EU) No. 461/2010 of May 27, 2010, on the Application of Article 101(3) of the Treaty on the Functioning of the European Union to Categories of Vertical Agreements and Concerted Practices in the Motor Vehicle Sector, 2010 O.J. (L 129) 52; Council Regulation (EC) No. 487/2009 of May 25, 2009, on the Application of Article 81(3) of the Treaty to Categories of Agreements and Concerted Practices in the Air Transport Sector, 2009 O.J. (L 148) 1.

478 I. Luc, *Exemption par catégorie (règlement d')*, *in* DICTIONNAIRE DE DROIT DE LA CONCURRENCE 432, 432 (M. Chagny & E. Combe eds., 2023).

479 This is what is provided for in the exemption regulations, *see* for example, Commission Regulation (EU) No. 330/2010 of Apr. 20, 2010, on the Application of Article 101(3) of the Treaty on the Functioning of the European Union to Categories of Vertical Agreements and Concerted Practices, 2010 O.J. (L 102) 1, art. 2(1): "This exemption shall apply to the extent that such agreements contain vertical restraints." The same sentence is reproduced throughout the aforementioned regulations.

480 Exemption is generally defined as "the act by which an authority frees a subject of law from an obligation that would normally be incumbent upon them, or removes them from the ordinary regime that would be applicable to them," VOCABULAIRE JURIDIQUE, *op. cit.* at 434. It is not unknown in criminal law, although it is very rare in this field, and of a different nature, since the exemption never defeats the finding of an offense, but only relieves the accused, otherwise convicted, of the obligation to undergo their sentence. Examples are few and far between: in the case of absolution, or in cases of terrorism, where the offender has "helped to avoid the commission of the offense and to identify, where appropriate, other culprits," officers may be exempted from punishment. This latter hypothesis, however, is closer to the leniency procedure in competition law than to the exemption provided for in agreement law. For a comparative analysis of exemption in criminal law, *see* Sénat, *L'exemption judiciaire de sanction pénale* (Feb. 1, 2007), available online at https://senat.fr.

481 *See* the aforementioned regulations, *supra*, no. 345 (footnote).

restrictions,"[482] i.e., a list of practices that withdraw the benefit of the exemption:[483] if the agreement contains none, it is presumed to be lawful.

At this stage, there are two ways to understand why a given practice is not deemed anticompetitive: on the one hand, through legal discourse, and on the other, through economic discourse. Like most texts issued by the Commission, exemption regulations adopt an economic perspective: in their preamble, they state that agreements are exempted because they are supposed to produce efficiency gains or positive effects that outweigh their anticompetitive effects,[484] all to the benefit of consumers.[485] From an institutional point of view, this makes sense: the said regulations presume that exempted agreements fulfill the conditions of article 101(3). Paragraph 3 is based on the idea that "certain restrictive agreements may generate economic benefits that outweigh the negative effects of the restriction of competition."[486] However, we know that the argument of efficiency gains or other pro-competitive effects is never received in practice on the basis of paragraph 3,[487] and this for a legal reason.

Indeed, in law, if the result is not a constitutive element of an infringement, it is not likely to justify conduct, and therefore to defeat a finding of infringement.[488] By analogy and for the same reasons, it is not efficiency gains or pro-competitive effects that explain why practices covered by exemption regulations are presumed to be lawful. They are so, quite simply, because their *primary aim is* not to restrict competition. Indeed, a careful study of the *ratio legis* of exemption regulations reveals that they are in fact based not on the invocation of positive effects, but on the existence of *legitimate grounds*, such as rationalizing production or distribution, engaging in a research and development policy, organizing a distribution system, increasing the quality or quantity of goods produced, encouraging the production of new products, or ensuring a higher standard of service.[489] While we can always write, for example, "such an agreement *has the effect of* fostering innovation," for the sake of consistency and conformity with legal reasoning, we should prefer expressions

482 "Hard-core restrictions" are those that exclude the benefit of the block exemption for the entire agreement, whereas "excluded restrictions" render the regulation inapplicable only to the clause deemed restrictive.

483 Given that the practices in question are those commonly deemed anticompetitive by case law, we will examine them in the next chapter, which deals with the definition of infringements.

484 *See* in particular Regulation (EU) 2022/720, recitals 6–7; Regulation (EU) No. 1217/2010 of Dec. 14, 2010, on the Application of Article 101(3) of the Treaty on the Functioning of the European Union to Certain Categories of Research and Development Agreements, 2010, O.J. (L 335) 36, recital 15.

485 *See* in particular Regulation (EU) 2022/720, recital 8; Regulation (EU) No. 1217/2010, recital 10.

486 EC Comm., Guidelines on the Application of Article 81(3) of the Treaty, 2004 O.J. (C 101) 97, "Key points."

487 *See supra*, no. 285.

488 *See supra*, nos. 279–281.

489 For other examples, *see* A. C. Witt, The More Economic Approach to EU Antitrust Law 161–62 (2019), and references cited.

such as "such an agreement *aims* to foster innovation."[490] Thus, as long as an agreement (i) is primarily aimed at achieving a legitimate objective, (ii) restricts competition only incidentally, is (iii) necessary and (iv) proportionate to the aim pursued, it is not anticompetitive – not because of a consequentialist and hypothetical economic analysis, but in application of the legal theory of legitimate grounds.

346. **Individual exemptions: once an artificial rationale, now devoid of any contentious significance.** Since 2003, no individual exemptions have been granted, as only efficiency gains are now taken into account at the paragraph 3 stage – a defense that is systematically deemed to be inoperative.[491] In fact, it is increasingly rare for companies to claim the benefit of an individual exemption.[492]

Prior to 2003, numerous individual exemptions were applied for and granted.[493] To do so, the Commission first characterized a restriction of competition on the basis of paragraph 1, before exempting the disputed agreement on the basis of paragraph 3.[494] René Joliet rightly remarked at the time that the analysis of the restriction of competition was mechanical and excessive – in a word, artificial.[495] In reality, the characterization of the restriction of competition was only a necessary, and quickly dispatched, step in order to be able to exempt the agreement.[496] As long as the objective pursued by the parties was lawful, it would have been appropriate to consider that competition was, quite simply, not restricted.

The examples are varied and could be multiplied. However, the golden thread linking each case is identical. In every case, the Commission finds that the agreement in question is *justified by a legitimate ground*: the development of a new technique;[497] the improvement of distribution and

490 If only because, when investing in R&D, you never know whether it will actually result in innovation. Moreover, overly frequent and inelegant use of the word "effect" in sentences that would retain the same meaning without it is commonplace in this field.

491 *See supra*, no. 285.

492 L. Idot, *L'intégration des considérations d'intérêt public dans le droit des ententes: Approche juridique*, Concurrences no. 2-2021, art. no. 99790, 12, 20, no. 39, and the numerous decisions cited.

493 Between 1965 and 1998, the Commission exempted 141 agreements on the basis of paragraph 3, *see* Witt, The More Economic Approach to EU Antitrust Law, *op. cit.* at 167.

494 By the formula, reproduced identically in all the decisions: "The provisions of Article 85(1) of the EC Treaty are declared inapplicable, in accordance with Article 85(3), to the Agreement."

495 R. Joliet, The Rule of Reason in Antitrust Law: American, German and Common Market Laws in Comparative Perspective 114 (1967).

496 As expressly recognized in the following judgment: Case 26/76, Metro, ECLI:EU:C:1977:167, para. 27.

497 Comm. EC, July 17, 1967, IV/26045, A.C.E.C. – Berliet, iii, 1: "Whereas one of the parties cannot reasonably be expected to undertake the effort of developing a new technique in collaboration with the other partner and then accept that the latter may subsequently exploit the results of its work with a third party; whereas, consequently, reciprocal exclusivity commitments are essential to achieving the favorable results of the agreement" (emphasis added) (unofficial translation).

after-sales service;[498] the need to ensure a regular supply;[499] the desire to enable small companies to compete with larger ones;[500] the need to put an end to or mitigate the harmful consequences of a crisis affecting the sector;[501] or the intention to put in place practices beneficial to the environment.[502]

347. **The implicit admission of the theory of legitimate ground on the basis of article 101(1) TFEU through the theory of ancillary restraints.** Legitimate grounds are also occasionally taken into account on the basis of article 101(1), but this has long been the subject of criticism, as some consider that they should only be accepted on the basis of article 101(3). Some rulings have thus been analyzed as "hidden exemptions"[503] reflecting the implicit importation of the American rule of reason[504] into Union law. Indeed, this is not an isolated phenomenon. The Court has often accepted certain grounds for ruling out the existence of an anticompetitive agreement, always subject to the proviso that they are legitimate, necessary and proportionate:[505] guaranteeing the proper practice of the legal profession;[506] taking account of the objectives of the common agricultural

498 Comm. EC, Dec. 13, 1974, IV/14 650, Bayerische Motoren Werke, para. 24.

499 Comm. EC, Dec. 19, 1974, IV/23 013, Goodyear Italia – Euram, para. 12.

500 Comm. EC, June 27, 1967, IV/223, Transocean Marine Paint Association, iv.

501 *Ex multis*: Comm. EC, July 19, 1984, IV/30.863, BPCL/ICI, para. 34; Comm. EC, July 4, 1984, IV/30.810, Synthetic Fibers, paras. 28–31: "[A]gainst the background of the overcapacity that existed in the synthetic-fibres industry in 1982 and that is still running at a high level . . . . The purpose of the agreement is to reduce capacity so that the capacity that remains can be operated at a more economic level. ...In the present case, however, market forces by themselves had failed to achieve the capacity reductions necessary to re-establish and maintain in the longer term an effective competitive structure within the common market. The producers concerned therefore agreed to organize for a limited period and collectively, *the needed structural adjustment*" (emphasis added); Comm. EC, Apr. 29, 1984, IV/34.456, Stichting Baksteen, paras. 18–21, esp. para. 19: "The agreement *aims* at reducing capacity in order to improve the rate of utilization of the capacity retained and gradually restore a lasting balance between supply and demand in the medium term" (emphasis added).

502 *Ex multis*: Comm. EC, Dec. 21, 1994, IV/34.252, *Philips-Osram*, para. 25: the contested agreement will result in "lower total energy usage and a better prospect of realizing energy reduction and waste emission programmes. In addition, the parties will concentrate their R& D activities in Philips' laboratories, achieving ... a concentration of effort to tackle properly the common challenge of developing lead-free materials"; Comm. EC, May 18, 1994, IV/33.640, Exxon/Shell, para. 68: the joint venture in question will make it possible to dispense with the transport of ethylene, and thus avoid "health and environmental risks connected with such transport"; Comm. EC, Jan. 14, 1999, IV.F.1/36.718, CEDED, para. 47: "The agreement is designed to reduce the potential energy consumption of new washing machines by at least 15 to 20%... ."

503 N. Petit, Droit européen de la concurrence 351 (3rd ed. 2020), no. 838.

504 It should be noted, however, that the United States has long been familiar with the theory of ancillary restraints, which is distinct from the rule of reason, *see* United States v. Addyston Pipe & Steel Co., 175 U.S. 211 (1899).

505 Indeed, the notion of ancillary restraint covers any restraint that is directly linked to, and necessary for, a principal transaction. It is therefore neither a question of balancing pro- and anticompetitive effects, nor of accepting a rule of reason. The reasoning is as follows: "If, without the restriction, the main operation is difficult or even impossible to implement, the restriction may be regarded as objectively necessary for its implementation," *see* Case T-112/99, Métropole télévision (M6), ECLI:EU:T:2001:215, paras. 104–105 and 110. *See also* EC Comm., Guidelines on the Application of Article 81(3) of the Treaty, 2004 O.J. (C 101) 97, paras. 28–31.

506 Case C-309/99, Wouters, ECLI:EU:C:2002:98, paras. 107–109.

policy;[507] the social policy aims pursued by collective agreements concluded between representative employers' and workers' organizations;[508] adopting anti-doping regulations aimed at ensuring the fair running of sporting competitions;[509] complying with national regulations;[510] setting up a compulsory pension fund benefiting all members of a liberal profession;[511] setting up a selective distribution system based on objective criteria,[512] or a franchising network;[513] preventing improper handling of seed varieties protected by plant breeders' rights;[514] ensuring the proper functioning of a purchasing cooperative in order to maintain its bargaining power vis-à-vis producers;[515] preserving the luxury image of cosmetic products;[516] or perhaps, if the Court follows the conclusions of its Advocate General, the preservation of the "European Sports Model."[517]

348. **Intermediate conclusion on the consideration of legitimate grounds under article 101 TFEU: unjustified complexity.** Competition law "has now reached a level of abstraction and complexity that tends to render it unreadable."[518] In fact, from the distinction between the examination carried out on the basis of paragraph 3, now exclusively focused on efficiency and the balancing of pro- and anticompetitive effects, and therefore insusceptible of calling into question a finding of infringement,[519]

---

507 *See* Regulation (EU) No. 1308/2013 of the European Parliament and of the Council of Dec. 17, 2013, establishing a Common Organisation of the Markets in Agricultural Products, 2013 O.J. (L 347) 671, pt. IV, ch. I, art. 2019 (1), (2) Concertation on prices or quantities, as well as exchanges of strategic information, may be exempted from the ban on agreements "if they are agreed between the members of the same producer organization … recognised by a Member State and are strictly necessary for the pursuit of one or more of the objectives assigned to the producer organisation," *see* Case C-671/15, Association des producteurs vendeurs d'endives, ECLI:EU:C:2017:860, answer to preliminary question. More generally, *see* Eur. Comm., *The Application of Union Competition Rules to the Agricultural Sector*, COM(2018) 706 final (Oct. 26, 2018).

508 Case C-67/96, Albany International, ECLI:EU:C:1999:430, para. 59; Case C-219/97, Maatschappij Drijvende Bokken, ECLI:EU:C:1999:437, para. 57; Case T-217/03, Fédération nationale de la coopération bétail et viande, ECLI:EU:T:2006:391, para. 98.

509 Case C-519/04 P, David Meca-Medina, ECLI:EU:C:2006:492, paras. 42–45.

510 *See, inter alia,* Case 40/73, Suiker Unie, ECLI:EU:C:1975:174, paras. 36–73; *adde,* Case C-198/01, Consorzio Industrie Fiammiferi, ECLI:EU:C:2003:430, para. 53.

511 Case C-180/98, Pavel Pavlov, ECLI:EU:C:2000:428, paras. 93–99.

512 Case 26/76, Metro SB-Grossmärkte, ECLI:EU:C:1977:167, paras. 20–21 and para. 27; *adde,* Case 31/80, L'Oréal, ECLI:EU:C:1980:289, paras. 15–16; Case 107/82, AEG-Telefunken, ECLI:EU:C:1983:293, paras. 33–43.

513 Case 161/84, Pronuptia de Paris, ECLI:EU:C:1986:41, paras. 16–22.

514 Case 27/87, Louis Erauw-Jacquery, ECLI:EU:C:1988:183, para. 10.

515 Case C-250/92, Gøttrup-Klim, ECLI:EU:C:1994:413, para. 35.

516 Case C-230/16, Coty Germany, ECLI:EU:C:2017:941, paras. 21–36. For application in French law: ADLC, decision no. 18-D-23 Oct. 24, 2018, regarding practices implemented in the retail of outdoor power equipment (Fr.); comm. D. Bosco, *Première décision 'post-Coty' de l'Autorité de la concurrence*, CONTRATS CONCURRENCE CONSOMMATION (Dec. 2018), comm. 204.

517 Opinion of Advocate General A. Rantos, Case C-333/21, European Superleague Compagnie, ECLI:EU:C:2022:993, paras. 85–123.

518 D. Bosco, *L'avocat général Rantos défend les fédérations sportives au nom de la spécificité du modèle sportif européen*, CONTRATS CONCURRENCE CONSOMMATION (Feb. 2023), comm. 30.

519 *See supra*, no. 285

through the theory of ancillary restraints, to the possibility of taking the said pro-competitive effects into consideration at the paragraph 1 stage to call into question the characterization of an infringement by object, without however mobilizing any rule of reason[520] – the superposition of apparently distinct methods of analysis makes the agreement characterization process excessively subtle,[521] muddled – in a word: unreadable. For this reason, some are now arguing in favor of doing away with the alternative between paragraphs 1 and 3 of article 101, so that the analysis can be carried out as a unit,[522] which would indeed be a first step towards a salutary simplification. The safest course would still be to accept the unitary theory of legitimate ground, which would be all the more relevant, as it is identical in the case of abuse of a dominant position.

349. **The implicit admission of the theory of legitimate ground under article 102 TFEU through the theory of objective justifications.** Abuse of a dominant position is, theoretically at least, subject to two distinct means of justification: a dominant undertaking may "*either* by demonstrating that its conduct is objectively necessary *or* by demonstrating that its conduct produces substantial efficiencies which outweigh any anti-competitive effects on consumers."[523] However, we know that this second argument, because it is based on proof of effects, is never accepted in practice.[524] Objective justification, on the other hand, has long been accepted,[525] and is sometimes referred to as "quasi-exemption,"[526] implying that once an abuse has been identified, it can be "exempted." However, just as it seems illogical to us to consider that the agreement is characterized and then exempted,[527] we consider *a fortiori*[528] that the abuse is not qualified and then justified.

---

520 Case C-307/18, Generics (UK), ECLI:EU:C:2020:52, paras. 103–104; *adde*, in the same sense, Opinion of Advocate General J. Kokott, Case C-307/18, Generics (UK), ECLI:EU:C:2020:28, para. 158; Case C-883/19 P, HSBC, ECLI:EU:C:2023:11, paras. 139–140; Case C-211/22, Super Bock Bebidas, ECLI:EU:C:2023:529, para. 36.

521 In this sense: C. Bovet, *ECJ: Discourse on Method*, CONCURRENCES, no. 2-2023, art. no. 112117, 2, 3.

522 This is also our position, *see infra*, no. 503. For a proposal advocating a "monistic" rewrite of article 101 – i.e., the removal of paragraph 3 – *see* L. Gyselen, *What Makes an Agreement Anti-Competitive: Lessons from the Past*, *in* THE NOTION OF RESTRICTION OF COMPETITION: REVISITING THE FOUNDATIONS OF ANTITRUST ENFORCEMENT IN EUROPE 111, 133–35 (D. Gerard, M. Merola & B. Meyring eds., 2017). *Adde*, *see* B. Hawk, *The American (Anti-Trust) Revolution: Lessons for the EEC?*, 9 EUROPEAN COMPETITION LAW REVIEW 53, 69 (1988): "The bifurcation of what ideally should be a single anti-trust analysis into the double test of Article 81(1) and Article 81(3) results in near anarchy." *Contra*, for an article in favor of greater mobilization of article 101(3), *see* D. Bailey, *Reinvigorating the Role of Article 101(3) Under Regulation 1/2003*, 81 ANTITRUST LAW JOURNAL 111 (2016).

523 Comm. EC, Guidance on the Commission's Enforcement Priorities in Applying Article 82 of the EC Treaty to Abusive Exclusionary Conduct by Dominant Undertakings, 2009 O.J. (C 45) 7, para. 28.

524 *See supra*, no. 288.

525 *Ex multis*: Case 85/76, Hoffmann-La Roche, ECLI:EU:C:1979:36, para. 90; cf. judgment: Case 311/84, CBEM, ECLI:EU:C:1985:394, para. 27; Case C-7/97, Oscar Bronner, ECLI:EU:C:1998:569, para. 41; Case C-457/10 P, AstraZeneca, ECLI:EU:C:2012:770, para. 134.

526 D. Bosco, *Abus de position dominante*, RÉPERTOIRE DE DROIT EUROPÉEN (Jan. 2019), no. 51.

527 *See supra*, no. 345

528 We write *a fortiori*, because this double step has no textual basis in terms of abuse of dominant position.

Indeed, it would be advisable to dispense with this double step, since in law, when a legitimate reason is admitted, there is no infringement.[529] The legitimate grounds that can be put forward are more or less identical to those that can be argued on the basis of article 101 TFEU.[530]

For example, in the *SABAM* case, a copyright management company holding a de facto monopoly was accused of a mismatch between the economic value of the service provided and its price.[531] In response to a preliminary question, the Court concluded that such practice did not constitute an abuse of a dominant position, provided that the prices were not excessive, and that there was no other pricing system capable of achieving the same "legitimate aim" – namely, the protection of the interests of authors, composers, and music publishers.[532] In another ruling, it held that an abuse could be justified by the "task" and "method of financing of public service undertakings."[533]

A third case, from French decision-making practice, is worth mentioning. In the *Immaculée Conception* case,[534] the Conseil de la Concurrence accepted that a legitimate reason could prevent a finding of infringement. This Cistercian congregation, based off the coast of Cannes on the island of Saint-Honorat, had reserved exclusive service to the island for itself through its own transport company – de facto ruling out any possibility of competition. However, the defendant's argument was tenable: its primary objective was not to exclude potential competitors, but to avoid an influx of visitors by controlling ticketing, in order to preserve the tranquility of the monastic site and the integrity of the listed site.[535] Indeed, when the service had been opened up to several other companies, the number of visitors had increased exponentially: the ground was trampled, and numerous disturbances to public order were reported. The Conseil de la Concurrence

---

529 This is also the opinion expressed in the Opinion of Advocate General F. G. Jacobs, Case C-53/03, Syfait, ECLI:EU:C:2004:673, para. 72: "[T]he two-stage analysis suggested by the distinction between an abuse and its objective justification is to my mind somewhat artificial. Article 82 EC, by contrast with Article 81 EC, does not contain any explicit provision for the exemption of conduct otherwise falling within it. Indeed, the very fact that conduct is characterised as an 'abuse' suggests that a negative conclusion has already been reached . . . . In my view, it is therefore more accurate to say that certain types of conduct on the part of a dominant undertaking do not fall within the category of abuse at all."

530 The president of the Court of First Instance listed a number of examples: improving the quality of products or services, offering new products or services, innovating, stepping up promotional efforts, developing services to accompany the sale or after-sales services, and so on. B. Vesterdorf, *Considérations sur la notion de "concurrence par les mérites"*, *in* La modernisation du droit de la concurrence 163, 170 (G. Canivet ed., 2006).

531 On the difficulties associated with the general characterization of excessive prices, *see infra*, no. 406.

532 Case C-372/19, SABAM, ECLI:EU:C:2020:959, reply to preliminary question.

533 Case C-52/07, Kanal 5, ECLI:EU:C:2008:703, para. 47.

534 Cons. conc., decision no. 05-D-60 of Nov. 8, 2005, on practices implemented by the Cisterian Order of the Immaculée Conception, the Planaria company and the municipality of Cannes (Fr.); comm. E. Claudel, *L'abus de position dominante peut être justifié !*, RTD com. 582 (2006).

535 Cons. conc., decision no. 05-D-60 of Nov. 8, 2005, on practices implemented by the Cisterian Order of the Immaculée Conception, the Planaria company and the municipality of Cannes (Fr.), para. 62.

examined whether there were other, less restrictive means of achieving the same objective.[536] It concluded that the exclusivity granted by the congregation was "justified by the particular geography of the site, the private nature of the island and the need to control the flow of visitors," and that "[n]o other solution, allowing the same objectives to be achieved but with fewer restrictions on competition," had been identified.[537] The charge of abuse of a dominant position was therefore dismissed.[538]

350. **Self-defense: a justification distinct from legitimate grounds and inoperative in anticompetitive practices law.** In the law of anticompetitive practices, while the argument of self-defense has long been admissible in theory,[539, 540] it has never been accepted in practice.[541] The explanation is simple: for the legitimate nature of the defense to be accepted, the company in question must itself be the victim of anticompetitive behavior; if this is the case, it is not entitled to retaliate by adopting anticompetitive behavior, but must report to the competent authorities the unlawful practice from which it claims to be suffering.[542] It follows that committing an infringement cannot be considered a necessary and proportionate response.[543]

*

* *

536 *Id.* paras. 63–67.

537 *Id.* para. 67 (unofficial translation).

538 In this respect, it is interesting to note that the abuse was not characterized or justified: the Conseil de la Concurrence directly concluded that there had been no infringement.

539 For a detailed study, *see* J.-P. Viennois, *La légitime défense en droit de la concurrence ou l'emprunt concevable d'une notion en droit pénal*, Revue de science criminelle et de droit pénal comparé 295 (2004). The author argues that the theory of self-defense is universal and can therefore logically be invoked in anticompetitive practices law. We believe, *a contrario*, that the scope of application of self-defense is limited to offenses of result (*see infra*, no. 248), which explains why this argument has never been accepted by the competition judge.

540 Self-defense was already recognized under the ECSC Treaty, *see* Case 16-61, Acciaerie Ferriere e Fonderi di Modena, ECLI:EU:C:1962:29, at 576–77. *Adde*, on the basis of the EC Treaty: Case 27/76, United Brands, ECLI:EU:C:1978:22, paras. 183–189.

541 *See ex multis*: Case 8, SA Musique Diffusion française, ECLI:EU:C:1983:15, paras. 89–90: the Court ruled out the claim of self-defense put forward by the applicant, since the commercial attacks it alleged were perfectly legal; Case C-235/92 P, Montecatini, ECLI:EU:C:1999:362, para. 60: the Court held that the arguments put forward by the company "which related in particular to the national political and social context ... were not such as to efface the unlawful nature of its conduct, since it could not be accepted that participation in an unlawful agreement constituted a legitimate form of self-defence."

542 *See* in particular Case T-30/89, Hilti, ECLI:EU:T:1991:70, para. 117. According to Advocate General Georges Cosmas, to accept another solution would be "indirectly to confer an individual right of 'self-determination' on undertakings enabling them to take appropriate steps to deal with competitions of unfair competition caused by the conduct of their competitor," *see* Opinion of Advocate General G. Cosmas, Case C-235/92, Montecatini, ECLI:EU:C:1997:362, para. 48, n.36.

543 In this sense, Case T-155/06, Tomra Systems, ECLI:EU:T:2010:370, para. 207: "[W]hilst the fact that an undertaking is in a dominant position cannot deprive it of its entitlement to protect its own commercial interests when they are attacked, and whilst such an undertaking must be allowed the right to take such reasonable steps as it deems appropriate to protect those interests, such behaviour cannot be allowed if its purpose is to strengthen that dominant position and thereby abuse it."

351. **Conclusion of Section 2: theorizing the effects-based approach and relativizing the role of economic analyses.** The study of the modalities of proof of intent provided an opportunity to address one of the most controversial themes in doctrine: the effects-based approach. It became clear that this approach does not imply a shift in the object of proof from the object – in other words, the goal pursued by the company – to the effect, i.e., the result. A contrary interpretation would be tantamount to admitting that a competition authority could sanction conduct on the basis of its unforeseeable effects, which would run counter to the principle of foreseeability. *De lege lata,* when a competition authority is faced with a practice whose anticompetitive nature is not certain, it sometimes resorts to the effects-based approach in order to *corroborate evidence of the* anticompetitive *object*. Nevertheless, it is a principle of law that when the infringing nature of the conduct is not established to the requisite legal standard, further proof is required. Consequently, the effects-based approach appears superfluous, as the evidentiary reasoning would be identical in its absence. Furthermore, the role of economic analyses in proving competition infringements has been relativized. While economic tests are ubiquitous in theory, in practice they are merely incidental clues. Conversely, arguments based on the existence of a legitimate ground are of major importance for companies, as they can, by demonstrating the absence of anticompetitive intent, defeat a finding of infringement.

*

* *

352. **Conclusion to Chapter 1: the discrepancy between the presentation of competition infringements and practical reality.** The roles have been reversed: while intent is generally presented as sometimes being relevant, but not required to prove the infringement, it is in fact a constitutive element, while economic effects and analysis ultimately play a much lesser role than is commonly attributed to them. This discrepancy between theory and practice is also found in the definition of competition infringements: while they are classically defined in terms of their effects, their definition is, in fact, based on intent.

*

* *

Chapter 2
THE ROLE OF INTENT IN DEFINING OFFENSES

353. **In search of a definition of competition infringements.** When the first regulations governing the application of competition rules were adopted in 1962, jurists were wondering what criteria could be used to judge behavior as anticompetitive – they are still asking the same question today.[1] Although attempts to define infringements have traditionally taken "restriction of competition" or, since the "more economic approach," harm to the consumer as their starting point, authors still struggle to define these concepts and reach a consensus on their meaning.[2] Nonetheless, according to the majority of doctrine, an anticompetitive practice is one that has a restrictive effect on competition, or a negative effect on the market or the consumer: the definition of infringements is thus generally based on effects (**Section 1**). Such proposals are unsatisfactory, however, insofar as they make it impossible to distinguish between lawful and unlawful conduct. However, the purpose of a definition is argumentation:[3] its function is to discover the essence of the thing studied, and to provide reasons for deciding. Thus, *de lege lata*, it appears that the *ratio decidendi* justifying

---

1 D. L. Holley, *EEC Competition Practice: A Thirty-Year Retrospective*, 16 Fordham International Law Journal 342, 364 (1992–1993).

2 In this sense, *see ex multis*: P. Stoffel-Munck, L'abus dans le contrat: Essai d'une théorie 451 (2000), no. 610; *see also* at 446, no. 602; D. Waelbroeck & D. Slater, *The Scope of Object vs Effect under Article 101 TFEU*, *in* Ten Years of Effects-Based Approach in EU Competition Law: State of Play and Perspectives 131, 138 (J. Bourgeois & D. Waelbroeck eds., 2012): "One might have assumed that more than fifty years after the entry into force of the Treaties, there would by now be a common agreement on what constitutes a '*restriction of competition*' or in other words a '*restrictive effect on competition*', which could guide undertakings and their advisors in the appraisal of individual situations. After all, this question is central to the application of competition rule. It is the '*DNA*' of the system, the one question which conditions all the others. However, the reality is that there is little consensus on consistency in this regard, be it in the Court's case-law or the Commission practice, making it impossible in practice to define a clear and coherent test to apply to individual cases."

3 F. Rouvière, Argumentation juridique 106–107 (2023), no. 99.

the characterization of competition infringements does not lie in considerations relating to the effects produced by the litigious behaviors, but in the intent that drives the companies. Indeed, anticompetitive practices can be defined as *a dol with market power* (**Section 2**), which makes it possible, on the one hand, to link the discipline to a general and transversal concept and, on the other hand, to group together all prohibited practices under a single concept, intelligible to any jurist.[4]

Section 1
Justifications for Adopting the Theory of Intent

354. **Unsatisfactory attempts at definition.** The *seemingly* central role attributed to effects in the characterization of infringements is matched by the prominent place they are given in attempts to define them (**Paragraph 1**). However, effects cannot be used as a compass to arrive at a satisfactory definition of anticompetitive practices (**Paragraph 2**).

Paragraph 1 – Effects, an omnipresent concept in the presentation of offenses

355. **The consequentialist interpretation of competition law and the elusive definition of infringements.** It has now become customary in doctrine to discuss the objectives of competition law,[5] which amounts to adopting a teleological interpretation of its rules.[6] The Court of Justice is no exception: in its solemn judgments defining abuse of a dominant position and agreements, it too frequently ventures onto the slippery slope of objectives. While teleological interpretation does not necessarily imply a consequentialist approach,[7] it has to be admitted that the repeated use of vocabulary focused on the word "effect" raises questions about the consequences the intervention of the competition authorities is intended to produce.

This is where the problem lies. Which effect should be taken into consideration when defining infringements? The effect on the consumer,

4 The definition of major legal concepts, such as *dol*, has "a fundamental and cross-cutting value for all subjects in which the defined concept is used," *see* J.-L. Bergel, Méthodologie juridique: Fondamentale et appliquée 348–49 (2018), no. 204.

5 The debate on the objectives of competition law will be discussed in detail *infra*, nos. 430 *et seq.*

6 On the notion of teleological interpretation, *see infra*, no. 474.

7 We would even argue that, because of its nature, teleological interpretation should not, in principle, presuppose consequentialist reasoning, *see infra*, nos. 473 *et seq.*

or the effect on competition? For authors, this subject is the golden apple of discord[8] – a conflict the Court is careful not to resolve, as it does not choose between one interpretation or the other but, revealing a lack of concern for coherence, allows both to coexist. And so the apple becomes a snowball: opinions abound, doctrinal output swells, and the debate draws ever more attention, particularly because in the absence of a clear jurisprudential stance, it cannot be definitively settled.

Whatever the position taken on this issue, the "effects doctrine" offers, in general, no satisfactory definition of infringements: despite their omnipresence in theory, the effect on consumers is devoid of any contentious significance (**I**), while the effect on competition is not conceptualizable per se, and therefore insusceptible of constituting a defining criterion (**II**). Any attempt at a definition based on the notion of effect therefore ends in failure: either because the definition incorporates a criterion that plays no part in judicial reasoning – it is therefore false – or because it incorporates a criterion that is itself undefinable – it is therefore inoperative.

I. The positive effect on consumers: the supposed objective of competition law

356. **Competition: a means of increasing consumer welfare?** In a now-famous article,[9] Professor Bonassies proposed a distinction between two visions of competition: "competition–means" and "competition–value." While the latter sees competition as an object of protection in its own right – the preservation of competition for competition's sake – the former subordinates competition law to the achievement of other objectives: competition is then seen only as a means of promoting economic progress, or even social progress.[10]

The law on anticompetitive practices has, seemingly, adopted the latter conception, setting itself the goal of improving "consumer welfare." Indeed, in a recent unequivocal ruling, the Court of Justice solemnly enshrined this ambition, declaring that "the well-being of both intermediary and final consumers must be regarded as the *ultimate objective*

8 I. Lianos, V. Korah & P. Siciliani, Competition Law: Analysis, Cases, & Materials 116–17 (2019). However, it remains customary in legal doctrine to consider that the implementation of rules should be aimed at achieving the objective of protecting consumer welfare. *See ex multis*: B. Sher, *The Last of the Steam-Powered Trains: Modernising Article 82*, 25 European Competition Law Review 243, 245 (2004); R. Nazzini, *Article 81 EC Between Time Present and Time Past: A Normative Critique of Restriction of Competition in EU Law*, 43 Common Market Law Review 497, 504 (2006); or else the objective of maximizing economic efficiency, *see* P. Akman, *The Tests of Illegality under Articles 101 and 102 TFEU*, 61 Antitrust Bulletin 84, 85 (2016) and references cited.

9 P. Bonassies, *Les fondements du droit communautaire de la concurrence: La théorie de la concurrence-moyen*, *in* Études dédiées à Alex Weill 51 (1983).

10 For the author, it is this latter conception of competition law that prevails in European Union law, *see id.* at 65.

warranting the intervention of competition law."[11] However, the place this objective occupies in theory (**A**) is not reflected in practice: consumer welfare is a criterion devoid of any normative scope (**B**).

A. Consumer welfare, a theoretically recognized objective

357. **Consumer welfare: a stated political objective, a controversial economic concept.** The Commission's political ambition has the merit of being clearly stated, asserted and repeated.[12] Indeed, there is not a single communication from the institution that does not remind us in one way or another, with ever-renewed fervor: *competition law is empowering the people*![13]

And the Court of Justice, perhaps in an effort to prove that it is neither detached nor indifferent to the spirit of the times, joins the chorus in singing the consumer's refrain. The litany, which is far from new, consists in refraining from positing competition rules as an end in themselves, instead declaring that they pursue a different purpose:[14] the rules are intended to "prevent competition from being distorted to the detriment of the public interest, individual undertakings and consumers,"[15] thus contributing to well-being in the Union; they aim "not only at practices which may cause prejudice to consumers directly, but also at those which are detrimental to them through their impact on an effective competition structure";[16] behavior is punishable "has the effect, to the detriment of consumers, of hindering the maintenance of the degree of competition existing in the market or the growth of that competition."[17] However, one must not forget that, after attending the mass, the jurist must recover their critical

---

11 Case C-377/20, ENEL, ECLI:EU:C:2022:379, para. 46 (emphasis added).

12 B. Wardhaugh, Competition, Effects and Predictability: The Rule of Law and the Economic Approach to Competition 113–15 (2020): the author notes that the Commission's unilateral reinterpretation of competition rules when adopting a "more economic" approach led to the belief that consumer welfare was the only normative objective to be pursued, which in practice would mean adopting classical price theory as the sole criterion for economic analysis, which would also compromise respect for the rule of law. On this subject, *see infra*, nos. 458–460.

13 Eur. Comm., *A Competition Policy Fit for New Challenges*, COM(2021)713 final (Nov. 18, 2021) at 1: "[V]igorous competition enforcement has served European consumers and customers – citizens and businesses – by empowering them to make choices in the market place and benefit from innovative products and services at affordable prices." *Adde, inter alia*: Eur. Comm., *A Dynamic and Workable Effects-Based Approach to Abuse of Dominance*, Competition Policy Brief no. 1, 1 (Mar. 2023). Beyond the Commission's communications, the notion of consumer welfare is also present in all its guidelines and in every exemption regulation.

14 This has been described by some authors as a "skillful reversal of objectives," *see* D. Bosco & C. Prieto, Droit européen de la concurrence 185 (2013), no. 198.

15 Case 136/79, National Panasonic, ECLI:EU:C:1980:169, para. 20; Case 46/87, Hoescht, ECLI:EU:C:1989:337, para. 25; Case 374/87, Orkem, ECLI:EU:C:1989:387, para. 36; Case C-52/09, TeliaSonera Sverige, ECLI:EU:C:2011:83, para. 22; Case C-377/20, ENEL, ECLI:EU:C:2022:379, para. 41.

16 Case 6/72, Continental Can, ECLI:EU:C:1973:22, para. 26; Case C-95/04 P, British Airways, ECLI:EU:C:2007:166, para. 106; Case C-202/07 P, France Télécom, ECLI:EU:C:2009:214, para. 105; Case C-280/08 P, Deutsche Telekom, ECLI:EU:C:2010:603, para. 176; Case C-209/10, Post Danmark, ECLI:EU:C:2012:172, para. 20.

17 Case C-209/10, Post Danmark, ECLI:EU:C:2012:172, para. 24; Case C-377/20, ENEL, ECLI:EU:C:2022:379, para. 44.

faculties and distinguish the effects of announcements and other empty phrases from genuine normative statements.

However, the notion of "consumer welfare" is not a legal concept. It is purely economic[18] – it is therefore interpreted according to economic theories, themselves underpinned by their necessary ideological foundations,[19] and obscured by numerous controversies.[20] For example, Robert Bork, famous for having made "welfare" the alpha and omega of any valid competition policy in his book *The Antitrust Paradox*,[21] has been criticized by some for having used this notion wrongly: if his theory has become politically correct,[22] it would be economically false.[23] Some also believe that, in economics, this notion is too broad to be compatible with the more restricted mission of competition law, so that it would be more appropriate to aim to maximize not welfare, but only "consumer surplus."[24] Others still prefer the "overall surplus of the economy" (including corporate profit and consumer surplus[25]), accusing competition authorities of having worked towards a shift towards "consumer surplus" alone in a populist logic.[26] In short, there is no consensus on how consumer harm should be measured,[27] nor on whether it can be estimated with any degree of precision or consistency.[28]

---

18 For a discussion of the different schools of thought on consumer welfare, *see* L. Lovdahl Gormsen, A Principled Approach to Abuse of Dominance in European Competition Law 20–58 (2010). For a legal perspective, *see* M. Malaurie-Vignal, *Droit, économie et politique de concurrence: Réflexions à partir de la notion de bien-être du consommateur*, JCP E nos. 15–16, 28 (Apr. 12, 2018), étude 1187.

19 On this subject, *see infra*, no. 429.

20 For a general study of the evolution of the notion of "consumer welfare" and related controversies, *see* F. Marty, *Le critère du bien-être du consommateur comme objectif exclusif de la politique de concurrence. Une mise en perspective sur la base de l'histoire de l'antitrust américain*, xxviii Revue internationale de droit économique 471 (2014).

21 R. H. Bork, The Antitrust Paradox: A Policy at War with Itself (1978).

22 For a critical discussion, *see* E. Fox, *The Efficiency Paradox*, *in* How the Chicago School Overshot the Mark: The Effect of Conservative Economic Analysis on U.S. Antitrust 77 (R. Pitofsky ed., 2008).

23 According to some, Robert Bork should have spoken of "consumer surplus" rather than "consumer welfare." In this sense, *see* in particular B. Orbach, *The Antitrust Consumer Welfare Paradox*, 7 Journal of Competition Law & Economics 133 (2011); K. Heyer, *Consumer Welfare and the Legacy of Robert Bork*, 57 The Journal of Law & Economics 19 (2014).

24 C. Bertin & E. Le Noan, *Faut-il sauver le bien-être du consommateur?*, Concurrences no. 1-2019, art. no. 88866, 2, 3.

25 We still need to agree on the notion of consumer, which can include both the end consumer and intermediaries, and therefore companies…

26 F. Jenny & J. Philippe, *Populisme et concurrence*, Concurrences no. 3-2018, art. no. 87447, 1.

27 As Catherine Prieto points out, "[s]ome economists themselves admit to being perplexed about the objectives to be assigned to competition policy, wavering between maximizing consumer surplus and overall surplus, as well as between short-term and long-term surplus. Thus, when the European Commission invokes consumer interest as the cornerstone of its competition policy, it is legitimate to question the depth and scope of the concept being invoked," *see* C. Prieto, *La sécurité juridique dans le droit de la concurrence*, *in* Sécurité juridique et droit économique 299, 312 (L. Boy, J.-B. Racine & F. Siiriainen eds., 2010).

28 R. O'Donoghue, *What Makes a Unilateral Conduct Abusive: The Legal Perspective*, *in* The Notion of Restriction of Competition: Revisiting the Foundations of Antitrust Enforcement in Europe 169, 221 (D. Gerard, M. Merola & B. Meyring eds., 2017); *adde*, in the same vein, P. Rey, *Concurrence par les mérites*, *in* La modernisation du droit de la concurrence 151, 153 (G. Canivet ed., 2006).

358. **The objective of consumer welfare, insusceptible of contributing to the definition of competition infringements.** In any case, *if* the aim of competition law is to promote consumer welfare, a teleological interpretation[29] of articles 101 and 102 TFEU necessarily leads to defining anticompetitive practices as those that have a negative effect on consumers, and do not create sufficient efficiency gains to compensate for this harm.[30] Infringements would then have to be determined in terms of the economic relevance of prohibiting them.[31] What is more, as we have seen, there are many economic tests whose function is to estimate, assess, and quantify the beneficial and harmful effects that consumers may sooner or later suffer, much like an accountant taking stock.[32]

However, for the law to accept an economic concept, and *a fortiori* to accept it as an element in the definition of an offense, the latter would have to be, if not determined, at least determinable with a reasonable degree of predictability.[33] Unless we are acting as apprentice sorcerers, this is not the case. It is therefore hardly surprising that, despite the prominence given to the notion of consumer welfare, the legal system rejects it as a foreign body, denying it any normative scope.

B. Consumer welfare, an objective without normative scope

359. **Textual argument: interpreting competition rules in the light of article 3 TFEU.** Case law frequently refers to article 3(1)(b) TFEU, which states that the objective of Union action is "the establish[ment] of the competition rules necessary for the functioning of the internal market,"[34] defined as "a system ensuring that competition is not distorted."[35] There is no trace here of the idea that competition is protected for something other than itself.[36]

---

29 This would, incidentally, be a somewhat contradictory view of the notion of teleology. In this sense, *see infra*, nos. 473 *et seq.*

30 L. Gyselen, *What Makes an Agreement Anti-Competitive: Lessons from the Past*, *in* The Notion of Restriction of Competition: Revisiting the Foundations of Antitrust Enforcement in Europe 111, 116 (D. Gerard, M. Merola & B. Meyring eds., 2017): "Assuming consumer welfare is the relevant standard, one can define an anti-competitive agreement as one that (i) has the potential to cause some form of consumer harm (e.g. higher prices) and (ii) fails to create efficiencies that compensate consumers for that harm in some other form (e.g. better quality of goods or services, more innovation)."

31 D. Spector, *Analyse économique et sécurité juridique: entre règles* per se *et règles de raison*, *in* Politiques de la concurrence 271, 276 (D. Encaoua & R. Guesnerie eds., 2006): according to the author, taking economic reasoning into account should make it possible to "improve per se rules to make the definition of prohibited practices more economically relevant."

32 *See supra*, no. 333.

33 On the principle of foreseeability, *see infra*, nos. 461–467.

34 *See inter alia*: Case 27/76, United Brands, ECLI:EU:C:1978:22, para. 63; Case 85/76, Hoffmann-La Roche, ECLI:EU:C:1979:36, para. 38; Case 322/81, Nederlandsche Banden Industrie Michelin, ECLI:EU:C:1983:313, para. 29; Case C-202/07 P, France Télécom, ECLI:EU:C:2009:214, para. 103; Case C-52/09, TeliaSonera Sverige, ECLI:EU:C:2011:83, para. 21; Case C-377/20, ENEL, ECLI:EU:C:2022:379, para. 42.

35 Protocol (No. 27) on the Internal Market and Competition, 2008 O.J. (C 115) 309.

36 We will, however, address the possibility of a teleological interpretation of the rules in the light of the more generously worded article 3 TEU, *infra*, no. 432.

360. **Jurisprudential argument: the *GlaxoSmithKline* case.** If consumer welfare seems to be the raison d'être and the foundation of competition law enforcement, some authors have already warned that the Court's rhetoric is no more than a facade, a papier-mâché décor that harbors no real rules, nor any obligation for the prosecuting authority to provide reasoning.[37]

The judges expressly recognized this in the *GlaxoSmithKline* case.[38] The Court of First Instance, no doubt inspired by the solemn declarations of the Court,[39] had stated that the aim of the law on anticompetitive practices "is to prevent undertakings, by restricting competition between themselves or with third parties, from reducing the welfare of the final consumer."[40] It went on to rule that the defendant was right to argue that, having proved that the disputed agreement restricted third parties' ability to act freely, the Commission still had to demonstrate how it "had the effect of restricting competition to *the detriment of the final consumer.*"[41] The Court annulled the decision, holding that competition rules aim "to protect not only the interests of competitors or of consumers, but also the structure of the market and, in so doing, *competition as such.*"[42] The Court therefore ruled that the Court of First Instance had erred in law "by requiring proof that the agreement entails disadvantages for final consumers as a prerequisite for a finding of anti-competitive object."[43]

---

37 On the subject of agreements, *see* A. C. Witt, The More Economic Approach to EU Antitrust Law 201 (2019): "According to the Commission's more economic approach, exclusionary effects should only be considered anticompetitive if they are likely to result in consumer harm. However, according to the existing case law, the Court considers the likelihood of exclusionary effects as such sufficient to make an agreement or unilateral conduct anticompetitive"; in the same vein, concerning abuse of a dominant position: R. Di Giovanni Bezzi, *A Tale of Two Cities: Effects Analysis in Article 102 TFEU Between Competition Process and Market Outcome*, 14 Journal of European Competition Law & Practice 83, 94 (2023); *adde*, A. Komninos, *The Consumer Welfare Standard: A 'Problem' to Fix in EU Competition Law?*, *in* The Transformation of EU Competition Law: Next Generation Issues 199, 212 (A. Claici, A. Komninos & D. Waelbroeck eds., 2023), and the numerous case law references examined in the article: "[T]here has been no 'tyranny' of the consumer welfare standard in EU competition law. Protection of an 'effective competition structure' has always been, and remains, a valid objective and is seen as a good proxy of the broader *consumer welfare* principle, which is the 'ultimate objective' of the competition rules but *does not amount to an operational-technical test that can be applied to specific cases*" (emphasis added).

38 *See* the commentary by J. Drexl, *La Constitution économique européenne – L'actualité du modèle ordolibéral*, xxv Revue internationale de droit économique 419, 446 (2011): "In this case, the jurisprudence has thus demonstrated tremendous ordoliberal stability against the influence of more recent economic theories."

39 *See supra*, no. 357.

40 Case T-168/01, GlaxoSmithKline, ECLI:EU:T:2006:265, para. 118.

41 *Id.*, para. 172 (emphasis added).

42 Case C-501/06 P, GlaxoSmithKline, ECLI:EU:C:2009:610, para. 63 (emphasis added).

43 *Id.*, para. 64. It could be argued that, given the alternative between object and effect provided for in article 101 TFEU, this applies only to "infringement by object," but that an "infringement by effect" would presuppose precisely that an effect on consumers has been duly established. We reject this view for the reasons already set out *supra*, nos. 277 *et seq.* In the same vein, Case C-377/20, ENEL, ECLI:EU:C:2022:379, para. 47: "[A] competition authority discharges its burden of proof if it shows that a practice of an undertaking in a dominant position could impair, by using resources or *means other than those governing normal competition*, an effective competition structure, *without it being necessary for that authority to prove that that practice may also cause direct harm to consumers*" (emphasis added).

361. **Logical argument: consumer welfare, an overly abundant definitional element, as it is systematically presumed.** When it states that the competition rules are "*not only* aimed at practices which may cause damage to consumers directly, but also at those which are detrimental to them through their impact on an effective competition structure,"[44] the Court seems to be opening the way to an alternative: a competition infringement would be defined as a practice that causes harm to the consumer, either directly or indirectly through a restriction of competition.

However, according to established case law, only the restriction of competition needs to be demonstrated, and not the effect on the market or consumers.[45] It follows that proof of consumer harm is not necessary: in practice, it is systematically deduced from the restriction of competition.[46] While this "presumption"[47] is not without its critics,[48] it must be admitted that in addition to being misleading in suggesting that consumer harm is a criterion for defining infringements, this alternative is devoid of any contentious scope.

II. Negative impact on competition: the supposed criterion for defining infringements

362. **Lack of a clear definition of the restrictive effect of competition.** More than sixty years after the entry into force of the competition rules, one might legitimately expect doctrine to have a clear and synthetic vision of the discipline's flagship concept, namely the "restriction of competition." However, this is not the case:[49] the problem "seems as essential as it is

44 Case 6/72, Continental Can, ECLI:EU:C:1973:22, para. 26; Case C-95/04 P, British Airways, ECLI:EU:C:2007:166, para. 106; Case C-202/07 P, France Télécom, ECLI:EU:C:2009:214, para. 105; Case C-280/08 P, Deutsche Telekom, ECLI:EU:C:2010:603, para. 176; Case C-209/10, Post Danmark, ECLI:EU:C:2012:172, para. 20 (emphasis added).

45 *See supra*, nos. 277 *et seq.*

46 Opinion of Advocate General J. Kokott, Case C-95/04 P, British Airways, ECLI:EU:C:2006:133, para. 89.

47 We use quotation marks because, since the effect on consumers is not a constituent element of infringements, it is not an object of proof and therefore need not be presumed.

48 *See inter alia*: A.-L. Sibony, *La preuve scientifique évitée. Inventaire de quelques techniques judiciaires*, *in* Preuve scientifique, preuve juridique 161, 174 (E. Truilhé-Marengo ed., 2011): "It may happen, however, that a presumption is not or no longer in line with a relevant scientific approach. This is the case ... for the – implicit – presumption that the behavior of a dominant firm harms consumers when it affects the structure of the market (i.e., when it tends to drive out a competitor). This view is not in harmony with contemporary economic doctrine, which argues that the exclusion of a competitor only really harms consumers if the foreclosed competitor is at least as efficient as the dominant firm. The contemporary economic approach would therefore require that, in order to punish an eviction practice by a dominant company, it must be demonstrated that the practice harms (or would harm if it continued to be implemented) consumers. Presuming this in all cases seems ill-founded. What is more, and this is what is most important here, this presumption precludes proof that, from an economic point of view, should be decisive: case-by-case proof of the effect of the practice in question on consumers."

49 In this sense, *see ex multis*: D. Waelbroeck & D. Slater, *The Scope of Object vs Effect under Article 101 TFEU*, *in* Ten Years of Effects-Based Approach in EU Competition Law: State of Play and Perspectives 131, 138 (J. Bourgeois & D. Waelbroeck eds., 2012); P. Ibáñez Colomo &A. Lamadrid De Pablo, *On the Notion of Restriction of Competition: What We Know and What We Don't Know We Know*, *in* The Notion of Restriction of Competition: Revisiting the Foundations of Antitrust Enforcement in Europe 333, 333 (D. Gerard, M. Merola & B. Meyring eds., 2017).

largely unresolved"[50] – the notion appearing indefinable (**A**). The impossibility of defining the effect on competition in an autonomous way is due to the fact that, on its own, i.e., considered independently of its cause, the effect means nothing, from which it follows that it is not possible to distinguish the pro-competitive effect from the anticompetitive effect (**B**) without referring to the behavior that has generated it.

A. The indefinable notion of "restrictive effect on competition"

363. **The supposed inadequacy of the legal approach: perennial criticism of the theory of freedom of action and the notion of competition on the merits.** For a long time, it was customary to present the restrictive effect of competition as a restriction on the freedom of action of companies[51] – which was, moreover, in line with the Commission's decision-making practice.[52] However, this theory has subsequently been criticized for its inability to distinguish between anticompetitive behavior and lawful practices. The criticism is as follows: if the reduction of freedom of action is the criterion, since any contractual commitment restricts it, then any contract is anticompetitive.[53] While such reasoning may be exaggerated, it has led to the idea that the law of anticompetitive practices is nothing more than a history of freedom[54] being consigned to the dustbin of history.

The fate of the notion of competition on the merits is no more prosperous.[55] Specialists seem to regard it as a vestige of the past,[56] to which the Court of Justice remains attached by tradition, but which, like a Mesopotamian jar, is no longer of much use.[57] Since, according to the majority doctrine, what matters most is the economic effect, competition

---

50 P. Stoffel-Munck, L'abus dans le contrat: Essai d'une théorie 451 (2000), no. 610; *see also* at 446, no. 602.

51 For a discussion and critique of the freedom of action doctrine, *see* D. Bosco, L'obligation d'exclusivité 81–87 (2008), nos. 72–77.

52 A. C. Witt, The More Economic Approach to EU Antitrust Law 114–18 (2019), and the numerous references cited.

53 *See, inter alia*, G. Marenco, *La notion de restriction de concurrence dans le cadre de l'interdiction des ententes*, *in* II Mélanges en hommage à Michel Waelbroeck 1217, 1220 and 1236–40 (1999) (*nota bene*: the author does not agree with the criticism).

54 We will revive this idea, *infra*, nos. 400 *et seq.*

55 C. Prieto, *Abus de position dominante – Notion d'abus en droit communautaire*, JurisClasseur Concurrence – Consommation (Feb. 2018) fasc. 561, no. 9: "According to a strong current of economists, highly critical during the consultations opened by the Commission to draw up the guidelines, this concept of competition on the merits has remained an empty formula. It failed to provide a readable framework for decision-making practice."

56 *Contra, see* G. Decocq, *La concurrence par les mérites*, *in* Les concepts émergents en droit des affaires 239, 246 (E. Le Dolley ed., 2010): "Can we really believe that competition on the merits should be definitively relegated to the status of an accessory to competition law? On the contrary, should we consider it to be the cornerstone of a truly competitive market economy? Only time will tell."

57 Like the Goldsmith's Jar discovered in Larsa, Iraq, we shall see that the notion of competition on the merits conceals many treasures, insofar as it reflects the need to prove recourse to an illicit means in order to characterize the offense. In this respect, *see infra*, nos. 400 *et seq.*

authorities need not concern themselves with the means employed.[58] Described as a "meaningless" concept by an OECD report,[59] it is now common practice either to consider it as just one of several qualification criteria,[60] or to define it in terms of economic analysis. Thus, even if the notion does not appear in any standard economics textbook,[61] "deserving" behavior is now commonly defined as behavior that does not harm consumers.[62] As a stowaway, consumer welfare has thus infiltrated, at least in theory,[63] the wagon of an old notion that was, and has remained, totally foreign to it.

364. **The replacement of general, abstract legal definitions by a multiplicity of economic tests.** Once the relevance of legal concepts in defining the restriction of competition had been rejected, we were forced to turn to economists, whose judgment on the merits of a given behavior is often presumed to be more legitimate than that of legal experts.[64] Even as the possibility of predicting the effects of a given behavior remains controversial within the scientific community,[65] doctrine, denouncing the "inadequacy of general definitions," has gradually replaced them with "specific tests."[66] The doctrinal production on the restrictive effect of competition thus consists

---

58 F. Castillo de la Torre, *Is the Effects-Based Approach Too Cumbersome? Taking Stock of Recent Practice and Case Law on Article 102 TFEU*, *in* The Transformation of EU Competition Law: Next Generation Issues 145, 149 (A. Claici, A. Komninos & D. Waelbroeck eds., 2023) (*nota bene*: the author does not endorse this view).

59 OECD, Competition on the merits, Policy Roundtables, DAF/COMP(2005)27 (Mar. 30, 2006), at 91: "Competition policy would be strengthened if courts and agencies abandoned the use of meaningless expressions such as 'competition on the merits'" (unofficial translation).

60 One author, for example, believes that behavior based on competition on the merits that produces undesirable effects on the structure of competition should be prohibited, as "the effects criterion then takes precedence over the legitimacy criterion," *see* B. Vesterdorf, *Considérations sur la notion de "concurrence par les mérites"*, *in* La modernisation du droit de la concurrence 163, 173 (G. Canivet ed., 2006).

61 In this sense, Rey, *Concurrence par les mérites*, *op. cit.* at 152.

62 *Id.* at 153; *adde, ex multis*: L. Peeperkorn, *Conditional Pricing and the AEC Test –A Happy Marriage or an Awkward Couple?*, Concurrences no. 2-2019, art. no. 90191, 40, 41, no. 8: "[T]he Court has demystified the vague expression 'dominant firms have a special responsibility to only compete on the merits'. ...[T]he Court equates competition on the merits with conduct that does not harm consumers"; A. Meij & T. Baumé, *Balancing Object and Effect Analysis in Identifying Abuses of a Dominant Position under Article 102 TFEU*, *in* Ten Years of Effects-Based Approach in EU Competition Law: State of Play and Perspectives 165 (J. Bourgeois & D. Waelbroeck eds., 2012): "In our view, the notion of competition on the merits can only be understood in the light of the classical aim of competition law. Because that concept is key to distinguishing what should be prohibited from what should be permitted or even ultimately promoted under competition law, competition on the merits is necessarily closely related to consumer welfare"; C. Bloud-Rey, *Loyauté et pratiques anticoncurrentielles, antinomie?* 234 Petites affiches 20 (Nov. 24, 2011), nos. 9–13.

63 The preceding discussion has shown that, despite the rhetoric attributing it a prime role, consumer welfare is neither a constituent element of infringements, nor a defining criterion for anticompetitive practices.

64 L. Idot, *La qualification de la restriction de concurrence: À propos des lignes directrices de la Commission concernant l'application de l'article 81, § 3 CE*, *in* La modernisation du droit de la concurrence 85 (G. Canivet & M.-A. Frison-Roche eds., 2006): "The definition of what constitutes a restriction of competition will mainly depend on the economists' judgment of the merits of the behavior."

65 *See supra*, nos. 114 *et seq.*

66 B. E. Hawk, *À propos de la "concurrence par les mérites": Regards croisés sur l'article 82 CE et la Section 2 du Sherman Act*, Concurrences no. 3-2005, art. no. 231, 33, 35, no. 18.

not in the search for a definition,[67] but in the enumeration of tests enabling the characterization of such or such subcategory of anticompetitive behavior.[68] And yet we know that these economic tests are never more than an accessory method of proof in practice.[69] It follows, on the one hand, that the substitution of economic analysis for the legal approach has failed to produce a definition of the restrictive effect on competition; and, on the other, that any attempt to define competition based on a generalization of the various economic tests would be misguided, insofar as they play only an evidentiary, and not a substantive, role.

The replacement of the theory of freedom of action and the notion of competition on the merits by a more economic approach has not, contrary to popular belief, led to a better understanding of the restriction of competition, but has merely increased the technicality and complexity of the subject. The restrictive effect of competition is like a distant cloud that clouds our eyes as soon as we try to get close to it. This is because, if we consider the effect independently of its cause, it is impossible to distinguish the anticompetitive effect from the pro-competitive effect.

B. The elusive distinction between procompetitive and anticompetitive effects

365. **The restrictive effect on competition, necessarily distinct from the effect on market *structure*.** Unlike merger law, the law on anticompetitive practices protects competition, and therefore prohibits *behaviors*. Its aim is not to regulate market structure. Consequently, the anticompetitive effect cannot be defined as that which leads to greater concentration in the relevant market.[70] Whether there is a single supplier – a monopoly situation – or only a few – an oligopoly – is not enough to qualify as a restriction of competition, since market structure can play a role in characterizing the infringement only as a contextual element.

366. **Logical argument: the effect is nothing without its cause.** According to Lalande, an effect is a "phenomenon produced by a cause."[71] Thus, the effect, considered in itself, means nothing. The "exclusionary effect," for

67 However, the definition proposed by two authors does not appear to offer a new perspective on the issue, since it is based on a consequentialist approach to competition infringements, and is therefore misaligned with the realities of litigation. *See* Ibáñez Colomo & Lamadrid De Pablo, *On the Notion of Restriction of Competition: What We Know and What We Don't Know We Know*, *op. cit.* at 370: "In essence, a restriction of competition can be defined as a practice that is presumed to have a net negative impact on firms' ability and incentive to compete. In other words, the notion refers to instances in which the anticompetitive effects are presumed to weigh more than any pro-competitive gains that may result from the practice."

68 For a critique of the possibility of developing "tests" to qualify particular categories of anticompetitive behavior, *see supra*, no. 331.

69 *See supra*, nos. 334–335.

70 The Court recently reiterated this point, *see* Case C-449/21, Towercast, ECLI:EU:C:2023:207, para. 52: "[T]he mere finding that an undertaking's position has been strengthened is not sufficient for a finding of abuse… ."

71 A. Lalande, Vocabulaire technique et critique de la philosophie 266 (2002).

example, cannot be considered anticompetitive in itself, because, as the Court expressly recognized: "Competition on the merits may, by definition, lead to the departure from the market or the marginalisation of competitors that are less efficient and so less attractive to consumers from the point of view of, among other things, price, choice, quality or innovation."[72]

In other words, in order to be an infringement, the exclusionary effect must be the consequence of anticompetitive behavior. If the competitor disappears naturally, i.e., as a result of the normal functioning of competition, no infringement can be characterized. It is therefore important to realize that the effects, when isolated from the behavior, do not in any way allow us to determine whether or not we are in the presence of an illicit practice. Here are a few examples to illustrate this point.[73]

Price uniformity is not necessarily an anticompetitive effect: it can be the natural consequence of a collusive equilibrium. In a transparent oligopolistic market, companies can intelligently align their prices by observing each other – which is perfectly legal, although it leads to the same result as a price-fixing agreement. Public price announcements are permitted, while the private exchange of price information is prohibited. Isn't the effect equivalent? Certain purchasing cooperatives are legal, while agreements are prohibited, yet the effect is identical: the price is determined by common agreement. A company sells its goods or services at an exorbitant price, but this is an anticompetitive effect only if such a pricing practice results from the exploitation of others:[74] in both cases, the consumer has paid a high price.

It is thus impossible to define the restrictive effect of competition autonomously, without taking into account the conduct that gives rise to it.[75] Failure to take this assertion as a premise leads to an "inconclusive" and "unsatisfactory" discussion of the notion of restriction of competition.[76] We must now corroborate it by explaining, using logical arguments, why the effect on competition and the effect on consumers are, in themselves, devoid of definitional scope.

---

72 In this sense, *inter alia*: Case C-209/10, Post Danmark, ECLI:EU:C:2012:172, para. 22; Case C-377/20, ENEL, ECLI:EU:C:2022:379, para. 45.

73 For further illustrations, *see* F. Costa-Cabral, Intent in EU Competition Law: The Judicial Assessment of Anti-competitive Strategies 10–11 (2014) (Ph.D. dissertation, King's College London).

74 However, it is very difficult to determine whether prices are excessive, *see infra*, no. 406.

75 In the same vein, *see* P. Stoffel-Munck, L'abus dans le contrat: Essai d'une théorie 447–48 (2000), no. 604: the author considers that the conditions of abuse and that of hindrance to competition "overlap," as "[e]ither the section on abuse consists of examples and historical details, while the section on obstruction contains the substantive developments, or vice versa. *However, it is hard to find substantive elements specific to either issue*. In the end, this leads us to consider that distinguishing between harm to competition and abuse leads to a relative impasse" (emphasis added).

76 In this sense, J. Temple Lang, *Restriction of Competition and Exclusionary Abuse Under Article 102 – The Solution, in* The Notion of Restriction of Competition: Revisiting the Foundations of Antitrust Enforcement in Europe 239, 240 (D. Gerard, M. Merola & B. Meyring eds., 2017).

Paragraph 2 – Effects: an extraneous concept to the definition of offenses

367. **Effects are not a criterion for defining anticompetitive practices.** Neither the effect on competition (**I**) nor the effect on the consumer (**II**) can be used as a criterion to define anticompetitive practices.

I. The absence of a defining scope for the effect on competition

368. **Competition: a concept that can be understood in its own right.** Today, competition is considered an autonomous notion, capable of being understood in and of itself. Economists have theorized it independently, as a *mechanism* by which supply meets demand, reaching a certain equilibrium price that varies according to the structure of the market in question.[77] Competition is thus often modeled, and apprehended through more or less sophisticated mathematical figures[78] – in this sense, it has become *autonomous* from the behavior that causes it, except for certain so-called heterodox schools, which are very much in the minority.[79]

369. **Restriction of competition, formerly confused with fraudulent behavior.** Conversely, in the past, competition had no existence of its own. This is due to the fact that economic science was not dissociated from other disciplines: for a long time, it was at one with philosophy and law.[80] This is not to say that competition did not exist: it was referred to as healthy rivalry,[81] or the freedom to contract and trade.[82] So, for the jurist of yesteryear, the reasoning was simpler, because it was binary: competition was hindered in the presence of a maneuver; it was free in its absence.[83] It was thus the notion of maneuver, and maneuver alone, that needed to be defined: on the basis of this notion, one knew whether or not to

---

77 A. Bienaymé, *Concurrence*, Encyclopædia Universalis.

78 For an overview, *see* E. Combe, Économie et politique de la concurrence 1–58 (2nd ed. 2020), nos. 1–33; and a reference work, D. Hildebrand, The Role of Economic Analysis in EU Competition Law: The European School (4th ed. 2016).

79 On this subject, no one has set out the Austrian perspective on competition better than Israel Kirzner, in particular by drawing a clear distinction, in the footsteps of Friedrich Hayek, between competition as a *process* and competition as a *result* of the process, and by emphasizing the role of entrepreneurial behavior in the emergence of healthy, lively competition. *See* I. M. Kirzner, Concurrence & esprit d'entreprise (R. Audoin trans., Economica 2005).

80 With Aristotle, and again with the Scholastics, *see supra*, no. 36 and no. 51

81 *See* Hesiod's *Theogony*, *supra*, no. 33.

82 *See supra*, no. 44, no. 60 and no. 74.

83 *See supra*, no. 77.

enter into a condemnation procedure. It follows that focusing on the "restriction of competition" and attempting to define it per se would have been meaningless – as it was deemed *equivalent* to fraudulent conduct. Consequently, to isolate competition and consider that certain practices have a "restrictive effect" on it would only have added an unnecessary step to the reasoning.

And yet, despite the contemporary autonomization of the notion of competition and its negative counterpart, the restriction of competition, the latter remains inseparable from conduct, as in the past (**A**), so that not only can it not be defined without reference to it, but above all, it is a superfluous notion, insofar as it adds nothing to the notion of anticompetitive conduct – for in its entirety, it is conflated with it (**B**).

A. The restriction of competition, inseparable from anticompetitive behavior

370. **A thought experiment: a criminal lawyer presents the constituent elements of competition infringements.** To see that, from a strictly legal point of view, the restriction of competition cannot be dissociated from conduct, we need to draw an analogy with criminal law. Let's begin with a brief review of criminal law reasoning, before comparing it with competition law reasoning.

Intentional offenses *stricto sensu* are made up of three elements: (i) intent in the strict sense, i.e., the will to achieve a result; (ii) the conduct; (iii) the result (actual, or only potential in the case of a formal offense).[84]

We know that only the first two are required as constitutive elements to characterize a competition infringement. Moreover, they are intrinsically linked, since intent is always presumed from conduct and circumstances.[85] In short, the criminal lawyer would consider that a competition infringement requires (i) anticompetitive behavior and (ii) the corresponding intent, and that (iii) the result is not required as a constituent element.

371. **A competition specialist's presentation of the constituent elements of competition infringements.** However, the classic presentation of competition infringements does not follow the criminal lawyer's schema. A distinction is commonly made between: (i) the anticompetitive behavior; (ii) the restriction of competition; (iii) the potential result on the market.

Based on this trichotomy, two causal links are then classically established: the first between the anticompetitive behavior and the restriction of competition – "such behavior has the effect of restricting

84 On the notion of formal offense, *see supra*, no. 272.

85 It should be noted that proof of conduct alone can sometimes lead to a presumption of intent. However, if the conduct is not sufficient to convince the judge, i.e., if it is somewhat ambiguous, it will be necessary to resort to the body of evidence method to establish intent to the requisite legal standard.

competition" – the second between the restriction of competition and the result on the market – "the restriction of competition has the potential effect of harming the consumer."[86]

We will demonstrate that *the first causal link does not exist*, and that *the second causal link is superfluous*. In the appendices, the reader will find several diagrams illustrating the following.[87]

372. **Applying competition law reasoning to poisoning.** Here again, it is relevant to illustrate the demonstration by reasoning by analogy with the poisoning offense.[88] Thus, it will be realized that examining the restriction of competition is not a necessary step in demonstrating a competition infringement.

Poisoning is the administration of a substance of such a nature as to cause death. It requires: (i) the administration of a lethal substance (the conduct), (ii) the corresponding intent, and (iii) the result is not required as a constituent element. However, if a criminal law specialist were to apply competition law reasoning to this offense, they would be led to distinguish: (i) the conduct, i.e., the administration of a lethal substance; (ii) *the endangerment of the life of another person*; (iii) the potential result on the victim, i.e., their death.

Two causal links could then be established: (i) "the administration of a lethal substance has the effect of endangering the life of another person"; (ii) "the endangerment of the life of another person has the potential effect of causing the death of the victim." It goes without saying that these steps are superfluous: it is obvious that the administration of a poison endangers the life of another person, with the potential consequence of death. The reasoning is absurd, insofar as it is not rational to artificially create unnecessary reasoning steps. Adopting these three subdivisions in criminal law, and recognizing the existence of these two causal links, would unnecessarily complicate the qualification process.

373. **The causal link between elements (ii) and (iii) is superfluous.** Firstly, since the victim's death is not a constitutive element, the intended result does not have to have been achieved – it can remain only *potential*.[89] However, endangering a person's life implies, by definition, the *possibility* of their death. The causal link between the two is therefore *automatic*. Similarly, in the law of anticompetitive practices, the result on the market is not a constitutive element, and a restriction of competition necessarily implies the *possibility* of an anticompetitive result on the market – this causal link is

86 We could also write: "the restriction of competition is the cause of such inefficient result," if we adopted the paradigm of economic efficiency.

87 *See infra*, Appendices nos. 3 to 5.

88 The analogy is appropriate because, as we demonstrated *supra*, nos. 272–275, poisoning and competition infringements have the same structure: they belong to the category of formal offenses.

89 In the sense that the offense is characterized independently of the actual occurrence of the result.

therefore, as in the case of poisoning, *automatic.*[90] It is sufficient to establish that competition has been endangered or restricted to demonstrate, without any further demonstration, that the potential result is the death of the victim or the effect on the market. As a result, taking this causal link into account in the reasoning is superfluous, since it does not need to be proven.

374. **There is no causal link between elements (i) and (ii).** Secondly, "endangering the life of another person" is itself already implicated in the "administration of a lethal substance." Indeed, as soon as the capacity of the substance administered to cause the death of the victim is established, there is "endangerment of the life of another person." The reasoning is identical for competition infringements: when conduct is deemed anticompetitive, there is a restriction of competition. What is important to understand here is that there is no causal link, but an *identity* between the two elements, as they designate and define the same thing: the prohibited conduct.

375. **Intermediate clarification: a test to identify or rule out the existence of a causal link.** In order to determine whether or not a causal link exists between two elements, three questions need to be asked: 1. "Is it impossible to reverse cause and effect without the proposition becoming absurd?" 2. "Is there a temporal succession between cause and effect?" 3. "Is randomness conceivable between cause and effect?" If all three answers are positive, there is a causal link; if all three are negative, there is no causal link.

Let's take a coin and a tennis ball and examine the following propositions.

"If my coin is copper red, then it is worth between one and five cents." The order of the two elements – the color and the value of the coin – can be completely reversed;[91] these two characteristics are simultaneous, they do not follow one another in time; finally, there is no randomness in their relationship: a copper-red coin is always worth between one and five cents. There is therefore no causal link between the color and the value of the coin: there is neither cause nor effect, since both are part of the description of the object in question – the coin.

Now consider the sentence: "The tennis ball breaks the glass." This time, the order cannot be reversed without altering the meaning of the sentence: the glass does not break the ball; there is a succession in time: the ball will take a few seconds to reach the glass; and we acknowledge the element of chance: by luck, the ball might not break the glass.

376. **Application of the previous test to competition infringements and poisoning offenses.** Subjecting the pairs "administration of a lethal substance – endangering the life of another person" and "anticompetitive behavior – restriction of competition" to the same test leads to three negative

---

90 This would not be the case if the required result were concrete, i.e., if the materialization of the feared result – i.e., the effect on the market (higher prices, lower quality, etc.) – were required as a constitutive element.

91 "If my coin is worth between one and five cents, then it is copper red."

responses. Indeed, it is possible to write "there is administration of a lethal substance when it endangers the life of another person" and "the life of another person is endangered when there is administration of a lethal substance"; as well as "in the presence of anticompetitive behavior, there is restriction of competition" just as "in the presence of a restriction of competition, there is anticompetitive behavior." The two elements do not follow one another in time, but occur at the same moment; there is no randomness.[92]

Thus, *there is no causal link between anticompetitive behavior and restriction of competition: the two are identical.* It follows that the restriction of competition cannot be defined independently of the anticompetitive behavior.

B. Restriction of competition conflated with anticompetitive behavior

377. **The logical consequence of the absence of a causal link between the anticompetitive behavior and the restriction of competition.** In the presence of a causal link, there are two truly distinct elements: the glass and the tennis ball are two different things.

In the absence of a causal link, two elements may be presented as distinct, but in reality they describe the same thing – namely, the object to which they both relate: the coin, the offense of poisoning, or the competition infringement.

These two elements[93] may be necessary to describe the thing. Sometimes, on the other hand, they can be redundant. For example, while it is interesting to know that a coin is both copper red and worth between one and five cents in order to know the nature of the thing, it is not necessary to specify that the administration of a lethal substance leads to the endangerment of the life of another person, or that anticompetitive conduct constitutes a restriction of competition – as this would be tantamount to giving the same information twice. In this sense, they are pleonastic propositions.[94] Pleonasm is an expression that adds repetition to what has already been stated, a sequence of words being pleonastic as soon

92 Conversely, all three answers are positive if we apply the test to the pairs "endangering the life of another person – potential death of the victim" and "restriction of competition – potential result on the market." It is the restriction of competition that causes the effect on the market, not the other way around; there is a time-lapse between one and the other; and a restriction of competition may produce no effect on the market: there is therefore randomness. But, as we have just seen, given that the required result is only potential, this causal link is automatic: it results directly and systematically from anticompetitive behavior or the administration of a lethal substance.

93 We write "two elements" to simplify the reasoning: obviously, there can be many more. For example, we could add to the description of the coin its weight, the alloy of which it is made, the design on the obverse side, the number on the tail side, and so on.

94 It should be noted that in law, a pleonasm may sometimes stem from a doctrinal stance: for example, the theory that the State and law are one and the same renders the expression "*État de droit*" pleonastic, since it assumes every State is, by definition, an "*État de droit*" (i.e., a rule-of-law State), *see* in this sense, M. Troper, *Hans Kelsen*, ENCYCLOPŒDIA UNIVERSALIS.

as the elements that make it up "are more numerous than is required to express a given content."[95]

While criminal lawyers rightly content themselves with the notion of "lethal substance," competition law adds the notion of "restriction of competition" to "anticompetitive behavior," even though the latter has no autonomous existence and adds no additional criteria. The effect on competition or the restriction of competition is thus of no defining significance, nor is the effect on consumers.

II. The absence of a definitional scope for the effect on consumers

378. **Logical arguments.** The result, whether an effect on consumers or on the market, is not a constituent element of competition infringements.[96] Nevertheless, as in the case of poisoning, it could have formed part of the definition of the offense. But this is not the case: since, unlike poisoning, which is an offense of result, competition infringements are offenses of means,[97] the result does not make it possible to distinguish between lawful and unlawful conduct – in this sense, it has no defining significance. Indeed, consumers only suffer harm if an *unlawful means* has been used (**B**), since it is the *cause* of the harm (**A**).

A. unlawful means: the cause of the damage suffered by consumers

379. **Reasoning by analogy with swindling: the result of the offense does not define the unlawful means.** Swindling is a "key offense" in criminal law, playing "the leading role both in common offenses outside the Penal Code and in offenses specific to companies and businesses."[98] It falls under the heading of cunning delinquency: the offender seeks to induce the delivery of the thing they covet by fraudulent means – trickery, deception or even lies.[99] In addition, as we have shown, this offense, like competition infringements, falls into the category of offenses of means.

---

95 TLFi

96 *See supra*, nos. 277 *et seq.*

97 The terms "offense of means" and "offense of result" are to be understood in the sense of our classification, *see supra*, no. 245 and no. 247, resp.

98 M. Delmas-Marty, 2 Droit pénal des affaires – Partie spéciale: Infractions 9–10 (3rd ed. 1990).

99 A. Lepage, P. Maistre du Chambon & R. Salomon, Droit pénal des affaires 41 (6th ed. 2020), no. 127.

As a reminder, offenses of means are offenses whose result is not unlawful in itself, but only because of the means used to achieve it; unlike offenses of result, whose result is unlawful in itself.[100] Thus, causing death is an unlawful result in itself, and the definition of poisoning presupposes the establishment of a material causal link between the poison administered and the potential for death: the result is therefore part of the definition of the means. Conversely, the result of a swindle – the delivery of a thing – is not unlawful in itself: it can be, and most often is, the lawful consequence of a contract. What renders the result unlawful is the use of a *fraudulent means* to achieve it. And no one would think of defining this fraudulent means on the basis of the notion of delivery,[101] which, in itself, means nothing: the delivery must have been *provoked by a maneuver* in order to be tainted by illegality. In the absence of a maneuver, the delivery is lawful – so it cannot shed any light on the notion of maneuver, let alone define it.

The same applies to the law on anticompetitive practices, since competition infringements and swindling fall into the same category:[102] since the effect on the consumer – e.g., *ex multis*, an increase in prices or a reduction in the number of companies operating in a market – can result from both lawful and unlawful behavior, it is not possible to define anticompetitive behavior based on the result.

B. The absence of prejudice suffered by consumers without recourse to unlawful means

380. **The unlawful means is the only element that needs to be defined.** In the same way that, in the case of swindle, it is inconceivable that a person who hands over property to another should suffer harm if they have not been induced to do so by a fraudulent maneuver, consumers suffer no harm if companies have not engaged in anticompetitive behavior.[103]

However, anticompetitive behavior is commonly defined as that which causes more or less direct harm to the consumer.[104] However, in the

100 Thus, causing death is an unlawful result in itself, and the definition of poisoning presupposes establishing a material causal link between the poison administered and the potential for death: the result is part of the definition of the means.

101 This is only useful for determining when the offense was committed, and is of no importance when the defendant is being prosecuted for attempted swindle.

102 *Compare with* the law on market abuse. As one author has remarked, "subject to *fraud against the law*, the speculator's enrichment has a legal cause: is this enrichment, which is said to be without cause, not the counterpart of the risk?," J.-F. Rougé, *La spéculation*: *Règles du jeu*, 94 Petites Affiches, 16, 20 (Aug. 6, 1993).

103 As one author has remarked, in matters of abuse and agreements, "determining fault comes down to identifying the actions that make the enrichment unjustified," *see* G. Decocq, *Leçon sur la responsabilité civile du fait d'une pratique anticoncurrentielle*, *in* Leçons de droit civil: Mélanges en l'honneur de François Chabas 197, 233 (N. Guimezanes ed., 2011).

104 *See supra*, no. 364.

absence of unlawful means, the consumer does not, by definition, suffer any harm.[105] Indeed, "the principle of free competition implies the legitimacy of competitive harm": the existence of harm is presumed from the unlawful conduct, which confers, "by extension," an unlawful character to the harm caused.[106]

On this point, the Court's case law, including the most recent, has not yielded to the current of modernization. It continues to state that committing an infringement consists in hindering competition, to the detriment of consumers, "*through recourse to means* or resources different from those governing normal competition."[107]

The problem is that economists and lawyers do not reason in the same way. The economist models reality, and determines, on the basis of their own assumptions, which are far from unanimous, the most efficient market structure and behaviors, or those most likely to contribute to consumer welfare. As a free rider, they proceed autonomously. It makes no difference to them whether the behavior in question constitutes a "maneuver" or an "unlawful means" in the legal sense of the term – economic theory does not take legal categories into consideration. For example, the economist will consider that collusive equilibria,[108] today facilitated by algorithms,[109] are harmful insofar as they lead to the same effect as a price-fixing agreement in the absence of any collusion. Lawyers, on the other hand, are not concerned with this result, because, in the absence of a concurrence of wills, there is no fraudulent means, and therefore no offense.[110] We should also mention predatory pricing: economic doctrine on the question of whether or not it is harmful to consumers has fluctuated,[111] while the law has remained constant: predation is not a matter of competition on the merits.

These differences in position are due to the fact that they do not pursue the same objective. The economist's objective is theoretical, while the jurist's is practical. The legal approach may appear more dogmatic, even

105 *See supra*, no. 379.

106 G. Decocq, *Observations sur le dommage concurrentiel*, 44 Journal des sociétés 39, 39–40 (June 2007), dossier: "L'évaluation du préjudice économique."

107 Case C-377/20, ENEL, ECLI:EU:C:2022:379, para. 44 (emphasis added); *adde*, Case C-680/20, Unilever Italia, ECLI:EU:C:2023:33, para. 39.

108 The notion of collusive equilibrium, coined by industrial economics and game theory, describes the phenomenon whereby firms coordinate their prices without resorting to explicit agreements, and without even communicating with each other. On this subject, *see* B. Jullien, *Économie industrielle*, Encyclopædia Universalis.

109 On this theme, *see* A. Ezrachi & M. E. Stucke, Virtual Competition: The Promises and Perils of the Algorithm-Driven Economy (2016); *adde*, F. Marty, *Algorithmes de prix, intelligence artificielle et équilibres collusifs*, xxxi Revue internationale de droit économique 83 (2017).

110 We will discuss, *infra*, no. 516, whether it is conceivable to consider algorithmic collusion as constituting a concurrence of wills.

111 *See infra*, no. 459

conservative, but to ensure the coherence of the law and the predictability of jurisprudential solutions, the jurist must remain within the established framework, and reason on the basis of it. They seek to understand judicial reasoning, to discover which arguments are likely to be heard by the judge. It is the discovery of the normative argument that interests them, not the construction of a theory independent of legal solutions.[112] However, the law of anticompetitive practices, even if its semantics sometimes seem to indicate the contrary, only takes into consideration, *de lege lata*, the means. It does not dwell on the question of the result: it excludes it from its reasoning, and de facto simultaneously rejects economic theories that take sides on the difficult question of the "best result."[113]

Consequently, jurists cannot take the result as the starting point for defining the offense, or if they do, they must make it clear that they are adopting a *de lege ferenda* approach. On the other hand, a careful reading of case law will lead them to maintain that, in positive law, it is the means alone that deserves their full attention.

*

* *

381. **Conclusion of Section 1: the central element in the definition of competition infringements – anticompetitive conduct.** While there appears to be a *de lege lata* causal link between the restriction of competition and the potential result on the market, this is not only automatic, but also superfluous, since it is not required to characterize the infringement. What is more, the restriction of competition, far from being an independent element of the infringement, is in fact totally at one with the anticompetitive behavior, so that the restriction of competition is not susceptible of an autonomous definition. It is therefore necessary to bypass two of the three elements in order to define an anticompetitive infringement – namely, the effect on the market and the restriction of competition. Thus, by process of elimination, only conduct should be the focus of attention.

The distinction between restriction of competition and anticompetitive behavior is, incidentally, a modern invention. In the past, competition infringement has always been defined solely in terms of behavior, and this has been the case since antiquity.[114] The parliamentary work of 1926, prior to the reform of article 419 of the Penal Code, attests to

112 This is the scientific aspect of law: jurists cannot totally emancipate themselves from reality and engage in acts of creation. They are constantly constrained by reality. So, if doctrine, as a critical examination, is indispensable, the science of law is its necessary prerequisite. In this sense, E. Picard, *'Science du droit' ou 'doctrine juridique'*, *in* L'UNITÉ DU DROIT. MÉLANGES EN HOMMAGE À ROLAND DRAGO 119, 122 (1996).

113 This is a difficult question, and probably insoluble, *see supra*, esp. no. 120.

114 *See* Part I, Title I, Chapter 1.

the fact that it was still considered impossible to define "gain that is not the result of the normal functioning of competition" in an autonomous way – this being nothing other than gain "resulting from fraudulent maneuvers."[115] Even today, it is on the side of the maneuver, and the corresponding intent, that we should look for a definition of anti-competitive practices.

*

* *

Section 2
Benefits of Adopting the Theory of Intent

382. **An unmarked path: the territory of indeterminate notions.** The most essential concepts, instruments of persuasion par excellence, are expressed through the most ambiguous notions of thought.[116] It is only through a gradual process of clarification, always left in abeyance, to be prolonged and perfected, that a definition likely to provide the judge with reasons to decide is likely to be proposed. Readers should not expect to find here definitive assertions, clear-cut distinctions or an exact science. They will be led into the realm of vagueness:[117] the life of the law is born from the vagueness of words.

383. **The distinction between precondition and constitutive element: to *want,* you still need to be *able*.** With his dark, serious gaze, she sometimes thinks his eyes are as pale blue as they are innocent; with his shoulders rolled up, curled up in his chair, he wishes he could make himself as straight as a statue. She can do nothing, but if he wants to, he can work on his posture: there is no intent worthy of the name except that which aims at an objective that the individual imagines as possible.[118] So, in order to undermine competition, a company must already be *capable* of doing so: a small newcomer, arriving in a market without innovating, cannot

---

115 *See* the reproduction of the legislative debates of 1926, *supra*, no. 127.

116 A point made with regard to "universal values" by C. Perelman & L. Olbrechts-Tyteca, Traité de l'argumentation 188 (2008).

117 René Demogue considers that "while we have no doubt that there is a natural law outside ourselves, an ideal law with variable content, we find it more difficult to discover it, and we have to admit that it is not very accessible," *see* Les notions fondamentales du droit privé: Essai critique 46 (1911).

118 C.-A. Vallier, De l'intention morale 73 (1882): intent presupposes a "firm desire for execution" and "belief in the possibility of this execution"; *adde*, in the same vein, G. E. M. Anscombe, L'intention 57–58 (M. Maurice & C. Michon trans., Gallimard 2002). Such an assertion is not contradicted by criminal law: the impossible offense is equated with the attempt precisely because of the agent's belief in the *possibility*, however mistaken, of carrying out their criminal purpose.

disrupt the meeting of supply and demand – it cannot form anticompetitive intent. The definition of anticompetitive intent (**Paragraph 2**) would therefore not be complete without a study of its prerequisite:[119] market power (**Paragraph 1**).

Paragraph 1 – A common prerequisite: market power

384. **A unitary vision of agreements and abuse of dominance.** It is customary to teach that only abuse of a dominant position requires a two-stage reasoning process: first, to establish dominance, which implies delimiting a "relevant market," and then to characterize an abuse. Agreements, by contrast, are most often apprehended without delimiting the market, or examining the position of companies in it.[120] However, this dichotomy in the characterization of infringements is only apparent. Agreements and abuse of a dominant position both presuppose the existence of market power, a prerequisite for the possibility of restricting competition. A general definition of power (**I**) and a theorization of market power (**II**) will thus make it clear that there is an inseparable link between this prerequisite and the infringement itself – for without the ability to influence competition, there can be no intent to distort it.

---

119 The notion of "precondition" originates from criminal law, and is attributed to Robert Vouin, who developed it in relation to breach of trust. *See* R. Vouin & M.-L. Rassat, Droit pénal spécial: Infractions contre les biens, les personnes, la famille, les mœurs et la paix publique 78 (5th ed. 1983) (1953), no. 59: the author considers it necessary to distinguish between the offense of breach of trust itself, which consists of fraudulent misappropriation, and three preconditions – namely, the existence of a contract, an object, and its delivery. This can be either a legal circumstance or a factual circumstance, *see* J.-P. Doucet, *La condition préalable à l'infraction*, Gazette du palais (1972), ii, doct. 726. For an overview, *see* B. Thellier de Poncheville, La condition préalable de l'infraction (2010). In addition, for articles 101 and 102 TFEU to be applicable, there must be an effect on trade between Member States. On the role of effects in assessing the criterion of effect on trade between Member States, *see* with interest: H. Mayras, *La théorie de l'effet dans le droit des ententes*, ix Jus Gentium: Diritto delle relazioni internazionali 41 (1973). More recently, one author has defended the idea that this assessment could involve taking into account intent as a relevant element, and that an error of law was admissible, *see* J. Blockx, *Mens Rea* in EU Antitrust Law: When Intentions Matter 138–41 (2020), nos. 453–463, and case law cited. For our part, we consider that the "qualified effects" criterion (*see* Case C-413/14 P, Intel, ECLI:EU:C:2017:632, paras. 40–65, esp. para. 49) is met provided that it is "*foreseeable* that the conduct in question will have an immediate and substantial effect in the European Union" (emphasis added). As we know, if a consequence is foreseeable, it is deemed to have been foreseen, and therefore intended. Similarly, in international law, *see* the following article: B. Stern, *Quelques observations sur les règles internationales relatives à l'application extraterritoriale du droit*, 32 Annuaire français de droit international 7, 31–32 (1986).

120 Market power is indeed considered negatively in the context of agreements: when the parties have low market shares, the cartel is deemed incapable of restricting competition, *see* D. Bosco, *Le problème du franchissement des seuils en parts de marché*, Concurrences no. 1-2014, art. no. 63014, 26, 26, no. 1: "[I]f the parties have a limited market share, they are, according to the usual formula, in a safe zone. The English expression refers to an image: a safe harbor, a secure, peaceful port, which preserves the parties from the turbulent waters of legal insecurity." *Adde*, on this theme: Case 5/69, Völk, ECLI:EU:C:1969:35, para. 7; Case C-215/96, Bagnasco, ECLI:EU:C:1999:12, para. 34; Case C-238/05, Asnef-Equifax, ECLI:EU:C:2006:734, para. 50; Case C-226/11, Expedia, ECLI:EU:C:2012:795, para. 16; and Eur. Comm., Notice on Agreements of Minor Importance which Do Not Appreciably Restrict Competition Under Article 101(1) of the Treaty on the Functioning of the European Union (De Minimis Notice), 2014 O.J. (C 291) 1, paras. 5 and 8.

I. The definition of power

385. **Semantic clarification.** Power is distinct from freedom (**A**), which is the presupposition of competition, because in a certain sense it is the ability to constrain the freedom of others (**B**).

A. The distinction between freedom and power

386. **The presupposition of competition: freedom.** To be autonomous is to establish one's own law,[121] to be able to decide for oneself. In philosophy, this moral freedom is opposed both to submission to impulses and to uncritical obedience to injunctions dictated by an external authority. However, the autonomous individual does not live without rules: they follow only those they have chosen after an examination undertaken with the help of their reason.[122]

Without autonomy, there can be no competition: if every entrepreneur followed the established order, imitating those who came before them, charging the same prices, civilization would not have evolved, and markets would have remained static.[123] If we speak of entrepreneurial freedom, it is because commerce implies novelty, because novelty is *creation*, and because all creation, insofar as it opposes the existent, presupposes freedom – the freedom not to be or do like others, the freedom to determine oneself.

387. **Comparison and distinction between freedom and power.** In the first sense, power is defined as the ability and possibility to carry out an action.[124] In this sense, it extends the notion of freedom: one who lacks the power to act cannot be free.

But power can also have a different meaning: it refers to *to influence and exercise control over someone.*[125] Of course, in a certain way, everyone acts on others, because human beings build their personality by imitating or rejecting the behavior and thoughts of those around them. We are influenced by our environment, the people we meet and our exchanges with others: our individuality is the sum of our experiences of accepting and rejecting what others propose to us. Otherness is part of freedom, in that it gradually enables us to discover who we are, and thus to be freer. Power is thus

---

121 A. Lalande, Vocabulaire technique et critique de la philosophie 101 (2002).

122 B.-M. Jacob, Devoirs: Conférence de morale individuelle et de morale sociale 25 (1908). The term "reason" is important, and deserves a comment: choosing one rule over another cannot, on principle and without further examination, be considered an act of freedom. The decision must be taken with reason, i.e., with an awareness of right and wrong.

123 This is what prompted F. A. Hayek to say that the more "imperfect" competition is (in reference to the static economic notion of pure and perfect competition), the more effective it actually is. *See* F. A. Hayek, *The Meaning of Competition*, 13 Econ Journal Watch 359, 371 (2016).

124 TLFi.

125 TLFi.

a natural phenomenon of interaction and reciprocal influence. However, there are different modalities and degrees of power. The ability to influence and exercise control over others can be conscious or unconscious, voluntary or spontaneous. It can consist in serving as a model or anti-model for others – in which case the decision remains the individual's: they remain autonomous – or in imposing something on others – in which case the decision is dictated by a third party.

However, even when certain things are enjoined by others, the freedom of the other is not, by this very fact, constrained.[126] Thus, the contract does not imply deciding for others, but obliging oneself, and if the aim of any negotiation is to influence the choices of the potential contracting party, the latter remains, in the last resort, the sole master of their will – except in cases of *dol*.[127] Think again of contracts of adhesion: their content is determined by only one of the parties, but the other remains free to contract or not to contract. Moreover, contract law theorists are no strangers to the figure of power. The raison d'être of certain contracts is precisely to enable an individual to choose for another, and to bind them by this decision. For example, the power of the principal to bind the agent, of the spouse to bind the community, or of the manager to bind the legal entity.[128] In these cases, the power to decide for another is legitimate, since it is foreseen, accepted and regulated.

Nevertheless, outside the contractual hypotheses[129] – in other words, cases where the transfer of decision-making power is agreed – power does not reside in the ability to *bind* others, but in the ability to *coerce* them. Power is thus distinct from freedom, because it *can* be the instrument of its annihilation.

B. Power: the ability to coerce others

388. **Power, or the ability to restrict the freedom of others.** Power is the ability to make one's own choice prevail, by restricting or suppressing the autonomy of others in order to impose a decision on them.[130] The holder

126 One view – too extreme in our opinion – is that the slave continues to act freely by accepting their status, a view reminiscent of Étienne de la Boétie's voluntary servitude, *see* P. Amselek, *Les règles juridiques en tant qu'objets mentaux*, 79 Archives for Philosophy and Social Philosophy 311, 319–20 (1993): "Even in the extreme case of master-slave relations, the master's authority actually derives from the slave's willingness to give allegiance and allow themselves to be led."

127 Here we use the term "*dol*" as understood *infra*, no. 400.

128 E. Gaillard, Le pouvoir en droit privé 139 (1985), no. 217.

129 Emmanuel Gaillard has developed a very fruitful theory of power, which excludes from its scope the hypothesis we are aiming at – namely, power as constraint. He considers that it does not cover cases where power takes the form of "pressure, influence or constraint which would not be exercised in the form of a legal decision taken by an individual empowered to do so," *see* Gaillard, Le pouvoir en droit privé, *op. cit.* at 144, no. 225.

130 *Compare with* Gaillard, Le pouvoir en droit privé, *op. cit.* at 138–39, no. 216; and *with* M. Weber, La domination 44 (I. Kalinowski trans., La Découverte 2014): the author defines domination as "the possibility of compelling others to adjust their behavior according to one's own will."

of power establishes their own rules, which will constrain others and encroach on their sphere of freedom[131] by overriding their agreement, or even disregarding their consent. However, it is a fundamental principle that the State has a monopoly on coercion: the only legitimate form of coercion is therefore that which requires everyone to submit to the law.[132]

And yet, alongside the supposedly benevolent power of the State, we need only open our eyes to see the existence of private powers. They exist in many forms: seductive power, hierarchical power, intellectual power, psychological power, money power, market power – there are many ways to establish domination and authority, to make oneself master of others, to make oneself obeyed by those under obligation, to exert a decisive influence on others, reduced to mere subjects, manipulated at will. While some forms of power are necessary – such as parental authority, without which children cannot learn to set healthy limits for themselves – others are *by their very nature* deleterious, for it is incumbent on those who know they are in a position to condition others to take the precaution of guarding against them. Power implies responsibility: the responsibility not to exercise it.

This does not mean that those who hold power must renounce it: power is acquired through superiority, which is a state of affairs. We would not dream of asking beauty to become ugly, success to fail, or intelligence to become stupid. Nor is there any question of requiring the one who dominates to benefit the other – this is a matter of grace, not of right[133] – nor of not continuing to be superior to them. Power is a circumstance: it can arouse admiration, even adulation, and is even useful insofar as it invites others to surpass themselves.[134] But as soon as it is put to use, power is diverted from itself, because it becomes *the tool* for controlling others – a harmful and malignant instrument, because it deprives others of their ability to act freely. The chessboard is like that: there are pawns and bishops, just as there is a queen and a king, but despite their power, they are never the ones who make the rules – for no one is entitled to impose the rules of their own game on others.

389. **Power: the prerequisite for all forms of *dol*.** Thus defined, power rubs shoulders with *dol* – it precedes and heralds it. It is a *potential dol.* One deceives their counterparty: even then, they must have the ability to lie, distort and manipulate, an aptitude that is inconceivable for good people.

131 *Id.* at 140, no. 218.

132 The discussion then moves on to another terrain, which is not our place to visit here – that of the eternal question: "What is law?" On this theme, *see* G. Vedel, *Indéfinissable mais présent*, 11 Droits: Revue française de théorie juridique 67, 70 (1990): "I began by saying that I did not know how to solve the problem of defining law. And now, I have just suggested that such a definition might not be very useful. Would this not, in a different domain, be akin to echoing Baudelaire's anathema: '*s'éprenant d'un problème insoluble et stérile*' ['of sheer futility the fatuous schemer']?"

133 And we know that these two orders, moral and legal, are (*partly*) separate, as were beliefs and law in the past, *see supra*, no. 25, and internal and external forums, *see supra*, no. 53.

134 *See* Hesiod's *Theogony*, *supra*, no. 33.

The other abuses a person in a state of weakness: how could they do so without first establishing their hold over them? The company abuses its power, individually or collectively, to impose its own conditions: how could it do so without economic power? Power confronts its holder with a dilemma: not to exercise it, and retain power by virtue of one's own qualities alone, or to exercise it, by attempting to establish domination over others. This is why, in anticompetitive practices law as in other disciplines, power always implies a *particular responsibility*. In short, market power is just one aspect of the much more general concept of power, which permeates the whole of law. A concept that, like so many others in competition law, has been interpreted through an economic lens, to the point that it obscures its *legal* nature – even though it remains a shared concern across multiple disciplines.

II. Theorizing market power

390. **Characteristics of market power.** Market power is a common prerequisite for agreements and abuses of dominant position (**A**), and is partly confused with anticompetitive intent (**B**).

A. A common condition for agreements and abuses of dominant position

391. **The original simplicity of characterizing market power.** For a long time, there was no need to theorize about the obvious. It is not possible to undermine competition without having the ability to do so. In a city flower market, would we criticize one vendor among ten others for raising their prices, accusing them of exploiting onlookers? And if they were to say to their neighbor, "Tomorrow, I'll sell my white lisianthus for more," would anyone think of denouncing such an exchange of information? Would Lysias have vilified the wheat merchants[135] if they had not been the masters of the market?

In 1810, the obvious became clear in article 419 of the Penal Code.[136] Not all coalitions were punished: only those formed between "the *principal holders* of the same kind of merchandize or provisions" were covered. This condition was assessed simply, and did not give rise to any difficulty of interpretation:[137]

---

135 On the speech by Lysias *Against the Corn Dealers*, *see supra*, no. 39.

136 Art. 419 of the 1810 Penal Code is reproduced *in extenso*, *supra*, no. 98.

137 Unlike the notion of "merchandise," which was the subject of much controversy. *In fine*, services and labor were judged to fall within the category of merchandise, thanks to an extensive interpretation of the text. For a detailed study and examples of case law, *see* A. Chauveau, F. Hélie & E. Villey, v Théorie du Code pénal 607–19 (1888), nos. 2391–2397.

the judge never prosecuted an insignificant agreement[138] – *de minimis non curat praetor*. However, the doctrine soon voiced a criticism of the incrimination, which proved to be perennial. Not only were merchants able, through their agreements, to manipulate prices upwards or downwards, but they were also able to evade prosecution by grouping together in trading companies.[139] In this way, hoarding by a single person – the legal person – escaped the rigors of criminal law. Such a solution broke with tradition: hoarding had always been regarded as synonymous with monopoly, and targeted both individual behavior and fraudulent associations.[140] In 1926, during the debates that preceded the reform of article 419, a senator had rightly taken the view that even when "hoarding is concealed under a legal mask," the offense must exist.[141] The new wording of the article has therefore extended the scope of the offense by expressly mentioning the possibility, alongside the collective offense, of its individual commission.[142] This shows that there was no difference in nature between what we now distinguish as agreement and abuse of a dominant position, but only a difference in the *way* the offense *was committed.*[143] Thus, *market power is a unitary concept:* it is simply held by one person in the case of abuse of a dominant position, or by several in the case of agreements.

What is more, while it used to be a prerequisite that the parties to a coalition were the "main holders of a given good,"[144] this condition did not and still does not have to be proven in the case of agreements,[145] whereas

---

138 *See*, for example, CA Grenoble, 1re ch., May 1, 1894, Dalloz Périodique, 1895, ii, pp. 221–22, at 221 (Fr.): the court of appeal ruled that the coalition was not illicit, notably because "the merchants who have thus contracted represent in the region, in terms of both number and significance, only a minority of the producers of the said goods" (unofficial translation). *Compare with* Case 5/69, Völk, ECLI:EU:C:1969:35, para. 7: "[A]n agreement falls outside the prohibition in Article 85 when it has only an insignificant effect on the markets, taking into account the weak position which the persons concerned have on the market of the product in question."

139 For commentary: H. Babled, Droit français: Les syndicats de producteurs et détenteurs de marchandise au double point de vue économique et pénal 134–35 (1892); H. Savatier, La concurrence déloyale, l'accaparement et l'organisation moderne du commerce et de l'industrie 19–20 (1896); C. Jannet, *Des syndicats industriels pour régler la production en France*, xxix La Réforme Sociale – Bulletin de la Société Économie Sociale 121, 143 (1895): the author castigates the fact that it is impossible to target the coalition conducted through a company, even though this marks "the absolute loss of autonomy" of merchants; L. Mazeaud, i Le régime juridique des ententes industrielles et commerciales en France 132–33 (1928).

140 *See supra*, no. 74.

141 Adoption of a Bill to Amend Articles 419 and 420 of the French Penal Code, JORF, Débats parl., Sénat, Nov. 19, 1926, pp. 1648–55, at 1650 (Fr.) (unofficial translation).

142 The new wording of article 419, which was not applied (for the reasons explained *supra*, no. 102), is as follows: "All those who … by exercising or attempting to exercise, either individually, or through assembly or coalition, an action on the market with the aim of obtaining a gain that would not be the result of the natural interplay of supply and demand … shall be punished."

143 When the prohibition of abuse of a dominant position was incorporated into domestic law in 1967 (*see supra*, no. 107 and references cited), the Commission Technique des Ententes et des Abus de Position Dominante itself recognized the existence of an "indivisible link between the action of the agreements and that of the dominant position," *see* L. Laugier, *La prohibition des abus de position dominante*, Gazette du Palais nos. 345–348, 1, 3 (Dec. 11–14, 1965).

144 This prerequisite was presumed, but the presumption was rebuttable.

145 As in the past, this is still a negative condition: it is presumed that the parties to the agreement have market power, with the onus on the defendant to prove the contrary, *see supra*, no. 391. Except in the case of an "effects-based" approach, *see* C. Prieto, *Ententes: Restriction de concurrence, JurisClasseur Europe Traité* (Oct. 2017), fasc. 1410, nos. 67–68. However, as the effects-based approach is in practice a myth (*see supra*), this is undoubtedly a hypothetical case.

today it requires a major and increasingly complex demonstration[146] in order to characterize an abuse of a dominant position, which begins with the definition of the relevant market.

392. **The increasing complexity of relevant market definition: a necessity?** In order to qualify an abuse, the competition authority must first characterize the company's dominant position. This begins with defining the relevant market. In the early days of Community case law, this process was relatively straightforward. In the *United Brands* case, for example, the reasoning was not the most scientific: it consisted in using common sense. The Court held that the relevant market was that for bananas, since they have "certain characteristics, appearance, taste, softness, seedlessness, easy handling, a constant level of production which enable it to satisfy the constant needs of an important section of the population consisting of the very young, the old and the sick," which distinguishes them from other fresh fruits. Is this reasoning any less insightful than today's sophisticated economic studies?[147] Do the latter enable us to grasp reality more accurately?[148] Or does our thirst for accuracy lead us to another of the chimerical oases of our time?

The issue is controversial: some have criticized the methodology used to define the relevant market,[149] while others have even suggested abandoning this step.[150] Indeed, the limits of this approach became apparent with the emergence of digital markets, which, because they are innovative, are deemed to be more "dynamic" than so-called traditional markets. New analytical frameworks were thus deemed necessary,[151] in order to better

---

146 *See* OECD, Market Definition, DAF/COMP(2012)13/REV1 (Sept. 21, 2012).

147 For an example of a more sophisticated definition of the relevant market, *see* Case T-342/99, Airtours, ECLI:EU:T:2002:146, para. 42. On this subject, A.-L. Sibony, *La preuve scientifique évitée. Inventaire de quelques techniques judiciaires*, *in* Preuve scientifique, preuve juridique 161, 166–67 (E. Truilhé-Marengo ed., 2011). It should also be noted that it is surprising, to say the least, that the method for defining the relevant market is common to both anticompetitive practices law and merger law – these two disciplines being, in their objectives and methods, if not opposed, at least radically different.

148 Nobel Prize-winner economist Jean Tirole writes: "There is no easy recipe for defining a market, as shown by the many debates between economists and antitrust practitioners regarding the degree of monopoly power in specific sectors. Several useful (although imperfect) criteria have nonetheless been proposed. …For the purposes of this book, this empirical difficulty of defining a market will be ignored." *See* J. Tirole, Théorie de l'organisation industrielle 26 (1993).

149 J. Drexl, *Anticompetitive Stumbling Stones on the Way to a Cleaner World: Protecting Competition in Innovation without a Market*, 8 Journal of Competition Law and Economics 507 (2012).

150 L. Kaplow, *Why (Ever) Define Markets?*, 124 Harvard Law Review 437 (2010); P. Anato & C. Le Grip, Rapport d'information déposé par la Commission des affaires européennes sur le droit européen de la concurrence face aux enjeux de la mondialisation No. 2451, 122 (Nov. 27, 2019), proposition no. 13: the authors of the report suggest abandoning the notion of "relevant market," which should be replaced by systematic use of the concept of "potential competition." *Contra*, on the unjustified and unrealistic nature of removing the definition of the relevant market, *see* OECD, Market Definition, DAF/COMP(2012)13/REV1 (Sept. 21, 2012) at 62–75, nos. 245–303.

151 Among the abundant literature on these issues, *see* N. Petit, Big Tech and the Digital Economy: The Moligopoly Scenario (2020). The Commission has also undertaken to revise its Market Definition Notice, notably to integrate the challenges of the ecological transition and the digital revolution, *see* V. Grac-Aubert, *Concurrence: La Commission européenne modernise sa manière de définir le 'marché pertinent'*, Dalloz Actualité (Dec. 13, 2022).

grasp market phenomena – this adaptation to what we like to think of as "new" having, as usual, led to an increase in complexity.[152]

And yet, if we dwell for a moment on the notion of innovation,[153] it becomes clear that innovation, since it lies at the heart of competition,[154] is neither new nor truly different from the past. All markets are innovative by nature, whatever the era or sector. It is thus artificial to claim that some markets are highly innovative, while others remain more "static" – the difference between yesterday and today has more to do with the *increased speed* of market evolutions linked to innovations, and the sometimes *disruptive* nature of the latter: only their speed and scale distinguish them from the past. These characteristics aside, innovation is on every entrepreneur's mind, so the criticisms directed at the definition of certain "modern" markets – i.e., digital – should be extended to all markets.

This is not the only inconsistency: how can we explain the fact that so much theoretical effort is expended to ensure the accuracy, precision, reality, veracity, and "solidity" of the concept of the relevant market, without which there can be no dominant position, no abuse, while the Autorité de la concurrence can simultaneously define a minuscule market limited to the Goûter refuge, located on the normal route of Mont Blanc, dear only to mountaineers?[155] Does not this show the method's inconsistency, and the arbitrary nature of this step? Is it not, after all, just a compulsory passage dressed up in clever calculations, leading – by happy chance – to the very place the authority had already decided to go?[156]

393. **The economization of the concept of market power.** *De lege lata*, the relevant market is defined with a view to characterizing the market power of the company in question. However, to say that the presentation of market power departs from our proposed definition of power[157] would be an understatement. Like so many other concepts, it has undergone economization. Economic theory understands it as a technical concept that can be measured using cost-benefit tests,[158] indices or even market share

152 *See* Eur. Comm. Press Release IP/22/6528, Competition: Commission Seeks Feedback on Draft Revised Market Definition Notice (Nov. 8, 2022); and Eur. Comm., Draft Commission Notice on the Definition of the Relevant Market for the Purposes of Union Competition Law, 2022. The draft in question is forty-six pages long, whereas the 1997 communication is nine pages long.

153 For a precise definition, *see* M. Cartapanis, Innovation et droit de la concurrence 9–11 (2018), nos. 5–7.

154 As competition presupposes creation and novelty, *see supra*, no. 386.

155 ADLC, decision no. 15-D-12 of July 30, 2015, on practices implemented by the Fédération française des clubs alpins et de montagne and the Compagnies de guides de Chamonix et de Saint Gervais in the high mountain guide sector (access to Mont Blanc via the Goûter refuge) (Fr.).

156 *See also* N. Petit, Droit européen de la concurrence 370 (3rd ed. 2020), no. 866, and case law cited: the author notes that the "notion of relevant market is not without subjectivity" and that it "allows, in certain cases, the control authorities to pursue strategic objectives under the guise of an objective methodology."

157 *See supra*, no. 388.

158 *See* in particular Comm. EC, DG Competition Discussion Paper on the Application of Article 82 of the Treaty to Exclusionary Abuses 10–12 (Dec. 2005), paras. 24–35.

calculations,[159] and sometimes considers it to be per se capable of compromising "market efficiency" and harming consumer welfare[160] – which is in contradiction with case law, since dominance in itself is not considered unlawful.[161] What is more, some commentators consider believe that there is no universal economic test for market power,[162] and a dominant position has never been characterized solely on the basis of the company's market share[163] or its costs[164] – these elements of proof[165] being no more than useful pieces of evidence, or convenient presumptions.[166] A gulf was thus created between theory and practice: the presentation of market power became so complicated that the purpose of the proof was lost sight of, while its definition in case law remained unchanged. The concept has remained legal: *power cannot be reduced to a figure.*[167]

394. **Market power: a legal concept.** In 1966, the Commission's landmark Memorandum defined market power as the ability of one or more undertakings to "substantially *influence the decisions of other* economic *agents* by means of an *independent strategy.*"[168] More recent statements by the Commission do not call into question this first definition.[169] Case law, for its part, has consistently remained faithful to its early rulings, whose

---

159 Comm. EC, Guidance on the Commission's Enforcement Priorities in Applying Article 82 of the EC Treaty to Abusive Exclusionary Conduct by Dominant Undertakings, 2009 O.J. (C 45) 7, para. 11: "The Commission considers that an undertaking which is capable of profitably increasing prices above the competitive level for a significant period of time does not face sufficiently effective competitive constraints and can thus generally be regarded as dominant."

160 For a detailed and nuanced presentation of the concept of market power, *see* Petit, Droit européen de la concurrence, *op. cit.* at 199–236, nos. 431–564; *adde*, N. Petit, *Understanding Market Power* 2–16 (Robert Schuman Centre for Advanced Studies, Working Paper No. 2022/14, 2022), https://ssrn.com/abstract=4148489; E. Arezzo, *Is There a Role for Market Definition and Dominance in an Effect-Based Approach?, in* Abuse of Dominant Position: New Interpretation, New Enforcement Mechanisms 21–54 (M.-O. Mackenrodt, B. C. Gallego & S. Enchelmaier eds., 2008).

161 Since a dominant position is not prohibited per se, *see* in particular. Case C-23/14, Post Danmark, ECLI:EU:C:2015:651, para. 70: "[A] finding that an undertaking has a dominant position is not in itself a ground of criticism of the undertaking concerned... ."

162 In this sense, R. S. Markovits, *Some Preliminary Notes on the American Antitrust Law's Economic Tests of Legality*, 27 Stanford Law Review 841 (1975).

163 Even after the modernization movement, *see* A. C. Witt, The More Economic Approach to EU Antitrust Law 221 (2019), and references cited.

164 In any case, as one author rightly noted, "to assess whether a company's profits are excessive, and, if so, indicative of significant market power, is to make a decision laden with subjectivity," Petit, Droit européen de la concurrence, *op. cit.* at 368, no. 880.

165 On the distinction between elements of proof and objects of proof, *see supra*, no. 261, and reference cited.

166 For an overview of the methods of proving the existence of a dominant position, *see* Petit, Droit européen de la concurrence, *op. cit.* at 382–91 nos. 921–960.

167 Figures are static, the market is dynamic, and far too complex to be encased in models, no matter how sophisticated.

168 Comm. EC, Le problème de la concentration dans le marché commun 22 (1966) (emphasis added) (unofficial translation).

169 *Compare* the quotation from the Memorandum *with*: Comm. EC, Guidance on the Commission's Enforcement Priorities in Applying Article 82 of the EC Treaty to Abusive Exclusionary Conduct by Dominant Undertakings, 2009 O.J. (C 45) 7, para. 10; *adde*, Comm. EC, Commission Notice on the Definition of Relevant Market for the Purposes of Community Competition Law, 1997 O.J. (C 372) 5, para. 2.

content largely mirrors that of the Memorandum – albeit in less precise terms.[170] For the Court of Justice, a dominant position is the "position of economic strength enjoyed by an undertaking which enables it to *prevent* effective competition" by virtue of "the *power* to behave to an appreciable extent *independently* of its competitors, customers and ultimately of its consumers."[171] Does this not embody the very spirit of the general definition provided by[172] – power as the possibility of making one's own choice prevails over that of others, by restricting their freedom?

And if the obligation to prove market power is reserved only for the law of abuse, is it not obvious that *a pari*, an agreement between several undertakings makes them independent of competition, and enables them to influence the decisions of other economic agents? How, then, can we justify mobilizing such vast resources on the basis of article 102 to demonstrate the existence of a dominant position, while based on article 101, market power is systematically presumed, and thus abstracted from litigation? After all, is not the greatest proof of power to be found in its exercise?[173] Put another way, is power not partly conflated with anticompetitive intent?

B. A condition partly conflated with anticompetitive intent

395. **Is the definition of market power distinct from the definition of anticompetitive intent?** In positive law, the concept of market power is approached in a fragmented manner: on the one hand, it is subject to differentiated legal treatment depending on whether the authority is pursuing an agreement or an abuse; on the other hand, on the basis of article 102, it requires a step prior to the characterization of the infringement itself.[174] Nevertheless, even if we adopt a *de lege lata* approach, if we look at definitions rather than litigation techniques, it must be acknowledged that market power describes nothing other than an incipient anticompetitive intent. As a result, it appears paradoxical that the law on abuse of a dominant position has been burdened with so many complications, even though, to prove market power as defined, it would suffice to prove intent. Put another way, proving abuse could, without requiring any further demonstration, demonstrate the existence of market power.

---

170 We consider the Court's definition to be less precise than the Memorandum's, as it places greater emphasis on the company's independence (i.e., autonomy) than on its power (the ability to coerce others).

171 Case 27/76, United Brands, ECLI:EU:C:1978:22, para. 65 (emphasis added). The formula was subsequently used identically, *see, e.g.*, Case 85/76, Hoffmann-La Roche, ECLI:EU:C:1979:36, para. 38; Case T-30/89, Hilti, ECLI:EU:T:1991:70, para. 90; Case C-250/92, Gøttrup-Klim, ECLI:EU:C:1994:413, para. 47; Case T-321/05, AstraZeneca, ECLI:EU:T:2010:266, para. 239; Case T-691/14, Servier, ECLI:EU:T:2018:922, para. 1595.

172 *See supra*, no. 388.

173 Think of the old English proverb: "The proof of the pudding is in the eating"!

174 *De lege ferenda*, we will argue in favor of a simple and unified approach to market power, *see infra*, no. 501.

This line of reasoning is not entirely foreign to U.S. antitrust law,[175] where the focus is more on anticompetitive behavior itself than on market power.[176] In European Union law, the idea was also put forward, more or less directly, by several authors.[177] And, even if the solution is old, and remained isolated, the Court of Justice recognized, in the *United Brands* ruling, that to characterize a dominant position, it is possible to "take account if need be of the facts put forward as acts amounting to abuses without necessarily having to acknowledge that they are abuses."[178] If abuse is proof of dominance, why prove it as if it were an autonomous condition?

396. **Logical argument: comparing definitions.** We know that anticompetitive behavior is that which "tends to," is "of such a nature as to" or is "likely to" restrict competition. However, power is nothing other than a capacity, a potentiality, that may never be exercised.[179] So what is the difference between one and the other? There is none, and it is rather in terms of boundaries that we should be thinking. Anticompetitive behavior presupposes the use of a power, but whereas this power may remain in abeyance, unused, asleep, committing a competition infringement involves the company waking it up, activating it, exercising it. It does not matter whether this results in a concrete effect, or whether the desired objective is achieved: there has been a *willingness to use it*. The parties to an agreements concentrate their powers in order to influence certain parameters of competition: a company lowers its prices in the hope of ousting another operator, or concludes exclusivity clauses to protect itself from competitors and restrict the freedom of its partners. They have the power to do so, but only contravene competition rules if they actually try to do so. However, intent can only exist if the agent conceives the objective pursued as possible:[180] it would therefore be sufficient to prove the implementation of the intention to demonstrate capacity. This is, moreover, the solution implicitly adopted in agreement cases, and no one is criticizing the fact

---

175 In this regard, *see* R. Joliet, *Monopolisation et abus de position dominante: Essai comparatif sur l'article 2 du Sherman Act et l'article 86 du Traité de Rome*, RTD Eur. 645, 654–57 (1969).

176 Petit, *Understanding Market Power*, *op. cit.* at 31–32; *adde*, O. Odudu, *The Role of Specific Intent in Section 1 of the Sherman Act: A Market Power Test?*, 25 World Competition 463, 476 (2002): "Specific intent can be used to predict outcomes because when a person has intent to bring about an outcome, they will act to bring about that outcome… . Specific intent is predictive, and its predictive nature allows it to function as an accurate predictive tool – as a market power test."

177 E. Cerexhe, *L'interprétation de l'article 86 du Traité de Rome et les premières décisions de la Commission*, Cahiers de droit européen 272, 287 (1972), no. 47: the author considers that market power could be deduced from the behavior of firms, since they "could impose their decisions without other economic agents having the possibility of reacting to this preponderant influence"; T. Eilmansberger, *Dominance – The Lost Child? How Effects-Based Rules Could and Should Change Dominance Analysis*, 2 European Competition Journal 15 (2006); *compare with* S. Weber Waller, *The Language of Law and the Language of Business*, 52 Case Western Reserve Law Review 283, 334 (2001): "Sophisticated corporations expend too many resources in their strategic planning and marketing decisions not to take seriously the results of that work."

178 Case 27/76, United Brands, ECLI:EU:C:1978:22, para. 68.

179 *See supra*, no. 388.

180 *See supra*, no. 383.

that market power is not the subject of specific demonstrations on the basis of article 101 in every case.

The definition of anticompetitive intent will only reinforce the idea that there is, if not an identity, at least a profound link between it and the notion of market power.

Paragraph 2 – A common criterion: anticompetitive intent

397. **A definition based on an indeterminate concept.** The chosen definition of anticompetitive intent, which consists in designating it as "*dol* with market power" (**I**), necessarily relies, as does the definition of any standard using indeterminate concepts (**II**), on terms that cannot achieve an extreme degree of precision, but that nonetheless have the advantage of being understood by all jurists.

I. Defining anticompetitive intent

398. **A link with general law reasoning.** Following the Aristotelian model, the function of a definition is to capture, by successive approximations, the essence of the object under study.[181] By providing a general definition of anticompetitive intent, we aim to show that the law of anticompetitive practices is not as detached as it seems from the reasoning of general law (**A**), before verifying whether the proposed definition explains the established jurisprudential solutions (**B**).

A. General definition of anticompetitive intent

399. **A preliminary clarification: the need to eliminate politicized or moral notions, circular notions, and the accumulation of terms designating the same thing.** It is all very well to criticize the words of jurists, to reproach them for their elusive nature and vaporous appearance, and then to aspire to replace them with the fixity and supposedly clear contours of numbers, believing that this will solve the problem.[182]

It is true, however, that the legal vocabulary has become considerably more obscure and cumbersome as a result of contemporary lawmaking.[183]

---

181 G. Cornu *Les définitions dans la loi, in* Mélanges dédiés à Jean Vincent 77, 79 (1981).

182 On this subject, *see infra*, nos. 448 *et seq.*

183 *See* P. Conte, *L'art de légiférer se perd-il? Réflexions en forme de pamphlet à partir de quelques illustrations de droit pénal, in* Études à la mémoire de Christian Lapoyade-Deschamps 307 (2003): the study lists "contemporary illustrations of legislation in disastrous form."

Legislators are rarely jurists. For several decades now, new terms have been proliferating in the law.[184] They are devoid of precedent,[185] devoid of tradition, sometimes devoid of content, and often tinged with good intentions that are as much political promises. The jurist confronted with them is at a loss: how to interpret them? The solution is often, for want of a better alternative, to wait for jurisprudence to do its work – which, for the doctrine, amounts to evading the problem. Another approach is possible: look beyond the words' veneer to uncover their meaning and, if they have none, or if they do not provide the necessary clarification to more classic, better-defined legal concepts with a long tradition, discard them. Once this has been done, criticism of jurists is bound to miss its target. As things stand, however, it has to be admitted that the "legal expressions" of competition law are not very enlightening, or even misleading.

Indeed, what are we to think of "competition on the merit," vaguely tinged with morality, and whose meaning has been so overused?[186] Does it require companies to help their fellow human beings, to behave with a view to the Good? What about the notion of equity,[187] which, understood as the vain wish to re-establish material equality between all, can become the Trojan Horse of a social policy disguised as market law? Do we expect economic players to redistribute wealth as if they were engaged in charity work? Is not there – and was not there even among theologians[188] – a clear distinction between what earthly justice imposes and what divine justice imposes, between what the law requires and what the moral rules we choose to set for ourselves impose on our conscience?[189]

---

184 Such is the case with the expression "for object or effect," which would not have been acceptable to any ancient jurist.

185 Think, for example, of the replacement, during the 2016 reform of contract law, of the notion of cause by other words that designate more or less the same thing, but under the veil of different terms that are not the subject of established case law… On this theme, *see* G. Chantepie & M. Latina, Le nouveau droit des obligations: Commentaire théorique et pratique dans l'ordre du Code civil 245–46 (2nd ed. 2018), no. 284; *adde*, D. Mazeaud, *Pour que survive la cause, en dépit de la réforme*, 240 Revue Droit & Patrimoine 38 (Oct. 2014).

186 *See supra*, no. 363. The expression was coined by the ordoliberals, who distinguished between "competition on the merits" ("*Leistungswettbewerb*") and "impediment competition" ("*Behinderungswettbewerb*"), *see* C. Mongouachon, *L'ordolibéralisme: Contexte historique et contenu dogmatique*, Concurrences no. 4-2011, art. no. 38770, 70, 76, no. 24. In this sense, competition on the merits is partly confused with the definition we are about to propose. However, we prefer to exclude this expression from our definition for two reasons: firstly, because it is recent and has no counterpart in other areas of law (yet we wish to show the link the discipline shares with general law); secondly, because it is subject to too much controversy, and is sometimes rejected outright by specialists.

187 It should be noted that fairness is sometimes more or less consciously confused with loyalty (since the English adjective "fair" can be translated as either "*équitable*" or "*loyal*"); indeed, there is a semantic shift from the idea of a "loyal exchange" toward that of an "equitable outcome," particularly evident in the Digital Markets Act, *see* P. Ibáñez Colomo, *The Draft Digital Markets Act: A Legal and Institutional Analysis*, 12 Journal of European Competition Law & Practice 561, 568–69 (2021). *Adde*, on the multiple meanings of the term "loyalty" in competition law, *see* M. Malaurie-Vignal, *La loyauté, l'égalité et l'équité en droit de la concurrence*, Contrats concurrence consommation (Feb. 2021), repère 2: the notion is sometimes confused with the word "*équité*," and sometimes, when considered in "its equality dimension," it can mean "that the rules of the game are the same for everyone."

188 *See supra*, no. 53

189 "*Ah! la charité, la charité, cette idée chrétienne devenue folle le jour où elle a épousé le droit*" ("Ah! Charity, charity – this Christian idea gone mad the day it married the law"), writes Dean Carbonnier in Essai sur les lois 311 (2nd 1992).

Alongside these first notions, which can be malleable in one direction or another, depending on the sensibility of the interpreter, we also find several circular notions. Loyalty: honoring commitments, keeping one's word – necessary to establish a relationship of trust with a view to concluding a contract, or to maintain it if it already exists.[190] It is an indeterminate concept, extremely useful and fruitful in contract law. But when it comes to competition, to whom has the company undertaken such an obligation?[191] Competition is a battle, and must certainly be "fair," but in the usual sense of the term, i.e., "n accordance with the requirements of the law."[192] But this second meaning of loyalty tells us nothing about what the law requires. The same criticism can be leveled at the term "abuse": to abuse is to use something excessively.[193] But what is excess? "threshold of the tolerable" – which, precisely, the law does not tolerate!"[194] We should also mention the expressions "normal competition" and "abnormal competition": what is normal is what conforms to the norm.[195] And each time, the line of reasoning spins endlessly on itself. This semantic journey concludes with the trio of "prevent," "restrict" and "distort." Why three terms for a single reality?[196] Is the jurist not the miser who carefully weighs each of them when they take up their pen?

If neither the economic analysis nor the terms just quoted allow us to arrive at a satisfactory solution, how will we get out of the impasse into which the delicate question of the definition of anticompetitive intent has led us? The answer is to link it to a legal concept that, from the outset, has underpinned every solution in competition law, and with which the law is so familiar: *dol*.[197]

400. **The definition of *dol* and its further development: the link between *dol* and free will.** Since Roman law,[198] *dol* has had a consistent definition[199]: classically,

---

190 *See* P. Brunswick, *Le devoir de loyauté, une norme générale de comportement oubliée puis retrouvée*?, Cahiers de droit de l'entreprise (Jan. 2016), dossier 1.

191 *A priori*, the company has no such duty towards anyone, unless we imagine an invisible contract between all companies and all consumers, *see infra*, no. 404.

192 TLFi.

193 Vocabulaire juridique 7 (G. Cornu ed., 11th ed. 2016).

194 *Id.* at 430.

195 *Id.* at 691. In a second sense, "normal" means "in fact, the most frequent, current, common, habitual," *id.*

196 The fact that these three terms do not designate three distinct things is not a matter of controversy among specialists. *See, inter alia*, J. A. Ellis, *L'interprétation du mot 'affecter' dans l'article 85, § 1er, du Traité de la Communauté économique européenne par rapport aux mots 'empêcher', 'restreindre', ou 'fausser' le jeu de la concurrence*, Recueil Dalloz 221, 224–25 (1963), chron. xxxiii.

197 The real definitions are, in fact, those "contained in general law, the only source capable of irradiating the entire legal system," F. Colonna d'Istria, *Le mythe des 'définitions dans la loi': Exemples de droit des obligations*, *in* Le droit entre autonomie et ouverture: Mélanges en l'honneur de Jean-Louis Bergel 61, 71 (J.-Y. Chérot et al. eds., 2013).

198 *See supra*, no. 30 and no. 190; *adde*, J. Gaudemet & E. Chevreau, Droit privé romain 384–85 (3rd ed. 2009), no. 132.

199 We leave aside here the second meaning of *dol*, understood as the mental element of intentional offenses (on this subject, for a critique of the different forms of *dol*, *see supra*, no. 190).

it refers to any ruse, feint, deception, or maneuver used to deceive or mislead someone, or to obtain their consent by surprise.[200]

We must push the reasoning further in order to clarify this initial outline. Since antiquity, law has *postulated* human free will.[201] This postulate is a constant, underpinning its most essential solutions: as soon as individuals are free, they must act voluntarily in order to commit themselves; they must intend wrongdoing in order to be punished. And since freedom cannot be demonstrated, it is a "negative concept": the law only incorporates it into its reasoning when it is lacking[202] – the legal apprehension of free will only appears when it disappears. Insanity, constraint and error are all causes of its annihilation: they invalidate the commitment and excuse the wrongdoing. This very general principle is the basis for a number of more specific rules. The prohibition of *dol* is one of them. Examining it allows us to grasp the essence of the concept, by discovering its connection to freedom.

Dol is the hallmark of offenses of means,[203] which, as a reminder, share several common features: (i) penalize the use of unlawful means, (ii) employed with the aim of obtaining an undue advantage, (iii) which ultimately serves to protect property.[204] In this respect, it is relevant to note that the Aristotelian theory of justice was largely developed on the basis of exchange.[205] Nothing could be more logical: any exchange presupposes freedom, for it alone enables commitment; and all justice is founded on freedom, for without it, neither reward nor blame would be conceivable.[206] Indeed, for Aristotle as for the scholastics, the conditions of exchange are just if they are the fruit of free will, for all that justice demands is the absence of fraud falsifying the transaction.[207] But why? Precisely because

---

200 J. Carbonnier, 4 Droit civil: Les obligations 99 (16th ed. 1992), no. 42; *compare with* Vocabulaire juridique 365 (G. Cornu ed., 11th ed. 2016).

201 *See supra*, no. 28.

202 Already in Aristotle, *see supra*, no. 29.

203 As a reminder, this category includes, *inter alia*, swindling, theft, breach of trust, deceit, pre-contractual *dols*, unfair competition, and anticompetitive practices, *see supra*, no. 245.

204 *See supra*, no. 246.

205 *See supra*, no. 35. This is not surprising: the distinction between yours and mine is consubstantial with the feeling of individuality. As soon as the human species became aware of its individuality, it sought to appropriate space, to invest it and possess it, in order to free itself – so far as possible – from physical constraint through mastery over the material world. If sedentism opens the way to art, politics, and justice, it is because it ensures greater stability in the means of subsistence; and if a state is formed, it is because everyone wants to secure their property, and have it protected by a third party arbitrator (*see supra*, no. 23). Property is a principle immanent to the most ancient civilizations, which undoubtedly precedes the emergence of earthly justice and constitutes its cause. On this theme, *see* L. Faucher, *Propriété*, *in* II Dictionnaire de l'économie politique: Contenant l'exposition des principes de la science 460, 461–64 (C. Coquelin & G.-U. Guillaumin eds., 1853); *adde*, F. A. Hayek, La Constitution de la liberté 102–103 (R. Audouin & J. Garello trans., Litec 1994).

206 *See supra*, Plato's speech between Clinias and the Stranger from Athens, no. 28

207 *See* in this sense, *supra*, resp. no. 37 and no. 64. *Adde*, F. A. Hayek, Droit, législation et liberté: Une nouvelle formulation des principes libéraux de justice et d'économie politique 467–68 (R. Audouin trans., PUF, 2nd ed. 2013), and references cited n.2; F. Chénedé, *De l'autonomie de la volonté à la justice commutative: Du mythe à la réalité*, 4 Droit & Philosophie: Annuaire de l'Institut Michel Villey 155,

fraud, deception, lies, maneuvers, artifice – in a word, *dol* – consist in suppressing the freedom of others in order to obtain a gain that would not have been acquired in their absence, because the gain has only been obtained through the abolition of the free will of one or more third parties, in other words, their capacity to determine themselves autonomously,[208] in full knowledge of the facts. As a result of fraudulent conduct, the victim is led to serve the intentions of another, instead of their own.[209] Thus, in law, there is an ancient and enduring link between the lawfulness and freedom of a transaction.[210] In short, *if one party's* dol *taints the exchange, it is because it annihilates the freedom of the other party, or parties.*

On the basis of this relationship between *dol* and freedom, it is still necessary to specify the three categories of *dol*, of which the reader will find a summary table in the appendix,[211] and which serve to clarify the mental element of all the offenses of means,[212] thus transcending the distinction between civil law and criminal law:[213] (i) either the free will of another is purely and simply ignored, (ii) or nullified by error, (iii) or coerced.

401. **First category of *dol*: ignoring free will.** The first and most serious category of *dol* consists in appropriating property without seeking the consent of others. The thief is punished because they have appropriated property without any regard for the owner's consent, which is purely and simply ignored: not only does the victim have no choice, but they have no control over the event – it remains external to them. The same is true of breach of trust: the agent entrusted with the power to manage property diverts it from its intended use in violation of the mandate conferred on them – the principal's decision is not respected.

---

172 n.74 (2012): the author notes, referring to a translation note by Jean Tricot, that according to Aristotle, the presumption of free determination of the justness of the contract? must be disregarded when *dol* or fraud taints the agreement. *Adde*, S. Trifilio, *The Economic Theory of the Scholastics as a Contractual Analysis*, 24 Journal des Économistes et des Études Humaines 1, 3 (2018): "In personal transactions, the respective value of the protagonists (their function within the City in particular) is irrelevant. Volition is the criterion of the *synallagmata*. Aristotle talks about involuntary relations for the transaction has not been initially accepted by at least one of the protagonists (such as in acts of violence or robbery."

208 On the notion of autonomy, *see supra*, no. 386.

209 This is Friedrich Hayek's definition of coercion, which he applies both to unjustified interference by the state, and to acts of fraud or deception. In the first case, coercion is of public origin, in the second, of private origin. *See* Hayek, La Constitution de la liberté, *op. cit.* at 98–106.

210 This is obviously not the only criterion, even less so today than in the past: morality, public order, general interest, balance, solidarity, equity, protection of the weaker party are all arguments that serve to justify judicial intervention in the contractual sphere, and challenging what the parties had freely agreed upon. On this subject, *see infra*, no. 427.

211 *See* Appendix no. 6 *infra*. This table establishes a symmetry between the three general categories of *dol*, and the three categories of *dol* with market power (in other words, the three categories of anticompetitive intent).

212 What follows applies, *ipso facto*, to all offenses falling into the category of offenses of means mentioned *supra*, no. 245, and not just to competition infringements.

213 While the notion of *dol* is well known to civil law practitioners, Marcel Planiol noted that, in criminal law, fraud and breach of trust are three offenses derived from theft (in other words, according to our classification, three offenses of means). According to the author, they share common features: in these offenses, "*dol* is the means," *see* M. Planiol, *Dol civil et dol criminel*, xx Revue critique de législation et de jurisprudence 545 & 643, 557 (1893).

402. **Second category of *dol*: free will nullified by error.** The second form of *dol* is well known to private law specialists, but its influence is not limited to contract law. It consists in appropriating property by giving others a false impression of reality in order to induce them to commit or give. Pre-contractual *dols*, like swindling or deception, consist in lying or deceiving in order to mislead another person and induce the victim to enter into a transaction that they would not have accepted had they known the truth. The exchange appears voluntary: it has the *appearance* of a freely consented act. The party has entered into a contract, and the victim of the fraud has handed over the thing. But since the error is excused, it eliminates the will[214] – the contract is annulled, and the fraudulent maneuver is punishable under civil or even criminal law. The process is identical in the case of a forgery. For example, if an individual draws up a false pay slip or certificate in order to obtain something, the forger will only obtain it because they have knowingly led others to believe in a falsified reality.

403. **Third category of *dol*: forced free will.** Finally, the last category of fraud covers cases where the will of the other party is coerced, either because the victim is in a state of weakness, or because the perpetrator of the fraud is in a position of strength, or both simultaneously. This is the case with economic violence, abuse of weakness, dependence, or authority. Here, consent is also apparent, but in reality non-existent, since it is nullified by the coercion exerted by the perpetrator of the *dol*, who exploits their control for personal gain. The victim, trapped in the situation, is left with no choice but to comply with the abuser's demands.

404. **Anticompetitive practices: *dol* with market power.** As competition infringements fall into the category of offenses of means,[215] they also involve *dol*.[216] However, this is a *special form of dol*, which differs from the *dol* just mentioned, not by its different nature, but *by the larger scale on which*

---

214 We can see here that the approach taken in criminal law for the perpetrator of an offense (the invincible error reduces or negates their intent to commit the offense) also applies to the victim of *dol* (the induced error nullifies their consent).

215 *See supra*, no. 271.

216 This is, moreover, the conclusion reached by certain older doctrinal proposals aimed at defining the abuse of a dominant position: L. Focsaneanu, *La notion d'abus dans le système de l'article 86 du Traité instituant la Communauté économique européenne*, *in* LA RÉGLEMENTATION DU COMPORTEMENT DES MONOPOLES ET ENTREPRISES DOMINANTES EN DROIT COMMUNAUTAIRE 324, 371–72 (J. A. Van Damme ed., 1977): the author proposes to define abuse of a dominant position as "the fact that an undertaking makes Improper OK *use of* its market dominance *in order to make profits or secure for itself excessive advantages* at the expense of its customers or suppliers" (emphasis added). *Adde*, E. Cerexhe, *Les règles de concurrence applicables aux entreprises*, *in* LES NOVELLES: DROIT DES COMMUNAUTÉS EUROPÉENNES 805, 838 (W. J. Ganshof van der Meersch et al. ed., 1969), no. 2093: for the author, an abuse is "the fact that one or more undertakings behave in the market in such a way that they *derive abnormal advantages* compared with those they would enjoy if they were subject to the pressure of competitive forces. The notion of abuse thus implies… that certain economic subjects will suffer *unjustified harm*" (emphasis added). *Compare with* the definition of "monopolization" proposed by René Joliet, in reference to U.S. law, *see* Joliet, *Monopolisation et abus de position dominante: Essai comparatif sur l'article 2 du Sherman Act et l'article 86 du Traité de Rome*, *op. cit.* at 670–71: for the author, the criterion is not "the mere desire to acquire a monopoly; rather, it lies in the *methods used* to obtain and maintain control of the market" (emphasis added). This is also the logical consequence of the definition proposed by the Commission's important Memorandum, *see* COMM. EC, LE PROBLÈME DE LA CONCENTRATION

it operates.[217] Indeed, whereas classic *dol* annihilates the victim's free will, and therefore acts *inter partes*, in competition law, *dol* potentially produces *erga omnes* consequences, with regard to all players in the market in question – companies and consumers alike.

To convince themselves of this, jurists may usefully draw inspiration from Adam Smith's famous symbol of the "invisible hand,"[218] to imagine the existence of an "invisible contract" between all actual and potential businesses, and all actual and potential consumers in a market. This is a fertile thought experiment: it involves recognizing that, by buying or refraining from buying, consumers allocate their resources to those who know best how to use theirs: this is their economic freedom – allocating their goods[219] to those they have chosen. Thus, everything happens as if companies were permanent agents of consumers: they are obliged (on pain of not growing, losing market share, or even disappearing) to leverage their resources to satisfy the current and future demand of as many principals as possible.[220] According to this hypothesis, the sovereign is the consumer,[221] or more precisely, the aggregate of all present and future consumers: market power belongs to this aggregate and to no other. The company must discover the relevant information[222] – What do consumers want? How much do they want? What price are they willing to pay? – in order to adapt to them.[223]

DANS LE MARCHÉ COMMUN 22 (1966): "In the opinion of the group, it must be admitted that there is abuse of a dominant position when the holder of that position *uses* the opportunities arising therefrom to *obtain advantages that he would not obtain* in the case of practicable and sufficiently effective competition" (emphasis added) (unofficial translation).

217 It should be noted that the following reasoning also applies to market abuse, which is historically linked with competition infringements, *see supra*, no. 209.

218 On this subject, the enlightening remarks of P. STOFFEL-MUNCK, L'ABUS DANS LE CONTRAT: ESSAI D'UNE THÉORIE 425 (2000), no. 568, can be read with profit: "It is natural that, once it has come to dominate the market, a company should wish to maintain its position: the Tarpeian Rock has never been kind to those elected to the Capitol. To do so, the dominant firm may seek to stabilize the market, notably by sharing it through an agreement, but above all it will seek to 'lock it down' by closing access to any new competition. In both cases, the aim is to *remove from the market's 'invisible hand' the power to determine its development, so as to direct it according to a deliberate will.* This is private dirigisme. Agreement offenses and abuse of dominance are thus linked in both spirit and purpose" (emphasis added).

219 The term "property" should be defined here as all things that have an economic value, which includes personal data. On this subject, *see infra*, no. 525.

220 The reasoning is that of L. von Mises, *Du caractère atavique de quelques idées économiques*, *in* LES FONDEMENTS PHILOSOPHIQUES DES SYSTÈMES ÉCONOMIQUES, TEXTS BY JACQUES RUEFF AND ESSAYS WRITTEN IN HIS HONOR 317, 318 (1966).

221 As Catherine Prieto has rightly remarked, "[l]oyalty toward some may degenerate into disloyalty toward consumers when the latter are deprived of their *legitimate expectation* in a market economy – *namely, to arbitrate the merits of companies,*" *see* C. Prieto, *Loyauté du commerce et droit européen de la concurrence*, REVUE DES AFFAIRES EUROPÉENNES NO. 2, 299, 311 (2011), no. 22 (emphasis added).

222 F. A. Hayek, *Competition as a Discovery Procedure* (M. S. Snow trans.), 5 THE QUARTERLY JOURNAL OF AUSTRIAN ECONOMICS 9 (2002), no. 3; *adde*, I. M. Kirzner, *Entrepreneurial Discovery and the Competitive Market Process: An Austrian Approach*, 35 JOURNAL OF ECONOMIC LITERATURE 60 (1997).

223 *See*, *inter alia*, I. M. KIRZNER, HOW MARKETS WORK: DISEQUILIBRIUM, ENTREPRENEURSHIP AND DISCOVERY 34–49 (1997).

This tacit contract implies compliance with *two* essential *rules*. Firstly, companies implicitly undertake to *anticipate consumer needs* (think)[224] and to *wager on a strategy* (take action). Secondly, they promise to accept the existence of a *game*, its necessary *randomness*, its inevitable *chance*:[225] allow competitors to act, and consumers to make their own choices. Companies must therefore admit that they will always be in a state of uncertainty, and come to terms with the fact that, whatever their efforts, they are certainly masters of their strategy, but conversely have no control over the results that will flow from it. If they fail to comply with the first rule, they will probably end up, in the more or less long term, naturally excluded from the market; if they fail to comply with the second, they will be guilty of a competition infringement.

Indeed, the essence of competition infringement is for its perpetrator(s) to place themselves, like an illegitimate demiurge, *above the game* in order to eliminate or reduce the element of chance. And yet, chance only exists if there is freedom:[226] if the future is placed under the control of one or more companies, the others – competitors and consumers – are no longer totally free, as they are forced to obey, in part, rules they have not chosen.[227] The will of one is then substituted for the spontaneous and unpredictable result of the decisions of all.[228] Put another way, the intent of the perpetrator of a competition infringement is to neutralize the ability of others to form their own: they unilaterally impose their own will on others[229]. In this hypothesis, the invisible pact is broken, and the supposedly sovereign power of consumers is monopolized. There can no longer be a "*natural* meeting of supply and demand," because *the conditions of exchange* are affected, directly or indirectly, by the action of the offending company, which diverts and deviates from the normal course of events for its own benefit.[230] The conditions of exchange then

---

224 Anticipation is what distinguishes the competitive game from games of chance.

225 Indeed, "economic life is essentially analyzed as a game (a competition *subject to a rule* and whose *outcome* remains *random*," this game being based on risk and the absence of any possibility of predicting the outcome in advance, *see* D. Villey, Notes de philosophie économique (1958–59): Le jeu des intérêts 166–67 (1965).

226 On this subject, the theory of the economist G. L. S. Shackle, which takes the time factor into account, is most interesting. L. S. Shackle, which takes the time factor into consideration, is most interesting, *see supra*, no. 84, and references cited.

227 *Compare with* our definition of autonomy, *supra*, no. 386.

228 In Friedrich Hayek's view, state sanction comes into play when behavior cannot be justified other than by "the intention of imposing a certain market conduct," as freedom of trade is impeded when a company forces others to conform to a behavior that it has itself determined, *see* F. A. Hayek, Droit, législation et liberté: Une nouvelle formulation des principes libéraux de justice et d'économie politique 759–63 (R. Audouin trans., PUF, 2nd ed. 2013).

229 Franz Böhm, one of the leading exponents of ordoliberalism, considered monopolists to be "akin to entities capable of unilaterally imposing their will, i.e., in reality to administrative law entities under" – which poses a problem, since the latter are not invested with a prerogative of public power, and are therefore unfounded in imposing their choices on others, *see* C. Mongouachon, *L'ordolibéralisme: Contexte historique et contenu dogmatique*, Concurrences no. 4-2011, art. no. 38770, 70, 72, no. 10.

230 Cf. the definition of monopoly provided by Muyart de Vouglans, *supra*, no. 74. *Adde*, Prieto, *Loyauté du commerce et droit européen de la concurrence*, *op. cit.* at 304, no. 13: "What is distorted competition if not organized cheating?"

become *artificial*,[231] i.e., fabricated, fake, counterfeiting nature[232] – because in nature, the course of things may be governed by a purpose, but nobody knows it, and nobody has any control over it.

In short, anticompetitive intent is a *dol* with market power, defined as "*a means, employed individually or collectively, intended to annihilate or diminish the free will of the players in a market, with the aim of obtaining an advantage that would not have been acquired in its absence.*"

We now need to verify the relevance of this definition in the light of case law, by comparing it with the various forms of behavior that constitute anticompetitive practices – which will also provide an opportunity to refine it.

B. The definition of anticompetitive intent verified in specific cases

405. **Correspondence between the general categories of *dol* and *dol* with market power.** Legal reasoning is unitary and transcends disciplines: competition law is not autonomous from general law. Thus, the three categories of *dol* described above are identical in the case of *dol* with market power.[233] They provide a new classification of anticompetitive practices, which has the advantage of capturing the *essence* of the infringements,[234] and thus of providing a more precise understanding of the reasons for their repression, unlike traditional classifications. Indeed, what contribution is made to understanding the *ratio decidendi* justifying the punishment of anticompetitive behavior by distinguishing between vertical and horizontal agreements: here, pricing practices, there, non-pricing practices? Or, on the one hand, predatory behavior, on the other, exploitative behavior?[235] Conversely, all three categories of *dol* are relevant to the presentation of all competition infringements, demonstrating that anticompetitive intent is an explanatory concept of the discipline.

406. **First category of *dol* with market power: free will ignored.** Since free will is the presupposition of competition, and that without autonomy there can be no competition,[236] companies are obliged to determine their commer-

231 Let's not forget that what we call "artifice" here was considered in ancient times to be a kind of spell enabling hoarders to manipulate prices – which is why these dishonest traders were called *dardanarii*, a word taken from the name of the magician Dardanus, *see supra*, no. 46.

232 TLFi.

233 *See* our summary table, Appendix no. 6.

234 Discovering the essence or nature of an institution being the primary objective of a definition, *see* F. Colonna d'Istria, *Le mythe des 'définitions dans la loi': Exemples de droit des obligations*, *in* Le droit entre autonomie et ouverture: Mélanges en l'honneur de Jean-Louis Bergel 61, 84 (J.-Y. Chérot et al. eds., 2013).

235 It should also be noted that these categories are porous: some anticompetitive practices are both tariff and non-tariff, and the line between predation and exploitation is sometimes difficult to draw.

236 In this sense, *see supra*, no. 386.

cial strategy on their own, individually. If they relinquish this necessary independence, they reduce or even eliminate economic uncertainty by replacing competition with the comfort of greater certainty about the future. They avoid having to wager on a strategy, and they do not have to try to be better than their competitors – the competition is played out in advance, with the aim of all competitors winning to the detriment of consumers. The result is a *direct effect on* trading conditions, which are *abnormally* favorable to companies. The infringement thus lies in *the appropriation of consumers' power to influence the conditions of exchange*: they remain partly excluded from the formation of those conditions,[237] and pay a surcharge or fail to benefit from more favorable terms as a result of the infringement. Thus, upstream, companies relinquish their autonomy, with the downstream consequence of depriving consumers of their market power,[238] in other words, preventing them from influencing the exchange process.

The most typical example of this type of behavior is price fixing,[239] whether the agreement is secret or not,[240] horizontal or vertical.[241] However, price is not the only parameter of competition likely to be affected: think of commercial conditions collectively imposed on distributors,[242] quotas for products manufactured or placed on the market,[243] or even restrictions on the use of a new technology favorable to the environment.[244] The prohibition of the exchange of information on prices or sensitive commercial information[245] follows the same logic: it is only punished insofar as it reduces the decision-making autonomy of companies.[246]

---

237 *Compare with* theft, *supra*, no. 401.

238 On consumer market power, *see supra*, no. 404.

239 *See* in particular. Case C-359/01 P, British Sugar, ECLI:EU:C:2004:255.

240 A case in point is the joint fixing of commissions and interest rates by competing banks in the following case: Case C-125/07 P, Erste Group Bank, ECLI:EU:C:2009:576

241 We are referring here to resale price maintenance, i.e., prices imposed by a supplier on its distributors with the aim of making prices uniform in the distribution market, thereby eliminating all price competition between the various sales outlets, *see* Cons. conc., decision no. 07-D-50 of Dec. 20, 2007, on practices implemented in the sector of toy distribution (Fr.); more recently, Case C-211/22, Super Bock Bebidas, ECLI:EU:C:2023:529.

242 For example, in the case: ADLC, decision 18-D-24 of Dec. 5, 2018, relating to practices implemented in the household appliances sector (Fr).

243 Comm. EC, Nov. 26, 1986, IV/31.204, MELDOC, para. 60.

244 Eur. Comm., July 8, 2021, C(2021) 4955 final, Car Emissions, paras. 121–122; comm. D. Bosco, *Droit de la concurrence et* green deal*: Sanction d'une entente limitant la concurrence sur l'innovation verte*, CONTRATS CONCURRENCE CONSOMMATION (Jan. 2022), comm. 14.

245 In particular, on prices and technological development capabilities, with the aim of curbing the decline in prices in the relevant market: Case C-99/17 P, Infineon Technologies, ECLI:EU:C:2018:773; or on the occupancy rate of Parisian luxury hotels and the average price applied during certain periods of the year: Cons. conc., decision no. 05-D-64 of Nov. 25, 2005, regarding practices implemented on the Paris luxury hotel market (Fr).

246 In this sense, Case T-35/92, John Deere, ECLI:EU:T:1994:259.

This category also includes abusive pricing, insofar as a dominant firm illegitimately uses its position as a "price maker" to impose excessive conditions on consumers, who are then unable to influence the conditions of exchange in the absence of credible competitors. However, the Scholastics were already warning that it was impossible, *ex nihilo* and *in abstracto*, for anyone to determine a market price.[247] Today, the very idea that prices could be "excessive" is controversial.[248] Indeed, for a competition authority to take a position on this point amounts to determining a pricing policy itself,[249] which is the antithesis of the spirit of competition law, based as it is on free competition and, consequently, the free determination of prices by businesses and businesses alone.[250] In fact, apart from the specific and strictly delimited case of a price that is *manifestly disproportionate* to the very low economic value of the service provided, over which the company had an *administrative monopoly*,[251] no decision has recognized the abusive nature of prices charged by a company in a dominant position, for lack of being able to establish to the requisite legal standard their unfair, unjustified and therefore illegitimate nature.[252]

407. **Special features of the second and third categories of *dol* with market power.** The second and third categories of *dol* with market power present an important difference from the first: the conditions of exchange are not affected directly by the anticompetitive behavior, but more often indirectly, due to the potential exclusion of a competitor or the fact that the perpetrators of the unlawful practice seek to protect themselves from the competitive pressure that could be imposed on

---

247 In fact, they called this prize the "*pretium mathematicum*," which, according to them, could only be known by God, *see supra*, no. 61.

248 For a critical study, *see* N. Wahl, *From Greek Olive Oil to Latvian Music: Is There Any Such Thing as Unfair Prices?*, Concurrences no. 2-2018, art. no. 86617, 1.

249 The question of what constitutes a "fair price" offers a "fine subject for meditation for econometricians in need of formulas…" according to A. Pirovano, *Justice étatique, support de l'activité économique – Un exemple: La régulation de l'ordre concurrentiel*, Justices: Revue générale de droit processuel no. 1, 15, 30 (Jan.-June 1995).

250 In this regard, *see* R. Joliet, *Monopolisation et abus de position dominante: Essai comparatif sur l'article 2 du Sherman Act et l'article 86 du Traité de Rome*, RTD Eur. 645, 683 (1969): "Under these conditions, *dirigisme* is inevitable, as it is difficult to see how the Community authority would not be led to substitute its own judgment for that of the company. …The line of reasoning that consists in attempting to calculate the prices that would have resulted from the interaction of anonymous market forces, had there been effective competition, is indeed an artificial exercise. It is tantamount to granting the administrative authority the power to authoritatively set prices in place of the dominant undertaking."

251 And even in this case, the abuse was not characterized in the *General Motors* case, since the company had swiftly reduced its prices and reimbursed its contractors: Case 26/75, General Motors, ECLI:EU:C:1975:150, paras. 11–24. For a rare example of excessive pricing being penalized, *see* Case 226/84, British Leyland Public Limited Company, ECLI:EU:C:1986:421, paras. 25–34. *Compare with* U.S. jurisprudence in this area, particularly Verizon Communications Inc. v. Law Offices of Curtis v. Trinko, LLP, 540 U.S. 398, 407 (2004): "The mere possession of monopoly prices … is not only not unlawful; it is an important element of the free-market system. The opportunity to charge monopoly prices – at least for a short period – is what attracts 'business acumen' in the first place; it induces risk taking that produces innovation and economic growth."

252 *See* the recent reasoning of the Court of Cassation in the *Sanicorse* case: Cass. com., July 7, 2021, no. 19-25.586 (Fr.).

them by others. The immediate victim of the infringement may then be distinct from the ultimate victim – the consumer – whose harm consists in the loss of opportunity to obtain more favorable market conditions, since the more suppliers, the tougher the competition, and the more likely the conditions of exchange are to benefit the consumer.[253]

408. **Second category of *dol* with market power: free will nullified by error.** Certain anticompetitive behaviors share the feature of *presenting a distorted or misleading image of reality in order to obtain an undue advantage.* This type of maneuver includes deception: consider the *AstraZeneca* case, in which the company obtained a patent term extension by means of misleading statements.[254] Bid rigging to obtain a public procurement contract or private contract is part of the same process – the aim is for several companies to agree on the bids to be submitted in order to obtain the contract. To this end, one of the parties to the agreement submits a so-called cover bid, whose conditions or price are deliberately inadmissible, so that the bidder designated in advance can submit a more favorable – but less attractive – offer than the one it would have submitted in the absence of the agreement.[255] In this way, the successful bidder wins the contract on advantageous terms only because the companies collectively distorted the award procedure. Lastly, very similar to the first two types of behavior is denigration, which consists in disseminating information that discredits a company or its products, for example, in the pharmaceutical sector, in order to delay the development of competing generic drugs.[256]

409. **Third category of *dol* with market power: constrained free will.** The last category of *dol* with market power seeks to prevent competitors from acting, in order to *protect themselves from competition by restricting their commercial autonomy, or even their ability to enter or remain active in a market.* The behaviors that fall into this category are extremely varied, but are all based on the same logic.

Predatory pricing consists in a company adopting an irrationally low pricing policy to exclude its competitors, and *in fine* enabling it to raise prices at will.[257] Exclusivity obligations, on the other hand, are anticompetitive insofar as they are practiced by a dominant company with

253 On this point, it should be noted that legal reasoning is fully in line with economic reasoning.

254 Case C-457/10 P, AstraZeneca, ECLI:EU:C:2012:770. On this judgment, *see supra*, no. 283.

255 For example: Case T-141/07, General Technic-Otis, ECLI:EU:T:2011:363; Cons. conc., decision no. 07-D-15 of May 9, 2007, on practices implemented in the public markets relative to Ile-de-France secondary schools (Fr.); ADLC, decision no. 22-D-08 of Mar. 3, 2022, concerning practices implemented in the waste collection and management sector in Haute-Savoie (Fr.)

256 *See* in particular the *Janssen-Cilag* case, Cass. com., June 1, 2022, no. 19-20.999 (Fr.).

257 *Ex multis*: Case C-62/86, Akzo, ECLI:EU:C:1991:286; Case C-333/94 P, Tetra Pak, ECLI:EU:C:1996:436; Case C-202/07 P, France Télécom, ECLI:EU:C:2009:214.

the aim of depriving buyers of "any possibility of choice" and "barring access to the market" for other producers.[258] In the context of a distribution system, exclusivity can also be a means of making it difficult for independent distributors to emerge, which is necessary for new competitors to gain access to the relevant market.[259] Similarly, a supplier's prohibition on its distributors importing or exporting contract products from one Member State to another is designed to prevent competition forming in the distribution market, leading to artificial territorial partitioning that generally benefits the supplier.[260] Loyalty rebates can also be misused to exclude a competitor of the dominant firm from the market.[261] Discrimination, which consists in imposing unequal terms on trading partners for equivalent services, results in some of them being placed at an unjustified disadvantage,[262] and may even lead to their elimination from the relevant market.[263] Another example is the collective boycott, an agreement by which companies cease to buy from a particular company, or to supply a particular customer,[264] with the aim of driving the operator in question out of the market in which it operates.[265] Pay-for-delay agreements, too, are designed to delay the market entry of generics in return for a transfer of value.[266] Similarly, tying enables a company that is dominant in one market to enter another where it is not yet dominant, illegitimately stifling competition.[267] A refusal to contract can also be anticompetitive when it has no rational explanation other than that of preventing others from developing an activity in a

258 *See inter alia*: Case 85/76, Hoffmann-La Roche, ECLI:EU:C:1979:36, para. 90; Case 322/81, Nederlandsche Banden Industrie Michelin, ECLI:EU:C:1983:313, para. 73. Even in *Intel*, the latter was accused of having adopted "an overall strategy aimed at foreclosing AMD's access to the most important sales channels," *see* Case C-413/14 P, Intel, ECLI:EU:C:2017:632, para. 55. The issue at stake in this case was evidentiary, and did not concern the definition of the conduct of which the respondent was accused (on this topic, *see supra*, no. 302).

259 Comm. EC, Dec. 23, 1992, IV/31.533, Schöller Lebensmittel, para. 68.

260 For a ban on exports: Comm. EC, Dec. 18, 1987, IV/31.503, Konica, paras. 41–45; Comm. EC, Dec. 19, 1974, IV/23.013, Goodyear Italiana – Euram, para. 8; and on imports: Comm. EC, Dec. 4, 1991, IV/33.157, Eco System v. Peugeot, para. 23. It should be noted that, while these practices are generally linked to the objective of "completing the internal market" – the aim of European integration being to prevent the re-fragmentation of markets by private undertakings following the dismantling of economic borders between Member States (on the importance of this objective, *see* Secrétariat du comité intergouvernemental, Rapport des chefs de délégation aux ministres des Affaires étrangères ["Spaak Report"], Brussels, Apr. 21, 1956) – they can also be linked to the concept of *dol* with market power, insofar as they restrict the freedom of certain partners to trade freely.

261 Case C-95/04 P, British Airways, ECLI:EU:C:2007:166.

262 Comm. EC, Dec. 17, 1975, IV/26 699, Chiquita, II, A, 3, b).

263 Case 27/76, United Brands, ECLI:EU:C:1978:22.

264 ADLC, decision no. 12-D-19 of Sept. 26, 2012, regarding practices in the teeth whitening and lightening sector. At issue in this case was a disparagement practice (Fr.), para. 134.

265 Cass. com., Oct. 22, 2022, no. 00-18.048 (Fr.).

266 Case C-307/18, Generics (UK), ECLI:EU:C:2020:52; on this type of practice, *see* W. Chaiehloudj, Les accords de report d'entrée: Contribution à l'étude de la relation du droit de la concurrence et du droit des brevets (2019).

267 Comm. EC, Mar. 24, 2004, COMP/C-3/37.792, Microsoft, paras. 622 and 841.

given market.[268] Favoritism[269] is also punishable only if its purpose is to protect oneself from competition by penalizing others.[270]

In all these examples, the intention behind the conduct is identical: to unduly alter the free formation of the conditions of trade by restricting the freedom of the players present in a given market.[271] While such a definition may appear imprecise, as it attempts to capture the essence of scattered jurisprudential pronouncements, it is not a source of legal uncertainty – anticompetitive intent is an indeterminate but determinable concept.

II. An indeterminate but determinable concept

410. **"Concepts with variable content."** One of the characteristics of major legal concepts is that they cannot be defined with absolute precision: they all contain an element of the ineffable (**A**). However, because these major concepts are familiar to every jurist, and appeal to an intuitive sense of justice, their praetorian interpretation remains predictable (**B**).

A. Legal indeterminacy: the ineffable part of any definition

411. **The inadequacy of words.** Think of the dreamer lost in the clouds: to describe them, they will list the clouds, the cirrus, the hazy veils, their shapes and their colors – but they will never be able to speak of the heavens except through imperfect metonymies.[272] Reality is too complex

---

268 Case C-42/21 P, Lietuvos, ECLI:EU:C:2023:12; comm. M. Cartapanis, *Infrastructures essentielles: La Cour de justice de l'Union européenne écarte le test Bronner lorsque le comportement abusif se manifeste par le démantèlement d'une infrastructure ferroviaire*, CONCURRENCES no. 2-2023, art. no. 112261, 74; Case C-241/91 P, Magill, ECLI:EU:C:1995:98.

269 On this new category of abuse of a dominant position, *see* D. Bosco, Google Shopping*: Avènement jurisprudentiel d'un abus par favoritisme*, CONTRATS CONCURRENCE CONSOMMATION (Feb. 2022), comm. 34.

270 *See* Case T-612/17, Google and Alphabet, ECLI:EU:T:2021:763; ADLC, decision no. 21-D-11 of June 7, 2021, regarding practices implemented in the online advertising sector.

271 *Compare with* the proposal of G. Marenco, *La notion de restriction de concurrence dans le cadre de l'interdiction des ententes*, *in* II MÉLANGES EN HOMMAGE À MICHEL WAELBROECK 1217, 1230, 1245 (1999): "It is therefore the *tendency* of the agreement to increase or restrict supply on the market that must be assessed, without prejudice to the question of whether the company's calculations are correct. The criterion of restriction of the parties' entrepreneurial freedom is particularly well suited to determining this tendency. When the company's commercial initiative is restricted by its own promise, the agreement prevents a potential offer from entering the market. On the other hand, clauses in the agreement that do not restrict the parties' freedom of action should be considered as aiming to organize additional supply." The author concludes that this thesis is "fruitful," and "provides a satisfactory solution to most of the more difficult problems of competition law"; on the link between freedom and protection of competition, *see also* J. Drexl, *La Constitution économique européenne – L'actualité du modèle ordolibéral*, XXV REVUE INTERNATIONALE DE DROIT ÉCONOMIQUE 419, 435–36 (2011); *adde*, A. Sen, *Markets and Freedoms: Achievements and Limitations of the Market Mechanism in Promoting Individual Freedoms*, 45 OXFORD ECONOMIC PAPERS 519, 524 (1993): according to the author, the preservation of freedom requires protecting individuals' decision-making autonomy and ensuring their immunity from external interference.

272 C. Baudelaire, *Conseils aux jeunes littérateurs* 15 (Mille et une nuits 1995): "E. Delacroix once said to me: 'Art is such an ideal and fleeting thing, that the tools are never clean enough, nor the means swift enough.'"

to be confined within the reductive cage of language.[273] Law, however, is based on the verb, and is thus condemned to remain partly "mute,"[274] suspended who knows where until the legislator, by passing a law, or the judge on the ephemeral occasion of a dispute, offers it a chance to speak. The researcher, on the other hand, will attempt a synthesis: they will try to reach the essence of the concept that occupies them. Is the quest in vain? Perhaps, in philosophy: a thousand words can be added to describe the Beautiful or the True, and a thousand others just as many, without the debate being able to be settled, without belief ever being able to be fixed.[275] In law, however, there are constants, rules, a reality that limits the creativity of the observer,[276] who must find the right balance between excessive indeterminacy, which would let the rule fly away, and excessive precision, which would confine it.

412. **A lure: precision for the imprecise.** Scientific thought has made precision its ideal – one it believes it both must and can achieve.[277] The quest for absolute knowledge, for the eradication of all errors, for automatic interpretation – in a word, for *control* – is the illusory ambition of the modern age. Forgetting that we are chasing a mirage, we go on, wandering in a desert, draining the law dry. Replacing its words, supposedly too vague, with a pileup of false details made up of figures, models, tests and technical terms, we have gradually forgotten that the law of anticompetitive practices is based on a classic notion: *dol.*

Like most concepts with variable content, whose importance in the legal system is matched only by their indeterminacy, *dol* is certainly defined by other equally general and abstract terms.[278] Yet, this definition is, and has always been, deemed satisfactory: can one imagine a private law scholar rejecting the relevance of willful misconduct, on the grounds of its insufficient precision, and the risks of judicial error that might follow? Pushed to its extreme, such

---

273 It is this observation that gave rise to Hart's famous formula, according to which the law has an "open texture," implying the existence of a margin of discretion for the judge, who must necessarily interpret texts that are too imprecise to allow for "automatic" application. *See* H. L. A. Hart, The Concept of Law 124–36 and 272–76 (3rd ed. 2012).

274 *See* the major study: R. Sacco, *Mute Law*, 43 The American Journal of Comparative Law 455 (1995); *adde*, in French, on what the author later preferred to call "*droit spontané*" rather than "*droit muet*," no doubt drawing inspiration from F. A. Hayek, *see* R. Sacco, Anthropologie juridique: Apport à une macro-histoire du droit 109–43 (2008). On the influence of F. A. Hayek on R. Sacco, *see* P. Legrand, *Questions à Rodolfo Sacco*, 47 Revue internationale de droit comparé 943 (1995). On spontaneous law, *see* B. Stern, *La coutume au cœur du droit international: Quelques réflexions*, *in* Mélanges offerts à Paul Reuter, Le droit international: Unité et diversité 479 (1981).

275 This is the criticism leveled by proponents of the pragmatic school against philosophy and theology, which they accuse of inevitably leading to sterile debates and purely verbal solutions, *see* S. Madelrieux, William James: L'attitude empiriste 185–87 (2008). In the final analysis, it seems to us that art is the only way to get close to pure ideas, because it is as indescribable as they are.

276 For a comparison on this point between law and economics, *see infra*, nos. 489–490.

277 C. Perelman & L. Olbrechts-Tyteca, Traité de l'argumentation 178 (2008).

278 What is freedom, a maneuver, a ruse, a feint, a constraint? We have tried, *supra*, nos. 400–409, to come up with a more complete definition of *dol*, but because it is expressed in words, it is still and always will be limited.

criticism becomes absurd: since no word fully captures the reality it seeks to designate, we would have to abandon the idea of using language to speak the law.[279] This may be the dream of some utopian minds, but no computing power, however "intelligent"[280] it may be, will ever be able to centralize and process all the data required for *jurisdictio*[281] – for one reason only: because it is human, and contains an element of contingency and sensitivity.[282]

This quest is not only illusory, but also futile. While advocates of precision fear arbitrariness and instability, indeterminate notions lead to neither. Indeed, *indeterminacy*, which belongs to the normal life of law,[283] does not invite contingency or instability; it is *indeterminability* that must be feared.[284] The difference between the two lies in the impossibility of giving a clear content to an indeterminable norm, whereas it is possible for the judge to interpret an indeterminate norm in a predictable manner.

B. Praetorian interpretation: the predictability of solutions

413. **A necessity: accepting the variability of the norm.** The legislator provides a definition, which the judge extends with solemn recitals. Has everything been said? Far from it: the lawyer's work has barely begun. They have to gather information, cross-check it, compare it, rule out inconsistencies and discover constants. This work of synthesis, necessary for any definition, which alone can touch the essence of a concept and clarify its normative

---

279 On this subject, *see* P. Roubier, Théorie générale du droit: Histoire des doctrines juridiques et philosophie des valeurs sociales 110–11 (2nd ed. 1951), no. 12. According to Paul Roubier, "by abandoning a system of rules that are too rigidly defined, the needs of justice would be better satisfied." Using liability for damage caused by fault as an example, the author writes that this is more than just a rule; it is a "principle of law, that is, the result of an effort of abstraction and generalization, which has a greater influence that of the ordinary rule, whose object is a particular and precise point."

280 On the notion of "artificial intelligence," *see infra*, no. 512.

281 A. Chouraqui, L'informatique au service du droit 70 (1970): norms "are modified as they evolve, notably through case law, for the same literal content. Sometimes, and even quite often, the relationship between several norms is not unequivocal, and to determine it, we have to resort to reasonings of a legal, historical, ethical, economic or other nature, based on a number of *factors that cannot be determined in advance, representing an infinite potential for 'nuances.'* In such cases, the relationships between *legal rules cannot be unequivocally determined by a finite number of finite logico-mathematical formulas*" (emphasis added); *adde*, on this theme, V.-L. Bénabou, *Un droit vivant: Manifeste pour des juristes incarnés et sensibles à l'heure de l'intelligence artificielle*, *in* Penser le droit de la pensée: Mélanges en l'honneur de Michel Vivant 715 (2020).

282 *Compare with* J. Carbonnier, *Les notions à contenu variable dans le droit français de la famille*, *in* Les notions à contenu variable en droit 98, 111–12 (C. Perelman & R. Vander Elst eds., 1984): Dean Carbonnier notes that the interpretation of a variable-content notion is not a simple "rational adaptation," but that it includes "at least some sentimental variability." He concludes: "Technical analysis has thus brought us into contact with an infinitely larger problem of philosophy: the role of sentiment in law. Law being human, and man being sensitive as well as intelligent, it would be human, not overly human, for the heart to have its place in law in the same way as reason." Cf. the notion of "sensualist morality," and its rejection by utilitarians, *supra*, no. 89.

283 Indeed, it would be "inaccurate to believe that law is based solely on known, predetermined and immutable concepts," J.-L. Bergel, *Le processus des concepts émergents*, *in* Les concepts émergents en droit des affaires 439 (E. Le Dolley ed., 2010).

284 S. Rials, *Les standards, notions critiques du droit*, *in* Les notions à contenu variable en droit 39, 46 (C. Perelman & R. Vander Elst eds., 1984).

structure, can only be *doctrinal.*[285] It requires us to be faithful to reality, to attempt to reveal it. In this way, the definition is part of the law, may express more than statutes and case law combined. It does not, however, express everything. To claim otherwise would be to deny the existence of the future: faced with a new case, the judge will adapt past experience to the present[286] to bring it into line with the present,[287] leaving it to the doctrine to update its definitions.[288] And when the legislator chooses to establish a vague notion as a rule of law, they introduce a variability that is anticipated and, because it is desired, is not left to chance: it constitutes a legislative technique, reflecting the choice to leave it to the judge to bring the text to life,[289] gradually adapting it to the new.[290]

Thus, indeterminacy is a quality when it is framed by correct definitions, which enable the application of the norm to be circumscribed; it is an evil when it becomes, under the effect of the activism of a judicial or administrative authority, or of doctrine, a source of confusion and ambiguity.[291] Concepts with variable content may be indeterminate when they are still suspended in the abstract, but they become determinable when they are put into practice. *Provided they are properly defined*, the praetorian solutions based on them are therefore predictable – for it is only the lack of rigor in the definition of the framework that is likely to lead to excessive variability in the content,[292] giving the impression that the implementation of the rule risks bordering on the arbitrary.

414. **Interpretation by the judge: a constrained and therefore predictable exercise.** The interpretative freedom of judges,[293] offered by the existence of a

---

285 F. Colonna d'Istria, *Le mythe des 'définitions dans la loi': Exemples de droit des obligations*, *in* Le droit entre autonomie et ouverture: Mélanges en l'honneur de Jean-Louis Bergel 61, 88–89 (J.-Y. Chérot et al. eds., 2013).

286 This past experience allows the selection of certain rules and the rejection of others, the persistence of certain rules, principles or definitions being explained by a phenomenon that several authors have called "sedimentation," *see* C. Atias, Théorie contre arbitraire 171–217 (1987); J.-L. Bergel, *Le processus de transformation de décisions de justice en normes juridiques*, Revue de la recherche juridique: Droit prospectif no. 4, 1055, 1059 (1993).

287 Carbonnier, *Les notions à contenu variable dans le droit français de la famille*, *op. cit.* at 101: "Who will vary the variable content? In practice, it will be the judge (before them, the commentator may have dreamed, but they did not act). The record will spin in the judge's hands. But it does not turn at random. There are directions, criteria for variability."

288 *See infra*, no. 504

289 Carbonnier, *Les notions à contenu variable dans le droit français de la famille*, *op. cit.* at 110.

290 In this sense, *see* G. Cornu, Droit civil: Introduction au droit 105 (13th ed. 2007), no. 188: the content of certain notions is intentionally left "vague." The vocation of indeterminate notions is to be "always determinable and remodelable" – indeterminacy being their means of adaptability. According to the author, this is particularly true of good faith, fraud and *dol.*

291 R. Legros, *Les notions à contenu variable en droit pénal*, *in* Les notions à contenu variable en droit 21, 30 and 36 (C. Perelman & R. Vander Elst eds., 1984). For a critique of the discrepancy between the discourse on competition law and the reality of litigation, *see infra*, nos. 484–495.

292 *Id.* at 33.

293 Let's note at the outset that this freedom is framed as "it is from the outset enmeshed in a web of concepts, representations, values, and practices," *see* F. Brunet, La normativité en droit 369 (2012).

general and abstract rule, does not confer them excessive power[294]: it does not permit arbitrariness. Indeed, indeterminate concepts such as *dol* are characterized by their reliance, for interpretation, on core principles of legal reasoning – the discretionary margin left to the interpreter in determining their content is limited and framed.[295] Moreover, the consistency argument, which plays a very important role in legal argumentation,[296] prevents the "falsification" of the qualification operation when the incompatibility of a conclusion with solutions already accepted in the past is highlighted,[297] thus further narrowing the judge's margin of discretion. Finally, European Union case law, like that of common law countries, is characterized by strong deference to its own past solutions.[298] Thus, the argument of precedent, through various interpretative techniques,[299] underpins the future coherence of case law, thereby ensuring the stability of its solutions, which have not been substantially modified since the creation of the Court of Justice.

*

* *

415. **Conclusion of Section 2: competition infringements, defined as *dol with market power*.** Like all offenses of means, abuse of a dominant position and agreement offenses require the use of an unlawful means to be characterized. By re-establishing the link between the law of anticompetitive practices and classical legal reasoning, competition infringements have been defined as a *dol*, which differs from that required by other branches of the law not in nature but in magnitude, since they presuppose the existence of market power. It is a legal criterion that unites all anticompetitive behaviors under the aegis of a single concept – the lowest common denominator of the various categories of practices – thus making it possible to grasp their essence, providing arguments to guide the judge's

294 We refer here exclusively to the judge, and not to the administrative authority, insofar as, in the law of anticompetitive practices, the Court of Justice takes a broad view of its control over the implementation of indeterminate concepts: it does not leave it to the Commission itself to define what is meant by a given term. Consequently, the interpretation of these indeterminate concepts is not the source of administrative discretion – discretion being reserved for the judge alone. On this subject, *see* H. Bauer-Bernet, *Notions indéterminées et droit communautaire*, *in* Les notions à contenu variable en droit 267, 275 (C. Perelman & R. Vander Elst eds., 1984).

295 C. Bouix, *Les notions indéterminées, entre adaptation et sécurité*, *in* Les rythmes de production du droit 271, 289 (M. Nicod ed., 2016).

296 N. MacCormick, Raisonnement juridique et théorie du droit 153–79 (J. Gagey trans., PUF 1996).

297 J. Verhaegen, *Notions floues et droit pénal*, *in* Les notions à contenu variable en droit 7, 15 (C. Perelman & R. Vander Elst eds., 1984).

298 L. Navel, L'argument de continuité jurisprudentielle dans la jurisprudence de la Cour de justice de l'Union européenne 38–53 (2021).

299 On this subject, *see* with interest: G. Leroy, La pratique du précédent en droit français: Étude à partir de l'avocat général à la Cour de cassation et des conclusions du rapporteur public au Conseil d'État 319–68 (2021) (Ph.D. dissertation, Aix-Marseille Université), nos. 294–329.

decision, and a compass for companies. Indeed, the definition of *dol*, like that of most major legal concepts, is indeterminate, but determinable: case law interpretation enables us, over time, to clarify its content and adapt it to new cases in a predictable manner.

*

* *

416. **Conclusion to Chapter 2: Intent as a factor in defining competition infringements.** Competition infringements are traditionally defined, in most legal literature, in terms of their effects on competition, the consumer or the market. These definitions rely on economic analysis, which, with its normative ambitions, is responsible for deciding, in place of the jurist, which behaviors should be sanctioned. However, case law shows that, in practice, effects have no defining significance. A comparison of the reasoning used in competition law and criminal law has also shown that the notion of restriction of competition is superfluous, insofar as it is confused with anticompetitive behavior. It has thus become clear that only behavior should be taken into account in defining anticompetitive practices. As a result, the scope of the economic and effects analysis is greatly diminished, since the proposed definition, based on a legal concept – *dol* with market power – is sufficient in itself to justify and explain the linkage of all behaviors prohibited by case law to the qualification of anticompetitive practices.

*

* *

417. **Conclusion to Title I: competition, a game like any other – reasoning by analogy with a sporting competition, soccer.** Soccer and competition are both “games”: players and companies alike engage in fierce competition to win the match. There are winners and losers: the referee and the competition authority never impose the *result of the match*, but only respect for the *laws of the game*. Every year, the International Football Association Board updates the body of rules governing sporting events:[300] these detail all the “fouls and misconduct” giving rise to sanctions.[301] Many of these are set out in precise terms in the regulation,[302] while others are drafted in more abstract terms, to enable the referee to penalize any disruption to the smooth running of the match. These are grouped together under the term

300 *Laws of the Game, 22/23* International Football Association Board, www.theifab.com.

301 *Id.* at 97–110.

302 *Id.* at 97–99.

"unsporting behaviour,"[303] defined as an "action/behaviour; punishable by a caution"[304] which may, in particular, consist of "attempt[ing] to deceive the referee," "interfere[ing] with or stop[ing] a promising attack," "den[ing] an opponent an obvious goal-scoring opportunity," "initiat[ing] a deliberate trick ... to circumvent the Law" and, more generally, "show[ing] a lack of respect for the game."[305] What all these acts have in common is that they are, firstly, indeterminate, and secondly, unfair in that they are intended to prevent the opposing team from winning the game by means not attributable to the players' own *merits*.

Any consideration other than *the way the game is played* is alien to the laws of soccer. The referee does not blow the whistle according to their preference as to the outcome of the match; the competition authority does not define an infringement based on its market outcome.[306] The referee does not seek to satisfy the fans of one team or the other: all but the sore losers will have appreciated having witnessed a fine confrontation – the beauty of the game fulfills their expectations. Competition law also assumes that preserving the competitive process leads to "consumer welfare."[307] If the match pits one very popular team against another that has been abandoned by its fans, the referee must, in any case, not favor one team or the other, depending on which part of the crowd is shouting the loudest from the stands, just as competition law cannot set itself the goal of favoring a certain category of consumer, either for political or ideological reasons. Any deviation from these principles on the part of the referee would result in being accused of breaching their duty of impartiality – and the same must apply to competition law. The rules of the game are not set based on the effects expected by the referee or the competition authority: it is not the result of the match that determines whether it has been well played. Unsportsmanlike conduct cannot be defined as that which results in a goal being scored, as this is also the

303 *Id.* at 103–104.

304 *Id.* at 167.

305 *Id.* at 103–104.

306 To argue the opposite, as Henri Lepage has written, would be tantamount to accepting that the referee could impose the outcome of the match, and would mark the advent of "a competition law at odds with ethics and the fundamental principles of law." The author continues: "What are we to think of a sporting competition in which the referees not only ensure that the contestants comply with the rules of the game, but also claim the right to judge the fairness of the results on the basis of whether or not they conform to the authorities' *a priori* idea of what the result should be, even before the competition begins? That would be a scandal." Yet this is the line of reasoning followed by competition law, in the "type of situation where referees, having defined the rules of the game, also arrogate to themselves the discriminatory power to decide whether the final result is 'fair' according to a pre-established reference standard that defines not so much who should be the winner, but how the finishers should be situated in relation to each other (the 'distribution' of the result). This is all the more absurd in that the particularity of this reference standard ('pure and perfect competition') in fact leads us to consider that the preferable result among all is one where ... everyone arrives at the same time, where there is neither first nor last, and where there is therefore no need for competition at all!," *see* H. Lepage, *Le droit de la concurrence, un bien ou un mal?*, *in* II Institut du Commerce et de la Consommation, Liberté d'entreprendre et concurrence: Comment rétablir un "État de droit"? 104, 105 (1986).

307 *See supra*, no. 361.

potential outcome of sportsmanlike conduct. The result cannot, therefore, be a criterion for qualifying either a foul or a competition infringement. Rule consequentialism is incompatible with the very status of a rule, and contrary to the spirit of the game.

And yet, although *de lege lata* intent plays a central role in competition law, both in the characterization of infringements and in their definition, it is currently only implicit. The discipline is marked by its utilitarian origins, which are in contradiction with its raison d'être and the types of reasoning it embraces. It is therefore appropriate to plead, *de lege ferenda*, for the abandonment of effects-based theories, and in favor of the adoption of the theory of intent.

*

* *

Title II

The desirable role of intent *de lege ferenda*

418. **A tension between two paradigms: respect for the law for its own sake and utilitarian approach to law.** Utilitarianism has had a profound influence on contemporary competition law. Indeed, the vast majority of economic theories, regardless of the schools to which the discipline has resorted over the years,[1] stem from the idea that the law aims to produce concrete, material results. From the adoption of the Penal Code in 1810, the existence of a fraudulent maneuver was no longer sufficient to justify punishment: it became necessary for the judge to characterize, in addition, an effect on prices.[2] In 1953, French competition law was conceived as a tool for economic policy aimed at maintaining attractive prices.[3] While the objectives pursued have fluctuated over time, the paradigm has remained the same: the idea that competition should be protected as an end in itself is no longer universally upheld.

Today, the discipline's supposed aim is to promote consumer welfare.[4] But how can such a vaguely defined goal provide a valid basis for competition policy? At opposite ends of the spectrum, do Richard Posner and

---

1 On the supersession of Chicago School theories in favor of the new industrial economics, *see* C. Prieto, *Source économique du droit de la concurrence: Quelle efficacité?*, Contrats concurrence consommation (June 2020), no. 6, dossier 3, esp. nos. 12–13. *Adde*, L. Idot, *Argument économique et argument sociologique*, *in* L'argument sociologique en droit: Pluriel et singularité 43, 59 (D. Fenouillet ed., 2015): "Within a single discipline, such as industrial economics, thought evolves. We know that there have been successive schools of thought. The Harvard School/Chicago School opposition has now been surpassed by the so-called new industrial economics. More interestingly, and less well known, economists themselves acknowledge the limitations of industrial economics analyses. Over the past decade or so, a new discipline has emerged: behavioral economics."

2 *See supra*, nos. 98–99.

3 As demonstrated by the inclusion in 1953 of article 59 *bis* prohibiting agreements in the 1945 pricing ordinance, *see supra*, no. 108.

4 Case C-377/20, ENEL, ECLI:EU:C:2022:379, para. 46.

his theory in favor of economic efficiency, and Lina Kahn and her fight against the concentration of economic power, not both advance arguments in support of consumer interests? Put another way, are these not theories that can only be distinguished by ideological bias? In short, utilitarianism has resulted in the *politicization* of competition rules and, consequently, in the emergence of debates that are less rigorous from a legal point of view, falling more within the realm of political science than law. Paradoxically, while the advent of the effects-based approach was supposed to put the discipline on a "scientific" footing, making it more objective and therefore more relevant, over the span of two centuries, it has ultimately burdened it with debates that have nothing to do with substantive issues, which are no longer really focused on the reasoning and principles received by jurisprudence, but on ideological quarrels. The ambition for accuracy, certainty and neutrality has thus led to "arbitrary and contingent choices."[5]

This discourse, which surrounds and weighs down competition law, has not, however, reached its roots: it is like loud music drowning out the quiet breath of tradition. As a result, two paradigms currently coexist: one noisily but superficially, while the other is as silent as it is profound. Now, since the theory of intent is implicitly received *de lege lata*, and enables us to account for the reasoning received in competition law, it would be appropriate, *de lege ferenda*, to bring legal reasoning to the surface by adopting the theory of intent (**Chapter 2**), which presupposes abandoning the effects-based theories (**Chapter 1**).

---

5 The expression is borrowed from B. Oppetit, Droit et modernité 179 (1998).

Chapter 1
REJECTING EFFECTS-BASED THEORIES

419. **The ailments affecting contemporary competition law.** Competition law today is propelled by a malaise that also affects other areas of law: legal utilitarianism and scientism. By subordinating the discipline to the achievement of ends other than freedom of competition, and by believing that these ends can be achieved through "scientific" analyses, competition law is being led astray, not only because this philosophical trend and these methods constitute a questionable foundation (**Section 1**), but also because they produce questionable consequences (**Section 2**). They undermine the readability and predictability of competition law, thereby compromising respect for the principles of the rule of law.

Section 1
A questionable foundation

420. **Utilitarianism and contemporary competition law.** The only time a movement can be grasped in its full breadth is when it emerges. When it becomes so widespread as to be omnipresent, it becomes a natural phenomenon that we hardly notice or no longer question – invisible and painless, like the air we breathe. It is therefore pertinent to note the progression of legal utilitarianism since the eighteenth century (**Paragraph 1**), before examining its influence on competition law in contemporary times (**Paragraph 2**).

Paragraph 1 – The progression of utilitarianism since the 18th century

421. **The progress of utilitarianism.** While the utilitarian movement has had an influence on the contemporary conception of law (**I**), its influence is especially pronounced in economic law – a discipline in which it has shaped the way we think about the objectives and modes of action of the State (**II**).

I. The rise of utilitarianism: a general movement

422. **A twofold revolution.** Over the last two centuries, individual freedom has gradually been subordinated to the realization of the general interest (**B**), leading to a proliferation of state rules that prescribe rather than prohibit, and to the expansion of special rights. At the same time, the very notion of the general interest has evolved: from the sum of common interests once guided by natural law as a compass, under the influence of the utilitarian current, the ends of law have gradually been reduced to the achievement of material objectives (**A**).

A. Expanding the role of the state, lowering the ends of the law to material issues

423. **The reduction of legal ends to material objectives.** From the eighteenth century onwards, utilitarians dismissed the ends of law as "anarchic principles," which were criticized for being based on indeterminate notions that were, in their view, inaccessible other than through intuition and the senses, to which a cold, calculating, and objective reason should be substituted.[1] They were thus blind to the nature of law – an organized system of higher principles around which specific rules are ordered,[2] the discovery of which calls for neither an arbitrary sensibility evading all scrutiny, nor any form of mysticism, but the recognition, analysis and hierarchization of the principles forming the legal order.[3] These principles, which constitute distinct ends, are placed at a high level of abstraction – they give law its grandeur – utilitarianism lowers it by replacing them[4] with material concerns:[5] it completes the shift from Ideas to objects.

1 *See supra*, nos. 88–90.

2 In this respect, the contemporary jurist would benefit from studying Domat's method, as transcribed by C. Prieto, *Domat et la mémoire du droit*, *in* Le droit dans le souvenir: Liber amicorum Benoît Savelli 119, 129–34 (1998).

3 R. Libchaber, L'ordre juridique et le discours du droit: Essai sur les limites de la connaissance du droit 194–95 (2013); *adde*, J. Rawls, Theory of Justice (1971), and J. Rawls, Théorie de la justice 60 (C. Audard trans., Points 2009).

4 Indeed, utilitarianism sets aside reflection on justice, insofar as it completely equates it with the maximization of happiness, *see* Rawls, Théorie de la justice, *op. cit.* at 50–51.

5 A. Kojève, *La spécificité et l'autonomie du Droit*, Commentaire no. 1, 122, 127 (1980), no. 9.

424. **The expansion of government missions.** These concerns have been transformed into a host of objectives – often vague and overly broad[6] – that the State sets itself and believes it must and can achieve. The law is then reduced to a technique for enacting rules to pursue concrete, immediate goals, and ensuring these rules effectively achieve their aims. And it would be futile to attempt to reason with the technician, convinced by their training of the State's ability to act on society,[7] that their techniques do not work, "and produce a host of unforeseen or undesired results": they may think of changing technique, but, as a blind optimist, they will remain "convinced of the instrumental character of their specialty"[8] – housing law to ensure that everyone has a home, consumer law to promote consumption, and so on.[9] The phenomenon reaches its climax in declarations of rights, where the most unrealistic promises find expression, as if we could create any state of affairs by decreeing that it must exist: has the right to work reduced unemployment? Has the right to health killed disease? Has the right to culture educated those who are indifferent to it?[10]

425. **Normative disorder and the decline of law.** Utilitarianism, which goes hand in hand with empiricism, has led to a profound change in the way legal rules are justified. Whereas in the past, the law was based on principles and tradition, it is now statistical surveys, paired with the social sciences, which provide the law with its objectives, inviting the legislator to adopt an ever tighter and more restrictive network of technical, precise rules, supposedly effective,[11] with the ambition of engineering a perfect society through a perfect system,[12] by fabricating from scratch "insecurities tied to expert dependence."[13] Public opinion begins to believe in the myth

---

6 M. Villey, *Critique de l'utilitarisme juridique*, REVUE DE LA RECHERCHE JURIDIQUE: DROIT PROSPECTIF 166, 170, 172 (1981–1982), no. VI-9.

7 J. CARBONNIER, DROIT ET PASSION DU DROIT SOUS LA V[E] RÉPUBLIQUE 19 (1996). Christian Atias considers, in this respect, that technique has led jurists to perceive their discipline as a science whose rigor and objectivity are unreflectively placed at the service of the State's will, even if it has gone astray, *see* C. ATIAS, SCIENCE DES LÉGISTES, SAVOIR DES JURISTES 69 (3rd ed. 1993). Bruno Oppetit, for his part, holds that utilitarianism – unworthy, in his view, of being called a philosophy – serves no purpose other than to act as an alibi for legal positivism – for the idea that law is an act of the will and not of knowledge. *See* OPPETIT, DROIT ET MODERNITÉ, *op. cit.* at 205.

8 P. Rémy, *Les civilistes français vont-ils disparaître?*, 32 MCGILL LAW JOURNAL 152, 156–57 (1986).

9 *Id.*

10 M. VILLEY, LE DROIT ET LES DROITS DE L'HOMME 11–12 (2nd ed. 2014); *adde*, F. A. HAYEK, DROIT, LÉGISLATION ET LIBERTÉ: UNE NOUVELLE FORMULATION DES PRINCIPES LIBÉRAUX DE JUSTICE ET D'ÉCONOMIE POLITIQUE 523–27 (R. Audouin trans., PUF, 2nd ed. 2013).

11 For illustrations, *see* G. RIPERT, LE DÉCLIN DU DROIT: ÉTUDES SUR LA LÉGISLATION CONTEMPORAINE 102–103 (1949).

12 Rémy, *Les civilistes français vont-ils disparaître?*, *op. cit.* at 158. *Adde*, P. Malaurie, *Le droit et l'esprit: Dernière leçon*, 67 COMMENTAIRE 609, 611 (1994): "Imagine even the unimaginable, a machine that would not only know everything, but would foresee everything: what will happen tomorrow, the day after tomorrow, and every day, every year, and every century to come: a prophetic machine, which guesses what is and what will be the moving action of the divine human comedy. It would not be able to create perfect law."

13 J. CARBONNIER, FLEXIBLE DROIT: POUR UNE SOCIOLOGIE DU DROIT SANS RIGUEUR 204–205 (10th ed. 2013).

that the law must adapt to the facts:[14] it demanded, in response to every grievance, that a new rule be adopted to appease it – and it would take courage for the State to refuse it this "symbolic satisfaction."[15] Today's legal system seems to be driven by the law of entropy: disorder increases and the legal system becomes more cumbersome. The more technical laws there are, the more technicians are needed, and the more technicians there are, the less the legislator hesitates to enact new technical laws.[16] However, the phenomenon is based on an illusion, which consists in believing that as the facts become more complex, it is inevitable to respond by making the law more complex.[17] *In fine*, legal principles are seen as a brake on action, a "strip that turns the administrator into a mummy," because the law, concerned with legality, is opposed to efficiency.[18] This phenomenon, inherited from utilitarian thinking, is both simultaneous with and tied to another: the subordination of individual freedom to the achievement of the general interest.

B. The subordination of individual freedom to the realization of the "general interest"

426. **From the common good to the general interest: from freedom as an end to freedom as a means.** The eighteenth century heralded a major shift: the common good of yesteryear, deemed to result spontaneously from the free action of individuals governed by natural law, was replaced by the notion of "general interest," understood as the *voluntary construction* of an order shaped by the raison d'état.[19] This shift led to a progressive narrowing of perspectives: from *good* to *interest*, from interest to *wealth*, from wealth to *money*.[20] However, the term has never been clearly defined. How could it be otherwise? It is like a Pandora's box inside which utilitarians, along with their allies the positivists, found it all too easy to slot in, under the guise of good intentions, each new objective they intended to pursue.[21]

---

14 C. Atias & D. Linotte, *Le mythe de l'adaptation du droit au fait*, Recueil Dalloz-Sirey 251, 258 (1977), chron. xxxiv.

15 J. Carbonnier, Essai sur les lois 312–13 (2nd ed. 1992).

16 *Id.* at 310.

17 *Id.* at 312–13.

18 J. Rivero, *L'État moderne peut-il être encore un État de droit?*, Annales de la faculté de droit de Liège 65, 75 (1957).

19 On this shift, *see* J. Broch, *L'intérêt général avant 1789. Regard historique sur une notion capitale du droit public français*, 95 Revue historique de droit français et étranger 59, 77–86 (2017).

20 D. Villey, Notes de philosophie économique (1958–59): Le jeu des intérêts 189–237, esp. 215 (1965).

21 Commenting on the theory that the social purpose of law is the measure of its just exercise, one author wrote that it errs "essentially on two points: an uncertain philosophical substratum,... masked and served by the use of a very vague criterion." The consequences of this theory are important, however: it leads us to consider that "the action would degenerate into abuse as soon as it deviated from the social purpose that the legislator imposes on almost all rights." *See* P. Stoffel-Munck, L'abus dans le contrat: Essai d'une théorie 391 and 397 (2000), nos. 510 and 520. For a critique of this approach, theorized in France by Josserand, *id.* at 408–21, nos. 548–562.

While it is therefore impossible to identify the content of the general interest with any precision, it is easy to understand its mechanism.

It consists in no longer recognizing the value of freedom as an *end in itself*, and reducing it to a mere *instrument* for the realization of other goals. To achieve this, the first step is to discredit freedom. Either by caricaturing it, claiming that it is the Trojan Horse of the liberals,[22] which would like to impose on everyone a right that favors the dominant class (freedom is blind: it rewards only merit[23]); or by distorting it, by declaring that freedom is the absence of rules (whereas it presupposes the existence of rules[24]); or by making it frightening, by decreeing that since individuals are not capable of self-determination, they need to be protected from themselves by the State[25] (which would mean placing them under its permanent guardianship). Once the meaning of freedom has been altered, its intrinsic value undermined, it is possible to place other, more important interests above it. The hierarchy of values is then reversed: it becomes desirable to restrict liberty whenever it is deemed to run counter to the general interest – it is thus reduced to a mere instrument serving it.[26]

Whereas the common good was conceived as the sum of individual wills, the general interest entails an arbitrary valorization of certain objectives to the detriment of others, which it assigns to all[27] because they are deemed to satisfy the greatest number. But the very idea of a "general" interest is based on a logical fallacy. Paul and Peter may have some interests in common, others incompatible. Add John to this duo, and the trio's zone of common interests will be even more restricted

---

22 C. Prieto, *La culture de concurrence: Une quête de sens et d'action*, *in* À QUOI SERT LA CONCURRENCE? 719, 720 (M. Behar-Touchais, N. Charbit & R. Amaro eds., 2014): the author notes that the expression "free competition" has been "demonized," then reasserts its value by demonstrating that its preservation does not presuppose the absence of rules, but on the contrary the framing of freedom. In the same vein and by the same author: C. Prieto, *Loyauté du commerce et droit européen de la concurrence*, REVUE DES AFFAIRES EUROPÉENNES NO. 2, 299, 299 (2011), no. 1: "The adjective '*free*' is the focal point of all tensions. In the caricatured image it is usually given, this European law of free competition is perceived as the instrument of pure, hard-line liberalism – godless and lawless. The only law it knows is 'the law of the jungle,' in other words, the law of the strongest, with the most devastating effects on social values."

23 Cf., in antiquity, the notion of isonomy, *see supra*, no. 35, and references cited.

24 *See supra*, no. 386; *adde*, D. VILLEY, NOTES DE PHILOSOPHIE ÉCONOMIQUE (1958–59): LE JEU DES INTÉRÊTS 145 (1965): according to the author, it is "false to believe that liberalism is reluctant to state involvement in economic life"; F. A. HAYEK, THE FATAL CONCEIT: THE ERRORS OF SOCIALISM 63 (W. W. Bartley ed., 1988): confusion has been created by "the common supposition that it is possible to have this kind of freedom without restraints. …General freedom in this sense is nevertheless impossible, for the freedom of each would founder on the unlimited freedom, i.e., the lack of restraint, of all others. …This can be secured by uniformly restricting the freedom of all by abstract rules that preclude arbitrary or discriminatory coercion by or of other people, that prevent any from invading the free sphere of any other."

25 *See*, for example, M. FABRE-MAGNAN, L'INSTITUTION DE LA LIBERTÉ 53–108 (2018): the author believes that the law is justified in intervening to protect individuals from their own servitude (for instance, from addictions or from what some moralists regard as "deviance"), and denounces the "illusions of absolute consent."

26 OPPETIT, DROIT ET MODERNITÉ, *op. cit.* at 181.

27 RAWLS, A THEORY OF JUSTICE, *op. cit.* at 49.

than it was initially. And the greater the number of people, the smaller the zone becomes – on the scale of a society, it becomes negligible.[28] This is why there is a fundamental difference, and in some cases even incompatibility, between freedom and the realization of the general interest. However, "[j]ustice denies that the loss of freedom for some is made right by a greater good shared by others," because the liberties guaranteed by justice cannot be subject "to political bargaining or to the calculus of social interests."[29] This gradual shift has nonetheless legitimized the power of state authority to define and impose, in the place of the individual, what constitutes pleasure or punishment[30]. Freedom only exists if each individual can autonomously value what is most important to them[31] – the general interest thus appearing as the "antithesis of freedom."[32] Nevertheless, despite its limitations, this approach to state action has had a particularly strong influence on economic law.

II. The rise of utilitarianism: a movement characteristic of economic law

427. **The methods of economic law: the interference of economics.** The freedom of contract, which the proliferation of special laws and solidarism[33] have sought to limit in the name of the general interest, to the point where the individual will is autonomous in name only,[34] is matched on a much larger scale by economic freedom, due to the power relationships it implies. Although both phenomena stem from

28 This example is provided by Villey, Notes de philosophie économique (1958-59): Le jeu des intérêts, *op. cit.* at 158.

29 Rawls, A Theory of Justice, *op. cit.* at 28.

30 M. El Shakankiri, La philosophie juridique de Jérémy Bentham 423 (1970). *Adde*, cf. P. Stoffel-Munck, L'abus dans le contrat: Essai d'une théorie 401–21 (2000), nos. 510–537.

31 F. A. Hayek, The Road to Serfdom (1944); *adde*, Villey, Notes de philosophie économique (1958-59): Le jeu des intérêts, *op. cit.* at 159: the theory of the general interest appears to the author as "substantially totalitarian," for "[i]f there were a determined general interest, how could one ever contest its automatic precedence over any particular interest? How could I have rights against a general interest?"

32 G. Farjat, L'ordre public économique 32 (1963) (*nota bene*: the author uses the expression in reference to economic public order).

33 Raymond Gassin, noting that special laws are enacted in response to changing ideas, economic data or political forces (at 92), allows us to see just how contingent, and therefore unstable, they are compared with rules of general law (at 95), *see* R. Gassin, *Lois spéciales et droit commun*, Recueil Dalloz 91 (1961), chron. xviii.

34 On the theme of the "myth of the autonomy of the will," *see* C. Atias, Précis élémentaire de contentieux contractuel 38–39 (2nd ed. 2003); *adde*, F. Chénedé, *De l'autonomie de la volonté à la justice commutative: Du mythe à la réalité*, 4 Droit & Philosophie: Annuaire de l'Institut Michel Villey 155 (2012). On the opposition between the two distinct conceptions of public order, one upholding the autonomy of the will, the other governing everything that positive law does not intend to abandon to the will of individuals, *see* J. Ghestin, *L'ordre public, notion à contenu variable, en droit privé français*, Les notions à contenu variable en droit 77, 82 (C. Perelman & R. Vander Elst eds., 1984).

the utilitarian movement, the latter has had a slightly different fate from the former: in the name of "economic public order,"[35] under the influence of various and contradictory ideologies, it has sometimes been a matter of advocating unrestricted economic freedom (which is therefore no longer a freedom) to promote "efficiency," and sometimes of restricting it excessively in a dirigiste perspective aimed at achieving utopian "social justice."[36] In both cases, the shift in the locus of decision-making has been definitively consummated – from the temple of legal art to the experts' minimarket (**A**). Since expertise is deemed to be "scientific," this major shift seemed to be an improvement: when science expresses itself, it produces a discourse regarded as true and objective, whereas the philosopher and the jurist combined would only be capable of making uncertain statements.[37] However, every economic theory is founded on an ideology that, while by its very nature debatable, is concealed beneath the veneer of neutrality of scientific discourse (**B**).

A. Assumed hegemony: the shift in decision-making to experts

428. **From the existence of higher values to an ideology masked by science.** Economic "science" leads, on the surface only, to a form of depoliticization. For state action to be "effective," it would suffice to give it the sole rule of conforming to the guidance of the knowledgeable. We are thus witnessing an inversion of the relationship of dependence between the expert, on the one hand, the politician on the other – who prides themselves on pursuing the right course because they rely on science – and the jurist – the latter becoming a mere "executing organ of a scientific *intelligentsia* that comes up with optimal strategies and programs."[38] This trend, known as technocracy, has led to a shift in the locus of decision-making.[39]

Whereas, in the past, the theories underpinning the legal order were intrinsically linked to values that were the subject of metaphysical or

35 For a recent study of the concept, tracing its history and evolution, *see* W. Chaiehloudj, *L'ordre public économique*, *in* LE DROIT ÉCONOMIQUE AU XXIE SIÈCLE: NOTIONS ET ENJEUX 527 (J.-B. Racine ed., 2020).

36 Did Dean Ripert not warn of the dangers of this notion as early as 1949, in the opening pages of his book on the decline of law? *See* RIPERT, LE DÉCLIN DU DROIT: ÉTUDES SUR LA LÉGISLATION CONTEMPORAINE, *op. cit.* at 7: "No doubt, we continue to affirm that justice must be achieved, but nowadays we speak of social justice. Le's beware of any qualifier added to justice. An ideal contains none."

37 *See supra*, nos. 84 *et seq.*

38 J. HABERMAS, LA TECHNIQUE ET LA SCIENCE COMME "IDÉOLOGIE" 100 (1973).

39 According to François Terré, "economics, as it was experienced in the business world until the second half of the twentieth century, under the traditional oversight of politics, has largely distanced itself – if not emancipated itself – from the latter. Hence a certain decline, or at least a crisis of the legal order," *see* F. Terré, *Concurrence et proportionnalité*, *in* MÉLANGES EN L'HONNEUR DU PROFESSEUR CLAUDE LUCAS DE LEYSSAC 467, 471 (2018).

ethical discussions, it would now be appropriate to acquiesce to a technique that hides under the carpet of logic "what is, however, in truth only politics, as it has always been done."[40] Make no mistake: the cut between values and science serves precisely to conceal the real interests underlying economic analysis.[41] When the latter is mobilized, the examination seems depersonalized, the question of values evacuated,[42] whereas it is an illusion to believe that economic analysis is independent.[43] The existence of ideological presuppositions in economic theories has already been demonstrated,[44] their risks denounced.[45] Yet these theories, whatever their obedience and the injunctions they formulate, appear – each in turn depending on political alternations – to be the falsely neutral yardstick of the success or failure of economic *law*, which is now difficult to distinguish from economic *policy*.

B. A masked ideology: the lack of axiological neutrality in economic expertise

429. **The ideological underpinnings of economic analysis.** The current sophistication of economic reasoning[46] should not obscure the obvious: the idea of a pure theory is illusory.[47] The origins of this mirage of objectivity date back to the seventeenth century,[48] and continue to influence the way we think about economic analysis today. Economic analysis has claimed to do without judgments and biases in order to become objective – i.e., axiologically neutral.[49] Modern economics has thus become "a science that

40 *Id.* at 103; *adde*, on this theme, R. Savatier, *L'ordre public économique*, Recueil Dalloz 37, 37 (1965), chron. vi.

41 Habermas, La technique et la science comme "idéologie", *op. cit.* at 142. *Nota bene*: the author's remark is not aimed specifically at economic analysis, but at science in general.

42 A.-L. Sibony, *Du bon usage des notions d'efficacité et d'efficience en droit*, *in* L'efficacité de la norme juridique: Nouveau vecteur de légitimité 82 (M. Fatin-Rouge Stefanini, L. Gay & A. Vidal-Naquet eds., 2012).

43 A. Jacquemin, *Le droit économique, serviteur de l'économie?*, Revue trimestrielle de droit commercial 283, 292 (1972).

44 M. Lao, 79 *Ideology Matters in the Antitrust Debate*, Antitrust Law Journal 649 (2014); J. Drexl, On the (A)political Character of the Economic Approach to Competition Law, in Competition Policy and the Economic Approach: Foundations and Limitations 312, 321–24 (J. Drexl et al. eds., 2011).

45 C. Koening & B. von Wendland, The Art of Regulation: Competition in Europe – Wealth and Wariness 37–38 (2017): "[P]roblems and dangers occur when the objectives [of public intervention] are used to justify state intervention and to hide that such intervention may be rather in the singular political interest of a certain politician or government but not in the long-term public interest."

46 Sophistication does not, however, make them any more accurate, *see supra*, nos. 114 *et seq.*

47 Habermas, La technique et la science comme "idéologie", *op. cit.* at 144.

48 *See supra*, nos. 80 *et seq.*

49 However, this is a chimera, *see* Villey, Notes de philosophie économique (1958-59): Le jeu des intérêts, *op. cit.* at 48: "The economist who aspires to 'guide the action' of governments or business leaders clearly cannot base their reasoning solely on automatic mechanisms, as analyzed in pure economic theory."

claims to be free of value judgments."[50] Economists gradually retreated into methodological quarrels, abandoning the ideological stakes of their theories. There has been a decline in economic *doctrine* to the benefit of *technique*.[51]

Yet the absence of doctrine is impossible: the choice of criteria for rendering reality objective is, precisely, a *choice* that emanates from the observing *subject*.[52] Consequently, these choices are inevitably the fruit of a certain vision of the world, which cannot be objective.[53] Thus, setting wealth maximization as an objective is not neutral, since such a goal presupposes a certain worldview. To claim that this is the result, without value judgment, of "scientific" observation is to pass off a normative approach as a descriptive one – a phenomenon that one author has called "smuggling normatives."[54] Moreover, since the discovery of Gödel's incompleteness theorem, it has been accepted that no formal system can escape "an irreducible share of the incalculable."[55] Consequently, the idea that it would be possible to control the course of things by means of precise, objective techniques is merely a fantasy.[56] So, from the moment we consider that economics offers to define an optimal social outcome – which is clearly not demonstrated – and that the aim of law is to achieve this *optimum*, it follows that a state authority will have the power to decide what the *optimum* is, and to impose it on everyone, based on a questionable method.[57] This scientifically enlightened despotism is particularly prevalent in competition law – the debate over its objectives being a topical manifestation of the drifts to which utilitarianism inevitably leads.

---

50 S. Trifilio, Esprit mathématique et pensée économique dans l'Antiquité et au Moyen Âge 103 (2010) (Ph.D. dissertation, Aix-Marseille University).The author continues (at 103–104): "But apart from the fact that such a position presupposes that only the end (not the means) is the object of a value judgment, if the economist (following utilitarian philosophy) has succeeded in sparing themselves any reflection or justification on the subject of the end, it is only by declaring the latter to be necessary and universal (necessity and universality being precisely, according to Aristotle – let us note in passing – the properties of what belongs to science *stricto sensu*). In reality, neoclassical economists evade the problem of the ends of action by arbitrarily positing or assuming that a certain end is scientific (necessary and general) rather than practical (accidental and individual). In so doing, however, they simply push the problem back upstream of their discipline. Yet it is precisely at this (exorbitant?) price – which Aristotle could not even imagine paying – that they have been able to develop a 'scientific' (and mathematical) approach to the questions that interest them."

51 D. Villey & C. Nême, Petite histoire des grandes doctrines économiques 232–36 (1996).

52 Moreover, even the hard sciences have now recognized that they leave room for a degree of subjectivity, *see supra*, no. 115.

53 Habermas, La technique et la science comme "idéologie", *op. cit.* at 152.

54 A. Allen, *Economic Analysis of Law: Some Realism about Nominalism*, 60 Virginia Law Review 451, 467 and 477 (1974).

55 On this subject, *see* A. Supiot, La gouvernance par les nombres: Cours au Collège de France (2012-2014) 340 (2015).

56 Habermas, La technique et la science comme "idéologie", *op. cit.* at 144.

57 This critique of utilitarianism is that of Oppetit, Droit et modernité, *op. cit.* at 179.

Paragraph 2 – The utilitarianism of competition law: the debate on its objectives

430. **Competition law subordinated to the pursuit of objectives other than the preservation of free competition.** The debate on the objectives of competition law is not new: it has appeared, disappeared and reappeared repeatedly for several decades.[58] It stems from a standpoint not to protect free competition as such, but to subordinate it to ends other than its own[59] in the name of a teleological interpretation of the objectives pursued by the discipline.[60] However, the discussion, although inexhaustible,[61] "often lacks rigor"[62]: it is a debate present "everywhere" while "it leads nowhere."[63] Initially, under the influence of the Chicago School, the aim of competition law in the age of "modernization" became to promote "economic efficiency" – the ambition being to make its implementation "economically correct" (**II**). The limits of this approach, at a time when the "all-economy" approach is increasingly criticized[64] and scientism seems

---

58 H. Hovenkamp, *Is Antitrust's Consumer Welfare Principle Imperiled?*, 45 The Journal of Corporation Law 65, 85 (2019). *Adde*, on this theme, A. Pirovano, *Progrès économique ou progrès social (ou les contradictions du droit de la concurrence)*, Recueil Dalloz-Sirey 145, 152–56 (1980), chron. xxii: the author already noted in 1980 that the economic aspirations of the discipline are difficult to reconcile with the achievement of social progress.

59 Cf. Pierre Bonassies' theory of "competition–means," discussed *supra*, no. 356.

60 However, such an approach is based on an erroneous vision of the notion of teleology, *see infra*, nos. 473–477.

61 Among a wealth of literature: for critical perspectives, A. Künzler, *Economic Content of Competition Law: The Point of Regulating Preferences*, *in* The Goals of Competition Law 182 (D. Zimmer ed., 2012); *adde*, F. Maier-Rigaud, *On the Normative Foundations of Competition Law – Efficiency, Political Freedom and the Freedom to Compete*, *in* The Goals of Competition Law 132 (D. Zimmer ed., 2012); for a position in favor of the pursuit of multiple goals and the advent of a "polycentric" competition law, I. Lianos, *Some Reflections on the Question of the Goals of EU Competition Law* (CLES Working Paper Series, 3/2013, Jan. 2013); and, by the same author, *Polycentric Competition Law* (CLES Research Papers Series, 4/2018, Sept. 2018); for a critical study focusing on American law, *see* B. Orbach, *How Antitrust Lost Its Goals*, 81 Fordham Law Review 2253 (2013); M. E. Stucke, *Reconsidering Antitrust's Goals*, 53 Boston College Law Review 551 (2012); and in French law, J.-C. Roda, *Réflexions sur les objectifs du droit français de la concurrence*, Recueil Dalloz 1504 (2018); *adde*, for a plea against the hegemony of "economism" and in favor of a "plurality of ends" integrating the "social finality of law," *see* N. Mathey, *Les finalités du droit de la concurrence: Essai de téléologie du droit*, Contrats concurrence consommation (Dec. 2020), dossier 13. Finally, for a statistical approach to the objectives formulated, based on a sample of around four thousand sources: K. Stylianou & M. Iacovides, *The Goals of EU Competition Law: A Comprehensive Empirical Investigation*, 42 Legal Studies 620 (2022).

62 D. Bosco, *La prise en compte d'intérêts publics dans la mise en œuvre des règles sur l'abus de position dominante*, Concurrences no. 2-2021, art. no. 99790, 31, 31, no. 1; *also*, D. Bosco, *La régulation concurrentielle des GAFA, le droit et les droits*, Gazette du Palais 42 (Sept. 15, 2021), special issue no. 2: the author notes the existence of a phenomenon of "de-judicialization of competition law" consisting in "the idea – which is a recent idea, but which is expressed so forcefully today that one comes to think that it is natural – that competition authorities are political authorities who must achieve political objectives."

63 D. Bosco, *Regard sur la postmodernisation de l'abus de position dominante*, *in* 1 Laurence Idot: Concurrence et Europe – Liber Amicorum 25, 33 (C. Lemaire & F. Martucci eds., 2022).

64 According to Christian Atias, the economic analysis of law "must make due allowance for Aristotelian prudence in the formation of law" and "conclusions drawn on the effects of rules must be relativized." Indeed, it cannot be accepted as an "indisputable postulate" that legislation "has the mission of regulating behaviors in accordance, notably, with their economic effects," which makes doubt "all the more permissible as the effectiveness of this regulation is hardly verified." Finally, according to the author, it is a mirage to think one

to have had its day, have led to a reconsideration of the modernization movement. However, what we are witnessing today is not a return to legal reasoning, but a politicization of debates: in the age of "postmodernity," competition law should now be "politically correct" (**I**).

I. Critique of a new injunction: conforming to the political doxa

431. **A paradox: the formulation of political objectives that must be considered through the prism of economic analysis.** After denouncing the excesses of economism, and to compensate for its shortcomings, the aim is now to broaden the scope of competition law objectives. The logic remains the same: competition rules should not aim to protect free competition in and of itself, but should contribute to building a better social order[65] (**A**). Paradoxically, however, the emphasis on these new goals does not change the existing frameworks of analysis: even if they are not economic in nature, these political objectives should be taken into account through the prism of economic analysis (**B**).

A. Competition authorities' ambition to build a better social order

432. **The entry into force of the Lisbon Treaty: the objectives set out in article 3 of the Treaty on European Union.** Following the entry into force of the Lisbon Treaty, the first articles of the Treaty on European Union were amended, and the objective of "undistorted competition" was, for political reasons, discreetly relegated to a less visible place: additional Protocol No. 27, which nevertheless has the status of primary law.[66] Article 2 sets out in

---

can erase the irrational aspect of law, *see* C. Atias, *Sur E. Mackaay et St. Rousseau,* Analyse économique du droit, *Paris, Dalloz, Éditions Thémis, 2008*, Revue de la recherche juridique: Droit prospectif 2469, 2470 and 2472–73 resp. (2008). Moreover, an analysis of the letter of the treaty does not suggest that wealth maximization was the sole aim of its drafters, *see* A.-L. Sibony, *Du bon usage des notions d'efficacité et d'efficience en droit, in* L'efficacité de la norme juridique: Nouveau vecteur de légitimité 77 (M. Fatin-Rouge Stefanini, L. Gay & A. Vidal-Naquet eds., 2012). *See*, for example, W. Kerber, *Should Competition Law Promote Efficiency? Some Reflections of an Economist on the Normative Foundations of Competition Law*, *in* Economic Theory and Competition Law 93, 118–19 (J. Drexl et al. eds., 2009): "The normative foundations of competition law is not well developed. ... 'Economic efficiency' – as it is usually defined – cannot be the final answer to this normative question. On the one hand, there are different concepts of efficiency, with their specific problems and deficits. On the other hand, the discussion in economics, which is narrowed down to 'total-welfare standard versus consumer-welfare standard', does not sufficiently grasp the complexity of normative problems."

65 D. Bosco, *L'avenir du droit de la concurrence*, Contrats concurrence consommation (Dec. 2020), dossier 15, no. 7: "Essentially, what is now expected of competition law is that it should no longer be satisfied with merely overseeing the competitive process, but that it should contribute to establishing a new social order; competition authorities should have a *worldview* and participate actively in a broader social project."

66 This means that while the objective of undistorted competition has been removed from the Treaty on European Union, its normative scope has remained intact, *see* D. Bosco & C. Prieto, Droit européen de la concurrence 183–85 (2013), no. 197. As Catherine Prieto rightly writes, the relegation of free competition to a protocol, whereas it was originally intended to be mentioned in the body of the Lisbon

no particular order the "values" on which the Union is founded – human dignity, freedom, democracy, equality, the rule of law, tolerance, justice, solidarity, etc. Article 3 goes on to set out the "aims" pursued by the Union, including, in paragraph 3, the establishment of an internal market. This is accompanied by other objectives, which are varied, to say the least, and sometimes contradictory: a highly competitive social market economy, full employment, social progress, sustainable development, economic growth, price stability, the fight against discrimination, solidarity between generations, cultural diversity, the development of our heritage[67] – in short, an ideal world. While the normative scope of these ambitious formulas is relative, if not non-existent,[68] they have nonetheless shaped thinking, and have undoubtedly played a major role in the evolution of *discourse* on the discipline.

433. **The disjointed broadening of the discourse on the aims of competition law to non-economic purposes.** The current debate on the aims of the law on anticompetitive practices gives the impression that no issue seems off-limits to the discipline: democratic pluralism, protection of personal data, of the consumer, of the environment, a driver of gender equality, the fight against powerful operators (especially when they happen to be foreign), a vehicle for market access for people from immigrant backgrounds, an instrument for advancing the digital transition,[69] fairness – few themes are spared.[70] However, in comparison with the previous trend, which focused solely on economic objectives, the merit of this recent enthusiasm lies in the fact that it cannot hide what it is: an accumulation of assumptions that vary according to the ideological sensibilities of its advocates.

And yet, despite its highly subjective nature, this politicized discourse has already made its way into the Commission's annual reports,[71] and into certain soft law texts.[72] Thus the guidelines accompanying the revised version

---

Treaty, constitutes a strong symbol, "even if no legal consequences can be drawn from it," *see* C. Prieto, *Loyauté du commerce et droit européen de la concurrence*, Revue des affaires européennes no. 2, 299, 299 (2011), no. 1.

67 For a commentary on the evolution of the Treaty on European Union following the entry into force of the Lisbon Treaty, *see* J. Drexl, *La Constitution économique européenne – L'actualité du modèle ordolibéral*, xxv Revue internationale de droit économique 419, 437–41 (2011).

68 Cf., in general, the illusory nature of declarations of law, *supra*, no. 424; and in particular, the lack of normative scope of the objective of "consumer welfare," *supra*, nos. 359–361. *A fortiori*, the objectives set out in article 3 of the Treaty on European Union, insofar as they are unrelated to competition, seem neither able nor entitled, in our view, to guide its policy.

69 Eur. Comm., *Shaping Europe's Digital Future*, COM(2020) 67 final (Feb. 19, 2020), at 9–10.

70 *See* references cited *supra*, no. 430 (footnote); *adde*, for an overview: A. C. Witt, The More Economic Approach to EU Antitrust Law 86–102 (2019).

71 *Id.* at 94–102.

72 Recently, *see* Eur. Comm., *Amendments to the Communication from the Commission Guidance on the Commission's Enforcement Priorities in Applying Article 82 of the EC Treaty to Abusive Exclusionary Conduct by Dominant Undertakings*, C(2023) 1923 final (Mar. 27, 2023), para. 1: articles 101 and 102 TFEU serve "Europe well by contributing to a level playing field where markets serve consumers. It can moreover contribute to achieving objectives that go beyond consumer welfare, such as plurality in a democratic society."

of the exemption regulation on horizontal agreements,[73] and those following the new exemption regulation on vertical restraints, which state that "[s]ustainable development is a core principle of the Treaty ... together with digitalisation and a resilient Single Market."[74] Competition law should therefore promote "sustainability,"[75] which implies "limiting the use of natural resources," "reducing waste," or "promoting animal welfare."[76] The Commission does not fail to provide examples: from now on, companies will be entitled to include in the selection criteria of their distributors the fact of ensuring that "goods are delivered via sustainable means, such as cargo bike"[77] – where the absurd rivals the comical. But while the politician talks, the lawyer asks: how are these new objectives supposed to be taken into account, if at all? And the Commission answers: "through the prism of economic analysis."

B. The paradoxical consideration of non-economic objectives through the prism of economic analysis

434. **Non-economic objectives must be translated into economic benefits.** Since the 2000s, the Commission has considered that non-economic objectives can be taken into account, provided that they can be translated into economic benefits.[78] The efforts of virtuous companies can be "taken into account as qualitative or quantitative efficiencies."[79] However, the Court did not follow the Commission's position, creating a divergence of interpretation between the two institutions that could compromise legal certainty.[80]

In fact, *some* of these aims have long been capable of playing a role, not as an objective of competition law, but either as a *parameter of competition* that can be restricted – as in the case of practice such as agreeing

73 Eur. Comm., *Guidelines on the Applicability of Article 101 of the Treaty on the Functioning of the European Union to Horizontal Co-operation Agreements*, 2023 O.J. (C 259) 1, para. 518: "Competition law enforcement contributes to sustainable development by ensuring effective competition, which spurs innovation, increases the quality and choice of products, ensures an efficient allocation of resources, reduces the costs of production, and thereby contributes to consumer welfare." We admit to struggling to grasp how, apart from green innovation, the stated benefits promote sustainable development.

74 Eur. Comm., Guidelines on Vertical Restraints, 2022 O.J. (C 248) 1, para. 8.

75 Note that the environment is one of the most thought-provoking topics, *see inter alia*: OECD, Environmental Considerations in Competition Enforcement, DAF/COMP(2021)4 (Nov. 19, 2021). For a balanced view, *see* W. Chaiehloudj, *Le droit de la concurrence est-il un frein à la protection de l'environnement?*, Contrats concurrence consommation (Apr. 2022), étude 6.

76 Eur. Comm., Guidelines on Vertical Restraints, 2022 O.J. (C 248) 1, para. 8.

77 *Id.*, para. 144.

78 A. C. Witt, *Public Policy Goals Under EU Competition Law – Now is the Time to Set the House in Order*, 8 European Competition Journal 443, 469 (2012).

79 Eur. Comm., Guidelines on Vertical Restraints, 2022 O.J. (C 248) 1, para. 9.

80 Witt, *Public Policy Goals Under EU Competition Law – Now is the Time to Set the House in Order*, *op. cit.* at 69–70.

not to innovate[81] – or as a *legitimate reason* to rebut a finding of infringement[82] – but in this case, it is the companies that are pursuing a "legitimate aim," not competition law.[83] This is nothing new: on the one hand, price is not the only relevant competition parameter;[84] on the other, the Commission has, from the very beginnings of its decision-making practice, exempted agreements on the basis of a variety of legitimate grounds.[85] In both cases, the companies' objectives are not subjected to the scrutiny of economic analysis. Nevertheless, these new goals coexist with the old ones: one normative demand, now relatively old, requires competition law to be "economically correct."

II. Critique of an enduring injunction: conforming to the economic doxa

435. **The split between economics and law, and the normative ambition of economic analysis.** The adoption of a more economic approach is based on a "chronic epistemological doubt" as to the relevance of legal reasoning, which would lead to erroneous or arbitrary results – a problem deemed to be resolvable by recourse to a series of economic tools.[86] The relationship between the legal and economic approaches to competition has thus been one of *tension* since the nineteenth century: while the law has remained stable, economic analysis has constantly sought to discredit its long-established[87] solutions – it has never concealed its normative ambitions (**B**). These frictions must, however, be put into perspective. They stem from the split between law and economics conveyed by the dominant school of thought in competition law. This approach is highly simplistic, in that it does not reflect the richness of economic theories (**A**). Indeed, other schools of thought, currently in the minority, have not treated economics as an autonomous discipline, separate from law, and offer insightful reflections compatible with legal reasoning.[88]

---

81 *See* in particular. Eur. Comm., July 8, 2021, C(2021) 4955 final, Car Emissions, paras. 121–122.

82 *See supra*, nos. 343–349

83 In this sense, *see supra*, no. 343.

84 F. Castillo de la Torre, *Is the Effects-Based Approach Too Cumbersome? Taking Stock of Recent Practice and Case Law on Article 102 TFEU*, *in* The Transformation of EU Competition Law: Next Generation Issues 145, 156 (A. Claici, A. Komninos & D. Waelbroeck eds., 2023).

85 *See supra*, no. 346.

86 Castillo de la Torre, *Is the Effects-Based Approach Too Cumbersome? Taking Stock of Recent Practice and Case Law on Article 102 TFEU*, *op. cit.* at 146.

87 As notes C. Prieto in *Source économique du droit de la concurrence: Quelle efficacité?*, Contrats concurrence consommation (June 2020), dossier 3, no. 10: "The return to classical liberalism, carried out by the Chicago School, was intended to discredit legal norms in the name of economic efficiency. …Economic analysis of law, far from remaining a mere tool of expertise, has become normative."

88 *See infra*, nos. 478–480

A. Competition law's reductive vision of economic analysis

436. **The separation between law and economics conveyed by the dominant economic trend in competition law.** The modernization of competition rules marks the end of the teachings of ordoliberalism, and the simultaneous triumph of "neoclassical" economic analysis, inherited from the Chicago School.[89] This school cemented the separation between economics and law, replacing the criterion of justice with that of efficiency.[90] In the past, economists were once *moralists* as well: economics had never attempted to separate itself from the other human sciences.[91] It was only at the end of the nineteenth century, under the influence of the marginalist revolution, which involved extensive mathematical modeling,[92] that the sophistication of analysis led to a disconnection between law and certain economic schools of thought[93] – the latter seeking to establish economics as an autonomous discipline.[94] However, their vision is considered reductive, artificially complex, and anti-historical[95] by some,[96] and these currents are often criticized for lacking critical self-reflection regarding their own methodology.[97]

The long-dominant – albeit now outmoded[98] – trend in competition law stems from such a split, which confines it to a closed, inward-looking analytical framework. However, it should not be forgotten that other schools

---

89 B. Wardhaugh, Competition, Effects and Predictability: The Rule of Law and the Economic Approach to Competition 96 (2020): "The Guidelines and expected method of analysis here could have been produced in Chicago. Freiburg's ordoliberal considerations are completely absent from this new approach." On the ordoliberal trend, *see infra*, no. 480.

90 C. Veljanovski, The Economics of Law 14 and 27–43 (2nd ed. 2006).

91 S. Schweitzer & L. Floury, Droit et économie: Un essai d'histoire analytique 113 (2015).

92 D. Villey, Notes de philosophie économique (1958-59): Le jeu des intérêts 52 (1965): "[P]olitical economy came to be reduced to economic mathematics, and it was claimed that only mathematical training truly qualifies the economist. Nothing is more false."

93 Schweitzer & Floury, Droit et économie: Un essai d'histoire analytique, *op. cit.* at 113 n.150.

94 On this theme, *see* T. Kirat, *Économie et droit: De l'analyse économique du droit à de nouvelles alliances?*, 49 Revue économique 1057 (1998).

95 As Daniel Villey notes: "The teaching of the history of economic thought once held a prominent place in the training of economists, particularly in France. The proliferation of new 'subjects' is now in the process of drowning it out entirely." Villey, Notes de philosophie économique (1958-59): Le jeu des intérêts, *op. cit.* at 138.

96 *See*, for example, H. Hovenkamp, *Law and Economics in the United States: A Brief Historical Survey*, 19 Cambridge Journal of Economics 331, 334 (1995); *adde* E. Mackaay, *La règle juridique observée par le prisme de l'économiste: Une histoire stylisée du mouvement de l'analyse économique du droit*, Revue internationale de droit économique 43, 70–72 (1986).

97 *Id.* at 347.

98 On this subject, *see* C. Prieto, *Source économique du droit de la concurrence: Quelle efficacité?*, Contrats concurrence consommation (June 2020), dossier 3, nos. 12–19: The author notes the hope of overcoming the mistrust of the Chicagoan approach thanks to the "post-Chicago" current known as the "New Industrial Organization" – the latter, however, suffers from excessive sophistication, which inevitably raises the question of its "administrability." It should be noted, however, that this new approach has not relinquished efficiency as the goal of competition law, and is therefore a continuation rather than a break with the methods of the Chicago School.

of thought, foremost among them the ordoliberal movement, have not severed the deep connection between law and economics,[99] which goes back to Aristotle,[100] and are more focused, not on interventionist or non-interventionist approaches aimed at maximizing economic efficiency, but on the question of the *institutional framework* enabling the emergence and structuring of a free market.[101] While this latter concern is much older, efficiency-based approaches are now in the majority.[102] Nevertheless, these approaches are incompatible with respect for certain legal principles[103] that the law has never intended to sacrifice, and never will. They are therefore difficult to integrate into legal reasoning, and make dialogue between jurists and economists difficult – a problem made all the more acute by the fact that this type of economic analysis has always clearly asserted its normative ambitions.

B. The normative aim of economic analysis in competition law

437. **"The decline of law as an autonomous discipline."** A famous article by Richard Posner, entitled "The Decline of Law as an Autonomous Discipline,"[104] perfectly illustrates the mindset of the Chicago School. According to Posner, legal thinking is too inward-looking and outdated, and the decline of "faith" in the law is due to the growing prestige and authority of the exact sciences,[105] from which it follows that it is imperative that law open up to the insights of economists and statisticians, who should play a much greater role in legal reforms.[106] While this rhetoric is well-honed, it nevertheless overlooks the fact that it is because Posnerian economic analysis is not easily compatible with legal reasoning – since it can

---

99 Has not one author remarked that "'economism,' which consists in opposing economic efficiency, a scientific and objective criterion, to the values traditionally embodied by law, from legal certainty to commercial loyalty, is, to a large extent, a delusion to which jurists all too readily fall prey"? *See* A. Jacquemin, *Le droit économique, serviteur de l'économie?*, Revue trimestrielle de droit commercial 283, 284 (1972). Indeed, the economic approach is only opposed to the legal approach when it conveys points of view incompatible with legal reasoning. Otherwise, law and economics can go hand in hand.

100 *See supra*, no. 37.

101 Q. Slobodian, Globalists: The End of Empire and the Birth of Neoliberalism 6 (2018).

102 A. Sen, *Markets and Freedoms: Achievements and Limitations of the Market Mechanism in Promoting Individual Freedoms*, 45 Oxford Economic Papers 519, 519 (1993).

103 W. Kerber, *Should Competition Law Promote Efficiency? Some Reflections of an Economist on the Normative Foundations of Competition Law*, *in* Economic Theory and Competition Law 93, 94 (J. Drexl et al. eds., 2009).

104 R. Posner, *The Decline of Law as an Autonomous Discipline: 1962–1987*, 100 Harvard Law Review 761 (1987).

105 Cf. *supra*, nos. 80 *et seq.*

106 Posner, *The Decline of Law as an Autonomous Discipline: 1962–1987*, *op. cit.* at 772–73: "A related reason for the decline of faith in law as an autonomous discipline is the continuing rise in the prestige and authority of scientific and other exact modes of inquiry in general. ...[T]he heart of legal thinking, when law is conceived as an autonomous discipline, seem to many younger scholars old-fashioned, passé, tired. ...[E]conomists, statisticians, and other social scientists should have a far more prominent role in efforts at legal reform."

be difficult to translate into rules that align with the legal system[107] – that jurists are unlikely to incorporate it blindly into their reasoning.

Yet, no doubt because a new theory always arouses curiosity,[108] and possibly because it served as a convenient scientific alibi to justify an anti-state political agenda in the USA,[109] Posner's ambition fascinated several generations of jurists, and gradually spread as far as Europe.[110] Thus, this form of economic analysis has become "one of the main foundations of competition policy" insofar as it would "provide a unique and optimal scientific answer to every question"[111] – which, *if we agree* to let it play this role, implies a profound transformation of legislative and jurisdictional methods.[112] The question, then, is whether it is appropriate to accept the postulate that economic theory should dictate the solutions to an entire field of law; in other words, whether it is desirable for economic theory to become the main normative source,[113] entailing the supersession of legal reasoning and the relegation of its traditional concepts to the past.

438. **"The decline of economic analysis as an autonomous discipline"?** *If, and only if*, this premise were accepted, then all that would be left for jurists to do would be to sign a blank check to economists, who would then be responsible for entirely substituting their views for those of competition authority members and magistrates.[114] Competition rules would then have to be designed solely on the basis of the findings of economic analysis, economic expertise would have to play a pre-eminent role in the implementation of the rules, and every divergence between the law and what economic analysis suggests would have to be regarded as a failure of the law.[115] Conversely, however, if efficiency is not the goal of competition law, there is no reason for it to be designed or applied according to this

---

107 *See* in particular *infra*, nos. 458–462.

108 Cf., for example, the idea of "no-fault liability," *supra*, no. 144 in tort law, no. 154 in criminal law, or the emergence of the theory of imputability, *supra*, no. 184

109 *Id.* Posner, *The Decline of Law as an Autonomous Discipline: 1962–1987*, *op. cit.* at 66.

110 On Richard Posner's influence on contemporary economic thought, particularly in Europe, *see* S. Hans-Bernd & M. Vatiero, *Fifty Years of Richard Posner's Economic Analysis of Law: An Introduction*, XXXI HISTORY OF ECONOMIC IDEAS 1, 7–10 (2023), https://ssrn.com/abstract=4547843.

111 M. Deschamps & F. Marty, *Les politiques de concurrence sont-elles réductibles à de la théorie économique appliquée? Réflexions autour de l'affaire Microsoft*, CAHIERS DE MÉTHODOLOGIE JURIDIQUE NO. 5, 2571, 2571–73 (2008) (*nota bene*: the authors do not endorse the statement); *adde*, in the same vein, M. E. Stucke, *Does the Rule of Reason Violate the Rule of Law?*, 22 LOYOLA CONSUMER LAW REVIEW 15, 21 (2009).

112 G. Canivet, *La pertinence de l'analyse économique du droit: Le point de vue du juge*, 99 PETITES AFFICHES 23 (May 19, 2005).

113 This is one of the questions raised by: M. Deschamps & F. Marty, *L'analyse économique du droit est-elle une théorie scientifique du droit?*, CAHIERS DE MÉTHODOLOGIE JURIDIQUE NO. 5, 2541, 2558 (2008).

114 G. Marenco, *La notion de restriction de concurrence dans le cadre de l'interdiction des ententes*, *in* II MÉLANGES EN HOMMAGE À MICHEL WAELBROECK 1217, 1231 (1999).

115 F. Jenny, *Competition Law Enforcement: Is Economic Expertise Really Necessary?*, *in* INTERNATIONAL ANTITRUST LAW & POLICY: FORDHAM CORPORATE LAW 185, 188 (1998).

approach.[116] And perhaps, in fact, there is nothing erroneous or undesirable about what economists identify as a "type I error" (an unwarranted condemnation, because science considers that there is no harmful economic effect), or a "type II error" (an error considered less serious: not condemning when there should have been). Why should it not be economists who, in certain cases, commit an error? The jurist can reverse the criticism, and point out to the economists that they go astray by failing to take into consideration other parameters that are nonetheless essential – such as respect for legal principles – which leads them to use their vocabulary, to forget that a society may wish to afford itself, at a certain "cost," the luxury of inefficiency to satisfy aspirations that are deeper than economic.[117] Chicago School analysis, like most utilitarian economic theories, categorically rejects certain legal concepts from its discourse,[118] and thus becomes closed in on itself, forgetting that its injunctions are only acceptable and desirable insofar as they take into consideration values that are and will always remain superior to it. In short, it would be desirable, in response to Richard Posner, for a jurist to publish an article entitled "The decline of economic analysis as an autonomous discipline."

*

*   *

439. **Conclusion of Section 1: the utilitarianism of contemporary competition law, a questionable foundation.** Contemporary competition law is a striking illustration of the continuous progress of legal utilitarianism since the eighteenth century. Methodologically, the discipline relies on expertise, and seems no longer willing to engage with classical legal reasoning, insofar as legal concepts are discarded in favor of a series of economic tests and theories. From a substantive point of view, competition law seems to have given up protecting freedom of competition as an end, in favor of a variety of increasingly politicized objectives. The omnipresence of the latter, whose normative scope is nonetheless uncertain, in the discourse on the discipline, generates strong uncertainty regarding the criteria for qualifying anticompetitive practices. A postulate, however questionable, has gradually become dogma: it is necessary to systematically mobilize economic analysis in order to understand the effects produced by litigious practices,

116 *Id.*

117 In this sense, R. Stones, EU Competition Law and the Rule of Law: Justification and Realisation 149–211, 210 (2018) (Ph.D. dissertation, London School of Economics): the author considers that in some respects, the implementation of competition rules does not take into account the political and economic interest represented by respect for the rule of law.

118 *See* M. E. Stucke, *Morality and Antitrust*, 2006 Columbia Business Law Review 443, 445–46 (2006): "Under the continued influence of the Chicago-school's neoclassical economic theories, antitrust analysis is primarily concerned with economic efficiency. Since terms like 'morality' and 'evil' are judgmental, not descriptive, they are deemed outside the discourse of economic theory."

so as to sanction only those that produce negative effects on the greatest happiness of the greatest number. This postulate has led to unprecedented complexity in the law on anticompetitive practices. Moreover, if it is not abandoned, it is likely to have questionable consequences with regard to the principles of the rule of law.

*

* *

Section 2
Questionable consequences

440. **The harmful consequences of utilitarianism in law on anticompetitive practices.** Whereas, if it were simpler, it could be more agile and therefore more "efficient,'" over the past twenty years, competition law has gradually become a behemoth, now struggling to move forward. The desire to subordinate it to the achievement of ends other than the preservation of freedom of competition has weighed it down excessively: now grappling with increasing complexity (**Paragraph 1**), it has become less accessible to its intended users (**Paragraph 2**).

Paragraph 1 – The increasing complexity of competition law

441. **The complexity of competition law, a pretext for adopting new rules.** While the aim of the modernization movement was to promote "efficiency" in the implementation of competition rules, it has, paradoxically, led to a reduction in their effectiveness by overcomplicating the discipline. And yet, "when a drawback is discovered, the fault lies with the shortcomings of the legislation," and "all we have to do is pass one more law,"[119] the discrediting of a law sometimes translates into "more recourse to the legislator."[120] This is precisely what happened: to the supposed inadequacies of the law on anticompetitive practices (**I**), it was deemed appropriate to respond with a new regulation – the Digital Markets Act – which will have no impact other than to complicate competition law even further, without proving any more effective than its traditional rules (**II**).

---

119 J. Carbonnier, Essai sur les lois 312–13 (2nd ed. 1992).

120 J. Carbonnier, Droit et passion du droit sous la Ve République 111 (1996).

I. The problem identified: the insufficient "effectiveness" of competition law

442. **Insufficient effectiveness exacerbated by indiscriminate use of commitment procedures.** To compensate for the lack of speed and the high cost of enforcing competition rules (**A**), it has now become commonplace to resort to commitment procedures (**B**), which are *supposed* to have many virtues, including reducing the burden of proof on competition authorities, and improving the speed of their intervention on the market.[121] However, the frequent use of this procedure is not without its critics. While substantive modernization has led to an increase in the burden of proof, giving rise to a great "luxury of controversy," at the same time, the possibility of using the commitment procedure, described as "procedural modernization," has enabled the authorities to dispense with a thorough analysis of the litigious conduct[122] – thus preventing jurisprudence from evolving and adapting to novel cases.

A. The high cost and lack of celerity in the enforcement of competition rules

443. **The paradox of modernizing competition law: the rising cost of enforcement.** Under the pretext of sanctioning only practices that have a harmful effect on competition or the market, in order to avoid prosecuting behavior that could potentially, albeit uncertainly, produce "beneficial results,"[123] the use of economic analyses has greatly increased tenfold, and the importance of their role in the process of characterizing infringements has been exaggerated.[124] They have sometimes been overused,[125] leading to intense, albeit unnecessary, litigation. The direct consequence of this complexity is an exponential increase in the length of decisions. Between 1979 and 1991, a Commission prohibition decision averaged sixty-eight paragraphs. This number rose to two hundred and thirty-four over the period from 1992 to 2004, and reached five hundred and two between 2005 and 2017. Put another way, the length of decisions has increased more than sevenfold since the original.[126]

---

121 E. Claudel, *Procédures négociées, accessoires ou alternatives à la sanction en droit de la concurrence: Raison garder!*, Concurrences no. 4-2015, art. no. 75896, 61, 64–67, nos. 8–9.

122 D. Bosco, *Le choc des modernisations du droit de la concurrence*, Contrats concurrence consommation (Oct. 2012), repère 9: according to the author, procedural modernization has almost canceled out the substantial modernization of competition law.

123 These are commonly referred to as "type i errors," i.e., "false positives."

124 *See supra*, nos. 331 *et seq.*

125 *See supra*, no. 333

126 P. Ibáñez Colomo & A. Kalintiri, *The Evolution of EU Antitrust Policy: 1966–2017*, 83 The Modern Law Review 321, 348–49 (2020); *compare with* statistics provided by A. C. Witt, The More Economic Approach to EU Antitrust Law 245 (2019).

In this way, the more economic approach, supposed to improve the "efficiency" of competition law, has led to the opposite result: by increasing the cost of implementing the rules, it has reduced, with constant resources, the number of cases that can be prosecuted, and has led to their chronic under-application. It has also led to an increased risk of Commission decisions being overturned by EU judges.[127]

444. **The weakening of Commission decisions by economic analysis.** Fernando Castillo de la Torre, principal legal adviser to the European Commission (DG COMP), recently noted and criticized a fundamental trend: the legality of Commission decisions is often assessed on the basis of what the authority claims to have proven.[128] Thus, if it considers that it has established actual effects, the General Court will verify that this is indeed the case; if it has implemented some kind of test, it will ensure that it has been "conducted rigorously."[129] Furthermore, it is now established case law that when a company produces an economic study, the competition authority cannot exclude its relevance without first examining its probative value.[130]

However, whenever the Commission ventures off the beaten path of the Court's jurisprudence, by demonstrating a point unrelated to the constituent elements of the infringements, the judges should set aside the relevance of the related debates. This, moreover, is what the Court did in a remarkable passage of the *Tomra* judgment. The judges began by recalling that "according to well-established case-law, where some grounds of a decision on their own provide a sufficient legal basis for the decision, any errors in other grounds of the decision have, in any event, no effect on its enacting terms."[131] In this case, the Commission had carried out, as has become its custom,[132] an excessively detailed examination of the effects of the disputed practices.[133] The General Court, taking the view, in line with the Court's case law, that this was not a

127 Castillo de la Torre, *Is the Effects-Based Approach Too Cumbersome? Taking Stock of Recent Practice and Case Law on Article 102 TFEU*, *op. cit.* at 198: "If some of the recent annulments are due to judges 'embracing' much of the 'more economic' approach that the Guidance was meant to embody, a realistic counterfactual is that the Commission would have been more successful in court if the Guidance had not been adopted."

128 *Id.* at 162, n.83.

129 Case T-604/18, Google, ECLI:EU:T:2022:541, para. 644, concerning the performance of an AEC test. We also recall the complexity of the debates concerning the counterfactual test implemented in the *O2* case: the Court of First Instance criticized the Commission for basing its reasoning on the single hypothesis that both operators (O2 and T-Mobile) would have been present and in a competitive situation, whereas it was appropriate, according to the judges, to also consider the situation where O2 could have been "entirely or partially absent from ... market." *See* Case T-328/03, O2 (Germany), ECLI:EU:T:2006:116, paras. 74–79.

130 Case C-680/20, Unilever Italia, ECLI:EU:C:2023:33, paras. 54–55, para. 60, and answer to the second question.

131 Case T-155/06, Tomra Systems, ECLI:EU:T:2010:370, para. 286.

132 *See supra*, nos. 299–300, and the references cited.

133 Comm. EC, Mar. 29, 2006, COMP/E-1/38.113, Prokent-Tomra, paras. 285 and 332. For an extract from the decision, *see supra*, no. 300.

constitutive element, held that it was appropriate to dismiss the plea "as ineffective and it is not necessary to consider whether the evidence adduced by the Commission demonstrated that the agreements in question had actually eliminated competition."[134] It also rightly added that "even if the Commission had made a manifest error of assessment, as the applicants allege, in holding that those agreements actually eliminated competition, the legality of the contested decision would not be affected."[135]

Conversely, admitting that an error of assessment concerning, for example, the characterization of current effects, can justify the annulment of a decision, amounts to substantially increasing, albeit unduly, the standard of proof – because *in law*, only proof of potential effects is required.[136] Since the adoption of the "more economic approach," this phenomenon has led to an increase in the number of decisions annulled by Union courts.[137]

The problem, however, is more pernicious and difficult to pin down than it seems. The complexity of competition law has reached new heights, and it is now a real challenge to distinguish accurately, after reading dozens or even hundreds of pages of a decision, between the arguments that played a decisive role in the qualification process, and those that were merely incidental, or even excessive. However, in order to respect the right to be heard, judges have no choice but to review the entire statement of reasons, when the arguments raised by the defendant companies invite them to do so, and there is doubt as to whether the point raised was important or not in the authority's reasoning. It follows that the most frequent grounds for annulment no longer relate to substantive issues, but to procedural questions.[138] Indeed, "rather than considering the Commission's assessment to be erroneous, the rulings instead find that the Commission did not 'sufficiently' or 'properly' take into account a (supposedly) relevant element, or note the presence of a shortcoming in the process of applying a test or economic model."[139] This perhaps explains why, in the most recent decisions, the Commission has ceased to engage in such detailed analyses of effects as it did at the time of the reform aimed at modernizing

134 Case T-155/06, Tomra Systems, ECLI:EU:T:2010:370, para. 290. The appeal against this judgment was dismissed in its entirety, *see* Case C-549/10 P, Tomra Systems, ECLI:EU:C:2012:221.

135 *Id.*

136 Castillo de la Torre, *Is the Effects-Based Approach Too Cumbersome? Taking Stock of Recent Practice and Case Law on Article 102 TFEU*, *op. cit.* at 162, n. 83: "In my view, the mere fact that in a decision the Commission may have focused on demonstrating 'actual' effects should not affect the threshold against which the judicial review is carried out. If the Commission does not provide enough evidence of actual effects but the evidence is good enough to prove, at least, potential effects, a decision should not be annulled."

137 *Id.* at 148: "Embracing an approach favoured by the Commission has, ironically, probably led to an increase of annulments of Commission decisions." According to the author, one of the reasons for this is that complexity "increases the angles of attack" (*id.* at 198).

138 *Id.* at 192.

139 *Id.*

the competition rules,[140] particularly with regard to cases taking place in digital markets.[141]

The increased cost of enforcing the rules and the risk of having a decision overturned following the modernization of competition law have also prompted authorities to engage more and more frequently in alternative procedures to sanction, which are not, however, a panacea.

B. A critical look at commitment procedures

445. **Excessive and ill-advised use of the commitment procedure.** The commitment procedure was designed to deal "more effectively" with practices for which there was established case law, and for which the competition authorities would not have considered it necessary to impose a penalty.[142] However, following the introduction of this alternative sanction procedure by article 9 of Regulation 1/2003, prohibition decisions gradually became the exception, and commitment decisions the norm.[143] Several authors have noted that this procedure can serve as a convenient shortcut to "close a case for lack of strong evidence";[144] and, in fact, the majority of cases resolved by means of commitments do not concern practices where the existence of an infringement was obvious.[145]

This is not the only criticism that can be leveled at commitment decisions. Indeed, as a "unilateral administrative act with negotiated content,"[146] they are supposed to establish a dialogue between the authorities and the companies, and enable negotiation on the most appropriate means of putting an end to the competition concerns identified. Companies are de facto encouraged to quickly concede the existence of a problem, and to actively try to participate in resolving it without too much discussion of its reality,

---

140 A. C. Witt, *The European Court of Justice and the More Economic Approach to EU Competition Law – Is the Tide Turning?*, 64 The Antitrust Bulletin 172, 213 (2019). The author adds that it is likely "the consequence of trying to find the appropriate balance between accuracy on the one hand and cost-efficient enforcement on the other."

141 *See infra*, nos. 517 *et seq.*

142 Eur. Comm., Commission Notice on Best Practices for the Conduct of Proceedings Concerning Articles 101 and 102 TFEU, 2011 O.J. (C 308) 6, para. 116; in the same vein, ADLC, Communiqué de procédure du 2 mars 2009 relatif aux engagements en matière de concurrence, paras. 6 and 11.

143 F. Jenny, *Worst Decision of the EU Court of Justice: The Alrosa Judgment in Context and Future of Commitment Decisions*, *Fordham* 38 International Law Journal 701, 702 (2015). For statistics on the use of commitment procedures in French law, *see* E. Claudel, *Procédures négociées, accessoires ou alternatives à la sanction en droit de la concurrence: Raison garder!*, Concurrences no. 4-2015, art. no. 75896, 61, 63, no. 4.

144 OECD, Summary of Discussion on the Roundtable on Commitment Decisions in Antitrust Cases, DAF/COMP/M(2016)1/ANN3/FINAL (Nov. 14, 2016), at 6.

145 P. Ibáñez Colomo, The Shaping of EU Competition Law 98–102 and 288–89 (2018); *adde*, Claudel, *Procédures négociées, accessoires ou alternatives à la sanction en droit de la concurrence : Raison garder !*, *op. cit.* at 76, no. 41: "The commitment procedure tends to be used by competition authorities beyond what should, in our view, be its natural boundaries, namely, practices that are clearly (but not seriously) anticompetitive, still in force and likely to be resolved more quickly by a negotiated rather than coercive route, or which, more generally, lend themselves well to freely accepted remedies."

146 ADLC, Les engagements comportementaux 15 (unofficial translation).

so as not to invite the competition authorities to push their investigations too far.[147] The latter have sometimes used their negotiating power to obtain commitments from companies that go beyond what would have been necessary and proportionate to resolve a problem that, because it has not been demonstrated, is never more than assumed – which, moreover, offers the authorities a considerable margin of discretion. The advantage of the procedure – that it does not involve any finding of an infringement, and therefore does not require an in-depth investigation – can then turn into a serious disadvantage when an authority illegitimately limits the commercial freedom of companies and, consequently, competition.[148] Doctrine has pointed out that the commitment procedure can lead to a blurring of boundaries between law and regulation.[149] Indeed, whereas law intervenes after an infringement has been committed (*ex post*), regulation intervenes beforehand (*ex ante*), even before an infringement can be identified.[150] What is more, if everything is negotiable in the minds of companies, the prophylactic function of competition law is reduced to a mere pittance,[151] even though it is already well known that in this field, the commission of an infringement, even when sanctioned by the normal means, can still prove lucrative.[152]

446. **Commitment procedures: an "effective" tool?** While no solution is perfect, a cost-benefit analysis is nonetheless essential. The commitment procedure is not without its shortcomings; at the very least, does it keep its promises? Has it improved the speed with which rules are implemented? Alas, the gain is not the greatest: the average time from initiation of proceedings to adoption of a decision is only seventeen percent longer for the prohibition procedure compared to the commitment procedure.[153] What is more,

---

147 F. Marty & M. Mezaguer, *Quelles garanties pour la procédure d'engagements en droit de la concurrence de l'Union européenne?*, XXX Revue internationale de droit économique 55, 62 (2016).

148 In this sense, *see* F. Jenny, *Worst Decision of the EU Court of Justice: The Alrosa Judgment in Context and Future of Commitment Decisions, Fordham* 38 International Law Journal 701, 755 (2015); OECD, Commitments Decisions: What Makes Them So Attractive? Note by Jean-François Bellis, DAF/COMP/WD(2016)53 (June 7, 2016), at 9; F. Wagner-Von Papp, *Best and Even Better Practices in Commitment Procedures after Alrosa: The Dangers of Abandoning the Struggle for Competition Law*, 49 Common Market Law Review 929, 956–58 (2012); ADLC, Les engagements comportementaux 33 (2019).

149 This risk is denounced, *inter alia*, by: OECD, Commitment Decisions in Antitrust Cases – Note By the BIAC, DAF/COMP/WD(2016)31 (June 8, 2016), at 3; D. Gerard, *Negotiated Remedies in the Modernization Era: The Limits of Effectiveness*, *in* European Competition Law Annual 2013: Effective and Legitimate Enforcement 139, 160–68 (P. Lowe, M. Marquis & G. Monti eds., 2016); F. Wagner-Von Papp, *Best and Even Better Practices in Commitment Procedures after Alrosa: The Dangers of Abandoning the Struggle for Competition Law*, 49 Common Market Law Review 929, 933 (2012); ADLC, Les engagements comportementaux *op. cit.* at 12.

150 On the distinction between these two modes of intervention, *see* N. Dunne, *Between Competition Law and Regulation: Hybridized Approaches to Market Control*, 2 Journal of Antitrust Enforcement 225, 228–31 (2014).

151 E. Claudel, *Procédures négociées, accessoires ou alternatives à la sanction en droit de la concurrence: Raison garder!*, Concurrences no. 4-2015, art. no. 75896, 61; in the same vein, D. Bosco, *What else? Le droit!*, Contrats concurrence consommation (Nov. 2014), comm. 253.

152 *See* G. de Moncuit de Boiscuillé, La faute lucrative en droit de la concurrence (2020).

153 M. Mariniello, *Commitments or Prohibitions? The EU Antitrust Dilemma*, Bruegel Policy Brief no. 1, 1, 4 (2014), no. 2.

monitoring compliance with commitments, sometimes over several years, is as complex as it is costly.[154] Finally, in the absence of a finding of infringement, the victims of anticompetitive practices find it extremely difficult to obtain compensation for the harm they have suffered, and are thus "marginalized."[155] For such a meager result, what have we not sacrificed?

Commitment decisions are adopted out of sight of the courts: since they do not establish an infringement or impose a penalty, they do not constitute an "indictment within the meaning of article 6, paragraph 1, of the European Convention on Human Rights,"[156] and therefore offer very few guarantees to companies. The judicial review carried out is reduced to its simplest form – the standard being that of a manifest error of assessment[157] – and some have stressed that the possibility of a commitment decision being successfully challenged is highly unlikely.[158]

What is more, when an authority can obtain commitments from companies without having to demonstrate the existence of an anticompetitive practice, it can go further than the healthy limits set by jurisprudence, by regulating practices that might not be considered as constituting an infringement by judges. This risk has been identified: the commitment procedure enables the administrative authorities to create a parallel "*soft* jurisprudence,"[159] which, moreover, escapes the minimum guarantees imposed by respect for the rule of law.[160] Advocate General Giovanni Pitruzzella rightly feared that the competition concerns identified by the Commission could be transformed into a "mere *petitio principii*" based on conjecture and general hypotheses, and stressed the risk of undermining the principles of predictability and legality,[161] and of excessive and abusive recourse to this procedure.[162]

---

154 ADLC, Les engagements comportementaux 11–12 (2019) (unofficial translation).

155 E. Claudel, *Procédures négociées, accessoires ou alternatives à la sanction en droit de la concurrence: Raison garder!*, Concurrences no. 4-2015, art. no. 75896, 61, 73–75, nos. 33–36.

156 ADLC, Les engagements comportementaux, *op. cit.* at 121; and in particular Cass. com., Nov. 4, 2008, no. 07-21.275 (Fr.): the preliminary assessment carried out by the competition authority as part of a commitment procedure is not an indictment, as "its purpose is not to prove the reality and imputability of infringements of competition law with a view to sanctioning them." (unofficial translation) *Adde*, on this subject, *see* L. Arcelin, *L'alliance raisonnable entre droit de la concurrence et CEDH*, Revue Lamy de la concurrence no. 11 (Apr. 1, 2017).

157 Case C-441/07 P, Alrosa, ECLI:EU:C:2010:377, para. 120; except where the interests of third parties are affected by the commitments entered into, *see* Case C-132/19 P, Groupe Canal +, ECLI:EU:C:2020:1007.

158 In this sense, *see* H. Schweitzer, *Judicial Review in EU Competition Law*, *in* Research Hanbook on EU Antitrust Law: Enforcement and Procedure 491, 521 (D. Gerard, I. Lianos eds., 2013).

159 W. P. J. Wils, "*Ten Years of Commitment Decisions Under Article 9 of Regulation 1/2003: Too Much of a Good Thing?*," Concurrences, 6th International Conference 'New Frontiers of Antitrust' 10 (2015), https://ssrn.com/abstract=2617580.

160 D. Waelbroeck, *The Development of a New 'Settlement Culture' in Competition Cases: What is Left to the Courts?*, *in* Alternative Enforcement Techniques in EC Competition Law: Settlements, Commitments and Other Novel Instruments 221, 223–24 (C. Gheur & N. Petit eds., 2009).

161 Opinion of Advocate General G. Pitruzzella, Case C-132/19 P, Groupe Canal +, ECLI:EU:C:2020:355, paras. 67 and 70.

162 *Id.*, para. 69.

447. **The pernicious effect of relying on commitment procedures: a renunciation of the development of case law.** In short, the procedural reform adopted in 2003, combined with the modernization movement, has made the law on anticompetitive practices much less clear, without making it more "effective." More perniciously, excessive recourse to the commitment procedure can also be perceived as a deleterious renunciation. Indeed, when competition authorities, by engaging less and less in prohibition procedures, no longer make an effort to substantiate a finding of infringement in the presence of new cases, they hinder a development that is nonetheless essential: the evolution of jurisprudence. The gradual adaptation of competition rules to contemporary issues has thus been compromised on the altar of a short-sighted "efficiency policy," which has also proved ineffective.

And if we are today pointing the finger at the inadequacies of the law on anticompetitive practices, and its inability to effectively resolve the problems posed by the digital economy, it is partly because, over the last twenty years or so, the competition authorities have not sufficiently developed case law solutions. If they had pursued new practices more often, and developed a rationale for linking them to existing legal categories, they would have made a useful contribution, under the supervision of the judges, to the adaptation of the rules to new cases, which would have led, over time, to a gradual alleviation of the burden of proof[163] – because when one form of behavior is the subject of clear case law, the rationale for subsequent cases of a similar nature is necessarily simplified.

However, instead of challenging the substantial complexity and procedural excesses affecting the law on anticompetitive practices, the remedy that was deemed appropriate was, once again, to complicate positive law even further, by adopting a new regulation designed to supplement the existing rules and make up for their alleged shortcomings.

II. The supposed remedy: new rules

448. **An illusory remedy.** For several years now, voices have been raised to denounce the inability of competition law to deal quickly enough with certain "new" practices,[164] in this case those of the powerful, mainly

163 For presumptions of jurisprudential origin, particularly in view of the importance and force of the argument of precedent in the case law of the courts of the European Union (*see supra*, no. 414), are rapidly becoming "quasi-legal presumptions" (on this concept, *see supra*, no. 198).

164 *See ex multis*: R. Podszun, *From Competition Law to Platform Regulation – Regulatory Choices for the Digital Markets Act*, 17 Economics 1, 5–6 (2023), J.-C. Roda, *Le Digital Markets Act (1re partie) – Contrôler les contrôleurs d'accès*, Communication Commerce électronique (Feb. 2023), étude 4, esp. nos. 8–9: the author remarks that the shortcomings pointed out are perhaps exaggerated and wonders whether the authorities are not accentuating these, in order to reinforce the legitimacy of the instrument.

American and Chinese, digital market operators. Despite a lack of consensus as to whether adopting new rules was the most appropriate course of action,[165] the Digital Markets Act came into force at the end of 2022[166] after a tedious legislative process, in order to "complete" the law on anticompetitive practices,[167] by helping to preserve competition in a specific sector.

Because it is the product of expert economic reports,[168] and because it is driven by the illusion that precise, technical rules are more effective than general, abstract ones, it is the culmination of the technocratic drift affecting competition law[169] (**A**). Where will it end? Once the need to turn to the legislator has been established, it is to be feared that every time there is a new development, the legislator will be called upon once again.[170] This is a slippery slope toward murky waters, insofar as this type of regulation, which will in no way prove more effective than traditional competition rules, compromises respect for the guarantees to which, in a state governed by the rule of law, companies are entitled[171] (**B**).

A. The digital markets act: a symbol of the spirit of contemporary competition law

449. **For every supposed novelty, a new law.** While case law on anticompetitive practices had yet to be developed to resolve the competition problems specific to the digital sector,[172] and the new rules introduced by the Digital Markets Act prohibit conduct some of which are reminiscent of cases

---

165 *Ex multis:* O. Budzinski & A. Stöhr, *Competition Policy Reform in Europe and Germany – Institutional Change in the Light of Digitization*, 15 European Competition Journal 15 (2018); W. Kerber, Updating Competition Policy for the Digital Economy? An Analysis of Recent Reports in Germany, UK, EU, and Australia (Sept. 14, 2019), https://ssrn.com/abstract=3469624; J. Crémer, Y.-A. de Montjoye & H. Schweitzer, Competition Policy for the Digital Era 4 (2019): "There is no general answer to the question of whether competition law or regulation is better placed to deal with the challenges arising from digitization of the economy."

166 Regulation (EU) 2022/1925 of the European Parliament and of the Council of Sept. 14, 2022, on Contestable and Fair Markets in the Digital Sector, 2022 O.J. (L 265) 1.

167 *Id.*, recital 10. Indeed, the respective fields of anticompetitive practices law and the Digital Markets Act overlap, *see* P. Larouche & A. de Streel, *The European Digital Markets Act: A Revolution Grounded on Tradition*, 12 Journal of European Competition Law & Practice 542, 543–45 (2021).

168 *See inter alia*: Crémer et al., Competition Policy for the Digital Era, *op. cit.*; F. Scott Morton et al., Committee for the Study of Digital Platforms: Market Structure and Antitrust Subcommittee, Stigler Center for the Study of the Economy and the State (July 1, 2019); J. Furman et al., Unlocking Digital Competition: Report of the Digital Competition Expert Panel (Mar. 2019); L. Cabral et al., The EU Digital Markets Act: A Report from a Panel of Economic Experts (2021).

169 According to one author, "the DMA represents an expansion of the administrative State," *see* N. Petit, *The Proposed Digital Markets Act (DMA): A Legal and Policy Review*, 12 Journal of European Competition Law & Practice 529, 531 (2021).

170 *See* L. Idot, *Protection des consommateurs – Un nouveau pas vers un droit européen de la concurrence déloyale*, Europe (May 2019), alerte 30.

171 For a more detailed study of the risks of non-compliance of the Digital Markets Act with the principles of the rule of law, *see* M.-S. Garnier, *The Rule of Law at Risk: The Dark Side of the Digital Markets Act*, 72–73 ORDO 302 (2022).

172 On this subject, *see infra*, nos. 517 *et seq.*

prosecuted or liable to be prosecuted on the basis of article 102 TFEU,[173] the European legislator chose a different path. This involved taking up some of the objectives already familiar to competition law – "fairness" and "contestability" – and defining new subjects – "gatekeepers"[174] – and subjecting them to a series of obligations drafted in a way that is as technical as it is precise. While it is easy to understand the motivations behind such a regulation, in many respects it is indicative of a contemporary trend: the adoption of increasingly meticulous, technical laws to apprehend what is considered a "novelty."[175]

450. **Economic expertise, the main source of inspiration for technical rules.** The Digital Markets Act has definitively shifted the locus of decision-making to the experts:[176] the rules formulated are not the result of legal debate structured around the question of what would or would not constitute fraudulent conduct,[177] but are aimed at sanctioning what some experts consider to be harmful to competition,[178] despite the absence of any consensus among economists as to whether the evils identified truly constitute problems, and the remedies envisaged actual solutions.[179] What is more, given that the regulation uses terms that have not been the subject of any case law, and which do not fall into the category of major legal concepts, they will be interpreted by the judge without any point of reference, so that their precision is, paradoxically, a source of uncertainty.[180]

451. **A paradox: the decision to abandon the effects-based approach.** Lastly, the Digital Markets Act bypasses the constraints associated with the implementation of articles 101 and 102 TFEU, which now seems to

---

173 In this regard, *see* the explanatory table proposed by M. Debroux, *Nature, objectifs et régime des obligations imposées aux contrôleurs d'accès: Des obligations ex ante et* per se, *vraiment?*, Conference Digital Market Act: Droit de la concurrence et géants du numérique, Concurrences no. 3-2022, art. no. 108068, 66, 69–71; *adde*, M. Behar-Touchais, *L'articulation du DMA avec les autres textes existants*, Conference Digital Market Act: Droit de la concurrence et géants du numérique, Concurrences no. 3-2022, art. no. 108068, 51, 52, no. 1; J. Blockx, The Expected Impact of the DMA on the Antitrust Enforcement of Unilateral Practices 3–4 (Jan. 27, 2023), https://ssrn.com/abstract=4341277.

174 On the author's "largely perfectible" definition of "gatekeepers," *see* D. Bosco, *À propos du concept de "contrôleur d'accès" dans le DMA*, Conference Digital Market Act: Droit de la concurrence et géants du numérique, Concurrences no. 3-2022, art. no. 108068, 61.

175 Cf *supra*, no. 237.

176 Cf. *supra*, no. 428.

177 *See supra*, nos. 404–409.

178 *See supra*, no. 448 (footnote): the aforementioned expert reports express themselves in terms such as "optimized competition system," "self-correcting capacity of digital markets," and seek to assess the "social welfare of advertising," or "measure consumer welfare in a behavioral world." On the economic logic of the Digital Markets Act, *see* G. Colangelo, DMA Begins 2–6 (Dec. 16, 2022), https://ssrn.com/abstract=4292049.

179 On the possible undesirable consequences, from an economic point of view, of the rules enacted by the Digital Markets Act, *see* P. Bentata, *Regulation "gatekeepers": Predictable "unintended consequences" of the DMA for users' welfare*, Competition Forum no. 0031 (2022), https://competition-forum.com.

180 On this topic, *see* J.-L. Bergel, Méthodologie juridique: Fondamentale et appliquée 348 (2018), no. 204. The authors of a report commissioned by the French National Assembly also considered that the text was "rendered illegible by confusing drafting," *see* C. Hennion, Rapport d'information déposé par la Commission des affaires européennes sur le *Digital Markets Act* no. 4409, 9 (July 22, 2021).

be criticized for involving an "individualised assessment" taking into consideration the "actual or potential effects" of behavior, and providing for the possibility for companies to justify them with "efficiency ... arguments."[181] Indeed, the regulation lays down rules enabling the practices of certain companies to be sanctioned "independently from [their] actual ... effects."[182] The offenses it contains fall into the category of commission offenses.[183] These are characterized by the fact that (i) they do not require any result as a constitutive element, and (ii) they do not admit contrary evidence once the material conduct has been established.[184] They are thus much more rigid than the offenses of means provided for in articles 101 and 102 TFEU.

Is it not surprising that the Commission, which worked so hard to make the "effects-based" approach a success, is now happy to scrap it? Would we have needed a supposedly "more effective" regulation if the effects-based approach had not made the law on anticompetitive practices "less effective"? The cure appears worse than the disease: its effectiveness seems illusory, and its implementation risks compromising respect for certain legal guarantees.

B. The digital markets act: a regulation that compromises legal guarantees

452. A regulation **granting significant discretionary power to the Commission and undermining the principle of legal certainty.** Articles 101 and 102 TFEU, articles 101 and 102 TFEU, by virtue of their reliance on general and abstract concepts, are highly flexible and can be easily adapted to novel cases, without generating legal uncertainty.[185] Articles 5 to 7 of the Digital Markets Act, on the other hand, list in detail the behaviors that are prescribed or proscribed. *A priori*, there are two advantages to precisely targeting prohibited practices: to serve an educational purpose by clearly establishing the rules, and to reduce the Commission's margin of discretion. However, the more precise a rule is, the more likely the company subject to it will seek ways to circumvent it.[186] This risk has been anticipated: that is why article 13(4) of the Regulation, entitled "Anti-circumvention," stipulates that gatekeepers must not engage in "any behaviour that undermines effective compliance with the obligations." The list of obligations

181 Regulation (EU) 2022/1925 of the European Parliament and of the Council of Sept. 14, 2022, on Contestable and Fair Markets in the Digital Sector, 2022 O.J. (L 265) 1, recital 10.

182 *Id.*, recital 11.

183 *See supra*, no. 236.

184 *See supra*, no. 237.

185 *See supra*, nos. 410 *et seq.*

186 A. C. Witt, *Platform Regulation in Europe – Per se Rules to the Rescue?*, 18 Journal of Competition Law & Economics 670, 683 (2022).

set out in the Regulation is therefore anything but stable or exhaustive. Furthermore, article 8(1) states that the onus is on the gatekeeper to demonstrate that it has complied with the Regulation, and that it is "effective in achieving the objectives of this Regulation and of the relevant obligation." This provision means that the companies concerned will have to comply not only with the letter of the text, but also with its spirit, even if the objectives in question are not specified.

In addition, because of their precision, the rules of the Digital Markets Act will not be flexible enough to adapt to new practices, which is particularly problematic in a fast-moving sector: the obligations imposed will quickly become outdated, making it necessary to adopt new rules once again. The Regulation thus offers only short-term legal certainty,[187] which has already been undermined for the reasons outlined above. In addition, and no doubt due to the long time needed for any reform through legislation,[188] the Regulation empowers the Commission to adapt, by means of delegated acts[189] and for a tacitly renewable period of five years, both the designation of the subjects of the Regulation and the content of the obligations.

In short, the Digital Markets Act is a monument to complexity designed to compensate for supposed "shortcomings" that the institutional system itself has created, and which confers, without really admitting it, such a wide margin of discretion on the Commission that it will have "a blank slate on which to define the scope of the regime,"[190] which will further reduce the scope of jurisdictional control exercised by the Union's judges.[191]

---

187 Cf. B. Leoni, La Liberté et le droit 33 (2006): "With legislation, we are far from achieving the ideal legal certainty. ... While legislation is almost always certain, i.e., precise and identifiable for as long as it remains in force, people can never be sure that the legislation in force today will still be in force the next morning. A legal system based on legislation means that other people (the legislators) can ... change the way they intervene every day. In this way, individuals are prevented from 'foreseeing the legal consequences of their conduct.'" *Adde*, P. Conte, *La distinction de la légalité formelle et de la légalité matérielle: Ses dits et ses non-dits*, Droit pénal (July 2020), étude 23, no. 8: "[C]utting legality from expediency creates the possibility of opposing them, and thus restores arbitrariness: for what is a solution improvised on the spur of the moment and that could not have been foreseen before the problem arose, but an arbitrary solution?"

188 Note that the Commission's initial proposal was published on December 15, 2020, *see* R. Podszun, Competition in the Digital Economy: What's Next After the Digital Markets Act? Statement for the Economic Committee of the German Parliament (Bundestag) (May 5, 2022), https://ssrn.com/abstract=4096357.

189 It should be noted that delegated acts were introduced into EU law following the adoption of the Lisbon Treaty, and are intended, under article 290 TFEU, to "supplement ... certain *non-essential* elements of the legislative act." However, it is questionable whether the "adaptations" that the Commission can make really concern points that are ancillary to the Digital Markets Act. In this respect, one author has argued that the repeated use of delegated acts has profoundly affected the institutional balance of the Union, as in practice it has involved a one-off transfer of legislative power from the European Parliament and the Council to the Commission, *see* S. Thiery, Les actes délégués en droit de l'Union européenne (2020).

190 P. Ibáñez Colomo, *The Draft Digital Markets Act: A Legal and Institutional Analysis*, 12 Journal of European Competition Law & Practice 561, 562 (2021).

191 *Id.* at 575.

Paragraph 2 – Lack of clarity in competition law

453. **Competition law and the rule of law.** The biggest problem affecting competition law is its lack of clarity: it has become difficult to know what criteria are *actually* taken into consideration to characterize an infringement – a fact that raises legitimate concerns with regard to the rule of law.[192] The problem is all the more worrying in that, in Union law, compliance with the principles it lays down is most often checked against the yardstick of a formalistic approach. The adoption of a law is thus presumed *proportionate* the moment it pursues objectives of general interest, without any substantial examination of the relevance of those objectives being necessary, given that the Union legislator is vested with a "broad discretion" involving "political, economic and social choices."[193] Similarly, a rule is deemed to satisfy the principle of legality on condition that it is in writing and the subject of interpretative case law, without the need for a concrete analysis of its accessibility, readability and conformity with more general principles.[194] There is then a great risk that the rule of law will become "a vague simulacrum."[195]

Indeed, if the principle of legality requires competition law to be intelligible and consistent with the principles of legal reasoning, these two requirements are compromised by the effects-based approach (**I**). While companies would theoretically be entitled to invoke non-compliance with this principle when the implementation of the rules does not appear sufficiently predictable, the argument of reasonable doubt as to the scope of the law is, in most cases, categorically rejected (**II**).

I. Competition law put to the test of the principle of legality

454. **The "effects-based approach": a myth and a dead end.** There are "reasons to believe that the economic approach has largely remained within the

192 This should give cause for concern, even among economists, given that respect for the rule of law is said to promote "economic efficiency." On this point, *see* the opinion published by the EESC, THE RULE OF LAW AND ITS IMPACT ON ECONOMIC GROWTH, ECO/511 (Feb. 20, 2020).

193 Case C-477/14, Pillbox 38 (UK), ECLI:EU:C:2016:324, para. 49; *adde*, on this theme, A. Portuese, *Principle of Proportionality as Principle of Economic Efficiency*, 19 EUROPEAN LAW JOURNAL 612 (2013).

194 According to Chaïm Perelman, a rule becomes arbitrary if it cannot be justified on the basis of the coherence of the system as a whole – i.e., by more general principles – *see* C. PERELMAN, DE LA JUSTICE 68–72 (1945). *Adde*, J. CARBONNIER, DROIT ET PASSION DU DROIT SOUS LA V[E] RÉPUBLIQUE 42 (1996): "If a government passes a law to ... institute expropriation judges who will find themselves mentally closer to the administration than to the citizens, it is not stepping outside the bounds of the rule of law, but it is disregarding its spirit."

195 M. Villey, *Aristote le Juste*, LE MONDE, Dec. 9–10, 1984, at XII.

doctrinal field."[196] Indeed, despite the apparent doctrinal shift and the omnipresence of the "effects-based approach" in the discourse on competition law, the latter has not succumbed to the sirens of modernity.[197] Nevertheless, the discrepancy between what is said about competition law and what competition law is – in other words, the gap that has opened up between theory and practice – seriously undermines the clarity of the rules and, consequently, legal certainty (**A**). Moreover, even if the "effects-based approach" were to be adopted in practice, i.e., if it were to be endorsed by the Court of Justice, it would infringe the principle of foreseeability – which, at a time when some are noting the "fundamentalization" of competition law "under the combined effect of the European Convention and the Charter of Fundamental Rights,"[198] gives rise to legitimate concerns (**B**). In short, the effects-based approach is, *de lege lata*, nothing more than a myth in which belief ought to be relinquished, and, *de lege ferenda*, a path that cannot be taken without compromising respect for the principles of the rule of law.

A. The gap between theory and practice: a source of opacity in competition rules

455. **Effects-based theory: myth or reality?** Let it be stated clearly: the effects-based approach is a myth masquerading as reality. The only time that effects played a real role was in the nineteenth century, when the *legislator* established them as a constitutive element of the offense of coalition in article 419 of the 1810 Penal Code – and we know the theoretical difficulties and practical ineffectiveness this led to.[199] Article 59 *bis* of the 1945 French ordinance no longer required proof,[200] and a study of the Commission's decision-making practice shows that the effects were never, and are not today, required to characterize the offense.[201] In short, in European competition law, effects are not a constituent element of competition infringements. Why has it taken so much development to

196 D. Bosco, *Regard sur la postmodernisation de l'abus de position dominante*, *in* 1 Laurence Idot: Concurrence et Europe – Liber Amicorum 25, 27 (C. Lemaire & F. Martucci eds., 2022). In the same vein, *see* O. Fréget, La concurrence: Une idée toujours neuve en Europe et en France 257 (2015): "For the most part, competition law, when it reaches the level of the Court of Justice, has been little influenced by these approaches. The Court consistently reaffirms that the purpose of competition law is to protect competition, conceding at most that the effect on competition must be established, but always in a very conceptual way."

197 However, the difference between the Commission's decision-making practice and the case law of the European courts is not new. As long ago as 1977, Lazar Focsaneanu criticized the discrepancy between case law and the Commission's "politico-economic exegesis," *see* L. Focsaneanu, *La notion d'abus dans le système de l'article 86 du Traité instituant la Communauté économique européenne*, *in* La réglementation du comportement des monopoles et entreprises dominantes en droit communautaire 324, 372 (J. A. Van Damme ed., 1977).

198 E. Claudel, *Les sources vives du droit de la concurrence (Étude du droit européen et français des pratiques anticoncurrentielles)*, *in* Mélanges en l'honneur du Professeur Claude Lucas de Leyssac 57, 106 (2018).

199 *See supra*, nos. 99–100; this is also the reason why article 419 was reformed in 1926, *see supra*, no. 102.

200 *See supra*, nos. 128–129.

201 *See supra*, no. 277.

demonstrate something so simple? For several decades now, there has been a profound discrepancy between theory and practice, between rhetoric and reality, in the law of anticompetitive practices – a discrepancy that has become even more pronounced with the modernization movement.

456. **The "modernization" of competition rules: a politico-economic ambition of the Commission with no normative scope.** With the modernization of competition rules, the "effects" seemed to take center stage: they have since monopolized the stage, attracting all the attention. But what are the *legal foundations* of "modernization"? They are inconsistent, to say the least, because they are "soft": the more economic approach has no other source than the positions taken by parts of doctrine, and by the Commission, which has never resorted to anything other than "soft law" in support of its reform ambitions. Indeed, the Commission never intended to propose a genuine reform of "hard law," i.e., articles 101 and 102 TFEU, which would have necessitated a legislative procedure,[202] and which was the only route likely to bring about in-depth changes to the definition and implementation of competition rules. Moreover, the very idea that such a far-reaching reform could be carried out by means of communications and guidelines is in itself open to criticism, insofar as, in compliance with democratic principles, it would necessarily have implied calling on the EU legislator.[203] However, the modernization of article 101 is based on guidelines,[204] which are supposed to clarify the interpretation of its paragraph 3; that of article 102 on "guidelines"[205] supposed to be only procedural and not substantive, aimed at informing companies on the use the institution intends to make of its discretionary power to initiate proceedings[206], and not at "constitute[ing] a statement of the law."[207]

457. **The practical implications of "modernization": undermining the clarity of competition rules.** These positions, by appearing to require proof of effects or advocating the systematic mobilization of certain economic tests, went further than the case law required to establish an infringement[208] – which

202 A. C. Witt, The More Economic Approach to EU Antitrust Law 250 (2019).

203 Recall the European Parliament's comments on the Commission's use of soft law, even before the publication of its Guidelines on abuse of a dominant position. *See* Eur. Parl., Motion for a Resolution on the Legal and Institutional Implications of the Use of 'Soft Law' Instruments, A6-0259/2007 (June 28, 2007), recital X: "[W]hereas, where the Community has legislative competence but there seems to be a lack of political will to introduce legislation, the use of soft law is liable to circumvent the properly competent legislative bodies, may flout the principles of democracy and the rule of law under Article 6 of the EU Treaty, and also those of subsidiarity and proportionality under Article 5 of the EC Treaty, and may result in the Commission's acting *ultra vires*."

204 Comm. EC, Guidelines on the Application of Article 81(3) of the Treaty, 2004 O.J. (C 101) 97.

205 Comm. EC, Guidance on the Commission's Enforcement Priorities in Applying Article 82 of the EC Treaty to Abusive Exclusionary Conduct by Dominant Undertakings, 2009 O.J. (C 45) 7.

206 *Id.*, para. 2.

207 *Id.*, para. 3.

208 *See* in particular A. C. Witt, The More Economic Approach to EU Antitrust Law 292 (2019): "*De facto*, if not *de lege*, the Guidance Paper reduces the scope of Article 102 in a manner that is incompatible with the Court's interpretation of the provision."

may have suggested that the Commission's decision-making practice was charting a different course than the Court's.[209] In truth, since modernization, the Commission has been placed in an uncomfortable position: it faces an intractable dilemma stemming from the ambiguity surrounding the normative scope of soft law.[210]

On the one hand, while the Commission's guidelines are not binding on EU judges or Member States,[211] the Commission is bound by the case law of the European Court of Justice.[212] The hierarchy of norms must not be overlooked: it is up to the judges to interpret competition infringements, to contribute to their definition, and to determine the criteria for their characterization.

But on the other hand, the Court considers that "although those measures may not be regarded as *rules of law* which the administration is always bound to observe, they nevertheless form *rules of practice from which the administration may not depart* in an individual case without giving reasons that are compatible with the principle of equal treatment."[213] This perhaps explains why the Commission has, in practice, reported evidence of effects that were not required by law: in reality, it had no choice but to be either unfaithful to case law in order to be faithful to its doctrine, or unfaithful to its doctrine in order to be faithful to case law… We know what this dilemma has led to: a drastic increase in the cost of implementing competition rules, and the concomitant weakening of Commission decisions.[214]

If modernization is anything to go by, it has led to a loss of clarity in the rules,[215] since it has contributed to casting a shadow of doubt over the *actual* constituent elements of offenses. This has led to three problems. Firstly, competition law has been reinterpreted by the Commission

---

209 L. Lovdahl Gormsen, Why the European Commission's Enforcement Priorities on Article 82 EC Should Be Withdrawn 1, 6 (2010), https://ssrn.com/abstract=2400402.

210 For an enlightened look at the normativity and legitimacy of soft law, *see*: E. Claudel, *Les sources vives du droit de la concurrence (Étude du droit européen et français des pratiques anticoncurrentielles)*, *in* MÉLANGES EN L'HONNEUR DU PROFESSEUR CLAUDE LUCAS DE LEYSSAC 57, 72–80 (2018).

211 Case C-360/09, Pfeiderer, ECLI:EU:C:2011:389, para. 21; Case C-226/11, Expedia, ECLI:EU:C:2012:795, para. 29.

212 *See* in particular the Opinion of Advocate General J. Kokott, delivered on Apr. 14, 2011, in Case C-109/10 P, Solvay, ECLI:EU:C:2011:256, paras. 20–21: the applicants had repeatedly relied on a Commission communication. The Advocate General rightly took the view that this "has no bearing on the assessment of the present appeal," since "even if its administrative practice were to change, *the Commission would still have to act within the framework prescribed for it by the Treaties as interpreted by the Court*" (emphasis added).

213 Case C-189/02 P, Dansk Rørindustri, ECLI:EU:C:2005:408, para. 209; Case C-167/04 P, JCB Service, ECLI:EU:C:2006:594, para. 207 (emphasis added).

214 *See supra*, no. 444.

215 Indeed, as some authors have noted, recourse to soft law "generates considerable legal insecurity among its recipients. Indeed, because [these soft law texts] emanate from authorities vested with sanctioning power, they create confusion among litigants, tossed back and forth between soft reality and the feeling of a hard law in the making," *see* E. Claudel & B. Thullier, *Regard sur le droit mou*, REVUE DE JURISPRUDENCE COMMERCIALE 4, 6 (Jan.-Feb. 2006).

outside any legislative procedure, which raises legitimate concerns about respect for the democratic process.[216] Secondly, this solitary revolution is, in some respects, in direct contradiction with the case law of the Court of Justice – which raises questions with regard to the principle of the rule of law and respect for the hierarchy of norms,[217] and makes it difficult both for companies to grasp their meaning, and for national competition authorities to interpret them coherently. Finally, the wave of modernization has brought with it a part of the legal doctrine. If we consider the role of legal doctrine in describing, organizing and presenting the rules,[218] it is regrettable that some authors were quick to accept this paradigm shift, without questioning its reality or relevance. The doctrine has thus participated, willy-nilly, in the recognition of the effects-based approach as the undisputed dogma of competition law reasoning.[219] Yet, this approach could have provoked a strong reaction from legal experts. Because it undermines the foreseeability of the rules, it should have been vigorously opposed.

B. The effects-based approach: a potential threat to the predictability of the standard

458. **The variability of economic theories on competition.** It hardly needs to be demonstrated that there has been a rapid succession of different, even contradictory, economic theories on competition. A glance at an economics textbook is enough to be persuaded. We learn that "while competition can be *defined by its consequences*, it is more difficult to identify its characteristics."[220] Indeed, from the model of pure and perfect competition to those of duopoly and oligopoly, from the structuralist approach to the contestability of markets, from the Harvard School to the Chicago School, from efficiency to wealth maximization, from consumer surplus to total welfare, from the holistic method to methodological individualism, from industrial economics to game theory, from the neoclassical current to the nebulous "more economic approach," from the "static" point of view to the "dynamic" perspective…[221] it is easy to get lost. Indeed, it has recently

---

216 B. Wardhaugh, Competition, Effects and Predictability: The Rule of Law and the Economic Approach to Competition 182 (2020).

217 *Id.* at 113–15.

218 It goes without saying that doctrine also has a role to play in proposing improvements to the legal system, but it should indicate that it is taking a *lege ferenda* approach.

219 On doctrinal production as an institutionalized practice, and the tendency of authors to follow the dominant paradigm, *see* P. Schlag, *Spam Jurisprudence, Air Law, and the Rank Anxiety of Nothing Happening (A Report on the State of the Art)*, 97 Georgetown Law Journal 803, 806 (2009): "I am afraid that many people do follow the dominant paradigm simply because … well, it is the dominant paradigm."

220 E. Combe, Économie et politique de la concurrence 1 (2nd ed. 2020) (emphasis added).

221 This is only a summary of the best-known theories. For an overview, *see* Combe, Économie et politique de la concurrence, *op. cit.* at 1–58. For more details, *see* D. Hildebrand, The Role of Economic Analysis in EU Competition Law: The European School (4th ed. 2016).

been suggested that reliance on a "complexity science" be considered to overcome the limitations of existing analytical frameworks.[222] It follows that, for a jurist, it is no sign of weakness to acknowledge that it is difficult to clearly understand the substance of the matter, for want of sufficient expertise. How could it be otherwise? Economists themselves do not agree, either on the definition or on the virtues and limits of competition.[223] What is more, while there is a growing body of economic thought, its increasing volume and rigor "fail to dispel the impression of a lack of robustness and the absence of a unified vision of all the dimensions of competition."[224]

While the instability of economic theories is not in itself open to criticism – any science progresses by calling into question its acquired knowledge[225] – their versatility nevertheless raises the question of whether a *standard* that, to deserve its name, needs stability[226] can rest on a basis as unstable as shifting sands. If competition rules were truly based on an "effects-based approach" of any kind, the discipline would quickly be faced with a major problem: its non-compliance with the principle of legal certainty.[227] Indeed, if this approach were to be adopted at the stage of defining the rules, their medium-term predictability would be compromised; if it were to guide their implementation entirely, legal certainty would be undermined in the short term, going so far as to call into question the existence of competition "rules."

459. **Medium-term predictability: the harmful consequences of the effects-based approach to defining infringements.** If the effects-based approach were to be used to identify anti-competitive behavior by creating normative presumptions of illegality, then the coherence of solutions and the permanence of qualification criteria would quickly be undermined. Indeed, despite modernization, the definition of infringements has remained based, since the origins of the discipline,[228] on a legal concept – *dol*.[229] This indeterminate notion is the common thread linking all decisions: it is *enduring*, and makes it possible to apprehend all anti-competitive behavior in *a unitary*

---

222 N. Petit & T. Schrepel, Complexity-Minded Antitrust (June 29, 2022), https://ssrn.com/abstract=4050536. For a critique of this proposal, *see* P. Bentata & P. Garello, Complexity-Minded Antitrust: Taking Theories Seriously (Feb. 28, 2023), https://ssrn.com/abstract=4368392.

223 D. Encaoua & R. Guesnerie, Politiques de la concurrence 10 (2006).

224 *Id.* at 13.

225 In economics, however, the problem is the lack of consensus on the criteria for refuting a theory, *see supra*, no. 117.

226 Indeed, the requirement of legal certainty and predictability "implies a certain stability of the law applicable to a given situation", *see* P. Beauvais, *Le droit à la prévisibilité en matière pénale dans la jurisprudence des cours européennes*, Archives de politique criminelle no. 1, 3, 11 (2007), no. 29.

227 On this subject, *see* C. Prieto, *La sécurité juridique dans le droit de la concurrence*, *in* Sécurité juridique et droit économique 299, 313–14 (L. Boy, J.-B. Racine & F. Siiriainen eds., 2010); *adde*, M. Malaurie-Vignal, *Logique économique et logique juridique*, Contrats concurrence consommation (Nov. 2005), étude 20.

228 *See supra*, esp. no. 77

229 *See supra*, nos. 404 *et seq.*

manner, in other words, to discover the *coherence* of solutions. However, if the infringement were defined by its effects, since these effects are determined by the yardstick of unstable theories, the corpus of jurisprudential solutions would itself be unstable, and the jurist would soon be unable to find any criterion enabling the various cases to be linked together.[230] This is because the effects-based approach and legal reasoning are based on a different logic, which sometimes makes it difficult to reconcile them.

Think of the Chicago School thesis, which argued that it was pointless to crack down on agreements. The idea was that if parties to an agreement were cheaters, they would eventually betray their own commitments – hence the short-lived nature of agreements and the economic inefficiency of spending resources to pursue them. However, subsequent analyses have shown that their existence can be sustained over time.[231] It follows that if jurists had adopted the economist's point of view, they would have refrained from prohibiting practices that are traditionally among the most serious.

The example of predatory pricing is also illuminating: this strategy was already condemned in the nineteenth century, as clearly contrary to the spirit of competition. Indeed, temporarily lowering prices in order to exclude a competitor, with the aim of subsequently raising them again and again, has always been deemed to constitute a *maneuver*. The legal analysis ends here. As for economists, they will ask whether such a strategy can have harmful effects.[232] In the absence of barriers to entry, once a competitor has been ousted, the high prices charged by the monopolist will immediately encourage other competitors to enter the market, thereby restoring competition. The repression of predatory pricing would therefore stem from a misunderstanding of the nature of competition, and would also enable "inefficient firms" to prevent the dominant firm from lowering its prices, and if necessary to file a complaint against the latter with the sole aim of obtaining compensation.[233] Two criticisms can be leveled at these arguments. Firstly, what about the harm suffered by the competitor who has been unfairly excluded? Admittedly, it may soon be succeeded by other companies, but was it not *entitled* to continue to exist and, once excluded from the market, to demand compensation? Secondly, economists have subsequently refined their views on predatory strategies and, by means of sophisticated models, now seem to agree on their potential

230 Cf. D. Danet, *Le droit antitrust doit-il être "économiquement correct"?*, Dalloz Affaires no. 43, 1370, 1374 and 1375–76 (1996).

231 On this subject, *see* C. Prieto, *Loyauté du commerce et droit européen de la concurrence*, Revue des affaires européennes no. 2, 299, 305 (2011), no. 14.

232 On "what economists see" when they observe case law, and the divergences between the economist's and the judge's gaze, *see* A.-L. Sibony, *La jurisprudence de la Cour au prisme de la science économique*, *in* Dans la fabrique du droit européen: Scènes, acteurs et publics de la Cour de justice des Communautés européennes 171, 185–90 (P. Mbongo & A. Vauchez eds., 2009), and the examples mentioned.

233 *See also* Combe, Économie et politique de la concurrence, *op. cit.* at 322–28, nos. 180–183.

harmfulness.[234] This means that if judges had listened to economic theories, they would have, within the space of a few decades, condemned, then acquitted, then condemned once again the same behavior.[235]

In reality, qualifying behavior by its consequences, when these consequences are determined by "scientific" theories or ideological biases,[236] necessarily leads to anarchy. Imagine a court composed successively of judges sympathetic to neo-Brandeisian theories, then of others of Chicago School persuasion, and finally of degrowth-oriented ecologists. They will have to decide whether a given practice is anticompetitive: each will put forward a different argument. If jurisprudence were formed in this way, would it still deserve the name of jurisprudence? There would be no stability, no predictability, no real criteria – discretion would be definitively replaced by arbitrariness. Behavior would be sanctioned sometimes because it had a negative effect on the structure of competition, sometimes because it contributed to the protection of the environment, then sanctioned again because it produced inefficiencies detrimental to consumer welfare, and finally valued because it was found to promote total welfare.

460. **Short-term predictability: the harmful consequences of the effects-based approach at the rule implementation stage.** While the effects-based approach would generate medium-term instability in the definition of offenses, it would, if used as an exclusive guide at the rule implementation stage, lead to the very existence of rules being called into question. Indeed, the existence of a rule presupposes a certain degree of abstraction and generality – the casuistic reasoning resulting from the confrontation between general principles and particular cases, these general principles themselves being able, in matters where jurisprudence plays an important role, to be inferred from the comparison between several particular cases. If every case were to be resolved by applying tests designed to prove that a particular behavior produces a particular consequence, by means of expert analysis, each decision, insofar as it would be based solely on criteria of expediency and circumstances that vary from case to case and are independent of the company's will, would collapse inward on itself:[237] it would be impossible to generalize, and it would become impossible to infer a

234 *Id.* at 328–48, nos. 184–191.

235 *Compare with* what happened in the U.S., *see* M. E. Stucke, *Does the Rule of Reason Violate the Rule of Law?*, 22 Loyola Consumer Law Review 15, 21 (2009): "Under the Court's flawed economic theories, antitrust standards will continue to stray further from rule-of-law principles. Evolving (and disputed) economic theory cannot provide the requisite rules of civil and criminal illegality …Each new economic 'wisdom' can affect criminal liability."

236 *See supra*, no. 429.

237 *See* O. Fréget, La concurrence: Une idée toujours neuve en Europe et en France 250 (2015); *adde*, O. Fréget, *Le respect de la concurrence libre et non faussée est-il une finalité ou un moyen*?, Concurrences no. 3-2016, art. no. 80007, 1, 3: "[T]he claim of a rule that adjusts depending on the effect produced by its violation is legally inconsistent – not to call it a 'legal oxymoron.' If the rule reveals itself in its violation, it means it either does not pre-exist, or exists only marginally, and thus is not a rule at all… . Wanting a flexible, self-adjusting rule can, in reality, amount to not wanting any rules whatsoever."

standard from it.[238] Companies would no longer be able to know whether or not a given behavior violated the rules, since it would be the unforeseen consequences of an act that would label it, on a case-by-case basis, black or white. It would be like a thief stealing from a safe only being judged guilty if the judge found treasure inside, or like fouls only being called depending on the outcome of the match. Moreover, the European Court of Human Rights has ruled that a criminal offense cannot be justified by a "utilitarian justification."[239] The growing recognition of fundamental rights also means that the principles of culpability, foreseeability and legality can be invoked by companies, which cannot therefore be penalized either on the basis of an unstable rule, or because of the unforeseeable consequences of their behavior.

II. Companies invoking the principle of legality

461. **Predictability and reasonable doubt regarding the law.** As a result of the convergence between common law and civil law systems, driven by the jurisprudence of the European Court of Human Rights, the notion of criminal legality has undergone a profound transformation: legality is no longer entirely embedded in the law but must now be perfected through case law interpretation. This development is not without legitimate cause for concern.[240] For this reason, the principle of legality implies, even more than in the past, respect for the principle of foreseeability,[241] which has long been the subject of attention,[242] and is currently receiving increasing attention under the influence of the growing importance of fundamental

---

238 This is what led Bruno Oppetit to write that competition law "follows, contrary to classical legal discourse, a factualist and inductive line of reasoning that leads to a decision of pure expediency,... yet we know to what arbitrariness, to what subjectivity, such casuistry leads," *see* B. Oppetit, Droit et modernité 180 (1998); report by C. Champaud, *Les caractères du droit de la concurrence*, JurisClasseur Concurrence consommation (1991), fasc. 30, no. 79: "The factualist and inductive approach of competition law poses a real fundamental problem with regard to our national and even continental legal traditions."

239 Neste v. Russia, App. no. 69042/01 (ECtHR June 3, 2004), at 10.

240 *See* P. Conte, *Principe de la légalité criminelle: Quelques airs nouveaux sur des paroles anciennes*, Droit pénal (June 2020), étude 17, no. 5: according to the author, the traditional conception of criminal legality has been "weakened," because whereas previously "the principle was considered to be respected only on condition that the criminal legislator enacted provisions allowing the citizen to know, without hesitation, the boundaries of prohibition," it is now the citizen's duty to fill the gaps left by the legislative process – including those stemming from its mediocrity – and to evaluate the '*risks*' of their conduct. Legality, once synonymous with certainty for the citizen, has been replaced by legality defined by doubt – if not arbitrariness.

241 R. Sicurella & M. Costa, *Legality*, *in* General Principles for a Common Law Criminal Framework in the EU: A Guide for Legal Practitioners 3, 12–13 (R. Sicurella et al. eds., 2017): legality also implies non-retroactivity, the prohibition of interpretation by analogy, and extensive interpretation. Previously, the Court of Justice had put in place "avoidance strategies," as well as "substitution strategies" aimed at not fully recognizing the full range of procedural and substantive guarantees for companies. On this phenomenon and the gradual abandonment of these strategies, *see* T. Bombois, La protection des droits fondamentaux des entreprises en droit européen répressif de la concurrence 64–83 (2012).

242 Its respect stems from recognition of the principles of the rule of law. On this theme, among a wealth of literature: for a list of rule of law criteria, *see* Venice Commission, Rule of Law Checklist, CDL-AD (2016) 007 (Mar. 18, 2016); for a historical perspective, *see* J.-Y. Morin, *La 'prééminence du droit' dans l'ordre juridique européen*, *in* Theory of International Law at the Threshold of the 21th Century: Essays in Honour of

rights.[243] In short, the aim is to ensure that the discretion inherent in any interpretation does not turn into arbitrariness, so that the addressees of the rule can know, at the moment they act, whether or not their conduct is lawful (**A**). Indeed, it would be artificial to consider that a rule has been intentionally infringed,[244] if its content is too unclear, or its implementation too unpredictable to be known – in which case, the excusable error regarding the prohibition must be recognized[245] (**B**). In view of the lack of clarity in competition law,[246] it is necessary to ask: if the implementation of the rules becomes so complex as to render them unintelligible and, consequently, unpredictable, can we still say that the principle of legality is genuinely upheld?

A. Requirements Relating to the Foreseeability of the Rule

462. **The importance of predictable rules in competition law.** "The very essence of the rule is to create order; the arbitrariness that dictates the solutions to individual cases leads, almost necessarily, to chaos."[247] The rule is a source of security and freedom: it enables each individual to know the sphere within which they can act freely,[248] and to anticipate the reactions of others.[249] And yet, freedom is the presupposition of competition:[250] it is therefore easy to understand the importance of rule predictability in this area. What is more, the clearer a rule is, the more it fulfills its pedagogical function, and the more likely it is to be respected – if individuals know what is forbidden, they are less inclined to break it.

Krzysztof Skubiszewski 643, 646–56 (1996); more particularly on the requirement of foreseeability, *see* P. Wachsmann, *La prééminence du droit dans la jurisprudence de la Cour européenne des droits de l'homme*, *in* Le droit des organisations internationales: Recueil d'études à la mémoire de Jacques Schwob 241, 664–77 (1997).

243 Sicurella & Costa, *Legality*, *op. cit.* at 11–12.

244 The mental element is required in anticompetitive practices law by Regulation 1/2003, and more generally in Union law, by the principle of culpability (*see supra*, no. 203), which derives from a cross-reading of arts. 7 and 6(2) ECHR and arts. 48(1) and 49 of the Charter of Fundamental Rights of the European Union. On this topic, *see* Opinion of Advocate General J. Kokott, Case C-501/11 P, Schindler, ECLI:EU:C:2013:248, paras. 114–115; *adde*, Case C-295/12 P, Telefónica, ECLI:EU:C:2014:2062, paras. 146–149.

245 R. Sicurella, Nulla poena sine culpa*: Un véritable principe droit européen?*, Revue de science criminelle et de droit pénal comparé 15 (2002).

246 *See supra*, nos. 455–457.

247 J. Rivero, *L'État moderne peut-il être encore un État de droit?*, Annales de la faculté de droit de Liège 65, 68 (1957).

248 *Id.*; *adde*, at 80: "[T]he more the administration undertakes, the more its actions shape the framework within which private activity operates, which can only flourish in a minimum of security; individuals commit themselves only when they can foresee and assess the consequences of their actions. Consequently, if the growing reach of the administration into daily life resulted in arbitrariness, i.e., the unpredictability of the consequences of the act performed by the individual, the results would be disastrous for "the functioning of society"; yet submission to the rule has the virtue of making the behavior of power, to a large extent, predictable."

249 On this subject, *see* B. Deffains & S. Ferey, Agir et juger: Comment les économistes pensent le droit 59–61 (2010).

250 *See supra*, no. 386.

Finally, since the threat of sanction is intended to influence the conduct of its addressees, it can only relate to those consequences of their actions that can be foreseen, since, by definition, the unforeseeable cannot be prevented.[251]

463. **Requirements relating to the quality of the rule of law.** The legal system requires that the addressee of a rule be able to foresee, to a reasonable degree, the consequences of a given act in order to regulate their conduct, in other words, to determine their behavior knowingly.[252] This assessment leads to a "shift in the center of gravity" of the analysis: foreseeability is evaluated not only by the existence of a written rule, but also by its capacity to be known and understood by its addressees.[253] In the *Sud Fondi* judgment, the European Court of Human Rights expressly recognized that article 7 of the Convention requires "a *link of an intellectual nature (conscience and will)*" to punish the perpetrator of an offense, as it would be "inconsistent, on the one hand, to require an accessible and foreseeable legal basis and, on the other, to allow a person to be considered 'guilty' and 'punished' when they were not in a position to know the criminal law."[254]

The principle of legality therefore requires "the law to define clearly offences and the penalties sanctioning them,"[255] clarity being assessed not only in terms of the text of the law, but also in terms of the case law interpreting it.[256] Article 7 therefore does not prohibit "the gradual clarification of the rules,"[257] unless the result of the interpretation was unforeseeable at the time the offense was committed[258] – the solution adopted must be "consistent with the essence of the offence."[259] Thus, the existence of a power of interpretation does not *in itself* run counter to the requirement of foreseeability, "provided that the scope of the discretion and the manner of its exercise are indicated with sufficient clarity, having regard to the legitimate

251 F. A. Hayek, Droit, législation et liberté: Une nouvelle formulation des principes libéraux de justice et d'économie politique 66 (R. Audouin trans., PUF, 2nd ed. 2013).

252 X. Souvignet, La prééminence du droit dans le droit de la Convention européenne des droits de l'Homme 286–87 (2012).

253 *Id.* at 287.

254 Sud Fondi v. Italy, App. no. 75909/01, ¶ 116 (ECtHR Jan. 20, 2009) (unofficial translation); for a commentary, *see* R. Sicurella, *Développer une culture pénale européenne: De l'européanisation des principes fondamentaux du droit pénal à une théorie "européenne" de la responsabilité pénale*, 1 Revue de science criminelle et de droit pénal comparé 1, 14–15 (2020).

255 Case C-413/08 P, Lafarge, ECLI:EU:C:2010:346, para. 94. On the relationship between the precision of penal rules and sentencing, *see* F. Palazzo, *Précision de la loi pénale et certitude de la peine: Principes et expériences*, in Humanisme et justice: Mélanges en l'honneur de Geneviève Giudicelli-Delage 633 (2016).

256 Case C-413/08 P, Lafarge, ECLI:EU:C:2010:346, para. 94.

257 Case C-189/02 P, Dansk Rørindustri, ECLI:EU:C:2005:408, para. 217; Case C-194/14 P, AC-Treuhand, ECLI:EU:C:2015:717, para. 41.

258 *Id.*, para. 218.

259 S.W. v. United Kingdom, App. no. 20166/92, ¶ 36 (ECtHR Nov. 22, 1995); Kononov v. Latvia, App. no. 36376/04, ¶ 185 (ECtHR May 17, 2010).

aim in question, *to give the individual adequate protection against arbitrary interference.*"[260]

This protection implies prohibiting the use of overly vague notions and criteria in the interpretation of a provision,[261] and the clear establishment of its constituent elements[262] – for if the law is excessively complex, it becomes unintelligible. It would then be unrealistic to claim that its implementation is foreseeable,[263] and it would then become necessary to accept the argument of reasonable doubt as to scope, should it be invoked by the company under scrutiny.

B. Acknowledging reasonable doubt as to the scope of the law

464. **A delicate balance between the presumption of knowledge of the law and the recognition of a legitimate doubt as to its scope.** If, in the early days of the Community, the concept of abuse of a dominant position was perceived by the drafters of the Treaty as a novelty[264] that would be difficult to distinguish from lawful behavior,[265] the scope of anticompetitive agreements was already well circumscribed. In any case, competition rules have now been interpreted by the Court for decades: thus, it may seem surprising at first glance that reasonable doubt could still persist as to their scope. However, the complexity of the subject raises the question of whether companies are still capable of assessing the lawfulness or unlawfulness of their strategies. Indeed, the predictability of competition law is "far from proven," particularly in view of the "economic analyses" used, which can "make the outcome of litigation uncertain"[266] and, above all, in view of the gap between the discourse on competition law and the reality of litigation.[267]

The situation is delicate: ideally, there should be "a clear correlation between the degree of foreseeability of a criminal-law provision and the

260 Case C-413/08 P, Lafarge, ECLI:EU:C:2010:346, para. 94.

261 Liivik v. Estonia, App. no. 12157/05, ¶¶ 96–104 (ECtHR, June 25 2009).

262 Dallas v. United Kingdom, App. no. 38395/12, ¶¶ 72–75 (ECtHR, Feb. 11, 2016).

263 Sicurella & Costa, *Legality*, *op. cit.* at 24–25.

264 This is rather surprising since, as a reminder, in the past no distinction was made between anticompetitive practices committed collectively or individually, *see* esp. *supra*, no. 74.

265 Cf. Eur. Parl., Committee on the Internal Market, Summary record of the meeting of Wednesday Jan. 10, 1962, Brussels, APE 7054, at 22 *bis*: "[T]he boundary between abuse of power, on the one hand, and initiatives and measures on the other is so blurred that the most qualified jurist, and *a fortiori* entrepreneurs, are unable to assess *a priori* what constitutes abuse of power and what does not. This is why it is recommend that the executive make very discreet and flexible use [of this regulation] until such time as we have some case law on the subject" (unofficial translation).

266 C. Smits & D. Waelbroeck, *Le droit de la concurrence et les droits fondamentaux*, *in* LES DROITS DE L'HOMME DANS LES POLITIQUES DE L'UNION EUROPÉENNE 135, 150 (M. Candela Soriano ed., 2006).

267 *See supra*, nos. 454–457.

personal liability of the offender."[268] However, while it is important to ensure that the rules are intelligible, so as not to turn the characterization of the mental element into an artificial exercise, taking into account reasonable doubt as to the scope of the law must not serve as a convenient excuse for companies that know perfectly well that they are acting outside the framework. The balance is all the more difficult to strike given that, although the notion of "company" is a unitary one, it covers very different realities.[269] A small or medium-sized enterprise does not have the same resources as a multinational, and is therefore less likely to understand the subtleties of competition law. Moreover, the criteria for accepting the argument that the rules are unpredictable are not the clearest.

465. **Lack of clarity regarding the criteria for admitting reasonable doubt as to the scope of the law.** In anticompetitive practices law, as in most Member States,[270] reasonable doubt as to the scope of the law is not an argument to challenge a finding of infringement: it is a mitigating circumstance that may lead to a reduction in the fine.[271]

However, the criteria for reducing the penalty, or even imposing a purely symbolic fine, are rather unclear: sometimes the Commission held that the application of the rules was "of such a specific nature as not to enable conclusions to be easily drawn from previous ... decisions"[272]; sometimes it recognized that the fact of classifying a consultancy firm as a party to the cartel constituted "to a certain extent a novelty"[273]; here, the Paris Court of Appeal reduced the fine on the grounds that "the law and case law applicable in this area were not clearly established"[274]; there, the Court took into consideration the existence of a statement by the Commission that "gave rise to doubts on the part of the applicants and led them to believe that their agreement was not unlawful"[275]; and the Court upheld

---

268 G.I.E.M. S.R.L. and others v. Italy, App. no. 1828/06, ¶ 242 (ECtHR June 28, 2018).

269 *See supra*, no. 171.

270 *See supra*, no. 196, and doctrinal references cited.

271 While the attenuating circumstance of reasonable doubt as to the existence of an infringement was expressly included in the 1998 guidelines (Comm. EC, Guidelines on the Method of Setting Fines Imposed Pursuant to Article 15(2) of Regulation No 17 and Article 65(5) of the ECSC Treaty, 1998 O.J. (C 9) 3, para. 3) it disappeared from the 2006 guidelines (Comm. EC, Guidelines on the Method of Setting Fines Imposed Pursuant to Article 23(2)(a) of Regulation No 1/2003, 2006 O.J. (C 210) 2). However, the General Court considered that this deletion was not sufficient "for the Commission automatically to reject its application as a mitigating circumstance," *see* Case T-472/13, Lundbeck, ECLI:EU:T:2016:449, para. 830. Moreover, as we know, this attenuating circumstance is sometimes confused with negligence, *see supra*, no. 269.

272 Comm. EC, July 20, 1999, IV/36.888, 1998 Football World Cup, para. 123. Only a symbolic fine of one thousand euros was imposed in this case, *see* para. 125.

273 Comm. EC, Dec. 10, 2003, COMP/E-2/37.857, Organic Peroxides, para. 15.

274 CA Paris, pôle 5, ch. 5–7, Mar. 13, 2014, no. 2013/00714 (Fr.) (unofficial translation).

275 Case T-86/95, Compagnie générale maritime, ECLI:EU:T:2002:50, para. 485.

the argument that the competition rules had never been clarified in relation to the conduct in question.[276]

Such grounds are insufficient: authorities and courts should specify that it is because the interpretation was *unforeseeable* that the mitigating circumstance in question is retained. Indeed, even when conduct is found to be an offense for the first time, the solution remains foreseeable if the offense is properly defined and the criteria for its qualification are clearly established.[277]

However, the predictability of developments in case law[278] has drawn criticism, and the Court of Justice appears relatively strict in that it generally refuses to accept the argument based on the absence of awareness of the unlawful nature of the conduct,[279] even when the company has sought the advice of legal counsel,[280] or has set up a compliance program.[281] Moreover, case law seems to have little sympathy for the argument based on a company size.

466. **Too little differentiation between small and large companies.** The scope of the principle of foreseeability is supposed to depend on the nature of its addressees.[282] Compliance with this principle does not prevent the person concerned from seeking "appropriate legal advice" in order to understand the norm, with the Strasbourg and Luxembourg courts specifying that

---

276 Case C-62/86, Akzo, ECLI:EU:C:1991:286, para. 163; for other examples, *see* Case T-217/03, Fédération nationale de la coopération bétail et viande, ECLI:EU:T:2006:391, para. 361; Eur. Comm., Apr. 29, 2014, C(2014) 2892 final, Motorola, para. 561.

277 Cf. *supra*, no. 198, and nos. 413–414.

278 *See* in particular G. Decocq, *Une entreprise de conseil qui facilite une entente est-elle complice du coauteur?*, Contrats concurrence consommation (Oct. 2008), 10, comm. 235.

279 As early as the *Hoffmann-La Roche* judgment, the Court refused to accept the plea of excusable ignorance (Case 85/76, Hoffmann-La Roche, ECLI:EU:C:1979:36, p. 501, para. 4 and paras. 128–132), while the Advocate General took the view that one "should not hesitate to speak in [the applicant's case] of a mistake of law excluding liability," and considered that one should at least hold "that the degree of guilt is so small that there [is] no ground for imposing a fine," *see* Opinion of Advocate General G. Reischl, Case 85/76, Hoffmann-La Roche, ECLI:EU:C:1978:162, at 597. For other examples, *see ex multis*: Case 193/83, Windsurfing International, ECLI:EU:C:1986:75, para. 107; Case T-43/92, Dunlop Slazenger International, ECLI:EU:T:1994:79, para. 143; Case T-37/05, Worlds Wide Tobacco España, ECLI:EU:T:2011:76, para. 160; Case C-681/11, Schenker, ECLI:EU:C:2013:404, para. 38; Case T-472/13, Lundbeck, ECLI:EU:T:2016:449, para. 831; Case T-612/17, Google and Alphabet, ECLI:EU:T:2021:763, paras. 649, 657 and 680. On this subject, *see also* Case C-266/06 P, Evonik Degussa, ECLI:EU:C:2008:295, para. 54: the Community judicature has "made it possible, through consistent and published case law, to clarify the indeterminate concepts that Article 15(2) of Regulation No. 17 might contain," including the expressions "deliberately" and "negligently" (unofficial translation); and the position supported in the Opinion of Advocate General N. Wahl, Case C-194/14 P, AC-Treuhand, ECLI:EU:C:2015:350, para. 25: "[W]here a rule of criminal law already satisfies the principle of *nulla poena sine lege certa* as a result of the clarity of its wording, there is no need to resort to interpretative case-law in order to ensure that that principle is observed."

280 Case 19/77, Miller International, ECLI:EU:C:1978:19, para. 18; Case C-681/11, Schenker, ECLI:EU:C:2013:404, answer to the first preliminary question. The solution nevertheless appears justified, as admitting that the fact that a company seeks legal advice constitutes an attenuating circumstance could open "the way to the production of opinions tailored to the interests of the undertaking." In this sense, *see* Opinion of Advocate General J. Kokott, Case C-681/11, Schenker, ECLI:EU:C:2013:126, para. 60 (the Advocate General nevertheless drew up a list of minimum requirements to be met for a legal opinion to be taken into account, paras. 62–73).

281 Case C-501/11 P, Schindler, ECLI:EU:C:2013:522, para. 90 and paras. 113–114. On this judgment, *see supra*, no. 175.

282 Case C-189/02 P, Dansk Rørindustri, ECLI:EU:C:2005:408, para. 219.

this is "particularly true in relation to persons carrying on a professional activity, who are used to having to proceed with a high degree of caution," as they can be "expected to take special care in assessing the risks" associated with their activity.[283]

"A large company has a multi-lobed brain: its legal department will register new texts with the indifference of specialists."[284] Perhaps this is why jurisprudence treats large companies so harshly. The sheer size of a company can lead to the presumption that it is familiar with the law,[285] even when it is complex, and can even increase the amount of the fine: as these behemoths have "legal and economic knowledge and infrastructures,"[286] it would be justified to "punish [them] more severely," as it is "presumed to have sufficient knowledge and structural resources to be aware that their conduct constitutes an infringement."[287] While the argument is understandable, it must not lead to a systematic rejection of the possibility of error: if the implementation of the rule becomes unpredictable even for a specialist, this would be an excessive solution.

If it seems appropriate not to give too much credence to the argument of error when invoked by a large company, conversely, can the same degree of severity be applied to a sole trader or an small or medium-sized enterprise (SME)?[288] Should we not consider that "the diligence expected of an undertaking in this regard depends on its size and its experience in competition matters"[289]? This is, incidentally, the solution adopted in customs law.[290] However, the Court never seems to have ruled on this essential point. For its part, the Commission has acknowledged, in the course of a dispute, that it is possible that some companies, particularly

---

283 *Id.* In the same vein, *see* Cantoni v. France, App. no. 17862/91, ¶ 35 (ECtHR Nov. 15, 1996); Kononov v. Latvia, App. no. 36376/04, ¶ 235 (ECtHR May 17, 2010).

284 J. Carbonnier, Essai sur les lois 309 (2nd ed. 1992).

285 *See inter alia*: Case T-202/98, British Sugar, ECLI:EU:T:2001:185, para. 128.

286 Case T-217/06, Arkema France, ECLI:EU:T:2011:251, para. 244.

287 Case T-279/02, Degussa, ECLI:EU:T:2006:103, para. 289.

288 Indeed, under domestic law, SMEs are just as liable to prosecution as large corporations, and subject to the same rules. On this subject, *see* C. Lucas de Leyssac, *PME et règles de protection du marché: Le regard du juriste*, *in* Les PME et le droit de la concurrence: Analyse critique, comparative et prospective 47, 79 (M. Baillat et al. eds., 2009): the author notes that "[t]he trend is towards the increasingly general subjection [of SMEs] to the common rule." However, it is worth noting the Autorité de la concurrence's commendable efforts to make competition rules more accessible to small businesses: it recently published a guide for SMEs and created a dedicated space on its website, *see* ADLC, Mieux comprendre les règles de concurrence: Guide à destination des PME (2020).

289 Opinion of Advocate General J. Kokott, Case C-681/11, Schenker, ECLI:EU:C:2013:126, para. 69. *Adde*, Case T-38/02, Groupe Danone, ECLI:EU:T:2005:367, para. 175: the Court of First Instance mentions "an additional need for deterrence," in the presence of an undertaking of international dimension, "by comparison with an undertaking without such resources," which suggests that the judge might show more leniency if faced with a smaller-scale undertaking.

290 In this respect, the Court considers that "the Court has consistently held" that account must be taken of "the nature of the error, the professional experience of the trader concerned and the degree of care which he exercised," *see* Case C-250/91, Hewlett Packard France, ECLI:EU:C:1993:134, para. 22; in the same sense, Case C-251/00, Ilumitrónica, ECLI:EU:C:2002:655, para. 54.

"the smaller ones, may well not have fully appreciated" that they were committing an infringement,[291] although it is not clear what weight this statement had on the calculation of the fine imposed.

467. **The distinction between formal and substantive assessment of foreseeability.** The case law concerning the consideration of reasonable doubt as to the scope of the law is strict and highly formalistic. The Court seems to consider that as long as there is a text and case law, the application of the rules is foreseeable. If this predictability is only a façade, the characterization of intent will necessarily be fictitious. Instead of a formal assessment, it would be preferable to adopt a substantive approach, which would take into account the diminished clarity of competition rules, and would recognize that, in the presence of such a technically complex law, companies of markedly different sizes cannot be treated in exactly the same way. The problem, however, lies in the fact that if we were to accept a more realistic approach to error of law, the preventive function of the law on anticompetitive practices could be compromised. This is why the solution lies in simplifying the rules: it would then become fully legitimate, and not artificial, to consider that error is no longer admissible, save in exceptional cases – which would be a healthier solution, and more appropriate in the presence of texts that have been subject to more than sixty years of jurisprudential interpretation.

*

* *

468. **Conclusion of Section 2: the questionable consequences of the effects-based approach.** Over the past twenty years, the effects-based approach has led to an unprecedented increase in the complexity of competition law, a rise in the cost of implementing it, and a weakening of the Commission's decisions. The solutions adopted to date have only exacerbated the problem: competition authorities have increasingly embarked on alternative procedures to sanctions, compromising the development of case law, and the legislator has adopted a new regulation intended to address shortcomings in the implementation of traditional rules, which has further increased the technical complexity of the field. Due to the discrepancy between the principles endorsed by case law and the discourse surrounding competition law, the latter has become difficult to understand, giving rise to legitimate concerns regarding the principles of predictability and legal certainty.

*

* *

291 Comm. EC, July 10, 1986, IV/31.371, Roofing felt, para. 109.

469. **Conclusion to Chapter 1: a return to the legal foundations of competition law – an imperative.** In light of this assessment, it seems more necessary than ever to propose a different approach. We should not expect economic analysis to replace legal reasoning, nor to task law with "the pursuit of preferable objectives."[292] The fact that the subject of the discipline is competition – an economic concept – does not mean that the substance of the rule should be defined by economics.[293] It is up to the jurist to define the concepts and establish the qualification criteria, with the support of economists, but not under their sway. Given the instability of economic science and the ideological stakes involved, its normative ambition cannot be accepted without compromising legal certainty. Yet, as Paul Roubier has rightly remarked, the gravest legal crises are precisely "those that threaten legal certainty," because "it is the most essential value."[294] If it disappears, "no other value can survive; the very word progress becomes a mockery, and the worst injustices multiply with disorder," as law gives way to politics, i.e., "pure considerations of expediency," so that the "jurisconsult no longer has anything to say."[295] It is therefore appropriate to call for a return to the forefront of legal reasoning, by advocating the adoption of the theory of intent.

*

* *

---

292 B. Oppetit, *Droit et économie*, *in* DROIT ET MODERNITÉ 181 (1998).

293 L. Boy & A. Pirovano, *Ambiguités du droit économique (éléments d'une méthodologie)*, PROCÈS: CAHIERS D'ANALYSE POLITIQUE ET JURIDIQUE NO. 7, 7, 9 (1981).

294 P. ROUBIER, THÉORIE GÉNÉRALE DU DROIT: HISTOIRE DES DOCTRINES JURIDIQUES ET PHILOSOPHIE DES VALEURS SOCIALES 333 (2nd ed. 1951), no. 38.

295 *Id.* at 333–34.

Chapter 2
EMBRACING THE THEORY OF INTENT

470. **A theory rooted in the legal tradition, and capable of resolving the current challenges facing competition law.** The theory of intent seems fully justified, insofar as it is consistent with the teleology of competition law, and would enable a return to vocabulary more accurately aligned with legal semantics (**Section 1**). Furthermore, restoring the effectiveness of competition rules undoubtedly depends on the primacy of legal reasoning,[1] i.e., *apolitical* considerations that ensure the stability of solutions and their adaptability to novel cases. Adopting this theory would simplify the discipline, making it not only more intelligible to its addressees, but also more readily adaptable to contemporary challenges, notably those posed by the practices of companies operating in digital markets (**Section 2**).

Section 1
Justifications for adopting the theory of intent

471. **An improvement from both a teleological and semantic standpoint.** Adopting the theory of intent would enable a reconnection with the roots of the discipline: in this sense, it is a theory consistent with the teleology of competition law (**Paragraph 1**). It would also serve as a vector of improvement in the discourse on competition law (**Paragraph 2**).

---

1 In the same spirit, *see* J.-B. Blaise, *Une construction inachevée: le droit français des ententes et des positions dominantes*, *in* Aspects actuels du droit commercial français: Études dédiées à René Roblot 159, 161 (1984): "The development and greater practical effectiveness of competition law undoubtedly require a restoration of the role of the norm."

Paragraph 1 – A theory consistent with the teleology of competition law

472. **The *ultimate aim* pursued by competition law.** Teleology, understood in its original sense, is a *philosophy* of *ends* (**I**). It is thus, by its very nature, largely incompatible with legal utilitarianism. And since competition law has never truly subscribed to the effects-based approach,[2] the question is not what objectives the discipline pursues, but rather what higher value it seeks to protect. It appears, in fact, that it has never abandoned its primary aim: the protection of freedom in competition, as an end in itself (**II**).

I. Teleology: a philosophy of ends

473. **Teleological interpretation in theory and practice.** Teleological and utilitarian interpretations are sometimes conflated, though they are in fact distinct (**A**): While all norms inherently pursue objectives of varying proximity, this does not necessarily mean that the objective in question is material in nature, nor that it is concretely predefined. In law, teleological interpretation is, in principle, broader and more ambitious – which is why the Court of Justice has used this technique only sparingly (**B**).

A. Distinction between teleological and utilitarian interpretations

474. **Definition of teleology.** In the philosophical sense of the term, teleology – an indispensable mode of reasoning in theology – is the pursuit of an end considered good *in itself*.[3] It is classically opposed to "mechanism," which is defined as a "philosophical theory admitting that a class of facts, or even all phenomena, may be reduced to a system of '*mechanical*' determinations."[4] Mechanism thus rests on the postulate that definite causal links can be established[5] – which, in the human "sciences," is an illusion.[6]

In law, teleological interpretation "refers to the interpretation that assumes that a rule must be applied in such a way as to fulfill its ends, and interpreted in light of its finalities."[7] But what is meant by "ends"? Some have lamented the "death of ends," the exclusion of final causes – rules

---

2 *See supra*, nos. 454–457.

3 A. Lalande, Vocabulaire technique et critique de la philosophie 1107 (2002).

4 *Id.* at 603 (emphasis added).

5 *Id.*

6 *See supra*, nos. 81 *et seq.*

7 Vocabulaire juridique 1018 (G. Cornu ed., 11th ed. 2016).

having been, for the most part, relegated in contemporary times to mere functions, to technical mechanisms aimed at predetermined objectives.[8] An "end" is not the material desire that human beings experience, nor the concrete goals they set for themselves. Finality stands above us; it is a good in itself[9] – and law is the art of coordinating these higher, ideal values.[10]

In this sense, teleology, understood in its primary sense, is opposed to an instrumentalist and utilitarian interpretation of legal rules, since where the latter determines concrete and precise objectives, the former implies interpreting the norm by the yardstick of a higher end or principle[11] – it raises it above its contingency, calling for a form of transcendence.[12]

However, it is always possible to explain a rule in two ways: top-down and bottom-up. For example, we might consider that murder is punished, not because it is a structural prohibition to which societies have always been attached, but because it leads to suboptimal results at the level of a country:[13] if murder were not effectively punished, the number of homicides would increase, the number of productive adults would symmetrically decrease, many would be afraid to leave their homes and would therefore go to work less, and they would also develop anxiety disorders that are costly for social security. Whatever the truth of the matter, it seems to us that punishment is more acceptable when it is based on an ethic shared by the whole of a social group rather than on calculations.

So the retreat from teleological interpretation in favor of utilitarian interpretation seems to us to be the result of a categorical rejection of mystery. Indeed, utilitarians reject the idea that there can be rules whose origin remains unexplained, that are not rationally justified, at least according to their own perception of rationality. They call traditional rules and secular values to account, and constantly ask: "Why this rule and not another?"

---

8 M. Villey, Philosophie du droit: Définition et fins du droit, Les moyens du droit 132–33 (reed. 2001), nos. 108-109. Cf. *supra*, nos. 422 *et seq.*

9 M. Villey, *Critique de l'utilitarisme juridique*, Revue de la recherche juridique: Droit prospectif 166, 171 (1981-1982), no. vi-9.

10 In this sense, *see* P. Roubier, Théorie générale du droit: Histoire des doctrines juridiques et philosophie des valeurs sociales 317 (2nd ed. 1951), no. 36: "[T]here is one notion that must govern the entire ordering of law, and that is the notion of 'value'; in the final analysis, law rests on a philosophy of values."

11 Moreover, one author has argued that the interpretation of a norm by means of a consequentialist analysis of the costs and benefits of its implementation is incompatible with the rule of law, insofar as it leads to a considerable increase in the interpreter's margin of discretion and denies that the law can be respected for its own sake, *see* E.-J. Mestmäcker, *The Development of German and European Competition Law with Special Reference to the European Commission's Article 82 Guidance of 2008*, *in* European Competition Law: The Impact of the Commission's Guidelines on Article 102, 25, 50–52 (L. F. Pace ed., 2011).

12 Thus, in ancient and scholastic models of justice, the "ultimate end of law was not the maximization of consumer enjoyment," but rather a form of transcendent justice, the pursuit of ends deemed just in themselves, *see* R. Sève, *Droit et économie: Quatre paradigmes*, 37 Archives de philosophie du droit 63, 63–66 (1992). The author rightly notes that the modern "Machiavellian" model has severed ties with any form of transcendence. Cf. *supra*, nos. 422 *et seq.*, on the reduction of legal ends to material realities.

13 Cf. the economic analyses of criminal law cited *supra*, no. 121.

"In the name of what is it imposed, what does it lead to?" – and the philosopher does not know what to answer, other than "who knows?"

This tension between the two types of interpretation is directly reflected in the opposition between the approach aimed at making competition an end in itself, and that aimed at making it produce other results distinct from itself. However, the Court of Justice has never had more than moderate recourse to teleological interpretation, and for the most part true to its primary meaning.

B. Moderate use of teleological interpretation by the European Court of Justice

475. **The search for the legislator's intention: an interpretative technique not used by the Court of Justice.** The debate on the "objectives" of competition law is based on and justified by the importance of the teleological interpretation of Union law by the Court of Justice. It would be a matter of discovering, or rather decreeing, that such and such a mission should be assigned to the rules.[14]

The authors' rhetorical device is frequently based on the classic argument of seeking the legislator's intention. Thus, even though the preparatory works for the Treaty of Rome are inaccessible, there are numerous attempts at historical contextualization. Their argumentative aim is to defend the idea that the rule should be interpreted in a certain way in the future, having regard to the presumed will of the European legislator. These works interpret the context of the time in order to ascertain what *political* influences prevailed at the time. Given the uncertain results of such an undertaking – all politics being by nature contingent and ephemeral – the scope of the investigation is sometimes extended to the Sherman Act. While the value of such research is undeniable, it seems questionable to us to base the interpretation of a rule on historical conjecture, which, given the strategic importance of competition in terms of both diplomacy and economic administration, is intertwined with important ideological issues. The Court of Justice has never used this interpretative technique, and the few documents published, such as the Spaak Report,[15] have never been mentioned, not even in its earliest decisions.[16]

476. **The different types of teleological interpretation.** When the debate on the purpose(s) of competition rules is based on teleological interpretation, it alters its meaning. There are three types of teleological interpretation:

---

14 *See supra*, nos. 430 *et seq.*

15 Secrétariat du comité intergouvernemental, Rapport des chefs de délégation aux ministres des Affaires étrangères ["Spaak Report"], Brussels, Apr. 21, 1956).

16 L. Focsaneanu, La jurisprudence de la Cour de justice des communautés européennes en matière de concurrence: Les règles applicables aux entreprises (Articles 85 et 86 du Traité de Rome) 24 (1977).

that which aims to preserve the effet utile of Union law ("systematic" interpretation), that which aims to complete a flawed or ambiguous rule so that it is coherent[17] ("*stricto sensu*" interpretation) and, finally, that which focuses on the *consequences* that will result from a decision ("consequentialist" interpretation).[18]

The consequentialist interpretation is the only one that could justify the interference of utilitarian objectives in the interpretation of rules. However, it is still necessary to distinguish between two forms of consequentialism[19] – one legal, the other extralegal.

The first is to consider the *legal consequences* of a decision[20] – for example, by asking whether it could disrupt the coherence of the legal system, for instance by treating two identical cases differently,[21] or by leading to a contradiction between several rules or principles.

The second is based on consideration of the *economic or social consequences* of a decision. Generally speaking, this approach does not lead to general, abstract rules, because for the consequentialist, it is the results of human action, and they alone, that decide on the virtue of an act, not the act itself: in this respect, extralegal consequentialism is utilitarianism. And as we know, the utilitarian cannot assert "this is permissible, that is not," but can only say "you must not provoke this, you must not provoke that."[22] Analysis is then entirely dependent, not on action, but on the future, i.e., on what no one can predict. For this reason, extralegal consequentialism can be incompatible with legal consequentialism. Indeed, how can we ensure consistency in the implementation of rules if they are interpreted according to their results?[23] Since two identical

---

17 For example, in the *Towercast* case, the Court of Justice ruled that Regulation no. 139/2004 should be read "in the light of its context," *see* Case C-449/21, Towercast, ECLI:EU:C:2023:207, para. 41.

18 K. Lenaertz & J. A. Gutierrez-Fons, Les méthodes d'interprétation de la Cour de justice de l'Union européenne 55–58 (2020), no. 59. For examples where the Court expressly resorts to this interpretative method, *see* esp. Case C-456/12, Minister voor Immigratie, ECLI:EU:C:2014:135, para. 37; Case C-377/13, Ascendi Beiras Litoral, ECLI:EU:C:2014:1754, para. 48.

19 For an in-depth discussion of the distinction between legal and extralegal consequentialism, *see* G. Leroy, *Vers une exposition raisonnée de l'argument conséquentialiste dans la motivation des arrêts de la Cour de cassation?*, Les Cahiers Portalis no. 9, 181, 183–84 (2020).

20 On this subject, *see* N. MacCormick, Raisonnement juridique et théorie du droit 153–79 (J. Gagey trans., PUF 1996).

21 F. Schauer, *Precedent*, 39 Stanford Law Review 571, 572–76 (1987): the author considers that precedent has a forward-looking aspect, insofar as it must fit into a larger normative whole and, as an argument, will condition, along with all other precedents, future decisions.

22 In this sense, and for a critical look, the following important study should be consulted with interest: G. E. M. Anscombe, *Modern Moral Philosophy*, xxxiii Philosophy 1, 12–13 (1958). Not listed in the bibliography

23 *See* F. Carbonnel, *Reasoning by Consequences: Applying Different Argumentation Structures to the Analysis of Consenquentialist Reasoning in Judicial Decisions*, *in* Legal Argumentation Theory: Cross-Disciplinary Perspective 1, 6 (C. Dahlman & E. Feteris eds., 2013): "Incorporation of consequences in judicial reasoning cannot ignore a crucial rule applicable to legal argumentation in general: that the legal answer 'always has to be capable of being framed in terms of the law, through interpretation of statues or of precedents, or of legal principles developed through reflection on law as practically coherent normative order.'"

cases may produce different economic or social consequences,[24] extralegal consequentialism will, on some occasions, lead to a breach of the formal rule of justice according to which two identical cases must be treated identically,[25] or even conflict with the general principle of legal certainty or the principle of equal treatment.

Extralegal consequentialism may also run counter to teleological interpretation *stricto sensu*, insofar as it would add to two articles designed to penalize restrictions of competition other objectives that derive neither from the letter nor from the spirit of the text. Indeed, as articles 101 and 102 TFEU are not incomplete,[26] they do not call for an extensive interpretation.

477. **The Court of Justice's cautious use of teleological interpretation.** The Court has always been cautious in its use of teleological interpretation:[27] its role is to carry out a *legal* interpretation – and if the judges were to make economic assessments in interpreting the rule, they would be "distorting the nature of [their] powers."[28] Moreover, when Judge Pierre Pescatore listed the objectives pursued by the European Economic Community, he confined himself to equality, non-discrimination, legal and political unity, and solidarity, and, in matters of competition, mentioned only freedom.[29] Similarly, Lazar Focsaneanu believes that the interpretation method used in competition law is necessarily *restrictive*, since state intervention limits commercial freedom, which is itself essential to competition.[30] Moreover, when two objectives are of equal importance but incompatible with each other, the Court must balance them in order to decide which should prevail over the others.[31] The pursuit of socio-economic objectives, such as consumer welfare, may restrict commercial freedom,[32] jeopardize the

---

24 Indeed, if the result X is sanctioned, the same behavior A, which may randomly produce results X Y Z, will be treated differently depending solely on the consequences of the act, which will not always have been foreseen or foreseeable; and a behavior B or C might just as easily produce a result X, so that consequentialism prevents rules of conduct from being determined.

25 F. Rouvière, *Le fondement du savoir juridique*, RTD Civ. 279 (2016).

26 Although the definition of competition infringements is indeterminate, it is nonetheless determinable, *see supra*, nos. 410 *et seq.*

27 R. Monaco, *Les principes d'interprétation suivis par la Cour de justice des communautés européennes*, *in* Mélanges offerts à Henri Rolin: Problèmes de droit des gens 217, 224 (1964). This is also borne out by the fact that the objectives mentioned *supra*, no. 430, have never had any real normative scope.

28 *Id.* at 225.

29 P. Pescatore, *Les objectifs de la Communauté européenne comme principes d'interprétation dans la jurisprudence de la Cour de justice: Contribution à la doctrine de l'interprétation téléologique des traités internationaux*, *in* II Miscellanea W. J. Ganshof van der Meersch: Studia ab discipulis amicisque in honorem egregii professoris edita 325, 346–47 (1972), on competition law.

30 Focsaneanu, La jurisprudence de la Cour de justice des communautés européennes en matière de concurrence: Les règles applicables aux entreprises (Articles 85 et 86 du Traité de Rome), *op. cit.* at 24. *See also supra*, no. 386

31 Lenaertz & Gutierrez-Fons, Les méthodes d'interprétation de la Cour de justice de l'Union européenne, *op. cit.* at 58, no. 60.

32 In this sense, L. Lovdahl Gormsen, A Principled Approach to Abuse of Dominance in European Competition Law 93–94 (2010).

principle of equal treatment or the principle of predictability, even though such an objective cannot be considered to be of equal importance to free competition, since, unlike the latter, it is not expressly mentioned in any text of primary law.[33]

From this point of view, the recent adoption by the Court of Justice of the objective of consumer welfare is open to criticism, insofar as this position contradicts its own reasoning – this objective having no normative scope.[34] It follows that this is not an interpretation in the true sense of the word, but a mere statement that undermines the intelligibility of the law, since it does not describe an element taken into account in the decision-making process.[35]

II. The teleology of competition law: freedom as an end, not a means

478. **A *continuum*, from Aristotelian theories to the present day.** From Aristotle to the Scholastics and ordoliberalism, there is only one step (**A**). What these three doctrines have in common is that they do not dissociate the economic perspective from legal reasoning, nor do they subordinate state intervention to any end other than freedom of exchange. To show that contemporary competition law has not renounced these ideals allows us to make a few remarks about the limits of the discipline, which cannot take on the task of achieving objectives already pursued by other areas of law (**B**).

A. Freedom, from Aristotle and the scholastics to ordoliberalism

479. **The link between Aristotle, the Scholastics and ordoliberalism.** Currents are never born independently of a broader history: they are the product of more or less conscious, and more or less ancient, influences.[36] While the roots of ordoliberalism are relatively unknown, its deep links with the doctrine of the Scholastics have been demonstrated.[37] We know how

---

33 *See supra*, no. 432.

34 In this sense, *see supra*, nos. 359–361.

35 However, the formulation of objectives in a law sometimes serves to justify the existence of a rule (though it is debatable in this regard to limit the rule's objective to consumers alone – free competition being beneficial to all market participants), and sometimes to make the norm clearer, a function that is not fulfilled in this case. On this subject, *see* C. Prieto & E. Putman, *Typologie matérielle et formelle des formulations d'objectifs dans les textes législatifs*, Revue de la recherche juridique: Droit prospectif no. 4, 879, 886–90 (1989).

36 D. Villey, Notes de philosophie économique (1958–59): Le jeu des intérêts 76 (1965). On the "quests of competition policy," *see* D. Bosco & C. Prieto, Droit européen de la concurrence 17–109 (2013), nos. 3–118.

37 W. Decock, Le marché du mérite: Penser le droit et l'économie avec Léonard Lessius 124–30 (2019); N. Goldschmidt, *Walter Eucken's Place in the History of Ideas*, 26 The Review of Austrian Economics 127, 142 (2013).

much these medieval thinkers owe to Aristotle[38] – and it is fair to say that ordoliberalism is much more than a current of ideas: it is the contemporary legacy of an ancient tradition, not the contingent intention of yesterday's legislator or today's and tomorrow's administrative authority. At different times, these doctrines are all based on the idea that the law, in the economic sphere, imposes a just division, namely, the rewarding of merit through voluntary exchange, which is itself just on the condition that it is consented to without fraud – competition law, therefore, is not meant to serve any purpose other than freedom of exchange.[39]

What they also have in common is the *recognition* of the existence of an *order*[40] that is binding on everyone, both legal subjects and states. In the case of the former, the aim is to lay down general, abstract rules to correct the excesses of the "invisible hand" of the market through the "visible hand of the law"[41]; in the case of the latter, the aim is to prevent the state from restricting fundamental rights and violating the principles of the rule of law, so that healthy state intervention does not turn into planning that undermines commercial autonomy.[42] Ordoliberals therefore conceive of state intervention as essentially "negative," i.e., as having the primary function of *preventing* excesses of economic power, rather than *prescribing* specific behaviors or outcomes.[43] It is the creation of a *framework* enabling individuals to exercise their *economic freedom* that is important, not the concrete consequences of the use of this freedom,[44] provided that this use does not lead to a lessening of the freedom of others.[45]

Finally, these schools of thought are similar in their method: ordoliberalism, like Aristotelian economic doctrine,[46] does not compartmentalize

---

38 In this sense, Villey, Notes de philosophie économique (1958-59): Le jeu des intérêts, *op. cit.* at 83; *adde*, *see supra*, no. 49

39 *See supra*, no. 400; *adde*, for an interesting comparison between Aristotle and Bentham, M. El Shakankiri, La philosophie juridique de Jérémy Bentham 245 (1970).

40 Note that the notion of order already appears in Hesiod's *Theogony*, *see supra*, no. 23; *adde*, for a contemporary perspective, R. Libchaber, L'ordre juridique et le discours du droit: Essai sur les limites de la connaissance du droit 195 (2013).

41 Q. Slobodian, Globalists: The End of Empire and the Birth of Neoliberalism 7 (2018).

42 J. Drexl, *La Constitution économique européenne – L'actualité du modèle ordolibéral*, xxv Revue internationale de droit économique 419, 453 (2011); A. Sen, *Markets and Freedoms: Achievements and Limitations of the Market Mechanism in Promoting Individual Freedoms*, 45 Oxford Economic Papers 519, 526–27 (1993). On this theme, *see* M. Foucault, Naissance de la biopolitique: Cours au Collège de France, 1978-1979, 105–33 (2004).

43 T. Ergen & S. Kohl, *Varieties of Economization in Competition Policy: Institutional Change in German and American Antitrust*, 1960–2000, 26 Review of International Political Economy 256, 274–76 (2019).

44 Indeed, for ordoliberals, "it is not the progress of well-being, but justice and freedom that constitute the values according to which the economic constitution must be oriented," L. Miksch, *Die sittliche Bedeutung der inneren Koordination*, 3 ORDO 70 (1950), quoted and translated by C. Mongouachon, *L'ordolibéralisme: Contexte historique et contenu dogmatique*, Concurrences no. 4-2011, art. no. 38770, 70, 75, no. 19.

45 Drexl, *La Constitution économique européenne – L'actualité du modèle ordolibéral*, *op. cit.* at 429; *see* our definition of *dol*, *supra*, no. 400.

46 *See supra*, no. 37.

disciplines. It rests on a holistic reflection that encompasses economics, law, and ethics, and does not oppose legal and economic analysis, but rather blends them into an overall line of reasoning.

In sum, ordoliberals recognize the value of freedom as an *end*, and even more so, as a *presupposition* of the rule of law, and not as a means of achieving other ends. With this simple idea, they have profoundly influenced the construction of the European Community.

480. **The "Constitution" of the European Union: the adoption of an ordoliberal conception of the market economy.** Although the ordoliberal inspiration of the European construction has been the subject of numerous studies,[47] this current remains far less studied than Chicagoan theories – no doubt due to the domination of legal utilitarianism in the world of ideas for decades.[48] Nevertheless, ordoliberalism has exerted a significant influence on Community jurisprudence since its inception. Indeed, while the members of the Commission were, from the outset, in favor of interventionism,[49] European judges interpreted competition rules solely with the aim of protecting competition in and for itself[50] – this end being considered by some as a "constitutional objective" of the Union, enabling the emergence of a "free economy,"[51] protected from abuses by private actors[52] as well as public authorities.[53] However, as

---

47 *Ex multis*: P. Commun, Les ordolibéraux: Histoire d'un libéralisme à l'allemande 227–389 (2016); D. J. Gerber, Law and Competition in Twentieth Century Europe: Protecting Prometheus 232–65 (2nd ed. 2001); D. Bosco & C. Prieto, Droit européen de la concurrence 89–99 (2013), nos. 96–106; L. Zenouvou, Les usages de la notion de concurrence en droit 27–37 (2012), nos. 67–90; Q. Slobodian, Globalists: The End of Empire and the Birth of Neoliberalism 204–12 (2018); K. K. Patel & H. Schweitzer, *Introduction*, *in* The Historical Foundation of EU Competition Law 1, 8 (K. K. Patel & H. Schweitzer eds., 2013), and the numerous references cited. *Contra*, some authors – albeit in the minority – have sought to relativize the idea that ordoliberalism played a major role in the construction of the European Community, *see* in particular. H. Buch-Hansen & A. Wigger, The Politics of European Competition Regulation: A Critical Political Economy Perspective 34–65 (2011); on the negotiations preceding the adoption of the Treaty of Rome, *see* Zenouvou, Les usages de la notion de concurrence en droit, *op. cit.* at 27–37, nos. 67–90. Finally, one author has defended, against the tide, the idea that competition law has, from its inception, pursued the objective of efficiency, *see* P. Akman, *Searching for the Long-Lost Soul of Article 82 EC*, 29 Oxford Journal of Legal Studies 267, 267–303 (2009).

48 In this sense, and for a lively critique, *see*: E.-J. Mestmäcker, A Legal Theory without Law: Posner v. Hayek on Economic Analysis of Law (2007).

49 Similarly, as early as the 1960s, we can note a tension between the desire to adopt a competition policy and the intention to pursue an industrial policy – the former ultimately prevailed over the latter – *see* L. Warlouzet, *Europe de la concurrence et politique industrielle Communautaire: La naissance d'une opposition au sein de la CEE dans les années 1960*, Histoire, économie & société no. 1, 47, 53 and 61, resp. (2008).

50 In this sense, *see* S. M. Ramírez Pérez & S. van de Scheur, *The Evolution of the Law on Articles 85 and 86 EEC* [Articles 101 and 102 TFEU], *Ordoliberalism and its Keynesian Challenge*, *in* The Historical Foundation of EU Competition Law 19, 20–21 and 38–43 (K. K. Patel & H. Schweitzer eds., 2013).

51 J.-L. Dewost, B. Lasserre & R. Saint-Esteben, *L'entreprise, les règles de concurrence et les droits fondamentaux: Quelle articulation?*, 35 Nouveaux cahiers du Conseil constitutionnel (Apr. 2012).

52 On this subject, *see* C. Mongouachon, *Le droit européen de la concurrence face à ses finalités: Un débat philosophique*, Revue de la recherche juridique: Droit prospectif 1945 no. 5, 1945, 1949–53 (2017).

53 F. Marty, *Concurrence et politique industrielle: Analyse de logiques distinctes*, *in* Entreprises stratégiques nationales et modèles économiques européens 131, 138 (V. de Beaufort ed., 2012) Not listed in the bibliography: according to ordoliberals, only rules that are "as immutable as possible can guarantee the protection of the market process and the stability of participants' expectations, in the face of the risks of coercion arising from choices dictated by the immediate interests of the sovereign"; *adde*, G. Amato, Antitrust and the Bounds of Power: The Dilemma of Liberal Democracy in the History of the Market (1997).

the Court of Justice has not deviated from its original reasoning, it has thus ensured the persistence of ordoliberal principles,[54] despite the upheaval of modernization.

It is clear, however, that economic freedom alone is not enough to constitute a company. This is why competition law is not the alpha and omega of law – indeed, if it were, it would be the only legal discipline in existence. Competition law has its limits, which are offset by other areas of the law.

B. Few remarks on the limits of competition law

481. **The scope of the law on anticompetitive practices ends where other laws begin.** The adage "One man's freedom ends where another's begins" can usefully be transposed to competition law. Thus, "the scope of the law of anticompetitive practices should end where that of other laws begins." These include consumer law, environmental law, urban planning law, immigration law, intellectual property law, restrictive practices law, personal data law, platform law, artificial intelligence law, tax law to ensure the redistribution of wealth, and public welfare policies.[55] So why not admit that, in the midst of this flood of state constraints, there might be an island of economic freedom? Have we so vilified the very notion of being (even occasionally) free?[56] Why should the enforcement of cartels and abuses of dominant position achieve the ends that legitimize the existence of other disciplines that already meticulously take care of them?

Competition rules should be recognized as *the common law of economic freedom*, just as contract law is the common law of contractual freedom.[57]

482. **The need to recognize the limits of competition law.** These questions call for a critical approach to the discourse that subordinates the existence and implementation of competition rules to ends other than freedom, on the one hand, because case law attests to the fact that these objectives are devoid of normative scope, and, on the other, because the existence of "instrumentalization strategies" for these rules on the part

---

54 Patel & Schweitzer, *Introduction*, *op. cit.* at 9–10; P. Marsden, *Some Outstanding Issues From the European Commission's Guidance on Article 102 TFEU: Not-So-Faint Echoes of Ordoliberalism*, *in* Competition Law and the Enforcement of Article 102, 53, 72 (F. Etro & I. Kokkoris eds., 2010).

55 In this regard, we fully endorse the assertion that "[c]ompetition law is indispensable for establishing the social market economy," but that it "needs additional social measures to achieve a satisfactory level of social security," *see* Drexl, *La Constitution économique européenne – L'actualité modèle ordolibéral*, *op. cit.* at 433. Moreover, even Friedrich A. Hayek – often (wrongly) labeled an "ultraliberal," a term so overused it has lost much of its meaning – believed that the state must provide social protection to individuals to ensure their subsistence, *see* F. A. Hayek, The Road to Serfdom (1944).

56 *See supra*, no. 426.

57 On the link between freedom as understood in contract law and competition law, *see* B. Oppetit, *La liberté contractuelle à l'épreuve du droit de la concurrence*, Revue des sciences morales et politiques 241, 242–43 and 249 (1995).

of the European Commission[58] opens the door to pressure from interest groups, whereas the pursuit of "a single objective, namely, the protection of competition" would guarantee greater impartiality on the part of the competition authorities.[59]

Paragraph 2 – A theory for improving the semantics of competition law

483. **The syncretism of competition law discourse.** The discipline's lack of legibility is partly due to the syncretism[60] of its discourse. This is the result of the interweaving of legal and economic reasoning: it accommodates ways of describing reality that are, in some respects, incompatible[61] (**I**). Adopting the theory of intent would lead to an improvement in the discourse on competition law, as it would invite us to stop using certain ambiguous formulas and to cease employing overabundant or imprecise words, in order to state the rules more faithfully and clearly (**II**).

I. The syncretism of discourse: a blend of law and economics

484. **The friction between economic and legal language.** If the economist wants to improve well-being, the jurist wants to ensure respect for principles; if the economist aims for efficiency,[62] the jurist is a fussy being obsessed with precision. The economist has their vocabulary; the jurist has their own. The mixing of genres is not without friction:[63] the use of expressions borrowed from economic analysis impoverishes legal language (**A**), and sometimes misunderstands the nature of the law, as illustrated by the artificial opposition between the "formal" and "effects" approaches (**B**).

---

58 C. Mongouachon & L. Zenouvou, *La place du Parlement européen dans le modèle institutionnel de concurrence de l'Union européenne*, Concurrences no. 3-2018, art. no. 87566, 67, 76, no. 29.

59 *Id.* at 77, no. 30, and doctrinal references (in German) cited.

60 Syncretism is the "factitious union of ideas or theses of disparate origin," under which "irreducible differences persist," *see* A. Lalande, Vocabulaire technique et critique de la philosophie 1087–88 (2002).

61 On the difficulties of translating certain economic words and expressions into legal language, *see* A.-L. Sibony, Le juge et le raisonnement économique en droit de la concurrence 168–76 (2008), nos. 231–244.

62 T. Kirat, *Économie et droit: De l'analyse économique du droit à de nouvelles alliances?*, 49 Revue économique 1057, 1066 (1998): according to the author, proponents of the normative approach to the economic analysis of law rely, for the most part, on an "overly economic view of the legal rule," based on an "uncertain notion of efficiency."

63 On this theme, *see* L. Idot, *Argument économique et argument sociologique*, *in* L'argument sociologique en droit: Pluriel et singularité 43, 56 (D. Fenouillet ed., 2015).

A. The use of non-legal expressions borrowed from economic analysis

485. **Language obscured or impoverished by imprecise terms.** Any legal demonstration implies the univocity of the terms on which it is based.[64] However, when a word covers several very distinct meanings, depending on the context in which it is used, the reasoning inevitably loses clarity. Such is the case with the word "test," which may refer at times to a method of proof,[65] at times to the operation of qualification,[66] at times to the definition of competition infringement itself.[67]

What can we say about the term "effect"? Not only does its use sometimes lead to inelegant pleonasms,[68] but it is also used to refer to very different things. In this case, it refers to the effect on competition, which is entirely conflated with anticompetitive behavior.[69] "Anticompetitive effect" is therefore not a useful expression for reasoning, as it is superfluous. What about the effect on prices? Or on consumers? Are these the same thing? Will we prefer to talk about effects on the environment, democracy, equity or the digital transition?[70] Does the jurist not perceive the inconsistency in using these expressions, given that competition infringements are formal and do not require any results?[71] Under the influence of the economic approach, even notions that appear more legal, such as competition on the merits or fairness, have lost their rigor, since they are most often defined, in terms of their effects, by economic tests.[72]

The words of economics have progressively undermined the intelligibility of legal reasoning, sometimes by feigning to ignore it: the opposition between the "formal" and "effects-based" approaches is the most convincing illustration.

B. An illustration: the artificial opposition between "formal" and "effects-based" approaches

486. **Legal reasoning is always formal.** Law is formal in two respects. Not only is legal interpretation strictly circumscribed,[73] but the rule of law

64 C. Perelman & L. Olbrechts-Tyteca, Traité de l'argumentation 161 (2008).

65 This is the case for a "cost test," or the "AEC test," although the latter may also, according to some, have a defining scope, *see supra*, no. 335.

66 Such is the case with the "Bronner test," which would, at the same, time help define the theory of essential infrastructure. For a critique, *see supra*, no. 331.

67 *See supra*, no. 364.

68 *See infra*, no. 297 and no. 377.

69 *See supra*, nos. 370 *et seq.*

70 *See supra*, nos. 432–433.

71 *See supra*, nos. 270 *et seq.*

72 *See supra*, nos. 363–364.

73 On this theme, *see* F. Schauer, *Formalism*, 97 The Yale Law Journal 509 (1988).

itself *is* inherently rigid. If law "cannot lay claim to the absolute of the straight line,"[74] it can only consist of dotted lines.[75] The more a legal rule relies on precise terms, the more rigid it is; when it is framed in general notions, it is more flexible.

It is therefore paradoxical that the implementation of articles 101 and 102 TFEU has been criticized for being too "formal,"[76] since these articles mobilize general and abstract notions, rather than more precise descriptions, such as those used in the Digital Markets Act.[77]

Clearly, certain behaviors are presumed to constitute anticompetitive practices,[78] just as lying is presumed to constitute swindling.[79] But is the interpretation of the notion of swindling too formalistic? Any rule – especially one that falls within the scope of criminal law[80] – "is formalistic or must lose its status as a rule."[81] Nevertheless, economists also criticized jurists for the excessive formalism of legal reasoning.

487. **Economists' misguided criticism: the formalism of the rule would lead to miscarriages of justice.** The opposition between the "effects-based" approach and the "formal" approach originated in the United States in the 1950s.[82] The idea was to criticize the legal approach, which was deemed too formal, judging that the latter, because it did not take into account the effects of disputed behavior, would lead to "type I errors" or "type II errors."[83]

It appears that economic reasoning is, in fact, more formal than legal interpretation, in that it never changes the prism of its analysis or its method of assessment: a behavior is either efficient or it is not, in application of a given economic model.[84] Conversely, the law can change the

---

74 J. Carbonnier, Flexible droit: Pour une sociologie du droit sans rigueur 8 (10th ed. 2013).

75 This is why the "rules *versus* standards" debate (L. Kaplow, *Rules versus Standards: An Economic Analysis*, 42 Duke Law Journal 557, 568 (1992)) is framed in terms that may be subject to criticism. Louis Kaplow distinguishes between rules and standards, arguing that the content of a rule is determined before it is applied to a specific case (*ex ante*), whereas the content of a standard is only known when it is implemented (*ex post*). Yet any norm, whether it takes the form of a precise rule or is based on general and abstract notions, must have "*ex ante*" content in order to be qualified as a norm. In this sense, *see* J. Lindeboom, *Formalism in Competition Law*, 18 Journal of Competition Law & Economics 832, 839 (2022).

76 The criticism being, according to some, caricatured, *see* D. Bosco & C. Prieto, Droit européen de la concurrence 477 (2013), no. 558.

77 On the disadvantages of using precise competition rules, *see supra*, nos. 448 *et seq.*

78 Always, however, context-dependent, so that there is, strictly speaking, no such thing as unlawful conduct per se, *see supra*, no. 320 and no. 322.

79 *See supra*, no. 379.

80 *See supra*, nos. 130 *et seq.*

81 O. Fréget, La concurrence: Une idée toujours neuve en Europe et en France 254 (2015); in the same vein, R. Whish, Intel v. Commission*: Keep Calm and Carry on!*, 6 Journal of European Competition Law & Practice 1, 1 (2015): "The expression 'form-based' is always used pejoratively, but laws by their very nature have 'form'."

82 Lindeboom, *Formalism in Competition Law*, *op. cit.* at 856.

83 *Id.* at 860. *Adde*, on this theme, *see supra*, no. 438; and D. A. Crane, *Rules versus Standards in Antitrust Adjudication*, 64 Washington and Lee Law Review 49 (2007).

84 On this theme, *see* Lindeboom, *Formalism in Competition Law*, *op. cit.* at 861–63.

definition of a norm when faced with a novel case.[85] Thus, the opposition between formalism and the effects-based approach stems from a misunderstanding of legal interpretation, and misses its target, since economic reasoning is no less formalistic than legal reasoning. On the contrary, as early as the 1950s, Paul Roubier warned that legal technique "hardens and freezes the law," preventing it from adapting "to the contours of facts and circumstances."[86] Economists reduce reality "to the mechanism of a few elementary cogs,"[87] and make the rule much more rigid than the jurist, whose reasoning is as fluid as it is lively. Above all, the intrusion of economic concepts into legal discourse compromises the intelligibility of the rule by suggesting, wrongly, that the source of competition law is economic, whereas the role of the jurist is to adopt a discourse that enables the addressees of the rule to understand it, so as to be able to respect it.

II. The role of legal discourse: access to the signified

488. **The need for clarity in legal discourse.** In law, "clarity expresses a degree of adequacy between the explicit terms of a normative system and its implicit terms."[88] When the discourse does not reflect reality, and the explicit contradicts the implicit, access to the norm is compromised. It is therefore absolutely essential to use language that *is faithful to positive law* (**A**), in order to improve the discourse on competition law (**B**).

A. The need to use language that is clear and faithful to positive law

489. **Different ways of describing reality.** There are a thousand and one ways of seeing the world. Does the depiction of a landscape seem more real when painted by a naturalist, than when the picture is the work of a surrealist? Is one vision more accurate than the other? That's not the question: the artist aims to go beyond reality, to sublimate it. The economic, sociological and psychological approaches are no less true than the legal perspective: they all superimpose mental constructs on reality.[89] And it is undoubtedly the multiplication of ways of accessing reality that enables

---

85 *See supra*, nos. 413–414; and *infra*, nos. 518 *et seq.* for illustrations.

86 P. Roubier, Théorie générale du droit: Histoire des doctrines juridiques et philosophie des valeurs sociales 109 (2nd ed. 1951), no. 12.

87 *Id.* (*nota bene*: the author does not specifically target economic analysis).

88 T. Ivainer, *Qu'est-ce qu'un texte clair?*, Histoire Épistémologie Langage no. 4, 23, 28 (1984).

89 On this theme, with regard to law, *see* P. Amselek, *Les règles juridiques en tant qu'objets mentaux*, 79 Archives for Philosophy and Social Philosophy 311(1993).

us to form a more interesting, because broader, idea of it – curiosity always expands perspective.

However, law has one important characteristic: it does not just describe things; it shapes them. It acts on them. And as it constrains reality, the jurist must himself be constrained. By contrast, artists have total freedom. Scientists are slightly less so: they are limited by their quest for truth. However, while they must observe certain principles, these may be swept aside from time to time by scientific revolutions. Moreover, in the human sciences, the multiplication of distinct, even competing schools of thought is proof of the relative freedom of discourse.

490. **The particularity of law: normativity.** The essential difference between law and the other human sciences is a difference of nature, which imposes a difference of method. Since law is the only normative discipline, it is also the only one that cannot deviate from its own principles, otherwise it would betray its essence. Law creates a rationality that falls in love with itself and never abandons itself.[90] Aren't periods in which principles are flouted called periods of "lawlessness"?

Law is close to philosophy, but the age prefers science. And jurists, legislators, civil servants and statesmen often succumb to the temptation to transform scientific knowledge, which is no more than description, into a host of prescriptions.

491. **The peculiarity of competition law: the evolution of discourse, the permanence of substantive rules and reasoning.** The situation in the law of anti-competitive practices is unique in that the general and abstract rules it imposes have not been altered in substance. *Only the discourse has changed*: economic discourse has penetrated legal discourse, without modifying the accepted solutions. The situation is highly paradoxical: economic knowledge has claimed a normative role, and although the legal system has denied it that status, it has nonetheless integrated economic language and vision into its discourse. As a result, two competing – and sometimes incompatible – styles coexist within legal language, leading to statements that are at times illogical and often difficult to interpret.

492. **The coexistence of two styles: one consequentialist, the other behavioral.** An individual picks up an angular stone and appears intent on throwing it at a bay window to shatter it into a thousand pieces. A stone, thrown with sufficient force, has the potential consequence of breaking a pane of glass.

One event, two narratives: in the first sentence, *human action* and *intent* are emphasized; in the second, the focus is on the causal relationship

90 For Denis Baranger's description of the common law, *see* W. Blackstone, *Sur l'étude du droit*, 23 Revue d'histoire des Facultés de droit et de la science juridique 196, 256 (2003) (D. Baranger trans.): it is an "old, thick-skinned beast which, like Roman law before it, abhors definitions and all reductions to first principles. Common law is highly rational, yet at the same time resists reason – understood as the dominion exercised over the world through knowledge of the world – because it is a reason unto itself, and an empire exercised over itself."

between the mechanical setting in motion of an *object* – the stone – and a *result*. The difference lies in the way the story is told, and the impression it leaves on the reader. If the author wishes to emphasize the breaking of the glass, they will emphasize the result: "the bay window could have exploded under the effect of a stone thrown at such speed!"; if they want the character to be remembered, they will dwell on the action: "seized with anger, Jérôme grabbed the largest stone he could find in his path, and prepared to propel it with the intention of breaking the glass…" A scene identical in every respect can be described in different ways.

Every action consists of three elements: intent, conduct and consequence.[91] Either the narrative emphasizes the subjectivity of the action, linking it in a few words to the individual; or it objectifies it by coldly analyzing its characteristics and results. However, law is not literature: the aim of the terms it employs is not to satisfy the aesthetic tastes of its readers, but to communicate the norm it imposes as clearly as possible – clarity of texts, clarity of decisions, clarity of reasoning. Yet the simultaneous use of two different styles to describe the same phenomenon poses a problem for the jurist, as it creates uncertainty about the definition of the norm and the criteria for its application. This is, however, a common practice in the law of anticompetitive practices: the consequentialist style coexists with the behavioral style, producing a pernicious effect – namely, the repeated suggestion that the law is more concerned with sanctioning outcomes than conduct, which is contrary to the reality of case law. While the novelist may, by virtue of artistic freedom, choose a depersonalized style – whether to elevate their novel to the status of a modern masterpiece or to denounce the erosion of the subject in contemporary society – the jurist must strive to align their writing with legal principles, which serve as constraints that limit their creative freedom.

B. Elements for improving the discourse on competition law

493. **For the deletion of certain expressions and phrases.** The use of less rigorous expressions such as "**infringements** by object," "per se," and "by effect" should be discontinued. Not only are they unintelligible to non-specialists, but even in competition law they could be removed without altering the established solutions. Moreover, doctrine and jurisprudence often resort to unfortunate expressions and formulas. What, for example, is gained by writing "discriminatory effect" instead of "discrimination"? Or "the conduct having this effect as its objective" instead of "the objective pursued"? Or, finally, by reasoning as follows: "anticompetitive conduct having as its effect a restriction of competition, itself producing

91 This is the analysis that emerges from the philosophy of action. For contemporary references, *see supra*, no. 183.

an anticompetitive effect," instead of focusing on the only element that truly counts, namely, the conduct?

494. **For a split between legal and economic discourse.** *Legal* discourse on competition law would gain clarity and intelligibility if the two possible approaches – economic and legal – were clearly dissociated. Economists speak about competition using their own reasoning methods and vocabulary.[92] Jurists, on the other hand, should limit the borrowing of economic concepts, and emphasize legal reasoning and concepts. This would make it possible to distinguish between insights from economics, whose role should be limited to being *descriptive*, and legal discourse, which is *normative*. For example, it is not appropriate *to justify in law* the prohibition of a particular practice by "theories of harm," insofar as what they describe – an effect on the market, on the dynamics of competition or on consumer welfare – is not a constitutive element of competition infringements. Similarly, the expressions "type I or type II errors" are not legal concepts, and to use them is, for a jurist, to signal that they accept that their discipline be evaluated according to economic standards.

495. **"Competition," the domain of economists; "*freedom* of competition," the domain of jurists.** Finally, the notion of competition, when considered in isolation, is specific to economists.[93] What interests jurists is "*freedom* of competition," not competition itself. In the final analysis, freedom of competition is no more than the ancient freedom of trade, protected since antiquity. Competition as an economist's object of modeling does not primarily concern the jurist, because the discipline protects the freedom of competition, just as contract law protects freedom of contract.

*

* *

496. **Conclusion of Section 1: the theory of intent, a theory in line with the teleology of competition law and legal semantics.** The theory of intent offers a return to more legal language, by setting aside certain notions and expressions that, because they stem from an economic vision of competition, should be excluded from the legal discourse on competition law. Moreover, because it focuses on the preservation of freedom of competition, and sets out the *legal* criteria for characterizing a restriction on this freedom, it is faithful to the original philosophy of the discipline, according to which freedom of competition must be protected in and for itself. In addition, the adoption of this theory would simplify and clarify the discipline, enabling it to adapt usefully to contemporary issues.

---

92 On this subject, *see* B. Deffains & S. Ferey, Agir et juger: Comment les économistes pensent le droit (2010).

93 *See supra*, no. 368.

*
* *

Section 2
Benefits of adopting the theory of intent

497. **Rediscover the essence of the law of anticompetitive practices to facilitate its adaptation to new cases.** Adopting the theory of intent would not revolutionize the law of anticompetitive practices. On the one hand, this theory is not innovative: it is based on classic legal reasoning, the product of a long tradition. On the other hand, it is already, for the most part, implicitly accepted *de lege lata* – it therefore makes it possible to present in a clear and systematic way reasoning already employed in practice. The adoption of this approach makes the case for simplifying the discipline (**Paragraph 1**), as it invites us to set aside certain superfluous theories that unnecessarily complicate competitive analysis. This theoretical simplification makes it possible to grasp the essence of infringements, and highlights the arguments justifying a decision one way or the other in the presence of a novel case: in this sense, it facilitates the adaptation of competition law to contemporary issues (**Paragraph 2**).

Paragraph 1 – Simplifying competition law

498. **The need for theoretical and practical simplification.** The more complex an object, the more necessary it is to discover its primary elements, so as to be able to communicate to others what it is. This is above all a theoretical task (**I**): it involves removing from the analysis certain excessively sophisticated or even unnecessary lines of reasoning, and clarifying the meaning of commonly used notions. Since law is rhetoric, and doctrine aims at improving the legal order, the proposed simplification is not without practical suggestions (**II**).

I. The theoretical implications of simplification

499. **Bringing together what has been separated.** The common thread running through this study can be summed up in one word: unification. The aim has been to identify false oppositions in order to highlight the unity of reasoning. As a result, it has become clear that abuse of a dominant position and cartels share a unity of nature (**A**), and that the law of anticompetitive practices borrows all its reasoning from general law (**B**).

A. A unitary approach to abuses of dominant positions and cartels

500. **Cartels and abuse of dominant position: offenses of the same nature.** Prior to the French decree of 1953 and the Treaty of Rome of 1957, monopoly was always considered synonymous with hoarding: the maneuvers of merchants were considered to be of the same nature – only the way in which they were perpetrated differed. Even today, both offenses are defined by a single concept: the notion of *dol*.[94] It should therefore be borne in mind that:

1. Anticompetitive intent is identical in the case of a cartel and an abuse of a dominant position. It is a means intended to annihilate or diminish the free will of market players, with the aim of obtaining an advantage that would not have been acquired in its absence.[95]

2. Both infringements fall into the same category: they are offenses of means,[96] which presuppose, in order to be characterized, unlawful conduct and the corresponding mental element. It is the means used, and the means alone, that constitute the offense, the result being unlawful only by virtue of the means employed to obtain it.[97]

3. Cartels and abuses of a dominant position are formal offenses, i.e., attempts to commit them are autonomous offenses.[98] Intent is therefore more important than result, the latter not being required as a constitutive element.[99]

4. The only difference is the time at which the offense is consummated. When committed collectively, the agreement is consummated as soon as it is formed, i.e., as soon as there is a concurrence of wills,[100] whereas when committed individually, the infringement presupposes a commencement of execution.[101]

501. **Demonstrating dominance as a precondition: an indispensable step?** Since competition infringements are identical in nature, we may well ask whether the difference between the two is relevant. Does the characterization of an abuse of a dominant position require proof of the dominant position? Why is it that competition authorities are required to provide evidence of a dominant position in the case of individual conduct, but are not required to demonstrate the collective market power of the parties to a cartel?

---

94 As defined *supra*, nos. 400 *et seq.*

95 *See supra*, no. 404.

96 *See* esp. *supra*, no. 245.

97 *See* esp. *supra*, no. 379.

98 *See supra*, no. 272.

99 *See supra*, nos. 277 *et seq.*

100 *See supra*, no. 280 and no. 327.

101 *See supra*, no. 283.

Could we not consider that, as soon as a unilateral practice potentially restricts the freedom of market players, abuse is sufficient proof of the existence of a dominant position? In other words, does abuse in itself imply dominance, or at the very least, constitute an important indicator of it?[102]

If we accept this premise, it becomes appropriate to dispense with the requirement of proof of a dominant position as a precondition.[103] The proposal is not new: the idea has already been put forward.[104] Such a unification of regimes would save time and lead to significant procedural economies, without increasing the risk of a judicial error. Indeed, it would involve adopting the same regime as that which already exists for cartel cases: a company prosecuted on the basis of article 102 TFEU would, therefore, be entitled to present evidence of its lack of market power.

It would also be appropriate, when companies contest their market power, to give greater consideration to their internal documents in order to identify the market or markets in which they operate or intend to operate, for the purpose of defining the relevant market.[105] Indeed, the substitutability criterion is extremely complex to apply in dynamic markets, which are evolving ever more rapidly and increasingly overlapping. Furthermore, this criterion is neither free from subjectivity nor from uncertainty.[106] Internal documents, by contrast, have the advantage of revealing the commercial strategy of the company in question in a manner that is difficult to dispute, and likely more reliable. This type of evidence would thus render the definition of the relevant market more predictable, fairer, and more precise.

B. Linking the law of anticompetitive practices to the reasoning of general law

502. **Is the law of anticompetitive practices a criminal law that fails to recognize itself as such?** The reasoning behind the characterization of competition

---

102 For the reasons given *supra*, nos. 391 *et seq.*

103 However, the Commission could choose, as part of its discretionary power, to prosecute only companies of a certain size, leaving it to the national competition authorities to prosecute smaller companies. Nevertheless, in theory, any company whose conduct acts *erga omnes*, and not just *inter partes* (*see supra*, no. 404), is liable to prosecution if it engages in anticompetitive behavior. This assertion has a significant deterrent value and would generally help ensure greater discipline across markets.

104 One author, for example, has proposed removing the condition of a dominant position, and characterizing abuse according to a single criterion, namely, an "appreciable and illegitimate restriction of competition," *see* A.-S. Choné-Grimaldi, Les abus de domination: Essai en droit des contrats et en droit de la concurrence 247–57 (2010), nos. 371–393. While we agree with the idea that a single criterion might suffice, instead of the current three or even four (dominant position, abuse, restriction of competition, and effect on the market or consumers), for the reasons given *supra*, nos. 354 *et seq.*, we consider that this single criterion lies in anticompetitive behavior and not restriction of competition. *See also* EAGCP, An Economic Approach to Article 82, 14 (July 2005): "Traditional modes of establishing 'dominance' by recourse to information about market structure are merely proxies for a determination of 'dominance' in any substantive sense, *i.e.*, the ability to exert power and impose abusive behavior on other market participants. If an effect-based approach provides evidence of an abuse which is only possible if the firm has a position of dominance, then no further separate demonstration of dominance should be needed."

105 This proposal has already been put forward by legal writers, *see supra*, no. 395 (footnote).

106 *See supra*, no. 392.

infringements is identical to that of criminal law. Contrary to the commonly held view that the discipline's methods and concepts are autonomous from general law, the law of anticompetitive practices has remained based on traditional legal principles and reasoning, which have been obscured by the emphasis on theories lacking normative force, a complex institutional framework, and the adoption of a technical vocabulary that is difficult to understand.

503. **Proposals for clarifying competitive analysis.** In order to improve the clarity of competitive analysis, the following proposals should be accepted:

1. The notion of restriction of competition is entirely conflated with anticompetitive behavior itself.[107] The two have been dissociated because of an economic approach to competition, with economists isolating the latter in order to study it, while jurists are primarily interested in behavior that restricts the freedom of action of market players.[108] Thus, dissociating anticompetitive behavior from the restriction of competition leads to unnecessary complexity of reasoning.

2. Depending on the context in which it is used, the notion of anticompetitive effect covers either the effect on competition, or the effect on the market or consumers. In the former case, it is confused with the restriction of competition – in which case, like the latter, it is redundant. In the second case, it refers to the actual or potential *result* of the infringement. In this case, the term "result" should be preferred to "effect," as it has a precise legal meaning – it refers to the outcome of the infringement.

3. The result is not required as a constituent element of competition infringements. The gain or advantage obtained by the offending undertakings is unlawful only by virtue of the means used to achieve it, from which it follows that the result cannot be used to infer the existence of an infringement.[109]

4. "Infringement by object," "restriction by object," "approach by object" or "approach per se" are conceptually indistinguishable from "infringement by effect," "restriction by effect" or "approach by effect." These terms only exist in competition law, and are legally meaningless. An infringement is always made up of the same constituent elements: it cannot be either intentional or unintentional, depending on the case. Effects cannot be used to punish the unforeseeable consequences of the conduct adopted by companies; and when effects are foreseeable, intent is presumed. The effects-based approach therefore adds nothing to the object-based approach.[110]

---

107 For the reasons given *supra*, nos. 367 *et seq.*

108 *See supra*, no. 404.

109 *See supra*, no. 379.

110 *See supra*, no. 303.

Case law seems to have linked this alternative to different standards of proof: examining effects would imply a greater burden of proof. Nevertheless, without the need for a written rule to specify this, the principle is that when there is doubt about the existence of an infringement, it is necessary to prove more.[111] There is therefore no need for the alternative between object and effect, and the latter is not useful insofar as evidentiary reasoning would be identical if it did not exist – its abandonment would not entail a lightening of the standard of proof. It should be dispensed with, as it leads to confusion over the constituent elements of the infringement, and leads to endless doctrinal and litigation debates that could be avoided.

5. The alternative between "intentionally" and "negligently" in article 23(1) and (2) of Regulation 1/2003 should be abandoned. The same infringement cannot be both intentional and negligent, as each infringement is based on a single mental element, which can be deduced from the structure of the incriminating text and, if necessary, its interpretation in case law. In practice, negligence is systematically confused with an error of law.[112] As the latter is taken into account without the need for a written rule, eliminating negligence would in no way change the solutions already accepted.

6. The expression "subjective intent" designates motives, not intent.[113] Motives may be relevant from time to time as a clue used to corroborate evidence of the infringement, or at the stage of determining the *quantum* of the penalty, as a mitigating or aggravating circumstance, but they are not a constitutive element.

7. The theory of legitimate grounds consists in admitting that conduct, which would otherwise be deemed unlawful, can be justified by the pursuit of an objective deemed lawful, provided that the conduct adopted is necessary and proportionate to achieving it.[114] This theory makes it possible to cover the full range of defenses accepted by the judge: objective justifications, individual and block exemptions, and ancillary restraints. Self-defense, on the other hand, is never accepted in anticompetitive practices law.[115]

8. A single article could usefully replace the current articles 101 and 102 TFEU, making it possible to punish abuses of dominant positions and cartels simultaneously:

---

111 *See supra*, nos. 292 *et seq.*

112 *See supra*, no. 269.

113 *See supra*, no. 267.

114 *See supra*, nos.337 *et seq.*

115 *See supra*, no. 350.

> Are prohibited, insofar as they are liable to affect trade between Member States and provided that they do not pursue a legitimate ground, conduct adopted by an undertaking aimed at restricting, individually or collectively, the free formation of the conditions of exchange, with the aim of obtaining an undue advantage.[116]

The adoption of a text of this type would make it possible to clearly bring out the structure of the infringement from a reading of the incriminating text. Such drafting would do away with the double analysis implied by paragraphs 1 and 3 of article 101:[117] since exemption regulations establish simple legal presumptions of lawfulness, the latter could be taken into account on the basis of the theory of legitimate grounds.[118]

9. The role of economic expertise should be presented with more measure: *de lege lata*, economic expertise is merely relevant but ancillary evidence, forming part of a much broader body of evidence.[119] They should only be used when they are useful in proving a constituent element of the infringement, and not to demonstrate an overabundance of evidence.[120]

10. Economic analysis should only ever be *descriptive*, not *prescriptive*: it has no right to dictate to the legal system the solutions it should adopt, whether in terms of formulating the objectives pursued by the norm, defining it, or implementing it.[121] At the very most, it can, like other sciences, help to grasp the facts, and stimulate certain debates.[122]

504. **A doctrinal reorientation.** In light of the foregoing, it would appear that doctrinal attention should be refocused on a question that seems to us to be among the most essential: what is fraudulent conduct in competition law? Since the evolution of a concept is the fruit of collective reflection,

---

116 This proposed wording is loosely based on article 419 of the French Penal Code, as amended in 1926: "All those who … by exercising or attempting to exercise, either individually, or through assembly or coalition, an action on the market with the aim of obtaining a gain that would not be the result of the natural interplay of supply and demand … shall be punished." On this reform, *see supra*, nos. 126–127.

117 This proposal has already been put forward by several authors, *see supra*, no. 348.

118 *See supra*, no. 345.

119 *See supra*, nos.331 *et seq.*

120 Which, *de lege lata*, is not always the case in practice, *see supra*, no. 333.

121 Cf. J.-C. Roda, *La crise du droit* antitrust, *in* Mélanges en l'honneur de Jacques Mestre 839, 847 and 848, resp. (2019): "As with the expert in a conventional civil trial, the judge should not be bound by the economists' observations," and "[i]f economic analysis truly is an empirical science, as is often claimed, it should not have a prescriptive role: in principle, it should simply be about describing what is and not indicating what ought to be."

122 In this sense, P. Maistre du Chambon & P. Conte, *Préface*, *in* Analyse économique du droit et matière pénale xiii, xiv (C. Claverie Rousset ed., 2018): economic analysis can "be useful in criminal law, at least insofar as it retains the role it ought to have – that of an aid to understanding certain forms of criminality, in the same way as history, psychology, sociology, etc. – and on the condition, therefore, of avoiding any hegemonic drift: criminality is a complex phenomenon, at once human and social, individual and collective, which by its very nature calls for examination from all angles."

admitting that a competition infringement consists of *dol with market power* invites specialists to debate the arguments for deciding whether certain practices fall into this category.[123] In the light of case law, the aim would be to identify the constants in the reasoning, and then to seize on borderline or novel cases to engage in a *disputatio* on the reasons justifying a decision one way or the other.

II. The practical consequences of simplification

505. **Two avenues for practical improvement.** Adopting the theory of intent would improve the reasoning behind decisions, and hence the readability of competition law (**A**), and would also encourage the Commission to make useful and reasoned use of exemption regulations and guidelines (**B**).

A. Improving the motivation of decisions and the legibility of the law

506. **Quality of motivation and clarity of the rule.** Motivation for decisions must make it possible to clearly identify the constituent elements of an infringement, and to infer from case law the reasons for a decision. At present, decisions are so long and complex that even specialists sometimes find it difficult to follow the Court's reasoning. Admittedly, the practices with which the competition authorities are dealing are becoming increasingly sophisticated, but complexity need not be met with greater complexity. On the contrary, to grasp what is complex, we need to set out in search of simplicity. While certain contentious debates – in particular those concerning evidence, procedural compliance, the competence of authorities, the definition of the undertaking's scope, and the duration of infringements – must continue to mobilize significant resources, as they contribute to the proper administration of justice, a simplification is both possible and necessary. Abandoning theories based on effects and simplifying reasoning would reduce the length of decisions and de facto improve their readability.

Would the authorities' decision-making practice and case law not be more intelligible if we were to remove the debates on effects, on the alternative between object and effects, on justifications based on efficiency gains and individual exemptions, as well as the statements of principle relating to consumer welfare? What if the judge were to write outright that the purpose of the evidence is to demonstrate *dol*, and if their reasoning were explicitly aimed at linking the disputed practices to this *legal* category by means of arguments of a *legal nature* – in other words, arguments that any jurist can understand without any difficulty whatsoever?

123 For illustrations based on behaviors adopted by digital companies, *see infra*, nos. 517 *et seq.*

The law on anticompetitive practices has all the qualities required for the implementation of a fair, clear and effective competition policy:[124] it is based on a general and abstract norm of conduct, subject to stable interpretation by the courts and adaptable to new cases. All that is required, therefore, is for decisions to be better reasoned, so that companies of all sizes know whether the conduct they intend to adopt is lawful or unlawful under competition rules. The cases in which it would be necessary to recognize the existence of a reasonable doubt as to the scope of the law would become extremely rare, if not exceptional, and the assertion that the company was aware that it was infringing the rules would no longer suffer from any reproach of artificiality, or even fiction.[125]

507. **Simplification, a source of greater efficiency in enforcing competition rules.** The simplification of the discipline would both generate significant procedural economies and improve the speed of justice, giving competition authorities the opportunity to increase the number of cases prosecuted, and respond to more complaints. In addition to public enforcement, the adoption of the theory of intent could also encourage private enforcement.[126] Indeed, while Directive 2014/104/EU[127] has encouraged the growth of private actions,[128] it still seems difficult for victims of anticompetitive practices to obtain compensation for the harm suffered in the absence of a prior decision by an authority finding the existence of an infringement. The fact that proof of effects, or even of a dominant position in the case of abuse, is no longer required, would make it possible to limit the need for costly economic analyses, as well as to circumvent the

---

124 It should be added that competition authorities may also conduct sector inquiries in order to gain a better understanding of the operation of certain markets, cf. W. Chaiehloudj, *Quels outils efficaces pour les autorités de concurrence dans l'économie numérique?*, Contrats concurrence consommation (Mar. 2020), étude 4, no. 9, and examples mentioned. Some authors, meanwhile, believe that sector inquiries "may well become, in the future, a multifunctional tool for market intervention, going beyond their original function of detecting infringements of competition rules," *see* N. Petit & C. Lousberg, *Le "couteau suisse" du droit européen de la concurrence?*, Concurrences no. 2-2010, art. no. 31031, 21, 32, no. 45. Competition authorities are also justified in adopting precautionary measures in order to intervene rapidly (*see*, for example, recently: ADLC, decision no. 23-MC-01 of May 4, 2023, on the request by the company Adloox for interim measures (Fr.); comm. M. Cartapanis, *L'Autorité de la concurrence prononce des mesures conservatoires pour mettre fin à des pratiques susceptibles de constituer un abus de position dominante dans le secteur de la publicité en ligne*, Concurrences no. 3-2023, art. no. 113346, 92).

125 On this subject, *see supra*, no. 467.

126 According to David Bosco, the future of competition law presupposes, among other things, a "revival of private enforcement of competition law," *see* D. Bosco, *L'avenir du droit de la concurrence*, Contrats concurrence consommation (Dec. 2020), dossier 15, no. 4.

127 Directive 2014/104/EU of the European Parliament and of the Council of Nov. 26, 2014, on Certain Rules Governing Actions for Damages under National Law for Infringements of the Competition Law Provisions of the Member States and of the European Union, 2014 O.J. (L 349) 1.

128 In particular, by introducing, for the benefit of victims of anticompetitive practices, a presumption of fault on the part of the judge when a competition authority characterizes an infringement, presumptions facilitating proof of damage, and by facilitating access to evidence held by third parties, in particular competition authorities. For an overview, *see* G. Decocq, *Leçon sur la responsabilité civile du fait d'une pratique anticoncurrentielle*, *in* Leçons de droit civil: Mélanges en l'honneur de François Chabas 197 (N. Guimezanes ed., 2011); J. Riffault-Silk, *Action et recours privés*, *in* Dictionnaire de droit de la concurrence 73 (M. Chagny & E. Combe eds., 2023); and for an in-depth study: R. Amaro & J.-F. Laborde, La réparation des préjudices causés par les pratiques anticoncurrentielles: Recueil de décisions commentées (2nd ed. 2020).

problem of access to certain evidence, which would encourage victims to take legal action.[129] However, as things stand at present, and given the porosity between anticompetitive practices and unfair competition,[130] it seems more plausible that a victim could obtain compensation on the basis of article 1240 of the Civil Code by attempting to extend the scope of unfair competition to new cases,[131] than by trying, on his or her own, to provide proof of an agreement or abuse.

B. For a useful and reasoned use of soft law and exemption regulations

508. **Toward a simplification of guidelines and exemption regulations.** Through the use of soft law instruments, the Commission has sought, on its own initiative, to bring about a change in the way in which anticompetitive practices are apprehended. The modernization drive, driven by the ambition to make implementation of the rules more efficient, has paradoxically led to a reduction in their effectiveness. By placing the emphasis on the effects of behavior, and by suggesting that companies could justify the adoption of infringing conduct by efficiency gains benefiting the consumer, it has taken a different path from that of the judges of the European Union.[132] Yet the function of guidelines is, or at least should be, to clarify the scope of the rules for the benefit of those to whom they are addressed, not to attempt to impose an economic or politicized vision of them, which in part runs counter to established case law. In this respect, the amendments recently made by the Commission to its communication on the priorities adopted in the field of abuse of a dominant position, while intended to "taking into account the experience gained through the Commission's enforcement practice" and "the clarifications provided by the case law of the Union Courts,"[133] in other words, to bring the Commission's soft law into line with case law, we feel that they

129 More effective collective redress mechanisms than those provided for by the Hamon law should also be introduced, as the Commission invited ten years ago, *see* Eur. Comm. Press Release IP/13/524, Commission Recommends Member States to Have Collective Redress Mechanisms in Place to Ensure Effective Access to Justice (June 11, 2013). This becomes particularly necessary in digital markets, insofar as anticompetitive practices result in a large number of victims, whose individual harm may not be particularly substantial (*see supra*, no. 132).

130 *See supra*, no. 149.

131 The recent Paris Court of Appeal ruling in the *UberPop* case (CA Paris, pôle 5, Oct. 4, 2023, no. 21/22383, *UberPop* (Fr.)), whereby the judges appear to be using the basis of unfair competition to punish an infringement of the free play of competition, invites us to reflect on this point, since in this case, the damage is not confined to certain players, but affects the market as a whole – as evidenced by the fact that the judges note that the disputed practices "*had the effect of disrupting the market* by placing the Uber group and the users of its services, whether occasional drivers or professional drivers, in an abnormally favorable situation compared with their taxi-driver competitors who comply with the regulations governing the paid transport of private individuals" (emphasis added) (unofficial translation).

132 *See supra*, nos. 284–288 and nos. 359–361.

133 Eur. Comm., Amendments to the Communication from the Commission Guidance on the Commission's Enforcement Priorities in Applying Article 82 of the EC Treaty to Abusive Exclusionary Conduct by Dominant Undertakings, Annex, C(2023) 1923 final, (Mar. 27, 2023), para. 1.

are still insufficient, insofar as they remain strongly inclined toward the objective and criterion of consumer welfare, and are still entrenched in a very (overly) economic approach.

Furthermore, exemption regulations would benefit from being based not on the idea that an infringement can be exempted following an assessment of its pro- and anticompetitive effects,[134] but on a simpler reasoning in line with case law. The idea would be to emphasize the fact that companies' conduct does not constitute an infringement of competition rules if it is necessary and proportionate to the achievement of legitimate objectives,[135] which the regulations would be designed precisely to set out – which would make it easier for companies to enact compliance programs and implement them properly. Finally, as Catherine Prieto has pointed out, it would be advisable "to be vigilant about the presence of confirmed jurists among the drafters of exemption regulations and guidelines, with a view solely to ensuring readability."[136]

509. **Reflections on prosecutorial discretion.** When the Commission published its Guidelines on abuse of a dominant position, it suggested that it would use its discretionary power to prosecute as a matter of priority infringements likely to have a negative impact on consumers, and it is well known that, in practice, the Commission mobilizes economic analyses to prioritize the cases it intends to take up.[137] Since the criterion for classifying competition infringements is not economic, but legal, how can we justify the fact that economic analysis plays such an important role in the selection of cases prosecuted? Does such an approach not risk opening the door to a selection process that appears, at times, to be driven more by a case's media potential[138] than by the seriousness of the behavior in question? The primary criterion ought to be the gravity of the conduct rather than its effects.[139]

Moreover, the Commission must not shy away from pursuing new practices, without recourse to the commitment procedure,[140] so as to enable case law to evolve and decide, in the course of appeals, which unprecedented conduct is detrimental to the free play of competition. Finally, as competition law is

---

134 *See supra*, no. 345.

135 *Id.*

136 C. Prieto, *Source économique du droit de la concurrence: Quelle efficacité?*, CONTRATS CONCURRENCE CONSOMMATION (June 2020), dossier 3, no. 21.

137 T. Valletti & B. Durand, *Tommaso Valletti (DG COMP) Economics in Competition Law – Working Together*, CONCURRENCES no. 4-2017, art. no. 84875, 11, 12.

138 Pierre Mazeaud forcefully asserted that legislators must "refrain from turning the law into an instrument of communication," and avoid a "degeneration of the law into an instrument of political spectacle," *see* P. Mazeaud, *Vœux du président du Conseil constitutionnel, M. Pierre Mazeaud, au Président de la République*, CAHIERS DU CONSEIL CONSTITUTIONNEL (July 2005), no. 18.

139 If only because these are difficult to establish, even more so before the investigation begins.

140 For the reasons given *supra*, nos. 445–447.

universal in its application, the desire to apply competition rules to digital markets must not lead to their under-enforcement in other sectors. The protection of victims is at stake, as is the dissuasive potential of discipline, because if companies know that their sector of activity is being ignored by the competition authorities, they may be encouraged to engage in illicit behavior.

510. **The opportunity offered by "soft law."** The possibility offered to the Commission of using soft law[141] would enable it to respond usefully and effectively to contemporary issues. While making it clear that such communications are not intended to establish the law, the Commission could inform companies that it will, in the future, consider certain borderline or novel cases to be anticompetitive. With the help of a legal team, it would then have to justify these assertions *against the yardstick and within the limits of* the Court's established case law, by arguing them in law. Such a practice would be likely to have the consequence, by informing companies of the conduct that the institution expects of them in the future, of encouraging them to comply with it in advance. The advantages of such a solution, compared with the adoption of specific regulations such as the Digital Markets Act, are manifold. Firstly, it does not require the mobilization of the legislator, and can be easily and rapidly adopted. Secondly, as it is only an interpretation of existing rules, it does not create legal uncertainty – provided that the Commission remains faithful to the spirit of the texts and interpretation in case law. Thirdly, given that the Commission's margin of discretion when implementing articles 101 and 102 TFEU is limited, and that its guidelines are not binding on the European courts, the latter would not deprive companies of genuine judicial control,[142] nor of the possibility of challenging the Commission's positions.

Paragraph 2 – Adapting competition law to contemporary challenges

511. **Two contemporary challenges: artificial intelligence and digital markets.** Competition law is currently confronted with two major challenges that the theory of intent can help to address: on the one hand, the legal treatment of potentially anticompetitive behavior committed by means of "artificial intelligence" (**I**), and on the other, the novel practices adopted by companies in the digital sector (**II**).

141 On the notion of soft law and its integration into the general theory of law, *see* C. Thibierge, *Le droit souple: Réflexion sur les textures du droit*, RTD Civ. 599 (2003). *Adde*, for a look at soft law in competition law, *see* E. Claudel, *Les sources vives du droit de la concurrence (Étude du droit européen et français des pratiques anticoncurrentielles)*, *in* Mélanges en l'honneur du Professeur Claude Lucas de Leyssac 57, 62–80 (2018).

142 By contrast, judicial review of commitment decisions is limited to manifest errors of assessment, in view of the wider margin of discretion conferred on competition authorities, *see supra*, no. 446; and the same may legitimately be expected of judicial review of decisions finding a breach of the rules of the Digital Markets Act.

I. The theory of intent and "artificial intelligence"

512. **Is the intelligent algorithm an "agent" in its own right, or a tool for which the company is responsible?** The algorithm[143] is as old as time itself: had Euclid not already devised a series of operations for calculating the greatest common divisor of two numbers around 300 BC? At the time, algorithms were a method of calculation used to improve mathematical knowledge. Since then, the perception of the algorithm has evolved to the point where it is now often considered not simply as a tool, but almost as an individual in its own right – an "artificial intelligence."[144] Having personified it in this way, can we now consider holding it responsible for the damage it causes? Should we, taking the anthropomorphic perspective to its logical conclusion, postulate the existence of algorithmic free will? Or, to put it another way, can it be said to have an intent of its own? Asking these questions implies taking a legal look at this contemporary issue (**A**), which will shed light on how competition law can apprehend the practices of companies mobilizing these digital tools (**B**).

A. A legal perspective: free will, responsibility and "artificial intelligence"

513. **Man-made intelligence: an ancient idea.** Is not the idea that humans might give *life* to a machine of their own making, designed according to their desires from inert matter, identical to the alchemist's quest to find the secret formula for transforming lead into gold? Such an ambition stems from the desire to rise above natural laws, to create for oneself a being or a precious material that exists in nature only by chance. It has always aroused fascination: from the earliest times, automata, i.e., devices that mechanically imitate the movements of a living being,[145] were produced to be used either for purely recreational purposes, or with a scientific aim.[146] These electronics and steel *devices* were perfected as technology advanced, and faith in progress knew no bounds, leading to the belief that the automaton would one day reach the decisive milestone: that of

---

143 According to the specialized literature, an algorithm is "an unambiguous, precise, list of simple operations applied mechanically and systematically to a set of tokens or objects," *see* OECD, Algorithms and Collusion DAF/COMP(2017)4 (June 9, 2017), at 6.

144 Artificial intelligence is defined as a field of computer science devoted to the study of "intelligent agents," i.e., "able to carry out tasks of significant difficulty in a way that is perceived as 'intelligent'," *see id.* at 7. According to the proposed European regulation on artificial intelligence, an "artificial intelligence system" is "software" capable of "generat[ing] outputs such as content, predictions, recommendations, or decisions influencing the environments they interact with," *see* Eur. Comm., *Proposal for a Regulation of the European Parliament and of the Council Laying Down Harmonised Rules on Artificial Intelligence (Artificial Intelligence Act) and Amending Certain Union Legislative Acts*, COM/2021/206 final (Apr. 21, 2021), art. 3(1).

145 A. Lalande, Vocabulaire technique et critique de la philosophie 98–99 (2002).

146 For a historical perspective, *see* J.-C. Beaune & A. Doyon, *Automate*, Encyclopædia Universalis.

intelligence, *consciousness*, *autonomy* – in other words, that it *would come to life* and be transformed into an *autonomous being*, almost like any other, but more rational and more efficient than the others.

First in the minds of science fiction writers, then in the collective unconscious, machines have become creatures – entities created out of nothing, by humans and for humans, which could help them by emancipating them from difficult or thankless tasks, seduce them by offering the promise of time savings, augment them by calculating what they are not powerful enough to conceive independently, assist them by whispering to them the optimum decisions. The figure of a docile assistant made of clay is not new: it recalls the mythical Golem, an embryonic being created by a wise man to serve him, which quickly became uncontrollable and threatening.[147] Here we see the darker side of the algorithm, and the crux of the problem, as it arises for the jurist: can this being, sometimes marvelous, sometimes monstrous, be held *responsible* when it causes damage?

514. **Should we postulate the free will of the "intelligent algorithm"?** The debate is not whether it is *possible* to admit the freedom of the algorithm, but whether such recognition would be *relevant*. Indeed, in law, the recognition of free will – whether of an individual or a legal person – has always been the result of pragmatic reflection. It has never been more than a *postulate*: no one can provide proof of the full autonomy of a human being,[148] and it is well known that attributing a will of its own to a legal person results from a legal *abstraction*.[149] These postulates are accepted not because they are true, but because they are relevant: they encourage compliance with the rules.

Freedom, and its corollary responsibility, implies one essential thing: *power*, understood in its original sense – the ability and possibility to act.[150] There are two things of which only human beings are capable: on the one hand, *sensation* – the pleasure of reward, the suffering of blame – and, on the other, the *intelligence* to understand what is forbidden and to avoid it. If a legal person is recognized as having a will of its own, it is because its culture, as well as its hierarchical and procedural framework, conditions the decisions of its members, and can, therefore, *influence* their behavior.[151] Although devoid of feelings, it nonetheless wields *power* over beings endowed with sentience.

---

147 For a parallel between mythology and artificial intelligence, *see* P. Bentata, *Ce que les mythes nous racontent de l'AI*, L'Opinion, July 20, 2023, at 8.

148 Cf. *supra*, no. 27.

149 *See supra*, no. 165.

150 *See supra*, no. 387.

151 *See supra*, no. 167.

Conversely, the algorithm, even if deemed intelligent, never has power over the individual: it is under the individual's control, or at the very least, it *must be* and remain so. This is borne out by the draft European regulation on the use of artificial intelligence, which prohibits the use of these tools to manipulate individuals, exploit their vulnerability or influence their behavior[152] – a clear indication that the legal system does not accept that artificial intelligence has any control over the human mind. Thus, it is up to the user to control the "intelligent" algorithm, and to ensure that it functions in accordance with its intended purpose. However, when algorithmic software is endowed with the ability to learn as it experiments, it seems to gain in "autonomy," insofar as its actions may not be determined in advance by its designer or user. The law is then faced with a singular situation: the machine's decision may not be a faithful expression of the will of the person who designed or uses it.[153] However, it is a general principle that the law holds individuals responsible for the foreseeable consequences of their actions, as well as for the consequences that *must be* foreseen. To accept that the user of an algorithm is not responsible for the damage caused by the tool they use would be to remove that responsibility, all the more so as it is now accepted that there are algorithmic auditing solutions that enable real-time monitoring of the software's correct operation, thus reducing the already limited autonomy of the machine to a bare minimum.

Consequently, the idea that artificial intelligence can *autonomously* be the cause of an infringement is based on faulty reasoning: even when the algorithm goes off course, and deviates from its intended purpose, this risk must have been foreseen by the user – hence, the decisions taken by the machine can be *deemed* to have been intended by the user, and to engage their individual liability.[154] It is therefore impossible to recognize any specific intention in a machine, since it is never more than

---

152 Eur. Comm., *Proposal for a Regulation of the European Parliament and of the Council Laying Down Harmonised Rules on Artificial Intelligence (Artificial Intelligence Act) and Amending Certain Union Legislative Acts*, COM/2021/206 final (Apr. 21, 2021), Title II.

153 *See* S. Mérabet, Vers un droit de l'intelligence artificielle 80–86 and 117–18 (2018) (Ph.D. dissertation, Aix-Marseille Université).

154 This is *a normative presumption*. When an intentional offense in the strict sense is committed due to the use of artificial intelligence, the decision taken by the latter must be deemed to have been intended by the user, who, depending on the case, should be able to engage the liability of the software supplier if it has been found defective. When an intentional offense in the broadest sense (in particular an offense of lack of foresight) is committed as a result of intelligent software – notably when an accident is caused by a vehicle equipped with "automated driving systems" (ADS) – the fault will rest with the manufacturer if the driver was not at the controls of the vehicle, as "the distance [between the manufacturer and] the offense does not exonerate them: they continue to act, if necessary wrongfully, through the ADS they have installed. In any case, the autonomous vehicle remains a 'thing,' and the artificial intelligence that drives it, devoid of legal personality, does not relieve the persons operating it of responsibility," *see* S. Detraz, *De la mauvaise conduite des véhicules autonomes en droit pénal*, Recueil Dalloz 1039 (2021). In civil law, on the adaptation of the liability regime for defective products and certain special compensation regimes to cover damage caused by artificial intelligence, *see* G. Loiseau, *Les responsabilités du fait de l'intelligence artificielle*, Communication Commerce Électronique (Apr. 2019), comm. 24.

a tool over which human beings must retain full control.[155] It follows that the issues raised by the use of algorithms by companies can be dealt with by applying the traditional reasoning of competition law.

B. The challenges arising from the use of artificial intelligence by companies

515. **Algorithms as a means of committing an infringement.** In their report on algorithms, the French and German competition authorities noted that they had already dealt with a "certain spectrum of cases involving algorithms, which have not raised specific legal difficulties."[156] The best-known example is the *Eturas* case, which involved the use of a common software to set the discount rates applied to customers on behalf of several travel booking agencies. The cartel was deemed to have been established, since the companies "could *reasonably assume* that all the other users of that system would also limit their discounts to a maximum of 3%."[157] In the *Pioneer* case, the Commission took into consideration the use of software, which, by monitoring retailers' price deviations, facilitated their control and thus prevented price erosion.[158] In terms of price discrimination, the use of algorithms will only be deemed infringement if it is aimed at unduly exploiting consumers[159] or foreclosing competition,[160] as in the *Google Shopping* decision.[161] If it were proven that the use of an algorithm had facilitated the implementation, monitoring or balancing of the cartel,[162] it would be appropriate for this circumstance to be taken into account as an aggravating circumstance. Nevertheless, in all these cases, the use of algorithms does not raise any real theoretical issues: they are merely the technical means by which infringements are committed, and such conduct is already covered by established case law.

---

155 *Contra*, for a viewpoint defending the idea that artificial intelligence should be granted legal personality and rights, *see* P.-J. Delage, *Les androïdes rêveront-ils de personnalité juridique*?, *in* SCIENCE-FICTION ET SCIENCE JURIDIQUE 165 (P.-J. Delage ed., 2013).

156 ADLC & Bundeskartellamt, Algorithms and Competition, Executive Summary (Nov. 2019), at 5.

157 Case C-74/14, Eturas, ECLI:EU:C:2016:42, para. 15.

158 Eur. Comm., July 24, 2018, C(2018) 4790 final, Pioneer, esp. para. 155; comm. D. Bosco, *Concurrence algorithmique et droit des ententes*, CONTRATS CONCURRENCE CONSOMMATION (Nov. 2018), comm. 194.

159 This hypothesis, according to which the price discrimination made possible by the ability to set personalized prices could lead to abusively high prices, has not attracted any particular interest from the competition authorities, which is no doubt due to the fact that the criteria for classifying prices as abusive are particularly stringent (*supra*, no. 406). In this respect, *see* M. Cousin, *L'algorithme au service de la politique tarifaire: Nouvelles pratiques, nouveaux risques?*, CONCURRENCES no. 4-2017, art. no. 84905, 17, 19. The use of pricing algorithms could, however, lead to "perfect" pricing discrimination (F. Marty, *Algorithmes de prix et discrimination parfaite: Une théorie concurrentielle en voie de trouver sa pratique?* (Science Po OFCE Working Paper, no. 31, Dec. 2017), but companies are reluctant to engage in such practices, as they damage their image and arouse consumer distrust (E. COMBE, VERS DES PRIX PERSONNALISÉS À L'HEURE DU NUMÉRIQUE? 38–39 (Oct. 2019)).

160 F. Marty, *Plateformes numériques, algorithmes et discrimination*, 164 REVUE DE L'OFCE 1, 16–18 (2019).

161 Eur. Comm., June 27, 2017, C(2017) 4444 final, Google Search (Shopping).

162 On this topic, *see* OECD, *Algorithms and Collusion*, DAF/COMP(2017)4 (June 9, 2017), at 29–36.

516. **Artificial intelligence, the imputation of a violation and the concurrence of wills.** What if the algorithm is not just a tool under the company's control, but becomes an independent agent making "autonomous" decisions? Even if the reality of such a possibility is still debated among experts,[163] it does not seem to create any insurmountable theoretical difficulties either. Two cases, for the moment purely hypothetical, can be mentioned here.

The first is that of the commission of an infringement of the competition rules, whatever it may be, by an intelligent algorithm that has not respected the function assigned to it. As we know, case law concerning the modalities for imputing an infringement to a company is very expansive: it is sufficient that an infringement was committed by any one or more of its agents for it to be attributable to the company, even if the main partners or managers were unaware of their actions.[164] This solution is based on the idea that it is the company's responsibility to ensure that its agents do not commit unlawful acts, and that it is legitimate for it to be held liable for them, all the more so when the fault is economically profitable for it. However, there is nothing to prevent artificial intelligence from engaging the responsibility of the company[165] in the same way as an agent, because if the company can and must control the acts of its employees, it can and must *a fortiori* ensure that it has control over the IT tools it uses – because a machine is more controllable than a human being. In any event, it must remain so, or cease to be used. The reasoning is simple: since an offense committed by an employee is imputed to the company, even if the employee acts *in an unforeseeable manner*, i.e., without having received orders to do so and without alerting their superiors,[166] there is no reason to consider that the faulty or unplanned operation of an "artificial intelligence" could exonerate the company from its responsibility[167] – since the company must ensure that the algorithm it uses functions in accordance with its intended purpose.[168]

163 As one author rightly points out: "The [AAI] issues will need to be discussed, tested, and resolved before the scenarios of AAI literature can be integrated in policy environments. To date, the EU Commission is in observational mode," *see* N. Petit, *Antitrust and Artificial Intelligence: A Research Agenda*, 8 Journal of European Competition Law & Practice 361, 362 (2017).

164 *See supra*, no. 172.

165 However, it seems unlikely that the algorithm designer or supplier would be held liable under competition law. This is because, under the principle of personal liability, the latter would have to be found to have had anticompetitive intent, whereas software designers and suppliers have no interest in restricting competition in their customers' markets. The only qualification that seems conceivable is that of cartel facilitator, subject to proving that the designer or supplier was aware of the possibility of using the software in question for anticompetitive purposes – but is that not a textbook case? *See* M. Malaurie-Vignal, *Algorithmes et concurrence*, Contrats concurrence consommation (June 2021), étude 6, nos. 18–29.

166 *See supra*, no. 172.

167 On this theme, *compare with* N. Zingales, *Antitrust Intent in an Age of Algorithmic Nudging*, 7 Journal of Antitrust Enforcement 386, 408–10 (2019).

168 Cf. the solutions adopted in cases of market abuse, when companies resort to high-frequency algorithmic trading techniques and are sanctioned on the basis of the offense of price manipulation, even when the use of the algorithm was dysfunctional. *See* F. Barrière, *L'algorithme fou*, Bulletin Joly Bourse no. 10, 410 (2016); F. Barrière, *Trading algorithmique et manipulation sur contrats financiers*, Bulletin Joly Bourse no. 2,

The second case involves the possibility of price coordination through the use of separate algorithms, without there being any concurrence of wills between the companies.[169] It seems just as hypothetical as the first, insofar as there is lively debate in the specialized literature as to whether tacit collusion is really possible between algorithms, outside of controlled laboratory experiments.[170] Following the same reasoning as above, however, it appears that if this type of algorithmic collusion is one day scientifically proven, the company will be, or at the very least should be, aware of the pricing uniformity that could result from the simultaneous use, by itself and its competitors, of algorithms capable of colluding with each other.[171] The use of this type of tool should then make it possible to presume the existence of a concurrence of wills between the different companies, since as the consequence of using this type of algorithm will be *known*, it will have to be *foreseen*, and may be deemed to have been *intended* by the company[172] – all the more so given that software tools aimed at monitoring the proper functioning of algorithms are expected to be developed,[173] and companies will be required to use them to ensure that their algorithms remain under control.

In short, the algorithm will never have any intention of its own, because it is – or at the very least must be and remain – under the control of the

---

102 (2017), and references cited; M. Nussenbaum, Trading *haute fréquence: Efficience des marchés ou manipulation de cours? Les sanctions récentes*, *in* Mélanges en l'honneur de Jean-Jacques Daigre: Autour du droit bancaire et financier et au-delà 593 (2017). For a more general study, *see* M. Teller, *Du droit et des algorithmes: Libres propos sur la notion d'algorithme, cet impensé du droit*, *in* 8 Droit bancaire et financier: Mélanges AEDBF France 263, 270 (B. Bréhier ed., 2018): the author notes that, in financial matters, the regulator has taken an interesting path – "it is working to enable algorithmic regulation. This has led to the development of RegTechs (*Regulatory Technologies*), which put information technology at the service of regulatory supervision: RegTechs are designed to automate governance and compliance processes efficiently and rapidly." *Compare with* J.-C. Roda, *L'entente algorithmique*, JCP G no. 28 (July 15, 2019), doctr. 785, no. 19: the author mentions the possibilities of "compliance by design," which would entail encoding clear principles that oblige artificial intelligence to comply with the rules.

169 This coordination could, according to some, exist in a number of ways, theorized in the form of scenarios by the following work, which has since been quoted extensively in the literature: A. Ezrachi & M. E. Stucke, Virtual Competition: The Promises and Perils of the Algorithm-Driven Economy 35–71 (2016).

170 *See*, *inter alia*, F. Marty, S. Harnay & J. Toledano, *Algorithmes et décision concurrentielle: Risques et opportunités*, 166 Revue d'économie industrielle 91, 103 (2019); E. Calvano et al., *Algorithmic Pricing: What Implications for Competition Policy?*, 55 Review of Industrial Organization 155 (2019); E. Calvano et al., *Artificial Intelligence, Algorithmic Pricing, and Collusion*, 110 American Economic Review 3267 (2020); A. Ittoo & N. Petit, *Algorithmic Pricing Agents and Tacit Collusion: A Technological Perspective*, *in* L'intelligence artificielle et le droit 241, 256 (H. Jacquemin & A. de Streel eds., 2017): "[T]he algorithmic tacit collusion conjecture should not presently be taken as a given. …At the time, [tacit collusion] is still an open research question."

171 In this spirit, *see* for example. A. Heinemann, *Algorithmes et économie numérique en droit de la concurrence*, *in* Droit et économie numérique 201, 215–16 (A. Richa et al. ed., 2021): the author considers that if a company provides a pricing algorithm, and the latter is adopted by its competitors, this could be considered a "pre-agreement," insofar as the company must be aware of the pricing uniformity to which their simultaneous use may lead; *adde*, M. Gal, Algorithms as Illegal Agreements 37 (May 2, 2018), https://ssrn.com/abstract=3171977.

172 The reasoning is the same as in the case of poisoning: if science teaches that a new substance is lethal, its administration constitutes poisoning; as long as this is not the case, the individual cannot be held liable, *see supra*, no. 320.

173 On this subject, *see* I. Lorenzoni, *An 'AI Whistle-Blower' to Monitor Algorithmic Infringements?*, 15 The Competition Law Review 31 (2023).

company using it. At present, artificial intelligence is only ever a tool at the service of conscious, voluntary corporate strategies. If, in the more or less near future, it is scientifically established that algorithms can exchange information with each other, or even agree with each other without any intervention on the part of the companies using them, such a risk will become foreseeable. It will therefore have to be foreseen, and carefully avoided, failing which companies will be deemed to have intended what the algorithms have done without sufficient oversight.

II. The theory of intent and digital markets

517. **A few avenues to facilitate the adaptation of competition law to the challenges of the digital age.** The theory of intent would make it simpler to grasp the practices of the "digital giants," which are currently the subject of numerous proceedings before the European Commission, providing the prosecuting authorities with grounds for decision (**A**), subject to simplifying the process of characterizing infringements, in particular by limiting recourse to economic expertise, clearly defining the legal criteria presiding over the qualification operation, and assuming greater recourse to presumptions (**B**).

A. An asset: legal arguments for decision-making

518. **The debate on digital markets: is the law of anticompetitive practices a relevant tool?** To say that the Commission is active in the digital arena would be an understatement[174] – the French Competition Authority is equally engaged.[175] At a time when the first decisions based on the Digital Markets Act are still awaited, doctrine is divided as to whether traditional competition rules were sufficient to "effectively" capture anticompetitive conduct by digital companies.[176] And it has to be admitted, along with the

174 For an overview, *see* J.-C. Roda, *Un an de droit de la concurrence dans l'univers numérique*, Communication Commerce électronique (Oct. 2022), chron. 12; *adde*, C. Prieto, *Numérique et abus de position dominante*, Cahiers de droit de l'entreprise no. 3 (May 2019), dossier 18; L. Arcelin, *Le droit de la concurrence mis à l'épreuve par le numérique*, JCP E no. 45, 1493 (Nov. 7, 2019).

175 *See inter alia*: ADLC, decision no. 21-D-11 of June 7, 2021, regarding practices implemented in the online advertising sector; ADLC, decision no. 22-D-13 of June 21, 2022, regarding practices implemented in the press sector; and, recently, ADLC Press Release, Advertising on iOS mobile applications: the General Rapporteur confirms having notified the Apple group of an objection (July 27, 2023).

176 Among a wealth of literature, *see* R. Podszun, *From Competition Law to Platform Regulation – Regulatory Choices for the Digital Markets Act*, 17 Economics 1, 4 (2023): "[I]t is hard to tackle new phenomena after an economic revolution such as the platform revolution with the established rules"; and *contra*, L. Idot, *Abus de position dominante et écosystèmes numériques*, Europe (Nov. 2022), comm. 384: the author notes that cases pursued on the basis of article 102 TFEU in the digital sector "once again illustrate that a provision with general scope and flexible concepts, such as article 102 TFEU, enables authorities to address diverse forms of conduct, in contrast to predetermined lists of obligations, which are readily circumvented"; *adde*, G7 Competition Authorities, Common Understanding of G7 Competition Authorities on "Competition and the Digital Economy (June 5, 2019), at 4: "Because of its flexible analytical framework, fact-based analysis, cross-sector application and technology-neutral nature, competition law can effectively apply to digital markets and to harmful anticompetitive behaviours emerging in the digital economy."

advocates of the adoption of special rules, that the (very) long duration of the proceedings initiated[177] over the last few years has undermined the principle of prompt justice.[178] However, it is unlikely that the Commission will be able to intervene more quickly on the basis of the new regulation adopted,[179] and it is well known that the lack of efficiency attributed to the implementation of articles 101 and 102 TFEU is largely linked to the increasing complexity of the law on anticompetitive practices, itself due to its "modernization."[180] And yet, the more complex markets and business strategies become, the more likely it is that having to prove anticompetitive effects will open the door to loopholes and other delaying tactics, all the more given the vast financial, legal, and economic resources available to digital giants, which enable them to challenge every step of the prosecuting authority's reasoning.[181]

519. **Towards a resurgence of the ordoliberal doctrine?** Some have noted a "reappearance of ordoliberal logic"[182] in the characterization of infringements committed in digital markets. Indeed, the notion of competition on the merits is often mobilized, but this time without always being underpinned by complex economic demonstrations.[183] This development raises questions. Has the time come, in practice, for simplification? Alas, this is not yet the case: decisions take an extremely long time,[184] and their motivation is sometimes obscure. Perhaps, however, we are beginning to realize that the complex theories of competition law make it inefficient, and that the solution lies in a return to fundamentals – that is, to legal reasoning.

520. **The challenge of qualifying novel cases, and the tension between economic and legal approaches.** Digital cases raise important questions of qualification,[185] insofar as they constitute unprecedented cases, or even

177 For an in-depth discussion of the temporality of competition rules, *see*: E. Claudel, *La temporalité des règles de concurrence est-elle adaptée au numérique*?, Cahiers de droit de l'entreprise no. 3 (May 2019), dossier 21.

178 To cite just one example, the *Google Shopping* investigation was launched in 2010 following a complaint from competitors. The Commission's decision was handed down in June 2017, the General Court's ruling in November 2021, and the case is currently pending before the Court of Justice.

179 *See supra*, nos. 448 *et seq.*

180 *See supra*, nos. 441 *et seq.*

181 This is all the more easy to contest given that most economic analyses are based on models whose conclusions are by their very nature conjectural, and therefore contestable, *see* in this sense *supra*, no. 332.

182 F. Marty, *L'approche plus économique en matière d'application des règles de concurrence* 1, 54–59 (GREDEG Working Papers Series, No. 2020-16).

183 *Compare with* the criticisms leveled at the notion, and the definition generally adopted, which paradoxically consists in approaching it through economic reasoning, *supra*, nos. 363–364.

184 The Commission's *Google Shopping* decision is 216 pages long, the Court's ruling 96; the Commission's *Google Android* decision is 328 pages long; the Court's ruling 179.

185 For the time being, this concerns primarily, if not exclusively, the characterization of abuse of a dominant position, since digital cases are all being pursued under article 102 TFEU. Indeed, the only procedure initiated under article 101 TFEU, involving a suspected agreement between Meta and Google, ended with the case being discontinued, *see* Eur. Comm. Press Release IP/22/1703, Antitrust: Commission Opens Investigation into Possible Anticompetitive Conduct by Google and Meta, in Online Display Advertising (Mar. 11, 2022) (Case AT.40774). The procedure was closed on December 19, 2022.

borderline cases. They also highlight long-standing tensions between advocates of a greater role for economic analysis and those who are primarily concerned with the quality of the legal reasoning behind decisions. On the occasion of the much-discussed *Google Shopping* case,[186] the former lamented the Commission's failure to provide a satisfactory "theory of harm," i.e., sufficiently "robust" economic analyses to establish that the disputed practices produce negative effects on the market, expressed indignation that "tests" drawn from previous cases had been set aside,[187] and denounced the risk of unpredictability stemming from the "creation of new types of abuse."[188] From a legal standpoint, the latter criticized the General Court for basing its reasoning on arguments that are difficult to convince, or that contradict the principle of free enterprise.[189]

In fact, the heart of the debate should focus above all on the quality of *legal* reasoning – improving it presupposes a simplification of reasoning. Indeed, the fragmentation of the abuse of a dominant position into numerous subcategories, to which different qualification tests would be applicable, leads to a loss of benchmarks. It should not be forgotten that the characterization of an infringement is, by definition, based on general criteria, which are now difficult to define.[190] Moreover, the digital economy reveals, more than ever, the hesitations of the economic perspective: analyses are increasingly complex, diverge widely depending on the experts consulted, and are grappling with major challenges, both diplomatic and ideological,[191] to such an extent that it appears difficult, if not impossible, to affirm that, in any given case, any particular "theory of

---

186 Eur. Comm., June 27, 2017, C(2017) 4444 final, Google Search (Shopping); Case T-612/17, Google, ECLI:EU:T:2021:763; case pending before the Court of Justice, Case C-48/22 P.

187 For a critical look at qualification "tests," *see supra*, no. 331.

188 *See inter alia*: R. Podszun, *From Competition Law to Platform Regulation – Regulatory Choices for the Digital Markets Act*, 17 Economics 1, 4 (2023): "[In *Google Shopping*], the European Commission failed to provide a clear-cut 'theory of harm'. The term 'theory of harm' in competition law stands for the economic reasoning why a behavior is deemed anti-competitive. …Economic reasoning is used to justify firm behavior or the prohibition of it. …Establishing a new type of abuse runs the risk of the judiciary pointing at missing precedent"; *adde*, in the same spirit, F. Bostoen, *The General Court's Google Shopping Judgment: Finetuning the Legal Qualifications and Tests for Platform Abuse*, 13 Journal of European Competition Law & Practice 75, 77–79 (2022).

189 D. Bosco, Google Shopping*: Avènement jurisprudentiel d'un abus par favoritisme*, Contrats concurrence consommation (Feb. 2022), comm. 34, esp. nos. 3–4: the author criticizes the fact that the General Court referred to the "universal vocation" of Google's search engine, since "in a system of free enterprise and market economy, private goods cannot have a 'universal vocation.' This premise that Google's services should be of common utility and that its use of them is contrary to 'normality' is deeply troubling."

190 One author has quite rightly asked: "How do the special criteria, listed practice by practice, relate to the general criteria emerging from the definition of abuse of a dominant position?", and noted that at present, "the approach is not general, but special, depending on the practice in question," *see* A.-S. Choné-Grimaldi, *Les abus de position dominantes dans le secteur numérique (réflexions à partir de la décision* Google-Android*)*, Recueil Dalloz 343 (2020), esp. no. 2 and no. 19.

191 *See*, in particular, the now-famous article, which is more political manifesto than legal analysis: L. Kahn, *Amazon's Antitrust Paradox*, 126 The Yale Law Journal 710 (2017).

harm" has been clearly established.[192] Everything becomes debatable, and the discussion is often not very legal. But if digital markets are revealing the limits of economic theories, they are also an opportunity to rediscover the stability and adaptability of legal reasoning.

The reflections that follow are intended to sketch out a few avenues, by demonstrating that the general definition of competition infringements proposed, based on the idea that they are a *dol* with market power,[193] offers a fertile basis for thinking about current and future business in the digital sector. Indeed, even if digital markets differ from traditional markets in several respects – they are virtual, their dynamism relies heavily on technological disruptions, the business model of certain companies is based on free access and capturing the attention of Internet users,[194] the accumulation of data produces significant network effects, giving their holders a major competitive advantage, etc.[195] – rivalry remains the same across all markets: sometimes companies focus on their own qualities; sometimes they try to prevent others from playing the game. Big digital companies are no exception to the rule, and their anticompetitive strategies are not fundamentally different from those of yesteryear.

521. **Stability of legal reasoning: connecting novel cases to the general definition of anticompetitive practices.** The behaviors singled out in the digital sector all stem from the same spirit, and can easily be linked to the general definition of anticompetitive practices.[196] For a company, this means using its power to prevent competitors from developing and growing freely.[197] In this way, companies protect themselves from serious competition, or even from the emergence of a new player likely to challenge their hegemony. They refuse to allow the cards to be reshuffled, seek to establish the status quo, and try to make competition more static for their own exclusive benefit. When entering markets they had not previously conquered – typically more open due to the lack of an established incumbent – they deploy their firepower to impose their own rules on others, distorting the game from the outset to ensure victory. Each case is thus bound by the same criterion: that

---

192 For an overview of the complexity and technicality of debates on the application of a given theory of harm to a case, and the tests that should be mobilized, *see, inter alia*, OECD, Abuse of Dominance in Digital Markets, DAF/COMP/GF(2020)4 (Dec. 3, 2020), at 27-67 and esp. at 58, concluding: "[W]here new theories depart from established theories, care may be needed given the impact on market participant certainty and the need to ground exclusionary concerns in economic analysis."

193 *See supra*, nos. 404 *et seq.*

194 On this subject, *see* M. Cartapanis, *Captures d'attention et droit de la concurrence*, RTD Com. 733 (2022).

195 The literature on the digital economy is abundant. *See, inter alia*: N. Petit, Big Tech and the Digital Economy: The Moligopoly Scenario (2020).

196 *See supra*, nos. 404 *et seq.*

197 They therefore fall into the third category of *dol* with market power: "constrained free will," *see supra*, no. 409; *adde*, our summary table, Appendix no. 6.

of a fraudulent maneuver. The company indirectly alters the free formation of exchange conditions to gain an advantage, by attempting to prevent rivals from competing freely. As with all other anticompetitive practices, the idea is that companies are free to adopt the strategies of their choice, provided that these do not infringe on the freedom of others. A study of the most emblematic cases, through a strictly legal prism, makes this clear.[198] These cases are grouped below according to their similarities.

522. ***Google Android*, *Google Search*, *Google Chrome*, *Google AdSense* and *Apple Pay*.** In the *Google Android* case,[199] Google is accused of requiring smartphone manufacturers to pre-install the Google Search application and the Chrome browser on all their phones, failing which they would be denied a license for the Play Store. Given that users tend to give priority to pre-installed applications, it is not unreasonable to assume that Google's behavior was aimed at preventing its competitors from attracting users.[200] Google defended itself by arguing that its application and browser were already preferred by consumers – but if that were true, why was it necessary to impose such contractual clauses? Similarly, why does it require manufacturers to agree not to develop or sell any device running an open-source version of Android,[201] except to ensure that no one might prefer an alternative system over its own? The same logic still drives the company when it acts as an intermediary between advertisers and web publishers via its AdSense service: Google initially signed exclusivity clauses with publishers, barring them from displaying rivals' ads, before relaxing its strategy, reserving for itself the most profitable spaces on websites and requiring their owners to display a minimum number of Google ads – thus preventing competing advertising agencies from either accessing the market, or the most profitable inserts.[202]

Finally, since Apple is aware of its customers' attachment, if not loyalty, to its products, operating system and applications, why does it prevent mobile wallet developers from accessing the hardware and software necessary to create alternative "contactless payment" solutions that could compete with Apple Pay? On the one hand, Apple opens the door to its ecosystem, via the App Store, to third-party developers, but at the same

198 As the cases mentioned below are all still in progress, we obviously do not prejudge their outcome. We are treating them as "cases," in order to check whether they are likely to fall within our definition.

199 Eur. Comm., July 18, 2018, C(2018) 4761 final, Google Android; Case T-604/18, Google, ECLI:EU:T:2022:541; case pending before the Court of Justice, Case C-738/22 P.

200 Comm. EC, Mar. 24, 2004, COMP/C-3/37.792, Microsoft; Case T-201/04, Microsoft, ECLI:EU:T:2007:289.

201 A so-called Android fork, such as Amazon's Fire OS.

202 Eur. Comm., Mar. 20, 2019, C(2019) 2173 final, Google Search (AdSense), case pending before the General Court (Case T-334/19); comm. C. Prieto, *Stratégie contractuelle d'exclusivité au profit de Google Search AdSense, troisième abus de Google condamné par la Commission européenne*, Revue des contrats no. 3, 92 (Sept. 2019).

time denies them access to the mobile wallet market to protect its Apple Pay solution from potential competition.[203]

523. **The *App Store* and streaming music applications.** Furthermore, how can Apple justify preventing developers of streaming music apps, such as Spotify, from informing consumers that they can pay less for their service if they do not go through the App Store to take out a subscription? Even if such a practice could result in a higher price for the consumer, as developers tend to pass on the 30% commission charged by Apple on the subscription price displayed on its store, the issue here is not the price itself.[204] It seems to us that the problem, in terms of competition rules, lies more in the existence of a restriction on the freedom of both consumers and developers. Firstly, Apple indirectly prevents them from selling their services through the distribution channel of their choice, by prohibiting them from communicating the different places where subscriptions can be taken out. It should also be remembered that Apple competes with these developers, as the company also offers a streaming music service, Apple Music – an application that comes pre-installed on all iPhones. To prevent an operator such as Spotify from informing consumers of the existence of a cheaper offer if it is subscribed outside the App Store is tantamount to granting itself an unfair advantage over its competitor, since the latter must either give up part of its margin or accept being more expensive than Apple Music. Secondly, such a practice aims to ensure that as many transactions as possible are carried out on the App Store, even though this is not the most advantageous solution for consumers, who potentially pay more for their subscription. If they were better informed of the options available to them, they would probably subscribe more frequently outside the Apple store,[205] which means that the company's behavior also restricts consumers' freedom of choice.

524. ***Amazon Buy Box* and *Google Shopping*.** When Amazon concludes clauses obliging publishers to offer the company conditions similar to, or more favorable than, those granted to its competitors,[206] isn't it clear that the latter are prevented from competing effectively with the platform,

---

203 Eur. Comm. Press Release IP/22/2764, Antitrust: Commission Sends Statement of Objections to Apple Over Practices Regarding Apple Pay (May 2, 2022) (Case AT.40452).

204 In the first statement of objections sent to Apple, the high commission charged by Apple for all subscriptions made via the App Store was also at issue. This grievance was eventually dropped (Eur. Comm. Press Release IP/21/2061, Antitrust: Commission Sends Statement of Objections to Apple on App Store Rules for Music Streaming Providers (Apr. 30, 2021) (Case AT. 40437)) – no doubt because of the difficulties involved in characterizing excessive prices (*see supra*, no. 406). Compare with the U.S. *Epic Games* case, *see* W. Chaiehloudj, *Le droit de la régulation numérique marginalisera-t-il le droit de la concurrence? Réflexions à la lumière de l'affaire* Epic Games c/ Apple, CONCURRENCES no. 3-2021, art. no. 101309.

205 Which might also encourage Apple to reduce the amount of commission it charges on the App Store…

206 This case was resolved by the adoption of a commitment decision, whereas it would, in our view, have been preferable for the Commission to engage in prohibition proceedings, *see* Eur. Comm., May 4, 2017, C(2017) 2876 final, E-book MFNs.

and differentiate themselves by offering more attractive prices? Amazon, which itself sells products on its platform and also provides logistics and delivery services, also welcomes third-party sellers. However, it has artificially increased the visibility and appeal of its own offers, as well as those of sellers using its "Fulfillment by Amazon" service.[207] Such behavior enables it not only to protect itself from competition from third-party sellers, but also to reduce the attractiveness of competing logistics and delivery service companies, insofar as sellers are strongly encouraged to use Amazon's services – as this is a *sine qua non* condition for being visible on the site.

This behavior is not unlike that at issue in the *Google Shopping* case.[208] When the company decided to create its price-comparison service, it systematically displayed the results of its own price-comparison service in its search engine – by far the most widely used – relegating those of competitors to later pages, where they were rarely consulted, thus preventing them from making themselves known to Internet users.

525. ***Meta* and *Amazon Marketplace*: massive data collection as a prerequisite to an anticompetitive strategy.** In digital markets, data is extremely important[209] – so much so that it is sometimes one of the pillars of a company's business model, as it seeks to collect as much of it as possible: to resell, to increase the value of its targeted advertising services,[210] or to develop the most profitable sales strategies possible. They have thus become a genuine parameter of competition, which must be taken into account when examining contentious behavior.[211] However, the inclusion of this new variable in the analysis does not alter the established reasoning, as shown by three recent cases, which follow a similar strategy.

---

207 Eur. Comm., Communication from the Commission published pursuant to Article 27(4) of Council Regulation (EC) No. 1/2003 in Case AT.40703 Amazon – Buy Box and AT.40462 – Amazon Marketplace, 2022 O.J. (C 278) 8, paras. 7–9. Here again, a commitment decision was preferred to a prohibition procedure, and Amazon undertook to apply non-discriminatory conditions and criteria for the selection of the featured offer, so that sellers on the platform and Amazon would operate on "a level playing field," *see id.*, paras. 12–13.

208 Eur. Comm., June 27, 2017, C(2017) 4444 final, Google Search (Shopping); Case T-612/17, Google, ECLI:EU:T:2021:763; case pending before the Court of Justice Case C-48/22 P.

209 On the definition of massive data and its treatment by competition law, *see* V. Giovannini, Données massives et droit de la concurrence (2022) (Ph. D. dissertation, Université d'Aix-Marseille); on the articulation between sector regulation and competition law, *see* M. Malaurie-Vignal, *Le droit de la concurrence, les données personnelles et le bien-être du consommateur – Réflexion sur l'articulation entre deux droits spéciaux*, Contrats concurrence consommation (July 2021), repère 7; M. Malaurie-Vignal, D. Heintz & M. Lécole, *Comment appréhender les abus et l'utilisation des données dans la relation d'une plateforme avec ses partenaires contractuels?*, Contrats concurrence consommation (Dec. 2020), dossier 16; C. Cizeron, *Droit de la concurrence et RGPD: Dénouement du contentieux Meta*, Contrats concurrence consommation (Oct. 2023), comm. 156.

210 Indeed, the more precisely Internet users are profiled, the higher the price at which the advertising service can be sold, since the advertising offer will primarily target consumers likely to be interested in the product or service in question, thereby increasing the conversion rate, i.e., the likelihood that the advertisement will result in a purchase, registration, or download. More broadly, on the economic ecosystem of big data, *see* OECD, Big Data: Bringing Competition Policy to the Digital Era, DAF/COMP(2016)14 (Oct. 16, 2016), paras. 30–41.

211 As evidenced by a recent Court ruling, "access to personal data and the fact that it is possible to process such data have become a significant parameter of competition between undertakings in the digital economy," Case C-252/21, Meta Platforms, ECLI:EU:C:2023:537, para. 51.

First, the company uses its power to collect a large amount of data, taking advantage of the captivity of its service users. Such behavior is akin to excessive pricing, with the difference that, instead of paying a high price, consumers consent to the collection of their data in order to access the service of their choice. However, it is well known that the criteria established in case law to determine the excessive nature of a pricing policy are extremely demanding, and that the very notion of "excessive pricing" may seem contrary to the spirit of free competition, insofar as a company must be able to determine its prices as it sees fit, leaving the consumer free to contract or not[212]. Consequently, and by analogy, it would be of little relevance if data collection, even if it may appear excessive in scale, could *on its own* constitute an abuse of a dominant position – it is up to special rules, such as those laid down by the General Data Protection Regulation (GDPR), to provide a framework for data collection and processing, in particular by establishing the conditions under which the user's consent is validly obtained.[213] Thus, it is rather *the maneuvering that this data collection enables* that is problematic, rather than the collection itself – the latter being merely a prerequisite for the adoption of an anticompetitive strategy.[214]

For example, when Amazon collected large quantities of non-public data from the activity of third-party sellers operating on its platform, it did so *for the purposes* of "identifying products to be launched, starting and ending their sale, identifying suppliers, negotiating wholesale prices and terms, planning and managing inventories, and setting the prices of Amazon's own retail offers."[215] In other words, the company took advantage of an information asymmetry, then used the successes and failures of its current or potential competitors to enter their markets when it felt it would be profitable to do so, while staying one step ahead of them, since the information gathered enabled it to identify business opportunities more easily, offer optimized prices and attract customers. As other sellers did not have the same information, they could no longer compete as effectively with the platform – and this is where the real restriction lay.

---

212 *See supra*, no. 406.

213 Regulation (EU) 2016/679 of the European Parliament and of the Council of Apr. 27, 2016. on the Protection of Natural Persons with Regard to the Processing of Personal Data and on the Free Movement of Such Data, 2016 O.J. (L 119) 1. *See* in particular the obligations relating to consent (as defined by the Regulation in art. 4(11), art. 6(1)(a), and art. 9(2)(a)). Think also of the Digital Services Act, which imposes transparency obligations on companies, offers the Commission extended powers of investigation for "very large online platforms" and "very large online search engines" (designated in art. 33), allowing it to request access in particular to its algorithms and data processing methods, *see* Regulation (EU) 2022/2065 of the European Parliament and of the Council of Oct. 19, 2022, on a Single Market for Digital Services, 2022 O.J. (L 277) 1, art. 69(2)(d).

214 In their joint study on data, the French and German competition authorities identified the various anticompetitive strategies that can be based on the massive collection of data, *see* ADLC & Bundeskartellamt, Competition Law and Data 20–25 (May 10, 2016).

215 Eur. Comm., Communication from the Commission published pursuant to Article 27(4) of Council Regulation (EC) No. 1/2003 in Case AT.40703 Amazon – Buy Box and AT.40462, 2022 O.J. (C 278) 8, para. 4.

Similar reasoning applies to the statement of objections recently sent by the Commission to Meta.[216] Among other things,[217] Meta is accused of imposing conditions on companies providing advertising services that advertise on Facebook or Instagram, authorizing Meta to use data relating to competing advertisements for the benefit of Facebook Marketplace – a service linked to its Facebook social network. Such a practice gives Facebook Marketplace an illegitimate advantage over other platforms of the same type, insofar as Meta uses the popularity of its social network to give itself a potentially decisive lead on the online advertising market, whereas other operators, who do not have access to the same volume of data,[218] could have proved to be credible competitors in the market pre-empted by Meta. Similarly, the fact that Facebook required users of its social network to consent to the company's ability to collect personal data about them, not only when using the network itself, but also the group's other services (such as WhatsApp or Instagram) as well as third-party applications and sites, certainly constituted a potential breach of the GDPR, but constitutes an abuse essentially because of the undue advantage that such a practice conferred on the company. Indeed, as Facebook's competitors on the targeted advertising market are not in a position to collect as much information, the company can consolidate or even increase its market share even though it obtained the data unlawfully.[219] Its position is therefore not the result of its own merits, but of the artificial creation of barriers to entry that disqualify its competitors.[220]

The situation created by Amazon's and Meta's behavior is similar to that which would exist if, in a trail race, only one competitor had access to a

---

216 Eur. Comm. Press Release IP/22/7728, Antitrust: Commission Sends Statement of Objections to Meta over Abusive Practices Benefiting Facebook Marketplace (Dec. 19, 2022) (Case AT.40684).

217 The other complaint seems less convincing: Meta's practice of linking its Facebook social network to its Facebook Marketplace advertising service, so that all Facebook users automatically have access to Facebook Marketplace. On the one hand, such a practice does not *in itself* put competitors offering similar services at a disadvantage, as consumers simply need to go online to find credible and easily accessible alternatives. On the other hand, it seems to us that it is legitimate for Meta to create an ecosystem integrating both a social network and a marketplace, and that prohibiting it from doing so would constitute excessive interference in its business model. Sanctioning Meta in this respect would also risk creating an inequality of treatment between it and other companies, such as Google and Apple, insofar as the latter are not criticized for linking some of their services together.

218 We know that the accumulation of data enables a company to strengthen its dominant position and prevents its competitors from gaining market share, *see* OECD, Big Data: Bringing Competition Policy to the Digital Era, *op. cit.*, para. 25.

219 From this point of view, it is moreover not certain that the fact that the data collection constitutes an infringement of the GDPR is ultimately such an important element in the reasoning governing the characterization of abuse, insofar as it is, at most, an indication of the existence of a maneuver, which the Bundeskartellamt could perhaps have done without.

220 The reasoning of the Bundeskartellamt is not unrelated to this assertion, *see* Bundeskartellamt, Feb. 6, 2019, B6-22/16, Facebook, at 11: "Facebook's conduct ... impedes competitors because Facebook gains access to a large number of further sources by its inappropriate processing of data and their combination with Facebook accounts. It has thus *gained a competitive edge* over its competitors *in an unlawful way* and *increased market entry barriers*, which in turn secures Facebook's market power towards end customers" (emphasis added).

map enabling them to know which paths were less hilly, took performance-enhancing drugs and equipped themselves with an assistant placing obstacles in the path of the others: the runner could make their way to the finish line more easily than the others – and some would consider the competition rigged.

526. **The *Towercast* ruling and "killer acquisitions."** Another contemporary issue has been much in the news over the past year: "killer acquisitions." This term, derived from merger law, refers to the acquisition of a dominant company of an innovative or promising operator in order to strengthen its position, prevent the emergence of a potential competitor, or even mothball the innovations it has developed.[221] The phenomenon is a cause for concern, insofar as such external growth strategies enable giants of the digital economy to grow still further, and diversify their business sectors to the point of becoming veritable conglomerates. While some would see no problem with this,[222] the Commission regretted that such acquisitions were not covered by Merger Regulation 139/2004.[223] It therefore decided, through a (highly questionable) speech by European Commissioner Margrethe Vestager, to announce that the institution was going to change its interpretation of article 22 of the said Regulation, in order to allow certain concentrations to be referred to the Commission even if they did not cross the thresholds set out in the text – one author rightly considered this to be "forcing the Regulation."[224]

In parallel with this development, another question has recently arisen: that of whether a killer acquisition could, where it has not been the subject of proceedings under merger law, be assessed on the basis of article 102 TFEU.[225] The aim was to mobilize once again a famous judgment, peacefully dormant since 1973: *Continental Can*. In this case, the Court of Justice held that "the acquisition of the majority holding in a competing company by an undertaking or a group of undertakings

221 C. Picart, *Killer acquisitions*, *in* Dictionnaire de droit de la concurrence 508, 508 (M. Chagny & E. Combe eds., 2023); *adde*, on this theme: ADLC, Contribution de l'Autorité de la concurrence au débat sur la politique de concurrence et les enjeux numériques 9–10 (Feb. 19, 2020). Facebook's takeover of WhatsApp and Instagram, and Google's acquisition of YouTube and DoubleClick are often cited as examples.

222 *See* in particular F. A. Hayek, 3 Law, Legislation, and Liberty 79 (1979): "Size has thus become the most effective antidote to the power of size: what will control the power of large aggregations of capital are other large aggregations of capital…."

223 This is because the sales of target companies are usually low or non-existent – hence they are not notifiable, *see* Council Regulation (EC) No. 139/2004 of Jan. 20, 2004, on the Control of Concentrations between Undertakings, 2004 O.J. (L 24) 1, art. 1.

224 D. Bosco, *Le 'nouvel' article 22, un forçage du règlement européen sur les concentrations*, Contrats concurrence consommation (Nov. 2020), no. 11, comm. 163, no. 4; *adde*, on the first application of this new interpretation, in the context of the "*Illumina/Grail* saga," *see* D. Bosco, Illumina-Grail, *the Threefold Error of the EU General Court*, Concurrences no. 4-2022, art. no. 109076; L. Idot, *Concurrence: Nouveaux épisodes dans la saga Illumina/Grail*, Europe (Apr. 2023), comm. 145.

225 On the relationship between article 102 TFEU and the Merger Control Regulation, *see* M. Cartapanis, *La notion de concentration – Droit européen et droit français*, JurisClasseur Concurrence – Consommation (Apr. 2023), fasc. 410, no. 3.

holding a dominant position" could constitute an abuse of a dominant position if the "degree of dominance reached substantially fetters competition, i.e. that *only undertakings remain in the market whose behaviour depends on the dominant one.*"[226] This solution, which allowed a form of control over market structures based on the prohibition of abuse of a dominant position, seemed obsolete following the introduction of merger control in 1989. However, it was recently invoked by several national competition authorities, including the French one, which considered that the *Continental Can* case law was no longer applicable.[227] The Paris Court of Appeal, unsure whether the existence of merger control law meant that it should be disregarded, referred a question to the Court of Justice for a preliminary ruling. In its *Towercast* ruling, the Court of Justice held that a concentration of undertakings below the *ex ante* control thresholds that has not been referred to the Commission under article 22 may be deemed to constitute an abuse of a dominant position.[228] The reasoning in *Continental Can*, which sets out the criteria for determining abuse in this context, has been taken up and clarified by the Court.[229]

In short, this ruling – in theory – allows competition authorities to tackle the problem of killer acquisitions, which is not without its reservations. Indeed, such a solution "opens the way to all kinds of intervention."[230] It also leads to a blurring of the lines between *ex ante* control of market *structure* and *ex post* sanctioning of anticompetitive *behavior*. What is more, the Court was hesitant as to the appropriate sanction to be imposed in the event of such an abuse: should the authorities simply impose a fine on the company, or can they enjoin it to dispose of the abusively acquired asset?[231] Such legal uncertainty is likely to dissuade certain transactions,[232] which is particularly problematic given that start-up founders often aim to have their start-ups bought out after a few years of development.

---

226 Case 6/72, Continental Can, ECLI:EU:C:1973:22, para. 28 and para. 26, resp. (emphasis added).

227 ADLC, decision no. 20-D-01 of Jan. 16, 2020, regarding a practice implemented in the digital terrestrial television broadcasting sector (Fr.); comm. D. Bosco, *Continental Can, c'est fini*, CONTRATS CONCURRENCE CONSOMMATION (Mar. 2020), comm. 51.

228 Case C-449/21, Towercast, ECLI:EU:C:2023:207, answer to preliminary question.

229 *Id.*, para. 52.

230 L. Idot, *La remise en cause des frontières du droit de la concurrence*, EUROPE (Nov. 2022), alerte 76. The author notes that the situation is all the more problematic "at a time when the decentralized application of articles 101 and 102 TFEU is also a matter for national courts under general law," due to the risk of fragmentation of decisions adopted in the various Member States.

231 On this subject, *see* I. Guittard, *Continental Can renaît de ses cendres! L'arrêt Towercast retient l'applicabilité de l'article 102 TFUE à une concentration 'sous les seuils'*, CONTRATS CONCURRENCE CONSOMMATION (May 2023), comm. 86, no. 7.

232 M. Cartapanis, *Seuils de notification: La Cour de justice de l'Union européenne restaure la jurisprudence* Continental Can *et juge que l'article 102 TFUE est susceptible de s'appliquer à une concentration non notifiable* (Towercast), CONCURRENCES no. 2-2023, art. no. 112272, 78, and references cited.

If the theoretical questions raised by the *Towercast* ruling are numerous and important, what will happen in practice? Advocate General Juliane Kokott considers article 102 TFEU to be a "weaker instrument" than merger law for catching killer acquisitions.[233] In our view, it could even turn out to be a "non-instrument," since a careful reading of the criteria laid down by the Court as early as the *Continental Can* ruling, and taken up by the *Towercast* ruling, reveals that the hypothesis in question is undoubtedly a textbook case. On the one hand, the acquisition must be aimed at a target operating in the market where the undertaking is dominant, which already severely restricts the scope of the solution, and on the other, the abuse cannot result solely from "the strengthening of an undertaking's position" following the acquisition, but must leave "only undertakings dependent" on the undertaking in question. If such a criterion seems unclear, it also appears, at first glance, extremely restrictive: since the analysis is restricted to the market in which the company is dominant, the remaining companies in this market are, by definition, competing companies. Can you imagine a company being dependent on its own competitor, even if it is dominant? And even if reference is made to existing competition in the main market and in adjacent markets, it would be difficult to take mere dependence into consideration – in civil law, it is the *abuse* of dependence that is punished, not the *situation* of dependence itself.

Although the *Continental Can* ruling is one of the best known in the field, it has never, to our knowledge, been used to characterize abuse, not even in 1973. Among the competition authorities that have recently invoked it, the Luxembourg authority rejected the complaint,[234] while its Italian counterpart considered that the acquisitions made by the company in question were part of a broader strategy of foreclosure – and it was this latter strategy that truly constituted the abuse.[235] Precisely, it is only on the condition that an acquisition forms part of a *more global anti-competitive strategy* that it can be used as a basis for characterizing an abuse of a dominant position.[236] To decide otherwise would be to confuse the control of market structure with that of behavior, and would therefore be contrary to the spirit of the law on anticompetitive practices.

---

233 In this sense, *see* Opinion of Advocate General J. Kokott, Case C-449/21, Towercast, ECLI:EU:C:2022:777, para. 48; for a critical commentary on these conclusions, *see* R. Saint-Esteben, *Un vrai-faux retour de l'arrêt* Continental Can*? (*Towercast*)*, CONCURRENCES no. 4-2022, art. no. 111085.

234 Conseil de la concurrence [Cons. conc.] du Luxembourg [Luxembourg Competition Authority], decision no. 2019-R-01 of Mar. 15, 2019, Fédération des Artisans (Fr.).

235 Autorita' Garante della Concorrenza e del Mercato [AGCM] [Italian Competition Authority], decision no. 28495 of Dec. 22, 2020, Ticketone v. Condotte Escludenti Nella Vendita di Biglietti (It.).

236 *Compare*, in the United States, *with* the famous case: Standard Oil of New Jersey v. United States, 221 U.S. 1 (1911). According to René Joliet, what justified the characterization of a violation of section 2 of the Sherman Act was not only the fact that Standard Oil had carried out a series of acquisitions, but also its "recourse to coercive or abusive tactics such as espionage practices, or systematic predatory pricing, or price discrimination designed to force weaker competitors to join the *holding* company or cease all activity." Put another way, the Supreme Court sought to demonstrate "the intention of the companies in question" and concluded that the "acts performed by the companies could not be explained ... by the desire to

B. A prerequisite: simplifying the characterization of offenses

527. **A return to general legal criteria.** The debates surrounding the characterization of abuse of a dominant position in digital markets focus mainly on the relevance of attaching a given case to certain categories, which have the peculiarity of being very narrow. Each category corresponds either to a "category of abuse" – here, it would be an abuse of leverage, there a refusal to contract, or perhaps a mixture of the two – or to a specific theory – as in the case of the "essential facilities" theory – or to a previous judgment, apprehended in the form of a "test" – think of the ubiquitous *Bronner* test.[237] And, as soon as the case in question does not fit into a pre-established box, it is deemed to be a "new form of abuse," or even an "unnamed abuse." Such an approach overlooks an important point: abuse is a unitary concept, and while it can be broken down into different types of behavior, these always relate to a general definition and are (or should be) characterized by general criteria applicable to all practices.

So, to stop systematically reasoning in terms of the "applicability" of such and such a category, test or theory to novel cases would greatly simplify debates, both doctrinal and contentious, by allowing us to focus on the essentials.[238] Jurists do not need boxes to describe, they are looking for arguments to convince. Most of the time, the categories or theories in question are descriptive: they do not provide information on what really counts – i.e., what constitutes an unlawful maneuver. For example, the theory of essential facilities[239] lays down four conditions: the refusal to contract must (i) relate to an indispensable good, (ii) be such as to eliminate competition, (iii) hinder the appearance of a new good, (iv) not be objectively justifiable. Conditions (i) and (ii) raise questions of fact, and conditions (iii) and (iv) provide no information on what can eliminate competition or be justified.[240] A further illustration is provided by the notion of "favouring," mentioned forty times by the General Court in

---

increase their commercial position by normal methods," but "revealed, on the contrary, *the intention to eliminate the other competitors* in this sector of activity, and *to encroach on their commercial freedom*," *see* R. Joliet, *Monopolisation et abus de position dominante: Essai comparatif sur l'article 2 du Sherman Act et l'article 86 du Traité de Rome*, RTD Eur. 645, 664 and 665, resp. (1969).

237 On this test, *see supra*, no. 331.

238 Not least because the theories in question sometimes seem ill-suited to grasp the novel behaviors of digital companies. For example, on the subject of essential facilities theory, *see* W. Chaiehloudj, *Quels outils efficaces pour les autorités de concurrence dans l'économie numérique?*, Contrats concurrence consommation (Mar. 2020), étude 4, no. 20: the author considers that the conditions it lays down seem to be "a brake on its application."

239 On this theory, *see* G. Canivet, *Le droit de propriété confronté à la théorie des infrastructures essentielles*, 658 Lamy Droit des Affaires 79 (2006).

240 Discussions of this theory quickly turn to questions of an economic nature, i.e., how important it is to strike a balance between the incentive to innovate protected by an intellectual property right, property rights, and the need to ensure that new entrants are not excluded from a market by barriers to entry. This type of debate is certainly interesting, but what about the legal arguments?

Google Shopping.[241] This does not shed any light on the *reasons* why the conduct in question is deemed anticompetitive. Moreover, the use of this term is misleading as to the reason for the finding of infringement, insofar as it implies that a dominant undertaking is prohibited from favoring itself; whereas it seems obvious that any undertaking, in order to survive and grow, has an obligation to favor itself! The establishment of an "abuse by favoritism,"[242] as if it were a new type of abuse, therefore seems neither relevant nor useful, since it is rather easy to perceive in Google's behavior a maneuver in line with previous solutions.[243]

So, when we set out the few emblematic cases currently underway involving digital markets, we deliberately avoided using technical terms and complex theories in order to show that the jurist can follow a more direct path from case to qualification. We may be criticized for the lack of precision and the risk of error involved in such an approach. But we are convinced, firstly, that simplicity actually enables a more accurate grasp of reality; and secondly, that the current approach means that many practices that jeopardize healthy competition go unpunished due to insufficient procedural speed. However, continuing to apply the same method will not produce different results. Abandoning the need to demonstrate the existence of a dominant position, and making greater use of legal presumptions, would make it easier to characterize the behavior of companies in the digital sector.

528. **In favor of abandoning the need to demonstrate the existence of a dominant position.** While we have already been critical of the definition of the relevant market and the economization of the proof of a dominant position,[244] these two steps are all the more difficult in digital markets.

Indeed, the risk that the definition of the relevant market may be tainted by artificiality is more acute here,[245] since the more complex a market,[246] the more the calculations involved at this stage may give rise to different or even opposing conclusions, depending on which variables are taken into account or disregarded. In *Google Android*:

---

241 Case T-612/17, Google, ECLI:EU:T:2021:763.

242 D. Bosco, Google Shopping*: Avènement jurisprudentiel d'un abus par favoritisme*, Contrats concurrence consommation (Feb. 2022), comm. 34.

243 Indeed, one author has argued that Google's strategy is to "stifle the merits" of its competitors, by preventing them from showcasing their innovations in the price comparison market, where the company's merits are weaker than in the general search market, *see* C. Prieto, *Les mérites étouffés des concurrents de Google ou l'abus par algorithme*, RTD Eur. 429 (2017).

244 *See supra*, nos. 393 *et seq.*

245 Some consider that, in traditional markets, reasoning is not free of subjectivity, *see supra*, no. 392.

246 Not least because the balance of power in this sector is unique: the major companies in the digital sector compete with each other to conquer new markets, using innovation to the full. As a result, even though they may appear to be in a monopoly position in their business segment, a "dynamic" analysis of the competitive pressure they face leads us to consider that they are in competition with each other. This is why one author has proposed the notion of "moligopoly," a neologism combining the words "monopoly" and "oligopoly," *see* N. Petit, Big Tech and the Digital Economy: The Moligopoly Scenario 169–71 (2020).

> Thus, in a digital "ecosystem," which brings together several categories of supplier, customer and consumer and causes them to interact within a platform, the products or services which form part of the relevant markets that make up that ecosystem may overlap or be connected to each other on the basis of their horizontal or vertical complementarity. ...Identifying the conditions of competition relevant to the assessment of the position of economic strength enjoyed by the undertaking concerned may therefore *require multi-level or multi-directional examination* in order to determine the fact and extent of the various competitive constraints that may be exerted on that undertaking.[247]

It is not difficult to foresee that such milestones will lead to further sophistication in the definition of the relevant market, without, however, making it possible to reach indisputable conclusions. It would seem more appropriate, and no less precise and no less fair, to rely on the simple idea that if there is an abuse, it is because there is an anticompetitive strategy resulting in *victims* who constitute proof of the existence of market power – the onus being on the company to rebut this presumption.

For example, in the *Apple Pay* case,[248] would it not be bogus to assert that economic analyses *objectively* and *accurately* lead to the definition of a market for "mobile wallets on iOS"?[249] Why not consider the relevant market for mobile wallets on all operating systems? As a defense, Apple will no doubt point to its business model, based on a "closed ecosystem," and produce a host of economic studies. There is also a good chance that Apple will invoke the principle of equal treatment. Indeed, how can the Commission justify restricting the market to Apple's operating system alone, whereas Google, because its ecosystem is "open," could benefit from a broader definition of the market in which it operates[250] – which might, in some cases, lead to the latter not being considered dominant?[251]

The real issue is whether preventing competitors from accessing the Apple ecosystem wallet market is justified by its business model – which raises the *legal* question, not of the relevant market or of dominance, but of the

---

247 Case T-604/18, Google, ECLI:EU:T:2022:541, paras. 116–17; comm. D. Bosco, *Délimitation du marché pertinent et économie numérique: Des jalons posés par le Tribunal dans l'affaire Android*, Contrats concurrence consommation (Nov. 2022), comm. 176.

248 *Nota bene*: we are reasoning here in a forward-looking manner, as the Commission has not yet issued its decision.

249 Eur. Comm. Press Release IP/22/2764, Antitrust: Commission Sends Statement of Objections to Apple Over Practices Regarding Apple Pay (May 2, 2022) (Case AT.40452).

250 One author has questioned whether such a difference in treatment is fair, *see* A.-S. Choné-Grimaldi, *Les abus de position dominantes dans le secteur numérique (réflexions à partir de la décision* Google-Android*)*, Recueil Dalloz 343 (2020), no. 5.

251 Moreover, it is undoubtedly because of the uncertainties linked to the definition of the relevant market in digital markets that the French Competition Authority has proposed "to broaden the qualification of the notion of dominant position in order to include certain players either in a situation of quasi-dominance or on the verge of tipping the market" (unofficial translation), *see* ADLC, Contribution de l'Autorité de la concurrence au débat sur la politique de concurrence et les enjeux numériques 5 (Feb. 19, 2020).

existence of legitimate ground justifying a strategy that would otherwise appear anticompetitive. It is around this question that the contentious debate should be directed, and that doctrinal discussions would benefit from focusing.[252] If the Commission's arguments fail to convince the General Court, this could leave unpunished a behavior that appears to be driven by an anticompetitive strategy.

529. **In favor of simple presumptions of unlawfulness.** It would also be appropriate to accept and increase the use of *simple presumptions of unlawfulness*, without lowering the standard of proof.[253] Indeed, if the context in which the conduct takes place shows that it falls within the general definition of the competition infringement, why not consider, as the criminal courts do when qualifying offenses such as swindling or misuse of corporate assets,[254] that the existence of a maneuver, even if "unspoken," is sufficient to characterize the material and mental elements of the infringement?[255]

Moreover, it is much easier to prove that a behavior "aims to" restrict the freedom of third parties than to demonstrate that it "has the potential or actual effect" of causing a certain result, particularly in sectors as complex as digital markets. For example, in the *Android* case, Google tried to argue that it had restricted the development of open-source versions of Android in order to prevent fragmentation of its ecosystem, which would have jeopardized the reliability of its applications. The Commission ruled, on technical grounds, that the argument was unjustified, and this was confirmed by the General Court.[256]

*

* *

530. **Conclusion of Title II: the theory of intent – restoring clarity and effectiveness to the implementation of competition rules.** Adopting the theory of intent would not only revive the original philosophy of competition law and improve the clarity of the discipline's discourse, but also make

252 For our part, as indicated *supra*, no. 523, we believe that it will be difficult for Apple to justify the disputed practice, insofar as it has opened the doors of its App Store to third-party developers, from which it follows that it does not appear rational to close it on the mobile wallet market. If the company had totally partitioned its system, it seems to us that it would have been able, on the contrary, to argue for the preservation of the image of its products and its business model, relying in particular on the solutions accepted in the field of selective distribution.

253 Which is that of reasonable doubt benefiting the respondent company, *see supra*, no. 321.

254 Like competition infringements, these violations fall within the category of offenses of means, and likewise rest on concepts with variable content.

255 For an illustration, *see* Raymond Gassin's enlightening commentary, *supra*, no. 198.

256 Case T-604/18, Google, ECLI:EU:T:2022:541, paras. 837–41, on the "anticompetitive nature of the *objectives pursued*," and paras. 876–92, esp. para. 892: according to the General Court, Google has not "demonstrated that the exclusion of non-compatible Android forks resulting from the AFAs [anti-fragmentation agreements] met a *legitimate objective*" (emphasis added). Note that the language used by the Court focuses on the intention that motivated the company being sued.

it simpler and, consequently, more effective and intelligible. Given the current complexity of the subject, such an evolution seems more necessary than ever. It would not, however, overturn the established solutions, insofar as it would only require the abandonment of theories that are, *de lege lata*, devoid of normative scope.

The only obstacle to its acceptance stems from the fact that jurists have been accustomed for several decades to accepting economic dogma and the vocabulary and reasoning associated with it, as well as the presence of a large number of economists in competition authorities.[257] While it is necessary for economists to provide their expertise in merger control, the relevance of their intervention in anticompetitive practices law is less obvious. It would therefore be advisable to ensure that cartel and abuse of dominance cases are handled primarily by jurists. Only then can a theory that is more respectful of legal reasoning be received in practice.

*

* *

531. **Conclusion to Part II: toward an explicit role for intent in competition law.** Contrary to traditional doctrinal presentations, this study has established the central role played, *de lege lata*, by the concept of intent, both at the stage of characterizing infringements, as a *constitutive element*, and at that of defining them, anticompetitive practices having been defined as presupposing *dol with market power*. While competition law may appear to be utilitarian in nature, concerned as it is with the effects of litigious practices on the market or consumer welfare, such a view is not in line with reality. There is a profound gap between the rhetoric of the discipline, and the principles and reasoning it embraces in practice. Yet the latter are far simpler than those associated with effect-based theories. Their rediscovery has made it possible to link competition law to general law, by showing the deep links that unite it with other areas of the law, and to demonstrate the conceptual unity that exists between cartels and abuses of dominant position.

De lege ferenda, the aim was to argue that the utilitarian foundation underpinning the discipline today is questionable in itself and, above all,

257 L. Idot, *Argument économique et argument sociologique*, *in* L'ARGUMENT SOCIOLOGIQUE EN DROIT: PLURIEL ET SINGULARITÉ 43, 50 (D. Fenouillet ed., 2015): "[E]conomists are increasingly numerous and sometimes in the majority within specialized authorities." At the Commission, "the last two directors-general of DG Competition are no longer jurists but economists. Similarly, the proportion of jurists in this directorate of some 400 people is tending to decrease. …An equivalent observation can be made for the French Competition Authority. For the college, and more particularly among the permanent members, it is considered essential to have at least one vice-president who is an economist. In the investigation departments, the number of rapporteurs with an economic background has risen considerably in recent years, the general rapporteur's aim being to achieve a balance between the various categories. Even more striking, the last ten years have seen the creation of specific functions reserved for economists. The movement was launched by Mario Monti, himself a professor of economics." It should also be noted that, for the first time in France, an economist, Benoît Cœuré, was appointed chairman of the French Competition Authority in January 2022.

that it produces debatable consequences. It is detrimental to the clarity of the subject, as the effects-based approach leads to the layering of complex theories, based on an unstable economic science grappling with strong ideological stakes, which are not only difficult to understand for non-specialists and businesses, but also lack normative force – giving rise to legitimate concerns regarding the principles of legal certainty, predictability and legality. In addition, these theories have led to less effective enforcement of competition rules, compromising the principle of promptness in justice and restricting the ability of competition authorities with limited resources to pursue the full range of cases that merit sanction. Faced with this situation, another approach was proposed. Explicitly adopting the theory of intent, which is already, for the most part, implicitly accepted by competition law *de lege lata*, would offer the possibility of theoretical streamlining and, while improving the compatibility of the matter with the principles of the rule of law, would restore its effectiveness. On the one hand, it would lead to an improvement in the reasoning of decisions, by providing *legal* criteria and arguments enabling judges to link unprecedented cases to established jurisprudence. On the other hand, by encouraging the use of presumptions, it would make it possible to exclude certain complex economic issues and analyses from contentious proceedings, and thus facilitate the finding of infringements, while offering companies the opportunity to defend themselves, either by contesting the anticompetitive nature of their behavior, or by invoking legitimate grounds to justify it. In short, intent has remained, since its origins, a cardinal concept for striking a balance between the effectiveness of repressive policy and the preservation of the rights of the defense.

*

* *

OVERALL CONCLUSION

532. **Intent and competition law: a fruitful alliance.** The encounter between intent and the law of anticompetitive practices is like that of two strangers who had hitherto studiously ignored each other – not out of mutual disinterest, but because they both perceived in each other the reflection of their own hesitations.

Intent did not dare venture into the realm of a law obsessed with economic effects, while the latter had no interest, at least in appearance, in a notion deemed eminently subjective and which, according to the majority opinion, was likely to lead to judicial errors, as well as compromising its effectiveness. Despite this relationship of mutual indifference, they were made to get along: only their respective complexity prevented them from realizing the long-standing, unknowing links between them. Along the way, however, this alliance allowed them to discover their true nature.

Intent appeared *simpler* than it seemed. Its supposed subjectivity, often criticized, turned out to be an unfair reproach: from the outset, it was *objectively inferred* on the basis of behavior and circumstances. It was not until the nineteenth century that the notion was gradually weighed down by a host of subcategories of *dol*, under the influence of a psychological perspective vainly attempting to grasp the subtleties of human volition. Thus, despite the reduction in the scope of intent in favor of new and competing notions such as imputability, it has remained the ethical foundation of state sanction, whose function is to approximate the state of mind of the accused at the time of the litigious acts in order to ensure that the punishment is as just as possible.

Transversal, intent has also emerged as a constant in legal reasoning, to be found in all areas of the law and in all countries analyzed. Its *balance* is *precarious*, however, for when meticulous laws multiply excessively, a presumption of intent can quickly turn into fiction. Notwithstanding the difficulty of the study, the impression of confusion that emerged at first gradually dissipated, thanks to a historical and comparative law approach.

This has enabled us to critically examine contemporary doctrinal theorizations and then, by means of an *attempt at general theorization*, to enclose this reputedly elusive notion within a unitary, precise and operative conceptual framework. A new quadripartite classification of offenses has been proposed, the scope of which goes beyond competition law alone. It is based on an analysis of the structure of the offenses, making it possible to identify the specific mental element required, offers the opportunity to point out important differences in regime and, we hope, constitutes a useful contribution to the theory of intent.

Once the concept had been clearly defined, its confrontation with a competition law that imagines itself objective and efficient brought it out of its loneliness, showing that its specific features do not prevent it from recognizing the deep ties that bind it to general law. Above all, it has shown that what is commonly said about competition law is far removed from reality.

Utilitarian? Superficially, perhaps – but not truly – while it may appear to be concerned only with the material consequences of its actions on the market, it is really only interested in the rectitude of behavior and the intention that drives it. As *the general law of economic freedom*, its sole mission is to preserve this freedom for its own sake, in the same way that the general law of contract is the guarantor of contractual freedom.

Objective, because *scientific*? Far from it. On the one hand, the role of economic analysis in the law of anticompetitive practices is vastly overestimated. Legal reasoning, through the use of presumptions, plays a far more decisive, albeit less visible, role than economic reasoning. On the other hand, economics cannot claim to be as objective as the hard sciences: debates about the foundations of the discipline reveal that it is at grips with strong *ideological* issues. The mirage of its objectivity is evaporating – the use of economic analysis implies significant political bias, disguised by a false scientific neutrality.

Does it at least keep its promises – is it *effective*? If this was the primary objective of the modernization that began in the 2000s; twenty years on, hopes have been disappointed. The European Commission has indeed sought to prove the economic effects of the practices it has had to deal with, but it has often done so in excess, going further than required by case law, thereby needlessly mobilizing precious resources and drastically increasing the cost of implementing the rules. Herein lies the great paradox: the Court of Justice, guardian of continuity, has not substantially varied its positions – it has consistently held that effects are not a constitutive element of competition infringements, and that economic analyses represent, at most, incidental evidence that is sometimes relevant, but not required to characterize an anticompetitive practice.

There is therefore a profound discrepancy between the rhetoric of the discipline and its practical reality, which the theory of intent has brought to light at an opportune moment. Today, competition law seems to be at a crossroads. On the one hand, some are proposing to safeguard existing rules, while retaining an economic prism whose limits are now well known; on the other, the solution has consisted, with the Digital Markets Act, in the adoption of special rules, wrongly assumed to be able to compensate for the alleged inadequacies of the prohibition of cartels and abuses of dominant position.

So, while the arrival of intent in the competitive equation was undoubtedly unexpected, their alliance deserves to be nurtured, as it offers a *third way* of reviving a *legal approach* to anticompetitive behavior.

533. **Intent and competition law: an alliance to be nurtured.** The theory of intent has raised the law of anticompetitive practices above the misleading appearance it conveys at first glance.

De lege lata, used as an innovative reading prism, it has made it possible to attest that, contrary to popular belief, intent plays *a role in the characterization* of anticompetitive practices as a *constitutive element*. Competition infringements being *formal* in nature, they are consummated independently of any result – they are attempts elevated to autonomous offenses. What is more, it has been shown that the alternative between "object" and "effect" makes no difference as regards the object of proof: the anticompetitive effects of disputed behavior never have to be proven. At the very most, the effects-based approach means, in practice, a heavier burden of proof in the case of behavior whose infringement is ambiguous. By analogy between competition law and criminal law, the notion of "restriction of competition" has been deemed superfluous, insofar as it merges entirely with anticompetitive behavior, which alone can and must be defined.

Yet, while competition infringements are commonly defined in terms of the effects they have on competition, the market or consumers, the study first established that these effects had no defining significance. A unitary definition of anticompetitive practices was then proposed: cartel and abuse of dominant position were then defined as *dol with market power*. This definition is faithful to positive law and reveals the link uniting the discipline and other areas of law, by showing that a classic concept, *dol*, is implicitly received by competition law.

De lege ferenda, a critical analysis of the utilitarian perspective currently pervading the discipline was undertaken, and its questionable consequences with regard to the principles of the rule of law were examined. It was asserted that it was not possible, without infringing the principle of foreseeability, to adopt an "effects-based approach," insofar as judging lawful or unlawful conduct on the basis of the economic effects it produces would necessarily lead, in certain cases, to sanctioning a company for consequences it had not foreseen, nor been able to foresee – which would transform the presumption of intent into a dangerous fiction. However, once it had been demonstrated that the effects-based approach was nothing more than a myth devoid of any effective normative scope, it was rather the mismatch between the presentation of anticompetitive practices law and its jurisprudential reality that gave rise to legitimate concern, since such dissonance unnecessarily complicates reasoning and gives a distorted image of the discipline. To untangle this Gordian knot, an alternative approach was proposed.

In this respect, adopting the theory of intent – the central proposition of the thesis – would simplify reasoning, without upsetting established case law solutions. It is consistent with the teleology of competition law, and would enable a qualitative improvement in its semantics. A number of proposals have been put forward, including: a unified approach to cartels and abuses of a dominant position, abandoning the stage of qualifying a dominant position, ceasing to use the notion of effect, and making reasoned use of the tools of soft law. In addition, the theory of intent makes it possible to clearly establish the constituent elements of competition infringements, provides legal arguments for deciding whether to classify new cases as anticompetitive practices, and encourages greater and more assertive use of presumptions. It would therefore provide a powerful basis for repressing new forms of anticompetitive behavior – particularly those perpetrated by digital companies – more quickly and more effectively, while respecting fundamental rights, without the need for sector-specific regulations.

Finally, at the end of the thesis, a more general conclusion is in order: as the comparison between intention and competition law has proved fruitful, it perhaps constitutes an alliance from which to draw inspiration.

534. **Intent and competition law: an alliance to draw inspiration from?** Sooner or later, young researchers will be faced with the thorny question of "how to talk about the law," which will lead them down the path of the eternal question: "What is the law?" With no fully satisfactory answer in sight, acknowledging the limited time available, and the critical volume of contemporary normative and doctrinal production, it seems tempting to limit oneself to a cold, technical and superficial analysis of what is. Indeed, attempting to uncover the underlying coherence of the legal order, which is often concealed, in order to order scattered, increasingly technical, sometimes contradictory or logic-defying norms, may seem a risky undertaking, if not doomed to failure. Yet, without claiming to solve the – ultimately philosophical – enigma of full knowledge of the object under study, to forego such a quest is certainly a regrettable renunciation: it implies tacit acceptance of the disorder, highly unsatisfactory to the mind, in which the law finds itself. But between excessive formalism and its opposite, reckless dogmatism, it is difficult to find a balanced path through criticism, to choose between adhering to one method or another, to decide between one vision of law, research and doctrine or another. If our work has taught

us anything, it is certainly the constancy of doubt, which does not fade with time, and, above all, the value of intuition. Intuition is what first enables us to formulate a hypothesis, and then, out of curiosity, leads us to temporarily leave the well-trodden paths and venture elsewhere, into the realms of philosophy, legal theory, history or comparative law – to move away from the subject, in the hope of dealing with it more effectively.

535. If intent has shed new light on the law of anticompetitive practices, it is because it is a major legal concept that appeared capable of explaining it – like the Rosetta Stone that deciphers a tower of glass and steel. We believe that, in law, there are other towers of Babel, and other concepts that are just as many keys to understanding, the study of which would have the merit, both of rationalizing certain areas of the law and of enabling their author to attempt, or at least hope, to contribute a small stone to the edifice, in permanent reconstruction, of fairness.

Appendix no. 1 – general theory of intent: quadripartite classification of offenses

Summa divisio Offenses:	Subcategories:	The law describes:	Examples:	Features:	Common features:
Offenses INTENTIONAL *LATO SENSU* *Knowledge and will regarding the conduct but not the result*	Type I **Offenses of commission** *Violations of so-called police regulations*	The will **to engage in a conduct** regardless of the result.	Infringements of so-called technical legislation, deliberate endangerment, procedural infringements of competition law, breaches of the Digital Markets Act, non-compliance with undertakings, gun jumping.	1/ Infractions not requiring a material result as a constituent element. 2/ No causal link to prove. 3/ Does not use any standard.	1/ Non-punishable attempt. 2/ Mental element *automatically presumed* upon proof of material element. 3/ Non-invocable error of fact. 4/ Legitimate grounds and self-defense non-invocable.
	Type II **Offenses of lack of foresight** *Unintentional harm to persons and property.*	The will to **engage in a conduct** *and* the occurrence of an **unintended** but **foreseeable result**.	Involuntary manslaughter, unintentional injury, unintentional fire, destruction, damage or deterioration of the property of others.	1/ Infractions requiring a material result as a constituent element. 2/ Need to establish a **material causal link** between the *result* and the *conduct*. **3/ Standard of due diligence**.	
Offenses INTENTIONAL *STRICTO SENSU* *Knowledge and will regarding the conduct and the result*	Type III **Offenses of means** *Infringement of property rights*	The **will** to engage in a conduct	Theft, deception, swindling, market abuse, breach of trust, criminal conspiracy**, cartels, abuse of dominant position**.	1/ No **causal link** to prove. 2/ Formal or material offenses. 3/ Invocable legitimate grounds. **4/ Loyalty standard**.	1/ Punishable attempt that can be made a separate offense. 2/ Invocable legitimate grounds *or* self-defense. 3/ Mental element *not systematically presumed* on proof of material element. 4/ Invocable factual error.
	Type IV **Offenses of result** *Intentional harm to persons and property.*	The **will** to engage in a conduct in order to obtain a **result that is unlawful in itself**.	Voluntary manslaughter, deliberate arson, intentional assault and battery.	1/ Need to establish an **intellectual causal link** between the *result* and the *conduct*. 2/ Formal or material offenses. 3/ Invocable self-defense. **4/ Rationality standard.**	

Appendix no. 2 – general theory of intent: relationships between the elements of the offense

Moral, material elements and result

	Constant presumption	**Offenses of commission**	***Variable relationship***	
Mental element Intent *lato sensu*	*presumed by* ←	Material element Prohibited conduct	×	Result (∅ of)
		Offenses of lack of foresight		
Mental element Intent *lato sensu*	*presumed by* ←	Material element Negligent conduct	*material causality* →	Result (always required)
		Offenses of means		
Mental element Intent *stricto sensu*	*presumed by* ←	Material elements Unlawful means + Circumstances	*presumes unlawfulness of* →	Result (not always required)
		Offenses of result		
Mental element Intent *stricto sensu*	*presumed by* ←	Material elements Conduct aimed at producing an unlawful result + Circumstances	*intellectual causal link* →	Result (not always required)

Appendix no. 3 – comparative diagram no. 1: competition infringements and poisoning

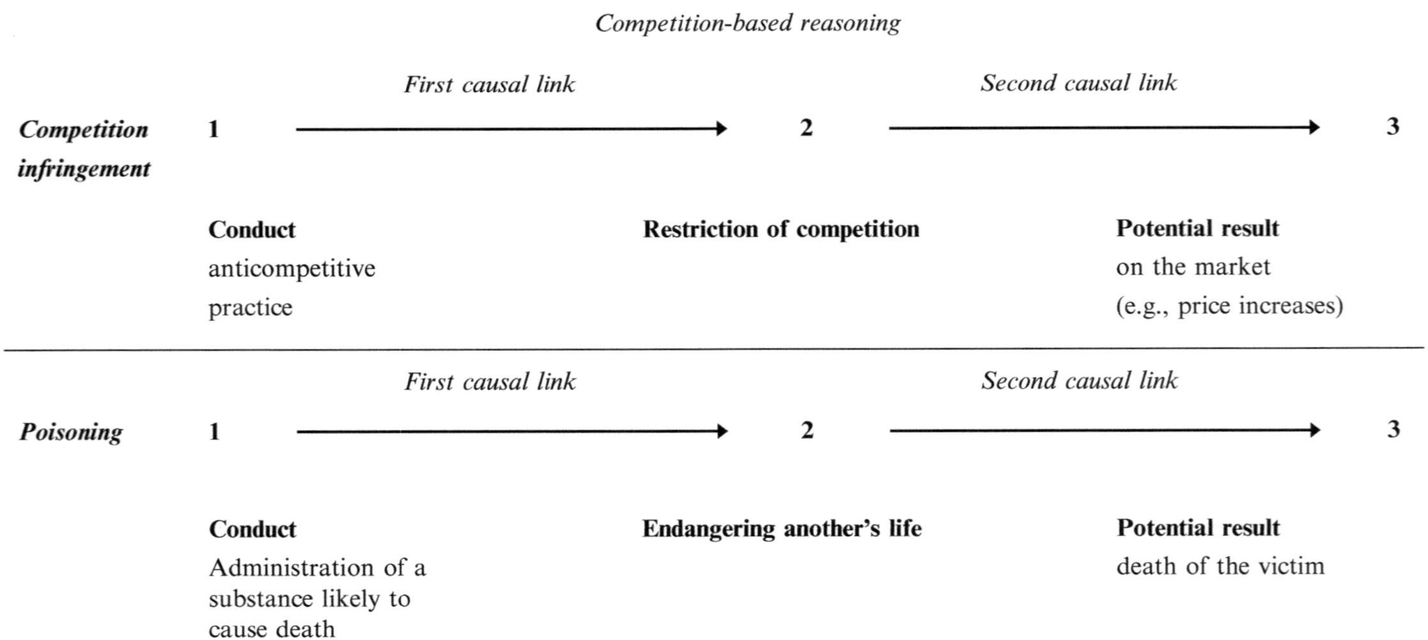

Elements nos. 1, 2 and 3 are combined.

In the case of competition infringements, the potential result on the market is the feared consequence of the restriction of competition, itself *automatically presumed* in the presence of anticompetitive conduct. In the case of poisoning, the potential death of the victim is the feared consequence of endangering another's life, *automatically presumed* if there has been administration of a substance likely to cause death.

The first causal link does not exist, as the elements nos. 1 and 2 are identical.

Endangering another's life is entirely contained in the administration of a substance likely to cause death. Similarly, the restriction of competition is one and the same with anticompetitive conduct. Elements nos. 1 and 2 are part of the same thing, i.e., the definition of the offending conduct: since they are one and the same, element n°. 2 is redundant.

The second causal link is superfluous, as element no. 3 is not required as a constitutive element.

The potentiality of the result is sufficient to characterize competition infringements and poisoning. Putting a person's life at risk can lead to death, and a restriction of competition can have an anticompetitive effect on the market. No special reasoning or analysis is required to demonstrate this, and indeed, given the formal nature of the offenses, no such demonstration is necessary.

Appendix no. 4 – comparative diagram no. 2: competition infringements and poisoning

Penal reasoning

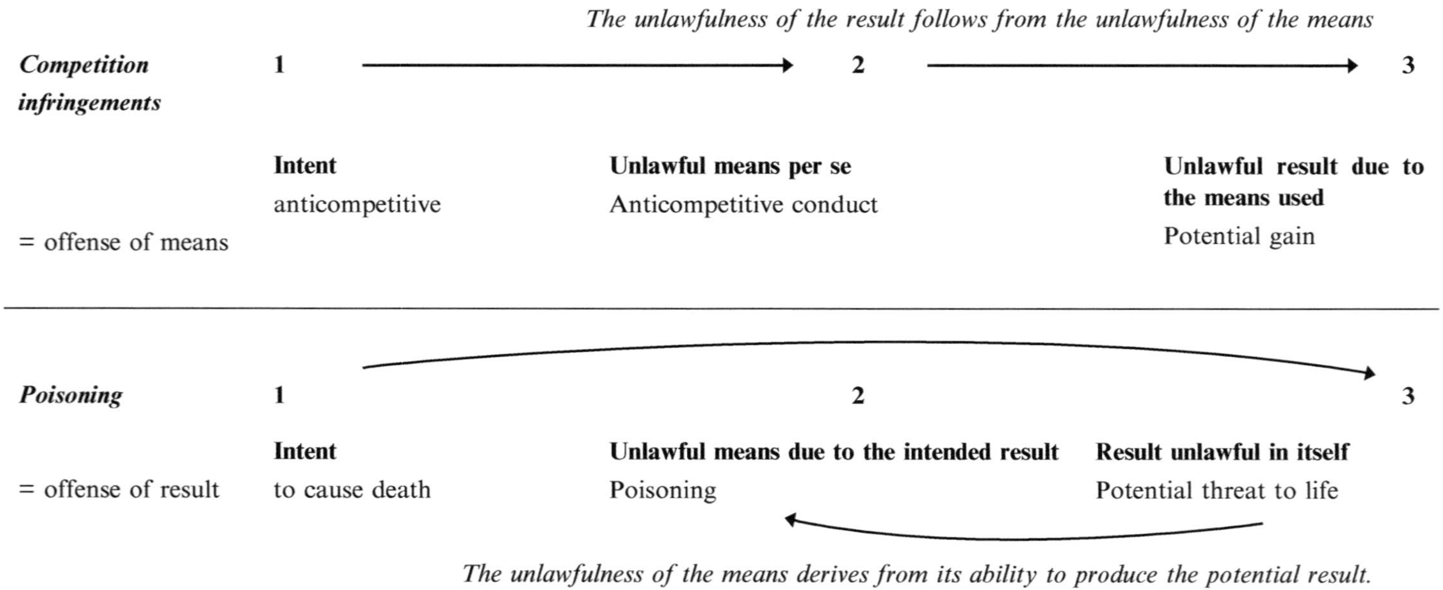

Anticompetitive intent is defined by reference to the means employed, since the result obtained is not unlawful in itself, but only because of the use of unlawful means to achieve it. A gain is undue only when obtained by unlawful means. This reasoning applies to all offenses involving means (theft, deceit, fraud, forgery, corruption, fraudulent bankruptcy, misuse of corporate assets, insider trading, unfair competition).

The intention to cause death is defined by reference to the intended result, since the means employed is unlawful only because it is intended to achieve a result that is unlawful in itself. Indeed, it is always unlawful to cause injury to life, limb or property. The reasoning is the same for all offenses of result (voluntary manslaughter, intentional assault and battery, arson).

It follows that anticompetitive intent is at one with the means employed, while *animus necandi* is at one with the intended result.

Appendix no. 5 – comparative diagram no. 3: competition infringements and swindling

Penal reasoning

			The unlawfulness of the result stems from the means		
Competition infringement	**1**		**2**		**3**
	Intent anticompetitive		**Unlawful means per se** Anticompetitive conduct		**Unlawful result due to the means used** Potential gain
= offense of means					

			The unlawfulness of the result stems from the means		
Poisoning	**1**		**2**		**3**
	Intent to defraud		**Unlawful means per se**		**Unlawful result due to the means used** Transfer of the item
= offense of means					

The relationship between the material and mental elements of the offense is identical in the case of competition infringements and swindling, insofar as they fall into the category of offenses of means. Their structure is therefore identical.

Appendix no. 6 – anticompetitive intent: *dol* with market power

THE GENERAL DEFINITION OF *DOL* *Maneuver* designed to annihilate or diminish *the free will* of another person in order to obtain an *advantage* that would not have been acquired in its absence.		
THE THREE CATEGORIES OF *DOL* ***Dol inter partes***. *Dol* affects the freedom of the victim alone.		
Free will ignored Appropriation of property without seeking the consent of others. *Theft*, *breach of trust*.	**Free will annihilated by error** Appropriation of property by giving others a false image of reality to induce them to transfer it. *Swindling*, *deception*, *pre-contractual* dols.	**Constrained free will** Appropriation of property by forcing others to transfer it. *Abuse of weakness, abuse of dependence, abuse of authority, economic coercion.*
Absence of consent The victim is forced into a situation to which they have not consented.	***Appearance of consent*** The victim apparently consents to the exchange, but in reality their will is not free, as it is vitiated by the existence of a maneuver.	
A SPECIFIC TYPE OF *DOL*: *DOL* WITH MARKET POWER, OR ANTICOMPETITIVE INTENT ***Dol erga omnes***. *Dol* has a potential impact on the freedom of all players in a given market: companies or consumers.		
Free will ignored Obtaining an advantage by directly preventing the free formation of the conditions of exchange. *Price fixing*, *exchange of information on prices or sensitive information*, *fixing of quotas*, *market sharing*, *resale price maintenance*, *excessive pricing*.	**Free will annihilated by error** Obtaining an advantage by misrepresenting reality in an attempt to drive others out of the market. *Deception*, *denigration*.	**Constrained free will** Obtaining an advantage by attempting to prevent others from participating freely in the market. *Predatory pricing*, *exclusive rebates*, *export bans*, *discrimination*, *pay-for-delay agreements*, *individual or collective boycotts*, *tying*, *favoritism*.
Direct alteration of the free formation of exchange conditions Consumers have conditions imposed on them that are not the result of a free meeting of supply and demand.	***Indirect alteration of the free formation of exchange conditions*** The conditions of exchange are not directly affected: competitors are potentially deprived of participating in the exchange, so consumers indirectly suffer a loss of chance of obtaining more favorable conditions.	

TABLE OF CASES

Court of Justice of the European Union

(Formerly: Court of Justice of the European Communities)

Judgments

July 12, 1962, Case 16-61, Acciaerie Ferriere e Fonderi di Modena, ECLI:EU:C:1962:29

June 30, 1966, Case 56-65, Société Technique Minière, ECLI:EU:C:1966:38

July 13, 1966, Case 56-64, Consten and Grundig, ECLI:EU:C:1966:41

December 12, 1967, Case C-23/67, Brasserie de Haecht, ECLI:EU:C:1967:54

July 9, 1969, Case 5/69, Völk, ECLI:EU:C:1969:35

July 15, 1970, Case 41/69, ACF Chemiefarma, ECLI:EU:C:1970:71

February 18, 1971, Case 40-70, Sirena, ECLI:EU:C:1971:18

May 6, 1971, Case 1-71, Cadillon, ECLI:EU:C:1971:47

June 8, 1971, Case 78-70, Deutsche Grammophon, ECLI:EU:C:1971:59

November 25, 1971, Case 22-71, Béguelin Import, ECLI:EU:C:1971:113

July 14, 1972, Case 48/69, Imperial Chemical Industries, ECLI:EU:C:1972:70

February 21, 1973, Case 6/72, Continental Can, ECLI:EU:C:1973:22

July 11, 1973, Case 8-74, Procureur du Roi, ECLI:EU:C:1974:82

November 13, 1975, Case 26/75, General Motors, ECLI:EU:C:1975:150

December 16, 1975, Case 40/73, Suiker Unie, ECLI:EU:C:1975:174

June 15, 1976, Case 96/75, EMI Records, ECLI:EU:C:1976:87

October 25, 1977, Case 26/76, Metro, ECLI:EU:C:1977:167

February 1, 1978, Case 19/77, Miller International, ECLI:EU:C:1978:19

February 14, 1978, Case 27/76, United Brands, ECLI:EU:C:1978:22

February 13, 1979, Case 85/76, Hoffmann-La Roche, ECLI:EU:C:1979:36

June 26, 1980, Case 136/79, National Panasonic, ECLI:EU:C:1980:169

October 29, 1980, Case 209/78, Van Landewyck, ECLI:EU:C:1980:248

December 11, 1980, Case 31/80, L'Oréal, ECLI:EU:C:1980:289

May 26, 1981, Case 157/80, Siegfried Ewald Rinkau, ECLI:EU:C:1981:120

June 7, 1983, Case 100/80, SA Musique Diffusion française, ECLI:EU:C:1983:158

October 25, 1983, Case 107/82, AEG-Telefunken, ECLI:EU:C:1983:293

November 8, 1983, Case 96/82, IAZ, ECLI:EU:C:1983:310

November 8, 1983, Case 96/102, IAZ International Belgium, ECLI:EU:C:1983:310

November 9, 1983, Case 322/81, Nederlandsche Banden Industrie Michelin, ECLI:EU:C:1983:313

November 16, 1983, Case 188/82, Thyssen, ECLI:EU:C:1983:329

February 21, 1984, Case 86/82, Hasselblad, ECLI:EU:C:1984:65

February 29, 1984, Case 270/82, Estel, ECLI:EU:C:1984:84

March 28, 1984, Case 29/83, Compagnie royale asturienne des mines, ECLI:EU:C:1984:130

July 12, 1984, Case C-170/83, Hydrotherm Gerätebau, ECLI:EU:C:1984:271

September 25, 1984, Case 117/83, Könecke, ECLI:EU:C:1984:288

January 30, 1985, Case 123/83, Bureau national interprofessionnel du cognac. ECLI:EU:C:1985:33

July 3, 1985, Case 243/83, Binon, ECLI:EU:C:1985:284

July 11, 1985, Case 42/84, Remia, ECLI:EU:C:1985:327

September 17, 1985, Case 25/84, Ford Werke, ECLI:EU:C:1985:340

October 3, 1985, Case 311/84, CBEM, ECLI:EU:C:1985:394

January 28, 1986, Case 161/84, Pronuptia de Paris, ECLI:EU:C:1986:41

February 25, 1986, Case 193/83, Windsurfing International, ECLI:EU:C:1986:75

April 23, 1986, Case 294/83, *Parti écologiste "Les Verts"*, ECLI:EU:C:1986:166

November 11, 1986, Case 226/84, British Leyland Public Limited Company, ECLI:EU:C:1986:421

January 27, 1987, Case 45/85, Verband der Sachversicherer, ECLI:EU:C:1987:34

November 18, 1987, Case 137/85, Maizenai, ECLI:EU:C:1987:493

April 18, 1988, Case 27/87, Louis Erauw-Jacquery, ECLI:EU:C:1988:183

May 4, 1988, Case 30/87, Corinne Bodson, ECLI:EU:C:1988:225

July 11, 1989, Case 246/86, Belasco, ECLI:EU:C:1989:301

September 21, 1989, Case 46/87, Hoescht, ECLI:EU:C:1989:337

October 18, 1989, Case 374/87, Orkem, ECLI:EU:C:1989:387

January 11, 1990, Case C-277/87, Sandoz Prodotti Farmaceutici, ECLI:EU:C:1990:6

July 10, 1990, Case C-326/88, Hansen & Soen, ECLI:EU:C:1990:291

February 28, 1991, Case C-234/89, Stergios Delimitis, ECLI:EU:C:1991:91

April 23, 1991, Case C-41/90, Klaus Höfner and Fritz Elser, ECLI:EU:C:1991:161

July 3, 1991, Case C-62/86, Akzo, ECLI:EU:C:1991:286

October 2, 1991, Case C-7/90, Paul Vandevenne, ECLI:EU:C:1991:363

March 31, 1993, Case C-89/85, Ahlström Osakeyhtiö, ECLI:EU:C:1993:120

April 1, 1993, Case C-250/91, Hewlett Packard France, ECLI:EU:C:1993:134

December 15, 1994, Case C-250/92, Gøttrup-Klim, ECLI:EU:C:1994:413

April 6, 1995, Case C-241/91 P, Magill, ECLI:EU:C:1995:98

March 25, 1996, Case C-137/95 P, SPO, ECLI:EU:C:1996:130

November 14, 1996, Case C-333/94 P, Tetra Pak ECLI:EU:C:1996:436

February 27, 1997, Case C-177/95, Ebony Maritime, ECLI:EU:C:1997:89

July 17, 1997, Case C-219/95 P, Ferriere Nord, ECLI:EU:C:1997:375

November 26, 1998, Case C-7/97, Oscar Bronner, ECLI:EU:C:1998:569

December 17, 1998, Case C-185/95 P, Baustahlgewebe, ECLI:EU:C:1998:608

July 8, 1999, Case C-49/92 P, Anic Partecipazioni, ECLI:EU:C:1999:356

July 8, 1999, Case C-235/92 P, Montecatini, ECLI:EU:C:1999:362

July 8, 1999, Case C-199/92 P, Hüls, ECLI:EU:C:1999:358

January 21, 1999, Case C-215/96, Bagnasco, ECLI:EU:C:1999:12

September 16, 1999, Case C-22/98, Jean Claude Becu, ECLI:EU:C:1999:419

September 21, 1999, Case C-67/96, Albany International, ECLI:EU:C:1999:430

September 21, 1999, Case C-219/97, Maatschappij Drijvende Bokken, ECLI:EU:C:1999:437

September 12, 2000, Case C-180/98, Pavel Pavlov, ECLI:EU:C:2000:428

November 16, 2000, Case C-294/98 P, Metsä-Serla Oyj, ECLI:EU:C:2000:632

November 16, 2000, Case C-286/98 P, Stora Kopparbergs Bergslags, ECLI:EU:C:2000:630

December 7, 2000, Case C-214/99, Neste Markkinointi Oy, ECLI:EU:C:2000:679

February 19, 2002, Case C-309/99, Wouters, ECLI:EU:C:2002:98

July 11, 2002, Case C-210/00, Käserei Champignon Hofmeister, ECLI:EU:C:2002:440

November 14, 2002, Case C-251/00, Ilumitrónica, ECLI:EU:C:2002:655

September 9, 2003, Case C-198/01, Consorzio Industrie Fiammiferi, ECLI:EU:C:2003:430

January 7, 2004, Case C-204/00 P, Aalborg Portland, ECLI:EU:C:2004:6

April 29, 2004, Case C-359/01 P, British Sugar, ECLI:EU:C:2004:255

February 15, 2005, Case C-12/03 P, Tetra Laval, ECLI:EU:C:2005:87

June 28, 2005, Case C-189/02 P, Dansk Rørindustri, ECLI:EU:C:2005:408

July 14, 2005, Case C-65/02 P, ThyssenKrupp Stainless, ECLI:EU:C:2005:454

April 6, 2006, Case C-551/03 P, General Motors, ECLI:EU:C:2006:229

July 13, 2006, Case C-74/04 P, Volkswagen, ECLI:EU:C:2006:460

July 18, 2006, Case C-519/04 P, David Meca-Medina, ECLI:EU:C:2006:492

September 21, 2006, Case C-167/04 P, JCB Service, ECLI:EU:C:2006:594

November 26, 2006, Case C-238/05, Asnef-Equifax, ECLI:EU:C:2006:734

March 15, 2007, Case C-95/04 P, British Airways, ECLI:EU:C:2007:166

May 22, 2008, Case C-266/06 P, Evonik Degussa, ECLI:EU:C:2008:295

June 3, 2008, Case C-308/06, Intertanko, ECLI:EU:C:2008:312

November 20, 2008, Case C-209/07, Beef Industry Development, ECLI:EU:C:2008:643

December 11, 2008, Case C-52/07, Kanal 5, ECLI:EU:C:2008:703

December 16, 2008, Case C-47/07 P, Masdar (UK) Ltd., ECLI:EU:C:2008:726

April 2, 2009, Case C-202/07 P, France Télécom, ECLI:EU:C:2009:214

June 4, 2009, Case C-8/08, T-Mobile Netherlands, ECLI:EU:C:2009:343

July 9, 2009, Case C-511/06 P, Archer Daniels Midland, ECLI:EU:C:2009:433

September 3, 2009, Case C-534/07 P, William Prym, ECLI:EU:C:2009:505

September 10, 2009, Case C-97/08 P, Akzo Nobel, ECLI:EU:C:2009:536

September 24, 2009, Case C-125/07 P, Erste Group Bank, ECLI:EU:C:2009:576

October 6, 2009, Case C-501/06 P, GlaxoSmithKline, ECLI:EU:C:2009:610

December 23, 2009, Case C-45/08, Spector Photo Group, ECLI:EU:C:2009:806

June 17, 2010, Case C-413/08 P, Lafarge, ECLI:EU:C:2010:346

June 29, 2010, Case C-441/07 P, Alrosa, ECLI:EU:C:2010:377

October 14, 2010, Case C-280/08 P, Deutsche Telekom, ECLI:EU:C:2010:603

February 17, 2011, Case C-52/09, TeliaSonera Sverige, ECLI:EU:C:2011:83

June 14, 2011, Case C-360/09, Pfeiderer, ECLI:EU:C:2011:389

September 29, 2011, Case C-521/09 P, Elf Aquitaine, ECLI:EU:C:2011:620

October 4, 2011, Case C-403/08, Football Association Premier League, ECLI:EU:C:2011:631

December 21, 2011, Case C-72/11, Mohsen Afrasiabi, ECLI:EU:C:2011:874

March 27, 2012, Case C-209/10, Post Danmark, ECLI:EU:C:2012:172

April 19, 2012, Case C-549/10 P, Tomra, ECLI:EU:C:2012:221

July 19, 2012, Case C-628/10 P, Alliance One International and Standard Commercial Tobacco, ECLI:EU:C:2012:479

December 6, 2012, Case C-441/11 P, Verhuizingen Coppens, ECLI:EU:C:2012:778

December 6, 2012, Case C-457/10 P, AstraZeneca, ECLI:EU:C:2012:770

December 13, 2012, Case C-226/11, Expedia, ECLI:EU:C:2012:795

February 7, 2013, Case C-68/12, Protimonopolny úrad Slovenskej republiky, ECLI:EU:C:2013:71

March 14, 2013, Case C-32/11, Allianz Hungária Biztosító, ECLI:EU:C:2013:160

June 18, 2013, Case C-681/11, Schenker, ECLI:EU:C:2013:404

July 11, 2013, Case C-429/11 P, Gosselin, ECLI:EU:C:2013:463

July 18, 2013, Case C-501/11, Schindler, ECLI:EU:C:2013:522

February 27, 2014, Case C-396/12, A.M. van der Ham, ECLI:EU:C:2014:98

March 12, 2014, Case C-456/12, Minister voor Immigratie, ECLI:EU:C:2014:135

June 12, 2014, Case C-377/13, Ascendi Beiras Litoral, ECLI:EU:C:2014:1754

July 10, 2014, Case C-295/12 P, Telefónica, ECLI:EU:C:2014:2062

September 11, 2014, Case C-382/12 P, MasterCard, ECLI:EU:C:2014:2201

September 11, 2014, Case C-67/13 P, Groupement des cartes bancaires, ECLI:EU:C:2014:2204

March 19, 2015, Case C-286/13 P, Dole Food Company, ECLI:EU:C:2015:184

June 24, 2015, Case C-293/13 P, Fresh Del Monte Produce, ECLI:EU:C:2014:2439

July 16, 2015, Case C-172/14, ING Pensii, ECLI:EU:C:2015:484

October 6, 2015, Case C-23/14, Post Danmark, ECLI:EU:C:2015:651

October 22, 2015, Case C-194/14 P, AC-Treuhand, ECLI:EU:C:2015:717

November 26, 2015, Case C-345/14, Maxima Latvja, ECLI:EU:C:2015:784

January 20, 2016, Case C-373/14 P, Toshiba Corporation, ECLI:EU:C:2016:26

January 21, 2016, Case C-74/14, Eturas, ECLI:EU:C:2016:42

May 4, 2016, Case C-477/14, Pillbox 38 (UK), ECLI:EU:C:2016:324

April 27, 2017, Case C-469/15 P, FSL, ECLI:EU:C:2017:308

September 6, 2017, Case C-413/14 P, Intel, ECLI:EU:C:2017:632

November 14, 2017, Case C-671/15, Association des producteurs vendeurs d'endives, ECLI:EU:C:2017:860

December 6, 2017, Case C-230/16, Coty Germany, ECLI:EU:C:2017:94

September 26, 2018, Case C-99/17 P, Infineon Technologies, ECLI:EU:C:2018:773

January 30, 2020, Case C-307/18, Generics (UK), ECLI:EU:C:2020:52

January 30, 2020, Case C-538/18 P, České dráhy, ECLI:EU:C:2020:53

April 2, 2020, Case C-228/18, Budapest Bank, ECLI:EU:C:2020:265

November 25, 2020, Case C-372/19, SABAM, ECLI:EU:C:2020:959

December 9, 2020, Case C-132/19 P, Groupe Canal +, ECLI:EU:C:2020:1007

January 27, 2021, Case C-595/18 P, The Goldman Sachs Group, ECLI:EU:C:2021:73

March 25, 2021, Case C-152/19 P, Deutsche Telekom, ECLI:EU:C:2021:238

March 25, 2021, Case C-614/16 P, Merck, ECLI:EU:C:2021:246

March 25, 2021, Case C-611/16 P, Xellia Pharmaceuticals, ECLI:EU:C:2021:707

October 6, 2021, Case C-882/19, Sumal SL, ECLI:EU:C:2021:800

May 12, 2022, Case C-377/20, ENEL, ECLI:EU:C:2022:379

January 12, 2023, Case C-42/21 P, Lietuvos geležinkeliai, ECLI:EU:C:2023:12

January 12, 2023, Case C-883/19 P, HSBC, ECLI:EU:C:2023:11

January 19, 2023, Case C-680/20, Unilever Italia, ECLI:EU:C:2023:33

March 16, 2023, Case C-449/21, Towercast, ECLI:EU:C:2023:207

June 29, 2023, Case C-211/22, Super Bock Bebidas, ECLI:EU:C:2023:529

July 4, 2023, Case C-252/21, Meta Platforms, ECLI:EU:C:2023:537

Opinions of Advocates General

March 23, 1966, Case 56-65, Société Technique Minière, ECLI:EU:C:1966:17, Opinion AG K. Roemer

April 27, 1966, Case 56-64, Consten and Grundig, ECLI:EU:C:1966:19, Opinion AG K. Roemer

December 19, 1968, Case 14/68, Walt Wilhelm, ECLI:EU:C:1968:55, Opinion AG K. Roemer

June 10, 1970, Case 41/69, ACF Chemiefarma, ECLI:EU:C:1970:78, Opinion AG J. Gand

June 16 and 17, 1975, Case 40/73, Suiker Unie, ECLI:EU:C:1975:78, Opinion AG H. Mayras

October 29, 1975, Case 26/75, General Motors Continental, ECLI:EU:C:1975:141, Opinion AG H. Mayras

September 19, 1978, Case 85/76, Hoffmann-La Roche, ECLI:EU:C:1978:162, Opinion AG G. Reischl

December 5, 1989, Case C-326/88, Hansen & Soen, ECLI:EU:C:1989:609, Opinion AG W. van Gerven

July 17, 1992, Case C-89/85, Ahlström Osakeyhtiö, ECLI:EU:C:1992:293, Opinion AG M. Darmon

October 19, 1996, Case C-177/95, Ebony Maritime, ECLI:EU:C:1996:445, Opinion AG F. G. Jacobs

July 15, 1997, Case C-235/92, Montecatini, ECLI:EU:C:1997:362, Opinion AG G. Cosmas

November 27, 2001, Case C-210/00, Käserei Champignon, ECLI:EU:C:2001:645, Opinion AG C. Stix-Hackl

October 28, 2004, Case C-53/03, Syfait, ECLI:EU:C:2004:673, Opinion AG F. G. Jacobs

October 25, 2005, Case C-551/03 P, General Motors, ECLI:EU:C:2005:639, Opinion AG A. Tizzano

December 8, 2005, Case C-105/04 P, FEG, ECLI:EU:C:2005:751, Opinion AG J. Kokott

February 23, 2006, Case C-95/04 P, British Airways, ECLI:EU:C:2006:133, Opinion AG J. Kokott

October 26, 2006, Case C-391/04, Ypourgos Ikonomikon, ECLI:EU:C:2006:669, Opinion AG P. Mengozzi

November 20, 2007, Case C-308/06, Intertanko, ECLI:EU:C:2007:689, Opinion AG J. Kokott

February 19, 2009, Case C-8/08, T-Mobile Netherlands, ECLI:EU:C:2009:110, Opinion AG J. Kokott

April 23, 2009, Case C-97/08 P, Akzo Nobel, ECLI:EU:C:2009:262, Opinion AG J. Kokott

September 10, 2009, Case C-45/08, Spector Photo Group, ECLI:EU:C:2009:534, Opinion AG J. Kokott

April 22, 2010, Case C-280/08 P, Deutsche Telekom, ECLI:EU:C:2010:212, Opinion AG J. Mazák

September 2, 2010, Case C-52/09, TeliaSonera, ECLI:EU:C:2010:483, Opinion AG J. Mazák

February 10, 2011, Case C-272/09 P, KME Germany, ECLI:EU:C:2011:63, Opinion AG E. Sharpston

April 14, 2011, Case C-109/10 P, Solvay, ECLI:EU:C:2011:256, Opinion AG J. Kokott

May 24, 2011, Case C-209/10, Post Danmark, ECLI:EU:C:2011:342, Opinion AG P. Mengozzi

November 16, 2011, Case C-72/11, Mohsen Afrasiabi, ECLI:EU:C:2011:737, Opinion AG Y. Bot

April 18, 2013, Case C-501/11 P, Schindler, ECLI:EU:C:2013:248, Opinion AG J. Kokott

October 24, 2013, Case C-396/12, A.M. van der Ham, ECLI:EU:C:2013:698, Opinion AG J. Kokott

March 27, 2014, Case C-67/13 P, Groupement des cartes bancaires, ECLI:EU:C:2014:1958, Opinion AG N. Wahl

May 21, 2015, Case C-23/14, Post Danmark, ECLI:EU:C:2015:343, Opinion AG J. Kokott

May 21, 2015, Case C-194/14 P, AC-Treuhand, ECLI:EU:C:2015:350, Opinion AG N. Wahl

June 25, 2015, Case C-373/14 P, Toshiba Corporation, ECLI:EU:C:2015:427, Opinion AG M. Wathelet

September 5, 2019, Case C-228/18, Budapest Bank, ECLI:EU:C:2019:678, Opinion AG M. Bobek

January 22, 2020, Case C-307/18, Generics (UK), ECLI:EU:C:2020:28, Opinion AG J. Kokott

May 7, 2020, Case C-132/19 P, Groupe Canal +, ECLI:EU:C:2020:355, Opinion AG G. Pitruzzella

December 9, 2021, Case C-377/20, ENEL, ECLI:EU:C:2021:998, Opinion AG A. Rantos

July 7, 2022, Case C-42/21 P, Lietuvos geležinkeliai, ECLI:EU:C:2022:537, Opinion AG R. Rantos

July 14, 2022, Case C-680/20, Unilever Italia, ECLI:EU:C:2022:586, Opinion AG A. Rantos

July 14, 2022, Case C-176/19 P, Servier, ECLI:EU:C:2022:576, Opinion AG J. Kokott

October 13, 2022, Case C-449/21, Towercast, ECLI:EU:C:2022:777, Opinion AG J. Kokott

December 15, 2022, Case C-333/21, European Superleague Compagnie, ECLI:EU:C:2022:993, Opinion AG A. Rantos

General Court of the European Union

(Formerly: Court of First Instance of the European Communities)

Judgments

October 24, 1991, Case T-1/89, Rhône-Poulenc, ECLI:EU:T:1991:56

December 12, 1991, Case T-30/89, Hilti, ECLI:EU:T:1991:70

March 10, 1992, Case T-12/89, Solvay, ECLI:EU:T:1992:34

March 10, 1992, Case T-15/89, Chemie Linz, ECLI:EU:T:1992:37

July 2, 1992, Case T-61/89, Dansk Pelsdyravlerforening, ECLI:EU:T:1992:79

July 7, 1994, Case T-43/92, Dunlop Slazenger International, ECLI:EU:T:1994:79

July 14, 1994, Case T-66/92, Herlitz, ECLI:EU:T:1994:84

July 14, 1994, Case T-77/92, Parker Pen, ECLI:EU:T:1994:85

October 27, 1994, Case T-35/92, John Deere, ECLI:EU:T:1994:259

April 6, 1995, Case T-143/89, Ferriere Nord, ECLI:EU:T:1995:64

April 6, 1995, Case T-141/89, Trefileurope, ECLI:EU:T:1995:62

April 6, 1995, Case T-142/89, Usines Gustave Boël, ECLI:EU:T:1995:63

April 6, 1995, Case T-144/89, Cockerill-Sambre, ECLI:EU:T:1995:65

April 6, 1995, Case T-148/89, Trefilunion, ECLI:EU:T:1995:68

October 8, 1996, Case T-24/93, Compagnie maritime belge transports, ECLI:EU:T:1996:139

March 11, 1999, Case T-141/94, Thyssen Stahl, ECLI:EU:T:1999:48

October 7, 1999, Case T-228/97, Irish Sugar, ECLI:EU:T:1999:246

March 15, 2000, Case T-25/95, Cimenteries CBR, ECLI:EU:T:2000:77

July 6, 2000, Case T-62/98, Volkswagen, ECLI:EU:T:2000:180

October 26, 2000, Case T-41/96, Bayer, ECLI:EU:T:2000:242

December 12, 2000, Case T-128/98, Aéroports de Paris, ECLI:EU:T:2000:290

July 12, 2001, Case T-202/98, British Sugar, ECLI:EU:T:2001:185

December 18, 2001, Case T-112/99, Métropole télévision (M6), ECLI:EU:T:2001:215

February 28, 2002, Case T-86/95, Compagnie générale maritime, ECLI:EU:T:2002:50

March 20, 2002, Case T-23/99, LR AF 1998, ECLI:EU:T:2002:75

June 6, 2002, Case T-342/99, Airtours, ECLI:EU:T:2002:146

March 19, 2003, Case T-213/00, CMA CGM, ECLI:EU:T:2003:76

September 30, 2003, Case T-203/01, Manufacture française des pneumatiques Michelin, ECLI:EU:T:2003:250

October 21, 2003, Case T-368/00, General Motors Nederland, ECLI:EU:T:2003:275

December 17, 2003, Case T-219/99, British Airways, ECLI:EU:T:2003:343

January 13, 2004, Case T-67/01, JCB Service, ECLI:EU:T:2004:3

July 8, 2004, Case T-44/00, Mannesmannröhren-Werke, ECLI:EU:T:2004:218

July 8, 2004, Case T-50/00, Dalmine, ECLI:EU:T:2004:220

July 8, 2004, Case T-67/00, JFE Engineering, ECLI:EU:T:2004:221

July 27, 2005, Case T-49/02, Brasserie nationale, ECLI:EU:T:2005:298

September 15, 2005, Case T-325/01, Daimler Chrysler, ECLI:EU:T:2005:322

October 25, 2005, Case T-38/02, Groupe Danone, ECLI:EU:T:2005:367

April 5, 2006, Case T-279/02, Degussa, ECLI:EU:T:2006:103

May 2, 2006, Case T-328/03, O2 (Germany), ECLI:EU:T:2006:116

September 27, 2006, Case T-322/01, Roquette Frères, ECLI:EU:T:2006:267

September 27, 2006, Case T-168/01, GlaxoSmithKline, ECLI:EU:T:2006:265

December 5, 2006, Case T-303/02, Westfalen Gassen Nederland, ECLI:EU:T:2006:374

December 13, 2006, Case T-217/03, Fédération nationale de la coopération bétail et viande, ECLI:EU:T:2006:391

December 14, 2006, Case T-259/02, Raiffeisen Zentralbank Österreich, ECLI:EU:T:2006:396

January 30, 2007, Case T-340/03, France Télécom, ECLI:EU:T:2007:22

September 17, 2007, Case T-201/04, Microsoft, ECLI:EU:T:2007:289

December 12, 2007, Case T-36/05, Coats, ECLI:EU:T:2007:268

July 8, 2008, Case T-99/04, AC-Treuhand, ECLI:EU:T:2008:256

July 8, 2008, Case T-53/03, BPB, ECLI:EU:T:2008:254

October 8, 2008, Case T-73/04, Carbone-Lorraine, ECLI:EU:T:2008:416

October 8, 2008, Case T-69/04, Schunk and Schunk, ECLI:EU:T:2008:415

May 26, 2009, Case T-127/04, KME Germany, ECLI:EU:T:2009:142

July 9, 2009, Case T-450/05, Automobiles Peugeot, ECLI:EU:T:2009:262

April 28, 2010, Case T-456/05, Gütermann and Zwicky, ECLI:EU:T:2010:168

July 1, 2010, Case T-321/05, AstraZeneca, ECLI:EU:T:2010:266

September 9, 2010, Case T-155/06, Tomra Systems, ECLI:EU:T:2010:370

March 8, 2011, Case T-37/05, Worlds Wide Tobacco España, ECLI:EU:T:2011:76

March 24, 2011, Case T-375/06, Viega, ECLI:EU:T:2011:106

June 7, 2011, Case T-217/06, Arkema France, ECLI:EU:T:2011:251

July 12, 2011, Case T-132/07, Fuji Electric, ECLI:EU:T:2011:344

July 13, 2011, Case T-141/07, General Technic-Otis, ECLI:EU:T:2011:363

October 5, 2011, Case T-39/06, Transcatab, ECLI:EU:T:2011:562

October 25, 2011, Case T-348/08, Aragonesas Industrias y Energía, ECLI:EU:T:2011:621

June 27, 2012, Case T-372/10, Bolloré, ECLI:EU:T:2012:325

December 12, 2012, Case T-332/09, Electrabel v. Commission, ECLI:EU:T:2012:672

March 14, 2013, Case T-587/08, Fresh Del Monte, ECLI:EU:T:2013:129

April 12, 2013, Case T-401/08, Säveltäjäin Tekijänoikeustoimisto Teosto, ECLI:EU:T:2013:170

April 12, 2013, Case T-442/08, CISAC, ECLI:EU:T:2013:188

September 13, 2013, Case T-566/08, Total Raffinage Marketing, ECLI:EU:T:2013:423

September 16, 2013, Case T-373/10, Villeroy & Boch Austria, ECLI:EU:T:2013:455

December 13, 2013, Case T-399/09, Holding Slovenske Elektrarne, ECLI:EU:T:2013:647

February 6, 2014, Case T-27/10, AC-Treuhand, ECLI:EU:T:2014:59

May 21, 2014, Case T-519/09, Toshiba, ECLI:EU:T:2014:263

June 12, 2014, Case T-286/09, Intel, ECLI:EU:T:2014:547

December 12, 2014, Case T-558/08, Eni, ECLI:EU:T:2014:1080

July 15, 2015, Case T-389/10, SLM, ECLI:EU:T:2015:513

September 9, 2015, Case T-104/13, Toshiba, ECLI:EU:T:2015:610

June 2, 2016, Case T-426/10, Moreda-Riviere Trefilerías, ECLI:EU:T:2016:335

June 30, 2016, Case T-491/07 RENV, Groupement des cartes bancaires, ECLI:EU:T:2016:379

September 8, 2016, Case T-472/13, Lundbeck, ECLI:EU:T:2016:449

December 12, 2018, Case T-691/14, Servier, ECLI:EU:T:2018:922

November 10, 2021, Case T-612/17, Google et Alphabet (Google Shopping), ECLI:EU:T:2021:763

January 26, 2022, Case T-286/09 RENV, Intel, ECLI:EU:T:2022:19

June 15, 2022, Case T-235/18, Qualcomm, ECLI:EU:T:2022:358

September 14, 2022, Case T-604/18, Google (Google Android), ECLI:EU:T:2022:541

Opinions of Advocates General

July 10, 1991, Case T-1/89, Rhône-Poulenc, ECLI:EU:T:1991:38, Opinion AG B. Vesterdorf

European Commission

(Formerly Commission of the European Communities)

July 17, 1967, IV/26045, A.C.E.C. – Berliet

June 27, 1967, IV/223, Transocean Marine Paint Association

July 16, 1969, IV/26.623, Entente internationale de la quinine

June 2, 1971, IV/26.760, GEMA

December 13, 1974, IV/14 650, Bayerische Motoren Werke

December 19, 1974, IV/23.013, Goodyear Italiana – Euram

December 17, 1975, IV/26 699, Chiquita

June 9, 1976, IV/29.020, Vitamins

December 1, 1976, IV/29.018, Miller International

December 22, 1976, IV/24.510, Gerofabriek

December 23, 1977, IV/29.146, BMW Belgium

September 21, 1978, IV/28.824, Breeders' rights – maize seed

December 12, 1978, IV/29.535, White lead

October 7, 1981, IV/29.491, Nederlandsche Banden-Industrie Michelin

September 28, 1981, IV/29.988, Italian flat glass

December 17, 1981, IV/29.995, NAVEWA-ANSEA

January 6, 1982, IV/28/748, AEG-Telefunken

December 7, 1982, IV/30.070, National Panasonic

November 16, 1983, IV/30.696, Distribution system of Ford Werke AG – interim measure

December 12, 1983, IV/30.389, Nutricia/de Rooij

April 29, 1984, IV/34.456, Stichting Baksteen

July 4, 1984, IV/30.810, Synthetic Fibers

July 19, 1984, IV/30.863, BPCL/ICI

December 7, 1984, IV/28.930, Milchförderungsfonds

December 10, 1984, IV/30.717, Uniform Eurocheques

December 18, 1985, IV/30.739, Siemens/Fanuc

July 12, 1985, IV/4.204, Velcro-Aplix

July 10, 1986, IV/31.371, Roofing felt

September 25, 1986, IV/31.143, Peugeot

November 26, 1986, IV/31.204, MELDOC

December 18, 1987, IV/31.017, Fisher-Price/Quaker Oats

December 18, 1987, IV/31.503, Konica

December 21, 1988, IV/39.979, Decca Navigator System
August 2, 1989, IV/31.553, Welded steel mesh
December 4, 1991, IV/33.157, Eco System v. Peugeot
February 5, 1992, IV/31.572, Building and construction industry in the Netherlands
December 23, 1992, IV/31.533, Schöller Lebensmittel
May 18, 1994, IV/33.640, Exxon/Shell
December 21, 1994, IV/34.252, Philips-Osram
January 14, 1999, IV.F.1/36.718, CEDED
July 20, 1999, IV/36.888, 1998 Football World Cup
May 16, 2000, IV/34.018, FETTCSA
December 10, 2003, COMP/E-2/37.857, Organic Peroxides
March 24, 2004, COMP/C-3/37.792, Microsoft
March 29, 2006, COMP/E-1/38.113, Prokent-Tomra
July 4, 2007, COMP/38.784, Wanadoo España v. Telefónica
October 3, 2007, COMP/D1/37860, Visa International
October 17, 2007, COMP/D1/38606, Groupement des cartes bancaires
December 19, 2007, COMP/34.579, MasterCard
January 30, 2008, COMP/B-1/39.326, E.ON Energie
May 13, 2009, COMP/C-3/37.990, Intel
March 11, 2008, COMP/38.543, International removal services
July 16, 2008, COMP/CE/38.698, CISAC
June 22, 2011, COMP/39.525, Telekomunikacja Polska
June 19, 2013, C(2013) 3803 final, Lundbeck
December 10, 2013, C(2013) 8870 final, Fentanyl
April 29, 2014, C(2014) 2892 final, Motorola
July 9, 2014, C(2014) 4955 final, Servier
May 4, 2017, C(2017) 2876 final, E-book MFNs
June 21, 2017, C(2017) 4100 final, Lighting Systems
June 27, 2017, C(2017) 4444 final, Google Search (Shopping)
October 2, 2017, C(2017) 6544 final, Baltic Rail
July 18, 2018, C(2018) 4761 final, Google Android
July 24, 2018, C(2018) 4790 final, Pioneer
January 22, 2019, C(2019) 241 final, MasterCard II
March 20, 2019, C(2019) 2173 final, Google Search (AdSense)
July 8, 2021, C(2021) 4955 final, Car Emissions

European Court of Human Rights

June 8, 1976, App. no. 5100/71, Engel v. Netherlands

February 21, 1984, App. no. 8544/79, Öztürk v. Germany

October 7, 1988, App. no. 10519/83, Salabiaku v. France

May 30, 1991, App. no. 11598/85, Société Stenuit v. France

November 22, 1995, App. no. 20166/92, S.W. v. United Kingdom

September 16, 1996, App. no. 17371/90, Gaygusuz v. Austria

November 15, 1996, App. no. 17862/91, Cantoni v. France

July 15, 2003, App. no. 32559/96, Fortum Corporation v. Finland

June 3, 2004, App. no. 69042/01, Neste v. Russia

November 23, 2006, App. no. 73053/01, Jussila v. Finland

June 25, 2009, App. no. 12157/05, Liivik v. Estonia

May 17, 2010, App. no. 36376/04, Kononov v. Latvia

September 27, 2011, App. no. 43509/08, Menarini Diagnostics v. Italy

February 11, 2016, App. no. 38395/12, Dallas v. United Kingdom

June 28, 2018, App. no. 1828/06, G.I.E.M. S.R.L. and others v. Italy

French Jurisprudence and Decision-Making Practice

Competition Council

March 22, 1994, decision no. 94-D-21 concerning practices by Office d'annonces, the exclusive manager of advertising in France Télécom directories (Fr.)

October 19, 2001, decision no. 01-D-67 relating to practices identified in connection with the award of public roadworks contracts in the Bouches-du-Rhône department (Fr.)

November 8, 2005, decision no. 05-D-60 on practices implemented by the Cisterian Order of the Immaculée Conception, the Planaria company and the municipality of Cannes (Fr.)

November 25, 2005, decision no. 05-D-64 regarding practices implemented on the Paris luxury hotel market (Fr.)

May 9, 2007, decision no. 07-D-15 on practices implemented in the public markets relative to Ile-de-France secondary schools (Fr.)

December 20, 2007, decision no. 07-D-50 on practices implemented in the sector of toy distribution (Fr.)

February 21, 2008, decision no. 08-D-03 concerning practices implemented by the Fédération Nationale des Gîtes de France and the Bienvenue à la ferme network (Fr.)

French Competition Authority

September 26, 2012, decision no. 12-D-19 regarding practices in the teeth whitening and lightening sector (Fr.)

April 21, 2015, decision no. 15-D-06 regarding practices implemented by Booking.com B.V., Booking.com France SAS and Booking.com Customer Service France SAS in the online hotel booking sector (Fr.)

July 30, 2015, decision no. 15-D-12 on practices implemented by the Fédération française des clubs alpins et de montagne and the Compagnies de guides de Chamonix et de Saint Gervais in the high mountain guide sector (access to Mont Blanc via the Goûter refuge) (Fr.)

October 24, 2018, decision no. 18-D-23 regarding practices implemented in the retail of outdoor power equipment (Fr.)

December 5, 2018, decision no. 18-D-24 relating to practices implemented in the household appliances sector (Fr.)

January 16, 2020, decision no. 20-D-01 regarding a practice implemented in the digital terrestrial television broadcasting sector (Fr.)

June 7, 2021, decision no. 21-D-11 regarding practices implemented in the online advertising sector

March 3, 2022, decision no. 22-D-08 concerning practices implemented in the waste collection and management sector in Haute-Savoie (Fr.)

June 21, 2022, decision no. 22-D-13 regarding practices implemented in the press sector

May 4, 2023, decision no. 23-MC-01 on the request by the company Adloox for interim measures (Fr.)

Court of Cassation

Cass. civ., June 18, 1828, Rec. Dalloz, 1833, t. XXXIII, pp. 174–175

Cass. crim., February 1, 1834, Rec. Sirey, 1834, t. XXXIV, pp. 81–84

Cass. crim., January 26, 1838, Rec. Sirey, 1838, t. XXXVIII, pp. 241-243

Cass. crim., August 31, 1838, Rec. Sirey, 1838, t. XXXIII, pp. 988–990

Cass. civ., June 26, 1850, Rec. Sirey, 1850, pp. 726–731

Cass. civ., May 3, 1911, Rec. Dalloz, 1912, pp. 32–45

Cass. civ., October 26, 1921, Rec. Dalloz, 1925, p. 120

Cass. crim., October 21, 1926, Sirey, 1927, pp. 33–35

Cass. crim., December 13, 1956, no. 55-05.772

Cass. com., April 18, 1958, no. 58-04.997

Cass. 2e civ., December 18, 1964, JCP, 1965, II, 14304

Cass. crim., May 8, 1968, no. 67-90.684

Cass. crim., December 10, 1970, no. 70-91.155

Cass. crim., June 25, 1979, no. 78-93.259

Cass. com., January 27, 1982, no. 80-14.175

Cass. com., March 1, 1982, no. 80-15.834

Cass. ass. plén., May 9, 1984, no. 80-14.994

Cass. com., October 17, 1984, no. 82-16.666

Cass. crim., June 18, 1991, no. 91-82.033

Cass. crim., July 12, 1994, no. 93-85.262

Cass. crim., February 29, 2000, no. 98-88.175

Cass. com., January 15, 2002, no. 99-21.547

Cass. com., March 11, 2003, no. 01-02.310

Cass. com., May 12, 2004, no. 02-19.199

Cass. crim., June 20, 2006, no. 05-85.255

Cass. crim., June 25, 2008, no. 07-80.261

Cass. crim., September 24, 2008, no. 08-80.113

Cass. com., November 4, 2008, no. 07-21.275

Cass. crim., December 6, 2011, no. 10-82.266

Cass. crim., March 22, 2016, no. 15-84.949

Cass. crim., January 23, 2018, no. 16-87.709

Cass. com., January 29, 2020, no. 18-10.967

Cass. crim., November 17, 2020, no. 19-82471

Cass. ass. plén., November 25, 2020, no. 18-86.955

Cass. com., June 9, 2021, no. 19-10.943

Cass. com., July 7, 2021, no. 19-25.586

Cass. ch. mixte, October 29, 2021, no. 19-18.470

Cass. com., June 1, 2022, no. 19-20.999

Cass. com., October 22, 2022, no. 00-18.048

Cass. com., March 1, 2023, no. 20-18.356

Council of State

November 21, 2001, no. 238214, Zhary

April 4, 2019, no. 429370, Hamon

Courts of Appeals

CA Grenoble, 1re ch. May 1, 1894, Dalloz Périodique, 1895, II, pp. 221–222

CA Grenoble, ch. corr. 1, April 30, 2007, C. and Sté Panzani (SAS) c/ UFC Que choisir de l'Isère

CA Limoges, ch. acc., May 14, 1991, no. 91-1048

CA Paris, pôle 5, ch. 7, December 20, 2018, no. 18/07722

CA Paris, pôle 5, October 4, 2023, no. 21/22383, UberPop

CA Paris, pôle 5, ch. 5–7, March 13, 2014, no. 2013/00714

Foreign Case Law and Decision-Making Practice

Germany

Reichsgericht

December 4, 1897, 38 RGZ 155

Bundeskartellamt

February 6, 2019, B6-22/16, Facebook

Italy

Autorità Garante della Concorrenza e del Mercato

December 22, 2020, decision no. 28495, Ticketone c/ Condotte Escludenti Nella Vendita di Biglietti

Luxembourg

Competition Council

March 15, 2019, decision no. 2019-R-01, Fédération des Artisans

United States

Supreme Court

United States v. Trans-Missouri Freight Association, 166 U.S. 290 (1897)

United States v. Addyston Pipe & Steel Co., 175 U.S. 211 (1899)

New York Central & Hudson River Railroad v. United States, 212 U.S. 481 (1909)

Standard Oil of New Jersey v. United States, 221 U.S. 1 (1911)

United States v. American Tobacco, 221 U.S. 106 (1911)

United States v. Socony-Vacuum Oil Co., Inc., 310 U.S. 150 (1940)

NCAA v. Board of Regents of University of Oklahoma, 468 U.S. 85 (1984)

Verizon Communications Inc. v. Law Offices of Curtis v. Trinko, LLP, 540 U.S. 398 (2004)

Court of Appeals for the Seventh Circuit

Olympia Equipment Leasing Co. v. Western Union Telegraph Co., 797 F.2[d] 370 (1986)

BIBLIOGRAPHY

I. General Works, Manuals and Treatises

Benabent, A. *Droit des obligations*. Domat droit privé. 19th ed. Paris: LGDJ, 2021.

Bernardini, R., and M. Dalloz. *Droit criminel.* Vol. II: *L'infraction et la responsabilité*. Paradigme. 4th ed. Brussels: Bruylant, 2020.

Blasselle, R. *Traité de droit européen de la concurrence.* Tome I. Manuels 2000. Paris: Publisud, 2002.

Bongert, Y. *Cours d'histoire du droit pénal.* Tome 1: *Le droit pénal français médiéval de la seconde moitié du XIIIe siècle à l'ordonnance de 1493*. Paris: Les cours de droit, 1973.

Bosco, D., and C. Prieto. *Droit européen de la concurrence.* Droit de l'Union européenne. Brussels: Bruylant, 2013.

Bouloc, B. *Droit pénal général.* Précis. 24th and 27th eds. Paris: Dalloz, 2015 and 2021.

Boutard Labarde, M.-C., and G. Canivet. *Droit français de la concurrence.* Droit des affaires. Paris: LGDJ, 1994.

Burst, J.-J., and R. Kovar. *Droit de la concurrence.* Droit des affaires et de l'entreprise. Paris: Economica, 1981.

Carbasse, J.-M. *Histoire du droit pénal et de la justice criminelle.* Droit fondamental. 3rd ed. Paris: PUF, 2014.

Carbonnier, J. *Droit civil.* Tome 4: *Les obligations.* Thémis Droit Privé. 16th ed. Paris: PUF, 1992.

Chantepie, G., and M. Latina. *Le nouveau droit des obligations: Commentaire théorique et pratique dans l'ordre du Code civil.* Dalloz. 2nd ed. Paris: Dalloz, 2018.

Combe, E. *Économie et politique de la concurrence.* Preface by G. Canivet. Précis. 2nd ed. Paris: Dalloz, 2020.

Conte, P. *Droit pénal spécial.* 6th ed. Paris: LexisNexis, 2019.

Conte, P., and P. Maistre du Chambon. *Droit pénal général.* U. 5th ed. Paris: Armand Colin, 2000.

De Biolley, S., H. Labayle, and A. Weyembergh. *Criminal Law of the European Union.* Codes essentiels. 4th ed. Brussels: Larcier, 2020.

De Laubadère, A., and P. Delvolve. *Droit public économique.* Précis. 5th ed. Paris: Dalloz, 1986.

Decocq, A. *Droit pénal général.* U. Paris: Armand Colin, 1971.

Decocq, A., and G. Decocq. *Droit de la concurrence: Droit interne et droit de l'Union européenne.* Manuel. 9th ed. Paris: LGDJ, 2021.

Delamare, N. *Traité de la Police.* Tomes I and II. Paris: Michel Brunet, 1705 and 1722.

Delmas-Marty, M. *Droit pénal des affaires.* Tomes 1 and 2. Thémis. 3rd ed. Paris: PUF, 1990.

Descamps, O., and R. Szramkiewicz. *Histoire du droit des affaires.* Droit privé. 2nd ed. Paris: Domat, 2013.

Desportes, F., and F. Le Gunehec. *Droit pénal général.* Corpus droit privé. 16th ed. Paris: Economica, 2009.

Domat, J. *Les loix civiles dans leur ordre naturel.* Tome IV: *Le droit public.* Paris: Pierre Emery, 1701.

Donnedieu de Vabres, H. *Traité élémentaire de droit criminel et de législation pénale comparée.* 2nd ed. Paris: Sirey, 1943.

Dreyer, E. *Droit pénal général.* Manuels. 6th ed. Paris: LexisNexis, 2021.

Frison-Roche, M.-A., and J.-C. Roda. *Droit de la concurrence.* Précis. 2nd ed. Paris: Dalloz, 2022.

Garçon, E. *Code pénal annoté.* Tomes I and III. 2nd ed. Paris: Sirey, 1952 and 1959.

Garraud, R. *Traité théorique et pratique du droit pénal français.* Tome I. 3rd ed. Paris: Sirey, 1913.

Gaudemet, J., and E. Chevreau. *Droit privé romain.* Domat droit privé. 3rd ed. Paris: Montchrestien, 2009.

Goldman, B. *Cours de droit du commerce et de la concurrence dans les communautés européennes.* Paris: Les cours de droit, 1964.

Goldman, B., A. Lyon-Caen, and L. Vogel. *Droit commercial européen.* Précis Droit Privé. 5th ed. Paris: Dalloz, 1994.

Grotius, H. *Le droit de la guerre et de la paix.* Tome II. Translated by J. Barbeyrac. Amsterdam: Pierre de Coup, 1724.

Guettier, C., P. Le Tourneau, C. Bloch et al. *Droit de la responsabilité et des contrats 2021/2022.* Dalloz Action. Paris: Dalloz, 2020.

Hélie, F., A. Chauveau, and E. Villey. *Théorie du Code pénal. Tomes I et V*. Paris: Marchal et Billard, 1887 and 1888.

Jeanclos, Y. *Droit pénal européen: Dimension historique*. Corpus – Histoire du droit. Paris: Economica, 2009.

Jeandidier, W. *Droit pénal des affaires*. Paris: Dalloz, 1991.

Jousse, D. *Traité de la justice criminelle de France*. Tome III. Paris: Debure, 1771.

Laingui, A. *Histoire du droit pénal*. Que sais-je? 2nd ed. Paris: PUF, 1993.

Larouche, P., E. Mackaay, A. Parent, and S. Rousseau. *Analyse économique du droit*. Méthodes du droit. 3rd ed. Paris: Dalloz, 2021.

Lebret, J. *Cours de droit pénal général et de procédure pénale*. Tome I. Aix-en-Provence: Centre régional de documentation pédagogique, 1964.

Lepage, A., P. Maistre du Chambon, and R. Salomon. *Droit pénal des affaires*. 6th ed. Paris: LexisNexis, 2020.

Lianos, I., V. Korah, and P. Siciliani. *Competition Law: Analysis, Cases, & Materials*. Oxford: Oxford University Press, 2019.

Merle, R. *Droit pénal général complémentaire*. Thémis. Paris: PUF, 1957.

Merle, R., and A. Vitu. *Traité de droit criminel*. 7th ed. Paris: Cujas, 1997.

Mommsen, T. *Le droit pénal romain*. Translated by J. Duquesne. Paris: Albert Fontemoing, 1907.

Muyart de Vouglans, P.-F. *Institutes au droit criminel*. Paris: Le Breton, 1757.

———. *Les loix criminelles de France dans leur ordre naturel*. Paris: Mérigot le jeune, Crapart, Morin, 1780.

Ortolan, M. *Éléments de droit pénal*. Tome I. 3rd ed. Paris: Henri Plon, 1863.

Petit, N. *Droit européen de la concurrence*. Précis Domat Droit Privé. 3rd ed. Paris: LGDJ, 2020.

Planiol, M. *Traité élémentaire de droit civil*. Paris: LGDJ, 1931.

Pradel, J. *Droit pénal comparé*. Précis. 4th ed. Paris: Dalloz, 2016.

———. *Droit pénal général*. Référence. 22nd ed. Paris: Cujas, 2019.

Pradel, J., and G. Corstens. *Droit pénal européen*. Précis. 2nd ed. Paris: Dalloz, 2002.

Pradel, J., and M. Danti-Juan. *Droit pénal spécial: Droit commun, droit des affaires*. Références. 8th ed. Paris: Cujas, 2020.

Puech, M. *Droit pénal général*. Paris: LITEC, 1988.

Rassat, M.-L. *Droit pénal général*. Droit fondamental. 2nd ed. Paris: PUF, 1999.

Rivero, J. *Droit administratif*. Preface by J. Waline. Bibliothèque Dalloz. Reprint of 1st ed. 1960. Paris: Dalloz, 2011.

Robert, J.-H. *Droit pénal général.* 6th ed. Paris: PUF, 2005.

Savigny, F. *Traité de droit romain.* Tome I. Translated by C. Guenoux. First ed. 1840. Paris: Firmin Didot Frères, 1855.

Starck, B., H. Roland, and L. Boyer. *Obligations.* Tome 1: *Responsabilité délictuelle.* 5th ed. Paris: LITEC, 1996.

Stasiak, F. *Droit pénal des affaires.* 2nd ed. Paris: LGDJ, 2009.

Terré, F., P. Simler, Y. Lequette, and F. Chénedé. *Droit civil: Les obligations*. Précis. 13th ed. Paris: Dalloz, 2022.

Villey, E. *Précis d'un cours de droit criminel.* 2nd ed. Paris: G. Pedone-Lauriel, 1880.

Vouin, R., and M.-L. Rassat. *Droit pénal spécial: Infractions contre les biens, les personnes, la famille, les mœurs et la paix publique*. Précis Dalloz. 5th ed. Paris: Dalloz, 1983.

Whish, R., and D. Bailey. *Competition Law*. 10th ed. Oxford: Oxford University Press, 2021.

II. Special Works, Monographs and Ph.D. Dissertations

Amalfitano, A. *La responsabilité pénale des personnes morales en Europe: Une recherche pour la construction d'un modèle commun*. Preface by J.-C. Saint-Pau. Bibliothèques de droit. Paris: L'Harmattan, 2015.

Ancel, M. *La défense sociale nouvelle.* Publications du centre d'études de défense sociale. 3rd ed. Paris: Cujas, 1981.

Andriychiuk, O. *The Normative Foundations of European Competition Law: Assessing the Goals of Antitrust Through the Lens of Legal Philosophy.* Cheltenham: Edward Elgar, 2017.

Anscombe, G. E. M. *L'intention.* Translated by M. Maurice and C. Michon. Bibliothèque de philosophie. Paris: Gallimard, 2002.

Arcelin, L. *L'entreprise en droit de la concurrence français et communautaire*. Preface by M.-D. Hagelsteen. Bibliothèque de droit de l'entreprise. Tome 61. Paris: LITEC, 2003.

Aristotle. *Économiques.* Translated by J. Tricot. Bibliothèque des textes philosophiques. Paris: Librairie philosophique J. Vrin, 2004.

———. *Éthique à Eudème.* Translated by V. Décarie. Bibliothèque des textes philosophiques. Paris: Librairie philosophique J. Vrin, 1978.

———. *Éthique à Nicomaque.* Translated by J. Tricot. Bibliothèque des textes philosophiques. Paris: Librairie philosophique J. Vrin, 2021.

———. *La politique.* Translated by J. Tricot. Bibliothèque des textes philosophiques. Paris: Librairie philosophique J. Vrin, 2019.

Arnould, D. *Les figures du destin dans l'épopée antique gréco-latine.* Kubaba. Paris: L'Harmattan, 2016.

Atias, C. *Épistémologie juridique*. Droit fondamental. Paris: PUF, 1985.

———. *Théorie contre arbitraire*. Les voies du droit. First ed. Paris: PUF, 1987.

———. *Le traitement des délinquants*. Bibliothèque criminologique. Paris: Vrin, 1991.

———. *Science des légistes, savoir des juristes*. 3rd ed. Aix-en-Provence: PUAM, 1993.

———. *Précis élémentaire de contentieux contractuel*. 2nd ed. Aix-en-Provence: Presses Universitaires d'Aix-Marseille, 2003.

———. *De la difficulté contemporaine à penser en droit: Leçons de philosophie du droit*. Droits, pouvoirs et sociétés. Aix-en-Provence: PUAM, 2016.

Audren, F., A.-S. Chambost, and J.-L. Halperin. *Histoires contemporaines du droit*. Méthodes du droit. Paris: Dalloz, 2020.

Aulu-Gelle. *Nuits Attiques*. Translated by R. Marache. Universités de France. Paris: Les Belles Lettres, 1978.

Babled, H. *Droit romain: De la cura annonae chez les Romains; Droit français: Les syndicats de producteurs et détenteurs de marchandises au double point de vue économique et pénal*. Paris: Arthur Rousseau, 1892.

Bachelard, G. *La formation de l'esprit scientifique*. Bibliothèque des textes philosophiques. 5th ed. Paris: Librairie philosophique J. Vrin, 1967.

———. *Le rationalisme appliqué*. Quadrige. Paris: PUF, 2004.

———. *Le nouvel esprit scientifique*. Quadrige. Paris: PUF, 2020.

Baker, J. B. *The Antitrust Paradigm: Restoring a Competitive Economy*. Cambridge: Harvard University Press, 2019.

Balat, N. *Essai sur le droit commun*. Preface by M. Grimaldi. Bibliothèque de droit privé. Tome 571. Paris: LGDJ, 2016.

Baranger, D. *Penser la loi: Essai sur le législateur des temps modernes*. L'esprit de la cité. Paris: Gallimard, 2018.

Beccaria, C. *Des délits et des peines*. Translated by M. Chevallier. Preface by R. Badinter. Paris: GF Flammarion, 1991.

Bentham, J. *A Fragment on Government*. Oxford: Oxford University Press, 1891.

———. *Traités de législation civile et pénale*. Preface by M. Bozzo-Rey, A. Brunon-Ernst, and E. de Champs. Bibliothèque Dalloz. Paris: Dalloz, 2010.

Bergel, J.-L. *Théorie générale du droit*. Méthodes du droit. 5th ed. Paris: Dalloz, 2012.

———. *Méthodologie juridique: Fondamentale et appliquée*. Thémis droit. Paris: PUF, 2018.

Bergson, H. *L'évolution créatrice*. Quadrige. Paris: PUF, 1941.

Bernardeau, L., and J.-P. Christienne. *Les amendes en droit de la concurrence: Pratique décisionnelle et contrôle juridictionnel du droit de l'Union.* Précis. Brussels: Larcier, 2013.

Bernardini, R. "L'intention coupable en droit pénal." Ph.D. diss., directed by R. Gassin, Université de Nice, 1974.

Berté Puel, S. "L'intention en droit pénal." Ph.D. diss., directed by P. Poncela, Université Paris X Nanterre, 2005.

Berthe, M. "Le rôle de la volonté en droit pénal." Ph.D. diss., directed by G. Danjaume, Université Paris VIII Vincennes, 2010.

Blackstone, W. *Commentaries on the Laws of England.* Oxford: Oxford University Press, 2016.

Blomsma, J. *Mens Rea and Defences in European Criminal Law.* School of Human Rights Research. Vol. 54. Cambridge: Intersentia, 2012.

Blockx, J. *Mens Rea in EU Antitrust Law: When Intentions Matter.* International Competition Series. Alphen-sur-le-Rhin: Wolters Kluwer, 2020.

Blondel, E. *Le problème moral.* Philosopher. Paris: PUF, 2000.

Bombois, T. *La protection des droits fondamentaux des entreprises en droit européen répressif de la concurrence.* Brussels: Larcier, 2012.

Bork, R. H. *The Antitrust Paradigm: A Policy at War with Itself.* New York: Basic Books, 1978.

Bosco, D. *L'obligation d'exclusivité.* Preface by C. Prieto. Série concurrence. Brussels: Bruylant, 2008.

Bossuet. *Traité du libre arbitre.* Le Philosophe. Paris: Éditions Manucius, 2006.

Brault, D. *L'État et l'esprit de concurrence en France.* Paris: Economica, 1987.

Browne, S. *The Laws Against Engrossing, Forestalling, Regrating, and Monopolizing: Containing All the Statutes and Adjudged Cases Concerning Them.* London: W. Griffin, 1767.

Brunet, F. *La normativité en droit.* Bibliothèque des thèses. Paris: Mare & Martin, 2012.

Buch-Hansen, H., and A. Wigger. *The Politics of European Competition Regulation: A Critical Political Economy Perspective.* Studies in Global Political Economy. London: Routledge, 2011.

Canguilhem, G. *La connaissance de la vie.* Bibliothèque des textes philosophiques. Paris: Librairie philosophique J. Vrin, 1992.

Carbonnier, J. *Essai sur les lois.* 2nd ed. Paris: Répertoire du notariat Defrénois, 1992.

———. *Droit et passion du droit sous la Ve République.* Essais. Paris: Champs, 1996.

Cartapanis, M. *Innovation et droit de la concurrence*. Preface by D. Bosco. Collection des thèses. Vol. 169. Paris: Institut Universitaire Varennes, 2018.

Castillo de la Torre, F., and E. Gippini Fournier. *Evidence, Proof and Judicial Review in EU Competition Law*. Elgar Competition Law and Practice. Cheltenham: Edward Elgar, 2017.

Chabas, F. *Responsabilité civile et responsabilité pénale*. Paris: Éditions Montchrestien, 1975.

Chabert, G. *Un nouveau pouvoir spirituel: Auguste Comte et la religion scientifique au XIXe siècle*. Caen: Presses Universitaires de Caen, 2004.

Chaiehloudj, W. *Les accords de report d'entrée: Contribution à l'étude de la relation du droit de la concurrence et du droit des brevets*. Preface by D. Bosco. Paris: Concurrences, 2019.

Chapoutot, J. *Libres d'obéir: Le management, du nazisme à aujourd'hui*. NRF Essais. Paris: Gallimard, 2020.

Choné-Grimaldi, S. *Les abus de domination: Essai en droit des contrats et en droit de la concurrence*. Preface by B. Teyssié. Recherches juridiques. Paris: Economica, 2010.

Cicero. *Traité du destin*. Translated by A. Yon. Universités de France. Paris: Les Belles Lettres, 2018.

Claudel, E. "Ententes anticoncurrentielles et droit des contrats." Ph.D. diss., directed by M.-C. Boutard-Labarde, Université Paris X Nanterre, 1994.

Colliez, A. *Les coalitions industrielles et commerciales d'aujourd'hui: Trusts, cartels, corners*. Paris: Guillaumin, 1904.

Commun, P. *Les ordolibéraux: Histoire d'un libéralisme à l'allemande*. Penseurs de la liberté. Paris: Les Belles Lettres, 2016.

Costa-Cabral, F. "Intent in EU Competition Law: The Judicial Assessment of Anti-Competitive Strategies." Ph.D. diss., directed by C. Townley and R. Whish, King's College London, 2014.

Dana, A.-C. *Essai sur la notion d'infraction pénale*. Preface by A. Decocq. Bibliothèque de sciences criminelles. Tome XXIII. Paris: LGDJ, 1982.

Datson, L., and P. Galison. *Objectivité*. Dijon: Les presses du réel, 2012.

Daury-Fauveau, M. "Des principes constitutionnels ou internationaux, protecteurs des droits de l'homme, considérés dans leur application aux mesures punitives prononcées par une autorité autre que la justice pénale." Ph.D. diss., directed by A. Decocq, Université Paris II Panthéon-Assas, 1992.

David, R., C. Jauffret-Spinosi, and M. Gore. *Les grands systèmes de droit contemporain*. Précis. 12th ed. Paris: Dalloz, 2016.

De Bracton, H. *On the Laws and Customs of England*. Translated by S. E. Thorne. Vol. 2. Cambridge: Harvard University Press, 1968.

De Molina, L. *De iustitia et de iure*. Vol. 2: *De contractibus*. Mainz: Mylius, 1602.

De Monneron, F. "Le déterminisme et la responsabilité morale." Ph.D. diss., directed by C. Michon, Université de Nantes, 2011.

De Roover, R. *La pensée économique des scolastiques: Doctrine et méthode*. Publications de l'Institut d'Études Médiévales de Montréal. Paris: Librairie J. Vin, 1971.

Decock, W. *Le marché du mérite: Penser le droit et l'économie avec Léonard Lessius*. Brussels: Zones Sensibles, 2019.

Decocq, A., and M. Pedamon. *L'ordonnance du 1er décembre 1986 relative à la liberté des prix et de la concurrence*. Paris: Éditions Techniques, 1987.

Deffains, B., and S. Ferey. *Agir et juger: Comment les économistes pensent le droit*. Paris: Éditions Panthéon Assas, 2010.

Delaporte, J.-B., and P. N. Riffé-Caubray. *Les pandectes françaises, ou recueil complet de toutes les lois en vigueur*. Paris: Bossance, Masson et Besson, 1806.

Dellis, G. *Droit pénal et droit administratif: L'influence des principes du droit pénal sur le droit administratif répressif*. Preface by Y. Gaudemet. Bibliothèque de droit public. Tome 184. Paris: LGDJ, 1997.

Delmas-Marty, M., ed. *Corpus Juris: Portant dispositions pénales pour la protection des intérêts financiers de l'Union européenne*. Paris: Economica, 1997.

Delmas-Marty, M., and C. Teitgen-Colly. *Punir sans juger? De la répression administrative au droit administratif pénal*. Paris: Economica, 1992.

Delmas-Marty, M., and J. A. E. Vervaele, eds. *La mise en œuvre du Corpus Juris dans les États membres: Dispositions pénales pour la protection des finances de l'Europe*. Vol. III. Antwerp: Intersentia, 2000.

Demogue, R. *Les notions fondamentales du droit privé: Essai critique*. Paris: Arthur Rousseau, 1911.

Depeyrot, G. *Le Bas Empire Romain: Économie et numismatique*. Hespérides. Paris: Errance, 1991.

Dequeux de Saint-Hilaire, M. *De l'influence du christianisme sur le droit pénal des romains*. Paris: A.-E. Rochette, 1861.

Dobre, V. "L'intention fautive en droit européen de la concurrence." Ph.D. diss., directed by J.-M. Thouvenin, Université Paris X Nanterre, 2020.

Dubois, C. *Responsabilité civile et responsabilité pénale: À la recherche d'une cohérence perdue*. Preface by Y. Lequette. Bibliothèque de droit privé. Tome 570. Paris: LGDJ, 2016.

Durant, W. *Histoire de la civilisation*. Paris: Rencontre, 1963.

Dworkin, R. *Taking Rights Seriously*. Cambridge: Harvard University Press, 1977.

El Khouri, A. "Le courant néo-classique dans la pensée et le droit pénal en France." Ph.D. diss., directed by A. Decocq, Université Paris II, 1994.

El Shakankiri, M. *La philosophie juridique de Jeremy Bentham*. Preface by M. Villey. Bibliothèque de philosophie du droit. Vol. XI. Paris: LGDJ, 1970.

Elewa Badar, M. *The Concept of Mens Rea in International Criminal Law*. Studies in International & Comparative Criminal Law. Oxford: Hart Publishing, 2013.

Érasme and Luther. *Luther: Du serf arbitre. Érasme, diatribe: Du libre arbitre*. Folio Essais. Paris: Gallimard, 2001.

Eugene Ulmer, H. C. *La répression de la concurrence déloyale dans les États membres de la Communauté économique européenne. Tome I: Droit comparé avec des propositions pour le rapprochement des législations*. Paris: Dalloz, 1967.

Ezrachi, A., and M. Stucke. *Virtual Competition: The Promises and Perils of the Algorithm-Driven Economy*. Cambridge: Harvard University Press, 2016.

Fabre-Magnan, M. *L'institution de la liberté*. Paris: PUF, 2018.

Farjat, G. *L'ordre public économique*. Bibliothèque de droit privé. Tome XXXIV. Paris: LGDJ, 1963.

———. *Droit économique*. Thémis Droit. 2nd ed. Paris: PUF, 1982.

Fauconnet, P. *La responsabilité*. Paris: Alcan, 1920.

Ferry, E. *La sociologie criminelle*. Translated by L. Terrier. Paris: Alcan, 1905.

Finley, M. *Économie et société en Grèce ancienne*. Textes à l'appui. Paris: La Découverte, 1984.

Focsaneanu, L. *La jurisprudence de la Cour de justice des communautés européennes en matière de concurrence: Les règles applicables aux entreprises (Articles 85 et 86 du Traité de Rome)*. Paris: Éditions techniques et économiques, 1977.

Foucault, M. *Naissance de la biopolitique: Cours au Collège de France, 1978–1979*. Hautes études. Paris: Gallimard, Seuil, 2004.

Frambéry-Iacobone, A. "La recherche de l'intention en droit pénal contemporain (XIXe–XXe siècles)." Ph.D. diss., directed by N. Hakim and M. Manikis, Université de Bordeaux, 2022.

François, S. *Le consentement de la personne morale*. Preface by B. Fages. Bibliothèque de droit privé. Tome 601. Paris: LGDJ, 2020.

Frank, L. *697 ministres: Souvenirs d'un directeur général des prix, 1947–1962*. XIXe et XXe siècles. Paris: Comité pour l'histoire économique et financière de la France, 1990.

Frede, M. *A Free Will: Origins of the Notion in Ancient Thought*. Sather Classical Lectures. Vol. 68. Berkeley: University of California Press, 2012.

Fréget, O. *La concurrence: Une idée toujours neuve en Europe et en France*. Paris: Odile Jacob, 2015.

Frion, J.-J. "L'agissement parasitaire." Ph.D. diss., directed by A. Lucas, Université de Nantes, 2001.

Gaillard, E. *Le pouvoir en droit privé*. Preface by G. Cornu. Droit civil. Paris: Economica, 1985.

Garçon, E. *Le droit pénal: Origines – évolution – état actuel*. Paris: Payot, 1922.

Genin, J.-C. "La répression des actes de tentative en droit criminel romain: Contribution à l'étude de la subjectivité répressive à Rome." Ph.D. diss., directed by R. Raplat, Université de Lyon, 1968.

Gény, F. *Science et technique en droit privé positif*. Part III: *Élaboration technique du droit positif*. Paris: Sirey, 1921.

Gerber, D. J. *Law and Competition in Twentieth Century Europe: Protecting Prometheus*. 2nd ed. Oxford: Oxford University Press, 2001.

Gernet, L. *Recherches sur le développement de la pensée juridique et morale en Grèce: Étude sémantique*. L'évolution de l'humanité. Paris: Albin Michel, 2001. First published 1917.

Giovannini, V. "Données massives et droit de la concurrence." Ph.D. diss., directed by D. Bosco, Université d'Aix-Marseille, 2022.

Girot, M. "La dépénalisation: Un instrument au service du droit pénal." Ph.D. diss., directed by G. Giudicelli-Delage, Université de Poitiers, 1994.

Goblot, E. *Essai sur la classification des sciences*. Paris: F. Alcan, 1898.

Goldenberg, N. "L'élément moral en droit pénal des affaires." Ph.D. diss., directed by D. Mayer, Université Paris I Panthéon-Sorbonne, 1995.

Gomez, E. "L'imputabilité en droit pénal." Ph.D. diss., directed by A. Giudicelli, Université de La Rochelle, 2017.

Gordon, B. *Economic Analysis Before Adam Smith: Hesiod to Lessius*. New York: Palgrave Macmillan, 1975.

Griffon, R. *De l'intention en droit pénal*. Paris: Sirey, 1911.

Guyomar, M. *Les sanctions administratives*. Systèmes pratiques. Paris: LGDJ, 2014.

Habermas, J. *La technique et la science comme idéologie*. Tel. Paris: Gallimard, 1973.

Haid, F. "Les notions indéterminées dans la loi: Essai sur l'indétermination des notions légales en droit civil et pénal." Ph.D. diss., directed by J.-L. Bergel, Aix-Marseille Université, 2005.

Hale, M. *The History of the Pleas of the Crown*. Vol. 1. London: Payne, 1800.

Halévy, E. *Le radicalisme philosophique*. Vol. 3: *La formation du radicalisme philosophique*. Éthique et philosophie morale. Paris: PUF, 1996.

Hamon, A. *Déterminisme et responsabilité*. Bibliothèque internationale de sciences sociologiques. Paris: Schleicher Frères, 1898.

Hannoun, C. *Le droit et les groupes de sociétés*. Bibliothèque de droit privé. Tome 216. Paris: LGDJ, 1991.

Hart, H. L. A. *The Concept of Law*. Clarendon Law Series. 3rd ed. Oxford: Oxford University Press, 2012.

Hausman, D. M. *The Inexact and Separate Science of Economics*. Cambridge: Cambridge University Press, 1992.

Hayek, F. A. *The Political Ideal of the Rule of Law*. National Bank of Egypt. Cairo: Cairo, 1955.

———. *Droit, législation et liberté: Une nouvelle formulation des principes libéraux de justice et d'économie politique*. Translated by R. Audouin. Quadrige. 2nd ed. Paris: PUF, 2013. First published 1973.

———. *Scientisme et sciences sociales: Essai sur le mauvais usage de la raison*. Translated by R. Barre. Agora. Paris: Plon, 1995.

———. *La Constitution de la liberté*. Translated by R. Audouin and J. Garello. Liberalia. Paris: LITEC, 1994.

———. *L'ordre sensoriel: Une enquête sur les fondements de la psychologie théorique*. Translated by R. Mach. Paris: CNRS Éditions, 2001.

———. *La route de la servitude*. Translated by G. Blumberg. Quadrige. 6th ed. Paris: PUF, 2013.

———. *La présomption fatale: Les erreurs du socialisme*. Translated by R. Audouin. Paris: Institut Coppet, 2019.

Head, S. *Mindless: Why Smarter Machines Are Making Dumber Humans?* New York: Basic Books, 2014.

Helvétius. *De l'homme, de ses facultés intellectuelles et de son éducation*. Tome I. London: Société Typographique, 1773.

Hésiode. *La Théogonie, Les Travaux et les Jours et autres poèmes*. Translated by P. Brunet. Classiques. Paris: Le Livre de Poche, 1999.

———. *Les Travaux et les Jours*. Translated by P. Mazon. Classiques en poche. Paris: Les Belles Lettres, 2018.

Hildebrand, D. *The Role of Economic Analysis in EU Competition Law*. International Competition Law Series. Alphen-sur-le-Rhin: Kluwer Law International, 2016.

Hume, D. *Enquête sur l'entendement humain*. Translated by M. Malherbe. Bibliothèque des textes philosophiques. Paris: Librairie philosophique J. Vrin, 2016.

Husserl, E. *La crise des sciences européennes et la phénoménologie transcendantale*. Translated and prefaced by G. Granel. Tel. Paris: Gallimard, 1989.

Homère. *L'Iliade et l'Odyssée*. Translated by L. Bardollet. Bouquins. Paris: Robert Laffont, 1995.

Ida, N. "La preuve devant l'Autorité des marchés financiers." Ph.D. diss., directed by H. Barbier, Université d'Aix-Marseille, 2019.

Jacob, B.-M. *Devoirs: Conférence de morale individuelle et de morale sociale*. Paris: Édouard Cornély et Cie, 1908.

Jacquemin, M. *Droit romain: De la loi Aquilia – Droit français: De l'intention en droit pénal*. Besançon: Paul Jacquin, 1888.

James, W. *Le pragmatisme: Un nouveau nom pour d'anciennes manières de penser*. Translated by N. Ferron. Classiques. Paris: Champs, 2007.

Jhering, R. *Études complémentaires de l'Esprit du droit romain*. Vol. III: *Du rôle de la volonté dans la possession: Critique de la méthode juridique régnante*. Translated by O. de Meulenaere. Paris: A. Marescq, 1891.

Joliet, R. *The Rule of Reason in Antitrust Law: American, German and Common Market Laws in Comparative Perspective*. Collection scientifique de la faculté de droit de l'Université de Liège. Vol. 26. Dordrecht: Springer, 1967.

Josserand, L. *Les mobiles dans les actes juridiques de droit privé*. Bibliothèque Dalloz. 2nd ed. Paris: Dalloz, 2006.

Justinien. *Les douze livres du Code de l'empereur Justinien*. Translated by P.-A. Tissot. Tome II. 2nd ed. Paris: A. Metz, 1807.

Kahn, L. "Étude sur le délit et la peine en droit canon." Ph.D. diss., Université de Nancy, 1898.

Kenel, P. *La responsabilité pénale des personnes morales en droit anglais: Un modèle pour la Suisse*. Geneva: Droz, 1991.

Kirzner, I. M. *How Markets Work: Disequilibrium, Entrepreneurship and Discovery*. London: The Institute of Economic Affairs, 1997.

———. *Concurrence & esprit d'entreprise*. Translated by R. Audoin. Paris: Economica, 2005.

Koening, C., and B. Wendland. *The Art of Regulation: Competition in Europe – Wealth and Wariness*. Cheltenham: Edward Elgar, 2017.

Kouamé-Koki, H. *Les droits fondamentaux des personnes morales dans la Convention européenne des droits de l'homme*. Tome I: *De l'impensable à l'indispensable*. Paris: L'Harmattan, 2014.

Kramer, S. N. *Le mariage sacré à Sumer et à Babylone*. Translated by J. Bottéro. Paris: Berg International, 1983.

———. *L'histoire commence à Sumer*. Histoire. Paris: Champs, 2017.

La Pergola, A., and L. Prete. "Burden of Proof in Competition Law: An Overview of EU and National Case Law." *e-Competitions* Special Issue (March 29, 2023), art. no. 111517, 1–20.

Lagueux, M. *Rationality and Explanations in Economics*. New York: Routledge, 2014.

Laingui, A. *La responsabilité pénale dans l'Ancien droit (xvie–XVIIIe siècles)*. Bibliothèque d'histoire du droit et droit romain. Tome XVII. Paris: LGDJ, 1970.

Lapidus, A. *Le détour de valeur*. Paris: Economica, 1986.

Larrieu, P. *Mythes grecs et droit: Retour sur la fonction anthropologique du droit*. Dikè. Laval: Presses Universitaires de Laval, 2017.

Laurent, P. "Contrat et droit pénal." Ph.D. diss., directed by G. Marino, Université d'Aix-Marseille, 2001.

Le Gousse, G. *Le pouvoir d'agir autrement: Essai sur le libre arbitre*. Philosophica. Rennes: Presses Universitaires de Rennes, 2017.

Le Magueresse, Y. *Des comportements fautifs du créancier et de la victime en droit des obligations*. Aix-en-Provence: PUAM, 2007.

Le Moal, R. "Contribution à l'étude d'un droit de la concurrence: Nature du droit sur les valeurs concurrentielles." Ph.D. diss., directed by M. R. Percerou, Université de Rennes, 1972.

Lebigre, A. *Quelques aspects de la responsabilité pénale en droit romain classique*. Sciences historiques. No. 11. Paris: PUF, 1967.

Leca, A. *La genèse du droit: Essai d'introduction historique au droit*. 2nd ed. Aix-en-Provence: Librairie de l'Université d'Aix-en-Provence, 2000.

Leeson, P. T. *WTF?! An Economic Tour of the Weird. Stanford*, CA: Stanford University Press, 2017.

Legeais, R. *Grands systèmes de droit contemporains: Approche comparative*. 3rd ed. Paris: LexisNexis, 2016.

Legros, R. *L'élément moral dans les infractions*. Liège: Desoer, 1952.

Lenaertz, K., and J. A. Gutierrez-Fons. *Les méthodes d'interprétation de la Cour de justice de l'Union européenne*. Droit de l'Union européenne. Brussels: Bruylant, 2020.

Leoni, B. *La liberté et le droit*. Bibliothèque classique de la liberté. Paris: Les Belles Lettres, 2006.

Leroy, G. "La pratique du précédent en droit français: Étude à partir de l'avocat général à la Cour de cassation et des conclusions du rapporteur public au Conseil d'État." Ph.D. diss., directed by F. Rouvière, Aix-Marseille Université, 2021.

Levitt, S. D., and S. J. Dubner. *Freakonomics: A Rogue Economist Explores the Hidden Side of Everything*. New York: William Morrow, 2005.

Levitta, C. *Précis de l'histoire du droit pénal allemand depuis la Caroline jusqu'à nos jours*. Translated by M. L. Bonneville de Marsangy. Paris: Cotillon, 1862.

Lianos, I. *La transformation du droit de la concurrence par le recours à l'analyse économique*. Preface by R. Kovar. Brussels: Bruylant, 2007.

Liautey, A. "La hausse des prix et la lutte contre la cherté en France au XVIe siècle." Ph.D. diss., Paris: Jouve et Cie, 1921.

Libchaber, R. *L'ordre juridique et le discours du droit: Essai sur les limites de la connaissance du droit*. Paris: LGDJ, 2013.

Ligny, V. *La responsabilité pénale du chef d'entreprise: Essai de théorisation d'une responsabilité pénale en mutation*. Droit privé et sciences criminelles. Paris: L'Harmattan, 2021.

Locré, J.-G. *La législation civile, commerciale et criminelle de la France*. Tome XXXI. Paris: Treuttel et Würtz, 1827.

Lovdahl Gormsen, L. *A Principled Approach to Abuse of Dominance in European Competition Law*. The Cambridge Antitrust and Competition Law Series. Cambridge: Cambridge University Press, 2010.

Lucretius. *De la nature*. Translated by C. Nissard. Paris: Firmin Didot, 1868.

Lysias. *Discours*. Tome II. Université de France. Paris: Les Belles Lettres, 1962.

MacCormick, N. *Raisonnement juridique et théorie du droit*. Translated by J. Gagey. Les voies du droit. Paris: PUF, 1996.

Mach, O. *L'entreprise et les groupes de société en droit européen de la concurrence*. Geneva: Georg, 1974.

Madelrieux, S. *William James: L'attitude empiriste*. Science, histoire et société. Paris: PUF, 2008.

Maine, H. S. *Ancient Law: Its Connection with the Early History of Society and Its Relation to Modern Ideas*. New York: Henry Holt and Company, 1906.

Maman, R. "Contribution à l'étude de l'élément intentionnel en droit pénal des affaires." Ph.D. diss., directed by C. Mascala, Université de Toulouse, 2007.

Maréchal, J.-Y. *Essai sur le résultat dans la théorie de l'infraction pénale*. Logiques juridiques. Paris: L'Harmattan, 2003.

Margaine, C. "La capacité pénale." Ph.D. diss., directed by P. Conte, Université Montesquieu Bordeaux IV, 2011.

Martin, X. *Beccaria, Voltaire et Napoléon: Ou l'étrange humanisme pénal des Lumières (1760–1810)*. Poitiers: Éditions Dominique Martin Morin, 2018.

Mazeaud, L. *Le régime juridique des ententes industrielles et commerciales en France*. Preface by R. Garraud. Le droit des cartels et des trusts dans les principales législations. Tome I. Paris: Sirey, 1928.

Merabet, S. "Vers un droit de l'intelligence artificielle." Ph.D. diss., directed by H. Barbier, Aix-Marseille Université, 2018.

Merle, P. *Les présomptions légales en droit pénal.* Preface by A. Vitu. Bibliothèque des sciences criminelles. Paris: LGDJ, 1970.

Merle, R. *La pénitence et la peine.* Éthique & Société. Paris: Cerf-Cujas, 1985.

Mestmäcker, E.-J. *A Legal Theory without Law: Posner v. Hayek on Economic Analysis of Law.* Beiträge zur Ordnungstheorie und Ordnungspolitik. Vol. 174. Tübingen: Mohr Siebeck, 2007.

Mestre, A. *Les personnes morales et le problème de leur responsabilité pénale.* Paris: Arthur Rousseau, 1899.

Meusy, N. *Code de la religion et des mœurs, ou Recueil des principales ordonnances, depuis l'établissement de la monarchie françoise, concernant la religion et les mœurs.* Paris: Humblot, 1776.

Michon, C. *Qu'est-ce que le libre arbitre?* Chemins philosophiques. Paris: Librairie philosophique J. Vrin, 2011.

Michoud, L. *La théorie de la personnalité morale et son application au droit français.* Introuvables. Paris: Éditions Panthéon-Assas, 2020.

Mises, L. *L'action humaine: Traité d'économie.* Translated by R. Audouin. Paris: Institut Coppet, 2011.

Morris, E. *Short Inquiry into the Nature of Monopoly and Forestalling, with Some Remarks on the Statutes Concerning Them.* London: T. Cadell and W. Davies, 1795.

Motulsky, H. *Principes d'une réalisation méthodique du droit privé: La théorie des éléments générateurs des droits subjectifs.* La Bibliothèque Dalloz. Paris: Dalloz, 2002.

Mourgeon, J. *La répression administrative.* Bibliothèque de droit public. Paris: LGDJ, 1967.

Nasri, A. "Contribution à l'étude de la notion de causalité en droit pénal." Ph.D. diss., directed by B. Bouloc, Université Paris I Panthéon-Sorbonne, 2006.

Navel, L. *L'argument de continuité jurisprudentielle dans la jurisprudence de la Cour de justice de l'Union européenne.* Thèses. Brussels: Bruylant, 2021.

Nazzini, R. *The Foundations of European Union Competition Law: The Objectives and Principles of Article 102.* Studies in European Law. Oxford: Oxford University Press, 2011.

Negrel-Filippi, F. "Le dol éventuel, vers la reconnaissance d'une intention atténuée." Ph.D. diss., directed by G. Giudicelli-Delage, Université Paris I Panthéon-Sorbonne, 2010.

Nietzsche, F. W. *Le crépuscule des idoles.* Translated by H. Albert. GF. Paris: Flammarion, 1985.

Odudu, O. *The Boundaries of EC Competition Law: The Scope of Article 81*. Studies in European Law. Oxford: Oxford University Press, 2006.

Olivi. *Traité des contrats*. Translated by S. Piron. Bibliothèque scolastique. Paris: Les Belles Lettres, 2012.

Olson, M. *Logique de l'action collective*. Translated by M. Levi. Fondamentaux. Brussels: Éditions de l'Université de Bruxelles, 2018.

Oppetit, B. *Droit et modernité*. Doctrine juridique. Paris: PUF, 1998.

Ost, F., and M. Van de Kerchove. *De la pyramide au réseau? Pour une théorie dialectique du droit*. Droit. Brussels: Publications des Facultés universitaires Saint-Louis, 2002.

Pages, M., M. Bonetti, V. de Gauléjac, and D. Descendre. *L'emprise de l'organisation*. Fondamentaux. 7th ed. Brussels: Éditions de l'Université de Bruxelles, 2019.

Pareto, V. *Cours d'économie politique*. Geneva: Librairie Droz, 1964.

Peirce, C. S. *À la recherche d'une méthode*. Translated by J. Deledalle-Rhodes and M. Balat. Études. Perpignan: Presses Universitaires de Perpignan, 1993.

Perelman, C. *De la justice*. Actualités sociales: Nouvelle série. Brussels: Office de publicité, 1945.

———. *Le raisonnable et le déraisonnable en droit: Au-delà du positivisme juridique*. Bibliothèque de philosophie du droit. Paris: LGDJ, 1984.

Perelman, C., and L. Olbrechts-Tyteca. *Traité de l'argumentation*. Fondamentaux. Brussels: Éditions de l'Université de Bruxelles, 2008.

Perreau, B. *De la qualification en matière criminelle*. Paris: LGDJ, 1926.

Petit, N. *Big Tech and the Digital Economy: The Moligopoly Scenario*. Oxford: Oxford University Press, 2020.

Picard, E. *La notion de police administrative*. Preface by R. Drago. Bibliothèque de droit public. Rouen: Publications de l'Université de Rouen, 1984.

Piettre, A. *Histoire de la pensée économique et des théories contemporaines*. Précis Dalloz. 7th ed. Paris: Dalloz, 1979.

Pignatel, L. "L'émergence d'un neurodroit: Contribution à l'étude de la relation entre les neurosciences et le droit." Ph.D. diss., directed by S. Cimamonti, Université d'Aix-Marseille, 2019.

Piotrowski, R. *Cartels and Trusts: Their Origin and Historical Development from the Economic and Legal Aspects*. London: George Allen & Unwin, 1933.

Pippin, R. B. *Hegel's Practical Philosophy: Rational Agency as Ethical Life*. Cambridge: Cambridge University Press, 2008.

Pirovano, A. *Faute civile et faute pénale*. Preface by P. Bonassies. Bibliothèque de droit privé. Tome LXX. Paris: LGDJ, 1966.

Pliny the Elder. *Histoire Naturelle*. Translated by E. Littré. Paris: J. Dubochet, 1850.

Poincaré, H. *La valeur de la science*. Paris: Flammarion, 1911.

———. *Dernières pensées*. Bibliothèque de philosophie scientifique. Paris: Ernest Flammarion, 1920.

Polanyi, K. *La subsistance de l'homme: La place de l'économie dans l'histoire de la société*. Bibliothèque des savoirs. Paris: Flammarion, 2011. First published 1977.

Posner, R. A. *Economic Analysis of Law*. 1st ed. Boston: Little & Brown, 1972.

———. *The Overcoming Law*. Cambridge: Harvard University Press, 1995.

———. *Antitrust Law*. 2nd ed. Chicago: University of Chicago Press, 2001.

———. *Frontiers of Legal Theory*. Cambridge: Harvard University Press, 2001.

Prigogine, I. *La fin des certitudes*. Paris: Odile Jacob, 1996.

Prothais, A. *Tentative et attentat*. Bibliothèque de sciences criminelles. Tome XXIV. Paris: LGDJ, 1985.

Rawls, J. *Théorie de la justice*. Translated by C. Audard. Empreintes. Paris: Points, 2009.

Rebut, D. "L'omission en droit pénal: Pour une théorie de l'équivalence entre l'action et l'inaction." Ph.D. diss., directed by Y. Mayaud, Université Jean Moulin Lyon III, 1993.

Rees, R. *Diocletian and the Tetrarchy*. Debates and Documents in Ancient History. Edinburgh: Edinburgh University Press, 2004.

Reix, M. "Le motif légitime en droit pénal: Contribution à la théorie générale de la justification." Ph.D. diss., directed by J.-C. Saint-Pau, Université Montesquieu – Bordeaux IV, 2012.

Revel, J.-F. *Histoire de la philosophie occidentale*. Agora. Paris: Pocket, 2003.

Ricoeur, P. *Philosophie de la volonté*. Tome II: *Finitude et culpabilité*. Essais. Paris: Points, 2009.

Ripert, G. *Le déclin du droit: Études sur la législation contemporaine*. Paris: LGDJ, 1949.

———. *Aspects juridiques du capitalisme moderne*. 2nd ed. Paris: LGDJ, 1951.

Rivière, Y. *Histoire du droit pénal romain: De Romulus à Justinien*. La roue à livres. Paris: Les Belles Lettres, 2021.

Romano, S. *L'ordre juridique*. Translated by L. François and P. Gothot. Bibliothèque Dalloz. 2nd ed. Paris: Dalloz, 2005.

Rostovtseff, M. *Histoire économique et sociale du monde hellénistique*. Paris: Robert Laffont, 1989.

Rothbard, M. N. *Economic Thought Before Adam Smith: An Austrian Perspective on the History of Economic Thought*. Vol. 1. Auburn: Ludwig von Mises Institute, 1995.

Roubier, P. *Théorie générale du droit: Histoire des doctrines juridiques et philosophie des valeurs sociales*. 2nd ed. Paris: Sirey, 1951.

Rousseau, F. *L'imputation dans la responsabilité pénale*. Preface by J.-C. Saint-Pau. Nouvelle Bibliothèque de Thèses. Vol. 89. Paris: Dalloz, 2009.

Rouvière, F. *Argumentation juridique*. Thémis Droit. Paris: PUF, 2023.

Sacco, R. *La comparaison juridique au service de la connaissance du droit*. Études juridiques comparatives. Paris: Economica, 1991.

———. *Anthropologie juridique: Apport à une macro-histoire du droit*. L'esprit du droit. Paris: Dalloz, 2008.

Sadin, E. *L'intelligence artificielle ou l'enjeu du siècle: Anatomie d'un antihumanisme radical*. Paris: L'Échappée, 2018.

Saint-Gérand, V. "La culpabilité dans la théorie de la responsabilité pénale." Ph.D. diss., directed by Y. Mayaud, Université Jean Moulin Lyon III, 2000.

Salomao Filho, C. *Histoire critique des monopoles: Une perspective juridique et économique*. Droit & Économie. Paris: LGDJ, 2010.

Savatier, H. *La concurrence déloyale, l'accaparement et l'organisation moderne du commerce et de l'industrie*. Paris: Librairie C. Poussielgue, 1896.

Schiavone, A. *Ius: L'invention du droit en Occident*. Translated by G. Bouffatigue and J. Bouffatigue. Paris: Belin, 2008.

Schmidt, C. *Neuroéconomie*. Économie. Paris: Odile Jacob, 2010.

Schopenhauer, A. *Essai sur le libre arbitre*. Translated by S. Reinach. Petite Bibliothèque. Paris: Rivages poche, 2018.

Schumpeter, J. A. *History of Economic Analysis*. New York: Oxford University Press, 1954.

Schütz, B. "Le principe de la personnalité des peines en droit pénal français." Ph.D. diss., Université de Nancy, 1967.

Schweitzer, S. *Le libéralisme: Autopsie d'une incompréhension*. Droits, pouvoirs & sociétés. Aix-en-Provence: PUAM, 2023.

Schweitzer, S., and L. Floury. *Droit et économie: Un essai d'histoire analytique*. Preface by P. Bonfils. Droits, pouvoirs & sociétés. Aix-en-Provence: PUAM, 2015.

Sélinsky, V. *L'entente prohibée, à travers les avis de la Commission technique des ententes et des abus de position dominante*. Bibliothèque de droit de l'entreprise. Paris: Librairies techniques, 1979.

Seneca. *Lettres à Lucilius*. Translated by J. Baillard. Paris: Hachette, 1914.

Shackle, G. L. S. *Time & Choice*. Vol. LXII. Proceedings of the British Academy. London: British Academy, 1976.

———. *Epistemics and Economics: A Critique of Economic Doctrines*. New York: Routledge, 2017.

Sibony, A.-L. *Le juge et le raisonnement économique en droit de la concurrence*. Preface by G. Canivet. Droit & Économie. Paris: LGDJ, 2008.

Sichel, L. *La gravité de la faute en droit de la responsabilité civile*. Bibliothèque de droit privé. Tome 614. Paris: LGDJ, 2022.

Silva-Romero, E. *Wittgenstein et la philosophie du droit*. Droit, éthique, société. Paris: PUF, 2002.

Slobodian, Q. *Globalists: The End of Empire and the Birth of Neoliberalism*. Cambridge: Harvard University Press, 2018.

Sobo, F. "L'article 121-3 du Code pénal." Ph.D. diss., directed by M. Massé, Université de Poitiers, 2006.

Soulignac, J.-L. "L'élément moral dans les infractions en droit pénal français." Ph.D. diss., directed by A. Vitu, Université de Nancy, 1955.

Starck, B. *Essai d'une théorie générale de la responsabilité civile considérée en sa double fonction de garantie et de peine privée*. Preface by M. Picard. Paris: L. Rodstein, 1947.

Stoffel-Munck, P. *L'abus dans le contrat: Essai d'une théorie*. Preface by R. Bout. Bibliothèque de droit privé. Tome 337. Paris: LGDJ, 2000.

Stones, R. "EU Competition Law and the Rule of Law: Justification and Realisation." Typed thesis, edited by P. Ibáñez Colomo, London School of Economics, 2018.

Stuart Mill, J. *L'utilitarianisme*. Translated by P.-L. Le Monnier. Paris: Alcan, 1889.

Supiot, A. *La gouvernance par les nombres: Cours au Collège de France (2012–2014)*. Poids et mesures du monde. Paris: Pluriel, 2015.

Sutherland, E. H. *White Collar Crime*. New Haven: Yale University Press, 1983.

Thellier de Poncheville, B. *La condition préalable de l'infraction*. Preface by A. Varinard. Institut de sciences pénales et de criminologie. Aix-en-Provence: PUAM, 2010.

Thévenon, J.-M. *L'élément objectif et l'élément subjectif de l'infraction: Contribution à l'étude de leurs définitions et de leurs rapports*. Lyon: Paquet, 1942.

Thiery, S. *Les actes délégués en droit de l'Union européenne*. Droit de l'Union européenne. Brussels: Bruylant, 2020.

Thomas, E. *L'entreprise contrevenante en droit des pratiques anticoncurrentielles: Variations autour de la distinction entre société et entreprise (Union européenne et France)*. Preface by L. Idot. Paris: Concurrences, 2021.

Thomas Aquinas. *Somme Théologique*. Translated by F. Lachat. 16 vols. First published 1266–1273. Paris: Louis Vivès, 1854–1861.

Tirole, J. *Théorie de l'organisation industrielle*. Économie et statistiques avancées. Paris: Economica, 1993.

Tournier, G. *Babel ou le vertige technique*. Les idées et la vie. Paris: Librairie Arthème Fayard, 1959.

Trifilio, S. "Esprit mathématique et pensée économique dans l'Antiquité et au Moyen Âge." Ph.D. diss., co-directed by G. Bramoullé and P. Garello, Université d'Aix-Marseille, 2010.

Valeur, R. *La responsabilité pénale des personnes morales dans les droits français et anglo-américains*. Paris: Marcel Giard, 1931.

Vallier, C.-A. *De l'intention morale*. Paris: Germer Baillière et Cie, 1882.

Van de Kerchove, M. *Le droit sans peines: Aspects de la dépénalisation en Belgique et aux États-Unis*. Brussels: Publications des Facultés universitaires de Saint-Louis, 1987.

Van Inwagen, P. *Essai sur le libre arbitre*. Translated by C. Michon. Analyse et philosophie. Paris: Librairie philosophique J. Vrin, 2017.

Veljanovski, C. *The Economics of Law*. 2nd ed. London: The Institute of Economic Affairs, 2006.

Veyne, P. *Comment on écrit l'histoire: Essai d'épistémologie*. L'univers historique. Paris: Seuil, 1971.

———. *Les Grecs ont-ils cru à leurs mythes?* Points. Paris: Seuil, 1983.

Vignon-Barrault, A. "Intention et responsabilité civile." Ph.D. diss., directed by D. Mazeaud, Université du Maine, 2000.

Villey, D. *Notes de philosophie économique (1958–59): Le jeu des intérêts*. Paris: Les Cours de droit, 1965.

Villey, D., and C. Neme. *Petite histoire des grandes doctrines économiques*. Paris: LITEC, 1996.

Villey, M. *Leçons d'histoire de la philosophie du droit*. Philosophie du droit. Paris: Dalloz, 1962.

———. *Philosophie du droit: Définitions et fins du droit, Les Moyens du droit*. Bibliothèque Dalloz. Paris: Dalloz, 2001.

———. *La formation de la pensée juridique moderne*. Quadrige. Paris: PUF, 2003.

———. *Le droit romain*. Quadrige. Paris: PUF, 2012.

———. *Le droit et les droits de l'homme*. 2nd ed. Quadrige. Paris: PUF, 2014.

Viney, G. *Le déclin de la responsabilité individuelle*. Bibliothèque de droit privé. Tome LIIIII. Paris: LGDJ, 1965.

Vogel, L. *Concurrence: 11 leçons*. 2nd ed. Brussels: Bruylant – Lawlex, 2020.

Waelbroeck, C.-F. *De la liberté des coalitions industrielles et commerciales en Belgique*. Brussels: A. Lacroix, Verboeckhoven et Cie, 1867.

Wagner, E. "La notion d'intention pénale dans la doctrine classique et la jurisprudence contemporaine." Ph.D. diss., directed by A. Vitu, Université de Clermont-Ferrand, 1976.

Wagner, M. *Les effets de l'infraction: Essai d'une théorie générale*. Preface by Y. Mayaud. Bibliothèque des sciences criminelles. Tome 50. Paris: LGDJ, 2011.

Walter, F. *Histoire du droit criminel chez les Romains*. Translated by J. Picquet-Damesme. Paris: A. Durand, 1863.

Wardhaugh, B. *Competition, Effects and Predictability: The Rule of Law and the Economic Approach to Competition*. Hart Studies in Competition Law. Oxford: Hart Publishing, 2020.

Weber, M. *La domination*. Translated by I. Kalinowski. Textes à l'appui. Paris: La Découverte, 2014.

Wigmore, J. H. *Un jalon vers une "science de la preuve": La représentation graphique des raisonnements probatoires*. Translated by O. Leclerc. Tiré à part. Paris: Dalloz, 2019.

Winiger, B. *Responsibility, Restoration and Fault*. Cambridge: Intersentia, 2018.

Witt, A. C. *The More Economic Approach to EU Antitrust Law*. Hart Studies in Competition Law. Oxford: Hart Publishing, 2019.

Wittgenstein, L. *Tractatus logico-philosophicus – Suivi de Investigations philosophiques*. Translated by P. Klossowski. Preface by B. Russell. Tel. Paris: Gallimard, 1961.

Zenati-Castaing, F. *Le savoir des lois: Essai sur le droit romaniste*. Méthodes du droit. Paris: Dalloz, 2021.

Zenouvou, L. *Les usages de la notion de concurrence en droit*. Preface by P. Brunet. Bibliothèque de droit public. Tome 272. Paris: LGDJ, 2012.

III. Articles, Studies, Contributions to Collective Works, Book Prefaces, Columns, Observations and Commentaries

Adam, S., N. Blaise, and C. Colette-Basecqz. "Conclusions." In *La responsabilité pénale des personnes morales en Europe*, edited by S. Adam, N. Colette-Basecqz, and M. Nihoul, 433–463. Brussels: La Charte, 2008.

Agretelis, D. "Mens Rea in Plato and Aristotle." *Issues in Criminology* 1, no. 1 (Autumn 1965): 19–33.

Akman, P. "Searching for the Long-Lost Soul of Article 82 EC." *Oxford Journal of Legal Studies* 29, no. 2 (2009): 267–303.

———. "The Role of Intent in the EU Case Law on Abuse of Dominance." *European Law Review* 39, no. 3 (June 2014): 316–337.

———. "The Tests of Illegality under Articles 101 and 102 TFEU." *Antitrust Bulletin* 61, no. 1 (2016): 84–104.

Al-Sanhoury, A.-A. "Le standard juridique." In *Recueil d'études sur les sources du droit en l'honneur de François Gény*. Tome II, 144–156. Paris: Sirey, 1934.

Allen, A. "Economic Analysis of Law: Some Realism about Nominalism." *Virginia Law Review* 60, no. 3 (March 1974): 451–482.

Alschuler, A. W. "Two Ways to Think About the Punishment of Corporations." *American Criminal Law Review* 46 (2009): 1359–1392.

Ambos, K. "Réflexions sur la théorie française de l'infraction pénale du point de vue allemand." In *Vers un nouveau procès pénal? Neue Wege des Strafprozesses*, edited by J. Leblois-Happe. Colloques. Vol. 9, 147–162. Paris: Société de législation comparée, 2013.

Amory, B., G. Van de Walle, and N. A. Smuha. "The Object-Effect Dichotomy and the Requirement of Harm to Competition: On the Road to Clarity After Cartes Bancaires?" In *The Notion of Restriction of Competition: Revisiting the Foundations of Antitrust Enforcement in Europe*, edited by D. Gerard, M. Merola, and B. Meyring. GCLC Annual Conference Series, 65–85. Brussels: Bruylant, 2017.

Amselek, P. "L'interpellation actuelle de la réflexion philosophique par le droit." *Droits*, no. 4 (1986): 123–135.

———. "Les règles juridiques en tant qu'objets mentaux." *Archives for Philosophy and Social Philosophy* 79, no. 3 (1993): 311–320.

Ancel, P. "Rapport de M. Ancel sur la responsabilité sans faute." *Travaux de l'Association Henri Capitant* (1946): 65–82.

Angeloff, C. "Developments in the Law: Criminal Conspiracy." *Harvard Law Review* 72, no. 5 (March 1959): 920–1008.

Angevin, H. "Atteintes volontaires à la vie." *JurisClasseur Pénal Code* (June 2021).

Anscombe, G. E. M. "Modern Moral Philosophy." *Philosophy* 33, no. 124 (1958): 1–19.

Arcelin, L. "L'alliance raisonnable entre droit de la concurrence et CEDH." *Revue Lamy de la concurrence*, no. 11 (April 1, 2017).

———. "La conquête du droit du marché par la notion d'entreprise." *RTD com.* (2018): 575.

———. "Le droit de la concurrence mis à l'épreuve par le numérique." *JCP E*, no. 45 (November 7, 2019): 1493.

Arezzo, E. "Is There a Role for Market Definition and Dominance in an Effect-Based Approach?" In *Abuse of Dominant Position: New Interpretation, New Enforcement Mechanisms?*, edited by M.-O. Mackenrodt, B. C. Gallego, and S. Enchelmaier. MPI Studies on

Intellectual Property and Competition and Tax Law. Vol. 5, 21–54. New York: Springer, 2008.

Atias, C. "Juris dictio: Redire l'inédit." *Recueil Dalloz* (1992): 281.

———. "Sur E. Mackaay et St. Rousseau, Analyse économique du droit." *Revue de la recherche juridique: Droit prospectif*, no. 5 (2008): 2469–2475.

Atias, C., and D. Linotte. "Le mythe de l'adaptation du droit au fait." *Recueil Dalloz-Sirey*, chron. XXXIV: 251–258.

Auguet, Y. "Droit pénal et droit de la concurrence: 'La transformation du fait répressif en droit de la concurrence'." In *Droit pénal et autres branches du droit: Regards croisés*, edited by J.-C. Saint-Pau. Actes et études, 279–300. Paris: Éditions Cujas, 2012.

Bailleux, A. "The Fiftieth Shade of Grey Competition Law, 'Criministrative Law' and 'Fairly Fair Trials'." In *Do Labels Still Matter? Blurring Boundaries Between Administrative and Criminal Law: The Influence of the EU*, edited by F. Galli and A. Weyembergh, 137–152. Brussels: Éditions de l'Université de Bruxelles, 2014.

Baan, P. A. "La notion de discernement au point de vue psychiatrique." In *Annales de la faculté de droit et de sciences politiques et économiques de Strasbourg*. Tome VIII, Travaux du colloque de philosophie pénale (12–21 janvier 1959) "La responsabilité pénale", 183–202. Strasbourg, 1961.

Babusiaux, C. "La répression et le contrôle administratif de la régulation concurrentielle." In *Les enjeux de la pénalisation de la vie économique*, edited by M.-A. Frison-Roche, 113–121. Paris: Dalloz, 1997.

Bacache, M. "Responsabilité civile: Une réforme a minima?" *JCP G*, no. 38 (September 14, 2020): art. 1007.

Bailey, D. "Restrictions of Competition by Object under Article 101 TFEU." *Common Market Law Review* 49, no. 2 (April 2012): 559–600.

———. "Reinvigorating the Role of Article 101(3) Under Regulation 1/2003." *Antitrust Law Journal* 81, no. 1 (2016): 111–144.

Bakouche, D. "Aléa et faute intentionnelle." *Responsabilité civile et assurances*, dossier 7 (March 2014): 26–32.

Barbry, P., and R. Plaisant. "Libre concurrence et ententes industrielles (Décret du 9 août 1953)." *Recueil Dalloz*, chron. XI (1954): 67–74.

Barrière, F. "L'algorithme fou." *Bulletin Joly Bourse*, no. 10 (2016): 410.

———. "Trading algorithmique et manipulation sur contrats financiers." *Bulletin Joly Bourse*, no. 2 (2017): 102.

Bartholomae, T. C. "The Common Law on Restraint of Trade." *The University Journal of Business* 1, no. 4 (August 1923): 451–466.

Batey, R. "Judicial Exploitation of Mens Rea Confusion, at Common Law and under the Model Penal Code." *Georgia State University Law Review* 18, no. 2 (Winter 2001): 341–414.

Batiffol, H. "Observations sur la preuve des faits." In *La preuve en droit*, edited by C. Perelman and P. Forier. Travaux du centre national de recherches logiques, 303–314. Brussels: Bruylant, 1981.

Bavasso, A. "The Role of Intent Under Article 82 EC: From 'Flushing the Turkeys' to 'Spotting Lionesses in Regent's Park'." *European Competition Law Review*, no. 11 (2005): 616–623.

Bayart, A. "Peut-on éliminer les fictions du discours juridique?" In *Les présomptions et les fictions en droit*, edited by C. Perelman and P. Forier. Travaux du centre national de recherches logiques, 27–42. Brussels: Bruylant, 1974.

Beaugrand, P. "Le temps, l'imagination, l'incertitude dans la théorie du professeur G. L. S. Shackle." *Revue économique* 33, no. 2 (1982): 297–322.

Beauvais, P. "Le droit à la prévisibilité en matière pénale dans la jurisprudence des cours européennes." *Archives de politique criminelle* 29, no. 1 (2007): 3–18.

Becker, G. "Crime and Punishment: An Economic Approach." *The Journal of Political Economy* 76, no. 2 (March–April 1968): 169–217.

Behar-Touchais, M. "Vers un retour à une conception stricte de la restriction par l'objet." *Concurrences*, Colloque du 17 avril 2015: "Restriction par objet, restriction par effet: Quelle portée encore accorder à cette distinction?"

———. "L'articulation du DMA avec les autres textes existants." *Concurrences*, no. 3-2022, Conference "Digital Market Act: Droit de la concurrence et géants du numérique," art. no. 108068 (2022): 51–60.

Bellis, J.-F., and T. Kasten. "Will Efficiencies Play an Increasingly Important Role in the Assessment of Conduct Under Article 102 TFEU?" In *Competition Law and the Enforcement of Article 102*, edited by F. Etro and I. Kokkoris, 129–137. Oxford: Oxford University Press, 2010.

Benabou, V.-L. "Un droit vivant: Manifeste pour des juristes incarnés et sensibles à l'heure de l'intelligence artificielle." In *Penser le droit de la pensée: Mélanges en l'honneur de Michel Vivant*, 715–730. Paris: LexisNexis – Dalloz, 2020.

Benillouche, M. "La subjectivisation de l'élément moral de l'infraction: Plaidoyer pour une nouvelle théorie de la culpabilité." *Revue de science criminelle et de droit comparé* (2005): 529.

Benmakhlouf, A., and F. Falletti. "Les Ordnungswidrigkeiten en République Fédérale d'Allemagne." *Archives de politique criminelle* 7 (1984): 74–83.

Bentata, P. "Regulation 'Gatekeepers': Predictable 'Unintended Consequences' of the DMA for Users' Welfare." *Competition Forum*, no. 0031 (2022). https://competition-forum.com.

———. "Ce que les mythes nous racontent de l'AI." *L'Opinion*, July 20, 2023: 8.

Bentata, P., and P. Garello. "Complexity-Minded Antitrust: Taking Theories Seriously." February 28, 2023. https://ssrn.com/abstract=4368392.

Benzoni, L. "Loyauté de la concurrence et économie: Une perspective historique." *Revue Lamy de la concurrence*, no. 66 (November 1, 2017): 4–10.

Beres, A. "Entretien sur l'économie avec Sir Karl Popper." *Revue française d'économie* 1, no. 2 (1986): 55–64.

Bergel, J.-L. "Différence de nature (égale) différence de régime." *RTD civ.* (1984): 255–272.

———. "La relativité du droit?" *Revue de la recherche juridique: Droit prospectif*, no. 3 (1986): 13–22.

———. "Le processus de transformation de décisions de justice en normes juridiques." *Revue de la recherche juridique: Droit prospectif*, no. 4 (1993): 1055–1062.

Bernardeau, L., and T. Étienne. "Principes généraux du droit et contrôle juridictionnel en droit de la concurrence – M. Jourdain: juge pénal?" *Cahiers de droit européen* (2016): 365–384.

Bernardi, A. "Stratégies pour une harmonisation des systèmes pénaux européens." *Archives de politique criminelle* 24, no. 1 (2002): 195–233.

———. "L'européanisation de la science pénale." *Archives de politique criminelle* 26, no. 1 (2004): 3–36.

Berréville, J. "Quelques réflexions sur l'élément moral de l'infraction." *Revue de science criminelle et de droit pénal comparé* (1973): 865–877.

Bertin, C., and E. Le Noan. "Faut-il sauver le bien-être du consommateur?" *Concurrences*, no. 1-2019, art. no. 88866 (2019): 2–5.

Bigot, J. "Faute intentionnelle, faute dolosive, faute volontaire: Le passé, le présent, l'avenir." *Revue générale du droit des assurances*, no. 2 (February 2015): 75.

Bishop, J. H. "Criminal Intent as Applied to Conspiracy Under the Sherman Act." *Virginia Law Review* XI, no. 6 (April 1925): 417–431.

Blackstone, W. "Sur l'étude du droit." Translated and postface by D. Baranger. *Revue d'histoire des Facultés de droit et de la science juridique*, no. 23 (2003): 196–256.

Blaise, J.-B. "Une construction inachevée: le droit français des ententes et des positions dominantes." In *Aspects actuels du droit commercial français: Études dédiées à René Roblot*, 159–180. Paris: LGDJ, 1984.

———. "La sanction pénale." *JCP E*, no. 12 (March 21, 2013): comm. 1170, 30–33.

———. "Ententes." *Répertoire de droit européen*, no. 495 (September 2017).

Blanc-Jouvan, G. "La frontière entre le volontaire et l'involontaire: L'exemple de la délinquance routière." In *Code pénal et Code d'instruction criminelle: Livre du bicentenaire*. Études, mélanges, travaux, 485–505. Paris: Dalloz, 2010.

Blockx, J. "Revaluing the Role of Intent Evidence in EU Antitrust Law." *European Competition and Regulatory Law Review* 3, no. 4 (2019): 354–362.

———. "The Expected Impact of the DMA on the Antitrust Enforcement of Unilateral Practices." January 27, 2023. https://ssrn.com/abstract=4341277.

Bloud-Rey, C. "Loyauté et pratiques anticoncurrentielles, antinomie?" *Petites affiches*, no. 234 (November 24, 2011): 20.

Bodenstein, H. D. J. "Phases in the Development of Criminal Mens Rea." *South African Law Journal* 36, no. 4 (1919): 323–349.

Bonassies, P. "Les fondements du droit communautaire de la concurrence: La théorie de la concurrence-moyen." In *Études dédiées à Alex Weill*, 51–67. Paris: Dalloz, 1983.

Bonfils, P. "Consécration de la dualité des fautes civile et pénale non intentionnelles." *Recueil Dalloz* (2004): 721.

Bosco, D. "Une 'amende de principe' pour une entente sans effets." *Contrats concurrence consommation*, no. 4 (April 2008): comm. 108, 39.

———. "Regards sur la modernisation de l'abus de position dominante." *Petites affiches*, no. 133 (July 3, 2008): 14.

———. "Le test de l'opérateur aussi efficace: Une nouvelle ère?" *Concurrences*, no. 3-2013, art. no. 53042 (2013): 12–15.

———. "Quarante millions d'euros pour un dénigrement abusif de médicaments génériques." *Contrats concurrence consommation*, no. 7 (July 2013): comm. 161.

———. "Le problème du franchissement des seuils en parts de marché." *Concurrences*, no. 1-2014, art. no. 63014 (2014): 26–29.

———. "La Cour de justice appelle une interprétation restrictive de la notion de restriction par l'objet." *Contrats concurrence consommation*, no. 11 (November 2014): comm. 250.

———. "Abuse de dominante position." *Répertoire de droit européen* (January 2019).

———. "L'arrêt Intel, un 'grand arrêt'?" *Contrats concurrence consommation*, no. 11 (November 2017): comm. 227.

———. "Concurrence algorithmique et droit des ententes." *Contrats concurrence consommation*, no. 11 (November 2018): comm. 194.

———. "Première décision 'post-Coty' de l'Autorité de la concurrence." *Contrats concurrence consommation*, no. 12 (December 2018): comm. 204.

———. "À propos de la notion de restriction par l'objet (encore...)." *Contrats concurrence consommation*, no. 11 (November 2019): comm. 183.

———. "L'avenir du droit de la concurrence." *Contrats concurrence consommation*, no. 12 (December 2020): dossier 15.

———. "Pénal et concurrence: La nouvelle donne." *Contrats concurrence consommation*, no. 2 (February 2020): reference 2.

———. "Continental Can, c'est fini." *Contrats concurrence consommation*, no. 3 (March 2020): comm. 51.

———. "Restriction 'par l'objet': Une histoire sans fin." *Contrats concurrence consommation*, no. 6 (June 2020): comm. 103.

———. "Le 'nouvel' article 22, un forçage du règlement européen sur les concentrations." *Contrats concurrence consommation*, no. 11 (November 2020): comm. 163.

———. "La prise en compte d'intérêts publics dans la mise en œuvre des règles sur l'abus de position dominante." *Concurrences*, no. 2-2021, Conference: "L'intégration des considérations d'intérêt public dans l'application des règles de concurrence," art. no. 99790 (2021): 31–34.

———. "Retour vers le futur de l'arrêt Bronner." *Contrats concurrence consommation*, no. 5 (May 2021): comm. 85.

———. "La Cour de justice confirme son approche des restrictions par l'objet applicable aux accords de règlement amiable dans l'affaire du Citalopram." *Contrats concurrence consommation*, no. 5 (May 2021): comm. 87.

———. "La régulation concurrentielle des GAFA, le droit et les droits." *Gazette du Palais*, hors série no. 2 (September 15, 2021): 42.

———. "Droit de la concurrence et green deal: Sanction d'une entente limitant la concurrence sur l'innovation verte." *Contrats concurrence consommation*, no. 1 (January 2022): comm. 14.

———. "Google Shopping: Avènement jurisprudentiel d'un abus par favoritisme." *Contrats concurrence consommation*, no. 2 (February 2022): comm. 34.

———. "Regard sur la postmodernisation de l'abus de position dominante." In *Laurence Idot Liber Amicorum – Concurrence et Europe*, vol. 1, edited by C. Lemaire and F. Martucci, 25–36. Paris: Concurrences, 2022.

———. "Illumina-Grail, the Threefold Error of the EU General Court." *Concurrences*, no. 4-2022, art. no. 109076.

———. "L'article 102 du TFUE, le réseau de distribution et la notion d'unité économique." *Contrats concurrence consommation*, no. 10 (October 2022): comm. 158.

———. "À propos du concept de 'contrôleur d'accès' dans le DMA." *Concurrences*, no. 3-2022, Conférence "Digital Market Act: Droit de la concurrence et géants du numérique," art. no. 108068 (2022): 61–65.

———. "Délimitation du marché pertinent et économie numérique: Des jalons posés par le Tribunal dans l'affaire Android." *Contrats concurrence consommation*, no. 11 (November 2022): comm. 176.

———. "L'avocat général Rantos défend les fédérations sportives au nom de la spécificité du modèle sportif européen." *Contrats concurrence consommation*, no. 2 (February 2023): comm. 30.

———. "Réseaux de distribution exclusive et abus de position dominante." *Contrats concurrence consommation*, no. 3 (March 2023): comm. 48.

———. "Nouvelles précisions sur le champ d'application du test Bronner." *Contrats concurrence consommation*, no. 3 (March 2023): comm. 49.

———. "Le préjudice de développement et le préjudice financier devant la Cour de cassation." *Contrats concurrence consommation*, no. 5 (May 2023): comm. 85.

Bostoen, F. "The General Court's Google Shopping Judgment: Finetuning the Legal Qualifications and Tests for Platform Abuse." *Journal of European Competition Law & Practice* 13, no. 2 (2022): 75–86.

Bouloc, B. "Présomption d'innocence et droit pénal des affaires." *Revue de science criminelle et de droit pénal comparé*, no. 3 (July–September 1995): 465–473.

———. "Nécessité de l'intention en droit pénal." *Revue de science criminelle et de droit pénal comparé* (1996): 847.

———. "Les techniques probatoires d'analyse des comportements économiques." In *Les enjeux de la pénalisation de la vie économique*, edited by M.-A. Frison Roche. Thèmes et commentaires, 81–92. Paris: Dalloz, 1997.

Bouscant, R. "La faute dans les infractions aux règles de concurrence en droit européen." *RTD Eur.* (2000): 67.

Brand, P. "The Beginnings of the English Common Law (to 1350)." In *The Oxford Handbook of European Legal History*, edited by H. Pihlajamäki, M. D. Dubber, and M. Godfrey, 430–473. Oxford: Oxford University Press, 2018.

Brickey, K. F. "Corporate Criminal Liability: A Brief History and an Observation." *Washington University Law Quarterly* 60, no. 2 (Summer 1982): 393–424.

Bringuier-Fau, S. "La volonté en droit de la concurrence." In *De la volonté individuelle*, edited by M. Nicod. Travaux de l'IFR, 166–176. Toulouse: Presses de l'Université Toulouse 1 Capitole, 2010.

Broch, J. "L'intérêt général avant 1789: Regard historique sur une notion capitale du droit public français." *Revue historique de droit français et étranger* 95, no. 1 (January–March 2017): 59–86.

Brochier, H. "La science économique est-elle une science?" *Les études philosophiques*, no. 2 (April–June 1978): 229–234.

———. "Les théories économiques sont-elles réfutables?" *Économies et sociétés*, no. 10 (October 1987): 107–118.

———. "Fondements idéologiques et visée scientifique en économie." *Économies et sociétés*, no. 10 (October 1988): 169–188.

Brook, O. "Struggling with Article 101(3) TFEU: Diverging Approaches of the Commission, EU Courts, and Five Competition Authorities." *Common Market Law Review* 56 (2019): 121–156.

Brown, D. K. "Criminal Law's Unfortunate Triumph over Administrative Law." *Journal of Law, Economics & Policy* 7, no. 4 (Summer 2011): 657–684.

Brunner, F. "Le dernier argument du 'Phédon' de Platon en faveur de l'immortalité de l'âme." *Revue des sciences philosophiques et théologiques* 70, no. 4 (October 1986): 497–520.

Brunswick, P. "Le devoir de loyauté, une norme générale de comportement oubliée puis retrouvée?" *Cahiers de droit de l'entreprise*, no. 1 (January 2016): dossier 1.

Budd, M., and A. Lynch. "Voluntariness, Causation and Strict Liability." *Criminal Law Review* (February 1978): 74–81.

Budzinski, O. "An Institutional Analysis of the Enforcement Problems in Merger Control." *European Competition Journal* 6, no. 2 (August 2010): 445–474.

Budzinski, O., and A. Stöhr. "Competition Policy Reform in Europe and Germany: Institutional Change in the Light of Digitization." *European Competition Journal* 15, no. 1 (2018): 15–54.

Byl, S. "Notule relative au glissement de sens de 'stelio'." *Latomus* 45, fasc. 1 (January–March 1986): 143–146.

Caeiro, P. "The Influence of the EU on the 'Blurring' Between Administrative and Criminal Law." In *Do Labels Still Matter? Blurring Boundaries Between Administrative and Criminal Law: The Influence of the EU*, edited by F. Galli and A. Weyembergh, 171–190. Brussels: Éditions de l'Université de Bruxelles, 2014.

Calvano, E., et al. "Algorithmic Pricing: What Implications for Competition Policy?" *Review of Industrial Organization* 55, no. 1 (2019): 155–171.

Candido da Silva, M. "L'économie morale carolingienne (fin VIIIe – début IXe siècle)." *Médiévales*, no. 66 (Spring 2014): 159–178.

Canivet, G. "Le droit de propriété confronté à la théorie des infrastructures essentielles." *Lamy Droit des Affaires*, no. 658 (November 2006): 79.

———. "La place des économistes dans les organes d'application du droit de la concurrence: Retour sur un malaise existentiel." *Concurrences*, no. 2-2019, art. no. 90116 (2019): 1–10.

Carbasse, J.-M. "Sécularisation et droit pénal." *Droits: Revue française de théorie juridique* 60, no. 2 (2014): 13–38.

Carbonnel, F. "Reasoning by Consequences: Applying Different Argumentation Structures to the Analysis of Consequentialist Reasoning in Judicial Decisions." In *Legal Argumentation Theory: Cross-Disciplinary Perspective*, edited by C. Dahlman and E. Feteris, 1–19. New York: Springer, 2013.

Cartapanis, M. "Captures d'attention et droit de la concurrence." *RTD com.* (2022): 733.

———. "La notion de concentration – Droit européen et droit français." *JurisClasseur Concurrence – Consommation*, fasc. 410 (April 2023).

———. "Seuils de notification: La Cour de justice de l'Union européenne restaure la jurisprudence Continental Can et juge que l'article 102 TFUE est susceptible de s'appliquer à une concentration non notifiable (*Towercast*)." *Concurrences*, no. 2-2023, art. no. 112272 (2023): 78–82.

———. "Infrastructures essentielles: La Cour de justice de l'Union européenne écarte le test Bronner lorsque le comportement abusif se manifeste par le démantèlement d'une infrastructure ferroviaire." *Concurrences*, no. 2-2023, art. no. 112261 (2023): 74–76.

———. "L'Autorité de la concurrence prononce des mesures conservatoires pour mettre fin à des pratiques susceptibles de constituer un abus de position dominante dans le secteur de la publicité en ligne." *Concurrences*, no. 3-2023, art. no. 113346 (2023): 92–94.

Cass, R. A., and K. N. Hylton. "Antitrust Intent." *Southern California Law Review* 74, no. 3 (January 2001): 657–746.

Castillo de la Torre, F. "Is the Effects-Based Approach Too Cumbersome? Taking Stock of Recent Practice and Case Law on Article 102 TFEU." In *The Transformation of EU Competition Law: Next Generation Issues*, edited by A. Claici, A. Komninos, and D. Waelbroeck, 145–198. Alphen-sur-le-Rhin: Wolters Kluwer, 2023.

Cavanagh, N. "Corporate Criminal Liability: An Assessment of the Models of Fault." *The Journal of Criminal Law* 75, no. 5 (October 2011): 414–440.

Cedras, J. "Le dol éventuel: Aux limites de l'intention." *Recueil Dalloz* (1995): 18.

Cerexhe, E. "Les règles de concurrence applicables aux entreprises." In *Les novelles: Droit des communautés européennes*, edited by W. J. Ganshof van der Meersch et al., 805–852. Brussels: Larcier, 1969.

———. "L'interprétation de l'article 86 du Traité de Rome et les premières décisions de la Commission." *Cahiers de droit européen*, no. 1 (1972): 272–298.

Chabas, F. "La notion de contravention." *Revue de science criminelle et de droit pénal comparé* (1969): 1–45.

Chacornac, J. "L'article 121-2 du Code pénal et les groupes de sociétés: Les sociétés mères sont-elles des personnes morales comme les autres?" In *Mélanges en l'honneur du Professeur Philippe Conte*, 271–284. Paris: LexisNexis, 2023.

Chaiehloudj, W. "L'ordre public économique." In *Le droit économique au XXIe siècle: Notions et enjeux*, edited by J.-B. Racine. Droit & Économie, 527–562. Paris: LGDJ, 2020.

———. "Quels outils efficaces pour les autorités de concurrence dans l'économie numérique?" *Concurrences*, no. 3-2021, art. no. 101309.

———. "Le droit de la concurrence est-il un frein à la protection de l'environnement?" *Contrats concurrence consommation*, no. 4 (April 2022): étude 6.

———. "La percée de la responsabilité civile dans le droit des pratiques anticoncurrentielles." *RTD civ.*, no. 1 (January–March 2023): 21–43.

Chavanne, A. "Le délit d'escroquerie et la politique criminelle contemporaine (Étude de jurisprudence)." In *Les principaux aspects de la politique criminelle moderne: Recueil d'études en hommage à la mémoire du Professeur Henri Donnedieu de Vabres*, prefaced by L. Hugueney. Institut de droit comparé de l'Université de Paris, 147–156. Paris: Cujas, 1960.

———. "Le problème des délits involontaires." *Revue de science criminelle et de droit pénal comparé* (1962): 241–250.

Champaud, C. "Contribution à la définition du droit économique." *Recueil Dalloz*, chron. XXIV (1967): 215–220.

———. "Les sources du droit de la concurrence au regard du droit commercial et des autres branches du droit applicable en France." In *Études offertes à Roger Houin: Problèmes d'actualité posés par les entreprises*, 61–107. Paris: Dalloz-Sirey, 1985.

———. "Les caractères du droit de la concurrence." *JurisClasseur Concurrence consommation*, fasc. 30, no. 79 (1991).

Charbit, N. "L'intention de la faute." *Petites affiches*, no. 53 (March 14, 2003): 14.

Chatriot, A. "Les ententes: Débats juridiques et dispositifs législatifs (1923–1953), La genèse de la politique de concurrence en France." *Histoire, économie & société*, no. 1 (2008): 7–22.

Chénedé, F. "De l'autonomie de la volonté à la justice commutative: Du mythe à la réalité." *Droit & Philosophie: Annuaire de l'Institut Michel Villey* 4 (2012): 155–181.

Choné-Grimaldi, S. "Les abus de position dominantes dans le secteur numérique (réflexions à partir de la décision Google-Android)." *Recueil Dalloz* (2020): 343.

Cizeron, C. "Droit de la concurrence et RGPD: Dénouement du contentieux Meta." *Contrats concurrence consommation*, no. 10 (October 2023): comm. 156.

Clarkson, C. M. V. "Kicking Corporate Bodies and Damning Their Souls." *The Modern Law Review* 59, no. 4 (July 1996): 557–572.

Claudel, E. "Rôle et place des mécanismes fondamentaux du droit civil en droit des affaires." *RTD com.* (1999): 291.

———. "L'abus de position dominante peut être justifié!" *RTD com.* (2006): 582.

———. "Procédures négociées, accessoires ou alternatives à la sanction en droit de la concurrence: Raison garder!" *Concurrences*, no. 4-2015, art. no. 75896 (2015): 61–84.

———. "Responsabilité au sein des groupes en droit de la concurrence: Un exemple à suivre?" *Cahiers de droit de l'entreprise*, no. 5 (September 2017): dossier 27.

———. "Les sources vives du droit de la concurrence (Étude du droit européen et français des pratiques anticoncurrentielles)." In *Mélanges en l'honneur du Professeur Claude Lucas de Leyssac*, 57–114. Paris: LexisNexis, 2018.

———. "La temporalité des règles de concurrence est-elle adaptée au numérique?" *Cahiers de droit de l'entreprise*, no. 3 (May 2019): dossier 21.

———. "Autonomie et notion d'entreprise." *Contrats concurrence consommation*, no. 6 (June 2020): dossier 7.

Claudel, E., and B. Thullier. "Regard sur le droit mou." *Revue de jurisprudence commerciale*, no. 1 (January–February 2006): 4–8.

Cléro, J.-P. "Le calcul benthamien des plaisirs et des peines: Calcul introuvable ou seulement indéfiniment différé?" *Archives de philosophie* 78, no. 2 (2015): 229–258.

Coffee, J. "No Soul To Damn, No Body To Kick: An Unscandalized Inquiry Into the Problem of Corporate Punishment." *Michigan Law Review* 79 (1981): 386–549.

———. "Does Unlawful Mean Criminal: Reflections on the Disappearing Tort / Crime Distinction in American Law." *Boston University Law Review* 71, no. 2 (March 1991): 193–246.

Cohen, C. "Le chef d'entreprise est-il délinquant ordinaire?" In *Les enjeux de la pénalisation de la vie économique*, edited by M.-A. Frison-Roche, 71–80. Paris: Dalloz, 1997.

Coing, H. "European Common Law: Historical Foundations." In *Nouvelles perspectives d'un droit commun*, edited by M. Cappelletti. European University Institute series, 31–44. Brussels: Bruylant, 1978.

Colangelo, G. "DMA Begins." December 16, 2022. https://ssrn.com/abstract=4292049

Colonna d'Istria, F. "Le mythe des 'définitions dans la loi': Exemples de droit des obligations." In *Le droit entre autonomie et ouverture: Mélanges en l'honneur de Jean-Louis Bergel*, edited by J.-Y. Chérot et al., 61–89. Penser le droit. Brussels: Bruylant, 2013.

———. "Qu'est-ce qu'un argument technique en droit? Étude aristotélicienne." In *Penser la technique juridique*, edited by A. Desrameaux and F. Colonna d'Istria, 169–187. Contextes. Paris: LGDJ, 2018.

Comanor, W. S., and H. E. Frech. "Predatory Pricing and the Meaning of Intent." *The Antitrust Bulletin* 38 (Summer 1993): 293–308.

Combacau, J. "L'illicite et le fautif." *Droits: Revue française de théorie juridique*, no. 5 (1987): 3–8.

Conte, P. "Droit pénal et concurrence." *JCP – Cahiers de droit de l'entreprise*, no. 3 (2000): 21–26.

———. "Le lampiste et la mort." *Droit pénal*, no. 1 (January 2001): chron. 2.

———. "L'art de légiférer se perd-il? Réflexions en forme de pamphlet à partir de quelques illustrations de droit pénal." In *Études à la mémoire de Christian Lapoyade-Deschamps*. Bordeaux: Presses universitaires de Bordeaux, 2003.

———. "La dépénalisation: Réalité ou mirage? L'exemple de l'élément moral des infractions d'affaires." In *Peines, dangerosité, quelles certitudes*. Essais de philosophie pénale et de criminologie, 23–34. Paris: Dalloz, 2010.

———. "Les Messieurs Jourdain dans les palais de la République: Variations sur l'article 121-3 du Code pénal et ses avatars." In *Mélanges en l'honneur du professeur Jacques-Henri Robert*, 137–144. Paris: LexisNexis, 2012.

———. "L'obscur article 121-3 du Code pénal." *Recueil Dalloz* (2014): 1317.

———. "Harcèlement moral – Éléments matériel et moral." *Droit pénal*, no. 4 (April 2016): comm. 58.

———. "Principe de la légalité criminelle: Quelques airs nouveaux sur des paroles anciennes." *Droit pénal*, no. 6 (June 2020): étude 17.

———. "La distinction de la légalité formelle et de la légalité matérielle: Ses dits et ses non-dits." *Droit pénal*, no. 7–8 (July 2020): étude 23.

———. "Le cas des fusions-absorptions de sociétés." *Droit pénal*, no. 1 (January 2021): comm. 2.

———. "Quelques observations sur la distinction des règles substantielles et des règles de preuve en droit pénal." In *Mélanges en l'honneur de Philippe Théry: Les coutures du droit*, 195–202. Paris: LGDJ – Dalloz, 2022.

Condorcet. “Dixième époque: Des progrès futurs de l’esprit humain.” In *Esquisses d’un tableau historique des progrès de l’esprit humain*, 265–296. Paris: GF Flammarion, 1988.

Conley, J., and W. O’Barr. “Crime and Custom in Corporate Society: A Cultural Perspective on Corporate Misconduct.” *Law and Contemporary Problems* 60, no. 3 (Summer 1997): 5–21.

Constant, J. “Dominique-François de Sohet, jurisconsulte liégeois.” *Journal des tribunaux*, no. 4761 (November 20, 1971): 673–684.

Cornu, G. “Aperçu de la pensée juridique française contemporaine.” *Annales de l’Université de Poitiers*, no. 1 (1960): 15–28.

———. “Les définitions dans la loi.” In *Mélanges dédiés à Jean Vincent*, 77–92. Paris: Dalloz, 1981.

Costa, J.-L. “Les infractions involontaires du point de vue de la responsabilité pénale en France.” *Revue de science criminelle et de droit pénal comparé* (1963): 731–749.

Coste-Floret, P. “L’interprétation des lois pénales.” *Revue de science criminelle et de droit pénal comparé*, no. 1 (1937): 4–20.

Cousin, M. “L’algorithme au service de la politique tarifaire: Nouvelles pratiques, nouveaux risques?” *Concurrences*, no. 4-2017, art. no. 84905 (2017): 17–24.

Currat, P. “L’interprétation du Statut de Rome.” *Revue québécoise de droit international* 20, no. 1 (2007): 137–163.

D’Angio-Barros, A. “Affaires économiques – Concurrence et pratiques anti-concurrentielles: 1931–1985.” *Service des archives économiques et financières* (May 2012). https://www.economie.gouv.fr/saef/affaires-economiques-concurrence-et-pratiques-anti-concurrentielles.

Danet, D. “Le droit antitrust doit-il être ‘économiquement correct’?” *Dalloz Affaires*, no. 43 (1996): 1370–1376.

Dannecker, G. “La responsabilité pénale pour les délits d’omission, notamment dans le domaine de l’économie et de l’environnement.” *Revue de science criminelle et de droit comparé* (April–June 1987): 379–395.

David, R. “Droit comparé et systèmes socio-politiques.” *Revue internationale de droit comparé*, no. 2 (1970): 263–268.

———. “Le droit continental, la Common Law, et les perspectives d’un jus commune européen.” In *Nouvelles perspectives d’un droit commun*, edited by M. Cappelletti. European University Institute, 113–135. Brussels: Bruylant, 1978.

De Champs, E. “Utilitarisme et liberté. La pensée politique de Jeremy Bentham.” *Archives de Philosophie* 78, no. 2 (2015): 221–228.

De Gauléjac, V. “L’emprise à IBM, 1979–2019: De l’adhésion à la répression.” *Nouvelle revue de psychosociologie* 1, no. 29 (2021): 13–22.

De Muizon, G. "Les tests de preuve économiques permettant de caractériser une pratique anticoncurrentielle." *Concurrences*, no. 4-2012, art. no. 49238 (2012): 25–28.

De Roover, R. "Monopoly Theory Prior to Adam Smith: A Revision." *The Quarterly Journal of Economics* 65, no. 4 (November 1951): 492–524.

———. "The Concept of Just Price: Theory and Economic Policy." *The Journal of Economic History* 18, no. 3 (December 1958): 418–434.

———. "La doctrine scolastique en matière de monopole et son application à la politique économique des communes italiennes." In *Studi in onore di Amintore Fanfani nel venticinquennio di cattedra universitaria*, tome I, 149–179. Milan: Giuffrè, 1962

De Soto, M. J. "Les philosophes du XVIIIe siècle et la Révolution française." In *Annales de la faculté de droit et de sciences politiques et économiques de Strasbourg*. Tome VIII, Travaux du colloque de philosophie pénale (12–21 janvier 1959) "La responsabilité pénale," 137–153. Strasbourg, 1961.

De Vel, G. "La responsabilité pénale des personnes morales dans les instruments juridiques du Conseil de l'Europe." In *La responsabilité pénale des personnes morales en Europe*, edited by S. Adam, N. Colette-Basecqz, and M. Nihoul, 343–371. Brussels: La Charte, 2008.

Deak, F. "Contracts and Combinations in Restraint of Trade in French Law – A Comparative Study." *Iowa Law Review* 21 (1936): 397–454.

Debré, M. "Pour une administration de l'économie française." *Sciences politiques* (June 1938): 246–269.

Debroux, M. "Restriction par objet: L'Avocat Général Bobek propose à la Cour de justice de l'Union européenne, saisie d'une question préjudicielle par la Cour suprême hongroise, une méthode d'analyse visant à déterminer si une pratique anticoncurrentielle peut être qualifiée de restriction par objet ou si l'examen de ses effets est nécessaire (*Gazdasági Versenyhivatal / Budapest Bank*)." *Concurrences*, no. 4-2019, art. no. 92206 (2019): 87–89.

———. "Nature, objectifs et régime des obligations imposées aux contrôleurs d'accès: Des obligations ex ante et per se, vraiment?" *Concurrences*, no. 3-2022, Conference "Digital Market Act: Droit de la concurrence et géants du numérique," art. no. 108068 (2022): 66–72.

Debuyst, C. "Les conceptions criminologiques de la criminalité." In *Annales de l'Université de sciences sociales de Toulouse*. Tome XXIV, fasc. 1 and 2 (1976): 151–172.

Decocq, A. "L'article 419 du Code pénal est-il devenu un texte historique." *Revue de jurisprudence commerciale* (1980): 77–97.

———. "De l'application de la Convention européenne aux procédures communautaires de concurrence pouvant aboutir à des amendes ou à des astreintes." In *Mélanges en hommage à Louis Edmond Pettiti*, 289–307. Brussels: Bruylant, 1998.

Decocq, G. "Leçon sur la responsabilité civile du fait d'une pratique anticoncurrentielle." In *Leçons de droit civil: Mélanges en l'honneur de François Chabas*, edited by N. Guimezanes, 197–233. Brussels: Bruylant, 2011.

———. "Observations sur le dommage concurrentiel." *Journal des sociétés*, no. 44 (June 2007), dossier: "L'évaluation du préjudice économique": 39–44.

———. "La concurrence par les mérites." In *Les concepts émergents en droit des affaires*, edited by E. Le Dolley. Droit & Économie, 239–246. Paris: LGDJ, 2010.

———. "Éthique et droit de la concurrence." *Contrats concurrence consommation*, no. 1 (January 2020): repère 1.

Delage, P.-J. "Les androïdes rêveront-ils de personnalité juridique?" In *Science-fiction et science juridique*, edited by P.-J. Delage. Les voies du droit, 165–184. Paris: IRJS Éditions, 2013.

———. "L'apport de la philosophie dans la théorisation du droit pénal." In *Faut-il rethéoriser le droit pénal*, edited by J. Leroy, 17–24. Paris: LexisNexis, 2017.

Delmas-Marty, M. "Le droit pénal, l'individu et l'entreprise: culpabilité 'du fait d'autrui' ou du 'décideur'?" *JCP G*, no. 45 (November 20, 1985): doctr. 3218.

———. "Pour des principes directeurs de législation pénale." *Revue de science criminelle et de droit pénal comparé* (1985): 225–229.

———. "Les problèmes juridiques et pratiques posés par la différence entre le droit criminel et le droit administratif pénal." *Revue internationale de droit pénal* 59 (1988): 15–19.

———. "Les standards en droit pénal." *Revue de la recherche juridique: Droit prospectif*, no. 4 (1988): 1019–1034.

———. "La preuve pénale." *Droits: Revue française de théorie juridique*, no. 23 (1996): 53–65.

Demogue, R. "La notion de sujet de droit: Caractères et conséquences." *RTD civ.* (1909): 611–655.

Deringer, A. "Les règles de la concurrence au sein de la C.E.E. (Analyse et commentaire des articles 85 à 94 du Traité)." *Revue du Marché Commun*, no. 32 (February 1963): 84–89.

Descamps, O. "Histoire du droit de la responsabilité dans le monde occidental." In *Prendre la responsabilité au sérieux*, edited by A. Supiot, 37–54. Paris: PUF, 2015.

Deschamps, M., and F. Marty. "L'analyse économique du droit est-elle une théorie scientifique du droit?" *Revue de la recherche juridique: Droit prospectif*, no. 5 (2008): 2541–2569.

———. "Les politiques de concurrence sont-elles réductibles à de la théorie économique appliquée? Réflexions autour de l'affaire Microsoft." *Revue de la recherche juridique: Droit prospectif*, no. 5 (2008): 2571–2593.

Detraz, S. "L'hypothèse d'une responsabilité pénale du fait des choses." In *Mélanges en l'honneur du professeur Jacques-Henri Robert*, 229–245. Paris: LexisNexis, 2012.

———. "L'intention coupable est-elle encore le principe?" In *Le nouveau Code pénal, 20 ans après: État des questions*, edited by L. Saenko, 63–78. Paris: LGDJ, 2014.

———. "De la mauvaise conduite des véhicules autonomes en droit pénal." *Recueil Dalloz* (2021): 1039.

Dewey, J. "The Historical Background of Corporate Legal Personality." *Yale Law Journal* 35, no. 6 (April 1926): 655–673.

Dewost, J.-L., B. Lasserre, and R. Saint-Esteben. "L'entreprise, les règles de concurrence et les droits fondamentaux: Quelle articulation?" *Nouveaux cahiers du Conseil constitutionnel*, no. 35 (April 2012).

Di Giovanni Bezzi, R. "A Tale of Two Cities: Effects Analysis in Article 102 TFEU Between Competition Process and Market Outcome." *Journal of European Competition Law & Practice* 14, no. 2 (2023): 83–94.

Dittert, D. "Abus de position dominante: Vers une approche 'plus économique'?" *Revue des affaires européennes*, no. 1 (September 2012): 197–205.

Dölling, D., and C. Laue. "Corporate Criminal Liability in Germany – A Never Ending Story?" In *La responsabilité pénale des personnes morales en Europe*, edited by S. Adam, N. Colette-Basecqz, and M. Nihoul, 25–46. Brussels: La Charte, 2008.

Donnedieu de Vabres-Tranié, L., and M. de Walsche. "Interprétation systématique de la notion d'entreprise et responsabilité pénale des personnes morales: Quand le droit de la concurrence bouscule le droit pénal des personnes morales." *Gazette du Palais*, no. 11 (May 5, 2022): 74–78.

Doucet, J.-P. "Une discussion sur l'erreur de droit." *Revue de science criminelle et de droit pénal comparé* (1962): 497–503.

———. "La condition préalable à l'infraction." *Gazette du Palais* II (1972): doct. 726.

Drexl, J. "La Constitution économique européenne – L'actualité du modèle ordolibéral." *Revue internationale de droit économique* XXV, no. 4 (2011): 419–454.

———. "On the (A)political Character of the Economic Approach to Competition Law." In *Competition Policy and the Economic Approach: Foundations and Limitations*, edited by J. Drexl et al., 312–336. Cheltenham: Edward Elgar, 2011.

———. "Anticompetitive Stumbling Stones on the Way to a Cleaner World: Protecting Competition in Innovation without a Market." *Journal of Competition Law and Economics* 8, no. 3 (September 2012): 507–544.

Dreyer, E. "Que reste-t-il du principe de responsabilité personnelle des personnes physiques?" In *Le nouveau Code pénal, 20 ans après: État des questions*, edited by L. Saenko, 97–106. Paris: LGDJ, 2014.

———. "La sanction de la faute lucrative par l'amende civile." *Recueil Dalloz*, no. 9 (2017): 1136.

———. "Harceler la fille, c'est aussi harceler la mère." *Gazette du Palais*, no. 40 (November 17, 2020): 47–48.

Dubber, M. D. "The Comparative History and Theory of Corporate Liability." *New Criminal Law Review* 16, no. 2 (Spring 2013): 203–240.

Dunham, W. "Cold Case Files: The Athenian Grain Merchants, 386 B.C." *Cato Journal* 28, no. 3 (Autumn 2008): 495–513.

Dunne, N. "Between Competition Law and Regulation: Hybridized Approaches to Market Control." *Journal of Antitrust Enforcement* 2, no. 2 (2014): 225–269.

Durand, P. "L'évolution de la condition juridique des personnes morales de droit privé." In *Le droit privé français au milieu du XXe siècle: Études offertes à Georges Ripert*. Tome I: "Études générales," 138–159. Paris: LGDJ, 1950.

Duvert, C. "Harcèlement moral." *JurisClasseur Pénal Code*, fasc. 20, no. 3 (December 2022).

Eckert, R. "Peine judiciaire, pénitence et salut entre droit canonique et théologie (XIIe s. – début du XIIIe s.)." *Revue de l'histoire des religions*, no. 4 (2011): 483–508.

Ehrlich, I. "The Deterrent Effect of Capital Punishment: A Question of Life and Death." *The American Economic Review* 65, no. 3 (June 1975): 349–417.

Eilmansberger, T. "How To Distinguish Good From Bad Competition Under Article 82 EC: In Search of Clearer and More Coherent Standards for Anti-Competitive Abuses." *Common Market Law Review* 42 (2005): 129–177.

———. "Dominance – The Lost Child? How Effects-Based Rules Could and Should Change Dominance Analysis." *European Competition Journal* 2 (2006): 15–30.

Elholm, T. "Guilt / Fault." In *General Principles for a Common Law Criminal Framework in the EU: A Guide for Legal Practitioners*, edited by R. Sicurella et al., 41–72. Milan: Giuffrè, 2017.

Ellis, J. A. "L'interprétation du mot 'affecter' dans l'article 85, § 1er, du Traité de la Communauté économique européenne par rapport aux mots 'empêcher', 'restreindre', ou 'fausser' le jeu de la concurrence." *Recueil Dalloz*, chron. XXXIII (1963): 221–228.

Epstein, R. A. "The Next Generation of Legal Scholarship." *Stanford Law Review* 30, no. 3 (February 1978): 635–660.

Eraly, A. "Le pouvoir sans l'incarnation: L'empire de la domination impersonnelle." *Nouvelle revue de psychosociologie* 1, no. 29 (2021): 223–234.

Ergen, T., and S. Kohl. "Varieties of Economization in Competition Policy: Institutional Change in German and American Antitrust, 1960–2000." *Review of International Political Economy* 26, no. 2 (2019): 256–286.

Erner, G. "La morale économique chrétienne: Le tournant médiéval." *Revue internationale des sciences sociales* 3, no. 185 (2005): 513–522.

Escudero, J. A. "L'historiographie générale du droit anglais." *Les Cahiers de droit* 9, no. 2 (1967–1968): 117–240.

Esmein, P. "La faute et sa place dans la responsabilité civile." *RTD civ.* (1949): 481–490.

Éveillard, G. "La vie privée des personnes morales." *Droit administratif*, no. 1 (January 2023): comm. 4, 38–42.

Faivre, P. "La responsabilité pénale des personnes morales." *Revue de science criminelle et de droit pénal comparé*, no. 3 (July–September 1958): 547–574.

Farjat, G. "La notion de droit économique." *Archives de philosophie du droit* 37 (1992): 27–62.

Faure, B. "Les droits fondamentaux des personnes morales." *Revue du droit public*, no. 1 (January 2008): 233.

Feldman, J. "Objectivité et subjectivité en science. Quelques aperçus." *European Social Science Journal* XL (2002): 85–130.

Ferguson, Y. "Puissance de calcul, force de l'emprise? Critique de l'organisation augmentée." *Nouvelle revue de psychosociologie* 1, no. 29 (2021): 157–169.

Figueira, T. "'Sitopolai' and 'Sitophylakes' in Lysias' 'Against the Graindealers': Governmental Intervention in the Athenian Economy." *Phoenix* 40, no. 2 (Summer 1986): 149–171.

First, H. "Is Antitrust 'Law'?" *Antitrust* 10, no. 1 (Autumn 1995): 9–12.

Fisse, B., and J. Braithwaite. "The Allocation of Responsibility for Corporate Crime: Individualism, Collectivism and Accountability." *Sydney Law Review* 11, no. 3 (1988): 468–513.

Focsaneanu, L. "Pour objet ou pour effet." *Revue du marché commun*, no. 87 (January 1966): 862–870.

———. "La notion d'abus dans le système de l'article 86 du Traité instituant la Communauté économique européenne." In *La réglementation du comportement des monopoles et entreprises dominantes en droit communautaire*, edited by J. A. Van Damme, 324–380. Bruges: De Tempel, 1977.

Foucault, M. "Le panoptisme." In *Surveiller et punir: Naissance de la prison*, 228–264. Tel. Paris: Gallimard, 1975.

Fox, E. "The Battle for the Soul of Antitrust." *California Law Review* 75, no. 3 (1987): 917–923.

———. "The Efficiency Paradox." In *How the Chicago School Overshot the Mark: The Effect of Conservative Economic Analysis on U.S. Antitrust*, edited by R. Pitofsky, 77–101. Oxford: Oxford University Press, 2008.

Frankfurt, H. G. "Alternate Possibilities and Moral Responsibility." *The Journal of Philosophy* 66, no. 23 (December 1969): 829–839.

Freget, O. "Le respect de la concurrence libre et non faussée est-il une finalité ou un moyen?" *Concurrences*, no. 3-2016, art. no. 80007 (2016): 1–3.

French, P. A. "The Corporation as a Moral Person." *American Philosophy Quarterly* 16, no. 3 (July 1979): 207–215.

Friedel, G. "À propos de la notion d'entreprise..." In *Études dédiées à René Roblot: Aspects actuels du droit commercial français*, 97–114. Paris: LGDJ, 1984.

Friedman, M. "The Methodology of Positive Economics." In *Essays in Positive Economics*, 3–43. Chicago: University of Chicago Press, 1996.

Frison-Roche, M. "Peut-on établir des analogies opératoires entre droit de la concurrence et droit boursier?" *Petites affiches*, no. 144 (July 21, 1999): 9.

Fumaroli, M. "Anciens et modernes, décadence ou progrès: Le 'retour à l'Antique' au XVIIIe siècle." In *Exercices de lecture: De Rabelais à Paul Valéry*, 498–531. NRF – Bibliothèque des idées. Paris: Gallimard, 2006.

Gal, M. "Algorithms as Illegal Agreements." May 2, 2018. https://ssrn.com/abstract=3171977

Gassin, R. "Lois spéciales et droit commun." *Recueil Dalloz*, chron. XVIII (1961): 91–98.

———. Note sous Cass. crim., December 10, 1970, no. 70-91.155. *JCP G*, II (1972): jurisprudence no. 17277.

Gaudemet, J. "Le problème de la responsabilité pénale dans l'Antiquité." In *Studi in onore di Emilio Betti*, vol. II, 483–508. Milan: Giuffrè, 1961.

Gautier, P.-Y. "Quelle langue parle le droit?" *Pouvoirs* 2023/3, no. 186 (2023): 99–110.

Gazzaniga, J.-L. "Les métamorphoses historiques de la responsabilité." In *Les métamorphoses de la responsabilité: Sixièmes journées René Savatier*, 3–18. Paris: PUF, 1997.

Geeroms, S. "La responsabilité pénale de la personne morale: Une étude comparative." *Revue internationale de droit comparé* 48, no. 3 (1996): 533–579.

Geradin, D., and I. Girgenson. "The Counterfactual Method in EU Competition Law: The Cornerstone of the Effects-Based Approach." In *Ten Years of Effects-Based Approach in EU Competition Law: State of Play and Perspectives*, edited by J. Bourgeois and D. Waelbroeck, 211–238. GCLC Annual Conference Series. Brussels: Bruylant, 2012.

Gerard, D. M. B. "The Effects-Based Approach Under Article 101 TFEU and Its Paradoxes: Modernisation at War With Itself?" In *Ten Years of Effects-Based Approach in EU Competition Law: State of Play and Perspectives*, edited by J. Bourgeois and D. Waelbroeck. GCLC Annual Conference Series, vol. 3, 17–41. Brussels: Bruylant, 2012.

Germain, M. "L'apport du droit de l'entreprise au droit des personnes." *JCP E*, suppl. 2 (1997): 11–15. Colloque du 25e anniversaire de la FNDE.

Gernet, L. "Le droit pénal de la Grèce Ancienne." In *Du châtiment dans la cité: Supplices corporels et peine de mort dans le monde antique*, Table ronde de Rome (9–11 novembre 1982), 9–35. Rome: École française de Rome, 1984.

Gervasoni, S. "Une différence de degré plus que de nature, qui impose une approche prudente et pragmatique de la distinction." *Concurrences*, Colloque du 17 avril 2015: "Restriction par objet, restriction par effet: Quelle portée encore accorder à cette distinction?"

Ghestin, J. "L'ordre public, notion à contenu variable, en droit privé français." In *Les notions à contenu variable en droit*, edited by C. Perelman and R. Vander Elst. Travaux du centre national de recherches logiques, 77–97. Brussels: Bruylant, 1984.

Giudicelli, A. "Incertitudes sur les frontières de l'intention." In *Dix ans après la réforme de 1994: Quels repères dans le Code pénal?*, edited by M. Danti-Juan. Travaux de l'Institut de sciences criminelles de Poitiers, vol. XXIV, 25–43. Paris: Cujas, 2005.

Glaser, S. "Élément moral de l'infraction internationale." *Revue générale de droit international public* (1955): 537–569.

Goldschmidt, N. "Walter Eucken's Place in the History of Ideas." *The Review of Austrian Economics* 26 (2013): 127–147.

Grac-Aubert, V. "Concurrence: La Commission européenne modernise sa manière de définir le 'marché pertinent'." *Dalloz Actualité* (December 13, 2022).

Green, N. "The Road to Conviction – The Criminalisation of Cartel Law." In *Annual Proceedings of the Fordham Corporate Law Institute: International Antitrust Law & Policy*, vol. 30, 13–29. New York: Juris Publishing, 2003.

———. "From Rome to Rome: The Evolution of Competition Law into a Twenty-First Century Religion." *Competition Law Journal* 9, no. 1 (2010): 7–25.

Green, S. P. "Why It's a Crime to Tear the Tag Off a Mattress: Overcriminalization and the Moral Content of Regulatory Offenses." *Emory Law Journal* 46, no. 4 (Fall 1997): 1533–1616.

———. "Moral Ambiguity in White Collar Criminal Law." *Notre Dame Journal of Law, Ethics & Public Policy* 18, no. 2 (2004): 501–520.

Grimaudet, F. "Traité des causes qui excusent de dol." In *Œuvres*, edited by Robert Foüet, 390–408. Paris, 1669.

Grynfogel, C. "Le concours de volontés entre entreprises, une notion protéiforme en droit communautaire des ententes." *Revue de jurisprudence de droit des affaires* (2005): 552.

———. "La notion d'"objet anticoncurrentiel' et la sécurité juridique des entreprises." *Revue de jurisprudence de droit des affaires*, no. 8–9, chron. (2014): 5–9.

Guenzoui, Y. "Entente et contrat: Le trouble notionnel." *RTD com.* (2006): 273.

Guittard, I. "Continental Can renaît de ses cendres! L'arrêt Towercast retient l'applicabilité de l'article 102 TFUE à une concentration 'sous les seuils'." *Contrats concurrence consommation*, no. 5 (May 2023): comm. 86.

Gyselen, L. "What Makes an Agreement Anti-Competitive: Lessons from the Past." In *The Notion of Restriction of Competition: Revisiting the Foundations of Antitrust Enforcement in Europe*, edited by D. Gerard, M. Merola, and B. Meyring. GCLC Annual Conference Series, 111–135. Brussels: Bruylant, 2017.

Haid, F. "Les classes et sous-classes d'arguments utilisables pour répondre à une problématique juridique de droit privé: Contribution à l'élaboration des fondamentaux épistémologiques de la formation des juristes à l'argumentation." *Revue de la recherche juridique: Droit prospectif*, 2021-3, no. 35 (2021): 1606–1678.

Halperin, J.-L. "L'approche historique et la problématique du jus commune." *Revue internationale de droit comparé* 52, no. 4 (October–November 2000): 717–731.

Hamdani, A., and A. Klement. "Corporate Crime and Deterrence." *Stanford Law Review* 61, no. 2 (November 2008): 271–310.

Hamel, J. "La personnalité morale et ses limites." *Recueil Dalloz*, chron. XXXIV (1949): 141–144.

Hans-Bernd, S., and M. Vatiero. "Fifty Years of Richard Posner's Economic Analysis of Law: An Introduction." *History of Economic Ideas* XXXI, no. 3 (2023). https://ssrn.com/abstract=4547843

Harno, A. "Intent in Criminal Conspiracy." *University of Pennsylvania Law Review* 89 (March 1941): 624–647.

Hart, H. L. A. "The Aims of the Criminal Law." *Law and Contemporary Problems* 23, no. 3 (Summer 1958): 401–441.

———. "American Jurisprudence Through English Eyes: The Nightmare and the Noble Dream." *Georgia Law Review* 11, no. 5 (September 1977): 969–990.

Hart, H. L. A., and S. Hampshire. "Decision, Intention and Certainty." *Mind* 67, no. 265 (January 1958): 1–12.

Hawk, B. "The American (Anti-Trust) Revolution: Lessons for the EEC?" *European Competition Law Review* 9 (1988): 53–87.

———. "À propos de la 'concurrence par les mérites': Regards croisés sur l'article 82 CE et la Section 2 du Sherman Act." *Concurrences*, no. 3-2005, art. no. 231 (2005): 33–41.

Hayek, F. A. "Competition as a Discovery Procedure." Translated by M. S. Snow. *The Quarterly Journal of Austrian Economics* 5, no. 3 (Autumn 2002): 9–23.

———. "Le simulacre de connaissance." In *Nouveaux essais de philosophie, de science politique, d'économie et d'histoire des idées*, translated by C. Piton, 53–68. Bibliothèque classique de la liberté. Paris: Les Belles Lettres, 2008.

———. "The Meaning of Competition." *Econ Journal Watch* 13, no. 2 (May 2016): 359–372.

Hazlitt, W. "Pourquoi les arts ne progressent-ils pas? – Un fragment." In *Sentiment et raison*, translated by J. Zanetta, 133–138. Mémoire de la critique. Paris: Sorbonne Université Presses, 2019.

Hébraud, P. "Rôles respectifs de la volonté et des éléments objectifs dans les actes juridiques." In *Mélanges offerts à Jacques Maury*, tome II, 420–476. Paris: Dalloz-Sirey, 1960.

Heinemann, A. "Algorithmes et économie numérique en droit de la concurrence." In *Droit et économie numérique*, edited by A. Richa et al., 201–226. Bern: Stämpfli Verlag, 2021.

Herzog, J. B. "La prévention des infractions involontaires contre la vie et l'intégrité de la personne humaine." In *La prévention des infractions contre la vie humaine et l'intégrité de la personne*, edited by A. Besson and M. Ancel. Publications du centre d'études de défense sociale, tome IV, vol. 1, 207–244. Paris: Cujas, 1956.

Hésiode. *Œuvres d'Hésiode*. Translated by M. A. Bignan. In *Les petits poèmes grecs*, edited by M. Aimé-Martin, 113–164. Paris: Auguste Desrez, 1838.

Heyer, K. "Consumer Welfare and the Legacy of Robert Bork." *The Journal of Law & Economics* 57, no. 3 (August 2014): 19–32.

Hirsch, H. J. "Rapport allemand." In *La criminalization du comportement collectif: XIVe Congrès international de droit comparé*, edited by H. De Doelder and K. Tiedemann, 31–69. The Hague: Kluwer Law International.

Holley, D. L. "EEC Competition Practice: A Thirty-Year Retrospective." *Fordham International Law Journal* 16, no. 2 (1992–1993): 342–411.

Hornman, M., and E. Sikkema. "Corporate Intent: In Search for a Theoretical Foundation for Corporate Mens Rea." In *Overarching Views of Crime and Deviancy: Rethinking the Legacy of the Utrecht School*, edited by F. De Jong. Willem Pompe Institute, 287–309. The Hague: Eleven International Publishing, 2015.

Houin, R. "Le problème des fictions en droit civil." *Travaux de l'Association Henri Capitant* (1947): 242–252.

Hovenkamp, H. "Law and Economics in the United States: A Brief Historical Survey." *Cambridge Journal of Economics* 19 (1995): 331–352.

———. "The Monopolization Offense." *Ohio State Law Journal* 61, no. 3 (2000): 1035–1049.

Huftier, M. "Libre arbitre, liberté et péché chez saint Augustin." *Recherches de théologie ancienne et médiévale* 33 (July–December 1966): 187–281.

Ibáñez Colomo, P. "Beyond the More Economics-Based Approach: A Legal Perspective on Article 102 TFEU Case Law." *Common Market Law Review* 53, no. 3 (June 2016): 709–740.

———. "The Draft Digital Markets Act: A Legal and Institutional Analysis." *Journal of European Competition Law & Practice* 12, no. 7 (2021): 561–575.

———. "The (Second) Modernisation of Article 102 TFEU: Reconciling Effective Enforcement, Legal Certainty and Meaningful Judicial Review." (October 2023). https://ssrn.com/abstract=4598161

Ibáñez Colomo, P., and A. Kalintiri. "The Evolution of EU Antitrust Policy: 1966–2017." *The Modern Law Review* 83, no. 2 (2020): 321–372.

Ibáñez Colomo, P., and A. Lamadrid de Pablo. "On the Notion of Restriction of Competition: What We Know and What We Don't Know We Know." In *The Notion of Restriction of Competition: Revisiting the Foundations of Antitrust Enforcement in Europe*, edited by D. Gerard, M. Merola, and B. Meyring. GCLC Annual Conference Series, 333–373. Brussels: Bruylant, 2017.

Ida, N. "Abus de marché et droit de garder le silence." *JCP E*, no. 16–17 (April 22, 2021): comm. 1226, 36–41.

Idot, L. "La qualification de la restriction de concurrence: À propos des lignes directrices de la Commission concernant l'application de l'article 81, § 3 CE." In *La modernisation du droit de la concurrence*, edited by

G. Canivet and M.-A. Frison-Roche. Droit & Économie, 85–104. Paris: LGDJ, 2006.

———. "Réflexions sur l'application de certains principes et notions du droit pénal en droit des pratiques anticoncurrentielles." In *Les droits et le droit: Mélanges dédiés à Bernard Bouloc*, 457–489. Paris: Dalloz, 2007.

———. "Le retour de l'objet anticoncurrentiel…" *Concurrences*, no. 4-2009, art. no. 29202 (2009): 1–2.

———. "Opérations d'initiés." *Europe*, no. 2 (February 2010): comm. 75.

———. "La responsabilité pénale des personnes morales: Les leçons du droit européen de la concurrence." *Concurrences*, no. 1-2012, art. no. 41768 (2012): 55–72.

———. "La Cour de Justice revient une nouvelle fois sur la notion d''objet anticoncurrentiel'." *Revue des contrats*, no. 3 (July 1, 2013): 955.

———. "Argument économique et argument sociologique." In *L'argument sociologique en droit: Pluriel et singularité*, edited by D. Fenouillet. Thèmes & commentaires, 43–59. Paris: Dalloz, 2015.

———. "Réflexions sur la notion d'infraction unique et continue en droit européen de la concurrence." In *Humanisme et justice: Mélanges en l'honneur de Geneviève Giudicelli-Delage*, 549–570. Paris: Dalloz, 2016.

———. "Mesures tarifaires d'adhésion à un groupement et effets anti-concurrentiels." *Europe*, no. 8–9 (August 2016): comm. 295.

———. "Les suites de l'arrêt dit 'des cartes bancaires': La distinction 'restriction de concurrence par objet / restriction par effet' toujours au cœur des débats sur l'article 101 TFUE." *RTD Eur.* (2016): 817.

———. "Réflexions sur l'évolution de la preuve des pratiques anticoncurrentielles devant les autorités de concurrence." *Concurrences*, no. 4-2017, art. no. 84879 (2017): 45–59.

———. "Une lecture de l'arrêt Intel." *Concurrences*, no. 1-2018, art. no. 86053 (2018): 15–22.

———. "La distinction restriction de concurrence par objet / restriction de concurrence par effet et l'article 101 TFUE: Un sujet de disputatio." In *Mélanges en l'honneur du professeur Claude Lucas de Leyssac*, edited by G. Parléani. Mélanges, 243–268. Paris: LexisNexis, 2018.

———. "Consumer protection – A new step towards a European law on unfair competition." *Europe*, no. 5 (May 2019): alerte 30.

———. "L'intégration des considérations d'intérêt public dans le droit des ententes: Approche juridique." *Concurrences*, no. 2-2021, art. no. 99790 (2021): 12–22.

———. "La remise en cause des frontières du droit de la concurrence." *Europe*, no. 11 (November 2022): alerte 76.

———. "Concurrence: Nouveaux épisodes dans la saga." *Europe*, no. 4 (April 2023): comm. 145.

———. "Abus de position dominante et écosystèmes numériques." *Europe*, no. 11 (November 2022): comm. 384.

Jannet, C. "Les syndicats industriels pour régler la production en France." *La Réforme Sociale* (January 1895): 121–149.

Jaulin, A. "Marx lecteur d'Aristote." *Les Études Philosophiques* 1, no. 161 (2016): 105–122.

Jeandidier, W. "L'élément moral des infractions d'affaires ou l'art de la métamorphose." In *Une certaine idée du droit: Mélanges en l'honneur d'André Decocq*, 369–383. Paris: LITEC, 2004.

———. "L'élément matériel des infractions d'affaires ou la prédilection pour l'inconsistance." In *Mélanges offerts à Raymond Gassin: Sciences pénales & sciences criminologiques*, 245–263. Aix-en-Provence: PUAM, 2007.

Jenny, F. "Competition Law Enforcement: Is Economic Expertise Really Necessary?" In *International Antitrust Law & Policy: Fordham Corporate Law*, 185–201. Huntington: Juris Publishing, 1998.

Jenny, F., and J. Philippe. "Populisme et concurrence." *Concurrences*, no. 3-2018, art. no. 87447 (2018): 1–2.

Jescheck, H.-H. "The Doctrine of Mens Rea in German Criminal Law: Its Historical Background and Present State." *Comparative and International Law Journal of Southern Africa* 8, no. 1 (1975): 112–120.

Jimenez de Asua, J. "La faute consciente et le 'dolus eventualis'." *Revue de droit pénal et de criminologie* (1959–1960): 603–616.

João Melícias, M. "Use and Abuse of Intent Evidence in Antitrust Analysis." *World Competition* 33 (2010): 569–594.

Joliet, R. "Monopolisation et abus de position dominante: Essai comparatif sur l'article 2 du Sherman Act et l'article 86 du Traité de Rome." *RTD Eur.* (1969): 645–696.

———. "La notion de pratique concertée et l'arrêt ICI dans une perspective comparative." *Cahiers de droit européen* (1974): 251–287.

Jones, A. "Left Behind by Modernisation? Restrictions by Object under Article 101(1)." *European Competition Law Journal* 6, no. 3 (December 2010): 649–676.

Jourdain, P. "Droit à réparation – Responsabilité fondée sur la faute." *JurisClasseur Notarial*, fasc. 120-10 (October 2022).

Kadish, S. H. "Some Observations on the Use of Criminal Sanctions in Enforcing Economic Regulations." *University of Chicago Law Review* 30, no. 3 (Spring 1963): 423–449.

Kahn, L. "Amazon's Antitrust Paradox." *The Yale Law Journal* 126, no. 3 (January 2017): 710–805.

Kaplow, L. "Why (Ever) Define Markets?" *Harvard Law Review* 124, no. 2 (December 2010): 437–517.

Khairallah, G. "Le raisonnable en droit privé français." *RTD civ.* (1984): 439–467.

Kenny, A. "Intention and Purpose." *The Journal of Philosophy* 63 (1966): 642–651.

Kerber, W. "Should Competition Law Promote Efficiency? Some Reflections of an Economist on the Normative Foundations of Competition Law." In *Economic Theory and Competition Law*, edited by J. Drexl et al. ASCOLA Competition Law Series, 93–120. Cheltenham: Edward Elgar, 2009.

———. "Updating Competition Policy for the Digital Economy? An Analysis of Recent Reports in Germany, UK, EU, and Australia." (September 14, 2019). https://ssrn.com/abstract=3469624

Kipping, M. "Concurrence et compétitivité: Les origines de la législation anti-trust française après 1945." In *Études & documents*, vol. VI, 429–455. Paris: Comité pour l'histoire économique et financière de la France, 1994.

Kirat, T. "Économie et droit: De l'analyse économique du droit à de nouvelles alliances?" *Revue économique* 49, no. 4 (1998): 1057–1087.

Kirshner, J. "Les travaux de Raymond de Roover sur la pensée économique des scolastiques." *Annales* 30, no. 2–3 (March–June 1975): 318–338.

Kirzner, I. M. "Entrepreneurial Discovery and the Competitive Market Process: An Austrian Approach." *Journal of Economic Literature* 35, no. 1 (March 1997): 60–85.

Knetsch, J. "La place de la responsabilité civile sans faute dans le système de responsabilité civile. Étude de droit comparé." *Revue des contrats*, no. 4 (December 2019): 196–209.

Kojève, A. "La spécificité et l'autonomie du Droit." *Commentaire* 1980/1, no. 9 (1980): 122–130.

Komninos, A. P. "Intel: The ECJ Finally Speaks – Time to Listen." *Competition Law & Policy Debate* 4, no. 2 (June 2018): 42–50.

———. "The Consumer Welfare Standard: A 'Problem' to Fix in EU Competition Law?" In *The Transformation of EU Competition Law: Next Generation Issues*, edited by A. Claici, A. Komninos, and D. Waelbroeck, 199–212. Alphen-sur-le-Rhin: Kluwer Law International, 2023.

Kotsiris, L. "An Antitrust Case in Ancient Greek Law." *International Lawyer* 22 (1988): 451–456.

Kovar, R. "Le droit de la concurrence et la règle de raison." *Revue trimestrielle de droit européen*, no. 2 (1987): 237–254.

Kovar, J.-P., and R. Kovar. "L'objet anticoncurrentiel au sens de l'article 101, paragraphe 1, du TFUE: Un objet difficile à identifier." *Concurrences*, no. 1-2016, art. no. 77266 (2016): 48–60.

Koyré, A. "De l'influence des conceptions philosophiques sur l'évolution des théories scientifiques." In *Études d'histoire de la pensée philosophique*, 253–269. Tel. Paris: Gallimard, 1971.

Kuenzler, A., and L. Warlouzet. "National Traditions of Competition Law: A Belated Europeanization Through Convergence?" In *The Historical Foundations of EU Competition Law*, edited by K. K. Patel and H. Schweitzer, 89–124. Oxford: Oxford University Press, 2013.

Künzler, A. "Economic Content of Competition Law: The Point of Regulating Preferences." In *The Goals of Competition Law*, edited by D. Zimmer. Ascola Competition Law Series, 182–213. Cheltenham: Edward Elgar, 2012.

Lagarde, G. "Propos de commercialiste sur la personnalité morale: Réalité ou réalisme?" In *Études offertes à Alfred Jauffret*, 429–446. Aix-en-Provence: Faculté de droit et de science politique d'Aix-Marseille, 1974.

Laingui, A. "Le premier grand traité de responsabilité pénale: Le 'De Poenis Temperandis' d'André Tiraqueau (1559)." In *Mélanges en l'honneur du Doyen Pierre Bouzat*, 179–203. Paris: A. Pédone, 1980.

———. "L'Homme criminel dans l'Ancien Droit." *Revue de science criminelle et de droit pénal comparé*, no. 1 (January–March 1983): 15–35.

———. "Le droit pénal canonique, source de l'ancien droit pénal laïc." In *Églises et pouvoir politique: Actes des journées internationales d'histoire du droit d'Angers*, 213–232. Angers: Presses de l'Université d'Angers, 1987.

———. "P. F. Muyart de Vouglans ou l'anti-Beccaria (1713–1791)." *Archives de philosophie du droit* 39 (1995): 169–179. Theme: "Le procès."

Laingui, A., and M. Crépin. "La philosophie du droit pénal dans l'Antiquité grecque et romaine." *Revue internationale de droit pénal* 53 (1982): 597–611.

———. "La philosophie du droit pénal du Moyen Âge à l'époque moderne." *Revue internationale de droit pénal* 53 (1982): 613–626.

Lallement, J. "Popper et le principe de rationalité." *Économies et sociétés*, no. 10 (October 1987): 25–40.

Lalou, H. "La gamme des fautes." *Recueil Dalloz*, chron. V (1940): 17–20.

Lande, R. H., and R. O. Zerbe. "The Sherman Act is a No-Fault Monopolization Statute: A Textualist Demonstration." *American University Law Review* 70 (2020): 497–588.

Lao, M. "Reclaiming a Role for Intent Evidence in Monopolization Analysis." *American University Law Review* 54 (2004): 151–213.

———. "Aspen Skiing and Trinko: Antitrust Intent and 'Sacrifice.'" *Antitrust Law Journal* 73, no. 1 (2005): 171–208.

———. "Ideology Matters in the Antitrust Debate." *Antitrust Law Journal* 79, no. 2 (2014): 649–684.

———. "No-Fault Digital Platform Monopolization." *William & Mary Law Review* 61, no. 3 (2020): 755–814.

Larguier, J. "Mort et transfiguration du droit pénal." In *Aspects nouveaux de la pensée juridique: Recueil d'études en hommage à Marc Ancel*, vol. II, 123–150. Paris: A. Pédone, 1975.

Larouche, P., and A. de Streel. "The European Digital Markets Act: A Revolution Grounded on Tradition." *Journal of European Competition Law & Practice* 12, no. 7 (2021): 542–560.

Lasserre Capdeville, J. "Discriminations." *JurisClasseur Pénal Code*, fasc. 20 (December 2022).

Laugier, L. "La prohibition des abus de position dominante." *Gazette du Palais*, nos. 345–348 (December 11–14, 1965): 1–4.

Laurent, P. "L'entente: Une catégorie juridique ambivalente." *Recueil Dalloz-Sirey*, chron. XLIII (1977): 307–318.

Laval, C. "Jeremy Bentham et le gouvernement des intérêts." *Revue du Mauss* 1, no. 27 (2006): 289–306.

Le Pen, C. "'Falsifiabilité' et théorie économique, ou comment rendre une théorie économique infalsifiable." *Économies et sociétés*, no. 10 (October 1987): 119–128.

Le Tourneau, P. "La verdeur de la faute dans la responsabilité civile." *RTD civ.* (1988): 505–518.

———. "Les métamorphoses contemporaines et subreptices de la faute subjective." In *Les métamorphoses de la responsabilité: Sixièmes journées René Savatier*, 19–33. Paris: PUF, 1997.

Lebohec, J.-B. "La responsabilité est-elle incompatible avec le déterminisme?" *Archives de philosophie du droit* 63, no. 1 (2021): 83–103.

Lebret, J. "Essai sur la notion de l'intention criminelle." *Revue de science criminelle et de droit pénal comparé* (1938): 438–484.

Lecuyer, H. "Des effets à la cause: La présomption maltraitée." In *Études en l'honneur du professeur Marie-Laure Mathieu – Comprendre: Des mathématiques au droit*, 425–433. Brussels: Bruylant, 2019.

Leduc, F. "Retour sur les fautes de l'assuré faisant disparaître l'aléa." *Revue des contrats*, no. 3 (September 2020): 59–61.

Legal, A. "La responsabilité sans faute." In *La chambre criminelle et sa jurisprudence: Recueil d'études en hommage à la mémoire de Maurice Patin*, 130–152. Paris: Cujas, 1965.

———. "La responsabilité pénale du fait d'autrui dans son application au chef d'entreprise." In *Mélanges offerts à Jean Brethe de la Gressaye*, 477–491. Bordeaux: Éditions Bière, 1967.

Legeais, D. "Concurrence déloyale et parasitaire." *JurisClasseur Commercial*, fasc. 254 (August 2021).

Legeais, R. "Les réponses du droit anglais et du droit allemand aux problèmes de la responsabilité pénale des personnes morales." Proceedings of the symposium *La responsabilité pénale des personnes morales*, April 7, 1993. *Revue des sociétés* (1993): 371–379.

Legrand, P. "Questions à Rodolfo Sacco." *Revue internationale de droit comparé* 47, no. 4 (1995): 943–971.

Legros, R. "L'influence des lois particulières sur le droit pénal général." *Revue de science criminelle et de droit pénal comparé* (1968): 233–261.

———. "Imputation pénale et entreprise économique." *Revue de droit pénal et de criminologie*, no. 5–6 (February–March 1969): 365–385.

———. "L'arrêt BMW et le droit pénal européen." *Cahiers de droit européen* (1980): 206–239.

———. "La preuve légale en droit pénal." In *La preuve en droit*, edited by C. Perelman and P. Forier. Travaux du centre national de recherches de logique, 149–173. Brussels: Bruylant, 1981.

———. "Les notions à contenu variable en droit pénal." In *Les notions à contenu variable en droit*, edited by C. Perelman and R. Vander Elst. Travaux du centre national de recherches logiques, 21–37. Brussels: Bruylant, 1984.

———. "Une lecture pénale de Grotius." *Bulletin de la classe des lettres et des sciences morales et politiques* 73 (1987): 424–457.

Leroy, G. "Vers une exposition raisonnée de l'argument conséquentialiste dans la motivation des arrêts de la Cour de cassation?" *Les Cahiers Portalis* 2020/1, no. 9 (2020): 181–190.

Levasseur, G. "Les personnes morales victimes, auteurs ou complices d'infractions en droit français." *Revue de droit pénal et de criminologie* (1954–1955): 827–847.

———. "Les sanctions dans le traité constitutif du Marché Commun." In *Les problèmes juridiques et économiques du Marché Commun*, edited by H. Batiffol et al., 95–119. Paris: Librairies techniques, 1960.

———. "Étude de l'élément moral de l'infraction." In *Annales de la faculté de droit et de sciences économiques de Toulouse*. Tome XVII, fasc. 1, Travaux du colloque de sciences criminelles (30–31 janvier, 1er février 1969): "Confrontation de la théorie générale de la responsabilité pénale avec les données de la criminologie," 81–97. Toulouse, 1969.

———. "L'imputabilité des infractions en droit français." *Revue de droit pénal et de criminologie*, no. 5–6 (February–March 1969): 387–408.

———. "Le droit de la preuve en droit pénal français." In *La preuve en droit*, edited by C. Perelman and P. Forier. Travaux du centre national de recherches de logique, 175–195. Brussels: Bruylant, 1981.

———. "Homicide volontaire: Animus necandi." *Revue de science criminelle et de droit pénal comparé* (1992): 73.

Lévêque, F. "Quel test de preuve pour l'article 82?" *Revue Lamy de la concurrence*, no. 11 (April 2007): 111.

Lévy-Bruhl, H. "Le point de vue de l'historien du droit." In *Annales de la faculté de droit et de sciences politiques et économiques de Strasbourg*. Tome VIII, Travaux du colloque de philosophie pénale (12–21 janvier 1959): "La responsabilité pénale," 35–48. Strasbourg, 1961.

Lianos, I. "Some Reflections on the Question of the Goals of EU Competition Law." *CLES Working Paper Series* 3/2013 (January 2013).

———. "Polycentric Competition Law." *CLES Research Papers Series* 4/2018 (September 2018).

Libchaber, R. "Le juriste et ses objets: Trois exemples de construction en droit privé." *Enquête* no. 7 (1999). http://enquete.revues.org/1583

———. "Réalité ou fiction? Une nouvelle querelle de la personnalité est pour demain." *RTD civ.* (2003): 166.

Lindeboom, J. "Formalism in Competition Law.", 18 *Journal of Competition Law & Economics* 832 (2022).

Lizée, M. "De la capacité organique et des responsabilités délictuelle et pénale des personnes morales." *McGill Law Journal* 41 (December 1995): 131–168.

Loiseau, G. "Les responsabilités du fait de l'intelligence artificielle." *Communication Commerce électronique*, no. 4 (April 2019): comm. 24.

Lorenzoni, I. "An 'AI Whistle-Blower' to Monitor Algorithmic Infringements?" *The Competition Law Review* 15, no. 1 (January 2023): 31–49.

Lottin, O. "La preuve de la liberté humaine chez saint Thomas d'Aquin." *Recherches de théologie ancienne et médiévale* 23 (July–December 1956): 323–330.

Louis-Lucas, P. "Vérité matérielle et vérité juridique." In *Mélanges offerts à René Savatier*, 583–601. Paris: Dalloz, 1965.

Lovdahl Gormsen, L. "Why the European Commission's Enforcement Priorities on Article 82 EC Should Be Withdrawn." (2010). https://ssrn.com/abstract=2400402

Luc, I. "La responsabilité pénale des personnes morales en droit de la concurrence." In *Dépénalisation de la vie des affaires et responsabilité pénale des personnes morales*, edited by M. Benillouche and M. Daury-Fauveau. CEPRISCA, 119–132. Paris: PUF, 2009.

Lucas de Leyssac, C., and M.-P. Lucas de Leyssac. "L'inquiétant article L. 420-6 du Code de commerce et comment se rassurer." In *Les droits et le Droit: Mélanges dédiés à Bernard Bouloc*, 651–680. Paris: Dalloz, 2006.

Mackaay, E. "La règle juridique observée par le prisme de l'économiste: Une histoire stylisée du mouvement de l'analyse économique du droit." *Revue internationale de droit économique* (1987): 43–88.

Maddalon, P. "Les utilisations des faits économiques dans le droit de l'Union européenne." In *Les utilisations des faits économiques dans le droit*

de l'Union européenne, edited by P. Maddalon. Cahiers européens, no. 3, 7–18. Paris: éd. Pedone, 2012.

Maier-Rigaud, F. "On the Normative Foundations of Competition Law – Efficiency, Political Freedom and the Freedom to Compete." In *The Goals of Competition Law*, edited by D. Zimmer. Ascola Competition Law Series, 132–168. Cheltenham: Edward Elgar, 2012.

Maistre du Chambon, P., and P. Conte. "Préface." In *Analyse économique du droit et matière pénale*, edited by C. Claverie Rousset, XIII–XVII. Paris: LexisNexis, 2018.

Malabat, V. "À la recherche du sens du droit pénal du harcèlement." *Droit social* (2003): 491.

———. "L'incrimination générale de faux." *Répertoire de droit pénal et de procédure pénale* (February 2017).

———. "Le droit pénal a-t-il encore une utilité?" In *Analyse économique du droit et matière pénale*, edited by C. Claverie Rousset, pref. P. Maistre du Chambon and P. Conte, 91–102. Paris: LexisNexis, 2018.

Malaurie, P. "Le droit et l'esprit: Dernière leçon." *Commentaire* 1994/3, no. 67 (1994): 609–612.

Malaurie-Vignal, M. "Logique économique et logique juridique." *Contrats concurrence consommation*, no. 11 (November 2005): étude 20.

———. "La Cour de cassation distingue l'action en concurrence déloyale et l'action en concurrence parasitaire." *Contrats concurrence consommation*, no. 6 (June 2014): comm. 127.

———. "Droit, économie et politique de concurrence: Réflexions à partir de la notion de bien-être du consommateur." *JCP E*, no. 15–16 (April 12, 2018): étude 1187, 28–33.

———. "La loyauté, l'égalité et l'équité en droit de la concurrence." *Contrats concurrence consommation*, no. 2 (February 2021): repère 2.

———. "Algorithmes et concurrence." *Contrats concurrence consommation*, no. 6 (June 2021): étude 6.

———. "Le droit de la concurrence, les données personnelles et le bien-être du consommateur: Réflexion sur l'articulation entre deux droits spéciaux." *Contrats concurrence consommation*, no. 7 (July 2021): repère 7.

Malaurie-Vignal, M., D. Heintz, and M. Lecole. "Comment appréhender les abus et l'utilisation des données dans la relation d'une plateforme avec ses partenaires contractuels?" *Contrats concurrence consommation*, no. 12 (December 2020): dossier 16.

Marenco, G. "La notion de restriction de concurrence dans le cadre de l'interdiction des ententes." In *Mélanges en hommage à Michel Waelbroeck*, vol. II. Études de droit européen et international, 1217–1245. Brussels: Bruylant, 1999.

Maréchal, J.-Y. "Plaidoyer pour une responsabilité pénale directe des personnes morales." *JCP G*, no. 38 (September 14, 2009): étude 249, 46–52.

———. "Élément moral de l'infraction." *JurisClasseur Pénal Code*, fasc. 20 (November 2022).

Markovits, R. S. "Some Preliminary Notes on the American Antitrust Law's Economic Tests of Legality." *Stanford Law Review* 27, no. 3 (February 1975): 841–858.

Marquis, M. "O2 (Germany) v Commission and the Exotic Mysteries of Article 81(1) EC." *European Law Review* 32 (2007): 29–47.

Marsden, P. "Some Outstanding Issues From the European Commission's Guidance on Article 102 TFEU: Not-So-Faint Echoes of Ordoliberalism." In *Competition Law and the Enforcement of Article 102*, edited by F. Etro and I. Kokkoris, 53–72. Oxford: Oxford University Press, 2010.

Marsden, P., and P. Whelan. "'Consumer Detriment' and Its Application in EC and UK Competition Law." *European Competition Law Review* 27, no. 10 (2006): 569–585.

Martin, X. "Du temps des Lumières à 1810: Anthropologie et droit criminel." In *Bicentenaire du Code pénal – 1810–2010*, 65–82. Paris: Les colloques du Sénat, 2010.

Marty, F. "Le critère du bien-être du consommateur comme objectif exclusif de la politique de concurrence. Une mise en perspective sur la base de l'histoire de l'antitrust américain." *Revue internationale de droit économique* XXVIII, no. 4 (2014): 471–497.

———. "Algorithmes de prix, intelligence artificielle et équilibres collusifs." *Revue internationale de droit économique* XXXI, no. 2 (2017): 83–116.

———. "Algorithmes de prix et discrimination parfaite: Une théorie concurrentielle en voie de trouver sa pratique?" *Science Po OFCE Working Paper*, no. 31 (December 2017).

———. "Plateformes numériques, algorithmes et discrimination." *Revue de l'OFCE*, no. 164 (2019): 1–40.

———. "L'approche plus économique en matière d'application des règles de concurrence." *GREDEG Working Papers Series*, no. 2020-16.

Marty, J.-P. "Les délits matériels." *Revue de science criminelle et de droit pénal comparé* (1982): 41–64.

Marty, F., S. Harnay, and J. Toledano. "Algorithmes et décision concurrentielle: Risques et opportunités." *Revue d'économie industrielle* 2019/2, no. 166 (2019): 91–118.

Marty, F., and J. Pillot. "Des critères de l'application de la théorie des facilités essentielles dans le cadre de la politique de concurrence européenne." *Reflets et perspectives de la vie économique* 2011/4, tome L (2011): 197–221.

Mathey, N. "Les finalités du droit de la concurrence: Essai de téléologie du droit." *Contrats concurrence consommation*, no. 12 (December 2020): dossier 13.

Matsopoulou, H. "Extension de l'imputabilité des personnes morales." In *Dix ans après la réforme de 1994: Quels repères dans le Code pénal*, edited by M. Danti-Juan. Travaux de l'Institut de sciences criminelles de Poitiers, vol. XXIV, 67–86. Paris: Cujas, 2005.

Maulin, R. "L'approche par les effets en droit de la concurrence: Le devoir d'inventaire." *Concurrences*, no. 3-2015, art. no. 73845 (2015): 24–39.

Mauss, M. "La religion et les origines du droit pénal d'après un livre récent." *Revue d'histoire des religions*, no. 34 (1896): 269–295.

Mayaud, Y. "La volonté à la lumière du nouveau Code pénal." In *Mélanges en l'honneur du professeur Jean Larguier: Droit pénal, procédure pénale*, 203–2018. Grenoble: Presses Universitaires de Grenoble, 1993.

———. "De l'article 121-3 du Code pénal à la théorie de la culpabilité en matière criminelle et délictuelle." *Recueil Dalloz* (1997): 37.

———. "L'intention dans la théorie du droit pénal." *Problèmes actuels de science criminelle* XII (1999): 57–66.

———. "Entre le dit et le non-dit, ou les leçons de droit pénal du Conseil constitutionnel." *Recueil Dalloz* (1999): 589.

———. "Retour sur la culpabilité non intentionnelle en droit pénal… (À propos de la loi no. 2000-647 du 10 juillet 2000)." *Recueil Dalloz* (2000): 603.

———. "Les délits non intentionnels en matière pénale." *Revue de droit sanitaire et social* (2008): 49.

———. "L'articulation des responsabilités pénales entre personne morale et personnes physiques – Une logique d'artifices…" *Actualité juridique Pénal* (2018): 546

Mayaux, L. "Faute intentionnelle, dolosive… ou frauduleuse: L'art d'ajouter du flou au flou." *Revue générale du droit des assurances*, no. 3 (March 2014): 147.

Mayer, D. "La notion de substance mortelle en matière d'empoisonnement." *Recueil Dalloz* (1994): 325.

Mayras, H. "La théorie de l'effet dans le droit des ententes." *Jus Gentium: Diritto delle relazioni internazionali* IX, no. 2 (April 1973): 41–61.

Mazeaud, D. "Pour que survive la cause, en dépit de la réforme." *Revue Droit & Patrimoine*, no. 240 (October 2014): 38–40.

Mazeaud, H. "Discussion du Rapport de M. Ancel sur la responsabilité sans faute." *Travaux de l'Association Henri Capitant* (1946): 76–77.

Mazeaud, P. "Vœux du président du Conseil constitutionnel, M. Pierre Mazeaud, au Président de la République." *Cahiers du Conseil constitutionnel*, no. 18 (July 2005).

Meij, A., and T. Baumé. "Balancing Object and Effect Analysis in Identifying Abuses of a Dominant Position under Article 102 TFEU." In *Ten Years of Effects-Based Approach in EU Competition Law: State of Play and Perspectives*, edited by J. Bourgeois and D. Waelbroeck. GCLC Annual Conference Series, 159–183. Brussels: Bruylant, 2012.

Melícias, M. J. "Did They Do It: The Interplay Between the Standard of Proof and the Presumption of Innocence in EU Cartel Investigations." *World Competition* 35, no. 2 (September 2012): 471–510.

Mercadal, B. "Recherches sur l'intention en droit pénal." *Revue de science criminelle et de droit pénal comparé* (January–March 1967): 1–47.

———. "Éthique financière." In *L'éthique des marchés financiers*, edited by J.-V. Louis and D. Devos. Études européennes series, 23–37. Brussels: Éditions de l'Université de Bruxelles, 1996.

Merle, R. "La culpabilité devant les sciences humaines et sociales." *Revue de science criminelle et de droit pénal comparé* (1976): 29–37.

Mestmäcker, E.-J. "The EC Commission's Modernization of Competition Policy: A Challenge to the Community's Constitutional Order." *European Business Organization Law Review* 1, no. 3 (September 2000): 401–444.

Metz. "La responsabilité pénale dans le droit canonique médiéval." In *Annales de la faculté de droit et de sciences politiques et économiques de Strasbourg*. Tome VIII, Travaux du colloque de philosophie pénale (12–21 janvier 1959): "La responsabilité pénale," 83–116. Strasbourg, 1961.

Michoud, L. "La notion de personnalité morale." *Revue du droit public et de la science politique en France et à l'étranger* (1899): 193–228.

Migeotte, L. "Le contrôle des prix dans les cités grecques." In *Économie antique: Prix et formation des prix dans les économies antiques*, edited by J. Andreau et al. Entretiens d'archéologie et d'histoire, tome 3, 33–52. Saint-Bertrand-de-Comminges: Musée archéologique départemental, 1997.

Mimin, P. "Les présomptions quasi-légales." *JCP G*, I, Doctrine, doctr. 578 (1946): 43–45.

———. "L'intention et le mobile." In *La chambre criminelle et sa jurisprudence: Recueil d'études en hommage à la mémoire de Maurice Patin*, 114–128. Paris: Cujas, 1965.

Mises, L. "Du caractère atavique de quelques idées économiques." In *Les fondements philosophiques des systèmes économiques*, texts by Jacques Rueff and essays written in his honor, 317–319. Bibliothèque économique et politique. Paris: Payot, 1966.

Mistretta, P. "Harcèlement." *Répertoire de droit pénal et de procédure pénale* (April 2022).

Moine-Dupuis, I. "L'intention en droit pénal: Une notion introuvable?" *Recueil Dalloz* (2001): 2144.

Monaco, R. "Les principes d'interprétation suivis par la Cour de justice des communautés européennes." In *Mélanges offerts à Henri Rolin: Problèmes de droit des gens*, 217–227. Paris: A. Pédone, 1964.

Mongin, P. "L'instrumentalisme dans l'Essai de M. Friedman." *Économies et sociétés*, no. 10 (October 1987): 73–106.

Mongouachon, C. "L'ordolibéralisme: Contexte historique et contenu dogmatique." *Concurrences*, no. 4-2011, art. no. 38770 (2011): 70–78.

———. "Le droit européen de la concurrence face à ses finalités: Un débat philosophique." *Revue de la recherche juridique: Droit prospectif* 2017-5 (2017): 1945–1965.

Mongouachon, C., and L. Zenouvou. "La place du Parlement européen dans le modèle institutionnel de concurrence de l'Union européenne." *Concurrences*, no. 3-2018, art. no. 87566 (2018): 67–77.

Montesquieu. "Des lois dans le rapport qu'elles ont avec la nature du climat." In *De l'esprit des lois*, tome II, 33–61. Paris: Dabo, 1824.

Moreau, J. "Aristote et la monnaie." *Revue des Études Grecques* 82, fasc. 391–393 (July–December 1969): 349–364.

Morin, A. "De l'étude des racines chrétiennes des droits pénaux français, britannique et canadien." *Revue générale de droit* 32, no. 2 (2002): 213–304.

Morvan, P. "La personne morale maltraitée par le droit pénal." In *Code pénal et Code d'instruction criminelle – Livre du bicentenaire*, 171–183. Études, mélanges, travaux. Paris: Dalloz, 2010.

Nazzini, R. "Article 81 EC Between Time Present and Time Past: A Normative Critique of Restriction of Competition in E U Law." *Common Market Law Review* 43, no. 2 (April 2006): 497–536.

Nussenbaum, M. "Trading haute fréquence: Efficience des marchés ou manipulation de cours? Les sanctions récentes." In *Mélanges en l'honneur de Jean-Jacques Daigre: Autour du droit bancaire et financier et au-delà*, 593–604. Paris: Joly Éditions, 2017.

Nuvolone, P. "La conception juridique italienne de la culpabilité." *Annales de l'Université de sciences sociales de Toulouse* XXIV, fasc. 1–2 (1976): 59–71.

———. "Lombroso et le droit pénal." *Revue de science criminelle et de droit pénal comparé* (1977): 291–301.

O'Donoghue. "What Makes a Unilateral Conduct Abusive: The Legal Perspective." In *The Notion of Restriction of Competition: Revisiting the Foundations of Antitrust Enforcement in Europe*, edited by D. Gerard, M. Merola, and B. Meyring. GCLC Annual Conference Series, 169–238. Brussels: Bruylant, 2017.

O'Grady, C. "The Role of Exclusionary Intent in the Enforcement of Article 102." *World Competition* 37, no. 4 (2014): 459–486.

Odudu, O. "Interpreting Article 81(1): Object as Subjective Intention." *European Law Review* 26 (2001): 62–75.

———. "Interpreting Article 81(1): The Object Requirement Revisited." *European Law Review* 26, no. 4 (2001): 379–390.

———. "The Role of Specific Intent in Section 1 of the Sherman Act: A Market Power Test?" *World Competition* 25, no. 4 (2002): 463–491.

———. "Restrictions of Competition by Object – What's the Beef?" *Competition Law Journal* 8, no. 1 (2009): 11–17.

Odudu, O., and D. Bailey. "Single Economic Entity Doctrine in EU Competition Law." *Common Market Law Review* 51, no. 6 (December 2014): 1721–1758.

Oehler, D. "La conception juridique allemande de la culpabilité." In *Annales de l'Université de sciences sociales de Toulouse*, tome XXIV, fasc. 1–2, 73–84. Toulouse, 1976.

Olbrechts, F. "The Concept of Restriction of Competition 'By Object': An Endless Debate." *Competition Forum*, no. 0011 (2021).

Ollard, R. "Essai sur l'élément qualifiant de l'infraction." In *Mélanges en l'honneur du Professeur Philippe Conte*, 605–621. Paris: LexisNexis, 2023.

Oppetit, B. "La liberté contractuelle à l'épreuve du droit de la concurrence." *Revue des sciences morales et politiques* (1995): 241–254.

———. "Le consentement sans l'échange: Le concours des consentements, le concours implicite." *Revue de jurisprudence commerciale*, Special Issue: "L'échange des consentements," no. 11 (November 1995): 69–73.

Orbach, B. "The Antitrust Consumer Welfare Paradox." *Journal of Competition Law & Economics* 7, no. 1 (2011): 133–164.

———. "How Antitrust Lost Its Goals." *Fordham Law Review* 81, no. 5, art. 6 (2013): 2253–2277.

Ottenhof, R. "Imputabilité, culpabilité et responsabilité en droit pénal." *Archives de politique criminelle*, no. 22 (2000): 71–83.

Pace, L. F., and K. Seidel. "Drafting and the Role of Regulation 17: A Hard-Fought Compromise." In *The Historical Foundations of EU Competition Law*, edited by K. K. Patel and H. Schweitzer, 54–88. Oxford: Oxford University Press, 2013.

Pageaud, P.-A. "La notion d'intention en droit pénal." *JCP G*, I, doctr. 876 (1950): 35–40.

Paillusseau, J. "Les apports du droit de l'entreprise au concept de droit." In *Colloque du 25ᵉ anniversaire de la FNDE. JCP E*, suppl. 2 (1997): 3–11.

Panebianco, G. "The Nulla Poena Sine Culpa Principle in European Courts Case Law: The Perspective of the Italian Criminal Law." In *Human Rights in European Criminal Law: New Developments in European*

Legislation and Case Law After the Lisbon Treaty, edited by S. Ruggeri, 47–78. New York: Springer, 2015.

Parain-Vial, J. "La nature du concept juridique et la logique." *Archives de philosophie du droit*, no. 11: "La logique du droit" (1966): 45–57.

Parcu, P. L. "Considerazioni sulla rilevanza del movente nella valutazione delle violazioni antitrust." In *Antitrust Between E U Law & National Law*, vol. IX, edited by E. A. Raffaelli, 341–383. Bruxelles/Milan: Bruylant/ Giuffrè, 2011.

Parcu, P. L., and M. L. Stasi. "The Role of Intent in the Assessment of Conduct under Article 102 TFEU." In *Abuse of Dominance in EU Competition Law: Emerging Trends*, edited by P. L. Parcu et al., 12–33. Cheltenham: Edward Elgar, 2017.

Parent, H. "Histoire de l'acte volontaire en droit pénal anglais et canadien." *McGill Law Journal* 45, no. 4 (2000): 975–1020.

———. "L'imputabilité pénale. Mort d'un mythe, naissance d'une réalité." *Revue juridique Thémis* 35 (2001): 191–239.

Parker, J. S. "The Economics of Mens Rea." *Virginia Law Review* 79, no. 4 (May 1993): 741–811.

Patel, K. K., and H. Schweitzer. "Introduction." In *The Historical Foundation of EU Competition Law*, edited by K. K. Patel and H. Schweitzer, 1–18. Oxford: Oxford University Press, 2013.

Patin, M. Note under Cass., crim., December 13, 1956, no. 55-05.772. *Recueil Dalloz*, II, Jurisprudence (1957): 349–350.

Paynot-Rouvillois, A. "Personne morale et volonté." *Droits: Revue française de théorie juridique*, no. 28 (1999): 17–28.

Peltier, V. "L'élément moral de la contrefaçon de marque." *Propriété industrielle*, no. 4 (April 2017): étude 12.

Peeperkorn, L. "Defining 'By Object' Restrictions." *Concurrences*, no. 3-2015, art. no. 74812 (2015): 40–50.

———. "Conditional Pricing and the AEC Test – A Happy Marriage or an Awkward Couple?" *Concurrences*, no. 2-2019, art. no. 90191 (2019): 40–53.

Percerou, J. "Des syndicats de producteurs: Essai sur leur fonctionnement et leur forme juridique." *Annales de droit commercial* (1897): 271–299.

Perelman, C. "Présomptions et fictions en droit, essai de synthèse." In *Les présomptions et les fictions en droit*, edited by C. Perelman and P. Foriers. Travaux du centre national de recherches de logique, 339–348. Brussels: Bruylant, 1974.

———. "La preuve en droit: Essai de synthèse." In *La preuve en droit*, edited by C. Perelman and P. Forier. Travaux du centre national de recherches logiques, 357–364. Brussels: Bruylant, 1981.

Perrier, J.-B. "La distinction culpabilité/imputabilité." In *Faut-il rethéoriser le droit pénal*, edited by J. Leroy, 69–80. Paris: LexisNexis, 2017.

Perrier, J.-B., and S. Cimamonti. "Perspectives européennes: L'avenir de la justice pénale de l'Union européenne." *Les nouveaux problèmes actuels de sciences criminelles* XXIV (2013): 139–162.

Perrier, J.-B., and J.-C. Roda. "Droit pénal et droit de la concurrence." In *Le droit pénal et l'éthique des affaires: Actes du colloque du 18 mars 2016*, edited by J.-B. Perrier, 127–146. Clermont-Ferrand: Centre Michel de l'Hospital, 2018.

Perrin, B. "Le caractère subjectif de la répression pénale dans les XII Tables." *Revue historique de droit français et étranger* 28 (1951): 383–405.

Pescatore, P. "Les objectifs de la Communauté européenne comme principes d'interprétation dans la jurisprudence de la Cour de Justice: Contribution à la doctrine de l'interprétation téléologique des traités internationaux." In *Miscellanea W. J. Ganshof van der Meersch: Studia ab discipulis amicisque in honorem egregii professoris edita*, tome II, 325–363. Brussels: Bruylant, 1972.

———. "Le recours, dans la jurisprudence de la Cour de justice des communautés européennes, à des normes déduites de la comparaison des droits des États membres." *Revue internationale de droit comparé* (1980): 337–359.

Petit, N. "The Guidelines on the Application of Article 81(3) EC: A Critical Review." *IEJE Working Paper*, no. 4/2009. https://ssrn.com/abstract=1428558

———. "From Formalism to Effects: The Commission's Communication on Enforcement Priorities in Applying Article 82 EC." *World Competition* 32, no. 4 (December 2009): 485–504.

———. "La rationalisation au long cours de la restriction de concurrence par 'objet' dans la jurisprudence de la Cour de justice de l'Union européenne." *AJ Contrats d'affaires – Concurrence – Distribution* (2015): 422.

———. "Antitrust and Artificial Intelligence: A Research Agenda." *Journal of European Competition Law & Practice* 8, no. 6 (2017): 361–362.

———. "The Proposed Digital Markets Act (DMA): A Legal and Policy Review." *Journal of European Competition Law & Practice* 12, no. 7 (2021): 529–541.

———. "Understanding Market Power." *Robert Schuman Centre for Advanced Studies Working Paper*, 2022/14. [URL incomplete in source]

———. "Épistémologie du droit de la concurrence." In *Laurence Idot: Concurrence et Europe – Liber Amicorum*, vol. I, edited by C. Lemaire and F. Martucci, 557–567. Paris: Concurrences, 2022.

Petit, N., and A. Ittoo. "Algorithmic Pricing Agents and Tacit Collusion: A Technological Perspective." In *L'intelligence artificielle et le droit*, edited by H. Jacquemin and A. de Streel, 241–256. Brussels: Larcier, 2017.

Petit, N., and T. Schrepel. "Complexity-Minded Antitrust." (June 29, 2022). https://ssrn.com/abstract=4050536

Pfister, L. "Contrat, libre concurrence et ordre public: La sanction des ententes dans la jurisprudence française du XIXe siècle." *Revue des contrats*, no. 2 (April 2012): 349.

Picard, E. "'Science du droit' ou 'doctrine juridique.'" In *L'unité du droit: Mélanges en hommage à Roland Drago*, 119–171. Paris: Economica, 1996.

Picod, F. "Droit du marché et droit commun des obligations: Rapport introductif." *RTD com.* (1998): 1.

Picod, Y. "Concurrence déloyale et parasitisme: L'indifférence de la nature intentionnelle de la faute." *Concurrences*, no. 1-2016, art. no. 77744 (February 2016): 1–3.

Picod, Y., and N. Dorandeu. "Concurrence déloyale." *Répertoire de droit commercial* (April 2022).

Pierre, P. "La place de la responsabilité objective: Notion et rôle de la faute en droit français." *Revue Juridique de l'Ouest*, no. 4 (2010): 403–423.

Pieth, M., and R. Ivory. "Emergence and Convergence: Corporate Criminal Liability Principles in Overview." In *Corporate Criminal Liability: Emergence, Convergence and Risks*, edited by M. Pieth and R. Ivory. Ius Gentium, vol. 9, 3–60. New York: Springer, 2011.

Pin, X. "La non-intention est-elle vraiment l'exception?" In *Le nouveau Code pénal, 20 ans après: État des questions*, edited by L. Saenko, 79–93. Paris: LGDJ, 2014.

Pinatel, J. "Responsabilité et criminologie." In *Annales de la faculté de droit et de sciences politiques et économiques de Strasbourg*, tome VIII, Travaux du colloque de philosophie pénale (12–21 janvier 1959): "La responsabilité pénale," 159–202. Strasbourg: Faculté de droit de Strasbourg, 1961.

———. "L'apport de l'ethnographie à la criminologie et au droit pénal." *Revue de science criminelle et de droit pénal comparé* XXI (January–March 1966): 646–653.

———. "La théorie pénale de l'intention devant les sciences de l'homme." In *L'évolution du droit criminel contemporain: Recueil d'études à la mémoire de Jean Lebret*, 181–191. Paris: PUF, 1968.

Pirenne-Delforge, V., and G. Pironti. "Les Moires entre la naissance et la mort: De la représentation au culte." *Études de lettres*, no. 3–4 (2011): 93–114.

Piron, S. "Marchands et confesseurs. Le Traité des contrats d'Olivi dans son contexte." In *L'argent au Moyen Âge*, 289–308. Série Histoire ancienne et médiévale. Paris: Publications de la Sorbonne, 1998.

Pirovano, A. "La concurrence déloyale en droit français." *Revue internationale de droit comparé* 26, no. 3 (July–September 1974): 467–504.

———. “Progrès économique ou progrès social (ou les contradictions du droit de la concurrence).” *Recueil Dalloz-Sirey*, chron. XXII (1980): 145–156.

———. “Justice étatique, support de l’activité économique – Un exemple: La régulation de l’ordre concurrentiel.” *Justices: Revue générale de droit processuel*, no. 1 (January–June 1995): 15–33.

Planiol, M. “Dol civil et dol criminel.” *Revue critique de législation et de jurisprudence* XX (1893): 545–616 and 643–663.

Platel, B., and T. Viala. “Le fabuleux destin du concept de harcèlement moral.” *JCP E*, no. 20 (May 16, 2002): 762.

Plato. “La République.” In *Œuvres de Platon*, translated by V. Cousin, tome X, 234–295. Paris: Pichon et Didier.

———. “Lois.” In *Platon: Œuvres complètes*, edited and translated by L. Brisson, 903–907. Paris: Flammarion, 2008.

Podszun, R. “Competition in the Digital Economy: What’s Next After the Digital Markets Act? Statement for the Economic Committee of the German Parliament (Bundestag).” (May 5, 2022). https://ssrn.com/abstract=4096357

———. “From Competition Law to Platform Regulation – Regulatory Choices for the Digital Markets Act.” *Economics* 17, no. 1 (2023).

Poirier, J. “Les caractères de la responsabilité archaïque.” In *Annales de la faculté de droit et de sciences politiques et économiques de Strasbourg*, tome VIII, Travaux du colloque de philosophie pénale (12–21 janvier 1959): “La responsabilité pénale,” 19–34. Strasbourg, 1961.

Polanyi, K. “Aristotle Discovers the Economy.” In *Trade and Markets in the Early Empires*, edited by K. Polanyi, C. M. Arensberg, and H. W. Pearson, 64–94. Glencoe: The Free Press, 1957.

Portuese, A. “Principle of Proportionality as Principle of Economic Efficiency.” *European Law Journal* 19, no. 5 (2013): 612–635.

Posner, R. A. “Utilitarianism, Economics, and Legal Theory.” *Journal of Legal Studies* 8, no. 1 (January 1979): 103–140.

———. “An Economic Theory of the Criminal Law.” *Columbia Law Review* 85, no. 6 (October 1985): 1193–1231.

———. “The Decline of Law as an Autonomous Discipline: 1962–1987.” *Harvard Law Review* 100 (1987): 761–780.

———. “Law and Economics is Moral.” *Valparaiso University Law Review* 24 (1990): 163–173.

Pouch, T. “La science économique sous le regard de Husserl.” *L’homme & la Société* 175, no. 1 (2010): 165–196.

Poullet, Y. “À propos de Free Will, Causality and Neuroscience.” *Archives de philosophie du droit* 62, no. 1 (2020): 565–572.

Pradel, J. "Les sanctions en matière de délinquance économique." In *The Sanctions in the Field of Economic Criminal Law*, 85–97. Bonn: International Penal and Penitentiary Foundation, 1984.

———. "Le défaut de prévoyance en droit pénal français." *Revue de droit pénal et de criminologie* (March–April 1994): 435–448.

———. "La responsabilité pénale en droit français depuis le Code pénal de 1994: Permanence ou changements?" In *Les métamorphoses de la responsabilité: Sixièmes journées René Savatier*, 155–176. Paris: PUF, 1997.

———. "La responsabilité des personnes morales en droit pénal comparé." In *Strafjustiz und Rechtsstaat: Justice pénale et État de droit*, edited by M. A. Niggli and N. Queloz, 49–68. Zurich: Schulthess, 2003.

———. "Les grandes tendances de l'européanisation des systèmes pénaux nationaux." *Les Cahiers de droit* 50, no. 3–4 (September–December 2009): 1015–1038.

Pralus, M. "Réflexions autour de l'élément moral des délits." *Droit pénal*, no. 12 (December 2002): chron. 41.

Prieto, C. "Domat et la mémoire du droit." In *Le droit dans le souvenir: Liber amicorum Benoît Savelli*, 119–135. Aix-en-Provence: PUAM, 1998.

———. "La généralisation de l'analyse fondée sur les effets." *Petites affiches*, no. 239 (November 29, 2007): 8.

———. "La sécurité juridique dans le droit de la concurrence." In *Sécurité juridique et droit économique*, edited by L. Boy, J.-B. Racine, and F. Siiriainen. Droit, Économie, International, 299–331. Brussels: Larcier, 2010.

———. "Loyauté du commerce et droit européen de la concurrence." *Revue des affaires européennes* 2011/2 (2011): 299–312.

———. "Les mérites étouffés des concurrents de Google ou l'abus par algorithme." *RTD Eur.* (2017): 429.

———. "Ententes: Restriction de concurrence." *JurisClasseur Europe Traité*, fasc. 1410 (October 2017).

———. "Abus de position dominante – Notion d'abus en droit communautaire." *JurisClasseur Concurrence – Consommation*, fasc. 561 (February 2018).

———. "Ententes: Concours de volontés." *JurisClasseur Europe Traité*, fasc. 1405 (October 2017).

———. "Numérique et abus de position dominante." *Cahiers de droit de l'entreprise*, no. 3 (May 2019): dossier 18.

———. "Source économique du droit de la concurrence: Quelle efficacité?" *Contrats concurrence consommation*, no. 6 (June 2020): dossier 3.

Prieto, C., and E. Putman. "Typologie matérielle et formelle des formulations d'objectifs dans les textes législatifs." *Revue de la recherche juridique: Droit prospectif* 1989-4 (1989): 879–893.

Prorok, J. "L'amende civile dans la réforme de la responsabilité civile: Regard critique sur la consécration d'une fonction punitive générale." *RTD civ.* (2018): 327.

Prothais, A. "Plaidoyer pour le maintien de l'incrimination spéciale de l'empoisonnement." *Recueil Dalloz-Sirey*, chron. XVIII (1982): 107–110.

Puech, M. "Scolies sur la faute pénale." *Droits: Revue française de théorie juridique*, no. 5 (1987): 77–86.

———. "De la mise en danger d'autrui." *Recueil Dalloz* (1994): 153.

Quinn, M. C. "Predatory Pricing Strategies: The Relevance of Intent Under Antitrust, Unfair Competition, and Tort Law." *St. John's Law Review* 64, no. 3 (Spring–Summer 1990): 607–628.

Rade, C. "L'impossible divorce de la faute et de la responsabilité civile." *Recueil Dalloz* (1998): 301–305.

Radulesco, J. "La responsabilité pénale des personnes morales." *Revue internationale de droit pénal*, no. 1 (1929): 286–306.

Rahl, J. A. "Symposium on 'Price Competition and Antitrust Policy': Price Competition and the Price Fixing Rule – Preface and Perspective." *Northwestern University Law Review* 57, no. 2 (May–June 1962): 137–150.

Ramírez Pérez, S. M., and S. Van de Scheur. "The Evolution of the Law on Articles 85 and 86 EEC [Articles 101 and 102 TFEU], Ordoliberalism and Its Keynesian Challenge." In *The Historical Foundation of EU Competition Law*, edited by K. K. Patel and H. Schweitzer, 19–53. Oxford: Oxford University Press, 2013.

Rassat, M.-L. "Escroquerie." *JurisClasseur Pénal des Affaires*, fasc. 10 (June 2022).

Raymond, G. "Le mulot mort était dans le sachet de pâtes alimentaires." *Contrats concurrence consommation*, no. 12 (December 2007): comm. 311.

Rebut, D. "Tentative." *Répertoire de droit pénal et de procédure pénale* (May 2009).

Rémy, P. "Critique du système français de responsabilité civile." *Droits et cultures* I (1966): 31–49.

———. "Les civilistes français vont-ils disparaître?" *McGill Law Journal* 32 (1986): 152–158.

Renoux-Zagame, M.-F. "Le droit commun entre providence divine et raison." In *Du droit de Dieu au droit de l'homme*, 50–76. Léviathan. Paris: PUF, 2003.

Rey, P. "Concurrence par les mérites." In *La modernisation du droit de la concurrence*, edited by G. Canivet. Droit & Économie, 151–161. Paris: LGDJ, 2006.

Rials, S. "Les standards, notions critiques du droit." In *Les notions à contenu variable en droit*, edited by C. Perelman and R. Vander Elst.

Travaux du Centre national de recherches de logique, 39–53. Brussels: Bruylant, 1984.

Richard, E. "'Mon nom est personne': La construction de la personnalité morale ou les vertus de la patience." *Entreprises et histoire* 4, no. 57 (2009): 14–44.

Rivero, J. "Droit public et droit privé: Conquête, ou statu quo?" *Recueil Dalloz* (1947): chron. XVIII, 69–72.

———. "Apologie pour les 'faiseurs de système.'" *Recueil Dalloz*, I, Doctrine (1951): chron. XXIII, 99–102.

———. "La présomption fatale: Les erreurs du socialisme." *Annales de la faculté de droit de Liège* (1957): 65–101; trans. R. Audouin. Paris: Institut Coppet, 2019.

———. "Vers un droit commun européen: Nouvelles perspectives en droit administratif." In *Nouvelles perspectives d'un droit commun*, edited by M. Cappelletti. European University Institute, 389–406. Brussels: Bruylant, 1978.

Robert, J.-H. "Imputation et complicité." *JCP G*, I, Doctrine, chron. 2720 (1975): 33–45.

———. "L'histoire des éléments de l'infraction." *Revue de science criminelle et de droit pénal comparé* (1977): 269–284.

———. "La faute et la peine dans la philosophie du nouveau Code pénal français." In *La faute, la peine et le pardon*, edited by J.-B. D'Onorio, 99–114. Paris: P. Téqui, 1999.

———. "Politique pénale: Ressorts et évolution." *Pouvoirs*, no. 128 (January 2009): 103–111.

Robert, P. "La crise de l'économie répressive." *Revue de science criminelle et de droit pénal comparé*, no. 1 (1986): 69–78.

Roda, J.-C. "Réflexions sur les objectifs du droit français de la concurrence." *Recueil Dalloz* (2018): 1504.

———. "La crise du droit antitrust." In *Mélanges en l'honneur de Jacques Mestre*, 839–853. Mélanges. Paris: LGDJ, 2019.

———. "L'entente algorithmique." *JCP G*, no. 28 (July 15, 2019): doctr. 785.

———. "Le standard de preuve: Réflexions à partir du droit de la concurrence." *Recueil Dalloz* (2021): 1297.

———. "Un an de droit de la concurrence dans l'univers numérique." *Communication Commerce électronique*, no. 10 (October 2022): chron. 12.

———. "Le Digital Markets Act (1re partie) – Contrôler les contrôleurs d'accès." *Communication Commerce électronique*, no. 2 (February 2023): étude 4.

Rosanò, A. "Some Developments of the Principle of Mens Rea in the Case Law of the Court of Justice of the European Union." *New Journal of European Criminal Law* 7, no. 3 (2016): 302–314.

Ross, A. "Tû-tû." Translated by E. Millard and E. Matzner. *Enquête*, no. 7 (1999): 263–279.

Roubier, P. "Théorie générale de l'action en concurrence déloyale." *RTD com.* (1948): 541–591.

Rouge, J.-F. "La spéculation: Règles du jeu." *Les Petites affiches*, no. 94 (August 6, 1993): 16–25.

Rousseau, F. "Projet de réforme de la responsabilité civile: L'amende civile face aux principes directeurs du droit pénal." *JCP G*, no. 24 (June 11, 2018): art. 686, 1177–1184.

———. "Tentative d'éclaircissements de l'obscur article 121-3, alinéa 4 du Code pénal." In *Mélanges en l'honneur du Professeur Philippe Conte*, 733–747. Paris: LexisNexis, 2023.

Rousseva, E. "Reflections on the Relevance and Proof of Efficiency Defences in Modern EU Antitrust Law." In *Ten Years of Effects-Based Approach in EU Competition Law: State of Play and Perspectives*, edited by J. Bourgeois and D. Waelbroeck. GCLC Annual Conference Series, 239–291. Brussels: Bruylant, 2012.

Rouvière, F. "Le fondement du savoir juridique." *RTD civ.* (2016): 279.

———. "La méthode casuistique: L'apport des cas critiques pour la construction des catégories juridiques." *Revue de la recherche juridique: Droit prospectif* 2018-5 (2018): 1985–1999.

Roux, J.-A. Observations under Cass. crim., October 21, 1926. *Sirey* (1927): 33–35.

Rubinstein, A. "Dilemmas of an Economic Theorist." *Econometrica* 74, no. 4 (July 2006): 856–883.

Ruelle, A. "Les responsabilités du fait d'autrui en droit romain dans la ligne de mire de Domat et de Pothier." In *Le fait d'autrui: Responsabilités contractuelles et extracontractuelles*, edited by C. Delforge and J. Van Zuylen. Université Saint-Louis Bruxelles, 9–41. Limal: Anthémis, 2021.

Sabato, E. "Le règne de la science et la révolte romantique." In *L'écrivain et la catastrophe*, 11–23. Paris: Seuil, 1986.

———. "Sur l'art abstrait." In *L'écrivain et la catastrophe*, 122–129. Paris: Seuil, 1986.

Sacco, R. "Droit commun de l'Europe, et composantes du droit." In *Nouvelles perspectives d'un droit commun*, edited by M. Cappelletti. European University Institute, 95–109. Brussels: Bruylant, 1978.

———. "Mute Law." *The American Journal of Comparative Law* 43, no. 3 (Summer 1995): 455–467.

Saint-Esteben, R. “Une repénalisation du droit de la concurrence en France? À propos de l’utilisation de l’article 40 du code de procédure pénale par les services d’instruction de l’Autorité.” *Concurrences*, no. 2-2019, art. no. 90001 (2019): 54–65.

———. “Un vrai-faux retour de l’arrêt Continental Can? (Towercast).” *Concurrences*, no. 4-2022, art. no. 111085 (2022).

Saint-Pau, J.-C. “Faut-il repenser la responsabilité pénale des personnes morales?” In *Faut-il rethéoriser le droit pénal*, edited by J. Leroy, 101–111. Paris: LexisNexis, 2017.

Salin, P. “L’école ‘autrichienne’ et l’esprit scientifique.” *Liberté économique & progrès social*, no. 177 (Autumn 2021): 2–9.

Salvage, P. “L’imprudence en droit pénal.” *JCP G*, no. 50 (December 11, 1996): 3984.

Salvaire, J. “Réflexions sur la responsabilité pénale du fait d’autrui.” *Revue de science criminelle et de droit pénal comparé*, no. 2 (April–June 1964): 307–315.

Savatier, R. “Personnalité et dépersonnalisation de la responsabilité civile. La foi en la liberté de la personne et la responsabilité fondée sur la faute.” In *Mélanges de droit, d’histoire et d’économie offerts à Marcel Laborde-Lacoste*, 321–344. Bordeaux: Bière, 1963.

———. “L’ordre public économique.” *Recueil Dalloz*, chron. VI (1965): 37–44.

Sayre, F. B. “Mens Rea.” *Harvard Law Review* 45, no. 6 (April 1932): 974–1026.

Schauer, F. “Precedent.” *Stanford Law Review* 39, no. 3 (February 1987): 571–605.

Schlag, P. “Spam Jurisprudence, Air Law, and the Rank Anxiety of Nothing Happening (A Report on the State of the Art).” *Georgetown Law Journal* 97 (2009): 803–835.

Schrepel, T. “Les position dominantes bientôt sanctionnées?” *JCP E*, no. 46 (November 15, 2018): 36–38.

———. “Pour une suppression en droit de la concurrence des restrictions ‘par objet’: L’innovation juridique peut aussi être conceptuelle.” In *L’innovation juridique et judiciaire: Méthodologie et perspectives*, edited by A. Masson and H. Bouthinon-Dumas, 321–337. Brussels: Larcier, 2019.

Schweitzer, S. “Du mécanicisme à l’émergence de l’humain dans la théorie contemporaine de la firme.” In *Éthique en entreprise*, 77–99. Éthique et déontologie. Aix-en-Provence: Librairie de l’Université, 2001.

Segonds, M. “Tentative.” *JurisClasseur Pénal Code* (November 2022).

Sen, A. “Markets and Freedoms: Achievements and Limitations of the Market Mechanism in Promoting Individual Freedoms.” *Oxford Economic Papers* 45, no. 4 (October 1993): 519–541.

Sériaux, A. "L'appréciation de la faute pénale d'imprudence en droit français contemporain." *Revue de science criminelle et de droit pénal comparé*, no. 2 (April–June 2017): 231–246.

Sève, R. "Droit et économie: Quatre paradigmes." *Archives de philosophie du droit* 37 (1992): 63–68.

Sher, B. "The Last of the Steam-Powered Trains: Modernising Article 82." *European Competition Law Review*, no. 5 (2004): 243–246.

Sibony, A.-L. "La jurisprudence de la Cour au prisme de la science économique." In *Dans la fabrique du droit européen: Scènes, acteurs et publics de la Cour de justice des Communautés européennes*, edited by P. Mbongo and A. Vauchez. Droit de l'Union européenne, 171–197. Brussels: Bruylant, 2009.

———. "La porosité du droit: À propos des relations du droit avec d'autres disciplines." *Revue de la Faculté de droit de l'Université de Liège* 2, no. 2010/2 (2010): 271–278.

———. "La preuve scientifique évitée. Inventaire de quelques techniques judiciaires." In *Preuve scientifique, preuve juridique*, edited by E. Truilhé-Marengo. Droit des technologies, 161–180. Brussels: Larcier, 2011.

———. "La CJUE précise la pertinence de l'intention pour la qualification d'abus de position dominante." *Concurrences*, no. 3-2012, art. no. 48339 (2012): 101–104.

———. "Du bon usage des notions d'efficacité et d'efficience en droit." In *L'efficacité de la norme juridique: Nouveau vecteur de légitimité*, edited by M. Fatin-Rouge Stéfanini, L. Gay, and A. Vidal-Naquet, 61–84. Brussels: Bruylant, 2012.

Sibony, A.-L., and E. Barbier de la Serre. "Charge de la preuve et théorie du contrôle en droit communautaire de la concurrence: Pour un changement de perspective." *RTD Eur.* 43, no. 2 (April–June 2007): 205–252.

———. "Expert Evidence before the EC Courts." *Common Market Law Review* 45, no. 4 (2008): 941–985.

Sicurella, R. "Nulla poena sine culpa: Un véritable principe de droit européen?" *Revue de science criminelle et de droit pénal comparé* (2002): 15.

———. "Développer une culture pénale européenne: De l'européanisation des principes fondamentaux du droit pénal à une théorie 'européenne' de la responsabilité pénale." *Revue de science criminelle et de droit pénal comparé*, no. 1 (2020): 1–25.

Siragusa, M. "Italy – New Forms of Abuse of Dominance and Abuse of Law." In *Abuse of Dominance in EU Competition Law: Emerging Trends*, edited by P. L. Parcu et al., 119–138. Cheltenham: Edward Elgar, 2017.

Smits, C., and D. Waelbroeck. "Le droit de la concurrence et les droits fondamentaux." In *Les droits de l'homme dans les politiques de l'Union européenne*, edited by M. Candela Soriano, 135–162. Brussels: Larcier, 2006.

Smulders, B. "The Bifurcated Approach and Its Practical Impact on the Establishment of Harm to Competition." In *The Notion of Restriction of Competition: Revisiting the Foundations of Antitrust Enforcement in Europe*, edited by D. Gerard, M. Merola, and B. Meyring. GCLC Annual Conference Series, 51–63. Brussels: Bruylant, 2017.

Sorice, R. "La rilevanza penale della colpa nel Medioevo: Ricerche sulla Doctrina Bartoli." *Rivista internazionale di diritto comune* 31 (2020): 199–229.

Spector, D. "Analyse économique et sécurité juridique: Entre règles *per se* et règles de raison." In *Politiques de la concurrence*, edited by D. Encaoua and R. Guesnerie, 271–285. Paris: La Documentation française, 2006.

Spencer, J. R. "La responsabilité pénale dans l'entreprise en Angleterre." *Revue de science criminelle et de droit pénal comparé* (1997): 289.

Spiteri, P. "L'infraction formelle." *Revue de science criminelle et de droit pénal comparé* (1966): 497–520.

Stasiak, F. "L'utilisation d'une information privilégiée par un initié primaire." *Revue de science criminelle et de droit pénal comparé*, no. 1 (2010): 156.

———. "Infractions boursières." *Revue de science criminelle et de droit pénal comparé* 2011, no. 1 (January–March 2011): 113–129.

———. "Droit pénal et droit de la concurrence: Regards croisés." In *Droit pénal et autres branches du droit: Regards croisés*, edited by J.-C. Saint-Pau. Actes et études, 267–278. Paris: Éditions Cujas, 2012.

Stasiak, F., J.-M. Brigant, and A. Bellezza. "Le droit répressif des abus de marché: Un exemple de confusion des genres?" *Revue de science criminelle et de droit pénal comparé* (2020): 375.

Steel, S. "Les défenses en matière de responsabilité contractuelle et extra-contractuelle en droit français." *Revue des contrats*, no. 4 (December 2019): 262–274.

Stern, B. "La coutume au cœur du droit international: Quelques réflexions." In *Mélanges offerts à Paul Reuter: Le droit international – Unité et diversité*, 479–499. Paris: A. Pedone, 1981.

———. "Quelques observations sur les règles internationales relatives à l'application extraterritoriale du droit." *Annuaire français de droit international* 32 (1986): 7–52.

Stigler, G. J. "The Optimum Enforcement of Laws." *Journal of Political Economy* 78, no. 3 (May–June 1970): 526–536.

Stoffel-Munck, P. Commentary under Cass. ch. mixte, October 29, 2021, no. 19-18.470. *JCP G*, no. 24 (June 20, 2022): doctr. 759.

Strowel, A. "Utilitarisme et approche économique dans la théorie du droit: Autour de Bentham et Posner." *Revue interdisciplinaire d'études juridiques* 18, no. 1 (1987): 1–45.

Stucke, M. E. "Morality and Antitrust." *Columbia Business Law Review*, no. 3 (2006): 443–547.

———. "Does the Rule of Reason Violate the Rule of Law?" *Loyola Consumer Law Review* 22, no. 1 (2009): art. 5, 15–27.

———. "Reconsidering Antitrust's Goals." *Boston College Law Review* 53 (2012): 551–629.

———. "Is Intent Relevant?" *Journal of Law, Economics & Policy* 8, no. 4 (Autumn 2012): 801–858.

Sun Beale, S. "A Response to the Critics of Corporate Criminal Liability." *American Criminal Law Review* 46, no. 4 (Fall 2009): 1481–1506.

Stylianou, K., and M. Iacovides. "The Goals of EU Competition Law: A Comprehensive Empirical Investigation." *Legal Studies* 42 (2022): 620–648.

Teller, M. "Du droit et des algorithmes: Libres propos sur la notion d'algorithme, cet impensé du droit." In *Droit bancaire et financier: Mélanges AEDBF France*, vol. 8, edited by B. Bréhier, 263–273. Paris: Revue Banque Édition, 2018.

Temple Lang, J. "Restriction of Competition and Exclusionary Abuse Under Article 102 – The Solution." In *The Notion of Restriction of Competition: Revisiting the Foundations of Antitrust Enforcement in Europe*, edited by D. Gerard, M. Merola, and B. Meyring. GCLC Annual Conference Series, 239–254. Brussels: Bruylant, 2017.

Terré, F. "Concurrence et proportionnalité." In *Mélanges en l'honneur du professeur Claude Lucas de Leyssac*, 467–471. Paris: LexisNexis, 2018.

Thibierge, C. "Le droit souple: Réflexion sur les textures du droit." *RTD civ.* (2003): 599.

Thomas, Y. "L'extrême et l'ordinaire: Remarques sur le cas médiéval de la communauté disparue." In *Les opérations du droit*, 207–237. Hautes études. Paris: EHESS-Gallimard-Seuil, 2011.

Tiedemann, K. "Tendances mondiales d'introduction de sanctions nouvelles pour les crimes en col blanc." *Revue internationale de criminologie et de police technique* XLIV, no. 2 (April–June 1991): 226–242.

———. "Introduction." In *La criminalisation du comportement collectif: XIV*[e] *Congrès international de droit comparé*, edited by H. De Doelder and K. Tiedemann, 6–30. The Hague: Kluwer Law International, 1996.

———. "La responsabilité pénale dans l'entreprise: Vers un espace judiciaire européen unifié?" Introductory report, Seminar of the Association de recherches pénales européennes, Paris (Cour de cassation, December 13, 1996). *Revue de science criminelle et de droit pénal comparé* (1997): 259.

Tilloy, C. “Concurrence déloyale.” *JurisClasseur Procédures* (January 2021): fasc. 10.

Townley, C. “The Concept of an ‘Undertaking’: The Boundaries of the Corporation – A Discussion of Agency, Employees and Subsidiaries.” In *EC Competition Law: A Critical Assessment*, edited by G. Amato and C.-D. Ehlermann, 3–23. Oxford: Hart Publishing, 2007.

Tremblay, L. “L’origine mythique de la primauté du droit: Hésiode et les dieux.” *Revue juridique Thémis de l’Université de Montréal* 52, no. 425 (2018): 425–519.

Trifilio, S. “The Economic Theory of the Scholastics as a Contractual Analysis.” *Journal of Economists and Human Studies* 24, no. 1 (June 2018): 1–6.

Trousse, P. E. “Le mobile justificatif.” *Revue de droit pénal et de criminologie* (1962–1963): 418–436.

Vallar, S. “Folie et droit romain – Quelques observations.” *Criminocorpus: Revue d’Histoire de la justice, des crimes et des peines* (2016). http://journals.openedition.org/criminocorpus/3146

Valletti, T. “Economics in Competition Law – Working Together.” *Concurrences*, no. 4-2017, art. no. 84876 (2017): 11–15.

Van de Kerchove, M. “Symbolique et instrumentalité: Stratégies de pénalisation et de dépénalisation dans une société pluraliste.” *Revue de l’Université de Bruxelles*, no. 1–3 (1984): 123–171.

Van der Woude, M. “A Curious Question: Why Bother with Economists?” *Concurrences*, no. 3-2015, art. no. 74831 (2015): 66–71.

———. “La métamorphose d’un droit.” *Concurrences*, no. 2-2022, art. no. 106134 (2022).

Vandewattyne, J., and D. Ndahabonimana. “Quarante ans après *L’emprise de l’organisation*: Un retour sur le terrain.” *Nouvelle revue de psychosociologie* 1, no. 29 (2021): 23–36.

Varinard, A. “Le déplacement des critères de la faute.” In *Dix ans après la réforme de 1994: Quels repères dans le Code pénal*, edited by M. Danti-Juan. Travaux de l’Institut de sciences criminelles de Poitiers, vol. XXIV, 45–66. Paris: Cujas, 2005.

Varinard, A., and E. Joly-Sibuet. “Les problèmes juridiques et pratiques posés par la différence entre le droit pénal et le droit administratif pénal.” *Revue internationale de droit pénal* 59 (1988): 189–215.

Vedel, G. “Indéfinissable mais présent.” *Droits: Revue française de théorie juridique*, no. 11 (1990): 67–71.

Verhaegen, J. “Faute pénale et faute civile.” *Archives de philosophie du droit* 28 (1983): 17–28.

———. "La définition de l'intention coupable dans les codes pénaux modernes." In *Liber amicorum Frédéric Dumon*, vol. I, 527–536. Antwerp: Kluwer, 1983.

———. "L'exigence de l'intention coupable dans les infractions aux lois et règlements particuliers." *Revue de droit pénal et de criminologie*, no. 12 (1986): 947–955.

———. "L'élément fautif en matière de contraventions aux règlements." *Revue de droit pénal et de criminologie*, no. 3 (1988): 289–297.

Verny, E. "Empoisonnement." *Répertoire de droit pénal et de procédure pénale* (December 2016).

———. "Fraudes: Tromperies et falsifications." *JurisClasseur Concurrence – Consommation* (June 2021): fasc. 1010.

Veron, M. "Recel d'abus de biens sociaux." *Droit pénal*, no. 11 (November 2008): comm. 139.

Vervaele, J. A. E. "La responsabilité pénale de et au sein de la personne morale aux Pays-Bas. Mariage entre pragmatisme et dogmatisme juridique." *Revue de science criminelle et de droit pénal comparé* (1997): 325.

Vesterdorf, B. "Considérations sur la notion de 'concurrence par les mérites.'" In *La modernisation du droit de la concurrence*, edited by G. Canivet. Droit & Économie, 163–175. Paris: LGDJ, 2006.

Viano, C. "Causalité et responsabilité chez Lysias et Aristote." In *Aitia: Causalité juridique, causalité philosophique*. Mètis: Anthropologie des mondes grecs anciens, 69–85. Paris: Éditions de l'EHESS, 2015.

Vidal, J. "La conception juridique française de la culpabilité." In *Annales de l'Université de sciences sociales de Toulouse*, tome XXIV, fasc. 1–2, 45–58. Toulouse, 1976.

Viennois, J.-P. "La légitime défense en droit de la concurrence ou l'emprunt concevable d'une notion en droit pénal." *Revue de science criminelle et de droit pénal comparé* (2004): 295.

Villey, E. "De l'intention en matière pénale." *La France judiciaire* I, Doctrine (1876): 1–8.

Villey, M. "Logique d'Aristote et droit romain." *Revue historique de droit français et étranger*, quatrième série, vol. 28 (1951): 309–328.

———. "La responsabilité chez St Thomas." In *Annales de la faculté de droit et des sciences politiques et économiques de Strasbourg*, tome VIII, Travaux du colloque de philosophie pénale (12–21 janvier 1959): "La responsabilité pénale," 117–133. Strasbourg, 1961.

———. "Critique de l'utilitarisme juridique." *Revue de la recherche juridique: Droit prospectif*, no. VI-9 (1981–1982): 166–174.

———. "La Doctrine du droit dans l'histoire de la science juridique." Preface to Kant's *Métaphysique des mœurs*, Part I: *Doctrine du droit.* Translated by A. Philonenko. Bibliothèque des textes philosophiques, 7–36. Paris: Librairie philosophique J. Vrin, 2011.

Viney, G. "Conclusions." Proceedings of the symposium *La responsabilité pénale des personnes morales*, April 7, 1993. *Revue des sociétés* (1993): 381–388.

———. "Rapport de synthèse." In *Les métamorphoses de la responsabilité: Sixièmes journées René Savatier*, 323–339. Paris: PUF, 1997.

Vitu, A., and D. Beauvais. "Participation à une association de malfaiteurs." *JurisClasseur Pénal Code* (August 2022): fasc. 20.

Vogel, L. "L'économie, serviteur ou maître du droit." In *Une certaine idée du droit: Mélanges offerts à André Decocq*, 605–614. Paris: LITEC, 2004.

———. "Une nouvelle venue sur la scène du droit de la concurrence: La restriction par objet." *Contrats concurrence consommation*, no. 5 (May 2015): dossier 2.

———. "Où va le droit de la concurrence?" In *Le droit français de la concurrence, trente ans après l'ordonnance du 1er décembre 1986: Rétrospectives et perspectives*, edited by C. Arens, M. Chagny, and J.-L. Fourgoux, 37–48. Paris: LGDJ, 2017.

Wacke, A. "Freedom of Contract and Restraint of Trade Clauses in Roman and Modern Law." *Law and History Review* 11, no. 1 (Spring 1993): 1–19.

Waelbroeck, D., and D. Slater. "The Scope of Object vs Effect under Article 101 TFEU." In *Ten Years of Effects-Based Approach in EU Competition Law: State of Play and Perspectives*, edited by J. Bourgeois and D. Waelbroeck. GCLC Annual Conference Series, 131–157. Brussels: Bruylant, 2012.

Wahl, N. "From Greek Olive Oil to Latvian Music: Is There Any Such Thing as Unfair Prices?" *Concurrences*, no. 2-2018, art. no. 86617 (2018): 1–9.

Warlouzet, L. "Europe de la concurrence et politique industrielle communautaire: La naissance d'une opposition au sein de la CEE dans les années 1960." *Histoire, économie & société*, no. 1 (2008): 47–61.

Weber, H. "L'adhésion des employés à l'organisation chez McDonald's." *Nouvelle revue de psychosociologie* 1, no. 1 (2006): 117–127.

Weber Waller, S. "The Language of Law and the Language of Business." *Case Western Reserve Law Review* 52, no. 1 (Fall 2001): 283–338.

Wells, C. "Corporate Criminal Responsibility." In *Research Handbook on Corporate Legal Responsibility*, edited by S. Tully, 147–158. Cheltenham: Edward Elgar, 2005.

Wendzel, B., M. Angelo, M. Jantz, and A. Peterson. "Corporate Criminal Liability." *American Criminal Law Review* 56, no. 3 (2019): 671–710.

Whelan, P. "Parental Antitrust Liability and the Pressing Issue of the Legitimacy of EU Competition Law." *Concurrences*, no. 2-2021, art. no. 100086 (2021).

Whish, R. "Anticompetitive Object vs. Anticompetitive Effects: Does It Really Matter?" *Concurrences*, no. 2-2012 (New Frontiers of Antitrust Conference – Paris, February 10, 2012), art. no. 45426 (2012): 59–60.

Wils, W. P. J. "La compatibilité des procédures communautaires en matière de concurrence avec la Convention européenne des droits de l'homme." *Cahiers de droit européen* (1996): 329–354.

———. "The Undertaking as Subject of E.C. Competition Law and the Imputation of Infringements to Natural or Legal Persons." *European Law Review* 25, no. 2 (2000): 99–116.

———. "Is Criminalization of EU Competition Law the Answer?" *World Competition* 28, no. 2 (2005): 117–159.

———. "The Increased Level of EU Antitrust Fines, Judicial Review and the ECHR." *World Competition* 33, no. 1 (2010): 5–29.

———. "Judgment of the EU General Court in Intel and the So-Called More Economic Approach to Abuse of Dominance." *World Competition* 37, no. 4 (December 2014): 405–434.

Witt, A. C. "The Enforcement of Article 101 TFEU: What Has Happened to the Effects Analysis?" *Common Market Law Review* 55, no. 2 (April 2018): 417–448.

———. "The European Court of Justice and the More Economic Approach to EU Competition Law – Is the Tide Turning?" *The Antitrust Bulletin* 64, no. 2 (2019): 172–213.

———. "Platform Regulation in Europe – Per se Rules to the Rescue?" *Journal of Competition Law & Economics* 18, no. 3 (September 2022): 670–708.

Wolff, M. "On the Nature of Legal Persons." *Law Quarterly Review* 54, no. 4 (October 1938): 494–521.

Wolowski, L. "La concurrence et la coalition." *Revue de législation et de jurisprudence*, tome X (April–September 1839): 367–371.

Wróblewski, J. "Structure et fonctions des présomptions juridiques." In *Les présomptions et les fictions en droit*, edited by C. Perelman and P. Forier. Travaux du centre national de recherches logiques, 43–71. Brussels: Bruylant, 1974.

———. "La preuve juridique: Axiologie, logique et argumentation." In *La preuve en droit*, edited by C. Perelman and P. Forier. Travaux du centre national de recherches logiques, 331–355. Brussels: Bruylant, 1981.

Zaibert, L. A. "Intentionality, Voluntariness, and Culpability: A Historical-Philosophical Analysis." *Buffalo Criminal Law Review* 1, no. 2 (January 1988): 459–500.

Zingales, N. "Antitrust Intent in an Age of Algorithmic Nudging." *Journal of Antitrust Enforcement* 7, no. 3 (October 2019): 386–418.

IV. Reports, Parliamentary Proceedings, Guidelines, Communications

Anato, P., and C. Le Grip. *Rapport d'information déposé par la Commission des affaires européennes sur le droit européen de la concurrence face aux enjeux de la mondialisation*, no. 2451 (November 27, 2019).

Antitrust Modernization Commission. *Report and Recommendations.* Washington, D.C. (April 2007).

Association internationale de droit pénal. "XIVe Congrès international de droit pénal (Vienne, 2–7 octobre 1989)." *Revue internationale de droit pénal* 86, no. 1 (2015): 129–146.

Bundeskartellamt (Competition Authority). *Competition Law and Data* (May 10, 2016).

———. *Algorithms & Competition – Executive Summary* (November 2019).

Cabral, L., et alii. *The EU Digital Markets Act: A Report from a Panel of Economic Experts.* Luxembourg: Publications Office of the European Union, 2021.

Commission of the European Communities. *Le problème de la concentration dans le marché commun.* Études, série Concurrence, no. 3. Brussels, 1966.

———. Tiedemann, K. "Principes généraux applicables aux sanctions communautaires: Projet de rapport général." In *Étude sur les systèmes de sanctions administratives et pénales dans les États membres des communautés européennes*, vol. II: *Rapports de synthèse*, 7–40. Brussels: Office for Official Publications of the European Communities, 1994.

———. *Guidelines on the Application of Article 81(3) of the Treaty.* 2004 O.J. (C 101) 97.

———. *Green Paper on the Approximation, Mutual Recognition and Enforcement of Criminal Sanctions in the European Union.* COM(2004)334 final (April 30, 2004).

———. *DG Competition Discussion Paper on the Application of Article 82 of the Treaty to Exclusionary Abuses.* December 2005.

———. *Guidelines on the Method of Setting Fines Imposed Pursuant to Article 23(2)(a) of Regulation (EC) No 1/2003.* 2006 O.J. (C 210) 2.

———. "Antitrust: Consumer Welfare at Heart of Commission Fight Against Abuses by Dominant Undertakings." Press Release IP/08/1877 (December 3, 2008).

———. *Guidance on the Commission's Enforcement Priorities in Applying Article 82 of the EC Treaty to Abusive Exclusionary Conduct by Dominant Undertakings.* 2009 O.J. (C 45) 7.

Commission of the European Union. *Observations under Article 15(3) of Regulation No. 1/2003.* No. 7764P, 2010.

———. *Guidelines on Vertical Restraints.* 2010 O.J. (C 130) 1.

———. *Commission Notice on Best Practices for Proceedings Concerning Articles 101 and 102 TFEU.* 2011 O.J. (C 308) 6.

———. "Best Practices for the Submission of Economic Evidence and Data Collection in Cases Concerning Articles 101 and 102 TFEU and in Merger Cases." Staff Working Paper, C(2011) 7329 final (November 17, 2011).

———. *Notice on Agreements of Minor Importance (De Minimis Notice).* 2014 O.J. (C 291) 1.

———. *Guidance on Restriction of Competition "By Object" for the Purpose of Defining which Agreements May Benefit from the De Minimis Notice.* C(2014) 4136 final (June 3, 2015)

———. *The Application of Union Competition Rules to the Agricultural Sector.* COM(2018) 706 final (October 26, 2018).

———. *Shaping Europe's Digital Future.* COM(2020) 67 final (February 19, 2020).

———. "Antitrust: Commission Sends Statement of Objections to Apple on App Store Rules for Music Streaming Providers." Press Release IP/21/2061 (April 30, 2021) (Case AT.40437).

———. *A Competition Policy Fit for New Challenges.* COM(2021) 713 final (November 18, 2021).

———. "Antitrust: Commission Opens Investigation into Possible Anticompetitive Conduct by Google and Meta, in Online Display Advertising." Press Release IP/22/1703 (March 11, 2022) (Case AT.40774).

———. "Antitrust: Commission Sends Statement of Objections to Apple Over Practices Regarding Apple Pay." Press Release IP/22/2764 (May 2, 2022) (Case AT.40452).

———. *Guidelines on Vertical Restraints.* 2022 O.J. (C 248) 1.

———. *Communication under Article 27(4) in Case AT.40703 Amazon – Buy Box and AT.40462 Amazon Marketplace.* 2022 O.J. (C 278) 8.

———. *Draft Notice on the Definition of the Relevant Market for Union Competition Law Purposes.* 2022.

———. "Competition: Commission Seeks Feedback on Draft Revised Market Definition Notice." Press Release IP/22/6528 (November 8, 2022).

———. "Antitrust: Commission Sends Statement of Objections to Meta over Abusive Practices Benefiting Facebook Marketplace." Press Release IP/22/7728 (December 19, 2022) (Case AT.40684).

———. *A Dynamic and Workable Effects-Based Approach to Abuse of Dominance. Competition Policy Brief*, no. 1 (March 2023).

———. *Amendments to the Communication on Enforcement Priorities Under Article 82 EC.* Annex, C(2023) 1923 final (March 27, 2023).

———. *Guidelines on the Applicability of Article 101 TFEU to Horizontal Co-operation Agreements.* 2023 O.J. (C 259) 1.

Commission Technique des Ententes. "Rapport au ministre chargé des affaires économiques: années 1954 et 1955." *JORF, Documents administratifs*, no. 1 (January 14, 1960): 1–14.

———. "Rapport au ministre chargé des affaires économiques: année 1956." *JORF, Documents administratifs*, no. 2 (January 14, 1960): 15–28.

Conseil de la concurrence. "Études thématiques: Objet, effet et intention anticoncurrentiels." In *Rapport d'activité 2003* (March 30, 2004): 55–78.

Corps législatif. "Exposé des motifs du Livre II du Code pénal dans la séance du Corps législatif du 3 février 1810." In J.-G. Locré, *La législation civile, commerciale et criminelle de la France*, tome XXIX, 260–268. Paris: Treuttel et Würtz, 1831.

———. "Rapport au Corps législatif: Séance du 9 février 1810." In *Archives parlementaires de 1787 à 1960*, 2nd série (1800 à 1860), tome X, du 21 janvier 1808 au 5 juin 1810, 549–556. Paris: Librairie administrative Paul Dupont, 1867.

Council of Europe. *Report on Decriminalization.* Strasbourg: European Committee on Crime Problems, Legal Affairs, 1980.

———. *Thematic Monitoring Review of the Conference of the Parties to CETS No.198 on Article 10 (1 and 2) ("Corporate Liability").* C198-COP(2021)6_HR (November 19, 2021).

Council of Europe, European Court of Human Rights. *Guide to Article 6 of the European Convention on Human Rights: Right to a Fair Trial (Criminal Section).* 2022.

Court of Justice of the European Communities. *Memorandum concerning the Accession of the EC to the Convention for the Protection of Human Rights and Fundamental Freedoms.* SJ/229/79 (1979).

Crémer, J., A. de Montjoye, and H. Schweitzer. *Competition Policy for the Digital Era.* Luxembourg: Publications Office of the European Union, 2019.

Encaoua, D., and R. Guesnerie, eds. *Politiques de la concurrence: Report to the Conseil d'Analyse Économique.* Paris: La Documentation française, 2006.

European Advisory Group on Competition Policy. "An Economic Approach to Article 82." July 2005.

European Economic and Social Committee. *The Rule of Law and Its Impact on Economic Growth.* ECO/511 (February 20, 2020).

European Parliament. *Minutes of the Meeting of the Internal Market Commission, May 24–25, 1962, Milan.* PE/V/62-6.

———. *Motion for a Resolution on the Legal and Institutional Implications of the Use of Soft Law.* A6-0259/2007 (June 28, 2007).

———. *Resolution of May 22, 2012, on a European Union Approach to Criminal Law.* 2013 O.J. (CE 264) 7.

French Competition Authority. "The Single, Complex and Continuous Offense." In *Annual Report 2015* (March 2016): 91–132.

———. *Communiqué relatif à la méthode de détermination des sanctions pécuniaires* (July 30, 2021).

G7 Competition Authorities. *Common Understanding of G7 Competition Authorities on "Competition and the Digital Economy"* (June 5, 2019).

Hennion, C. *Rapport d'information déposé par la Commission des affaires européennes sur le Digital Markets Act*, no. 4409 (July 22, 2021).

Organisation for Economic Co-operation and Development. *Competition on the Merits, Policy Roundtables.* DAF/COMP(2005)27 (March 30, 2006).

———. *Roundtable on Facilitating Practices in Oligopolies.* DAF/COMP(2008)24 (September 5, 2008).

———. *Market Definition.* DAF/COMP(2012)13/REV1 (September 21, 2012).

———. *The Role of Efficiency Claims in Antitrust Proceedings.* DAF/COMP(2012)23 (May 2, 2013).

———. *Big Data: Bringing Competition Policy to the Digital Era.* DAF/COMP(2016)14 (October 16, 2016).

———. *Algorithms and Collusion.* DAF/COMP(2017)4 (June 9, 2017).

———. *Abuse of Dominance in Digital Markets.* DAF/COMP/GF(2020)4 (December 3, 2020).

Secretariat of the Intergovernmental Committee. *Rapport des chefs de délégation aux ministres des Affaires étrangères ("Rapport Spaak").* Brussels (April 21, 1956).

Sénat. "Adoption d'un projet de loi relatif à la modification des articles 419 et 420 du Code pénal." *Journal Officiel de la République Française, Débats parlementaires, Sénat*, Séance du 19 novembre 1926: 1648–1655.

Venice Commission. *Rule of Law Checklist.* CDL-AD (2016) 007 (March 18, 2016).

Vermeulen, G., W. De Bondt, and C. Ryckman. *Liability of Legal Persons for Offences in the EU.* DG Justice (JLS/2010/JPEN/PR/1009/E4), 2012.

Villani, C., ed. *Donner un sens à l'intelligence artificielle: Rapport de mission parlementaire.* 2018.

V. Dictionaries and Encyclopedias

Bailey, D. "Règle de raison." In M. Chagny and E. Combe, eds., *Dictionnaire de droit de la concurrence*, 730–732. Paris: Concurrences, 2023.

Beaune, J.-C., and A. Doyon. "Automate." *Encyclopædia Universalis.*

Boutot, A. "Science et philosophie." *Encyclopædia Universalis.*

Brochier, H. "Rationalité économique." *Encyclopædia Universalis.*

Cherbuliez, A.-F., and C. Coquelin. "Coalitions." In C. Coquelin and G.-U. Guillaumin, *Dictionnaire de l'économie politique: Contenant l'exposition des principes de la science*, tome I, 382–388. Paris: Librairie Guillaumin et Cie, 1852.

Coquelin, C. "Concurrence." In C. Coquelin and G.-U. Guillaumin, *Dictionnaire de l'économie politique: Contenant l'exposition des principes de la science*, tome I, 448–455. Paris: Librairie Guillaumin et Cie, 1852.

Clément, A. "Accaparement." In C. Coquelin and G.-U. Guillaumin, *Dictionnaire de l'économie politique: Contenant l'exposition des principes de la science*, tome I, 5–8. Paris: Librairie Guillaumin et Cie, 1852.

Cornu, G., ed. *Vocabulaire juridique.* Quadrige. Paris: PUF, 11th ed., 2016.

———. *Droit civil: Introduction au droit.* Domat Droit Privé. Paris: LGDJ, 13th ed., 2007.

D'Argis, B. "Stellionat." In *L'Encyclopédie de Diderot et d'Alembert*, tome XV, 509. Paris, 1751.

Daremberg, C., E. Saglio, and E. Pottier. *Dictionnaire des Antiquités grecques et romaines*, tome II. Paris: Hachette, 1892.

De Jaucourt, L. "Loi." In D. Diderot, *Encyclopédie, ou dictionnaire raisonné des sciences, des arts et des métiers*, tome IX, 643–678. Paris: Briasson.

Decocq, G. "Facilité essentielle." In M. Chagny and E. Combe, eds., *Dictionnaire de droit de la concurrence*, 443–444. Paris: Concurrences, 2023.

Faucher, L. "Propriété." In C. Coquelin and G.-U. Guillaumin, *Dictionnaire de l'économie politique: Contenant l'exposition des principes de la science*, tome II, 460–473. Paris: Librairie Guillaumin et Cie, 1853.

Fieffé-Lacroix. *La clef des lois romaines, ou dictionnaire analytique et raisonné de toutes les matières contenues dans le Corps du Droit.* Paris: C. Lamort, 1810.

Gaudemet, J. "Justice distributive." *Encyclopædia Universalis.*

Grimal, P. *Dictionnaire de la mythologie grecque et romaine.* 15th ed. Paris: PUF, 2002.

Jullien, B. "Économie industrielle." *Encyclopædia Universalis.*

Lalande, A. *Vocabulaire technique et critique de la philosophie.* Quadrige. Paris: PUF, 1st ed., 2002.

Luc, I. "Exemption par catégorie (règlement d')." In M. Chagny and E. Combe, eds., *Dictionnaire de droit de la concurrence*, 432–435. Paris: Concurrences, 2023.

Picart, C. "Killer Acquisitions." In M. Chagny and E. Combe, eds., *Dictionnaire de droit de la concurrence*, 508–511. Paris: Concurrences, 2023.

Rouquette, R. *Dictionnaire du droit administratif.* Paris: Éditions du Moniteur, 2002.

Saint-Bonnet, F. "Arbitraire." In J. Andriantsimbazovina et al., eds., *Dictionnaire des droits de l'homme*, 58–61. Paris: PUF, 2008.

Schmidt, J. *Dictionnaire de la mythologie grecque et romaine.* Références. Paris: Larousse, 1993.

Troper, M. "Hans Kelsen." *Encyclopædia Universalis.*

ALPHABETICAL INDEX

(Numbers refer to paragraph numbers)

A

D

E

F

G

H

I

J

K

L

M

N

O

Q

R

S

T

U

V

W

TABLE OF CONTENTS